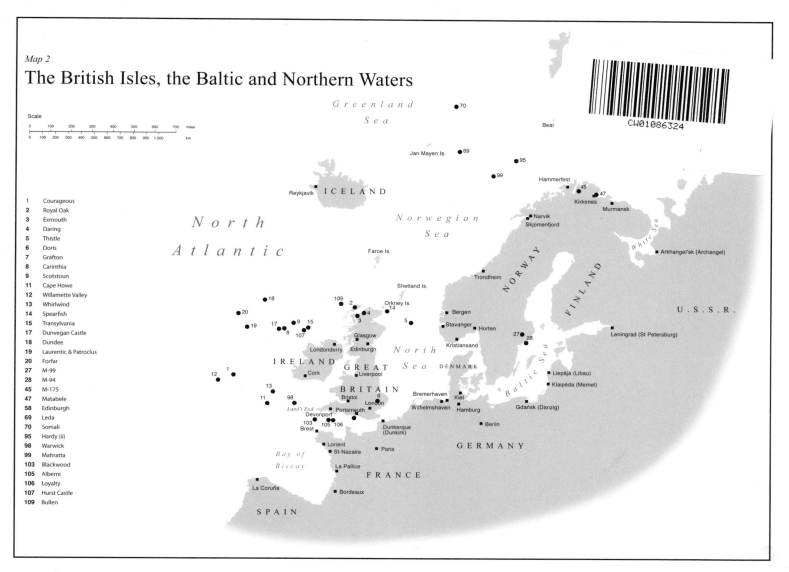

Map 2

The British Isles, the Baltic and Northern Waters

Scale

1	Courageous
2	Royal Oak
3	Exmouth
4	Daring
5	Thistle
6	Doris
7	Grafton
8	Carinthia
9	Scotstoun
11	Cape Howe
12	Willamette Valley
13	Whirlwind
14	Spearfish
15	Transylvania
17	Dunvegan Castle
18	Dundee
19	Laurentic & Patroclus
20	Forfar
27	M-99
28	M-94
45	M-175
47	Matabele
58	Edinburgh
69	Leda
70	Somali
95	Hardy (ii)
98	Warwick
99	Mahratta
103	Blackwood
105	Alberni
106	Loyalty
107	Hurst Castle
109	Bullen

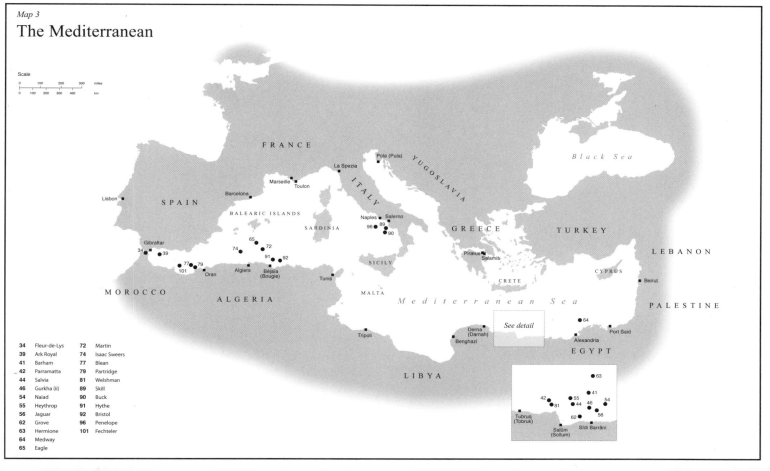

Map 3

The Mediterranean

Scale

34	Fleur-de-Lys	72	Martin
39	Ark Royal	74	Isaac Sweers
41	Barham	77	Blean
42	Parramatta	79	Partridge
44	Salvia	81	Welshman
46	Gurkha (ii)	89	Skill
54	Naiad	90	Buck
55	Heythrop	91	Hythe
56	Jaguar	92	Bristol
62	Grove	96	Penelope
63	Hermione	101	Fechteler
64	Medway		
65	Eagle		

U-BOAT ATTACK LOGS

Auftauchen! – a rare shot of the bows of a Type VIIC U-boat breaking the surface as seen through her own periscope. *DUBMA*

U-BOAT ATTACK LOGS

A Complete Record of Warship Sinkings
from Original Sources 1939–1945

Daniel Morgan & Bruce Taylor

With a foreword by
Professor Jürgen Rohwer

Seaforth
PUBLISHING

In memory of all those treated in these pages
who went to sea and never came back,
and to those they left behind to mourn the loss

Copyright © Daniel Morgan and Bruce Taylor, 2011

First published in Great Britain in 2011 by Seaforth Publishing
An imprint of Pen & Sword Books Ltd
47 Church Street, Barnsley
S Yorkshire S70 2AS

www.seaforthpublishing.com
Email info@seaforthpublishing.com

British Library Cataloguing in Publication Data
A CIP data record for this book is available from the British Library

ISBN 978-1-84832-118-2

Typeset and designed by Palindrome
Printed and bound in China by 1010 Printing International Limited

Contents

Acknowledgements

No lengthy exercise in historical research can reach completion without the help of a disproportionately large number of people and institutions and this book has perhaps incurred a greater debt than most. In addition to assistance with specific entries offered by many individuals throughout the world (listed below), the authors would like to begin by recording their particular gratitude to a number of specialists and institutions who have been invaluable to the project as a whole for more than a decade.

Under the stewardship of Capt. Christopher Page the Naval Historical Branch of the Ministry of Defence in Portsmouth (formerly London) has provided full access to its *U-Boot-Waffe* collection including the microfilmed *Kriegstagebücher* which form the heart of this volume. In particular, Kate Brett (formerly Tildesley), Curator of the NHB, has spent countless hours tracking down related Allied material from that institution's wider collections while offering her professional insight into the many problems raised by the project. This book could not have assumed its present dimension without her active assistance and the personal interest she has taken in it, and it's our hope that she will find the result to be an adequate recompense for her generosity over so many years.

Thomas Weis, head of the Marinearchiv of the Bibliothek für Zeitgeschichte at the Württembergische Landesbibliothek in Stuttgart, has made a similar contribution from the German side, not only devoting much time to our visits but also supplying documents and photos from his collections while providing access to the Sammlung Rohwer, the accumulation of naval material assembled by Professor Jürgen Rohwer over many decades at the BfZ. Beyond many other kindnesses Prof. Rohwer has done us and our work the honour of writing the Foreword. Elsewhere in Germany, the authors are indebted to Horst Bredow, founder of the remarkable Deutsches U-Boot Museum-Archiv (formerly U-Boot-Archiv) in Cuxhaven-Altenbruch, Lower Saxony, a unique collection of private records and published sources filed by U-boat. This material has offered an essential complement to the formal primary documentation of the period and our thanks to him and to his erstwhile colleague Horst Schwenk for making it available to us on many occasions. Our gratitude also to the Bundesarchiv-Militärarchiv in Freiburg im Breisgau (especially Jana Brabant and Andrea Meier) and to the Bildarchiv of the Bundesarchiv, Koblenz (especially Aileen Tomcek). A particular word of thanks to Guðmundur Helgason and his remarkable uboat.net for much generous assistance down the years. On the Allied side, our thanks also to Michael McAloon, Stephen Prince and Jock Gardner at the NHB, to Jenny Wraight and Iain MacKenzie at the Admiralty Library, and to the staff of The National Archives (formerly The Public Record Office) at Kew, London; the Imperial War Museum, Lambeth, London; the Royal Naval Museum, Portsmouth; the Naval Studies Library of Plymouth City Library; the Service Historique de la Marine, Paris (especially Mme Patricia Dussard); the National Archives of Canada, Ottawa (especially Ken McLeod); the Naval Historical Center, Washington, DC (especially Ms. Heidi Myers); and the National Archives and Records Administration at College Park, Maryland where Patrick Osborne and Dr. Tim Mulligan went to great lengths to locate documentation on US sinkings for us. Information and assistance on the three Soviet entries was kindly provided by Miroslav Morozov of Moscow, and on Royal Navy sinkings in the Arctic by Cdr W. E. Grenfell RN of Havant, Hants. And UCLA's Young Research Library has again proved a superb and generous resource of secondary material. To them all our thanks and gratitude.

Equally, the process of translating the *Kriegstagebücher* could not have been accomplished without much assistance over many years and from many quarters. Our thanks go to Horst Bredow, Kate Brett, Oblt.z.S. Claus-Peter Carlsen, Walter Cloots, Rainer Kolbicz, Dr Tim Mulligan, Kptlt Kurt Petersen, Herbert Ritschel, Professor Jürgen Rohwer, the late Vizeadmiral Horst von Schroeter, Jak P. Mallmann Showell, Jürgen Weber and Thomas Weis. Our particular thanks to Glyn Jones who performed a valuable and painstaking bilingual edit of each excerpt, and to Jak Showell for most generous assistance with technical matters as the volume came full term. The maps were rendered by Yee-Ping Cho of Los Angeles, Calif. who in addition lent much technical assistance with photos. Great as the help has been, it goes without saying that any remaining errors are ours and ours alone.

Beyond those mentioned above, assistance and information has been gratefully received in connection with specific entries from the following individuals: *Alysse* (**51**) Commandant André Guenais FNFL (survivor), Marcelin Hellequin and Charles Salou; *Andania* (**10**) Commodore Ronald W. Warwick and Harold Woods; *Avenger* (**75**) Jason Pilalas of San Marino, Calif.; *Broadwater* (**36**) Sir Hooky Walker KCMG; *Buck* (**90**) Klaus Zaepfel of Virginia Beach, Va.; *Camito* (**25**) Mrs June Bateley of Pacific Paradise, Queensland; and Alan Dowling of Caldicot, Monmouthshire; *Colombia* (**82**) Theo Burgers of Schiedam and Joop Romkema of Leeuwarden, the Netherlands; *Cossack* (**37**) Keith Batchelor and Peter Harrison; *Courageous* (**1**) the late Professor Sir Peter Russell; *Daring* (**4**) David Axford; *Dunedin* (**40**) Lt Cdr Chris Broadway RN (Retd) of Torquay, Devon; the late Harry Cross (survivor); Bill Gill (survivor) of Brighton, Sussex; Stuart Gill of Beckenham, Kent; Johann Mohr *fils* of Frankfurt, Germany; and Dr Jonathan R. Winkler, Wright State University, Dayton, Ohio; *Eagle* (**65**) Capt. John Rodgaard USN (Retd) of Burke, Va.; *Fechteler* (**101**) interview with former crewmen of *U380* at UBAC (now DUBMA), Cuxhaven-Altenbruch, May 2001; *Fiske* (**104**) Richard Jagodowski of Tucson, Ariz., and Cdr E. Andrew Wilde, Jr USN (Retd) of Needham, Mass.; *Gladiolus* (**35**) Rainer Kolbicz; *Grafton* (**7**) Barrie Austin of Chippenham, Wilts.; *Grove* (**62**) Dr Guy Blanchard of the University of Cambridge; *Hecla* (**73**) Charlie Brierley of Rochdale, Lancs.; Bill Forster; Dr Tim Mulligan of College Park, Md.; and Capt. John Rodgaard; *Hermione* (**63**) Steve Brotherton of Warrington; and John Roberts; *Heythrop* (**55**) Richard Green; *Isaac Sweers* (**74**) Eline Embrechts of Baden, Switzerland; Joop Romkema of Leeuwarden, the

Netherlands; J. van der Avert and Dr A. P. van Vliet of the Instituut voor Maritieme Historie, The Hague; *Jacob Jones* (**53**) Cdr E. A. Wilde Jr; *Leary* (**93**) Brigadier General John H. Morrison, Jr of McLean, Va., and Cdr E. A. Wilde, Jr; *Leopold* (**100**) CPO W. Scott Epperson USCG of Los Angeles, Calif., and Scott T. Price USCG of Washington, DC; *Martin* (**72**) Tom Barnes of Sutton-in-Ashfield, Notts.; Jill Barnett and Rear-Admiral J. W. D. Cook RN (Retd) of Farnham, Surrey; *Medway* (**64**) Lt Ron Wallingford RNVR of Southampton, Hants.; *Mimosa* (**61**) Charles Salou; *Montbretia* (**76**) Kontreadmiral G. A. Steimler KNM (Retd) (survivor) of Sandvika, Norway; *Naiad* (**54**) the late Vice-Admiral Sir Louis Le Bailly RN (survivor); *P615* (**84**) the late Vizeadmiral Horst von Schroeter; *Parramatta* (**42**) Dr Nicholas Lambert of Canberra, Australia; *Picotee* (**29**) Geoff Smith of Rotherham, S. Yorks.; *Polyanthus* (**87**) Dr Friedrich Curio of Ahorn bei Coburg, Germany and Guðmundur Helgason of Reykjavik, Iceland; *Salvia* (**44**) Richard Green of Burnaby, British Columbia; *Springbank* (**33**) Phillip Tatum of Beckenham, Kent; *Veteran* (**71**) Bill Ellis of Dulverton, Somerset; *Welshman* (**81**) interview with former crewmen of *U380* at UBAC (now DUBMA) in May 2001.

Finally, we would like to thank our families and friends past and present who have shared the journey over many years and through many vicissitudes, and who in their different ways have each helped bring the ship into harbour. Mention of friends of course puts each author in mind of the other, separated always by geography and occasionally by trenchant disagreement but forever joined by that which gave the project life and brought it to completion. *Dein wahrer Freund ist, wer dich sehn lässt deine Flecken und sie dir tilgen hilft, eh' Feinde sie entdecken.*

DANIEL MORGAN AND BRUCE TAYLOR
LONDON AND LOS ANGELES

Authors' Note

Citations from documents and reproductions of images held by The National Archives, Kew, London are Crown Copyright. Photos credited *IWM* are reproduced by permission of the Imperial War Museum, Lambeth, London. The copyright of much of the remainder rests either with their authors or their descendants. Citations from these and from books and articles are acknowledged by inclusion in the *Select Bibliography*, the list of *Sources* at the close of each entry and/or in the *Acknowledgements* above. Credits are given after each photo where it has been possible to establish either the source or the copyright with certainty. Extensive efforts have been made to locate copyright holders and these are invited to contact the authors with proof of copyright.

Abbreviations

1/c First Class (USN)
2/c Second Class (USN)
3/c Third Class (USN)
AA Anti-Aircraft
AB Able Seaman (RN)
Act. Acting (RN)
AMC armed merchant cruiser
AOB angle on the bow (relative inclination of the target)
AP Armour-Piercing (shells)
A/S Anti-Submarine
ATW ahead-throwing weapon (Hedgehog spigot mortar)
BAMA Bundesarchiv-Militärarchiv, Freiburg-in-Breisgau
B.d.U. *Befehlshaber der Unterseeboote*
BEF British Expeditionary Force
BEM British Empire Medal
BfZ Bibliothek für Zeitgeschichte, Stuttgart
bhp brake horsepower
BK Bundesarchiv, Koblenz
BS Battle Squadron (RN)
Capt. Captain
cbm cubic metres (of diesel fuel)
C.C. Capitaine de corvette (French navy); Capitano di corvetta (Italian navy)
C. de G. Croix de Guerre
Cdr Commander (RN or USN)
Cdre Commodore (RN)
CEA Chief Electrical Artificer (RN)
CERA Chief Engine Room Artificer (RN)
C.F. Capitaine de frégate (French navy)
Ch.Yeo.Sigs. Chief Yeoman of Signals (RN)
cm centimetre
CO Commanding Officer
Co. Company; County (Ireland)
CortDiv [Destroyer] Escort Division (USN)
CPO Chief Petty Officer
CS Cruiser Squadron (RN)
(D) Destroyers (RN)
dc depth charge(s)
DesRon Destroyer Squadron (USN)
DF Destroyer Flotilla (RN)
DP dual-purpose
DSC Distinguished Service Cross (RN)
DSO Distinguished Service Order (RN)
DUBMA Deutsches U-Boot Museum-Archiv (formerly U-Boot-Archiv), Cuxhaven-Altenbruch, Lower Saxony
(E) Engineering (RN)
EG Escort Group (RN/RCN)
Eng. English
ERA Engine Room Artificer (RN)

FAT *Federapparat-Torpedo*
F.d.U. *Führer der Unterseeboote*
ff following
Flt Lt Flight Lieutenant (RAF)
FNFL Forces Navales Françaises Libres
Fregkpt. Fregattenkapitän
ft feet
(G) Gunnery (RN)
G7a standard Kriegsmarine compressed-air torpedo
G7e standard Kriegsmarine electric torpedo
Ger. German
GMT Greenwich Mean Time
GNAT German Naval Acoustic Torpedo (the *Zaunkönig* acoustic homing torpedo)
GRT Gross Register Tons
HE High-Explosive (shells)
HF/DF (properly H/F D/F) High-Frequency Direction Finder/Finding
HHellMS His Hellenic Majesty's Ship
HM His Majesty's [ship]
HMAS His Majesty's Australian Ship
HMCS His Majesty's Canadian Ship
HMNZS His Majesty's New Zealand Ship
HMS His Majesty's Ship
HMSAS His Majesty's South African Ship
HMS/m His Majesty's Submarine
HMSO His/Her Majesty's Stationery Office
HMT His Majesty's Trawler
HNorMS His Norwegian Majesty's Ship (Royal Norwegian Navy in exile)
HrMs Hare Majesteits (KM)
IWM Imperial War Museum, London
I.WO *Erster Wachoffizier* ('First Watch Officer')
II.WO *Zweiter Wachoffizier* ('Second Watch Officer')
(jg) junior grade (USN)
Kapt.Lt Kapteinlöytnant (KNM)
Kapt.z.S. Kapitän zur See
KBF *Krasnoznamenny Baltiiskii Flot* (Red Banner Baltic Fleet, Soviet navy)
KCL, LHCMA King's College, London, Liddell Hart Centre for Military Archives
kg kilogram
kHz kilohertz
klt kapitan-leitenant (Soviet navy)
KM Koninklijke Marine (Royal Netherlands Navy)
Kmdt Kommandant
KNM Kongelige Norske Marine (Royal Norwegian Navy)
Korvkpt. Korvettenkapitän
Kptlt Kapitänleutnant

KTB   *Kriegstagebuch*
Ktz   Kapitein ter zee (KM)
LCT   Landing Craft (Tank)
L.I.   Leitende Ingenieur ('Chief Engineer')
lit.   literally
LST   Landing Ship (Tank)
Lt   Lieutenant (RN, USN; Löytnant in KNM)
Lt Cdr   Lieutenant Commander (RN/USN)
Lt (jg)   Lieutenant (junior grade) (USN)
Lt.z.S.   Leutnant zur See
LUT   *Lagenunabhängiger-Torpedo*
L.V.   Lieutenant de vaisseau (French navy)
m   metre
Mar.   Marine (Kriegsmarine)
mb   millibars (of barometric pressure)
MF   Minesweeping Flotilla (RN)
MG   machine gun(s)
MinRon   Mine Squadron (USN)
mm   millimetre
MM   Machinist's Mate (USN)
MN   Marine nationale (French navy); Merchant Navy (GB)
MOMP   Mid-Ocean Meeting Point
M.Qu.   Marine Quadrat
ms   manuscript
MS   Motor Ship
MTB   Motor Torpedo Boat
MY   Motor Yacht
n.   note
NAC   National Archives of Canada, Ottawa, Ont.
NA   National Archives, College Park, Md.
N.A.   Navio Auxiliar (Brazilian navy)
NEF   Newfoundland Escort Force (RCN)
NF   Navire Français
NHB   Naval Historical Branch, Ministry of Defence, Portsmouth, Hants. (formerly London)
NHC   Naval Historical Center, Washington, DC
NMM   National Maritime Museum, Greenwich, London
np   no place of publication stated
NS   *Nahschuss* (G7a and *Zaunkönig* torpedoes)
NZO   *Nachtzieloptik* (night binoculars)
OBE   Officer of the Order of the British Empire
Oblt   Oberleutnant
Oblt.z.S.   Oberleutnant zur See
OBV   ocean boarding vessel
OD   Ordinary Seaman (RN)
ORP   Okręt Rzeczypospolitej Polskiej ('Ship of the Polish Republic')
O.Sig.   Ordinary Signalman (RN)
pdr   pounder
PG   'Pinched German' (NHB/NARA archival abbreviation for Kriegsmarine documentation)
PO   Petty Officer
PoW   prisoner(s) of war
Q/mtre   Quartier-maître (French navy)
Qu.   Quadrat
RAAF   Royal Australian Air Force
RAF   Royal Air Force

RAN   Royal Australian Navy
RCAF   Royal Canadian Air Force
RCN   Royal Canadian Navy
RCNR   Royal Canadian Naval Reserve
RCNVR   Royal Canadian Naval Volunteer Reserve
RDF   Radio Direction Finding (radar)
Ret'd   Retired
Rev.   Reverend
RFA   Royal Fleet Auxiliary
RG   Record Group (NAC, NARA)
RMS   Royal Mail Ship
RN   Royal Navy
R.N.   Regia Navale (Italian navy)
RNASBR   Royal Naval Auxiliary Sick Berth Reserve
RNM   Royal Naval Museum, Portsmouth, Hants.
RNR   Royal Naval Reserve
RNSM   Royal Navy Submarine Museum, Gosport, Hants.
RNVR   Royal Naval Volunteer Reserve
RNZN   Royal New Zealand Navy
rpm   revolutions per minute
R.Smg.   Regia Sommergibile (Italian navy)
SANF   South African Naval Forces
SF   Submarine Flotilla (RN)
SG   Support Group (RN)
SHM   Service Historique de la Marine, Paris
SKL   Seekriegsleitung (German Naval War Staff)
SOE   Senior Officer of the Escort
SS   Steam Ship; *Schnellschuss* (G7a and *Zaunkönig* torpedoes)
st. l-t   starshii leitenant (Soviet navy)
Sub-Lt   Sub-Lieutenant (RN)
(T)   Torpedoes (RN)
T1   the compressed-air G7a torpedo
T2   the electric G7e torpedo
T3a   a development of the electric G7e torpedo
T4   the *Falke* acoustic torpedo
T5   the *Zaunkönig* acoustic homing torpedo
TCG   Türkiye Cumhuriyeti Gemisi ('Ship of the Turkish Republic')
Temp.   Temporary
TF   Task Force (USN)
TG   Task Group (USN)
TNA   The National Archives, Kew, London (formerly The Public Record Office)
TR   torpedo report
tt   torpedo tube(s)
USAAF   United States Army Air Forces
USCG   United States Coast Guard
USN   United States Navy
USS   United States Ship
UZO   *Überwasserzieloptik* (target bearing indicator)
VMF   *Voenno-Morskoi Flot* (Soviet navy)
WLEF   Western Local Escort Force (RCN)
WRNS   Women's Royal Naval Service
WS   *Weitschuss* (G7a and *Zaunkönig* torpedoes)
W/T   Wireless Telegraphy
yds   yards

Glossary

Action Stations In British and empire warships, the first state of combat readiness when an engagement is ongoing or believed to be imminent and requiring the entire crew to be at their posts and all hatches and watertight doors to be sealed; called *Gefechtsstationen* in German and translated as 'Battle Stations' in the KTB excerpts.

Aldis light *or* **lamp** A hand-held lamp used for morse signalling

Aphrodite German radar decoy introduced in September 1943 consisting of hydrogen-filled balloons to which four-metre strips of aluminium or tin foil were attached. Once launched they were intended to hover above the water secured by a sheet anchor.

Asdic Echo-location apparatus fitted in British and empire warships for purposes of submarine detection; known in the US Navy and generally since the Second World War as **Sonar**

Ato (also known as the T1) Kriegsmarine shorthand for the **G7a** torpedo powered by compressed air as distinct from the electric **G7e** (see **Eto**)

B-Dienst (*Beobachtung-Dienst* – 'Monitoring Service') The Kriegsmarine's radio monitoring and intelligence service

bearing The position of a ship or feature either relative to true north or as an angle from the observing vessel's head

beta In torpedo-aiming calculations the angle separating the target bearing at the time of launch and its anticipated point of interception; also known as the aim-off angle

Bolde, properly *Kobold* ('goblin'); known as *Bold* or *Pillenwerfer* ('pill-thrower') Calcium-zinc discharge that replicated the echo produced by an **Asdic** submarine contact by generating large masses of bubbles from the stern of the U-boat

Carley float Invertible liferaft in widespread use during the Second World War, composed of copper or steel tubing bent into an oval ring surrounded by kapok or cork and covered with a layer of waterproof canvas. The floor of the raft consisted of wood or webbing grating to which boxes containing paddles, water, rations and survival equipment were lashed. Survivors could either sit around the edge of the raft or cling to rope loops strung around its edge. The largest model could accommodate up to fifty men, half inside the raft and the rest holding onto the loops in the water.

CAT Counter-Acoustic Torpedo or Canadian Anti-Acoustic Torpedo device in the form of a towed array

Cruising Stations In British and empire warships, the third state of combat readiness, generally kept during daylight hours with a third of the crew at their posts

Defence Stations In British and empire warships, the second state of combat readiness, generally kept at night with half of the crew at their posts

draught (US: **draft**) The vertical distance between the waterline and the bottom of the hull (keel)

Echolot German echo-sounding device patented by the Atlas-Werke firm and used largely to measure the distance from keel to seabed in unfamiliar waters

eel(s) (*Aal/Aale* in German) U-boat slang for a torpedo of any sort

E-boat Allied term for the German motor torpedo boat (*S-Boot*)

Enigma Alternative name for the German *Schlüssel-M* electromechanical cipher machine used for encoding and decoding radio traffic, and by extension the entire Kriegsmarine enciphering system together with its intelligence-bearing product

Eto (also known as the T2, later variant T3a) Kriegsmarine shorthand for the electric **G7e** torpedo as distinct from the **G7a** which was powered by compressed air (see **Ato**)

Federapparat-Torpedo (**FAT** – 'spring apparatus'; erroneously *Flächenabsuchender-Torpedo* – 'shallow-searching torpedo') Torpedo design employed against large formations of ships which began with a preset straight run before pursuing a meandering trajectory of 800 or 1,600 metres with course alternations of 180 degrees

Flugabwehrkanonen (**Flak** – 'aircraft defence cannon'); also *Fliegerabwehrwaffen*, *Flawaffen* ('air-defence weapons') Anti-aircraft armament

Foxer British anti-acoustic torpedo device in the form of a towed array

FXR US anti-acoustic torpedo device in the form of a towed array

Gröner Recognition manual for the merchant fleets of the world compiled by Erich Gröner and standard issue aboard U-boats

Gruppenhorchgerät (**GHG** – 'group listening apparatus') The Kriegsmarine's standard hydrophone apparatus as developed by the Atlas-Werke company. In the case of U-boats it consisted of a cluster of sound-receiver diaphragms on the outer hull. Capable of picking up a surface vessel at a range of ten miles, further in the case of a convoy.

Hedgehog ahead-throwing weapon (**ATW**) British anti-submarine weapon introduced in 1942 and widely deployed in Allied escorts as a supplement to the depth charge. Hedgehog consisted of twenty-four contact-fuzed spigot mortar bomblets fired from spiked fittings which gave the weapon its name. The beginning of an important line of anti-submarine weapon development which included the Squid depth-charge mortar; see p. xxxi.

Heulboje ('whistling buoy') Term used by the *U-Boot-Waffe* to describe the Allied **Foxer**, **FXR** and **CAT** noise-making devices whose sound was likened to that of a nautical whistling buoy

High-Frequency Direction Finder/Finding (**HF/DF**, properly **H/F D/F**) British device introduced in 1942 for finding the direction of a radio source; deployed in Allied escorts, aircraft and some merchantmen for gaining directional or triangulation fixes on U-boats from their transmissions

Lage (abbreviated from *Lagenwinkel* – 'positional angle') In torpedo fire control, the relative inclination of the target to the U-boat (expressed in degrees); see p. xxiv

Luftzielsehrohr Sky search periscope; another name for the *Nachtzielsehrohr*

Metox U-boat radar-detection device, found ineffectual against the Allied Mk-III centimetric radar when this was introduced in the spring of 1943

Nachtzieloptik (NZO – 'night search optic') Target bearing indicator in the form of night binoculars; essentially another name for the *Überwasserzieloptik* (UZO) as used for surface attacks at night

Nachtzielsehrohr Night search periscope; another name for the *Luftzielsehrohr*

Nahschuss (NS – 'close fire') One of the three run settings of the **G7a** and *Zaunkönig* torpedoes. In the former case this involved setting the torpedo to run at 40 knots over 8,000 metres. In the latter case the setting was intended for use against retiring targets, being designed to pursue a straighter, less erratic track towards the target until it picked up a noise contact, altering course accordingly.

Naxos U-boat radar-detection device introduced in the autumn of 1943 and effective against both airborne and seaborne apparatus; the successor of the **Metox** device

patrolling station (zigzagging) Evasive manoeuvring performed both by warships and merchantmen, usually to a set though irregular pattern, intended to frustrate efforts by an attacking U-boat to take up a firing position

Pi-1 Detonator pistol fitted to the **G7a** and **G7e** torpedoes which allowed either contact or magnetic detonation

Pi-4 Detonator pistol fitted to the *Zaunkönig* acoustic homing torpedo

Pillenwerfer see **Bolde**

Runddipol ('round dipole') The antenna of the *Naxos* radar detector; it replaced the wooden Biscay Cross, a rudimentary device strung with wires which had to be dismantled before diving

Quadrat (**Qu.** or **M.Qu.** – '[marine] quadrant') At six miles on each side (36 square miles), the smallest of the four squares used in the Kriegsmarine's *Marine Quadratkarte* system and the main positioning data used in the logs; see pp. xxxiv–xxxv.

S-Boot (*Schnellboot* – 'fast boat') Kriegsmarine shorthand for the motor boat; German examples of the type were known as E-boats by the Allies

Schnellschuss (SS – 'quick fire') One of the three run settings of the **G7a** and **Zaunkönig** torpedoes. In the former case this meant setting the torpedo to its maximum speed of 44 knots over 6,000 metres. In the latter case this involved disarming the acoustic mechanism to permit the T5 to function like a conventional straight-running torpedo.

Schnorchel (called 'Schnorkel' by the RN, 'Snort' or 'Snorkel' by the USN) Valved air pipe and breathing apparatus protruding above the surface which permitted a U-boat both to recharge its batteries and thereby proceed underwater on diesel rather than electric power. Introduced operationally in the spring of 1944.

S-Gerät (*Sondergerät* – 'special apparatus' or *Such-Gerät* – 'search apparatus') A form of active sonar technology which enabled U-boats to detect minefields or targets; standard equipment on the Type-VII boats

Snowflake British illuminant introduced in late 1941 in the form of a magnesium flare discharged from the main armament before beginning a slow ascent by parachute; slowly replaced **Starshell**

Sonar The name given by the US Navy to echo-location technology and related shipborne apparatus installed for submarine detection; known as **Asdic** by the British

Starshell Illuminant in the form of a shell discharged from the main armament before beginning a slow descent by parachute; occasionally used as an incendiary and eventually replaced by **Snowflake**

Überwasserzieloptik (UZO – 'surface search optic') The main bridge target bearing indicator in the form of water- and pressure-resistant binoculars; connected to the *Vorhaltrechner* (torpedo data computer)

Very pistol Handheld gun designed to fire flares as a distress signal or for other signalling purposes at sea

Vorhaltrechner ('aim-off calculator') In torpedo fire control, the device which computed the correct aim-off the weapon and in its *Lage laufend* ('inclination running') mode could generate automatic adjustments to target range and inclination until firing; see p. xxiv.

Wanz, Wanze ('bug'; abbreviated from *Wellenanzeiger* – 'wave indicator') U-boat radar-warning device devised by the Hagenuk company; replaced the outdated **Metox** apparatus in the autumn of 1943

Weitschuss (WS – 'remote fire') One of the three run settings of the **G7a** and *Zaunkönig* torpedoes. In the former case this meant setting the torpedo to its maximum possible range of 12,500 metres at a speed of 30 knots. In the latter case the torpedo was set to assume a labile or erratic snaking track towards its target until it picked up a noise contact, altering course accordingly.

Weyer (*Weyers Taschenbuch der Kriegsflotten*) Recognition manual for the warships of the world edited by Bruno Weyer from 1900 to 1933; standard issue aboard U-boats

Zaunkönig ('wren'; also known as the T5; called GNAT by the Allies) Acoustic homing torpedo introduced in the autumn of 1943; see pp. xxvi–xxvii and HMCS *St Croix* (**86**)

zigzagging *see* **patrolling station**

Foreword

Daniel Morgan and Bruce Taylor have spent many years assembling a significant corpus of documentation on the sinking of Allied warships by German U-boats. A glance at the Acknowledgements section of their work reveals a long list of contributors that not only encompasses some of those who participated in the events related but also staff in the key German and Allied naval archives that make their collections available to researchers, along with many individuals who have helped identify details or provided information on those U-boat attacks which resulted in the loss of Allied warships. Among these names can be found my own.

In the late 1940s I provided assistance to a former German naval officer, Günter Hessler, who was then engaged in writing a history of the U-Boat War from 1939 to 1945 on behalf of the British Admiralty.[1] This involved extensive use of the war diaries of the *Befehlshaber der Unterseeboote* (Commander-in-Chief Submarines – B.d.U.) from which I was able to extract information on successes reported by U-boats against both warships and merchantmen. I was then allowed to compare this data with *B.R. 1337 (Restricted): British and Foreign Merchant Vessels Lost or Damaged by Enemy Action during the Second World War*, issued by the Admiralty's Naval Staff (Trade Division) on 1 October 1945. Together with access to other printed and archival material and the assistance of former U-boat men along with numerous sailors, seamen and marine enthusiasts from many countries, this research formed the basis of my *Die U-Boot-Erfolge der Achsenmächte, 1939–1945* published in 1968.[2] A revised version was published in 1993 under the title *Axis Submarine Successes of World War Two* by Greenhill Publishing in London and Naval Institute Press in Annapolis, with a further revision offered by the same houses in 1999. Together, these volumes have largely made good what was initially an unsatisfactory listing of warship losses.

Daniel Morgan and Bruce Taylor have now completed their own study and in so doing have closed a significant gap in the documentation relating to U-boat successes against warships. Drawing on archives now accessible in Germany, the United Kingdom, the United States, Canada and a number of other Allied nations, they have assembled a huge body of material relating to the sinking of warships by the *U-Boot-Waffe*. As well as analysing this material, the authors have reproduced and translated into English the corresponding excerpts from the surviving U-boat war diaries. The result is a detailed account of attacks on warships, including all relevant technical data, the background of

the attack and the sinking of each vessel, drawing not only on official reports but also on the testimony of survivors. Each entry is rounded off by a list of sources and supplementary literature.

The work begins in 1939 with the sinkings of the British aircraft carrier *Courageous* on 17 November and the battleship *Royal Oak* on 14 October. Twenty sinkings are then covered in 1940, including two French submarines in addition to the British warships lost. In 1941 twenty-three losses are detailed, including one Australian, one Canadian, one Norwegian and one US warship, as well as two Soviet submarines. Thirty-six sinkings are analysed in 1942, with the victims here including three Canadian, two Free French, one Dutch, one Norwegian and six American warships, together with a third Soviet submarine. For 1943 fourteen vessels are treated, including one Dutch, one Canadian, and five American, while in 1944 a further fifteen are analysed, including three Canadian and three American before the main body of the work ends with the sinking of the British frigate *Bullen* on 9 December 1944.

The inclusion of a particular warship sinking in the main part of this book is dependent on the survival of the U-boat war diary in question (lacking towards the end of the war or when the U-boat was itself sunk during the same cruise) and the warship meeting certain size and type criteria. Although the main body of the work does not therefore cover every U-boat warship sinking, those vessels excluded are listed separately in a Gazetteer. For these vessels and for those damaged by U-boat but not sunk, the field therefore remains open, as indeed it does for those warships sunk by submarines of the Finnish, Italian and Japanese navies. Irrespective of these exclusions, this very comprehensive and well-documented volume with its detailed source listings represents a key addition to the historiographical canon. It also contains a number of important corrections to existing publications, such as the entry for the mysterious sinking of the British corvette *Gladiolus* in the battle for convoy SC48. Was she lost to a torpedo fired by *U553*, *U558* or *U432*? Or – another possibility – did she disappear without trace as a result of an unexplained accident?

In short, we can only congratulate the authors on their accomplishment in this book, while also extending our thanks to its many contributors for their invaluable assistance.

JÜRGEN ROHWER
WEINSTADT, BADEN-WÜRTTEMBERG

---

1   Fregkpt. Günter Hessler, *The U-Boat War in the Atlantic, 1939–1945* (3 vols, London: HMSO, 1989).
2   Munich: J. F. Lehmanns Verlag, 1968.

Introduction

The present work describes the sinking of individual warships by the *U-Boot-Waffe* during the Second World War. Whereas a majority of these sinkings have hitherto been approached largely from the Allied point of view, this study is based on original research in both primary and secondary sources from all of the combatants involved, and where possible using both official and private material. In each case the key document is the log or war diary (*Kriegstagebuch* – KTB) of the attacking U-boat, and great care has been taken not only in the layout, translation and annotation of the relevant excerpts but in the comparison of these with Allied sources in an effort to provide as clear an interpretation of events as permitted by the evidence. If in doing so this book also reveals something of the nature of U-boat operations and the harsh realities of submarine warfare as it was visited on the men and vessels of all sides, then it will have served its purpose.

Scope of the work

The main body of this volume contains 109 entries, one of which (**19**) concerns the destruction by *U99* of HM armed merchant cruisers *Laurentic* and *Patroclus* in the same engagement, meaning that a total of 110 warship sinkings receive detailed treatment in its pages. The criteria for according a vessel a full entry is the survival of the U-boat log recording the sinking of

> *either* (*a*) a surface unit in excess of approximately 600 tons' displacement (excluding trawlers, navy tankers, landing ships, troop transports and miscellaneous vessels)
> *or* (*b*) a submarine of whatever size.

Those sinkings not meeting these criteria are listed in the Gazetteer, which together with the main entries means that a total of 246 vessels are treated in this volume. Although practically all of the units covered belonged to the Allied cause during the Second World War, three did not: they are the Spanish Republican submarine *C3*, torpedoed by *U34* in December 1936 and included as the first entry in the Gazetteer (**G1**), and the Vichy French submarine *Sfax* and naval tanker *Rhône*, sunk in error by *U37* in the same engagement in December 1940 (**21 and G6**). The rest provide a cross-section of fighting ships, of campaigns and theatres, and like these three of death and survival against the relentless backdrop of sea and ocean.

I   The sources

The capture of German naval records

With the war at sea won and the Allies sweeping through Germany, one of the key objectives of the British Admiralty in the spring of 1945 was the capture of high-grade naval intelligence.[1] Prior to the invasion of

Normandy it had been agreed with the United States that such material would fall under joint US and British ownership but be held in custody by the Admiralty's Naval Intelligence Division, Section 24 (NID 24). This in turn led to the formation of a joint committee, the Target Intelligence Committee (TICOM), which was charged with identifying the key locations of material in all military areas and intercepting personnel and documentation believed to be evacuating Berlin before the Allied advance. From the naval perspective the breakthrough came on 10 April when a tip-off led a small naval intelligence team (NTS 55) commanded by Lt Cdr T. J. Glanville RNVR to a building occupied by the German Naval War Staff (*Seekriegsleitung* – SKL) in Bad Sulza, twenty miles east of Weimar. The target, a former technical college not on TICOM's list, turned out to be one of many such occupied by the SKL and at first promised little, with 'all the rooms ankle-deep in papers, broken glass, clothes and sundry other items. In the cellar and in the courtyard there was evidence of the burning of documents.' However, among the wreckage a charred piece of paper was found providing a list of other SKL outposts, including one by the name of Tambach. It was to be a critical find.

The most obvious Tambach, a town in nearby Thuringia, gave no sign of having been an SKL outpost. However, perusal of a cultural gazetteer turned up another possibility: a remote settlement overlooked by a castle near Coburg in Bavaria. The team arrived shortly before nightfall on 25 April 1945 to find that while Coburg had been occupied by the Americans two weeks before, Tambach and its castle had escaped scrutiny. Entering the castle unannounced, Glanville and his team first accepted the surrender of a bewildered German naval rating and then performed a cursory search which revealed a haul beyond their wildest dreams. They had captured, virtually intact, the central archive of the German navy from 1850 to 1945, the records having been removed from Berlin in November 1943 as the Allied blitz intensified. Despite the protestations of Admiral Walter Gladisch, the senior German naval officer present, that the records had been spared destruction because 'Dönitz had ordered they be preserved and handed over to the Allies as evidence that the Kriegsmarine had acted throughout in accordance with humanitarian principles and the traditions of the sea', the preservation of the material was by no means a *fait accompli* and Glanville had to take urgent steps to secure the trove with the few men at his disposal. Not only had Gladisch removed certain classified papers to his headquarters in a nearby farmhouse for protection, but several SKL women auxiliaries had attempted to burn some records. Although this fire was extinguished Glanville feared further such attempts with the possible assistance of SS units still believed to be in the area. A battalion of troops was deployed

1   See R. M. Coppock, *Capture of the German Naval Archive at Tambach in 1945* (NHB, T.57475, 1995), Howard M. Ehrmann, 'The German Naval Archives (Tambach)' in Robert Wolfe, ed., *Captured German and Related Records: A Naval Archives Conference* (Athens, Ohio: Ohio University Press, 1974), pp. 157–72, and Paul Heinsius, „Der Verbleib des Aktenmaterials der deutschen Kriegsmarine. Das ehemalige Marinearchiv, Marinegerichtsakten und Personalakten, Krankenakten sowie Druckschriften und Bibliotheken" in *Der Archivar* VIII (April 1955), pp. 75–86.

The page from Korvkpt. Ernst-August Rehwinkel's log covering *U578*'s attack on the USS *Jacob Jones* on 28 February 1942 (**53**), together with the torpedo report (*Schussmeldung*) corresponding to the hits which sank her. *NHB*

The Kriegstagebücher

to guard the castle and in an operation supervised by officers from the Admiralty's Naval Intelligence Division – including one Cdr Ian Fleming RNVR who later found fame as an author – the documentation from the Third Reich was packed into beer crates and transported to Britain in the first few weeks of May. Such was the volume of material that the packing of the rest took several more months.

By July 1947 an exhaustive cataloguing and microfilming process led by the US Navy's Office of Naval Intelligence at 20 Grosvenor Square in London had resulted in the production of several thousand miles of film catalogued under the NID's archival acronym PG – 'Pinched German'. Copies were initially held by the US National Archives and the British Admiralty. Following a series of formal requests for restitution by the Federal German government, the original documentation was returned to Germany between 1959 and 1977, the documents relating to the *U-Boot-Waffe* being among the last to be repatriated. The original *Kriegstagebücher* are now housed in the Bundesarchiv-Militärarchiv in Freiburg-in-Breisgau, Baden-Württemberg where they are available for consultation by historians and researchers.

The *Kriegstagebücher* represent the main record produced by individual units such as U-boats and surface vessels as well as high-command organisations such as the *Seekriegsleitung*, the *Befehlshaber der Unterseeboote* (Commander-in-Chief Submarines – B.d.U.) and such local operational command centres as *Führer der Unterseeboote Norwegen* (Commander of Submarines Norway – F.d.U. Norwegen), etc. The KTBs of the various shore commands offer a wider context of events in the war at sea, but for the historian researching the sinking of Allied warships by submarines the key sources are those from individual U-boats, which were generated by each cruise and then archived ashore on completion of the operation. To these can be added a number of ancillary documents that are often though not always appended to the KTB. These include navigational track charts (*Wegekarten*), attack sketches (*Gefechtsskizzen* or *Angriffsskizzen*), listings of key incoming and outgoing radio signals (*Funkkladdenauszüge*), and above all the torpedo reports (*Schussmeldungen*) which were prepared by the torpedo officer, normally the First Watch Officer (*Erster Wachoffizier* – I.WO). The torpedo reports are occasionally found together with their respective KTBs but can otherwise be consulted in the Bibliothek für Zeitgeschichte in Stuttgart, though in this case the collection extends only to April 1943. The inconsistency of this ancillary material apart, the only significant gaps in this corpus of material before December 1944 are those resulting from the loss of the boat together with the KTB of the cruise in question, an increasingly common state of affairs as the war went on. After December 1944 German recordkeeping and archiving gradually breaks down and the survival of material becomes much more sporadic. Although the KTBs for certain command centres such as *F.d.U. Norwegen* survive as late as April 1945, the same is not true of B.d.U. itself for which no records are extant after 15 January 1945. Nor is it true of those for individual U-boats, which begin to peter out in December 1944 and with a few exceptions are unavailable after January 1945. But for these twin circumstances of war attrition and organisational disintegration this book might have contained 138 full-length entries rather than 109.[2]

Unlike the U-boat KTBs of the Great War which were set down in the challenging *Fraktur* (lit. 'broken') script, those for 1939–1945 were submitted in typescript on pre-printed sheets – a great advance in legibility, whatever the textual implications of a fair copy. The logs are in a three-column format with heads set in Blackletter type in which the salient aspects of each cruise are usually commented on in a chronological sequence indicated in the left-hand column (*Datum und Uhrzeit* – 'Date, time'), from sailing (or earlier) to docking at the end of the cruise. In the next column the KTB provides regular four-hour positional data (using the Kriegsmarine's quadrant system) together with natural conditions summarised in the column title: *Angabe des Ortes, Wind, Wetter, Seegang, Beleuchtung, Sichtigkeit der Luft, Mondschein usw.* ('Details of position, wind, weather, sea, light, visibility, moonlight, etc.').[3] The third column, the most important, was simply labelled *Vorkommnisse* – 'Incidents' – and frequently offers a detailed narrative of events supported by extensive data. More detail on the content and translation of these columns can be found in Reading the *Kriegstagebücher*.

Although various officers contributed data to a U-boat KTB – including the navigator, radio officer, supply officer and torpedo officer, each of whom kept their own logs – the final draft for the cruise in question was composed by the commanding officer (*Kommandant*) who placed the impress of his character on it and held sole responsibility for its content. A KTB might therefore range in tone from the prolixities of one Otto – Schuhart, vanquisher of HMS *Courageous* (**1**) – to the clipped phrasing of another – Kretschmer, 'Silent Otto' – who accounted for HMSs *Daring* (**4**), *Laurentic* and *Patroclus* (**19**) and *Forfar* (**20**). However, the burden of a commander's responsibility was constant and is reflected in his signature, often found at the end of each day's narrative of the cruise, as well as in the frequent use of

the first person singular in addition to the first person plural. Phrases such as 'I go to 160 m' in the case of a boat diving or 'I fire a spread of three torpedoes' in the event of a surfaced attack at night (when the torpedo officer would in fact be doing the firing) are common and reflect the commander's sense of his vessel as an extension of his will. In the way of submarine warfare, the logs also reflect the fact that he was frequently the only member of the crew with any visual record of events and consequently the only individual aboard who could regard himself as being in full possession of the evidence, such as it was. Submitted to B.d.U. for scrutiny and copied for a variety of other parties such as the parent flotilla, U-Boat Operations Division and the *Seekriegsleitung*, the KTB was the critical element in the review of a U-boat patrol and the evaluation of its commander.

The original diary was kept in manuscript and then typed up either on return to harbour, or – particularly later in the war, when U-boats spent many monotonous days submerged to avoid air attack – towards the end of the cruise itself. It should be noted that the final versions are not free of occasional handwritten amendments since a review of the fair typescript would often prompt the commander to make corrections or amendments in pen or pencil. Regrettably, archivists working on the originals in London after the war added their own marginalia and it is not always easy to distinguish between contemporaneous and subsequent additions. The KTB describing the sinking of HMS *Royal Oak* (**2**) by *U47* is a case in point, containing as it does a variety of marginal additions which may represent any combination of Kptlt Günther Prien himself, B.d.U. Operations staff and post-war archivists. All such annotations are captured in the translations that follow.

The language used in the KTBs is standard High German. Differences in individual compositional styles aside, a majority of the text employs the past tense as well as the terse use of past participles, e.g. 'Surfaced.' However, this often changes to the present tense during attack sequences with many commanders adopting a stream of consciousness narration that reflects the heightened state of the crew as a whole. The following example comes from Kptlt Otto Schuhart's log of the sinking of the *Courageous* (**1**):

> Gradually, and keeping close watch all the while, we get closer. I estimate her to be proceeding at about medium speed. Air escort no longer visible; I look equally in vain for an outlying destroyer escort. The close escort is now evident: a destroyer ahead, another astern, and one on each side.

An unusual deviation from these norms appears in Kptlt Siegfried Strelow's log of the sinking of HMS *Leda* (**69**) where the use of the pluperfect underlines the retrospective nature of KTB composition:

> During the previous night's shadowing I had come to the conclusion that the relatively bright night-time conditions […] and the very strong side and forward escort made a surface attack impossible.

Although often referred to as 'logs' in this book, the U-boat KTBs therefore offer rather more information than might be expected of an ordinary ship's deck log, and indeed rather more information than could be cogitated and set down within the immediate aftermath of the events recorded. This state of affairs, and the sense in which the KTBs often represent an evolved account of events based on subsequent information and assessment, in turn raises problems of a textual nature where their interpretation is concerned. More on this below.

---

2   This number of 138 plainly excludes those ships which would in any case have been omitted from the main part of the book by reason of size or type; see p. xiv. The twenty-eight eligible vessels for which no KTB record survives are captured in the Gazetteer.

3 From the Autumn of 1943 a number of KTBs have the head of the second column abbreviated to *Ort, Wetter* ('Position, weather'). The first instance of this in this volume comes in *U952*'s log of the sinking of HMS *Polyanthus* (**87**) on 20 September 1943. In the interests of consistency none of the entries concerned have been modified to reflect this change.

The Kriegstagebücher *as source material*

From 1945 the KTBs provided the Allies with a comprehensive body of material that permitted a much fuller appreciation of the war at sea than could ever have been gleaned from Allied sources alone. In particular, they formed the basis for detailed analysis of key incidents and events deemed to be of national importance by the successor body to NID 24, the Admiralty's Foreign Documents Section – a service also performed for foreign governments. In the late 1940s assistance was received from German archival and naval specialists, notably Fregkpt. Günter Hessler (decorated commander of *U107* in which he sank HMSs *Crispin* and *Manistee* (**22** and **23**) and son-in-law of the wartime head of the *U-Boot-Waffe*, Karl Dönitz), the senior naval archivist Korvkpt. Peter Handel-Mazetti, and a civilian counterpart, Walther Pfeiffer, whose pencilled marginalia pre-dating the microfilming process survives on many KTBs. The legacy of Hessler's involvement was *The U-Boat War in the Atlantic, 1939–1945*, eventually published in 1989.[4]

With the release of the KTBs into the public domain after declassification by the British in 1978, notably through the US National Archives at College Park, Maryland, historians and researchers were able to begin the process of sifting through the many thousands of attacks made by the 1,100 U-boats that participated in the Second World War.[5] Over the following decades groundbreaking work on U-boat operations was carried out by a former naval officer, Jürgen Rohwer, in collaboration with historians and archivists from all the Allied nations. In 1968 Rohwer published the fruit of this research in *Die U-Boot-Erfolge der Achsenmächte, 1939–1945*, translated into English as *Axis Submarine Successes of World War Two* in 1983.[6] Revised in 1999, this volume lists chronologically and by theatre of operations every Axis submarine attack delivered by torpedo or gunfire. In recent years work on the KTBs has yielded other important contributions, including Kenneth Wynn's two-volume *U-Boat Operations of the Second World War* (1997–8) which provides a digest of every U-boat cruise, and Rainer Busch and Hans-Joachim Röll's five-volume *Der U-Boot Krieg, 1939–1945* (1996–2003), volume III of which tabulates sinkings by individual U-boat.[7] Other studies have drawn on the KTBs to examine campaigns in the various theatres including the eastern seaboard of the United States and Canada, the Caribbean, the Mediterranean, the Arctic, the Baltic and the Indian Ocean.[8] KTB extracts from individual boats and higher commands can

be found on a number of websites, including uboat.net, ubootwaffe. net and uboatarchive.net, the latter (at the time of writing) offering a valuable introduction to the *Kriegstagebuch* and its contents as well as the translation of several excerpts.

In contrast to the Allied side (see below), personal memoirs, letters and diaries make up a comparatively insignificant part of the German source material for this book, to which, post-war circumstances apart, the reduced number of men who served in the *U-Boot-Waffe* and their terrible attrition provides a ready explanation, quite apart from the fact that keeping a diary was a court-martial offence. Much of the available personal material is held at Horst Bredow's remarkable Deutsches U-Boot Museum-Archiv (formerly the U-Boot Archiv) at Cuxhaven-Altenbruch in northern Germany.

Allied sources

Where the Allied side is concerned, the principal source of information rests in the official enquiry which almost always followed the sinking, notable exceptions being HMSs *Dunedin* and *Eagle* (**40** and **65**) for which boards of enquiry seem never to have been convened, and the Soviet entries (*M-99*, *M-94* and *M-175*, **27**, **28** and **45**) which are based on material contained in secondary sources. Where applicable, the official enquiries usually involved detailed questioning of the surviving officers together with senior ratings or enlisted men until a full picture had been formed of the attack, of the measures taken to save the vessel and then abandon her, and of the fate of her company, though this last was never the first priority. In cases of a loss on convoy duty the senior officer of the escort would also be questioned as to the dispositions of his command at the time of the attack and the steps taken to engage the perpetrator. The commanders and officers of ships sailing in company would also be summoned as witnesses as circumstances permitted. The aim was not only to establish the state of readiness and efficiency of officers and men but to gather information about the enemy and make recommendations for future procedure and modifications of a technical and tactical nature. These sources, which are sometimes very extensive, can be supplemented by the reports, letters, memoirs and published accounts of the participants which form an important prop in building a picture of events, particularly from the human perspective which was never a priority of the official enquiry. Often prepared many years or decades after the fact, these private records are certainly more reasoned and ordered in their perceptions but generally less accurate to the moment in their detail or emotional tone. The survival of this material on the Allied side, which is voluminous in the case of some sinkings, contrasts strongly with the situation on the German side where comparable sources are for various reasons (discussed above) few and far between. Taken all round, and subject to the analysis below, the KTBs therefore have an immediacy which

---

4 Three vols, London: HMSO, 1989.

5 See Timothy P. Mulligan, *Guides to the Microfilmed Records of the German Navy, 1850–1945*, No. 2: *Records Relating to U-Boat Warfare, 1939–1945* (Washington, D.C.: National Archives and Records Administration, 1985).

6 Munich: J. F. Lehmanns Verlag, 1968; London/Annapolis, Md.: Greenhill Books/Naval Institute Press, 1983.

7 Respectively 2 vols, London: Chatham Publishing, 1997–8, and 5 vols, Hamburg: Mittler, 1996–2003.

8 Homer H. Hickam, *Torpedo Junction: U-Boat War off America's East Coast* (Annapolis, Md.: Naval Institute Press, 1989); Michael Gannon, *Operation Drumbeat: The Dramatic True Story of Germany's First U-Boat Attacks along the American Coast in World War II* (New York: Harper & Row, 1990); Michael L. Hadley, *U-Boats against Canada: German Submarines in Canadian Waters* (Kingston, Ont., and Montreal: McGill-Queen's University Press, 1985); Marc Milner, *North Atlantic Run: The Royal Canadian Navy and the Battle for the Convoys* (Toronto: University of Toronto Press, 1985); Gaylord T. M. Kelshall,

The U-Boat War in the Caribbean (Port of Spain, Trinidad: Paria, 1988); Lawrence Paterson, *U-Boats in the Mediterranean, 1941–1944* (Annapolis, Md.: Naval Institute Press, 2007); Richard Woodman, *Arctic Convoys, 1941–1945* (London: John Murray, 1996); Vice-Admiral Sir Ian Campbell and Capt. Donald Macintyre, *The Kola Run* (London: Frederick Muller, 1958); Miroslav Morozov, *Podvodniye lodki VMF SSSR v velikoi otetchestvennoi voine 1941–1945. Part I: Krasnoznammenny Baltiiskii Flot: Letopis boevykh pokhodov* (Moscow: Izdatel'stvo Poligon, 2001); and Lawrence Paterson, *Hitler's Grey Wolves: U-Boats in the Indian Ocean* (London: Greenhill Books, 2004).

is necessarily lacking in most of the official Allied documentation, though much of the human drama of each sinking reposes in the personal records of the participants, often penned with the sobriety and perspective that only time and age can bring.

Problems of interpretation

Despite what is often an abundance of material from both sides and the broad concurrence of German and Allied primary sources in the case of many sinkings, a number of the entries in this book pose as many questions as they answer. In particular, comparison of sources frequently throws up significant discrepancies in data where individual attacks are concerned and occasionally with respect to the identity of the perpetrator. What is the nature of these discrepancies and what do they tell us about the material and its authors?

Errors of observation and memory are hardly to be avoided in any primary account of military conflict. The chaotic nature of battle, the confusion and time compression frequently experienced by those recalling momentous events and the impossibility of compiling an accurate record in the face of the enemy are problems common to any combat situation, and the Second World War at sea is no exception. In the case of the Allies, the errors to be found in many sinking accounts can be attributed to 'bewildered confusion' as most of the attacks analysed in this volume came unheralded, giving the victims a significantly narrower grasp of the context of events than their attacker. On the other hand, a U-boat commander's appreciation of the state of his victim after he had struck her was often very limited and frequently non-existent, and those studying U-boat attacks must prepare themselves for a shift in the relative value of the source material from the perpetrator to the victim once the torpedo has found its mark.

For all this, it is clear that errors are more prevalent on the German side, and not simply because the KTBs had a single author whereas Allied records usually (though not always) offer the perspective of several witnesses, either from the vessel attacked or from ships in company. Taken as a whole, submarine records are constrained by the fact that attacks were often delivered while the vessel was either fully or partially submerged (i.e. at periscope depth). In the former case the commander was reliant solely on acoustic data, whether gathered by hydrophone apparatus and interpreted by his radio staff or simply with the benefit of his own ears. Hydrophone and naked aural data provided both tactical and 'chronicling' information to the commander, but acoustic data often lent itself to misinterpretation as is evident in many attacks with the *Zaunkönig* homing torpedo (see below). Even at periscope depth the submarine's 'eye on the world' was often a very limited one, the apparatus providing a view of events to a single observer through a magnifying lens that was frequently washed down in the prevailing swell or as a consequence of poor trim. Then there was the hazard of periscope misting as during *U431*'s attack on HrMs *Isaac Sweers* (**74**) when detailed observation proved impossible. Even when surfaced, for example during a night attack on a convoy, a U-boat would be able to count on just six pairs of eyes (of which four pairs scanned a particular 90-degree section of the horizon) against the dozens that a surface escort might have in place. This inequality was accentuated by the fact that the superior height of a surface vessel allowed for a greater visual range and ensured that lookouts were much less likely to be hindered by spray and waves than their U-boat counterparts. Though galling, this inferior vantage point was the price for the benefit of concealment offered by the U-boat's low silhouette and ability to submerge, together with the tactical advantage of surprise which is the defining characteristic of submarine warfare. Not for nothing did the Royal Navy Submarine Service adopt the motto *Veniat non videor* – 'We come unseen'.

The U-boat KTBs also contain errors beyond those of a purely observational nature. Simple typographical errors are common, the result of carelessness either by the commander or his typist. Torpedo firing data is often incorrectly entered, as revealed by comparisons with torpedo reports for the same incident. Data provided to the commanding officer by the navigator such as the marine quadrant would also occasionally be in error, and even where positions were deemed to be correct at the time of entry subsequent amendments were common; Kptlt Joachim Preuss's KTB for the attack on HMS *Salvia* (**44**) is a case in point, a series of reassessments in the day or so after the event placing the sinking twenty-six miles west of the position originally recorded. However, in this respect it should be noted that the recorded positions of even surface vessels could frequently be fifty or more miles out after weeks at sea in the Atlantic – see HMS *Camito* (**25**) – meaning that the sinking coordinates for any warship lost on the high seas should be regarded as conjectural at best, whichever side's data is taken.

Discrepancies between German and Allied accounts in this volume are treated on a case-by-case basis. Where a log appears to be in error, this is pointed out in the notes or in the supporting essays. As a rule, the Allied version of events is given priority over the German where separate Allied reports agree the point. Often, however, the information comes uncorroborated from the KTB alone. In cases such as the sinking of the decoy ship USS *Atik* (**57**), lost with all hands after a prolonged engagement with *U123*, the KTB is the only record of the sinking. But occasionally there are instances such as HMS *Gladiolus* (**35**) in which the victim disappeared without trace and the KTB data from as many as three U-boats is so slender and obscured as to provide no firm basis for drawing conclusions on the sinking or even the identity of the perpetrator or perpetrators.

Textual issues and the 'a posteriori' entry

Sometimes problems of interpretation extend beyond inaccuracy and discrepancy in observation and recordkeeping to the structure and preparation of the KTB itself, for the U-boat *Kriegstagebücher* were not logs in the sense of a sequential and above all contemporaneous record. Rather, they were discursive documents, for the most part set down chronologically but necessarily prepared by the commander at some remove from the events described and on the basis of collated data and evidently with the benefit of hindsight. To this can be added the fact that the KTBs as they have come down to us are not original documents *per se* but fair copies typed up and annotated at the end of the cruise in question on the basis of an assessment of the entire operation and its permutations. The textual issues implied by this state of affairs are critical to any sober assessment of the KTBs and their value as evidence, whether taken as a whole or in the context of a given episode such as the individual sinkings covered in this book. This is not to question the worth of the KTBs as source material, but as with any documentation those handling it should be mindful of the circumstances under which it was composed and the form in which it has come down to us. It should be stated that most of the excerpts reproduced in this book show no overt sign of subsequent amendment and give every indication of being a faithful record and description of events, but there are sufficient indications to suppose that much subsequent information and interpretation was seamlessly worked into the final versions. Plainly, some commanders took greater care or showed greater competence or integrity in this than others while many are perfectly candid in their use of subsequent data. A straightforward example of what might be called an *a posteriori* entry – i.e. the tendency of a commander to inform or modify his log on the basis of subsequent data or assessment – comes in Kptlt Hans Heidtmann's record of *U559*'s attack on HMAS *Parramatta* (**42**). His entry for 0012 on 27 November 1941 opens as follows: 'Spread of three torpedoes fired at both vessels; inclination 80°, enemy speed 8 knots, range 2,000 m. All miss. This is inexplicable as the next attack with just a single torpedo involves the same coordinates and this hits from 1,500 m.'

Often, as here, the later interpretation is acknowledged and its permutations confined to a simple reassessment of the event under review. On other occasions information subsequently obtained is used to fill in gaps or correct errors, as in Kptlt Hans Cohausz's log for the sinking of HMS *Andania* (**10**) which evidently began by identifying his victim as the liner *Scythia* but adjusts this following a signal from B.d.U. containing the correct information. There are cases, however, when subsequent data is used in a much more contrived way. An example comes in one of the three KTB excerpts included in the entry for HMS *Gladiolus* (**35**), that of Oblt.z.S. Heinz-Otto Schultze of *U432*. His entry for 0346 on 17 October 1941 contains the following *a posteriori* deduction based on cogitations at least a day after that time:

> 25 sec. after our first torpedo hits (or 2 min. 55 sec. after this torpedo is fired) there is a detonation against a steamer in the column beyond the one we first attacked. I initially considered this to be a hit scored by another boat because my double salvo unquestionably missed its intended target. Therefore <u>no further observations made</u> and no mention of this in my W/T transmission reporting our successes [i.e. on the 18th, almost a day after this entry]. But subsequent assessment of the torpedo data led us to conclude that one of the eels [i.e. torpedoes] from our double salvo probably went on to hit this other ship fortuitously. Whether or not it actually was our hit or that of another boat should be easy enough to establish upon return to base.

Plainly, reconsideration by Schultze of his own firing data and angles together with the absence of any reported attack by another boat in the intervening period made him confident of putting in a follow-up claim. However, there are also cases in which the *a posteriori* nature of composition is so pervasive as to cloud the entire account of an event. The most singular example in this volume is contained in the excerpt from *U652* which describes the loss of HMS *Jaguar* (**56**) in March 1942. Here Oblt.z.S. Georg-Werner Fraatz provides what at first glance would appear a straightforward description of events. On closer inspection, however, Fraatz's repeated but inconsistent overlaying of present events with *ex post facto* rationalisation makes it almost impossible to follow or even reconstruct the exact train of events as experienced by him, to separate recorded fact from subsequent deduction.

Tonnage and exaggeration

As discussed, although some of the data was supplied by his subordinate officers, the commander had sole responsibility for the content of his KTB which loomed large in the evaluation of his performance on his return to port. The vast majority of front-line cruises concluded in a debrief by the Flotilla Commander, a senior member of B.d.U. Operations, and usually when the U-boat high command was based at Kernevel near Lorient, by the *Befehlshaber der Unterseeboote* himself, Karl Dönitz. Since this process required the KTB to be gone through in painstaking detail it can be supposed that the incentive to put a positive gloss on events must have been considerable, with tonnage exaggeration the readiest means of doing so.

In the introduction to his *Axis Submarine Successes of World War Two* Professor Jürgen Rohwer addresses the issue of inflated data for both the *U-Boot-Waffe* and other submarine services of the era. Disputing the notion that submarine commanders routinely exaggerated sinking reports, he argues that 'gross errors' were relatively unusual while misinterpretation of acoustic phenomena was often the cause of sinkings being recorded where none took place. The latter point is not disputed, nor was this problem unique to the *U-Boot-Waffe*: in the later stages of the war in the Pacific the US Submarine Service ceased giving credit for sinkings based on acoustic data alone. As any reader of the later entries in this volume will appreciate, German acoustic torpedo technology was plagued by persistent faults, among them the tendency of torpedoes to explode in the wake of their targets, with many a false sinking being recorded in consequence.

However, Rohwer also gives the U-boat commanders the benefit of the doubt where the recording of their victims' tonnage is concerned, observing that 'most such reports and overestimates resulted primarily from the difficult external circumstances surrounding an attack and the consequently reduced opportunity for close visual observation'.[9] While lack of experience and the difficulties of estimating the size of ships from a submarine conning tower cannot be denied, this would hardly explain the frequency with which tonnages were exaggerated as against underestimated.[10] The point being that a commander's natural desire to account for a larger target had a predictable effect on his assessment of its size, a tendency that can most charitably be described as 'the angler's weakness'. A good example of this comes in September 1942 with the attack on convoy RB1 by U-boats of the *Vorwärts*, *Pfeil* and *Blitz* packs which claimed HM destroyer *Veteran* (**71**). Believing that they had savaged a troop convoy, the Germans claimed 48,000 tons of passenger liners sent to the bottom whereas, *Veteran* apart, they had in fact despatched three coastal and river steamers displacing less than a quarter of that figure. As Fregkpt. Victor Oehrn (see **16**) admitted in his unpublished memoirs, 'Gauging [the size of the enemy vessel] correctly is greatly impeded by the ship's degree of ballast, conditions of light, defensive manoeuvres by escorts, the desire to see the target as large as possible, etc.' but there is more to it than that.[11] Although

---

9 Rohwer, *Axis Submarine Successes*, 2nd edn, xi.
10 Among the few exceptions recorded in this book are those of Kptlt Klaus Scholtz vis-à-vis HMS *Rajputana* (**24**) and Kptlt Hartmut Graf von Matuschka vis-à-vis HMS *Hurst Castle* (**107**).
11 *Navigare Necessum Est*, typescript, DUBMA. Oehrn accounted for HMS *Penzance* (**16**) while commander of *U37* before going on to hold a number of senior staff positions.

tonnage exaggeration can readily be understood as a facet of human nature, the fact that the *U-Boot-Waffe* based the award of the Knight's Cross and to some extent its system of promotion on tonnage accrual makes this also a cultural problem from which it was hard to escape in either good times or bad. There were many ways in which Admiral Dönitz's men prosecuted his *Tonnageschlacht*, or 'tonnage war'.

Not that the issue of tonnage exaggeration went unrecognised, even in the earliest days of the Battle of the Atlantic. The U-boat men themselves coined a term for exaggerated tonnage estimates: *Schepke-Tonnage*, based on the notorious penchant of Kptlt Joachim Schepke (*U3*, *U19* and *U100*) for magnifying the size of his merchant victims, to which his alleged bet with Prien and Kretschmer as to who could top the tonnage tables no doubt owed something. Reprimanded by Dönitz who warned other commanding officers against following his example, Schepke is not represented in this volume but two equally notorious 'tonnage kings' are: Fregkpt. Albrecht Brandi and Korvkpt. Adalbert 'Adi' Schnee. On the basis of his claims – which included the incontestable sinkings of HMSs *St Issey*, *Welshman* and *Puckeridge* together with USS *Fechteler* (**G44**, **81**, **G59** and **101**) – Brandi became one of only two U-boat officers (out of a total of twenty-seven recipients) to receive the Knight's Cross with Oak Leaves, Swords and Diamonds, the highest German military decoration of the Second World War. Impressive though his accomplishments were, they were a shadow of what he claimed them to be. In the words of David Brown, late Director of the Admiralty's Naval Historical Branch, 'Brandi in fact received the honour more for the unquenchable optimism of his claims against warships in the Mediterranean; Brandi survived, but so did two-thirds of the ships which he believed he had hit.'[12] Nor was he the worst offender: 'In a different league, however, was the Atlantic C.O. who so consistently overclaimed that his final total was 100,000 tons in excess of reality'. The commander in question was 'Adi' Schnee who sank HMS *Springbank* (**33**) while in command of *U201*.

Other entries in this volume suggest exaggeration on such a scale that invention would seem a more appropriate word. On the night of 4 April 1943 *U188* attacked convoy ON176 in what Kptlt Siegfried Lüdden's log describes as 'good visibility' (**83**). His war diary goes on to describe the sinking of four merchantmen in crisp detail for what he estimates is a total of 23,000 GRT. Although one of these sinkings was definitely that of HM destroyer *Beverley* (displacing 1,190 tons), there is nothing in Allied records to corroborate the loss of any merchantmen at this juncture. As Lüdden put it in his log, 'I could never have dared hope that my first attack on a convoy would run so smoothly' but it is easier to equate his version of events with a concern to impress B.d.U. on this his maiden war patrol. If so the ploy worked as Lüdden was lionised on his return to Lorient and credited with all of his 23,000 tons. Equally, Kptlt Günther Prien's claim, signalled nearly two days after the sinking of HMS *Royal Oak* (**2**), to have inflicted damage on the battlecruiser *Repulse* (32,000 tons) as well is curious since the only other large vessel present was the seaplane carrier *Pegasus* which displaced just 3,300 tons and bore no resemblance whatever to a capital ship. Here too B.d.U. itself could on occasion take a hand with *U751*'s sinking of HMS *Audacity* (8,600 tons) in December 1941 (**43**) interpreted at Kernevel as having claimed the

light carrier *Unicorn* (16,510 tons) whereas Kptlt Gerhard Bigalk's accurate description of his victim should have disqualified any such interpretation. The official propaganda line, meanwhile, had him sinking a Formidable-class carrier (23,207 tons). Although B.d.U. often found state propaganda an embarrassing nuisance, there is a degree to which the tendency to exaggeration was a phenomenon which could trickle down from the top, as was shown again in the optimistic interpretation of *Zaunkönig* acoustic torpedo data later in the war (see below). Small wonder that post-war analysis of German records found B.d.U. to have overestimated its successes by approximately one third over the course of the war as a whole.[13]

Falsification, collusion and beyond

If those handling the KTBs should be mindful that many of the *U-Boat-Waffe*'s 1,400 seagoing commanders had recourse at one time or another to various degrees of massaging or exaggeration to put a gloss on their performance, they should also be alert to the possibility of out-and-out log falsification, invariably to conceal events of an undesirable or unsavoury nature. That said, there is no evidence to suggest that the U-boat KTBs were falsified on any but the rarest occasions. Indeed, taken generally their value as primary material is beyond question and the data and interpretations contained in them frequently stand up to corroboration in Allied sources. However, falsification or concealment did occur, a corollary of the highly sensitive diplomatic permutations of U-boat operations, from *U34*'s destruction of the Republican *C3* during the Spanish Civil War (**G1**) to the sinking of the liner *Athenia* at the hands of Oblt.z.S. Fritz-Julius Lemp in *U30* (see **G3**) on 3 September 1939. The first was a flagrant breach of Germany's declared neutrality, the second a direct contravention of standing orders and of great embarrassment to the German High Command. The *C3* incident apparently resulted in the destruction of *U34*'s log while the *U-Boot-Waffe*'s involvement in the sinking of the *Athenia* had to be vigorously denied throughout the war, Lemp being ordered to erase all mention of the incident from his KTB. Another instance of log falsification which has come to light is Dönitz's directive to Oblt.z.S. Reinhard Hardegen (see **57**) to expunge all mention in *U123*'s log of the sinking of the neutral Portuguese freighter *Ganda* on 20 June 1941.[14]

Apart from the post-war allegations of Funkmaat Heinz Guske as they touch on Oblt.z.S. Hanskurt von Bremen's command of *U764* (see HMS *Blackwood*, **103**), only one entry in this volume provides an unequivocal example of log falsification, that concerning the attack on the Vichy French submarine *Sfax* by *U37* in December 1940 (**21**). In this case an ill-judged decision by Oblt.z.S. Nicolai Clausen resulted in the sinking of a friendly warship and a naval tanker sailing in company in broad daylight and excellent visibility. Not only does Clausen's KTB make no mention whatsoever of the incident but the cover-up resorted to – altering *U37*'s positional data – is so inept as to place her deep in the Algerian Sahara. Although this degree of incompetence supports the view that the *U-Boot-Waffe* was not much versed in the business of log falsification, it inevitably provides ammunition for those who would put the most nefarious interpretation on certain unanswered conundrums in the war at sea. In the case of HMS *Fidelity*, sunk by

---

12 David Brown, 'The Ebb and Flow of the Battle: The U-Boat Aces', NHB, FDS 444, p. 1.

13 Jak P. Mallmann Showell, *The U-Boat Century: German Submarine Warfare, 1906–2006* (London: Chatham Publishing, 2006), p. 14.
14 Gannon, *Operation Drumbeat*, p. 52.

U435 in December 1942 (**80**), Kptlt Siegfried Strelow's record of a signal from B.d.U. to the effect that 'Strelow to report whether survivors are in boats or whether their destruction can be counted on given the state of the weather' has prompted an allegation that 'hundreds of survivors' were massacred after the sinking.[15] Although the signal is nothing if not sinister, the claim is not one which can be substantiated from the available evidence. In this respect it should be recalled that documented cases of German submarine massacres are few (there is only one proven case during the Second World War) and that chivalry, though understandably rare in the unremitting sphere of submarine warfare, was by no means unknown in the *U-Boot-Waffe*: witness the rescue and fair treatment of AB William Pester of HMS/m *Spearfish* (**14**) and the two survivors of the USS *Cythera* (**59**) by *U34* and *U402* respectively.[16] That said, the incident in September 1942 during which U-boats were attacked by a US aircraft while assisting POW survivors of the troopship *Laconia* (**G34**) prompted a shift in mood among many in the *U-Boot-Waffe*, men already hardened by what all recognised was a struggle to the death. Kptlt Walter Göing's matter-of-fact description of the pitiful survivors of USS *Muskeget* (**66**), sunk three days before the *Laconia* on 9 September 1942, is a case in point, though his callousness might as readily have been reciprocated had the tables been turned.

II Tactics, trigonometry and torpedoes: Anatomy of a U-boat attack

As technical documents it should come as no surprise that the KTBs make frequent and often abbreviated reference to procedures, equipment and data of a complex nature which few readers could be expected to grasp without assistance.[17] To remedy this, each log excerpt in this book is supported by a number of notes which, together with the Glossary and the Abbreviations, are designed to provide sufficient information for a detailed picture of the attack to be formed. Nonetheless, as practically all the KTBs allude to procedures which are taken as understood by their intended audience, it may be useful to offer a more detailed picture of these, particularly as they touch on the tactics, fire control and torpedo armament involved in a U-boat attack from approach to firing.[18]

The approach

Once a target had been sighted the priority for a U-boat commander was to gain an accurate fix of its course and speed before taking up a firing position. This usually involved manoeuvring on the surface and ideally under cover of night until the boat was ahead (*vorsetzen*) and on a parallel course with the target. In sufficiently favourable conditions of light (i.e. with the moon or sun on the far side of the target) the U-boat would enjoy the maximum freedom of manoeuvre, but this was uncommon and circumstances frequently called for greater stealth. For example, a U-boat might be obliged to forgo the most efficient line of interception and adopt the *Hundekurve* ('pursuit curve'), so named for the line taken by a dog chasing down its prey. In a naval context this allowed the U-boat to present its smallest profile to the enemy while still remaining on the surface, with all the tactical advantages implied by this. With slight variations depending on the type in question, the U-boats treated in the main part of this book could only manage an underwater speed of about eight knots as opposed to a maximum of around eighteen knots on the surface, making it impossible for a submerged boat to keep up with any but the slowest convoys – let alone warships sailing alone or in company whether zigzagging or not. Remaining on the surface also provided six pairs of eyes – the commanding officer, torpedo officer and four lookouts – whereas in a submerged attack the commanding officer was the only visual party to events on the surface via the restricted view of his periscope.

In the event of sighting a convoy and receiving permission to attack – not always granted since U-boats were sometimes required to issue a radio beacon signal and await the arrival of other boats – the commander's first task was to penetrate the escort screen. While there was a significant difference between slow and fast convoys (the former allowing penetration from the rear as well as on the beam and from ahead), the determining factor in a U-boat's ability to engage a convoy effectively was the composition and expertise of its escort, which varied greatly depending on the route and of course the period in question. In the cases of HMSs *Penzance* and *Dundee* (**16** and **18**), both sunk in the North Atlantic in the autumn of 1940, *U37* and *U48* encountered only one and four escort vessels respectively when attacking convoys SC1 and SC3. How different from the predicament of *U990* which was confronted with no less than nineteen escorts when attacking JW57 in the Arctic in February 1944 and had to settle for an attack on HMS *Mahratta* (**99**).

In many of the attacks described in this volume daylight conditions ruled out the possibility of the boat remaining on the surface as a target or targets approached. As U-boat commanders were reminded in their handbooks, 'the submarine must not endanger its most valuable asset, invisibility. In daytime, in clear weather, the submarine should not therefore be able to see more of the enemy than just the tops of his masts (crow's nest on the mast, rangefinder in the foretop)' before submerging. Even then there was no guarantee that a simultaneous sighting by the enemy would not occur, as was the case prior to *U124*'s attack on the lone cruiser HMS *Dunedin* in November 1941 (**40**), and before *U804*'s on the USS *Fiske* in the Atlantic convoy lanes

---

15 Alan Burn, *The Fighting Commodores: Convoy Commodores in the Second World War* (Barnsley, S. Yorks.: Leo Cooper, 1999), pp. 172–6.

16 For examples involving merchantmen, see Timothy P. Mulligan, *Neither Sharks nor Wolves: The Men of Nazi Germany's U-Boat Arm, 1939–1945* (Annapolis, Md.: Naval Institute Press, 1999).

17 See Reading the *Kriegstagebücher*.

18 For tactics, see Earl J. Coates, ed., *The U-Boat Commander's Handbook* (Gettysburg, Pa.: Thomas Publications, 1989), essentially a reprint of the US Navy's 1943 translation of the 1942 edition of the *Handbuch für U-Boot-Kommandanten*. On fire control, the key primary technical source in English is *The U-Boat Torpedo Firing Handbook*, vol. 3: *Fire Control on U-Boats Type VII and IX* (NHB, T.18402), a post-war Admiralty translation of the original *U-Boot-Waffe* document of 1941. However, the subject is best approached in Clemens Brechtelsbauer, „Wie funktioniert eigentlich . . . Der Torpedovorhalterechner [sic]" in *Das Archiv*, no. 15 (October 2000), pp. 27–9, Eng. trans. 'How does it work . . . ? The Torpedo Data Computer' in *The U-Boat Archive*, no. 5 (December 2000), pp. 15–18. The key secondary source for torpedo technology is Eberhard Rössler, *Die Torpedos der deutschen U-Boote : Entwicklung, Herstellung und Eigenschaften der deutschen Marine-*

Torpedos (Hamburg: Mittler, 2005). For a torpedo rating's perspective, see Heinz Trompelt, *Ein andere Sicht: Tatsachenbericht eines Torpedo-Obermech. Maat und Fähnrich zur See* (Norderstedt: Books on Demand, 2006).

in August 1944 (**104**). Once submerged, the commander's only view of the world was through the periscope, difficult enough even if the target were not heading away from the U-boat. Though hydrophone data might give a broad picture of the bearing of a target and even its course to a skilled operator, visual contact was vital if accurate firing data were to be obtained. Essentially, the periscope was meant to be raised only when the U-boat was proceeding at reduced speed to avoid producing the wake and conspicuous *Wasserfahne* (lit. 'water plume') that might quickly reveal its position. This was particularly the case in the Mediterranean where the phenomenon of a *spiegelglatte See* ('mirror-smooth sea') was a frequent and unwelcome reality. No surprise, therefore, that daytime attacks in this theatre tended to result from fortuitous approaches by the enemy rather than stealth by the U-boat, with HMSs *Barham*, *Gurkha*, *Heythrop* and *Eagle* (**41**, **46**, **55** and **65**) all falling into this category.

Specifications of U-boat types featured in the main entries*

Type	IA	IIA	IIB	IIC	IID	VIIA	VIIB	VIIC	IXA	IXB	IXC	IXC-40
Displacement (tons)												
Surfaced												
	862	254	279	291	314	626	753	769	1,032	1,051	1,120	1,120
Submerged												
	983	303	328	341	364	745	857	871	1,152	1,178	1,232	1,232
Dimensions (feet)												
Length												
	237.5	134.2	140.1	144	144.4	211.6	218.2	220.1	251	251	252	252
Beam												
	20.4	13.4	13.4	13.5	16.4	19	20.3	20.3	21.3	22.3	22.3	22.6
Draught (standard)												
	14.1	12.5	12.8	12.5	12.8	14.4	15.4	15.7	15.4	15.4	15.4	15.4
Maximum speed (knots)												
Surfaced												
	17.8	13	13	12	12.7	17	17.9	17.7	18.2	18.2	18.3	18.3
Submerged												
	8.3	6.9	7	7	7.4	8	8	7.6	7.7	7.3	7.3	7.3
Endurance (miles)												
Surfaced @ 8 or 10 knots												
	7,900/10	1,600/8	3,100/8	3,800/8	5,650/8	6,200/10	8,700/10	8,500/10	10,500/10	12,000/10	13,450/10	13,850/10
Submerged @ 4 knots												
	78	35	35	42	56	94	90	80	78	64	63	63
Armament												
Torpedo tubes (bow + stern)												
	4 + 2	3 + 0	3 + 0	3 + 0	3 + 0	4 + 1	4 + 1	4 + 1†	4 + 2	4 + 2	4 + 2	4 + 2
Torpedoes carried (normal)												
	14	5	5	5	5	11	14	14	22	22	22	22
Deck gun (mm)												
	1 × 105	–	–	–	–	1 × 88	1 × 88	1 × 88	1 × 105	1 × 105	1 × 105	1 × 105
Standard AA armament (mm)												
	1 × 20	2 × 20	2 × 20	2 × 20	2 × 20	1 × 20	1 × 20	1 × 20	1 × 37	1 × 37	1 × 37	1 × 37
									1 × 20	1 × 20	1 × 20	1 × 20
Complement												
	44–46	22–24	22–24	22–24	22–24	42–46	44–48	44–52	48–56	48–56	48–56	48–56

* For *UA*, see HMS *Andania* (**10**).

† Note that two of the Type-VIIC boats featured in the main entries, *U331* (HMS *Barham*, **41**) and *U431* (HMS *Martin* and HrMs *Isaac Sweers*, **72** and **74**), were completed without the stern tube.

Sources: uboat.net; Jak P. Mallmann Showell, *U-Boats Under the Swastika* (Shepperton, Surrey: Ian Allan, 1973); Eberhard Rössler, *Geschichte des deutschen Ubootbaus* (2nd edn, 2 vols, Koblenz: Bernard & Graefe, 1986–7); and Robert C. Stern, *Type VII U-Boats* (Annapolis, Md.: Naval Institute Press, 1991).

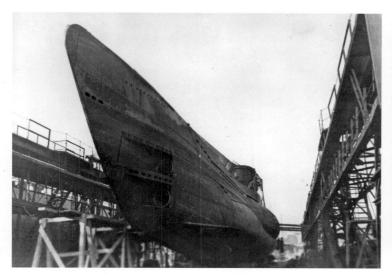

Loading a G7e torpedo in the forward compartment
of the Type-IXB *U103*, 1942. *BK*

The business end of a Type-VIIC boat showing two of its five torpedo tubes.
Note the characteristic vents forward and the saddle tanks abreast the
conning tower, on which the snorting bull emblem of the 7th *U-Flottille* can
just be made out. This photo, taken in dry dock under camouflage netting,
dates from May 1943. *BK*

German torpedoes in the Second World War

Although U-boats were fitted with a variety of ordnance including
an 88- or 105-mm deck gun, an array of anti-aircraft armament and
occasionally mines, the key weapon – and the one used against every
warship treated in the main part of this volume – was of course the
torpedo. These were fired from bow tubes (Tubes I, II and III in the
Type IIs, with a Tube IV in the Type-I, Type-VII and Type-IX boats)
and from the stern compartment (Tube V in the Type VIIs, Tubes V and
VI in the Type-I and Type-IX boats), thereby giving the commanding
officer the tactical freedom to engage from either end. A U-boat would
leave harbour with all its torpedo tubes loaded and as many spares as
could be carried, usually two in the early Type IIs, between six and
nine in the Type VIIs, and up to sixteen in the Type IXs. These were
stored internally at the expense of the crew who suffered extremely
cramped conditions until they were expended. The Type VIIs and IXs
were also modified to accommodate external reloads (two and four
torpedoes respectively) between pressure hull and deck casing, though
the fact that the boats had to be surfaced for several hours to effect the
transfer made it an impractical option as the war progressed.

For the first four years of the war the main weapons used by
the *U-Boot-Waffe* were two straight-running torpedoes, the G7a
(nicknamed the 'Ato') and the G7e ('Eto') which together accounted
for every vessel covered in the main part of this volume until HMCS
St Croix was destroyed by a *Zaunkönig* acoustic torpedo in September
1943 (**86**). The letter 'G' (short for *Geradlaufapparat* – 'straight-running
apparatus') referred to the model number and denoted a diameter of
533 millimetres (21 inches), while the '7' referred to its approximate
length in metres (actually 7.18 metres or 23½ feet). Whereas the 'a' in
G7a denotes the sub-model type, it being the first in that particular
series (followed by a 'B-to' and 'C-to'), the 'e' in G7e refers to its electric
mode of propulsion.

Designed in the early 1930s and refined shortly before the outbreak

of war, the G7a was a development of the standard German torpedo,
itself based on the original Whitehead torpedo. It was powered by a
reciprocating engine driven by super-heated steam produced by the
ignition of compressed air, petrol and water in a combustion chamber.
The G7a was capable of a maximum speed of 44 knots and a range of
6,000 metres on its *Schnellschuss* (SS – 'quick fire') setting. It could also
be set to run at 40 knots on the *Nahschuss* (NS – 'close fire') setting with
an increased range of 8,000 metres, or set to the maximum possible
range of 12,500 metres at a speed of 30 knots with the *Weitschuss*
(WS – 'remote fire') setting. Although the G7a was the fastest torpedo
employed by the *U-Boot-Waffe* during the Second World War, the
exhaust gases given off as a consequence of its form of propulsion
resulted in a visible trail of bubbles – a distinct tactical disadvantage in
relatively calm conditions in daylight or on well-lit nights.

Although conceived in the 1920s, the all-electric G7e torpedo did
not enter service until 1936, after which it too received a number of
significant enhancements before the war. Powered by lead acid wet

Fish out of water: stowing (or unstowing) a G7e torpedo
in a Type-II U-boat, 1941. *BK*

cell batteries, its existence was unknown to the British until fragments of one were recovered from the bottom of Scapa Flow following the sinking of the *Royal Oak* by *U47* in October 1939 (**2**). The advantages of the G7e rested in its relative simplicity and cheapness of manufacture (around half the cost of the G7a) together with the absence of that trail of bubbles which characterised the G7a. However, there were also two clear drawbacks: the G7e required far more onboard maintenance than the G7a, those stored in torpedo tubes having to be removed for servicing at regular intervals and their batteries ideally preheated to 30°C (86°F) before firing; and it had no setting beyond the fixed range of 5,000 metres at 30 knots.

The respective merits and drawbacks of these types led to the U-boats being stowed with a mix of torpedoes for each cruise. At the start of the war the G7a and the G7e were supplied in their basic configurations as the T1 and T2 respectively, both fitted with the Pi-1 pistol which could be set for contact or magnetic detonation. As the war progressed these configurations and the pistol design itself underwent a number of modifications, the G7e benefitting from an increase in range to 7,500 metres when introduced as the T3a in late 1942. Aside from the differences indicated above, the G7a and G7e were similar and largely interchangeable weapons, both equipped with a warhead containing 300 kilograms (661 pounds) of the increasingly obsolete hexanite explosive (a combination of hexanitrodiphenylamine and trinitrotoluene developed for the *Kaiserliche Marine* before the Great War) with an admixture of aluminium.[19] Above all, as straight-running torpedoes they both relied on an identical torpedo fire-control system.

The Vorhaltrechner

As with any conventional ordnance aimed at a moving target, an assessment of the correct aim-off – i.e. the point that has to be selected ahead of the target in order to secure a hit – was key to the success of a torpedo attack. To achieve the correct firing solution from the available data each U-boat was fitted with an analogue electro-mechanical attack computer, the *Vorhaltrechner* (lit. 'aim-off calculator') or torpedo data computer.

Developed for the Kriegsmarine by Siemens in the 1930s, the *Vorhaltrechner* was installed in the commander's control room in the conning tower of each U-boat. It was responsible for computing all optically obtained data concerning the course, speed and relative inclination of the target into settings for the U-boat's *Torpedoschussempfänger* (torpedo launch receivers), which would in turn program the required gyro angle into the relevant torpedo tubes. This required the *Vorhaltrechner* to be linked both to the boat's gyro compass and the key optical instruments used in the attack sequence. These were the *Überwasserzieloptik* ('surface attack optic' – UZO) device for surface attacks – the main bridge target bearing indicator in the form of water- and pressure-resistant binoculars attached to a rotating bracket with a ring marking off degrees of the compass – or one of the two periscopes in the event of a submerged attack, usually the attack periscope (*Angriffssehrohr*) in the cramped confines of the conning tower, or less frequently the control room periscope known as the *Nachtzielsehrohr* ('night search periscope') or *Luftzielsehrohr* ('sky search periscope'), the latter due to its role in identifying nearby enemy aircraft.

So much for the U-boat's fire-control equipment. But how were its torpedoes brought to target? Apart from target speed – most simply assessed by assuming a parallel course to the target for a brief period and obtaining a match – the critical piece of data was the relative inclination of the target known as the *Lagenwinkel* ('positional angle') though usually referred to by its abbreviation '*Lage*'. The *Lage* was the cornerstone of the trigonometric formula used by the *Vorhaltrechner* to calculate a firing solution. It is expressed as follows:

$$\beta = \arcsin ((v_g/v_t) \sin \gamma)^{20}$$

whereby β (beta) indicates the aim-off to be calculated (*Vorhalt*), v_g the speed of the target (v = velocity; g = *Gegner* 'enemy'), and v_t the velocity of the torpedo (t = *Torpedo*), and γ (gamma) the relative inclination of the target (*Lage*; also known in English as 'angle on the bow' – AOB). The *Lage* is provided in almost every KTB excerpt in this volume, usually enhanced either by the terms *Bug links* ('bows left') or *Bug rechts* ('bows right') – to indicate the target's general orientation with respect to the boat – or simply 'red' or 'green' meaning that the target was showing its port or starboard side. A *Lage* of 0° meant a target bow-on to the U-boat (often the case in the unwelcome scenario of a closing destroyer); 180° meant a target sailing directly away from the U-boat, while a 90° angle (be it *Bug links* or *Bug rechts*) indicated a target that was broadside on. Other data entered into the *Vorhaltrechner* included target range (E = *Entfernung*), target bearing, U-boat course and speed, and the angle of spread (*Streuwinkel*) or individual angle of dispersion between torpedoes in the event of two or more being fired.

The attack

To understand how this data fits together, consider the attack by *U431* (Kptlt Wilhelm Dommes) on HMS *Martin* in the Western Mediterranean on the night of 10 November 1942 (**72**). Dommes's torpedo report provides the key data entered into the *Vorhaltrechner*:

- the relative inclination of the target (γ, gamma): red 80° ('red' means that the target is showing its port side)
- target range (E/'Emil' – *Entfernung*): 40 hectometres (= 4,000 metres)[21]
- the target bearing (ω, omega): 27.2° (not shown on the plot below)
- target speed (v_g): 15 knots
- torpedo speed (v_t): 30 knots (i.e. the G7a set for its maximum run of 12,500 meters)
- angle of dispersion (ψ, psi): 1.8°.

Of the key pieces of data required for this calculation, the target bearing and torpedo speed were 'knowns' which could be determined with a high degree of accuracy, whereas target speed and relative

---

19 Warhead weights of between 280 and 380 kilograms are given in a variety of sources. The figure of 300 kilograms is that provided in Rössler's authoritative *Die Torpedos der deutschen U-Boote*, pp. 63 and 71, and is corroborated by Admiralty tests conducted in 1944 and late 1945.

20 This formula may also be expressed as $\sin \beta = (v_g/v_t) \sin \gamma$.
21 The running time provided in the torpedo report indicates that *U431* overestimated the range by around 1,000 metres. Apart from the impressive accuracy of Dommes's calculations, this would explain why so many torpedoes hit, the spread not having run far enough to fan out beyond *Martin's* hull length.

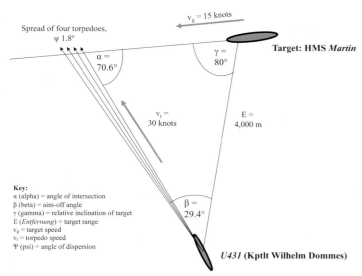

Key:
α (alpha) = angle of intersection
β (beta) = aim-off angle
γ (gamma) = relative inclination of target
E (*Entfernung*) = target range
v_g = target speed
v_t = torpedo speed
Ψ (psi) = angle of dispersion

Spread of four torpedoes, ψ 1.8°
v_g = 15 knots
α = 70.6°
γ = 80°
v_t = 30 knots
E = 4,000 m
Target: HMS *Martin*
β = 29.4°
U431 (Kptlt Wilhelm Dommes)

U431's attack on HMS *Martin*, 10 November 1942 (**72**)
Torpedo tracks are shown emanating from their points of trigonometric
calculation in the control room rather than from the point of launch in
the bow tubes. As the U-boat is closely aligned with the line of fire, only a
minimum parallax adjustment is required (see main text).

inclination had to be assessed to the best of the commanding officer's
(or torpedo officer's) ability. The aggregation of all this data permitted
the *Vorhaltrechner* to calculate an aim-off angle for the torpedoes
(β, beta) of 29.4°, giving an angle of intersection (α, alpha) of 70.6°.
At 0354 German time *U431* fired a spread of four G7a torpedoes
which obtained three hits on *Martin* at a range of 3,100 metres. A
trigonometric illustration of the attack is provided above.

Although range played no part in the trigonometric calculation
since the aim-off angle would be unchanged so long as the target held
both its course and speed, a value for range was nonetheless entered
into the *Vorhaltrechner*. There were three reasons for this. First, the
range at point of intersection was an important calculation in its
own right due to the limited extent of a torpedo run; plainly, no shot
could be fired if the point of intersection was calculated to lie beyond
the range of the torpedo. Second, the *Vorhaltrechner* required range
information in order to calculate the angle of dispersion for torpedoes
fired in a salvo. Third and most important, the computer was required
to make the necessary parallax adjustment given that the trigonometric
triangle of the attack was not 'pure'. Just as the positioning of gun
turrets along the hull of a ship gave each a slightly different perspective
of the target relative to the firing vessel, the same was true of torpedoes
fired from either the bow or the stern, a distance in the Type-VII
boats of approximately 27 metres (89 feet) and 32 metres (105 feet)
respectively from their trigonometric points in the main control
room (*Operationszentrale*, or simply *Zentrale*) and conning tower
where the UZO and periscopes were located. Moreover, torpedoes
were often fired not in line with the head or stern of the vessel but
set to turn up to 90 degrees from the head of the boat (giving a side
angle – *Seitenwinkel* – or relative bearing of the target to the U-boat's
course line ω, omega), while torpedoes could also be fired on the turn.
In such situations the torpedo would cover the first 9.5 metres in a
straight line before assuming a circular movement with a radius of 95

The page from Kptlt Heinz Walkerling's log recording *U91*'s attack on
HMCS *Ottawa* on 13 September 1942 (**68**). Note the fire-control notation
at the beginning of the entry for 0205. *NHB*

metres which would gradually bring it onto a straight-running course
towards the target. In such cases range assumed an added significance
since the *Vorhaltrechner* required this data in order to calculate the
parallax adjustment (δ, delta) and subsequent angle of fire (ρ, rho).
This explains why U-boat commanders were exhorted 'always to fire
at the minimum angle in order to avoid misses resulting from false
convergence values', as once the theoretical and the actual tracks
converged at the entered range they would then diverge with every
extra metre travelled. This, too, is why the problem of convergence was
greater over shorter ranges.[22]

Once the attack sequence was underway and the initial data had
been entered the *Vorhaltrechner* could be set to automatic update mode
so long as target course and speed remained constant. This situation,
called *Lage laufend* ('inclination running'), involved taking account
of the changes in the relative movements of both vessels and making
corresponding alterations to the relative inclination as time passed;
see *U443*'s attack on HMS *Blean* for an example of this (**77**). While

---

22 Coates, ed., *U-Boat Commander's Handbook*, p. 59.

this gave the commanding officer the tactical freedom to determine the optimum firing moment, the automatic update function depended on the key underlying data remaining constant during the entire sequence. Any change in target speed or course (through zigzagging for example) would render this function null and void and all data would have to be manually re-entered from scratch.

Another item of data that had to be determined was the running depth of the torpedo or torpedoes fired, which was entered manually into the tubes themselves. While this had no bearing on the trigonometric calculations discussed above, it did present the U-boat commander with another variable to factor in and therefore another opportunity for error. The Pi-1 detonator pistol and those of its successors which were fitted in the G7a and G7a torpedoes from the beginning of the war allowed either for contact detonation on striking the target or for magnetic detonation whereby the firing circuit was closed under the influence of an external magnetic field such as that generated by the hull of a ship. All else being equal, a magnetic detonation was the more desirable as the explosion of a single torpedo below the keel of a ship was a surer way of sinking it than a contact detonation on its side. U-boats were provided with detailed listings of the standard draughts of Allied merchantmen and warships, but this required an assessment of the condition of vessels in ballast together with accurate identification of smaller warship silhouettes if errors were to be avoided – no easy task on the high seas in anything less than good conditions. For magnetic detonations the ideal depth was two metres under the hull while that for contact detonation had obviously to be much shallower – between two and six metres depending on the size of the target. Examples of commanders misjudging their calculations and wasting good torpedoes are to be found in the attacks on USS *Gannet* and HMS/m *P615* (**60** and **84**).

Evidently, some U-boat commanders and their torpedo officers had a greater gift for calculating the *Lage* and related torpedo data than others, which – technical failures aside – was the most likely reason for a torpedo to hit or miss its target. To minimise the possibility of this, both watch officers (I.WO and II.WO) were encouraged to offer their estimates for target speed, range and inclination, the commander judging which was the most correct. However, errors were common, especially at night when there was a tendency on the part of data observers to underestimate target inclination. Once an erroneous estimate of either target speed or inclination was embedded in the calculations it would be augmented with every metre covered by the torpedo. Commanding officers were therefore instructed to fire a spread (or fan) of torpedoes not only against such high-value units as HMSs *Barham* or *Eagle* (**41** and **65**) – targeted with four apiece from virtually point-blank range – but also if the target range demanded it, as in the case of HMS *Martin* (**72**) which was engaged with a full salvo at an estimated range of 4,000 metres. A salvo of at least two torpedoes was expected for any unaccompanied vessel at a range in excess of 1,000 metres, the angle of dispersion being entered manually based on the estimated length of the target and with the firing fixed at 2.3 seconds between torpedoes. Even then misses were common, spread or no spread. There were, however, occasions when miscalculation was accompanied with fortune to such a degree that a commander might strike and sink a ship quite different from that initially targeted. Such was the case of Kptlt Friedrich Guggenberger after a significant

miscalculation of the speed and range of his intended target (HMS *Malaya*) yielded *Ark Royal* instead when the latter made an obliging turn to land aircraft (**39**).

Miscalculations apart, German torpedoes were dogged by a number of technical problems during the first months of the war which affected those set both for magnetic and contact detonation. These culminated in the Norwegian Campaign in April 1940 during which the *U-Boot-Waffe* obtained a succession of hits on units of the Royal Navy with torpedoes that failed to explode. With morale at rock bottom B.d.U. was obliged to suspend front-line operations while the problem was looked into. As so often, there was no single answer. Not only was the magnetic detonator found to be unreliable at northerly latitudes or in the vicinity of a significant deposit of iron ore or other metal, but the high pressure in a submerged U-boat affected the depth-keeping mechanism of the G7e itself, which explained why problems were experienced even with contact detonation settings.

Enter the Zaunkönig

In addition to solving problems with the *U-Boot-Waffe*'s torpedoes, the *Torpedoversuchsanstalt* (Torpedo Experimentation Facility) in Gotenhafen was charged with developing weapons with capabilities well beyond those of the G7a and G7e. In particular, a 'pattern-running' type was sought with the capacity to weave back and forth, thereby increasing the probability of a hit when fired into a convoy. The first of these, the *Federapparat-Torpedo* ('spring apparatus torpedo' – FAT), sometimes referred to as the *Flächenabsuchender-Torpedo* or 'shallow-searching torpedo', appeared in late 1942. Based on the G7e, it incorporated a steering mechanism that allowed the torpedo to assume a pre-set 'ladder' pattern. A more sophisticated version of this weapon appeared in 1944, the *Lagenunabhängiger-Torpedo* ('any inclination torpedo' – LUT), which not only added the capability of setting a change of course at the end of the initial straight run but could be fired from depths of up to fifty metres (165 feet).

However, the holy grail of torpedo design in the battle against Allied warships on the high seas was the realisation of a concept that predated the outbreak of war: a torpedo with acoustic sensors that would be attracted by the noise of a target's propellers, thereby obviating the need to obtain a favourable angle of fire. One of the great weaknesses of the U-boat before the autumn of 1943 was its lack of defensive options in the event of being sighted and closed by an Allied escort. As the *Lage* or relative inclination of such targets was inevitably 0° (bow on) or thereabouts, there was no realistic chance of achieving a hit with a straight-running torpedo. An effective acoustic homing device would clearly be a very different proposition.

The first of the acoustic designs to achieve operational readiness was the T4 torpedo, a modification of the G7e known as the *Falke* ('falcon'). Though put into service in March 1943, its subsequent development was overtaken by events. The appalling losses of April and May led Dönitz to withdraw all U-boats from the Atlantic and that summer saw feverish efforts to bring an improved version of the T4 into front-line service. This was the T5 or *Zaunkönig* ('wren') acoustic homing torpedo which became known to the Allies by the acronym GNAT (German Naval Acoustic Torpedo). Fitted with a 273-kilogram (600-pound) warhead (slightly less than that of the conventional torpedoes due to the need to accommodate the homing mechanism), it ran on a single speed setting of 24.5 knots to a maximum of 5,000 metres (5,750 if preheated). In many of the KTB excerpts involving the T5 the attack data includes information on the settings which match those for the G7a, though in name only (see above). In this case the *Schnellschuss* (SS) setting had the effect of deactivating the acoustic homing mechanism so that the torpedo followed a straight course, while the *Nahschuss* (NS) and *Weitschuss* (WS) settings, involving slight differences in the T5's *Ente* ('duck') steering control mechanism, were used against retiring and closing targets respectively; see HMSs *Itchen* and *Mahratta* (**88** and **99**) for more on this.

With its unprecedented ability to engage from a bow-on inclination the *Zaunkönig* significantly altered the risk profile of an escort attacking a U-boat. A look at the attrition of Allied warships will give some idea of the impact of the *Zaunkönig* as the *Zerstörer-Knacker* (lit. 'destroyer cracker') it was intended to be.[23] Between January 1943 and the introduction of the *Zaunkönig* in September of that year the *U-Boot-Waffe* accounted for just eleven escorts in all theatres. When battle was rejoined in September the *Leuthen* group sank three Allied escorts and rendered another a total constructive loss within the space of a week; see HMCS *St Croix*, HMS *Polyanthus* and HMS *Itchen* (**86–88**). By the end of the year a further seven had been lost to this cause in 1943 including HMS *Hythe* (**91**) and the US destroyers *Buck* and *Bristol* (**90** and **92**) over a four-day period in the Mediterranean, together with USS *Leary* and HMS *Hurricane* (**93** and **94**) in the North Atlantic. Before the war was over a total of seventy-seven warships had been struck by a *Zaunkönig*, of which at least forty never returned to harbour.

However, the Germans were again let down by technical flaws and here the haste with which the T5 was put into service took a hand, it having originally been scheduled for final testing in January 1944. A particular problem was the sensitivity of the Pi-4 pistol which caused premature detonation in a large number of cases due to the extreme turbulence encountered by the torpedo when crossing a target's wake. 'End of run' detonations were also common for reasons not altogether clear. Meanwhile, the Allies discovered that the dropping of a single depth charge could prompt a detonation, though this required advance warning of an attack. In addition, interrogation of captured submariners soon provided the Allies with the optimum frequency at which the T5's acoustic sensor became effective against would-be targets, namely those cruising at around fifteen knots – the typical operational speed of a convoy escort. By making significant alterations in speed and avoiding cruising between eight and twenty knots, an escort was reckoned to emit a sound frequency that was much less likely to attract the *Zaunkönig*; see HMS *Hurricane* (**94**). Most effective of all were the various anti-torpedo noise arrays developed by the Allies and towed behind the escort: the British Foxer, the US FXR and Fanfare, and the Canadian CAT device (Counter-Acoustic Torpedo or Canadian Anti-Acoustic Torpedo). This apart, the *Zaunkönig* had the alarming propensity to home in on the firing vessel if inexpertly used, and at least two U-boats had been lost to this cause by the end of the war. There is also evidence that, in its haste to introduce the

---

23 Jürgen Rohwer, *Die Entwicklung des Zaunkönigs : die Kriegsgeschichte als Hilfswissenschaft der Wehrtechnik, dargestellt am Beispiel der zielsuchenden Torpedos* (BfZ, Sammlung Rohwer, „T-5: Manuskripte und Auswertung" folder).

Zaunkönig, the *U-Boot-Waffe* devoted insufficient time to training U-boat commanders in the complexities of the new weapon, of which *U616's* attack on the USS *Buck* (**90**) may provide evidence, successful though it was. All played their part in ensuring that the T5's success rate against escorts was a fraction of the figure estimated by B.d.U., which produced optimistic extrapolations of sinking data from U-boat reports; see below. Though undoubtedly a great technical accomplishment, the *Zaunkönig* did not make the decisive contribution to victory at sea which the Kriegsmarine had hoped.

Analysis of *Zaunkönig* performance

Total fired: 464

Hits	77 (16.6%)	Misses 387 (83.4%)
Ships sunk	40+ (52%+)	90 detonations close to target but no hit (23.3%); of these 37 deemed decoy-related and 32 depth-charge related;
		21 no data
		11 premature detonations (2.8%)
		146 end-of-run detonations (37.7%)
		140 no detonation heard (36.2%)

Note   Percentages relate to the **bold** number in the *preceding* section.
Sources   Jürgen Rohwer, *Auswertung der Zaunkönig-Frontschüsse (September 1939–Mai 1945)* (BfZ, Sammlung Rohwer, „T-5: Manuskripte und Auswertung" folder) together with author data.

III   Punch and counterpunch: The conflict between the *U-Boot-Waffe* and the Allied navies

Although this volume focuses on the sinking of Allied warships, it should be made clear from the outset that, with a handful of exceptions, these were never the principal targets of those U-boats thrown into front-line operations. For the man who spearheaded Germany's submarine war, Admiral Karl Dönitz, there was only one measure of success in the war at sea: *Tonnageschlacht*, or 'tonnage war' against the merchant shipping which represented the lifeblood of the Allied war effort. As in 1917, the U-boat war of 1939–1945 was therefore intended as a *guerre de course* in the classic sense of that term. The first step towards unrestricted submarine warfare came with the issue of *Ständiger Kriegsbefehl* (Standing War Order) no. 154 in November 1939, though it was not put into full execution until August 1940. Aware that the war had come too early for the Kriegsmarine's surface fleet to assert itself against the might of the Royal Navy, Dönitz devoted much energy to persuading Hitler and the *Seekriegsleitung* that in the *U-Boot-Waffe* Germany possessed a war-winning weapon which had to be given absolute priority in pursuit of one overriding objective: the destruction of merchant shipping in the Atlantic to the point where Britain would be forced to sue for peace. But his efforts were unavailing in their main purpose and Dönitz spent the early years of the war in the frustrated conviction that neither the number of U-boats nor the pace of new construction nor the Luftwaffe's air support was all that it could be for the Battle of the Atlantic. Although no one knew it, by the time Dönitz gained daily access to Hitler after replacing Grossadmiral Erich Raeder as Commander-in-Chief of the German navy in January 1943, the opportunity for the *U-Boot-Waffe* to deliver victory at sea had passed.

The *U-Boot-Waffe*'s campaign against Allied shipping has been

treated in great detail on many occasions and in many places.[24] Rather than adding a further iteration this introduction will instead focus on the various phases and dimensions of the conflict as it touched the vessels which form the core of this book. It is a measure of how far-reaching was the U-boat war that those reading the main entries sequentially or chronologically by theatre or campaign will be able to follow the progress of almost the entire conflict in the 'Background of the Sinking' and other essays which appear in each.

Restricted operations and theatres: September 1939–May 1940

Quite apart from the restrictions on U-boat operations as they applied to merchant shipping around the British Isles in the early months of the war, the opening of the *U-Boot-Waffe*'s campaign against Britain and France was characterised by significant strategic limitations together with the reduced number of U-boats available for operations (only thirty-nine on the outbreak of war) – a state of affairs that persisted well into 1941. Until the surrender of Norway and France in June 1940 the approaches to Britain's Atlantic ports – namely the North Channel and the Western Approaches – lay a formidable distance from the main U-boat bases of Kiel and Wilhelmshaven. With the English Channel declared too dangerous following the loss of three units attempting the passage in October 1939, the U-boats could only gain the broad Atlantic via the North Sea, which required the expenditure of several days and a significant proportion of their available diesel fuel. To give the example of *U34*'s (see **13** and **14**) first wartime patrol from August to September 1939, Kptlt Wilhelm Rollmann had to undertake a journey of 1,700 miles before reaching his operations area in the Western Approaches, which at between 9 and 11 knots would take at least nine days and expend twenty tons of fuel – approximately a third of her capacity.[25] It was therefore in the North Sea that the U-boats now claimed a majority of their warship pennants for the only time in the war. Here the victims were vessels assigned either to coastal convoy duties – such as HMSs *Exmouth* and *Daring* (**3** and **4**) – or deployed in response to developments ashore, such as MN *Doris* and HMS/m *Thistle* (**5** and **6**) during the Norwegian Campaign and HMS *Grafton* (**7**) during the evacuation of Dunkirk. In many of these cases B.d.U. was assisted by *B-Dienst*, the Kriegsmarine's radio monitoring and intelligence service, which had cracked the British Admiralty's administrative code before the war (providing general information on the sailing and dispositions of warships and convoys until a more difficult code was introduced in August 1940) and made considerable progress against both the code and the super-enciphering of Naval Cipher No. 1 and the Naval Code. This period is also notable for two spectacular successes against capital ships: the sinking of the carrier *Courageous* in the Western Approaches (**1**) and the daring penetration of Scapa Flow by *U47* which resulted in the destruction of the battleship *Royal Oak* (**2**), both with heavy loss of life. Though the propaganda value of these events was huge and the elimination of one of the Royal Navy's six fleet carriers in particular a serious setback, neither event formed part of any wider trend, with the vulnerability that led to each

being rapidly addressed by the Admiralty. However, analysis of U-boat KTBs during this period makes it equally clear that the Royal Navy's losses were much less than they might have been had the Germans been using fully efficient ordnance. The 'torpedo crisis' that dogged the U-boat arm in the early months of the war – involving problems of depth-keeping and pistol operation (see above) – nullified attacks on the carrier *Ark Royal* and the battleships *Nelson* and *Warspite* together with those on more than twenty cruisers, destroyers and other vessels. This was particularly true of the Norwegian Campaign in the spring of 1940, which caused heavy attrition to the German surface fleet without a commensurate toll being taken of the Royal Navy.

The fall of France, the first 'happy time' and the slaughter of the AMCs: June 1940–February 1941

As Dönitz put it in the memoirs he wrote after a decade of post-war incarceration, the fall of France in June 1940 and the opportunities this opened up to the *U-Boot-Waffe* from its new bases at Lorient, St-Nazaire, Brest and La Pallice on the Atlantic represented an 'outstanding improvement in our strategic position in the war at sea' and provided the basis for what was proportionately the most successful period of U-boat operations of the war.[26] In what came to be known as the *glückliche Zeit* ('happy time'), hundreds of convoyed ships were sunk in the Atlantic by a few dozen U-boats, including those commanded by such famous tonnage aces as Otto Kretschmer, Heinrich Liebe and Joachim Schepke. This was also the period in which the number of ships sunk per U-boat at sea reached its highest level of almost 5.5 per month in October 1940, one that never came close to being regained. It was only the comparative shortage of operational U-boats – with an average of fewer than thirty at sea during this period – that saved the Allies from truly crippling losses.

Savage though the attrition was to the Allies, from a strictly naval perspective the battle was therefore far from the frenzy it later became. With scant Allied intelligence of U-boat dispositions, limited air cover, escorting vessels few in number after the attrition of Dunkirk and their radar, training and tactics still in a rudimentary state of development, the U-boats encountered comparatively few obstacles in their efforts to send merchantmen and their cargoes to the bottom. The most audacious commanders such as Kretschmer took to penetrating the heart of the merchant columns from where they were able to sink several vessels in a matter of minutes. With convoy escorts unable to provide effective defence, few fell victim to submarine attack while the merchantmen around them were being massacred. Indeed, the destroyer HMS *Whirlwind* (**13**) and HM sloops *Penzance* (**16**) and *Dundee* (**13**, **16** and **18**) were the only escort vessels to succumb to U-boat attack between the sinking of HMS *Daring* in February 1940 (**4**) and that of HMS *Picotee* in August 1941 (**29**). Plainly, the time had not yet come when a U-boat commander might resort to attacking a convoy escort out of frustration at his inability to penetrate its defences. In naval terms, this period is characterised by the toll taken of British armed merchant cruisers (AMCs), ten of which were sunk by U-boats between June 1940 and May 1941; all have entries in this book from *Carinthia* (**8**) to *Salopian* (**26**). These converted passenger ships, usually accounted for while sailing unescorted on

---

24 The fundamental sources are Günter Hessler, *The U-Boat War in the Atlantic, 1939–1945* (3 vols, London: HMSO, 1989) and Clay Blair, *Hitler's U-Boat War* (2 vols, New York: Random House, 1996–8).

25 This analysis is owed to Jak P. Mallmann Showell, to whom we extend our thanks.

26 *Memoirs: Ten Years and Twenty Days* (London: Greenhill Books, 1990), p. 110.

blockade duty, had few anti-submarine capabilities and made easy prey for the U-boats thanks to their large size and limited speed and manoeuvrability. Not only this, but as Kptlt Hans Cohausz's account of the sinking of HMS *Andania* (**10**) shows, the patrol lines of the AMCs became known to German intelligence in the summer of 1940 and a heavy toll taken as a consequence. The only shred of consolation for the British was the large number of torpedoes it frequently took to sink an AMC thanks to their stout construction and cargo of sealed wooden barrels – torpedoes that might otherwise have despatched so many merchantmen. Kretschmer, for instance, needed ten to dispose of HMSs *Laurentic* and *Patroclus* (**19**) in the same engagement. The AMCs were gradually withdrawn and repurposed from 1941, but the hazardous nature of their work is well shown in the fate of two of the ocean-boarding vessels which were introduced to replace them: HMSs *Manistee* and *Camito* (**23** and **25**), both lost in February 1941. The Admiralty also resorted to another ploy of Great War vintage, the submarine decoy or Q-ship, which resulted in the loss of two vessels in a week in June 1940, HMSs *Cape Howe* and *Willamette Valley* (**11** and **12**) – sunk with nothing in return. The same adventurous spirit animated the US Navy in 1942, though with no better results; see USS *Atik* (**57**).

New theatres of operations: March–December 1941

Although the Allies had yet to reach the nadir of their fortunes in the Battle of the Atlantic, the spring of 1941 represents a significant turning point in a number of respects. Using a mixture of captured intelligence, painstaking deduction and rare genius, the codebreakers at Bletchley Park in England for the first time penetrated the sophisticated encryption technique of the *Schlüssel-M* ('Enigma') machine with far-reaching consequences for the war at sea. It would take more than thirty years for the intelligence breakthroughs of May 1941 to become widely known, but already in March of that year the removal of three leading U-boat commanders from the game within the space of ten days provided a first indication to the world at large that the *U-Boot-Waffe* was not to have it all its own way. The loss of Otto Kretschmer, Günther Prien and Joachim Schepke together with their crews was more than a heavy blow to German pride and morale. It reflected the progress made by the Royal Navy in convoy protection and U-boat detection, at once the product of hard-won experience, improved training and significant technological advance quite unconnected with the intelligence effort. To give one example, the introduction of the Type-271 centimetric radar in March 1941 gave a growing number of escorts the ability to detect surfaced U-boats at night and thereby disrupt the tactical advantage hitherto enjoyed by the Germans. The 'happy time' of U-boats being able to cruise in and out of convoys practically at will was over, and with it came an increased focus on the escort as a foe to be reckoned with rather than a hapless observer of nocturnal depredations. On the other hand, the spring and summer of 1941 saw a significant increase in the number of U-boats at sea and the resulting ability of the *U-Boot-Waffe* to put its long-planned *Rudeltaktik* ('pack tactic') into full effect. The time of the wolfpacks had come. Battle between escort and U-boat was now joined in earnest, but the spate of escort sinkings in the Atlantic from August 1941 does not in itself illustrate any swing in favour of the *U-Boot-Waffe*. If anything the U-boats' advantage was much diminished and

the number of escort victims – none between January and July 1941 and twenty between August and the end of the year – a measure of the degree to which the Allies were able to interdict them in their main purpose. Of course, this was scant consolation to the victims and their companions, particularly during the chaos of night convoy attacks during which such vessels as *Picotee* (**29**) and her sister *Gladiolus* (**35**) were lost with all hands and without a single ship in company aware of their fate.

It was in this period, too, that the Royal Navy ceased to carry the weight of the U-boat war on its own and that the word 'Allied' now became a more appropriate term for those confronting the grey wolves, with the losses of the Soviet *M-99* in the Baltic (**27**), the Norwegian-manned escort destroyer *Bath* in the Atlantic (**30**) and the Australian sloop *Parramatta* in the Mediterranean (**42**) a reflection of what had truly become a world war on the high seas. In October 1941 came the sinking of the USS *Reuben James* (**38**) with the loss of 100 men which marked a turning point in US–German relations. Meanwhile, on 19 September HMCS *Lévis* (**32**) became the first ship lost to enemy action by the fledgling Royal Canadian Navy, destined to make a significant contribution to the Battle of the Atlantic.

But Hitler's wider ambitions were also complicating the task of the *U-Boot-Waffe*. At U-boat high command Dönitz was powerless to prevent a number of unwanted distractions from the Atlantic convoy lanes, namely the opening of new theatres of operations in the Baltic (from June 1941), the Barents and Norwegian seas with the introduction of British convoys to Russia (August 1941), and the Mediterranean (from September 1941). In the Baltic the ill-prepared Soviet navy lost three M-class submarines within weeks of Hitler invading Russia (**27**, **28** and **G7**), although the low importance attached by U-boat high command to this theatre is apparent from the antiquated Type-II boats it assigned there. Where the Mediterranean is concerned, the spectacular sinkings of the battleship HMS *Barham* (**41**, with heavy loss of life) and the carrier HMS *Ark Royal* (**39**, with practically none) announced the arrival of the *U-Boot-Waffe* in that theatre, but the sinking of the sloop HMAS *Parramatta* (**42**) in November 1941 was in its way a much more potent augury of things to come, marking as it does the onset of a prolonged battle which made the waters off Cyrenaica a graveyard for Allied warships. Nor was the Central Atlantic safe from the U-boat threat, as shown by the agony of the light cruiser HMS *Dunedin* and her men in November 1941, for long one of the overlooked tragedies of the war at sea (**40**).

Height of the conflict in the Atlantic, the Mediterranean and the Arctic: January 1942–March 1943

In terms of mercantile tonnage, 1942 yielded exceptional returns for the U-boat arm with around 1,000 ships sent to the bottom for a total of almost six million tons. The opening of a key new theatre of operations played a large part in this inflated figure: Operation PAUKENSCHLAG ('Drumbeat'), which unleashed the U-boats against the eastern seaboard of North America as the United States found itself at war in the world's two largest oceans. With US coastal defence initially lacking in both organisation and experience, the *U-Boot-Waffe* entered its second 'happy time' of conspicuous success; see USSs *Jacob Jones*, *Atik* and *Cythera* (**53**, **57** and **59**). In addition to the rich pickings enjoyed off the US coast until the inception of partial convoying in May, the U-boats also sank hundreds of merchantmen on the so-called 'Newfie–Derry run', aided by an intelligence blackout for the Allies between February and November 1942 once the Germans introduced a fourth rotor to their *Schlüssel-M* encryption machine; among the naval casualties were HMCS *Spikenard*, FNFL *Mimosa*, HMCS *Ottawa*, HMS *Veteran* and HNorMS *Montbretia* (**52, 61, 68, 71** and **76**). This 'Triton' key it would take Bletchley Park ten months to crack and a year to master. Meanwhile, *B-Dienst* penetration of Admiralty Naval Cipher No. 3 in February 1942 allowed most Allied naval signals in the Atlantic to be decrypted until June 1943, though only around ten per cent were read in time to be of operational use.

Despite a number of famous convoy victories for the U-boats as the wolfpack era reached its zenith, it would be a mistake to judge the success of the *U-Boot-Waffe* during this period on the basis of merchant sinkings alone. The average number of U-boats in the Atlantic passed 100 by the late summer of 1942 and continued to climb into 1943, but the number of merchantmen sunk per U-boat at sea during this period averages just over 1.0, a fraction of that attained during the first 'happy time' of late 1940. Convoys were now much more stoutly defended and although the Battle of the Atlantic was understood to be reaching a climax the attrition of merchantmen no longer came close to overtaking Allied construction as the industrial might of the US began to assert itself. Moreover, the losses suffered by the *U-Boot-Waffe* were now mounting alarmingly. Among other factors, the high-frequency direction-finding antennae (HF/DF or 'Huff-Duff') being fitted to escorts made it possible to track down any U-boat transmitting the radio signals that were essential to prosecuting the wolfpack strategy. Now it was the *U-Boot-Waffe*'s turn to suffer attrition, with U-boat losses rising from approximately eleven a month in the second half of 1942 to almost twenty a month in the first half of 1943; see the graph on p. xxxii.

Of course, for the seamen and sailors manning and escorting the convoys this subtle swing in favour of the Allies was imperceptible. Those involved with convoys HX229 and SC122 in March 1943 would have been bemused by any assertion of Allied superiority as they were put to the sword by no less than forty-three U-boats from three wolfpacks, suffering the loss of twenty-two merchantmen for a total in excess of 145,000 tons. Equally imperceptibly to those taking part, the Battle of the Atlantic had developed from being largely a U-boat assault on convoyed merchantmen to a savage encounter between the *U-Boot-Waffe* and the wide assortment of naval vessels and aircraft charged with defending them. In November 1942 the number of operational U-boats reached 200 for the first time but this milestone has to be set against the increasing number of escort vessels and the highly evolved training, tactics and technology which they now brought to bear. Despite continued attrition to merchantmen, it was naval vessels which now bore the brunt of the Battle of the Atlantic, with mounting losses to U-boats and Allied warships alike. Sometimes this attrition is reflected in the loss of unaccompanied vessels – USS *Jacob Jones*, USS *Muskeget* and HMS *Fidelity* (**53, 66** and **80**) – at others it extends to those lost in the confusion of battle with none aware of their demise until any but a fraction of the crew could be saved: HMCS *Spikenard*, FNFL *Mimosa* and HMS *Veteran* (**52, 61** and **71**).

In other theatres the remarkable endurance of the Type-IX boat made itself felt as the *U-Boot-Waffe* brought the battle to Canadian waters,

of which the sinking of HMCS *Charlottetown* (**67**) in the St Lawrence River in September 1942 and later that of HMCS *Shawinigan* (**108**) in the Cabot Strait at the close of 1944 are represented in the main part of this volume. The heavy toll taken of warships in the Mediterranean in 1942 (eighteen in all) represents the highest rate of sinking per U-boat in any major theatre, with the losses of HMSs *Heythrop*, *Medway*, *Eagle* and *Partridge* (**55, 64, 65** and **79**) all illustrating the problems of Asdic detection associated with these waters. Three vessels – HMS *Martin*, HMS *Hecla* and HrMs *Isaac Sweers* (**72–74**) – were lost against the background of Operation TORCH – the Allied landings in North Africa – to which HMS *Avenger* (**75**) and five naval transports (**G38–42**) also fell victim on the Atlantic side in what was otherwise a disappointing episode for the *U-Boot-Waffe*. Dramatic and sudden losses like those of HMSs *Barham*, *Jaguar* and *Eagle* (**41, 56** and **65**) aside, sinkings were often characterised by a comparatively low fatality rate that reflected the higher water and air temperature together with the generally placid sea conditions characteristic of the Mediterranean. In the Arctic, by contrast, the losses of HMSs *Matabele* and *Somali* (**47** and **70**) lay at the other end of the survival spectrum, forerunners of the grim fate awaiting the many Allied sailors who suffered immersion at these latitudes as the *U-Boot-Waffe* contested the passage of war supplies to Russia.

The U-boats defeated: April–September 1943

Notwithstanding its remarkable successes in March 1943, between January and May that year the *U-Boot-Waffe* was rewarded with little more than half the number of merchant sinkings that had crowned its efforts in the same period of 1942 – this despite the deployment of *twice* the number of U-boats. There were many reasons for this, including the timely decryption of Enigma signals; the introduction of improved Asdic and anti-submarine weaponry such as the Hedgehog spigot mortar; advances in training and organisation (of which the work of HMS *Western Isles*, the anti-submarine training school under the formidable Cdre Gilbert Stephenson at Tobermory, Scotland is an example); and the introduction of new tactics for convoy escort and support groups such as the 'creeping attack' developed by Capt. F. J. 'Johnnie' Walker. Along with the growing number, effectiveness and lethality of escorts from three navies was the development of Allied air power which began to play a decisive role in the matter. While the largest-ever assembly of U-boats was feeding on the ill-fated HX229 and SC122, RAF Wellington aircraft were for the first time being fitted with ASV Mk-III centimetric radar, a development that boded ill for U-boats crossing the Bay of Biscay and against which the German Metox radar detector proved ineffectual. US aircraft were also acquiring state-of-the-art radar in the summer of 1943 by which time the Liberator bomber had finally closed the 'air gap' in the Atlantic. It was at this juncture that the number of U-boats lost during front-line operations began to mount decisively. 'Black May' itself (as May 1943 came to be known) cost the Kriegsmarine forty-one U-boats at sea and is recognised as the point at which the Battle of the Atlantic ceased to be a meaningful competition. This savage attrition – in which the destruction of experienced crews was every bit as disastrous as the loss in *matériel* – was approximately three times that of the previous worst month (February 1943) and matched the number of U-boats lost in 1941 as a whole. Aware of the futility of battling against such odds, Dönitz withdrew his boats from the Atlantic convoy lanes, the first operational acknowledgement that the dream of *Tonnageschlacht* victory had gone. From now on the number of merchantmen lost to the *U-Boot-Waffe* collapses, with the sinking rate for each month averaging around ten per cent of the record tally notched up in May and June 1942. Even more revealing is the new strategy adopted by the Allies having finally broken the 'Triton' code. By April 1943 they were for the first time using positional data gleaned from decrypts not to reroute convoys away from the wolfpacks but to strengthen the convoys running into them.

The Allied victory in mid-1943 is also reflected in the spread of warship sinkings over the first nine months of that year. Indeed, with the exception of HMS *Beverley* (**83**), the warship losses covered in the main section of this book paint a picture of isolated successes far from the key convoy lanes of the Atlantic: the loss of HMS *Welshman* (**81**) in the Mediterranean and the Dutch depot ship HrMs *Colombia* (**82**) in the Indian Ocean, the sinking of HM submarine *P615* (**84**) off West Africa and that of USS *Plymouth* (**85**) off the Virginia coast. Although these losses continued to show the global reach of the *U-Boot-Waffe*, in their own way they reflect the Allies' mastery of the sea channels that really counted in the context of total war. Indeed, not even the withdrawal of U-boats from the Atlantic convoy lanes could halt the attrition, the *U-Boot-Waffe* losing more boats in July and August 1943 combined than it had in May, yet with even fewer merchant pennants to show for it. Given this outcome, it is ironic that the loss of the USS *Gannet* (**60**) in June 1942 should reflect local cooperation between the British and US navies at its very worst because it was the efficiency of that union and the sharing of intelligence, tactics and technology between these two and the RCN that had done so much to turn the tide.

The German response and the Zaunkönig: *September 1943– November 1944*

From their naval intelligence in the otherwise relatively quiet summer of 1943 the Allies gathered that something was afoot and so it proved: the return of the *U-Boot-Waffe* to the fray in September with a confidence afforded by a lethal new weapon: the T5 acoustic homing torpedo, known to the Germans as the *Zaunkönig* ('wren') and to the Allies by its acronym GNAT (German Naval Acoustic Torpedo); see above. To this was added an array of measures against radar such as the *Wanze* warning system and, rather less effectively, the *Aphrodite* decoy device. The *Zaunkönig* was first fired in anger by U-boats from the *Leuthen* pack in September 1943 and with devastating results: within seventy-two hours three escorts had been sent to the bottom – HMCS *St Croix*, HMS *Polyanthus* and HMS *Itchen* (**86–88**) – another rendered a constructive total loss (HMS *Lagan*) along with six freighters sunk and two damaged in the first mauling of an Atlantic convoy since May. Although the U-boats continued to live dangerously and the toll on merchant shipping remained low, the experience of Canadian Stoker William Fisher in September 1943 – sunk twice by *Zaunkönig* in three days – hardly constituted evidence of Allied supremacy at sea.

The majority of warship losses covered in the main part of this volume from September 1943 onward are therefore victims of the *Zaunkönig* torpedo. Indeed, it should be noted that the toll taken of Allied warships in 1944 rivals even that of Allied merchantmen, an unthinkable ratio in the early years of the war and proof both of the effectiveness of convoy defence and of the extent to which the U-Boat War had become a naval conflict in the fullest sense. But if the toll on warships remained high, there are also echoes of the German torpedo crisis of 1940 in the failure of the *Zaunkönig* to inflict even greater damage on the Allied navies. Though the delivery of such a formidable weapon into front-line operation was an undeniably impressive achievement, the persistent flaws of the T5 (including an over-sensitive detonator liable to be triggered in a vessel's wake) resulted in a success rate against escorts of just 16.6 per cent, less than half B.d.U.'s estimated kill rate of 40 per cent; this compares with an eventual kill rate by war's end of 25 per cent for the Hedgehog anti-submarine spigot mortar and an absolute kill rate of 34 per cent for the Squid depth-charge mortar. A particularly telling episode for the *U-Boot-Waffe* during this period was its attempt to counter NEPTUNE, the naval side of the Normandy landings. Despite a force of forty-three U-boats deployed from French bases (including twelve with the new *Schnorchel* apparatus that allowed for greater submerged speed and range) and blood-curdling battle orders from Dönitz, it was able to sew pennants for only seven war vessels between June and August 1944 (including HMS *Blackwood*, **103**) and a dozen merchantmen out of 5,339 vessels taking part in the operation. Moreover, these nineteen successes cost the *Landwirt* group twenty of its own number, a dismal return for an increasingly sombre B.d.U. with almost no cards left to play. With the loss of the *U-Boot-Waffe*'s French bases from September 1944 onward, the Battle of the Atlantic was effectively over and the strategic focus shifted to the North Sea, the Northern Theatre and British coastal waters.

The spread of warships sunk during this period reflects at once the strength of the Allied naval coalition and the gradual contraction of U-boat operations. In addition to the sinking of the destroyer *St Croix* in the mid-Atlantic (**86**), the contribution of the Royal Canadian Navy in both home and European waters is illustrated by the losses of HMCSs *Shawinigan* (**108**) and *Alberni* (**105**) in the autumn of 1944, while the emergence of the US Navy as the most powerful in the world is hinted at not only in its ongoing commitment to the Atlantic theatre where it suffered the loss of USSs *Leary* (**93**), *Leopold* (**100**) and *Fiske* (**104**) together with the destroyer escort *Borie* (**G65**) and the escort carrier *Block Island* (**G81**) – the largest US naval victim of a U-boat – but also in its support of Allied operations in the Mediterranean, from which USSs *Buck*, *Bristol* and *Fechteler* (**90**, **92** and **101**) never returned. Meanwhile, losses of smaller Soviet vessels in the Barents Sea and the Gulf of Finland make up a substantial proportion of the Gazetteer. Like its efforts on land, the Russian contribution to the Allied cause at sea was a long and lonely one with a disproportionately sparse coverage in post-war historiography in the West, though this can partly be explained by limited access to primary sources.

The unchronicled denouement: December 1944–April 1945

To scan the table of contents of this book would be to gain the impression that the war at sea ended in December 1944. But as a review of the Gazetteer will show, the U-boat war was far from over even if the outcome was by now evident to all the protagonists. However, the absence of U-boat documentation from this date makes it impossible to analyse further warship sinkings with the benefit of

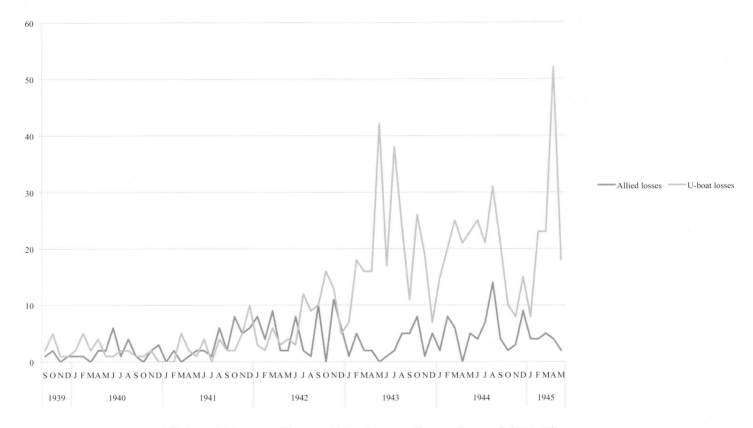

Allied warship losses to U-boats vs U-boat losses to all causes, by month (1939–45)

the U-boat KTB (see above), and HMS *Bullen* (**109**), sunk by *U775* on 6 December 1944, is therefore the last to receive a full entry in this volume. All warships claimed by the *U-Boot-Waffe* from here until the end of the war, mainly in far northern latitudes, are confined to the Gazetteer. The trials of such unfamiliar names as the Soviet escort destroyer *Deyatel'ny* (Arctic, January 1945; **G121**), the Norwegian trawler *Nordhav II* (North Sea, March 1945; **G128**) or the British trawler *Ebor Wyke* (Icelandic waters, May 1945; **G135**) must therefore await another time and place. But like the anonymously named Norwegian minesweeper *NYMS 382* (**G136**), sunk by *U1023* in the English Channel even as Germany was surrendering on 7 May 1945,

these vessels and dozens like them remind us of a recurring element in the pages of this book: that the size or importance of a vessel has no bearing on the human drama attending her sinking, with an overlooked incident like the loss of the Soviet submarine *M-94* (**28**) in the Baltic having as much or more to engage the emotions as that of a vessel many times her size and infinitely better known. Within the wider context of strategy, tactics and technology it is easy to forget the centrality of the human experience of war and combat; easy to forget that it was men rather than vessels which made the U-boat war of 1939–1945 the most bitterly contested in naval history.

Reading the Kriegstagebücher

The entries of which this volume is composed are themselves based on the U-boat *Kriegstagebuch* (KTB) excerpts which form the centrepiece of each. While the textual issues raised by the KTBs are covered in the Introduction, the purpose of this section is to provide a reader's guide to the excerpts and to the related apparatus which appears at the head of each entry, together with other features common to the book as a whole. Beyond helping readers navigate what is a large yet unified volume of material, the aim is to impart a sense of the KTBs as complex technical documents and convey the problems of translation they have brought in their train.

I   *Layout of the entries*

Data supplied for each ship

Entry number   This is cross-referenced throughout the volume and in the map section in bold, e.g. (**51**); **G-** and **X-** numbers refer to entries in the Gazetteer.

Commander's name   A † indicates that the commanding officer lost his life in the attack.

Sinking details   The date of sinking per *Allied* or ship's own timekeeping; a spread of dates indicates the period elapsed between initial hit(s) and eventual sinking.

Theatre   This is the theatre or campaign in which or during which the sinking occurred, with reference to the corresponding map.

Coordinates   The position of the attack, usually based on Allied data but occasionally derived from the Kriegsmarine's *Quadrat* code (see below); the sinking position is provided in the main text if significantly different.

Kriegsmarine code   The position of the attack given in the Kriegsmarine's *Quadrat* code as recorded in the log; '*(TR)*' here indicates that the data is taken from the torpedo report.

U-boat timekeeping   Relative timekeeping between the Allies and the attacking U-boat; any data given pertains to the U-boat.

Fatalities and survivors   A number with 'and' before it in this section refers to passengers and/or rescued individuals *not* of the ship's company.

Displacement   Standard displacement is provided for warships; the size of requisitioned merchantmen is stated both in deadweight tons and Gross Register Tons (GRT).

Dimensions   Maximum length × maximum beam × standard draught.

Maximum speed   Data shows the vessel's notional best speed at the time of the sinking.

Armament   Data shows armament fit at the time of the sinking.

Kriegstagebuch *(KTB) excerpts*

Each log excerpt in this book opens with the beginning of the attack sequence and closes as the routine of the U-boat returns to normal at the end of the engagement. Occasionally a later reference to the attack such as a signal to U-boat headquarters reporting the sinking requires the addition of a separate extract; such additions are indicated by ✗.

Incidents   A dotted line indicates that the first entry shown is *not* the first of the day. Radio transmissions and manuscript additions are always set in *italics*. The commanding officer's signature at close of day is shown **bold italics**, e.g. **Schuhart**.

There are explanatory notes as required for the KTB; points are developed under the heading *The sinking* that follows the KTB text.

II   *Column by column: The* Kriegstagebücher *in detail*

As with any serious exercise in translation, the objective in rendering the *Kriegstagebuch* excerpts into English has been to provide as faithful a reflection as possible of the original while at the same time offering a final body of text that is comprehensible to the reader. The endeavour has presented many problems with respect to the more esoteric aspects of the German, particularly in the realm of technical abbreviation. The following paragraphs explain the approach which has been adopted in dealing with such issues while providing some context for those elements common to all KTBs which are essential to an appreciation of the excerpts as a whole.

Column 1   Date and time

Each log excerpt begins with the date, which has been rendered in standardised form from a variety of different formats (e.g. **23.xii** for 23 December). Although some commanders were in the habit of repeating the date at the head of each page of their war diary, most provided it only at the beginning of each calendar day. Times are given in the twenty-four-hour clock, both in the original KTBs and in the translations. U-boat timekeeping was based on the Kriegsmarine's adoption of German official or 'legal' time (*Deutsche Gesetzliche Zeit* – DGZ) which varied according to the season as well as for other reasons. The variants were *Mittlere Greenwich-Zeit* (MGZ – Greenwich Mean Time/GMT), *Mitteleuropäische Zeit* (MEZ – Central European Time: GMT +1) and *Deutsche Sommerzeit* (DSZ – German Summer Time: GMT +2). The timekeeping observed by the *U-Boot-Waffe* during the Second World War was as follows, though it should not be regarded as absolute since there were departures from it at certain times and in certain waters, not to mention a number of irregularities specific to individual U-boats.

Dates	Timekeeping
3 September 1939–1 April 1940	either MGZ (GMT) or MEZ (GMT +1)
1 April 1940–2 November 1942	DSZ (GMT +2)
2 November 1942–29 March 1943	MEZ (GMT +1)
29 March–4 October 1943	DSZ (GMT +2)
4 October 1943–3 April 1944	MEZ (GMT +1)
3 April–2 October 1944	DSZ (GMT +2)
2 October 1944–2 April 1945	MEZ (GMT +1)
2 April 1945 onwards	DSZ (GMT +2)

To contextualise the German and Allied accounts of the sinking, the timekeeping differential between the two (or parity as the case may be) is provided at the head of each entry, with the value given indicating the extent to which U-boat timekeeping varied (or not) from the Allied. It should be noted that Allied timekeeping varies not only from navy to navy but occasionally from source to source, with surviving documentation employing two, three and even four timekeeping standards in describing the same action. The timekeeping preferred in the entries on the Allied side is generally that of the ranking officer who prepared the sinking report, though there are times when this cannot be determined from the available information, either because the senior officer went down with his ship or because the vessel was sailing independently or was lost with all hands. Inevitably, confusion could and did occur in practice, sometimes with serious consequences as in the case of HMS *Camito* (**25**) in which a timekeeping differential had a bearing on her sinking. Generally speaking, timekeeping in the Royal Navy was zone-based and referenced to its relationship to GMT (known as 'Z' or 'Zulu time'), although official reports usually revert to GMT itself. The Royal Canadian Navy's timekeeping varies from source to source, with warship sinkings generally reported in local time whereas the deliberations of Boards of Inquiry were usually based on GMT, even when this was at considerable variance with local time. The sinking of HMCS *Charlottetown* in the St Lawrence River (**67**) is a case in point, though that of *Valleyfield* off Newfoundland (**102**) was reported in local time throughout. Commonwealth and foreign navies serving under operational control of the Admiralty followed local RN practice. Like the RN, the US Navy reported in the zone time relevant to the action as referenced to GMT (known as 'Z' or 'Zebra time'), with other zones having letters denoting their relationship to 'Z' time.

Column 2   *The naval Quadratkarte*

B.d.U. required the position of every U-boat at sea to be recorded in the KTB at four-hourly intervals corresponding with the watchkeeping changes at 0000, 0400, 0800, etc., as well as beside those entries covering significant events such as convoy sightings or attacks on enemy vessels, and this was usually done. The positions in question, which are provided in the second column, are not rendered in coordinates of latitude and longitude but in the form of a *Quadrat* (quadrant – abbreviated to 'Qu.' or 'M.Qu.') that relates to a coded grid system designed for the Kriegsmarine before the war. Known as the *Marine Quadratkarte* ('naval quadrant map'), this consisted of quadrants of approximately equal size that encompassed all the oceans and coastal areas of the world.[1]

The *Marine Quadratkarte* was based on the principle of subsuming several square units of equal size into one larger unit. The basic large squares or *Grossquadrate* averaged 486 nautical miles on each side (236,196 square miles) and were denoted by a 'bigram' of two letters – e.g. 'AL' – whereby the first letter provided a very general estimate of latitude and the second an indicator of longitude. As the example above shows, the indicator of latitude was the more consistent of the two, although this too 'jumped' from ocean to ocean. These large squares were in turn subdivided into an average of nine rows and nine

columns of smaller squares measuring 54 miles on each side (2,916 square miles) and denoted by two numbers following the bigram of the large square – e.g. 'AL 52'. These indicated the position of the subsquare within the larger square, whereby '11' would be extreme top left and '99' extreme bottom right. However, the intervening numbers were not in numerical sequence but in a subcode such that the top row read 11, 12, 13, 21, 22, 23, 31, 32, 33 from left to right – a system which placed '52' just above the centre of the subsquare.[2] These squares in turn break down into another nine rows and nine columns of smaller squares – the *Quadrate* proper – measuring six miles on each side (36 square miles) and denoted by a further two letters indicating the position within the larger square – e.g. 'AL 5214'.[3] The system also allowed for the spherical nature of the earth at extreme longitudes with the use of *Grossquadrate* of ten as against nine subunits that included filler squares as well as those of irregular shape.

Although these six-digit quadrant positions take the place of coordinates in the KTBs and in all radio transmissions, it should be noted that they do not offer the precision of coordinates in degrees and minutes, denoting as they do a position anywhere within an area of 36 square miles. If a U-boat commander wished to give a more specific position, as was often the case when cruising inshore, the quadrant could be refined with one of twenty-nine abbreviations indicating the relative position within this smallest quadrant. These abbreviations are purely descriptive, encompassing terms such as l.o.E. (*linke obere Ecke* – 'upper left corner'), r.K.u. (*rechte Kante unten* – 'lower right edge'), and so on; the logs describing the sinkings of HMS/m *Thistle* and USS *Alexander Hamilton* (**5** and **48**) are cases in point.[4] Where they appear in the original, these abbreviations are rendered in full in the translations.

British naval intelligence had been quick to gather information on the *Marine Quadratkarte*, obtaining part of it in December 1939 and more in early 1940. By the summer of that year they had pieced together sectors of the North Atlantic, the North Sea and the Baltic, a picture which was completed in May 1941 with the capture of complete grid charts for the North Atlantic and Mediterranean. The simultaneous breaking of the German *Schlüssel-M* ('Enigma') encryption system briefly afforded the British the position of every U-boat at sea which sent in a positional report. Unfortunately for the Admiralty, over-zealous responses to early decrypts of Enigma-encoded messages soon aroused B.d.U.'s suspicions of a security breach relating not to the *Schlüssel-M* system itself (which was deemed unbreakable) but to the widespread dissemination of U-boat positional data *en clair* within the Kriegsmarine at large, to the Luftwaffe and to various overseas stations.[5] This prompted the introduction of a makeshift 'reference-point system' in June, to be replaced by a set of *Fluss* ('flux') substitution tables in September of that year. These in turn gave way to a more sophisticated *Adressbuch* ('address book') cipher system introduced in November 1941 and modified in September 1943. The *Adressbuch* system blinded

---

1   See Jeffrey K. Bray, ed., *Ultra in the Atlantic, V: The German Naval Grid and its Cipher* (Walnut Creek, Calif.: Aegean Park Press, 1994). The Wehrmacht and the Luftwaffe had their own distinct grid systems.

2   It was also possible to create a box 162 miles on each side (26,244 square miles) with the addition of a single letter.

3   Or three letters for a square with 18 miles on each side (324 square miles).

4   For a full list of these abbreviations and their relative positions in the squares, see http://www.uboatarchive.net/KTBNotesNavigation.htm

5   See [Fregkpt. Günter Hessler,] *The U-Boat War in the Atlantic, 1939–1945*, I, p. 79.

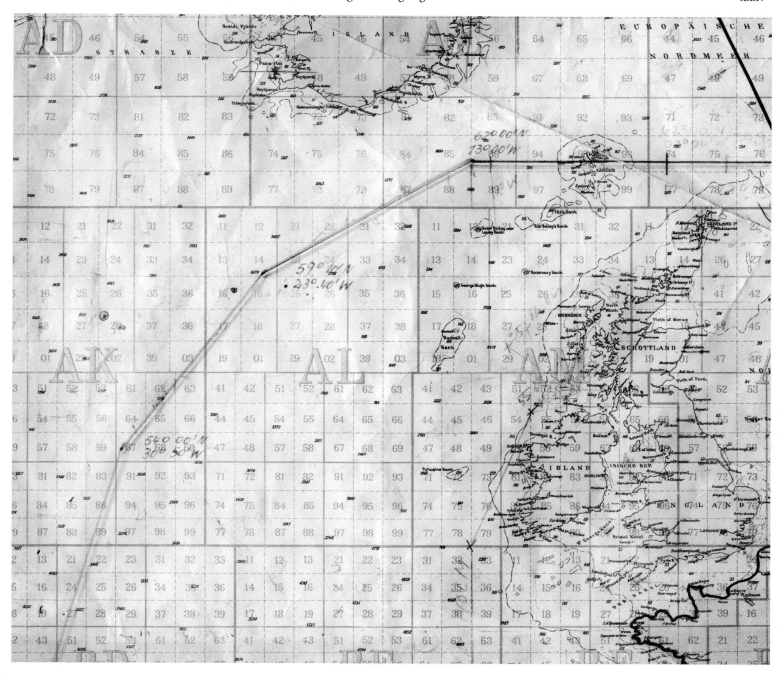

The portion of the *Marine Quadratkarte* covering the eastern Atlantic and the approaches to the British Isles, seen here from a captured copy in the collections of the Naval Historical Branch. This example shows the 'AK', 'AL' and 'AM' *Grossquadrate* together with the numbered subsquares into which each was divided. *NHB*

the Allies once again to German positions, not least because of the intelligence blackout which followed the introduction of a fourth rotor to the *Schlüssel-M* encryption machine for U-boat traffic in February 1942. When this 'Triton' addition was cracked later that year the way was paved for British and US intelligence to piece together the *Adressbuch* system. The key breakthrough came in the spring of 1943, a development which contributed to the *U-Boot-Waffe*'s unprecedented attrition during 'Black May'. However, the new cipher systems used to

encode grid coordinates from June 1941 onwards do not extend to the actual KTBs, in which commanding officers continued to enter the *Quadrat* positions unencrypted. The same applies to positions stated in incoming and outgoing signals as they appear in the KTB. The only alteration made in the translations is the occasional reinsertion of the initial *Grossquadrat* bigram where this has been left out of the original entry; such additions are made in brackets.

Column 2   Meteorological and sea data

The Kriegsmarine applied standardised systems of notation to indicate the state of the wind, weather and sea, with appropriate abbreviations. Where wind is concerned, the Beaufort Wind Scale (as internationally standardised in 1923) is used to describe its strength on a scale of 0 to 12, whereby 'o' indicates a flat calm and '12' a full hurricane. The compass direction of the wind is almost always recorded in the logs, with abbreviations similar to those employed in English into which they are translated directly.

Beaufort Wind Scale

0	Calm	5	Moderate breeze	9	Gale
1	Light air	6	Fresh breeze	10	Strong gale
2	Light breeze	7	Strong breeze	11	Whole gale
3	Slight breeze	8	High wind	12	Hurricane
4	Gentle breeze				

The data for wind is usually followed by that for the prevailing sea where a similar numeric scale is used. The scale employed is a matter of debate, with the now-obsolete Douglas Sea Scale (using a scale of 0 to 9) being favoured in some quarters, though if so the question arises as to which of the two Douglas codes is being applied, that for sea or that for swell, even if the difference is more descriptive than numerical. Since many commanding officers go on to describe the *Dünung* (swell), it must be supposed that it was the sea rather than the swell code that was initially being applied. Analysis of the KTBs is complicated by the use of any of five data annotations and inconsistent usage in the same log, but the evidence is that the wartime *U-Boot-Waffe* employed the *Petersen Seegangskala* (Petersen Sea State Scale).[6] Devised by a German sea captain in the late 1920s and accepted by international convention in 1939, the Petersen Sea Scale was essentially a modified version of the Beaufort Wind Scale, though like the Douglas Sea Scale it ended at 9 (the equivalent of 12 on the Beaufort Scale). Both scales are virtually identical with respect to 'sea' descriptions, the difference being more marked in descriptions of swell. Irrespective of the scale used, the sea state is rendered in the translations with the word 'sea' placed before

the data provided. The table below shows the comparison between the systems.

The log usually (though not always) goes on to provide details of the weather. Although U-boat commanders were free to enter any observation they saw fit – and frequently did just that – here too they relied on a system devised by Sir Francis Beaufort, the Beaufort Weather Notation System, which was adopted by the Royal Navy in 1833 and standardised by international convention in 1935. What is interesting about the use of this system in the *U-Boot-Waffe* is that the notation employed preserves the letter-based abbreviations of the *English* words, e.g. 'd' for drizzle, 'f' for fog, 'l' for lightning, 'p' for passing shower, 't' for thunder, and so on, rather than the initial letters of their German equivalents as one might expect of a military arm of the Third Reich; others match the German term owing to its close relationship with English, notably 'r' = *Regen* (rain), 's' = *Schnee* (snow) and 'h' = *Hagel* (hail).[7] All such abbreviations are resolved into the English word in full in the translations. A letter from this system that occurs with great frequency is 'c' – cloud. The extent of cloud cover is frequently described using a fractional system of decimals. Sometimes a number between 1 and 10 is given, or else a fractional format is employed: 1/10, 2/10, etc.; where this occurs the Beaufort letter 'c' is resolved to 'cloud' and the fraction left as it appears in the original.

In addition to the above, the second column of the KTB is sometimes used to record other natural phenomena such as the brightness of the moon or the presence of sea phosphorescence, particularly when these might have implications for the commander's tactical options during the attack sequence. These are translated directly along with the occasional references to barometric pressure in millibars (*Millibar* – mb). By contrast, on the rare occasions where a measurement of temperature is given, the abbreviation for Celsius (C) is added to the data where necessary, and the equivalent in Fahrenheit supplied in brackets. Finally, the commander frequently used this column to record the prevailing visibility in qualitative form – good, average, poor, etc. – and/or quantitatively through an estimate in nautical miles. The latter is almost always abbreviated in the German to 'sm'

Comparison of sea and swell scales

	Douglas Sea Scale	*Douglas Swell Code*	*Petersen Sea Scale*	*Petersen Swell Code*
0	Calm (glassy)	No Swell	Smooth	None
1	Calm (rippled)	Very low (short and low wave)	Calm	Rippled
2	Smooth	Low (long and low wave)	Gentle motion	Short
3	Slight	Light (short and moderate wave)	Slightly agitated	Small, white horses
4	Moderate	Moderate (average and moderate wave)	Moderately agitated	Long, white horses, breaking
5	Rough	Moderate rough (long and moderate wave)	Rough	Large, wave crests creating large white areas of foam
6	Very rough	Rough (short and heavy wave)	Very rough	Breaking
7	High	High (average and heavy wave)	High	Huge waves, spray, strips of foam, rolling
8	Very high	Very high (long and heavy wave)	Very high	Mountainous waves with long breaking crests, sea white with foam
9	Phenomenal	Confused (wave length and height indefinable)	Exceptional	Mountainous waves, ships disappearing in wave troughs, sea white with foam

---

6   Peter Petersen, „Zur Bestimmung der Windstärke auf See. Für Segler, Dampfer und Luftfahrzeige" in *Annalen der Hydrographie und Maritimen Meteorologie* no. 55 (March 1927), pp. 69–72.

7   For a glossary of the commonest German weather terms, see http://www.uboatarchive.net/KTBNotesWeather.htm

(*Seemeilen* – nautical miles), for which 'nm' is used to distinguish this from another frequently used measure of distance (and length), metres (m).

Column 3   Abbreviations

The heart of the KTBs rests in the third column under the catch-all title *Vorkommnisse* ('Incidents'); see p. xvi. Much of the information contained here will be readily understood by most readers, with the balance being explained either in the notes or with reference to the technical information provided in Part II of the Introduction, especially with respect to torpedo fire control (pp. xxiv–xxvi); other issues are dealt with in the Glossary. Inevitably, the translations resolve many of the German abbreviations that appear in the original into their English equivalents, where these exist. Although this implies a sacrifice of the original notation, it is hoped that this expedient and others like it in the translations will help to clarify the logs as a whole. These abbreviations usually concern depth-keeping, the range and bearing of other vessels, and the various speeds of which a U-boat was capable. These topics are treated in turn in the paragraphs that follow.

(a) Depth-keeping
Naturally enough, any cruise would involve a U-boat diving for purposes of stealth, testing the integrity of the hull, obtaining better hydrophone conditions or avoiding enemy attack from surface or airborne units. In the event of enemy attack the depth or depths reached during the process of evasion would be recorded in the KTB. This data was frequently set down in a specific formula that used a base depth denoted by the letter 'A' which in this context stood for 80 metres (262 feet). Thus, in the case of *U136*'s sinking of HMS *Arbutus* (**50**), where Kptlt Heinrich Zimmermann's log has *Ich höre noch vier Salven beim Schliessen des Turmluks. Gehe langsam auf A + 80 m.* ('As I'm closing the hatch I hear another four salvoes. I go slowly to A + 80 m.'), a depth of 80 + 80 = 160 metres (525 feet) is in fact being indicated. All instances of this notation in the logs are resolved in the translations with the actual depth in metres.

Nor is the letter 'A' the only depth-keeping conundrum for the reader of the U-boat *Kriegstagebuch*. A number of excerpts in this volume employ the letter 'T' in the same context – e.g. 'We go to T = 20' in *U132*'s attack on the USS *Alexander Hamilton* (**48**).[8] Since the German word for 'depth' is *Tiefe* it might be supposed that some U-boat commanders simply used this notation to indicate that a measure of depth was being recorded, this being faithfully transcribed in the typed fair copy of the log. However, analysis of the KTBs suggests that things may not be so simple. The unavoidable implication is that, like 'A', 'T' denotes some kind of base depth, though the precise figure has proved elusive. At least one U-boat veteran has suggested that 'T' simply represents depths beyond 'A', so that the above example of 'T = 20' would indicate a depth of 100 metres (i.e. 80 + 20 metres). However, it is equally likely that 'T' represents a deeper base depth altogether. In the excerpt documenting *U331*'s attack on HMS *Barham* (**41**), Oblt.z.S. Hans-Diedrich Freiherr von Tiesenhausen records the

failure to activate a depth gauge in the control room when he ordered an emergency dive after unleashing his salvo. No sooner was this oversight noticed and corrected than the gauge swung to 'T = 130 m', von Tiesenhausen immediately taking steps to bring *U331* to a safer depth, which she did after some hesitation. A reprimand duly followed from B.d.U. for the great danger in which the boat and its crew had been placed through the inattention of one man. However, this reprimand would hardly have been issued had von Tiesenhausen merely signified a depth of 130 metres (426 feet) – above the Type VIIC's operational safe depth of approximately 150 metres (492 feet) and well within its design crush depth of approximately 250 metres (820 feet). However, when survivors of *U331* were interrogated by British intelligence following the loss of their boat a year later it was revealed that *U331* had inadvertently dived to 270 metres (885 feet) during this episode, a figure, later revised to 267 metres, which was confirmed post-war.[9] An extrapolation of this data (i.e. 130 + 140 = 270 metres) would therefore suggest that 'T' represents depths beyond 140 metres (460 feet), the figure in metres subsequently given indicating the depth in excess of that value. By extension, 'T' itself can be equated to the design safe operational depth of the Type VIIC which lay in that vicinity. For all this, the 'T' question remains open and it is quite possible that this notation may have different meanings in different KTBs.

(b) Range and bearing
Abbreviations in the third column relating to a target's range and bearing have also been resolved in the translations. When a vessel is sighted, the KTB will usually provide either its relative bearing ('Vessel sighted at 30° on the port bow') or its absolute compass bearing. In the latter case the data is preceded by the abbreviation 'rw.' (*rechtweisend* – lit. 'true pointing') in the original. In English the custom is simply to place the word 'true' after the bearing in question, which convention is followed in the translations. However, some commanders are wont to express compass positions not in individual degrees but in 'Dez.' (*Dezimale* – decimals), namely units of ten degrees. In such cases a relative bearing of 30 degrees would therefore be recorded as '3 Dez.' The translations simply multiply this figure by ten to provide the bearing in standard degree format. Similarly, instances where ranges are recorded in 'hm' (*Hektometer*, where 1 hectometre = 100 metres) are given in metres, so a range expressed in the original as '15 hm' is rendered as '1,500 m' in the translation. Apart from nautical miles, practically all measurements are given in the metric system, for which a conversion table is provided below. When imperial equivalents are provided in parentheses in the logs and elsewhere, these are usually rounded up or down to the nearest whole number (see table overleaf).

(c) Speed
Other abbreviations in the third column include those for speed. Unlike the commander's estimate of target speed, which is almost always given in knots, only exceptionally was the U-boat's own speed recorded in knots. The commander instead relied on abbreviations of standard engine-room telegraph settings which are shown in the table below. When translating these abbreviations, the norms applied by

---

8 The excerpts in question are HMS *Rajputana*/*U108* (**24**); HMS *Springbank*/*U201* (**33**); HMS *Gladiolus*/*U553* and *U432* (**35**); HMS *Cossack*/*U563* (**37**); HMS *Ark Royal*/*U81* (**39**); HMS *Barham*/*U331* (**41**); the Soviet *M-175*/*U584* (**45**), and USS *Alexander Hamilton*/*U132* (**48**).

9 It should be noted, however, that design specifications are notably cautious and that there are a number of cases on record of U-boats surviving even greater depths, including at least one beyond 300 metres (984 feet).

Imperial weights and measures

Measure	Imperial equivalent	Decimal equivalent
inch (in/")	—	2.54 cm
foot (ft/')	= 12 in	30.48 cm
yard (yd)	= 3 ft	91.44 cm
fathom (fm)	= 6 ft	1.83 m
cable (British)	= 100 fm/200 yd	182.88 m
(US)	= 120 fm/240 yd	219.46 m
nautical mile (nm)	= 6,080 ft	1,853.18 m
pound (lb)	= 16 oz	453.6 g
ton (long)	= 2,240 lb	1,016 kg

Decimal weights and measures

Measure	Decimal equivalent	Imperial equivalent
millimetre (mm)	—	—
centimetre (cm)	10 mm	0.394 in
metre (m)	100 cm	39.37 in
	1,000 mm	3 ft 3.37 in
kilometre (km)	1,000 m	1,093.61 yd
hectometre (hm)	100 m	328.08 ft
	10 hm	3,280.84 ft
kilogram (kg)	1,000 g	2 lb 3.27 oz
metric tonne	1,000 kg	2,205 lb

the Admiralty in its evaluation of the Type-VIIC *U570* (captured by the British in August 1941 and renamed HMS/m *Graph*) have been employed with adjustments made for slight misunderstandings of the German settings. It should be noted that the revolutions per minute and speed in knots yielded by these settings depended not only on the U-boat type (the Type-IX, for example, generated slightly higher speeds at slightly lower revolutions), but also on whether diesel, electric or combined propulsion was being referred to, and whether the movement was ahead or astern.[10] Moreover, these technical settings should not be confused with the various non-technical descriptive terms for speed also found in logs such as 'high speed'.

	German telegraph setting in full	Literal translation	Admiralty equivalent
K.F.	*Kleine Fahrt*	Small speed	Dead slow
L.F.	*Langsame Fahrt*	Slow speed	Slow
H.F.	*Halbe Fahrt*	Half speed	Half speed
2 × H.F.	*Zweimal halbe Fahrt*	2 × half speed	⅗ speed
G.F.	*Grosse Fahrt*	Great speed	¾ speed
2 × G.F.	*Zweimal grosse Fahrt*	2 × great speed	⅘ speed
A.K.	*Äusserste Kraft*	Extreme speed	Utmost speed
2 × A.K.	*Zweimal äusserste Kraft*	2 × extreme speed	Emergency speed

---

10 Further details can be found in *U570: Interrogation of Survivors, October 1941* by the Admiralty's Naval Intelligence Division (TNA, ADM 186/806).

1 HMS *COURAGEOUS*

Capt. W. T. Makeig-Jones, RN†
Sunk by *U29* (Type VIIA), Kptlt Otto Schuhart, 17 September 1939
Western Approaches, 190 nm WSW of Bolus Head, Kerry (Ireland)

Courageous under way before the war. Tactical misuse by the Admiralty and two torpedoes from *U29* brought a premature end to her career. *Wright & Logan*

Theatre	Western Approaches (Map 2)	*Displacement* 22,500 tons
Coordinates	50° 10' N, 14° 45' W	*Dimensions* 786.25' × 90.5' × 24'
Kriegsmarine code	Quadrat BE 3198	*Armour* 3" belt; 1–3" horizontal; 2" bulkheads; 0.75" casings and uptakes
U-boat timekeeping	identical	*Maximum speed* 29.5 knots
Fatalities 518	*Survivors* 698	*Armament* 16 × 4.7" AA; 24 × 40 mm AA
		Air wing 48 aircraft (Swordfish) served by two lifts and two catapults

Career

Laid down in March 1915 as the first in a class of light battlecruisers, HMS *Courageous* and her two sisters were the ultimate expression of Admiral Lord Fisher's obsession with the primacy of speed and gunpower afloat. In particular, the class was designed as the spearhead of Fisher's Baltic Project which proposed an amphibious landing on the Pomeranian coast followed by a thrust to Berlin that would end the war. However, Fisher's departure from the Admiralty in 1915 and the disaster that befell the British battlecruisers at Jutland the following year greatly diminished the role this increasingly preposterous trio might play in the fleet. Launched at Armstrong Whitworth's Walker yard in February 1916 and completed with four 15-inch guns in January 1917, *Courageous* served with the 3rd Light Cruiser Squadron and then the 1st Cruiser Squadron of the Grand Fleet. In November of that year she was involved in an engagement with German forces in the Heligoland Bight, emerging with slight damage. In 1919 *Courageous* was reduced to the role of gunnery training ship and her future left uncertain but the signing of the Washington Treaty in 1922 and the allowance contained within its terms for 135,000 tons of British aircraft-carrier construction provided the necessary reprieve. The last member of her class to undergo reconstruction, *Courageous* was paid off into dockyard control at Devonport in June 1924 and did not emerge until February 1928. Briefly assigned to the Mediterranean Fleet, in 1929 she was allocated to the Atlantic Fleet (renamed Home Fleet in 1932) with which she remained until 1935. A year's detachment

to the Mediterranean from 1935 to 1936 was followed by a major refit at Portsmouth which lasted until June 1938. Apart from a few months in the Reserve Fleet in 1939 the rest of her career was spent with the Home Fleet based on Devonport.

Background of the attack

Despite having only thirty-nine operational vessels at the outbreak of hostilities, the *U-Boat-Waffe* immediately made its presence felt, *U30* sinking the liner *Athenia* within hours of the declaration of war on 3 September. The Admiralty, which had an exaggerated confidence in the efficacy of the Asdic submarine-detection apparatus, had yet to establish a coherent strategy for combating the submarine threat. At the instigation of the aggressive new First Lord, Winston Churchill, the Admiralty deployed *Ark Royal* (**39**) and *Courageous* in 'Hunter Killer' groups to seek out and destroy U-boats in key approaches to home waters while a large number of unconvoyed ships were still making for British ports. It was to prove a disastrous tactic. With *Ark Royal* already at sea off the Orkneys, on the evening of 3 September HMS *Courageous* sailed from Plymouth to patrol the Western Approaches for enemy submarines with the destroyers *Inglefield*, *Intrepid*, *Ivanhoe* and *Impulsive* as close escort. On 14 September *Ark Royal* was attacked by *U39* whose torpedoes exploded in her wake. This early indication that the role of hunter and hunted might easily be reversed did not have time to be heeded, while the sinking of *U39* and the capture of her crew by *Ark Royal*'s escort only enhanced the Admiralty's misplaced confidence in its anti-submarine capability. Three days later it was an older carrier's turn to be tested when *Courageous* was sighted by *U29* shortly after 1800 while zigzagging back to Devonport. Already at 1545 her destroyer screen had been depleted by the dispatch of *Inglefield* and *Intrepid* to investigate a U-boat attack on the freighter *Kafiristan* 130 miles to the west, leaving her with just *Ivanhoe* and *Impulsive* for company. However, it took two hours' pursuit and an obliging alteration of course from his quarry just as she seemed to be escaping him before Kptlt Otto Schuhart was presented with one of the greatest targets ever to fill the lens of a U-boat periscope.

War Diary of *U29*, patrol of 16 August–26 September 1939: PG 30026, NHB, reel 1,061, pp. 531–3

Date, time	Details of position, wind, weather, sea, light, visibility, moonlight, etc.	Incidents
17.ix		
	Wind E 2, sea 2–3, long flat swell, clear, sunny, excellent visibility	Lying in wait on American shipping route.
1605		Steamer approaches from the west. The sun is right behind it, making it difficult to discern properly until quite late. Our boat appears to be more or less on her general course line – course 80°, speed 13–14 knots.
1617		Dived. Vessel is zigzagging so must be English. A freighter capable of carrying passengers. But what is it? Size roughly 10,000 tons, Manchester Line? Spends a long time on one leg of zigzag, so the range at which she will pass us is quite considerable, perhaps 5,000 m. Only now do I see that she is flying a reddish flag, which makes me wonder about nationality – American maybe? Suddenly I see an aircraft flying low off the steamer's quarter, so clearly either a troop transport or carrying war matériel. Decision taken to fire torpedo. However, steamer zigzags away from me just as I'm ready to fire, which makes angle too wide.
		Intend to surface once the vessel is out of sight, maintain contact and attack under cover of night; at the same time I authorise W/T report to be transmitted to submarines operating further east. Course 80°. Because of the air cover I submerge to 20 m.
1800		Full sweep of horizon at 13 m. Angular cloud of black smoke on the horizon off the port bow: no, not a cloud of smoke, an aircraft carrier. Assume *Ark Royal*.[1]
		Range more than 10,000 m, course SW. Has escort; ahead of carrier I can discern the masts of a destroyer.It now becomes obvious that the aircraft I saw alongside the freighter was not hers but came from *Ark Royal*.
		Gradually, and keeping close watch all the while, we get closer. I estimate her to be proceeding at about medium speed. Air escort no longer visible; I look equally in vain for an outlying destroyer escort. The close escort is now evident: a destroyer ahead, another astern, and one on each side.[2] The ones ahead and astern would appear to be stationed about 1,000 m from carrier, but it's too difficult to gauge the distance of those abeam.
1845		The carrier herself is zigzagging on a westerly course of ~~270°~~;[3] I alter to 0°. Decision taken to fire three Etos with a minimal angle of dispersion in order to achieve preferably two hits – practically half way between a straight multiple salvo and a spread, at a depth of 6 m.[4] Since the *Neptunia* experience I've lost confidence in magnetic detonation.[5] I see two aircraft circling the force at irregular intervals.
1900		At 90° inclination her range is too great (roughly 7,000 m). As we progress I suddenly realise her speed is quite high (20 knots). Continue to track zigzagging carrier, keeping her under constant periscope

---

1 Actually HMS *Courageous*, though *Ark Royal* had also been deployed on anti-submarine duty; see above.

2 British sources are unanimous that *Courageous* had only two destroyers escorting her at this juncture, *Ivanhoe* on the port bow and *Impulsive* on the starboard bow. The rest of *Courageous*'s close escort, *Inglefield* and *Intrepid*, had been dispatched to chase down a U-boat contact at 1545.

3 The original has '270°' crossed out with 'XXX'.

4 Schuhart's decision to have a minimal differential between torpedoes of this salvo is plainly dictated by the lengthy range of his target at this juncture. The Type-VII U-boats could fire a salvo of up to four torpedoes from the forward torpedo compartment at intervals of 2.3 seconds, the angle of dispersion being entered manually for each salvo. However, it should be noted that no torpedoes were fired by *U29* until over an hour later at 1950, by which time the range was down to approximately 2,000 metres. 'Eto' was Kriegsmarine shorthand for the electric G7e torpedo as distinct from the compressed-air G7a torpedo known as an 'Ato'.

5 On 13 September a salvo of torpedoes armed with magnetic pistols had failed to detonate on the hull of the British minesweeper *Neptunia* requiring Schuhart to despatch her with gunfire. Having lost confidence in magnetic detonators Schuhart this time selects contact pistols.

		observation. From previous observations of English zigzagging there is no need to give up hope of getting her just yet.

1922   Carrier has been getting further and further away but now suddenly alters course by at least 70°, embarking on southerly leg of zigzag (225°), medium speed. A little later she shifts again, this time to 180°. Things now start happening very fast. Aim-off is calculated for 90° inclination and speed of 15 knots; I estimate she will pass the 90° angle at a range of 3,000 m, but have decided to fire at greater range; I can expect the Etos to run for 4,000–5,000 m. I have nothing to help me determine the range since the carrier is enormous, and her flat profile gives me nothing to gauge this by. What's more, I'm looking right into the sun, which makes it trickier to work out her inclination. Periscope is often awash as boat is broadside on to the run of the sea. Engines only running slow or dead slow due to risk of being detected.

Attack depth: 14 m. Attack course 240°.

1950   Lat. = 50° 5' Long. = 14° 20'   Three torpedoes fired while turning hard astarboard; 100° inclination. Target points: 20 m ahead of bow, amidships and 20 m astern. On firing I see carrier's port destroyer 500 m ahead of the boat. Turn hard astarboard to 0°, utmost speed ahead with both engines, dive quickly to 50 m. The boat barely rose after the three torpedoes were fired and is firmly under the control of the *Leitender Ingenieur*.[6]

1953   Hits of two torpedoes are clearly heard throughout the boat with a monitored running time of 2 min. 15 sec. = 2,160 m. A major detonation immediately after the second hit followed by several smaller ones. So loud are the noises that I feared some damage might be done to the boat. Jubilation aboard, albeit tinged with tangible concern as to what will happen to us now.

Behaviour of carrier between 1900 and 1922 leaves me perplexed; possibly there was a rotation in the air cover at this time during which she made a deliberate effort to slow down.[7] However, I myself saw nothing which would corroborate this.

Meanwhile boat has dropped to 60 m, and since this depth has no appreciable effect on either the outside or the inside of the boat we go to 80 m. Due to flooding (shaft glands etc.), the limitations imposed on the engines and our using the pumps only sparingly for fear of being heard, the boat is briefly so heavy that she sinks to 105 m. She then stabilises perfectly.

From 100 m depth we start hearing a bubbling sound on the upper deck which we attribute to pursuit using echo-ranging sets,[8] but was probably caused by the pressure of the 100-m depth. Throughout the pursuit course remains 80°, both engines dead slow, or at slow speed as necessary.

1959[9]   Powerful propeller noises rapidly close the boat and pass overhead; four depth charges are released which detonate right over the boat (at 60 m) but well above us. Boat is rocked by huge tremors – I am standing in the tower and feel everything shake. No deep-water convulsions, however. A few minutes later six more depth charges produce a similar effect but in a third attack they detonate somewhat further away so we don't feel the powerful tremors of the previous two attacks.

We are held down until about 2200 – the boat right in the middle of this concert of depth charges and propeller noises that keep coming and going. Over the period as a whole they move further away. By 2200 the boat has managed to put approximately four miles between herself and the point from which she fired her torpedoes, but not until 2400 can we reckon with a fair degree of certainty that our pursuers have been shaken off. From here on I give more specific observations made during this period.

1950[10]   *Ship's bearing*: _____[11] *Range*: 2,500 m *Depth*: 14 m   Three torpedoes fired.

1952   *Ship's bearing*: 170° *Range*: 2,500 m *Depth*: _____   Propeller noises of carrier.

---

6 *U29*'s Chief Engineer (*Leitender Ingenieur*), Oblt (Ing.) Lauf.

7 Schuhart is correct in attributing the change of course to aircraft rotation, *Courageous* having turned into the wind to land aircraft and thereby given *U29* her chance.

8 Asdic. Schuhart's account was no doubt of great interest to B.d.U. since this was among the U-boat arm's first operational exposures to the Royal Navy's submarine echo-location technology.

9 Manuscript addition in pencil.

10 The break in the chronological sequence here reflects the original.

11 This and succeeding entries so denoted indicate blanks in the original.

Date, time	Details of position, wind, weather, sea, light, visibility, moonlight, etc.	Incidents
1953	*Ship's bearing*: ____ *Range*: 2,500 m *Depth*: 40 m	First torpedo hits on the port side. Second hit is much more powerful and followed by a number of subsequent detonations.
1959	155°–330°, 600 m, 60 m	Propeller noise of approaching destroyers from starboard astern to starboard ahead. Two destroyers pass overhead. Four powerful depth-charge detonations along the boat from stern to stem. At the same time, and at similar intervals, weaker detonations can be heard on either side of the boat. It seems that the destroyers are proceeding in line abreast.
2001	____, increasing, 80 m	Destroyers are getting further away. Prolonged sound of detonations both nearby and further off.
2003	280°, decreasing, 90–100 m	Two destroyers approaching. One passes overhead between conning tower and bow. Six strong detonations. Again it seems destroyers are in line abreast.
2004–2007	Not detectable, remains same, 80–100 m	Throughout the boat we can feel a clear pinging against the side of the boat like the pulse of a transmitter. A powerful bubbling that resembles boiling water can be heard through the hydrophones.[8]
2008–2020	____, not determined	Destroyers approaching. Detonations close to boat and some above but the depth charges now appear to have been set at shallower settings.
2020–2041	Not determined, 80–100 m	Destroyers have stopped and are dropping depth charges over a wider area.
2041–2156	____, 200–6,000 m, 80–100 m	Destroyers appear to be forming a search group. Numerous detonations. It sounds as if 40–50 depth charges are being dropped in just one area, though this area is far away from the boat.
2156–2321	____, ____, 80 m	Propeller noises move astern. Bearings registered every so often at 291° and 75°.
2321–2340	250°, 4,000 m, 80 m	Propeller noises become louder then shift astern. Boat turns 10° to starboard. Noise shifts to 140° and then becomes fainter. Only sporadic detonations can now be heard.
2356	____, ____, 60 m	Propeller noises become fainter and we no longer get an accurate fix on them.
0135[12]		Boat surfaces.
	Anything else to note? F.[?][13]	In summary, I would say that the position from which we fired appears to have been noticed immediately by the destroyers. However, the fact that the boat was overrun three times is less likely the result of the enemy getting a fix on us than a search formation carried out without hydrophone intercept data. Sound pulses similar to those of our *S-Gerät* were not confirmed.[14] A pinging felt on the port side was unexplained but would appear to have been random sound waves.[15] As regards our own speed during the pursuit, for both engines this remained dead slow or occasionally slow speed. These observations were made by Ob.Fk.Gefr. Schröter through the group listening apparatus with icy calm and admirable sang-froid, even at the most critical moments.[16]

As regards the boat herself, I must first commend the *Leitender Ingenieur*, Oblt (Ing.) Lauf, who had her totally under control for all the many hours we spent submerged. His calm and steady bearing quickly imposed itself not just on the men in the central control room but also on the entire crew. The overall composure of the crew was good; if anyone thought they knew what to expect from reading war literature, such fictional impressions were doubtless overtaken by reality. The men were quite exhausted by a pursuit lasting so many hours and it took much of the next day for them to recover.

In my opinion the destroyer I saw when firing the torpedoes must have gauged our position by seeing the two detonations strike on the port side of the carrier. She was doubtless alerted to the position of the attack by the expulsive surge caused by the firing of the three torpedoes. Hence the first depth charges dropped in this area. Together with the rear escort she then took up the pursuit but without ever getting a proper fix on the boat's position after the initial series of depth charges. An alternative explanation for the destroyer picking up the boat's trail is that the torpedoes were spotted as they ran beneath her. In the clear, light Atlantic water the red warheads must be visible to a depth of 10 m at the very least.

---

12 The break in the chronological sequence here reflects the original.
13 Manuscript addition in pen.
14 The *S-Gerät* (*Such-Gerät* – 'search apparatus') was a new form of active sonar technology which enabled U-boats to detect minefields or targets.
15 See n. 8.
16 By 'group listening apparatus' – *Gruppenhorchgerät* (GHG) in the original – Schuhart is referring to *U29*'s hydrophone. The rating of *Oberfunkgefreiter* equates to Leading Telegraphist in the Royal Navy and Radioman 3rd Class in the US Navy.

18.ix

0100	Wind E 2, sea 2, clear bright night then sunny day, good visibility	Propeller noises have faded out of earshot astern, nothing of note has been heard for an hour. Boat slowly rises to 23 m. At this point a sharp clang can be heard which is doubtless the exterior of the boat expanding.
0135		Tower hatch open. Course 340°, 13 knots. I intend to get well clear of the position of the sinking between now and first light and only then subject boat to inspection. Inspection reveals that, apart from the attack periscope, the boat seems to have emerged completely unscathed. The upper deck shows no sign of any damage from either depth charges or water pressure. The attack periscope is full of water, which can only have entered through the collar. After 24 hours drying out we find that all mirrors are covered in grease and dirt, and the periscope is no longer serviceable.
		So the question now arises as to whether *U29*'s attack proved successful. To turn about and renew the attack on what might only be a badly damaged ship is not something I can countenance since
	Three lines deleted![17] *Schuhart*	1. The boat's offensive weapons are expended and the attack periscope disabled; all we have left in the torpedo tubes are a G7a and one Eto; what fuel we have is sufficient only to sail directly for home.[18]
		2. The general conviction is that the ship was destroyed. The detonations we observed were so strong that the ship must either have broken up and been set on fire or else been blown out of the water.
1000		Set course for home. At midday I hear confirmation via English radio of *U29*'s success. We gather we destroyed *Courageous*, not *Ark Royal*. What's more, we're supposed to have been destroyed ourselves.[19] Great joy throughout the boat.
		Speed for return journey set at 10 knots.
		At night, with the sea calm, the water is so phosphorescent that the boat must be visible for miles around despite her low speed. It's as if the waterline around the boat is lit up by glowing bulbs. The same light allows us to see great shoals of fish around the boat.
		Schuhart

---

17 Manuscript addition in pen.

18 This point 1 has been set down over three lines of text which have been blacked out. 'Eto' was Kriegsmarine shorthand for the electric G7e torpedo.

19 A submission to the Board of Enquiry on 27 September by Cdr Basil Jones, commanding HMS *Ivanhoe*, estimated that there was a '60% chance' that the offending U-boat had been sunk, a point reiterated by the Commander-in-Chief Western Approaches, Admiral Sir Martin Dunbar-Nasmith. Evidently, these statements were made in ignorance of Schuhart's return to Wilhelmshaven the previous day.

The sinking

Schuhart's log covers the sinking in unusual detail, from *U29*'s sighting and tracking of *Courageous* on the afternoon of the 17th through to the attack and then the immediate counter-attack by her escorts that continued long into the night. The British were unaware of any danger until the two torpedoes struck *Courageous* in quick succession on the port side abaft the bridge. The detonations and the ensuing flooding had two immediate consequences: the destruction of one of the ship's main dynamos which plunged her into almost total darkness, and a rapid heel of twenty degrees to port. Communications were not only limited to word of mouth but greatly hampered by the activation of the steam siren which both deafened the crew to verbal orders and sapped the morale of those trying to save the ship. Together this meant that many steps to limit flooding, including the sealing of internal 'Y' doors, were never fully taken. Meanwhile, the ship's uneven topweight and the displacement of aircraft and heavy equipment in the hangars accentuated the list and soon brought the port side of the flight deck to within a few feet of the sea. When after ten minutes the list had increased to forty-five degrees Capt. Makeig-Jones reluctantly conceded that 'those who wish to leave the ship may do so'. Shortly afterwards great 'cracking noises' were heard, an indication that bulkheads were collapsing. Sinking by the bow, *Courageous* was in her death throes and it was not long before she slipped beneath the waves altogether, only nineteen minutes after the attack.

While accepting that the speed of the sinking was probably due to uncontrolled flooding, the Board of Enquiry found that 'a possible catastrophe of this magnitude was either not foreseen or not provided for'. The Second Sea Lord, Admiral Sir Charles Little, inferred an unacceptable lack of preparation against underwater attack and recommended that the carrier's Executive Officer, Cdr C. W. G. M. Woodhouse, share some of this responsibility and be informed of the Board's displeasure. This was rejected by Churchill who, mindful no doubt of his own responsibility in the affair, took the wider view that the Navy as a whole had much to learn from the incident. Neither was he prepared to make a scapegoat of a man whose spinal injuries, sustained during the sinking, had forced to him to request being invalided out of the Service. The Board of Enquiry concluded that 'We consider the behaviour of both Officers, and the ship's company in general, in circumstances which could hardly have been worse, was very good.' Meanwhile, any expectation that the offending U-boat had been destroyed by *Courageous*'s escort evaporated in the fanfare surrounding *U29*'s return to Wilhelmshaven on 26 September.

For his part, Konteradmiral Karl Dönitz took the sinking of *Courageous* as a propitious sign of his enemy's vulnerability to U-boat attack. Asdic, it turned out, was by no means infallible. As he made plain in a report following *U29*'s cruise,

Courageous a few minutes after taking two hits from U29, already listing heavily but still with way on. She sank within twenty minutes of the attack. IWM

It is not true that England has the technical means to neutralise the U-boats. Their experience so far confirms that the English anti-submarine apparatus is not as effective as they claim it to be.

Not for some time would he have cause to reassess that judgement.

Fate of the crew

Why the order for Abandon Ship Stations was never given remains something of a mystery. When asked why Capt. Makeig-Jones had refrained from doing so Cdr Woodhouse suggested that he may have been reluctant to harm the morale of the ship's company while still uncertain as to the extent of the damage. As word gradually got round that every man should decide as he saw fit increasing numbers abandoned ship, many admitting afterwards that they simply followed the rest. A number of submissions to the Board testified that this had been carried out cheerfully and without panic, many Royal Marines in particular distinguishing themselves by their discipline and bearing as the disaster unfolded. However, as this general exodus reached a climax as *Courageous* entered her death throes many swimmers found themselves sucked down with her, only those lucky enough to grab onto flotsam returning alive to the surface. Matters were not helped by a shortage of lifejackets while many Carley floats were found to be stuck down by layers of peacetime paintwork. Further ordeals awaited many who managed to get clear of the ship. The water was covered in a thick layer of oil which coated all who swam through it. A number of men were knocked out and subsequently drowned as a result of flotsam bursting up from the depths at speed. Others struck out towards the accompanying destroyers but Admiralty orders that escorts give priority to finding and attacking the enemy meant that many were killed by the depth-charge patterns directed against *U29*. Some had to swim for almost an hour until they were rescued, but for others ten minutes in the water brought them to safety. They were rescued by the steamers *Dido* and *Collingsworth*, together with the Holland-America liner *Veendam* which closed after witnessing the disaster. The survivors were eventually transferred to HM destroyer *Kelly* (commanded by Capt. Lord Louis Mountbatten) and rushed to Devonport where fleets of ambulances and doctors awaited them. A Devonport ship, news of *Courageous*'s loss brought an anxious crowd

to the main gate of the naval barracks to scan lists of survivors.

Some 518 were lost out of a complement of 1,216 men, a figure which reflects both the speed of the sinking and the number of elderly members of the Royal Naval Reserve among the crew. Capt. Makeig-Jones was not among the rescued. The product of an earlier generation, he remained on the bridge saluting the ensign as his ship went down.

U29 and Otto Schuhart

Built by AG Weser at Bremen and commissioned in November 1936, *U29* served with five different flotillas during the war, though as a Type-VIIA boat she was on frontline duty only until December 1940. She sank eleven ships in nine cruises under Otto Schuhart but none approached the significance of this her first war patrol, which began before the outbreak of hostilities. The attack on *Courageous*, the first major naval sinking of the war by the *U-Boot-Waffe*, was described by Hitler as 'a wonderful success' and earned Schuhart the Iron Cross First Class with the Second Class being awarded to the rest of the crew, these conferred by the Führer himself when *U29* berthed at Wilhelmshaven on 26 September. Following an extensive refit, *U29* was transferred to training duties in January 1941, remaining in this

Schuhart seen on the casing of *U29* later in 1939 or 1940. *DUBMA*

capacity until being scuttled in Kupfermühlen Bay on the Baltic coast of Schleswig-Holstein in April 1945.

Otto Schuhart was awarded the Knight's Cross in May 1940 before being assigned to shore duties in early 1941, first as an instructor in the 1st *Unterseeboots-Lehr-Division* and then as Commander of the 21st Flotilla. He joined the post-war Bundesmarine, retiring in the rank of Kapitän zur See in 1967. He died in February 1990.

Sources

Admiralty, *Board of Enquiry into Loss of HMS* Courageous *Following Submarine Attack: Court of Enquiry* (TNA, ADM 156/195)

Brittain, Lt Norman, RNVR, letter to P. E. Russell, Southampton, 15 November 1939 (manuscript, Bruce Taylor collection)

Court-Hampton, Lt Edgar Arthur, letter to his family, 1 October 1939 (manuscript, IWM, 99/75/1)

Anon., 'Sinking of *Courageous*: British Admiralty Releases Pictures' in *Life* (12 February 1940), pp. 28–9

Brook, Peter, *Warships for Export: Armstrong Warships, 1867–1927* (Gravesend, Kent: World Ship Society, 1999)

Gibbings, Peter, *Weep for Me, Comrade* (London: Minerva Press, 1997)

Hughes, Terry, and John Costello, *The Battle of the Atlantic* (London: Collins, 1977)

Jones, Geoffrey, *U Boat Aces and Their Fates* (London: William Kimber, 1988)

Lamb, Cdr Charles, *War in a Stringbag* (London: Cassell, 1977); extracted in Max Arthur, ed., *The Navy: 1939 to the Present Day* (London: Hodder & Stoughton, 1997)

Poolman, Kenneth, *The British Sailor* (London: Arms and Armour Press, 1989)

Roskill, *War at Sea*, I, pp. 105–6

Rotherham, Capt. G. A., *It's Really Quite Safe!* (Belleville, Ont.: Hangar Books, 1985)

Winton, John, ed., *The War at Sea* [vol. I of *Freedom's Battle, 1939–45*] (London: Hutchinson, 1967)

War career of HMS *Courageous*: http://www.naval-history.net/xGM-Chrono-04CV-Courageous.htm

Sinking of HMS *Courageous*: http://www.uboataces.com/battle-courageous.shtml

2   HMS *ROYAL OAK*
Rear-Admiral H. E. C. Blagrove, RN†, Capt. W. G. Benn, RN
Sunk by *U47* (Type VIIB), Kptlt Günther Prien, 14 October 1939
Scapa Flow, Orkney (Scotland)

Royal Oak in 1938 or 1939. The prominent anti-torpedo bulge seen along her hull availed her not on the night of 14 October when Günther Prien registered four hits on the starboard side. *IWM*

Theatre   British home waters (Map 2)
Coordinates   58° 55' N, 02° 59' W
Kriegsmarine code   Quadrat AN 1610
U-boat timekeeping   identical
Fatalities   836   *Survivors*   375

Displacement   29,150 tons
Dimensions   620.5' × 102' × 28'
Armour   4–13" belt; 1–5.5" horizontal; 4–6" bulkheads; 3–13" turrets
Maximum speed   21.75 knots
Armament   8 × 15"; 12 × 6"; 4 × 4" AA; 4 × 47 mm AA; 16 × 40 mm AA; 4 × 21" tt

Career

The fourth unit of the Revenge class, the battleship HMS *Royal Oak* was laid down at Devonport Dockyard in January 1914, launched in November of that year and completed in May 1916. The Revenges were the last British battleships designed with provision for coal firing, though Lord Fisher's return to the Admiralty in 1914 caused all boilers to be fitted with oil burners prior to completion. Commissioning for the 4th Battle Squadron of the Grand Fleet in May 1916, *Royal Oak* appeared soon enough to participate in the Battle of Jutland on the last day of that month, scoring several hits on the battlecruiser *Derfflinger* and emerging unscathed from the encounter. Subsequently assigned to the 1st BS, in 1919 she joined the 2nd BS of the Atlantic Fleet on the dissolution of the Grand Fleet. Here she remained until passing into dockyard hands at Portsmouth in September 1922 during which she was fitted with anti-torpedo bulges. This completed, *Royal Oak* recommissioned for the 1st BS, Mediterranean Fleet in July 1924 and it was on this station that she provided the backdrop for the so-called 'Royal Oak affair', a farcical dispute between senior officers which originated in the musical accompaniment to a ship-board dance in January 1928. Service continued in the Mediterranean until May 1934 when *Royal Oak* paid off for a major refit at Devonport which saw improvements to her underwater protection, armour and anti-aircraft armament. The entire Revenge class was in fact in need of complete reconstruction but in view of design strictures and their slow speed the Admiralty decided that the limited funds and dockyard facilities available would be better applied to rebuilding more capable vessels, especially the preceding Queen Elizabeth class. Though more work was done on her than any of her sisters, it was as a somewhat obsolete unit that *Royal Oak* recommissioned with the 2nd BS, Mediterranean Fleet in August 1936. She saw service off Spain in the first half of 1937, coming under attack from Republican aircraft in February, but left the theatre on being assigned to the Home Fleet in July. In November 1938 *Royal Oak* was given the honour of conveying the body of Queen Maud of Norway from Portsmouth to Oslo and recommissioned for service with the Home Fleet in June 1939. The outbreak of war found her with the 2nd BS at Scapa Flow. Little can her crew have imagined that the Navy's greatest anchorage would prove her final resting place.

Background of the attack

The audacious plan to penetrate the Royal Navy's main anchorage at Scapa Flow was conceived by Kommodore Karl Dönitz himself as head of the U-boat arm in conjunction with his staff officer for operations, Kptlt Victor Oehrn (see **16**). Despite two failed attempts to breach its defences during the Great War, aerial intelligence gathered in September 1939 together with a detailed reconnaissance of the approaches to Scapa Flow by *U14* and reports by *U16* on prevailing currents (which were usually stronger than the maximum speed of a submerged U-boat) persuaded Dönitz and Oehrn that the operation was worth another try. Their choice for the mission was Kptlt Günther Prien, commander of *U47*, who was given all the necessary charts and reports at the beginning of October and instructed to think over the operation for forty-eight hours, accepting or declining it as he saw fit. Prien accepted. To maintain secrecy only Grossadmiral Erich Raeder, commander-in-chief of the German navy, was informed, and he solely by word of mouth from Dönitz who left no stone unturned in his efforts to facilitate Prien's task. As the War Diary of *F.d.U. West* recorded, 'To lessen suspicion, five U-boats operating around the Orkneys were withdrawn from these waters on 4 October in order to avoid potential disturbances in the Orkney sea area and thus potentially alert the English. Everything was being staked on the one card.'

The night chosen for the attack was that of 13–14 October when it was hoped that slack water and a full moon would provide favourable conditions for the attempt. Prien sailed from Kiel on the morning of 8 October and after an uneventful crossing of the North Sea found himself off Scapa Flow on the afternoon of the 13th. The previous afternoon a German reconnaissance plane had reported the presence of an aircraft carrier, five heavy ships and ten cruisers in Scapa Flow, including the exact positions of *Royal Oak* and the nearby *Repulse*. This intelligence was relayed to the *U-Boot-Waffe* as a matter of course and immediately transmitted by Dönitz to *U47*, though as it turned out Prien did not receive it until after the operation. In any case, the bulk of the Home Fleet including *Repulse* sailed from Scapa Flow that night and with it most of Prien's would-be targets. However, one rich prize remained and after some hair-raising obstacles of navigation *U47* entered the flow to find herself confronted with the silhouette of HMS *Royal Oak* lying peacefully at anchor, together with another vessel partly obscured beyond. Assigned the duty of Anti-Aircraft Guard Ship to add her firepower to the permanent defences ashore, the danger to *Royal Oak* was to come from quite another quarter.

War Diary of *U47*, patrol of 8–17 October 1939: PG 30044, NHB, reel 1,064, pp. 557–8

Date, time	Details of position, wind, weather, sea, light, visibility, moonlight, etc.	Incidents
13.x		
	East of the Orkney Islands. Wind NNE 3–4, light cloud cover, very bright night, northern northern horizon.	0437 the boat settled on the seabed at 90 m – rest for the crew. Reveille sounded at 1600, followed by breakfast. Then at 1700 preparations made for operation in Scapa Flow. Two torpedoes placed in quick-load position in front of Tubes I and II. Explosive charges set up in boat in case we need to scuttle her. The morale of the crew is excellent.
		At 1915 we surface. After a hot supper for the whole crew we make our way towards Holm Sound. Everything goes according to plan until 2307, shortly before Rose Ness, when we have to dive before a steamer. Despite the very bright night and the burning lights I can't make out the steamer in either of the two periscopes. We surface again at 2331 and enter Holm Sound. The current is behind us. As we

get closer the sunken vessel in Skerry Sound can easily be made out; this makes me think that we're already in Kirk Sound and I bear in that direction. The *Obersteuermann*[1] ascertains from dead reckoning that we're turning too fast and at the same time I see my error – only the one ship is sunk in the defile. By turning hard astarboard we manage to avoid the danger in our path. A few moments later we have a clear view of Kirk Sound ahead of us. It's just as well that I learnt the map off by heart beforehand because we now make passage though the Sound at phenomenal speed. During the transit I decide to veer to the north past the blockships. We pass the two-masted schooner at a distance of 15 m and at 270° – she is lying at 315° to the actual boom. A moment later the boat yaws in the current and is swung round to starboard. At the same time we discern the forward anchor chain of the northern blockship at an angle of 45°. By stopping the port engine, moving slowly forward on the starboard engine and with the rudder hard aport the boat starts moving, slowly at first and scraping the bottom. The pre-flooded ballast and diving tanks are blown, the boat turns further and further. Again the stern touches the anchor chain, the boat is free but is dragged round to port. She can only be brought back on course with harsh and rapid manoeuvres, but:

> A sinister sight. All the land is dark, but the Northern Lights flickering in the sky mean that the bay – surrounded by quite high mountains – is directly illuminated from on high.[2] The blockships in the sound look like part of a ghostly theatre set.

14.x

0027

We are in Scapa Flow!!!

It is sickeningly bright.[2] Though this does mean a fabulous view of the whole bay. Nothing to be seen south of Cava but we proceed in that direction. Then to port I see the Holm Sound guard post which in a few seconds will be presented with a perfect target in the form of our boat.[3] This would be a pointless risk, particularly as no ships can be made out south of Cava. This despite a view that allows us to see everything quite clearly at a great distance.

0055?[4]

So I make a decision. There is nothing south of Cava so before taking any risks that would jeopardise any chance of success we must seek out opportunities that can be exploited more easily. Accordingly I make a 180° turn to port and follow the coast northwards. There I discover two battleships with destroyers anchored further inshore.[5] No cruisers to be seen so I go for the two big fellows. Range 3,000 m. Torpedoes set at a depth of 7.5 m, impact detonators.

According to map:[6]

0116?[4] *0058 (Repulse d. B— [?])*   One shot at the northern ship, two at the southern. After a good 3½ mins. one torpedo detonates
 (Royal Oak)   against the northern ship, but nothing can be seen of the other two! Turn about! A stern torpedo shot,

0121?[4] *approx. 0102*   then load two bow tubes, then turn again!

0123 *0122*[6]   Three bow shots. Barely three minutes after firing they detonate against the nearer of the two ships. This is followed by tremendous rocking motions, explosions, crashes and rumblings. First columns of water shoot up, then columns of fire and fragments of the ship fly through the air. Then the bay bursts into life, lights come on in the destroyers and morse signals start frantically tapping from all quarters. Ashore, about 200 m from me, cars start whizzing up and down the roads. One battleship sunk, another damaged, but the devil himself has taken three of our eels.[7] All torpedo tubes are now empty. I decide to quit the scene on the grounds that:

1) I can't carry out any submerged attacks at night – <u>see experiences on entering</u>.[8]

2) On such a bright night I can't hope to navigate on the calm mirror-like surface without being seen.

---

1 The chief navigator, usually a warrant officer.

2 Prien's description of a well-illuminated anchorage is contradicted by British reports which record the 13th–14th as a dark night though the Northern Lights were noted by both sides.

3 Prien, who had long since cleared Holm Sound, is almost certainly referring to Hoxa Sound here.

4 The question marks are manuscript additions in pencil, possibly by the civilian archivist Walther Pfeiffer who was brought to Britain to work on the logs post-war.

5 *Royal Oak* was the only capital ship in Scapa Flow on the night of 13–14 October and there were no destroyers nearby; see the discussion below. That said, it is unclear how HM seaplane carrier *Pegasus* (3,300 tons and partly obscured by *Royal Oak*) could be mistaken for the battlecruiser *Repulse* (32,000 tons) or the drifter *Daisy II* (alongside *Royal Oak*) likewise for a destroyer in what is earlier described as a well-illuminated anchorage (see n. 2). In fact, the evidence is that visibility was much worse than the log marginalia suggests and silhouettes no doubt hard to distinguish against the darkened hills. More to the point, aerial reconnaissance the previous day had placed *Repulse* in the vicinity of *Royal Oak*. In any event, *Pegasus* emerged unscathed from the attack.

6 These entries, added in manuscript by a German hand other than Prien's (possibly Walther Pfeiffer; see n. 4), include the log's only reference to HMS *Repulse*, for which see the discussion below. It is also possible that they were added by B.d.U. staff, not least since the phrase 'According to map' may refer to the aerial reconnaissance on the 12th which identified *Repulse* in the vicinity, or indeed Prien's own plot of the attack. Whatever the case, *Repulse*'s continued and undamaged existence would soon invalidate Prien's claim.

7 'Eel' (German = *Aal*) was U-boat slang for torpedo.

8 Prien is presumably referring to his entry of 2307 on the 13th in which he records both periscopes as being out of action.

Date, time	Details of position, wind, weather, sea, light, visibility, moonlight, etc.	Incidents
		3) I have to presume that I was seen by a driver who stopped his car right abeam and who turned round and made off to Scapa at great speed.[9]
		4) I can't contemplate heading further north due to the presence of the destroyers I earlier discerned against the shoreline, and they themselves are well concealed from my sight.
0128		Set exit course with both engines at ⅗ speed. First to Skildaqoy Point[10] – that's the easy bit. Then the fun starts again. It is now low tide and the current is incoming. I try to get out using slow and dead slow speeds. I have to get through the defile on the southern side where the water is deep enough. More problems with eddying swirls. With course set at 58° and half speed at 10 knots we simply hold our position. At dead slow we struggle past the southern blockship. The helmsman does a first-rate job. We finally get free of the blockship by alternating between ⅗ speed, ¾ speed and finally utmost speed – only to be confronted by a mole! With some extreme wheel manoeuvring we round this too and finally we are out at 0215. A shame that only the one ship was destroyed.
		The torpedo misses I put down either to their not running straight, failures in their speed or their hitting the seabed. One torpedo got stuck in Tube IV.
		The crew acquitted themselves magnificently throughout the operation. Early on the 13th water was discovered in the lubricant – some 7–8%. Everyone got down to some hard work, either changing the oil or removing the water, as well as insulating the leaking area. The torpedo crew reloaded the torpedo tubes with remarkable speed. The boat was in such good shape that I was able to switch on to charge [the batteries] in the harbour and pump up air.
0215		Set south-easterly course for return journey. I still have five torpedoes for any merchant targets that might come our way.[11]
0630	57° 58' N 1° 03' W	Settled boat on seabed. The glow from Scapa could be seen for a long time; they would appear to be dropping depth charges.
1935	Wind ENE 3–4, slight cloud cover, sporadic showers, landward visibility bad, otherwise fine	Continued on course of 180°. I've chosen this course in the hope of sinking something along the coast, as well as avoiding *U20*.[12]
		signed Prien[13]

War Diary of *F.d.U. West*, 1–15 October 1939: NHB, reel 1,051, pp. 75–6

Date, time	Details of position, wind, weather, sea, light, visibility, moonlight, etc.	Incidents
	15.x[14]	
1100[14]		Report received concerning sinking of *Royal Oak*, presumably by U-boat.[15] No details of position given. Around 370 survivors. Can only have been *U47*.
2300[14]		Incoming W/T transmission from *U47*: *Mission accomplished per plan. Royal Oak sunk. Repulse damaged. Request Approach Route I on evening of 16.10 as no longer have other route information on board.*

---

9 No evidence has ever emerged to confirm this suspicion.
10 Should read Skaildaquoy Point. Prien exited the flow by the same route he had entered it, Kirk Sound, though taking the southern as against the northern channel past the blockships.
11 None did before *U47* made Wilhelmshaven on the 17th.
12 Kptlt Karl-Heinz Moehle.
13 This is not a holograph signature but simply typescript.
14 The position of these entries in the columns concerned reflects the original.
15 This is presumably from a British radio broadcast or decrypted signal; the figure for survivors is only five short of the actual number.

The sinking

As the war diary indicates, Prien's first attack, aimed at two separate targets, failed to have the desired effect. The torpedo fired at *Royal Oak* struck her at 0104 on the starboard side forward but without any dramatic explosion. The effect was likened by Paymaster Lt Cdr E. G. S. Maclean, then watching the Northern Lights on deck, to a 'muffled gong [. . .] which shook the ship from stem to stern'. This Maclean attributed to a detonation in the Inflammable Store, others to bottles of carbon dioxide exploding in the refrigerated compartment. Making his way towards the Inflammable Store with his Chief Petty Officer (Supply), Maclean found smoke issuing from the hatch leading down to it, the effect of floodwater reacting with the calcium flares kept in that compartment. Though both the commander and the captain appeared and asked various questions, the possibility of submarine attack was never entertained and as late as 0116 Capt. Benn was quoted as saying that he had 'no uneasiness about the safety of the ship'. The flooded compartments were sealed and many of those woken by the shudder of the first torpedo returned to bed. However, there was nothing ambiguous about the next salvo of torpedoes which struck the ship on the starboard side amidships at around 0120 (the precise time is unclear in both British and German official sources). All three detonated, the effect on *Royal Oak* being described by the Board of Enquiry as 'immediate and catastrophic'. Hits were registered abreast 'A' and 'B' shellrooms, the Forward Boiler Room and the Starboard Wing Engine Room which examination of the wreck later discovered to have been ruptured by holes approximately fifty by forty feet in each case. Listing immediately, *Royal Oak* was swept by fire, fumes and smoke. With all power lost and lights extinguished there was no opportunity to issue formal instructions to abandon ship. Shaken by a series of internal explosions, she capsized and sank bow first at 0129, twenty-five minutes after the first hit and approximately ten after the second salvo.

The triumphant press conference held in Berlin on 18 October together with the overblown (and apparently much regretted) account of the sinking scripted by the Propaganda Ministry in Prien's name (see below) gave rise to suspicions that he had exaggerated events. The published account, which omits certain elements such as the torpedo duds, refers to a chase by a destroyer which never took place, and enlists his First Watch Officer, Oblt.z.S. Engelbert Endrass (see **8** and **17**) in asserting a positive identification of *Repulse* – this despite the fact that she was then at sea with the Home Fleet. It reiterates Prien's comments in Berlin where he declared that 'Although the ships merged into the black background of the landlocked harbour, I am quite certain that one was *Repulse* because she and *Renown* are the only ships of the type with two funnels.' Although these statements might be taken as providing a clearer case for imperfect warship recognition than for fabrication (*Repulse* and *Renown* being battlecruisers rather than battleships and *Hood* having a similar two-funnel silhouette – one funnel more than the vessel actually spotted, HM seaplane carrier *Pegasus*), examination of the log and surviving documentation indicates otherwise, not least since the log proper makes no reference to *Repulse*, which is mentioned only in a manuscript addition in a hand other than Prien's (see note 6). The question remains as to when Prien settled on the identity of the ships struck. That he did so before returning to Germany is evident from his signal of 2300 on the 15th (see above), nearly two days after

the attack, in which *Repulse* is reported as damaged and *Royal Oak* sunk. It must be supposed that in the interim Prien had received the information – accurate on the afternoon of the 12th but invalidated within hours by the exodus of ships from Scapa Flow that night – that *Repulse* and *Royal Oak* had been sighted lying abeam of each other and made the corresponding inference.

Exaggerated or not, there can be little doubt that Prien's was, in Churchill's words, 'a feat of arms' and indeed one of the greatest exploits in the history of submarine warfare. Equally, no amount of exaggeration could disguise the fact that the manner of the sinking was a huge embarrassment to the Admiralty and accusations of negligence and complacency were rife. Ironically, the blockship designed to obstruct the very passage through which *U47* had penetrated Kirk Sound, the *Lake Neuchâtel*, reached Scapa Flow the following day. A victim of the subsequent enquiry was Vice-Admiral Sir Wilfred French, Flag Officer commanding the Orkneys and Shetlands, who was placed on the retired list.

Fate of the crew

The death toll from the *Royal Oak* was very high. The eventual figure was 836 men – more than two thirds of the ship's company – the majority of whom perished within the space of a few minutes. The tragedy was made the more poignant by the loss of over 100 Boy seamen under the age of eighteen, the largest such attrition in the history of the Royal Navy. Aside from the devastating impact of Prien's second salvo, which detonated abreast the Stokers', Boys' and Marines' mess decks and prompted a complete loss of electrical power, the scale of the disaster can in part be attributed to a general conviction that Scapa Flow was invulnerable to underwater attack. Only this can explain why the initial detonation was never suspected as having been the work of an enemy submarine. To this was added an assumption in some quarters that *Royal Oak* was the target of an air attack, many heading below deck to take cover. Others simply returned to bed, leaving most of the crew ill-prepared to react to the mortal damage inflicted by Prien's subsequent attack. Moreover, this found the ship in a poor state of watertight integrity, to which her rapid capsize can partly be attributed. Lying at Air Defence Stations, many hatches, doors and ventilators were open that would have been sealed under different circumstances. Cases of cordite ignited in the magazines causing an immense deflagration that seared through the ship, incinerating everything in its path, and few if any members of the engine and boiler room watches can have survived the explosions and fumes. Loss of life was also heavy on deck as the ship rolled over, those attempting to abandon ship to starboard being hampered by falling debris and many were killed by equipment breaking free from its fastenings. Debris from the foretop destroyed a launch full of men about to cast off while others were sucked into the funnel when it met the water. Those who made it into the Flow did so mainly from the port side where Rear-Admiral Blagrove was last seen urging men to jump overboard further forward and away from the propellers. There they spent up to two and a half hours in waters whose coldness was mitigated only by the large quantities of oil that had leaked into it. Surgeon Lt Dick Caldwell paints a vivid picture of *Royal Oak*'s final moments and the predicament of those left in the water in words that might attach to almost any ship treated this book:

Prien presents his crew to Hitler in the Reich Chancellery in Berlin on 18 October 1939 as Raeder looks on on the left. The entire crew was awarded the Iron Cross 2nd Class with the exception of Prien who received the Knight's Cross. *BK*

The ship suddenly increased her list more and more rapidly. We were now on the ship's side and as she slid over, turning turtle, I lost my footing, fell, tried frantically to scramble up and dive clear and was thrown headlong into the sea. ('I'll be sucked down – that's what they say happens – what a fool I was not to jump sooner.') I seemed to go down and down and started fighting for breath. Then, as I came to the surface, the stern and propeller soared above me, then slipped slowly into the water and disappeared. A rush of water swept me head over heels, it seemed, and I went under again and came up in oil, thick black oil. I gulped it and retched at the filthy taste of it in my throat; oil, thick black oil smarting in my eyes. I swam and floundered about, hoping to find some support in the darkness. None of us had lifebelts. I heard cries round me, saw black heads bobbing, and I swam frenziedly again. I tried to wriggle out of my jacket, but found it heavy and slimy with oil. I repeatedly went under until quite suddenly I gave it up and thought, 'I'm going to drown.' Perfectly dispassionately 'I'm going to drown' and in a way which I cannot explain I wondered how to. And I thought of all the people I wanted to see, and things I wanted to do – that was all I thought of – and then I saw a group of heads and then threshed my way towards them.

Some made it dry-shod into one of the ship's picket boats but this was twice capsized by the crush of men attempting to find a berth in her and eventually it joined *Royal Oak* on the bottom. The majority of the survivors were picked up by the *Royal Oak*'s own drifter *Daisy II* and by the seaplane carrier *Pegasus*. The former had been moored alongside *Royal Oak* but raised steam after the first explosion and managed to cast off after being caught on her torpedo bulge as she capsized. She then steamed the length of the ship picking up oil-soaked survivors while *Pegasus* lowered her boats to render assistance. *Daisy II* was responsible for rescuing most of the survivors and her skipper John Gatt RNR given the Distinguished Service Cross, the only award made in connection with the disaster. A number of men struck out for the shore but only a handful survived the 850-yard swim to make their way to Kirkwall. The dazed survivors, accommodated either in *Pegasus* or in an assortment of ships about the Flow, were put through

further ordeals in the form of heavy bombing raids over the next few days before Capt. Benn succeeded in applying sufficient pressure for them to be transferred to the safety of Thurso on the mainland.

The Navy, meanwhile, was left to deal with consequences. Within a day of the sinking nets were spread over the ship to catch floating bodies. Divers descending to inspect the wreck were greeted with the horrific sight of suspended corpses and men found jammed in portholes in a vain attempt at escape. HMS *Royal Oak* lies capsized at an angle of forty degrees from the vertical in twenty-five metres of water. Her upturned hull, only five metres beneath the surface, is visible as a shadow in the water in good light. Although the ship is classified as a war grave and the ban on approaching her strictly enforced beyond the annual remembrance dive conducted by the Royal Navy, permission was granted for two weeks of diving in September 2000 from which a complete picture of her condition has emerged. Seventy years on, a grim reminder of the ship continues to rise from the depths in the form of fuel oil leaking from her tanks although steps have been taken to drain these since 2006. Apart from the wreck itself the principal memorials are to be found in St Magnus's cathedral in Kirkwall where the ship's bell and one of her nameplates have been preserved, together with a Garden of Remembrance at Scapa Flow.

U47 and Günther Prien

Built by Germaniawerft of Kiel and commissioned in December 1938, *U47* spent her entire career under Kptlt (later Korvkpt.) Günther Prien. She operated as leader of the 7th *U-Flottille*, initially from Kiel and subsequently from St-Nazaire. Her prolific tally began on the third day of the war but it was the sinking of *Royal Oak* on her second wartime cruise that brought *U47* and her audacious commander to prominence. The crew was awarded the Iron Cross Second Class for this exploit while Prien received the First Class (swiftly upgraded by Hitler to the Knight's Cross, the first of the war to be awarded to a U-boat commander) and were given an audience with the Führer in the Reich Chancellery in Berlin. Held in the highest regard by Dönitz, it was the failure of four of *U47*'s torpedoes to detonate against stationary British transports and cruisers in Bygdenfjorden during Operation HARTMUT in April 1940 that persuaded him to suspend U-boat operations while the problem was investigated. Often the first to locate convoys and bring in other boats to the attack, *U47* went on to sink nearly 200,000 tons of Allied shipping, Prien adding the Oak Leaf cluster to his Knight's Cross in October 1940. He was promoted Korvettenkapitän on 1 March 1941, days before *U47*'s career ended in unexplained circumstances off Rockall on or shortly after the 7th. For many years it was thought that *U47* had been destroyed in a depth-charge attack by HMS *Wolverine* but it is now conjectured that she fell victim to one of her own torpedoes. The mystery surrounding her loss gave rise to persistent though baseless rumours that Prien had fallen out with the High Command and been sent to a labour camp on charges of mutiny.

Sources

Admiralty, *Loss of HMS* Royal Oak: *Report of Board of Enquiry* (TNA, ADM 1/9840)

—, *Report on Sinking of HMS* Royal Oak: *Report by Director of Naval Branch E. G. N. Rushbrooke* (NHB, July 1945, NID 24/T16/); also on: http://www.uboatarchive.net/U-47RoyalOak.htm

Maclean, Paymaster Lt Cdr E. G. S., letter containing account of the sinking, 4 November 1939 (RNM, 2002/36)

Arthur, Max, ed., *The True Glory: The Royal Navy, 1914–1939* (London: Hodder & Stoughton, 1996)

—, *The Navy: 1939 to the Present Day* (London: Hodder & Stoughton, 1997)

Burt, R. A., *British Battleships of World War One* (London: Arms and Armour Press, 1986)

—, *British Battleships, 1919–1939* (London: Arms and Armour Press, 1993)

Churchill, Winston S., *The Second World War* (6 vols, London: Cassell & Co., 1948–54), I, pp. 489–91

Dönitz [Doenitz], Grossadmiral Karl, *Zehn Jahre und Zwanzig Tage* (Bonn: Athenäum-Verlag, 1958); English trans.: *Memoirs: Ten Years and Twenty Days* (London: Lionel Leventhal, 1990)

Frank, Wolfgang, *Enemy Submarine: The Story of Günther Prien, Captain of U47* (London: William Kimber, 1954)

Hewison, W.S., *The Great Harbour: Scapa Flow* (2nd edn, Kirkwall: The Orkney Press, 1990)

Jones, J. Farragut, *The Scourge of Scapa Flow* (New York: Dell Publishing, 1977)

Korganoff, Alexandre, *The Phantom of Scapa Flow: The Daring Exploit of the U-47* (London: Ian Allan, 1974)

Kurowski, Frank, *Jäger der Sieben Meere: Die Berühmtesten U-Boot-Kommandanten des II. Weltkriegs* (Stuttgart: Motorbuch Verlag, 1994)

McKee, Alexander, *Black Saturday: The Tragedy of the* Royal Oak (London: Souvenir Press, 1959)

Navy News, February 2001, p. 2

Prien, Korvkpt. Günther, *Mein Weg nach Scapa Flow* (Berlin: Deutscher Verlag, 1940); English trans.: *I Sank the* Royal Oak (London: Gray's Inn Press, 1954)

Raven, Alan, and John Roberts, *British Battleships of World War Two: The Development and Technical History of the Royal Navy's Battleships and Battlecruisers from 1911 to 1946* (London: Arms and Armour Press, 1976)

Roskill, *War at Sea*, I, pp. 73–4

Sarkar, Dilip, *Hearts of Oak: The Human Tragedy of HMS* Royal Oak (London: Amberley Publishing, 2010)

Snyder, Gerald, *The Royal Oak Disaster* (London: William Kimber, 1976)

Stern, Robert C., *Battle Beneath the Waves: The U-Boat War* (London: Arms and Armour Press, 1999)

Thompson, Major-General Julian, *The Imperial War Museum Book of the War at Sea: The Royal Navy in the Second World War* (London: Imperial War Museum, 1996)

Turner, David, *Last Dawn: The* Royal Oak *Tragedy at Scapa Flow* (Glendaruel, Argyll: Argyll Publishing, 2008)

Vause, Jordan, *Wolf: U-Boat Commanders in World War II* (Annapolis, Md.: Naval Institute Press, 1997)

Weaver, H. J., *Nightmare at Scapa Flow: The Truth About the Sinking of the* Royal Oak (n.p., Oxon.: Cressrelles, 1980)

HMS *Royal Oak* website:
   http://www.hmsroyaloak.co.uk/
Career history of HMS *Royal Oak*:
   http://www.naval-history.net/xGM-Chrono-01BB-Royal%20Oak.htm
U47 website:
   http://www.u47.org/english/index.asp

3   HMS *EXMOUTH*

Capt. R. S. Benson, DSO RN†
Sunk by *U22* (Type IIB), Kptlt Karl-Heinrich Jenisch, 21 January 1940
North Sea, 21 nm SE of Noss Head, Caithness (Scotland)

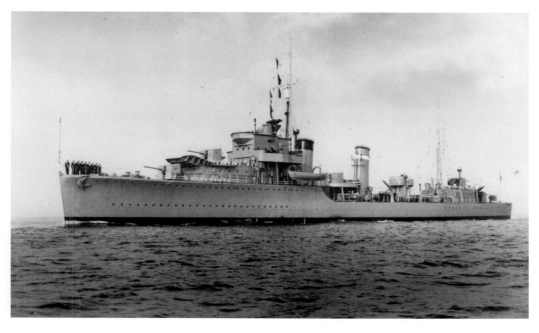

Exmouth seen entering Portsmouth as leader of the 5th Destroyer Flotilla, July 1935. She was lost with all hands to a single torpedo from *U22*.
Wright & Logan

Theatre British home waters (Map 2)	*Displacement* 1,495 tons
Coordinates 58° 18' N, 02° 29' W	*Dimensions* 343' × 33.75' × 8.75'
Kriegsmarine code Quadrat AN 1684	*Maximum speed* 36 knots
U-boat timekeeping differential +1 hour	*Armament* 5 × 4.7"; 8 × .5" AA; 5 × .303" AA; 8 × 21" tt
Fatalities 190 *Survivors* none	

Career

Approved under the 1931 estimates, the flotilla leader HMS *Exmouth* was laid down at Portsmouth Dockyard in May 1933, launched in January 1934 and commissioned in November of that year. Her design was based on that of HMS *Codrington*, leader of the 'A'-class destroyers. The eight 'E'-class destroyers that constituted her flotilla were completed between August and November 1934 and commissioned as the 5th Destroyer Flotilla, Home Fleet with *Exmouth* as leader. In August 1935 the Abyssinian Crisis brought the 5th DF to the Mediterranean where it remained until returning to Britain in March 1936. However, the Spanish Civil War took them south once more with intermittent patrol duty in the Bay of Biscay and Mediterranean between September 1936 and January 1938. Service in home waters continued until November when *Exmouth* was taken in hand for refitting at Portsmouth, emerging from this in time to rejoin her flotilla for the annual combined fleet exercises at Gibraltar in January 1939. These completed, the 5th DF was dispersed in April with *Exmouth* reduced first to the role of Boys' training ship and then assigned to aircraft co-operation duties with Portsmouth Command. The 'E' class was briefly reconstituted as the 12th DF, Home Fleet on the outbreak of war before *Exmouth* was assigned first to Western

Approaches Command at Milford Haven in December and then Rosyth Command in January 1940. Her war was to be over almost before it began.

Background of the attack

On the afternoon of 20 January 1940 HMS *Exmouth* received orders to rendezvous with the small freighter SS *Cyprian Prince* off Aberdeen and escort her and her cargo of searchlights, anti-aircraft guns, trucks, cars and ammunition to Scapa Flow. Once the two ships had established contact *Exmouth* flashed the signal 'Follow us. Speed 10 knots. Course 070', and proceeded to lead *Cyprian Prince* northwards with a bright stern light as her guide. As the night wore on their course took them directly into the patrol area south-east of the Orkneys assigned to Kptlt Karl-Heinrich Jenisch's *U22*. In a remarkable sequence of events, it is clear that Jenisch might have remained unaware of their presence had they not steamed directly across his line of sight while he had three Scandinavian steamers under observation. As his war diary shows, Jenisch showed no hesitation in shifting target and after tracking *Exmouth* and *Cyprian Prince* for over an hour managed to fire a torpedo at each in quick succession.

War Diary of *U22*, patrol of 15–24 January 1940: PG 30019, NHB, reel 1,060, pp. 168–74

Date, time	Details of position, wind, weather, sea, light, visibility, moonlight, etc.	Incidents
20.i		
1910	Wind SSE 5, sea 4, bright moonlight	Surfaced. To the south-east a lit-up steamer sighted heading north-west. Tracked and overhauled her. Steamer is being followed by two escorts.[1] To start with the bright moonlight prevents an attack; when the moon later passes temporarily behind light cloud I make three attempts to close. Moon keeps reappearing during approaches making it impossible to carry out an undetected attack.
2224	Qu. [AN] 1643 lower right	Abandon further attacks as ship's position is uncertain, the Pentland Skerries are only 11 miles off by dead reckoning and the moon now reigns unchallenged over a cloudless sky. We are sighted by the steamer when withdrawing to about 2,500 m; steamer turns towards us, the escorts form a line abreast and the group begins U-boat hunting. So clearly this was a U-boat hunter group with the steamer
2328	Qu. [AN] 1628 lower edge middle, moonlit	acting as a decoy.[2] More escorts appear from the south as I follow an easterly course, forcing me to detour to the north. By making further detours involving a variety of courses to the north, west and south I eventually shake off pursuit and can resume patrolling the same hunting grounds as this morning.
		K.-H. Jenisch
21.i		
0425	Qu. [AN] 1684 middle.	Three small illuminated steamers sighted heading north-west.[3] After my recent experiences I'm fairly suspicious of them. Just as I try to get a better look at them two large shadows loom up in my line of

---

1 The identities of these three ships have not been established.

2 Though reiterated by Jenisch in his post-cruise report, no evidence has been found to corroborate this incident. However, it might be conjectured that Jenisch exaggerated the matter in order to justify his attack on a neutral ship at 0711 on the following day (see n. 9).

3 The identities of these ships have not been established, though it is possible that they included the Danish SS *Tekla*, sunk by *U22* the following night (see n. 9).

	Moon setting and obscured by cloud.	sight – a destroyer and another steamer. The inclination is initially difficult to gauge so I turn and track them. I can't overhaul the destroyer.
0535	Qu. [AN] 1684 upper middle	While turning to attack the steamer we fire at the destroyer at a range of 1,500 m with an inclination of 110°. This hits after a running time of 2 min. 35 sec.[4] Dark smoke cloud observed during detonation.
0538	*Destroyer Exmouth, Pfeiffer 2/9/54*[5]	We then fire a torpedo at the steamer – estimated size approximately 4,000 tons – from a range of 1,000 m with an inclination of 80°.[6] A dud or a miss, perhaps due to change in course or speed of steamer in response to the first detonation; second torpedo explodes after 4 min. 7 sec.[7]
until 0627	Qu. [AN] 1681 & [AN] 1673. Very dark night.	Again hunting the steamer. At one point we have to run both engines at utmost speed in reverse so as not to ram the turning steamer. But no further chance of a shot presents itself as steamer makes off on a westerly course towards the coast at not less than 12.5 knots. At 0640 we hear the following message on the 600-m waveband delivered at great speed from either the destroyer or the steamer: *SOS Sinking in latitude 58° 18' N longitude 02° 25' W.* The radio station at Wick (gkr) repeats at 0650: *SOS unknown vessel sinking in position 58° 18' N, 02° 25' W.*[8]
0711	Qu. [AN] 1681 lower middle	While withdrawing on an easterly course we sight, approach and torpedo a steamer.[9] Size of steamer approximately 1,500 tons; she sinks in about 3 min.
0830	Qu. [AN] 1686 middle. Wind SSW 3, sea 1.	Dived.

4 Jenisch adds the following in his torpedo report: 'Hit noted forward, thick black cloud of smoke. Sinking not witnessed.' This report also records that the torpedo which sank *Exmouth* was fired by *U22*'s First Watch Officer, Oblt.z.S. H. J. Schroth, as was normal procedure in U-boat surface attacks. The running time equates to a range of around 2,350 metres rather than the 1,500 originally estimated by Jenisch, the difference at least partially explained by the oblique inclination of the target (110°).

5 Manuscript addition in pencil by the civilian archivist Walther Pfeiffer who was brought to Britain to work on the logs post-war.

6 This was the SS *Cyprian Prince* of 1,988 GRT and 2,900 deadweight tons.

7 Jenisch did indeed miss the *Cyprian Prince*. The detonation he heard was almost certainly *Exmouth*'s magazine.

8 'GKR' was the radio callsign for Wick. Cardinal points and degree and minute signs supplied to both sets of coordinates for clarity.

9 This was the Danish freighter *Tekla* of 1,469 GRT. It is unclear whether *Tekla* was illuminated at this stage (as she had been at 0425, assuming that she had indeed been spotted by *U22* at that juncture), or if the encounter related at 2224/2328 on the 20th had any bearing on Jenisch's decision to attack a neutral vessel; see n. 2.

The sinking

Having observed the impact of his first torpedo against *Exmouth*'s starboard side Jenisch immediately turned to attack *Cyprian Prince* – unsuccessfully as it turned out. Since *Exmouth* was lost with all hands and as neither *U22* nor *Cyprian Prince* saw her go down the precise circumstances of her loss remain unclear. However, the testimony of those in *Cyprian Prince* provides some clue to her end. At 0444 a detonation was heard in *Cyprian Prince* which the deck watch attributed to *Exmouth* dropping depth charges. Capt. Benjamin Wilson was immediately roused from his bunk, reaching the bridge in time to be greeted at 0448 by a 'terrific explosion, much louder than the first'. Though not appreciated in *Cyprian Prince* at the time, it would seem that *Exmouth* had suffered the detonation of one of her magazines approximately five minutes after being struck by Jenisch's first torpedo. This conjecture was borne out when the wreck was discovered lying in 160 feet of water on 24 June 2001, the ship upturned and her bows demolished by a major explosion.

An Admiralty Board of Enquiry held in the spring could shed little light on the sinking, though the identity of the perpetrator may have been revealed thanks to the capture of documents following the sinking of *U55* (Kptlt Werner Heidel) in the Western Approaches on 30 January. Whatever the case, it found Capt. Benson's instructions to the *Cyprian Prince* at the start of the voyage to have been inadequate and ruled that he should neither have been showing such a bright stern light nor leading his charge, this being the reverse of current convoy

practice. The Board also observed that neither ship was zigzagging. Although this would certainly have made *Exmouth* a greater test of Jenisch's marksmanship, it is clear from *U22*'s log that the discovery of this little convoy owed more to chance than any Board member might have allowed.

Fate of the crew

By the time *Cyprian Prince* had slowed her engines to look for survivors *Exmouth* had already disappeared, barely two minutes after the final explosion. At the Board of Enquiry it emerged that Capt. Wilson of the *Cyprian Prince* had attempted to locate the ship and the survivors, being forced to turn hard aport to avoid what he initially thought was *Exmouth*'s hull, but which, as Jenisch's log suggests, was as likely *U22* herself. Wilson then ordered full speed towards a number of flashing lights that were apparently interpreted as coming from survivors' lifejackets. Cries could be heard, a number of men were identified in the water and lifeboats were readied. However, Wilson now resolved not to stop for the survivors and instead steamed on towards Kirkwall at his best speed: 'I decided it was impossible to render assistance to the men in the water without sacrificing the *Cyprian Prince*.' This decision, taken within ten minutes of the sinking, was carefully scrutinised by the Board of Enquiry. Despite strong feeling in some quarters there was no escaping the fact that Wilson had acted in accordance with the Admiralty Defence of Merchant Shipping regulations which stated that merchantmen should not stop in the event of a submarine attack

U22 seen off the naval memorial at Laboe while serving with *U-Flottille Lohs* in the Baltic in 1938. *BK*

on a convoy. For all that, his decision was adjudged 'correct, although counter to the normally accepted custom at sea'. In fact Wilson's action is fully vindicated in Jenisch's war diary: the same decision that condemned *Exmouth*'s survivors quite clearly spared *Cyprian Prince* a similar fate at the hands of *U22*. Wilson, much affected by the incident, did not resume his command.

HMS *Exmouth* has the unfortunate distinction of being the first surface warship to be lost with all hands during the Second World War. Perhaps because she was not referred to by name, the distress signal sent first by *Cyprian Prince* and then relayed from Wick seems never to have been acted upon. Nor did attempts to alert Noss Head, Duncansby Head and Muckle Skerry by Aldis lamp obtain any response and it was not until *Cyprian Prince* reached Kirkwall at 1300 that day that the Admiralty responded to the sinking. An assortment of ships led by the destroyer *Sikh* and including the Wick lifeboat were sent out late that afternoon but to no avail. A ship's lifebuoy was found among the flotsam but no survivors were rescued and it was recalled at the Board of Enquiry that it had been a particularly bitter winter's night. It has been suggested that the Danish freighter *Tekla* was sunk by *U22* while attempting to rescue survivors of the *Exmouth* but no evidence has been found to support this, nor do her nine survivors appear to have related as much to the Admiralty. The bodies of eighteen sailors were washed up on the mainland a week later and a mass funeral was held at Wick on 31 January, a memorial being raised in memory of the ship's company in the Old Parish Church there in August 2005.

U22 and Karl-Heinrich Jenisch

One of the last Type-IIB boats, *U22* was built by Germaniawerft in Kiel and commissioned in August 1936. Based at Kiel throughout her career, she accounted for seven ships, all of them under her second commander Karl-Heinrich Jenisch. The majority fell victim to mines sown by her off the north-east coast of England, the torpedoing of HMS *Exmouth* being undoubtedly her greatest success. However, within weeks of this triumph *U22* was no more. Towards the end of March 1940 she went missing in the North Sea on Jenisch's fifth patrol, the suspected victim of a mine off the Danish coast. There were no survivors.

Sources

Admiralty, *Loss of HMS* Exmouth *whilst Escorting SS* Cyprian Prince: *Board of Enquiry* (TNA, ADM 1/10733)

Baird, R. N., *Shipwrecks of the North of Scotland* (Edinburgh: Birlinn General, 2003)

English, John, Amazon *to* Ivanhoe: *British Standard Destroyers of the 1930s* (Kendal, Cumbria: World Ship Society, 1993)

Kinghorn, D., and B. Hargreaves, 'Destroyers of the Royal Navy: Leaders of the "A"–"I" Classes' in *Warships*, Supplement no. 13 (September 1968), pp. 13–22

Lombard-Hobson, Capt. Sam, *A Sailor's War* (London: Orbis Publishing, 1983)

'Resting place of warship finally found' in *The Orcadian*, 28 June 2001; also on: http://www.orcadian.co.uk/archive/restingplace.htm

Scottish Daily Mail, 21 January 2002

Career history of HMS *Exmouth*:
   http://www.naval-history.net/xGM-Chrono-10DD-20E-Exmouth.htm

Website of HMS *Exmouth* 1940 Association:
   http://www.hmsexmouth.com/

Description of dive on wreck of HMS *Exmouth*:
   http://www.divernet.com/Travel_Features/travel_features_uk/157767/the_wild_east.html

4   HMS *DARING*

Cdr S. A. Cooper, RN†

Sunk by *U23* (Type IIB), Kptlt Otto Kretschmer, 18 February 1940
North Sea, 45 nm ENE of Noss Head, Caithness (Scotland)

Daring seen early in the war wearing the lighter shade of grey favoured for service in the Mediterranean.
Within a few weeks she had become Kretschmer's first warship victim. *BfZ*

Theatre	British home waters (Map 2)	*Displacement*	1,375 tons
Coordinates	58° 40' N, 01° 40' W	*Dimensions*	329' × 33' × 8.5'
Kriegsmarine code	Quadrat AN 1692	*Maximum speed*	35.5 knots
U-boat timekeeping differential	+1 hour	*Armament*	4 × 4.7"; 3 × 40 mm AA; 8 × .5" AA; 5 × .303" AA; 8 × 21" tt
Fatalities 156	*Survivors* 5		

Career

Built under the 1930 estimates, the 'D'-class destroyers, of which HMS *Daring* was the third unit, were virtual repeats of the preceding 'C'-class (see HMCS *Ottawa*, **68**), though with additional depth-charges and improved anti-aircraft armament. Their appearance just as the impressive Japanese Fubuki class was taking to the water provided the first indication that Britain had lost her lead in destroyer design, while austerity measures meant that four of the class, *Daring* included, could not initially be fitted with the new .5-inch machine gun. Laid down at John I. Thornycroft's yard at Woolston, Southampton in June 1931, *Daring* was launched in April 1932 and commissioned in November of that year. On completion the class entered service as the 1st Destroyer Flotilla, Mediterranean Fleet, *Daring* joining her sisters in January 1933. Here they remained with the exception of a brief sojourn in the Red Sea and Persian Gulf in the autumn of 1933 until ordered back to Britain for refitting in August 1934, *Daring*'s being carried out at Sheerness. Already in April of that year *Daring* had become the first command of Cdr Lord Louis Mountbatten, the future Earl Mountbatten of Burma. In December 1934 the 1st DF sailed for the China Station where Mountbatten reluctantly turned over his command on arrival at Singapore. Renumbered the 8th and then the 21st Flotilla, the class spent the remaining years of peace based on Hong Kong until ordered back to European waters on the outbreak of war. However, *Daring* was retained at Aden for escort and patrol duty in the Red Sea until November 1939 and never rejoined her sisters.

After docking and repairs at Malta, *Daring* sailed north, reaching Belfast on 7 January 1940 having escorted the armed merchant cruiser HMS *Dunnottar Castle* from Gibraltar. Additional repairs at Portsmouth followed, on completion of which she made for Scapa Flow to join the 3rd DF, Home Fleet on 10 February. The association lasted scarcely longer than a week.

Background of the attack

On 17 February 1940 *Daring* was ordered to join convoy HN12 ('Homeward Norway') transporting iron ore between the Norwegian port of Bergen and Methil on the Scottish coast. HN12 consisted of twenty ships deployed in columns of six or seven vessels each, a destroyer at each quarter and the submarine *Thistle* (**5**) astern. In the early hours of 18 February HN12, then making 7½ knots, had reached a point forty-five miles east of Wick on the north-east coast of Scotland and just over fifty miles south-east of the Orkneys. HMSs *Daring* and *Ilex* were keeping station on its port and starboard quarter, with *Delight* and *Inglefield* on the port and starboard bow respectively. Since *B-Dienst*, the Kriegsmarine's radio monitoring and intelligence service, had broken the administrative code used by the Royal Navy to transmit information on convoy sailings, it is reasonable to suppose that B.d.U. was informed of HN12's existence and that the subsequent encounter was not entirely fortuitous. Whatever the case, Kptlt Otto Kretschmer had been forewarned of the approach of HN12 by *U19* (Kptlt Joachim Schepke) a few hours earlier and his lookouts duly sighted the forward units of the convoy shortly after midnight. Unable on this occasion to employ his preferred tactic of breaking into the convoy itself, Kretschmer instead selected a straightforward target in the rear of the convoy against which he fired a single torpedo from a range of 800 metres. His task was made easier by the fact that although the advance escorts were zigzagging, the rear ones were not. Within minutes HMS *Daring* was no more.

War Diary of *U23*, patrol of 9–28 February 1940: PG 30020, NHB, reel 1,060, pp. 275–6

Date, time	Details of position, wind, weather, sea, light, visibility, moonlight, etc.	Incidents
18.ii		
0000	Qu. [AN] 1832	
0107		Two destroyers sighted heading south-west. Must relate to earlier W/T transmission from *U19*[1] (053/0015/18/1: *Enemy convoy sighted Qu. 1494, enemy steering southerly course*). I steer in this direction.
0305	[Sketch of attack]	Convoy heaves into sight at bearing 0° true. I manoeuvre ahead of it to eastward in order to have the dark horizon at my back and to avoid the unwanted attentions of the moon. The convoy, comprising twenty ships, is sailing in three columns with a destroyer at each corner; those on the port and starboard bows are zigzagging to and fro ahead of the wings of the convoy. The rear destroyers are maintaining a steady course.
		Astern of and between these two is an 'L'-class submarine.[2] While attempting to penetrate the convoy from the east and fire a shot at one of the steamers sailing in the middle I get caught between the two
	Moon setting	portside destroyers, so decide to attack the one in the rear of the convoy.
0354	Qu. [AN] 1692	Torpedo fired from 800 m at 0354. Torpedo no. E 2749. An initial detonation when it hits the destroyer followed by a second. Destroyer breaks in two. Stern section towers up and sinks until only a small section can be seen above the surface of the water. Fore part capsizes. Convoy holds its course, paying no heed to the wreckage.
		According to news broadcast at 2000 on 19 February this was the 'D'-class destroyer *Daring* (1,375 tons).
0400	Qu. [AN] 1692	Immediately afterwards attack submarine. Torpedo no. E 2953. Misses.
0521		Outgoing W/T transmission 812/0310/1815. Repeated by [radio] control centre. *Enemy convoy sighted Qu. 1692, heading south.* Alter course to 310°. A destroyer is following, though without having seen the boat.
		Took up position.[3]
0755	Qu. [AN] 1660	Dived. Five powerful depth-charge detonations.
0800	Qu. [AN] 1639	
1200	Qu. [AN] 4117, upper right	Day's run: 76 nm surfaced, 22 nm submerged.

---

1   Commanded by Kptlt Joachim Schepke, *U19* was operating further to the north-east.
2   HMS/m *Thistle*, which in fact belonged to the 'T' class. A First World War design, the 'L'-class overseas submarines had mostly been scrapped by 1939 but Kretschmer's mistake is understandable since both types had a forward gun mounted high in an elongated conning tower.
3   Manuscript addition in pencil.

The sinking

Kretschmer's torpedo struck *Daring* on the port side aft at around 0255 ship time, the initial explosion being seen as a dull red glow from *Thistle*. As Kretschmer observes, this was followed by a second explosion, probably in her after magazine, to which *Daring*'s rapid demise can be attributed. Here is the account of the youngest survivor, Ordinary Seaman William Edward Woodnut:

> I was at one of the gun stations on the middle watch looking forward to the time when very shortly I should be in my hammock, when suddenly there was a terrific explosion. The ship broke in half. I was thrown to the deck and saw the funnel falling towards me. Luckily it hit the gun and bounced over into the water. Then I went down with the ship as there was a second explosion. I remember rising to the surface to find the sea covered with oil.

The only officer survivor, Lt L. A. Rogers, reported to the Court of Enquiry that she simply 'shuddered, listed to port, and turned bottom up in less than 30 seconds'. Kretschmer's observations are corroborated in British accounts: her back broken, *Daring*'s forward section took at least half an hour to sink while the stern immediately stood up before subsiding until only the tip remained on the surface.

The loss of HMS/m *Thistle* with all hands on 10 April (5) prevented the holding of a more formal Board of Enquiry. Nonetheless, the sinking prompted the Commander-in-Chief Home Fleet, Admiral Sir Charles Forbes, to order that the standing instructions against escorts zigzagging when stationed astern of the convoy be amended forthwith.

Fate of the crew

HMS *Ilex* was the first to pass the wreckage at 0335 (about forty minutes after the sinking), signalling *Thistle* to rescue survivors while she attempted to locate the U-boat with her Asdic set. Perplexed at this order and apparently ignorant of Kretschmer's attack on his own vessel six minutes after that on *Daring*, *Thistle*'s CO (Lt Cdr W. F. Haselfoot) requested that *Ilex* lower a boat to assist in the search for survivors. However, *Ilex*'s Asdic sweep had already taken her out of visual range and she never received the signal. Commenting on the sinking, Admiral Forbes declared that, in the absence of a firm Asdic contact, *Ilex* should not have abandoned the scene without first launching a boat. By the time *Thistle* closed the wreckage a short while later only three survivors were in sight, one in the water (who promptly disappeared), another clinging to the upright stern section, and a rating clutching onto a raft who indicated that he had a broken arm. With no boat to assist the work of rescue *Thistle* manoeuvred as close as she dared to the raft while Lt R. P. N. Ennor dived into the water with a line. Misunderstanding instructions, the rating let go of the raft and clung on to his would-be rescuer, both sinking immediately. Resurfacing separately, Ennor made another attempt at rescue but both were now slick with oil and the sailor slipped from his grasp and disappeared. Attention now turned to the man on the stern section who was rescued at 0430 with the help of two whalers from *Ilex* which had returned to the scene without gaining any firm contact on *U23*.

Meanwhile, four other men had managed to get into a Carley float and clear of the wreck before drifting for several hours. One of them was OD Woodnut:

> An air-lock beneath my oilskins enabled me to keep afloat, and I swam round until I came across two [actually three] seamen clinging to a Carley float. One of them clambered aboard and pulled me and the other man up. It was dark, and we could hear the shouts of other men, but could not see them.

Seeing a submarine, they hailed it believing it was *Thistle* but desisted when the possibility arose that it was German; Kretschmer's log makes no reference to the matter. They were eventually picked up by HMS *Inglefield* after 0645, bringing the number of *Daring*'s survivors to five. *Ilex* detached for Rosyth on the 19th and *Inglefield* for Scapa Flow on the 20th, surviving crewmen being landed in each case.

U23 and Otto Kretschmer

Built by Germaniawerft in Kiel and commissioned in September 1936, in October 1937 *U23* became the second command of Oblt.z.S. (Kptlt from June 1939) Otto Kretschmer, first as part of *U-Flottille Weddigen* until December 1939 and subsequently with the 1st Flotilla until she was relegated to training duties in June 1940. However, *U23*'s frontline duty was not over, and in September 1942 she was allocated for service in the Black Sea. As with all boats earmarked for that theatre, *U23* was dismantled and then transported piecemeal to Romania by canal, river and road. Some successes were scored against Soviet vessels by Kptlt Rolf-Birger Wahlen, including the anti-submarine patrol boat *TSC-578/Shkval* in August 1943 (**G57**), but her career ended when Rumania fell to the Russians in the summer of 1944. An attempt to sell the three remaining boats to Turkey proved fruitless and in September 1944 *U23* was scuttled off the Turkish coast and her crew interned for

Kretschmer on his return from a successful patrol later in the war. *DUBMA*

the duration of the war. In late 2007 the wreck was discovered by a Turkish team lying three miles off Agva at a depth of 160 feet.

Kretschmer's tally in *U23* was eight ships for a total of 27,000 tons but he was destined for much greater things. In April 1940 he was given command of *U99* in which he proceeded to sink a record 234,000 tons of Allied shipping, including HMSs *Laurentic*, *Patroclus* and *Forfar* (**19** and **20**).

Sources

Admiralty, *Loss of HMS* Daring *by Enemy Action: Reports of HMS* Thistle *and* Ilex (TNA, ADM 1/10667)
—, *Torpedo Attacks on HM Ships, 1939–1941* (TNA, ADM 199/157)
—, *Trade Division, Scandinavian Convoys, 1939–1940* (TNA, ADM 199/2110)

Enders, Gerd, „Das Ende der 30. Flottille im Schwarzen Meer" in *Schaltung Küste* 154 (September 1994) pp. 30–1
English, John, *Amazon to Ivanhoe: British Standard Destroyers of the 1930s* (Kendal, Cumbria: World Ship Society, 1993)
Hough, Richard, *Mountbatten: A Biography* (London: Weidenfeld & Nicolson, 1980)
Kurowski, Frank, *Jaeger der Sieben Meere: Die Berühmtesten U-Boot-Kommandanten des II. Weltkriegs* (Stuttgart: Motorbuch Verlag, 1994)
Robertson, Terence, *The Golden Horseshoe* (London: Evans Brothers, 1955)
The War Illustrated, II, no. 26, 1 March 1940, p. 192, and no. 27, 8 March 1940, pp. 220–1
Ziegler, Philip, *Mountbatten* (London: Collins, 1985)

Career history of HMS *Daring*:
    http://www.naval-history.net/xGM-Chrono-10DD-19D-Daring.htm
Website devoted to the loss of HMS *Daring*:
    http://www.axfordsabode.org.uk/darfo102.htm
Article concerning discovery of wreck of *U23*:
    http://www.telegraph.co.uk/news/main.jhtml?xml=/news/2008/02/03/whitler103.xml

5 HMS/m *THISTLE*

Lt Cdr W. F. Haselfoot, RN†

Sunk by *U4* (Type IIA), Oblt.z.S. Hans-Peter Hinsch, 10 April 1940

Boknafjorden, 25 nm WNW of Stavanger (Norway)

A newly commissioned *Thistle* seen under way shortly before the outbreak of war.
A prolonged game of cat and mouse with *U4* ended with her at the bottom of Boknafjorden. *BfZ*

Campaign	Norwegian Campaign (Map 2)	*Displacement*	1,090 tons surfaced,	1,575 tons submerged
Coordinates	59° 17' N, 05° 06' E	*Dimensions*	275' × 26.5' × 12'	
Kriegsmarine code	Quadrat AN 2989	*Maximum speed*	15.25 knots surfaced	8.75 knots submerged
U-boat timekeeping differential	+1 hour	*Armament*	10 × 21" tt (16 torpedoes carried); 1 × 4" AA; 3 × .303" AA	
Fatalities	53 *Survivors* none			

Career

Fitted with ten torpedo tubes, the 'T'-class patrol submarines, of which fifty-three were eventually built in various sub-classes, boasted the heaviest broadside of any British design. A unit of the first group of the class, HMS/m *Thistle* was laid down at Vickers-Armstrong's yard at Barrow-in-Furness in December 1937, launched in October 1938 and completed in early July 1939. *Thistle* commissioned with the 5th Submarine Flotilla of the Home Fleet at Portsmouth in May 1939, a month before her sister *Thetis* sank with heavy loss of life in Liverpool Bay. On 26 September *Thistle* joined the 2nd SF at Dundee and spent the early months of the war on patrol and interception duty in the North and Norwegian Seas, including an unsuccessful mission to sink the liner *Bremen* in the Skaggerak in November. February 1940 found her in the unusual role of close escort to convoy HN12 between the Norwegian port of Bergen and Methil on the Scottish coast, narrowly escaping being torpedoed by Kptlt Otto Kretschmer in *U23* on the same night that he despatched HMS *Daring* (**4**). *Thistle* rescued one of the survivors. She remained in these waters for the rest of her brief career.

Background of the attack

The clash between *U4* and HMS/m *Thistle* in the early evening and night of 9–10 April 1940 took place against the background of WESERÜBUNG, the German invasion of Norway, and Operation WILFRED, the intended mining of the Norwegian Inner Leads by the British to interrupt the passage of Swedish iron ore between Narvik and Germany. WESERÜBUNG was fixed for 9 April and WILFRED for the 8th. *U4*, instructed to operate off Stavanger, was one of a large number of boats ordered to provide support at key landing points between Oslo and Narvik or to patrol the approaches to these as part of Operation HARTMUT, the naval side of WESERÜBUNG. Oblt.z.S. Hans-Peter Hinsch learnt of these intentions after opening sealed orders at sea on 6 April. *Thistle*, meanwhile, had sailed from Scapa Flow on the 7th with orders to patrol off the same port in the event of a German countermove against WILFRED, and otherwise to attack any enemy target that presented itself. Thus, though the British suspected that plans were afoot for an attack on Norway, the scale and imminence of the threat was not appreciated until the German offensive was well in train and Operation WILFRED effectively forestalled.

Shortly after 1600 on the 9th HMS/m *Thistle*, then submerged, came across *U4* in the approaches to Stavanger and put in an attack. In a signal made soon after, Lt Cdr Haselfoot reported that *Thistle* had 'expended six torpedoes on inward bound U-boat at entrance to Stavanger fjord at 1604. Result unconfirmed due to enemy air activity. Intend to carry out orders [to dive into Stavanger harbour] tomorrow Wednesday with remaining two warheads, air activity permitting.' However, prompted no doubt by strategic developments, the Admiralty altered *Thistle*'s orders to patrol off Skudeneshavn twenty miles to the north-west, though these were destined never to be carried out. To add a further twist, though Haselfoot had clearly taken *U4* by surprise, it seems likely that B.d.U. was informed of the presence of a British submarine in these waters thanks to the decryption of the Admiralty Naval Code and Naval Cipher No. 1 by *B-Dienst*, the Kriegsmarine's radio monitoring and intelligence service, assisted no doubt by Haselfoot's use of radio that day. Whatever the case, Haselfoot's was to prove a costly miss. In the war diary that follows Hinsch describes *Thistle*'s attack before relating how the roles of hunter and hunted were dramatically reversed after the two submarines surfaced later that night.

War Diary of *U4*, patrol of 4–14 April 1940: PG 30003, NHB, reel 1,057, pp. 850–5

Date, time	Details of position, wind, weather, sea, light, visibility, moonlight, etc.	Incidents
9.iv		
1600	Qu. [AN] 2997, wind NNW 2, sea 1, clear, good visibility	Nothing to report.
1705		Torpedo trail seen off the port quarter. Evasive manoeuvre hard astarboard, 12 knots. A trail of bubbles passes 10 m before the bows. Alarm! We dive to 40 m. As we are diving we hear the sounds of another three torpedoes, followed by four detonations.[1]
2000	Qu. [AN] 3131	Repeated electric engine noises heard.[2] It occurs to me that the coast offers an excellent dark background against which even a large submarine might remain unobserved. So we head further out to benefit from a better horizon. Moreover, I doubt the enemy would remain in the same confined area at night.
2217		Surfaced.
2400	Qu. [AN] 3131, wind NNW 3, sea 2, dark night, good visibility	Nothing to report.
		Hinsch
10.iv		
0157	Qu. [AN] 3123, upper left corner	A submarine on the starboard bow – in fact too close for me to fire at immediately. Bows right, inclination 140°. We turn to starboard with both engines at 4/5 speed, and present our stern to the enemy. Tubes I and III ready. After withdrawing about 600 m I alter onto a reciprocal course. Enemy seems to me to have stopped. First torpedo (G7a) fired with no aim-off. Using the trail of bubbles as a yardstick I deduce that enemy's bows are shifting to starboard and that she is actually still slightly under way. So the first torpedo misses. Immediately fire second torpedo (G7e) from a range of approximately 400 m, with aim-off allowing for speed of 5 knots and an inclination of 70°. A hit amidships.[3]
0213	Qu. [AN] 2989, lower left corner	Huge patch and all-pervading smell of oil. In the darkness we see nothing to fish out of the water. We remain at the scene for some time then head off at 3 knots, course 330°. W/T signal transmitted, not acknowledged by [radio] control centre.
0330		Passed position of sinking again. 15 minutes cruising around the patch of oil.
0400	Qu. [AN] 3123, wind NW 3, sea 2–3, clear, good visibility	Nothing to report.

---

1 As Lt Cdr Haselfoot's last signal indicates, *Thistle* had actually fired six of her torpedoes in an attempt to hit *U4*.

2 *Thistle* had presumably dived for cover from the 'air activity' referred to in her last report, hence the sound of her electric engines.

3 In his torpedo report Hinsch adds that he saw 'brief, bright flames up to about conning tower height, then everything shrouded in cloud'.

The Type-IIA *U4* under way in 1938. *BK*

The sinking and fate of the crew

Given that *Thistle* sank instantly with all hands Hinsch's is the only source that can shed light on the incident. Striking her amidships, the torpedo probably killed or injured all those on the conning tower, thus rendering the slender chance of there being any survivors even more remote. Why *Thistle* had surfaced despite having every reason to suppose that a U-boat was in the vicinity remains a mystery, though like *U4* she could not remain submerged indefinitely since her batteries needed periodic recharging. Fearing that his exploit might go unacknowledged, Hinsch returned to the scene an hour and a half later to gather evidence of the sinking for B.d.U. He needn't have worried. Thanks to *B-Dienst* decrypts Dönitz was able to tell Hinsch much more about his probable victim than he himself knew. Nonetheless, this success was but small consolation for the *U-Boot-Waffe* which had suffered repeated cases of torpedo failure during the campaign.

Across the Norwegian Sea *Thistle*'s fate remained a matter of speculation at the Admiralty for several days. Though presumed lost after failing to report in on both 10 and 11 April, it was only after *U4*'s return on the 14th and the subsequent broadcast of an account of her success in English that *Thistle*'s demise was recorded. This no doubt explains why her loss is occasionally stated as having occurred on the latter date.

Hinsch as a Fähnrich zur See (midshipman or ensign), about 1935. *DUBMA*

U4 and Hans-Peter Hinsch

Built by Deutsche Werke at Kiel, *U4* was commissioned in August 1935 and employed on training duties until the outbreak of hostilities. Four operational patrols were carried out in the first eight months of the war, all of them in the North Sea either off the Scandinavian coast or those of Germany and Holland. Modest success attended these patrols, the last two of which were made under the command of Oblt.z.S. Hans-Peter Hinsch in March and April 1940. HMS/m *Thistle* was Hinsch's only success before *U4* and other training boats were recalled from frontline service. Reassigned to the 21st Flotilla at Pillau, *U4* resumed training duties until being decommissioned in August 1944.

Hinsch went on to two further U-boat commands. The first of these, *U140* (see **28**), was a Type-IID boat in which he sank three ships in a tenure lasting from August 1940 to June 1941. Though given command of the Type-VIIC *U569*, six patrols between August 1941 and January 1943 yielded Hinsch only two sinkings, a tally which prompted his transfer to shore duties. He died in April 1967.

Sources

Admiralty, Flag Officer Submarines, *Attacks on Allied Submarines: Royal Navy Ship and Submarine Losses* [operational career of HMS/m *Thistle*] (TNA, ADM 199/1925)

HMS/m *Thistle* file (RNSM)

Trierweiler, A., *Versenkung des eng. U-Bootes* Thistle *durch Unterseeboot 4 während der Besetzung von Norwegen am 10.04.1940*, December 1984 (typescript, DUBMA, *U4* file)

Beesley, Patrick, *Very Special Intelligence: The Story of the Admiralty's Operational Intelligence Centre, 1939–1945* (London: Hamish Hamilton, 1977)

Bendert, Harald, *U-Boote im Duell* (Hamburg: Mittler, 1996)

Evans, A. S., *Beneath the Waves: A History of HM Submarine Losses, 1904–1971* (London: William Kimber, 1986)

Hezlet, Vice-Admiral Sir Arthur, *The History of British and Allied Submarine Operations During World War II* (2 vols, Gosport: Royal Navy Submarine Museum, 2002; published as *British and Allied Submarine Operations in World War II* on CD-ROM, 2003)

Hudson, B., and J. J. Colledge, 'British Submarines in World War II: Triton Class' in *Warships*, Supplement no. 90 (Autumn 1987), pp. 25–33

Jones, Geoffrey, *Submarines Versus U-Boats* (London: William Kimber, 1986)

Roskill, *War at Sea*, I, pp. 156–65 and 266–7

Career history of HMS/m *Thistle*:
http://www.naval-history.net/xGM-Chrono-12SS-07T-Thistle.htm

6 NF *DORIS*

C.C. J. E. M. Favreul, MN†
Sunk by *U9* (Type IIB), Oblt.z.S. Wolfgang Lüth, 8 May 1940
North Sea, 35 nm W of Den Helder (The Netherlands)

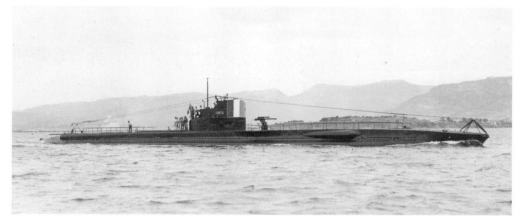

Doris under way off Toulon in July 1937. The *Tricolore* painted on the conning tower denotes her participation
in the Nyon Patrol off Spain during the civil war. *BfZ*

Campaign	Norwegian Campaign (Map 2	*Displacement*	615 tons surfaced 776 tons submerged
Coordinates	52° 47' N, 03° 49' E	*Dimensions*	216.5' × 16' × 12.5'
Kriegsmarine code	Quadrat AN 8511	*Maximum speed*	14 knots surfaced 7.5 knots submerged
U-boat timekeeping differential	+2 hours	*Armament*	7 × 550 mm tt (8 torpedoes carried); 1 × 75 mm; 1 × 13.2 mm AA
Fatalities	45 *Survivors* none		

The French navy (Marine nationale)

Although France had long been a great naval power and played her full part in the technological revolution of the nineteenth century, the primacy of the army in French military planning and financial restrictions both before and after the Great War conspired to hinder the development of the Marine nationale into a truly modern force. It was not until the late 1930s that the French navy began to emerge as a viable counterbalance to Italian aspirations in the Mediterranean, though much of its new construction lay unfinished at the time of the Armistice in June 1940 and its potential was destined never to be realised. However, those ships that were operational participated fully in the early campaigns of the war, first on convoy and patrol duty and then off Norway and Dunkirk. Among these was the *Doris*, which in being lost was nonetheless spared the long agony of the French navy that stretches from the Mers-el-Kebir tragedy of July 1940 to the scuttling of the Vichy fleet at Toulon in November 1942.

Career

Last of the four units of the Circé class of coastal submarines ordered under the 1923 programme, *Doris* was laid down at Chantiers Schneider et Cie in Bordeaux in February 1924 and launched in November 1927. Fitted out at Toulon, she was not fully commissioned into the French navy until January 1930. *Doris* is recorded as joining the IIIe escadrille de sous-marins at Toulon in 1933 and then the Ve escadrille in 1935. Fitted with Schneider diesels of German design and manufacture, these not only proved unreliable but led to a chronic

lack of spares once relations between the two countries deteriorated towards the end of that decade. The entire class was refitted at Toulon and La Ciotat (Provence) in 1939, following which they quit Toulon for Bizerte in February 1940 to carry out training duties in the Gulf of Tunis as the 13e division of the Ve escadrille. At the end of March they were dispatched to Brest and there given orders to take the battle to the Germans in the North Sea.

Background of the attack

In the first days of April 1940 Allied plans for an intervention against Norway to interdict the passage of Swedish iron ore between Narvik and Germany brought three divisions of French submarines north to the British Isles. Placed under the operational command of the formidable Vice-Admiral (Submarines) Sir Max Horton, these were divided between the North Sea ports of Dundee and Harwich. The four-strong 2e division was based on Dundee for service in the Norwegian Sea while the eight boats of the 13e and 16e divisions, including *Doris*, *Amazone* and the submarine depot ship *Jules Verne*, were assigned to Harwich for operations in the Heligoland Bight and the southern North Sea. In the event, the German attack on Denmark and Norway on 9 April gave the Allied submarine forces an even more urgent remit than that originally conceived.

On 19 April *Doris* sailed on her first war patrol off Heligoland though defects to her port diesel compressor soon had her back at Harwich for repairs. The limited shore facilities available to the French at Harwich, who had to rely largely on *Jules Verne* and spares sent from Cherbourg, no doubt contributed to these repairs never being fully carried out, but strategic developments also took a hand in the matter. With the German descent on Holland believed imminent, on 6 May Horton ordered all available units to put to sea and the following afternoon *Doris* sailed from Harwich in company with HMS/m *Shark* and *Amazone* of the 16e division. Their orders were to join a further ten submarines – four French, four British and two Polish – in forming a patrol line off the Dutch coast where U-boats were known to be operating. Indeed, the patrol area for which *Doris* was responsible coincided with that to which *U9* (Oblt.z.S. Wolfgang Lüth) had been

assigned following her departure from Kiel on the 5th. The fact that the Germans had broken several of the Royal Navy's operational and administrative ciphers suggests that this disposition may not have been coincidental. Whatever the case, shortly before midnight on the 8th *U9* sighted *Doris* to the east and immediately began manoeuvring to make an attack. Though the date of the sinking is often given as 9 May (per Lüth's log), the timekeeping both of the British Admiralty to which *Doris* was operationally attached (2215) and that of the French navy (2315; *Amazone* 2318) place her loss firmly on the 8th.

War Diary of *U9*, patrol of 5–30 May 1940: PG 30007, NHB, reel 1,057, pp. 1,031–3

Date, time	Details of position, wind, weather, sea, light, visibility, moonlight, etc.	Incidents
8.v		
2227	Qu. AN 8271, starlit, average visibility, wind E 2, new moon	We surface – landward to the east are the lights of 10 to 20 fishing boats.
2350	Qu. AN 8277, starlit, good visibility, sea phosphorescence, yet dark new moon night	Silhouette of a blacked-out submarine to the east on our port side, illuminated before the fishing boats. Range 3,000–4,000 m. We approach to attack but unfortunately I have to contend with a bright horizon off to the west. Enemy is steering reciprocal course of roughly 320°, then alters to parallel course 140°, cruising for a while at high speed so that her bow wave is clearly visible. Just as I am manoeuvring for a shot enemy alters course directly towards me. I turn away and put some distance between us. Enemy now proceeding on north-westerly course.
		Lüth
9.v		
0014	North of Ijmuiden. Qu. AN 8511, strong sea phosphorescence.	Double salvo – G7e set at 2 m depth, G7a at 3 m and [speed of] 30 knots, range 700 m, enemy speed 5 knots, inclination 80°.[1] Points of aim 20 m from the bow, 30 m from the stern. Own speed dead slow on port electric engine, bow wave clearly illuminated. After 52 sec. (= 780 m) a powerful detonation. Tracks of both torpedoes clearly visible. That of the G7e is revealed by its propeller ripples, G7a strikes abaft the conning tower.[2]
		First detonation gives way to a second even more powerful one.[3] This is followed by a searing column of flame 25 m high, white at the bottom and red at the top, then a 30–50-m high shower of sparks, and finally a 100-m high cloud of smoke. Pieces of debris fly in all directions, some landing within 50 m of our boat. We can make out a patch of oil about 500 m in diameter. We head over there but there is nothing left to see, just a strong smell of powder and oil. Submarine appeared to be about 1,000 tons with a conning tower that from sideways on looked to be relatively low but quite long.[4] Maybe Grampus class. Single deck gun was not evident.[5]
0026		Second detonation audible, but there is nothing to be seen. This must have been the G7e at the end of its run after 12 minutes' running time.
		We continue our course towards Scheveningen to fix ship's position.
0100	Qu. AN 8549, wind E 2, average visibility	At a distance of 12 nm we still can't see any lighthouse on the Dutch mainland. All lights are blacked out.

---

1   The assessments of enemy range and speed given here differ slightly from those in the separate torpedo report, which registered figures of 800 metres and three knots respectively. The torpedoes were fired by *U9*'s First Watch Officer, Lt.z.S. Frank Gramitzky. 'G7e' refers to the electric torpedo as distinct from G7a weapon powered by compressed air. The bracketed text is a pencilled addition to the log.

2   Lüth and Gramitzky's torpedo report records the G7e torpedo passing ahead of its target. The miss is confirmed lower down in the entry for 0026 on the 9th.

3   The detonation of *U9*'s G7a torpedo evidently triggered a secondary explosion.

4   *Doris* in fact displaced 615 tons on the surface and 776 tons submerged.

5   Although both had proportionately long conning towers, the British Grampus-class submarines were half as long again as *Doris* and had more than twice her displacement. Apart from the difficulties inherent in submarine recognition in view of their sparse superstructure, Lüth's failure to notice *Doris*'s gun no doubt reflects his having caught only fleeting glimpses of his victim.

0140	Qu. AN 8581	Dived due to approach of fishing boats.
0400		Settled on the bottom at 20 m.
1115	Wind E 2, sea 0–1	Lifted off the bottom, steered towards coast. Ship's position determined [from] Hook of Holland.[6]

6   The bracketed text is a pencilled addition to the log.

The sinking

The log apart, *Doris*'s last minutes are lost to us and there is no indication that she was ever alerted to *U9*'s presence. Even had she been so the odds would have been against Capitaine de corvette Jean Favreul whose orders of engagement from Vice-Admiral Horton constrained him from attacking any vessel until it was positively identified as belonging to the enemy. These strictures were owed not only to the amount of neutral shipping in the vicinity but to the two Polish submarines (*Orzeł* and *Wilk*) operating in these waters alongside the Allies together with the boats of the as-yet neutral Royal Netherlands Navy based at Den Helder. In any event, *Doris* evidently came to the immediate and terrible end described in Lüth's log. She was expected at Harwich at 1500 on 13 May and when signals asking her to confirm her time of arrival went unanswered the worst was feared. Already on the 9th a German communiqué had announced the sinking of an Allied submarine in the North Sea and on the 15th Horton gave it as his opinion that *Doris* had probably succumbed to a U-boat torpedo. However, as she was patrolling an area known to be mined her loss to that form of underwater warfare was officially presumed until post-war access to German records proved otherwise.

This, however, was not quite the last of the *Doris*. In June 2003 reports of fishermen losing their nets on an unknown wreck brought two Dutch divers to a marked position thirty-five miles off Den Helder. There in twenty-six metres of water they found the shattered wreck of the *Doris*, identifiable by an inscription bearing her name on a metal shard found near the remains of the conning tower. This identification was confirmed by the French minesweeper *Cassiopée* in November of that year and a service of remembrance held over the site on 16 July 2004. Analysis of the wreck not only confirmed a hit abaft the conning tower but revealed a secondary detonation of the torpedoes in the two midships tubes, to which Lüth's log description lends support. Moreover, the orientation of the boat – pointing north-west – not only confirms Lüth's observations but suggests that *Doris* was heading back to her patrol box having strayed two miles south of it at the time of the attack. The boat's 75-mm gun has been salvaged and at the time of writing is undergoing restoration in Brest for display in a museum which it is planned to dedicate to the French submarine service.

Fate of the crew

It must be supposed that *Doris*'s company (forty-two Frenchmen together with a Royal Navy liaison officer, Yeoman of Signals and Telegraphist) perished instantaneously. However, their fate is given a macabre twist by Pierre Menezo, an electrical artificer in the *Amazone*. In an undated and anonymous post-war account lodged in the Deutsches U-Boot Museum-Archiv at Cuxhaven-Altenbruch, Menezo recalled a disturbing encounter with a French naval chaplain in the *Jules Verne* shortly before *Doris* and *Amazone* sailed on 7 May during which the latter spoke of a strong premonition that neither would return from the coming patrols. The chaplain asked Menezo to inform his shipmates and those in *Doris* that he would pray for the forgiveness of their sins and issue a final blessing *in articulo mortis* ('at the point of death'). However, when both crews gathered for pre-patrol drinks in the *Amazone* Menezo was so struck by the dejected mood of *Doris*'s men that he deemed it inappropriate to pass on the message. Unlikely as it may sound, there is anecdotal evidence to suggest that their melancholia may have been owed to the knowledge that *Doris* would have difficulty diving in view of the compressor problem alluded to above, thus diminishing her prospects for a safe return. Whatever the facts of the matter, *Amazone* defied the chaplain's premonition but when a column of fire was spotted on the horizon at 2318 on the 8th (*Amazone*'s recorded time) few of her crewmen had any doubt who the victim had been. *Doris* and her men are remembered on a plaque erected in Bray-Dunes on the Channel coast of France.

U9 and Wolfgang Lüth

Heir to a name made famous by Lt.z.S. Otto Weddigen in the Great War, *U9* was built by Germaniawerft at Kiel and commissioned in August 1935. She spent the first phase of her wartime career as part of the 1st Flotilla at Kiel and Wilhelmshaven. Aside from a brief reconnaissance mission, all her frontline patrols with the 1st Flotilla were made under Oblt.z.S. Wolfgang Lüth and encompassed both minelaying duties and participation in Operation HARTMUT, the naval side of the Norwegian Campaign. *U9* accounted for seven ships in addition to *Doris* before

Lüth seen wearing the Knight's Cross he received in October 1940. *DUBMA*

being relegated to training duties at Danzig (Gdansk) in July 1940. In May 1942 she became the second Type-IIB U-boat to be transferred to the Black Sea, being partially dismantled before making a tortuous journey via canal, road and river to the Romanian port of Galati. *U9*'s twelve patrols in the Black Sea yielded several successes before she was sunk during a Soviet air raid on Konstanza on 20 August 1944. Salvaged by the Russians, she gave two years' service as the *TS-16* before being broken up.

Lüth left *U9* when she was withdrawn from the 1st Flotilla but spent the next three years as a frontline commander in *U138*, *U43* and *U181* before becoming the youngest-ever Commander of the Marineschule (Naval College) at Flensburg-Mürwik. Eventually promoted Kapitän zur See, he was the first (and one of only two) officers in the *U-Boot-Waffe* to be awarded the Knight's Cross with Oak Leaves, Swords and Diamonds. Lüth was killed in bizarre circumstances on 13 May 1945, shot by one of his own Marineschule sentries after failing to respond to a challenge late at night. Staunchly loyal to the Nazi cause (rather unusual among prominent U-boat commanders), Lüth ranks as the second most successful U-boat commander of the war after Otto Kretschmer (see **4**, **19** and **20**), having sunk well over 200,000 tons of Allied shipping.

Sources

Ministère des armées, *Liste Nominative du personnel du Sous-marin "Doris" disparu en mer le 7 [sic] Mai 1940* (SHM, *Doris* file)

Hervieu, Réné G., *Perte du Sous-Marin français La DORIS le 8 Mai 1940* (typescript; Nantes, 1995; SHM, *Doris* file)

Anon., *Der Verlust der* Doris (undated typescript; DUBMA, *U9* folder)

—, *Notice historique sur le sous-marin* La Doris (SHM, *Doris* file)

—, *Notice sur les bâtiments ayant porté le nom de* Doris (SHM, *Doris* file)

Alman, Karl, *Wolfgang Lüth: Der erfolgreichste U-Boot-Kommandant des Zweiten Weltkrieges. Mit vier Booten 609 Tage in See* (Friedberg, Hessen: Pozdun Pallas Verlag, 1988)

Auphan, Contre-amiral Paul, and Jacques Mordal, *The French Navy in World War II* (Annapolis, Md.: Naval Institute Press, 1959)

Beesley, Patrick, *Very Special Intelligence: The Story of the Admiralty's Operational Intelligence Centre, 1939–1945* (London: Hamish Hamilton, 1977)

Bendert, Harald, *U-Boote im Duell* (Hamburg: Mittler, 1996)

Bertrand, Michel, *La Marine Française au combat, 1939–1945* (2 vols, Paris: Charles-Lavauzelle, 1982–3)

Enders, Gerd, *Deutsche U-Boote zum Schwarzen Meer: Eine Reise ohne Wiederkehr* (Hamburg: Mittler, 2001)

Favreul, Capitaine de vaisseau Jacques, *La Doris: Histoire d'un sous-marin perdu* (Rennes: Marines Éditions, 2009); summarised on: http://www.marines-editions.fr/boutique/images_produits/f79990_1.pdf

Huan, Capitaine de vaisseau Claude, *Les Sous-marins français, 1918–1945* (Rennes: Marines Éditions, 2004)

Le Masson, Henri, *The French Navy* (2 vols, London: Macdonald, 1969)

—, *Les Sous-marins français des origines (1863) à nos jours* (Brest: Éditions de la Cité, 1981)

Le Masson, Philippe, *La Marine Française et la guerre, 1939–1945* (Paris: Jules Tallandier, 1991)

Roskill, *War at Sea*, I, pp. 266–7

Vause, Jordan, *U-Boat Ace: The Story of Wolfgang Lüth* (Annapolis, Md.: Naval Institute Press, 1992)

Webpage dedicated to NF *Doris*: http://perso.orange.fr/sous-marin.france/Q135.htm

van der Sluijs, Ton, 'Discovery of *Doris*' posted 10 March 2005: http://www.uboat.net/articles/?article=58

7   HMS *GRAFTON*

Cdr C. E. C. Robinson, RN†

Sunk by *U62* (Type IIC), Oblt.z.S. Hans-Bernhard Michalowski, 29 May 1940

English Channel, 25 nm NE of Dunkerque (Dunkirk), Nord (France)

A peacetime shot of *Grafton* wearing the lighter shade of grey favoured for service in the Mediterranean. She came to a chaotic end off Dunkirk. *Abrahams*

Campaign	Evacuation of Dunkirk (Map 2)	*Displacement*	1,350 tons
Coordinates	51° 24' N, 02° 49' E	*Dimensions*	323' × 33' × 8.5'
Kriegsmarine code	Quadrat AN 8758	*Maximum speed*	35.5 knots
U-boat timekeeping differential	+1 hour	*Armament*	4 × 4.7"; 8 × .5" AA; 5 × .303" AA; 8 × 21" tt
Fatalities	16 and 35 troops	*Survivors*	about 130 and about 750 troops

Career

Ordered under the 1933 estimates, HMS *Grafton* was the third unit of the 'G'-class destroyers. The class differed little from the two which preceded it (see HMSs *Exmouth* and *Firedrake*, **3** and **78**) except in propulsion where the cruising turbine was dispensed with and the Admiralty boiler replaced by a lighter Thornycroft design in *Grafton*'s case. *Grafton* was laid down at John I. Thornycroft's yard at Woolston, Southampton in August 1934, launched in September of the following year and completed in March 1936. The class entered service as the 20th Destroyer Flotilla, Mediterranean Fleet and that summer saw service off Spain following the outbreak of the Civil War. Renumbered the 1st DF in September 1936, here it remained on humanitarian and patrol duty until 1939, though for *Grafton* there was a balmy interlude escorting King Edward VIII's yacht *Nahlin* (with Mrs. Simpson aboard) in the Adriatic in the autumn of 1936. The outbreak of war found *Grafton* refitting at Malta from where she was assigned to anti-submarine patrol duty with Western Approaches Command at Plymouth in October. On 29 October she rescued seventy survivors from the British steamer *Malabar*, sunk by *U34* (see **13** and **14**) in the Western Approaches. In November she was reassigned to the 22nd DF with Nore Command at Harwich before joining a reconstituted 1st DF on patrol and boarding duty in the North Sea in January 1940. A brief refit at Hull between March and April was followed by service off Norway as part of the Home Fleet, *Grafton* rejoining Nore Command on 24 May to participate in Operation DYNAMO, the evacuation of the British Expeditionary Force during the German offensive in the West. Within hours *Grafton* was bombarding enemy positions off Calais while under heavy air attack and two days later escorted the cruisers *Arethusa* and *Galatea* on a similar mission in the same waters. However, the moment when she began ferrying troops herself was almost upon her.

Background of the attack

On 27 May *Grafton* joined the 900 vessels destined to become engaged in Operation DYNAMO, the rescue of Allied troops from the Channel coast. The following day she lifted 860 men from the beaches of De Panne and Braye and landed them at Dover in the late afternoon. That evening she returned to Bray-Dunes where the best part of 800 troops were embarked, *Grafton* shaping course for Dover via the tortuous but supposedly less dangerous Route Y. This led first north and then east to the Kwinte Bank buoy where a clear route west to the Kent coast opened up once the sandbanks had been negotiated. It was a calm night, which was greatly to the advantage of the German *Schnellboote* (E-boats) and U-boats which owned the hours of darkness as much as the Luftwaffe dominated the day. Even as *Grafton* was making her way towards the Kwinte Bank buoy the German navy was claiming its first major victim of the Dunkirk episode, the destroyer *Wakeful* whose fate was to be inextricably linked with her own. Laden with troops and already damaged by air attack the previous evening, *Wakeful* had just reached the Kwinte Bank buoy at 0045 GMT on the 29th (0145 German time) when she was ambushed by *S30* and hit by a torpedo which detonated in the forward boiler room with a 'brilliant white flash'. The impact rent *Wakeful* in two, both halves sinking immediately until the severed ends grounded in only nine fathoms of water. With them went most of the 650 soldiers *Wakeful* had embarked at Dunkirk. Around fifty survivors were left in the water but many were swept away from the wreck by a strong tide. A majority, including *Wakeful*'s commanding officer, Cdr R. L. Fisher, were gradually picked up by two Scottish drifters bound for Dunkirk, *Nautilus* and *Comfort*. The master of *Comfort* agreed to Fisher's request to return up-tide towards the wreck where he thought he had seen men clinging to the stern section of his ship, part of which was still above water. On reaching the scene shortly after 0240 *Comfort* saw that HMS *Grafton* had already approached the wreck and was lying stopped in order to pick up men found in the water, her boats having been lowered for this purpose. But no sooner had *Comfort* come along *Grafton*'s starboard side and Fisher shouted a warning to Cdr C. E. C. Robinson of the danger of torpedoes than 'some sort of grenade' exploded on *Grafton*'s bridge, killing Robinson and three of his officers and leaving the compass platform and Asdic control hut a jumble of tangled metal. The origin of this explosion has never been established but it may be that *Grafton* was struck by an explosive 20-mm round from one or other of the German craft subsequently noted in the vicinity. Scarcely had the smoke begun to clear than *Grafton* was convulsed by a huge detonation at around 0250, the result of a torpedo striking the opposite side to where *Comfort* was lying. For many years this was attributed to an E-boat torpedo similar to that which had accounted for *Wakeful*. However, closer inspection of Kriegsmarine records by Jürgen Rohwer revealed that it was almost certainly fired by *U62* which had been patrolling the route via the Kwinte Bank buoy and seized the opportunity which presented itself.

War Diary of U62, patrol of 18 May–4 June 1940: PG 30059, NHB, reel 1,068, p. 236

Date, time	Details of position, wind, weather, sea, light, visibility, moonlight, etc.	*Incidents*

29.v

0000	Qu. [AN] 8758, sea/swell 1, wind 0, dark night	Very good weather for attacking, with only the bright wake a problem. Boat positioned to the west of the flashing buoy which is apparently being used as a navigational aid for the north and west transport route. Based on all our observations so far there would appear to be two separate routes.[1]
0005	Qu. [AN] 8758	Emerging from the warning area[2] heading north-east, and from there 1. to the east (their favoured route)[3] 2. continuing to the north-east towards what must be the Thornton Bank buoy. From 0000 we discern a number of different flashing navigation lights as well as morse light exchanges.
0035		In warning area we come across a small vessel with a green top lamp.[2] Presumably for warning other vessels away.
0045		A steamer with running lights, flanked on either side by a smaller vessel showing a white light. Moderate speed, extreme range. At the buoy she turns north-east, not west as expected. I don't run in to attack as another vessel is approaching from the south-west which also has running lights. She is exchanging morse signals with other vessels in the vicinity but I can't make these out. Vessel halts by the Kwinte Bank buoy, then puts on her searchlights and repeatedly lights up the water and the ship's side. Other vessels approach having now shown their running lights. We can't make out how many of these smaller vessels there are. Judging by the height of their top lights they would appear to be tugs or similar. We refrain from closing in to attack as troop embarkation is expected in the roads.[4]
0155		Boat runs in to attack stationary transport.[5] Two E-boats approach from the south-west and head towards vessel. They are illuminated by searchlights and head off in a northerly direction, apparently enemy E-boats.[6] Our boat is standing right in the area lit up by searchlight so we turn and withdraw to the west. More small vessels approach the buoy, briefly showing their running lights. Boat manoeuvres to the edge of the illuminated area.
0330	Qu. as above, dawn approaching, misty	It's misty, which makes the stationary vessel by the buoy hard to discern precisely. It looks like a warship in so far as it has high fo'c's'le superstructure and an elongated stern. To the left of this vessel is a blacked-out destroyer which also appears to be between the vessel and our boat. Destroyers are moving dead slow and zigzagging.[7]
0348	*Was British destroyer Grafton. Pfeiffer 6/10/54*[8]	Boat positions herself for attack, though has to fire from 2,000 m as a destroyer is turning towards us. Two Etos, set to a depth of 3 m, running time 2 min. 10 sec.[9] A hit aft and a huge detonation cloud which for a moment shrouds everything. Then fire breaks out and we observe a thick cloud of smoke on the quarterdeck. Alarm! Destroyer heading in direction of torpedo at high speed. Turn to the north and head off on one engine at dead slow speed. Four destroyers take part in pursuing us using

---

1   Michalowski goes on to describe these routes in the next entry. There were in fact three official routes, all leading to Dover: Route Z leading due west along the French coast, Route X leading north-west towards Margate and around the Goodwin Sands, and finally Route Y, which is that on which *Wakeful* and *Grafton* met their fates. As a result of the incidents described in this entry, Route Y was altered with effect from 0630 on the 29th (i.e. within a few hours of the sinkings) so that ships no longer steered as far east as the Kwinte Bank Buoy.

2   The 'warning area' (*Warngebiet* in the original) described by Michalowski almost certainly refers to the French minefield west of the Kwinte Bank buoy and due east of *U62*'s position.

3   Michalowski's entry of 0045 in which he describes a steamer turn 'north-east, not west as expected' supports the conjecture that he intended to write 'west' rather than 'east' here, or any rate originally did so before a subsequent emendation. In any event, 'east' is correct here.

4   Presumably the Dunkirk roads.

5   This entry, referring to a transport (to which Michalowski seems to refer again at 0330), perhaps explains why *U62*'s attack of 0348 on *Grafton* was initially considered by B.d.U. to have been on the French freighter *Douaisien*, which was in fact lost on a mine.

6   These were less likely British MTBs than German *S-Boote* (known as E-boats by the Allies) perhaps those which attacked HMS *Wakeful* within the next hour. Although this is no more than a supposition, Michalowski's decision to withdraw at this point may explain his failure to notice the attack on *Wakeful* (at 0145 log time) in the same position as his own on *Grafton* at 0348.

7   It is unclear quite how many vessels Michalowski is describing here though one of them was clearly *Grafton*. However, as *Wakeful* had been sunk two hours earlier and *Grafton* was by all accounts stopped it is possible that Michalowski had either confused the minesweeper *Gossamer* (about to leave the scene) and the minelayer *Lydd* (just arriving at the scene) for destroyers, or was counting *Wakeful*'s two hull sections as separate ships. He might also be referring to the drifters *Comfort* and *Nautilus* which appeared at about this time.

8   Manuscript addition in pencil by the civilian archivist Walther Pfeiffer who was brought to Britain to work on the logs post-war.

9   'Eto' is the Kriegsmarine's standard abbreviation for the electric G7e torpedo as distinct from G7a weapon powered by compressed air ('Ato').

hydrophones and at one point one of them passes directly overhead.[10] Twenty-eight depth charges, but their only effect is to shake the boat and cause some erratic steering. Estimated range of depth charges 500 m. Boat escapes to the north.

1200   Qu. [AN] 8752   Day's run: 28 nm on the surface, 43 nm submerged.

---

10 Though four ships were on the scene, Michalowski's suggestion that *U62* was hunted by as many destroyers cannot be reconciled with British accounts of the episode, not least since they appear to have attributed the attacks to surface vessels. The evidence is that the British were too busy either firing on each other or rescuing survivors to engage in a submarine pursuit, though it is conceivable that Michalowski mistook the 'all-British Battle of the Kwinte' (see below) for a depth-charge attack.

The sinking

U62's torpedo struck just forward of the port propeller, the detonation wrecking the after part of the ship, disabling the turbines and leaving 'the deck … a mass of twisted steel and bodies'. Despite being well down by the stern, *Grafton* did not appear in any immediate danger of sinking though the nature and extent of the damage could not immediately be assessed as panicked soldiers began spilling out on deck. However, more bitter than enemy action was what the British now inflicted on each other. The loss of Cdr Robinson and his officers on *Grafton*'s bridge, the almost simultaneous detonation of *U62*'s torpedo and the appearance of the minelayer *Lydd* in addition to *Nautilus* and *Comfort* conspired to produce a tragic sequence of events out of the reigning chaos. *Comfort* was rocked by the torpedo detonation which washed many including Cdr Fisher of *Wakeful* overboard. Leaving the scene at high speed, *Comfort* returned fifteen minutes after the attack to find herself taken as the villain of the piece by both *Grafton* and *Lydd*, which proceeded to decimate her crew and most of *Wakeful*'s survivors with concentrated gunfire at point-blank range. Circling round, *Lydd* then bore down on *Comfort* at full speed and rammed her amidships, cutting her in two. Indeed, so convinced was *Lydd* that *Comfort* was an enemy vessel that they fired on those of her men who tried to jump over her guard rail upon ramming, all to hearty cheers from those looking on. Even without this dispiriting episode the salvage of *Grafton* herself was made impossible by the broader context of events and it was decided to scuttle her before daylight. Once the many hundreds of crewmen and passengers had been transferred *Grafton* was finished off by three shells from the destroyer *Ivanhoe*, fired from a range of 500 yards.

Fate of the crew

The reckoning for *Grafton* was not comparable to that borne by *Wakeful*, from which only thirty men survived of the nearly 800 who had left Dunkirk. Losses to *Grafton*'s ship's company were confined to Cdr Robinson and three others on the bridge from the first explosion together with twelve ratings as a result of the torpedo detonation. However, the death toll exceeded fifty as *Grafton*'s wardroom was packed with army officers, thirty-five of whom perished. The greatest threat in the aftermath of the torpedoing was panic bordering on hysteria among soldiers fearful of being trapped in a sinking ship. Bursting up onto the forecastle and with few if any of their own officers to control them, they had to be quietened first by megaphone and then at gunpoint by the First Lieutenant, Lt H. C. J. McRea, and other officers. By the time McRea's repeated assurances that *Grafton* was in no danger of sinking had been heeded and order restored the so-called 'all-British Battle of the Kwinte' was over.

The surviving ship's company and approximately 750 troops were

taken off at dawn on the 29th by the empty cross-Channel packet *Malines* which had immediately responded to distress signals. By midday they were at Dover, the wounded and *Grafton*'s men having been transferred to *Ivanhoe*. Much the doughtiest survivor was Cdr Ralph Fisher of HMS *Wakeful* whose fate summarises the fortunes of the British that night: sunk in *Wakeful*, washed overboard from *Comfort* by the torpedo hit on *Grafton* and then pitched back into the sea as *Comfort* was rammed by *Lydd* after being swept with gunfire, Fisher spent another two hours in water 'littered with wreckage and bodies'. He was eventually rescued by the Norwegian tramp steamer *Hird*, bound for Cherbourg with a load of Senegalese troops, which lowered a boat for him and a badly injured survivor from *Wakeful*. The latter subsequently died and Fisher was able to transfer to a minesweeper making for Dover. Nor was his ordeal over. Having reported the entire sequence of events to Admiral Sir Bertram Ramsay he was given a car to take him to Chatham later that day, but narrowly escaped serious injury when it was forced into a ditch by an army lorry.

Michalowski (in white cap) seen on *U62*'s conning tower in the spring of 1940. *DUBMA*

The Kwinte Bank débâcle was a bitter blow to the Royal Navy and led to an immediate order forbidding destroyers from stopping to rescue survivors for the remainder of the operation. Although this disaster must be set against the wider achievement of Operation DYNAMO which rescued nearly 340,000 troops to fight another day, it provides a grim reminder of the sacrifice made by the RN which lost six destroyers and had another nineteen damaged during the evacuation of France.

U62 and Hans-Bernhard Michalowski

Built by Deutsche Werke at Kiel and commissioned in November 1940, *U62* undertook five frontline patrols under Oblt.z.S. Hans-Bernhard Michalowski. These included Operation HARTMUT in support of the German invasion of Norway (April 1940) and then off Dunkirk the following month. *Grafton* was her first sinking of any note, the next being SS *Pearlmoor* north-west of Arran on her final operational patrol in July 1940. Outclassed by the Type-VII submarines then entering service in large numbers, *U62* was reassigned to training duties in October 1940, serving in this capacity until shortly before the end of the war. She was scuttled at Wilhelmshaven in early May 1945. Hans-Bernhard Michalowski (promoted Kapitänleutnant in January 1941) died of natural causes in a German military hospital on 20 May 1941 while still nominally commander of *U62*.

Sources

Admiralty, *Events Surrounding the Sinking of HMS Grafton in Operation Dynamo* (TNA, ADM 199/157)

Mallory, Capt. G. G., *Escape from Rotterdam and the Evacuation of Dunkirk (Operation Dynamo): Master's Letters/Reports 12th May to 11th June 1940* (miscellaneous typescript papers, IWM, 96/21/1)

Admiralty, *The Evacuation from Dunkirk: 'Operation Dynamo', 26th May–4th June 1940: A Naval Staff History* (London: Frank Cass, 2000)

Atkin, Ronald, *Pillar of Fire: Dunkirk 1940* (London: Sidgwick & Jackson, 1990)

Bartlett, Capt. Sir Basil, Bart, *My First War: An Army Officer's Journal for May 1940* (London: Chatto and Windus, 1940)

Collier, Richard, *The Sands of Dunkirk* (London: Fontana, 1974)

Divine, David, *The Nine Days of Dunkirk* (London: Faber & Faber, 1951)

English, John, *Amazon to Ivanhoe: British Standard Destroyers of the 1930s* (Kendal, Cumbria: World Ship Society, 1993)

Fisher, Rear-Admiral R. L., *Salt Horse: A Naval Life* (privately, about 1980; copy in KCL, LHCMA, GB99 Fisher)

Hogg, Lt Cdr Anthony, *Just a Hogg's Life: A Royal Navy Saga of the Thirties* (Chichester, W. Sussex: Solo Mio Books, 1993)

Kinghorn, D., and B. Hargreaves, 'Destroyers of the Royal Navy: "G" Class' in *Warships*, Supplement no. 8 (May 1967), pp. 17–24

Roskill, *War at Sea*, I, pp. 219–28

War career of HMS *Grafton*:
http://www.naval-history.net/xGM-Chrono-10DD-25G-Grafton.htm

Webpages concerning sinkings of HMSs *Wakeful* and *Grafton*:
http://www.24hourmuseum.org.uk/nwh/ART22986.html
http://www.navynews.co.uk/articles/2004/0407/0004072701.asp

8   HMS (ex RMS) *CARINTHIA*

Capt. J. F. B. Barrett, RN Ret'd
Sunk by *U46* (Type VIIB), Oblt.z.S. Engelbert Endrass, 6–7 June 1940
North Atlantic, 80 nm W of Tory Island, Donegal (Ireland)

An indistinct photo which nonetheless shows *Carinthia* in January 1940, four months after being requisitioned into the Royal Navy as an armed merchant cruiser. Comparison with pre-war photos shows little change in her appearance; one of her eight 6-inch mountings is visible just forward of the foremast. Endrass sank her with a single torpedo on the port side aft. *BfZ*

Theatre North Atlantic (Map 2)	*Deadweight* 12,936 tons
Coordinates (of attack) 55° 13' N, 10° 38' W	*Gross tons* 20,277
Kriegsmarine code (of attack) Quadrat AM 5432	*Dimensions* 624' × 73.75' × 32.75'
U-boat timekeeping differential –1 hour	*Maximum speed* 16 knots
Fatalities 4 *Survivors* about 330	*Armament* 8 × 6"; 2 × 3" AA

The armed merchant cruisers

With war imminent, in August 1939 the Admiralty requisitioned the first of fifty-seven cargo and passenger liners to serve as armed merchant cruisers. As in 1914, the outbreak of hostilities found the Royal Navy with a severe shortage of cruisers to meet its worldwide commitments in trade defence, and as then the unsatisfactory solution would be the refitting and commissioning of merchant shipping under the White Ensign. The ships selected were all of approximately 8,000–22,000 GRT, had a range of at least 4,500 miles, a top speed of fifteen knots or better and offered suitable positions for mounting at least six 6-inch guns, some of which were of 1895 vintage. Many of these had been earmarked for war service long before the outbreak of hostilities and stiffened for the installation of guns at the government's expense. Manned largely by reservists, in the early months of the war the AMCs gave valuable service enforcing the blockade of Germany and capturing enemy shipping on the high seas, but the limitations of the type against the new breed of German surface raider were made manifest in the destruction first of HMS *Rawalpindi* by the battlecruisers *Scharnhorst* and *Gneisenau* in November 1939 and then of the *Jervis Bay* by the *Panzerschiff Admiral Scheer* a year later, both ships sunk with heavy loss of life. But the hammer of the AMCs was to be the U-boat, which claimed ten of the type in the year separating the loss of *Carinthia* in June 1940 and the destruction of *Salopian* in May 1941 (**26**). In this the Kriegsmarine was initially assisted by the cracking of several of the Admiralty's administrative and operational codes by *B-Dienst*, its radio monitoring and intelligence service, which provided B.d.U. with much actionable data until August 1940. Already in the summer of that year the increasing demands being placed on the AMCs and the steady attrition they were suffering had prompted the introduction of ocean boarding vessels (see HMS *Crispin*, **22**) which began relieving the AMCs of the Western Patrol of their boarding and interception duties in late 1940. The double sinking of HMSs *Laurentic* and *Patroclus* (**19**) in November prompted the withdrawal of the AMCs from the Northern Patrol and their reassignment to the Western Patrol and the Halifax Escort Force with responsibility for covering the Denmark Strait. When HMS *Forfar* (**20**) was lost a month later Admiral Sir Charles Forbes, Commander-in-Chief Home Fleet, called for the remaining ships of the type to be withdrawn altogether until they could be provided with proper anti-submarine escorts. The Admiralty cited a lack of resources in ruling out both these measures but steps were taken to assign the AMCs to duties further west.

Nonetheless, these developments together with the disappearance of most German and much neutral merchant shipping from the high seas following the German occupation of Western Europe pointed towards the gradual redisposition of the AMCs from their assigned role. From 1941 many were converted for trooping and other purposes and by January 1943 only eighteen remained in service as such. This number had dropped to eight by the beginning of the following year as the Royal Navy hastened to commission the escort carriers under construction in the United States. The last active unit – HMS *Canton* –

was withdrawn in April 1944. Though the large hulls of the AMCs had given valuable and valiant service on blockade, escort and boarding duty in mountainous seas during the winter of 1939–40, they were inefficient in their intended role and a luxury the British could ill afford as the depredations of the *U-Boot-Waffe* put merchant tonnage at a premium.

The log excerpt below describing this and other AMC sinkings generally refers to the type as *Hilfskreuzere* ('auxiliary cruisers'), the name given by the Kriegsmarine to the disguised commerce raiders it dispatched across the oceans of the world in the first years of the war. Though the German *Hilfskreuzer* was also taken up from trade, the British armed merchant cruisers belong to a different ship type since no effort was ever made to disguise their armament or status as warships.

Career

Originally named the *Servia*, the liner RMS *Carinthia* was laid down for the White Star Line at Vickers-Armstrong & Co., Barrow in 1924, launched in February 1925 and completed that August. She embarked on her maiden voyage between Liverpool and New York on 22 August 1925, remaining on this route until 1931. Following an extensive refit, *Carinthia* carried out a world cruise during 1933, transferring briefly to the Southampton–New York run in 1934, the year the White Star Line merged with its rival Cunard. In 1935 she reverted to the Liverpool–New York service, remaining in this capacity until being requisitioned as an armed merchant cruiser on 17 September 1939. Refitted on the Clyde and assigned to the Northern Patrol between Britain and Iceland, HMS *Carinthia* made her maiden cruise under the White Ensign on 18 January 1940. Here she served, enforcing the distant blockade of Germany in the waters between Iceland and the British Isles until a collision off Donegal with the AMC *Cilicia* on 20 March brought her limping into Liverpool for repairs. It was not until late May that *Carinthia*, freshly stowed with 14,000 oil drums, returned to the fray.

Background of the attack

Believing that Italy was about to enter the war against the Allies, in April 1940 the Admiralty began to detach units of the Home Fleet to the Mediterranean theatre. Among those sent south was *Carinthia* and four other armed merchant cruisers, all with orders to intercept any Italian ships entering the Mediterranean in the event of war. However, with France out of the war and Britain left in serious danger following the evacuation from Dunkirk, the Western or Italian Patrol was cancelled and *Carinthia* ordered back to the Clyde in early June. Meanwhile, *U46* (Oblt.z.S. Engelbert Endrass) had sailed from Kiel on 1 June with orders to operate off Cape Finisterre. Avoiding the perils of the English Channel, *U46* rounded the British Isles through the Shetlands–Faroes gap en route to her patrol area off north-western Spain. In the early hours of 6 June she caught sight of HMS *Carinthia*, zigzagging on a mean west-north-west course off the Donegal coast of Ireland.

War Diary of *U46*, patrol of 1 June–1 July 1940: PG 30043a, NHB, reel 1,064, pp. 72–3

Date, time	Details of position, wind, weather, sea, light, visibility, moonlight, etc.	Incidents
6.vi		
0400	Qu. AM 5256, wind SE 2, sea 0, cloud 5, good visibility	Cruising speed.
0800	Qu. AM 5273	Cruising speed.
1200	Qu. AM 5199	Cruising speed.
1227	Qu. [AM] 5432	Alarm – steamer in sight ahead. Prepare for attack despite her evidently being a passenger vessel, since:

            1. She has camouflage painting
            2. She is fitted with guns
            3. She is steering a zigzag course

1313[1] fired single torpedo from roughly 1,300 m, inclination 70°, estimated speed of target = 13 knots.[2] Detonation after 53 sec., a hit 50 m from stern. After the hit I note a list of 40° to port and a large amount of smoke. Vessel circles, rudder is clearly damaged. Then out of the blue we are shelled. At first we assume it must be an aircraft. But then through the periscope I see that the vessel is firing in all directions from her stern. I circle the vessel which is now totally shrouded in smoke. After about half an hour the smoke has dispersed and the vessel, though still circling, has settled much deeper. I close to give her a *coup-de-grâce* shot but this allows the enemy to spot my periscope (the sea is smooth as a mirror) and open fire. Every time I try to raise my periscope I receive a fresh salvo. The barrages are only faintly audible from the boat and seem to have been very poorly aimed. After the sixth salvo I manage to fire a torpedo but it misses. This is the second time in this war (the first was during an Atlantic cruise in September 1939 with *U47*) that I have managed to miss a circling steamer.[3] The distance the vessel may cover after firing really needs to be worked out more carefully that one might think; it's no good just doing a rough calculation. I can't bear to waste another torpedo; besides, the vessel is sinking ever deeper. Ten minutes later the boats are swung out, crewed and lowered. I cover three miles submerged, then surface. The ship is still lying there, still smoking, listing to port and down by the stern. I head west on the surface – the enemy has no doubt radioed once more for urgent assistance and I don't see any point in waiting for the hounds. From the conning tower we subsequently see a number of explosions from abaft the funnel of the vessel – assume her boiler has gone up. Shortly afterwards the vessel disappears from sight and we resume course of 227°. I didn't witness the sinking but am convinced the ship couldn't have remained afloat much longer. She had eight boats on each side, a <u>single</u> funnel (black), and six or eight guns. 14,000 to 16,000 tons.[4]
<u>Note</u>: We sank the English auxiliary cruiser *Corinthia* [*sic*], 22,300 tons.

| 1600 | Qu. AM 5421 | Cruising speed. |

---

1   Aside from the hour's difference between the German and British sides, which, unusually, has the German account recording an earlier time than the British (see Reading the *Kriegstagebücher*, p. xxxiii), there appears to have been a disparity of around seven minutes between Endrass's chronometer and the times given at the Board of Enquiry.

2   Lt J. C. Blake hazarded a guess at the Board of Enquiry that *Carinthia* was making sixteen knots (her best speed) when she was hit.

3   As First Watch Officer (I.WO) of *U47* Endrass had been Günther Prien's second-in-command before receiving his own command of *U46*. His service under Prien had included the sinking of the *Royal Oak* at Scapa Flow (2). As the I.WO almost always served as the torpedo officer Endrass would have had responsibility for firing torpedoes during surface attacks and he is clearly referring to such an incident here.

4   *Carinthia*, which mounted eight 6-inch guns, was in fact of 20,277 GRT and 12,936 deadweight tons.

The sinking

Despite having nine men on submarine lookout duty, the first *Carinthia*'s crew knew of the presence of the enemy was when Endrass's torpedo struck her on the port side aft shortly after 1400, those on deck seeing a 'column of smoke and debris being thrown to half the height of the funnel'. Immediate flooding of the engine room brought on a complete power failure and within minutes the ship had taken a heavy list to port. Capt. Barrett, who had been on the sick list for a week with severe gastritis, left his cot and headed for the bridge to take command. Despite the severity of the damage initial assessments made Barrett confident enough to add in a wireless transmission to Rosyth at 1420 that 'if seaplanes can be sent to keep submarine away I think ship can be brought in'. This confidence was perhaps bolstered by a sighting of *U46* at 1415, whereupon *Carinthia* kept up a persistent fire to keep her attacker's periscope down. Endrass's parting shot was seen to pass just ahead of the ship at 1435. In response to Barrett's signal,

Survivors of the *Carinthia* none the worse for their ordeal at Greenock on 9 June. *IWM*

Endrass (in white cap) brings *U46* in to Lorient on 13 June 1941. The damage to the conning tower and attack periscope resulted from a collision with the British tanker *Ensis* following an unsuccessful attack on the 8th.
U46 wears the famous snorting bull emblem borrowed from *U47*, Endrass having served as her First Watch Officer under Günther Prien. Endrass had himself painted this device on *U47*'s conning tower after the sinking of the *Royal Oak* in October 1939 (**2**) and by tradition brought it with him first to *U46* and then to *U567*. *DUBMA*

air cover was supplied three hours later and the arrival of the HM minesweeper *Gleaner* and the destroyers *Volunteer* and *Wren* early on the 7th found *Carinthia* still afloat. HM tug *Marauder* joined *Gleaner* in the towing effort that afternoon but steady flooding through the bulkheads sealed *Carinthia*'s fate. Shrouded in a dense fog, the ship was abandoned at 1925 and had broken up and sunk by 2140. Her estimated final position of 55° 12' N, 09° 30' W was some forty miles east of that in which she had been attacked. No blame was apportioned at the subsequent Board of Enquiry, though it was felt that a larger number of oil drums would have increased her chances of staying afloat, a conclusion borne out by subsequent experience (see HMSs *Laurentic* and *Patroclus*, **19**).

Fate of the crew

The torpedo detonation claimed two officers and two ratings in the engine room, the only casualties of the entire episode. At 0800 on 7 June the vast majority of the ship's company – 303 men – began boarding an assortment of whalers and skiffs to transfer to *Gleaner* and *Wren* (173 and 130 men respectively), while the towing party (handpicked as practically the entire ship's company had volunteered to stay) was taken off by HM trawler *British Honduras* – standing by for precisely this purpose – before *Carinthia* sank later that evening. Capt. Barrett later characterised the abandon ship as having been 'cool and ordered, calm and methodical' and commended his men on having behaved 'in the best traditions of the Service' throughout the ordeal. *British Honduras* immediately turned for Rosyth but those rescued by *Gleaner* had to make a detour to rescue survivors of SS *Eros*, sunk by *U48* off Tory Island in the early hours of the 7th, before being landed at Greenock on the 9th. Meanwhile, those picked up by *Wren* were landed at Gourock in time to hear the BBC report of the loss of their ship on the 6 o'clock news that same evening. Their gratitude to their rescuers, whose leave had been delayed, was expressed by an offer to paint the ship for them. History does not recount whether the offer was accepted.

U46 and Engelbert Endrass

Built by Germaniawerft of Kiel and commissioned in November 1938, *U46* spent her operational career with the 7th *U-Flottille* at Kiel and St-Nazaire. She was commanded until April 1940 by Kptlt Herbert Sohler but his tenure yielded only two sinkings from five patrols. Things changed dramatically when Oblt.z.S. Engelbert Endrass was transferred from Günther Prien's *U47* (see **2**) in May 1940, sailing on his first patrol on 1 June. This yielded over 44,000 tons of shipping including *Carinthia*. Over the next sixteen months Endrass took this figure well past 100,000 tons including a second armed merchant cruiser, HMS *Dunvegan Castle* in August 1940 (**17**). These successes earned Endrass the Knight's Cross in September 1940 to which the Oak Leaf cluster was added later. See HMS *Dunvegan Castle* for details of *U46*'s and Endrass's subsequent careers.

Sources

Admiralty, *HM Ships Damaged and Lost: Loss of HMS* Carinthia *and Board of Enquiry* (TNA, ADM 1/10806)

—, *Blockade History, Atlantic Area, September 1939–December 1941* (TNA, ADM 199/2116)

—, *Torpedo Attacks on HM and Merchant Ships, 1939–1941* (TNA, ADM 199/157)

Hampshire, A. Cecil, *The Blockaders* (London: William Kimber, 1980)

Haws, Duncan, *Cunard Line* [Merchant Fleets, no. 12] (2nd edn, Hereford, Hereford and Worcester: TCL Publications, 1989)

Osborne, Richard, Harry Spong and Tom Grover, *Armed Merchant Cruisers, 1878–1945* (Windsor, Berks.: World Ship Society, 2007)

Poolman, Kenneth, *Armed Merchant Cruisers* (London: Leo Cooper, 1985)

9 HMS *SCOTSTOUN* (ex SS *CALEDONIA*)

Capt. S. K. Smyth, RN Ret'd
Sunk by *U25* (Type IA), Kptlt Heinz Beduhn, 13 June 1940
North Atlantic, 85 nm W of Barra, Outer Hebrides (Scotland)

The Anchor Line's SS *Caledonia* seen before the war. Her conversion to armed merchant cruiser entailed the removal of the forward and after derricks and all save the middle funnel, together with the mounting of eight 6-inch guns. Beduhn's first hit, registered on the port side aft (nearest the camera), left her crippled. *Bruce Taylor collection*

Theatre	North Atlantic (Map 2)	*Deadweight*	10,400 tons
Coordinates	57° 00' N, 09° 57' W	*Gross tons*	17,046
Kriegsmarine code (TR)	Quadrat AM 0217	*Dimensions*	578.5' × 70.25' × 29'
U-boat timekeeping differential	+1 hour	*Maximum speed*	16 knots
Fatalities 7	*Survivors* 340+	*Armament*	8 × 6"; 2 × 3" AA

Career

For background on the armed merchant cruisers, see HMS *Carinthia* (**8**).

Ordered by the Anchor Line, the liner SS *Caledonia* was laid down at Alexander Stephen's yard at Linthouse on the Clyde in 1922. However, construction was delayed and the ship not launched until April 1925, being completed later that year. Intended like her sister *Transylvania* (**15**) for the Glasgow–New York run, she embarked on her maiden voyage on 3 October 1925 and served in this capacity for the bulk of her peacetime career. *Caledonia* was requisitioned by the Royal Navy on 25 August 1939 and taken in hand for refitting as an armed merchant cruiser at Harland & Wolff of Belfast on 1 September, being renamed *Scotstoun* to avoid confusion with the Boys' training ship at Rosyth. On 17 October she sailed from Scapa Flow to join the Northern Patrol in the Denmark Strait in company with HMSs *Transylvania* and *Rawalpindi*. It proved to be an eventful first cruise. Three days later *Scotstoun* stopped and captured the German *Biscaya*, dispatching her to Leith with a prize crew. On the 21st she intercepted the cargo liner *Poseidon* which escaped in a snowstorm to be captured by the *Transylvania* on the 25th. Holed by ice and shipping water in mountainous seas, on 17 November *Scotstoun* was making for the Clyde when she intercepted the German freighter *Eilbek*, boarding and capturing her the following day. Service continued in northern waters,

10 January 1940 finding her hove to in a howling gale rolling forty-one degrees to port and thirty-eight to starboard. The damage was made good later that month and ballasting completed on the Clyde in May. Though under less trying circumstances, *Scotstoun* remained a bulwark of the Northern Patrol to the end of her days.

Background of the attack

On 8 June 1940 *U25* sailed from Wilhelmshaven with orders to join one of the early U-boat packs being mustered under Kptlt Günther Prien in *U47* (see **2**) in an operational area south-west of Ireland. However, *U25* had some work to do en route. As Kptlt Heinz Beduhn's log indicates, the U-Boot-Waffe had been alerted by radio to the departure of an 'auxiliary cruiser' from the Firth of Clyde the previous day, fruit of the decryption of Admiralty codes by *B-Dienst*, the Kriegsmarine's radio monitoring and intelligence service, which also contributed to the interception of HMS *Andania* three days later (**10**). It was not therefore a complete surprise when *U25* sighted a large vessel early on the 13th while on passage west of the Hebrides. The ship in question was HMS *Scotstoun* which had left Greenock in the early afternoon of the 12th for another stint on the Northern Patrol south of Iceland. Zigzagging routinely at fifteen knots, her mean course brought her within 500 metres (550 yards) of Beduhn's submerged *U25*.

War Diary of *U25*, patrol of 8–29 June 1940: PG 30022, NHB, reel 1,061, pp. 285–6

Date, time	Details of position, wind, weather, sea, light, visibility, moonlight, etc.	Incidents
13.vi		
0400	Swell	Position Qu. [AM] 2876.[1]
0608		Qu. [AM] 0218, tip of a mast sighted approaching at bearing 150° true. Turns out to be a large passenger liner, course 335°, inclination 20°. Estimated speed 13 knots. We dive – a clear chance to attack. Through the periscope I observe that the enemy is zigzagging. Estimated size 13,000 tons, speed roughly 13 knots.[2] No flag, no markings. I position myself for a stern attack. A single G7a torpedo fired from 500 m detonates aft.[3] The vessel stops, her stern settling a little in the water. We approach, still submerged. The vessel is flying a British war flag from the stern post and another from the after masthead. On the ship's fo'c's'le I can make out four guns, two on each side, roughly 15-cm calibre.[4] The vessel opens fire at what she takes to be our periscope. She's an auxiliary cruiser. Judging by Lloyd's Register she is the *California* or *Tuscania*, 17,000 GRT.[5]
0729		As vessel is not settling any deeper I fire a *coup-de-grâce* shot – a G7e from Tube VI – from 500 m, inclination 35°. Misses. Try again, this time from Tube IV from 1,200 m, inclination 90°.[6] Detonation abaft funnel. Auxiliary cruiser lists rapidly, settling deeper by the stern. Boats launched, guns
0824		abandoned. Vessel sinks stern first. Bow remains above water for about a minute at 45 degrees. Can hear the propeller noises of motorized lifeboats then a strong detonation nearby, perhaps a depth charge from one of them?[7] Dive to 30 m. Stop! Torpedo team stop![8]
0846		We surface. There are six fully loaded lifeboats 3,000 m off. The weather is good, SSW 2–3, some swell. Feign departure from scene, then resume course for operational position (210°). Vessel was sailing at perhaps 15 knots – hence torpedo hit aft.[9] It must have been the auxiliary cruiser destined for Iceland reported by B.d.U. as having left the Firth of Clyde on 12 June.[10]
1200	Wind SSW 2–3, variable visibility, sea 4, swell	Position Qu. [AM] 2997. Day's run: surfaced 287 nm. Submerged 8 nm. Incoming W/T transmission from B.d.U.: *Amendment to U25's attack orders – BE 5382 not BE 6385.1*[11]
1600		Position Qu. [AM] 5145.
↗		
14.vi		
0700		In response to B.d.U. W/T transmission: *Using short signal, who sank English auxiliary cruiser Skotstown [sic] early on 13.6 in AM 0718?*[12] I respond: Am stationed west of Ireland, have executed supplementary task 1.[13]

---

1 Here and elsewhere in the log Beduhn ignores the convention of placing positional data in the second column.

2 *Scotstoun* was actually of 17,046 GRT and making 15 knots, as correctly reassessed by Beduhn lower down.

3 Fired at 0716 log time according to the torpedo report.

4 *Scotstoun* was indeed fitted with 6-inch guns.

5 Although a sister of the two vessels mentioned, this was in fact the *Scotstoun* (ex SS *Caledonia*), all of which were of approximately the tonnage stated. In view of his earlier tonnage estimate it may be supposed that this reassessment was based on subsequent information as to the exact identity of the ship.

6 Fired at 0747 log time according to the torpedo report.

7 As no depth-charge detonations are recorded in British accounts this is more likely to have been a boiler explosion as the ship went under.

8 *U25*'s crew had clearly begun the torpedo reloading process, a laborious yet delicate procedure that needed perfect stability in the boat. Although it appears that Beduhn was simply overreacting to a detonation accompanying *Scotstoun*'s sinking, this was no time to reload if *U25* were about to come under attack.

9 Beduhn is referring to his first torpedo hit. To allow for an equal margin of error in either direction he would have aimed to hit *Scotstoun* amidships, so he is assuming (correctly) that he underestimated *Scotstoun*'s speed.

10 Although no such signal appears anywhere in the log or the appended signals list, Beduhn's intelligence was accurate, *Scotstoun* having sailed from Greenock on the afternoon of the 12th to resume the Northern Patrol south of Iceland.

11 Indicating that Beduhn should sail to hunting grounds 150 miles further west than originally ordered in order to join a U-boat pack assembling to intercept convoy HX48.

12 B.d.U. presumably learnt of the sinking of *Scotstoun* and then signalled to discover the perpetrator. A curiosity in this signal is the naval grid reference AM 0718, more than 100 miles south of the attack position. As Beduhn's coordinates tally precisely with those given in *Scotstoun*'s attack report this discrepancy can be attributed to a typist's error for AM 0218, just a few miles from where Beduhn first hit *Scotstoun* and the quadrant in which he had sighted her (see entry for 0608).

13 While his failure to signal news of his success at the first opportunity may be regarded as significant, Beduhn's response here presumably refers to his having intercepted and sunk the 'auxiliary cruiser' reported leaving the Clyde on the 12th (see n. 10) and subsequently identified as the *Scotstoun*. The misspelling can be accounted for by the fact that B.d.U. probably learnt the identity of his victim by means of a British radio broadcast and, finding no vessel of that name in either the Gröner or Weyer ship-recognition manuals (*Caledonia* having been renamed *Scotstoun* on the outbreak of war), produced the phonetic transcription seen in this signal.

The sinking

Beduhn's first torpedo, which detonated on the port side aft at 0618 British time, was sufficient to flood *Scotstoun*'s steering compartment, rip off the port propeller shaft and render her helpless to escape her attacker, the ship circling slowly under port wheel and starboard engine. It also brought down the W/T aerial and tore open hold No. 7, discharging much of her buoyancy cargo of oil drums into the Atlantic. Lookouts in *Scotstoun* reported observing the trails of two further torpedoes pass the ship by a narrow margin some time after 0635, though *U25*'s log and corresponding torpedo report record only one miss and no other U-boat was in the vicinity; reports published soon after of *Scotstoun*'s gunners diverting torpedoes away from their ship with 6-inch salvoes should be treated with the greatest scepticism. Nor did repeated shelling by *Scotstoun* between 0630 and 0647 at 'various sighted periscopes' prevent Beduhn firing a second *coup-de-grâce* shot which was registered aboard his victim as a 'double explosion' on the starboard side aft. This dramatically increased the rate of flooding and list as well as causing the release of noxious cordite fumes, leaving Capt. Smyth no alternative but to give the order to turn out the boats at 0652. The end came soon after. As Signalman Ronald Gold recalled, 'She reared bow up, slowly, and then started down very gently. The water reached a funnel, which went over with a bang towards the bridge in a shower of sparks.' By 0730 the *Scotstoun* had disappeared, just over an hour after the first hit.

No blame was apportioned by the subsequent Board of Enquiry. A recommendation was made for improved securing of oil drums used for buoyancy, another that all armed merchant cruisers should have extended air cover in the approaches to the Clyde. The 'double explosion' noted by various witnesses was attributed to the magnetic pistol detonating on the final torpedo prior to it dealing *Scotstoun* her death blow. As yet unaware that its ciphers had been broken, the sinking of *Scotstoun* and *Andania* (**10**) in the space of three days raised the suspicions of the Commander-in-Chief Home Fleet, Admiral Sir Charles Forbes, that the Northern Patrol had been deliberately targeted in preparation for a German breakout into the Atlantic, the cruisers *Newcastle* and *Sussex* being dispatched to plug the supposed gap in the Denmark Strait. The truth would have been even more unpalatable.

Fate of the crew

As with *Carinthia* (**8**) the previous week, *Scotstoun* sank with relatively little loss of life. Two members of the stern high-angle gun crew were confirmed to have been killed by the first explosion and there were four casualties aft as a result of Beduhn's second torpedo strike at 0647. In calm seas and good light all nine boats got away within twenty minutes without loss of life leaving just fifteen officers and men on board to serve the guns, these remaining at their posts until water was lapping round the mountings. Most of them escaped into Carley floats as water reached the upper deck. Only the captain and an engineering officer remained, to be washed overboard as *Scotstoun* entered her death throes. Capt. Smyth was pulled into a Carley float but Sub-Lt (E) Thomas Martin RNR was never seen again.

The first indication received by the survivors that help was at hand came at 1230 when the ship's boats were overflown by aircraft of RAF Coastal Command. By 1430 they had been picked up by HM destroyer *Highlander* and were at length returned to Greenock. As

U25 returning to Wilhelmshaven on 29 June 1940, sixteen days after sinking the *Scotstoun*. The photo shows damage to the conning tower and attack periscope suffered in a collision with a merchantman on the 19th. The toadstools were added during Beduhn's brief tenure. *DUBMA*

with *Carinthia*, *Scotstoun*'s final patrol had lasted under twenty-four hours.

U25 and Heinz Beduhn

Built by AG Weser of Bremen and commissioned in April 1936, *U25* operated as part of the 2nd *U-Flottille* from Wilhelmshaven for the duration of her short wartime career. From the outbreak of war until May 1940 she was commanded by Korvkpt. Viktor Schütze, destined to become one of the leading U-boat aces of the war with a tally in excess of 180,000 tons of Allied shipping. Schütze accounted for seven ships as commander of *U25* and made several attacks on British destroyers at Narvik during Operation HARTMUT, being denied only by ongoing torpedo problems. In May 1940 Schütze was reassigned to *U103* and succeeded as commander of *U25* by Kptlt Heinz Beduhn. *Scotstoun* was Beduhn's only confirmed success, her efforts to intercept convoy HX48 with the 'Prien' pack on the same patrol coming to nothing as no contact was made, the boat returning to Wilhelmshaven after colliding with a merchantman on 19 June. Early in her next patrol, and still under Beduhn's command, *U25* was lost with all hands on 3 August after entering a minefield laid by British destroyers off the Dutch coast.

Sources

Admiralty, *Loss of HMS* Scotstoun: *Board of Enquiry* (TNA, ADM 1/10808)

—, *Blockade History, Atlantic Area, September 1939–December 1941* (TNA, ADM 199/2116)

Kriegsmarine, *U443*, Torpedo reports of *U25*, 0717 and 0747 on 13 June 1940 (BfZ, Schussmeldung Collection)

Bishop, CPO Frederick George, and O.Sig. Ronald Gold, 'The *Scotstoun*'s Last Fight' in *Life* (15 July 1940), pp. 84–6

Hampshire, A. Cecil, *The Blockaders* (London: William Kimber, 1980)

Haws, Duncan, *Anchor Line* [Merchant Fleets, no. 9] (2nd edn, Burwash, E. Sussex: TCL Publications, 1988)

Michie, A., and W. Graebner, *Their Finest Hour: The War in the First Person* (London: Allen & Unwin, 1940)

Osborne, Richard, Harry Spong and Tom Grover, *Armed Merchant Cruisers, 1878–1945* (Windsor, Berks.: World Ship Society, 2007)

Poolman, Kenneth, *Armed Merchant Cruisers* (London: Leo Cooper, 1985

Roskill, *War at Sea*, I, p. 267

10   HMS (ex RMS) *ANDANIA*

Capt. D. K. Bain, RN Ret'd

Sunk by *UA* (ex TCG *Batiray*), Kptlt Hans Cohausz, 15–16 June 1940

North Atlantic, 100 nm S of Höfn (Iceland)

Andania in happier times, here while serving with the Cunard Line in the 1920s. Her wartime appearance changed little beyond the addition of deck guns. *Bruce Taylor collection*

Theatre	North Atlantic (Map 1)	*Deadweight*	11,776 tons
Coordinates	62° 36' N, 15° 09' W	*Gross tons*	13,950
Kriegsmarine code	Quadrat AE 8278	*Dimensions*	540' × 65.25' × 31.5'
U-boat timekeeping differential	+1 hour	*Maximum speed*	15 knots
Fatalities none	*Survivors* 353	*Armament*	8 × 6"; 2 × 3" AA

Career

For background on the armed merchant cruisers, see HMS *Carinthia* (8).

One of a class of six small liners built for the Cunard Line, RMS *Andania* was launched at Hawthorn Leslie of Hebburn-on-Tyne in November 1921 and completed in May of the following year. She sailed on her maiden voyage from Southampton to Montreal on 1 June 1922, transferring to the Hamburg–New York run in 1924. From 1927 she sailed on the Liverpool–Greenock–Belfast–Quebec–Montreal service in conjunction with the Anchor and Donaldson Lines. However, the onset of the Depression brought with it a decline in trade which caused *Andania* to be laid up in the autumn of 1932. By the time she resumed service in 1934 Cunard had merged with the White

Star Line and *Andania* spent the rest of her peacetime career on the Liverpool–New York run with the exception of a period under repair following a collision with the tanker *British Statesman* in December 1937. *Andania* was requisitioned by the Royal Navy on 2 September 1939 and taken in hand for conversion to an armed merchant cruiser at Cammell Laird's yard at Birkenhead. After fitting out in the Alfred Dock and trials in Liverpool Bay *Andania* sailed for Greenock where in late November she joined the Northern Patrol between Britain and Iceland. Aside from spells on the Clyde being fitted with a buoyant ballast of 15,000 oil drums between February and March 1940 and having her gearing attended to in May of that year, *Andania* spent the rest of her brief career serving on this station.

Background of the attack

Early breakthroughs in the decryption of Admiralty codes by *B-Dienst*, the German radio monitoring and intelligence service, provided the Kriegsmarine with the dispositions of a number of ships on the Northern Patrol in the spring and summer of 1940, notably the anticipated patrol lines of several armed merchant cruisers. (An earlier victim of this effort was HMS *Scotstoun*, sunk on 13 June; **9**.) Dispatched to Icelandic waters to make good this intelligence, *UA* was on the lookout for HMSs *Salopian* (**26**) and *Andania*, eventually coming across the latter south of Iceland on 13 June. However, *UA* was unable to close her down and *Andania* disappeared to the north-east. Dogged by squalls and bad visibility, Kptlt Hans Cohausz was again unable to put in an attack when *Andania* reappeared that evening, sailing back along her previous course. On the third encounter, late on

the morning of 14 June, Cohausz took up an attack position at a range of about 2,500 metres but his prey kept disappearing into the mist and a spread of three torpedoes missed their target. Nonetheless, *Andania's* sailing pattern confirmed to Cohausz the accuracy of his intelligence – namely, that the armed merchant cruisers of the Northern Patrol were steaming along set courses which were reversed every twelve hours. Sure enough, on the morning of the 15th *Andania* reappeared at much the same time as on previous days. A range of 5,000 metres combined with high speed in heavy seas prevented Cohausz making an attack, but he was content to await another chance. *Andania* duly obliged at midnight, passing *UA* for the sixth time in just over seventy-two hours. Though still 2,500 metres off, she was silhouetted in the half-light of an Icelandic June night giving Cohausz the chance to claim the victim he had stalked so patiently.

War Diary of *UA*, patrol of 6 June–30 August 1940: PG 30889, NHB, reel 1,144, pp. 444–5

Date, time	Details of position, wind, weather, sea, light, visibility, moonlight, etc.	Incidents
13.vi		
1200	Qu. AE 8465 bottom left, wind S 2, sea 2	Day's run: 220 nm.
1524		At 30° on the port bow a large steamer appears out of a cloud of rain, initially with an inclination of 25°. One funnel, two masts. Alarm dive before they have a chance of sighting us – no opportunity to haul ahead on the surface. Once submerged we have a brief opportunity to identify the vessel in a big squall at a range of 7,000 m and inclination of 90°. From her outline it's clear that she's a large passenger liner.[1]
1600	Qu. AE 8439, submerged, rainy squalls	
1713		After another period of clear visibility we surface and follow the vessel's wake, thereby establishing enemy course of 60° and speed of around 15 knots. We lose contact at 1850, but by now we have ascertained that we are dealing with a patrolling steamer (auxiliary cruiser).
2000	Qu. AE 8287, wind SE to S 2, sea 2, south of Iceland	
2203		Alarm dive. Our auxiliary cruiser of the morning promptly returns on a reciprocal course.[2] We initially have a favourable position but over the course of our underwater approach, which lasts until 2309, strong enemy zigzags of up to 40° away from us as well as smaller zigzags every 10 minutes make our position steadily more unfavourable to the point where no attack is possible. But we'll plug on until we've bagged this fellow.
2400	Qu. AE 8289, wind S 3, sea 2, overcast, squalls	*Cohausz*
14.vi		
0010		Surfaced, enemy soon lost from sight in a dark cloud whereas our boat now stands silhouetted against a bright, clear and unfavourable horizon.
0400	Qu. AE 8514 middle right, wind SW to S 2, sea 1–2	
0800	Qu. AE 8456 upper middle, wind SW 3, sea 2, variable visibility, overcast, fine rain	
1113		Enemy reappears over the horizon at a favourable inclination, once again sailing on a reciprocal course.

---

1 HM armed merchant cruiser *Andania*.
2 Cohausz means 'afternoon' rather than 'morning' since *Andania* had been sighted at 1524.

1205		We dive. At around 1130 I spot powerful squalls initially around the target and then close by. Visibility now down to 2–3,000 m. Our enemy has had unbelievable luck with the weather through continual variation from squalls to clear visibility. Not until 1205 does the shadow of the enemy appear in sight at a range of around 2,500 m, and even then as a barely discernible shadow through the rain. We run in to attack. We can only improve our position minimally on her beam. Although enemy (*Andania*, 14,000 tons) remains rather blurred in the squall, I fire a spread of three torpedoes, enemy speed 10 knots, inclination 80°, range 2,500 m.[3] All miss. Presumably a misjudgement of target speed and as a result of the zigzagging that makes observation particularly difficult in the hazy visibility. But this prey is worth any amount of perseverance.
1200	Qu. [AE] 8473 upper right, submerged	Day's run: 223 nm.
1557		Submerged, reloading and retrimming.
1600	Qu. AE 8449 lower right, south of Iceland	In the 5th line of the Northern Patrol.[4]
2000	Qu. AG[5] 8439 upper middle, wind SE 4, sea 3–4	As above.
2400	Qu. [AE] 8449 lower left, wind 6, sea 5	As above.
		Cohausz

15.vi

0400	Qu. AE 8458, wind WSW 7, sea 6	Heavy seas and a sudden change in the weather. This Icelandic weather is more unpredictable than the mood of an elderly aunt, changing all the time!
0538–0810		Dived ahead of an escort vessel that appears further to the south. Given the prevailing sheer sea we have no opportunity to get within striking distance.
1129		Just like clockwork, our zigzagging auxiliary cruiser returns from the limit of her patrol line (evident reversals of course at 1100 and 2300). We haul ahead and dive. Due to the heavy sea and high swell, the first sight we have of her in the periscope and first hydrophone bearing are both at around 6,000 m. Sea now 5–6. So there's a zone of around five miles in which we are operating blind. Despite our immediately responding to the hydrophone effect and first periscope sighting, we just can't get to her. Enemy passes ahead of us at a range of 5,000 m. This chap has clearly entered into an alliance with the weather gods but we won't be denied! As always, enemy is steering a basic course line of 60 or 240°, reaching the middle of her patrol line at around 1500 or 0300.
1200	Qu. AE 8711, south of Iceland, wind SW 6, sea 5–6	Day's run: 129 nm.
1600	Qu. AE 8458, wind SW 4–5, sea 4, heavy swell	In the 5th line of the Northern Patrol.[4]
2320		Our auxiliary cruiser is back again. But this time, despite steep and rough seas, we manage to complete the advance manoeuvre ahead of the enemy who is zigzagging every 10 minutes.

16.vi

0029	Qu. AE 8278, wind SW 5, sea 4–5, steep short swell	At 0029 I fire a double salvo from Tubes I and IV. Range 2,000 m, enemy speed 15 knots, inclination 80°.[6] After a short time there is a detonation against the auxiliary cruiser *Andania* abreast the after mast. A tall white detonation cloud hangs for several seconds. A few minutes later[7] there is a second even stronger explosion, apparently from within the vessel. Ship appears to settle heavily by the stern and immediately loses speed. She is apparently incapable of manoeuvring. I immediately fire a G7a at what is now an almost stationary vessel, though she simultaneously opens a suppressing fire with her

---

3   *Andania* was in fact of 13,950 GRT. The torpedo report records the spread as being fired at 1217.

4   Cohausz is here referring to the five lines of the Northern Patrol operated by the Royal Navy south of Iceland, the details of which, together with the patrol areas themselves, had been revealed through decryption of Admiralty signals by *B-Dienst*.

5   The 'AG' quadrant cited is clearly a typist's error for 'AE', as otherwise *UA* would have suddenly shifted to a position on the Scandinavian mainland 1,000 miles to the east.

6   An extremely accurate assessment when the corroborative data is taken into consideration. Cohausz's assessment of *Andania*'s speed, 15 knots, matches that reported by Capt. Bain to the Board of Enquiry. The torpedo report corrects the firing time to 0027, which given the running time of 2 min. 37 sec. matches British data precisely.

7   In his torpedo report this is corrected to 'a few seconds later'. Cohausz considers it possible that his second torpedo struck its target. As discussed below, this remains an outside possibility despite the different points of contact resulting from interval firing.

Date, time	*Details of position, wind, weather, sea, light, visibility, moonlight, etc.*	*Incidents*

guns.[8] The G7a has no effect – there is just a metallic clanging sound similar to that heard immediately before the first detonation. Pistol failure? Keeping the boat's trim at our depth is a huge task in such a sheer sea (sea 4–5, steep short swell). Every so often the boat is suddenly seized roughly and either thrown forwards or up towards the surface. The Chief Engineer and depth-keeper both do a superb job of maintaining the boat's trim despite the challenge of keeping the boat from breaching and so offering an easy target for a broadside of the enemy's guns. Boat is much too unstable in such heavy seas and is prone to make sudden lurches in inclination.

We now circle our stricken prey and approach from the opposite course to fire our second *coup-de-grâce* shot, this time a G7e.[9] But even here they seem to obtain a fix on us, probably through hydrophones though perhaps we've been sighted. Either way, there is more suppressing fire from three or four guns. Torpedo fired dead ahead at stationary target, aimed amidships. All that happens is that suddenly the torpedo shoots out of the swell directly ahead of the boat before plunging beneath the surface once more. In view of this failure, and despite strong suppressing fire, I again square up to the enemy. She is lying astern in the half light but I have a clear shot abaft the funnel and fire a G7a – my third *coup-de-grâce* shot – from the stern tube.[10] All the while the enemy is firing heavy salvoes to scare me away – not badly aimed, either.

But this time we hear nothing of the torpedo. Three *coup-de-grâce* shot failures? Most likely depth failures due to the excessive swell, but perhaps they could be pistol failures?[11] It's too much to bear given the wholly favourable nature of the situation. Or perhaps, given the incessant salvoes from all round the ship, there might have been a detonation which went unnoticed by us? (Range 1,500 m.) As enemy is well down by the stern and increasingly listing, I am inclined to think that the prevailing wind and sea conditions will prevent her ever seeing land again. Our boat now has only seven torpedoes left for the rest of her cruise. After three fruitless *coup-de-grâce* shots I am beginning to think that our remaining torpedoes could be put to greater offensive use elsewhere. So I decide to leave the ship to her fate, which in my view is beyond all doubt. We therefore steer south-west via Areas III and IV towards Areas I and II of the Northern Patrol where we're likely to find the southernmost escorts patrolling.

At 0425 we transmit our first W/T report of the sinking to B.d.U. Later on B.d.U. announces the sinking of the auxiliary cruiser *Andania* (not *Scytia* [*sic*])[12] as part of its area report. For good measure this is followed by a report from the British Admiralty announcing the same loss.

0400	Qu. AE 8514, wind WSW 3–4, sea 3, ocean area south of Iceland	

---

8 According to his torpedo report this was fired at 2337 from a range of 1,400 metres. The torpedo was seen by men on board *Andania* to be hissing and moving erratically.

9 According to the torpedo report, fired at 0118 from 1,400 metres.

10 According to the torpedo report, fired at 0150 from 2,000 metres.

11 The likelihood is that Cohausz simply missed with his second and third torpedoes. He fired at what he thought was a stationary vessel with no aim-off, but Capt. Bain (who reported three torpedoes passing astern at times corresponding exactly to those in *UA*'s torpedo reports) observed that *Andania* was actually under way at this time, her engines still turning despite being submerged.

12 Cohausz is apparently referring to the liner *Scythia* which had been requisitioned from the Cunard-White Star Line in August 1939 for service as a troopship. Indeed, it would seem that this was how Cohausz originally identified his victim and that the references to *Andania* at 1205 on the 14th and 0029 on the 16th were added later with the benefit of subsequent information.

The sinking

Although Capt. Bain's report to the Board of Enquiry refers to his ship being convulsed by 'heavy explosions' at 2330 on the 15th (British time), it remains unclear whether one or (as Cohausz believed) both of *UA*'s torpedoes had found their mark. If they did both strike *Andania* – and the extent of the damage raises the possibility that she was the victim of two – they did so in the same place, on the starboard side abreast the bulkhead separating No. 5 and No. 6 holds. Whatever the case, the effect was devastating, with 'B' and 'C' decks ripped open, the after magazine and shaft tunnels immediately flooded, and subsequent immersion of the generators leaving the ship without power. The main wireless aerial was blown down in the explosion, fouling the emergency one as it did so, but these two were soon disentangled and a distress signal transmitted at 2345. *Andania*'s guns were immediately brought to bear, the beginning of three hours' continual fire from their crews. However, aiming them remained a matter of intelligent guesswork until *UA*'s periscope was sighted at a range of 1,500 yards following the launch of her second torpedo. This and Cohausz's third and fourth torpedoes were noted by those ranged on *Andania*'s upper deck to pass astern – one by just fifty feet. Those not essential to saving the ship or manning the guns were evacuated into boats at 0115 on the 16th, to be set adrift an hour later. By 0210 the ship was down by the stern at an inclination of ten to fifteen degrees and with a gradual list to port. Despite the use of all available pumps and herculean efforts by the Engineering Department it proved impossible to stem the flow of water which eventually reached the pumps themselves. The engine spaces were evacuated at 0230 and ten minutes later Capt. Bain ordered all remaining crewmen off the ship, an operation that was completed by 0310. For *Andania* the end came quite suddenly at 0655, the ship disappearing within the space of a minute. She was the third armed merchant cruiser to be lost in ten days and, like *Carinthia* before her, was considered to have had insufficient oil drums in her holds to keep her buoyant in the event of attack.

Fate of the crew

Despite the great damage inflicted by Cohausz, the detonations caused no fatalities and only four men were wounded. Help, too, was close at hand. Though standing orders barred the armed merchant cruiser HMS *Derbyshire* from stopping to pick up survivors, she could see *Andania* on the horizon and was able to intercept the Icelandic trawler *Skallagrímur* and persuade her to render assistance. *Skallagrímur* reached the scene five minutes after *Andania* went down and proceeded to take aboard the entire ship's company without incident. However, her appearance wasn't universally welcomed, it initially being thought that she was Norwegian, thereby raising the possibility that a Quisling crew might turn the rescued over to the Germans. The destroyer *Forester* arrived shortly after, but as the weather was by now too severe to contemplate a transfer she remained in escort until conditions moderated later that afternoon. Following a successful transfer the crew was landed at Scapa Flow shortly before midnight on the 17th. Over the next few weeks Sub-Lt W. E. Warwick RNR discharged his final duties as treasurer of *Andania*'s wardroom mess fund, dispensing £3 4s 0d to each of its fifty members from the £160 he had recovered before she went down. Of these fifty, thirty-one acknowledged reimbursement, Warwick retaining the receipts for the rest of his life.

Batiray on launching under the Turkish ensign at the Krupp Germaniawerft yard at Kiel on 28 September 1938. A year later she was taken over by the Kriegsmarine and commissioned as *UA*. DUBMA

UA

Displacement   1,128 tons surfaced   1,248 submerged
Dimensions   284.5 × 22.25 × 13.5
Maximum speed   18 knots surfaced   8.5 knots submerged
Armament   6 × 21" tt (4 bow + 2 stern); 24 torpedoes carried; 1 × 105 mm; 2 × 20 mm AA; 40 mines
Endurance   13,100 nm surfaced @ 10 knots, 130 nm submerged @ 3 knots
Complement   130

UA and Hans Cohausz

Ordered by the Turkish navy as an ocean-going minelayer and laid down in February 1937, the *Batiray* was built by Germaniawerft of Kiel based on designs for the Type-IX boats planned for the Kriegsmarine. As in the Great War, the Turks were unfortunate in having a number of vessels building in foreign yards on the outbreak of hostilities and *Batiray*, then in the final stages of fitting out, was quickly taken over by the German government. (For another case, see HMS/m *P615*, **84**.) Initially named *Optimist*, she was renamed *UA* on commissioning in September 1939.

Of the fourteen foreign submarines commissioned into the *U-Boot-Waffe* during the Second World War, *UA* was not only the first but also much the most successful, sinking seven ships for some 40,000 tons, all under Kptlt Hans Cohausz during her maiden war patrol. The geographical spread of *UA*'s victims on this cruise bears witness to her impressive endurance, the Icelandic sinking of *Andania* being followed by successes off Cape St Vincent, Cape Verde, Madeira, Morocco, the Azores and finally Rockall on the return journey to Kiel. *UA* sank no further ships but saw plenty of action, notably when assisting *U68*, *U124* (see **40** and **61**) and *U129* in the rescue of survivors from the raider *Atlantis* and the supply ship *Python* off Ascension on 1 December 1941 after the latter was sunk by HMS *Dorsetshire*, which *UA* had earlier missed with five torpedoes (see HMS *Dunedin*, **40**). *UA* was also to play a pioneering role as a mid-Atlantic tanker for U-boats sailing to and from the North American coast in March and April 1942. The slaughter of the Type-XIV *Milchkühe* submarine tankers that followed and her close resemblance to British submarines with the main gun faired into the conning tower no doubt prompted her transfer to training duties in July 1942. *UA* was scuttled at Kiel in May 1945.

Cohausz's first tenure in command of *UA* ended after just two patrols with his appointment in command of the 1st *U-Flottille* first at Kiel and then at Brest. After two more patrols in *UA* in the spring of 1942, Cohausz (by now Korvettenkapitän) was given command of the

11th *U-Flottille* at Bergen in May 1942. Promoted Fregattenkapitän, Cohausz was appointed commander of the torpedo school at Mürwik in December 1944. He was captured at the end of the war and spent three months in detention before being released in August 1945.

Sources

Admiralty, *Loss of HMS* Andania *by Enemy Torpedo: Board of Enquiry* (TNA, ADM 1/10897)

—, *Blockade History, Atlantic Area, September 1939–December 1941* (TNA, ADM 199/2116)

—, *Torpedo Attacks on HM and Merchant Ships, 1939–1941* (TNA, ADM 199/157)

Beesley, Patrick, *Very Special Intelligence: The Story of the Admiralty's Operational Intelligence Centre, 1939–1945* (London: Hamish Hamilton, 1977)

Hampshire, A. Cecil, *The Blockaders* (London: William Kimber, 1980)

Haws, Duncan, *Cunard Line* [Merchant Fleets, no. 12] (2nd edn, Hereford: TCL Publications, 1989)

McCart, Neil, 'Cunard's "A" Class Liners of 1922' in *Ships Monthly* 33 (1998), no. 7, pp. 32–5

Osborne, Richard, Harry Spong and Tom Grover, *Armed Merchant Cruisers, 1878–1945* (Windsor, Berks.: World Ship Society, 2007)

Poolman, Kenneth, *Armed Merchant Cruisers* (London: Leo Cooper, 1985)

Roskill, *War at Sea*, I, p. 267

Wien, Hermann, „*UA* – Was war das für ein Boot?" in *Schaltung Küste* 156 and 157 (January and March 1995), pp. 251–79

11   HMS (ex SS) *CAPE HOWE* ('SS *PRUNELLA*')

Cdr E. L. Woodhall, DSO MVO RN†
Sunk by *U28* (Type VIIA), Kptlt Günter Kuhnke, 21 June 1940
Western Approaches, 120 nm WSW of Land's End, Cornwall (England)

Left: A survivor's photo of *Cape Howe* sinking around midday on 21 June. Men can be seen abandoning ship into a boat alongside. Note the sealed buoyancy barrels floating abreast the forward derrick. *TNA, ADM 199/150*
Right: *Cape Howe*'s after well deck awash a short while later. More of her buoyancy barrels can be seen amidst the wreckage. *TNA, ADM 199/150*

Theatre	Western Approaches (Map 2)	*Deadweight*	7,300 tons
Coordinates	49° 44' N, 08° 52' W	*Gross tons*	4,443
Kriegsmarine code	Quadrat BF 1561	*Dimensions*	388' × 53' × 23'
U-boat timekeeping differential	+1 hour	*Maximum speed*	10.5 knots
Fatalities	57 *Survivors* 40	*Armament*	7 × 4"; 4 × .303" AA; 4 × 21" tt

The decoy ships

The concept of the decoy vessel, or Q-ship as it came to be known, was first tested in November 1914. The aim was to tempt a U-boat into a surface attack against an apparently defenceless merchantman where it could then be engaged by a battery of guns hidden aboard its would-be victim. Should the U-boat announce its presence by means of a torpedo attack, a 'panic party' would abandon ship in the hope of tempting the assailant to finish her off with her deck gun and so give the 'freighter' a chance to reply in kind. Though it enjoyed a measure of success in the First World War and was reintroduced by its leading exponent, Vice-Admiral Gordon Campbell VC, at the beginning of the next conflict, this particular *ruse de guerre* was by now ill-suited to the U-boats' own method for prosecuting the war at sea. The widespread arming of British merchantman at the outset of the war dissuaded the U-boats from engaging in the surface attacks that had accounted for such a high proportion of their victims during the earlier conflict. Together with the greater destructive power of the new German torpedo, this not only prevented the Q-ships from scoring any successes but also saw them lose two of their number to U-boats, both of which are covered in this volume (see also HMS *Willamette Valley*, **12**). Following an Admiralty enquiry, operations were abandoned and the eight surviving vessels of the Special Service Squadron withdrawn in March 1941 (see **12** for more background on this), though four of these remained in service as armed merchant cruisers, and decoy vessels continued to be commissioned locally, including the two-masted schooner *Farouk*, despatched by gunfire from *U83* off Lebanon in June 1942 (**G29**). These dismal results did not prevent the US Navy beginning its own Q-ship programme in January 1942 though with no better success (see USS *Atik*, **57**).

Career

Completed for the Ottoman Line at Lithgow's of Port Glasgow, Scotland in 1930, the coal-fired freighter SS *Knight Almoner* spent her first years laid up in Newport, a victim of the economic depression. From this she was rescued by the Lyle Shipping Co. which purchased her in January 1934, and as the *Cape Howe* spent the remaining years of peace on general tramping duties, especially between Vancouver and ports in north-west Europe. On 15 September 1939 *Cape Howe* was requisitioned for conversion to a 'special service freighter' and fitted out at Portsmouth under the cover name of RFA *Prunella*. After working up in nearby waters *Cape Howe* made her first cruise in the Western Approaches on 7 April 1940. Like all ships in the Special Service Squadron she was manned with picked men and volunteers who were paid an additional four shillings *per diem* in recognition of the hazardous nature of their work. The Squadron operated in great secrecy and strenuous efforts were made to preserve the actual function of its vessels, even in the event of a boarding by friendly forces. With the German invasion of Norway on 9 April *Cape Howe* transferred to the Norwegian Sea, remaining astride the convoy routes until early June when she made for Scapa Flow to refuel. It was to be her last port of call.

Background of the attack

On 14 June HMS *Cape Howe* sailed from Scapa Flow and began trailing her cape in the North Channel, feigning an unescorted vessel plying the convoy routes between the Clyde and North America. After a few days without attracting a U-boat she proceeded down the west coast of Ireland towards the South-Western Approaches and into the English Channel. On 20 June she came across a derelict merchantman, the Norwegian SS *Altair*, which had been torpedoed by *U32* two days earlier and was still ablaze. Having ensured that it was in fact abandoned, Cdr Woodhall took the opportunity to give his gun crews some practise with the poop-deck 4-inch gun, though *Altair*'s cargo of timber proved impervious to his shells. Ordered into the Western Approaches late on the 20th, *Cape Howe* made further sweeps before picking up a distress signal from the SS *Otterpool*, torpedoed by *U30* some eighty miles south of the Scilly Isles. *Cape Howe* altered course accordingly, hoping to encounter the offending U-boat. She did indeed encounter a U-boat south of Ireland on the morning of the 21st, though not *U30* but Kptlt Kuhnke's *U28*.

War Diary of *U28*, patrol of 20 May–6 July 1940: PG 30025, NHB, reel 1,061, p. 473

Date, time	Details of position, wind, weather, sea, light, visibility, moonlight, etc.	Incidents
21.vi	Exit to Western Approaches	
0000	Qu. BF 1834, wind NNE 2, cloudy and misty	
0400	Qu. BF 1591	
0800	Qu. BF 1561	Submerged, we approach to attack an armed steamer of about 5,000–6,000 tons with the Swedish national emblem on her sides.[1]
1200	Qu. BF 1561	She is keeping to a mean north-easterly course and zigzagging.
	Lat.: 49° 44.8' N	Salvo of two torpedoes fired.[2] Inclination 90°, enemy speed 10 knots, range 600 m. Depth set at 3 m.
	Long.: 8° 47' W	One hit on the starboard side at forward end of the bridge. Vessel turns hard aport, stops and swings

---

1   The issue of *Cape Howe*'s neutral markings is discussed below.

2   Unusually, Kuhnke does not state the firing times and leaves his description of the episode to the standard midday entry, though the torpedo report gives these as 0846 and 0847. Also unusual is his decision not to fire an angled spread but to launch successive torpedoes with the same aim-off after an unspecified interval. This was described by the *Torpedo-Inspektion* (Torpedo Inspectorate) in the torpedo report as 'a spread of two by means of relocation of point of aim'.

Date, time	Details of position, wind, weather, sea, light, visibility, moonlight, etc.	*Incidents*
	Day's run: 130 nm	out boats. Second torpedo probably misses due to violent manoeuvre to port.[3] However, two detonations heard in quick succession. Second torpedo not observed as boat briefly dips below surface. Half an hour later I fire a *coup-de-grâce* shot from the stern tube, 600 m, depth again set at 3 m.[4] Detonates abreast engine room on the port side. Ship's side is ripped apart, vessel settles heavily by the bow and lists to port. However, she takes a good while to sink, hanging on for over two hours. She would seem to have a very buoyant cargo.[5] We withdraw.
1330		Surface briefly, but immediately forced to submerge again by search vessels.[6]
1600		Spotted by small English warship (large trawler or gunboat). She closes us but releases no depth charges.
1700		Surfaced.
2000	Qu. BF 1582	Reload torpedo tubes.

---

3 There is no evidence that *Cape Howe* made any turn to port at this juncture though it is possible that her steering had been affected by the blast (see below).

4 Kuhnke again fails to specify a firing time and that provided in the torpedo report is blurred to the extent that only the initial '09' is legible. However, the addition of 'half an hour' to his opening salvo gives a time of approximately 0915, which equates with *Cape Howe*'s second distress signal. The torpedo report also specifies a range of 650 metres rather than the 600 recorded here.

5 Kuhnke was right. *Cape Howe*'s holds were filled with the standard ballast for decoy ships and armed merchant cruisers: sealed empty barrels. By contrast, Kuhnke's observation that she remained afloat for another two hours is not borne out in British reports which record a period of 5½ hours.

6 The precise identity of these ships and the vessel referred to at 1600 is uncertain, though it seems likely that they were HM corvettes *Calendula* and *Gardenia* in the first instance and HM sloop *Scarborough* in the latter, all searching for *Cape Howe*.

The sinking

Shortly before 0800 *Cape Howe*'s Asdic operator, Sub-Lt Chaplin, detected the discharge of *U28*'s torpedoes but *Cape Howe* had already been hit by one of these by the time the alarm could be raised. The torpedo, which struck on the starboard side abreast No. 2 mess deck, did not inflict mortal damage but wrecked both the Asdic set and the control rods of the steering engine leaving *Cape Howe* in no position to detect or evade her assailant. Hoping to lure the U-boat to the surface, Cdr Woodhall ordered a 'panic party' to abandon ship under his navigation officer Lt Cdr Pottinger in the role of 'master'. But Kuhnke, who had quite likely spotted the armament of what he describes as a neutral vessel, clearly had no intention of surfacing nor was his periscope ever sighted. Half an hour after the first a *coup de grâce* torpedo from *U28* ended *Cape Howe*'s slim chance of making a fight of it. The torpedo struck amidships, blasting away the shutters concealing Port No. 1 gun and leaving the mounting exposed for all to see. The floodwaters gradually outstripped the capacity of the pumps, causing the ship to settle by the head and requiring the gun and torpedo tube positions to be abandoned. *Cape Howe* sank bow first at around 1315 British time, the ship's company watching her stern reach almost vertical before subsiding into the depths, 5½ hours after the first hit.

Not the least interesting aspect of the sinking of HMS *Cape Howe* is the circumstance under which Kptlt Kuhnke felt justified in attacking a ship his log begins by describing as armed and wearing the markings of a Swedish neutral. Some in the Admiralty felt that Cdr Woodhall had brought ruin on his ship by opening fire on the *Altair*, thus revealing his vessel's true nature to a would-be attacker. Though his impromptu gunnery practice was probably ill-advised, there is no evidence in Kuhnke's log that the *Altair* episode had any bearing on his engaging *Cape Howe* unless Woodhall had failed to stow his poop-deck gun or even the pair of Lewis machine guns mounted on the fo'c's'le head. Indeed, it might be supposed from a *prima facie* reading of Kuhnke's description of *Cape Howe* as an 'armed steamer' that either this was not done or her covert status otherwise revealed. Where the issue of Swedish markings is concerned, James Kane (see below) asserts that Woodhall ordered them to be painted on the ship's side on hearing of the loss of the *Otterpool* the previous day. Though no mention of any disguise has been found in British official sources, this confirmation of Kuhnke's observation raises the question of *Cape Howe*'s precise role on the morning she was sunk. While neutral disguises were occasionally worn by the Special Service Squadron, there is no clear evidence that this was resorted to while its units were operating specifically in the Q-ship role. Certainly, for the British to have employed this particular *ruse de guerre* for offensive purposes was to court major diplomatic repercussions. On the other hand, it seems unlikely that *Cape Howe* would have been zigzagging as reported by *U28* if she had been attempting to pass as a neutral vessel. However, there is evidence that, in early June at least, *Cape Howe* was acting in an intelligence-gathering role for which this may have been the cover, it being common for U-boats to surface to investigate such vessels. Perhaps most pertinent of all is the message sent by Admiral Sir Charles Forbes, Commander-in-Chief Home Fleet, to the Admiralty on 14 June upon sighting *Cape Howe* sailing from Scapa Flow for the last time:

> I met *Prunella* at sea this afternoon. There is every likelihood of her being sunk by mistake if I am not kept informed of her movements as everybody who closes her sees she is not what she pretends to be.

The conclusion to be drawn from this is that *Cape Howe*'s disguise was rather less convincing than it might otherwise have been, of which Kptlt Kuhnke may have gained a fatal appreciation on the morning of 21 June. The most likely scenario would seem to be that of a freighter disguised as a Swedish neutral for intelligence purposes but given away by poorly concealed armament, her crew shifting to Q-ship drill following Kuhnke's unheralded attack. Whatever the case, the precise details of *Cape Howe*'s appearance and purpose must be a matter for conjecture in the absence of definitive information. Equally, despite the evidence presented in his war diary, the question of exactly how and when Kuhnke decided that *Cape Howe* was a legitimate target remains unresolved. Certainly, to have sunk a Q-ship would have been an altogether more impressive feather in his cap than an armed merchantman garbed in bogus neutrality, and his failure to elaborate on the matter in his war diary might be regarded as significant. To that extent the loss of HMS *Cape Howe* bears more than a passing resemblance to that of another decoy ship, *Willamette Valley*, sunk a week later (**12**).

Fate of the crew

One man was killed and another severely injured when the first torpedo struck abreast No. 2 mess deck, but ninety-six got clear of the ship in two lifeboats, a jolly boat, a raft and two Carley floats. Much was in the survivors' favour: distress signals had been sent (and received) after both the first and second hits, and conditions remained good with warm sunshine and calm seas. However, things soon began to go wrong. Though HM corvettes *Calendula* and *Gardenia* and HM sloop *Scarborough* had been dispatched to the scene following receipt of the signal at 0816, the survivors received no sign of rescue on the 21st. The group was still together as night fell but in the early hours of the 22nd the lifeboat (Lt Cdr Pottinger and about thirty men) and raft (Lt Sharp and about fifteen men) lost touch with the jolly boat, the two Carleys and the second lifeboat (including Cdr Woodhall) in rising seas. By 1100 that day the weather had deteriorated to the point where sails could no longer be set in the lifeboat. Moreover, heavy seas and the number of men on the raft caused the rope connecting it to the lifeboat to part on at least four occasions, contact being lost altogether at 1430 that afternoon. With hail and rain making the lifeboat increasingly unseaworthy, Pottinger took steps to lighten its load by ordering everything put overboard except the most essential provisions, his zeal extending to £3,000 in cash. An unexpected contributor to this process was a radio officer who leapt overboard and vanished without trace. A destroyer was sighted at 2100 but the survivors were unable to attract its attention despite the use of flags, revolver shots and Lewis gun tracer bullets. The following morning, the 23rd, the boat was circled several times by aircraft and then sighted at 1400 by the French steamer *Casamance*, sailing from Bordeaux for Britain with a large number of refugees. The survivors were landed at Falmouth on the 24th.

Those on the raft had a rougher time of it, and the wounded OSig. Henry Kane soon died. They too sighted a ship on the 23rd (considered a passenger liner of the Union-Castle Line) but also failed to attract its attention. That afternoon the raft capsized, depriving the occupants of cigarettes, matches, the Lewis gun and its ammunition. For a further ninety-six hours they drifted in intermittently poor weather, sighting but not being sighted by numerous vessels, until on the morning of the 27th they were terrorised by the appearance of an unknown U-boat. Able Seaman G. Rhodes:

> We then threw over the one remaining rifle, and ammunition, thinking we were not in any position to do otherwise, as we saw the U-Boat had a machine-gun trained on us. After slowing his speed he just waved, and at

Officers of *U28* on return from patrol in 1940. Kuhnke is the right-hand figure in the second row. *DUBMA*

the rate of about sixteen knots left us and headed north. We were very pleased and celebrated by having a double ration of water.

After six days on the high seas an increasingly feeble band of thirteen men was rescued shortly before midday on the 27th by HM destroyer *Versatile* which immediately turned for Devonport, thereby bringing the total number of survivors to forty.

None of the four craft that lost touch with Pottinger and Sharp during the first night (including that containing Cdr Woodhall) was ever seen again, and the fifty-one men in question were only listed Missing, Presumed Killed after another five months had elapsed.

U28 and Günter Kuhnke

Built by AG Weser at Bremen and commissioned in September 1936, *U28* was one of the first Type-VIIA boats to be completed. Her frontline career lasted from September 1939 to November 1940 during which Kptlt Günter Kuhnke sank fourteen ships for a total of over 60,000 tons, earning him the Knight's Cross. In December 1940 *U28* was assigned to training duties, remaining in this capacity until clumsily handled on approaching the U-boat pier at Neustadt, into which she collided and sank with the loss of a crew member on 17 March 1944. Though salvaged for the 3rd U-boat training division at Neustadt, she was decommissioned in August of that year.

Kuhnke was briefly in command of *U125* before being promoted Korvettenkapitän and taking charge first of the 10th U-boat Flotilla at Lorient and then of the 33rd Flotilla at Flensburg. He was one of several ex-U-boat commanders who joined the newly formed Bundesmarine, retiring as a decorated Konteradmiral in 1972. Günter Kuhnke died in October 1990.

Sources

Admiralty, *Service Squadron of Merchant Vessels Armed and Fitted Out as Admiralty Freighters for Anti-Submarine and Anti-Raider Duties: Sailing Orders and Instructions, Reports of Proceedings* (TNA, ADM 199/146, 147, 148, 149, 150 and 151)

Pragnell, P. R., *Gramps Goes to War* (undated typescript memoir, IWM, 02/30/1)

Hampshire, A. Cecil, *On Hazardous Service* (London: William Kimber, 1974)

Kane, James S., *In Peril on the Sea: The Naval Career of Signalman Henry Kane* (Armagh, Co. Armagh: Ulster Society, 1994)

Middlemiss, Norman L., *Travels of the Tramps: Twenty Tramp Fleets*, vol. I (Newcastle upon Tyne: Shield Publications, 1989)

Roskill, *War at Sea*, I, pp. 136–7 and 197

Smith, James R., 'Decoys and Dummies of the Second World War' in *Sea Breezes* 68 (1994), pp. 875–7 and 918

__, 'Decoys and Dummies of World War Two' in *Warships*, Supplement no. 143 (May 2002), pp. 20–31

Smith, Peter C., *Hit First, Hit Hard: The Story of HMS* Renown*, 1916–1948*

(London: William Kimber, 1979), pp. 118–19

Stearns, Patrick, *Q Ships, Commerce Raiders and Convoys* (Staplehurst, Kent: Spellmount, 2004)

Webpages relating to sinking of HMS *Cape Howe*:
http://www.bbc.co.uk/ww2peopleswar/ (assorted material accessible under search term 'Cape Howe')
http://www.roll-of-honour.com/Ships/HMSCapeHowe.html
http://www.wartimememories.co.uk/ships/prunella.html (includes photo of survivor group following rescue)

Website devoted to Capt. Duncan Cameron Kennedy (survivor):
http://www.mikekemble.com/ww2/merchantnavy6.html

12   HMS (ex MS) *WILLAMETTE VALLEY* ('RFA *EDGEHILL*')

Cdr R. E. D. Ryder, RN

Sunk by *U51* (Type VIIB), Kptlt Dietrich Knorr, 28 June 1940

Western Approaches, 250 nm WSW of Cape Clear, Cork (Ireland)

An indistinct view of *Willamette Valley* following her commissioning as a decoy ship in February 1940.
Three torpedoes from *U51* put paid to her brief career but spared her CO, Cdr R. E. D. Ryder, to fight another day. *BfZ*

Theatre	Western Approaches (Map 2)	*Deadweight*	8,705 tons
Coordinates	49° 27' N, 15° 25' W	*Gross tons*	4,702
Kriegsmarine code	Quadrat BE 3476	*Dimensions*	401' × 54.25' × 25'
U-boat timekeeping differential	+3 hours	*Maximum speed*	12 knots
Fatalities 68	*Survivors* 25	*Armament*	9 × 4"; 1 × 3" AA; 4 × .303" AA; 4 × 21" tt

Career

For the tactics and operational employment of the decoy ships, see HMS *Cape Howe* (**11**).

Completed for the Reardon Smith Line at Napier & Miller Ltd of Old Kilpatrick on the Clyde in 1928, the motor ship *West Lynn* was transferred to a Reardon Smith subsidiary, the Oakwin Steamship Co., as the *Willamette Valley* in 1931, being reregistered to Reardon Smith in 1937. Requisitioned for conversion to a decoy ship on 17 September 1939, *Willamette Valley* was fitted out at Chatham and commissioned under the cover name of RFA *Edgehill*. On 25 February 1940 she sailed from Sheerness to work up in the Solent before heading out on her first sortie off Bermuda, Brazil and Sierra Leone. Following reports of U-boats operating off the French coast, *Willamette Valley* was ordered to the trade routes between Gibraltar and the English Channel in the

spring of 1940. There she passed an uneventful few weeks varying her nationality from Dutch to Greek, refraining from zigzagging and radioing her position in plain language whenever a stricken vessel sent out a distress signal. These tactics failed to attract any enemy attention, however, and the first recorded sighting of her by a U-boat on 28 June would be purely a matter of coincidence.

Background of the attack

On 6 June *U51* left Kiel to operate as part of a six-strong wolfpack north-west of Cape Finisterre under Kptlt Günther Prien in *U47* (see **2**). Its aim was to intercept the eastbound HX48 but a rerouting of the convoy made this impossible and the pack was dissolved after ten days at sea, Kptlt Dietrich Knorr making for an operational area south-west of Ireland. Here he carried out a series of attacks on merchant shipping, sinking the British tanker SS *Saranac* (see below) and freighter SS *Windsorwood* on the 25th. Moving south, *U51* had an uneventful few days before sighting a vessel on the evening of the 28th that Knorr estimated to be 'roughly 10,000 tons'. *U51* had in fact stumbled across the decoy ship HMS *Willamette Valley*, patrolling the Western Approaches in the hope of precisely this kind of enemy attention. It is possible that Knorr had the added good fortune of doing so at almost precisely the time of day that *Willamette Valley*'s gun crews were accustomed to close up at Action Stations, drop the shutters and expose her concealed armament. However, like Kptlt Günter Kuhnke with HMS *Cape Howe* (**11**) a week earlier, Knorr's log fails to make clear exactly what he saw, and when.

War Diary of *U51*, patrol of 6 June–5 July 1940: PG 30048, NHB, reel 1,066, pp. 53–4

Date, time	Details of position, wind, weather, sea, light, visibility, moonlight, etc.	Incidents
28.vi		
2000	Qu. BE 3475	
2145		Large steamer in sight at bearing 0° true, bows left, inclination 90°. Size roughly 10,000 tons.[1] Armed.[2] We haul ahead.
2308		We dive and prepare to attack. Both visibility and depthkeeping conditions are proving very tricky.
		Knorr
29.vi		
0000	Qu. BE 3476	
0012		Torpedo (G7a) fired from Tube I, inclination 70°, enemy speed 7 knots, range = 600 m, depth set at 4 m.[3] Detonation after 20 sec. – a hit amidships. Bright sheet of flame. Vessel comes to an immediate stop, clearly struck in the engine room, and remains stopped with a slight list to port.[4] Crew start making their way into boats.
0053		We surface. I can now determine for certain that the vessel is larger than previously thought. 180 m long, a minimum of 14,000 GRT.[5] Room for 80 passengers I should say. I can't make out the name on the side in the darkness. Perhaps she's an auxiliary cruiser.[6]
0106		*Coup-de-grâce* shot fired. An enormous tongue of flame, presumably a hit in the magazine. We can now smell the distinct aroma of powder. But still she doesn't sink.
0124		Second *coup-de-grâce* shot, producing a tall black detonation cloud. Vessel sinks very slowly stern first, but bows remain afloat, full of air and pointing vertically upwards. We can see plenty of oil on the surface. Depth charge detonations heard.[7]
		When comparing her to the 12,100-ton *Saranac* sunk on 25 June I would say this vessel was considerably larger. In my estimation 14,000 GRT.[5] As we've now expended all our torpedoes apart from the two in the upper deck containers we set course for home and transmit message accordingly.
0400	Atlantic, Qu. BE 3444, wind W 6, sea 5, average visibility, high swell, overcast	Cruising speed.

---

1 Actually 4,702 GRT and 8,705 deadweight tons; see n. 5.

2 This may well be an *a posteriori* addition since there is no evidence that *Willamette Valley* was showing her armament at this stage. However, Ryder did order the shutters covering the gun mountings lowered as part of a daily gun drill two hours later at around 2350 log time (2050 British time), approximately twenty minutes before Knorr fired his first torpedo at 0012.

3 The torpedo report indicates that this G7a was fired with its *Nahschuss* ('close fire') setting, whereby the torpedo ran at a speed of 40 knots over 8,000 metres.

4 *Willamette Valley* had actually been hit abreast a cargo hold rather than in the engine room though the fact that she came to an immediate stop explains Knorr's initial assessment. However, his torpedo report notes that this hit had 'minimal effect'.

5 Knorr's revised tonnage estimate which exaggerates the size of his target by a factor of three is surprising, to say the least; in addition, *Willamette Valley* measured 122 metres (401 feet), not 180 metres (591 feet) as Knorr states. This misjudgement might be explained either by unfavourable visibility or by his identification of the ship as an armed merchant cruiser (see n. 6), most of which displaced well over 10,000 GRT. Whatever the case, whereas Knorr was able to make an accurate identification of the tanker *Saranac* (see the entry for 0124) he plainly failed to do likewise with *Willamette Valley*.

6 Knorr uses the term *Hilfskreuzer* (auxiliary cruiser) with which the Kriegsmarine described the British armed merchant cruiser type.

7 This sentence was added subsequent to the rest of the log using a different typewriter.

The sinking

U51's first torpedo struck *Willamette Valley* abreast No. 2 cargo hold shortly after 2100 ship time on the 28th, but despite Knorr's belief that she had been hit in the engine room his quarry had not in fact been seriously damaged. However, her ability to seek out her attacker and manoeuvre accordingly had been fatally impaired, the detonation having put the Asdic equipment out of action. Hoping that the U-boat would reveal herself, Cdr Ryder resorted to the ploy of dispatching a 'panic party' in two boats while lying stopped to give the impression of a hapless victim, *Willamette Valley*'s gun crews standing by to open fire should the attacker surface. Kptlt Knorr plainly had other ideas. As the log shows, *U51* did indeed surface after the first attack but Knorr evidently gathered that his target was armed and the torpedo report shows him withdrawing to a range of 900 metres (985 yards) before launching his next attack. Some time after the first hit (twenty to thirty minutes according to British sources but fifty minutes in Knorr's log) *Willamette Valley* was dealt a mortal blow as *U51*'s second torpedo struck abreast the engine room and started an uncontrollable blaze. Although this did not cause *Willamette Valley*'s magazine to detonate as Knorr suggests, the ensuing fire required all available hands to suppress the blaze or move ammunition out of reach and left each gun served by a single crewman should the attacker reveal herself. In the event, *U51* betrayed her position only with her third torpedo, fired at 0126 on the 29th German time (2226 on the 28th British time) from a range of approximately 1,000 metres (1,095 yards). This struck abreast the mainmast with which *Willamette Valley* immediately capsized to port and began to sink by the stern. British records indicate that *Willamette Valley* sank rapidly; Knorr, well placed to judge and with nothing to gain by claiming a slow sinking, testifies otherwise.

As with *Cape Howe* a week earlier (**11**), the unanswered question in the sinking of *Willamette Valley* is quite at what stage Kptlt Knorr established that his victim was armed and – despite his references to an auxiliary cruiser – precisely what kind of ship he deemed her to be before launching his first torpedo. Indeed, as Ryder concluded in his report,

> The point of particular interest which has been in my mind as I have written this is the question of whether or not the enemy suspected our identity. I think that there is no definite evidence to conclude that we were suspected, although three torpedoes are more than is usually expended on a Merchant Ship . . . I feel that if the enemy had good evidence that they had sunk a ship of our class they would give it publicity as propaganda to justify their unrestricted sinkings.

Ryder's final point appears incontestable but the loss of two special service vessels in seven days was nonetheless a cause of grave concern to the Admiralty. On 11 July the officer in command of special service operations, Rear-Admiral G. W. Taylor, wrote to inform the commanders of his remaining decoy ships of a number of instances which 'may or may not have given away to the Submarine Commanders that the ships were other than they appeared to be'. Among these were efforts to sink a derelict steamer (*Cape Howe*) and hands going to Action Stations with gun shutters dropped before darkness had set in (*Willamette Valley*). His letter concluded with this exhortation:

> I can only stress the necessity for ship, Officers, and crew, to act at all times as a ship of the Merchant Navy is likely to do: to remember that, unless there is very good reason to think otherwise, it is

Knorr seen on the conning tower of *U51* in 1940. *DUBMA*

possible that you are being watched by a submarine. To refrain from carrying out Target Practice unless you are convinced that you are many miles away from positions where submarines are known to be working. You may well say 'How can we train our crews?' but surely they can be partially trained at the D[efensively]E[quipped] M[erchant]S[hip] gun, which should be sufficient for what is likely to be a point-blank scrap. I fully realize you require the patience of Job at your game and I wish you the best of luck.

Unfortunately for Rear-Admiral Taylor and the Special Service Squadron, not even the patience of Job would avail them in their wait for an obliging U-boat, and the Q-ship experiment was wisely abandoned in March 1941.

Fate of the crew

An inspection by the First Lieutenant (Lt E. F. M. Seymour RN) after the first hit revealed that only one crew member was missing. The casualties caused by the second torpedo are not recorded but a majority of the ship's company were aboard when the third struck, many of them still battling to bring the fires under control. It is not known how many got clear of the wreck, but only eleven of those still on board survived to be rescued after *Willamette Valley* capsized. Nine of them – a sub-lieutenant and eight ratings – were plucked off a raft by one of the panic party lifeboats the following morning. Fully supplied with food and water, its twenty-three men were picked up by the French trawler *Donibone* on 4 July having rowed and sailed towards Penzance for the best part of a week, being landed there the following day. However, the other two survivors, Cdr Ryder and Able Seaman Roberts, had a lonelier time of it. Each found himself alone on a piece of flotsam, but while Ryder was rescued by a ship from convoy BXH32 on 2 July and eventually landed at Plymouth, it was not until the 6th that AB Roberts was saved, his existence sustained by a full ration of water. The rest of the ship's company was never seen or heard of again.

A number of men were recommended for Mention in Despatches by Cdr Ryder. Those of a posthumous nature included Lt Seymour who lost his life following repeated attempts to rescue men from the inferno raging around the ship's engine room control platform; Surgeon-Lt Hamish Wallace RNVR and Leading Sick Berth Attendant W. A. Keyse RNASBR, who refused to abandon their charges in the Sick Bay; and 2nd Radio Officer P. R. Starkey MN who was in the Emergency Wireless Office below No. 1 Hold and gave up his chance of surviving by remaining at his post. Ryder himself went on to win the

Victoria Cross while in command of naval forces during the raid on St-Nazaire in March 1942. He died in 1986.

U51 and Dietrich Knorr

Built by Germaniawerft in Kiel and commissioned in August 1938, the early Type-VIIB *U51* made only four frontline patrols after the commencement of hostilities, all under Kptlt Dietrich Knorr. During the first of these in January 1940 she sank two Scandinavian vessels in the North Atlantic. In March and April she participated in Operation HARTMUT, the naval side of the German invasion of Norway, during which a number of unsuccessful attacks were made on British warships, notably the cruiser HMS *Cairo*. Her next cruise, which claimed *Willamette Valley* and two merchantmen, was her most successful but there was to be no return from her fourth patrol. On 16 August 1940 *U51* was heavily damaged by an RAF Sunderland off Rockall and then destroyed in a surface attack by HMS/m *Cachalot* in

the Bay of Biscay while making for Lorient in the early hours of the 20th. There were no survivors.

Sources

Admiralty, *Service Squadron of Merchant Vessels Armed and Fitted Out as Admiralty Freighters for Anti-Submarine and Anti-Raider Duties: Sailing Orders and Instructions, Reports of Proceedings* (TNA, ADM 199/149, 150 and 151)

—, *Awards Following Sinking of HMS* Willamette Valley (TNA, ADM 1/11660)

Hampshire, A. Cecil, *On Hazardous Service* (London: William Kimber, 1974)

Heaton, P. M., *Reardon Smith Line: The History of a South Wales Shipping Venture* (Pontypool, Gwent: privately, 1984)

Smith, James R., 'Decoys and Dummies of the Second World War' in *Sea Breezes* 68 (1994), pp. 875–7 and 918

—, 'Decoys and Dummies of World War Two' in *Warships*, Supplement no. 143 (May 2002), pp. 20–31

13   HMS *WHIRLWIND*

Lt Cdr J. M. Rodgers, RN

Sunk by *U34* (Type VIIA), Kptlt Wilhelm Rollmann, 5 July 1940

Western Approaches, 75 nm SSE of Cape Clear, Cork (Ireland)

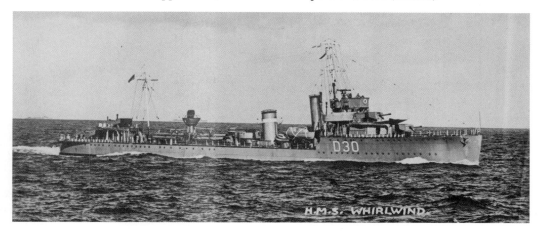

Whirlwind seen on the outbreak of war wearing the darker shade of grey favoured for ships of the Home Fleet. She lost her bow and over a third of her company to a torpedo from *U34*. *Bruce Taylor collection*

Theatre Western Approaches (Map 2)		*Displacement* 1,100 tons	
Coordinates 50° 17' N, 08° 48' W		*Dimensions* 312' × 29.5' × 8.5'	
Kriegsmarine code Quadrat BF 1286		*Maximum speed* 34 knots	
U-boat timekeeping differential +1 hour		*Armament* 4 × 4"; 1 × 40 mm AA; 5 × .303" AA; 6 × 21" tt	
Fatalities 57 *Survivors* 57			

The 'V & W'-class destroyers

First laid down in May 1916, the 'V & W'-class destroyers grew out of the Royal Navy's battle experience during the Great War. With a fine balance of armament, strength, speed, endurance and seakeeping qualities, the 'V & Ws' and their leaders of the Shakespeare and Scott classes proved to be the most influential design in the history of the type and laid the foundation for all subsequent British destroyers and many in foreign navies. Moreover, the seventy-five 'V & Ws' which were built earned a record of service over twenty-five or even thirty

years which gives them a special place in the annals of both the Royal Navy and the Royal Australian Navy whose famous 'scrap iron flotilla' was composed of a leader and four units. Though ten had been stricken from the Navy List by 1939 and most were twenty years old by the outbreak of the Second World War, the sixty-nine survivors (to include the leaders) gave yeoman service in every theatre and a quarter had been lost or written off by war's end, including HMSs *Veteran* and *Warwick* (**71** and **98**).

Career

HMS *Whirlwind* was laid down at Swan Hunter & Wigham Richardson's yard at Wallsend-on-Tyne in May 1917, launched in December of that year and completed on 15 March 1918. She belonged to what was known as the Admiralty 'W' or Repeat 'V' group of the class. Joining the Dover Patrol, *Whirlwind*'s first action came with the attack on Zeebrugge on 23 April 1918 followed on 10 May by the assault on Ostend after which she helped her heavily damaged sister *Warwick* (**98**) back to Dover. Details of *Whirlwind*'s inter-war service are few but 1921 found her serving in the 1st Destroyer Flotilla, Atlantic Fleet, renumbered the 5th DF in 1925. By 1929 she had been partially disarmed and refitted as a minelayer, service continuing with the 5th DF in home waters until she was put into reserve at the Nore in October 1934. However, in June 1939 *Whirlwind* was recommissioned with a crew drawn largely from the Royal Fleet Reserve and the RNVR, being assigned in September to the 11th DF for convoy defence under Western Approaches Command of the Home Fleet. Escort duty in the South-Western Approaches continued until April 1940 when she was detached for service with the Home Fleet proper following the German invasion of Norway. As the Norwegian Campaign unfolded her duties changed from escorting military convoys to supporting operations ashore and finally participating in the evacuation of Allied troops in May and June. By the end of June *Whirlwind* had resumed escort duty in the Atlantic with Western Approaches Command. Already on 30 October 1939 *Whirlwind* and *Walpole* had been obliged to sink the freighter *Brontë* with gunfire after she had been crippled by *U34* south-west of Fastnet. Little can *Whirlwind*'s men have imagined that the day would come when they themselves would enter the crosshairs of *U34*'s periscope.

Background of the attack

On 3 July 1940 convoy OB178 sailed from Liverpool with forty-nine merchantmen, her course south-west through the Western Approaches before an intended division in mid-Atlantic on the 7th. The convoy itself reached that point on time and in good order but a unit of its escort had been left in its wake. On the afternoon of the 5th *Whirlwind* had been ordered by HM sloop *Leith* (Senior Officer of the Escort) to run down a submarine sighting west-north-west of the convoy. At 1300 *Whirlwind* discerned a submarine conning tower several miles off on the starboard bow and course was altered accordingly. This was Kptlt Wilhelm Rollmann's *U34*, then two weeks out of Wilhelmshaven on her seventh and final war patrol. Though the subsequent Board of Enquiry was informed that *Whirlwind*'s Asdic was in good working order, it is clear both from Rollmann's log and from survivor testimony that no contact was ever obtained in a hunt lasting several hours. This technical failure on the part of the hunting vessel gave *U34* not one but two chances to inflict mortal damage on her pursuer from relatively close range.

War Diary of *U34*, patrol of 22 June–3 August 1940: PG 30031, NHB, reel 1,062, p. 335

Date, time	Details of position, wind, weather, sea, light, visibility, moonlight, etc.	Incidents
5.vii		
0800	Lat.: 50° 37' N, Long.: 9° 58' W, Qu. BF 1241, bottom left, wind WNW 3–4, sea 2–3, overcast, occasional showers, average visibility, 1,005 mb, air temp. 15° [C; 59°F], water 16° [C; 61°F]	Dived in the morning to load lower bow torpedo tubes.
1200	Lat.: 50° 28' N, Long.: 8° 49.5' W, Qu. BF 1267, top right, wind NNW 3, sea 2, overcast, good visibility, 1,003 mb, air and water 16°[C; 61°F]; south of Ireland	Day's run = 142 nm. At 1200, 1245, 1334, 1427, 1458 alarms caused by a Sunderland aircraft, typically flying east to west. At 1530 a destroyer approaches from the east, course 300°, alarm sounded. I take up an attacking position. Enemy alters course to 200° so we only get to within 3,000 m. She is a 'W'-class destroyer, D30, *Whirlwind*.[1] Enemy alters course to 110°, then 70°, 0°, 40°, 215°.[2]
1713	Qu. BF 1286, bottom left corner	I close once again and at 1713 manage to fire an angled double salvo from 800 m. I think due to my own error the angle of fire was not entered into the tubes as the bow torpedo team thought that a

---

1　While correct, Rollmann's identification is interesting since British sources record *Whirlwind*'s pendant number as having changed from D30 to I30 in May 1940. It must supposed that Rollmann either misread the first letter, made an inference or else added this identification after the fact having consulted the Weyer ship recognition manual.

2　The '40°' has been inserted in pencil.

		straight bow shot was intended – two misses.[3] Torpedoes clearly heard through listening apparatus. For over 5 minutes before firing a high-pitched fizzing sound (high short note) is heard at intervals of approx. 1.2 seconds.[4] Enemy speed estimated at 10 knots. No course alteration by enemy following salvo.
1826	Lat.: 50° 17.5' N, Long.: 9° 6' W, Qu. BF 1286, upper middle	At 1800 the destroyer turns about, new course 35°. At 1826 I get the chance for another shot. Inclination 90°, speed 17 knots, range 1,100 m. One Eto – bow shot, set at a depth of 2 m.[5] No sound of enemy detection apparatus at this time. Detonation forward close to bridge. Immediate blaze of burning oil and thick black clouds of smoke. At the same time fore part of the ship is torn off before the bridge and sinks within 10–15 sec., soon obscured by main body of the ship which is still moving. Bridge is a heap of ruins. Rest of ship is still under way, albeit settled deep in the water.

1835 Sunderland flying boat reappears above the destroyer. As I consider it certain that the rest of the ship cannot but sink after such damage, I fire no further torpedo and retire under water. 2050 resurface briefly but flying boat approaches yet again. There are now two of them up there, circling as low as possible and forcing us to remain under water.[6] At 2310 we resurface.

Following receipt of a radio signal from B.d.U. regarding a Gibraltar convoy I head south at full speed to intercept convoy.[7] British Admiralty warns of U-boat Qu. BF 1295 close to position of sinking of destroyer.[8]

W. Rollmann

---

3 Bow torpedoes could either be fired straight, i.e. in line with the head of the boat, or be adjusted to adopt a preset course a few seconds after launch. This is the misunderstanding to which Rollmann is referring.

4 This was probably *Whirlwind*'s Asdic.

5 'Eto' was Kriegsmarine shorthand for the electric G7e torpedo as distinct from the compressed-air G7a torpedo known as an 'Ato'.

6 British sources record only the one Sunderland, which kept on returning to the scene.

7 OG36, formed at sea off Land's End on 3 July.

8 The signal picked up by *U34* plots a more westerly position than the coordinates given by Rollmann in the margins of his log. Even allowing for a small element of drift in the hours before *Whirlwind* sank, the difference of over ten miles between the Admiralty and Kriegsmarine coordinates (see head of entry) is typical of the discrepancies that characterise the data and interpretations given by each side.

The sinking

It is not clear on which side Rollmann's torpedo struck *Whirlwind*, but the detonation demolished her fore part practically to the bridge. In his testimony to the Board of Enquiry Lt Cdr Rodgers stated that 'there would appear to be good reason to suspect the forward magazine having been hit and exploding'. However, the magnitude of the event failed to upset the composure of the ship's Chief Engineer, Commissioned Engineer D. J. B. Cock, who noted that 'I went along the upper deck to the engine room, and looking over the port side I saw an object passing by. I came to the conclusion that it was the bow of the ship and then realised that something must have happened.' Not only had *Whirlwind* lost her bows but her back was broken, the deck and side plating being 'folded in for about a foot, exactly across the ship abaft the lips of the after [torpedo] tubes and thence vertically down the side to the water line'. Damage control availed little as water rapidly gained in the boiler and engine rooms, a survey of the latter's after bulkhead showing it to be near collapse. Two hours after the attack HMS *Westcott* (Lt Cdr W. F. R. Segrave) came alongside and the question of what to do next arose. With Lt Cdr Rodgers incapacitated by a severe blow to the head, Segrave sought the opinion of Commissioned Engineer Cock who declared her to have at most four hours before sinking. As a tug dispatched from Falmouth was not expected to arrive for fifteen hours Segrave had little hesitation in deciding to hasten her end. But finishing *Whirlwind* off proved unexpectedly difficult, a tribute to the quality of her design and construction. Neither armour-piercing nor high-explosive shell had much effect, requiring *Westcott* to fire

a torpedo at 2145 which, however, ran erratically and passed astern. More rounds were fired, starting a number of blazes on board but with no fatal consequence. Finally, at 2245 *Westcott* fired a second torpedo which struck *Whirlwind* abreast her after funnel. Within two or three minutes she had disappeared, members of her ship's company looking on in tears.

After extensive questioning of all officers and a number of ratings, the Board of Enquiry criticised the regular nature of *Whirlwind*'s zigzagging while chasing down the contact but ceded that a search for a U-boat by a single destroyer was a 'task of the greatest difficulty'. Though it approved of the scuttling of *Whirlwind* it was not satisfied from the evidence that she could not in fact have been salved by tugs. No blame was apportioned, however, and it considered that Lt Cdr Segrave's decision not to use his vessel to tow *Whirlwind* was only prudent under the circumstances. All ranks and ratings were considered to have acted in the best traditions of the Service.

Fate of the crew

At least fifty of the ship's company were accounted for by *U34*'s torpedo which wrecked the living spaces forward. Two survivors from the bow section were Lt Cdr Rodgers himself, who had just left the bridge and received head wounds, and the Officer of the Watch, Lt C. R. Bax, who survived despite being blasted from the bridge to the deck abreast the after funnel. The Chief Petty Officers' mess, the watchkeepers' mess deck, the galley flat and much of the forward seamen's mess were either destroyed or flooded by water or fuel oil from No. 1 tank. Shortly

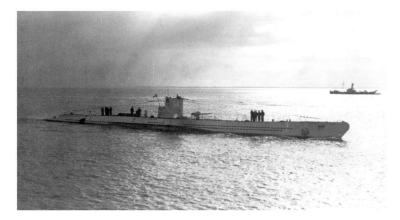

U34 seen before the war. In December 1936 she became the first U-boat to sink a naval vessel since the Great War, claiming the submarine *C3* of the Spanish Republican navy in the Mediterranean (**G1**). *DUBMA*

after the attack Signalman M. Y. French-Williams RNVR sighted a wounded shipmate about a cable from the ship, deposited there by the detonation. Diving overboard, French-Williams reached the man and kept him afloat until he could be recovered by volunteers in a Carley float. Though still alive upon being brought aboard *Whirlwind* this man eventually succumbed to shock, a sad return for French-Williams whose courage was nonetheless commended by the Board of Enquiry. In the two hours or so that elapsed before *Westcott* arrived on the scene lookouts were posted, the after guns loaded and manned and attempts made to assist the wounded, of whom two died. However, once the fifty-seven survivors, including seven badly injured men, had been got aboard *Westcott* and their ship given the *coup de grâce*, Lt Cdr Segrave abandoned any idea of hunting the perpetrator and turned for Falmouth where the wounded were landed the following day, the rest being turned over to Devonport barracks.

U34 and Wilhelm Rollmann

Built by Germaniawerft in Kiel and commissioned in September 1936, *U34* was soon in action during the Spanish Civil War under her first commander, Kptlt Harald Grosse. On a covert mission christened Operation URSULA, Germany's short-lived attempt to provide naval assistance to Franco's Nationalist revolt, *U34* torpedoed and sank the Republican submarine *C3* off Málaga on 12 December 1936 (**G1**). Her six operational patrols between August 1939 and August 1940 were all made under Kptlt Wilhelm Rollmann, who had assumed command in August 1938. *U34*'s war service began briskly with two merchantmen being sunk within five days of the commencement of hostilities, the first of over 100,000 tons of shipping accounted for by Rollmann in the first year of the war. Another merchantman, the Norwegian SS *Snar*, was captured on 9 November 1939 and sailed to Germany by a prize crew where she was refitted as a minelayer. *U34* laid mines of her own, one of which claimed the British tanker *Caroni River* off Falmouth on 20 January 1940. In April she took part in Operation HARTMUT in support of the German invasion of Norway during which Rollmann was able to finish off the Norwegian minelayer *Frøya* (**G4**) after she had been beached in Stjørnfjorden on the 13th. Five days later he apparently hit the battlecruiser *Repulse* with a salvo of torpedoes but these, like so many during this campaign, failed to detonate. For further details

Rollmann seen wearing the Knight's Cross which he was awarded following the patrol which claimed both *Whirlwind* and HMS/m *Spearfish* (**14**). *DUBMA*

of Rollmann's career and the rest of *U34*'s final operational patrol and subsequent fate, see HMS/m *Spearfish* (**14**).

Sources

Admiralty, *Loss of HMS* Whirlwind: *Board of Enquiry* (TNA, ADM 1/11217)

Blair, *Hitler's U-Boat War*, I, p. 172

Brennecke, Jochen, „Das U-Boot, das den Zerstörer *Whirlwind* in die Tiefe schickte: Kapitänleutnant Wilhelm Rollmann erzählt" [article in unknown newspaper] 13 August 1940 (DUBMA, *U34* file); Eng. trans. 'The U-Boat Which Sent the Destroyer *Whirlwind* into the Depths: Kptlt Wilhelm Rollmann Tells the Story' in *The U-Boat Archive* no. 1 (October 1998); reprinted in Jak P. Mallmann Showell, ed., *The U-Boat Archive: Early Journals Reprinted (1998–2000)* [U-Boat Archive Series, vol. 6] (Milton Keynes, Bucks.: Military Press, 2004), pp. 15–18

Chapman, Tom, '*Water, Water Every Where!': The Life Story of HMS* Westcott, *February 1918–June 1946* (Northaw, Herts.: Aedificamus Press, 1996)

Fairweather, Cliff, *Hard Lying: The Story of the "V & W" Class Destroyers and the Men Who Sailed in Them* (Chelmsford, Essex: Avalon Associates, 2005)

Preston, Antony, '*V & W' Class Destroyers, 1917–1945* (London: Macdonald, 1971)

Raven, Alan, and John Roberts, '*V' and 'W' Class Destroyers* [Man o'War, no. 2] (London: Arms and Armour Press, 1979)

War career of HMS *Whirlwind*: http://www.naval-history.net/xGM-Chrono-10DD-09VW-Whirlwind.htm

Vega, Julio de la, '"Operation Ursula" and the Sinking of the Submarine *C-3*' posted on 24 March 2005: http://uboat.net/articles/index.html?article=59

14 HMS/m *SPEARFISH*

Lt Cdr J.H. Forbes, DSO RN†

Sunk by *U34* (Type VIIA), Kptlt Wilhelm Rollmann, 1 August 1940

North Sea, 110 nm SE of Sumburgh Head, Shetland

Spearfish under way before the war. She met a violent end at the hands of *U34* in the North Sea,
just one man surviving. *DUBMA*

Theatre	North Sea (Map 2)	*Displacement*	670 tons surfaced 960 tons submerged
Coordinates	58° 28' N, 01° 06' E	*Dimensions*	208.75' × 24' × 10.25'
Kriegsmarine code	Quadrat AN 4281	*Maximum speed*	13.75 knots surfaced 10 knots submerged
U-boat timekeeping differential	+1 hour	*Armament*	6 × 21" tt (12 torpedoes carried); 1 × 3" AA; 1 × .303" AA
Fatalities	41 *Survivors* 1		

Career

Well armed, with good endurance and excellent manoeuverability, the 'S'-class patrol submarines, of which sixty-two were eventually completed in various sub-classes, represented the first truly capable design to enter service in the Royal Navy. A unit of the second group of the class, HMS/m *Spearfish* was laid down at Cammell Laird of Birkenhead in May 1935, launched in April 1936 and commissioned in September that same year. She entered service with the 5th Submarine Flotilla at Portsmouth before being assigned to the 6th SF at Portland in May 1937. Commanded by Lt T. H. Eaden, on 25 August 1939 *Spearfish* sailed from Portland on what became her first war cruise, a patrol off Obrestad (Norway) which resulted in an attack by an unidentified U-boat east of Egersund on 3 September. It was the start of a brief but eventful war. Two days later she joined the 2nd SF at Dundee and on the 20th sailed to take up her allotted station in the Kattegat between Norway and Denmark. On 22 September she suffered a prolonged depth-charging by German anti-submarine trawlers off the Horns Reef. After many hours on the bottom she surfaced and steered for home on one electric motor, unable to dive and with her radio temporarily out of action. When the Admiralty finally learnt of her predicament on the 25th the full might of the Home Fleet sailed to bring her in. On 26 September *Spearfish* was met and

escorted to Rosyth by the 2nd Cruiser Squadron and six destroyers while the major units of the Home Fleet were given their first taste of aerial attack at sea. Repaired at Newcastle upon Tyne and placed under the command of Lt Cdr J. H. Forbes, *Spearfish* spent the second half of March 1940 working up at Scapa Flow before joining the 6th SF at Blyth. Returning to German waters, on 11 April she caught the 'pocket battleship' *Lützow* off Hantsholm in the Skagerrak, wrecking her stern with a single torpedo and putting her out of action for almost a year. *Spearfish* survived a determined hunt by *Lützow*'s escort to reach Blyth in a damaged state on the 17th. Three further patrols from Blyth yielded a brace of Danish fishing vessels near the Dogger Bank on 20 May before *Spearfish* joined the 3rd SF at Rosyth in July. On the 31st *Spearfish* put to sea from Rosyth with orders to patrol off Stavanger. A tumultuous career was drawing to a close.

Background of the attack

The sinking of HM destroyer *Whirlwind* (**13**) south of Ireland on 5 July heralded the start of a remarkable spell for *U34* in the Western Approaches during which Kptlt Wilhelm Rollmann destroyed a further seven ships in the space of nine days. This run of success may partly be accounted for by the fact that *B-Dienst*, the Kriegsmarine's radio monitoring and intelligence service, had broken several of the

Admiralty's administrative and operational ciphers. Whatever the case, putting in at Lorient to take in fresh torpedoes and supplies on the 18th, *U34* proceeded to sink another four ships from convoy OB188 to the west of Ireland before turning for Wilhelmshaven with just a single torpedo remaining. The opportunity to use it came on 1 August, mid-way between Norway and Scotland. Shortly before sunset *U34* spotted an enemy submarine cruising on the surface on a converging course. This was HMS/m *Spearfish* which had sailed from Rosyth the previous day to resume patrolling off the Norwegian coast and was now unwittingly in mortal danger from a submerged foe.

War Diary of *U34*, patrol of 22 June–3 August 1940: PG 30031, NHB, reel 1,062, p. 358

Date, time	Details of position, wind, weather, sea, light, visibility, moonlight, etc.	Incidents
1.viii		
1436		Alarm. Two aircraft sighted.
1817		A slender object sighted on the horizon by the starboard watch, looking very much like a periscope. At 1819 we dive.[1] I soon discern a submarine sailing towards us, 0° inclination. The slender line first seen over the horizon turns out to be the two tall periscope standards in aligned bearing.
1848		Gradually the conning tower of the submarine comes into sight. Enemy course is 30°. Difficult to make out what type she is. I position myself ahead for an attack. Identify her as a Sterlet-class submarine, but inclination and speed are now extremely difficult to establish.[2]
1904	Lat.: = 58° 28' N Long.: = 01° 06' E Qu. AN 4281 upper left	At 1904 I fire a bow shot having first closed at ¾ speed and then utmost speed, the range being too great. Torpedo depth 2 m, enemy speed 9 knots, inclination 100°, hits 20 m from the bow. Running time of 1 min. 46 sec., equating to a range of 1,610 m. Immense pall following the explosion, the detonation of which can be felt in our U-boat despite the great distance. I assume the submarine's torpedoes must have gone up simultaneously. She sinks within 2–3 seconds and great pieces of wreckage fly through the air. 1905 we surface and immediately head towards the scene of the sinking. We find one man swimming, and bring him on board at 1910. At 1908 a powerful air bubble rises to the surface. There's very little oil to be seen, and just a few pieces of wooden debris floating about. The submarine sunk was *Spearfish* – other statements by the prisoner, Able Seaman (torpedo) <u>Pester</u>, Williams [*sic*] Victor, can be found in the appendix.[3] There is nothing else of note to be found in the vicinity. Sinking reported by radio. At 2250 alarm following sighting of three aircraft.
		W. Rollmann

---

1   Rollmann here deviates from the convention of recording times in the first column provided for this data; further down he fails to treat incidents as separate entries.
2   Rollmann's identification is correct, though the sub-class to which both *Sterlet* and *Spearfish* belonged was named after HMS/m *Shark*.
3   Rollmann means William Victor Pester. Regrettably, this appendix is absent from the war diary.

The sinking and fate of the crew

Little can be said by way of elaboration to Rollmann's log which makes it quite clear that *Spearfish* came to an immediate and catastrophic end when *U34*'s torpedo found its mark. The fact that the detonation was strongly felt nearly a mile off gives some idea of the force of the explosion which destroyed her.

The bewildered survivor, AB William Pester of Bournemouth, had just joined *Spearfish* on a 'pierhead jump'. Pester recalled that the bridge watch consisted of himself, Lt Cdr Forbes and another officer when *Spearfish* was hit, the time of the attack going unrecorded. The detonation blasted both officers over the conning tower hatch and Pester had just bent down to render assistance when what remained of *Spearfish* slid beneath the waves. Pester attempted to reach the surface but the strap of his binoculars caught on the gyro repeater travel bar and he was dragged deep with the wreck. Just when he had given up hope a large air bubble emerged from the conning tower, its force at such depth being sufficient to part the strap and propel him to the surface. Picked up by *U34*, Pester recalled being well treated aboard *U34* (especially for his neck injuries) before being transferred to Wilhelmshaven naval barracks and then a succession of prisoner-of-war camps. The next five years gave Pester ample opportunity to recount his tale to fellow prisoners. Repatriated to Britain in June 1945, the Australian-born Pester did not have long to enjoy his freedom. He was killed on 3 July when the motorcycle he had purchased with part of the gratuity received on demobilisation was in collision with a Bournemouth trolley bus. His girlfriend, who was riding pillion, also lost her life.

U34 and Wilhelm Rollmann

For details of *U34*'s earlier career and successes, see the preceding entry for HMS *Whirlwind* (**13**).

Spearfish was *U34*'s last victory, crowning a patrol during which thirteen vessels were sent to the bottom and for which Rollmann was awarded the Knight's Cross and fêted by the German media. On returning to Wilhelmshaven *U34* was allocated to training duties in the Baltic where she remained until sunk in a collision with the U-boat

Sole survivor: AB William Pester of the *Spearfish*, seen here in a press photo, comes ashore following *U34*'s return to Lorient on 3 August 1940. *DUBMA*

depot ship *Lech* off Memel (now Klaipėda, Lithuania) on 5 August 1943, with the loss of four of her crew. Though subsequently raised she never put to sea again.

Following *U34*'s last operational patrol Rollmann was transferred to shore appointments for the next three years, being promoted

Korvettenkapitän in December 1940. Given command of the new *U848* and advanced to Fregattenkapitän in November 1943, Rollmann did not long survive his appointment. *U848* was destroyed on her maiden cruise after prolonged attacks by US aircraft north-west of Ascension Island on 5 November. Men were seen in the water and rafts dropped from the air but only a single crewman survived to be picked up after a month adrift. Within a few days he too was dead.

Sources

Admiralty, Admiral Submarines, *Attacks on Allied Submarines: Royal Navy Ship and Submarine Losses* [operational career of HMS/m *Spearfish*] (TNA, ADM 199/1925)

HMS/m *Spearfish* file (RNSM)

Beesley, Patrick, *Very Special Intelligence: The Story of the Admiralty's Operational Intelligence Centre, 1939–1945* (London: Hamish Hamilton, 1977)

Bendert, Harald, *U-Boote im Duell* (Hamburg: Mittler, 1996)

Evans, A. S., *Beneath the Waves: A History of HM Submarine Losses, 1904–1971* (London: William Kimber, 1986)

Hezlet, Vice-Admiral Sir Arthur, *The History of British and Allied Submarine Operations During World War II* (2 vols, Gosport: Royal Navy Submarine Museum, 2002; published as *British and Allied Submarine Operations in World War II* on CD-ROM, 2003)

Hudson, B., and J. J. Colledge, 'British Submarines in World War II: Shark Class' in *Warships*, Supplement no. 89 (Summer 1987), pp. 1–8 and 11

Jones, Geoffrey, *Submarines Versus U-Boats* (London: William Kimber, 1986)

Poolman, Kenneth, *Allied Submarines of World War Two* (London: Arms and Armour Press, 1990)

Roskill, *War at Sea*, I, pp. 68, 177 and 266–7

15   HMS (ex SS) *TRANSYLVANIA*

Capt. F. N. Miles, RN Ret'd

Sunk by *U56* (Type IIC), Oblt.z.S. Otto Harms, 10 August 1940

North Atlantic, 55 nm W of Islay, Inner Hebrides (Scotland)

Theatre	North Atlantic (Map 2)	*Deadweight*	10,060 tons
Coordinates	55° 50' N, 08° 03' W	*Gross tons*	16,923
Kriegsmarine code	Quadrat AM 5357	*Dimensions*	578.5' × 70.25' × 29'
U-boat timekeeping differential	+1 hour	*Maximum speed*	16.5 knots
Fatalities 36	*Survivors* 300+	*Armament*	8 × 6"; 2 × 3" AA

Career

For background on the armed merchant cruisers, see HMS *Carinthia* (**8**).

Ordered like her sister *Caledonia* (later HMS *Scotstoun*, **9**) for the Anchor Line, the liner *Transylvania* was laid down at Fairfield, Govan in 1923, launched in March 1925 and completed later that same year. For appearance's sake the pair were fitted with three funnels though only the middle of these ever issued smoke. Intended for the Glasgow–New York service, *Transylvania* embarked on her maiden voyage on 12 September 1925 and served out her peacetime career without incident. On 7 September 1939 she was requisitioned into the Royal Navy and taken in hand for refitting as an armed merchant cruiser on the Clyde. Reduced to the single funnel, she was commissioned on 8 October and immediately joined the Northern Patrol between Britain and Iceland, *Transylvania*, *Scotstoun* and *Rawalpindi* being the first converted liners

to enter service in this role. Her maiden operational patrol took her to the Denmark Strait where on 20 October she stopped and captured the tanker *Bianca*, the first of several such incidents in the distant blockade of Germany. Five days later she intercepted the German cargo liner *Poseidon* off Iceland though mountainous seas prevented the capture being made good and *Transylvania* had to sink her by gunfire on the 26th. On 21 November the German freighter *Tenerife* was intercepted in heavy seas but managed to scuttle herself, followed on 28 March 1940 by the steamer *Mimi Horn* with the same result. Refitted in February and repaired at Belfast and on the Clyde between May and June, *Transylvania* remained in northern waters for the rest of her days, sailing from Greenock on her eleventh patrol shortly after midday on 9 August 1940.

The Anchor Line's *Transylvania* sailing from New York in August 1930. Her conversion to armed merchant cruiser nine years later entailed the removal of the forward and after funnels together with the mounting of eight 6-inch guns. Harms sent her to the bottom with a single torpedo. *Bruce Taylor collection*

Background of the attack

On 25 July 1940 *U56* sailed from Lorient with orders to patrol a small area off the southern coast of Ireland, though these were rescinded after several days during which a lone fishing boat represented the sum total of enemy shipping sighted. Steering round the west coast of Ireland, Oblt.z.S. Otto Harms found the Atlantic exit of the North Channel separating Northern Ireland and Scotland an altogether more fertile hunting ground. Much to his annoyance, and hindered no doubt by the slow surface speed of his Type-IIC boat, Harms was unable to mount a prolonged attack on convoy OB193 having made contact on 4 August, being fortunate to pick off SS *Boma* at the rear of the convoy having aimed at a larger vessel. A frustrating series of sightings with no opportunity for attack followed until the 9th when a shadow was spotted shortly before midnight. It was the unescorted *Transylvania*, zigzagging towards her patrol area at her best speed of 16½ knots.

War Diary of *U56*, patrol of 25 July–14 August 1940: PG 30053, NHB, reel 1,067, p. 139

Date, time	Details of position, wind, weather, sea, light, visibility, moonlight, etc.	Incidents
10.viii		
0045	Qu. [AM] 5357, wind W 4–5, sea 4, high swell, showers, variable visibility	A shadow appears at bearing 90° true. A large vessel that rapidly disappears to port. We attempt to out-steam her with a view to gaining an advance position. Ship approaches quite fast. She has an angled bow, superstructure rising to two levels and a single, somewhat raked funnel.
0100	Wind veering gradually to starboard, freshening somewhat	Torpedo fired from 500 m, inclination 85°, estimated speed of target 14 knots.[1] After 45.5 sec. we see a blaze of fire following a detonation about 20–30 m abaft the funnel. Torches appear shortly after and can be seen shining around the area where the torpedo hit, surrounded by dense clouds of smoke. The ship stops, her stern settling in the water. Navigation lights come on though after a while these are gradually extinguished. A great deal of red starshell is fired. A W/T transmission is sent on the 600-m band but we fail to pick it up. Vessel settles still deeper by the stern. The dark pall of black smoke is illuminated every so often by the glow of flame. The crew appears to be busy preparing boats. No torpedoes left for a *coup-de-grâce* shot and we can't linger to await her sinking due to visibility, heavy

---

1 *Transylvania*'s speed as reported to the Board of Enquiry was 16½ knots.

seas and low battery levels,[2] so we slowly head south and begin our return to Lorient. Short signal transmitted.

0140 Vessel now out of sight surrounded by this cloud of smoke – tiny white lights can be seen dotted around, doubtless from ship's boats. We head off at ¾ speed to recharge batteries.

0400 Qu. [AM] 5372, wind WNW 5, sea 5, high swell

---

2 Harms is referring to the effect of having been submerged for a prolonged period during which *U56* would have relied on her electric engines. The batteries would gradually run down, having to be recharged by running the main diesel engines at full speed when next cruising on the surface. The tactical limitations implied by this were largely addressed by the introduction of the *Schnorchel* device in 1944.

The sinking

Both German and British sources confirm that *Transylvania* was struck just after midnight on the 10th British time, the Officer of the Watch describing the explosion as a 'flash aft which silhouetted the mainmast . . . the ship seemed to shudder as if a large wave had hit her'. She had been hit on the port side abreast No. 4 6-inch gun, close to the engine room. Capt. Miles, noting the almost instantaneous cessation of the engines, hurriedly left his bunk for the bridge and ordered a distress signal to be sent immediately – no doubt the same reported by Harms. All lights, including emergency lighting, failed within a few minutes and reports from the engine room revealed it to be flooded. *Transylvania* had by now assumed a list of about six degrees to port and was unable to raise steam. By 0230 the flooding had reached 'B' deck, the water from the engine room having spread through the ship. Shortly before 0300, with the list increasing and *Transylvania* settling by the stern, Capt. Miles gathered his officers on the bridge, thanked them and the nearby ratings for their services and passed the order to abandon ship. The boats were ordered away, the evacuation left unmolested by *U56* which had no torpedoes left to finish her off. *Transylvania* was observed to disappear at 0450 British time, nearly five hours after the attack.

The Board of Enquiry was somewhat perplexed at the speed with which *Transylvania* flooded after a single torpedo strike. On the one hand it found that 'no effort on the part of the Captain or any other officers and ship's company could have saved the ship on account of the rate of flooding of the engine room'. On the other it noted that 'insufficient attention was paid to the shutting of certain bulkhead valves [in the engine room], with the result that flooding spread to other compartments'. Though the Board of Enquiry absolved any individual of blame for the sinking, Rear-Admiral E. J. Spooner commanding the Northern Patrol noted its observation concerning the bulkhead valves and requested that three of *Transylvania*'s engineers be removed from active service. It was left to the Commander-in-Chief Home Fleet, Admiral Sir Charles Forbes, to assess the wider picture. Concerned at the loss of a third AMC in these waters in the space of two months, Forbes requested the allocation of destroyer escort to these ships in the North-Western Approaches. The Admiralty's reply was that none could be spared while England lay under threat of German invasion.

Fate of the crew

Although the damage caused by a single torpedo was sufficient to sink *Transylvania*, no lives were lost as a result of the detonation. A staggered evacuation took place from 0325 onwards which coincided with the arrival on the scene of HM destroyers *Achates*, *Fortune* and *Antelope*. However, hampered by winds that increased to gale force as the night wore on, the disembarkation soon began to take a toll of the crew. A boat containing five men was slipped prematurely, never to be seen again. Those who had been queuing for this one crowded into another, causing it to capsize in heavy seas. Yet another capsized alongside *Achates*, resulting in many being drowned or crushed against the ship's side. The last men, including Capt. Miles, were clear of the ship by 0425, shortly before she sank. The survivors were landed at Greenock early that evening.

U56 and Otto Harms

Built by Deutsche Werke in Kiel and commissioned in November 1938, *U56*'s spent her operational career as part of the 1st Flotilla based at Kiel, Wilhelmshaven and finally Lorient. A Type-IIC boat lacking the speed and manoeuvrability of the new Type VIIs that were to form the backbone of the *U-Boot-Waffe*, her offensive capabilities were further limited by a payload of just five torpedoes. This may partly explain why *U56*'s thirteen frontline patrols yielded only four sinkings, of which *Transylvania* was much the greatest success. *U56*'s profile might

Harms seen on the conning tower of *U56* in the summer of 1940. *DUBMA*

have been considerably greater had three hits on the battleship HMS *Nelson* off Cape Wrath in October 1939 not been nullified by dud torpedoes, the likely consequence of pistol failure which dogged the *U-Boot-Waffe* in the first year of the war. *U56* was withdrawn from frontline service a month after the sinking of *Transylvania*, spending the rest of the war on training duties in the Baltic. She was eventually destroyed in an Allied bombing raid over Kiel on 28 April 1945 which also claimed six of her crewmen.

Transferred from *U56* in September 1940, Harms spent the next two years assigned to training duties before being recalled to frontline duty as commander of the new *U464*. Making for Newfoundland in late August 1942, *U464* was heavily damaged by a US Catalina west of the Faroe Islands. Kptlt Harms and most of his crew were rescued by an Icelandic fishing vessel, spending the rest of the war as prisoners.

Sources

Admiralty, *Loss of HMS* Transylvania: *Board of Enquiry* (TNA, ADM 1/10889)

Hider, Lt D. J. C. [Jack], RNVR, *Recollections of Lt D. J. C. Hider* (word-processed memoirs, IWM, 97/24/1)

Arthur, Max, ed., *The Navy: 1939 to the Present Day* (London: Hodder & Stoughton, 1997)

Hampshire, A. Cecil, *The Blockaders* (London: William Kimber, 1980)

Haws, Duncan, *Anchor Line* [Merchant Fleets, no. 9] (2nd edn, Burwash, E. Sussex: TCL Publications, 1988)

Osborne, Richard, Harry Spong and Tom Grover, *Armed Merchant Cruisers, 1878–1945* (Windsor, Berks.: World Ship Society, 2007)

Poolman, Kenneth, *Armed Merchant Cruisers* (London: Leo Cooper, 1985)

16   HMS *PENZANCE*

Cdr A. J. Wavish, RN†
Sunk by *U37* (Type IXA), Kptlt Victor Oehrn, 24 August 1940
North Atlantic, 700 nm W of Islay, Inner Hebrides (Scotland)

Penzance returns to Portsmouth to pay off in May 1938 after seven years' foreign service. She was an early victim of the *U-Boot-Waffe*'s assault on the Atlantic convoy system, destroyed with much of her crew by a torpedo from *U37*. *Wright & Logan*

Theatre	North Atlantic (Map 1)	*Displacement*	1,025 tons
Coordinates	56° 16' N, 27° 19' W	*Dimensions*	266.25' × 34' × 8.75'
Kriegsmarine code	Quadrat AK 6333	*Maximum speed*	16.5 knots
U-boat timekeeping differential	+3 hours	*Armament*	2 × 4" AA; 4 × .5" AA
Fatalities 90 *Survivors* 18			

The sloops

Of destroyer size but sacrificing the speed of that type for greater endurance, the sloop was recast during the First World War to counter the threats posed to merchant shipping by mines and torpedoes, tasks for which it proved well equipped. The Royal Navy's slender provisions for convoy defence had also rested on the sloop during the inter-war period, but the onset of the German U-boat offensive

in 1940 demonstrated the pressing need for large numbers of escort vessels, something which had been foreseen before the outbreak of hostilities. Though they continued to be built, the sloop represented a lavish option at a time when sophistication counted for less than hulls in the water, and the brunt of convoy defence was therefore borne first by corvettes and escort destroyers and eventually by frigates. But for much of the war there were few ships better fitted for long-range trade defence than the sloop and thirty-eight were laid down for the Royal, Indian and Australian Navies between 1939 and the end of hostilities.

Career

Ordered under the 1928 estimates, the Hastings-class escort sloop *Penzance* was laid down at Devonport Dockyard in July 1929, launched in April 1930 and completed in January 1931. *Penzance* spent the next seven years east of Suez, serving successively in the Persian Gulf, the Red Sea and then on the Africa Station between Mombasa and Simon's Town. It was not until May 1938 that she returned to Britain, being immediately assigned to the Fishery Protection Squadron. In June 1939 she transferred to the America and West Indies Station, first at Bermuda and then at Trinidad where the outbreak of war found her on patrol and contraband control duties. Here she stayed until March 1940 when the introduction of the BHX convoys taking ships north to join the main convoy route from Halifax, Nova Scotia to Britain brought her back to Bermuda as a local escort. However, the extension of U-boat operations further west began to make 'end-to-end' convoy escort imperative, and for this purpose the Admiralty instigated a cycle of slow convoys between Nova Scotia and Britain in August 1940. Sloops were among the few ships with the requisite endurance which could be spared and it fell to HMS *Penzance* to escort the first of these, SC1.

Background of the attack

When B.d.U. learnt from *B-Dienst*, the Kriegsmarine's radio monitoring and intelligence service, of the departure of SC1 from Nova Scotia, *U37* (Kptlt Victor Oehrn) was ordered from her operational area in the Western Approaches to a position further west where it was correctly anticipated that the convoy's protection would be at a minimum. With only HMS *Penzance* for escort, SC1 sailed from Sydney, Cape Breton Island on 15 August 1940, two days before Hitler announced a policy of unrestricted submarine warfare around the British Isles. Though the convoy was intended to steam at 7½ knots, a combination of bad weather and the inability of several vessels to maintain this speed meant that by the afternoon of 24 August it was proceeding at barely 6½ knots. That evening the convoy began zigzagging and the number of lookouts in *Penzance* was increased with a view to bringing her to an optimum state of readiness by the time she passed into the anticipated danger zone at longitude 20 degrees West on the 27th. But danger lay much closer at hand than Cdr Wavish or any on the British side suspected. With its new bases on the Atlantic coast the *U-Boot-Waffe* was now ranging much further into the Atlantic and barely half an hour after commencing her zigzag *Penzance* was in *U37*'s sights. At 1735 *Penzance*, then steaming ahead of the convoy at eight knots, had just completed a leg of her zigzag when the port lookout shouted 'Torpedo in sight bearing 125°!'

War Diary of *U37*, patrol of 17–30 August 1940: PG 30034, NHB, reel 1,062, pp. 632–4

Date, time	Details of position, wind, weather, sea, light, visibility, moonlight, etc.	Incidents
24.viii		
1600	Qu. AK 6312, wind NW 4, sea 3–4, cloud 3	
1905		Large tanker in sight on the starboard bow, inclination 40°, proceeding at high speed. Boat has difficulty maintaining visual contact.
1920		A number of smoke plumes to port.
1936		Boat has to dive because there is nowhere for it to go. Convoy is fine on the port bow so manoeuvring into advance position presents no problem. Three columns about 1,100 m apart comprising some 30 medium-sized steamers with just the odd one of about 8,000 tons. A single destroyer ahead, otherwise no escorts in sight.[1] Convoy initially steers course of 90°, then 40°. Boat now positioned immediately
2000	Qu. AK 6333	ahead and likely to penetrate between the centre and left-hand columns. Destroyer moves back and forth at either medium or slow speed, her inclination changing all the while. Several times she bears straight towards me, remaining at 0° inclination for 600–800 m before turning away. A few seconds of tension – is she turning again, is she yawing, has she got a fix on us? I'm ready to fire and ready to dive.
2038		Her inclination widens; she's turning further away. I fire from 380 m. A hit aft, in the after third of the ship.[2] She is literally rent asunder and sinks before the pall of smoke has time to clear. The crew give full vent to their jubilation, almost forcing me to lash out to restore order. Then I have a look round with the periscope and see that the boat is well positioned to penetrate the convoy – the forward steamers are now at a bearing of 60–70°, but still some 1,200 m away.
2046		Just as I'm looking for the easiest and choicest targets we suddenly hear the sound of a violent detonation somewhere nearby. I make a full 360° sweep – nothing. I assume it must have been one of the destroyer's depth charges, of which she no doubt had several primed on deck, and am able to announce 'no danger to the boat'.

---

1 HM sloop *Penzance*.
2 The torpedo in fact struck her amidships.

Date, time   *Details of position, wind,*
            weather, sea, light,
            visibility, moonlight, etc.   *Incidents*

But I decide to dive to 30 m all the same, if only for a short period. However unlikely it may seem, I can't rule out an aircraft attack.[3] Suddenly at 25 m, just as I am descending and almost down the ladder, there are crashing and splintering sounds all around us. The lights go partially out. In the control room water is spurting and hissing, the boat becomes heavy at the bows, the tower watch descend and make their report: water is entering, there must be leaks, and as a precaution they have evacuated the tower. All manometers and display instruments have stopped working with the exception of the manometers and the Papenberg in the control room.[4] The forward hydroplane is jammed in full dive position. Boat becomes 25° bow heavy. The noise of spurting water is so great that we have to shout to make ourselves heard. The ear gets no sense of increasing pressure, however, and I receive no reports of serious flooding.[5]

These are seconds of the greatest physical tension; the realisation that in the next few moments the most rapid decisions may be required consumes me completely. I'm standing in the control room trying to get an overview of the situation. Everyone is at their allotted station, mucking in, doing their bit and keeping their mouths firmly shut. Precise reports emerge from both bow and stern compartments.

The crew may have been dependent on me up until now but now it's my turn to depend on them. Gradually the spurting and hissing subsides. The boat rights herself. Calm spreads to every corner. The impact was not as severe as that produced by the aerial bomb north of Scotland, but it had a commensurately greater effect in terms of damage to glass and display instruments.[6]

What most impressed me though was the attitude of my crew. I can only describe them as having been unfazed by it all, with no one having lost his nerve.

I think it must have been aerial bombs.

The convoy steams over us and away while we get the boat back into reasonable working order.

---

3   Despite Oehrn's suspicion of air attack, there can be little doubt that the damage was owed to the heavy explosion that followed the sinking of *Penzance*'s stern section, probably as a result of depth charges detonating. In any event, *U37*'s experience illustrates the risks run by U-boats in attacking warships at short range.
4   The manometers were pressure gauges displaying the boat's depth at any given time. One of these, the Papenberg beside the hydroplane controls in the control room, was used for maintaining the boat at periscope depth.
5   Any serious rupture would cause the pressure inside the U-boat to rise sharply, with marked effects on the eardrums.
6   During her previous patrol in early August 1940, *U37* had come under aerial attack about fifty miles north-west of Westray in the Orkneys while in transit from Wilhelmshaven to her new base at Lorient.

The sinking

Hearing the port lookout's warning, the Officer of the Watch, Lt J. W. Draisley, immediately ordered *Penzance* hard astarboard and full speed ahead. But it was too late. *U37*'s torpedo struck her on the port side abreast the foremast, the resulting explosion 'splitting the ship in two'. On the starboard side aft Sub-Lt D. G. Boyle instinctively grabbed the deck rail as the torpedo detonated, surviving a 'terrific explosion as flames and smoke shot up in the air round the bridge'. *Penzance* immediately heeled to starboard, her back broken by the force of the explosion and what appears to have been the detonation of the forward magazine. She seems then to have capsized to starboard though none of the few survivors whose accounts are available formed any clear impression of what happened next. The general consensus is expressed in a joint report by two of *Penzance*'s officers: 'The ship rapidly turned turtle, the bows and stern coming up in the air, and the 'midships section, where she had been hit, going down. The bow section disappeared first and then the stern, the latter probably sinking about five minutes after the torpedo had struck the ship.' The disappearance of the stern section was followed by a number of heavy underwater

detonations, probably *Penzance*'s inventory of depth charges which, as Oehrn's log relates, came close to accounting for her assailant.

Fate of the crew

The manner in which *Penzance* met her end ensured that none survived below decks. Those on the bridge who lived to record their experiences were all blown clear of the ship. Lt Draisley, the ranking survivor, lost consciousness as a result of the explosion, to have it restored by the shock of cold water after being pitched into the ocean a hundred yards from his ship. The other survivors were those like Sub-Lt Boyle who had been on deck when the torpedo struck and were able to get clear as she capsized, the ship still under way on one propeller; as Boyle recalled, 'the screws were still turning, and the port one being, of course, in the air and the starboard one taking the ship forward still and away from me'. Depleted by the same underwater explosions that damaged *U37*, only nineteen members of *Penzance*'s ship's company survived to be picked up by SSs *Fylingdale* and *Blairmore* over the next few hours. One, Paymaster Sub-Lt R. A. S. MacDonald, died in *Fylingdale* and was committed to the deep in position 57° 55' N, 14°

Oehrn (right), then on Dönitz's staff at B.d.U., seen with Korvkpt. Viktor Schütze of *U103* at Lorient in October 1940. *DUBMA*

U37 and Victor Oehrn

The first of the larger Type-IXA boats, *U37* was commissioned in August 1938 and had a brisk start to the war, sinking six ships on her first offensive patrol in October 1939 under Korvkpt. Werner Hartmann. Her profile was to rise yet further following Operation HARTMUT when faulty torpedoes caused Dönitz to recall the U-boats after they had failed to register a single success in no fewer than forty attacks on Allied warships and transports off Norway. With the morale of senior commanders at rock bottom, in May 1940 Dönitz turned to his senior staff officer, Victor Oehrn, for a confidence-boosting patrol to demonstrate that success was still possible. Retrained and given command of the modern *U37* with a seasoned crew, Oehrn sank ten ships and damaged another at a time when his and Wolfgang Lüth's *U9* (see **6**) were the only U-boats at sea. The German propaganda machine went into full swing on his return, making much of 'the most successful U-boat patrol ever' which earned its author the Iron Cross First Class. Oehrn commanded *U37* for another three patrols, sinking *Penzance* on the second of these and receiving the Knight's Cross before being succeeded by his First Watch Officer, Nicolai Clausen, in October 1940. For the rest of *U37*'s career, see NF *Sfax* (**21**).

Victor Oehrn went on to serve on the staff of B.d.U., being promoted Korvettenkapitän in September 1941 and then appointed *F.d.U. Italien* (Officer Commanding U-Boats, Italy) in November. His service was interrupted by a spell as a prisoner of the British on the Suez Canal after being badly wounded and then captured in North Africa in July 1942. After several weeks starving himself to present the picture of a man at death's door Oehrn managed to secure release as part of a prisoner-exchange programme in November 1943. Promoted Fregattenkapitän in May 1944, he served out the war in a succession of staff appointments. However, Victor Oehrn is also remembered for an incident the day before *Penzance* was lost, 23 August 1940. This was the sinking of the British freighter *Severn Leigh* which Oehrn torpedoed and then finished off with *U37*'s deck gun in circumstances which prompted post-war accusations that he was a war criminal. He died in December 1997 at the age of ninety.

55′ W on the 29th. The rest required treatment for an assortment of broken bones, shock, burns, scalding and exposure. Provided with a thousand cigarettes from HMS *Highlander* to assist their recovery, they were landed at Lough Foyle without further incident on the 30th. However, for the seven crewmen picked up by the *Blairmore* the ordeal was not yet over. Five hours after the sinking of *Penzance*, *Blairmore* was herself torpedoed by a reinvigorated *U37* which had little difficulty in catching up with the plodding SC1 once she had surfaced and repaired her damage. The Swedish MS *Eknaren* picked up the remnant of *Blairmore*'s crew together with all seven *Penzance* men the following afternoon, the survivors eventually landed at Baltimore. Those lost in *Penzance* are commemorated on memorials in St George's Church, Chatham, and Port-of-Spain Cathedral, Trinidad.

Sources

Admiralty, *Torpedo Attacks on HM and Merchant Ships, 1939–1941* (TNA, ADM 199/157)

Oehrn, Victor, *Navigare Necesse Est: Der 2. Weltkrieg September 1939–November 1943: Meine Wege durch das Leben* (typescript memoirs, DUBMA)

Hague, Arnold, *Sloops: A History of the 71 Sloops Built in Britain and Australia for the British, Australian and Indian Navies, 1926–1946* (Kendal, Cumbria: World Ship Society, 1993)

Roskill, *War at Sea*, I, pp. 343–5

Vause, Jordan, *Wolf: U-Boat Commanders in World War II* (Annapolis, Md.: Naval Institute Press, 1997)

—, 'Victor Oehrn: The Ace with No Name' in Theodore P. Savas, ed., *Silent Hunters: German U-Boat Commanders of World War II* (Annapolis, Md.: Naval Institute Press, 2003), pp. 109–35

War career of HMS *Penzance*:
http://www.naval-history.net/xGM-Chrono-18SL-Penzance.htm

17 HMS (ex MS) *DUNVEGAN CASTLE*

Capt. H. Ardill, RN Ret'd
Sunk by *U46* (Type VIIB), Oblt.z.S. Engelbert Endrass, 27–28 August 1940
North Atlantic, 60 nm NW of Erris Head, Mayo (Ireland)

The motor liner *Dunvegan Castle* of the Union-Castle Mail Steamship Co. seen under way shortly before the war. Three torpedoes from Endrass ended her brief career. *Real Photographs*

Theatre	North Atlantic (Map 2)	*Deadweight*	10,489 tons
Coordinates	55° 05' N, 11° 00' W	*Gross tons*	15,007
Kriegsmarine code (TR)	Quadrat AM 5482	*Dimensions*	560' × 72' × 28.25'
U-boat timekeeping differential	–1 hour	*Maximum speed*	14.5 knots
Fatalities 27	*Survivors* 277	*Armament*	7 × 6"; 2 × 3" AA

Career

For background on the armed merchant cruisers, see HMS *Carinthia* (8).

Ordered for the Union-Castle Mail Steamship Co., the liner *Dunvegan Castle* was laid down at Harland & Wolff of Belfast and launched in March 1936, being completed in August that same year. Powered with diesel engines, she was designed for the Round-Africa service on which she served for the duration of her peacetime career. In September 1939 *Dunvegan Castle* was requisitioned by the Royal Navy and, like her sister *Dunnottar Castle*, taken in hand for refitting as an armed merchant cruiser at the same yard in which each had been built. This completed, in December she was assigned first to the South Atlantic and then to the West Africa Station based on Freetown, Sierra Leone where she remained on convoy escort duty until engine defects

required her to return to Belfast for repairs in August 1940.

Background of the attack

On 11 August *Dunvegan Castle* sailed from Freetown with the Liverpool-bound convoy SL43, escorting it as far as the Western Approaches before proceeding independently for Belfast. Dusk on the 27th found her approaching Bloody Foreland on the north-west coast of Ireland, zigzagging and maintaining her best speed of 14½ knots. Patrolling these waters after an uneventful week in the Atlantic was *U46* which caught sight of her in the fading hours of daylight, Oblt.z.S. Engelbert Endrass finding the ideal opportunity to close her on the surface and make his attack under cover of night.

War Diary of *U46*, patrol of 8 August–6 September 1940: PG 30043a, NHB, reel 1,064, pp. 160–1

Date, time	Details of position, wind, weather, sea, light, visibility, moonlight, etc.	Incidents
27.viii		
1600	Qu. AM 4637	Cruising speed.
1908	Qu. AM 5447	
		A steamer in sight on the starboard beam. Her mean course is between 70° and 90° with strong zigzags up to 80°. She is cruising at high speed (15–16 knots).[1]
		We haul ahead of her. Now that dusk is falling we can close her. Enemy is a large passenger liner, light

---

1 *Dunvegan Castle*'s speed as reported to the Board of Enquiry was 14½ knots.

[Qu. AM 5482][3]

grey, 15–20,000 tons, armed, presumably an auxiliary cruiser.[2] Even though she's sailing very fast her extreme zigzags make it easy for us to stay ahead of her. As night begins to fall enemy reduces speed, the very powerful sea phosphorescence making her bow wave and stern wash as clear as shadows. We prepare to attack. Right up until we fire there's a dilemma as to whether we opt for a bow or stern shot – enemy is zigzagging wildly, and in short bursts. Single torpedo fired at 2147, range 400 m, detonates abreast after end of the bridge.[4] No noticeable effect, enemy sails slowly on, starts circling. I prepare for second attack but dive as we think we see enemy manning his guns. Submerged we can see nothing. We retire and surface 10 minutes later. Enemy astern of us, and apparently still under way, circling. At 2212 we make another surface attack, a single torpedo which hits abreast the engine room.[5] We look on in anticipation of what will happen next. Nothing to be seen but we are suddenly fired upon, so alarm dive.[6] We retire under water for half an hour then resurface. Enemy is now stopped but seems to be holding up relatively well. Again we approach and fire a third torpedo at 2251 which hits forward of the bridge.[7] Enemy now ablaze, settling rather deeper in the water and well down by the stern. She must have had enough now – even the stoutest vessel can't take three torpedoes and a fire on board for very long. As we sail off we observe a series of further detonations for two whole hours afterwards, some of them extremely powerful.[8] In appearance this ship looked very much like the *Strathmore*, which is also grey or white; however, whether or not this was our victim could not be established with certainty.[9] The following day the British Admiralty announces the sinking by a U-boat of the auxiliary cruiser *Dunvegan Castle* (15,007 GRT) by radio. I take it that this must have been the auxiliary cruiser we sank.

2300	Qu. AM 5485	Set course 200°.
2400	Qu. AM 5721	Cruising speed.

Endraß

---

2   As Endrass notes lower down, *Dunvegan Castle* was of 15,007 GRT. Having served on the South Atlantic station she was presumably painted in Admiralty light grey (AP507C) or medium grey (AP507B) rather than the much darker hue of AP507A (Home Fleet dark grey) used in northern waters.

3   This quadrant does not appear in the log itself but is provided in Endrass's torpedo report.

4   The timing of the torpedo is significant. Despite Endrass's observation in the preceding sentence Capt. Ardill had ordered *Dunvegan Castle* to cease zigzagging at 2240 (2140 log time).

5   The torpedo report states this to have been fired from a range of 800 metres.

6   Though her guns were manned there is no record of *Dunvegan Castle* firing on *U46* at any stage.

7   The torpedo report states this to have been fired from a range of 2,500 metres.

8   Endrass's torpedo report estimated that *U46* could still discern these explosions at a range of twenty miles.

9   Though larger, the P&O liner RMS *Strathmore* (23,428 GRT), converted for trooping in March 1940, did indeed bear a close resemblance to *Dunvegan Castle*. The wording of this sentence suggests that *Strathmore* had been Endrass's original identification, corrected on the 28th by the Admiralty's announcement.

The sinking

Endrass's first torpedo, which struck *Dunvegan Castle* at 2250 British time (2150 German time), detonated abreast the refrigerator and generating rooms, stopping the engines and cutting all power in the ship. Though the emergency generator restored power for lights, pumps and steering, there was no restarting the main engines and a distress signal was sent out to this effect. *U46* had meanwhile been sighted about a quarter of a mile to starboard but the activity on the gun platforms was spotted by Endrass's lookouts and he immediately dived. However, he need not have worried since *Dunvegan Castle*'s gun crews could not in any case bring their weapons to bear. Lookouts in *Dunvegan Castle* sighted the track of Endrass's second torpedo twenty-five minutes after the first but Capt. Ardill, his ship virtually dead in the water, could do nothing to avoid a hit in the engine room. With *Dunvegan Castle* now little more than a sitting target Ardill had no choice but to pass the order to abandon ship. This process was almost complete when *U46*'s third torpedo struck just abaft the engine room half an hour later, causing an explosion so powerful that Ardill later informed the Board of Enquiry that he believed it to have been caused by two torpedoes. The dozen men still on board were unable to lower the last undamaged boat, which had slipped in its davits and was hanging at an extreme angle. With all others either destroyed or heavily laden they spent an anxious hour struggling to release it, mindful not only of the possibility of further attack but that the inferno raging aboard had prevented the magazines being flooded. Eventually the boat's falls were slipped and the men got clear just as diesel spewing from the ship began to ignite. After a series of explosions caused by the detonation of her magazines and depth charges over the next four or five hours (recorded by Endrass in his war diary), *Dunvegan Castle* disappeared at 0555 British time.

The Board of Enquiry absolved Capt. Ardill and his officers of any blame but observed that zigzagging should not have ceased after nightfall in view of the ship's low maximum speed. Unlike the armed merchant cruisers sunk earlier that summer, *Dunvegan Castle* was fully stowed with 23,225 steel drums, 2,700 wooden barrels and 440 tons of timber. These could not save her from three torpedoes, but the extra ballast fitted in this and other AMCs during 1940 required U-boat commanders to expend many more torpedoes in order to make good their attacks, as Otto Kretschmer was to discover against HMSs *Laurentic*, *Patroclus* and *Forfar* (**19** and **20**) later that year. Although

Endrass (in white cap) receiving the Knight's Cross on reaching Lorient in *U46* on 6 September 1940, nine days after the sinking of *Dunvegan Castle*.
DUBMA

this was not the case with *Dunvegan Castle*, her loss prompted the Commander-in-Chief Western Approaches, Admiral Sir Martin Dunbar-Nasmith VC, to suggest that Liverpool-bound AMCs remain in convoy until past the Mull of Kintyre and that outgoing ships be escorted whenever possible. In this he was echoing recommendations made by Admiral Sir Charles Forbes (Commander-in-Chief Home Fleet) after the loss of HMS *Transylvania* (**15**) that AMCs be provided with destroyer escorts in the North-Western Approaches. As earlier, the threat of German invasion kept any would-be escorts far to the south until the danger had passed, which it had by October.

Fate of the crew

Neither Capt. Ardill's report nor the records of the Board of Enquiry elaborate on how *Dunvegan Castle*'s twenty-seven fatalities were incurred, though all but three are listed as Missing, Presumed Killed, a clear indication that the manner of their death was not established. The fire and smoke produced by the second and third torpedoes prevented a complete search of the ship being made and it is quite probable that several men perished as a result of these explosions in addition to the three known to have done so. However, the majority of casualties were suffered after the order was passed to abandon ship at about 2315 on the 27th. This process was carried out over the next half hour but at least two rafts were overloaded to the point of being submerged and a number of men rescued later were taken directly from the water. In a follow-up letter to the Admiralty Ardill rued the inability of the boats

and rafts to keep together despite instructions to do so and it seems that some rafts were never found. The appearance of bodies on the shores of Aran (Co. Galway) some time later lends support to this, the remains being interred in the island graveyard. The 277 survivors were rescued from 0330 on 28 August by HM corvette *Primrose* (181 survivors) and HM destroyer *Harvester* (96 survivors; see **G49**), to be landed later that day at Gourock Pier on the Clyde.

U46 and Engelbert Endrass

For details of *U46*'s and Endrass's early career, see HMS *Carinthia* (**8**).

For a year following the sinking of the *Dunvegan Castle U46* continued to operate successfully under Endrass, destroying a further sixteen ships and earning him the Knight's Cross to which the Oak Leaves were added in June 1941. However, neither Endrass nor *U46* went on to greater things when they parted company that September. Already promoted Kapitänleutnant, Endrass was appointed in command of *U567* in which he was lost together with his entire crew while attacking convoy HG76 off the Azores in December 1941; see HMS *Audacity* (**43**). Having successfully attacked the Norwegian freighter SS *Annavore*, *U567* was located and sunk on the 21st by depth charges from HM sloop *Deptford* and HM corvette *Samphire* (**X2**).

After Endrass's departure *U46* was used first as a training boat and then as a moored practice torpedo-firing vessel before being scuttled at Kupfermühlen Bay, an inlet on the Baltic coast of Schleswig-Holstein, in May 1945.

Sources

Admiralty, *Loss of HMS* Dunvegan Castle: *Board of Enquiry* (TNA, ADM 1/10812)

—, *Torpedo Attacks on HM and Merchant Ships, 12/9/39–1/12/40* (TNA, ADM 199/957)

Haws, Duncan, *Union, Castle & Union-Castle Lines* [Merchant Fleets, no. 18] (Hereford, Hereford and Worcester: TCL Publications, 1990)

Newall, Peter, *Union-Castle Line: A Fleet History* (London: Carmania Press, 1999)

Osborne, Richard, Harry Spong and Tom Grover, *Armed Merchant Cruisers, 1878–1945* (Windsor, Berks.: World Ship Society, 2007)

Poolman, Kenneth, *Armed Merchant Cruisers* (London: Leo Cooper, 1985)

Topp, Erich, 'In Memoriam Engelbert Endrass: Castor mourns Pollux' in Theodore P. Savas, ed., *Silent Hunters: German U-Boat Commanders of World War II* (Annapolis, Md.: Naval Institute Press, 2003), pp. 1–17

Webpage devoted to sinking of HMS *Dunvegan Castle* and Sub-Lt John Sidney Brew (survivor):
http://brew.clients.ch/JohnDunC.htm
also on:
http://ubootwaffe.net/articles/dunvegancastle.html

18   HMS *DUNDEE*

Capt. O. M. F. Stokes, RNR
Sunk by *U48* (Type VIIB), Kptlt Heinrich Bleichrodt, 14–15 September 1940
North Atlantic, 265 nm W of Tiree, Inner Hebrides (Scotland)

Dundee returns to Portsmouth from the America and West Indies Station to pay off in March 1938.
She was another early casualty of the German campaign against the Atlantic convoy system. *Wright & Logan*

Theatre   North Atlantic (Map 2)
Coordinates (of attack)   56° 50' N, 15° 04' W
Kriegsmarine code (of attack)   Quadrat AM 1998
U-boat timekeeping differential   +2 hours
Fatalities   12   *Survivors*   110

Displacement   1,060 tons
Dimensions   281.25' × 35' × 8.25'
Maximum speed   16.5 knots
Armament   2 × 4" AA; 4 × .5" AA

Career

For notes on the sloop type, see HMS *Penzance* (**16**).

Ordered under the 1930 estimates as a unit of the Falmouth class, the escort sloop HMS *Dundee* was laid down at Chatham Dockyard on 1 December 1931, launched in September 1932 and completed in March 1933. Practically her entire career was spent on the America and West Indies Station based on Bermuda and eventually Trinidad, from where she was operating on the outbreak of hostilities. The first months of the war were given over to patrol duties from Trinidad before she was taken in hand for refitting at Bermuda in July 1940. In August the Admiralty introduced a cycle of slow convoys between Sydney, Cape Breton Island and Britain, the first of which claimed *Dundee*'s near-sister *Penzance* (**16**) on the 24th. It was to join the third of these, SC3, that *Dundee* sailed from Bermuda on 27 August.

Background of the attack

On 8 September *U48* left Lorient to take up a position on the anticipated route of the SC convoys that had begun crossing the Atlantic from Nova Scotia the previous month. Sailing under Kptlt Heinrich Bleichrodt for the first time, *U48* encountered SC3 north-west of Ireland after nightfall on the 15th and soon acquired a highly favourable attacking position on the port bow of the convoy. Bleichrodt's task was made easier by the slow speed of his quarry, the SC convoys being limited to eight knots – considerably less than their HX counterparts – and on this occasion SC3 was making no more than seven knots. The convoy, which had sailed from Sydney on 2 September with *Dundee* as its sole initial escort, was reinforced on the 7th by HM destroyers *Wanderer* and *Witch*, and late on the 14th by the Canadian destroyer *St Laurent*. A few hours after *St Laurent*'s arrival Bleichrodt began his assault on the convoy with an attack on HMS *Dundee*, then zigzagging irregularly some six cables (1,200 yards) ahead of the starboard columns of the convoy.

War Diary of *U48*, patrol of 8–25 September 1940: PG 30045b, NHB, reel 1,065, pp. 42–3

Date, time	Details of position, wind, weather, sea, light, visibility, moonlight, etc.	Incidents
14.ix		
2000	NW of Ireland, wind WNW 6, sea 5, overcast, good visibility	Position: Qu. AM 1976
2020		Convoy in sight, course 90°–100°, speed approx. seven knots. We haul ahead, ensuring that we remain on the side where the moon won't give us away. A single gunboat appears to be the sum total of convoy's escort so far.[1]
2357		Outgoing W/T transmission: *Convoy in sight AM 1955, course 90°. Speed 8 knots.*
2400	NW of Ireland, wind WNW 3, sea 3, cloudy but clear, very good visibility, bright full moon, minimal swell	Position: Qu. AM 1994, bottom right corner.

Bleichrodt |
| **15.ix** | | |
| 0024 | | Position: Qu. AM 1998.
Torpedo fired from Tube I at two overlapping steamers. A hit after 215 sec. running time on the outermost vessel, size about 5,000 tons.[2] Vessel engulfed in a huge pall of smoke from the detonation. Approximately eight seconds later another powerful detonation, presumably depth charges going up. |
| 0026 | [Data crossed out here; illegible] | As I turn I fire a G7a from Tube IV, again at a column of overlapping vessels. A detonation after 230 sec. running time.[3] Vessel size 5,000 tons.[4] After firing I turn ahead to keep pace with the convoy. I now see that the escort includes an additional three destroyers.[5] |
| 0123 | | Position: Qu. AM 1998 bottom right corner.
Torpedo fired from Tube I at a steamer from the front column.[6] Again a detonation against a ship on the other side. Running time 155 sec., size of vessel 6,000 tons.[7] Sinking clearly observed. |
| 0124 | | Torpedo fired from Tube II. A miss. The convoy is turning towards us now, assuming we are on the other side.
On the 600-m wave we pick up radio traffic being exchanged between ships in the convoy. (Warning of a U-boat on the surface, etc.) |
| 0300 | | Torpedo fired from Tube II at one of the leading ships in the convoy. Detonates after 135 sec. running time, 40 m from the stern. Torpedo breaches the surface on a number of occasions. Size of steamer 7,000 tons.[8] The stern of the ship is already awash within the space of about a minute.
After this shot we close on a vessel in the middle of the column, but she opens fire with her deck gun as we come within range.
I turn away and alter course to that of the convoy to keep pace with it. The three destroyers that make up the convoy's escort have now switched over to this side and are cruising back and forth at high speed. No sign of the gunboat. |
| 0312 | | Outgoing W/T transmission: *Scattered convoy, Qu. AM 1998.* |
| 0350 | | Outgoing W/T transmission: *Convoy scattered, Qu. AM 0174, general course 100°.* |

---

1   Almost certainly HMS *Dundee*, the only escort in an advance position at this point. This and all subsequent torpedoes were fired by *U48*'s I.WO (First Watch Officer), Oblt.z.S. Reinhard Suhren (see **31**).

2   HMS *Dundee*, which was the first victim of the night. The torpedo running time equates to 3,200 m. Bleichrodt is mistaken both as to the size of the vessel and the speed of her demise, though the error may be owed to his attention having been diverted to another target. However, the succession of detonations he records is strikingly similar to those recalled in *Dundee*.

3   The torpedo running time suggests a range of 3,400 m.

4   Though a case could be made for this being the actual attack on *Dundee* there is no record of any other ship in SC3 being struck at this time, and the claim more nearly equates to the second detonation in *Dundee* following the torpedo hit two minutes earlier.

5   These were HMSs *Witch* and *Wanderer*, respectively two miles on the starboard and port beams of the rearmost ships of SC3's outer columns, and the newly joined HMCS *St Laurent*, which was two miles off the port beam of the leading ship in the port column.

6   By 'column' Bleichrodt probably means 'row'.

7   SS *Alexandros*, 4,343 GRT.

8   SS *Empire Volunteer*, 5,319 GRT.

0510	Bright moonlight	As moon is about to be hidden behind a thick bank of cloud I look to get ahead of the convoy and transfer to the other side.
0528		As we are switching sides the front sweeper stationed at the head of the convoy suddenly bears down on us at high speed. He must have picked up a hydrophone bearing or seen our wake in the bright moonlight. We dive as there's no chance of a surface escape.
		Estimated range when we dive still about 2,000 m.
1050		Surfaced.

The sinking

U48's torpedo was recalled by Capt. Stokes as having struck *Dundee* at 2234 (though other British sources suggest this may have been as early as 2228), the explosion being followed by two further detonations within a matter of seconds. The effect was to wreck the after part of the ship as far forward as the mainmast, which was itself demolished. Years later Able Seaman R. J. Morry recalled the scene:

> Making my way along the deck aft to the action station, I saw there was nothing aft of the main mast but a tangled mess of mangled, twisted and smoking steel. The stern of the ship was gone, along with the Officer's [*sic*] Quarters, including personnel.

Steam supply was ordered to be cut and the main engines stopped, though the engine room remained dry and 'the after bulkhead was holding'. However, a preliminary inspection below decks concluded that *Dundee* would not remain buoyant for very much longer. With Capt. Stokes suffering from a dislocated shoulder, the decision to abandon ship was made by the ranking uninjured officer, Commissioned Gunner Oak, though he did so with Stokes's approval. All boats and rafts were safely away by 2315, but as the night wore on and help arrived in the shape of the destroyers *Wanderer* and *St Laurent* it became apparent that *Dundee* had been prematurely abandoned. On reboarding at 0325 on the 15th it was found that the after engine room bulkhead was holding and that there was only two to three feet of water in the engine room itself. As *Dundee* showed no sign of settling further she was taken in tow by *St Laurent* at 0535. This proved disastrous, however, the ship assuming a 'crab-wise' progress with her bows deviating twenty degrees to starboard and her reserve of buoyancy fatally compromised. By 1000 she was settling by the stern and the effort had to be abandoned. *Dundee* eventually sank at 1300 in position 56° 45' N, 14° 40' W.

The Board of Enquiry took a highly critical view of the matter, censuring both Capt. Stokes and Gunner Oak for their premature decision to abandon ship. It further criticised the boarding party for not exploring the option of bringing the steam-driven pumping plant into operation, whose capacity of eighty tons per hour was noted by the Board. Had such a course of action been taken, the Board found, 'the ship would, so far as can be determined, have continued to float'. The commander of the *St Laurent* also received criticism for having 'assumed too readily that *Dundee* would keep afloat' under tow, and not exploring the pumping option.

Fate of the crew

The initial and secondary detonations took a heavy toll of *Dundee*'s officers in their cabins aft. The injured Capt. Stokes apart, this left a sub-lieutenant and the Officer of the Watch, Commissioned Gunner Oak, as the sole survivors of the wardroom. Once the order to abandon ship had been passed the crew made it into the boats and rafts, all of which were successfully lowered apart from the motor boat. Not all proved seaworthy, however, including an overladen skiff which soon foundered leaving its occupants to fend for themselves in the water. However, there are no reports of fatalities in the two hours it took for the work of rescue to be carried out, though as AB Morry recalled further tribulations awaited before deliverance came in the shape of four ships:

> I decided to swim along at my own speed, and as the pickup ship was going in circles I felt sure it would close in on me. Some time after making this decision I suddenly found myself hanging grimly to the bottom step of a 'Jacob's Ladder'. Every time the ship rolled I would find myself swinging in the air and as she rolled back I would be doused under the surface. Just to my left, at a distance of twenty feet, was the top of the propeller blade, turning very slowly, resulting in me increasing my grip on the ladder. After making some progress in ascending the ladder, I was suddenly grasped by a large hand and bodily lifted over the ship's rail and dumped unceremoniously on the steel deck.

The rescuing ships were SS *Fido* (which picked up 41 men) and the Norwegian steamers *Granli* (20) and *Vigsnes* (6), together with HMS *Wanderer* (43) in which all 110 survivors were gathered before they were landed in Northern Ireland.

Capt. Stokes was transferred to administrative duties with the recommendation that he should not be given another seagoing command. Responding to the findings, Stokes requested that the Board refrain from censuring Gunner Oak as the decision to abandon ship had been made with his acquiescence and thus remained his responsibility. Given that the Board recorded that he was 'in extreme pain, and clearly exhausted' throughout the whole affair, and deprived of his key officers who were killed in the initial blast, this gesture is perhaps worthy of note. *Dundee*'s lost crewmen are remembered in the Scottish National War Memorial in Edinburgh Castle.

U48 and Heinrich Bleichrodt

Built by Germaniawerft at Kiel and commissioned in April 1939, *U48* was one of the first Type-VIIB submarines to enter service. As part of the 7th Flotilla she became the most successful U-boat of the war, sinking over fifty ships for a total in excess of 300,000 GRT. The lion's share of these was achieved under the command of Kptlt Herbert Schultze (September 1939–May 1940 and December 1940–July 1941), but both Korvkpt. Hans Rudolf Rösing and Kptlt Heinrich Bleichrodt earned Knight's Crosses following brief spells in command.

'Ajax' Bleichrodt, previously Wilhelm Rollmann's First Watch Officer in *U34* (see **13** and **14**), could hardly have dreamt that his maiden patrol in *U48* would be crowned with such outstanding success. HMS *Dundee* was one of eight ships sunk (including three other vessels from convoy SC3) with a ninth damaged by the time *U48* reached Lorient on

Bleichrodt seen wearing the Knight's Cross with Oak Leaves he was awarded in September 1942. *DUBMA*

25 September. Though Bleichrodt ended the war in command of the 22nd Flotilla having added the Oak Leaves to his Knight's Cross, his career as a frontline commander was not unblemished. Appointed in command of *U109* in June 1941, Bleichrodt's final patrol of December 1942–January 1943 had to be abandoned after he suffered a mental breakdown. In 1945 he was detained on a charge of war crimes for his attack on the liner *City of Benares*, which went down on 13 September

1940 with the loss of 245 passengers and crew including seventy-seven child evacuees. However, no evidence could be adduced to support the allegation that Bleichrodt, then in command of *U48*, had been given secret orders to sink the ship because of the number of Jewish passengers embarked and the case never went to trial. He died in January 1977.

U48 had the fortune to be withdrawn from frontline duty in the summer of 1941 long before the odds turned irrevocably against the *U-Boot-Waffe*. After two years on training duties she was decommissioned in October 1943 and scuttled at Neustadt on the German Baltic coast in May 1945.

Sources

Admiralty, *Loss of HMS* Dundee *as the Result of Enemy Submarine Attack: Board of Enquiry* (TNA, ADM 178/250)

—, Anti-Submarine Warfare Division, *Analysis of Attacks by a U-boat on Convoy SC3, 14th–18th September 1940* (TNA, ADM 199/1976)

Morry, AB R. J., memoirs (typescript, IWM, 05/6/1)

Barker, Ralph, *Children of the* Benares: *A War Crime and its Victims* (London: Methuen, 1987)

Brustat-Naval, Fritz, and Teddy Suhren, *Nasses Eichenlaub: Als Kommandant und F.d.U. im U-Boot-Krieg* (Hamburg: Koehler, 1998)

Hague, Arnold, *Sloops: A History of the 71 Sloops Built in Britain and Australia for the British, Australian and Indian Navies, 1926–1946* (Kendal, Cumbria: World Ship Society, 1993)

Hirschfeld, Wolfgang, and Geoffrey Brooks, *Hirschfeld: The Story of a U-Boat NCO, 1940–1946* (London: Leo Cooper, 1996)

Köhler, Kapt.z.S. Otto, 'In Memoriam Heinrich Bleichrodt: Das Leben eines Seemannes und Soldaten' in *Deutsches Soldatenjahrbuch, 1978* (Munich: Schild Verlag, 1977), pp. 323 ff

War career of HMS *Dundee*:
   http://www.naval-history.net/xGM-Chrono-18SL-Dundee.htm

Website concerning rescue of survivors of HMS *Dundee* and SS *Empire Volunteer*:
   http://www.warsailors.com/singleships/granli2.html

19   HMS (ex SS) *LAURENTIC* and HMS (ex SS) *PATROCLUS*

Capt. E. P. Vivian, RN Ret'd and Capt. G. C. Wynter, DSO RN Ret'd†
Sunk by *U99* (Type VIIB), Kptlt Otto Kretschmer, 3–4 November 1940
North Atlantic, 160 nm W of Slyne Head, Galway (Ireland)

Theatre   North Atlantic (Map 2)
Coordinates   53° 53' N, 14° 40' W
Kriegsmarine code   Quadrat AM 4796
U-boat timekeeping differential   +1 hour
Laurentic   *Fatalities*   51   *Survivors*   367
Patroclus   *Fatalities*   56   *Survivors*   230

Laurentic
Deadweight   11,710 tons
Gross tons   18,724
Dimensions   603' × 75.5' × 29.25'
Maximum speed   16.5 knots
Armament   7 × 5.5"; 3 × 4" AA; 4 × .303" AA

Patroclus
Deadweight   11,405 tons
Gross tons   11,314
Dimensions   517.75' × 62.25' × 30.75'
Maximum speed   15 knots
Armament   6 × 6"; 2 × 3" AA

Laurentic under way. The house flag of the White Star Line flying from the mainmast dates the photo to 1927–32. *Real Photographs*

Careers

For background on the armed merchant cruisers, see HMS *Carinthia* (**8**).

HMS *Laurentic*

Ordered by the White Star Line from Harland & Wolff of Belfast, the *Laurentic* was launched in June 1927 and embarked on her maiden voyage in November of that year. Cheaply built, she was among the last cruise liners to be fitted not only for coal firing but also with triple-expansion engines. After a brief spell on the Liverpool–New York run *Laurentic* transferred to her intended route, the Liverpool–Quebec–Montreal service, though her career was interrupted by a collision with the steamer *Lurigethan* in the Strait of Belle Isle in October 1932. Meanwhile, the White Star Line had fallen into serious financial difficulty, finding itself obliged to merge with the rival Cunard Line in 1934. The following year *Laurentic* was reduced to short-range cruising and it was during one of these voyages that she suffered a major collision with the SS *Napier Star* in the Irish Sea on 18 August 1935, six of her crew being killed. Though repaired at Liverpool, *Laurentic* spent much of the next few years laid up first at Southampton and then at Falmouth where she was requisitioned for conversion to an armed merchant cruiser in August 1939. Dilapidated though she was, the refit was completed at Devonport Dockyard in October and on 2 November *Laurentic* joined the Northern Patrol between Britain and Iceland. Her most notable action came on 22–23 November when she stopped and eventually sank the German blockade runner *Antiochia*. The new year began inauspiciously for *Laurentic*, the ship grounding off Islay on 6 January, but the opportunity was taken to improve her armament during a six-week refit at Harland & Wolff of Belfast. This completed, she returned to the Northern Patrol in May before being assigned to the Western Patrol (see HMS *Carinthia*, **8**) off Gibraltar in the summer of 1940, remaining on this station until being ordered to the Clyde in early November.

HMS *Patroclus*

Commissioned by the Blue Funnel Line (Alfred Holt & Co.) of Liverpool for the Far Eastern service, the passenger steamer *Patroclus* was launched at Scott's of Greenock on 17 March 1923 and completed that May. Though *Patroclus* was only coal-fired, the ships of the Blue Funnel Line were traditionally built to the highest standards and the sturdiness of her construction was to stand her and her men in good stead in their hour of need. *Patroclus* served uneventfully throughout the inter-war years on the company's principal routes between Liverpool and the Orient, especially Singapore, Hong Kong, the Dutch East Indies and the Chinese treaty ports. Requisitioned into the Royal Navy as an armed merchant cruiser on 2 September 1939, *Patroclus* was fitted out at Liverpool and like others of her type immediately allocated to the Northern Patrol, sailing in late December 1939. Here she remained until a boiler clean at Liverpool in early May 1940 heralded reassignment to the Western Patrol. With the exception of a refit at Birkenhead in August (prolonged by an accidental fire aboard), *Patroclus* continued patrol, escort and trooping duty until being recalled to Liverpool in November.

Background of the attacks

The remarkable chain of events of 3–4 November 1940 in which three ships sailing unaccompanied fell victim to the same U-boat in the same vicinity followed the arrival of *U99* in her assigned operational area 150 miles west of Galway Bay (Ireland). Late on the afternoon of the 3rd one of *U99*'s lookouts spotted the Elders & Fyffes banana boat SS *Casanare* steaming east-north-east. Kptlt Otto Kretschmer duly manoeuvred *U99* into position and torpedoed her. In his war diary Kretschmer rues the fact that *Casanare* had managed to transmit a distress signal before sinking, assuming no doubt that this would scupper his chances of picking off another unescorted ship. How wrong he was. Fortunately for Kretschmer this signal, in which *Casanare* broadcast her position

HMS *Patroclus* lying at anchor in February 1940, much as Kretschmer will have seen her on the night of 3–4 November.
Four of her six 6-inch mountings can be made out along the upper decks. *BfZ*

in plain language, was transmitted too late to serve as a warning for his next victim, HMS *Laurentic*, and proved an irresistible call to duty for HMS *Patroclus*, both of which were sailing independently to Britain to refuel. *Laurentic*, belching smoke from her coal-fired boilers and suffering from a faulty gyro compass, unwittingly found herself at the scene about thirty miles adrift from Capt. Vivian's reckoning. Even this Vivian might have rectified but for the failure of his ship's signal staff to inform him promptly of *Casanare*'s distress signal and the enemy submarine report accompanying it. As it turned out, no sooner had Vivian begun to weigh his options with respect to *Casanare* than he crossed Kretschmer's line of fire. On board *Patroclus*, meanwhile, the arrival of *Casanare*'s signal was the cause of heated debate among her

officers. Capt. G. C. Wynter immediately decided to alter course and go to the rescue of those in need. His officers, led by Cdr R. P. Martin, were unanimous in their objections, arguing that such an action would imperil both their vessel and its crew, Martin even going to the lengths of showing his captain an order of 13 July 1940 that forbade armed merchant cruisers from stopping unless there were exceptional mitigating circumstances. Wynter was adamant, however, and would permit no other course of action. *Patroclus* reached the scene within the hour, dropped a pattern of depth charges and prepared to take on board survivors from such boats as could be discerned. As her officers had feared, however, such immobility made her a gift target for Kretschmer, still lurking on the scene.

War Diary of *U99*, patrol of 30 October–8 November 1940: PG 30095, NHB, reel 1,078, pp. 309–10

Date, time	*Details of position, wind, weather, sea, light, visibility, moonlight, etc.*	*Incidents*
3.xi		
1200	Qu. [AM] 7468 upper right, wind N 3, sea 3, cloud 0	Day's run: surfaced 206.5 nm.
1530		Trail of smoke at bearing 310° true; turns out to be coal-fired freighter steering a zigzag course of approx. 60°.[1]
1600	Qu. [AM] 7185 upper right, wind N 3, sea 3, cloud 6	
1713		While manoeuvring into a position ahead of her another ship's smoke trail appears at bearing 285° true.[2] She seems to be steering a similar course.
2000	Qu. [AM] 7211 upper	

---

1   SS *Casanare*.

2   The identity of this second ship has not been established, though she seems to have turned and made off at high speed following the torpedoing of the *Casanare*, presumably to avoid sharing the same fate.

	middle, wind N 3, sea 3, cloud 3, moon and starlit night	
2140	Qu. [AM] 4875 'C a s a n a r e' British 5,376 GRT	Torpedo fired at first steamer, range 1,200 m, detonation beneath after mast.[1] Ship settles by the stern. Head immediately towards second vessel which has now disappeared in the darkness. It would be best to close her quickly before she notices the vessel just torpedoed. The latter is now showing lights as her crew begin abandoning ship and is unfortunately also now transmitting a radio signal. She is the British steamer *Casanare*, 5,376 GRT.
2202		Second steamer reappears at a bearing of 240° true and at the same time a third steamer appears at 300°.[3]
		Second vessel then turns about and heads away on a straight course at high speed. I close the third vessel which ploughs on.[3] As we close it becomes evident that she is a passenger liner with two funnels and a foremast. The after mast is stepped. Presumably an auxiliary cruiser. In the bows some of the scuttles have not been plated over so definitely a warship.[4] She is not proceeding at full speed.
2250	Qu. [AM] 4796 'L a u r e n t i c' British auxiliary cruiser 18,724 GRT	Torpedo fired at 1,500 m. Detonates below the funnel. Ship broadcasts *en clair*: *Torpedoed engine room, all fires out*, so she won't be able to move though she's not settling any deeper. Deck lights come on, lots of red starshell is fired from the bridge; boats are lowered. She is the 18,724-GRT British passenger liner *Laurentic* which has no doubt been requisitioned into service as an auxiliary cruiser. Second vessel reappears and remains in vicinity.[5]
2328		*Inexplicable miss of further torpedo fired at stopped* Laurentic.
2337		*Coup-de-grâce shot from 580 m. Detonates below the foremast. Has no obvious effect.*
2340		*Laurentic fires a well-aimed starshell followed by rapid salvoes of the same. I head off at utmost speed towards the second vessel which has stopped and is picking up men from a lifeboat.*
2400	Qu. [AM] 4796 lower right, wind N 2–3, sea 2, cloud 4	*Kretschmer*

4.xi

0002	Qu. [AM] 4796 lower right, 'P a t r o c l u s' British auxiliary cruiser 11,314 GRT	Torpedo fired at the vessel which has stopped, range 1,200 m.[6] Detonates forward of the bridge. Ship broadcasts her name and position *en clair* and lowers boats. She is the British passenger vessel (now probably auxiliary cruiser) *Patroclus*, 11,314 GRT.
0022		Second torpedo fired at *Patroclus*, range 1,200 m. Detonates aft. Has no obvious effect. The ship is laden with barrels and a number of empty ones spew out.
0044		Third torpedo fired at *Patroclus*, range 950 m, detonates beneath bridge. More barrels escape. The ship, now broadside to us, has settled slightly deeper and is now also heeling over to starboard. I decide to finish her off with gunfire.
0058		Four 8.8-cm shells fired from 1,000 m of which two hit their target, one apparently setting fire to ammunition which is stowed for use on the superstructure. But then I have to turn away and head off because *Patroclus* is returning our fire and her time-fuze shells are well aimed.
0118		Fourth torpedo fired at *Patroclus*, detonating beneath the foremast. No obvious effect apart from the appearance of yet more barrels. It will take the crew a good while to reload torpedoes so I use the enforced break to sail past *Laurentic* – which is still afloat and even more buoyant if anything – to the scene of *Casanare*'s torpedoing.
0215		I start questioning the crew of one of the five lifeboats in the position in which *Casanare* sank but am suddenly interrupted as an illuminated Sunderland appears and starts circling us on a radius of about 500 m.
0239		We dive.

---

3   This 'third steamer' is HMS *Laurentic*.

4   This statement is curious since one might have expected the scuttles to have been plated over in wartime rather than the reverse. Possible typist's error.

5   Though Kretschmer assumed this to be the second steamer he had spotted at 1713 (see n. 2), her movements in fact correspond to those of *Patroclus*, in all probability the fourth vessel *U99* had sighted that night.

6   HMS *Patroclus*.

Date, time	Details of position, wind, weather, sea, light, visibility, moonlight, etc.	Incidents
0400	Qu. [AM] 4874 middle, wind W 4, sea 3, cloud 5	
0404		Surface once reloading of torpedoes is complete.
		As we make our way back towards the auxiliary cruisers an escort is sighted.[7] We must sink these two before she can arrive on the scene.
0453		Second *coup-de-grâce* shot fired at *Laurentic*. Range 1,400 m. Detonates aft. After a few [missing word] ship sinks by the stern, her depth charges immediately exploding.
0516		Fifth torpedo fired at *Patroclus*. Detonation in the forward hold. Other than yet more barrels it has no obvious effect.
0525		Sixth torpedo fired at *Patroclus*. Detonates amidships in engine room. Ship breaks in two abaft the foremast. The stern section capsizes and sinks rapidly. The forward section sinks slowly. I head off quickly because the escort is now arriving on the battlefield and has begun illuminating the area with searchlights, and then from 0605 to 0900 fires starshell.
0605		
0800	Qu. [AM] 4782 lower left, wind W 4, sea 3, cloud 7, raining	
1118		Dive to avoid aircraft approaching at bearing 110° true which then drops a bomb far off.

---

7   HM destroyer *Achates*.

The sinkings

As Kretschmer's war diary relates, both *Laurentic* and *Patroclus* were laden with barrels to increase their reserve of buoyancy in the event of a torpedoing. Simple targets though they were to a commander renowned for his accuracy, it required no fewer than nine hits (plus one dud) to sink them. Apart from interrupting Capt. Vivian's cogitation in the charthouse, *Laurentic*'s first torpedo struck amidships in the boiler room, tearing a large hole in her hull. Vivian's subsequent signal, which was made *en clair*, informed Kretschmer that she was unable to raise steam so he had no need to hurry either his second shot (a probable dud) or his third, which to Kretschmer's frustration had no visible effect other than oblige Vivian to abandon ship. Prior to doing so, however, fire was returned from a 4-inch gun in *Laurentic* which had spotted *U99*'s conning tower, whereupon Kretschmer immediately turned his attention to the newly arrived *Patroclus*, now stopped in order to pick up survivors.

Patroclus was an easy target but proved a stubborn one. Shortly after 2300 GMT (midnight German time) Capt. Wynter's vessel took the first of six torpedoes from *U99*. Though this first detonation caused great damage abreast the forward well deck it did not affect her capacity to manoeuvre. For the second time that night Cdr Martin suggested that *Patroclus* could still take evasive action, Capt. Wynter again refusing though this time with greater reason: men from his own ship were in the water together with those from *Laurentic* and *Casanare*. A retired officer who had won the DSO in command of HM destroyer *Magic* during the night action at Jutland, Wynter would not countenance what he evidently considered a betrayal of the high tradition of the Royal Navy. However, *U99*'s second and third torpedoes, which struck *Patroclus* twenty and then forty minutes after the first, obliged a reluctant Wynter to pass the order to abandon ship. In the chaos caused by the third torpedo a number of men, Cdr Martin included,

found themselves stranded on board with no boats left to lower. In response to *U99*'s shellfire (Kretschmer having now resorted to his 88-mm gun to preserve torpedoes) this group set itself to man the starboard 3-inch gun, successfully forcing him to take evasive action. His gunnery option thwarted, Kretschmer fired his remaining loaded torpedo at *Patroclus*. To his dismay this – her fourth – also failed to achieve the desired result. The armed merchant cruisers remained afloat for another two hours, gaining some respite as *U99* was forced to dive by a Sunderland flying boat. Boats and rafts gradually filled with men confident that help would arrive within a few hours while Kretschmer loaded his five remaining torpedoes. Only *Patroclus* was manned, the dozen or so men who remained around the gun finding the hulk a preferable berth to the cold night waters of the Atlantic.

When Kretschmer resurfaced at 0300 he was able to attend to unfinished business without hindrance. With all five of *U99*'s tubes reloaded, the Sunderland having disappeared and no escort in sight, the long November night allowed him to manoeuvre on the surface at will. A third torpedo into *Laurentic*'s hull sank her shortly before 0500 but *Patroclus* required a fifth and sixth before the bridge structure collapsed and her back was finally broken. She sank at around 0550 GMT giving *U99* just enough time to make good her escape as the destroyer *Achates* arrived on the scene. Within twenty-four hours of reaching his operational area Kretschmer had sunk a merchantman and two armed merchant cruisers in virtually the same position. *U99* was back at Lorient within ten days of setting out, Dönitz dryly assessing the cruise as having been crowned with great fortune as well as skill.

Fate of the crews

Despite the destruction of two lifeboats by the second torpedo, *Laurentic*'s crew abandoned ship without great loss of life and Capt.

Vivian was seen making strenuous efforts to ensure that all his men disembarked safely. The majority of *Laurentic*'s casualties were incurred when first No. 1 cutter and then No. 5 lifeboat were destroyed by successive torpedoes as they came alongside *Patroclus*. Many of *Laurentic*'s survivors spent hours in the water clinging to wreckage but the majority were picked up by rescue ships arriving shortly before dawn and were landed at Greenock the following day. So distraught was Vivian at the loss of his ship and men that he was admitted to hospital following his appearance before the Board of Enquiry. This found him responsible for the unacceptable delay in his being handed *Casanare*'s distress signal but the First Sea Lord, Admiral of the Fleet Sir Dudley Pound, had good reason to withhold its judgement. By the time the Board had concluded its deliberations he was in possession of a medical report from the Royal Naval Hospital at Lancaster stating that Vivian was suffering from 'acute melancholia' and was considered to be a suicide risk. As Vivian was therefore due to be invalided out of the Service the letter of censure was considered to serve no useful purpose.

A number of those who abandoned HMS *Patroclus* were never seen again, Capt. Wynter among them, but the majority were picked up at dawn along with survivors from the *Laurentic*. Most dramatic of all was the experience of the small group left stranded on *Patroclus* after the third torpedo strike. Still aboard when Kretschmer registered his sixth and final hit, most resorted to pieces of wreckage in an effort to avoid being sucked under. The majority survived to be picked up by HMSs *Achates* and *Active* but Cdr Martin had a while longer to wait: the last to climb up the destroyer's side and grasp a friendly arm, he was then pitched back into the sea as the destroyer surged full ahead with both engines having suddenly received a fixed Asdic contact. Martin narrowly avoided drowning and was later picked up by the destroyer *Hesperus*. The following September he was a survivor of the sinking of HMS *Springbank* (**33**).

The late Capt. Wynter was considered by the Board of Enquiry to have been grievously at fault, first for having gone to the rescue of survivors and then for not having steamed away after the first torpedo had struck his ship. Admiralty Instructions were clarified in the aftermath of the enquiry, orders being issued on 4 December 1940 to the effect that 'No large ship is to go to the assistance of a ship that has been torpedoed [. . .] without a direct order from an Admiral.'

U99 and Otto Kretschmer

Built by Germaniawerft of Kiel and commissioned in April 1940, *U99* spent her career under Kptlt Otto Kretschmer, the most successful U-boat commander of the war in terms of tonnage sunk. Apart from her first cruise, during which she was damaged on 21 June 1940 by an Arado Ar196 floatplane from the battlecruiser *Scharnhorst* after being mistaken for a British submarine, all of her eight patrols were marked by great success. A marksman second to none both in training and in frontline operations, Kretschmer was highly critical of the wastefulness of firing more than one torpedo at a time and coined his own motto of 'one torpedo, one ship', though the sinkings of the well-

Kretschmer in his quarters at Lorient on 14 November 1940. He wears the Oak Leaves to the Knight's Cross awarded for sinking *Laurentic* and *Patroclus* just ten days earlier. *BK*

ballasted *Laurentic* and *Patroclus*, which took ten torpedoes between them, clearly tested this conviction somewhat. Nonetheless, in pursuit of this maxim Kretschmer pioneered the technique of sailing between escorts into the centre of a convoy from where he could pick off targets at close range. Kretschmer had previously commanded *U23* in which he sank the destroyer HMS *Daring* (**4**); see HMS *Forfar* (**20**) for details of his subsequent career with *U99*.

Sources

Admiralty, *Loss of HM Ships* Patroclus *and* Laurentic: *Board of Enquiry* (TNA, ADM 1/11215)

Jobling, Lt Cdr Thomas, *The Sinking of HMS* Patroclus, *4th November, 1940* (University of Leeds, Liddle Collection, no. 031)

Falkus, Malcolm, *The Blue Funnel Legend: A History of the Ocean Steam Ship Company, 1865–1973* (London: Macmillan, 1990)

Hampshire, A. Cecil, *The Blockaders* (London: William Kimber, 1980)

Haws, Duncan, *Cunard Line* [Merchant Fleets, no. 12] (2nd edn, Hereford, Hereford and Worcester: TCL Publications, 1989)

—, *White Star Line (Oceanic Steam Navigation Company)* [Merchant Fleets, no. 19] (Hereford, Hereford and Worcester: TCL Publications, 1990)

Middlemiss, Norman L., *Blue Funnel Line* [Merchant Fleets, no. 42] (Newcastle upon Tyne: Shield Publications, 2002)

Osborne, Richard, Harry Spong and Tom Grover, *Armed Merchant Cruisers, 1878–1945* (Windsor, Berks: World Ship Society, 2007)

Poolman, Kenneth, *Armed Merchant Cruisers* (London: Leo Cooper, 1985)

—, *The British Sailor* (London: Arms and Armour Press, 1989)

Robertson, Terence, *The Golden Horseshoe* (London: Evans Brothers, 1955)

Worsley, John, and Kenneth Giggal, *John Worsley's War: An Official War Artist in World War II* (Shrewsbury, Salop: Airlife Publishing, 1993)

Website devoted to the sinking of HMSs *Patroclus* and *Laurentic*: http://homepage.ntlworld.com/annemariepurnell/patroclus.html

Memoir of AB Alfred Miles (survivor of HMS *Patroclus*): http://barry-miles.tripod.com/

20   HMS *FORFAR* (ex SS *MONTROSE*)

Capt. N. A. C. Hardy, RN†
Sunk by *U99* (Type VIIB), Kptlt Otto Kretschmer, 2 December 1940
North Atlantic, 295 nm W of Slyne Head, Galway (Ireland)

SS *Montrose* of the Canadian Pacific Line seen before the war. Five hits from Kretschmer's *U99* sent her to the bottom of the Atlantic.
Bruce Taylor collection

Theatre	North Atlantic (Map 2)	*Deadweight*	8,050 tons
Coordinates	54° 35' N, 18° 18' W	*Gross tons*	16,402
Kriegsmarine code	Quadrat AL 6581	*Dimensions*	575.25' × 70.25' × 28'
U-boat timekeeping differential	+3 hours	*Maximum speed*	17 knots
Fatalities	176 *Survivors* 159	*Armament*	8 × 6"; 2 × 3" AA

Career

For background on the armed merchant cruisers, see HMS *Carinthia* (**8**).

One of a class of three liners built for the Canadian Pacific Line, the *Montrose* originated as the *Montmorency*, being laid down at Fairfield, Govan in 1919, launched as the *Montrose* in December 1920 and completed in March 1922. Destined for the Liverpool–Montreal–Quebec run, she embarked on her maiden voyage on 5 May that year. Later she transferred to the Antwerp–Montreal and then the Hamburg–Montreal services following repairs to damage suffered during a collision with an iceberg in 1928. In 1931 the *Montrose* was fitted with geared turbines at Harland & Wolff of Belfast, returning to the transatlantic run and making the first of forty-six pleasure cruises the following year. In May 1937 she was chartered by the Royal Empire Society to attend the Coronation Review off Spithead. On 6 September 1939 the *Montrose* was requisitioned by the Admiralty along with her sister *Montcalm* (HMS *Wolfe*) for service as an armed merchant cruiser. Renamed *Forfar* to avoid confusion with the elderly Scott-class destroyer HMS *Montrose*, she was converted at Fairfield's and assigned to the Northern Patrol in late November 1939. Apart from the installation of a buoyant cargo on the Clyde from the end of March and repairs to her propellers at Liverpool in late May, *Montrose* spent the rest of her career on this station together with a brief stint on the Western Patrol in November.

Background of the attack

At midday on 30 November 1940 HMS *Forfar* sailed from the Clyde for the mid-Atlantic, escorted initially by HMC destroyer *St Laurent*, with orders to meet convoy SC14 and bring it into Liverpool. The assignment was owed to a shortage of Revenge-class battleships to which the task of heavy support was usually entrusted against the possibility of a surface attack by German raiders. At 2300 on 1 December *St Laurent* was ordered to return to harbour but as reports began reaching Western Approaches Command that same night of a U-boat concentration around Liverpool-bound HX90 she was instructed to strengthen the escort of that convoy instead. An hour later *Forfar* was ordered to steer south of 54° 23' N, 20° 11' W where a U-boat had apparently been sighted. At 0220 on the 2nd the Officer of the Watch, Lt Robert Antrobus RNR, called Capt. Hardy to the bridge having sighted a 'suspicious object, possibly a submarine'. No action was taken as neither Hardy nor the other officers present could see anything and since, in the words of the ranking survivor, Cdr R. G. Arnot RN (Ret'd), 'Lieutenant Antrobus was of an imaginative nature and rather apt to get excited. On previous occasion[s] when he made reports these subsequently turned out to be unjustified.' On this occasion, however, the cry of wolf was surely genuine, for one of the most notorious wolves of the era had sighted *Forfar* just minutes earlier and was now closing to attack. Five days out of Lorient, Kptlt Otto Kretschmer was about to notch up his first victim since expending ten torpedoes on the armed merchant cruisers *Laurentic* and *Patroclus* (**19**) three weeks before.

War Diary of *U99*, patrol of 27 November–12 December 1940: PG 30095, NHB, reel 1,078, p. 332

Date, time	Details of position, wind, weather, sea, light, visibility, moonlight, etc.	Incidents
2.xii		
0315		We can't make headway against the sea even at ¾ speed, boat at one point dipping completely below the surface despite the fact that even the rear hydroplane was set at an upwards inclination of 5°. The conning-tower hatch closed itself so there was no great deluge of water.
0400	Qu. [AL] 6586 middle, wind NW 3, sea 3, cloud 4, high swell from the W	There is a severe drop in air pressure in the boat due to diesel fumes.[1] The bridge watch is safe and sound as they were lashed on.[2] Even with engines at maximum speed against the sea we only proceed at the equivalent of half speed.
0514		A large shadow looms up at a bearing of 70° true. We close in to attack. She's a large auxiliary cruiser – a modern passenger liner with two funnels and a foremast. Aftermast is stepped.
0540		An approaching destroyer heaves into sight from the east, bearing down on us at high speed. This
0546		forces us to fire just a single shot (G7a) at the auxiliary cruiser from a great range (3,600 m) and then dive. Destroyer steams right overhead – she's presumably heading to join the convoy now reported in the neighbouring quadrant.[3] Torpedo detonates after 2 min. 59 sec.; assume a hit. We can no longer hear the auxiliary cruiser.
0612		Surface. Auxiliary cruiser is lying motionless in a huge patch of oil – so we did hit her.
0625		Successive detonations heard far off, presumably torpedoes from our own boats striking the convoy.[4]
0639		Second torpedo fired at auxiliary cruiser, range 930 m, strikes amidships. No particular effect. Ship fires starshell and red distress signals.[5]
0643		Third torpedo fired at auxiliary cruiser, range 1,215 m. Hits beneath the after funnel. No particular effect. Ship has not lowered any boats, appears to be quite buoyant.
0650		Fourth torpedo fired at auxiliary cruiser, range 1,060 m. Hits a third of ship's length forward from stern. Ship settles more heavily by the stern.
0657		Fifth torpedo fired at auxiliary cruiser, range 1,140 m. Hits aft. Stern sheers off and sinks under the detonations of its depth charges; then fore part of the ship sinks.
0704	Qu. [AL] 6581 middle, British auxiliary cruiser ~~Caledonia, 17,046 GRT~~ *Forfar* (16,418 GRT, ex *Montcalm*)[7]	Auxiliary cruiser has presumably gone down with the majority of her crew.[6] She was of the Duchess of Atholl class, Canadian Pacific.

---

1   Like all U-boats in the early years of the war, the Type VIIBs could not run their more powerful diesel engines below the surface given the backflow of noxious gas into the boat. Not until the development of the *Schnorchel* device could this problem be addressed in part.

2   Enemy action and torpedo accidents apart, being washed overboard was the greatest threat to U-boat crews and many lost their lives in this manner. However, being lashed on was not always favoured because of the attendant risks in the event of an emergency dive.

3   The destroyer appears to have been HMS *Viscount* which had been detached from OB251 to support HX90 and was in almost exactly the same position as *Forfar* at this time. Contrary to his remarks here, Kretschmer's torpedo report describes her as *Forfar*'s escort, which was not the case. It seems remarkable that this destroyer, assuming it was indeed *Viscount*, failed to note the detonation of *U99*'s first torpedo against *Forfar*, but her CO Lt V. J. St Clair-Ford made no mention of sighting her in his testimony to the Board of Enquiry.

4   This timing corresponds closely with SS *Dunsley* (a straggler from nearby HX90) receiving eleven 88-mm shells from Kptlt Günther Prien's *U47* (see **2**).

5   Starshell was fired to illuminate the surrounding area with the aim of revealing a U-boat's position or forcing it to dive. The red distress signals were Very lights, fired from a hand-held pistol.

6   Kretschmer's assessment of the likely attrition is interesting; in fact his attacks cost the lives of slightly more than half of *Forfar*'s ship's company.

7   Kretschmer's initial identification of *Forfar* as the *Caledonia* is curious since this ship, fitted out as an armed merchant cruiser and renamed HMS *Scotstoun* (**9**), had been sunk by *U25* on 13 June. Plainly, *U99*'s Weyer had yet to be updated despite the fact that the Germans appear to have made a positive identification of that vessel. Nonetheless, the error was realised on *U99*'s return to Lorient and the correct identification inserted in pencil here and typed out in the appended torpedo report. It should, however, be noted that *Forfar* had earlier been the *Montrose* rather than her sister *Montcalm* which received a similar conversion and entered service as HMS *Wolfe*. Though built to a similar design for the same Canadian Pacific Line, the Duchess of Atholl-class ships were considerably larger at over 20,119 GRT.

Date, time	Details of position, wind, weather, sea, light, visibility, moonlight, etc.	Incidents
0712		Another vessel approaches and am forced to take evasive action since all torpedo tubes are empty. No possibility of reloading on the surface.[8]
0725		Dive to reload five tubes.
0800	Qu. [AL] 6581 middle right	

8 Reloading torpedoes required the utmost care and every effort was made to avoid sudden jolts or excessive movement. In view of the heavy seas described it is clear why Kretschmer chose to submerge for reloading.

The sinking

U99's first torpedo (fired by Oblt.z.S. Klaus Bargsten; see **37**) struck on the starboard side abreast the engine room at 0250 ship time, bringing down the main aerial and leaving *Forfar* unable to make steam. The Chief Engineer reported all engines out of action as well as flooding in the engine room', the after shaft tunnels and the diesel room. While a distress signal was being sent on the emergency set, Capt. Hardy and Cdr Arnot conferred on the bridge, the latter still optimistic about *Forfar*'s prospects. Quantities of starshell and Very lights were fired in an attempt to drive the U-boat from the scene while boats stowed with blankets, whisky and cigarettes were lowered as a precaution.

Although the appearance of HMS *Viscount* forced *U99* to dive, her departure left *Forfar* at Kretschmer's mercy. Bargsten's second and third torpedoes struck *Forfar* in quick succession, Capt. Hardy soon passing the order to abandon ship though matters were by now well beyond his control. Cdr Arnot was making his way from the bridge to supervise the order to abandon ship when the third torpedo hit:

> I was then proceeding along the boat deck when a third torpedo hit the ship again on the port side, and as far as I could see in very nearly the same place. After this there were ominous signs of breaking metal, grinding, and so on, and I myself fell from the boat deck through a cavity and arrived on the promenade deck. I had just picked myself up and gone off to where the cutters were when there was a fourth explosion, and this appeared to me to simply crumple the ship up. It was again on the port side and in more or less the same vicinity. It appeared to me then that the ship's back was broken . . .

Mindful of the six torpedoes which *Patroclus* (**19**) had taken before sinking (his frustrated 'no particular effect' comment being repeated after several hits on *Forfar*), Kretschmer had already ordered Bargsten to launch *U99*'s fifth torpedo, the last she had loaded. Although it may have detonated the after magazine this strike barely affected the issue. The two sections sank shortly after the fifth hit, the stern remaining afloat a few seconds longer than the bows. Capt. Hardy remained on his bridge and went down with the ship.

The Board of Enquiry weighed up a large amount of testimony from survivors and found 'that no negligence is attributable to any individual so far as the incidents we been able to investigate are concerned'. That the *Forfar*, sailing alone, was doomed to a slow death once disabled by Kretschmer's first torpedo was evident, her sinking equally so given that there was 'no doubt that the impact of no fewer than five torpedoes in the engine room region absolutely shattered that part of the ship'. But in addition to making suggestions regarding life-saving equipment and commending the behaviour of her ship's

company, the Board reserved its final paragraph to the alarm raised by Lt Antrobus, who did not survive the sinking: 'It is, however, our opinion that unless he had the most definite reasons for disregarding the report of the suspicious object made by Lieutenant Antrobus, the Captain should have given the order to turn away and to proceed at maximum speed, immediately the report was made.' Posthumous vindication for Antrobus, but whether *Forfar* could have eluded *U99* for long is another matter.

In view of the fact that *Forfar* was the fifth armed merchant cruiser lost to U-boats on the Northern and Western Patrol since early August, Admiral Sir Charles Forbes, Commander-in-Chief Home Fleet, proposed that the remaining ships of the type be withdrawn until proper anti-submarine escorts could be provided for them. Though the Admiralty again ruled that they could not be spared, the survivors were assigned to duties further west and their place on the Western Patrol eventually taken by the new ocean boarding vessels (see HMS *Crispin*, **22**).

Fate of the crew

Few men were killed or injured by the first torpedo. However, the second and third, which struck in almost exactly the same place just a few minutes apart, inflicted immense damage and casualties. Part of the boat deck collapsed onto the promendade deck killing many of those fallen in at their abandon-ship stations and destroying the vessels stowed on it. Kretschmer's fourth torpedo broke the ship's back making an orderly abandonment impossible. By now all but one of the ship's boats on the port side was either smashed or unseaworthy due to splinter damage from the detonations, the fourth torpedo having exploded close to the remaining cutter, blasting it to pieces and pitching its twenty or so occupants into the sea. Many had no option but to leap overboard and endeavour to get clear of the wreck as bow and stern began rising out of the water, though with large amounts of dangerous flotsam this proved a hazardous undertaking. For the majority of the ship's company who did get clear in eight Carley floats (subsequently lashed together) and the two salvageable lifeboats, the ordeal was far from over, only those in the lifeboats having the luxury of access to food, blankets, whisky and cigarettes. However, the survivors were fortunate in that the night was a relatively mild one for the time of year. The freighter SS *Dunsley* reached the scene at daybreak having fought off *U47* (see **2**) a few miles away and now stopped to pick up eighty-seven survivors in flagrant contravention of the Defence of Merchant Shipping Regulations. Mindful of the safety of his vessel, *Dunsley*'s master then made a hasty departure while the remaining survivors looked on aghast, though he took care to signal

A rare shot of *U99*, here seen at the outset of her final patrol on 22 February 1941. A month later she was no more, sunk by HM destroyers *Vanoc* and *Walker* on 17 March. *DUBMA*

Kretschmer seen at an award ceremony, perhaps that in which the Crossed Swords were added to the Knight's Cross with Oak Leaves in December 1940, three weeks after the sinking of HMS *Forfar*. *DUBMA*

their position to the destroyers escorting convoy HX90. Such was the havoc wreaked on the thinly defended HX90 that night (six ships sunk and three damaged) that resources could ill be spared and it was not until *Forfar*'s original escort *St Laurent* and would-be escort *Viscount* appeared at around 1400 that the remaining seventy-two men could be rescued. Injury, exposure and particularly the ingestion of fuel oil had accounted for many in the intervening period. The survivors, numbering a total of 159 men, were landed variously at Oban (*Dunsley*, on the 5th), Liverpool (*Viscount*, also on the 5th) and Gourock (*St Laurent*, on the 7th).

U99 and Otto Kretschmer

For details of *U99*'s and Kretschmer's earlier career, see HMSs *Laurentic* and *Patroclus* (**19**).

HMS *Forfar* was the first victim of *U99*'s eighth patrol, to which three merchantmen were later added. However, none of *U99*'s patrols compared to that which followed it between February and March 1941, during which 60,000 tons of shipping was sent to the bottom and Kretschmer's career tally taken past a quarter of a million tons – a record for any submarine commander during the Second World War. Yet for all its success this patrol was also to be Kretschmer's last. On 17 March the sinking of MS *Korshamm* prompted a heavy depth-charge attack from HMSs *Vanoc* and *Walker* of the 5th Escort Group which forced *U99* to the surface, Kretschmer ordering her abandoned under fire from the same destroyers. All but three of her crew survived to be rescued by *Walker*, one of whom had been ordered back by Kretschmer to ensure the scuttling of the boat. Earlier that evening *Vanoc* and *Walker* had accounted for *U100* and her ace commander Kptlt Joachim Schepke. After spending the next six years in captivity, mainly in Canada, Kretschmer joined the nascent Bundesmarine in 1955, retiring in 1970 as a Flottillenadmiral. He died in Bavaria in August 1998.

Sources

Admiralty, *Loss of HMS* Forfar *(late* Montrose)*: Board of Enquiry* (TNA, ADM 1/11216)

—, *Enemy Attacks on Merchant Shipping, 1939–1945* (TNA, ADM 199/144)

—, *Interrogation of German Naval Survivors, 1941* (TNA, ADM 186/806)

Ministry of Defence, 'Sinking of HMS *Forfar*', typescript letter from Kate Tildesley (Curator) to the Scottish Maritime Museum, Irvine (NHB, D/NHB/22/2)

Blair, *Hitler's U-Boat War*, I, pp. 210–11

Hampshire, A. Cecil, *The Blockaders* (London: William Kimber, 1980)

Haws, Duncan, *Canadian Pacific* [Merchant Fleets, no. 23] (Hereford, Hereford and Worcester: TCL Publications, 1992)

Herzog, Bodo, *Otto Kretschmer: Der erfolgreichste U-Boot-Kommandant des Zweiten Weltkrieges* (Norderstedt: Patzwall, 2001)

Kurowski, Frank, *Jäger der Sieben Meere: Die Berühmtesten U-Boot-Kommandanten des II. Weltkriegs* (Stuttgart: Motorbuch Verlag, 1994)

Macintyre, Capt. Donald, *U-Boat Killer* (London: Weidenfeld and Nicolson, 1956)

Osborne, Richard, Harry Spong and Tom Grover, *Armed Merchant Cruisers, 1878–1945* (Windsor, Berks.: World Ship Society, 2007)

Poolman, Kenneth, *Armed Merchant Cruisers* (London: Leo Cooper, 1985)

Robertson, Terence, *The Golden Horseshoe* (London: Evans Brothers, 1955)

Career information on SS *Montrose*: http://www.theshipslist.com/ships/descriptions/ShipsMM.html

Memoirs of Allan W. Kerr (survivor): http://www.bbc.co.uk/ww2peopleswar/stories/01/a1954901.shtml

21 NF *SFAX*
L.V. M. J. M. Groix, MN†
Sunk by *U37* (Type IXA), Kptlt Nicolai Clausen, 19 December 1940
North Atlantic, 80 nm NE of Cap Juby (Morocco)

Sfax seen before the war. She was struck aft by *U37* and blew up taking all but four crewmen to the bottom with her. The sinking of a Vichy submarine and tanker sailing in company was an acute embarrassment to the *U-Boot-Waffe* which resorted to an inept cover-up. *Bruce Taylor collection*

Theatre North Atlantic (Map 1)	*Displacement* 1,379 tons surfaced 2,084 tons submerged
Coordinates 28° 30' N, 11° 40' W	*Dimensions* 302.75' × 26.75' × 15.5'
Kriegsmarine code (as calculated from	*Maximum speed* 18 knots surfaced 10 knots submerged
French coordinates) Quadrat DJ 7432	*Armament* 9 × 550 mm tt; 2 × 400 mm tt (13 torpedoes carried);
U-boat timekeeping differential unknown	1 × 100 mm; 1 × 37 mm AA; 2 × 13.2 mm AA
Fatalities 65 *Survivors* 4	

Career

For background on the French navy, see NF *Doris* (**6**).

Ordered under the 1930 estimates, the submarine *Sfax* belonged to the third and final series of the thirty-one-strong Redoutable class of ocean-going submarines. She was laid down at Ateliers et Chantiers de la Loire at St-Nazaire in July 1931, launched in December 1934 and eventually completed for service in September 1936. Career details are scarce before the beginning of 1939 by which time she was part of the 2e division of the 1re escadrille based on Brest. Refitted there between February and April of that year, *Sfax* served on patrol duty in the Atlantic and the Mediterranean, the outbreak of war finding her division at Toulon. The first weeks of the conflict were spent off the Spanish port of Vigo in a vain wait for German blockade runners. Thereafter *Sfax* and her three companions of the 2e division were assigned to Atlantic convoy duty, sailing from Brest to Halifax, Nova Scotia on 14 November. This duty, which continued through the winter of 1939, was not only a misuse of the fighting potential of the submarine but proved to be one for which they were materially ill-equipped. On 15 April the onset of the Norwegian Campaign took *Sfax* from Brest to Narvik which she reached on the 17th. Following a two-week patrol *Sfax* turned for Dundee from where she operated

together with other French boats off Norway until sailing for Brest on 4 June. With the fall of France imminent, on the 19th *Sfax* was ordered to Casablanca, spending the rest of her career on patrol duty in the Atlantic.

Background of the attack

At noon on 17 December 1940 the Vichy naval tanker *Rhône* sailed from Casablanca bound for the Senegalese capital Dakar loaded with munitions and 3,500 tons of oil. At 1600 that afternoon she was overhauled by the *Sfax*, also bound for Dakar to relieve the submarine *Bévéziers* on that station and belatedly ordered to act as *Rhône*'s escort en route. The voyage passed uneventfully until the pair reached a position between Cap Juby and Fuerteventura at 1640 on 19 December, *Sfax* stationed 400 metres on *Rhône*'s starboard quarter and both vessels proceeding at around eight knots. By now they had entered the sights of Kptlt Nicolai Clausen in *U37*, who, apparently failing to identify them as Vichy French, proceeded to destroy both within the space of an hour. For obvious reasons Clausen's log for the day in question has been purged of all references to this event, devoting itself largely to an encryption issue with the boat's Enigma machine.

War Diary of *U37*, patrol of 28 November 1940–7 January 1941: PG 30034, NHB, reel 1,062, p. 473

Date, time	Details of position, wind, weather, sea, light, visibility, moonlight, etc.	Incidents
19.xii		
0000	Qu. DH 6982,[1] wind E to NE 2, sea 1–2, cloud 3, bright moon, very good visibility	
0045		Short signal retransmitted.
0400	Qu. DJ 9313	
0621		Incoming W/T transmission from B.d.U.: *0206 and 0241 short signals received, but indecipherable.* The 0241 signal is ours, while that of 0206 must be from another boat. We check it again carefully, but there's been no error on our part. The short signal group from the *M-Offz.* has presumably fallen into the hands of a fellow who hasn't a clue where to start.[2]
0800	Qu. DJ 9262, wind ESE 2, sea 1–2, cloud 1. Air: +17°[C; 63°F] Water: +19°[C; 66°F]	
1145		Short signal retransmitted yet again.
1200	Qu. DJ 9294, wind ESE 2, sea 1, cloud 1, very good visibility	Day's run = 181.5 nm.
1419		Incoming W/T transmission from B.d.U.: *Query short signal A x B M.*
1600	Qu. DJ 9285	Nothing to be seen.[3]
1923		Outgoing W/T transmission to B.d.U.: *Short signal A x B M as per setting 101.*
2000	Qu. DJ 9228, wind SSE 2, sea 0–1, cloud 0, good visibility	In the meantime we realise our mistake: we should have confirmed with a short signal. The latter two were filler letters. Keyed in wrongly – how annoying.
2400	Qu. DH 9231,[1] wind E to N 2, sea 1–2, cloud 3, very good visibility	*Clausen*

---

1   It is singular that the first and last entries on the 19th record *U37* as having been in quadrant DH whereas the intervening ones place her in quadrant DJ. The distance between quadrant DH 6982 (0000 on the 19th) and DJ 9313 (0400) is approximately 600 miles, almost ten times the range of a surfaced U-boat in a four-hour period. Even more pertinently, DJ 93 is a land quadrant some 350 miles from the sea.

2   An unusual reference to the Enigma cipher procedure in a U-boat log. By *M-Offz.* Clausen is referring to *Der Funkschlüssel M-Verfahren: M-Offizier und M-Stab* (*The Enigma Officer and Staff Procedure*) of April 1940, a guide for the use of short-signal encryption.

3   As probably the closest log entry to the time the *Sfax* was sunk (1640 French time), this non-statement speaks volumes.

The sinking

No survivor account has been found which might shed light on the sinking of the *Sfax* from the crew's perspective, but her demise was predictably swift. Eyewitnesses on *Rhône*'s bridge reported that at 1640 'a huge column of smoke then diesel oil erupted from the stern section of the *Sfax*, accompanied by two violent explosions. Within 30 seconds the submarine had disappeared, sinking by the stern at an angle of 40°'. In the absence of any evidence to the contrary, the commanding officer of the *Rhône*, Capitaine de corvette P. P. Clavery, formed the impression that the *Sfax* had fallen victim to an accidental torpedo exposion in her stern tubes which had in turn detonated the after fuel tanks, but it is unlikely that this conclusion much outlasted the *Rhône*'s own demise forty minutes later (see below).

As the log extract shows, Clausen's war diary has been purged of references to any attack on the day in question leaving little more than the details of a trivial signal misunderstanding. However, there is no doubt that *U37* was responsible for sinking both *Sfax* and *Rhône* since Clausen transmitted the following signal two days later on 21 December, possibly as the result of an inquiry from B.d.U. It does not of course appear in his log but was subsequently extracted from the Naval High Command war diary: 'A torpedo fired at a tanker of the Kopbard type (7329 [GRT]), gyro failure, and probably hit an Amphitrite submarine in the tanker's convoy. Tanker burnt out. Spanish steamer *St. Carlos* [*sic*] (300 [tons]) without distinguishing marks [sunk] by concentrated gunfire. Nine torpedoes left.' Clausen therefore claims to have hit *Sfax* in error after a torpedo aimed at the *Rhône* went awry, while providing no explanation for how the latter 'burnt out', even though he plainly remained on the scene long enough to observe as much. By 'Kopbard' Clausen was plainly referring to the French merchant tanker *Kobad* which bore more than a passing resemblance to the *Rhône*, but not the

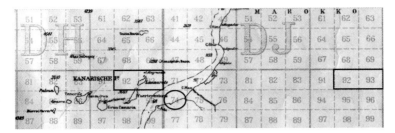

The *Quadratkarte* covering the Canary Islands and part of Spanish Morocco and Algeria. Although Clausen sank *Sfax* and *Rhône* in square DJ 74 (circled), his log places *U37* in squares DJ 92 and DJ 93, 300–350 miles inland. It must be supposed that this was simply an error for squares DH 92 and DH 93 off Lanzarote in which *U37* had been cruising on the morning of the sinking and to which Clausen now anxiously wished to return her. *NHB*

An undated photo of Clausen who had plenty of explaining to do after his first patrol in *U37* during which he sank a neutral Spanish fishing boat and two vessels of the Vichy navy. *DUBMA*

least interesting aspect of this version of events is how – and when – he made the submarine identification in particular.

It must be supposed that Clausen only learnt the identity of his victims after the fact since it is difficult to credit that a German U-boat commander would knowingly target a Vichy French vessel, let alone two, even if Clausen's sinking of a neutral Spanish fishing vessel (the *San Carlos*) suggests that he was in a bellicose frame of mind. In any event, no sooner had the identity of Clausen's victims become known to the German High Command than a communiqué was issued indicating the line to be followed by Axis diplomacy: 'We shall continue to maintain to the outside world that there is no question of a German or Italian submarine in the sea area in question being responsible for the sinkings.' All this information was pored over at length by Allied prosecutors investigating German war crimes at the Nuremberg Trials. For the naval historian, meanwhile, Clausen's log offers proof not only that the *Kriegstagebücher* could be and occasionally were falsified when the need arose, but that this could be carried out with utter incompetence since the log shows a distance of 350 miles between *U37*'s positions at 0000 and 0400 on the 19th. Still more inept were the actual quadrants to which *U37* supposedly decamped during this period, coordinates which place her deep in the Algerian Sahara where the only ships go on four legs.

Fate of the crew

Believing that *Sfax* had succumbed to an internal explosion and with no reason to think that his ships were under submarine attack, Capitaine de corvette Clavery of the *Rhône* closed the scene and ordered the engines stopped. Within half an hour of the sinking two whalers from the *Rhône* had picked up five men including *Sfax*'s commanding officer, Lieutenant de vaisseau Groix, who was found 'lifeless and severely wounded' and never regained consciousness. The survivors of this disaster were the bridge watch, consisting of Q/ mtre canonnier R. Vinchon; Q/mtre électricien O. Gouezou, Matelot radio R. Rittel, and Q/mtre de manoeuvre M. Kernogoret. However, the ordeal of *Sfax*'s four survivors was by no means over. At 1720, forty minutes after *Sfax* had been destroyed and before they had even boarded the tanker, *Rhône* was rocked by a violent explosion as 'a torpedo detonated forward of the bridge in hold no. 4, full of diesel oil which caught fire immediately'. Efforts were made to douse the blaze but when the fire began to approach the forward magazine with its

160 100-mm shells Clavery passed the order to abandon ship, the crew crowding into the two whalers and a rowing boat of unknown type. It was not possible to release the ship's motor boat but shortly after 1800 Clavery, aware that the boats were perilously overloaded, changed his mind about the danger of a magazine explosion and assembled a party of nine volunteers to reboard the ship. An hour's labour was rewarded with the lowering of the motor boat, but by the time this was done night had fallen and the other vessels were nowhere to be seen. The hulk of the *Rhône* did not sink until 1500 on the 20th.

Rescue for Clavery and the volunteer party came quickly in the shape of a Spanish trawler which brought them aboard at 2000 that evening and took the motor boat in tow. At 2300 they were transferred to the French freighter *Fort Royal* from which a signal was transmitted to Vichy naval command in Casablanca. This failed to reach its intended destination but was received by another French freighter, the *François L-D*, which altered course to the scene of the sinking and took Clavery and his party aboard before dispatching a motor whaler on a vain sweep to the south-east for more survivors. Turning south-west herself, at 0745 on the 20th the *François L-D* sighted one of the two whalers ten miles from the wreck of the *Rhône*, rescuing six men. The search continued but no more had been found by the time she turned for Agadir at 1830 that day, nor did sweeps of the area by air and surface craft locate any further survivors. Meanwhile, the rowing boat made landfall near Hassi Chbiki in Spanish Sahara (now Morocco) at 1700 that same evening, the survivors beginning a route march north towards Ifni. The second whaler came ashore near Chbika, not far north of Hassi Chbiki, at noon on the 21st after thirty-six hours on the open sea. In this way the two parties of survivors, numbering forty-three men, were reunited before being picked up by a Spanish army truck and taken to Xenel Marsa. The French destroyer *Brestois* was able to put its medical officer ashore to treat the wounded here but heavy surf prevented any embarkation of survivors who were first taken to the military outpost of Tan-Tan and eventually flown to Cap Juby or trucked to Guelmim in French Morocco. It is unclear how the four survivors of the *Sfax* were distributed between each of the three boats. The death toll of the *Sfax* was sixty-five men, that of the *Rhône* came to eleven.

L.V. Groix was posthumously promoted Capitaine de corvette 'on exceptional grounds and for feats of war' having earlier been commended for his efforts during the Norwegian Campaign of April–May 1940. He is remembered by a street named in his honour in his native town of Brest.

U37 and Nicolai Clausen

For details of *U37*'s earlier career, see HMS *Penzance* (**16**).

Victor Oehrn's departure in October 1940 brought *U37* under the command of his First Watch Officer, Kptlt Nicolai Clausen. Clausen's three operational cruises in the Atlantic yielded ten victims in addition to two about which he was sworn to silence, *Sfax* and *Rhône* of the Vichy navy. *U37*'s frontline career ended in March 1941, the boat being assigned first to training duties and then relegated to experimental work in June 1944. She was scuttled in Sønderborg Bay off the Baltic coast of Denmark in May 1945. Clausen had two further commands, the Type-IX-C *U129* in which he earned the Knight's Cross after sinking seven vessels in the Caribbean between February and March 1942, and the Type-IX-D *U182* from June of that year. *U129*'s medical officer, Dr Armin Wandel, later recalled Clausen's exceptional popularity with his crew, who 'would have walked through fire with him', and records that he gave up his commander's bunk to the Chief Engineer, preferring to sleep in the officers' wardroom on the grounds that the latter's job was much more important than his own. *U182*'s maiden patrol to the Cape and the east coast of South Africa began well, Clausen bagging five merchantmen for a total of over 30,000 tons in the first months of 1943. But her luck didn't hold. On 16 May *U182* was located off Madeira by the escort of convoy UGS8 and despatched by the US destroyers *Lamb* and *MacKenzie*. There were no survivors.

Sources

Ministère de la Défense, *Notice caractéristique concernant le sous-marin «Sfax»* (SHM, *Sfax* file)

—, Assorted cuttings relating to the Pétrolier *«Rhône»* (SHM, *Rhône* file)

British War Crimes Executive and US Chief of Counsel, *Excerpts from SKL War Diary collated and translated for the Nuremberg Trials by N.I.D. 24* (NHB)

Anon., '*U129*'s Second War Cruise and the Fate of the Submarine Supply Ship *Kota Pinang*' in *The U-Boat Archive* no. 1 (October 1998); reprinted in Jak P. Mallmann Showell, ed., *The U-Boat Archive: Early Journals Reprinted (1998–2000)* [U-Boat Archive Series, vol. 6] (Milton Keynes, Bucks.: Military Press, 2004), pp. 3–12

Caroff, Capitaine de vaisseau René Pierre Eugène, *Le Théatre Atlantique. Tome II, vol. II: Le Théatre Atlantique après le 25 juin 1940* (Paris: Marine nationale, 1959)

Huan, Capitaine de vaisseau Claude, *Les Sous-marins français, 1918–1945* (Rennes: Marines Éditions, 2004)

Le Masson, Henri, *Les Sous-marins français des origines (1863) à nos jours* (Brest: Éditions de la Cité, 1981)

Webpage dedicated to NF *Sfax*:
http://perso.orange.fr/sous-marin.france/Q182.htm

Transcript of interrogation of Grossadmiral Erich Raeder, Nuremberg War Trials, 13th[?] May 1946:
http://avalon.law.yale.edu/imt/05-13-46.asp
also on:
http://www.nizkor.org/ftp.cgi/imt/tgmwc/tgmwc-13/ftp.py?imt/tgmwc/tgmwc-13//tgmwc-13-128.09

Webpage relating to rescue of *Rhône* survivors by *Fort Royal*:
http://www.frenchlines.com/ship_fr_169.php

22   HMS (ex SS) *CRISPIN*
Cdr B. Moloney, DSO DSC RNR†
Sunk by *U107* (Type IXB), Kptlt Günter Hessler, 3–4 February 1941
North Atlantic, 475 nm W of Coll, Inner Hebrides (Scotland)

SS *Crispin* of the Booth Steamship Co. seen in the late 1930s. A torpedo from *U107* brought an end to her brief wartime career. *BfZ*

Theatre North Atlantic (Map 1)	*Deadweight* 7,920 tons
Coordinates 56° 38' N, 20° 52' W	*Gross tons* 5,051
Kriegsmarine code Quadrat AL 0249	*Dimensions* 412.25' × 55.75' × 25.75'
U-boat timekeeping differential +1 hour	*Maximum speed* 12.5 knots
Fatalities 20 *Survivors* 129	*Armament* 1 × 6"; 1 × 3" AA; 4 × 40 mm AA; 4 × 20 mm AA

The ocean boarding vessels

By the summer of 1940 the increasing demands being placed on the Royal Navy's armed merchant cruisers and the steady attrition they were suffering (see HMS *Carinthia*, **8**) led to the introduction of a new type of auxiliary warship, the ocean boarding vessel. The Admiralty's aim was to relieve the AMCs of the Western Patrol of their boarding and interception duties, and between 1940 and 1941 a total of sixteen small and mostly coal-fired freighters were requisitioned for this purpose. In the event, the German occupation of Western Europe and the consequent closure of many commercial markets meant that the arrival of the first OBVs coincided with a declining need for their services. As a result, the OBVs were gradually assigned to other duties, including as fighter catapult ships for convoy escort duty, with most of the survivors being returned to trade in 1941–2. Attrition continued to be high and six succumbed to enemy action, but the OBV could be regarded as an expendable commodity at a time when the large hulls of the AMCs had not only proved inefficient in their intended role but were increasingly in demand for trooping and other purposes.

Career

The coal-fired freighter *Crispin* was completed for the Booth Steamship Co. of Liverpool by Cammell Laird of Birkenhead in March 1935 and requisitioned into the Royal Navy in 1940. She was fitted out for war service at Dalmuir and worked up off Greenock. Details of her brief career are few, but this included periods on the Northern and Western Patrols based on Largs, Ayrshire before being assigned to convoy duty in the North Atlantic, possibly in an anti-aircraft capacity and suitably rearmed.

Background of the attack

Until the introduction of the long-range Type IXB brought the entire North Atlantic into the sphere of German U-boat operations in early 1941, it was customary for westbound convoys to scatter after reaching 20 degrees West, the point beyond which the British assumed their ships to enjoy relative immunity from submarine attack. Among the last to follow this procedure was OB280, part of whose escort detached itself at 2100 on 3 February in order to join the more weakly defended SC20, which was reckoned to be at greater risk of attack. However, as Kptlt Günter Hessler's war diary shows, it was OB280 that was in the most immediate danger, *U107* having made contact on the evening of the 3rd. Although dogged by bad weather and initially forced to keep her distance by the escort, later that evening *U107* began to trail the portion of the escort assigned to SC20 as it detached itself from OB280, comprising HM armed yacht *Philante*, HM corvette *Arbutus* (**50**), *Crispin* and the convoy rescue ship SS *Copeland*. For several hours this detachment had been the subject of delay and debate while reports that the U-boats had 'a major group' under observation filtered through from Western Approaches Command in Liverpool. However, Capt. H. S. Bowlby in *Philante* eventually persuaded the Senior Officer of the Escort, Lt Cdr M. Thornton in HMS *Harvester* (**G49**), of the need for his force to detach that evening if it were to rendezvous with SC20 before nightfall on the 4th given the prevailing weather and visibility. When it finally came at around 2100 (2200 log time) the detachment gave *U107* her chance. Reasonably enough in the circumstances, Kptlt Hessler mistook *Crispin* for a merchantman and attacked her with a single torpedo as midnight approached.

War Diary of *U107*, patrol of 24 January–1 March 1941: PG 30103, NHB, reel 1,080, p. 212

Date, time	Details of position, wind, weather, sea, light, visibility, moonlight, etc.	Incidents
3.ii		
1905	Qu. AL 0264	Convoy in sight at a bearing of 140° true.[1] Convoy consists of about 10 steamers and two or three destroyers. Destroyer on the starboard side forces *U107* to keep her distance.
1952		Outgoing W/T transmission: *Convoy in sight Qu. AL 0264. Enemy steering SW course. U107.*
2000	Qu. AL 0255, wind S 7, sea 5–6, overcast, rain and hail showers	Advance manoeuvre proves very difficult as waves crest over the boat even when proceeding slowly in this heavy sea. I try to get to windward of the convoy (see sketch) as it's now futile to try to fire against this sea.[2] Despite sailing blind we manage to gain an advanced position then reduce to slow speed for purposes of observation. All that can be seen of the convoy is a leading group consisting of two destroyers and one steamer.
2213		Outgoing W/T transmission: *Convoy Qu. [AL] 0257. U107.* I get the feeling that the convoy has split up or been scattered.
2150[3]		*Have reached advanced position but am forced to retire on several occasions as outlying destroyer comes too close for comfort.*

---

1   OB280.

2   The sketch has not survived.

3   The break in the chronological sequence here reflects the original.

2310		Commence run-in towards leading steamer. She is escorted by two destroyers stationed on her port and starboard bows.[4]
2333	Qu. AL 0249	Torpedo fired from Tube I, range 1,800 m, depth 3 m, inclination 85°, enemy speed 7 knots. A hit in the engine room. Vessel is a large freighter, perhaps 140 m long, roughly 7,000 GRT.[5] I retire, initially with the swell abeam, then directly into it. Steamer settles in the water.
2340		We hear a detonation. Vessel can no longer be seen. Destroyers start firing starshell but they don't get any fix on us. Despite the horizon being well lit up we can see no more of the convoy. Starshell is kept up for about two hours forcing the boat to maintain her distance.
2400	Qu. AL 0249, wind S 8, sea 6, very rough, squalls	No counter measures.

Heßler

---

4   The 'steamer' was *Crispin*, the 'destroyers' the armed yacht *Philante* and the corvette *Arbutus*.

5   *Crispin* was in fact of 5,051 GRT; Hessler's estimate of her length was not inaccurate, the actual figure being 126 metres (412.25 feet).

The sinking

Other than the findings of the Board of Enquiry, no detailed account of the sinking from *Crispin*'s perspective has come to light and the evidence from the Allied side lies mainly in two separate reports from Capt. Bowlby of the *Philante*, stationed seven cables off *Crispin*'s port bow at the time she was hit. *U107*'s torpedo struck her on the port side abreast or just forward of the bridge at 2235 ship time. Subsequent analysis concluded that it did sufficient damage to the transverse and watertight bulkheads between the reserve bunker and No. 2 Hold to permit flooding of both compartments, the bilges and eventually the boiler and engine rooms. Together with the resulting loss of steam this made it impossible either to operate the pumps or take any concerted steps to stem the entry of water. Plunged into darkness, *Crispin* could do little more than issue a distress signal at 2246 to the effect that she was sinking and required immediate assistance. However, the ship still had way on and her parlous state was not immediately apparent to the other vessels in company. As time passed she began to lose stability and an hour after sending the signal the order was given to abandon ship as the sealed barrels stowed to improve her buoyancy began spewing out of the holds. At 0145 she suddenly capsized and sank, her boilers exploding as the waves engulfed her. The fact that Hessler was well away from the scene when *Crispin* succumbed suggests that his reference to the vessel having 'disappeared' just seven minutes after he had launched his torpedo owes less to visual confirmation than to his confidence that her sinking and the corresponding tonnage credit could be taken for granted in the prevailing conditions. In the event, he was proved correct.

Fate of the crew

Although *Crispin*'s fate was sealed the moment *U107*'s torpedo detonated against her hull, the tribulations of her crew were prolonged by a succession of oversights among her companions which for some time prevented their recognising her predicament. Lt D. J. MacKillop RNVR, Officer of the Watch in *Philante*, reported a vivid flash astern in *Crispin*'s position and then noticed a number of lights which he interpreted as electric torches, but neither he nor any of his shipmates heard a detonation. In darkness and heavy seas it appeared that *Crispin* still had way on (as was indeed the case), and a subsequent distress signal picked up in mercantile rather than naval code was assumed to have come from a merchantman from OB280 and consequently ignored. Turning about and sailing down *Crispin*'s port side, *Philante*'s

bridge watch concluded that she was proceeding normally, her increasingly vulnerable state no doubt masked by a heavy swell and poor visibility. Meanwhile, HMSs *Harvester*, *Erica* and *Abelia*, all of which had seen the attack from a clearer line of sight, began to illuminate the area astern of OB280 with the salvoes of starshell noted by Hessler. Rather than bringing *Crispin*'s predicament to his notice, this had the effect of drawing Bowlby's attention back to the convoy he had just left. With *Crispin* not reckoned to be in any need of assistance, Bowlby decided to turn back with *Arbutus* and *Copeland* in order to lend his support to OB280's depleted escort. Meanwhile, *Crispin* was wallowing beyond salvage, her crew abandoning ship and in urgent need of rescue in heavy seas.

Several lives were lost in the torpedo detonation but a majority of the crew was able to get clear of the ship in an assortment of rafts together with at least one of the thirty-two-foot cutters, capable of accommodating upwards of fifty men. Ironically, it was not one of her companions but *Harvester* that went to *Crispin*'s aid having decrypted her distress signal. After rescuing 121 survivors *Harvester* signalled the returning *Copeland* and *Philante* (finally alerted to the situation) to proceed immediately to the listing wreck as several men had inadvertently been left on board. However, even as this message was being sent *Crispin* capsized and sank leaving *Copeland* and *Philante* to recover just eight more survivors and a corpse after a two-hour search.

A number of criticisms were levelled at the protagonists by the subsequent Board of Enquiry. The absence of effective cooperation between *Harvester* and *Philante* was regretted, confusion in communications having arisen from the fact that Lt Cdr Thornton was Senior Officer of the Escort yet Capt. Bowlby of *Philante* the ranking naval officer. Also censured was the failure of leadership and organisation in *Crispin* which allowed men to be left on board after the order was passed to abandon ship – this despite the fact that a roll call had been taken in the wardroom. A particular object of displeasure was the unnamed Leading Telegraphist in *Philante* who not only failed to decode *Crispin*'s signal until the following day, but insisted to Capt. Bowlby on the night in question that it could not have been *Crispin* in view of its mercantile origin. While greatly regretting his negligence, the Board observed that the Telegraphist's point was a valid one, nor was *Crispin* the last ocean boarding vessel to suffer the consequences of such disjunctures (see HMS *Camito*, **25**). A more practical recommendation with respect to future procedure was that all ships working with convoys be equipped with emergency lighting,

Hessler seen wearing the Iron Cross First Class which dates the photo to the spring or summer of 1941. *DUBMA*

the lack of which had proved a severe handicap during *Crispin*'s last hours afloat.

U107 and Günter Hessler

Commissioned in October 1940, *U107* was one of nine large Type-IXB boats to roll off the production line of AG Weser of Bremen as bases for Atlantic operations were falling into German hands in France. With its enhanced fuel, water and food capacity, the Type IXB afforded the U-boat arm a greater range than the more manoeuvrable Type-VII boats that had spearheaded Germany's opening offensive against the Atlantic convoys. *U107* was commissioned in October 1940 and sailed on her maiden operational cruise in January 1941, spending her first three patrols under Kptlt (Korvkpt. from September 1941) Günter Hessler. Hessler was unusual in having served neither as a U-boat watch officer nor as a commander-in-training prior to his appointment, though as a career officer in the Kriegsmarine since 1927 and with lengthy experience in torpedo boats he was evidently well equipped for the task. He also had other good cause to be embraced by the U-boat fraternity, having married Dönitz's daughter in 1937.

For more on *U107*'s successes and fate as well as further details on Günter Hessler, see HMS *Manistee* (**23**).

Sources

Admiralty, *Convoys OB280 and SC20, February–March 1941* (TNA, ADM 237/22)
—, *Enemy Submarine Attacks on HM Ships, 1941* (TNA, ADM 199/160)
—, *North Atlantic, Details of Shipping Losses, November 1940–June 1941* (NHB, CIV report, Atlantic Ocean)
—, Department of the Director of Naval Construction, *Damage Reports: Torpedo and Mine, 1940–1942* (TNA, ADM 267/92)

Poolman, Kenneth, *The Winning Edge: Naval Technology in Action, 1939–1945* (Stroud, Glos.: Sutton Publishing, 1997)
Rohwer, Jürgen, *Kriegsmarine U-107* [Warships in Profile, no. 8] (Windsor, Berks.: Profile Publications, 1970)
Roskill, *War at Sea*, I, pp. 265–6

Memoirs of George Woodley (survivor):
    http://www.bbc.co.uk/ww2peopleswar/stories/43/a7303943.shtml
Defunct website devoted to Lt Cdr Stephen Whiteside (fatality):
    http://homepage.ntlworld.com/howard.martin/Whiteside.html

23   HMS (ex SS) *MANISTEE*

Acting Cdr E. H. Smith, RNR†
Sunk by *U107* (Type IXB), Kptlt Günter Hessler, 23–24 February 1941
North Atlantic, 460 nm W of Lewis, Outer Hebrides (Scotland)

SS *Manistee* lying at Avonmouth in about 1937. Requisitioned by the Admiralty in 1940, she exchanged bananas for the perils of service as an ocean-boarding vessel, being lost with all hands to torpedoes from *U107*. *NMM*

Theatre North Atlantic (Map 1)	*Deadweight* 6,390 tons
Coordinates (of first attack) 58° 13' N, 21° 33' W	*Gross tons* 5,360
Kriegsmarine code (first attack; TR) Quadrat AL 2598	*Dimensions* 400.25' × 51' × 17'
U-boat timekeeping differential +1 hour	*Maximum speed* 13.5 knots
Fatalities 141 *Survivors* none	*Armament* 2 × 6"; 1 × 3" AA; 4 × .303" AA

Career

For background on the ocean boarding vessels, see the preceding entry for HMS *Crispin* (**22**).

Built by Cammell Laird of Birkenhead for Elders & Fyffes Shipping, SS *Manistee* was launched in October 1920 and completed in January 1921. A coal-fired banana boat, the *Manistee* spent her peacetime career plying her trade between the Caribbean and ports in Britain and northern Europe. In 1940 she was requisitioned by the Admiralty and refitted as an ocean boarding vessel, entering service that December or early 1941. Her operational career lasted fewer than a hundred days.

Background of the attack

Having torpedoed the ocean boarding vessel HMS *Crispin* (**22**) on the night of 3–4 February, *U107* went on to sink the SS *Maplecourt*, a straggler from convoy SC20, on the 6th. The next fortnight was unproductive as *U107* and others formed a patrol line to intercept convoy OB287 south of Iceland. This convoy was never located and the operation called off on the 21st. Low on fuel, Kptlt Günter Hessler was left hoping that the next convoy, OB288, would pass near enough to be intercepted by *U107*, then sailing at half speed for Lorient. It was at this point, late on the 23rd, that a steamer was sighted heading west-south-west. This was the ocean boarding vessel *Manistee*, sailing unescorted having recently detached herself from the same convoy Hessler was hoping to intercept. *Manistee* spent the next few hours being hunted not only by *U107* but by the Italian submarine *Michele Bianchi* (Capitano di corvetta Adalberto Giovannini). As Hessler's war diary makes clear, both were eager to get the first shot in.

War Diary of *U107*, patrol of 24 January–1 March 1941: PG 30103, NHB, reel 1,080, pp. 216–18

Date, time	Details of position, wind, weather, sea, light, visibility, moonlight, etc.	Incidents
23.ii		
1600	Qu. AL 2696	
1805	Qu. AL 2671	A cloud of smoke in sight at a bearing of 343° true. A steamer with two masts and a single funnel. We begin advance manoeuvres – making contact with the convoy is no certainty and this steamer is a bird in the hand so we duly commence our approach.[1]
1822		*U95* in sight. Morse exchange.[2]
		Steamer is zigzagging most erratically on a general course of 250°, initially at 13 knots and then at 11 knots. The additional mileage we've covered on this cruise means that there is insufficient fuel to haul ahead in time for a submerged daylight attack.
2000	Qu. AL 2675, wind NW 2, sea 1–2, 5/10 overcast	
2055		Italian submarine in sight ahead.[3] She too appears to be targeting the steamer. As the fuel situation means that this vessel will be my last chase of the cruise I decide to outmanoeuvre the Italian boat.
	It.: 'Bianchi'[4]	Gradually I gain a position between Italian submarine and steamer.
2232		We begin our approach as the Italian submarine is also turning to attack. In the ensuing battle to windward between the two boats I manage to get into a firing position first.
2240	Qu. AL 2838[5]	Vessel appears to have observed approach since she turns just as we are about to fire and appears to stop.

---

1 The convoy in question was OB288, to which *Manistee* had recently been attached.

2 Hessler no doubt made it clear to the commander of *U95* (Kptlt Gerd Schreiber) that his fuel situation did not permit him to chase the convoy and that *U95* should therefore leave this unaccompanied vessel to *U107*. *U95* did not miss out on the action, however; she caught up with the convoy that evening and sank three of its number during the night.

3 R.Smg. *Michele Bianchi*.

4 Manuscript addition in pencil.

5 This and the subsequent AL 28XX grid references are clearly incorrect, being well east of *U107*'s previous positions and those recorded by her the following morning. *U107* could only have covered 50-odd miles from the position given at 2000 (AL 2675) at her best surface speed of 18 knots, and in any case she reports *Manistee* heading on a westerly course, not due east. Possible typist's error. The correct quadrant (AL 2598) is given in Hessler's own torpedo report and confirmed both in the position given by *Michele Bianchi* and that radioed by *Manistee* herself.

Date, time	Details of position, wind, weather, sea, light, visibility, moonlight, etc.	Incidents
2242	Qu. AL 2838	Spread of torpedoes fired: Tubes IV and III, depth 3 m, inclination 65°, enemy speed 11 knots, range 1,200 m.[6] A hit in the engine room. Steamer loses way, takes on a list of 15° to port. We wait a while. She doesn't settle any further. No boats are lowered.
2258	Qu. AL 2838	*Coup-de-grâce* shot: Tube II, depth 3 m, angle of shot 0°, range 800 m. An unexplained miss, must have run under. Tube I, depth 3 m, angle of shot 0°, range 900 m. No explanation for what happens to this either. Missing a stationary steamer of a good size is just not possible. Torpedo failure. Vessel raises steam once more and gradually gets under way but being careful to keep her stern to our boat.
2317	Qu. AL 2838	We dive so as to close the steamer and deliver the *coup-de-grâce* from a submerged position at point-blank range. For no apparent reason boat loses trim and becomes stern heavy, first by 5° then by 15°. We surface.
2342	Qu. AL 2838	Stern shot from Tube V, depth 2 m, inclination 80°, enemy speed 3 knots, range 1,000 m. Misses. Torpedo twice breaches the surface and then veers off to starboard. We retire to work on the boat's trim and to load the last two torpedoes. The ponderousness at the stern is now explained by mechanical failure in the trim switch whereby all the trim water was directed aft.
2400	Qu. AL 2838, wind SW 1–2, sea 1, 3/10 overcast, bright night with Northern Lights above a bright sky	Torpedoes reloaded, trim problem resolved. *Heßler*
24.ii		
0050		Test dive.
0100		We approach to sink steamer. Vessel has meanwhile raised sufficient steam for 9 knots. The night is very bright thanks to the usual Northern Lights which means that only in brief patches is it possible to gain the benefit of a dark horizon. An uncommonly poor night for attacking, and I can't get any closer than 2,000 m. Vessel notices our approach and takes evasive action, which makes it clear that a skilful and tenacious captain is in command. Steamer is steering with wild zigzags of up to 180° to each side, constantly either increasing and decreasing speed, as well as going into reverse. Vessel always
0400	*Qu. AL 2648. Bright night, Northern Lights, scattered clouds.[7]*	manoeuvres to ensure that it is never facing a dark section of horizon. To sink the steamer with gunfire would appear a formidable task as well as dangerous at night with a convoy not far off. The search for attacking opportunities continues for 6½ hours. Vessel appears to have hydrophone equipment since she turns away every time the boat moves in to attack. As I run in at 0729 she turns away at almost 160°. I nonetheless follow through with attack approach and am fortunate in that the vessel slowly turns 90° to starboard soon after.
0758	Qu. AL 2657, wind E 0, sea 1, 1/10 overcast	Multiple salvo, Tubes III and IV. Range 2,000 m, inclination 80°, enemy speed 6 knots, a hit 40 m from the stern by the after cargo hold. Steamer gradually settles by the stern. But there's something not quite right about this steamer. As she is armed I can't work out why she didn't open fire during our earlier approaches. I wonder if she was biding her time, simply waiting for *U107* to get in close.[8] Steamer sends a radio transmission following this hit. She is the *Manistee*, 5,300 GRT.[9] She is sending continuous distress signals.
0841		As the fuel situation won't allow us to carry out any further pursuit we head off without waiting for her to sink, which looks certain based on our final observations. Course 152°, destination Lorient.
0919		Outgoing W/T transmission: *Total haul four steamers for 21,000 GRT. Out of torpedoes, Qu. AL 2654. U107.* Cruising at half speed.

6 This and all subsequent torpedoes were fired by Oblt.z.S. Hanschel, *U107*'s First Watch Officer. In this case Hanschel selects a wide angle of dispersion (6°) which suggests considerable uncertainty as to target inclination and/or speed.

7 Manuscript additions in pencil.

8 Hessler raises a significant point, one which has never been answered.

9 Actually 5,360 GRT; possible typist's error.

The sinking

Hessler recorded his first torpedo striking *Manistee* on the port side amidships at 2142 British time. However, Giovannini's *Michele Bianchi*, which Hessler's log shows to have been vying with *U107* to strike the first blow on *Manistee*, also reported a hit some fifteen minutes later, though his claim must be regarded as doubtful since *Manistee*'s first transmission was sent within a few minutes of *U107*'s attack and she reported no further hits until Hessler's second the following morning. What is certain both from *Manistee*'s subsequent radio transmissions and from Hessler's log is that she was still able to raise steam. At 2245 *Manistee* reported flooding in the main coal bunker but added that the damage was otherwise under control, Hessler subsequently paying an unusual tribute to the skill with which Cdr Smith handled his ship. At 0405 *Manistee* gave her position as 58° 55' N, 21° 00' W and her speed as 7½ knots. The extent of the damage done her by *U107*'s second torpedo shortly after 0700 (0800 log time) on the 24th is impossible to ascertain, though Hessler's log indicates that she gradually sank by the stern. Shortly after the hit *Manistee* signalled that she had been attacked in position 58° 55' N, 20° 50' W. This seems to have been the last that was ever heard of her.

Fate of the crew

Manistee's first wireless transmission to the effect that she had been torpedoed on her port side was acted on immediately by the new Commander-in-Chief Western Approaches, Admiral Sir Percy Noble who detached HM corvette *Heather* to render assistance. Before long the destroyers *Churchill* and *Leopard* were ordered to the scene, the former estimating that she would reach her position by 0500 the following morning. However, when both OB288 and OB289 came under sustained attack from a number of U-boats the destroyers were directed to reinforce the convoys instead, which lost a dozen ships that night. *Heather*, by now the sole rescue vessel, reached the position given by *Manistee* shortly after 1000 on the 24th and conducted a wide search until dark. She found no trace either of *Manistee* or her men. It is possible that some catastrophic event befell *Manistee* after *U107*'s last hit such as that which overtook the cruiser HMAS *Sydney* nine months later, but nothing has ever emerged to explain her demise and that of her ship's company, who were eventually reported Missing, Presumed Killed.

U107 and Günter Hessler

For information on the earlier careers of *U107* and Kptlt Günter Hessler, see HMS *Crispin* (**22**).

Hessler's three patrols in command of *U107* netted almost 120,000 tons of Allied shipping. Following her successful maiden patrol during which *Crispin* and *Manistee* were sunk, *U107* sailed from Lorient on what became the most successful U-boat cruise in history, fourteen ships being sunk for a total of nearly 90,000 tons. Hessler had more than enough tonnage to earn his Knight's Cross by the time of his third and last patrol in *U107* during September and October 1941, but Karl Dönitz, whose son-in-law he was, was reluctant to approve the decoration on grounds of favouritism and it was Raeder himself who had eventually to sign the necessary authorisation. However, *U107* was to be Hessler's only U-boat command. In December 1941 he was appointed to the operations staff of B.d.U., serving with it for the duration and reaching the rank of Fregattenkapitän. Hessler's fate was

Dönitz congratulating the crew of *U107* at Lorient on 2 July 1941. Hessler is behind him in the white cap. *DUBMA*

closely tied to the Allies after the war, first as a prisoner of the British and then as principal contributor to *The U-Boat War in the Atlantic, 1939–1945*, the classified three-volume history which the Admiralty ordered prepared from original sources. He died in April 1968, twelve years before his father-in-law.

Hessler was succeeded as commander of *U107* by Oblt.z.S. (Kptlt from April 1942) Harald Gelhaus, who continued her remarkable run of success by sinking over 100,000 tons of shipping in six patrols over the next twelve months. He too received the Knight's Cross before being assigned to staff duties with Kriegsmarine High Command. His replacement in May 1943, Oblt.z.S. (Kptlt from January 1944) Volker Simmermacher, proved less successful with no confirmed sinkings in three patrols. *U107*'s last commander was Lt.z.S. Karl-Heinz Fritz who sailed from Lorient on 16 August 1944 with orders to take her to La Pallice. On the 18th she was sighted by an RAF Sunderland in the Bay of Biscay and destroyed by a pattern of six depth charges. There were no survivors.

Sources

Admiralty, *Enemy Submarine Attacks on HM Ships, 1941* (TNA, ADM 199/160)

—, *North Atlantic, Details of Shipping Losses, November 1940–June 1941* (NHB, CIV report, Atlantic Ocean)

U107, Torpedo report of 2242 hrs on 23 February 1941 (BfZ, Schussmeldung collection)

Baveystock, Flt Lt Leslie, *Wavetops at My Wingtips: Flying with RAF Bomber and Coastal Commands in World War II* (Shrewsbury, Salop: Airlife Publishing, 2001)

Haws, Duncan, *Elders & Fyffes and Geest* [Merchant Fleets, no. 31] (Ridgewood, E. Sussex: TCL Publications, 1996)

McCutcheon, Campbell, *Elders & Fyffes* (Stroud, Glos.: Tempus Publishing, 2006)

Rohwer, Jürgen, *Kriegsmarine U-107* [Warships in Profile, no. 8] (Windsor, Berks.: Profile Publications, 1970)

24 HMS (ex SS) *RAJPUTANA*

Capt. F. H. Taylor, DSC RN
Sunk by *U108* (Type IXB), Kptlt Klaus Scholtz, 13 April 1941
Denmark Strait, 145 nm WNW of Reykjavik (Iceland)

Rajputana following her conversion to armed merchant cruiser. Two of her eight 6-inch mountings can be seen, most of which went into action against *U108* on the morning of 13 April 1941. *BfZ*

Theatre   North Atlantic (Map 1)
Coordinates (of first attack)   64° 50′ N, 27° 25′ W
Kriegsmarine code (of first attack)   Quadrat AD 5582
U-boat timekeeping differential   +2 hours
Fatalities   42   *Survivors*   275+

Deadweight   7,521 tons
Gross tons   16,644
Dimensions   570′ × 71.25′ × 28.75′
Maximum speed   17 knots
Armament   8 × 6″; 2 × 3″ AA

Career

For background on the armed merchant cruisers, see HMS *Carinthia* (**8**).

Built by Harland & Wolff of Greenock for the Peninsular & Oriental Steam Navigation Co., the liner *Rajputana* was launched on 6 August 1925 and completed in January of the following year. Destined for an uneventful career on the company's Far East service, the outbreak of war found *Rajputana* at Yokohama from where she was ordered to Esquimalt, British Columbia for refitting as an armed merchant cruiser on 4 September 1939. By now reduced to a single funnel, she was commissioned into the Royal Navy on 16 December, just weeks after her sister *Rawalpindi* had succumbed to German gunfire in the Iceland–Faroes gap. *Rajputana*'s first duties were on the America and West Indies Station where she remained until joining the Bermuda Convoy Escort Force (subsequently Bermuda and Halifax Escort Force) in May 1940, and finally the North Atlantic Escort Force the following spring.

Background of the attack

On 27 March 1941 *Rajputana* sailed from Halifax, Nova Scotia in company with HMS/m *Tribune*, the pair serving as the initial escort to convoy HX117 bound for the Clyde. Having handed the convoy over to the main escort at longitude 25 degrees West on the evening of 9 April *Rajputana* altered course north-west towards her assigned patrol area in the Denmark Strait. Also in the Denmark Strait was Kptlt Klaus Scholtz in *U108*, patrolling with special instructions to attack armed merchant cruisers. *U108* first sighted *Rajputana* early on the 11th and the log excerpt which follows describes no fewer than five separate attacks on her by Scholtz over the next two days. These were made possible because the armed merchant cruisers tended to patrol along fixed courses which were reversed every twelve hours, a regularity of operation that had helped account for HMS *Andania* (**10**) the previous June. The first two attacks went undetected by *Rajputana* though on each occasion Capt. Taylor unwittingly frustrated his pursuer by assuming a zigzag course and maintaining speeds that either spoilt Scholtz's aim or left him trailing in her wake. However, Scholtz was not be denied and *U108*'s sixth and eighth torpedoes finally spared his blushes on the morning of the 13th.

War Diary of *U108*, patrol of 3 March–2 May 1941: PG 30104, NHB, reel 1,080, pp. 636–8

Date, time	Details of position, wind, weather, sea, light, visibility, moonlight, etc.	Incidents
11.iv		
0945	Qu. AD 5352	A plume of smoke in sight at a bearing of 0° true which we attempt to close. A steamer, inclination 180°, which presently alters course to starboard, new course 60°. We haul ahead. Visibility is extremely variable due to rain showers and for a while the vessel disappears from sight. When she reappears she is sailing on a reciprocal course. Again we attempt to haul ahead. I assume she is an auxiliary cruiser on Denmark Strait patrol.[1]
1200	Qu. AD 5327, wind SW 4, sea 4, strong swell, good visibility, squalls	Day's run: 190 nm on the surface, 5 nm submerged = 195 nm.
1300		Vessel once again alters course by 180° or so, thereby confirming my assumption that she is an auxiliary cruiser. As it is pointless trying to haul ahead I take up position behind her, trying to follow the same course line.
1600	Qu. AD 5319, wind SW 3, sea 3, partly overcast, intermittent squalls, medium to good visibility	Auxiliary cruiser disappears from sight in a squall. I plough on.
1723		Auxiliary cruiser re-emerges from the squall, inclination 80°, range some 8,000 m. Alarm dive so as to remain unsighted. At periscope depth I establish that the vessel has altered course further in our direction, with an inclination of perhaps 40°. I decide to attack; sea is smooth, minimal swell, not a breath of wind.
1808	Qu. AD 5321	A twin salvo (both G7e) from range of 2,000 m, inclination 100°, enemy speed 13 knots, not possible to get closer given the great initial inclination of the target. They both miss; by hydrophone it appears they passed ahead of her so we must have overestimated her speed. She is an auxiliary cruiser of roughly 10,000 GRT,[2] camouflage painting, single funnel, two high masts, passenger superstructures amidships, four cargo hatches, a small derrick on the fo'c's'le. Bridge is set some distance from the funnel. Perhaps 130 m in length – quite similar to M.S. No. 328/*Nector* [*sic*].[3] Auxiliary cruiser has not noticed torpedoes and soon after turns away to port.
1940		Surfaced.
2000	Qu. AD 5324, wind W 4, sea 3, partly overcast, good visibility	
2025		Our boat lies directly on the auxiliary cruiser's course, inclination 0°. We dive in preparation for attack. Just as the range closes to around 5,000 m the auxiliary cruiser alters course to starboard by 90°. Attack has to be abandoned.
2239		We surface and pursue target's wake. Auxiliary cruiser temporarily disappears from sight.
2340		Alarm dive – auxiliary cruiser sighted at 30° on the starboard bow, inclination 10°, bows right, emerging from the mist. Attack attempted, but the night attack periscope is out of action and I can see nothing with the main attack periscope. It's now getting dark. Hydrophone contact is of poor quality, making it impossible to gain a clear picture of the enemy's various courses.
2400	Qu. AD 5323, wind SSW 4, sea 4, partly overcast, intermittent showers, visibility otherwise good	*Scholtz*

---

1   HM armed merchant cruiser *Rajputana*.

2   A rare case of a U-boat commander dramatically underestimating the size of his target, *Rajputana* being of 16,664 GRT.

3   Scholtz may be referring to the Ocean Steamship Co.'s *Nestor*, though at 14,629 GRT and 580 feet in length she was considerably larger than the 10,000 GRT and 130 metres (427 feet) stated here, even if much closer to *Rajputana*'s actual size. A more probable alternative is the freighter *Nestor* (2,446 GRT), converted by the Kriegsmarine in 1941 to a *Sperrbrecher* ('barrage breaker') magnetic-mine clearance vessel used to escort surface vessels and U-boats in the approaches to their bases. Although Scholtz's 'M.S.' abbreviation (*Minenschiff* – 'minelayer') and *Nestor*'s length (110 metres, 360 feet) lend some support to this identification, it should be stated that *Nestor*'s *Sperrbrecher* code number was 21 rather than the 328 mentioned here.

Date, time	Details of position, wind, weather, sea, light, visibility, moonlight, etc.	Incidents
12.iv		
0022		We surface as we can neither see nor hear anything. We dive again immediately; auxiliary cruiser is positioned at a relative bearing of 110°, range 3,000 m, inclination 90° bows right, our boat silhouetted against the bright western horizon. We withdraw.
0047		We surface. Auxiliary cruiser no longer in sight. A summary of the day: given the changing courses and speeds of the auxiliary cruiser a daylight attack can only be carried out if luck is on our side given that the enemy alters course constantly, usually reversing her course before our boat has completed her manoeuvre from the limit of visual range to a satisfactory submerged firing position. Where our twilight attack is concerned, our impressions on surfacing are that this would have succeeded had the night attack periscope been serviceable. As the night is too bright for a surface attack, with a full moon blazing through the clouds, yet is at the same time too dark for an underwater attack with the main attack periscope, I decide to use the hours of darkness to withdraw to the north and charge the batteries, so that we are well placed to seek contact once again and attempt a further daylight attack.
0400	Qu. AE 1771, wind ENE 3, sea 3, partly cloudy, good visibility, hail and squalls	Boat has reached her most northerly latitude of 66° 43' N. Indeed, the watch officer only just manages to avoid an ice floe that sticks up some 2 m above the surface. We turn about due to dangers posed by ice.
0800	Qu. AD 2995	
1000	Qu. AD 2997	Enemy in sight. Visibility is at first impaired due to showers but is then very good, about 15 nm.
1200	Qu. AD 5321, wind NE 5, sea 4, swell, snow and squalls, good visibility	Day's run: surface 135 nm, submerged 17 nm = 152 nm total.
1300		Enemy alters course towards us, inclination 10°.
1305		Dive to commence attack.
1325		Enemy changes course by 90°. Given my range of approx. 5,000 m I find myself once more in a hopeless position. Still submerged, I retreat.
1453		We surface. Enemy no longer in sight. I set off in pursuit.
1600	Qu. AD 5324, wind ENE 5, sea 6, cloudy, squalls, good visibility	I intend to re-establish contact before dark and then attempt a night attack.
1700		Auxiliary cruiser once again in sight, course roughly 200°.
1850	Qu. AD 5316	Enemy no longer in sight. Again, set off in pursuit.
2000	Qu. AD 5318, wind NE 4, sea 5, partly overcast, good visibility	Once again we encounter substantial ice floes which lie mainly beneath the surface.
2014		Enemy in sight, inclination 10°, bows right. We dive to attack.
2046		We fire third torpedo, a G7e, inclination 105°, enemy speed 8 knots, from a range of approx. 1,000 m. Either I miss or the torpedo runs under the target.
2048		We fire fourth torpedo, also a G7e, inclination 120°, enemy speed 5 knots, range roughly 800 m. This too misses, either because of a misjudgement of the vessel's speed or because torpedo runs under the target. But from this range the shots should have hit even with substantial coordinate errors. Gauging enemy's speed has become very difficult. As we ascertain by following in her wake, auxiliary cruiser is altering her speed constantly, and the changes are often substantial. Due to the strong swell I opted for a depth setting of 4 m but this may also have caused the torpedoes to run under the target. We reload torpedoes.
2308		We surface. Enemy no longer in sight.
2400	Qu. AD 5346, wind NE 4, sea 3, medium swell, cloudy, good visibility	*Scholtz*
13.iv		
0030		Enemy in sight ahead, sailing at high speed. We try to cling on to her wake. No chance of gaining advance position due to enemy's high speed. She temporarily disappears from sight despite our making 14 knots.

0400	Qu. AD 5536, wind NE 4, sea 3, swell, overcast, good visibility	
0715		Auxiliary cruiser in sight dead ahead, now sailing reciprocal course.
0740		Dive to attack. 5th torpedo, a G7e, inclination 90°, enemy speed 8 knots, range 800 m. Misses.
0743		6th torpedo, a G7e, inclination 120°, enemy speed 12 knots, range 600 m. A hit between the after mast and funnel. Huge flames accompany the detonation. After part of the ship is burning accompanied by clouds of smoke. Later this abates.
		On attacking we experienced strong variations in trim due to heavy swell and had to run at half speed to keep the boat stable. After the detonation the auxiliary cruiser fires at the periscope with her deck guns – we can hear the impacts inside the boat. I can see the shots being fired from the promenade deck above, presumably 8.8- and 2-cm calibre.[4]
		Auxiliary cruiser now only just has way on, holding same course.
0800	Qu. AD 5582, wind ENE 5, sea 4, mainly overcast, average visibility, freshening	They also seem to be using hydrophones to direct their fire whenever our periscope is lowered. Impacts heard all around the boat.
0823		7th torpedo, G7a, inclination 113°, enemy speed 3 knots, range 1,800 m. A dud. Torpedo could be heard with hydrophones for only five seconds, whereas all the others could be heard clearly for the duration of their runs. So clearly headed towards the seabed after 100 m of its run.
0930		8th torpedo, G7e. A *coup-de-grâce* shot for the stopped auxiliary cruiser. Hits. Impact not observed as boat briefly dips below surface. I manoeuvre around her bows. Vessel assumes heavy list to port and settles deeper by the stern. They've stopped firing. I take the view that no further torpedo is called for and that the ship will sink, particularly in these heavy sea conditions.
		I decide to head off, course 250°, and have another look later from the far horizon. Further cruising at periscope depth can't be justified given the difficult conditions for holding the boat's trim, not to mention the obviously expected air surveillance. Particularly in the absence of a sky search periscope.[5]
1101		Loud detonation nearby. As the possibility of aircraft can't be ruled out I dive to T = 45 m, though judging by the sound it can't have been a depth charge or aerial bomb.[6] We hear nothing else. I assume that it must have been an explosion on board the auxiliary cruiser (magazine).[7]
1200	Qu. AD 5559	Day's run: surface 161 nm, submerged 23 nm. Total = 184 nm.
1300		Propeller noises at a bearing of 240°, high revolutions, presumably a destroyer.[8]
1400		Propeller noises have shifted astern and died away.
1456		We surface 9 nm from scene of sinking. I head in her direction. Dead ahead a single high mast appears, followed by another at 300° on the starboard bow. Doubtless destroyers at scene of sinking.[9] No sign of the auxiliary cruiser. She must have sunk.
1518		We head off in the opposite direction.
1520		Alarm dive due to approaching aircraft, though she didn't spot us. I assume that flying boats from Reykjavik are searching for us in wide circles around the scene of the sinking.

4   *Rajputana* was armed with 6-inch mountings together with a pair of 3-inch ('12-pounder') guns which would equate with Scholtz's '8.8-cm calibre'. The 20-mm Oerlikon gun was not mounted.

5   The sky search periscope (*Luftzielsehrohr*) was another name for the night search periscope (*Nachtzielsehrohr*), which Scholtz earlier reports as being unserviceable.

6   By 'T = 45 m' Scholtz seems to be recording a dive of 185 metres (607 feet); for a full discussion of the 'T =' notation, see Reading the *Kriegstagebücher*, p. xxxvii.

7   As this entry corresponds with the time *Rajputana* sank, the detonation recorded by Scholtz could be attributed to a boiler explosion as she went down.

8   Presumably HMS *Legion*; see below.

9   *Legion* is the only vessel recorded by the British as reaching the scene of the sinking.

The sinking

Following a 'phenomenal crash' on her port side *Rajputana* came to an immediate stop, losing all power and assuming an immediate list of about ten degrees. The torpedo had struck abreast the engine rooms, tearing a large hole in her side which rapidly flooded both these and the after boiler room. A number of distress signals were transmitted to the Admiralty reporting that the engines were disabled and both engine rooms, the after stokehold and No. 4 hold flooded. Although a mine was initially suspected, the duty chief yeoman of signals spotted *U108*'s periscope four minutes after the hit and *Rajputana* immediately opened fire with her 6-inch guns. As Scholtz's log makes clear, these maintained a spirited volume of fire practically to the end. In contrast

A survivor's view of *Rajputana* going down shortly before 0800 (British time) on the morning of 13 April.
The second shot shows the final plunge with men visible among the flotsam in the foreground. *Bruce Taylor collection*

to the seven that preceded it, the torpedo that finished *Rajputana* off at 0730 (0930 log time) was spotted approaching at a leisurely pace by those on deck; so slowly, in fact, that an unsuccessful attempt was made to detonate it with the starboard 12-pounder. Striking between No. 4 and 5 holds, the explosion opened up the starboard side to the upper deck and immediately flooded the after part of the ship. At 0750 Capt. Taylor made another signal requesting 'immediate assistance, abandoning ship' in position 64° 50′ N, 27° 01′ W. Barely had the last of *Rajputana*'s men got clear than she sank by the stern with 'a tremendous rush of water'. It was just before 0800 British time, a little over two hours after the first hit.

B.d.U. commended Scholtz for his exemplary tenacity in pursuing *Rajputana*, though in light of six misses was less complimentary about his marksmanship which was considered to require 'further attention'.

Fate of the crew

Scholtz's sixth torpedo instantly claimed the lives of three of the engine room staff. Another man believed missing was later found swimming beneath the gratings, and an advert for Eveready batteries subsequently placed in the American media recorded how Stoker 1st Class Frank C. Davidson of Truro, Nova Scotia had used a torch to rescue shipmates from a flooded compartment. It is not known how many casualties were sustained as a result of the second hit. The speed of the sinking complicated efforts to get the port side boats away, some of them wallowing back under the promenade deck as *Rajputana* drifted to leeward. When she disappeared some minutes later the water was strewn with the boats, oil drums, wreckage and struggling men shown in the photos above, but most of those in the water found a berth. Thanks to the prompt and accurate transmission of distress signals by Capt. Taylor, a search was immediately instigated and a majority of the survivors were spotted by a Sunderland flying boat later that morning. Picked up by HM destroyer *Legion* that afternoon, they were safely in Reykjavik by evening though Lt Daniel Hanington RCNR recalling having shivered off twenty-nine pounds of his girth in the intervening period. It has not proved possible to corroborate the claim by Charles Hocking (see below) that thirty-four men were rescued by a second vessel and eventually returned to Canada. However, one of the ship's boats was never seen again and among those lost was *Rajputana*'s peacetime master, Cdr C. T. O. Richardson RNR, retained as the ship's navigating officer following her conversion for war service.

U108 and Klaus Scholtz

Built by AG Weser of Bremen and commissioned in October 1940, *U108* was commanded for her first eight frontline patrols by Kptlt (Korvettenkapitän from November 1941) Klaus Scholtz. The combination was a highly successful one, *U108* sinking twenty-five ships for a total of over 125,000 tons between February 1941 and August 1942. The good endurance of the Type-IXB boats served *U108* well and she scored heavily in US and Caribbean waters during Operation PAUKENSCHLAG. Awarded the Knight's Cross in December 1941 (to which the Oak Leaf cluster was added on leaving *U108* in September 1942), Scholtz was given command of the 12th Flotilla based on Lorient, which office he held until this force was disbanded in August 1944. He attempted to get his men back to Germany but they were captured in France in September, Scholtz spending the next nineteen months in US captivity. He later joined the newly created Bundesmarine, retiring in 1966 as a Kapitän zur See. Klaus Scholtz died in May 1987.

U108 enjoyed scant success in her last three patrols under Korvkpt. Rolf-Reimar Wolfram, being assigned to training duties in September 1943. She was sunk in a US bomber raid on Stettin on 11 April 1944, and though raised was decommissioned and eventually scuttled there on 24 April 1945.

Sources

Admiralty, *Enemy Submarine Attacks on HM Ships, 1941* (TNA, ADM 199/160)
—, *Reports of HX Convoys* (TNA, ADM 199/178)

Hocking, Charles, *Dictionary of Disasters at Sea during the Age of Steam Including Sailing Ships and Ships of War Lost in Action, 1824–1962* (2 vols, London: Lloyd's Register of Shipping, 1969), pp. 577–8
Kerr, George F., *Business in Great Waters: The War History of the P. & O., 1939–1945* (London: Faber and Faber, 1951)
Middlemiss, Norman L., *P. & O. Lines* [Merchant Fleets, no. 44] (Newcastle upon Tyne: Shield Publications, 2004)
Osborne, Richard, Harry Spong and Tom Grover, *Armed Merchant Cruisers, 1878–1945* (Windsor, Berks.: World Ship Society, 2007)
Poolman, Kenneth, *Armed Merchant Cruisers* (London: Leo Cooper, 1985)

Westell, Dan, 'Memoirs Offer a Personal Glimpse into Navy Battle' [obituary of Rear-Admiral D. L. Hanington, survivor]: http://www.craigmarlatt. com/canada/security&defence/navy-news2.html

25 HMS (ex SS) *CAMITO*

Cdr A. A. Barnet, RNR

Sunk by *U97* (Type VIIC), Kptlt Udo Heilmann, 6–7 May 1941

North Atlantic, 600 nm W of Land's End, Cornwall (England)

The Elders & Fyffes banana boat SS *Camito* seen leaving Avonmouth in the 1930s. The survivor of a U-boat attack in the First World War, she succumbed to *U97* in the Second. *Bruce Taylor collection*

Theatre   North Atlantic (Map 1)
Coordinates (of attack)   50° 40' N, 21° 30' W
Kriegsmarine code (of attack)   Quadrat BE 1372
U-boat timekeeping differential   +2 hours
Fatalities   2 in *Camito,* 26 in *Sangro*   *Survivors*   126

Deadweight   6,750 tons
Gross tons   6,833
Dimensions   426.25' × 54.25' × 17'
Maximum speed   15.5 knots
Armament   2 × 6"; 1 × 3" AA; 4 × .303"

Career

For background on the ocean boarding vessels, see HMS *Crispin* (**22**).

Built for Elders & Fyffes Shipping by Alexander Stephen & Sons of Linthouse, Glasgow, the coal-fired banana boat SS *Camito* was launched in April 1915, entering service as an escort vessel that same year. She had an eventful career, beating off an attack from *U82* on 15 June 1917 and striking a mine laid by *U79* off Aran Island, County Galway on 13 August. After the Great War *Camito* took up the cargo and passenger duties between Britain and the Caribbean for which she had been designed, serving in this capacity throughout the interwar period. In 1940 she was again requisitioned by the Admiralty and refitted as an ocean boarding vessel, thus making her one of the handful of merchantmen to have seen naval service in both world wars.

Background of the attack

On the evening of 3 May 1941 HMS *Camito*, then patrolling in the Western Approaches, intercepted the Italian tanker SS *Sangro* which quickly struck her colours and surrendered. Laden with fuel oil, the 6,466-ton *Sangro* was a valuable prize and Cdr Barnet lost no time in sending aboard a prize crew of twenty-six men and notifying the Admiralty of his capture. He was ordered to make for position 50° 00' N, 20° 22' W to rendezvous with HM corvettes *Orchis* and *Heather* on the evening of the 5th. However, the passage of *Camito* and *Sangro* to the meeting point proved to be a difficult one. *Sangro* had problems with her steering gear and the vessels twice came close to colliding in poor visibility on the night of 4–5 May. Similar difficulties were experienced the following night. The resulting delay might not have affected the issue except that *Camito*, keeping British Summer Time, had been sending her position in GMT, while *Orchis* and *Heather* were using Mid-Atlantic Standard Time (GMT –2 hours). The efforts of the two corvettes to make the rendezvous with *Camito* were therefore frustrated first by an inaccurate assessment of her relative position and then by poor visibility. The matter was complicated by difficulties in signalling, with *Camito* apparently working not in Auxiliary Code but in Fleet Code, which only *Heather* could decipher, all signals having to be re-encrypted in order that *Orchis* could read them. Subsequent investigation revealed that *Camito* should in this instance have been using standard naval codes and timekeeping. Whatever the case, all this unwittingly played into the hands of Kptlt Udo Heilmann whose war diary for 5 May reveals that *U97* sighted first *Heather* and *Orchis* heading south-south-west and then *Sangro* and *Camito* steering north-east just twenty minutes later, the vessels having clearly missed each other. Still en route to his assigned patrol area, Heilmann baulked at the prospect of attacking *Heather* and *Orchis* while they sailed in company but had no such qualms where *Camito* and her prize were concerned.

War Diary of *U97*, patrol of 1–30 May 1941: PG 30093, NHB, reel 1,077, pp. 131–2

Date, time	Details of position, wind, weather, sea, light, visibility, moonlight, etc.	Incidents
5.v		
1600	Qu. [BE] 1611, wind N 5, sea 3–4, overcast, variable visibility, 1,007 mb	
1625		An improvement in visibility. We surface and head towards our allotted operational area.
1725	Qu. [BE] 1298	A vessel heaves into sight at an acute inclination of 40° on the starboard bow, course roughly 210°. Shortly after sighting this vessel we see a second one steering the same course. We can identify both vessels as small escort types, apparently a U-boat hunter pairing.[1] They keep altering course. I turn away and withdraw to the south.
1745	Qu. [BE] 1532	A steamer appears at an acute inclination dead ahead. I now turn to the west to ascertain whether it is part of a convoy or sailing on its own. Further observation reveals a pair of steamers sailing in company, course north-east.[2] Because of the U-boat hunter group nearby I decide to maintain remote contact and only move in to attack on the surface under cover of darkness.
2000	Qu. [BE] 1531	Maintaining contact is becoming difficult due to the rapidly changing visibility and the heavy seas breaking over the boat. Contact temporarily lost as a result.
2057		Alarm! The two steamers loom up out of a wall of rain. Our boat is very close and is forced to dive. Both vessels are steering strong zigzag courses. It's quite possible that we've been spotted.[3]
2122		Surface and re-establish contact. While the first steamer is maintaining a consistent course and speed, the second vessel is constantly altering speed, and sometimes veering off at bearings that diverge up to 90° from the mean course.[4] Once dusk falls the two steamers start zigzagging more consistently as well as less frequently.
2400	Qu. [BE] 1299, wind N 5, sea 4, overcast, visibility variable, light showers, 1,010 mb	
		Heilmann
6.v		We establish course and speed of rear steamer while hauling ahead.
0202	Qu. [BE] 1372	Attack on rear steamer (size approx. 5,000 GRT).[5] <u>Spread of two torpedoes fired</u> (G7e). Shot coordinates: enemy speed 7 knots, inclination 89.6°, range 800 m. Two misses because enemy speed overestimated. Enemy apparently noticed our approach and reduced speed. I turn away immediately so as to get a stern shot in. <u>Single shot</u> (G7a). Shot coordinates: enemy speed 5 knots, inclination 93°, range 600 m. Misses as vessel stops and goes astern. Again I manoeuvre ahead and attack once more.
0240	Qu. [BE] 1372	<u>Single shot</u> (G7a). Shot coordinates: enemy speed 2 knots, inclination 78.7°, range 800 m. 48 seconds later a very powerful, high-pitched detonation with a large column of flame. It strikes slightly abaft of amidships. It seems as though torpedo must have struck on the waterline, or just slightly below, because the column sent up by the explosion and detonation were abnormal. We noted up to three separate detonations in the boat. Steamer continues at slow speed, then turns gradually towards us. A number of different lights are showing on deck. The torpedo doesn't seem to have made a great deal of difference to the steamer – she's not settling any deeper, or listing. Based on these observations and the behaviour of the vessel during the day I assume that she is a U-boat decoy.[6] So I decide to abandon my efforts with this vessel and work my way over towards the other one.
0353	Qu. [BE] 1348	Attack on 6,000 GRT tanker.[7]

---

1   These two were almost certainly HMSs *Heather* and *Orchis*, vainly trying to rendezvous with *Camito* and *Sangro*. Interestingly, while *U97* sighted both groups within twenty minutes of each other, the corvettes did not locate survivors from the *Sangro* until more than twenty-four hours had passed.

2   SS *Sangro* and HMS *Camito* respectively.

3   It is clear from Admiralty records that *U97* had not in fact been spotted.

4   SS *Sangro* showing the effects of her defective steering gear.

5   HMS *Camito* of 6,833 GRT. This and all subsequent torpedoes were fired by *U97*'s First Watch Officer, Kptlt Burkhard Hackländer, who went on to sink HMS *Matabele* while in command of *U454* (see **47**).

6   *Camito* was in fact an ocean boarding vessel.

7   SS *Sangro* of 6,466 GRT.

Single shot (G7e). Shot coordinates: enemy speed 5 knots, inclination 82°, range 500 m. Hits amidships after 30 seconds with a powerful detonation. Immediately after the explosion tanker is clearly observed to be blazing brightly. The glow of flame can be seen for a long time afterwards, even from a great distance. I now return to the position from which I attacked the first steamer. She's still there – steering back and forth at very slow speed, her course constantly altering. There are a large number of empty drums floating in the water that have clearly come from the steamer. So she probably was a decoy vessel or something similar which should be treated with a great deal of caution. As such, I decide against sacrificing more torpedoes and head off to the south-east, altering to the south-west once dawn breaks.

0503   Weather report transmitted to B.d.U.

The sinking

Despite Heilmann's fears there is no evidence that Cdr Barnet had any idea he was being stalked by a U-boat until *Camito* was struck on the starboard side abreast No. 3 hold at 0050 ship time. No casualties were inflicted nor did *Camito* initially appear to have suffered fatal damage. Though the port engine was disabled, the starboard unit remained serviceable and early reports suggested that its damaged twin could be quickly repaired, which proved to be the case. Of greater concern was the steady flooding of the shaft tunnels, while water was also entering through the main engine room bulkheads. Course was initially set to regain contact with *Sangro* when a huge explosion ahead revealed that she too had been torpedoed. Cdr Barnet recalled 'a sheet of flame high in the sky illuminating the sea for many miles around'. Incorrectly assuming that the entire crew had perished in the conflagration, he immediately altered course and made off on both engines at a speed of seven knots to avoid a similar fate. However, it was the ocean rather than *U97* that proved to be *Camito*'s undoing, Heilmann having long since disappeared to the south. By the afternoon of the 6th the wind had reached Force 7 and the sea was 'breaking unremittingly on the deck'. Fearing a second torpedo, at daybreak on the 7th Cdr Barnet ordered *Camito*'s lifeboats to be lowered with the majority of the ship's company while he remained on board with a skeleton crew. By early afternoon *Camito* had shipped so much water that he had no option but to pass the order to abandon ship. According to *Orchis*'s timekeeping, she sank at around 1430, approximately in position 50° 14' N, 21° 45' W and about twenty miles south-west of where *Sangro* had met her fate.

The Officer Commanding Northern Patrol, Rear-Admiral E. J. Spooner, made much of *Camito*'s failure to position herself at a safe distance from *Sangro* prior to the attack and questioned her slow speed, a point reiterated by the Court of Enquiry, which also commended Cdr Barnet and his ship's company for doing all in their power to save the ship. However, the confusion which resulted in three ships spending almost a day trying to locate each other in the same area of ocean without realising that they were using different timekeeping to relay their positions (with an additional code complication) seems to have passed without comment. That this situation should recur after the rescue of survivors of HMS *Crispin* (**22**) had been delayed by comparable disjunctures in February suggests either a significant failure of organisation or more likely the Admiralty's determination to keep the operation of its ocean boarding vessels secret.

Fate of the crew

In view of Heilmann's extreme caution when dealing with British

Heilmann (in white cap) brings *U97* back to St-Nazaire on 30 May 1941 from the patrol during which *Camito* was sunk. To the right the pennant corresponding to *Camito* reads *U-Boot Falle* ('U-boat trap [ship]'), as recorded in the log. Note *U97*'s seahorse emblem on the conning tower. *BK*

warships, the fact that he elected to attack *Camito* at all no doubt had much to do with the failure of *Heather* and *Orchis* to effect a timely rendezvous with her on 5 May. On the other hand, *Orchis*'s appearance at 1520 on the 7th was just as instrumental in saving the majority of her crew in what were now appalling conditions. After rescuing Cdr Barnet and his skeleton crew from their rafts, *Orchis* proceeded at full speed to the estimated position of the lifeboats which had been set adrift with the bulk of the ship's company more than seven hours earlier. The first was sighted at 1645 and the last (showing her position in increasingly poor visibility with an Aldis lamp) at 1830. All those who abandoned ship on the 6th were saved, a remarkable achievement in the prevailing conditions. However, the two men who went down with *Camito* did so in particularly regrettable circumstances. Taking advantage of damage to the wardroom bar and a relaxation of ordinary supervision, the ratings in question found two bottles of whisky and proceeded to drink themselves into an insensible condition. As they could neither be roused nor safely lowered when the time came for *Camito*'s skeleton crew to abandon ship, they were reluctantly left to their fate as the vessel foundered. For her part, *Heather* was sent ahead to rescue the crew of the *Sangro* though not one of *Camito*'s prize crew of twenty-six men survived the ordeal. The four men rescued by *Heather* not far from where *Sangro* sank were all members of her Italian complement.

U97 and Udo Heilmann

Built by Germaniawerft at Kiel and commissioned in September 1940, *U97* did not sail on her maiden operational patrol until February 1941. Commanded by the experienced Kptlt Udo Heilmann, she enjoyed conspicuous success on this cruise, sinking three vessels from OB289 and damaging a tanker from the same convoy on only her seventh night at sea. *U97*'s run of success continued, though the sinking of *Camito* and *Sangro* during her third patrol was overshadowed by her vain efforts to help the crippled battleship *Bismarck* as the Royal Navy closed in for the kill on 26 and 27 May. In September 1941 Heilmann took *U97* into the Mediterranean but sinkings were much harder to come by in this theatre and six patrols yielded only two small merchantmen. Heilmann left *U97* in May 1942 which continued to ply a lean trade in Mediterranean waters, her only major success coming with the sinking of the large tanker *Athelmonarch* off Palestine on 15 June 1943. The following day she was sighted on the surface by an RAAF Hudson and sunk south of Cyprus with the loss of over half her crew, including her commander Kptlt Hans-Georg Trox. The

Royal Navy picked up twenty-one survivors.

After *U97* Heilmann was assigned to training duties ashore in which he remained for the duration of the war. He died in November 1970.

Sources

Admiralty, Department of the Director of Naval Construction, *Damage Reports: Torpedo and Mine, 1940–1942* (TNA, ADM 267/92)

—, *Enemy Submarine Attacks on HM Ships, 1941* (TNA, ADM 199/160)

—, *Loss of HMS* Camito *and Captured Italian SS* Sangro (TNA, ADM 1/11546)

Barnet, Cdr A. A., correspondence with Mrs E. L. Townley, Largs, Ayrshire, 23 May–15 July 1941 (June Bateley collection)

Gibson, Mrs Helen, correspondence with Mrs E. L. Townley, Milliken Park, Renfrewshire, 12–20 May 1941 (June Bateley collection)

Haws, Duncan, *Elders & Fyffes and Geest* [Merchant Fleets, no. 31] (Ridgewood, E. Sussex: TCL Publications, 1996)

McCutcheon, Campbell, *Elders & Fyffes* (Stroud, Glos.: Tempus Publishing, 2006)

26   HMS *SALOPIAN* (ex MS *SHROPSHIRE*)

Capt. Sir John Alleyne, Bart, DSO DSC RN Ret'd
Sunk by *U98* (Type VIIC), Kptlt Robert Gysae, 13 May 1941
North Atlantic, 240 nm SE of Uummannarsuaq, Greenland

The Bibby Line's *Shropshire* seen in her peacetime livery. It required five of *U98*'s torpedoes to send her, as HMS *Salopian*, to the bottom of the Atlantic, a tribute to the stoutness of her construction on the Clyde. *Bruce Taylor collection.*

Theatre	North Atlantic (Map 1)	*Deadweight*	10,192 tons
Coordinates	56° 43' N, 38° 57' W	*Gross tons*	10,549
Kriegsmarine code	Quadrat AJ 3825	*Dimensions*	502' × 60.25' × 29.75'
U-boat timekeeping differential	+4 hours	*Maximum speed*	15.5 knots
Fatalities 3	*Survivors* 278	*Armament*	6 × 6"; 2 × 3" AA; 4 × .5" AA; 4 × .303" AA

Career

For background on the armed merchant cruisers, see HMS *Carinthia* (8).

Laid down for the Bibby Line at Fairfield's yard at Govan on the Clyde, the motor liner *Shropshire* was launched in June 1926 and completed in October that year. Her peacetime career was spent

transporting passengers and cargo on the company's service between Liverpool and Rangoon. *Shropshire* was requisitioned by the Royal Navy on 25 August 1939 and taken in hand for refitting as an armed merchant cruiser at Birkenhead, being renamed *Salopian* to avoid confusion with the County-class cruiser of the same name. Stripped of a funnel, two of her four masts and all her cabin fittings, on 29 September *Salopian* sailed into Scapa Flow with seven other armed merchant cruisers for duty on the Northern Patrol in the Iceland–Faroes gap. Manned to a considerable extent by reservists, her captain, Sir John Alleyne, already a recipient of the DSC, had won the DSO as navigator of the *Vindictive* at Zeebrugge in 1918. Still not fully worked up, on 17 October she joined the general exodus from Orkney which followed the sinking of the *Royal Oak* (2) three days earlier, being assigned to the Freetown Escort Force in November. Subsequently she was in collision with the Finnish freighter *Saimaa*, an accident that kept her in dock until 20 January 1940 though the opportunity was taken to carry out alterations to her fore bridge and to install a buoyant cargo. *Salopian* spent the rest of her career alternating patrol duty with convoy escort assignments in the Atlantic, serving with the Northern Patrol between February and August 1940 and the Western Patrol between November 1940 and February 1941; the intervening period was presumably taken up with a refit. In March 1941 she was transferred from the Freetown to the Bermuda and Halifax Escort Force before taking up her final assignment with the North Atlantic Escort Force in May.

Background of the attack

On 1 May 1941 *U98* sailed from St-Nazaire for operations in the North Atlantic, joining three other boats in a patrol line south-east of Greenland on the 11th. The following afternoon HMS *Salopian* handed over convoy SC30 to a destroyer escort on the threshold of the supposed U-boat danger zone south-west of Iceland and was on her way back to Halifax when she was sighted by *U98* early on the 13th. Few U-boat war diaries provide more detailed treatment of an attack than Kptlt Robert Gysae's on *Salopian*, yet questions remain. Not the least detailed or curious of these is Gysae's prolonged observation of *Salopian*'s gun crews responding to his first torpedo hit – so prolonged in fact as to hazard his boat. That no such response is recorded in British sources at this time makes his account the more mystifying.

War Diary of *U98*, patrol of 1–29 May 1941: PG 30094, NHB, reel 1,077, pp. 443–5

Date, time	Details of position, wind, weather, sea, light, visibility, moonlight, etc.	Incidents
13.v		
0400	[Qu.] AJ 3565, cloudy, wind W 2, sea 2	
0410		At 30° on the port bow we identify a shadow and head towards it. Battle Stations. Shadow gradually becomes larger – a passenger liner sailing alone.[1] No running lights, strong zigzags, general course appears to be southwards. We're unfavourably positioned with regard to the moon so we haul off at high speed and try to work round to the other side. This takes quite a while because the steamer is also sailing at high speed – 12 knots for sure. Finally we reach the other side but are now somewhat astern so we haul ahead again while at the same time attempting to shorten the range. The zigzag of the vessel is easy to determine against the moon. I can't get an accurate fix on her speed because there's simply no chance of my tracking her zigzag at the rate of knots she's making.
		I intend to fire a double salvo at the first favourable opportunity using estimated coordinates. Because of the target's great length I hope that at least one will hit so that the ship will at least be forced to reduce speed or even stop.
0530	[Qu.] AJ 3568	Double salvo, Tubes I and II.[2] Range approx. 1,500 m. Point of aim 50 m from bow and stern respectively. Shortly after the shots are fired the enemy zigzags away at 90°. They therefore miss. Despite the brightness of the night I don't think she has seen me and consider her evasive manoeuvre coincidental. The torpedoes were fired with a 0° line of bearing because the UZO had become waterlogged and had been disconnected.[3]
		Again we measure the length of her zigzag with the stopwatch. Every 7 or 15 min. she changes leg, turning approximately 90° each time. We haul away again at maximum speed and by keeping roughly to her base course we gradually pull ahead. I intend to fire another double salvo the moment she starts the next leg of her zigzag. I still have an Ato and an Eto ready in the bow tubes.[4]
		When she alters course to starboard – roughly southwards – I go on to maximum speed and manoeuvre to attack, slowing to half speed just before firing the first torpedo. Conditions are exceptionally favourable for once. Steamer lies between us and the moon, her inclination can be precisely determined and behind us we have the dark, almost black horizon covered in thick cloud.

---

1   HMS *Salopian*.

2   These torpedoes and all others up to and including those discharged at 0725 were fired by *U98*'s First Watch Officer, Oblt.z.S. Friedrich-Hermann Praetorius.

3   Always abbreviated, UZO was the *Überwasserzieloptik*, a target bearing indicator. It consisted of a pair of binoculars attached to a rotating bracket providing the relative bearing of the target. These were in turn connected mechanically to the *Vorhaltrechner* (torpedo data computer). The binoculars were in the possession of the duty watch officer on the bridge and, being unwaterproofed, were not to be left there when the boat submerged.

4   Kriegsmarine shorthand for the compressed-air G7a and electric G7e torpedoes respectively.

Date, time	Details of position, wind, weather, sea, light, visibility, moonlight, etc.	Incidents
0619	[Qu.] AJ 3595	Torpedo fired from Tube III. An Ato. Range about 1,200 m. Enemy speed 12 knots.
		We have to take this opportunity to fire despite an inclination of 130°. As the bearing rate changes the inclination becomes even greater. But this is our last chance to attack the vessel on the surface without being spotted because it is gradually becoming lighter. After the first torpedo is fired the vessel turns
0622		slightly towards us, so that the second torpedo (Eto), fired at 0622, can be launched at an inclination of 90°. This zigzag may not be in keeping with the pattern so far, but I still don't believe it was an evasive manoeuvre. Otherwise the steamer would have turned away on seeing the G7a trail. After firing the second torpedo I turn about so as to bring Tube V into play if need be. But the angle is now too great. These two torpedoes have also missed. This is not easily explained because even a 2-knot error in calculating vessel speed (as indeed we later determine) would not make us miss given a target length of 180 m (see torpedo report).[5]

With all the turning and reduction in speed I am now settling considerably by the stern. The vessel, clearly sailing faster than our last estimate, some 14 knots, is steering a course of 180° and gets gradually smaller until she is finally lost in the mist.

I've no more torpedoes left in the bow tubes. Luck has deserted us – four torpedoes gone and our steamer has got away. Our mood can be imagined. Nonetheless, I follow her last southerly course with both engines at 4/5 speed, although the extra 2 knots that has to be factored in hardly makes it a promising venture. At the same time we try to reload two of the torpedo tubes en route. Actually this works fine and in the meantime it has now become quite light in every direction. Only a few isolated patches of fog remain in the direction taken by our steamer. There is thus no doubt that we can be seen from quite a distance. By 0700 daylight is now fully established. Nothing can be seen of the enemy. I stand the men down from Battle Stations but keep ploughing on. Suddenly, at 0720, the lookout on the port quarter, Matr.Ob.Gefr. Meyer, spots the steamer through the mist on the port beam.[6] Steering a parallel course to our own at a range of 2,000–3,000 m, she is sailing through a patch of fog that completely covers her at the height of her bridge and superstructure. The hull of the ship below is easily distinguished, as are her masts and funnel. But the veil of mist is not that long and they'll emerge from it in a matter of minutes. It's now or never!

I turn towards the target for a daylight surface attack with both engines at 4/5 speed. Reloading has just been completed. Tube flooding is underway but it seems to take an eternity. Meanwhile we're getting closer and closer. The cloud is gradually thinning – surely we've been spotted by now. One of the bridge watches thinks he can spot muzzle flash. Finally the tubes are flooded. Now just the bow caps. That too takes forever because at our high speed it requires four men to open them. It's going to have to be like a torpedo-boat attack. But if we don't get her we're a sitting target. In the meantime the steamer has turned slightly towards us. Inclination is between 90° and 100°. We're only 500–600 m away so I reduce engines to half speed.

| 0725 | [Qu.] AJ 3825 | I get the word to fire. But the target bearing is shifting dramatically. With full rudder and outer engine at 3/5 speed we can only just turn to follow her, so quickly is she passing. First torpedo is therefore fired as soon as line of sight shows in the middle. Then we turn back to fire the second at her mainmast. We get the shot away but not quite on target. Then I turn away abruptly and order everyone below – we must have been seen. The vessel's guns (15-cm calibre) can be clearly discerned both aft and forward but they still aren't manned. I'll wait a moment longer. Suddenly the first torpedo detonates amidships with a powerful effect above the waterline (depth set at 2 m). The second detonates under the bows immediately after. Steamer stops and remains motionless, listing slightly to starboard. Her bows settle deeper in the water. The alarm is given, I get the bridge watch back up. The ship bursts into life and only now do they actually see us for the first time. Men start scurrying around the deck, boats are readied and the guns are manned. While all this is going on we are lying off the port quarter of the steamer which still shows no sign of sinking. Our position gives us a clear view of activity around the after guns, how she is crewed, how the covers and tompions are removed, and how the gun is trained round in our direction. Time to go. |

---

5 *Salopian* was in fact only 153 metres (502 feet) long. Her last recorded speed was 14½ knots, 2½ knots faster than the estimated speed entered into the torpedo data computer by Gysae at 0619 and thereby exceeding his 2-knot margin of error.

6 The rating of *Matrosen-Obergefreiter* equates to Leading Seaman in the Royal Navy and Petty Officer 3rd Class in the US Navy.

0730	[Qu.] AJ 3825	Alarm. Just as we are sealing the hatch two impacts are felt in the vicinity of the boat. A splinter clatters against the side of the hull.[7] Despite the great changes in weight and trim caused by all the torpedoes fired we are soon trimmed into diving position and down to periscope depth. Steamer is still afloat. Some of the boats have already been lowered and there are large numbers of boxes and barrels floating all around. Clearly there was a deliberate surplus of these to aid buoyancy. From the upper deck there is a great deal of machine-gun fire at our dive position from a number of different positions. But I'm long gone from there and now withdraw somewhat so that I can inspect the vessel properly.

My intention is to fire a *coup-de-grâce* shot from Tube V.

The vessel is a large Cunard Line steamer, approx. 20,000 GRT.[8] Given her silhouette and superstructure probably of the Franconia class. She is painted like a warship with a disruptive camouflage. As we cruise past the bows of the ship I can distinguish a large hole forward – the second torpedo ripped away the ship's bottom. The bulkhead there seems to have held, however, as the ship is not settling any lower. Up above we can clearly see the bow gun. The crew are at their stations – albeit already wearing lifejackets – and all gun barrels are trained to port because that's where they saw us dive. More boats have now been lowered. One of them has been lowered to starboard and is dangling from her davits. Bridge, control positions and guns remain manned and ready for action. They're now raising a huge warship ensign on the foremast; we'll have to see about lowering that. As they are clearly all expecting a port attack I manoeuvre round to the starboard side and close to roughly 300 m.

0800	[Qu.] AJ 3825	Torpedo fired from Tube V.[9] Hits just abaft the funnel abreast the boiler room. Steamer settles deeper but still doesn't sink. Once again I've nothing left in the tubes and have to reload.
0845		An Eto is ready to be fired from Tube I. This time I'm going to change the depth setting to 5 m because their effect so far has been negligible.
0850	[Qu.] AJ 3825	Torpedo fired from Tube I, range 375 m. Point of aim 60 m from stern, hits about 20 m forward of the mainmast. An enormous concussion can be felt in our own boat. The steamer remains afloat but there are more than ten boats in the water by now, each fully laden (30–40 men per boat). To a man the crew are wearing oilskins and have lifejackets on; no sign of any panic. I am forced to raise my periscope quite high when tacking between them. This results in someone spotting the periscope, whereupon they all starting pointing at me excitedly, obviously trying to alert the gun crews. The boats are equally divided around the ship. I dive deep and steal round back to the other side. Again I am forced to reload.

I now intend to load all remaining bow eels, and then fire successive single shots: amidships, foremast and mainmast, starting with depth setting of 6 m and increasing from there.[10] That British battle ensign is still flying from the foretop. A considerable period has now elapsed since this began and the steamer will certainly have radioed for assistance. But no destroyer noises are audible yet. While submerged I prepare a radio message to be sent in the event that we don't manage to sink the steamer with our three remaining torpedoes, so that other boats can immediately be alerted to her position.

1035		Reloading complete. At periscope depth I can make out several motor boats screening the ship with smoke-making apparatus. But the densest fug is on the starboard side where they're expecting the next attack, which hardly bothers me on the port side as I prepare to fire.
1043	[Qu.] AJ 3825	Torpedo fired from Tube II. Depth set at 6 m, range 1,400 m. Hits amidships. Monstrous detonation, followed by another. Boilers, magazine and depth charges have all gone up. Merchant cruiser is torn apart, masts collapse against one another, funnel is left standing. Bow and stern sink in separate sections, both sticking up sharply in the air. The latter remains afloat longest. Then it's all over apart from another sudden detonation which all in all is the most powerful of the lot. My initial thoughts are of destroyers and depth charges but I can't see any danger though the periscope.
1054		We surface. Lifeboats are now quite some distance from the position of the sinking, arranged into two columns and stepping masts to sail away from the scene. We disappear on a feigned north-westerly course then set course towards our assigned attack position in the reconnaissance line.

I have intentionally not ventured anywhere near the boats again for fear of encountering boat guns or other weapons. Besides, I think we've established our victim's identity sufficiently.

⚡

---

7 It is curious that Gysae records being engaged by *Salopian*'s guns at this time. Alleyne's report states that *Salopian*'s guns did not open fire until shortly before the third hit at 0400 ship time.

8 As so often, the estimate is exaggerated. *Salopian*, formerly of the Bibby Line, was actually of 10,549 GRT.

9 This torpedo and those launched at 0850 and 1043 were fired by Gysae himself.

10 'Eels' (German = *Aale*) was U-boat slang for torpedoes.

Date, time	Details of position, wind, weather, sea, light, visibility, moonlight, etc.	Incidents

15.v

| 0031 | | Outgoing W/T transmission to B.d.U.: *English auxiliary cruiser, approx. 20,000 GRT, sunk 13 May in Quadrant AJ 3825. Still 3 torpedoes below deck. 75 tons oil.* |

Gysae

The sinking

Gysae's first four torpedoes clearly went quite unnoticed by *Salopian*'s lookouts and it was only during *U98*'s third attack that the officer of the watch sighted a suspicious object on the starboard beam. Action Stations was sounded and the helm put hard aport to present a smaller target. However, this measure came too late and both Gysae's torpedoes struck *Salopian* on the starboard side at 0330 British time. Of these it was the first that inflicted critical damage, bringing down the wireless aerials and fracturing steam mains which caused the engines to stop. Despite the extensive damage noted by Gysae, the second torpedo, which exploded under the fo'c's'le, had only a marginal effect by comparison. Preemptive action on the part of the Senior Engineer, Temp. Lt Cdr (E) Bill Nisbet RNR prevented the ship being plunged into darkness once the generators drained of power, but Gysae's third and fourth strikes overwhelmed the emergency bilge pump and sealed *Salopian*'s fate. After the second hit Capt. Alleyne saw only one course of action open to him: to put all his men into lifeboats except key officers, damage-control parties and gun crews in the hope that the U-boat would attempt to finish her off by gunfire. Though Gysae was foolhardy enough to let *U98* suffer splinter damage while observing his handiwork at close quarters (even if this broadside finds no mention in primary sources on the Allied side, and is cited as having occurred between the second and third torpedoes in secondary sources), he was never likely to take on *Salopian*'s guns in a surface action. Instead he alternated between the port and starboard sides of his victim until his torpedoes had the desired effect. After four misses and four hits (six hits by Alleyne's reckoning), *Salopian* eventually succumbed to *U98*'s ninth torpedo. There is little to add to Gysae's account; *Salopian* broke her back, both ends disappearing within the space of a minute at 0645 British time, more than three hours after the first hit.

After unavailing efforts to assist the stricken *Bismarck* as she struggled to evade the vengeance of the Royal Navy for the loss of HMS *Hood* (see below), Gysae returned to St-Nazaire to a hero's welcome for the uncommon feat of sinking an enemy warship in excess of 10,000 tons. On behalf of Dönitz, Konteradmiral Eberhard Godt extolled an 'excellent and coolly executed patrol', noting that 'the Commanding Officer owes his fine success to his decisive, tenacious and carefully considered conduct. His observation of the sinking of the ship is to be lauded.' Whether or not Godt chose to ignore the fact that Gysae's penchant for observation had brought him and his boat perilously close to disaster is unclear.

Fate of the crew

U98's first salvo killed Acting Sub-Lt (E) Harold Holland RNVR and Fireman Henry McCaffrey MN in the evaporator compartment in No. 4 hold, while a third man, Leading Seaman J. L. Penton RNR, was later assumed to have been washed overboard by the column of water thrown up by the initial blast. Remarkably, this was the extent of *Salopian*'s casualties. Most of the ship's company was transferred to boats early on and the rest got away between the fourth and the fifth hits in an exemplary, even leisurely fashion, Sub-Lt (E) Bert Poolman RNR finding the time to rescue some valuables and change into his best uniform before abandoning ship. However, their survival owed a great deal both to mild conditions at sea and the fact that all escaped immersion as they took to the boats. Rescue was delayed both by drifting and considerations of security. With the ship's aerials down, the crew had been forced to rely on an old wireless set in *Salopian*'s motor boat to transmit their distress signal. This was received by a single vessel, *Empire Confidence*, which due to the imposition of radio silence was obliged to wait twenty-four hours before relaying it to the Admiralty. After a night on the high seas, on the morning of the 15th Capt. Alleyne dispatched the motor boat south to intercept a convoy from Halifax expected to be in the area. It was immediately sighted by HM destroyer *Icarus*, one of a number of ships searching for the survivors. Together with her sister *Impulsive*, *Icarus* began the work of rescue before proceeding to Reykjavik. As they went on survivors' leave at the end of the month *Salopian*'s men had occasion to compare the number of their dead with those rescued from the battlecruiser *Hood* sunk eleven days after their own ship: three in each case. They had indeed been fortunate. No Board of Enquiry was held for HMS *Salopian*, a terse entry in the Admiralty War Diary for 15 May stating that it would serve no purpose 'under the present circumstances', a decision that clearly owed much to the enormous strain placed on the Admiralty by events both in the Mediterranean and the Atlantic. A summary of findings was submitted by an Admiralty tribunal on 21 May on the basis of reports received, but it had no cause to censure any individual for the loss of *Salopian*, observing that 'the Commanding Officer took all possible action for the safety of the ship and subsequently his ship's company, and in such action he was well supported by the officers and the ship's company, whose conduct was in keeping with the best traditions of the Service.'

U98 and Robert Gysae

Built by Germaniawerft at Kiel and commissioned under Kptlt Robert Gysae in October 1940, *U98*'s maiden frontline cruise in March and April 1941 yielded four merchantmen. Her second cruise claimed *Salopian* together with SS *Rothermere* from convoy HX126 on 21 May but her return to St-Nazaire having expended the last of her torpedoes was delayed by wider events in the Atlantic. One of a number of U-boats assigned to support the breakout of *Bismarck* and *Prinz Eugen* into the Atlantic, the cancellation of the operation following damage to the former during the Battle of the Denmark Strait on 24 May caused a hasty redeployment. Ordered to form part of a new patrol line to find *Bismarck* and then escort her to Brest, *U98*

Gysae seen wearing the Oak Leaves to his Knight's Cross which he was awarded in May 1943 during the second of his two lengthy patrols in command of *U177*. DUBMA

her on two highly successful patrols in the South Atlantic and Indian Ocean which earned him the Oak Leaves to his Knight's Cross. Shore-based appointments and a brief spell in captivity at the end of the war were followed by two years in German minesweepers and then service in the post-war Bundesmarine in which he reached the rank of Flottillenadmiral. Robert Gysae died in April 1989.

Sources

Admiralty, *Damage to HM Ships by Torpedo and Mine, 1940–1942* (TNA, ADM 267/92)

—, War Diary for May 1941 (TNA, ADM 199/2227), pp. 391, 414, 440–1, 468, 499, 533 and 600

Osborne, Richard, Harry Spong and Tom Grover, *Armed Merchant Cruisers, 1878–1945* (Windsor, Berks.: World Ship Society, 2007)

Poolman, Kenneth, *Armed Merchant Cruisers* (London: Leo Cooper, 1985)

—, *The British Sailor* (London: Arms and Armour Press, 1989)

Watson, Nigel, *The Bibby Line, 1807–1990: A Story of Wars, Booms and Slumps* (London: James & James, 1990)

Defunct website containing memoirs of Cdr Tom Foden (survivor): http://www.petmac.co.uk/beer.html

waited in vain in mountainous seas while the Royal Navy hunted its quarry. Only when news came of her loss on the 27th did *U98* turn for St-Nazaire. *U98* made four more cruises in the Atlantic under Gysae before his departure in February 1942 though these yielded just four merchantmen. *U98* was lost on her first cruise under Oblt.z.S. Kurt Eichmann, sunk south-east of Cape St Vincent by HM destroyer *Wrestler* on 15 November 1942. There were no survivors.

In April 1942 Gysae was appointed to the Type-IXD *U177*, leading

---

27 *M-99*

st. l-t B. M. Popov, VMF†
Sunk by *U149* (Type IID), Kptlt Horst Höltring, 27 June 1941
Gulf of Finland, 35 nm NW of Cap Ristna, Hiiumaa (Estonia)

Theatre	Baltic Sea (Map 2)	*Displacement*	210 tons surfaced 261.5 tons submerged
Coordinates	59° 20' N, 21° 12' E	*Dimensions*	146' × 10.75' × 10'
Kriegsmarine code	Quadrat AO 2982	*Maximum speed*	13.5 knots surfaced 7.7 knots submerged
U-boat timekeeping differential	–1 hour	*Armament*	2 × 21" tt (2 torpedoes carried); 1 × 45 mm AA; 1 machine gun
Fatalities	20 *Survivors* none		

The Soviet navy (Voenno-Morskoi Flot)

The dawn of Russian seapower comes in the middle decades of the seventeenth century but it was not until the personal rule of Peter the Great (1694–1725) and the pursuit of Russian ambitions in the Black Sea and the Baltic that a seagoing navy came into being. In July 1696 a large force of Russian ships built on the Voronezh assisted in the capture of the Turkish fortress of Azov on the Black Sea and 10 October that year marks the foundation of the imperial Russian navy. Next Peter turned his attention to the Baltic and the outbreak of the Great Northern War with Sweden (1700–21) saw the establishment of several shipyards and a fleet base in the city he founded to make good this enterprise: St Petersburg. For all these developments Peter and his successors placed heavy reliance on foreign specialists, commanders and men until native expertise came to the fore in the nineteenth century. For all that it became a dominant naval power in the Baltic and the Black Sea, the early Russian navy enjoyed only limited success in battle and it was not until 1770 that it claimed its first major victory when a fleet commanded by Rear-Admiral John Elphinstone (seconded from the Royal Navy) defeated the Turks off Çeşme in the Aegean. Although the Russian navy played a role in the French Revolutionary Wars and together with the British and French inflicted another crushing defeat on the Turks at

Navarino in 1827, subsequent neglect left it unable to meet the challenge presented by the Crimean War (1853–6) during which the Black Sea Fleet found no option but to scuttle itself. Out of this ignominy came a new navy incorporating many of the technological advances of the day but hampered by poor training, inadequate planning and the inefficiency of Russian industry. With the Russo-Japanese War of 1904–5 came the Russian navy's baptism of fire against a first-class naval power on the high seas. A series of military reverses in the Far East culminated in the destruction of the Baltic Fleet at Tsushima in the Sea of Japan on 27–28 May 1905 after a nightmare voyage around the Cape of Good Hope. In June the navy's remaining prestige dissolved with the mutiny in the battleship *Knyaz Potemkin Tavrichesky* of the Black Sea Fleet, later immortalised by Sergei Eisenstein's silent film.

Although efforts were made to recover from these disasters Russia entered the First World War with much the weakest navy of the great powers and made relatively little impression in the war at sea. The October Revolution of 1917 brought the bulk of the fleet (if not its personnel) into Soviet hands as the Workers' and Peasants' Red Fleet but its strength was further depleted by Allied action in support of the White cause during the Civil War (1917–23). By the mid-1920s the outlook for the Soviet navy was bleak, particularly in light of the

A pair of Type-XII Malyutka-class coastal submarines seen in the Baltic in September 1941. *BfZ*;
Starshii leitenant B. M. Popov, commander of *M-99*. *Miroslav Morozov*

anti-Soviet Kronstadt Mutiny of 1921. However, increasing industrial capacity and a commitment to international revolution brought on a fresh perspective and a succession of initiatives led the Second Five-Year Programme of 1933 to authorise construction of over 550 vessels including 355 submarines. Meanwhile, a Pacific Fleet was established in 1932 and a Northern Fleet the following year. As with most other navies whose reconstruction began in the 1930s, the new Red Fleet was only partially built by the outbreak of hostilities but the ground had been laid for a significant contribution in the coming war.

Career

In 1933 the Soviet Union embarked on the most ambitious submarine-construction programme undertaken by any nation between the wars. By June 1941 the Soviet navy was in possession of the world's largest submarine fleet, consisting of over 200 units in twelve classes built mostly from 1930 onwards. In addition to large and medium-sized submarines, work had begun in 1932 on a class of small coastal boats of limited range (1,600 miles) and extremely modest torpedo armament (two bow tubes and two torpedoes). Designated the Malyutka ('M') class (*maly* meaning 'small' in Russian), the initial Type-VI prototype was expanded into the Type XII from 1934. A unit of this latter class was *M-99*, built at Leningrad's Yard No. 196 (Sudomekh), launched in April 1940 and assigned to the *Krasnoznammenny Baltiiskii Flot* (Red Banner Baltic Fleet – KBF) in July of that year. Her working-up period was curtailed by the onset of winter and the annual freezing over of the Gulf of Finland. On the outbreak of hostilities with Germany in June 1941 *M-99* formed part of the 8th Division of the 2nd Brigade of KBF submarines operating from the Soviet base of Hanko (Swedish: Hangö) in southern Finland, though a lack of repair facilities there meant that she probably spent at least a month at Tallinn preparing for sea-going operations. *M-99* sailed from Tallinn on her maiden patrol on 21 June under the newly appointed starshii leitenant (senior lieutenant) B. M. Popov, returning the following evening with the onset of Operation BARBAROSSA. On the night of the 24th *M-99* was assigned to a position between the islands of Utö (Finland) and Hiiumaa (Estonia) at the mouth of the Gulf of Finland ('position no. 7'), placing her among the first Soviet naval units to commence hostilities against Germany.

Background of the attack

At the beginning of the Great Patriotic War – the term still used by the Russians to describe the conflict with Germany that began on 22 June 1941 – the Soviet Union enjoyed a huge numerical advantage over its adversaries in submarines. In addition, the annexation of the Baltic states and the cession of Hanko and the Karelian Isthmus in southern Finland in 1940 afforded the Soviet navy an enhanced strategic position in the Baltic theatre. Yet this in no way translated into initial superiority. Quite aside from the fact that the Russians had deployed barely a third of their submarine strength in the Baltic (this being only one of four theatres for submarine operations), the suddenness of the German attack meant that large numbers of Soviet boats were unfit for war. The Gulf of Finland had only just become fully navigable after the spring thaw and the order to move to the first state of operational readiness was not passed to the KBF from Admiral V. I. Kuznetsov, *Narodny Kommissar* (National Commissar) and Chief of Staff of the Soviet navy, until shortly before midnight on 21 June – the eve of the German attack. As such, some vessels were not even seaworthy and a number of crews had yet to complete their basic training. This was particularly the case of the larger and medium-sized submarines of the 1st and 2nd Brigades, thus leaving the smaller Malyutkas to bear the brunt of initial operations.

With the majority of U-boats assigned to Atlantic operations and the bulk of the German surface fleet confronting the Royal Navy, the German Naval High Command had relatively few resources at its disposal to prosecute a naval campaign in the *Ostsee* – the Baltic. The chief strategy employed to prevent incursions from surface vessels and submarines alike was thus that of containment, beginning with the laying of extensive minefields at key strategic points. These encompassed the three *Wartburg* fields stretching from Klaipėda (Ger.: Memel) in Latvia to the Swedish island of Öland, as well as the *Weimar*, *Erfurt*, *Eisenach*, *Coburg* and *Gotha* fields blocking the entrances to the Latvian ports of Liepāja (Ger.: Libau) and Ventspils (Ger.: Windau), the Irbe Strait, and the Soela and Moon Sounds respectively. As was the case with the *Corbetha* and *Apolda* fields laid further west, this was completed without arousing the suspicions of the KBF despite numerous Soviet surface craft being recorded in plain view while the operations were carried out.

Five of the small Type-IID coastal boats were all that B.d.U. could muster to patrol the waters around these minefields. *U140* (see **28**) and

U144 were deployed off Liepāja and Ventspils, U142 was positioned south of Gotland, U145 west of the Baltic Islands and Kptlt Horst Höltring's U149 west of the *Apolda* minefield. U144 struck the first blow of the submarine conflict, sinking *M-78* as the latter sailed from Liepāja only forty-eight hours after the outbreak of war (G7), though U144's loss on 10 August left B.d.U. with only a brief signal to record

the accomplishment. Three days after the sinking of *M-78* and 250 miles to the north U149 sighted a small shadow at the mouth of the Gulf of Finland shortly after 0100 on 27 June. Kptlt Höltring quickly identified it as a Soviet 'M'-class submarine, though several hours were to pass before U149 found herself in a position to end *M-99*'s brief career in the white night of a northern summer.

War Diary of *U149*, patrol of 18 June–11 July 1941: PG 30138, NHB, reel 1,085, p. 79

Date, time	Details of position, wind, weather, sea, light, visibility, moonlight, etc.	Incidents
27.vi		
0113	Qu. [AO] 2985 middle right	After starboard lookout reports: 'Shadow at 10° on the port quarter.'[1] Through the mist we can make out a faint projection on the horizon. At 0120 we alter course towards it, going on to ¾ speed.
0125	To the W & S the horizon is wholly overcast whereas to the N & E it is bright. A misty haze covers the entire horizon, wind SSW 2–3, sea 1–2, light swell. Average visibility, 5–8 nm.	Both engines at ⅘ speed. We make for the dark horizon at a right angle to our line of sight.
0134		We sail ahead of the shadow with a view to intercepting it later. Through the NZO we discern it as the silhouette of a submarine.[2] Enemy now withdrawing at low speed, bows right.
0150		Enemy alters course hard aport.
0151	Qu. [AO] 2985	We dive as it's too light for a surface attack.
0210		Though the periscope initially takes a while to clear, a Russian 'M'-class submarine then appears at bearing 340° true. Enemy course 220°, speed 10 knots, range 2,000 m. We alter course hard aport to 270°. We go to ¾ speed. As a result of lowering the periscope it is then some five minutes before the mist and haziness clears upon raising it again. We therefore lose sight of enemy.
0256		'Propeller noises at 320°.' Enemy reappears, proceeding course 60°, passing us at high speed at a range of 200 m on our port beam. We alter course hard astarboard to 60°. Port engine at ¾ speed. After completing course alteration enemy then turns about 150 m ahead of us and withdraws at an inclination of 180°. A huge disappointment. Enemy is an improved 'M' class with partially enclosed conning tower.[3] It had three lookouts, all of whom were looking away to port but without using their binoculars. No lookouts at all on the starboard side.
0332		We alter course to 90°. Port engine dead slow, periscope depth. Enemy submarine gives the impression of patrolling to and fro along a NE–SW course line. So we will await its return.
0355	Bright, but cloudy, wind SW 2, sea 1–2, light swell from the SW	Enemy lost in the mist again, course 80°. Inclination 180°.
0420		Ob.Strm.[4] (on periscope watch duty) reports 'Submarine again in sight!'
0423		Prepare a single shot from Tube III using the torpedo data computer. Torpedo speed 30 knots, depth 2 m, enemy speed 8 knots, inclination 35°, bows left, range 600 m. Inclination now being automatically updated by computer.
0424		Enemy is steering a straight course; I order the boat hard aport, starboard engine at ¾ speed. Enemy course 215°. We haul ahead of the enemy in order to keep the parallax angle small.
0426		Shortly before firing we enter new coordinates for enemy speed of 5 knots. Range is 500 m.
0427		Tube III fire!! We fire with rudder kept hard aport so that the enemy bearing is always 350°–10° ahead.

1   It is to be presumed that Höltring is referring to a 190° *relative* bearing which can reasonably be expected to have fallen within the after starboard lookout's field of responsibility.

2   'NZO' is here an abbreviation for *Nachtzieloptik* ('night search optic') though Höltring is here simply referring to the UZO, the main bridge binocular and bearing indicator which was connected to the torpedo data computer.

3   Having obviously done his homework in Soviet submarine recognition, Höltring correctly discerns his target as the later XII series rather than the earlier Type-VII Malyutkas.

4   Short for *Obersteuermann*, the chief navigator (usually a warrant officer).

Date, time	Details of position, wind, weather, sea, light, visibility, moonlight, etc.	Incidents
		Data upon firing: enemy speed 5 knots, inclination 70°, bows left, range 500 m, aim-off angle 8.7°. No aim-off adjustment made for Eto as enemy speed is fairly slow.[5]
		After running time of 34.7 sec. (= 520 m) a detonation. A huge explosion cloud can be seen with pieces of wreckage flying up into the air. Nothing more to be seen of enemy vessel, only a large patch of oil and bubbles.
0429	Qu. [AO] 2982 lower middle	We retire steering course 90°, port engine dead slow.

---

5   'Eto' was Kriegsmarine shorthand for the electric G7e torpedo.

The sinking and fate of the crew

As Höltring's war diary makes clear, *M-99* met a sudden and catastrophic end following a close-range attack. In his torpedo report Höltring expands on the log by noting a 'massive, powerful impact on the target, submarine blown to smithereens. A high, brownish explosion cloud in which we can see large dark patches, presumably pieces of the wreck. Sinking immediate, slight reverberation felt in boat.' The Soviet navy had no knowledge of what had befallen *M-99*, the last contact being a sighting off Cap Ristna (the most westerly tip of the island of Hiiumaa) on the 25th. The worst was feared after a succession of radio signals went unanswered and she failed to make a rendezvous five miles east of Cap Ristna on 3 July. *M-103*, which had been patrolling an adjacent sector to *M-99*, reported a major explosion in the area on the 28th, at least a day after *U149*'s attack. A view widely held by the staff of the 2nd Brigade was that *M-99* had fallen victim to a mine but post-war details of German minelaying and Höltring's war diary leave little doubt as to her true fate.

It must be supposed that St. l-t Popov and his nineteen-man crew died instantly in the huge explosion described by Höltring.

U149 and Horst Höltring

Built by Deutsche Werke at Kiel and commissioned in November 1940, the Type-IID *U149* was destined for a career as a training boat with the 22nd Flotilla based at Wilhelmshaven and Gotenhafen (now Gdynia). The exception was her single front-line patrol under Kptlt Horst Höltring to coincide with the beginning of Operation BARBAROSSA, during which she claimed *M-99*, her only victim. Returning to training duties, she saw out the war unscathed, being

scuttled as part of Operation DEADLIGHT in July 1945.

Höltring left *U149* in November 1941, subsequently making six front-line patrols in command of *U604* during which six merchantmen were sunk for a total of nearly 40,000 tons. Heavily damaged by a succession of Allied aircraft attacks off Brazil in July and August 1943, *U604* was scuttled on 11 August and her surviving crew taken on board *U172* and *U185*. The latter was herself sunk by aircraft from the US escort carrier *Core* on 24 August and though there were many survivors Kptlt Höltring was not among them. Coming across two badly wounded veterans of *U604* in the bow torpedo compartment as *U185* filled with chlorine gas, Höltring obliged them in their pleas to put them out of their misery with a pistol before turning the weapon on himself. He was a posthumous recipient of the German Cross in Gold.

Sources

Admiralty Naval Historical Team, *Russian Submarines in the Baltic* [Bremerhaven, August 1949] (typescript, BfZ, Sammlung Rohwer)

Siivonen, Korvkpt. Eino, *Der U-Boot-Krieg in den Finnischen Gewässern* (manuscript, BfZ, Sammlung Rohwer)

Basov, A. V., *Flot v Velikoi Otechestvennoi Voine 1941–45* (Moscow: Akademiya Nauk SSSR, 1980)

Bendert, Harald, *U-Boote im Duell* (Hamburg: Mittler, 1996)

Blair, *Hitler's U-Boat War*, II, p. 394

Chirva, Yevgeny, *Podvodnaya voina na Baltike, 1939–1945* (Moscow: Yauza/ Eksmo, 2009)

Ignatyev, E. P., *Podvodniye lodki XII Serii* (St Petersburg: Izdatel'stvo Gangut, 1996)

Maksimov, Y. A., and S. N. Khakhanov, *Bor'ba za zhivuchest' podvodnikh lodok VMF SSSR v Velikoi Otechestvennoi voine 1941–1945 pri vozdeistvii oruzhiya protivnika*, Part III (Moscow: Minister'stvo Oborony [Ministry of Defence] [restricted circulation], 1965)

Morozov, Miroslav, *Podvodniye lodki VMF SSSR v velikoi otetchestvennoi voine 1941–1945*. Part I: *Krasnoznammenny Baltiiskii Flot: Letopis boevykh pokhodov* (Moscow: Izdatel'stvo Poligon, 2001)

Piterskij, N. A., *Die Sowjetische Flotte im Zweiten Weltkrieg* (Hamburg: Gerhard Stalling, 1966)

Platonov, A. V., *Entsiklopediya sovetskikh podvodnykh lodok, 1941–1945* (Moscow: Izdatel'stvo Poligon, 2004)

Polmar, Norman, and Jurrien Noot, *Submarines of the Russian and Soviet Navies, 1718–1990* (Annapolis, Md.: Naval Institute Press, 1991)

Rohwer, Jürgen, „Die sowjetische U-Bootswaffe in der Ostsee 1939–1945" in *Wehrwissenschaftliche Rundschau* 6 (1956), pp. 547–68

Rohwer, Jürgen, and M. S. Monakov, *Stalin's Ocean-Going Fleet* (London: Frank Cass, 2001)

Webpage devoted to *M-99*:
http://www.town.ural.ru/ship/ship/m99.php3

Höltring wearing the Iron Cross First Class, probably taken in 1942 or 1943. He took his own life in desperate circumstances on 24 August 1943. *DUBMA*

28 *M-94*

st. l-t N. V. D'yakov, VMF
Sunk by *U140* (Type IID), Oblt.z.S. Hans-Jürgen Hellriegel, 21 July 1941
Eastern Baltic, 6 nm S of Cap Ristna, Hiiumaa (Estonia)

One of the Type-XII Malyutka-class coastal submarines in the Baltic. *Miroslav Morozov*
Jonah: Starshii leitenant Nikolai Vasil'evich D'yakov, commander of *M-94* and sunk four times in submarines. *Miroslav Morozov*

Theatre Baltic Sea (Map 2)		*Displacement* 210 tons surfaced 261.5 tons submerged	
Coordinates 58° 54' N, 22° 02' E		*Dimensions* 146' × 10.75' × 10'	
Kriegsmarine code Quadrat AO 6139		*Maximum speed* 13.5 knots surfaced 7.7 knots submerged	
U-boat timekeeping differential –1 hour		*Armament* 2 × 21" tt (2 torpedoes carried); 1 × 45 mm AA; 1 machine gun	
Fatalities 8 *Survivors* 11			

Career

For background on the Soviet navy and design notes on the Malyutka class, see *M-99* (**27**).

M-94, a unit of the Malyutka-class coastal submarines, was completed at the Sudomekh yard in Leningrad in September 1939. Assigned to the Red Banner Baltic Fleet (KBF) that December, she was initially commanded by kapitan-leitenant (lieutenant-commander) V. A. Ermilov. Though attached to the 26th Division of the KBF's 2nd Brigade during the 'Winter War' against Finland and transferred to the Estonian port of Paldiski in December 1939, *M-94* was not deployed due to ice conditions and did not see frontline service until the outbreak of hostilities with Germany in June 1941. In October 1940 Ermilov was replaced by starshii leitenant (senior lieutenant) N. V. D'yakov and the following March the 26th Division became the 8th Division in the reorganisation of the Baltic Fleet's submarine units. Based at Tallinn, *M-94* sailed on her maiden war cruise on 23 June 1941 with orders to patrol an area south of Helsinki in the Gulf of Finland. It was to prove an eventful six days. On the 27th she was sighted by surface units of the Finnish navy and hunted for several hours though managed to escape without damage. The following day she narrowly evaded the German *Corbetha* minefield south-west of Porkkala (Finland), reaching Tallinn on the 29th. However, her reservoir of luck had run dry.

Background of the attack

For background on Soviet submarine operations in the Baltic, see *M-99* (**27**).

Soviet plans to prosecute a naval war against Germany in the Baltic were thwarted not only by extensive German minefields (see *M-99*) which claimed large numbers of Soviet submarines and surface craft in the first few weeks of hostilities, but also by developments on land. The lot of the KBF's 1st Brigade is a case in point. Though the bulk of the Brigade was transferred to the Latvian port of Daugavgrīva (Russian: Ust-Dvinsk; Ger.: Dünamünde) at the end of May 1941, the speed of the German advance through the Baltic states required the scuttling at Liepāja (Latvia; Ger.: Libau) of five submarines whose unseaworthy condition prevented them being moved to safety. Similar evacuations of Ventspils (Ger.: Windau) and Riga were effected on 1 July, several more submarines being either scuttled or lost to mines during the withdrawal. However, from this point on the KBF began to reassert itself, clearing mines, sowing its own and dispatching destroyers to the Irbe Strait (separating the Estonian island of Saaremaa and eastern Latvia) and into the Gulf of Riga to contest German efforts to supply their troops by sea.

On 20 July *M-94* and her sister *M-98* (klt I. I. Bezzubikov) were ordered to sea to patrol the mouth of the Gulf of Finland, the former being assigned a patrol area south of the Swedish island of Utö ('position no. 7'). However, their route would first take them though the Soela Sound separating the Estonian islands of Hiiumaa (Swedish: Dagö; Ger.: Dagden) and Saaremaa (Ger.: Ösel). Their passage through Trigi-Lakhti Bay had been carefully prepared, both commanders being briefed with sketches of the area in which U-boats had been sighted. As a precaution they were to be escorted to open water by Izhorets-class minesweepers No. 23 and No. 27 (redesignated *T-23* and *T-27* in early 1944) but the passage was to be fraught with difficulty. The task of minesweeping reduced the flotilla's speed to four knots, forcing *M-94* and *M-98*, which were sailing in line astern, to switch to their electric engines. This continued for several hours until 0300 when the minesweepers unexpectedly altered course to starboard. Assuming that he was supposed follow their lead, D'yakov ordered a corresponding alteration only to run aground on a sandbank in ten feet of water. After unsuccessful attempts to free his vessel (and expending much of *M-94*'s remaining electrical battery supply), D'yakov was forced to signal *M-98* for assistance while No. 23 returned to Trigi-Lakhti Bay in

search of a tug. Despite problems of her own in the shallow water, *M-98* finally managed to free *M-94* with a steel hawser, these two resuming their passage astern of the minesweepers once No. 23 had rejoined. Shortly before 0730 the escorts hauled in their sweeps and signalled the submarines to proceed independently. D'yakov's request for the escorted passage to continue as far as the Ristna light was declined and the minesweepers duly turned about. At this point the submarines assumed station in line abreast, *M-98* keeping to the Estonian coast in shallower waters while *M-94* proceeded in deeper water. Adopting a regular fifteen-degree zigzag, D'yakov remained on the surface, anxious to recharge his batteries before daylight proper arrived. As 0800 approached *M-94* was still on the surface, six or seven cables off *M-98*'s port beam, both vessels within sight of Soviet observation posts on the easternmost tip of Hiiumaa. However, none of the parties had sighted Oblt.z.S. Hans-Jürgen Hellriegel's *U140* which had taken up a submerged position barely an hour before and was waiting for just such a target to cross her path.

War Diary of *U140*, patrol of 7–24 July 1941: PG 30130, NHB, reel; 1,084, p. 444

Date, time	Details of position, wind, weather, sea, light, visibility, moonlight, etc.	Incidents
21.vii		
0145	Qu. [AO] 6138	Course altered to 10° so as to be as close as possible to advance position by daybreak.
0309	Qu. [AO] 6138	Dived so as to complete passage to intended position submerged.
0400	Qu. [AO] 6138	Cruising under water.
0620	Qu. [AO] 6139	Ahead two outbound submarines heave into sight.[1] I am stationed between enemy course and the barrage. I turn towards the barrage and assume an attack course. The submarines are zigzagging. The first one crosses my line of fire with an inclination of 80°, speed 11 knots.
0656		I fire a single torpedo, point of aim the bridge. After 1 min. 56 sec. it rips through submarine just abaft the conning tower, 20 m from the stern. Fore part of the boat rises 8–10 m out of the water.[2]
0706		The second submarine stops. I fire a single torpedo with no aim-off, point of aim 20 m from the bow. But she turns so for obvious reasons it misses. There are three men standing on the wreck of the boat we hit, presumably remnants of the bridge crew. A lifeboat makes its way from land and takes off the survivors. I set an exit course because they are probably forming a gradual picture of where our boat must lie. Once I get beyond the barrage I head off under water, course 265°.
1000		Astern, the second submarine ('C'-class) surfaces on the other side of the barrage, range 4 nm.[3] At high speed she makes for the other submarine which is lying flooded close to the coast. It's impossible not be drawn to this choice morsel. I turn about and head back towards the two submarines.
1115		From the coastline close by an S-boat heaves into sight.[4]
1126		Depth charge detonations!
		Through the periscope I see the S-boat closing us at high speed. As the chart shows soundings of 20 m at this point I attempt to dive to 18 m but run aground at 14 m. Forced therefore to enjoy a two-hour series of depth-charge attacks from above at depths of between 14 m and 20 m. Then I withdraw on courses of 200° and 210°.
		Results of depth charges:
		1. 3 lights no longer functioning
		2. The torpedo tube caps, especially on Tube I, will no longer close properly

---

1   *M-94* and *M-98* respectively.

2   In his torpedo report Hellriegel adds: 'Bows reared up 8 m above the water and stuck fast on seabed. Sank 3½ hours later'. Russian sources record the bows disappearing after nearly two hours.

3   Hellriegel's torpedo report refers to the submarines sighted during this attack as 'Schtsch-Klasse'. At almost 600 tons (700 submerged), the 'Shch (Щ)'-class submarines (Types III, V and X) were significantly larger than the Malyutkas. The identity of the submarine sighted by Hellriegel at 1000 is unclear from Russian sources as *M-98* had long since headed inshore to raise the alarm (hence the arrival of the S-boat and the attack on *U140*), making for open water thereafter.

4   *Schnellboot*, the German term for motor torpedo boat (known as E-boats by the Allies).

3. The insulation of Air Vent 3 is leaking
4. The after hydroplane will no longer go below 15°
5. The side hydroplanes are leaking in the stern compartment and are not responding.
I head west then alter to the south-west.

1200   Day's run: 71.5 nm

The sinking

Striking *M-94* in the stern section, Hellriegel's torpedo caused a powerful explosion and a huge column of water noted in *M-98*. Though *M-94* was not broken in two, a hole was blasted in her hull abaft the conning tower and she began to sink by the stern. Believing they had blundered into a German minefield, klt Bezzubikov in *M-98* immediately ordered both engines full speed in reverse. It was at this point, with *M-98* virtually stationary, that Hellriegel ordered the firing of a second torpedo, but in the intervening minutes Bezzubikov and his lookouts had discerned *M-94*'s bows rearing out of the water at forty-five degrees. Discarding the possibility of a mine explosion, Bezzubikov turned towards the coast, dispatching an inflatable dinghy to *M-94* when – like Hellriegel – he spotted some men perched on her casing. Only this manoeuvre prevented *M-98* sharing the same fate as her companion, *U140*'s torpedo being heard to explode harmlessly on the seabed shortly after. Meanwhile, the remains of *M-94*'s stern had settled at a depth of twenty metres, but the shallowness of the water and a reserve of buoyancy kept the bows above the surface for almost two hours before they disappeared at 0940 Soviet time.

In his report on the loss of *M-94*, the commander of the 2nd Brigade, kapitan 2nd class A.E. Orel, drew attention to the series of tactical errors that had afforded *U140* such an easy target. He particularly criticised st. l-t D'yakov's decision to proceed on the surface as well as his adherence to a regular zigzag in waters he had every reason to suspect were patrolled by enemy submarines. Nor, it was emphasised, should he have expected the minesweepers to act as anti-submarine escorts.

Fate of the crew

The crew of *M-94* can be divided into three different categories of misfortune: those who were blasted off the bridge, those in the stern compartments who were either killed by the detonation or subsequently drowned, and those trapped in the central control room and forward compartments. Of the bridge watch, shturman (navigator) Shpakhovsky, starshina motoristov (chief electrical engineer) Laptev and signal'shchit (signalman) Kompaneyets were hurled twenty yards from the submarine while D'yakov was dragged under the conning tower casing before managing to free himself and reach the surface. While his three companions recovered from the shock, a badly injured Shpakhovsky remained struggling in the water. Laptev went to his aid, but Shpakhovsky grabbed hold of his would-be rescuer and they both went under. Only with great difficultly did Laptev manage to free himself and resurface. He could do no more for Shpakhovsky who surfaced, spluttered incomprehensibly and disappeared forever. D'yakov and Laptev then swam to a struggling Kompaneyets and dragged him towards the hull onto which they eventually managed to clamber. Sighting *U140*'s periscope, D'yakov urgently attempted to warn *M-98* of the danger, transmitting by semaphore 'Turn to shore, enemy submarine attacking you.' It is doubtful whether Bezzubikov

and his bridge watch either received this signal or had need of further warning: *M-94*'s intact bows made it quite obvious that she had struck no mine.

Over the next half hour D'yakov tried repeatedly to elicit signs of life from inside *M-94* by banging on the forward section of the hull with his boot but no response had been received by the time *M-98*'s dinghy came alongside at around 0840, nearly an hour after the attack. However, some forty minutes after the survivors from the bridge had been rescued, and with the dinghy about a mile from the scene, D'yakov spotted three more men on the diagonally slanting bows. This resulted in the rescue not only of these three but of five more of *M-94*'s men in what is the most remarkable tale of escape recounted in this volume.

Of the fifteen men inside *M-94* when the torpedo struck, eight survived, all in the forward section. Four men were in Compartment III (the central control room), three in Compartment II, and another in the bow torpedo compartment, though the latter, torpedist (torpedoman) Golikhov, soon abandoned this fearing an inrush of water through the damaged inner hull. That they survived at all was due to starshii rulevoi (leading helmsman) Kholodenko who was stationed in the conning tower to relay orders between the bridge and the central control room when the torpedo struck. Despite striking his head on the upper hatch cover Kholodenko managed to seal it just before a torrent of Baltic water made this impossible. He then clambered down to the control room, closing the lower hatch as he did so. Having caught their breath the survivors took steps to assess the damage and halt the flooding of Compartment III by plugging the vents with signal flags.

The chief engineer, inzhener-kapitan-leitenant V. S. Shilyaev (who outranked D'yakov himself), quickly took control of the situation, ordering men back to the forward compartment to retrieve the boat's ISA-M life-saving apparatus. He then ordered everyone into Compartment III as Compartment II began filling with noxious chlorine gas released as water reached the electric batteries. With all eight gathered in the central control room, a further assessment of their situation was made. Attempts to communicate with the stern compartments proved fruitless, no sign of life being evident either through the glass spy-holes between the compartments or via the voice pipe from which only air and then diesel fuel emerged. Looking through the periscope, Shilyaev ascertained from the light blue-green colour that filled his field of vision that they could not be very far beneath the surface; moreover, the forty-five-degree angle that the wrecked submarine now assumed also indicated that the bows were above water. Shilyaev calculated that the only way of saving their lives was for all eight to squeeze into the chamber between the lower and upper tower hatches and for this to be flooded until such time as a reduction in the pressure differential permitted the upper hatch to be opened. However, this could not be attempted immediately since not all knew how to operate the ISA-M devices nor had all rehearsed such a procedure. After a brief demonstration Shilyaev decided on the order

Hellriegel on the bridge of *U96* in 1942 or early 1943. *DUBMA*

of evacuation on the basis of the men's physical and mental condition, placing himself last. The men then gathered in the chamber, sealed the lower hatch and began to flood it through the vents.

The first to leave once the signal was given, starshina rulevykh (chief helmsman) Trifonov dived under the waterproof tarpaulin, climbed the ladder, opened the atmospheric tap on the cover of the hatch, and, pushing it open, emerged onto the top of the conning tower. Here he attempted to release the buoy rope of the emergency life-ring as instructed. Unable to free it completely, he swam to the surface unaided. Trifonov was followed by the head of acoustics, Malyshenko, who also made it to the surface unaided. Kholodenko, the third to emerge, noticed that the life-ring was still stuck under the casing of the conning tower. Together with Golikov, the next to emerge, he managed to release it, and the evacuation was then completed, Shilyaev surfacing last to see four of his shipmates on the bow of the submarine and the other three close by in the water.

Their ordeal was not quite over. One of the last to surface, komandir otdeleniya tryumnikhov (chief mechanician) Lynkov, did so bleeding from ears and nose having prematurely removed his ISA-M device. Unconscious upon surfacing, he was dragged by his companions onto the wreck to receive artificial resuscitation. However, *M-94* was now sufficiently flooded as to sink altogether, leaving the eight men treading water a good six miles offshore. For over an hour the survivors struggled to remain buoyant, with Lynkov kept afloat by Shilyaev and Kholodenko and starshii rulevoi (leading helmsman) Shipunov, who was a poor swimmer, assisted by Malyshenko. Only at 1100, three hours after the attack, did the launch sent from the Ristna light reach the scene, fishing the exhausted men out of the water three hours after the attack. They were then transferred to the local hospital at Kyardla.

Cruel fates lay in store for the survivors of *M-94*. The majority were reassigned to a battalion of Marines in which most were killed in the fighting ashore. Shilyaev, commended for his courage and leadership on the morning of 21 July, was transferred to the Northern Fleet as the 4th Division's Engineer-in-Chief, later being given a sea-going appointment in *M-175* (**45**). Despite being censured following the loss of *M-94*, D'yakov was given command of the larger submarine *SHCH-408* which was lost following a collision with the netlayer *Onega* off Kronstadt in September 1941. D'yakov's next boat, the medium

submarine *S-9*, foundered off Utö in a violent storm in November, D'yakov being among the few to reach Kronstadt. Appointed in January 1942 to command the Malyutka *M-97*, and no doubt by now regarded as something of a Jonah, D'yakov's ill-starred career ended when she struck a mine off Helsinki in September of that year, being lost with all hands. This unenviable record makes Nikolai Vasil'evich D'yakov perhaps the only submariner in history to have survived the loss of three vessels, and to have been sunk in four.

U140 and Hans-Jürgen Hellriegel

Built by Deutsche Werke at Kiel and commissioned in August 1940, *U140* made just three frontline patrols. The first of these saw her sink three merchantmen in the Atlantic under Oblt.z.S. Hans-Peter Hinsch (see **5**) in November 1940. After a brief spell as a training boat with the 22nd Flotilla she returned to frontline duty under Oblt.z.S. Hans-Jürgen Hellriegel, whose three attacks on Soviet submarines yielded just the one sinking: that of *M-94*. In July 1941 *U140* returned to training duties, serving in this capacity until shortly before the end of the war. She was scuttled at Wilhelmshaven in May 1945.

After leaving *U140* Hellriegel assumed command of the Type-VIIC *U96*, enjoying a year of mixed fortune before being appointed to the Type-IXC *U543*. Neither his rare experience as commander of each of the three main U-boat types nor the Knight's Cross awarded in February 1944 availed him in the face of overwhelming Allied air power at sea. On 2 July 1944 *U543* was destroyed during her second patrol by an Avenger torpedo bomber from the escort carrier USS *Wake Island*. There were no survivors.

Sources

Basov, A. V., *Flot v Velikoi Otechestvennoi Voine 1941–45* (Moscow: Akademiya Nauk SSSR, 1980)

Bendert, Harald, *U-Boote im Duell* (Hamburg: Mittler, 1996)

Chirva, Yevgeny, *Podvodnaya voina na Baltike, 1939–1945* (Moscow: Yauza/Eksmo, 2009)

Ignatyev, E. P., *Podvodniye lodki XII Serii* (St Petersburg: Izdatel'stvo Gangut, 1996)

Maksimov, Y. A., and S. N. Khakhanov, *Bor'ba za zhivuchest' podvodnikh lodok VMF SSSR v Velikoi Otechestvennoi voine 1941–1945 pri vozdeistvii oruzhiya protivnika*, Part III (Moscow: Minister'stvo Oborony [Ministry of Defence] [restricted circulation], 1965)

Morozov, Miroslav, *Podvodniye lodki VMF SSSR v velikoi otetchestvennoi voine 1941–1945*. Part I: *Krasnoznammenny Baltiiskii Flot: Letopis boevykh pokhodov* (Moscow: Izdatel'stvo Poligon, 2001)

Piterskij, N. A., *Die Sowjetische Flotte im Zweiten Weltkrieg* (Hamburg: Gerhard Stalling, 1966)

Platonov, A. V., *Entsiklopediya sovetskikh podvodnykh lodok, 1941–1945* (Moscow: Izdatel'stvo Poligon, 2004)

Polmar, Norman, and Jurrien Noot, *Submarines of the Russian and Soviet Navies, 1718–1990* (Annapolis, Md.: Naval Institute Press, 1991)

Rohwer, Jürgen, „Die sowjetische U-Bootswaffe in der Ostsee 1939–1945" in *Wehrwissenschaftliche Rundschau* 6 (1956), pp. 547–68

Rohwer, Jürgen, and M. S. Monakov, *Stalin's Ocean-Going Fleet* (London: Frank Cass, 2001)

Webpage devoted to *M-94*:
http://www.town.ural.ru/ship/ship/m94.php3

29   HMS *PICOTEE*
Lt R. A. Harrison, RNR†
Sunk by *U568* (Type VIIC), Kptlt Joachim Preuss, 12 August 1941
North Atlantic, 80 nm SE of Vík (Iceland)

Picotee seen during her brief year of life. A torpedo from *U568* abreast the bridge and inaction among ships sailing in company sealed her fate and that of her entire crew. *BfZ*

Theatre	North Atlantic (Map 1)	*Displacement*	940 tons
Coordinates	62° 09' N, 18° 01' W	*Dimensions*	205.25' × 33' × approx. 11.25'
Kriegsmarine code	Quadrat AE 7665	*Maximum speed*	16 knots
U-boat timekeeping differential	+1 hour	*Armament*	1 × 4"; 4 × .303" AA
Fatalities	67 *Survivors* none		

The Flower-class corvettes

The Flower-class corvettes originated in March 1938 with an Admiralty requirement for a small coastal escort vessel capable of being built quickly and in quantity. With the heavy strain already imposed on the British shipbuilding industry this translated into a simple yet sturdy vessel that could be constructed to mercantile as against naval standards in smaller civilian dockyards. The resulting design was produced by Smith's Dock Company of Middlesbrough on the basis of plans for the whalecatcher *Southern Pride*. Though well found, the Flowers would as Nicholas Monsarrat memorably put it 'roll on wet grass', and lengthy convoy duty in severe weather made life wretched for their crews who were paid 'hard-lying' money in recognition of the arduous nature of their service. The first of the class, HMS *Gladiolus* (**35**), was completed at Middlesbrough in January 1940 and a further 287 had been built in British and Canadian yards by 1944, including fifty-two to a modified design with somewhat improved seakeeping and habitability. Equipped with Asdic, twenty-five (later forty) depth charges and a 4-inch deck gun, the Flower class held the line in the U-boat war until the Hunt-class escort destroyers and above all the frigates that followed them began entering service in numbers from 1941. As such they made a significant contribution to Allied victory in the Battle of the Atlantic and by war's end had claimed forty-seven U-boat sinkings for the loss of thirty-six of their own to various causes.

Career

HMS *Picotee* was laid down at Harland & Wolff of Belfast in March 1940, launched in July and completed on 5 September that same year. After working up at HMS *Western Isles*, she was assigned to the 4th Escort Group of Western Approaches Command at Greenock, joining her first convoy, OB218, at the end of September. *Picotee* quickly found herself in action, making an unsuccessful depth-charge attack against *U32* after the latter had sunk SS *Empire Ocelot* south-west of Rockall on 28 September. Escort duty, mainly on the Iceland–UK run, continued until April 1941 when she passed into dockyard hands for repair and refit, returning to the fray in June. On 7 August she departed Greenock to join convoy ON4.

Background of the attack

On 3 August *U568* sailed from Trondheim on her maiden operational patrol, at length taking up a position astride the convoy routes south of Iceland. On the evening of the 11th Kptlt Joachim Preuss's patience was rewarded with the appearance of the Iceland-bound portion of slow convoy ON4, weakly escorted by the anti-submarine trawler *Ayrshire* on its port bow and HMS *Picotee* (Senior Officer of the Escort) to starboard. Just before 0200 GMT *Picotee* appeared to acquire a submarine contact, quite probably *U568* herself. *Ayrshire* noted her dropping back along the starboard side of the convoy, followed shortly after by the sound of depth charges exploding. It was the last *Ayrshire* saw of *Picotee*, and not even a growing inkling of disaster prompted *Ayrshire* to make any effort to discover what might have befallen her.

War Diary of *U568*, patrol of 3 August–10 September 1941: PG 30604, NHB, reel 1,061, p. 473

Date, time	Details of position, wind, weather, sea, light, visibility, moonlight, etc.	Incidents
11.viii		
2000		[Qu.] AE 8716
2015		Alpha Alpha. Enemy position Qu. AE 8725. Escorts have white-painted crow's nests which are difficult to make out against the bright sky.
2400		[Qu.] AE 8447
12.viii		
0113		Alpha Alpha. Convoy position AE 8448.
		After a long northward zigzag by the convoy I am now stationed to the south, darkness having fallen in the meantime. As the sky to the south-east is totally clear and the moon rises at 0115, I work my way round the convoy (currently sailing in line ahead, course 310°) until I am on its northern side. In doing so we ascertain the convoy's speed as 7 knots. Just as I am about to attack the last ship of the convoy, a largish tanker, a corvette steams up from astern. I attack these simultaneously.
0311	[Qu.] AE 7665, bright moon	First torpedo fired at tanker, inclination 80°, bows right, 7 knots, range 1,200 m, depth 3 m. Second torpedo fired at corvette, inclination 89°, bows right, 7 knots, range 1,200 m, depth 2 m. Point of aim set at 20 m from bow as corvette is sailing at more than 7 knots. After 1 min. 13 sec. a hit on the corvette abreast the bridge, whereupon she is rent asunder and sinks immediately as her own depth charges detonate (five or six of them). Hit on the tanker not witnessed because corvette is directly aligned. We heard two torpedoes detonating from inside the boat but tanker hasn't sunk. New attack launched on tanker which now occupies penultimate position in the convoy.
0320		Attack data: inclination 101°, bows right, speed 7 knots, range 2,000 m. A miss. Inclination and range both overestimated. Convoy takes no action. Steering a course of 330° I again haul ahead but gradually position myself further out on the beam due to the very bright moon. New attack on the third-last ship (freighter of approx. 4,000 GRT) and penultimate ship (tanker of approx. 4,000 GRT).
0356		First attack (tanker): inclination 89°, bows right, 7 knots, range 800 m, depth = 3 m. Second attack (freighter): inclination 84.5°, bows right, 7 knots, range 800 m, depth = 3 m.[1] Two misses. As the attack data was certain and the angles of attack minimal (we were bow on), the misses must be due to the torpedoes underrunning their targets, or to the enemy stopping, but nothing of the sort was witnessed. Sea 4. Boat was sighted shortly after the attack. The convoy is now firing rockets. I haul ahead with a view to diving by dawn, reloading and then launching another attack when night returns. I still have one torpedo in the stern tube but hold no expectation of success tonight. This moon is preventing any further attack from within 1,000 metres and the element of surprise is no longer on my side. The sea is now too strong for us to reload on the surface.
0400	[Qu.] AE 7665	
0615		Outgoing W/T transmission to B.d.U.: *Convoy AE 7668 steering west, maintaining contact. 1 corvette sunk, still have 7 + 2 eels and 80 cubic metres.*[2] *U568*.
0800	[Qu.] AE 7624	The boat is positioned ahead of the convoy to the north-west, at the very limit of visibility.

1   There are several inconsistencies in this attack data. At 0320 Preuss records opening the range between himself and the convoy from 2,000 metres due to an unfavourably bright moon, yet his subsequent attacks were made from a range of 800 metres. Even allowing for his admission that 2,000 metres had been an overestimation, this is much closer than his earlier attacks. That apart, the attacks of 0356 appear to reverse the target order listed at 0320 (freighter, tanker) whereas it would be logical for him to begin by engaging the foremost ship (i.e. the freighter).

2   Translates as nine torpedoes (probably seven G7e and two G7a weapons as the Type VIIC was usually supplied with a greater proportion of the former) and 80 cubic metres of diesel fuel remaining.

The sinking

Since none survived the loss of HMS *Picotee*, Kptlt Preuss's account remains the principal source on her demise. The only Allied witnesses of note were the W/T officer and second officer of the Danish freighter SS *Delaware* who reported having seen what they interpreted as a pall of smoke accompanied by a hissing sound (similar to escaping steam) emanating from *Picotee* at about 0200. When the smoke cleared they discerned the 'unmistakable' profile of the 'corvette's bows rising out of the water at 45°, followed by a series of dull thuds, consistent with depth-charge detonations.

Fate of the crew

That no member of *Picotee*'s crew was ever rescued may well be owed to the unfortunate catalogue of neglect, confusion and incompetence that

Preuss (in white cap) and his crew gathered on the casing of *U568* at Trondheim, probably on sailing on their maiden war patrol on 3 August 1941. Nine days later *Picotee* became their first victim. *DUBMA*

now ensued, and which extended not only to elements of the convoy and her remaining escort but also to British naval command at Reykjavik.

Much of the initial confusion was understandable. Several vessels recorded hearing depth charges between 0200 and 0215, attributing them to an attack by *Picotee* rather than the explosions that Preuss records accompanying her sinking. Though the master of the convoy flagship, *Discovery II*, saw a 'red flash and black and white smoke', he claimed to have seen *Picotee* apparently intact only minutes later before having his view obscured by other ships in the column. For their part, the officers of the *Delaware* assumed that the Yugoslav freighter SS *Tsrat*, whose course took her directly past the scene of the sinking, would attempt to rescue survivors. However, *Tsrat* later claimed to have seen nothing though in this respect the evidence of her crew was dismissed as 'unreliable'. The SS *Akershus*, meanwhile, saw smoke astern of *Picotee*'s supposed position and at 0200 claimed to have sighted a submarine, immediately firing the rockets noted in Preuss's log. The only other action taken with respect to *Picotee* that night was by the convoy commodore in *Discovery II*, Capt. G. N. Jones RNR, who at 0415 signalled *Ayrshire* 'Have you seen corvette?' To this Lt L. J. A. Gradwell RNVR sent the reply 'Corvette can take care of herself', a response which neatly summarises *Picotee*'s fate. Despite both escorts' radio communications recorded as 'working perfectly' up to that point, *Ayrshire* made no attempt to establish what had happened to the Senior Officer of the Escort over the next twenty-four hours and Gradwell subsequently reported his assumption that *Picotee* had dropped back to hunt for U-boats.

However, *Ayrshire*'s inaction was only part of the fiasco, for *Picotee*'s disappearance then went unacknowledged for four days. On reaching Reykjavik at 0600 on 13 August the crucial evidence from the merchantmen that might have explained *Picotee*'s disappearance from the convoy was 'for various reasons' not brought to the attention of the authorities. The observation by the W/T officer in *Delaware*, the only Allied vessel to have conclusively witnessed *Picotee*'s demise, was not forwarded to Senior Officer Iceland, Rear-Admiral F. H. G. Dalrymple-Hamilton, by the Military Security Police, nor was the exchange of signals between Capt. Jones and Lt Gradwell mentioned in either officer's debrief with Dalrymple-Hamilton. In the absence of this information, *Picotee* was assumed to have joined an HX convoy though no steps were taken to verify this. The final chapter of this lamentable episode involved the instigation of an air search on the 16th (more than ninety-six hours after the sinking) after Western Approaches Command requested information as to why *Picotee* was not responding to signals. The search led to the discovery of an empty raft and dinghy in the early hours of the 17th. Whether these belonged to *Picotee* will never be known.

U568 and Joachim Preuss

Built by Blohm & Voss of Hamburg and commissioned in May 1941, *U568* made five patrols in a career lasting nine months, all under Kptlt Joachim Preuss. Her maiden patrol in August 1941 yielded only *Picotee*, after which she joined the *Kurfürst* group in its unsuccessful attempt to intercept convoy OG73. In her second patrol in October 1941 *U568* formed part of the large concentration of U-boats which attacked convoy SC48, Preuss accounting for SS *Empire Heron* on the 15th and damaging the destroyer USS *Kearny* early on the 17th after the latter had joined the escort following appeals by the hard-pressed British. The attack on the *Kearny*, which had a silhouette not dissimilar to a pre-war British destroyer, was a significant moment in the undeclared war between the United States and Germany in the North Atlantic. Attacks on SC48 also resulted in the loss of HMSs *Gladiolus* and *Broadwater* (**35** *and* **36**). On her third patrol *U568* was sent through the Straits of Gibraltar to operate in the Mediterranean; for details of her subsequent career, see HMS *Salvia* (**44**).

Sources

Admiralty, *Loss of HM Ships by Enemy Action* (TNA, ADM 199/621)
—, *Details of Convoy O.N.4* (NHB, ON Convoys Box)
Ruegg, R. A., *Flower-Class Corvettes* (typescript, IWM, 13(41).245/5, 1987)

Morison, *History of United States Naval Operations*, I, pp. 92–3
Preston, Antony, and Alan Raven, *Flower Class Corvettes* [Ensign, no. 3] (London: Bivouac Books, 1973); reprinted as Man o'War, no. 7 (London: Arms and Armour Press, 1982)

Website devoted to the sinking of HMS *Picotee*: http://www.hms-picotee.co.uk/

30   HNorMS *BATH* (ex USS *HOPEWELL*)

Cdr C. F. T. Melsom, KNM†
Sunk by *U204* (Type VIIC), Kptlt Walter Kell, 19 August 1941
North Atlantic, 460 nm WSW of Land's End, Cornwall (England)

USS *Hopewell* seen off Guantanamo Bay in January 1920, a world away from the Battle of the Atlantic
which claimed her as HNorMS *Bath* twenty years later. *BfZ*

Theatre	North Atlantic (Map 1)	*Displacement*	1,060 tons
Coordinates	49° 20' N, 17° 30' W	*Dimensions*	314.25' × 31.75' × 8.5'
Kriegsmarine code	Quadrat BE 2647	*Maximum speed*	35 knots
U-boat timekeeping differential	+1 hour	*Armament*	1 × 4"; 1 × 3" AA; 2 × 20 mm AA; 3 × 21" tt
Fatalities	82 *Survivors* 42+		

The Royal Norwegian Navy (Kongelige Norske Marine)

The seafaring heritage of the Norwegian people needs little introduction, but the Royal Norwegian Navy *per se* traces its origins to the force founded by Hans, union king of Denmark and Norway, in 1509. By tradition a majority of the Dano-Norwegian navy was made up of Norwegians and its greatest exploit, the attack on the Swedish fleet at Dynekilen during the Great Northern War in 1716, was led by Peter Tordenskjold of Trondheim at the head of a force composed largely of his countrymen. The dissolution of the union with Denmark in 1814 saw the establishment of a separate Norwegian navy which maintained its independence during the subsequent union with Sweden. However, no significant investment was forthcoming except during the 1870s, a state of affairs that not even Norway's independence in 1905 and the development of a great merchant marine could reverse. Although a number of vessels were on the stocks in April 1940, neutrality during the Great War and inertia after it meant that the Kongelige Norske Marine met the German onslaught with scarcely a score of seagoing units younger than twenty years old. Only thirteen vessels, five aircraft and 500 men escaped to Britain, but the Norwegian government in exile laid the foundations of a new navy which by the end of the war numbered fifty-eight ships and 7,500 men, much of it based on the revenue and personnel of the Norwegian merchant marine. Operating under control of the British Admiralty, the Royal Norwegian Navy gave distinguished service in northern waters, in the Atlantic, in the Mediterranean and off Normandy, suffering the loss of forty-five vessels and 933 men before the last shot had been fired. Indeed, one of

these, the minesweeper *NYMS 382*, has the melancholy distinction of being the last vessel lost to a U-boat, sunk by *U1023 after* the German surrender on 7 May 1945 (**G136**). The two RNorN sinkings treated in the main part of this volume (see also HNorMS *Montbretia*, **76**) accounted for fifteen per cent of its operational casualties.

The 'four-pipers'

The onset of the Battle of the Atlantic soon revealed the desperate shortage faced by the Royal Navy in vessels for convoy defence. Accordingly, in May 1940 Churchill sent a proposal to the US Government offering leases on a number of British bases in the Caribbean and Newfoundland in return for the loan of fifty elderly destroyers laid up on the east coast of the United States. Political considerations made it an offer Roosevelt could not accept, but a month later, with France defeated, the British Expeditionary Force expelled from the Continent and no less than twenty-five British destroyers sunk or damaged off Dunkirk, a renewed plea received a more favourable hearing. Without consulting Congress, on 2 September 1940 Roosevelt signed an executive order transferring fifty units of the Caldwell, Wickes and Clemson classes to the Royal Navy in return for ninety-nine-year leases on British bases in Bermuda, Newfoundland and the West Indies. Of these, seven were assigned to the Royal Canadian Navy while the rest entered service in the RN bearing the names of towns common to the British Commonwealth and the United States. Dilapidation, poor steering and manoeuvrability, design quirks and severe rolling in the Atlantic seaway made the 'four-pipers' rather unpopular in RN service and required extensive refitting and maintenance in British yards, but there could be no doubting the importance of the gesture which greatly eased the pressure on the Allies until purpose-built escorts began to enter service in numbers in 1941.

The Wickes-class destroyers

The Wickes-class destroyers, of which 111 were built in US yards from 1917, were based on the preceding Caldwell class, the first of the so-called 'flush-deckers' of which a total of 273 ships were built in three sub-classes. The flush-deckers were designed with an armament of four 4-inch guns, one 3-inch weapon and twelve torpedo tubes, though in the case of the Wickes and Clemson sub-classes (see HMS *Broadwater*, **36**) the maximum speed was increased from thirty to thirty-five knots to permit them to operate with the new Omaha-class scout cruisers and the US Navy's projected battlecruiser programme. Though capable ships, the flush-deckers were soon eclipsed by advances in destroyer design and thirty-two of the Wickes class were disposed of (largely as a result of chronic boiler defects) once US destroyer construction resumed in 1932, but fifty saw service in various guises with the wartime US Navy. A total of twenty-seven were transferred to Britain in 1940 where improvements were made to stability and anti-submarine armament along with modifications to command arrangements on the bridge.

Career

USS *Hopewell* (DD-181) was laid down at Newport News Shipbuilding Co., Virginia as the 107th unit of the Wickes class in January 1918 and launched the following June, being commissioned into the US Navy in March 1919. In April of that year she joined the 3rd Destroyer Squadron with which she served until placed in reserve at Charleston, South Carolina in October 1921. In April 1922 *Hopewell* was ordered to Philadelphia where in July she was put into mothballs in accordance with the terms of the Washington Treaty. Here she remained until recommissioned in June 1940, subsequently joining the US Navy's Neutrality Patrol in the Atlantic. However, in September 1940 *Hopewell* was transferred to Halifax, Nova Scotia as one of the fourth group of US destroyers to pass into British service, being commissioned into the Royal Navy as HMS *Bath* on the 23rd. After a brief refit at Devonport Dockyard, the end of October found *Bath* with the 1st Minelaying Squadron at the Kyle of Lochalsh, acting as cover for six minelaying sorties before the year was out. *Bath* was also earmarked for convoy duty with Western Approaches Command when available and in this capacity escorted three military convoys before docking at Chatham for refitting in January 1941. Still at Chatham, on 8 April *Bath* was recommissioned by a largely Norwegian crew for escort duty in the Atlantic under Western Approaches Command. A collision while running trials on the 16th required a month's repair on the Tyne, following which *Bath* made her way to HMS *Western Isles*, the Royal Navy's anti-submarine training establishment at Tobermory, Scotland. On 5 June she was allocated to the 5th Escort Group at Liverpool for service on the Liverpool–Gibraltar run, an assignment which claimed her on her sixth convoy.

Background of the attack

The first two weeks of August 1941 were to prove unusually lean for German U-boats in the Atlantic, a consequence of the speed with which Enigma messages were being decrypted by Bletchley Park and convoys rerouted around wolfpacks following the capture of *U110* on 9 May. This no doubt helps explain the urgency with which Dönitz exhorted all available units to attack the Gibraltar-bound convoy OG71 when it was first sighted by a Kondor aircraft on the 17th. However, the 5th Escort Group, consisting of the destroyers *Bath* and *Wanderer*, supported by the corvettes *Bluebell*, *Campanula*, *Campion*, *Hydrangea*, *Wallflower* and *Zinnia* (see the next entry, **31**), as well as the trawler *Lord Nuffield*, managed to drive off *U201* (Kptlt Adalbert Schnee; see **33**) that evening and the Germans struggled to maintain contact over the next twenty-four hours. But B.d.U. was determined that OG71 should not slip through, of which Kptlt Walter Kell's log gives ample evidence, and at 2115 on the 18th *U204* picked up the convoy on her hydrophones. After an abortive attack on a corvette shortly after midnight, at 0200 on the 19th Kell sighted HNorMS *Bath* stationed two miles astern of the convoy and lost no time in engaging. His choices were fully in accordance with Dönitz's standing orders that the escorts of the Gibraltar convoys be the first targets of any attack.

War Diary of *U204*, patrol of 22 July–22 August 1941: PG 30192, NHB, reel 1,090, p. 460

Date, time	Details of position, wind, weather, sea, light, visibility, moonlight, etc.	Incidents
18.viii		
2010	Qu. BE 2295	At a bearing of 90° true several clouds of smoke in sight, 15–20 nm away. Qu. BE 2374.
2035		Dived away from flying boat at bearing 90° true, heading straight towards us.
2043		Surfaced.
2045		Flying boat at bearing 90° true, heading straight towards us.
2048		Dived.
2115		U-boat heard through hydrophones at bearing 260° true.
		Convoy heard through hydrophones at bearing 100°–140° true.
2132		Surfaced.
2138		Incoming W/T transmission 2102/18/178 from *U559*: *Air cover, BE 2614.*
2145		Incoming W/T transmission 2056/18/181 from B.d.U.: *Take any attacking opportunity that presents itself. Spare no torpedoes. All boats to provide full contact reports at regular intervals as soon as enemy movements are available.*

Date, time	Details of position, wind, weather, sea, light, visibility, moonlight, etc.	Incidents
2148		Dived away from flying boat heading towards us.
2241		Surfaced.
2245		Incoming W/T transmission 2214/18/184 from *U201*: *BE 2532*.
2257		Incoming W/T transmission 2151/18/183 from B.d.U.: *According to B-Dienst convoy was in BE 2347 at 1915.*[1]
2324		Incoming W/T transmission 2211/18/185 from B.d.U.: *If contact should be lost and independent searching yields nothing, fan out and search between 180°–260°, starting from last known position. Divide up in the following order: Suhren, Kell, Heidtmann, Oesten, endeavouring at all costs to get ahead of the enemy by daybreak.*[2]

Kell

19.viii

Date, time	Details of position, wind, weather, sea, light, visibility, moonlight, etc.	Incidents
0000	Qu. BE 2539, North Atlantic, wind WNW 3, sea 2–3, visibility 3,000 m, overcast, 1,021 mb	Steering a course to south of convoy.
0038	Qu. BE 2644	Shadow at bearing 50°, convoy vessel (corvette) sailing very slowly, course 220°, inclination 60°.
0040		Battle Stations manned.
0043		Single torpedo fired from Tube II at corvette.[3] Depth 2 m, inclination 80°, enemy speed 3 knots, range 800 m. It turns out to be a surface runner, which she outmanoeuvres. The bow cap of Tube I wouldn't open properly (1½ turns short of fully open), couldn't get shot away. We head west. A further four corvettes heave into sight steaming in line abreast, steering 220°.[4] The rearguard presumably.
0107		Outgoing W/T transmission 0055/19/187: *Enemy position BE 2644. U204.*
0107		I head SE so as to position myself on the starboard side of the convoy, which I assume to be at a bearing of 200°–220°.
0113		Tube II reloaded.
0114		Another corvette in sight.
0140		Outgoing W/T transmission 0104/19/188: *From U201. BE 2563 lower edge middle, course 180°.*
0138		Course now set to south-west towards what I presume is the position of the convoy.
0200		I come across five corvettes sailing in line astern at 200–300 m intervals.[4]
0203		A shadow to port veers towards us. Bows right, inclination 30°. I stop. A large destroyer steering 240°, proceeding slowly.[5]
0205	Qu. BE 2647	Single torpedo fired from Tube I at Afridi-class destroyer.[6] Depth 2 m, inclination 90°, enemy speed 8 knots, range 700 m. (For the first 200 m or so torpedo ran on surface.) A hit just abaft amidships, running time 47 sec.[7] Torpedo detonation is followed by several subsequent detonations, probably depth charges or boilers.
0208		*Coup-de-grâce* shot from Tube V, depth 2 m, range 800 m. Torpedo probably passed beneath target. Target gradually settles deeper by the stern, great clouds of steam billow out of her. She capsizes to port; shortly before sinking we see a bright glow of flame. Destroyer sank in 5 min. 20 sec. With regard to her appearance, she had two funnels of differing thickness and twin gun mountings.[8]
0212		Heavy starshell fire; I am forced to withdraw to the north.
0215		I head south to haul ahead.

---

1   *B-Dienst* was the Kriegsmarine's radio monitoring and intelligence service.

2   Commanders of *U564* (see **31**), *U204*, *U559* (see **42**) and *U106* respectively.

3   The identity of this vessel is not known.

4   Six corvettes were present: *Bluebell, Campanula, Campion, Hydrangea, Wallflower* and *Zinnia.*

5   HNorMS *Bath.*

6   Both this and the *coup-de-grâce* were fired by Oblt.z.S. Wichler, *U204*'s First Watch Officer. It is hard to think of two destroyer types in British service less alike than the Tribal class, of which HMS *Afridi* was a member, and *Bath* of the US-built Wickes class.

7   Kell's torpedo report describes the hit as being between the second funnel and after superstructure. However, *Bath* in fact had four funnels; see n. 7.

8   Although it is possible that two funnels were toppled by the detonation, *Bath* had the four stacks for which her class was known. She also had single mountings rather than the twin arrangements described by Kell.

The sinking

Though Kell could not have known it, Cdr Melsom sighted *U204* from the bridge of HNorMS *Bath* at 0107 convoy time, the very moment that *U204* was launching her first torpedo (the hour's difference aside, *Bath*'s timekeeping deviated from the German by two minutes or so). Melsom ordered the helm thrown hard astarboard with the intention of ramming but his ship had not yet begun to turn when *U204*'s torpedo struck the starboard side abreast the forward engine room. *Bath* was at Action Stations with all watertight doors shut but the effect was catastrophic, the ship immediately heeling to port before righting herself shortly after with fires raging around the point of impact. Two minutes later her back broke, the fore part sinking within the space of another two minutes and the stern following it a minute later. The Board of Enquiry found no failure in *Bath*'s personnel, attributing her loss solely to enemy action.

Fate of the crew

Bath's demise came too quickly for any orderly evacuation to be effected. Though some rafts were launched none of the ship's boats could be lowered and the survivors had to get clear as best they could. Several men were relieved to note an absence of suction from the sinking parts of the ship but her disappearance was followed by a series of huge explosions. One of these was powerful enough to blow a loaded raft right out of the water. As testimony submitted to the Board of Enquiry makes clear, many experienced a temporary loss of sensation in their legs, others sustaining serious groin and abdominal injuries. One equated the experience to being 'cut in two parts'. The survivors were unanimous in attributing the detonations to two of the ship's depth charges but the Board, noting that all depth charges had been set to safe and that the characteristic fountain of water was not observed, attributed these to a second torpedo hit. The matter is settled by Kell's log which clearly states that his would-be *coup de grâce* torpedo not only failed to detonate but was fired before *Bath* sank. His torpedo report, meanwhile, attributes the subsequent explosions to a combination of depth-charge and boiler explosions.

Over the next four hours forty-nine survivors were rescued by HM destroyer *Wanderer* and HM corvette *Hydrangea*, many in a critical condition. Later that day thirty-three of those fit enough to be moved were transferred to HNorMS *St Albans* and landed at Liverpool. There were no survivors among the executive officers.

U204 and Walter Kell

Built by Germaniawerft and commissioned in March 1941, *U204* spent her three cruises in the forefront of Atlantic operations. Commanded throughout by Kptlt Walter Kell (previously *Kommandant* of the Type-IIB *U8*, albeit not on frontline duties), *U204* sank HNorMS *Bath* and

Commissioning day for *U204* on 8 March 1941, Kell shown second from right. As the shield on the conning tower indicates, the boat had been adopted by the city of Krefeld in the Ruhr. *DUBMA*

six merchantmen for a total of 25,000 tons. Her career ended following a successful attack on the British tanker *Inverlee* off Cape Spartel at the entrance to the Straits of Gibraltar on 19 October 1941. *U204* was immediately located and depth charged by HM sloop *Rochester* and HM corvette *Mallow*. There were no survivors.

Sources

Admiralty, *Loss of His Norwegian Majesty's Ship* Bath: *Board of Enquiry* (TNA, ADM 1/12024)

Abelsen, Frank, *Norwegian Naval Ships, 1939–1945* (Oslo: Sem & Stenersen AS, 1986)

Berg, Ole F., *I skjærgården og på havet: Marinens krig 8. april 1940–8. mai 1945* (Oslo: Marinens krigsveteranforening, 1997)

Blair, *Hitler's U-Boat War*, II, pp. 337–9

Churchill, *The Second World War*, II, pp. 398–416

DANFS, III, pp. 359–60 (USS *Hopewell*); also on: http://www.history.navy.mil/danfs/h7/hopewell-i.htm

Hague, Arnold, *Destroyers for Great Britain: A History of 50 Town Class Ships Transferred from the United States to Great Britain in 1940* (London: Greenhill Books, 1990)

Sly, Jeremy, 'Torpedoed!: The Brief but Active Career of HMS *Bath*' [reference not known]

Website titled *The Norwegian Navy in the Second World War*: http://www.resdal.org/Archivo/d00000a5.htm

Career history of HNorMS *Bath*: http://www.naval-history.net/xGM-Chrono-11US-Bath.htm

31 HMS *ZINNIA*

Lt Cdr C. G. Cuthbertson, RNR
Sunk by *U564* (Type VIIC), Oblt.z.S. Reinhard Suhren, 23 August 1941
North Atlantic, 80 nm WNW of Cabo Mondego (Portugal)

Probably not *Zinnia*, for which no photo has been found, but nonetheless an evocative shot of a Flower-class corvette quartering the sea while on convoy escort duty in the Atlantic. *BfZ*

Theatre	North Atlantic (Map 1)	*Displacement*	940 tons
Coordinates	40° 25' N, 10° 40' W	*Dimensions*	205.25' × 33' × approx. 11.25'
Kriegsmarine code (TR)	Quadrat CG 2783	*Maximum speed*	16 knots
U-boat timekeeping differential	+1 hour	*Armament*	1 × 4"; 4 × .303" AA
Fatalities 50 *Survivors* 15			

Career

For design notes on the Flower-class corvettes, see HMS *Picotee* (**29**).

By the close of 1939 the French government had placed orders for ten corvettes with Smith's Dock Company of Middlesbrough and nine more in an assortment of British and French yards. Of these construction had started on six at Middlesbrough by the time France surrendered in June 1940. The Smith's Dock order was immediately taken over by the Royal Navy and the keel of what would become HMS *Zinnia* laid on 20 August that year. *Zinnia* was launched on 28 November 1940 and sailed from Middlesbrough on 2 April 1941. After working up through April and May she was assigned to Western Approaches Command and joined her first convoy at Liverpool on 11 June. The drudgery of escort duty in the North Atlantic filled the rest of her short life, though not without incident: on 5 July she attempted to ram *U372* (see **64**) in defence of convoy SL88 250 miles west of Ireland. On 15 August HMS *Zinnia* sailed from Liverpool for the last time to escort convoy OG71 to Gibraltar.

Background of the attack

For additional background on convoy OG71, see the preceding entry for HNorMS *Bath* (**30**).

On 17 August 1941 *U201* (Kptlt Adalbert Schnee) made contact with the Liverpool–Gibraltar convoy OG71 shortly after it had exited the North Channel into the Atlantic. B.d.U. rapidly marshalled all available units to the attack, so beginning a prolonged battle in which OG71 lost eight of its twenty-two ships despite the eventual provision of no fewer than eleven escorts for its defence. After initial setbacks, the Germans claimed their first victim in the early hours of the 19th when *U204* torpedoed the Norwegian destroyer *Bath* (**30**). This was followed by three merchant sinkings before the U-boats lost contact later that day, the Admiralty reinforcing OG71 with two destroyers equipped with the latest HF/DF radio-detection device, HMSs *Gurkha* (**46**) and *Lance*. When a German aircraft sighted the convoy again on 21 August further U-boats were ushered into action, among them Oblt.z.S. Reinhard Suhren's *U564*. The log below chronicles *U564*'s sighting of OG71 on the afternoon of the 22nd and the attacks she made on it that night, culminating in a torpedo salvo against a cluster of ships including HMS *Zinnia* at 0425 on the 23rd (British time). Although *Zinnia* had been keeping close station on the port beam of the convoy since 0400 and was zigzagging at fourteen knots, *U564* was out of range of her Asdic and the dark night stacked the odds heavily in favour of the attacker.

War Diary of *U564*, patrol of 16–27 August 1941: PG 30598, NHB, reel 1,121, pp. 234–5

Date, time	Details of position, wind, weather, sea, light, visibility, moonlight, etc.	Incidents
22.viii		
1200	Qu. CG 1276	Day's run: 246.5 nm surfaced, 3.5 nm submerged
1250	Almost no swell, clear skies, visibility in	Five plumes of smoke visible at bearing 115° true. Course around 120°. An aircraft in sight at bearing 115° true, roughly the same course.

	excess of 20 nm clear skies, visibility in excess of 20 nm	
1330		An aircraft in sight, probably a Sunderland.
1340		A U-boat in sight at bearing 60° true.[1] Closing.
1450		A Sunderland in sight at bearing 180° true. Course perhaps 130°. Then turns about and retraces its course.
1455		U-boat now disappears at bearing 0° true.
1500		An aircraft in sight at 230° true, reciprocal course.
1503	Qu. CG 1565	A plume of smoke visible at bearing 100° true. Soon further plumes of smoke appear over the horizon, making four in total. It's the convoy, and about time too after all this searching.[2] The D/F bearings from the aircraft continue to produce an uncertain picture.
1550		An aircraft in sight at bearing 130°. A great distance away.
1600	Qu. CG 1593, wind WSW 1, sea WSW 0–1, sporadic clouds, very good visibility	I provide continual contact reports by radio, and a further beacon signal as requested for the Luftwaffe. The convoy's air escort has been appearing at regular intervals and on one occasion comprised two aircraft flying together.
2000	Qu. CG 1918	
2321	Minimal wind and sea, sporadic clouds, rather dark night	I move in to attack intending to fire four bow torpedoes followed by a stern torpedo after turning. Unfortunately the bow cap of Tube II doesn't open.
2331		I fire with Tubes I, III and IV at three steamers and then after turning fire a further torpedo from Tube V at another steamer that was somewhat detached from the rest. Four detonations heard after 6 min. 50 sec., 7 min. 8 sec. and 5 min. 40 sec.[3] We withdraw to reload torpedoes and haul away to the opposite side of the convoy. Escorts are firing starshell but these are very poorly directed.
		Suhren

23.viii

0000	Qu. CG 1953, no change in weather, somewhat darker night	
0200	Qu. CG 2744	Run in for second attack. Just before we reach our firing position a U-boat appears between us and the convoy.[1] We turn away as the field of fire is no longer open. As we move away we see a tanker burning brightly and before this another steamer was seen to sink. The destroyers are firing starshell rather wildly. The whole horizon is brightly lit and we can see the convoy filing past the burning tanker. We can make out fourteen vessels in all.
0322		We run in once again.
0335	Qu. CG 2772	Four torpedoes fired from the same tubes. After 3 min. 10 sec. we see a torpedo detonation and a great flash.[4] A burst of starshell follows immediately which this time lights up exactly the right area but it appears that our boat has not been observed. Withdraw to reload torpedoes.
0400	Qu. CG 2775, night becoming even darker	
0515		Run in for third attack. At this point a destroyer sails quite close, forming a contiguous target with two other steamers.
0525	Qu. CG 2781[5]	Three torpedoes fired from Tubes I, III and IV at two steamers and one destroyer. Powerful detonations after 2 min. 54 sec., 2 min. 57 sec. and 3 min. 5 sec. respectively, each accompanied by a glow of flame. One steamer capsizes within about two minutes, another – presumably a destroyer or other escort

1   Almost certainly Kptlt Adalbert Schnee's *U201* (see **33**).
2   Convoy OG71 which B.d.U. had been tracking for almost a week.
3   Only three torpedo run times are given by Suhren for the four detonations mentioned by him. Two of these are thought to have sunk the SS *Empire Oak* and the SS *Clonlara*. Three burning ships are noted in the torpedo report, but no other appears to have been damaged or sunk.
4   A torpedo struck SS *Spind*, damaging but not sinking her. *Spind* was finished off three hours later by *U552* (see **38**).
5   In his torpedo report the attack is recorded as taking place in Qu. CG 2783. Both of these place the German assessment of the position to the west of that reported by Lt Cdr C. G. Cuthbertson, commanding HMS *Zinnia*.

Date, time	Details of position, wind, weather, sea, light, visibility, moonlight, etc.	Incidents
		vessel – is blown out of the water by subsequent detonations accompanied by a huge pall of smoke, while the third steamer sinks with her stern rearing up sharply towards the sky.[6]
		The counter-attack this time is very slow off the mark and feeble as well, consisting of a single escort shining a solitary searchlight.
		I withdraw from the convoy.
0655		Report successes to B.d.U. via W/T, requesting permission to return to port.[7]
0735		Test dive.

6   HMS *Zinnia* was presumably the 'destroyer or other escort vessel' but there is no evidence of other ships being sunk in this encounter.

7   Suhren's request was due to *U564* having fired her last torpedo but was turned down by B.d.U. which ordered her to remain at sea for a while longer to provide position reports on the convoy.

The sinking

Though extra lookouts had been posted following two recent attacks on the convoy, *U564*'s attack from 3,000 metres came without warning. Her torpedo struck *Zinnia* at 0421 (the hour's difference aside, British timekeeping differed from the German by a few minutes) while she was under ten degrees of helm as part of a routine alteration to her broad and irregular zigzagging pattern. As *Zinnia*'s commanding officer Lt Cdr Cuthbertson reported to the Commander-in-Chief Western Approaches, Admiral Sir Martin Dunbar-Nasmith VC, the detonation had a devastating effect on his ship:

> I was stepping out of the Bridge Asdic House and facing the funnel and about 25 feet from the explosion. The Asdic House collapsed and parts of the ship were thrown into the air. She immediately heeled over on to her starboard beam ends, and in five seconds had capsized through 120 degrees.

Cuthbertson was one of a number of men pitched into the sea as *Zinnia* turned over. His next recollection, having surfaced after what he estimated to have been within twelve seconds of the detonation, was of the bows rising vertically out of the water before subsiding into the ocean. With the passage of another twelve seconds HMS *Zinnia* had disappeared leaving a number of survivors bobbing in a patch of oil.

Fate of the crew

Rapid though her sinking was, rather more of *Zinnia*'s men managed to get clear of the wreck than might have been expected in the circumstances. All of these had been above deck when the torpedo struck, either on the bridge, in the crow's nest, in the wheelhouse or on the pom-pom platform. Writhing in oil-covered water, they had to endure a series of underwater explosions after *Zinnia* went down which were later attributed to boiler explosions, further torpedoes or depth charges. The survivors were left clinging to any flotsam they could find to escape the worst of the oil, Lt Cdr Cuthbertson resorting to a corpse:

> I heard many cries for help in the water, and estimated there were about 40 men floating. I could do nothing to help them. The water was thick with fuel oil, and it was all I could do to keep my balance in the swell, and my nose and mouth above the oil. I remained afloat 40 minutes before finding the trunk of a body which had been blasted and was buoyant, this kept me afloat for the remaining 30 minutes.

A number of ships were on hand but the would-be rescuers had only the briefest opportunity to identify *Zinnia*'s position before she disappeared and survivors proved hard to locate in the darkness. For over two hours HM corvettes *Wallflower*, *Campion* and *Campanula* searched a broad area, rescuing seventeen men including Lt Cdr Cuthbertson:

> One corvette passed close without sighting me. Eventually at 0530 I was picked up by a boat from another corvette, HMS *Campion*. I had to be hoisted inboard, could only crawl along the deck and was completely blinded. I was still fully clothed.

They were landed at Gibraltar that evening on the heels of the badly mauled OG71. Aside from treating injuries the main task on board the rescue ships was the removal of oil from the men's bodies, effected with paraffin for the body and petrol for the eyes. Two of those rescued died later, the first in *Campion* shortly after being picked up, the other in Gibraltar after two unsuccessful blood transfusions, thereby bringing the death toll from HMS *Zinnia* to fifty.

Cuthbertson's report contained a number of suggestions to improve the prospects of survivors in the water, including the supply of lights and whistles for them to indicate their position and the need for escorts to drop rafts whenever possible. A number of these suggestions were forwarded to the Committee on Life-Saving at Sea which as a result included 'the provision of a short-range buoyant automatically operated light for attachment to rafts which are likely to float off or be got overboard most readily' as well as 'the attachment of ordinary service torches to every lifesaving raft, etc. carried on board' among its recommendations.

U564 and Reinhard Suhren

Built by Blohm & Voss at Hamburg and commissioned in April 1941, *U564* was the first command of Oblt.z.S. Reinhard Suhren and made her maiden operational patrol in April of that year. Few men were better qualified for a first command than Suhren who had achieved the unique feat of winning the Knight's Cross despite being only First Watch Officer of *U48* (see **18**). Successes for *U564* were plentiful over the next eighteen months, comprising nineteen ships sunk for a total of just under 100,000 tons, achieved on both sides of the Atlantic. The only blot for Suhren during this period, which saw him add the Oak Leaves and Swords to his Knight's Cross, was the sinking of the neutral tanker SS *Potrero del Llano* off Florida on 14 May 1942. She had apparently been fully lit up, with spotlights illuminating the Mexican flag. The sinking of a second tanker, the SS *Faja de Oro*, by *U160* on the 20th prompted the Mexican government to declare war on Germany

Suhren as commander of *U564* in 1941 or 1942.
Note the boat's famous black cat emblem on his cap. *DUBMA*

that same day. *U564*'s run of success came to an abrupt halt with Suhren's departure. Her next five patrols under Oblt.z.S. Hans Fiedler yielded no sinkings and she was badly damaged in air attacks off Cape Finisterre on 13 and 14 June 1943. She sank later on the 14th while under tow with the loss of twenty-eight of her crew.

The high esteem in which Suhren was held by B.d.U. is reflected in his promotion from Oberleutnant zur See to Fregattenkapitän, a rise of three ranks in the space of two and a half years. After leaving *U564*

Suhren became an instructor with the 2nd U-Boat Training Division before transferring to the 22nd *U-Flottille* as Chief of Staff. He spent the last year of the war as *F.d.U. Norwegen* (Officer Commanding U-Boats, Norway; redesignated *F.d.U. Nordmeer* – Northern Waters – in September 1944). Released from captivity in May 1946, Reinhard Suhren died in Hamburg in August 1984.

Sources

Admiralty, *Enemy Submarine Attacks on HM Vessels* (TNA, ADM 199/621)
Bates, N. W. J., *The Second World War Papers of N.W.J. Bates. No. 2: Gibraltar Convoy* (manuscript, IWM, P188)
Ruegg, R. A., *Flower-Class Corvettes* (typescript, IWM, 13(41).245/5, 1987)

Bailey, Chris Howard, *The Royal Naval Museum Book of the Battle of the Atlantic: The Corvettes and Their Crews: An Oral History* (Stroud, Glos.: Sutton Publishing, 1994)
Blair, *Hitler's U-Boat War*, I, pp. 337–9
Brustat-Naval, Fritz, and Reinhard [alias Teddy] Suhren, *Nasses Eichenlaub: Als Kommandant und FDU im U-Boot-Krieg* (Hamburg: Koehler, 1998); Eng. trans.: *Teddy Suhren: Ace of Aces. Memoirs of a U-Boat Rebel* (Annapolis, Md.: Naval Institute Press, 2006)
Harris, Paul, 'The Assassins Under the Waves' in *The Daily Mail*, Thursday, 15 March 2001; see also: http://www.uk-muenchen.de/berichte/reportagen_u564.htm
Paterson, Lawrence, *U-Boat War Patrol: The Hidden Photographic Diary of U 564* (London: Greenhill Books, 2004)
Preston, Antony, and Alan Raven, *Flower Class Corvettes* [Ensign, no. 3] (London: Bivouac Books, 1973); reprinted as Man o'War, no. 7 (London: Arms and Armour Press, 1982)

---

32   HMCS *LÉVIS* (i)
Lt G. W. Gilding, RCNR
Sunk by *U74* (Type VIIB), Kptlt Eitel-Friedrich Kentrat, 19 September 1941
North Atlantic, 160 nm E of Uummannarsuaq, Greenland

Lévis seen following *U74*'s attack on 19 September, her bows severed and hanging off forward of the deck gun.
As the bridge is vacant the photo seems to have been taken after she was finally abandoned that morning. *NAC*

Theatre   North Atlantic (Map 1)
Coordinates (of attack)   60° 07' N, 38° 37' W
Kriegsmarine code (of attack)   Quadrat AD 9458
U-boat timekeeping differential   +4 hours
Fatalities   18   *Survivors*   40+

Displacement   940 tons
Dimensions   205.25' × 33' × approx. 11.25'
Maximum speed   16 knots
Armament   1 × 4"

The Royal Canadian Navy

The Royal Canadian Navy traces its origins to the Naval Services Act of 1910 by which the dominion government provided for the establishment of a permanent force constituted along British lines. By the end of that year two elderly cruisers had been acquired from the Royal Navy to which a pair of submarines was added on the eve of the Great War. Although it reached a strength of 9,000 men and a hundred ships during that conflict, the immediate post-war period saw a drastic reduction in funding, personnel and equipment which left the RCN struggling to find a peacetime role for itself. The long-term survival of the force was assured with the establishment of the Royal Canadian Naval Volunteer Reserve in 1923 which in turn led to the raising of Naval Reserve divisions in fifteen cities. It was not until 1931 that the RCN took possession of two truly modern ships, the British-built destroyers *Saguenay* and *Skeena*, but the outbreak of the Second World War found her with a strength of only six destroyers, four minesweepers and approximately 3,500 men including reserves. Nonetheless, the RCN now began a spectacular expansion which placed her as the third-largest navy in the world on the cessation of hostilities with 375 vessels in commission. Although the RCN suffered from deficiencies in training and equipment in the early years of the war it eventually took over responsibility for the entire north-western sector of the Atlantic theatre and made a significant contribution to victory in the Battle of the Atlantic, accounting for thirty U-boats sunk by VE Day.

Career

For design notes on the Flower-class corvettes, see HMS *Picotee* (**29**).

Between 1941 and 1944 some 111 Flower-class corvettes were commissioned into the Royal Canadian Navy, a reflection of the major contribution made by this force to the Battle of the Atlantic. Canadian shipbuilders were kept equally busy, producing a total of 124 corvettes in thirteen yards over the same period, including all but two of those commissioned into the RCN along with fifteen others: eight for the US Navy and seven for the Royal Navy. Unlike their British sisters, most of the Canadian Flowers were named after local towns and ten were lost during the war, seven to U-boats.

The first of these casualties was HMCS *Lévis*, laid down at G. T. Davie of Lauzon, Quebec in March 1940, launched in September of that year and completed in May 1941 at the height of Canadian corvette construction. It is a measure of how desperate was the situation in the Atlantic that *Lévis* was rushed into service with a largely untrained crew and after only the briefest of work-ups, which began on her arrival at Halifax on 29 May. Not only did *Lévis* have the misfortune to be struck by a Quebec ferry, but she sailed for war lacking vital equipment and missing her anti-aircraft armament, the absence of which was never made good. Commissioned by Lt G. W. Gilding, RCNR, *Lévis* completed her work-up at Halifax, Nova Scotia in June and immediately joined the 19th Escort Group of the Newfoundland Escort Force based at St John's. But *Lévis*'s poor luck was set to continue, the ship becoming separated from her charges in heavy weather during her first eastbound convoy to Iceland. A brief and ill-starred career ended on only her second eastbound convoy.

Background of the attack

After a relatively lean July and August the U-boat arm reaped a rich harvest of sinkings in September 1941. The havoc wreaked by the *Markgraf* ('margrave') group east of Greenland on convoy SC42, which lost sixteen of its number, was the undoubted highlight from the German perspective, and convoy SC44, which sailed from St John's on 13 September, therefore had every reason to expect trouble despite an improved escort comprising HM destroyer *Chesterfield* (Senior Officer) and the corvettes *Honeysuckle* (RN), *Agassiz*, *Lévis*, *Mayflower* (all RCN) and *Alysse* (Free French navy; **51**). As it turned out, this slow eastbound convoy got off lightly as only five boats of the subsequently formed *Brandenburg* group were able to make contact. The first to do so was *U74* late on the 18th. Kptlt Kentrat's war diary indicates that the five torpedoes he fired from 0603 onwards (German time) took a heavy toll of the convoy; in fact there was only one victim, HMC corvette *Lévis* stationed to port of SC44 with her Asdic equipment out of action.

War Diary of *U74*, patrol of 8–26 September 1941: PG 30070, NHB, reel 1,071, pp. 494–5

Date, time	Details of position, wind, weather, sea, light, visibility, moonlight, etc.	Incidents
18.ix		
2100	[Qu.] AD 9758	At 30° off the starboard bow a number of smoke plumes in sight. As they come nearer we can identify them as an eastbound convoy. Vessels seem well strung out.
2330		*Alpha, Alpha. Enemy convoy in sight. Qu. AD 9761. Course NE, moderate speed. U74.*
2400	[Qu.] AD 9764 lower right, wind SW 3–4, sea 4, cloud 1–2/10, fairly bright night, Northern Lights, visibility 4–6 nm	Since 0530 on 18 September reception on the short-wave band has been very poor and it gradually cuts out altogether. We try absolutely everything but without success. I hope the other Brandenburg boats can receive me.[1]
		As dusk begins to fall I close in on the convoy, gradually getting myself into position on its starboard side. Convoy is composed of 20 steamers sailing in line ahead, two columns with substantial gaps between ships.[2] Escort comprises four corvettes and two destroyers.[3]
		Kentrat

---

1   B.d.U. received none of Kentrat's signals announcing his contact with SC44 though the other Brandenburg boats did.

2   There were in fact three columns totalling 51 ships.

3   The escort actually consisted of a destroyer and five corvettes.

19.ix

0200		*Alpha, Alpha. Enemy convoy, course 60°, moderate speed, Qu. AD 9739. U74.*

Shortly after darkness falls the Northern Lights begin shining brightly. Visibility is now 10–12 nm; might as well be broad daylight. Escorts have stationed themselves well out and several times I attempt to get into an attacking position from the starboard side only to be driven off by corvettes.[4] In these conditions we can probably be seen from about 6,000 m.

0400 [Qu.] AD 9813 upper middle, wind W to S 3, sea 3, cloud 2/10, very bright Northern Lights, visibility up to 7 nm, gentle SW swell

However, corvettes don't pursue me for long. I now work my way behind and round to the port side of the convoy where the Northern Lights are less bright.

No other Brandenburg boat has yet reported in. I must find out at all costs whether or not my signal was picked up and forwarded to B.d.U. by other boats nearby. I therefore send out the following radio signals, first to my neighbour on the patrol line (*U94*) and then to all other Brandenburg boats:

0425 *Alpha, Alpha. U94 – convoy located Qu. AD 9479.[5] U74.*

0450 *Brandenburg boats report in immediately. U74.*

0603 From about 3,000 m I fire a spread of four aimed at a large tanker of about 8–10,000 GRT sailing in fifth place in the column together with an overlapping steamer of about 6–7,000 GRT.

While turning I then fire a stern shot at foremost destroyer of port-side escort.[6]

Four detonations. One of these observed amidships on the large steamer.[7] About 50-m high column of explosion forming mushroom-shaped cloud.

Steamer then disappears shortly afterwards. The second steamer receives a hit abaft the bridge, flashes a green light several times and briefly transmits the morse signal 'Help'.

I head off at high speed on the surface. Destroyer initially takes no action whatsoever, then we see her silhouette narrowing but she doesn't seem to close us. There is a brief period of frenzied morsing between the escort ships, then silence.

0623 As we head off we hear the sound of 22 depth charges exploding.[8]

0631 A detonation is heard from the bridge.

0800 [Qu.] AD 9565 upper middle

0810 I set general course 60° to haul ahead and once again transmit a contact report.

---

4 Kentrat's claim that he was sighted and driven off by corvettes both here and at 0400 is not borne out in Allied sources. At no point prior to his attack of 0603 had he been sighted nor was any submarine contact reported by the escort.

5 *U94* was commanded by Oblt.z.S. Otto Ites.

6 HMCS *Mayflower* was the leading corvette on the port side with *Lévis* some distance astern. Though consistent with his style elsewhere in the war diary, Kentrat's use of the first person singular both here and in the earlier attack is misleading since all torpedoes were fired by *U74*'s First Watch Officer, Oblt.z.S. Adolf Friedrichs.

7 There is no evidence of damage to any vessel other than *Lévis* at this time.

8 This was presumably *Mayflower*'s attack on a supposed contact, though quite evidently a false one.

The sinking

From Kentrat's war diary it would seem that *Lévis* fell victim to a random strike by one of the five torpedoes launched by *U74* between 0603 and 0605 German time. There is no evidence for a hit on a merchantman at this point and it is difficult to know what to make of Kentrat's claims to have witnessed the sinking of two large freighters during this attack. An attack on a destroyer is indicated (0605 in the torpedo report) but this is unlikely to have been *Lévis* for two reasons: not only does Kentrat fail to claim to a hit, but he describes his target as the foremost destroyer on the port side of the convoy, which would equate to HMC corvette *Mayflower* rather than her sister *Lévis* which was keeping station further astern. But that *Lévis* was hit by one of Kentrat's torpedoes is beyond all doubt. At 0205 ship time she was struck on the port side about forty feet from the stem, the explosion almost removing her bows. Her ship's company were initially under the impression that they had struck a mine but the torpedo had been spotted by an officer in *Mayflower*. Lt Gilding was below decks when the torpedo struck but emerged and gave the order to abandon ship almost immediately, 'as it appeared in the darkness that the ship was sinking rapidly by the head'. The engineering staff obeyed, extinguishing the boilers but leaving the diesel generator running for power and light. Concerns that *Lévis* had been prematurely abandoned set in almost as soon as the survivors had got clear, and the First Lieutenants of both *Mayflower* and *Lévis* reboarded her at 0415 to see if the bulkhead abaft the wreckage was likely to hold. Their verdict was sufficiently optimistic for a full boarding party to be raised and at 0540 *Lévis* was taken in tow by *Mayflower* with the intention of reaching Iceland across 300 nautical miles of ocean. Progress was slow; the first hawser parted after little more than an hour and by mid-morning concerns over *Lévis*'s stability led to the boarding party being removed. *Lévis* continued to settle and eventually sank shortly after 1700, the tow from *Mayflower* having been slipped at that hour. The boilers, still hot, exploded with some violence as she slipped under.

A Board of Inquiry held at St John's three weeks after the sinking

An undated shot of Kentrat in command either of *U74* or *U196*. DUBMA

expressed its dissatisfaction over the premature abandonment of *Lévis*. While neither the absence of proper damage control material nor perhaps even poor organisation among *Lévis*'s ship's company could be wholly laid at his door, Gilding's conduct was roundly condemned. Rear-Admiral L. W. Murray, Flag Officer Newfoundland Force, concurred in the Board's findings, noting that 'the action of the Commanding Officer in ordering "Abandon Ship" without inspection of the damage or a search for wounded men, and in leading the Ship's company by leaving in the first boat, and not returning with the reboarding party, is considered far below the standard expected of a naval officer'. However, Gilding escaped a court-martial, Murray concluding that 'any charge of "cowardice" or "conduct not becoming an officer" could probably be circumvented by pleading shock'. By contrast, a number of men were given letters of commendation for their conduct, and Sub-Lt Hatrick's efforts to raise the alarm, rescue injured men and set the depth charges to safe did not go unnoticed, though his DSC was not gazetted until 1946. A legacy of the sinking was that all future ship contracts made the builder responsible for the provision of damage-control equipment. The name *Lévis* was revived in a River-class frigate of the Royal Canadian Navy laid down at the same Lauzon yard as her forebear in March 1943.

Fate of the crew

U74's torpedo, which detonated in the stokers' and seamen's mess decks, killed sixteen ratings of the Royal Canadian Navy and one of the Royal Navy, while injuring several more. A majority of the casualties were on the stokers' mess deck. The survivors made it safely into *Lévis*'s two seaboats and several Carley floats to be picked up by *Mayflower* and *Agassiz*, in which a sailor subsequently died of wounds. No further casualties were incurred, and indeed the roll of survivors increased when Ordinary Telegraphist Émile Beaudoin was found badly wounded in a corner of one of the mess decks by the boarding party at daybreak on the 19th. Once responsibility for escorting the convoy had been handed off to the Royal Navy south of Iceland the 19th Escort Group turned for Reykjavik to land the survivors, those fit enough to do so returning to Halifax just over a week later. Beaudoin was sunk again in HMC destroyer *Athabaskan* in 1944, an account of which he published later (see below).

U74 and Eitel-Friedrich Kentrat

Built by Bremer Vulkan at Vegesack, *U74* was commissioned in September 1940 under Kptlt Eitel-Friedrich Kentrat, whose command of *U8* had ended following an onboard accident which kept him hospitalised for three months. *U74*'s first five patrols under Kentrat yielded five sinkings in the Atlantic (including *Lévis*), but she is remembered as the only U-boat to have rescued survivors from the battleship *Bismarck* following her destruction on 27 May 1941. In December Kentrat was awarded the Knight's Cross on a low tonnage score, the same month in which he took *U74* into the Mediterranean where she failed to add to her tally in two patrols. As so often, a change of command in March 1942 boded ill for the boat in question, *U74* succumbing on her first patrol under her former Second Watch Officer Oblt.z.S. Karl Friederich (not to be confused with former First Watch Officer Oblt.z.S. Adolf Friedrichs, who fired the torpedoes which sank *Lévis*). The end came off Spain on 2 May 1942 after *U74* was bombed by an RAF Catalina and then depth charged by HM destroyers *Wishart* and *Wrestler*. There were no survivors.

After a spell at the headquarters of the Second Admiral of U-Boats, Kommodore Hans-Georg von Friedeburg, Kentrat – by now promoted Korvettenkapitän – was given command of the long-range Type-IXD-2 *U196* and ordered to the Indian Ocean. At 225 days her first patrol was the longest in the history of the *U-Boot-Waffe*, though only two ships were sunk. Kentrat left *U196* in Penang after her third patrol in August 1944 to serve out the war in a series of staff appointments in Tokyo; *U196*, meanwhile, shared the fate of *U74* and was lost on her next cruise. One of the last U-boat commanders to be released from captivity, Kentrat did not return to Germany until October 1947. He died in January 1974.

Sources

Admiralty, *Convoy Reports for ON17 and SC44* (TNA, ADM 237/68)

Royal Canadian Navy, Newfoundland Command Records, *Board of Inquiry into Loss of HMCS* Lévis (NAC, RG 24, D12, vol. 11930, file 1156-331/53)

Blair, *Hitler's U-Boat War*, I, pp. 361–7

Burrow, Len, and Émile Beaudoin, *Unlucky Lady: The Life and Death of HMCS* Athabaskan, *1940–1944* (Stittsville, Ont.: Canada's Wings, 1982)

Douglas, William A. B., Michael J. Whitby, Roger Sarty et al., *The Official Operational History of the Royal Canadian Navy in the Second World War*, vol. II, part 1: *No Higher Purpose, 1939–1943*; vol. II, part 2: *A Blue Water Navy, 1943–1945* (St Catharines, Ont.: Vanwell Publishing, 2002–7)

Goodeve, George, 'Naval Interlude' in *Lead and Line: Journal of the Naval Officers' Association of Vancouver Island* 15, no. 6 (June 2001), p. 7

Lamb, James B., *The Corvette Navy: True Stories from Canada's Atlantic War* (2nd edn, Toronto: Stoddart, 2000)

—, *On the Triangle Run: More True Stories of Canada's Navy by the Author of* The Corvette Navy (Toronto: Macmillan of Canada, 1986)

Lynch, Thomas G., *Canada's Flowers: History of the Corvettes of Canada, 1939–1945* (Halifax, Nova Scotia: Nimbus Publishing, 1981)

—, ed., *Fading Memories: Canadian Sailors and the Battle of the Atlantic* (Halifax, Nova Scotia: The Atlantic Chief and Petty Officers' Association, 1993)

Harbron, John D., *The Longest Battle: The RCN in the Atlantic, 1939–1945* (St Catharines, Ont.: Vanwell Publishing, 1995)

Johnston, Mac, *Corvettes Canada: Convoy Veterans of WWII Tell Their True Stories* (Toronto and Montreal: McGraw-Hill Ryerson, 1994)

McKee and Darlington, *Canadian Naval Chronicle*, pp. 37–9

Macpherson and Burgess, *Ships of Canada's Naval Forces* (3rd edn), p. 78

Macpherson, Ken, and Marc Milner, *Corvettes of the Royal Canadian Navy, 1939–1945* (St Catherines, Ont.: Vanwell Publishing, 1993)

Milner, Marc, *Canada's Navy: The First Century* (Toronto: University of Toronto Press, 1999)

Preston, Antony, and Alan Raven, *Flower Class Corvettes* [Ensign, no. 3] (London: Bivouac Books, 1973); reprinted as Man o'War, no. 7 (London: Arms and Armour Press, 1982)

History of the Royal Canadian Navy: http://www.navy.gc.ca/project_pride/history/history_e.asp

33   HMS (ex MS) *SPRINGBANK*

Capt. C. H. Godwin, RNR

Sunk by *U201* (Type VIIC), Oblt.z.S. Adalbert Schnee, 27 September 1941

North Atlantic, 560 nm WSW of Land's End, Cornwall (England)

Springbank at sea in 1941 during her six-month career. Note her twin 4-inch mountings and Fairey Fulmar fighter on its catapult. *IWM*

Theatre	North Atlantic (Map 1)	*Deadweight*	8,876 tons
Coordinates	49° 10' N, 20° 05' W	*Gross tons*	5,155
Kriegsmarine code	Quadrat BE 1939	*Dimensions*	434' × 54' × 25.75'
U-boat timekeeping differential	+1 hour	*Maximum speed*	12 knots
Fatalities 32	*Survivors* 314	*Armament*	8 × 4" AA; 8 × 40 mm AA; 6 × 20 mm AA; 8 × .5" AA
		Aircraft	1 aircraft (Fairey Fulmar Mk II on catapult)

Career

Ordered by the Bank Line (Andrew Weir Shipping & Trading Co. Ltd), the Inverbank-class passenger freighter *Springbank* was launched at Harland & Wolff's yard at Govan on 13 April 1926. Following service on the company's worldwide shipping routes, *Springbank* was requisitioned by the Royal Navy in November 1939 and selected for conversion as a seagoing auxiliary anti-aircraft vessel, for which role she was armed practically to cruiser standard, first at Cammell Laird of Birkenhead and then at Harland & Wolff of Belfast. The creation of this new class of vessel on merchant hulls reflects the recognition by the Admiralty of the increased threat of air attack to the convoy system, and the eight ships so converted represented a valuable contribution to their defence. While this conversion was taking place a memorandum prepared in September 1940 by the Royal Navy's Director of Air Material, Capt. M. S. Slattery, resulted the following March in the addition of a cordite-powered catapult and aircraft amidships, *Springbank* being redesignated a fighter catapult ship. The fighter in question was a two-seater Fairey Fulmar, a pre-war design lacking the

requisite speed for full-scale naval operations but found adequate for the task of beating off German land-based bomber and reconnaissance aircraft, especially the Focke-Wulf Kondor. Though it enjoyed some success, this system was wasteful of aircraft and occasionally of men. Unless the aircraft was launched within range of land the pilot had to ditch once his fuel ran out, making his a somewhat hazardous duty. The fighter catapult ships and the catapult-armed merchantmen that followed them were no more than a stop-gap until escort carriers began providing permanent air cover for convoys towards the end of 1941 (see HMS *Audacity*, **43**), but an important step had been taken.

Thus equipped, *Springbank* was commissioned in March 1941 and began convoy escort duty in the North Atlantic in April. On 17 September convoy HG73 sailed from Gibraltar, *Springbank* among her escort. The following day the appearance of a Kondor prompted the launch of the Fulmar, though Petty Officer Shaw was denied a kill when faulty ammunition caused his guns to jam. The Fulmar reached Gibraltar safely but *Springbank* was destined never to make harbour.

Background of the attack

Fresh from their successes against convoy OG74 when five merchantmen were sunk for a total of 25,000 tons on 20 and 21 September, Oblt.z.S. Adalbert Schnee's *U201* and Kptlt Johann Mohr's *U124* (see **40** and **61**) were joined over the next few days by *U203* (Kptlt Rolf Mützelburg) and *U205* (Kptlt Franz-Georg Reschke; see **63**) for a combined attack on HG73. Despite a strong escort the convoy lost five of its number to *U203* and *U124* on the night of the 25th–26th. The assault was renewed at 2335 German time on the 26th with an attack by *U124* on the Norwegian freighter *Siremalm* which quickly sank with her cargo of iron ore. Then it was *U201*'s turn. Finding himself in an excellent position shortly after 0200 on the 27th, Schnee records firing five torpedoes at as many ships within the space of three minutes. This spree has been the source of much post-war confusion, though two indisputable casualties were the British freighter *Cervantes* and HMS *Springbank*. At 0210 *Springbank* had picked up a hydrophone bearing and witnessed a ship being torpedoed in a column to port and nearer the head of the convoy, followed a few minutes later by the sighting of a submarine wake on her port bow. Barely had the order been given to turn hard aport and fire starshell than *Springbank* was struck aft and amidships by a pair of torpedoes, the track of the first having been spotted by the Officer of the Watch shortly before impact.

War Diary of *U201*, patrol of 14–30 September 1941: PG 30189, NHB, reel 1,089, p. 388

Date, time	Details of position, wind, weather, sea, light, visibility, moonlight, etc.	Incidents
27.ix		
0000	[Qu.] BE 1937 lower middle, wind NW to W 5, sea 4–5, cloud 9, 1,001 mb	
0021		Alarm dive.
0052		Resurface and set off in pursuit.
0152		Convoy once again in sight to starboard. As escorts are stationed on the beam close to the steamers, which are sailing in two columns, we penetrate the convoy and fire from between the two columns of steamers.
0208	[Qu.] BE 1939 lower edge right	A double spread fired at the column of ships to starboard, in which two vessels are overlapping; a freighter of 5,000 GRT and an escort vessel stationed directly beyond but some distance away. Two hits. The freighter sinks immediately, the escort vessel emits a large tongue of flame and a cloud of smoke.[1] No further observation could be made because of other shot opportunities that immediately present themselves. The type of vessel was not discerned but in seas like this her sinking must be considered probable. Shot coordinates: two Etos, range 480 and 600 m, depth 4 m, enemy vessel speed 7.5 knots, inclination 100°, aim-off 14.5°.
0209	[Qu.] BE 1939 lower edge right	Single shot fired from stern tube at port-column 3,000-ton freighter. Misses, probably because depth setting of 4 m was too great; the ship was only half laden and the torpedo was fired against the sea. Shot coordinates: one Eto from stern tube, range 400 m, enemy speed 7.5 knots, inclination 90°, aim-off 13.5°.[2]
0211	[Qu.] BE 1939 lower edge right	Launch another attack on starboard column of ships. A spread of two fired at two overlapping targets, the closest of which is a 3,000-ton freighter. Both torpedoes hit the nearer freighter, however, because the angle of spread selected was too small.[3] The two hits on the freighter occur at almost exactly the same moment that the boat is forced to dive due to dramatic starshell which lights up the scene of the crime. Though not what I had intended, they must both have struck the same vessel because the hits occurred at exactly the same time, whereas the second freighter targeted was some 400–500 m behind the first. There is no question of the vessel not sinking given two hits and the heavy seas. Shot coordinates: two Etos, range 650 m, depth 4 m, enemy speed 7.5 knots, inclination 90°, aim-off 14.5°.
0315		Alarm dive. Hydrophone pursuit and a well-placed depth charge at T = 70 m which does some modest

---

1   This attack was long considered to have been that in which *Springbank* was struck. Though the tonnage assessment points to this being the case, *Springbank* was neither the victim of a single torpedo nor did she sink immediately. In fact, Allied records point to this being the *Cervantes* (1,810 GRT). Despite Schnee's claim both here and in his 0657 signal, no escort was hit in this attack.

2   'Eto' was Kriegsmarine shorthand for the electric G7e torpedo as distinct from G7a weapon powered by compressed air.

3   HMS *Springbank*. Although cases have been made for this being *Siremalm* (2,468 GRT) or *Cervantes* (see n. 1), it was *Springbank* which not only took hits from a double salvo but recorded a torpedo attack on another ship in the convoy (*Cervantes*) *before* being struck herself.

		damage to the boat.[4]
0358		Surfaced and set off in pursuit of convoy to use up my two remaining eels.[5] But despite contact reports from Mohr I can't re-establish contact with convoy. As dawn begins to break I therefore assume a parallel course and hope to regain contact with it during the day.
0400	[Qu.] BE 1939 lower left, wind WNW 5, sea 5, cloud 5, 1,005 mb	
0657		Outgoing W/T transmission 0632/27/140 to B.d.U.: *Two freighters sunk totalling 8,000 tons. An escort vessel probably also sunk; hauling ahead. Wind WNW 5, sea 5, clear visibility, 1,005 mb. U201.*
0800	[Qu.] BE 2489 lower left, wind NW 6, sea 6, cloud 3, 1,007 mb	

---

4   By 'T = 70 m' Schnee seems to be recording a dive of 210 metres (689 feet); for a full discussion of the 'T =' notation, see Reading the *Kriegstagebücher*, p. xxxvii.

5   'Eels' (German = *Aale*) was U-boat slang for torpedoes.

The sinking

Capt. Godwin did not mince his words at the subsequent Board of Enquiry. What with *Springbank*'s screws and rudder blown off, severe flooding in the engine rooms and elsewhere, and a failure of all communication and lighting, 'the ship was doomed'. However, despite the heavy seas *Springbank*'s demise was far from immediate and it was not until 0330 Allied time, more than two hours after the attack, that she was abandoned by a majority of her ship's company after flooding reached the pumps themselves. At 0500 she gave a dramatic lurch to port and by 0800 the derelict was listing and settling by the head. With salvage deemed impossible, Capt. Godwin ordered HM corvette *Jasmine* to sink her with depth charges and then by 4-inch gunfire when this proved unsuccessful. In doughty fashion *Springbank* withstood this as well as the atrocious conditions, a tribute both to the quality of her construction and the hundreds of sealed metal drums with which her holds had been packed. She finally gave up the ghost at 1915 on the evening of the 27th. The Board of Enquiry approved all steps taken with regard to *Springbank*'s last hours afloat.

Fate of the crew

The initial explosions claimed the lives of three or four men together with another who eventually succumbed to head injuries. For the rest it was a matter of awaiting events until the decision was made at 0300 to disembark as many of the crew as possible (approximately 200 from a complement of 346). These were evacuated into boats and rafts that had been lowered shortly after the attack, volunteer boatkeepers standing by in each to prevent their being smashed against the side in the heavy swell. As it transpired, the 140 who remained on board had the best of it, being taken off between 0530 and 0800 by HMSs *Jasmine* and *Fowey* which risked damage by coming alongside in pitch darkness and heavy seas so that the men could leap to safety. Though a number of men mistimed their leap and fell between the two vessels and others sustained injuries upon landing, most of *Springbank*'s casualties were inflicted during the ordeal suffered by the boats and rafts after they were set adrift at 0300, several of which were never recovered. Few details of this have emerged, but one of those rescued at sea, Cdr R. P. Martin, was a survivor of the armed merchant cruiser *Patroclus* the previous November (**19**). Among the testimony given to the Board of Enquiry is his poignant observation that those in one group were last heard singing 'Roll out the Barrel'.

U201 and Adalbert Schnee

Built by Germaniawerft at Kiel and commissioned in January 1941, *U201* was commanded for her first seven patrols by Oblt.z.S. Adalbert Schnee, who had served two years under Kretschmer in *U23* (see **4**). The combination was a successful one; *U201* sank almost 100,000 tons of Allied shipping under Schnee (including *Springbank* and HM minesweeping trawler *Laertes*, **G32**) and earned her commander both the Knight's Cross and the Oak Leaves, though post-war comparisons of tonnage claimed versus tonnage sunk indicate Schnee to have been among the more optimistic war diarists. When *U201* and Schnee (now Kptlt) parted company in September 1942 the change augured ill for the former, which was lost with all hands on her third patrol under Oblt.z.S. Günther Rosenberg, the probable victim of a depth-charge attack by HMS *Viscount* on 17 February 1943.

Schnee joined the staff of B.d.U. where his seagoing experience was drawn on in planning operations against Allied convoys. Promoted Korvettenkapitän, he returned to operational duty in the very last days of the war, taking the new Type-XXI *U2511* on her first and only patrol. In October 1945 Schnee was summoned to Hamburg to

Schnee (left) seen with Korvkpt. Hans Cohausz (see **10**), commanding the 1st *U-Flottille*, on *U201*'s return to Brest from patrol in May or August of 1942. *DUBMA*

give evidence for the defence in the war-crimes trial of Kptlt Heinz-Wilhelm Eck. Under questioning, however, Schnee felt obliged to state that he would not have acted as Eck had in machine-gunning survivors of the Greek freighter SS *Peleus* off Sierra Leone in March 1944. Eck, who had been in command of *U852* at the time of the atrocity, was subsequently executed. After a career in commerce Schnee retired to become director of a sailing school on the island of Elba. He died in Hamburg in November 1982.

Sources

Admiralty, *Loss of HMS* Springbank: *Board of Enquiry* (TNA, ADM 1/11300)

—, *Director of Anti-Submarine Warfare: Attacks on Convoys, 1941* (TNA, ADM 199/1708)

Blair, *Hitler's U-Boat War*, I, pp. 289–91

Poolman, Kenneth, *The Catafighters and Merchant Aircraft Carriers* (London: William Kimber, 1970)

—, *The Winning Edge: Naval Technology in Action, 1939–1945* (Stroud, Glos.: Sutton Publishing, 1997)

Roskill, *War at Sea*, I, pp. 476–7

Fleet Air Arm Archive webpage devoted to HMS *Springbank*: http://www.fleetairarmarchive.net/Ships/SPRINGBANK.html

Memoirs of OD John V. Bales (survivor): http://www.bbc.co.uk/ww2peopleswar/stories/55/a6065255.shtml

Webpage devoted to convoy HG73: http://www.amhinja.demon.co.uk/archive/HG73.htm

Kolbicz, Rainer, 'Convoy HG-73: Reassessment of U-Boat Attacks during the Nights of 25/26 and 26/27 September 1941' posted 3 August 2009: http://www.uboat.net/articles/index.html?article=71

---

34   HMS *FLEUR-DE-LYS* (ex NF *LA DIEPPOISE*)
Lt A. Collins, RNR†
Sunk by *U206* (Type VIIC), Kptlt Herbert Opitz, 14 October 1941
Straits of Gibraltar

A rare though poor shot of *Fleur-de-Lys*. She fell victim to a daring foray into the Straits of Gibraltar by *U206*. *BfZ*

Theatre	North Atlantic (Map 3)	*Displacement*	940 tons
Coordinates	35° 59' N, 05° 40' W	*Dimensions*	205.25' × 33' × approx. 11.25'
Kriegsmarine code	Quadrat CG 9592	*Maximum speed*	16 knots
U-boat timekeeping differential	+1 hour	*Armament*	1 × 4"; 4 × .303" AA
Fatalities 70	*Survivors* 3		

Career

For design notes on the Flower-class corvettes, see HMS *Picotee* (**29**).

HMS *Fleur-de-Lys* originated as one of the four Flower-class corvettes authorised by the French government in April 1939 and ordered from Smith's Dock Company of Middlesbrough in August of that year. *La Dieppoise* (as she was to have been called) was laid down in January 1940 and launched on 21 June, the day before France requested an armistice with Germany. The ship was immediately taken over by the Royal Navy and completed with the appropriate name of *Fleur-de-Lys* on 26 August. After working up at the Navy's anti-submarine school at Tobermory she began duty with the Northern Escort Force of Western Approaches Command, joining her first convoy in September. On 7 November she was among the ships ordered to search for merchantmen of convoy HX84 which had scattered after being attacked by the 'pocket battleship' *Admiral Scheer*

in the North Atlantic. In December *Fleur-de-Lys* was reallocated to the 7th Escort Group based on Liverpool and on 19 January 1941 got to grips with the enemy for the first time, delivering three attacks on a U-boat in defence of convoy OB275, though without success. After repairs following a grounding incident in Liverpool, *Fleur-de-Lys* and the 7th Escort Group shifted to the heavily engaged Britain–Gibraltar convoy route in March. At the end of September she participated in Operation HALBERD, one of the embattled supply convoys to Malta, escorting the damaged battleship *Nelson* back to Gibraltar in the first days of October.

Background of the attack

On 8 October 1941 HM destroyers *Lance*, *Wild Swan* and *Croome* and HM corvettes *Jonquil* and *Fleur-de-Lys* were ordered to sail from Gibraltar to bolster the escort of convoy OG75, then approaching after a turbulent voyage from Liverpool. The convoy had been harried by U-boats since being sighted by a Kondor in the North Channel between Northern Ireland and Scotland on the 2nd. Aided by bad weather, OG75 reached port without loss on the 13th, though with U-boats snapping at its heels until it was virtually under the shadow of the Rock. However, the continued U-boat presence meant that the work of the Gibraltar escort force was not over. On the night of 13–14 October they were sent out on individual patrols following a U-boat sighting by HM anti-submarine trawler *Lord Hotham* off Gibraltar. The boat in question was almost certainly *U206* which had pursued OG75 past Cadiz and whose commander, Kptlt Herbert Opitz, had decided on a speculative foray into the Straits while awaiting further instructions from B.d.U. His boldness was rewarded with a shot at one of his hunters in the early hours of the 14th.

War Diary of *U206*, patrol of 30 September–28 October 1941: PG 30194, NHB, reel 1,090, pp. 762–3

Date, time	Details of position, wind, weather, sea, light, visibility, moonlight, etc.	Incidents
14.x		
0000	[Qu.] CG 9572, wind SE 2–3, sea 1–2, cloud 3, good visibility	I decide to venture right up to the Straits of Gibraltar and reconnoitre as far as Algeciras Bay. The easterly course and speed are then set so that by the time the moon comes up I find myself virtually on the Cape Trafalgar–Cape Spartel line. The lights are shining brightly ashore. On several occasions we have to make evasive manoeuvres to avoid lit-up merchantmen.[1]
		A very faint shadow appears on the starboard bow. We increase speed as it is so slow to gain in size. Steering a similar course to our own. I head towards the African coast so as to put the shadow between us and the moon. A destroyer silhouette, two funnels – assume she is Tribal class.[2] Gradually turns broadside on. Suddenly the destroyer alters course to starboard and towards us, and is now at a range of 2,000 m with an inclination of 0°. Fortunately she then alters course once again. We've got to shoot now just as she sails into the path of the moon.
		Coordinates set for a spread of three torpedoes: enemy speed 5 knots, range 800 m, target width 120 m, depth 2 m, inclination 75°.[3]
0336	[Qu.] CG 9593	Torpedoes released. I immediately order a sharp turn so that Tube V can be ready to fire just as a precaution. After 92 sec. – equivalent to about 1,300 m – two enormous detonations, one directly after the other. An extremely dark pall of smoke followed by a hissing crack and a glowing red tongue of flame, which is presumably the magazine going up. The after part of the ship then rises up and sinks at an angle, forward first. The easterly wind blows a huge burning cloud of smoke towards us that reeks of petroleum and oil. I take advantage of this cloud to head off at maximum speed towards Cape Spartel with a view to rounding the boom defence and escaping to the south-west. As we withdraw another shuddering detonation felt in the boat. My assumption is that the right-hand and middle eels of the spread struck the target, while the third eel detonated against a cliff face when sinking at the end of its run – this torpedo shot had the narrowest part of the straits as its backdrop.[4]
		I couldn't see what kind of anti-submarine activity ensued because the pall of smoke completely obscured the view towards Europe.
0350	[Qu.] CG 9594	From 0350 we observe starshell fired off to starboard.
0400	Wind E 4–5, sea 3, cloud 2, moonlit	
0515	W/T no. 65	When I reach the sanctuary of the open sea I transmit a short signal to warn other boats that the enemy is aware of our presence. Short signal confirmed by B.d.U. along with congratulations.
0800	[Qu.] CG 9571	

---

1 These would be neutral merchantmen, always brightly illuminated at night and clearly marked for daylight recognition.

2 This was in fact the single-funnelled corvette *Fleur-de-Lys*.

3 Opitz has over-estimated the size of his target by a factor of almost two, *Fleur-de-Lys* being only 63 m (205 ft) long against the 120 m (394 ft) stated here. However, the figure given by Opitz may well simply be that indicated in his Weyer for the Tribal-class destroyer he thought he was attacking, all of which measured 115 m (377 ft).

4 'Eel' (German = *Aal*) was U-boat slang for torpedo.

The sinking

Such official data as exists regarding the end of *Fleur-de-Lys* was forwarded to the Admiralty following an interview with an unnamed coxswain who was one of three survivors of the sinking. His observations bear out those in Opitz's war diary: *Fleur-de-Lys* was 'torpedoed on the port side under the bridge: the magazine exploded and the ship broke in half and sank'. Anecdotal information suggests that a number of those who got clear of the wreck perished in the detonation of the ship's depth charges. No board of enquiry was called in view of the catastrophic nature of the sinking, the absence of any

Commissioning day for *U206* with crew and assorted Nazi dignitaries on the casing at Kiel on 17 May 1941. Opitz is the tall figure just left of centre.
DUBMA

officer survivors and the relative certainty that *Fleur-de-Lys* had succumbed to U-boat attack.

Fate of the crew

Though it is hard to believe that the violent end of *Fleur-de-Lys* just a few miles off the Spanish coast was not witnessed either from the shore or by other vessels in the Straits, Opitz's log makes it clear that a stiff *Levante* breeze was blowing from the east which no doubt served to muffle the sound of an explosion. The first intimation the British had of her loss appears to have come by means of a radio signal received at Gibraltar at 1013 that morning, 14 October, eight hours after the event. This signal, sent by the Spanish freighter *Castillo Villafranca*, reported that she had three *Fleur-de-Lys* survivors on board, two of

them injured. One was evidently the coxswain referred to above. Ships were immediately dispatched from Gibraltar to search for further survivors but though 'wreckage was found in the vicinity of Tarifa Point and [HM trawlers] *Returno* and *Burke* recovered a few bodies', those rescued by *Castillo Villafranca* remained the only members of their ship's company to survive Opitz's attack.

U206 and Herbert Opitz

Built by Germaniawerft at Kiel and commissioned in May 1941, *U206*'s brief career consisted of three patrols under Oblt.z.S. (Kptlt from September 1941) Herbert Opitz, who joined the *U-Boot-Waffe* following peacetime service in the light cruiser *Emden*. *U206*'s first patrol resulted in the sinking of a fishing vessel south-east of Iceland and the rescue of six RAF airmen found in a dinghy after their Whitley bomber had suffered engine failure over the Atlantic. Her second patrol yielded *Fleur-de-Lys* on 14 October and the freighter *Baron Kelvin* in almost exactly the same position five days later. *U206* was lost with all hands on 30 November 1941 shortly after setting out from St-Nazaire on her third patrol. She is presumed to have struck a mine in the Beech Garden field sown by RAF aircraft in the Bay of Biscay after the fall of France in the summer of 1940.

Sources

Admiralty, War Diary for October 1941 (TNA, ADM 199/2232), pp. 328 and 344

—, *Submarine Attacks on Merchant Shipping 1939–1945 and Loss of HMS Cossack* [*sic*; *Fleur-de-Lys* documentation misfiled] (TNA, ADM 199/1197)

Ruegg, R A., *Flower-Class Corvettes* (typescript, IWM, 13(41).245/5, 1987)

Preston, Antony, and Alan Raven, *Flower Class Corvettes* [Ensign, no. 3] (London: Bivouac Books, 1973); reprinted as Man o'War, no. 7 (London: Arms and Armour Press, 1982)

Defunct webpage containing information on loss of HMS *Fleur-de-Lys*: http://www.candoo.com/ncot/discussion/posts/292.html

---

35   HMS *GLADIOLUS*

Lt Cdr H. M. C. Sanders, RD RNR†

Sunk either by *U553*, Kptlt Karl Thurmann; by *U558*, Kptlt Günther Krech; or by *U432*, Oblt.z.S. Heinz-Otto Schultze (all Type VIIC)

16 or 17 October 1941

North Atlantic, approx. 600 nm W of Tiree, Inner Hebrides (Scotland)

Theatre North Atlantic (Map 1)	*Displacement* 940 tons
Approx. coordinates 57° 00' N, 25° 00' W	*Dimensions* 205.25' × 33' × approx. 11.25'
Approx. Kriegsmarine code Quadrat AL 19XX	*Maximum speed* 16 knots
U-boat timekeeping differential +2 hours	*Armament* 1 × 4"; 1 × 40 mm AA; 4 × .303" AA
Fatalities 64 and 1 *Survivors* none	

Career

For design notes on the Flower-class corvettes, of which HMS *Gladiolus* was the first to be completed, see HMS *Picotee* (**29**).

HMS *Gladiolus* was laid down at Smith's Dock Company, Middlesbrough, in October 1939, launched in January 1940 and completed in April that year. After working up she was assigned to the 2nd Escort Division of Western Approaches Command at Plymouth

and joined her first convoy on 12 May. On 30 June, while escorting convoy OA175, *Gladiolus* had her first major U-boat encounter which ended in the scuttling of *U26* 200 miles south-west of Cape Clear. Although HM sloop *Rochester* and an RAAF Sunderland had a hand in the matter, *U26* was the first of forty-seven U-boats to be sunk by the Flower-class corvettes in the Second World War. In October *Gladiolus* was transferred to the 1st Escort Group at Liverpool, undergoing a

Gladiolus refuelling at sea in 1940 or 1941. Her loss can be attributed to any of three or possibly four U-boats. IWM

substantial refit at Birkenhead between November 1940 and January 1941. Rejoining the 1st EG at Londonderry, *Gladiolus* resumed convoy duty in the North Atlantic, assisting in the sinking of *U65* on 28 April and then in that of *U556* on 27 June. Allocated to the newly formed Newfoundland Command in the same month, *Gladiolus* joined the Canadian 20th Escort Group (EG-C20) in July. On 22 September *Gladiolus*'s ship's company learnt that she would soon go into refit at Charleston, South Carolina, but the urgent need for escorts after one of the most telling months yet for the *U-Boot-Waffe* in the Atlantic required this to be deferred on 4 October, *Gladiolus* being deemed 'quite capable of one more escort cycle before refit'. Assigned to Task Unit 4.1.5, on 9 October she weighed anchor at St John's to join convoy SC48 which had sailed from Sydney, Cape Breton Island on the 5th.

Background of the attack

Despite Enigma intelligence of German dispositions in the Atlantic, the thirteen-boat patrol line formed by B.d.U. in mid-October 1941 proved too great an obstacle for the slow convoy SC48 to avoid. On the night of 14–15 October the convoy ran into Kptlt Karl Thurmann's *U553* which despatched two of its number shortly before dawn. *U553*'s most important action, however, was the transmission of the convoy's position and course to all other boats within range, including *U558* (Kptlt Günther Krech), *U432* (Oblt.z.S. Heinz-Otto Schultze), and *U568* (Kptlt Joachim Preuss; see **29** and **44**), all of which closed in over the next thirty-six hours. SC48's original escort, consisting of HMC destroyer *Columbia* (Senior Officer of the Escort), and the corvettes *Gladiolus*, *Mimosa* (Free French; **61**), *Baddeck*, *Shediac*, *Camrose*, *Rosthern* and *Wetaskiwin* (all RCN) was far too weak to defend her against the expected onslaught, particularly as three of its members had to turn back for lack of fuel. *Gladiolus* herself was soon in action, driving off *U568* on the evening of the 15th after she had sunk *Empire Heron*. As still more U-boats closed in, desperate measures were taken by the Allies to stiffen the defence of SC48. At noon on the 16th the escort was reinforced by five American destroyers (USS *Plunkett* leading *Kearny*, *Decatur*, *Livermore* and *Greer*) from convoy ON24, but the US Navy was as yet inexperienced in the business of convoy

protection and at a technical disadvantage in having no radar. The onslaught finally came on the night of 16–17 October as eight U-boats jostled for position, the chaos of vessels on the scene being added to by the arrival of HM corvettes *Abelia* and *Veronica* at around 2300 on the 16th, by that of HM destroyers *Highlander* (which took over as Senior Officer at some point that night), *Broadwater* (**36**) and *Sherwood* about an hour later, and that of the Canadian corvettes *Pictou*, *Brandon* and *Weyburn* by daybreak on the 17th. Seven ships were sunk that night and the USS *Kearny* damaged with serious implications for US relations with Germany. The number of protagonists and victims raises significant problems in matching victim to perpetrator, not least *Gladiolus* whose last known movements came when she was ordered to investigate a radar contact approaching the convoy from the southwest at 1230 on the afternoon of the 16th. The contact in question turned out to be the USS *Plunkett*, with which *Gladiolus* presumably rejoined the convoy. Aside from a brief radio contact that evening nothing survives to document *Gladiolus*'s continued existence, and her failure to report in over the next seventy-two hours led the Admiralty to conclude that she had been lost. The precise cause of *Gladiolus*'s loss has defied all attempts to identify it but close analysis of attacks recorded that night allows cases to be made for three of the U-boats present: (A) *U553*, (B) *U558* and (C) *U432*.

The sinking

There are few Allied warship sinkings about which less is known than that of HMS *Gladiolus*. Indeed, no compelling data exists to document her demise from either side, while the large body of often contradictory information in Allied sources points to utter chaos on the night in question. The last *confirmed* contact with *Gladiolus* was made by HMC corvette *Wetaskiwin* after 1930 Allied time (2130 U-boat time) on the 16th, though its subject is not known. As there is no record of any *direct* attack on a warship in either German or Allied sources, the answer to *Gladiolus*'s disappearance would appear to rest in the multiple attacks made by the trio of U-boats that harried SC48 relentlessly between 0000 and 0400 German time on the 17th. The pages that follow set out the cases for and against each of these

U-boats, taken in the order in which they engaged SC48 that night. First concerns what British post-war analysis came to regard as the prime suspect: Kptlt Karl Thurmann's *U553*.

A The case for *U553*

In 1990 Dr R. M. Coppock, then Head of the British Ministry of Defence's Naval Historical Branch, undertook an investigation into the loss of HMS *Gladiolus* 'in some detail, since our records indicate that no particularly satisfactory investigation has previously been undertaken'. He concluded that the likely perpetrator was *U553*, whose log extract describes a series of attacks beginning at 0000 on the 17th U-boat time (2200 on the 16th Allied time), including one at 0007 which resulted in a hit on a vessel Kptlt Thurmann describes

as a tanker. Key to Coppock's conclusion that *Gladiolus* fell victim to this attack was the timing of a mysterious signal. Just as Thurmann was beginning his attack *Wetaskiwin* received a signal apparently from *Gladiolus* asking for a transmission on 325 kHz, presumably for direction-finding purposes. Uncertain of its authenticity, *Wetaskiwin* sent a request for identification which went unanswered. No further signal, confirmed or unconfirmed, was ever received from *Gladiolus*. The inference drawn by Coppock was that *Gladiolus* was unable to reply having blown up following a hit obtained by *U553*'s attack of 0007, the sheet of flame described by Thurmann in his log being evidence not of the tanker he thought he had struck but of a corvette magazine detonation.

War Diary of *U553*, patrol of 7–22 October 1941: PG 30590a, NHB, reel 1,119, pp. 77–8

Date, time	Details of position, wind, weather, sea, light, visibility, moonlight, etc.	Incidents
16.x		
2153		Outgoing W/T transmission: *Convoy at 2115 Qu. [AL] 1992, well strung out. Starboard side has two destroyers, one corvette.*[1]
2226		Outgoing W/T transmission: *Driven off by destroyer immediately after last report. Convoy disappeared in the rain. Visibility now down to half a mile. We adopt a general course of 30°. Convoy positions given refer to the leading group.*
		The onset of darkness is accompanied by heavy and persistent squalls. We turn about as a destroyer appears 1,500 m ahead of us; we remain unseen. Persistent rain, absolutely pitch-black night. We head towards the convoy with both engines at slow speed, course 340°. Crew ordered to Battle Stations. Towards 2330 visibility improves slightly, first to 500 m, then 1,000 m.
2330		Shadow to port just 150 m away turns out to be a destroyer. Crosses our bows. I'm now in the middle of the leading group. Convoy sailing 90°, 5 knots, we get in among the convoy with both engines dead slow. We take stock of the situation: at least 10 tankers between 6,000 and 9,000 GRT. We turn to attack the port side of the convoy.[2] Further off to port there are several small shadows, corvettes and so on.
2400	[Qu.] AL 1962, wind SW 4, overcast with rain, sea 5, visibility variable from 100 m to 2 nm, long medium swell from the SW	*Thurmann*
17.x		
0000–0007		At our leisure we fire Tubes I, II and IV one after the other, each aimed at a different tanker. Inclination 90°, target speed 5 knots, range between 500 and 700 m. No success. That despite clear firing-angle data on each occasion. They can only have underrun their targets. Depth setting changed from 3 m to 2 m. Then we fire from Tube III at a fourth tanker, a hit amidships, gigantic sheet of flame typical of a tanker hit.[3] We turn hard about so as to position the freighter between ourselves and a destroyer. The

---

1 Allied sources do not record the dispositions of the escort that night. This is not surprising given the chaos that reigned both in the face of sustained U-boat attack and as a consequence of the large number of escorts joining the convoy. Thurmann's observation here that SC48 was 'well strung out' is echoed in his reference to a 'leading group' in the signal transmitted at 2226, and repeated at 0205 on the 17th and in a further signal sent to B.d.U. at 0433. The latter describes the convoy as 'divided into 5–6 groups of 6–10 ships, the groups being separated from one another by a distance of several thousand metres'. SC48 was indeed divided into five rows of 8–11 ships, but what is curious about these repeated observations is that Allied sources make no reference to any loss of formation, whereas Kptlt Günther Krech in *U558* (see below) records the convoy being 'staggered . . . [with] . . . several steamers further ahead in a loose formation'. Together this suggests that the first row of the convoy had moved well ahead of the rest.

2 None of the merchantmen lost that night appear to have been sailing on the port side of any of the convoy's five rows so Thurmann may actually be referring to the starboard side: he had penetrated the convoy from ahead and was sailing in the opposite direction, meaning that the vessels referred to were on *his* port side.

3 This explosion may have come from HMS *Gladiolus*. The first tanker casualty of the night was not incurred until the SS *W. C. Teagle* was hit by *U558* at 0131 German time, almost 90 minutes after this attack. In his torpedo report, Thurmann states that the torpedo detonation was 'heard' in the boat while the sheet of flame was actually sighted, though the torpedo report makes plain that he did not actually see the vessel in question.

latter, which has a clearly identifiable twin gun mounting on the fo'c's'le, turns towards us at a range of 400 m.[4] Alarm! We steady the boat at T = 35 m, then go to T = 90 m; outstanding work by the L.I., everything proceeds quickly yet smoothly.[5] Three depth charges dropped at the point we dived but they explode well above us.[6] The only consequence is that we have problems expelling the air from the quick-diving tanks upon surfacing. The destroyer may well have had to dodge freighters; no Asdic pursuit. We wait another 20 minutes before surfacing, making sure we do so somewhat to the south.

0100   Outgoing W/T transmission: *Convoy Qu. [AL] 1965, 90°, 5 knots, at least 10 medium-sized and large tankers in its ranks. Two Trible-class [sic] destroyers.*[7] *Note beacon signals.*

0140   Regular beacon signals transmitted.

0205   Outgoing W/T transmission: *Qu. [AL] 1966, 6,000 GRT tanker sunk. Forced to submerge by destroyer, depth charges, no damage. A second boat has now taken up the tanker torch.*

Convoy now around 1,500 m abeam to port and has become very strung out. Appears to have been assembled into individual groups that are keeping a fair distance from one another. This impression strengthens as the night wears on. Starshell being fired far astern. We load the last two eels but this is no easy task given the state of the sea.[8] Men performing superbly. A tanker goes up in flames on the port bow. Another U-boat crosses our bows from starboard to port just a couple of boat lengths away, typical Nazi silhouette. Visibility improves.

0433   Outgoing W/T transmission: *Qu. [AL] 0146 convoy strung out in 5 to 6 groups of 6–10 ships several thousand metres apart.*

On the port bow a huge flame, another tanker going up. Occasional starshell fired ahead and astern. I decide to catch up with the leading group once reloading is complete.

---

4   Judging by his signal of 0100, Thurmann believed the escort to have included two Tribal-class destroyers (which were armed with 4.7-inch guns in twin mountings). This was not the case, nor was any escort present with the convoy at this juncture fitted with twin mountings.

5   By 'T = 35' and 'T = 90 m' Thurmann seems to be recording dives of 175 metres (575 feet) and 230 metres (755 feet) respectively. For a full discussion of the 'T =' notation, see Reading the *Kriegstagebücher*, p. xxxvii. 'L.I.' stands for *Leitender Ingenieur* – Chief Engineer.

6   It is not clear which, if any, of the escorts was dropping depth charges at this point, but upon witnessing an attack on the convoy at 2205 convoy time (0005 U-boat time) HMC corvette *Baddeck* fired starshell to the NNE and SSE while carrying out an RDF sweep 'ahead of convoy at about 2,000 yards between eighth column and port bow'.

7   No Tribal-class destroyers were present on this convoy.

8   'Eels' (German = *Aale*) was U-boat slang for torpedoes.

U553: pro and contra

Prof. Jürgen Rohwer's *Axis Submarine Successes of World War II* attributes *Gladiolus*'s loss to *U558* or *U432* later on the 17th (see below), with *U553*'s attack of 0007 deemed to have accounted for the Panamanian freighter SS *Bold Venture*. However, examination of all Admiralty records relating to SC48 makes it highly probable, though not certain, that *Bold Venture* was sunk by *U432* hours later at around 0340 U-boat time. If this was indeed the case then the argument for *U553* having sunk *Gladiolus* rather than a merchantman at this juncture becomes much stronger. Certainly, the evidence for a catastrophic hit at this point would appear incontrovertible, Thurmann's observations being corroborated (all times given in U-boat reckoning) not only by Krech in *U558* (a 'column of fire': 0015) and Schultze in *U432* ('starshell and detonations': 0010) but also by HMCS *Columbia* (a 'ship observed to be hit in the rear of the convoy': 0012), the tanker SS *W. C. Teagle* (a 'loud explosion' and a 'ship on fire astern': 0015) and the freighter SS *Rym* (an 'explosion astern of convoy': 0000), these two being themselves sunk over the next two hours. Of equal significance is the fact that *Rym* was the rearmost vessel in her column (third from the starboard side), suggesting that the victim could not be a merchantman unless she was a straggler.

However, the case for the victim being *Gladiolus* is not without its question marks, nor is she the only candidate for destruction at this time. For one thing, there is a marked discrepancy between Thurmann's account of sinking a vessel from the forward row of the convoy and the Allied sources cited above which are unanimous in recording a detonation astern. Moreover, there is evidence to suggest that it was in fact the Greek freighter SS *Evros*, listed by Rohwer as sunk by *U432* at 0343 German time but identified in one Allied source as being sunk at 2000 convoy time (0000 U-boat time) which would equate with Thurmann's attack in the first minutes of 17 October. Surviving documentation does not permit certainty on this point nor did any survive from *Evros* to settle the matter, but the fact that she was unquestionably at the rear of her column would *prima facie* make her a more likely victim of *U553*'s 0007 torpedo than *Gladiolus* whose last recorded position was fixed almost twelve hours earlier.

B   The case for *U558*

Kptlt Günther Krech carried out four attacks in the small hours of the 17th, at 0128, 0131, 0149 and 0214 U-boat time. The second, third, and fourth of these attacks can be equated with a fair degree of certainty to fatal hits on the British tanker *W. C. Teagle* and the Norwegian freighters SS *Erviken* and SS *Rym* respectively. The only unanswered question here is the fate of *U558*'s first torpedo.

War Diary of *U558*, patrol of 11–25 October 1941: PG 30593a, NHB, reel 1,119, pp. 585–8

Date, time	Details of position, wind, weather, sea, light, visibility, moonlight, etc.	Incidents
17.x		
0000	West of Ireland, Qu. AL 1991, wind W 3, sea 2–3, 10/10 overcast, good visibility, raining	
0015	Qu. AL 1967	Column of fire in sight at bearing 90° true.[9] We head towards it. This is followed by great bursts of starshell spread over a wide area.
0115	Qu. AL 1965	Three shadows in sight at bearing 65° true. One tanker, two freighters and possibly an escort vessel on the other side but I can't be sure about the latter.[10]
	Qu. AL 1966	The ships are drawn up in echelon, course 70°. Other steamers in loose formation further ahead. I haul ahead with a view to targetting the tanker and then turn to attack. At this point the rearmost steamer of the group ahead gets in the way.
0128		Torpedo fired from Tube I: torpedo speed 30 knots, depth 3 m, enemy speed 8 knots, range 2,000 m, inclination 90°.
		Steamer targeted was not hit.
		After 4 min. 47 sec. (= 4,400 m) a detonation was observed from the boat. Assume we hit another steamer in the group ahead.[11]
0131		In the meantime we turn to make another attack on the tanker from Tube II: torpedo speed 30 knots, depth 3 m, enemy speed 8 knots, range 800 m, inclination 80°.
		A hit 30 m from the stern after 50 sec. (= 780 m), bright sheet of flame rises from the stern. Fire spreads forward along the waists.[12]
0135	Qu. AL 1966	Sinks quickly stern first. Estimated 7,000 GRT.
		A slick of coal tar spreads out at the scene of the sinking.[13] One of the other merchantmen stops, presumably to pick up survivors.[14]
0149	Qu. AL 1966	Attack. Torpedo fired from Tube V: torpedo speed 30 knots, depth 3 m, enemy speed 0 knots, range 900 m, inclination 90°.
		A hit amidships after 49 sec. (= 760 m). Steamer immediately settles on an even keel, estimated 7,000 GRT.
		We then approach a third steamer of this group. Steamer turns directly towards us, hence short range upon firing.[15]
0214		Torpedo fired from Tube III: torpedo speed 30 knots, depth 3 m, enemy speed 8 knots, range 300 m, inclination 80°.
		A hit after 12 sec. (= 180 m) amidships, powerful detonation causing a high blast column.
		At such a short range the torpedo probably struck the target close to the waterline before the depth setting had activated. Steamer is showing evidence of a list to starboard, also settling by the head. Two escort vessels we had earlier observed rescuing survivors from a sunken steamer now close our position forcing us to withdraw at utmost speed.[16] As a result, sinking not witnessed but deemed probable.
		We set off in pursuit of the forward group of steamers as per their last observed course.

9 Possibly *U553*'s successful attack on the SS *Evros* or the SS *Bold Venture* – or indeed *Gladiolus*; see '*U553*: pro and contra' above, but also '*U432*: pro and contra' below.

10 Possibly *Gladiolus*.

11 Unless the torpedo detonated before the end of its run or exploded in a ship's wake it is possible that it in fact found its mark on *Gladiolus*'s hull. Despite being fired three minutes before the attack of 0131 it should be noted that this detonation (after a running time of 4 min. 47 sec.) must have come *after* the 0131 hit on the *W. C. Teagle* (running time 50 sec.).

12 This attack tallies in almost every detail with Allied accounts of the sinking of the *W. C. Teagle* (9,552 GRT).

13 *W. C. Teagle* was laden not with coal tar but 9,000 tons of phosphate.

14 This was the SS *Erviken* (6,595 GRT). Contrary to Krech's belief that she had stopped to pick up survivors, *Erviken* had in fact slowed to avoid colliding with the SS *Rym* which had gone to *W. C. Teagle*'s aid instead.

15 SS *Rym* (1,369 GRT), which had contributed to the loss of *Erviken* by slowing to pick up survivors of the *W. C. Teagle*. As confirmed by Krech's torpedo data, *Rym* had raised steam to an estimated 7 knots in a vain effort to regain the convoy at the time she was struck.

16 The identity of these 'escort vessels' is unclear. Most of the survivors of the *W. C. Teagle*, *Erviken* and *Rym* were picked up by HM corvette *Veronica* several hours later.

0437	West of Ireland, Qu. AL 0144, wind W 2–3, sea 2–3, 9/10 overcast, good visibility	We load the remaining two torpedoes. Starshell at very different points off to starboard. We duly alter course in that direction. Convoy would appear to have altered course by 20° to starboard.

U558: pro and contra

Krech's supposition that his first torpedo of 0128 eventually registered a hit might at first glance appear a typical case of U-boat commander's optimism, not least since it comes in the form of a reassessment of the event. Indeed, Dr Coppock is quick to discard the possibility of this torpedo having registered a hit on *Gladiolus* or any other ship for that matter:

> Although after 4 minutes 47 seconds it would not normally be expected to have reached the end of its run, when German torpedoes had a tendency to explode, I suspect this may have been the case. A torpedo could, in any event, have quite feasibly detonated without hitting a ship. The possibility that it went on to strike *Gladiolus* is so remote as to be discounted.

Overall, the authors find this assessment of *U558*'s credentials to be overly dismissive. Ships in convoy were frequently struck by torpedoes missing their intended targets and the possibility that *Gladiolus* was accounted for by a stray torpedo is no more remote than the cases made for *U553* above and *U432* below, both of which aimed at and claimed hits on tankers. Moreover, what sets Krech's log sequence apart from those of Thurmann and Schultze is a possible escort sighting among the ships attacked a few minutes later (see his entry for 0115).

C   The case for *U432*

An hour and a half after Kptlt Krech fired his last torpedo at SC48 Oblt.z.S. Heinz-Otto Schultze made the first of five attacks against the convoy, *viz.* 0343, 0344, 0346, 0400 and 0448 U-boat time. Only the last two of these can be unequivocally linked to Allied records, the Norwegian tanker SS *Barfonn* being struck at 0400 and finished off by Schultze within the hour. Despite the minute-by-minute chronology set out by Schultze, conflicting data in Allied reports makes it impossible to assign his first three attacks to specific ships, one of which could be *Gladiolus*.

War Diary of *U432*, patrol of 11 October–2 November 1941: PG 30486, NHB, reel 1,108, pp. 3–4

Date, time	Details of position, wind, weather, sea, light, visibility, moonlight, etc.	Incidents
17.x		
0000	West of Ireland, [Qu.] AL 1991, wind WSW 4, sea 3–4, overcast, 996 mb, +11°[C; 52°F]	
0010		Starshell and detonations across the whole of the northern horizon from WNW to N to ENE.[1] We alter course to intercept what we presume to be the most easterly group.
0130		In the east, torpedo detonations against a tanker.[2] Plume of smoke visible against the sky for a prolonged period. We alter course accordingly.
0210		Shadow of the convoy in sight.
0230		A straggler behind the convoy is torpedoed by another boat just as we are about to run in to attack ourselves.[3] We circumvent the two port-side destroyers and get in between the leading destroyer (American four-funnel type) and the convoy proper.[4] This is made up of about ten columns, each of four to five ships. The distances between the different columns do not appear to be very consistent. General course east.
0332		We run in to attack from the front of the convoy, penetrating the two middle columns.
0343		Torpedo fired from Tube I at the forward steamer in the next-but-one column to the south. 6,000 tons. Inclination 90°, enemy speed 7 knots, range 2,000 m, depth setting 3 m.[5]
0344		Double salvo from Tubes III and II at the second steamer sailing in the column immediately south of me. Inclination 90°, enemy speed 7 knots, range 400 m. 6–7,000 tons.
0346		Torpedo fired from Tube V at the 3rd and 4th ships of the column immediately to my north. As the range for firing was initially too close after the bow shots I withdraw slightly to the south. 7,000 tons,

---

1   Consistent with Thurmann's attack of 0007 (possibly on *Gladiolus*; see '*U553*: pro and contra' above) and *Baddeck*'s responding with starshell; see the entry for 0000–0007 in the log excerpt from *U553* above and n. 6 to the same.

2   Consistent with Krech's successful attack on the tanker SS *W. C. Teagle*; see the entries for 0131 and 0135 in the log excerpt from *U558* above.

3   Can be equated to Krech's successful attack on the freighter SS *Rym* though Schultze records this incident sixteem minutes later; see the entries for 0149 and 0214 in the log excerpt from *U558* above.

4   The latter destroyer must presumably have been HMCS *Columbia* or HMS *Broadwater*, both ex-US Navy flushdeckers

5   The identity of this vessel and those targeted in Schultze's subsequent attacks of 0344 and 0346 is unclear. This problem is treated below.

Date, time	Details of position, wind, weather, sea, light, visibility, moonlight, etc.	Incidents
		five holds, four masts, and several derricks. Inclination 90°, enemy speed 7 knots, range 800 m, depth setting 3 m.
	6,000 tons	The first steamer targeted is hit after 2 min. 30 sec. Sinks stern first within minutes.
		Double salvo misses. Given the very close range (approx. 500 m), the programmed gyro angle probably didn't have a chance to take effect so the inclination entered was around 30° too great.
	7,000 tons	The stern shot hits its target amidships after 1 min. 20 sec. The steamer breaks in two amidships and sinks immediately.
	5,000 tons??	25 sec. after our first torpedo hits (or 2 min. 55 sec. after this torpedo is fired) there is a detonation against a steamer in the column beyond the one we first attacked. I initially considered this to be a hit scored by another boat because my double salvo unquestionably missed its intended target. <u>Therefore no further observations made</u> and no mention of this in my W/T transmission reporting our successes. But subsequent assessment of the torpedo data led us to conclude that one of the eels from our double salvo probably went on to hit this other ship fortuitously.[6] Whether or not it actually was our hit or that of another boat should be easy enough to establish upon return to base.[7]
		After our stern shot we make our way through the columns before lining up a tanker at the rear of a middle column whose striking size (12,000 tons) invites our attention.
0400		Torpedo fired from Tube IV. Inclination 90°, enemy speed 7 knots, range 600 m, depth 3 m.
	<u>Tanker, 12,000 tons</u>[8]	After a running time of 41 sec. a hit aft in the engine room area. Tanker burns for a short while then settles by the stern right up to the deck rail.
		No more torpedoes loaded.
		We stop close to the tanker (which still has way on) and reload Tube II in the face of considerable difficulties caused by the strong swell.
0448		*Coup-de-grâce* shot fired from Tube II (depth setting 4 m), running time 31 sec., a hit amidships below the bridge. An enormous sheet of flame then a short-lived fire aboard. Tanker capsizes and sinks immediately apart from the bows which remain standing in a vertical position some 20 m above the surface. It seems pointless wasting another torpedo on this wreck, but equally with this sea we can't use the gun efficiently so we leave the scene and head off in pursuit of the convoy once more.
0530		While shrouded in a very dark bank of cloud we suddenly find ourselves right in the presence of a stationary destroyer which is obviously listening for U-boats with hydrophones. She pursues me at high speed. No chance of shaking her off so I sound the alarm for an alarm dive with the enemy just 250–300 m off.[9] We go deep as fast as we can. At T = 45 [m] the first well-aimed depth charges go off.[10] They cause considerable damage: hydroplanes, rudder and electric engines all put out of action, and all depth gauges in the control room go awry. The problems are dealt with quickly and efficiently, but not before the boat has gone much deeper at a sharp angle (bow heavy). Blowing the tanks finally does the trick and we take the boat back up to T = 70 [m].[11] We make off at silent speed against the sea. Depth charges gradually become fainter.
0730		Just as boat reaches 20 m and is about to resurface we again experience very heavy depth-charge reverberations.[12] We've obviously been located by the hunting group. This is either due to our going on to high speed and turning on the bilge pump before surfacing, or (as becomes apparent later) because a tell-tale slick of oil has given me away. Luckily I get to 70 m and then gradually manage to elude my pursuers. Further depth-charge attacks heard throughout the morning but they're all a fair distance off.
1300		Surfaced.

---

6   'Eels' (German = *Aale*) was U-boat slang for torpedoes.

7   As Schultze observes, his W/T report to B.d.U. at 0130 on the 18th made no reference to this *ex post facto* deduction, nor is it made plain when this 'subsequent assessment' took place. It must be supposed that reconsideration by Schultze of his own firing data and angles together with the absence of any reported attack by another boat over the next couple of days made him confident of putting in a follow-up claim.

8   The Norwegian tanker SS *Barfonn*, 9,739 GRT, 14,800 deadweight tons.

9   It is not clear from Allied sources which escort was responsible for these attacks.

10 By 'T = 45 [m]' Schultze seems to be recording a dive of 185 metres (605 feet); for a full discussion of the 'T =' notation, see Reading the *Kriegstagebücher*, p. xxxvii.

11 Possibly 210 metres (690 feet); see n. 10 above.

12 Dropped by HMS *Broadwater*. The depth charges referred to later in this entry were probably dropped by HMS *Abelia*.

0130

Outgoing W/T transmission to B.d.U.: *In [Qu. AL] 2755. 3 ships sunk from convoy for 25,000 GRT, including tanker of 12,000. Prolonged pursuit with depth charges. Junkers out of action.*[13] *Electric compressors semi-functional, port shaft coupling of only limited use. 2 leaks in fuel oil ballast tank. Still 6 E-torpedoes.*[14] *In pursuit at 11 knots.*

13 'Junkers' refers to the boat's air compressors.
14 Krech is here referring to the G7e torpedo.

U432: pro and contra

The key area of interest in Schultze's log lies in his descriptions of the attacks made from 0343 in which he records a pair of tankers definitely struck then and at 0344, together with another ship hit in a column beyond after a twin salvo fired at 0346 missed its intended target. It might be argued that Schultze was exaggerating the number of vessels struck at this juncture or else succumbing to the giddy optimism implied by his *ex post facto* deductions. However, one major Allied source suggests otherwise. At 0330 U-boat time HMCS *Columbia* recorded three separate hits in a manner consistent with *U432*'s log: 'One ship in starboard wing column observed to be hit, followed very soon after by one fairly near the 3rd or 4th column, and immediately by one in the rear of about the 7th column.' At first glance 0330 would appear too early, coming as it does between thirteen and sixteen minutes before *U432*'s observation, but the difference is consistent with Schultze's timekeeping which was already lagging sixteen minutes behind Krech's earlier that morning (see note 3 above). Moreover, not only is this the first attack recorded by either side since *U558*'s on *Rym* at 0214 and *U432*'s at 0343, but *Columbia*'s accounts bear out Schultze's description both of a succession of hits and the torpedoing of three different ships in as many columns. However, if the claims of other boats are taken into consideration then the evidence for three sinkings would leave a shortage of vessels to be despatched at this juncture. Taking into account the attack made by *U553*'s Kptlt Thurmann at 0007 (see '*U553*: pro and contra' above) in which the loss of one Allied ship seems beyond doubt, and assuming that, as posited there, his victim was *Evros* and not *Bold Venture* or *Gladiolus* herself, it may be inferred that it was the last two which fell victim to Schultze's salvoes, the latter an unwitting target of his final attack of the night.

Summary

Extensive as it is, the documentation relating to convoy SC48 in the British National Archives provides no clear picture of events on the night of 16–17 October 1941. Indeed, the opposite appears closer to the mark with many Allied accounts and files conflicting – often wildly – as to the times of merchantmen sunk, particularly with respect to the loss of the *Evros* and *Bold Venture*. Moreover, the relative positions of ships in the convoy are far from clear, with plenty of evidence that the cruising orders for SC48 had been deranged by the night in question as U-boat attacks, course alterations and stragglers gradually took their toll. As such it seems impossible to establish beyond reasonable doubt which of the multiple attacks delivered on the night *Gladiolus* went missing was responsible for her demise. Whichever of *U553*, *U558* or *U432* struck her presumably did so with a stray torpedo and in this respect there appears no reason to consider any of the above cases more or less likely than another, though the *prima facie* evidence

for *U432* being the perpetrator is perhaps stronger than for either of the others.

However, it should be pointed out that it is only a matter of probability rather than certainty that *Gladiolus* fell victim to an enemy submarine at all. Aside from the involvement of *U568* in this episode (which attacked two escorts that night, damaging the USS *Kearny* but missing HMCS *Pictou* which immediately counter-attacked), it has also been suggested that *Gladiolus* foundered owing to a loss of stability following her refit at Birkenhead, or otherwise fell victim to some other internal catastrophe. Though not beyond the bounds of possibility, a foundering seems unlikely in view both of the unexceptional weather conditions prevailing and the fact that not a single Flower-class corvette of the 280 that saw action in the Atlantic is recorded as having met such a fate in five years of unremitting war service. Whatever the case, the absence of conclusive evidence from either side requires the file on *Gladiolus* to be left open.

Fate of the crew

All that is known with respect to HMS *Gladiolus*'s crew is that they were lost with their ship in the Atlantic some time between 1930 Allied time on 16 October and dawn on the 17th. The absence of information reporting *Gladiolus* as having been attacked or otherwise in dire need prevented any assistance being rendered. Questions regarding her whereabouts were exchanged by escorts throughout the following day but the lingering presence of the enemy inevitably took precedence over the failure of a corvette to respond to signals. The need to defend the convoy (which suffered the loss of HMS *Broadwater* the following night; see **36**) with the available resources prevented a comprehensive search for a vessel not yet established as lost and with no confirmed last position. Not until the afternoon of the 21st (nearly five days after the sinking) did Admiral Sir Percy Noble, Commander-in-Chief Western Approaches, make his urgent concern known to the Canadian authorities at St John's, her last point of departure: 'Am now in anxiety over *Gladiolus*. Will signal again after interrogation of escorts.' This of course failed to clarify the situation. Though reluctant to write off a ship whose fate remained a complete mystery, Noble was forced to concede that 'no information can be obtained which can throw any light on her last movements', and on 26 October 1941 the Admiralty officially recorded *Gladiolus* as a total loss. The dead were presumed to include the sole survivor of the SS *Empire Heron* rescued in the early hours of the 16th, who was thereby claimed by his second sinking in twenty-four hours.

U553 and Karl Thurmann

Built by Blohm & Voss at Hamburg and commissioned in December 1940, *U553* made all of her nine frontline patrols under Kptlt (Korvkpt.

Thurmann and his crewmen catch up on the news on *U553*'s return to St-Nazaire with victory pennants flying on 24 June 1942. Note the boat's sea turtle emblem on their caps. *DUBMA*

U432 entering Brest with victory pennants flying on 19 September 1941, a month before the loss of *Gladiolus*. *DUBMA*

from August 1942) Karl Thurmann, a career naval officer whose pre-war service included appointments to the light cruisers *Emden* and *Köln*. *U553* claimed two merchantmen on her maiden patrol before playing a key role in decimating SC48 on her third. Another seven patrols added eight merchantmen to *U553*'s tally and brought her the distinction of being the first U-boat to penetrate the Gulf of St Lawrence in May 1942, Thurmann earning the Knight's Cross in August. *U553* sailed from La Pallice for the last time on 16 January 1943. Four days later she reported a problem with her periscope, the last that was ever heard from her. She was declared '*verschollen*' (missing) on the 28th, her fate unknown.

U558 and Günther Krech

Built by Blohm & Voss at Hamburg and commissioned in February 1941, *U558*'s career was spent in the thick of Atlantic action under her only commander, Kptlt Günther Krech. Her wartime record comprised twenty-three ships sunk for a total of over 100,000 tons, the bulk of which was accounted for in pack operations against convoys, though she also chalked up notable successes in the less heavily defended waters off the United States and the Caribbean, including HM anti-submarine trawler *Bedfordshire* in May 1942 (**G28**). These accomplishments were rewarded with a Knight's Cross for Krech in September 1942. *U558*'s run of success ended in the fateful summer of 1943. Frustrated in her attempts to locate convoys off the Azores in May and June, *U558* was eventually ordered to patrol in the Bay of Biscay. Here she was damaged by an RAF Liberator on 17 July and then sunk on the 20th by a combination of strafing and bombs from a USAAF Liberator and an RAF Halifax. Krech, his chief engineer and three crewmen survived the attack to spend five days adrift in a dinghy before being spotted from the air and rescued by the Canadian destroyer *Athabaskan* on 25 July. Günther Krech died in June 2000.

U432 and Heinz-Otto Schultze

Built by F. Schichau at Danzig (Gdansk) and commissioned in April 1941, *U432* undertook eight frontline patrols in the Atlantic, all but the

last under Oblt.z.S. (Kptlt from November 1941) Heinz-Otto Schultze, whose father Otto had been a U-boat ace during the Great War. *U432* sank around twenty vessels during Schultze's tenure (the *Evros* and *Bold Venture* claims being disputed) including the requisitioned trawler FNFL *Poitou* in December 1942 (**G43**). These success earnt Schultze the Knight's Cross in July 1942 and he went on to sink a total of over 60,000 tons in *U432*. In February 1943 Schultze turned command of *U432* over to Kptlt Hermann Eckhardt but the change boded ill for all concerned. Sailing from La Pallice under Eckhardt for the first time on the 14th, *U432* spent three weeks in the mid-Atlantic without success before encountering HM destroyer *Harvester* (**G49**) on the morning of 11 March. Crippled after ramming *U444* the previous night, *Harvester* was despatched with a pair of torpedoes but *U432* was located within the hour by the Free French corvette *Aconit* which exacted revenge with a combination of depth charges, gunfire and ramming. Twenty survivors of *U432* were picked up but Eckhardt was not among them.

Assigned to the new Type-IXD *U849* in October 1943 and ordered to the Indian Ocean, Schultze was lost with his entire crew on 25 November 1943 when she was caught on the surface by a US Liberator based on nearby Ascension Island and destroyed in a low-altitude bombing attack. A large number of men were seen to have abandoned ship as she foundered and a life raft was dropped from the air but no survivors were ever rescued.

Sources

Admiralty, War Diary for October 1941 (TNA, ADM 199/2232), pp. 393, 417, 494, 517, 569, 622 and 640

—, *HX and SC Convoys, 1940–1942: Reports* (TNA, ADM 199/55)

—, *SC Convoys, 1940–1946: Reports* (TNA, ADM 199/56)

—, *Enemy Submarine Attacks on Merchant and US Ships, 1941–1942: Reports* (TNA, ADM 199/1195)

—, *Director of Anti-Submarine Warfare: Attacks on Convoys, 1941–1942* (TNA, ADM 199/1709)

—, *Individual Atlantic Convoys, 1941–1942* (TNA, ADM 199/2099)

—, *Reports of Proceedings for SC Convoys* (TNA, ADM 237/187)

Correspondence between Dr R. M. Coppock and Capt. W. C. Dawson, August–October 1990 (NHB, F.D.S. case 463)

Ruegg, R A., *Flower-Class Corvettes* (typescript, IWM, 13(41).245/5, 1987)

Kolbicz, Rainer, 'U-Boat attacks on the Convoy SC-48 and the Mysterious Loss of HMS *Gladiolus* during the Night of 16/17 October 1941' posted January 2010: http://uboat.net/articles/73.html

Macpherson and Burgess, *Ships of Canada's Naval Forces* (3rd edn), p. 186

Preston, Antony, and Alan Raven, *Flower Class Corvettes* [Ensign, no. 3] (London: Bivouac Books, 1973); reprinted as Man o'War, no. 7 (London: Arms and Armour Press, 1982)

Ruegg, R. A., 'The War of the Flowers, 1939–1945: *Gladiolus*' in *Warships*, Supplement no. 101 (Summer 1990), pp. 22–4

Webpage devoted to convoy SC48: http://www.uboat.net/ops/convoys/battles.htm?convoy=SC-48

Reminiscences of Leading Stoker Dick Turner (crewman, 1940–1): http://www.hmshood.com/crew/biography/dickturner_bio.htm ; also on: http://www.bbc.co.uk/ww2peopleswar/stories/95/a8923395.shtml

---

36   HMS *BROADWATER* (ex USS *MASON*)

Lt Cdr W. M. L. Astwood, RN

Sunk by *U101* (Type VIIC), Kptlt Ernst Mengersen, 18 October 1941

North Atlantic, 380 nm W of Tiree, Inner Hebrides (Scotland)

USS *Mason* seen while serving with the US Navy between 1920 and 1922.
Twenty years and a change of name and navy saw her sunk under the White Ensign by *U101*. *BfZ*

Theatre   North Atlantic (Map 1)
Coordinates   56° 58' N, 18° 30' W
Kriegsmarine code   Quadrat AL 3951
U-boat timekeeping differential   +2 hours
Fatalities   45 and 11   *Survivors*   95+

Displacement   1,190 tons
Dimensions   314.25' × 31.75' × 9.25'
Maximum speed   35 knots
Armament   1 × 4"; 1 × 3" AA; 2 × 20 mm AA; 3 × 21" tt

The Clemson-class destroyers

Last of the so-called 'flush-deckers', the Clemson-class destroyers, of which no fewer than 156 were built in US yards from 1917, were based on the preceding Wickes class (see HNorMS *Bath*, **30**) though with improved endurance. The flush-deckers were all armed with four 4-inch guns, one 3-inch weapon and twelve torpedo tubes, though in the case of the Wickes and Clemson sub-classes the maximum speed was increased from thirty to thirty-five knots to permit them to operate with the latest units planned for the US fleet. Though capable ships for their time, the flush-deckers were soon outdated by advances in destroyer design and fifty-seven of the Clemson class were stricken once US destroyer construction resumed in 1932. However, ninety-one saw service in various guises during the Second World War, including twenty transferred to Britain in 1940 where steps were taken to improve stability, anti-submarine armament and command arrangements on the bridge.

Career

For details of the circumstances under which HMS *Broadwater* joined the Royal Navy, see HNorMS *Bath* (**30**).

USS *Mason* (DD-191) was laid down at Newport News Shipbuilding Co., Virginia in July 1918, launched in March of the following year and commissioned into the US Navy in February 1920. Having shaken down off Norfolk, Virginia, *Mason* served along the east coast until July 1922 when she was put into mothballs at Philadelphia in compliance with the terms of the Washington Treaty. Here she remained until recommissioned in December 1939 following the outbreak of the Second World War. In September 1940 she was one of the fifty US destroyers transferred to British service at Halifax, Nova Scotia as part of the 'Destroyers for Bases' deal signed earlier that month, being commissioned as HMS *Broadwater* on 2 October. Refitted at Devonport and Cardiff between November that year and January 1941, *Broadwater* was assigned to the 11th Escort Group for local escort duties under Western Approaches Command, joining her first convoy in February. Recurrent boiler trouble and other mechanical difficulties kept her in and out of harbour until June, after which she was allocated to the Newfoundland Escort Force, initially on the St John's–Iceland run and eventually as a mid-ocean escort.

Background of the attack

For background on convoy SC48, see the preceding entry for HMS *Gladiolus* (35)

Despite having her speed reduced by engine defects, in early October 1941 *Broadwater* sailed from Liverpool and joined the destroyer HMS *Highlander* on escort duty in the Atlantic, initially with Canadian troop convoy TC14. On 15 October the pair were rerouted

as information reached the Admiralty of concerted U-boat attacks against slow convoy SC48 bound for Liverpool. On the evening of the 16th *Broadwater* took station on the port bow of SC48, sighting and attacking a U-boat the following morning. However, as related in the preceding entry for HM corvette *Gladiolus*, a heavy toll was taken of the convoy which had lost seven ships by the time dawn broke on the 17th. The night of 17–18 October was quieter as continuous air cover by RAF Catalinas from Iceland was boosted by the arrival of the 3rd Escort Group. *U101*, which had joined the fray earlier that evening, was the only U-boat to press home her attack that night, her task made easier by the fact that her victim had not only fallen unaccountably far astern of the convoy but had stopped zigzagging.

War Diary of *U101*, patrol of 11 October–16 November 1941: PG 30097, NHB, reel 1,079, p. 219

Date, time	Details of position, wind, weather, sea, light, visibility, moonlight, etc.	Incidents
18.x		
0257	Qu. AL 3942	Outgoing W/T transmission 0235/18/160/203: *Qu. AL 3942. One escort, one destroyer, probably the rearguard pickets. Mengersen.* Two more small shadows can be made out to port of the corvette, with yet another to starboard. They are presumably also corvettes or gunboats. What a superb night it is – difficult to form any clear picture.[1] In this light drizzle it's only at the very closest range that one can pick out the vessels at all. You fiddle around with your binoculars, having no idea if you're looking at the sky or at the sea, until suddenly another shadow rears up. I'm constantly trying to pass the corvette on her starboard bow because I assume the convoy must be positioned ahead of her. But as soon as I get abreast of her with the diesel engines at half speed she turns straight towards me. Can she hear me through her hydrophones? The facts point to this being the case so I'm constantly forced to switch to the electric engines. I consider attacking her but then settle for the more valuable target I saw earlier behind the corvette, abeam and away to port. It seemed to be a destroyer; I presume her to be the final escort.[2]
0417		Run in to attack destroyer. The sea is now calm, almost oily. There's no chance of her seeing me, at most she might pick me up on the hydrophones. I therefore manoeuvre using the electric engines. Visibility has significantly improved now that the rain has abated.
0420	Qu. AL 3951	Spread of four torpedoes fired at destroyer.[3] Coordinates entered: enemy speed 7 knots, inclination 80°, range 1,800 m, angle of dispersion 2°, depth 2 m. The torpedoes run true as can be seen by their illuminated bubble tracks. I fear that she'll turn away but she remains beam on to me with no change in inclination. After 2 min. 30 sec. (2,300 m) a hit aft. A very bright tongue of flame shoots out of the after part of the ship (depth charges and magazine going up), then a large pall of smoke that shrouds the destroyer. As this gradually lifts we can see the destroyer settling by the stern. Some of the after structures are glowing white. Destroyer sends up two rockets.[4] From behind the cloud of smoke another destroyer emerges at an inclination of 0°. I withdraw at 180° using electric engines only. However, she then alters course towards the scene of the sinking, her fellow destroyer having sunk about 90 seconds earlier. She turns searchlights onto the area of the sinking and seems to be picking up survivors. A shame that we have no more bow torpedoes loaded; firing a stern shot from this range would be too much of a gamble. Besides, she's now circling and turning back towards us. But what's this? A number of smaller vessels astern on our starboard side. So ours wasn't the rearmost escort; these appear to be corvettes or other escorts. Four of them have formed a line abreast and are sailing right towards us. They are exchanging morse signals. One vessel flashes a light in our direction every so often. I'm now at all times using only the electric engines, course 210°.
0510		Escorts are now moving further away. I alter course slightly to the south, switching to diesels so as to

---

1 Mengersen's use of the word 'superb' (German = *toll*) is obviously meant ironically.
2 HMS *Broadwater*.
3 Torpedoes fired by the First Watch Officer, Oblt.z.S. Wilhelm-Heinrich Graf von Pückler und Limburg.
4 These were actually fired by HM trawler *Angle*, still some distance away.

		charge the batteries, and reload four torpedoes.
0555		Outgoing W/T transmission to B.d.U. 0450/18/205: *Qu. [AL] 3951 several destroyers and escorts steering eastwards, probably attached to convoy. One destroyer sunk, am forced to retire. Mengersen.* The type couldn't be made out because visibility was too poor. My impression is that she was a destroyer of the Churchill class, or a small cruiser.[5] Either way her silhouette was clearly longer than that of the other destroyer.
0925		Test dive. Fuel has penetrated the battery bilge. Fuel Bunker 2 is leaking. Starboard shaft is making an ugly noise. Starboard electric engine shut down.
1200	Qu. AL 0297	Day's run = 206 nm. Finish repairs and surface.

---

5   Mengersen's first deduction was correct. The Kriegsmarine often referred to the fifty destroyers transferred to British service from the US Navy as the 'Churchill class', a reference to one of their number, HMS *Churchill* (ex USS *Herndon*), and presumably a nod to he who clinched the deal. The smallest cruiser in the Royal Navy had nearly four times the displacement of HMS *Broadwater*, and none possessed her four funnels.

The sinking

That the destroyer *Broadwater* was fatally damaged at 0225 GMT by one of Mengersen's spread of four torpedoes appears beyond all doubt. However, for all its vivid evocation of frontline operations, few war diary extracts are less in accordance with the known facts than Mengersen's in this instance. Not only does he consistently refer to a hit aft when the detonation in fact removed *Broadwater*'s bows, but his torpedo report describes as taking 'a little more than a minute' a sinking which actually lasted eleven hours. These statements are the result either of misjudgement on his part or more likely a concern to ensure that the ship was credited to him whether he witnessed its demise or not, to which his suggestion that he may in fact have sunk a light cruiser lends additional support. Whatever the case, Mengersen's torpedo inflicted mortal damage on *Broadwater*. The bows were torn off as far back as the upper bridge, taking with them the front of the wheelhouse, the seamen's mess deck, the wardroom and the officers' cabins forward. The foremast sheered off with the impact, collapsing towards the stern, and the decks were severely buckled. All engines and dynamos stopped immediately. The ship settled in the water, kept afloat by the forward engine-room bulkhead. Efforts at saving her were quickly recognised to be futile and the rest of the night was spent evacuating the surviving ship's company. Informed by the commanding officer of HM trawler *Cape Warwick* that *Broadwater*'s back was broken and the chances of salvaging her nil, the injured Lt Cdr Astwood authorised her to be sunk by gunfire. The *coup de grâce* was administered by HM trawler *St Apollo* which despatched *Broadwater* with her 4-inch gun shortly after midday on the 18th.

The only significant question raised (though never answered) at the Board of Enquiry was why HMS *Broadwater* was so far off station. She was estimated to have fallen at least twelve miles astern of the convoy when Mengersen made his attack. Lt Cdr Astwood, who had fallen asleep over his charts shortly after midnight, was never woken and informed why this situation had arisen, though the fact that *Broadwater* was sailing in company with several other escorts suggests that it was more than a simple watchkeeper's error.

Fate of the crew

Though a second torpedo was spotted passing astern by a lookout positioned on the after 3-inch platform, *Broadwater* was not at Action Stations when the attack came. The torpedo detonated the forward magazine and took a heavy toll of those off watch on the seamen's mess deck, at least thirty men losing their lives here. Similarly, all in the wardroom and the officers' cabins were killed with the exception of Lt (E) C. E. A. Vann who was flung into an oil tank beneath his cabin and survived his ordeal with severe shock and a few broken ribs. The impact of the explosion blasted a number of men off the bridge, depositing them on the deck sixty feet away. Lt Cdr Astwood sustained head injuries in the blast which left him incapable of supervising the evacuation of the ship. He delegated this task to the navigating officer, who at that stage was reckoned to be the only other executive officer to have survived the attack. Though HM trawlers *Cape Warwick* and *Angle* were quickly on the scene, the ferrying of survivors in *Broadwater*'s whaler and other boats provided by the trawlers took the rest of the night. The evacuation was complicated by rising wind and heavy seas, with smashed and jagged plates hampering efforts to manoeuvre against the ship's side as she rolled in a beam sea. Sub-Lt Brooke-Smith and twelve ratings who had insisted on remaining aboard in the hope of salvaging the ship were ordered off at dawn as the weather deteriorated. Three of those rescued subsequently died of their injuries, the rest being landed at Londonderry. The list of those Missing, Presumed Killed included two survivors from the Norwegian SS *Erviken* and nine more from the British tanker *W. C. Teagle*, sunk by *U558* the previous night (see HMS *Gladiolus*, **35**).

Among the officer complement of HMS *Broadwater* was Lt John Parker RNVR of Boston, Massachusetts. On 15 June 1941, in defiance of the Neutrality Act, Parker and two others became the first US citizens to enter the Royal Naval College at Greenwich. Posted appropriately enough to one of the ex-American destroyers, Parker was among those killed on the bridge of HMS *Broadwater* on 18 October, thereby joining the select band of Americans to lose their lives in British service in the Second World War. Of these, twenty-three perished while serving in the RNVR between the outbreak of war and the attack on Pearl Harbor.

U101 and Ernst Mengersen

Built by Germaniawerft at Kiel and commissioned in March 1940, *U101* spent eighteen months in the thick of convoy action in the Atlantic, first under Kptlt Fritz Frauenheim and then under Kptlt Ernst Mengersen from November 1940. HMS *Broadwater* was to be *U101*'s last victim, the boat being reduced to training duties in January 1942 and finally decommissioned at Neustadt on the Baltic in October of the following year. Mengersen went on to command the Type-VIIB *U607* before being given a series of shore appointments, including

training duties and spells in charge of both the 15th and 20th Flotillas. Awarded the Knight's Cross following the sinking of HMS *Broadwater* and taken prisoner at war's end, Mengersen entered civilian life after his release in 1946. He died in 1995.

Sources

Admiralty, *Loss of HMS* Broadwater *18/10/41: Board of Enquiry* (TNA, ADM 1/12013); report on rescue of survivors by HM trawler *Cape Warwick* posted on: http://users.erols.com/sepulcher/broadwater.html

Blair, *Hitler's U-Boat War*, I, pp. 368–71
Cherry, Cdr A. H., *Yankee RN* (London: Jarrolds, 1951)
DANFS, IV, p. 262 (USS *Mason*); also on: http://www.history.navy.mil/danfs/m6/mason-i.htm
Hague, Arnold, *Destroyers for Great Britain: A History of 50 Town Class Ships Transferred from the United States to Great Britain in 1940* (London: Greenhill Books, 1990)

Career history of HMS *Broadwater*:
    http://www.naval-history.net/xGM-Chrono-11US-Broadwater.htm
Defunct website devoted to HMS *Broadwater*:
    http://pages.britishlibrary.net/chalkywhite/index.html

Mengersen (centre) seen with Kptlt Erich Topp (left) and Kptlt Georg-Wilhelm Schulz, commander of the 6th *U-Flottille*, at St-Nazaire in August 1942. *DUBMA*

---

37   HMS *COSSACK* (i)

Capt. E. L. Berthon, DSC RN†
Sunk by U563 (Type VIIC), Oblt.z.S. Klaus Bargsten, 23–27 October 1941
North Atlantic, 85 nm SW of Cape St Vincent (Portugal)

Cossack seen entering Portsmouth as leader of the 1st Tribal Flotilla in July 1938. The recognition stripes painted on 'B' mounting indicate her participation in the Nyon Patrol off Spain during the civil war. *Wright & Logan*

Theatre North Atlantic (Map 1)		*Displacement* 1,960 tons	
Coordinates (of attack) 35° 56' N, 10° 04' W		*Dimensions* 377' × 36.5' × 9'	
Kriegsmarine code (of attack) Quadrat CG 8813		*Maximum speed* 36 knots	
U-boat timekeeping differential +2 hours		*Armament* 6 × 4.7"; 2 × 4" AA; 4 × 40 mm AA; 8 × .5" AA; 4 × 21" tt	
Fatalities 159 *Survivors* 115+			

The Tribal-class destroyers

Displacing nearly 2,000 tons, the Tribals were much the largest destroyers hitherto designed for the Royal Navy and a total of twenty-seven were built including eleven for the Royal Canadian and Australian Navies. Designed in response to the large destroyers entering service in the major navies of the world in the mid-1930s, the class was initially to have carried no fewer than ten 4.7-inch guns in automatic mountings together with a substantial anti-aircraft armament and appropriate fire control. However, war service demonstrated the designed AA provisions to be inadequate and these were augmented at the expense of heavier armament. The class saw extensive service in all theatres and only fifteen survived the conflict.

Career

The lead ship of the class, HMS *Cossack* was ordered under the 1935 estimates and laid down at Vickers-Armstrong's yard at Walker-on-Tyne in June 1936, launched in June 1937 and completed in June 1938. *Cossack* was commissioned as leader of the 1st Tribal Flotilla, Mediterranean Fleet in June 1938 and began her career patrolling off Spain during the Civil War. She was still in the Mediterranean in September 1939, being ordered home with the rest of the now renamed 4th Destroyer Flotilla on 2 October. *Cossack's* war began inauspiciously with a collision with the steamer *Borthwick* in the Forth on 7 November which claimed the lives of five of her men. However, the next two years saw her carve her name as one of the great destroyers of the Second World War. Her reputation was made under Philip Vian who joined the ship as Captain (D) of the 4th DF as she completed repairs at Leith, Scotland in January 1940. While patrolling off the Norwegian coast on 16 February Vian was ordered to intercept the German tanker *Altmark* which had been reported off Bergen at noon the previous day. As the supply vessel of the 'pocket battleship' *Admiral Graf Spee* which had scuttled herself off Montevideo on 14 December, the *Altmark* was a ship of more than ordinary interest to the British. During his three-month cruise Kapitän zur See Hans Langsdorff of the *Admiral Graf Spee* had sunk nine British merchantmen and taken 300 of their crews prisoner. It was these men who now filled the holds of the *Altmark* as she made her way back to Germany. On the afternoon of the 16th Vian's force sighted *Altmark* and followed her into Jøssingfjorden thirty miles south of Stavanger. When the two Norwegian escorts accompanying her refused to permit a search of the ship Winston Churchill, then First Lord of the Admiralty, ordered Vian to put a boarding party on *Altmark* and free her prisoners despite the flagrant breach of Norwegian neutrality implied by such an act. After a brief action during which she damaged her bow coming alongside *Altmark*, *Cossack* sailed from Jøssingfjorden, her decks crammed with 299 merchant seamen. The exploit created a diplomatic row, turned Vian into a national hero and made *Cossack* a household name in Britain.

After further repairs at Leith *Cossack* returned to Norwegian waters where on 9 April she was caught up in Operation HARTMUT, the naval side of the German invasion of Norway. By day's end she was towing the destroyer *Kashmir* into Leith Harbour, but five days later was in action at the Second Battle of Narvik during which *U64* and eight German destroyers were sunk by a force led by the battleship *Warspite*. *Cossack*, however, was seriously damaged by nine 5-inch shells from the destroyer *Diether von Roeder* which cost her eleven men killed and twenty-nine wounded, and she ended the

battle aground on a submerged wreck. Lifted off by the tide, she sailed stern-first to Skjelfjord in the Lofoten Islands for emergency repairs before making for Scapa Flow. Repairs kept *Cossack* at Thornycroft's yard in Southampton until June when she was among the ships selected to escort the cruiser *Enterprise* to Canada with £130 million in British bullion and securities. August found her escorting the 1st Minelaying Squadron as it sowed the northern section of the East Coast Mine Barrier. Service with the Home Fleet continued into 1941, though broken by two months under repair at Rosyth in the autumn of 1940 with a further spell at Southampton early the following year as a result of hull damage in the North Atlantic. In March and April 1941 she was again with the 1st MS, this time covering the laying of the Northern Barrage. The rest of her career was spent mainly on convoy duty, and it was while escorting convoy WS8B that *Cossack* and the 4th DF, still commanded by Capt. Vian, was ordered to intercept the German battleship *Bismarck* as she made for Brest on 26 May. Vian made contact with *Bismarck* at 2200 and harried her through the night until dawn brought destruction at the hands of the Home Fleet. In July *Cossack* returned to the Mediterranean under a new commander, Capt. E. L. Berthon, where she participated in the SUBSTANCE, STYLE and HALBERD convoys to Malta before joining Force H at Gibraltar in September.

Background of the attack

On 17 October 1941 B.d.U. formed the *Breslau* group of U-boats to operate in the approaches to Gibraltar. (For background on this, see HMS *Fleur-de-Lys*, **34**.) One of its number, *U204* (see **30**), was destroyed on the 19th, but the remaining six boats held their positions in the Straits of Gibraltar to await the next convoy, attacking stragglers and naval shipping in the meantime. Informed of this concentration by Enigma decrypts, the Admiralty delayed the sailing of the Liverpool-bound HG75 by almost a week and it was not until 22 October that it left Gibraltar with a powerful thirteen-ship escort led by HMS *Cossack*. The convoy was almost immediately sighted by German aircraft and then by *U71* and *U563* on the 23rd. *U563* (Oblt.z.S. Klaus Bargsten) was quick to respond to the reports, making contact with HG75 that evening. Shortly after 2200 GMT the corvette *Carnation* reported a submarine sighting and the entire escort went to Action Stations. When the tentative Asdic contact faded and nothing more was sighted Capt. E. L. Berthon brought *Cossack* down to the second degree of readiness and his ship took station astern of the convoy. About fifteen minutes later a torpedo was seen approaching the port side, Berthon ordering an immediate course alteration to starboard. However, this manoeuvre was only sufficient to avoid one of the pair of torpedoes fired by *U563* and at 2238 British time *Cossack* was dealt a fatal blow.

War Diary of *U563*, patrol of 4 October–1 November 1941: PG 30597, NHB, reel 1,121, pp. 51–2

Date, time	Details of position, wind, weather, sea, light, visibility, moonlight, etc.	Incidents
24.x		
0000	Qu. CG 8821, wind NNW 2, sea 1–2, 5/10 overcast, 1,016 mb, visibility 3 nm	

Date, time	Details of position, wind, weather, sea, light, visibility, moonlight, etc.	*Incidents*

0014 — Four torpedo detonations heard in boat. We sight explosion cloud and shining lights at bearing 285° true.[1]

0018 — Several steamers in sight at bearing 285° true. We alter course towards them. Precise formation cannot yet be determined but we fire a spread of two torpedoes at the largest of them, range 3,500 m. Due to a switching error we only get one torpedo away. After 4 min. 30 sec. there is a detonation together with a huge sheet of flame followed shortly after by an explosion. Explosion cloud rises 80–100 m. My impression is that this torpedo detonation occurred on the far side of the steamer, and that it was not mine but another boat's torpedo which struck.[2] A large number of starshell and rockets are then fired towards the dark side which I have now vacated.

0030 — Ahead of me, with an inclination of 70°, bows left, appears a destroyer, range about 1,000 m.[3] She is illuminating the area on the far side of her with a searchlight. Immediately behind her and overlapping is a medium-sized steamer. Destroyer alters course, now has an inclination of 90°, bows right.[4]

0038 — Spread of two torpedoes fired. After about 30 sec. she alters course once again. At first I assume this is towards us at a bearing of 0° because we can make out the white foam from her bow. It turns out that she was turning away from us and what we saw was her propeller wake. I now find myself completely illuminated by starshell, which is being fired across the entire horizon on my side.

0039 — Emergency dive. As we are diving we hear two powerful torpedo detonations. Boat sinks to T = 45 m and we have difficulty bringing her back up.[5] It becomes apparent that the flooding valve of the torpedo compartment was leaking. Running time of my torpedo 1 min. = 900 m. So we evidently hit the steamer.[6]

0110 — We surface. Nothing more to be seen of the steamer. While we were submerged we heard the cracking noises typical of a sinking merchantman, as well as two explosions that sounded like they came from boilers going up. At a bearing of 20° true we can see a burning vessel with a destroyer and another escort vessel nearby; the destroyer is illuminating the area about her as a precaution.[7] I assume they are taking survivors on board.

0130 — Single torpedo fired from Tube V at the burning ship. No success. We then head off on a north-westerly course to catch up with the convoy.

0211 — Incoming W/T transmission from *U71*: *Convoy Qu. 8827 heading north*

---

1 Since no other ship was hit Bargsten may be mistaking depth-charge attacks carried out by *Carnation* following a contact obtained at around this time. However, the night in question was also characterised by a high degree of confusion among the convoy escort which is reflected in conflicting data in British reports of the action.

2 There are no records of attacks by other *Breslau* boats at this time so Bargsten may once again be confusing anti-submarine activity elsewhere in the convoy. This and subsequent torpedoes were fired by *U563*'s First Watch Officer, Oblt.z.S. Klaus Petersen.

3 HMS *Cossack*.

4 British and German sources cannot be reconciled on this point. Bargsten's plot of the attack confirms the log data which indicates that he fired when *Cossack* was beam on to him on her starboard side. By contrast, British records (which make no reference to any starshell being fired prior to *Cossack* being hit) are unanimous that the torpedo was sighted on her port side, where it struck despite a course alteration to starboard.

5 By 'T = 45 m' Bargsten seems to be recording a dive of 185 metres (607 feet); for a full discussion of the 'T =' notation, see Reading the *Kriegstagebücher*, p. xxxvii.

6 Actually *Cossack* since no other ship is recorded as having been attacked at this juncture.

7 *Cossack*, which burned for much of the night. The ships standing by are HM destroyer *Legion* and HM corvette *Carnation*.

The sinking

U563's torpedo struck *Cossack* on the port side abreast 'B' mounting and wrecked the fore part of the ship, probably as a result of the detonation of the forward magazine. A fire was ignited at the after end of the fo'c'sle which spread along the port side of the ship assisted by ready-use pom-pom ammunition stowed on the bridge structure. Of the two boiler rooms in operation, No. 1 was immediately flooded and No. 2 abandoned and its boiler subsequently shut down by the Chief Engineer, Cdr (E) R. B. Halliwell, fearing an oil fire. The senior surviving executive officer, Lt B. C. Moth, who was injured by the blast, consulted Cdr Halliwell and Warrant Officer Gunner (T) M. G. Foster before passing the order to abandon ship. His decision, which was later endorsed by the Board of Enquiry, was taken against the possibility that the forward magazine might explode. With a raging fire preventing access to what remained of the fo'c'sle Moth could not have known that it had almost certainly already done so.

Once the crew had abandoned ship unavailing attempts were made to combat the fire with hoses directed first from *Legion*'s and then *Carnation*'s fo'c'sle, but only when the former managed to secure herself alongside and run a hose along *Cossack*'s deck was the blaze extinguished. With the wreckage of the bows having sheared off, the 'Cossacks' reboarded their ship on the morning of the 24th. The boarding party was able to raise some steam but progress towards Gibraltar was slow and little headway was made that day due to the drag on the wrecked forward end, even when stores and equipment were jettisoned to reduce the draught. The arrival of the salvage tug *Thames* on the 25th afforded no improvement in the situation. The weather had by now taken a turn for the worse and the entry of water over the decks hampered efforts to pump her out. The bad weather continued and late on the afternoon of the 26th it was decided that the risk to those on board outweighed any advantage of their remaining in the ship, the boarding party being taken off by HM corvette *Jonquil*. Abandoned for the night, *Cossack* was still afloat at daybreak on the 27th but so low in the water that it was decided not to reboard her. She sank later that morning watched by much of her surviving company, the White Ensign still flying at the gaff.

No blame was attached to any individual for her loss and the conclusion of both the Board of Enquiry and the officers commanding Force H (Vice-Admiral Sir James Somerville) and North Atlantic (Vice-Admiral G. F. B. Edward-Collins) was that Lt Moth, a lieutenant of only six months' seniority, had made the right decision to abandon ship in the circumstances. Records reveal some disenchantment over the efficiency of *Cossack*'s pumps, the inability to supply her with further pumping gear and the delayed arrival of the *Thames* on the 25th, though no consensus was reached on any of these points nor was any censure meted out. Perhaps the most pertinent comment came from Vice-Admiral Somerville who observed that 'the employment of these large and valuable ships for slow convoys is obviously undesirable'.

Fate of the crew

U563's torpedo took a severe toll of *Cossack*'s company but the very high casualty rate must in part be attributed to the number of those taking passage in her to Britain. Virtually all those in the fore part of the ship and the bridge structure perished in the initial detonation. Capt. Berthon and other officers on the fore bridge were killed instantly leaving Lt Moth as the ranking survivor. Moth himself survived because the explosion came while he was resting beside the rangefinder support in the after part of the bridge. In addition to those killed many were badly injured by the force of the blast or suffered burns as fires raged unchecked. The act of abandoning ship was hampered by damage to *Cossack*'s motorboat and whaler, leaving the survivors to make do with the remaining Carley floats, the men leaping into the sea after them. Not all made it onto a float and small groups formed in the oil-covered water waiting for help to arrive. Although lives were no doubt lost in the water, *Legion* and *Carnation* were on the scene relatively quickly, lowering their ship's boats and dropping scrambling nets for men to clamber up. After a shower and a few hours' sleep there was no shortage of volunteers to reboard *Cossack* in the effort to save her.

The survivors were landed as soon as circumstances permitted though some had the misfortune of being torpedoed again, this time in the fighter catapult ship HMS *Ariguani* to which many of the wounded had been transferred on around 25 October. However, *Ariguani* survived to reach Gibraltar whose medical facilities were kept busy with a large number of burn cases together with those suffering from

Cossack seen minus her bows, probably on 24 October. She lingered another three days before foundering on the morning of the 27th.
HMS Cossack Association

fuel ingestion. Among the latter was Boy 1st Class K. F. W. Rail who was put on a week-long diet of water and charcoal powder, taken six times daily.

The sinking of the *Cossack* came at a time of terrible attrition for the Royal Navy, but her fighting career was not forgotten and in March 1943 a 'CO'-class destroyer bearing the name was laid down at the same Walker yard where construction had begun on Vian's ship seven years before. The dead are remembered on a plaque in Portsmouth Cathedral and in 'Instead of Tears', an elegy by the women's rights activist Marie Stopes whose friend Lt William Rose, *Cossack*'s First Lieutenant, was among the lost. Another casualty was the ship's dog Pluto, a veteran of the *Altmark* and *Bismarck* episodes and posthumous recipient of the Dickin Medal, the animals' Victoria Cross. R.I.P.

U563 and Klaus Bargsten

Built by Blohm & Voss of Hamburg and commissioned in March 1941, *U563* sailed on her maiden frontline patrol in late July. Her crew had every reason to be optimistic about their novice commander. As Kretschmer's First Watch Officer in *U99*, Oblt.z.S. Klaus Bargsten had sunk as many ships as any in the *U-Boot-Waffe*. However, Bargsten enjoyed much less success as commander in his own right and *Cossack* was *U563*'s only victim before she was heavily damaged by an RAF Whitley bomber on 1 December 1941 and put out of action for the best part of a year. She returned to the fray in October 1942 under Kptlt Götz von Hartmann who sank three merchantmen in as many patrols. Subsequently commanded by Oblt.z.S. Gustav Borchardt, *U563* was sunk in the Bay of Biscay by a Halifax and two Sunderlands of the RAF and RAAF on 29 May 1943, one of forty U-boats lost by the Kriegsmarine that month. There were no survivors.

Bargsten went on to moderate success as commander of the Type-IXC *U521*, sinking HM anti-submarine trawler *Bredon* in February 1943 (**G48**), but her career ended after the US patrol craft *PC-565* depth charged her to the surface on 2 June that year. Bargsten, the first to emerge upon surfacing, was the only survivor as *U521* was lashed with gunfire and finished off with a further pattern of depth charges. He spent the rest of the war in captivity, being released in 1946. He died in August 2000.

available in part in *Submarine Attacks on Merchant Shipping 1939–1945 and Loss of HMS* Cossack (TNA, ADM 199/1197)

—, *Monthly Anti-Submarine Reports, 1941*, vol. II (TNA, ADM 199/2058)

MacLeod, K. M., *All at Sea or MacLeod's War* (typescript, IWM, 96/56/1)

Rail, K. F. W., *One Man's Memories of War* (typescript, IWM, 03/14/1)

Blair, *Hitler's U-Boat War*, I, pp. 391–3

Brice, Martin H., *The Tribals: Biography of a Destroyer Class* (London: Ian Allan, 1971)

English, John, *Afridi to Nizam: British Fleet Destroyers, 1937–43* (Gravesend, Kent: World Ship Society, 2001)

HMS *Cossack* Association, *HMS* Cossack *1938–1941: Some Survivors' Narratives* (n.p.: HMS *Cossack* Association, 1998)

—, *Newsletters*, especially 2000, no. 3, pp. 6–7, and no. 4, pp. 10–13

Lyon, David, *HMS* Cossack [Warships in Profile, no. 2] (Windsor, Berks.: Profile Publications, 1971)

Stopes, Marie Carmichael, *Instead of Tears: In Memoriam for Officers and Men Who Went Down with HMS* Cossack (London: Alexander Moring, 1947)

Career history of HMS *Cossack*:
   http://www.naval-history.net/xGM-Chrono-10DD-34Tribal-Cossack1.htm

HMS *Cossack* Association website:
   http://www.hmscossack.org/

Biography of Kptlt Klaus Bargsten:
   http://en.wikipedia.org/wiki/Klaus_Bargsten

Bargsten as commander of *U563* some time between March 1941 and March 1942. *DUBMA*

Sources

Admiralty, *HG Convoys, January 1941–January 1942* (TNA, ADM 199/932)

—, *Loss of HMS* Cossack: *Board of Enquiry* (TNA, ADM 1/11846); also

---

38   USS *REUBEN JAMES* (i)

Lt Cdr Heywood L. Edwards, USN†

Sunk by *U552* (Type VIIC), Kptlt Erich Topp, 31 October 1941

North Atlantic, 625 nm W of Dursey Island, Cork (Ireland)

Reuben James seen traversing the Kiel Canal in October 1921 or February 1922. Her appearance had changed little by the time Kptlt Topp sank her in the North Atlantic twenty years later with serious implications for US–German relations. *BfZ*

Theatre   North Atlantic (Map 1)

Coordinates   51° 59' N, 27° 05' W

Kriegsmarine code   Quadrat AK 9922

U-boat timekeeping differential   +3 hours

Fatalities   100   *Survivors*   45

Displacement   1,190 tons

Dimensions   314.25' × 31.75' × 9.25'

Maximum speed   35 knots

Armament   4 × 4"; 1 × 3"; 12 × 21" tt

Career

For design notes on the Clemson-class destroyers, of which *Reuben James* was one of seventy-eight units to see service in the Allied fleets during the Second World War, see HMS *Broadwater* (**36**).

The USS *Reuben James* (DD-245) was laid down at New York Shipbuilding Corp., Camden, New Jersey in April 1919, launched on 4 October, and commissioned into the US Navy on 24 September 1920. Assigned to the Atlantic Fleet, on 30 November *Reuben James* sailed for the Mediterranean where she spent the next year operating from the Yugoslav ports of Zelenika (Montenegro) and Gruž (Dubrovnik, Croatia) on humanitarian duty in Asia Minor. In October 1921 she participated with the protected cruiser USS *Olympia* in the ceremonies attending the return of the Unknown Soldier to the United States from the French port of Le Havre. The end of that month found her at Gdansk (Danzig) in Poland where she assisted the American Relief Administration in its humanitarian work in the Baltic until February 1922. After a further stint in the Mediterranean *Reuben James* left Gibraltar for the US on 17 July 1922, being based thereafter at New York in the 3rd Naval District. Early 1926 found her patrolling the Nicaraguan coast against the supply of weapons to the Liberal party in its ongoing struggle against the US-backed Conservative regime which came to be known as the Constitutionalist War. Fleet duties continued until the ship decommissioned for refitting at Philadelphia on 20 January 1931. Spared the cull of over fifty of her sisters with chronic boiler defects, *Reuben James* rejoined the Atlantic Fleet in March 1932. She saw service in the Atlantic and particularly the Caribbean where an uprising against the dictator Gerardo Machado y Morales kept her in Cuban waters between September 1933 and January 1934. Later that year she was allocated to the Pacific Fleet and on 19 October sailed from Norfolk, Virginia for her new homeport of San Diego, California, where she remained until rejoining the Atlantic Fleet in January 1939. September 1939 brought *Reuben James* into the Neutrality Patrol which had been established on the outbreak of war 'to emphasize the readiness of the United States Navy to defend the Western Hemisphere'. Despite grounding at Lobos Cay, Cuba in November and suffering a collision with the tug *Wicomico* in Hampton Roads in February 1940, this assignment kept her busy guarding the approaches to the US Atlantic and Gulf shores until she was transferred to the so-called Support Force in March 1941 with orders to escort supply convoys destined for Britain. On 23 October 1941 she sailed from the new US base at Argentia, Newfoundland with four other destroyers to escort eastbound convoy HX156.

Background of the attack

In March 1941 Congress passed the Lend-Lease Act to facilitate the supply of arms and war *matériel* to the United Kingdom and other democracies facing the Axis onslaught. This circumstance led in turn to the creation of a US Navy force based at the Icelandic anchorage of Hvalfjörður charged with escorting the resulting convoys as far as an agreed Mid-Ocean Meeting Point (MOMP) from which the Royal Navy would see them into British ports. However, as time passed US destroyers began to join the British Newfoundland–Londonderry run,

a policy which not only placed further strain on US–German relations but brought closer the moment when an American vessel fell prey to a U-boat, with all that that implied for America's involvement in the war. That moment came on 21 May when the freighter *Robin Moor* was sunk by *U69* (Kptlt Jost Metzler) in the South Atlantic. B.d.U. had issued stringent instructions against deliberate attacks on American shipping but as President Roosevelt's chief critic Wendell Wilkie warned, 'If we load our ships with contraband of war and send them into combat zones they will most certainly be sunk'. Nor could the US Navy itself expect to remain immune from attack. On 4 September Oblt.z.S. Georg-Werner Fraatz (see **55**) came close to torpedoing the USS *Greer* when the latter took it upon herself to engage in a sonar pursuit after *U652* was spotted by an RAF Hudson. The result of this incident was Roosevelt's institution of a 'shoot-on-sight' policy against any vessel attempting to interfere with US shipping. As Samuel Eliot Morison put it in his official history of the US Navy during the Second World War (see *Sources*), 'From the date of the *Greer* incident, 4 September 1941, the United States was engaged in a *de facto* naval war with Germany on the Atlantic Ocean'. The naval war began in earnest on 17 October when the destroyer *Kearny* was hit by a torpedo from *U568* (Kptlt Joachim Preuss; see **29**) which claimed eleven lives and almost sank her. The escalation continued. On 30 October the Navy oiler USS *Salinas* was damaged by *U106* (Oblt.z.S. Hermann Rasch) and the following day, 31 October 1941, the US Navy lost her first warship of the Second World War: the *Reuben James*.

The night of 30–31 October 1941 found USS *Reuben James* as part of Task Unit 4.1.3 escorting convoy HX156, then eight days out of Halifax, Nova Scotia. With HX156 just a day's steaming from the agreed MOMP, it became apparent that she was being shadowed by a U-boat – Kptlt Erich Topp's *U552* as it turned out. TU 4.1.3, which consisted of the destroyers *Niblack*, *Tarbell*, *Benson*, *Hilary P. Jones* and *Reuben James*, was ill-equipped to deal with the threat as the only unit with effective radar was the *Niblack*, then keeping station astern of the convoy. So primitive was her equipment that *Niblack* had to position herself in the direction of the desired sweep in order to obtain a contact. Shortly after 0530 on the 31st (convoy time) Topp abandoned his attempts to reach a dawn attacking position and turned his attention to the destroyer on HX156's port quarter: *Reuben James*. At 0525 *Tarbell* (acting as RDF guardship) intercepted a U-boat signal from that side of the convoy – almost certainly one of a series of medium-wave beacon signals (see note 1) put out by *U552* as the only member of the *Stosstrupp* ('raiding party') group in touch with HX156 – and reported the contact to the rest of the escort. From the accounts of survivors it appears that *Reuben James* had received this information and begun turning to port on Lt Cdr Edwards' orders while he hastened back to his cabin to change out of his bath robe. But *Reuben James* was already the target of two torpedoes fired by *U552* and at a time variously estimated between 0525 and 0540 (see note 4) received a hit on the port side almost identical to that inflicted on the *Kearny* two weeks earlier. However, the effect of this on an elderly unit was of infinitely greater consequence.

War Diary of *U552*, patrol of 25 October–26 November 1941: PG 30589a, NHB, reel 1,118, p. 306.

Date, time	Details of position, wind, weather, sea, light, visibility, moonlight, etc.	Incidents
31.x		
0400	Qu. AK 9982, wind S 1–2, overcast, brightly moonlit night, sea 1	
0510		Convoy sighted in the bright moonlight, lying roughly 5 nm to the east. Large ships.
0556		Outgoing W/T transmission: *Convoy in sight Qu. AK 9973, enemy steering northerly course, speed 10 knots. U552.*
0630		Outgoing W/T transmission: *Enemy in Qu. AK 9957, course 10°. Speed 8 knots. U552.*[1]
0708		Outgoing W/T transmission: *Convoy in sight Qu. AK 9951, course 30°, 9 knots. U552.*
0700[2]		We move in to attack now that the moon has set. Even so, visibility is too good for comfort thanks to the Northern Lights and the stars. The escort vessels are stationed at a distance from the convoy but they are so numerous that we'll never manage to slip through in the short time that remains before daybreak.[3]
0800	Qu. AK 9927	0800 and still all we come up against are escort vessels.
0834[4]		From a range of 1,000 m we attack destroyer silhouette with a spread of two torpedoes and sink her.[5] Both torpedoes hit.[6] A huge tongue of flame. The wreck is blown to smithereens by the detonation of her own depth charges.[7] We then retire somewhat, unable to press home another attack because of the gathering light. We haul ahead.
1010		We come across Endrass.[8] A brief situation report via megaphone then we both resume contact with convoy on the port side.
1059		Outgoing W/T transmission: *Qu. AK 9686 course 30°. U552.*

---

1   This signal was recorded by Kptlt Engelbert Endrass as having been received by *U567* two hours later at 0830, just as Topp was in the final stages of his attack on the *Reuben James*. Since the time of Topp's transmission (0630) is consistent both with *U552*'s position at the time (well south of the attack on *Reuben James*) and the course of the convoy, it must be supposed that either Endrass's recordkeeping is faulty or else *U567*'s timekeeping was different. Whatever the case, it is difficult to equate this signal with the transmission intercepted by USS *Tarbell* at 0525 convoy time (0825 German time) since, apart from the reasons given above, it is extremely unlikely that Topp would have risked betraying his position to send a high-frequency signal during an attack sequence. As stated in the *Background* essay, *Tarbell* had probably detected one of the series of medium-wave beacon signals put out by *U552* to draw other boats to the convoy.

2   The break in the chronological sequence here can be explained by Topp's desire to record the radio signals in unbroken sequence before going on to describe his attack on the convoy.

3   The forty-two vessels of HX156 could hardly be considered to have had a 'numerous' escort. From his side of the convoy Topp could only have seen the USS *Hilary P. Jones* on the port beam, *Reuben James* on the port quarter and possibly *Niblack* astern. *Benson* and *Tarbell* occupied the equivalent positions to *Hilary P. Jones* and *Reuben James* on the starboard side of the convoy.

4   The final printed '0' is crossed out in pencil and a '4' written in its place, presumably to be consistent with the time of 0834 stated in Topp's torpedo report. US sources do not agree on the time *Reuben James* was hit, though the 0535 that can be inferred from *U552*'s log fits in the middle of the range of recorded times.

5   In his torpedo report Topp records the range as 2,500 metres. In the same box, however, he records the torpedo running time at 67 seconds, which equates to approximately 1,000 metres at the 30-knot speed of the G7e torpedo. His assessment of 2,500 metres can therefore be assumed either to be an error or, as is perhaps more likely, to refer to the range originally entered into the *Vorhaltrechner* (torpedo data computer) which then automatically generated a succession of adjustments to target range and inclination until the torpedo was launched. As was common practice in night attacks on the surface, the torpedoes were fired not by Topp himself but by his First Watch Officer Siegfried Koitschka who went on to sink the USS *Buck* (**90**) and the British *LCT 553* (**G62**) when in command of *U616*.

6   *U552*'s torpedo report also states that both torpedoes hit but in a post-war recollection of the incident Topp ceded that only one did. The fact that the torpedo in question almost certainly triggered a secondary detonation of the forward magazine may account for this error. The US Navy Board of Investigation found that thirty survivors attributed the loss of the ship to a single detonation and thirteen to two.

7   Topp's torpedo report adds several details to his succinct log entry. The two G7e torpedoes were fired with an angle of spread of 2.2 degrees, estimating *Reuben James*'s speed to be 8 knots whereas the US Navy assumed it to have been that of the convoy: 8.8 knots. Topp records the first striking near the bridge and the second detonating aft, though later admitted that only one torpedo had hit (see n. 6).

8   Kptlt Engelbert Endrass (see **8** and **17**), here in command of *U567* which had made contact with the convoy thanks to *U552*'s beacon signals; see n. 1. Friends before the war and famously inseparable during it when not on patrol, Topp and Endrass were known in St-Nazaire as Castor and Pollux after the twins of Greek mythology. Endrass was lost with *U567* in December 1941 (see **43**) and later in the war Topp composed a memoir of him whose title says it all: 'Castor Mourns Pollux: In Memoriam Engelbert Endrass'.

The sinking

Having reviewed a large body of witness and survivor testimonies, the Board of Investigation held at Hvalfjörður on 3 and 4 November 1941 determined that *Reuben James* had suffered 'one or more violent explosions accompanied by a lurid orange flame, and a high column of black smoke visible for several minutes at some miles'. Although no conclusion was reached on the matter, it is now generally accepted that the sheet of flame seen amidships marked the detonation of the forward magazine. Its effect was to sever the ship in two between No. 3 and No. 4 stacks, Kptlt Topp recalling the fore part 'flying into the air amidst a black explosion cloud'. The fore part sank within a matter of seconds taking most of the ship's officers with it, but the stern section was kept afloat while the forward engine-room bulkhead held, the wreck awash as far aft as the after deck house. At around 0540 the 'ship's stern lifted high – almost straight up in the air, and then slid quickly under, bow first', the sea boiling with the detonation of her depth charges. Within six or seven minutes of being torpedoed the stern section of the 'Rube' was following her bows to the bottom of the Atlantic.

Half a dozen US merchantmen had been lost since the beginning of the war but the sinking of the *Reuben James* had an effect on the United States not equalled by any incident before Pearl Harbor. While there was no question of a declaration of war, the event eased the transfer of the US Coast Guard to naval control on 1 November and prompted both the arming of merchantmen and the lifting of the restrictions that had hitherto denied European waters to American shipping, thereby permitting Lend-Lease goods to be escorted directly to British ports. Within two weeks of the sinking Congress and the Senate had repealed the 1939 Neutrality Act and America found herself on the brink of war with Germany. As significant was the strength of feeling stirred up by the folk ballad composed by Woody Guthrie under the title 'The Sinking of the *Reuben James*', and within a year a destroyer escort bearing the name had been laid down at Norfolk Navy Yard. From an operational standpoint it was obvious that an escort not patrolling station (zigzagging) was needlessly exposed to submarine attack, though as Capt. Louis E. Denfeld, Chief of Staff of the Atlantic Fleet, put it 'the question of patrolling stations at night is a difficult one as it frequently involves the use of extra fuel which can ill be spared'. Additional fuel tanks were fitted in older destroyers, the US Navy having assumed a more vigorous posture in the Atlantic by the time hostilities were formally opened with Germany on 11 December 1941.

Well debriefed, Topp escaped official censure from B.d.U. Though very unfortunate, no U-boat commander could be expected to identify as American a vessel that was not only escorting a UK-bound convoy blacked out at night, but belonged to a class of ship no less than fifty units of which had been transferred to Britain in September 1940. Besides, Hitler was in bellicose mood in the first months of the war against Russia and the markedly unconciliatory line followed by the German Chancellery on the sinking of the *Reuben James* reflects intense irritation with a stance that was correctly perceived as anything but neutral. If there were no attacks on convoys in the Western Atlantic in November 1941 this therefore owed less to German embarrassment than to the exigencies of war as U-boats were ordered to the Mediterranean theatre – much to Dönitz's disgust. In private, however, the incident was a source of considerable dismay, not least to Topp who was keenly aware of 'how politically explosive the sinking of the destroyer might become'. Indeed, his post-war memoirs and correspondence reveal his difficulty reconciling the fact that he 'felt no qualms whatsoever as far as international law was concerned' with his remorse at having accounted for so many lives from what was technically a non-combatant nation. Nor did the passage of time do anything to assuage that sentiment, the incident kept alive in post-war research and discussions with American veterans which troubled Topp to the end of his days: 'The passing of decades does not cushion anything. These images continue to haunt me; they take away my sleep.'

Fate of the crew

The experience of Fireman 2/c Parmie G. Appleton, one of only two men to survive from the fore part of the ship, goes some way to explaining the magnitude of the event that overtook the *Reuben James*:

> I was thrown off my feet by the terrific blast of the explosion. My head hit the overhead and I fell back and bounced off the bulkhead and back toward the wheel. Just as I grabbed the wheel the second explosion occurred, which ripped open the overhead of the bridge and threw me out through the opening in the overhead. While I was in the air I could see that the ship was broken in half and No. 1 stack falling toward the port side. I landed in the water on the starboard side of the forecastle, about 10ft from the ship abreast of the capstan.

The other survivor from this section, Coxswain Gerald J. Delisle, was dragged under while clinging to the signal halliards and reached the surface only with the greatest difficulty. A number of those in the engine room close to the point at which *Reuben James* broke in two found themselves 'covered from head to foot by a fuel oil shower' as the tanks ruptured but still lived to tell the tale. One was Shipfitter 1/c Fred Zapasnik:

> I then tried to make my way up the ladder to reach the maindeck, but a torrent of water cascaded down the hatch and knocked me down to the floorplates. When it stopped, I rushed up the ladder and, since it was still dark, I could not see what had happened. After my eyes adjusted to the darkness, I was horrified to see that there wasn't anything left of the ship forward of the fourth stack, which was lying across the deck right in front of me.

With the ship's whaler hopelessly shattered and the gig held fast, there was little those who congregated on deck could do to help themselves before deck fires and then the foundering of the stern section drove them into waters thick with oil. Only a few rafts were got away, and men either clambered into these or clutched the life ropes, vomiting and choking on fuel oil. Others succumbed to injuries and burns, or were claimed by the depth charges that now began to explode with murderous effect. Due to the safety forks being tied to the racks, two depth charges armed themselves as they rolled off when the stern section stood up prior to the final plunge. The ensuing carnage was witnessed by the approaching USS *Niblack*, whose Lt Cdr Griffith B. Coale recalled 'two grunting jolts' which tossed 'debris and men into the air'. Engine-Room Mate 2/c Thomas P. Turnbull, who suffered severe abdominal injuries, was even closer:

> Then the first depth charge exploded, then I rose up in the air, out of the water and went right down again. The explosion of the first depth charge rendered me almost unconscious. I was just breaking through the surface when the second depth charge went off. The explosion of the 2nd depth

Topp composes a signal in his cabin aboard *U552* in October 1941, the month he sank the *Reuben James*. The opened copy of Gröner's recognition manual of merchant shipping beside him leaves little doubt as to the subject of the signal. Not too much should be made of the portrait of Hitler on the bulkhead, which was standard U-boat issue. *BK*

charge threw me high into the air, I was on the edge of the spout caused by the 2nd explosion. I was unconscious momentarily and then I found myself swimming.

Rafts were blasted from the water and flipped over as splinters claimed further lives. For those who survived it was like 'being drug through hell by the devil himself'. *Niblack* was soon joined at the scene by *Hilary P. Jones* but 'rescue operations were hampered by the large amount of oil on the water, the presence of the submarine, darkness, and the hysterical and shocked condition of survivors'. The rescue was also interrupted by fears that the perpetrator was still lurking (not borne out by the log) and the recovery of forty-seven men was surprisingly high under the circumstances. Of these one man was found to be dead and another succumbed in the *Niblack* two days later leaving forty-five survivors. Though there are reports of a third survivor perishing after being landed in Reykjavik this is not corroborated in official records. There was not a single officer survivor.

A number of issues were highlighted in the submissions made to the Board of Investigation. Chief among them was the heavy loss of life to depth charges, estimated in one source to have been as many as fifty men. Where the survivors were concerned, *Niblack*'s medical personnel observed a high incidence of 'unique and similar abdominal injuries', their severity varying with the victim's proximity to the blast. Another observation from the *Niblack* was that, with two exceptions, 'every man who left his raft and struck out for the ship was lost by drowning'. A number of survivors questioned the suitability of a vessel of *Reuben James*'s vintage for convoy duty, a sentiment with which several thousand Allied sailors would have been in wholehearted agreement. In his submission to the Board, Fireman 2/c Roy V. Bush

spoke for many when he asserted that 'I hope in the future I never get duty on a four-stacker destroyer again because they are regular death traps'. His lost shipmates – 100 in official records though secondary sources vary considerably on this point – are remembered on a memorial overlooking Casco Bay near Portland, Maine.

U552 and Erich Topp

Built by Blohm & Voss at Hamburg and commissioned in December 1940, the famous 'red devil' boat *U552* made fifteen frontline patrols in the North Atlantic during which thirty-two ships were sunk for a total of over 160,000 tons. All but two of these were accounted for during the tenure of her first commander Oblt.z.S. Erich Topp whose prodigious success saw him promoted Kapitänleutnant (September 1941), Korvettenkapitän (August 1942) and eventually Fregattenkapitän (December 1944). Topp's substantial haul off the US coast in early 1942 earnt him the Oak Leaves (April 1942) and then the Swords (August 1942) to the Knight's Cross he had been awarded in June 1941. In September 1942 Topp was assigned to training duties ashore, taking command of the 27th *U-Flottille* (where new crews received tactical instruction) until August 1944. Topp was subsequently involved in the commissioning of the new Type-XXI boats whose battle instructions he wrote before himself taking command of *U3010* in March 1945 and *U2513* the following month. The end of the war found him at sea in *U2513*, which he surrendered in Norway as the third most successful U-boat commander of the war having sunk nearly 200,000 tons of enemy shipping. After periods in captivity and then in civilian life Topp joined the Bundesmarine in 1958, retiring with the rank of Konteradmiral in December 1969 to become an industrial consultant. In 1990 he published one of the most philosophical and reflective accounts of the U-boat war ever written (see *Sources*). He died in December 2005 at the age of ninety-one.

Between September 1942 and April 1944 *U552* undertook another five patrols under Kptlt Klaus Popp, but only the first of these enjoyed any success, HM anti-submarine trawler *Alouette* being accounted for off Portugal in September 1942 (**G35**) and the freighter *Wallsend* off Cape Verde in December. In April 1944 *U552* joined the 22nd *U-Flottille* at Gotenhafen where she served as a training boat until transferred to Wilhelmshaven late in the war, being scuttled there on 2 May 1945.

Sources

Admiralty, *Convoy HX156* (NHB, HX convoys box)

Navy Department, Office of the Judge Advocate General, *Board of Investigation into the Sinking of the USS* Reuben James (NHC, Box 667)

—, Office of Naval Records and Library, *Action Reports: Report of Commander Task Unit 4.1.3 Following the Sinking of USS* Reuben James (NA, RG 38, Series 023, 11/3/41, and Series 03, 2/10/42, Box 82, 370/44/20/3; also in NHC, Box 667)

—, Office of the Chief of Naval Operations, Division of Naval History, *USS* Reuben James *(DD 245)* (NHC, Box 667)

—, Bureau of Naval Personnel, Casualty lists for USS *Reuben James* (NA, RG 24, 3(A1))

Topp, Erich, letter to Jack Aloes, 20 January 1987 (manuscript, DUBMA, *U552* folder)

Coale, Lt Cdr Griffith B., *North Atlantic Patrol: The Log of a Seagoing Artist* (New York: Farrar & Rinehart, 1942); see also:

http://www.electricedge.com/griff/nap/nappage3.htm
http://www.electricedge.com/griff/nap/nappage4.htm
DANFS, VI, p. 85; also on:
http://www.history.navy.mil/danfs/r5/reuben_james-i.htm
Friedman, Norman, *US Destroyers: An Illustrated Design History* (2nd edn, Annapolis, Md.: Naval Institute Press, 2004)
Kurowski, Frank, *Jaeger der Sieben Meere: Die Berühmtesten U-Boot-Kommandanten des II. Weltkriegs* (Stuttgart: Motorbuch Verlag, 1994)
Morison, *United States Naval Operations*, I, p. 94
Parkin, Robert Sinclair, *Blood on the Sea: American Destroyers Lost in World War II* (New York: Sarpedon, 1995)

Roscoe, *US Destroyer Operations*, pp. 39–40
Topp, Erich, *The Odyssey of a U-Boat Commander*, trans. Eric C. Rust (Westport, Conn.: Praeger, 1992)
Vause, Jordan, *Wolf: U-Boat Commanders in World War II* (Annapolis, Md.: Naval Institute Press, 1997)

Website devoted to *U552*: http://www.u552.de/
Oral history and memoir of Torpedoman 3/c Robert J. Howard (survivor): http://www.aarp.org/fun/radio/pt_postscript/reuben_james_survivor.html [defunct]
http://www.ussholder.com/DD819-pas1-Howard.html

39   HMS *ARK ROYAL*
Capt. L. E. H. Maund, CBE RN
Sunk by *U81* (Type VIIC), Kptlt Friedrich Guggenberger, 13–14 November 1941
Western Mediterranean, 35 nm E of Gibraltar

Ark Royal seen at the time of her commissioning in November 1938. She played a key role in demonstrating the offensive capabilities of air power afloat.
Wright & Logan

Theatre	Mediterranean (Map 3)	*Displacement*	22,000 tons
Coordinates (of attack)	36° 03' N, 04° 45' W	*Dimensions*	800' × 94.75' × 22.75'
Kriegsmarine code (of attack)	Quadrat CG 9652	*Armour*	4.5" belt; 2.5–3.5" horizontal; 1.5–2.5" bulkheads
U-boat timekeeping differential	+1 hour	*Maximum speed*	30.75 knots
Fatalities 1 *Survivors* 1,748		*Armament*	16 × 4.5" DP; 50 × 40 mm AA; 32 × .5" AA
		Air wing	60 aircraft (Swordfish and Skuas) served by two lifts and three catapults

Career

Although the Royal Navy had pioneered the aircraft carrier concept during the First World War, HMS *Ark Royal* was only its second vessel to be designed as such from the keel up. Approved under the 1934 estimates, she was laid down at Cammell Laird of Birkenhead on 16 September 1935, launched in April 1937 and completed in December of the following year. The design incorporated a number of innovations that were to become standard in British carrier construction, including closed hangars on two levels forming part of the hull structure, an enclosed 'hurricane' bow and a pronounced overhang aft that added almost eighty feet to the ship's waterline length. She was also the first

capital ship in the Royal Navy in which extensive use was made of welding. The result was a capable and influential design though one which would see considerable improvement in subsequent classes.

Ark Royal commissioned with a Portsmouth crew in November 1938 and received her first aircraft in January 1939. She was sent to the Mediterranean to work up before joining the Home Fleet in British waters. On the outbreak of war she and *Courageous* (1) were deployed in 'Hunter Killer' groups to seek out and destroy U-boats in the Western and North-Western Approaches. The first indication that this tactic might prove disastrous came when *Ark Royal* was attacked by *U39* off St Kilda on 14 September. The subsequent destruction of

U39 by *Ark Royal*'s escort after the torpedoes exploded in her wake preserved the Navy's faith in the tactic and it was not until *Courageous* was sunk with heavy loss of life on the 17th that carriers were put to more constructive use. On 26 September *Ark Royal* was given a first taste of what she would eventually mete out when the Home Fleet was bombed in the North Sea by Junkers 88s having sortied to cover the rescue of HMS/m *Spearfish* (**14**). *Ark Royal* was near-missed by a 2,000-pound bomb but Dr Goebbels claimed a sinking in a propaganda stroke he would soon regret. 'Where is the *Ark Royal*?' asked Lord Haw-Haw in his broadcasts from Berlin. Though the Prime Minister Neville Chamberlain was obliged to confirm *Ark Royal*'s continued existence to Parliament, her subsequent exploits created amusement in Britain, damaged Goebbels' credibility and apparently brought Leutnant Adolf Francke, who had been awarded the Iron Cross for sinking her, to the brink of suicide.

Between October 1939 and February 1940 *Ark Royal* operated with the battlecruiser *Renown* as part of Force K against German raiders and supply ships in the South Atlantic. In April the German attack on Scandinavia threw her into the Norwegian Campaign during which Blackburn Skuas of her air wing (though flying from Hatston in the Orkneys) bombed and sank the German light cruiser *Königsberg* in Bergen harbour, the first instance of a major vessel succumbing to air attack. After the evacuation of Norway *Ark Royal* sailed south to Gibraltar where she joined Force H under Vice-Admiral Sir James Somerville at the end of June. She participated in the attack on the French fleet at Mers-el-Kebir on 4 July and again on the 7th when her Swordfish wrecked the beached battlecruiser *Dunkerque*. Over the next few months *Ark Royal* spearheaded Somerville's frequent incursions into the Western Mediterranean, attacking Italian air bases and covering supply convoys to Malta and Alexandria, one of which led to the inconclusive battle of Cape Spartivento on 27 November. On 9 February 1941 Force H carried out an audacious air and sea bombardment of Genoa, La Spezia and Livorno which inflicted heavy damage on Italian shore installations. Nor were 'the Ark's' activities confined to the Mediterranean. Already in September 1940 she had participated in Operation MENACE, the abortive attack on Dakar in Vichy-held Senegal, and in March 1941 her reconnaissance aircraft sighted the battlecruisers *Scharnhorst* and *Gneisenau* in the Atlantic though no interception could be made and Admiral Günther Lütjens reached Brest on the 22nd. When *Ark Royal*'s aircraft met Lütjens again two months later the stage was set for her greatest exploit: the attack on the battleship *Bismarck* on 26 May. Following an afternoon of extraordinary confusion during which her Swordfish came close

to sinking the cruiser *Sheffield*, two torpedo hits were registered on the *Bismarck* including one which jammed her rudders and left her unmanoeuvrable. When *Bismarck* died under a withering fire the following morning it was *Ark Royal* that the Home Fleet had to thank for delivering her into their hands. Convoy and flying-off operations continued in the Mediterranean through the summer and autumn of 1941, and it was while returning from one of these that *Ark Royal*'s remarkable career came to an end.

Along with *Illustrious* and her sisters, HMS *Ark Royal* was the first carrier to demonstrate the offensive capabilities of air power afloat. Her place in naval history is assured.

Background of the attack

On 10 November 1941 Force H, consisting of the battleship *Malaya* (wearing the flag of Vice-Admiral Sir James Somerville), the carriers *Ark Royal* and *Argus*, the cruiser *Hermione* (**63**) and seven destroyers, sailed from Gibraltar and headed eastward into the Mediterranean to carry out Operation PERPETUAL. Their mission was a familiar one for Force H: to fly off thirty-seven Hurricane fighters and seven Blenheim medium bombers for the defence of Malta. Having accomplished this task on the 12th Force H turned for home under the eyes of shadowing Italian aircraft. Early on the 13th Somerville received reports of enemy submarine activity east of Gibraltar, whereupon six Swordfish were flown off from *Ark Royal* to sweep the area ahead of the force. The reports were accurate. On the night of 11–12 November the first two boats of the *Arnauld* group, *U81* (Kptlt Friedrich Guggenberger) and *U205* (Kptlt Franz-Georg Reschke; see **63**), had forced the Straits of Gibraltar and entered the Mediterranean. Late on the 12th B.d.U. alerted the newcomers to the movements of Force H on the basis of Italian aerial reconnaissance. Within a few hours Reschke had Force H in his sights north of Oran, firing three torpedoes at *Ark Royal* in the early hours of the 13th. Hits were recorded in his war diary but the closest *U205* came was the detonation of a torpedo in the wake of the destroyer *Legion*. However, the *Arnauld* group had not finished with Force H and *U81*'s moment came as Somerville's ships neared Gibraltar that afternoon. Having observed the movements of the force for just over an hour Guggenberger fired a spread of four torpedoes at *Malaya* from a range logged at 3,000 to 4,000 metres. Although he had underestimated the range and above all the speed of the force by two knots, Guggenberger's spread nonetheless registered a hit on *Ark Royal* which was not only stationed well astern of his intended target but had just turned into the wind to land aircraft.

War Diary of *U81*, patrol of 4 November–10 December 1941: PG 30075a, NHB, reel 1,074, pp. 615–6

Date, time	Details of position, wind, weather, sea, light, visibility, moonlight, etc.	Incidents
12.xi		
2220	Wind W 4, sea 3, short swell, clear night with good visibility	We surface. Incoming W/T transmission: *To . . . and Guggenberger.*[1] *At 1500 Italian air reconnaissance reports English group consisting of battleship, aircraft carriers, cruisers and destroyers in Qu. AD 9148 or 9412.*[2]

1   The blank space here probably refers to Kptlt Franz-Georg Reschke of *U205* (see **63**) which had accompanied *U81* into the Mediterranean thirty-six hours earlier.

2   Guggenberger no doubt ignored the letters AD (the Denmark Strait off Iceland), realising that CH coordinates were intended, thereby indicating that Force

Course 270 degrees, speed approximately 15 knots.
Incoming W/T transmission: *To . . . Guggenberger.*[1] *Return of English group expected north of Qu. CG 9593. Guggenberger to occupy same attack area as Reschke.*

2400	[Qu.] CH 7751, wind W 5, sea 4, moderate swell, almost overcast, dark night, 1,011 mb	I intend to head northwards and as far west as possible. The closer we are to Gibraltar the better our chance of having a clear sight of a shot.

13.xi · *Guggenberger* ·

0400	[Qu.] CH 7459, wind NW 3–4, sea 3, moderate swell, partially overcast, good visibility, 1,012 mb	The prevailing sea conditions won't allow us to attain higher speeds.
0506		Incoming W/T transmission from Reschke: *English force in Qu. [CG] 7623, westerly course.*[3]
0800	[Qu.] CH 7445, wind NW 3, sporadic high clouds, good visibility	At speed of 16 knots the boat should intercept the group at around 1700.
0824 to 1201		Test dive and wholly essential repairs to the diesel-reverse mechanism, exhaust pipe and Junkers compressors.
1200	[Qu.] CG 9666	Day's run: surface 92.2 nm, submerged 21.7 nm = 113.9 nm
1212		Alarm due to aircraft. Boat now positioned some 25 nm off Gibraltar.
Around 1330		English torpedo boat in sight, outward bound from Gibraltar heading east, passes boat to the south and then turns about. We alter course to the south.
Around 1515		A flying boat in sight to the south-east. She is flying in circles. Shortly afterwards a number of aircraft in sight, fighters for the most part.
1550		Force of English warships in sight at a bearing of 120°. Alarm!
1600	[Qu.] CG 9652, wind S 5, sea 1–2, good visibility	English group consists of one battleship of the Revenge or Malaya class, an aircraft carrier of the Ark Royal class, the carrier *Furious*, three or four large destroyers of the very latest design and a further three destroyers.[4]
		Group is on a westerly course, and steering in line ahead with a 40-degree stagger to port *in the order set out above.*[5] Every 15 minutes or so they make a turn of up to 50°. The destroyers are drawn up in screen formation against U-boat attack, with one stationed 8,000 m on the group's starboard bow, presumably as distant lookout. Around 15–20 aircraft are circling the group at an altitude of about 100 m – float planes as outer escort, wheeled aircraft flying in formations of three and two providing immediate cover.
1636	[Qu.] CG 9655	A spread of four torpedoes fired between the distant and close escorts at the English battleship, point of aim 10 m from the bows, inclination 82°, bows right, enemy speed 16 knots, range 3,000–4,000 m, width of spread 150 m, depth 5 m.
		On firing boat threatens to breach the surface.[6] I order all men to the bows of the boat and dive to T=,5,35 m [*sic*] at high speed.[7] Because of the danger of aircraft I then dive to T = 40 m.[8]
		After 6 min. 06 sec. a hit (very powerful detonation) against the battleship. After 7 min. 43 sec. we hear another torpedo detonation, probably against one of the port-side destroyers, or the Ark

---

H was north of Algiers at the time the message was sent. See HMS *Gurkha* (**46**) for similar plotting errors in the Mediterranean. In addition, it must be supposed that the two middle digits of one or other positional square (i.e. 14 and 41) have been erroneously transposed since CH 9148 and CH 9412 are many miles apart.

3 Thereby informing Guggenberger that Force H was still the best part of 200 miles east of Gibraltar.

4 Though the battleship was indeed *Malaya* this vessel in fact belonged to the Queen Elizabeth class. Guggenberger appears to have mistaken *Argus* for the carrier *Furious*. The anti-aircraft cruiser *Hermione* (**63**) he seems not to have spotted.

5 Manuscript addition in pen by Guggenberger.

6 The simultaneous firing of all four bow torpedoes entailed the lightening of the bows by 6,432 kilograms (nearly 6½ tons) in a matter of seconds, with dramatic consequences for the boat's stability. The trim was best restored by flooding the tanks beneath the torpedo tubes in combination with the less sophisticated expedient of sending men to the forward compartments. *U81* evidently managed to maintain her trim better than *U331* on the 25th which surfaced on firing a similar spread at HMS *Barham* (**41**) and narrowly escaped being rammed and sunk.

7 An apparent error in redaction makes it unclear what data Guggenberger is recording here but if the intent was to record T = 35 metres then this might equate to a depth of 175 metres (574 feet). For a full discussion of the 'T =' notation, see Reading the *Kriegstagebücher*, pp. xxxvii.

8 Possibly 180 metres (591 feet); see n. 7.

Date, time	Details of position, wind, weather, sea, light, visibility, moonlight, etc.	Incidents
		Royal-class carrier.[9] Range of vessel for second hit would have been around 6,500 m allowing for the gradual deceleration of the Eto.[10]
	Western Mediterranean	Dive to T = 60 m.[11] Gyroscope and cooler turned off, lighting power reduced to 90 volts, depth gauge dials switched off, outer vents secured. We go down to T = 65 m, later back up to T = 50 m, withdraw to north-east.[12]
1725–2220		162 depth charges counted from three destroyers, no adverse effects. Depth charges gradually fade astern. We head north.
2222	Wind SW 1, sea 0, partially covered, dark night, good visibility	Surfaced. Destroyers are roughly 8,000–10,000 m astern. Nothing in sight apart from lighthouses on the Spanish coast. Absolutely no sign of the steamer or escort that hydrophone operator has identified as being very close to us. We head off to the north-east at slow speed. Strong sea phosphorescence.

↗
14.xi

| 2224 | | Incoming W/T transmission: *To Reschke and Guggenberger: 'Reuter' [sic] reports sinking of* Ark Royal. *Please provide confirmation of success or any other observations.* |

↗
15.xi

| 0553 | | Outgoing W/T transmission: *From U81: 13 November 1636, spread of four at battleship,* Ark Royal, Furious. *First hit probably*[13] *on battleship, second hit but target uncertain. Qu. [CG] 7645.*[14] |

↗

| 2000 | | From Wehrmacht report as well as other reports we learn that the first hit on 13 November left *Malaya* crippled while *Ark Royal* was sunk by the second.[15] Enemy speed was apparently 17 knots. |

---

9 Guggenberger had dived by this time so his assertion in the previous sentence that he had hit *Malaya* was inference, not observation. The times recorded for these detonations place the victim much further away than the 3,000–4,000 metres he had calculated for *Malaya*. Although he had significantly underestimated the range, it was his miscalculation of target speed by two knots that caused *U81*'s salvo to pass well astern of *Malaya* and into *Ark Royal*'s path. Moreover, despite Guggenberger's assertion to the contrary, a comparison of British and German sources suggests that it was the first torpedo detonation which marked the hit on *Ark Royal* at a range in excess of 5,000 metres, the second probably doing so against the seabed at the end of the 6,500-metre run acknowledged in the following sentence. It should be added that Guggenberger's reference to 'the Ark Royal-class carrier' is an *a posteriori* addition to the log since he only considered the possibility of having hit this vessel once news reached him on the 14th that Reuters had reported her sinking.

10 'Eto' is Kriegsmarine shorthand for the electric G7e torpedo which would run at a constant 30 knots for 5,000 metres (some six minutes into its run), gradually losing speed thereafter.

11 Possibly 200 metres (656 feet); see n. 7.

12 Possibly 205 metres (673 feet) and 190 metres (623 feet) respectively; see n. 7.

13 Manuscript addition in pen by Guggenberger.

14 Despite his claims, Guggenberger had as the log shows in fact targetted only *Malaya*; the addition of *Ark Royal* can no doubt be attributed to B.d.U.'s signal of 2224 on the 14th; see n. 9.

15 For all Guggenberger's surprise, this Wehrmacht radio report was no more than an extrapolation of his signal of 0553.

The sinking

The Board of Enquiry which followed the loss of *Ark Royal* learnt of an 'almighty explosion' on the starboard side abreast the bridge at precisely 1541. Since neither U-boat nor torpedo tracks were ever sighted it was initially believed that the bomb room had been the scene of an internal explosion. This, however, was dismissed in Capt. Maund's report which stated that 'it is unlikely that an internal explosion could have caused a column of water to rise up and wreck the starboard sea boat, as actually happened'. Uncertainty there may have been but Guggenberger's torpedo had done damage sufficient to sink the ship. The concussion caused her to whip so violently that aircraft parked at the fore end of the flight deck were repeatedly jolted into the air. However, that was the least of it. *Ark Royal* had been struck while the ship was heeled over during a rapid turn to port, the torpedo detonating beneath the protection system and causing extensive damage along more than 120 feet of hull. The explosion flooded the Starboard Boiler Room, blew open the bomb lift doors beneath the bridge and buckled many yards of armour plating. Also affected were the Damage Control headquarters and the main switchboard where the circuit-breakers on the ship's electrical ring main had been activated by the concussion but could not be reset once the compartment flooded. Lighting therefore failed and in the absence of diesel generators the crew had for many hours to perform damage control with just thirty-five battery-operated lanterns for the entire ship.

Ark Royal immediately assumed a ten-degree list to starboard which within three minutes had increased to twelve degrees as she ploughed on at eighteen knots, worsening the damage and flooding. With the telephone system out of action and the engine room

Legion stands by to take off the majority of *Ark Royal*'s ship's company less than an hour after she was hit by a torpedo from *U81*. *IWM*

The *Ark Royal*'s flight deck on the afternoon of 13 November. Part of her air wing of Swordfish torpedo bombers can be seen parked forward. A few hours later they were pitched into the Mediterranean when she capsized. *BfZ*

telegraphs jammed, Capt. Maund was obliged to make his way down to the main engine room control platform in order to put the turbines to half astern and take measures to halt the list by counter-flooding and pumping oil to the port side. However, the implementation of these and subsequent measures was hampered by lack of light and a breakdown in communication facilities, which required orders to be transmitted by chains of messengers between the flight deck (where Maund now set up his control centre) and the main control platform, and between the latter and its two adjacent engine rooms. But of far greater consequence to the survival of the ship was the flooding of the Starboard Boiler Room which was abandoned before the watertight hatches in the fan intakes above it had been fully closed off. This not only deprived the Starboard Engine Room of steam power but stilled the dynamos upon which the main pumps in that sector of the ship depended. This would not in itself have proved decisive except that, owing to the fact that the partitioning did not extend far enough up the funnel casing, the flooding of the starboard uptake also implied the flooding of the adjacent ones as the ship continued her list to starboard. The result of this major design fault was that the Port and Centre Boiler Rooms beneath the uptakes flooded as well, eventually cutting power to the entire ship and so defeating all efforts to save her. But this *dénouement* lay hours in the future. Within twenty minutes of the attack the list had increased to seventeen degrees and Maund, fearing that she might capsize at any moment, passed the order for all those not regarded as essential to the survival of the ship to abandon her. At around 1600 the destroyer *Legion* was ordered alongside and over the next three-quarters of an hour 1,487 men – eighty-five per cent of the ship's company – made their way to safety over the port side. The great majority of these were indeed of no use to the damage-control effort but among them were many technical ratings who could have restored electrical power at a critical juncture in the fight to save her. By the time eighty engine-room, electrical and shipwright specialists began reboarding from the destroyer *Laforey* at 2140 it was too late.

Indeed, the crew had been fighting a losing battle for some time. By 1700 the Centre Boiler Room was flooded and the list was depriving the Port Boiler Room of the suction needed to draw in sufficient feed water to keep steam up, which in turn deprived the ship of electrical

power for pumps, ventilation and auxiliary lighting. Having been reduced to fourteen degrees the list now slid back to seventeen as *Laforey* came alongside with electrical leads to restore power and forty tons of feed water to get up steam and resume pumping. None of this would have been necessary had *Ark Royal* been provided with diesel-powered generators and pumps operating independently of the ship's steam propulsion plant. Nor, indeed, would it have been so had the port boiler and engine rooms been flooded immediately after the torpedo hit, and in later years it was standard in British damage-control training to show how doing so would have allowed *Ark Royal* to be righted and brought safely into Gibraltar. By the time this measure came to be considered the ship was already so flooded that it would have caused her to founder immediately. And so *Ark Royal* was left to struggle against her fate. The fleet tug *St Day*, sent out from Gibraltar, made a 'pitiable exhibition' of taking the ship in tow and it was 2035 before the salvage tug *Thames* had her under way at two knots, battling against the powerful eastward current. Enough steam had been raised in the Port Boiler Room to get two dynamos working by 2150 but the distribution of electric power took rather longer than expected once *Laforey* had cast off and left *Ark Royal* to her own resources. By the early hours of the 14th a motley assortment of pumps (including equipment transferred or operated from *Hermione* and *Laforey*) had brought the list back to fourteen degrees – a considerable achievement in view of the brutal conditions prevailing in the unventilated engine spaces – while *St Day* had returned to the fray and joined *Thames* in the effort to bring *Ark Royal* in. If these developments gave Capt. Maund grounds for hoping that his ship might be saved he was soon to be disappointed. At around 0200 smoke and steam began to emerge from the Port Boiler Room which had soon to be abandoned. With the flooding of the last funnel uptake the furnace gases had no means of escape except into the boiler room itself. As this space became untenable *Ark Royal* lost the last of her steam power. Attempts by *Laforey* and the corvette *Pentstemon* to provide pumps and electrical power were defeated by the progressive flooding of the ship which by 0400 was listing to twenty-seven degrees. Informed by the Chief Engineer, Cdr (E) Hugh Dixon, that there was no more to be done, Maund gave the order to abandon ship and 250 men slid down ropes onto *St Day*. The remainder now came up from below and by 0430 the last man was over the side. *Ark Royal* did not sink until 0610, capsizing first to forty-five degrees and then hanging with the flight deck vertical with the water once the island reached the sea. She then rolled over and sank 14½ hours after being struck. Among those looking on was the commander of Force H, Admiral Sir James Somerville:

> It was the blackest of days when I saw my poor Ark sink at 6 a.m. this morning. Just a blur in the dark as she lay on her side for some time and then slowly, slowly she turned over like a tired and wounded ship going to sleep . . . I am rather cut up about this because I was so proud and so fond of my Ark.

Apart from the Board of Enquiry a court-martial was convened in February 1942 to try Capt. Maund on a charge of negligence. He was found guilty on two counts, one of failing to ensure that properly constituted damage-control parties had remained on board after the general evacuation, and another of failing to ensure that the ship was in an adequate state of readiness to deal with possible damage. He completed his career in a succession of shore appointments.

It has been written of the sinking of *Ark Royal* that 'everything went wrong' and it is hard to disagree with that verdict. In the final analysis the ship was lost due to major design faults, inadequate damage-control procedures and equipment, premature abandonment and unusually severe internal damage. These factors together permitted a major unit of great prestige to succumb to a single torpedo within sight of Gibraltar. From the German perspective the sinking of *Ark Royal*, reported by Reuters on the 14th, was greeted with disbelief in *U81* but jubilation at the Naval High Command. Guggenberger, convinced that his attack had been delivered against *Malaya*, reportedly declared to his First Watch Officer, Oblt.z.S. Johann-Otto Krieg, that 'This is the equivalent to giving birth whilst still a virgin!' when passed B.d.U.'s signal of 2224 on the 14th (see above). For the High Command, meanwhile, it came as a distinct relief to have finally disposed of the Royal Navy's prize carrier two years after Dr Goebbels had first reported her sinking. Although B.d.U. awarded Guggenberger the Knight's Cross together with its 'highest recognition' for the 'calm, surety and skill' with which he had seized his opportunity, the latter must also be considered extremely fortunate for he had completely missed his intended target.

In December 2002 the wreck of the *Ark Royal* was discovered at a depth of 2,950 feet some thirty miles east of Gibraltar – rather further from the Rock than estimated by the Admiralty (twenty-two miles) and evidence of how little progress she had made in the hours after the attack. The depth at which she sank was insufficient to permit the ship to right herself during the descent and the hull struck the seabed on its port side. A 65-foot (20-metre) section of the bow was severed from the hull and came to rest upside down south of the main section. Lying nearby are the remains of the funnel and bridge structure together with an extensive debris field including the remains of numerous aircraft.

Fate of the crew

The torpedo strike immediately plunged *Ark Royal* into darkness, causing much confusion as men responded to the call for Action Stations passed by bugle and word of mouth. There was no panic, however, and indeed there appears to have been a widespread confidence that this was just another incident 'the Ark' would take in her stride. The order to abandon ship, issued shortly after 1600 on the 13th, was therefore greeted with some disbelief. HMS *Legion* was ordered to close on the port side aft and a majority of the ship's company disembarked, some leaping onto hammocks arranged on the fo'c's'le, others using lines rigged from *Ark Royal*. Among the rescued were the ship's cats while owners of mess deck canaries brought their cages up on deck and liberated the occupants. Three of the ship's boats and a number of floats and dinghies were also slipped but were not much used. Overall, the evacuation seems to have been a high-spirited affair, so much so that Capt. Maund had recourse to a whistle to obtain silence. As Maund commented later, 'it was certainly not a time for a picnic as they seemed to think' though a number of men took the opportunity to sink a few bottles of beer before the Mediterranean claimed them. The atmosphere was given a further boost when a heavy suitcase belonging to the Paymaster Commander became snagged while being lowered and plopped into the sea: 'Willing hands attempted a rescue with boat hooks, but their efforts ended when the case burst open showering the contents over a few men swimming in the water. Their surprise equalled ours when the manna from heaven proved to be exactly that, treasury notes! Just how many were diverted to improper use was never discovered.' The request for additional specialist ratings at 1945 brought a flood of volunteers but only eighty men were allowed to return, bringing the total of those still aboard to 250. These were taken off by *St Day* between 0400 and 0430, again without loss. Capt. Maund was the last off.

The death toll from the sinking of *Ark Royal* was a single man, AB Edward Mitchell. However, there is some controversy as to how he met his end, the damage-control report suggesting that one of those in the flooded Damage Control headquarters had been drowned while other sources indicate that he had succumbed while asleep below decks. The rest were able to pay their respects to a much-loved ship in a memorial football match between the *Ark* and the Black Watch garrison at Gibraltar.

U81 and Friedrich Guggenberger

Built by Bremer Vulkan at Vegesack and commissioned in April 1941, *U81*'s first war patrol under Oblt.z.S. (Kptlt from September 1941) Friedrich Guggenberger took her to the Kola coast in the Soviet Arctic in early August, among the very first boats to operate in these waters. Following a patrol in the Atlantic during which two merchantmen were sunk from convoy SC42, *U81* was assigned to the Mediterranean theatre and sailed from Brest on 29 October. The following day she was spotted by a Catalina and a Hudson of the RAF in the Bay of Biscay and subjected to a depth-charge attack which forced her back to Brest. However, her second attempt to gain the Mediterranean not only brought her unscathed through the Straits of Gibraltar on the night of 11–12 November but led thirty-six hours later to arguably the greatest prize of this or any other U-boat: the carrier *Ark Royal*. *U81* made a further thirteen patrols in the Mediterranean during which fourteen vessels were sunk including the Free French anti-submarine trawler *Vikings* in April 1942 (**G27**). Guggenberger was succeeded as commander by Oblt.z.S. Johann-Otto Krieg in December 1942 whose

Guggenberger and the crew of *U81* celebrating their return to La Spezia after a Mediterranean patrol on 4 March 1942. *DUBMA*

eight cruises in the Mediterranean yielded fifteen sinkings. *U81*'s career ended at Pola (now Pula, Croatia) in the Adriatic where she was sunk by US bombers on 9 January 1944 with the loss of two crewmen.

After a spell on the staff of B.d.U. Guggenberger assumed command of the Type-IXC *U513* in May 1943. His first patrol yielded four vessels off Brazil before *U513* was sunk in her turn by a Mariner flying boat of the US Navy on 19 July. Guggenberger was one of seven men picked up by the seaplane tender USS *Barnegat* and spent the rest of the war in a succession of prisoner-of-war camps punctuated by two short-lived bids for freedom. He joined the Bundesmarine in 1956, becoming Deputy Chief of Staff of NATO AFNORTH (Allied Forces, Northern Europe) before retiring in the rank of Konteradmiral in 1972. Guggenberger went missing in unexplained circumstances in a forest near his home town of Erlenbach am Main, north-western Bavaria, in May 1988; his body lay undiscovered until 1990.

Sources

Admiralty, *Wartime Damage to H.M. Ships: Report Concerning the Loss of HMS* Ark Royal (TNA, ADM 199/2066)

—, *Director of Anti-Submarine Warfare: Monthly Reports 1941* (TNA, ADM 199/2058)

—, Report of Second Bucknill Committee relating to loss of HMS *Ark Royal*, 1941–2 (Liddell Hart Centre for Military Archives, King's College, London, Admiral Sir Thomas Binney Collection, 3.5.4)

Dutton, Mechanician Raymond, *What! No Isambard? Or, a Sort of Autobiography* (typescript, IWM, 85/49/1)

Evans, Signalman R. F., Journal (1941–2) (typescript IWM, 04/2/1)

Friend, Lt C., Memoir (typescript, IWM, 86/37/1)

Scott, Surgeon-Cdr W. I. D., Memoir (typescript, IWM, 99/12/1)

Smith, Signalman E., Memoir (1981) (typescript, IWM, P461)

Admiralty, Ark Royal: *The Admiralty Account of Her Achievement* (London: HMSO, 1942)

Apps, Michael, *The Four* Ark Royals (London: William Kimber, 1976)

Arthur, Max, ed., *The Navy: 1939 to the Present Day* (London: Hodder & Stoughton, 1997)

Brown, David K., 'HMS *Ark Royal*. Part 1: Design' in *Warship*, no. 2 (April 1977), pp. 38–44

—, Nelson *to* Vanguard, pp. 168–9

Eades, K. A., 'HMS *Ark Royal*' in *Warships*, Supplement no. 28 (November 1972), pp. 1–6

Jameson, Rear-Admiral William, Ark Royal, *1939–1941* (London: Rupert Hart-Davis, 1957)

Jones, Geoffrey, *U Boat Aces and Their Fates* (London: William Kimber, 1988)

McCart, Neil, *Three* Ark Royals: *1938–1999* (Liskeard, Corn.: Maritime Books, 2005)

Paterson, Lawrence, *U-Boats in the Mediterranean, 1941–1944* (Annapolis, Md.: Naval Institute Press, 2007)

Poolman, Kenneth, Ark Royal (London: William Kimber, 1956)

Robertson, Lt R. G., 'The Wartime *Ark Royal*' in *Ships Monthly* 20 (1985) no. 9, pp. 24–8, and no. 10, pp. 35–9

Rossiter, Mike, Ark Royal: *The Life, Death and Rediscovery of the Legendary Second World War Aircraft Carrier* (London: Bantam Press, 2006)

Russell, Sir Herbert, and Cdr Harry Pursey, Ark Royal: *The Story of a Famous Ship* (London: Bodley Head, 1942)

Rust, Eric C., 'Fritz Guggenberger: Bavarian U-Boat Ace' in Theodore P. Savas, ed., *Silent Hunters: German U-Boat Commanders of World War II* (Annapolis, Md.: Naval Institute Press, 2003), pp. 75–107

Simpson, Michael, ed., *The Somerville Papers: Selections from the Private and Official Correspondence of Admiral of the Fleet Sir James Somerville, G.C.B., G.B.E., D.S.O.* [Navy Records Society, vol. 134] (Aldershot: Scolar Press, 1995)

The War Illustrated, V, no. 115, 20 December 1941, pp. 337, 342–3 and 358–9

Career history of HMS *Ark Royal*:
http://www.naval-history.net/xGM-Chrono-04CV-Ark%20Royal.htm

40 HMS *DUNEDIN*

Capt. R. S. Lovatt, RN†

Sunk by *U124* (Type IXB), Kptlt Johann Mohr, 24 November 1941

Central Atlantic, 250 nm NE of Saint Peter and Saint Paul Rocks

Dunedin capturing the German supply ship *Lothringen* in the Central Atlantic on 15 June 1941. Note her camouflage, designed to give the impression of a smaller vessel. A terrible fate awaited her and her company on and after 24 November. *Dunedin Society*

Theatre Central Atlantic (Map 1)		*Displacement* 4,850 tons	
Approx. coordinates 03° 00' N, 26° 00' W		*Dimensions* 472.5' × 46.25' × 14.5'	
Kriegsmarine code Quadrat ES 7985		*Armour* 1.5–3" belt; 1" decks and bulkheads	
U-boat timekeeping differential +2 hours		*Maximum speed* 29 knots	
Fatalities 419 *Survivors* 67		*Armament* 6 × 6"; 3 × 4" AA; 6 × 20 mm AA; 4 × .5" AA; 12 × 21" tt	

Career

Designed with the benefit of war experience, the Danae class of light cruisers, of which HMS *Dunedin* was the fifth of eight units to be completed, was based on the preceding 'C' class though with an extra twenty feet of hull to accommodate a further 6-inch mounting abaft the bridge. *Dunedin* was laid down at Armstrong Whitworth's yard at Walker-on-Tyne in November 1917, launched the following November and completed at Devonport Dockyard in October 1919. She served with the 1st Light Cruiser Squadron in the Atlantic from 1920–3, accompanying it as far as New Zealand on the Empire Cruise of 1923–4. With the exception of refits at Chatham in 1927 and 1931–2, *Dunedin* remained with the New Zealand Division of the Royal Navy for the next thirteen years, showing the flag and rendering notable assistance to victims of the Apia typhoon of February 1928 and the Napier earthquake of February 1931. In 1937 she returned to Britain and became flagship of the Reserve Fleet at Portsmouth, serving as a Boys' sea training ship and as an aircraft target vessel. Under normal circumstances this would have signalled the end for what was now an elderly and well nigh obsolete unit but the international situation dictated otherwise. Reactivated as part of the 12th Cruiser Squadron

in August 1939 and manned largely by Reservists, *Dunedin* was assigned to the 11th CS of the Home Fleet on the outbreak of war and began several months' boarding and interception duty on the Northern Patrol. The 'D'-class proved to be unsuited for this task and *Dunedin* was taken in hand for refit and weather damage repairs at Belfast in December having spent no fewer than ninety-two days under way since the outbreak of war. Transferred to the 8th CS on the North America and West Indies station in January 1940, on 2 March *Dunedin* caused the MS *Heidelberg* to scuttle herself off Haiti and then captured another German merchantman, the MS *Hannover* (later HMS *Audacity*, **43**), off Santo Domingo on the 8th. April and May found her engaged in convoy defence in the Atlantic but by June she was back in the Caribbean area as Senior Officer, Jamaica Force.

Returning to the fray following refits on the Clyde and at Portsmouth between September and December together with a spell of anti-invasion duty with Portsmouth Command, on Christmas Day 1940 *Dunedin* narrowly escaped engaging the heavy cruiser *Admiral Hipper* off the Azores while escorting troop convoy WS5A bound for Suez via the Cape. Convoy duty in the Atlantic continued in the new year, the ship generally assigned as distant cover. After docking at Devonport in

March 1941 *Dunedin* was transferred to the West Africa station based on Freetown, which she reached at the end of April. As part of Force F, one of the raider hunting groups charged with eliminating the supply vessels dispatched in support of the battleship *Bismarck*'s ill-fated breakout into the Atlantic, she participated on 15 June in the capture of the German supply ship *Lothringen*, a success which not only owed much to the decryption of Enigma traffic but yielded material of use to British codebreaking efforts. *Dunedin* went on to capture a trio of Vichy French vessels including the *Ville de Tamatave* east of Saint Peter and Saint Paul Rocks on 30 June, the *D'Entrecasteaux* on 1 July and the *Ville de Rouen* which was intercepted in the Indian Ocean off Natal on the 22nd. Returning to the West Africa station, *Dunedin* continued to traverse the Atlantic on convoy duty and in search of raiders and supply ships ahead of a planned conversion to an anti-aircraft cruiser, one destined never to be realised.

Background of the attack

In November 1941 HM cruisers *Devonshire*, *Dorsetshire* and *Dunedin* were dispatched from Freetown following Enigma intelligence of the presence of two German ships in the mid-Atlantic – *Schiff 16* (the commerce raider *Atlantis*) and the supply vessel *Python*. Enigma decrypts revealed that a number of U-boats heading for South African waters (the *Kapstadt Gruppe* – 'Cape Town Group') would attempt to refuel from these vessels but as the location was not known the cruisers were assigned to different patrol areas which in *Dunedin*'s case lay off the oceanic outcrops known as Saint Peter and Saint Paul Rocks 550 miles off Brazil. On 22 November *Devonshire* found and sank *Atlantis* 350 miles north-west of Ascension Island while *Dorsetshire* went on to account for *Python* on 1 December. However, the *U-Boot-Waffe* was

to exact a measure of revenge for in the early hours of 23 November *U68* (Kptlt Karl-Friedrich Merten) and *U124* (Kptlt Johann Mohr) of the *Kapstadt Gruppe* were directed by B.d.U. to assist in the rescue of survivors of the *Atlantis*, the latter's alteration of course taking her across the path of the lone *Dunedin* at noon on the 24th.

As the log indicates, *Dunedin*'s upper works were sighted as she appeared over the horizon at 1356 German time and Mohr spent the next three-quarters of an hour observing her approach before diving and taking up an attacking position. This apart, the situation aboard *U124* in the forty minutes leading up to the attack seems to have been far from normal. Unconfirmed reports in the German wartime press suggest that *U124* suffered problems with her diving planes as she submerged to attack at 1443. Though the log makes no mention of it, these reports might be borne out by reports from the British side that a mast-like object was sighted at approximately the time Mohr dived, *Dunedin* altering course accordingly while *U124* unwittingly manoeuvered herself into a position ahead of her target's original course. This alteration would account for the fact that Mohr, who had initially planned to attack *Dunedin*'s port side once her course converged with his own, ended up firing at her starboard side and at extreme range. Whatever the case, at 1521 German time Mohr launched a spread of three torpedoes from a stated range of 4,000 metres, managing two hits. In fact, the running times of 5 min. 37 sec. and 5 min. 55 sec. equate to an immense strike range of more than 5,000 metres, exceeded only by Kptlt Friedrich Guggenberger's against *Ark Royal* eleven days earlier (**39**). In this case, however, the torpedoes struck their intended target rather than chancing against the hull of another.

War Diary of *U124*, patrol of 30 October–29 December 1941: PG 30114, NHB, reel 1,082, pp. 58–60

Date, time	Details of position, wind, weather, sea, light, visibility, moonlight, etc.	Incidents
24.xi		Between Freetown and Pernambuco.
0800	Qu. ES 7657, wind SE 3, cloud 1, average visibility, sea 2, light swell	Morning health check of crew by doctor.
1200	Qu. ES 7953	Carried over: 83 4,186 23rd/24th 0 251 83 4,437[1]
1356	Qu. ES 7995	Foretop of a warship sighted to the north-east. Advance manoeuvre to west.
1443		Dived. Enemy identified as 'D'-class English cruiser. Raised fo'c's'le. Guns between the fore funnel and tripod mast. Zigzag course, general course 250°. Speed 18 knots.[2]
1521		<u>Three torpedoes launched.</u> Range = 4,000 m. Inclination 85°.[3]

---

1 The columns of figures relate to diesel fuel reserves (in cubic metres) and miles covered respectively, in both cases updated from midday of the previous day. It is unclear why there has been no meaningful change in the former given that *U124* had sailed 251 miles over the previous twenty-four hours.
2 Mohr's assessment is remarkably accurate, Lt Cdr A. O. Watson later recording *Dunedin* as having altered from 287 to 230 degrees with a 25-degree zigzag on sighting the mast, her speed increasing from 15 to 18 knots.
3 The torpedo report records the inclination as 75 degrees, not 85 degrees. It also gives running times of 5 min. 37 sec. and 5 min. 55 sec. respectively, suggesting torpedo runs in excess of 5,000 metres – at the very limit of the G7e's range.

Date, time	Details of position, wind, weather, sea, light, visibility, moonlight, etc.	Incidents
		Impact below the bridge. Very powerful detonation. Whole cruiser enveloped in thick yellow cloud of explosion.
		Impact (18 sec. later) below the main mast. Powerful detonation. Wreckage from the ship flies high into the air.
		Cruiser veers to port and circles with a heavy list to starboard then stops.
1546		*Coup-de-grâce* torpedo – a miss.
1551	Qu. ES 7985	Cruiser capsized to starboard, sank by the stern.
1553		Surfaced.[4]
		A large oil slick in the area of the sinking as well as six emergency boats or rafts, two of which have capsized.[5]
		Feigned movement off to the north.
1600	Qu. ES 7986	
1700		Southerly course resumed, heading once more towards Bauer.[6]
1732		Following two vain attempts to contact Africa station and Norddeich, W/T signal to Africa station finally transmitted and understood:[7] *To B.d.U.: English 'D'-class cruiser sunk. Qu. 7985 ES. Continuing south. Mohr.*
2000	Qu. FD 1363, wind SSE 2, cloud 2–3, good visibility, sea 1, light swell	
2030		Incoming W/T transmission: *To U124: The Moor has done his duty. B.d.U.*[8]
2218–2250		Reloading completed.
		Test dive.

4 *Dunedin*'s survivors recalled *U124* surfacing close to the wreck immediately before it went down. A crewman was reported to have shot film footage of the scene from *U124*'s conning tower.

5 British records indicate that seven Carley floats and a raft were left at the scene of the sinking together with a waterlogged whaler and other flotsam.

6 Kptlt Ernst Bauer, commander of *U126*.

7 The location of the Africa radio station is unclear but Norddeich is on the coast of Lower Saxony. His difficulty in transmitting this signal may have had more to do with the disruption of the earth's electromagnetic field by sunspot activity than any shortcomings in *U124*'s radio. Though the cause was only determined post-war, this phenomenon had a sporadic but telling effect on both radar and radio transmissions in 1941–2 and was attributed on both sides to successful attempts at jamming by the enemy.

8 The original reads *Der Mohr hat seine Schuldigkeit getan.* This was the second time in Mohr's career that Dönitz had recourse to a pun on his name using this German proverb meaning 'you've served your purpose (and I've no further use for you)', the word *Mohr* being German for 'Moor' in its Muslim sense.

The sinking

Dunedin was struck twice on her starboard side, the first torpedo detonating against the forward boiler room at 1526, the next seconds later abreast the wardroom flat aft. As the ranking survivor Lt Cdr A. O. Watson reported, 'the explosion from the second torpedo had torn up the Quarterdeck, dislodged No. 6 6" gun, and blown off the port propeller'. An immediate list of fifteen degrees to starboard increased to thirty-five degrees within five or six minutes. Efforts were made to close hatches and doors on the upper deck but a number were found to have been buckled by the explosions. Capt. R. S. Lovatt, who was on the bridge at the time of the attack, seems to have had little doubt that his ship was finished and immediately made his way to the flag deck to originate a distress signal, passing the order to abandon ship while this was being transmitted. Anxious to finish off such a rare prize, Mohr closed and fired a *coup-de-grâce* torpedo at 1546. This missed but did not alter the issue as *Dunedin* disappeared five minutes later at 1351 British time, around twenty-five minutes after the first hit. Chief Electrical Artificer E. J. Stevenson recalls the end:

The bows continued to rise until the visible part of the hull was vertical. She hung in that position for what seemed to be an interminable period of time, during which the great rumbling came from within the hull as equipment and fittings broke loose from their fastenings. This was accompanied by a loud, clanking, metallic roar as both anchor cables ran out of the chain locker through the naval pipes to hang, in a cloud of brownish-red rust particles, perpendicular and parallel to the fo'c's'le deck. Then, almost silently, the ship began to slip stern first below the surface of the ocean. As the bows disappeared from sight there came from the men in the water a sound that will haunt me for the remainder of my life – they gave *Dunedin* three hearty cheers.

For these men, however, the ordeal was only just beginning.

Fate of the crew

From first-hand accounts it appears that around half the ship's complement – over 200 men – lost their lives either in the successive detonations or in the chaos that reigned as *Dunedin* rolled on to her beam ends. Although little has survived to record it, the carnage below was perhaps less than it might otherwise have been since a large number of men were on deck against the possibility of *Dunedin*

Johann Mohr seen on *U124*'s conning tower on her return to Lorient on 29 December 1941 following the cruise during which *Dunedin* was sunk. The pennants record the sinking of the then-neutral US freighter *Sagadahoc* on 3 December and, uppermost, that of *Dunedin* on 24 November.
Johann Mohr fils

encountering the *Python*. However, getting clear of the wreck was no guarantee of salvation since, as Lt Cdr Watson reported, none of the ship's boats survived the sinking in serviceable condition:

> The whalers, which were stowed in chocks on deck, were freed and one of them was seen, after *Dunedin* had sunk, in the water in a water-logged condition, with a few ratings both inside and outside the boat. The remaining boats, a 25 ft. motor boat and a 14 ft. dinghy, were freed, but as the ship heeled over to 90 deg. before sinking, they could hardly have floated off.

Much worse awaited the ship's cutter and those unfortunate enough to have boarded her. CEA Stevenson:

> The cutter, filled to the gun'les with men, many of whom were gravely wounded or injured, scraped down the ship's side plating as it was lowered from its davits on the high, sloping port side. The boat lurched and tilted crazily as it crashed over the exposed port bilge keel before dropping into the water. The cutter's falls were slipped and the boat bumped and slithered along the ship's bottom plating towards the shattered stern end of the cruiser. The port propeller shaft, grotesquely bent, free of its supporting 'A' bracket, with two of the four propeller blades broken off short but still revolving slowly, carved its way through the tightly packed mass of men in the cutter. All that remained on the surface of the sea were a few splintered planks of wood and a small number of men swimming desperately away from the thrashing shaft, which was adding to the general confusion and noise caused by the roar of escaping steam, the shouts and cries of the men struggling in the sea and the crash and rumble of equipment breaking loose below decks, by hammering against the ship's side as it slowly revolved.

Those remaining in the water – estimated at 145 men by one rough tally (later deemed 'almost certainly incomplete') – gathered on and around seven overloaded Carley floats, a raft and other flotsam. One of the Carleys soon drifted apart from the rest, never to be seen again, while Capt. Lovatt and Lt Cdr R. M. H. Sowdon were last spotted clinging to a large box and spar respectively. So it was that *Dunedin*'s survivors found themselves adrift in the mid-Atlantic with practically no food or water, far removed from the main shipping lanes and with the nearest British vessel more than 200 miles off and ignorant of their plight. With the main W/T office wrecked by the second torpedo, efforts had been made to transmit a distress signal on the emergency set but there was little confidence that it had got through despite being repeated six or seven times. Subsequent discussions also revealed that the position transmitted, 03° 00' N, 21° 00' W, was five degrees east of that indicated by the ship's plot at the time of the sinking: 03° 00' N, 26° 00' W. In the event, no signal was ever picked up, leaving a dwindling band of survivors to face the full horror of a sinking in the tropics. Lt Cdr Watson records their predicament:

> The first night on the rafts was fairly comfortable, there being no rain. The swell gave the rafts a considerable motion which made it difficult at times to keep on them, but the men got some sleep by huddling together and the night did not seem unduly cold. Many of the men were scantily clad and some were naked. Some were without lifebelts. Most of the badly wounded cases died during the first night, and a number of uninjured suffered from delusions… Sharks were very numerous but gave little trouble. On the other hand, an unknown type of small fish [black durgon, *Melichthys niger*] was extremely ferocious. They were less than a foot long and blunt nosed, quite unlike barracuda. During the first and each successive night many men sustained deep bites from these fish. The bites were clean cut and upwards of an inch or more deep, and were mostly in the soles of the feet, although in some cases the fish sprang out of the water and bit into the men's arms. Frequently the bites resulted in severed arteries and many men died from this cause. The gratings and nettings of the rafts did not prevent the fish from attacking from inside the rafts.

However, the first night was but a foretaste of what lay ahead as larger marine predators including Portuguese men o'war (*Physalia physalis*, which apparently claimed at least one life) joined the black durgon in attacking the hale and the wounded alike. Joiner Thomas Moore:

> And so into the second day, with thoughts of rescue after a nightmare endured during darkness. We soon began to sense our terror of daylight. Sharks, the bull-nosed ones, about twelve feet long [probably oceanic whitetip, *Carcharhinus longimanus*]. We kept them at bay as they swam close to our raft. The day wore on, we were slowly losing confidence of being picked up, and the heat on our bare heads was telling on us . . . Men began to stand up in the raft and scream and shout and say they were going back to the ship to call a taxi and jump off the raft. The tropical sun was intense and beating down on our heads and bodies and slowly was sending us raving mad. We soon lost what water we had left, salt water filtered into it… So the second night approached and, even more bitter to all[, m]any were bitten by Barracudas, and we soon realised that those bitten died within an hour or sooner, and by the third morning our number was halved.

Just three men survived from Moore's raft.

The first official inkling of disaster came late on 25 November with the decryption of Mohr's Enigma signal to B.d.U. of 1732 reporting the sinking (see log). The Admiralty responded by ordering the armed merchant cruiser *Canton* and the sloop *Bridgewater* to a search area suggested by Mohr's ES 7985 quadrant but nothing was found. However, help came in the shape of the US freighter SS *Nishmaha* which happened across the survivors late on the afternoon of the 27th in position 03° 30' N, 21° 30' W, the rafts having drifted almost 300 miles towards Africa. A total of seventy-two men were rescued after eighty hours in the water, many delirious or *in extremis*. Despite tireless efforts by crewmen of the *Nishmaha*, five succumbed to their injuries within twelve hours of rescue leaving sixty-seven of a ship's company of 486 to be landed at Port of Spain, Trinidad on 7 December. As Capt. O. H. Olsen of the *Nishimaha* later reported, those who lived to see dry land again did so by the greatest good fortune:

> As I look back on this occurrence, it is realised how fortunate we were in being the instrument of rescue for these unfortunate men. It was 5.00 pm when we first sighted a raft, and pitch dark when the final rescue was accomplished. From the condition of the men when taken aboard my ship I feel sure that, had they been obliged to spend another twelve hours without rescue, none of them would have survived.

The sinking of the *Dunedin* was not without heroism, Lt Cdr Watson recording the forty-eight hours spent by Sergeant H. M. King RM supporting a wounded member of the Marine detachment, and how AB D. Fraser left his raft to swim through shark-infested waters to the aid of a drowning man. Then there was AB J. W. C. Moore, who

> showed great strength of character, both by his unstinted expenditure of energy on various tasks and by the cheering and steadying influence he exerted on the remainder of the crew of his raft. It was probably owing to the former that he succumbed on the day of the rescue.

The loss of over 400 men and the circumstances of their death place the sinking of the *Dunedin* among the most harrowing – and least known – British naval disasters of the Second World War. Despite the scale of the tragedy, no Board of Enquiry seems to have been called, a likely consequence of the time elapsed before the survivors were repatriated, attrition of the senior officers and the succession of disasters which befell the Royal Navy in the weeks and months following her loss. Although Lt Cdr Watson was gazetted with the OBE in July 1942, these circumstances go some way toward explaining the oblivion into which the fate of *Dunedin* and her company fell for the next sixty years. The ship and her men are recalled in a plinth placed by the *Dunedin* Society in the National Memorial Arboretum at Alrewas, Staffordshire.

U124 and Johann Mohr

Built by AG Weser of Bremen and commissioned in June 1940, *U124* served with the 2nd *U-Flottille*, initially at Wilhelmshaven and then at Lorient. The nucleus of her crew was drawn from survivors of *U64* which had been sunk at Narvik by a Swordfish floatplane from HMS *Warspite* on 13 April 1940, an incident which claimed the lives of eight men. As the rescue of the crew had been achieved with the assistance of alpine troops of *Gebirgsjäger Regiment* 139, *U124* adopted their edelweiss emblem as her own. Until September 1941 she was commanded by Kptlt Georg-Wilhelm Schulz, who had been awarded the Knight's Cross in the summer of that year before being assigned to shore duties.

At only twenty-five, Schulz's First Watch Officer and successor Kptlt Johann Mohr was exceptionally young for his rank at this stage of the war. An officer of great skill and daring and a firm favourite of Dönitz, Mohr's first cruise in command despatched six freighters in the space of a week during September 1941. An eventful second cruise yielded first *Dunedin* and then the neutral freighter *Sagadahoc* on 3 December, the fourth US merchantman to be lost before America's entry into the war. However, the offensive side of the cruise ended with the rescue of survivors of the raider *Atlantis* and the supply ship *Python* off Ascension after the latter was sunk by HMS *Dorsetshire* on 1 December, an endeavour requiring the cooperation of eight submarines over 5,000 miles of ocean. On her next patrol in the spring of 1942 *U124* sank almost 50,000 tons off Cape Hatteras, North Carolina during Operation PAUKENSCHLAG ('drumroll'), earning Mohr the Knight's Cross.

For the rest of *U124*'s and Mohr's joint career, see FNFL *Mimosa* (**61**).

Sources

Admiralty, *Actions with the Enemy (3). HMS* Dunedin *Sunk: Awards to Personnel and Expression of Board's Gratitude to Mr O. H. Olsen, Master of S.S.* Nishmaha *for Rescue of Survivors* (TNA, ADM 1/12272)

—, *Casualty Lists for H.M. Ships, 1941* (NHB)

Watson, Lt Cdr A. O., Report on sinking of HMS *Dunedin*, Piarco, Trinidad, 28th January 1942 in *Wartime Damage to Ships: Reports, 1941–1942* (TNA, ADM 199/2067); available on: http://www.hmsdunedin.co.uk/watson_report.htm

Moore, Joiner Thomas, *The End of a Great Ship: The* Dunedin *Drama* (typescript, privately held)

Stevenson, Chief Electrical Artificer E. J., *HMS* Dunedin: *Being a Short History of the Ship . . .* (typescript, c.1975, RNM, 1981/742)

Wood, Ch. Yeo. Sigs. S. R., *Shipwrecked: Memoir of a* Dunedin *Survivor* (typescript, privately held)

Brook, Peter, *Warships for Export: Armstrong Warships, 1867–1927* (Gravesend, Kent: World Ship Society, 1999)

Busch, Harald, „Meisterlich getroffen" in *Kriegsmarine*, April 1942

—, *U-Boats at War* (New York: Ballantine, 1955)

Dietrich, Hans, „Mit rotem Siegeswimpel am Turm" in *Bremer Nachrichten*, 4 March 1942

Gasaway, E. B., *Grey Wolf, Grey Sea* (New York: Ballantine, 1970)

Gill, Stuart, *Blood in the Sea: HMS* Dunedin *and the Enigma Code* (London: Weidenfeld & Nicolson, 2003)

Morgan, Daniel, *EOU: The Naval Career of Commander EO Unwin RN* (London: privately, 2001)

Olsen, Capt. O. H., 'Official report of Captain [O. H. Olsen], Master of the Lykes Lines S.S. [*Nishmaha*]' in *Lykes Fleet Flashes*, February 1942; also available on: http://www.hmsdunedin.co.uk/olsen_report.htm

Ransome, George, "'D' Class Cruisers' in *Marine News* 30, no. 8 (August 1976), pp. 296–9

Raven, Alan, and John Roberts, *British Cruisers of World War Two* (London: Arms and Armour Press, 1980)

Roskill, *War at Sea*, I, pp. 47, 276, 291 and 546

Turner, L. C. F., H. R. Gordon-Cumming and J. E. Betzler, *War in the Southern Oceans, 1939–45* (Cape Town: Oxford University Press, 1961)

War career of HMS *Dunedin*: http://www.naval-history.net/xGM-Chrono-06CL-Dunedin.htm

Website of *Dunedin* Society: http://www.hmsdunedin.co.uk/

41 HMS *BARHAM*

Vice-Admiral H. D. Pridham-Wippell, CB CVO RN, Capt. G. C. Cooke, RN†
Sunk by *U331* (Type VIIC), Oblt.z.S. Hans-Diedrich Freiherr von Tiesenhausen, 25 November 1941
Eastern Mediterranean, 60 nm NNE of Sîdi Barrâni (Egypt)

Barham, probably at Scapa Flow in the summer of 1940. *U331* registered three torpedo hits on her port side
between the funnel and 'Y' turret. Within five minutes she had disappeared with almost two-thirds of her ship's company. *IWM*

Theatre Mediterranean (Map 3)	*Displacement* 31,350 tons
Coordinates 32° 34' N, 26° 24' E	*Dimensions* 643.75' × 104' × 31.25'
Kriegsmarine code Quadrat CO 6858	*Armour* 4–13" belt; 1–5" horizontal; 2" bulkheads; 3–13" turrets
U-boat timekeeping identical	*Maximum speed* 24 knots
Fatalities 863 *Survivors* 445+	*Armament* 8 × 15"; 12 × 6"; 8 × 4" AA; 32 × 40 mm AA; 12 × .5" AA
	Aircraft 1 Supermarine Walrus and catapult

Career

The fourth unit of the Queen Elizabeth class, the battleship HMS *Barham* was laid down at John Brown of Clydebank on 24 February 1913 and completed in August 1915. *Barham* and her sisters were the first battleships to be designed exclusively for oil firing, the saving in bunkerage, space and weight of plant permitting the installation of twenty-four boilers giving a best speed of twenty-four knots. This together with the new 15-inch gun – the largest ordnance then mounted at sea – and a good balance of protection and seakeeping made the Queen Elizabeth class the *ne plus ultra* of pre-First World War dreadnought design and a high point in warship construction. *Barham* commissioned into the 5th Battle Squadron of the Grand Fleet with which she served as part of Vice-Admiral Sir David Beatty's Battle Cruiser Fleet at Jutland on 31 May 1916. In a ferocious engagement lasting two hours *Barham* received six heavy shell hits which killed twenty-six men and wounded thirty-seven others but a similar measure of punishment was meted out to Konteradmiral Hipper's battlecruisers. She rejoined the fleet on 4 July following repairs at Cromarty. Service with the Grand Fleet continued until it was disbanded in April 1919, *Barham* becoming flagship of the 1st Battle Squadron, Atlantic Fleet with which she remained until transferring to the Mediterranean in 1924. After a refit at Portsmouth between 1927–8 she rejoined the Atlantic Fleet before paying off for a three-year modernisation between 1930–3, again carried out at Portsmouth Dockyard. A spell with the 2nd BS, Home Fleet ended when *Barham* joined the 1st BS in the Mediterranean, where she served until ordered home in December 1939.

Barham's war started badly. Sailing to join the Home Fleet, on 13 December 1939 she rammed and sank the destroyer *Duchess* which had been escorting her off the Mull of Kintyre. The incident cost the lives of a rating in *Barham* and 135 members of *Duchess*'s ship's company. Fifteen days later she was torpedoed by *U30* off the Butt of Lewis but managed to reach Liverpool under her own steam. Following repairs at Cammell Laird's yard at Birkenhead between January and April 1940, *Barham* returned to Scapa Flow to join the 2nd BS with which she remained until assigned to Force M in August for Operation MENACE, the abortive attack on Dakar in French Senegal. The operation, which took place from 23–25 September, saw *Barham* repeatedly hit by Vichy shore batteries. Her damage made good at Freetown, *Barham* joined the Mediterranean Fleet in November 1940 and was immediately in action, escorting convoys to Malta and Alexandria, covering carrier and surface operations, bombarding the Libyan port of Bardia on 3 January 1941 and participating in the Battle of Cape Matapan on 28 March during which three Italian heavy cruisers were destroyed.

Barham and *Malaya* were the only members of their class never to receive a complete reconstruction and by 1941 had come to be regarded as secondary units. With the military situation in North Africa looking increasingly dire, on 15 April it was suggested by the Admiralty that *Barham* should be run aground as part of a combined blocking and bombardment operation off Tripoli, the main Axis supply port in North Africa. Admiral Sir Andrew Cunningham, Commander-in-Chief of the Mediterranean Fleet, balked at a plan that would have cost the lives of much of her crew for no certain result, but reluctantly assented to a fleet bombardment. This was successfully carried out on 21 April, *Barham* in attendance, but as it turned out she had been spared the Admiralty's machinations for an even worse fate. Meanwhile, service continued in the Eastern Mediterranean and on 27 May she was heavily damaged by German aircraft during the withdrawal from Crete and sent to Durban for repairs, rejoining the Fleet at Alexandria in August.

Background of the attack

On 12 November 1941 *U331* sailed from Salamis to carry out Operation HAI ('shark') the landing of a party of seven soldiers near Râs Gibeisa on the Libyan coast with orders to blow up the railway line supplying British forces between Salûm (Sollum) and Alexandria. On the night of 17–18 November Oblt.z.S. Hans-Diedrich Freiherr (Baron) von Tiesenhausen put the soldiers and one of his wireless operators ashore in a dinghy and then stood out to sea to await their return. Though the charges were successfully laid, the demolition party returned to the beach to find that the men they had left there as sentries (including the wireless operator) had been captured by the British. The remainder found the dinghy intact but capsized it while attempting to make their rendezvous with *U331* and in doing so lost the green Very pistol which

was their only hope of alerting von Tiesenhausen of their whereabouts. By the time von Tiesenhausen reluctantly moved off the following morning the entire party had been rounded up and the charges defused. Turning east, von Tiesenhausen spent a week patrolling the waters between Salûm and Mersa Matrûh. With not a ship to her credit so far, *U331* was given a spectacular opportunity to hoist her first pennant on the afternoon of the 25th when a large squadron of British warships was sighted heading west from Alexandria. This was Force A consisting of the battleships *Queen Elizabeth*, *Barham* and *Valiant* sailing in line ahead with an escort comprising HM destroyers *Decoy*, *Griffin*, *Hasty*, *Hotspur*, *Jackal*, *Jervis*, *Kimberley*, *Kipling*, *Napier* and *Nizam*, the group acting as distant cover for the cruisers of Force B which had sailed from Alexandria on the 24th to intercept an Italian convoy bound for Benghazi. Von Tiesenhausen watched in disbelief as Force A altered course on its zigzag, bearing down on *U331*'s position and giving him a thrilling opportunity to sail straight through the oncoming destroyer screen. Thanks in part to the extremely high converging speed, *U331* penetrated the screen undetected and von Tiesenhausen was able to fire four torpedoes at point-blank range at the second battleship in line, HMS *Barham*.

War Diary of *U331*, patrol of 12 November–3 December 1941: PG 30402, NHB, reel 1,098, p. 607

Date, time	Details of position, wind, weather, sea, light, visibility, moonlight, etc.	Incidents
25.xi		
1430		Faint plumes of smoke at bearing 60° true.
1441		Mast of a destroyer in sight at bearing 70° true. Range 12 nm, course 60°, ¾ speed.
1500	Qu. CO 6857	At bearing 15° true three battleships (identifiable by their masts) at a range of 10–11 nm, steering southerly course. Masts are at first very hard to make out but gradually become larger and more distinct.
1532		At bearing 125° true an aircraft appears 10 nm away, flying in an easterly direction. The battleships are now dead ahead and two of them have their yards full on to me. Evidently they've altered onto a westerly course.
1543	d i v e d	As the range is decreasing steadily we turn and continue our approach under water. The battleship group bears directly down on us. The three battleships themselves are in close order in the middle of the group with a number of destroyers on either side. The exact formation is as follows: in the centre the three battleships, sailing in line ahead but each slightly off the port quarter of the preceding ship. They are flanked on each side by three or four destroyers sailing in line abreast.
1600[1]	Qu. CO 6855	
1547		Battle Stations! Our opportunity has come – it's now or never. Two of the port-side destroyers are hauling ahead and stationing themselves on the port bow of the battleships. Clearly the destroyers have drawn themselves up in such a way as to provide protection against torpedo bombers. At periscope depth we were able to get between these two destroyers.[2] The range from each was 250 m. I don't get a chance to attack the first battleship because maximum angle of shot was exceeded.[3] So by turning sharply I square up to the second without the time to identify her class. I manage to fire despite

1 The break in the chronological sequence here reflects the original.
2 Both the Board of Enquiry and subsequent British analysis found these to have been *Jervis* (which appears to have made a contact) and *Griffin* (which did not). Given that *Jervis* made this contact on her port side it may fairly be assumed that *U331* was on *Griffin*'s starboard beam, though von Tiesenhausen's plot suggests that he may in fact have passed on *Griffin*'s *port* side. That *Jervis* made the contact can be explained by the fact that *U331* would have been moving more slowly relative to her position than to those of other closer destroyers.
3 By the time von Tiesenhausen was ready to fire at Cunningham's flagship *Queen Elizabeth* his torpedo calculator had informed him that the angle from the bow tubes had already past its maximum of 90°.

		maximum angle exceeded, the sun behind me.[4]
1619	Qu. CO 6858, wind NNE 2, sea 2, cloud 7, sun, good visibility	Spread of four fired at battleship. Range 375 m (established via running time of 24 sec.). Depth settings as follows: Tube I, 3 m; Tube III, 4 m; Tube II, 5 m; Tube IV, 4 m. Inclination 70°, torpedo course 295°. After 24 sec. we hear three detonations, spaced at intervals equating to the firing of the torpedoes. A fourth is heard, but somewhat later.[5]

In the hydrophones this last torpedo's bearing merges with the noises coming from the battleship. The detonations are followed by cracking sounds suggesting that the bulkheads are giving way. The three detonations themselves were not particularly strong. I can't observe their effect as the boat threatens to breach the surface as a dangerous consequence of our having turned so hard.[6] At 9.5 m the boat is brought back under again. As the third battleship was stationed immediately astern of the one we torpedoed there is the worry that we will be rammed by the former.[7] I have the tower evacuated and the bulkhead closed. Fortunately we then manage to dive again at utmost speed. But no matter what we do we can't get her below 80 m. I then have the front depth manometer read, and it turns out that the large depth gauge in the central control room (and therefore the tank manometers as well) has been turned off, as have the side valves.[8] Four of the valves are hard to get at and in the heat of the moment the wrong one was turned off. So when the intakes to the large manometer and tank pressure gauges are opened up, the needle swings all the way across the entire dial. Once it finally settles into position the boat turns out to be at a depth of T = 130 m.[9] Immediately we blow the tanks and pump out until finally – with the needle motionless and shaking – the boat begins to rise again. The hull holds up well: just some slight leaks on the after access hatch (six different places), and both periscopes also leaking badly. Diving Tank III is leaking in three different places along the welded joint, while the port base valve of the electric engine is also leaking. Because of the pressure and high engine speed the clutch is slipping badly on the housing rings. The resulting overheating is contained by using the fire extinguisher. However, the boat behaves in an exemplary fashion – a glowing testimony to Nordseewerke Emden.[10] We bring the boat back to T = 80 m.[11] Not for some time after the torpedoes hit do the destroyers start dropping depth charges. I withdraw first to the north and then to the east. Destroyer noises and dropping of depth charges at the same bearing as that on which we fired torpedoes suggest that the battleship was probably hit. We can't establish any position for the main group.

1830–1840		Depth charges: 4 dropped at bearing 250° true, 8 at 200°, 12 at 190°, 2 at 260°. Medium range.
2000		
2039		We surface.
2106		To the south a fiery glow.
2226		As we sail north several shadows appear in sight ahead. We alter course to 120° as reloading of torpedo tubes is not yet complete. Range 6 nm. The idea is to avoid being seen by this group in the path of the moon.
2253	D i v e d	Course altered to 300°.
2329		Surfaced.
2131[1]		W/T report 2100 transmitted on resistor-capacitor wave: *23rd U-Flottille. 1619 Qu. CO 6855 battleship torpedoed.*[12] *Tiesenhausen.*

---

4   *U331*'s instruments have again failed to adjust to her hard turn to port; von Tiesenhausen simply overrides them. One of the spread appears to have passed astern of *Barham*.

5   This fourth detonation heard 'somewhat later' is probably *Barham* blowing up at approximately 1623 though may conceivably be an end-of-run detonation.

6   Although von Tiesenhausen attributes it to his hard turn at 1547, the effect of simultaneously firing 6,432 kg (nearly 6½ tons) of torpedoes from the four bow tubes would have the effect of forcing the bows to the surface unless the Chief Engineer had unusual skill in maintaining the trim of his boat. In this case *U331* broke the surface 150 yards ahead of HMS *Valiant*, too close for her to depress her guns sufficiently to hit. Assisted by the simple but effective measure of sending most of the crew to the bow, *U331* submerged once more and made good her escape, passing just fifty yards along *Valiant*'s starboard side as she did so.

7   HMS *Valiant*.

8   This error almost caused the loss of *U331* which was taken to the immense depth of 267 metres (876 feet), beyond her design crush depth of approximately 250 metres and well in excess of the safe operational depth of approximately 150 metres (492 feet). Despite being praised on his return to Salamis, von Tiesenhausen therefore received a stern reprimand from B.d.U. given that 'the boat was placed in great danger by the failure to turn the manometer valve correctly. It shows how the most terrible consequences can result from the error of just one man.'

9   By 'T = 130 m' von Tiesenhausen seems to be recording a dive of 270 metres (885 feet), subsequently revised to 267 metres (see n. 8); for a full discussion of the 'T =' notation, see Reading the *Kriegstagebücher*, p. xxxvii.

10   Nordseewerke Emden were the builders of *U331*.

11   Possibly 220 metres (722 feet); see n. 9.

12   The sinking quadrant provided here contradicts that recorded in the entry in question (CO 6858); possible typist's error.

Barham explodes four minutes after taking three hits from *U331*. She lies on her beam ends having capsized to port and men can be seen scrambling across her hull. The photo is a still from the famous footage shot from *Queen Elizabeth* by John Turner of Gaumont British News. *BfZ*

The sinking

Von Tiesenhausen scored three hits against *Barham* between the funnel and 'Y' turret with devastating consequences for the ship and her men. The Board of Enquiry's assessment of the damage was that 'the ship's side over a considerable length of her hull was blown in, thus opening her vitals to the sea, causing her to list heavily to port immediately on being hit, and with a slight pause at an angle of heel of about 40° to continue the list until in about four minutes' time the beam end position was reached,' water being seen to enter the funnel. However, the worst was yet to come. Watched by the entire squadron, *Barham* suddenly disintegrated in an enormous explosion, the wreck shrouded by a huge pall of smoke. The sight left an indelible impression on all who witnessed it, not least Admiral Cunningham looking on in *Queen Elizabeth*: 'It was ghastly to look at, a horrible and awe-inspiring spectacle when one realized what it meant.' Captured on film by Gaumont British News cameraman John Turner, the sinking of the *Barham* remains one of the enduring images of the Second World War at sea.

The Board of Enquiry convened in HMS *Woolwich* at Alexandria concentrated on two issues: the failure of the destroyer screen to detect *U331* and the cause of the explosion which destroyed *Barham*. Of the destroyers in a position to obtain a contact it was the furthest from *U331*, HMS *Jervis*, which actually did so, confirmation that Asdic was not an effective means of locating an enemy closing bow-on at high speed. The echo obtained was not reconfirmed because *Jervis* continued to sweep forward, whereas *U331* had soon passed through the screen. As such, the operator was instructed by the Officer of the Watch to disregard the echo and carry on with a forward sweep. The Board made the point that the possibility of a U-boat sailing rapidly through a destroyer screen was not sufficiently emphasised in operators' handbooks and that anti-submarine schools should take note. It was also established that owing to operational requirements *Jervis* had performed only one anti-submarine exercise during the preceding year. Writing to the First Sea Lord, Admiral of the Fleet Sir Dudley Pound, Cunningham offered no excuses: 'If there is

anything to be learnt from it, it is that our anti-submarine vessels are sadly out of practice. I am withdrawing the [submarine] *Otus* from operational duty to run her as a "clockwork mouse"' for training purposes. Subsequent experience demonstrated that the efficiency of Asdic was often compromised by the salinity and variation in water-temperature layers which are characteristic of the Mediterranean (see HMSs *Medway* and *Partridge*, **64** and **79**), but maybe there was something in the opinion of A/S specialist Lt Cdr John Mosse that 'the anti-submarine warfare standard in the Mediterranean had then been low and that the ships were always looking upwards, obsessed by the constant threat of air attack, to the detriment of their attention to the threat from underwater'. If so, events would bring a change of focus as the *U-Boot-Waffe* began to assert itself in this theatre.

As regards the fatal explosion no final conclusion was arrived at by the Board, and theories ranged from a major boiler explosion after water entered the funnel to the detonation of the ship's main magazines. Though the precise cause of the explosion has never been established, there can be little doubt that HMS *Barham* experienced the detonation of her after 15-inch magazines. The deflagration of 110 tons of cordite vented through the upper deck and the starboard side of the ship in a vast ball of flame and smoke. It was plausibly suggested that a fire in the after port 4-inch magazine had spread to the main magazine but it remains for a forensic analysis of the wreck to prove this.

Fate of the crew

Having lurched to starboard under the impact of the three torpedoes, *Barham* took on a rapid list to port before she settled on her beam ends and blew up. In the intervening minutes the efforts of perhaps 1,000 men to get on deck and then clear of the ship were complicated not only by the list but by the fact that *Barham* ploughed on, her speed relatively unimpaired by the progressive heel to port. The torpedo strikes were accompanied by a complete failure of all internal lighting and communication systems. Below decks men began to swarm round ladders while the ship assumed an impossible angle and loose fittings and equipment added to the mounting chaos. Bryan Samuels' experience was no doubt typical: 'The galley deck was tiled and hot greasy food and water was sloshing down the sloping deck. Fortunately overhead rails were within my reach and I was able to haul myself hand over hand up and across the galley and clamber out of the starboard door onto the main deck in the Marines' Battery.' Most were not so lucky. On the boat deck one of the ship's motor boats came off its crutches and fell over a hatch through which men were trying to escape. Others scrambled down from the superstructure to find the unearthly spectacle of their ship capsizing towards ninety degrees; officers on the bridge were seen 'hanging on as if on parallel bars'. Those on the higher starboard side of the ship had to climb the glacis outside the casemated 6-inch battery, normally flat but now vertical to the water. Having negotiated this obstacle the survivors, then sitting or standing on the ship's armour belt, were confronted with her bilge keel and barnacle-encrusted hull. Mid. Gwyn Grogan recalls his escape:

> I saw Lt Cdr Cobham cutting down some floats and there were a lot of men in the water already so I reluctantly took off rather a good pair of shoes and we scrambled down on our backsides to the glacis… We then had to slither down the area between the glacis and the bilge keel which was covered in barnacles which cut into our arms, legs and backsides. I realised

Von Tiesenhausen greeted on reaching La Spezia at the end of *U331*'s fourth patrol on 28 February 1942. It was during this patrol that the British announced the loss of the *Barham* during her previous sortie three months before, von Tiesenhausen being immediately awarded the Knight's Cross. The outsize version he wears around his neck was a gift from the crew. Note too *U331*'s snake emblem on his cap. *DUBMA*

> I would have to get into the water aware the ship would sink and we would be sucked down with it. It was suddenly every man for himself. At 20, life seems very precious. I took a header off the bilge keel as far out as I could point myself . . .

Others, however, dived off only to break their necks on submerged sections of the hull. ERA Denis Muskett, meanwhile, made the decision to abandon ship over the bows:

> The ship then seemed to roll over and I stood up and ran over to the bottom of the ship which was covered in razor sharp barnacles. I ran for'ard, sensing the end. I did not feel any pain as my feet were being deeply cut, just ran on and dived into the sea over the bows and immediately on touching the water tried to swim away from the ship.

Then came the explosion. Samuels:

> Suddenly I saw a tremendous flash and the whole after section seemed to blossom outwards. In a split second I saw men and metal hurtling into space, and then I too was flying. It happened so quickly, one moment in space, the next I was under water, going down, down, down.

The magazine detonation four minutes after the torpedoes struck accounted for much of the ship's company, and not just those still trapped in the ship. Many were tossed off the hull, killed by falling debris or sucked down as the ship disappeared altogether. Samuels was fighting for his life:

> My lungs were bursting. 'This is it,' I thought, surprisingly calm. I had heard of 'La panoramie de la vie passée' and now I had experienced it. I could hold my breath no longer and opened my mouth, expecting to take in water, amazingly it was air. I must have been in the wave caused by the ship sinking and been sucked down, round and up again.

By the time most reached the surface nothing was left of *Barham* but a huge pall of smoke and the uncanny silence that often follows a major disaster. Dotted across a large oil slick were a few pieces of debris and hundreds of bobbing heads clinging to flotsam or struggling to reach one of the few Carley floats that had been released before the ship blew up. In one of these Vice-Admiral Pridham-Wippell was trying to keep

spirits up with choruses of *There'll Always Be an England*. Help was at hand in the shape of the destroyer *Hotspur* which lowered boats and scrambling nets to minimise the chance of running men down. By the time she turned for Alexandria at nightfall 337 survivors were aboard. She was followed by *Nizam*, *Jervis* and *Jackal* which searched for survivors until dawn on the 26th. Their efforts brought the total of those rescued to approximately 445 men.

Virtually every man rescued was black with oil and vomiting from having swallowed it, a severe challenge to the medical officers and sick berth attendants of the rescuing ships. Cotton waste and hot baths dealt with the former but oil ingestion kept many in hospital for some time. Others had perforated eardrums, broken or missing limbs and severe internal injuries which claimed several lives before the ships reached Alexandria at noon on the 27th. The survivors were hospitalised or cared for in the repair ship *Resource* before being sent to a variety of camps and billets ashore. That so many were saved was as great a surprise to the rescuers as it must be to any who has watched footage of the disaster. Among the rescued was Vice-Admiral Pridham-Wippell, recognisable only by the gold braid on his jacket, but Capt. Cooke (who remained on his bridge) and 862 of *Barham*'s company went down with her. In his submission to the Board of Enquiry Lt G. M. Wolfe paid the following tribute to his shipmates:

> The general behaviour of the men was of the highest standard. In the ship they were cheerful, quiet and tried to help each other and in the water this was so too. They talked to each other quietly and waited patiently for the rescuing boats. There was no rushing the whaler from *Hotspur* which was nearest to me but an orderly queue of men waiting their turn.

Those they left behind are commemorated by a memorial book and a pair of gilt candlesticks on the nave altar of Westminster Abbey in London, donated largely through the tireless efforts of the captain's widow, Mrs Constance Cooke.

The loss of the *Barham* came at a desperate time in the history of the Royal Navy and in the interests of morale the scale of the tragedy was not admitted by the Admiralty until 27 January 1942, two months after the event. The subject was one on which the Admiralty remained extremely sensitive and few sinkings can have had so strange a coda as *Barham*'s. In December 1941, a month before the official communiqué announcing her loss, Helen Duncan, a prominent spiritualist, aroused official suspicion after she claimed to have conjured up a sailor wearing a *Barham* cap tally during a séance in Portsmouth. Duncan was placed under surveillance and later sentenced to nine months in gaol against fears that she might 'see' the landing sites of the D-Day invasion in 1944. In Berlin, meanwhile, the announcement of the sinking brought von Tiesenhausen the Knight's Cross, no surprise since *Barham*, though his first kill, remains the largest warship ever claimed by a German U-boat.

U331 and Hans-Diedrich von Tiesenhausen

The first wartime U-boat built by Nordseewerke of Emden (to which von Tiesenhausen pays generous tribute in his log), *U331* was commissioned in March 1941. On the night of 29–30 September *U331*'s second patrol took her through the Straits of Gibraltar and into the Mediterranean, one of six U-boats to do so as part of the *Goeben* group (including *U559*; see **42**). Commanded through all her ten patrols by Oblt.z.S. (Kptlt from January 1942) Hans-Diedrich von Tiesenhausen,

U331 sank only two ships in sixteen months. That one of these was the battleship *Barham* secured her place in history and saw von Tiesenhausen summoned to Berlin in triumph even before the sinking was confirmed. *U331*'s other kill was the derelict troop transport USS *Leedstown* on 9 November 1942 which had been abandoned after being bombed by the Luftwaffe off Algiers (**G37**). However, *U331*'s own career was drawing to a close in what had become an increasingly hostile environment for U-boats. On 17 November von Tiesenhausen raised the white flag after attacks by a succession of RAF Hudson bombers had left *U331* incapable of diving. Despite a circling Hudson and the impending arrival of the destroyer HMS *Wilton*, aircraft from the carrier *Formidable* saw *U331* stopped in the water and attacked with gunfire and torpedoes, sinking her and killing much of the crew. Von Tiesenhausen was one of seventeen survivors who spent the duration of the war as prisoners, first in England and then in Canada. Unable to settle in post-war Germany, von Tiesenhausen returned to Canada in 1951 where he at length struck up a friendship with Cdr J. A. J. Dennis, First Lieutenant of HM destroyer *Griffin* whose screen he had penetrated in November 1941. He died in Vancouver in August 2000.

Sources

Admiralty, *Loss of HMS* Barham: *Report of Board of Enquiry* (TNA, ADM 1/11948)

Dennis, Cdr J. A. J., *Memoirs of Cdr J. A. J. Dennis* (IWM, 95/5/1)

Anon., 'HMS *Barham*' in *Hard Lying: The V & W Magazine* no. 11 (June 2001), pp. 18–20

Arthur, Max, ed., *The Navy: 1939 to the Present Day* (London: Hodder & Stoughton, 1997)

Burt, R. A., *British Battleships of World War One* (London: Arms and Armour Press, 1986)

—, *British Battleships, 1919–1939* (London: Arms and Armour Press, 1993)

Connell, G. G., *Mediterranean Maelstrom: HMS* Jervis *and the 14th Flotilla*

(London: William Kimber, 1987)

Cunningham of Hyndhope, Admiral of the Fleet Viscount, *A Sailor's Odyssey* (London: Hutchinson & Co., 1951)

Herzog, Bodo, „Von Russland nach Canada : Ein „vergessener" U-Boot-Kommandant – Kapitänleutnant Hans-Diedrich Freiherr von Tiesenhausen (1913–2000) zum Gedächtnis" in *Militaria* 5 (2001), no. 2, pp. 53–9, and no. 3, pp. 84–7

Humphries, Steve, ed., *The Call of the Sea: Britain's Maritime Past, 1900–1960* (London: BBC, 1997)

Johnson, Bill, 'HMS *Barham*' in *Warship World* 5, no. 7 (Summer 1996), pp. 18–20

Jones, Geoffrey, *Battleship* Barham (London: William Kimber, 1979)

—, *U Boat Aces and Their Fates* (London: William Kimber, 1988)

Mościński, Jerzy, and Sławomir Brzeziński, *Brytyjski Pancernik* Barham [Profile Morskie, no. 44] (Wyszków: Wydawniczo Handlowa, 2002)

Muskett, Lt Denis, RNVR, *Tubal Cain: The Sinking of HMS* Barham (Lewes, Sussex: The Book Guild, 1986)

Paterson, Lawrence, *U-Boats in the Mediterranean, 1941–1944* (Annapolis, Md.: Naval Institute Press, 2007)

Raven, Alan, and John Roberts, *British Battleships of World War Two: The Development and Technical History of the Royal Navy's Battleships and Battlecruisers from 1911 to 1946* (London: Arms and Armour Press, 1976)

Turner, John, *Filming History: The Memoirs of John Turner, Newsreel Cameraman* (London: British Universities Film & Video Council, 2001)

Wade, Frank, *A Midshipman's War: A Young Man in the Mediterranean Naval War, 1941–1943* (Vancouver, B.C.: Cordillera Publishing, 1994)

Whinney, Capt. Bob, *The U-Boat Peril: An Anti-Submarine Commander's War* (Poole, Dorset: Blandford Press, 1986)

War career of HMS *Barham*:
http://www.naval-history.net/xGM-Chrono-01BB-Barham.htm
HMS *Barham* Association:
http://www.hmsbarham.com/
Webpage devoted to R. C. J. Jerrard (fatality):
http://www.rjerrard.co.uk/royalnavy/barham/barham.htm

---

42   HMAS *PARRAMATTA*

Cdr J. H. M. Walker, MVO DSC RAN†
Sunk by *U559* (Type VIIC), Kptlt Hans Heidtmann, 27 November 1941
Eastern Mediterranean, 40 nm ENE of Tubruq (Tobruk) (Libya)

Theatre	Mediterranean (Map 3)	*Displacement*	1,070 tons
Coordinates	32° 20' N, 24° 35' E	*Dimensions*	265' × 34' × 7.25'
Kriegsmarine code (TR)	Quadrat CO 6774	*Maximum speed*	16.5 knots
U-boat timekeeping	identical	*Armament*	3 × 4" AA; 4 × .5" AA
Fatalities	137 and 10	*Survivors*	about 25

The Royal Australian Navy

Despite repeated urgings from the British government and the Admiralty in the name of imperial defence, Australia was the only imperial dominion in possession of a significant naval force prior to 1939. Founded in 1911, the Royal Australian Navy entered the First World War with the battlecruiser HMAS *Australia* and seven other ships including the light cruiser *Sydney* which ended the career of the German raider *Emden* in the Cocos (Keeling) Islands in November 1914. Within a few months the submarine *AE2* was operating in the Dardanelles while the light cruiser *Pioneer* gave stalwart service off

East Africa in 1915–16. If the RAN distinguished itself in the Great War it truly came of age during the second conflict. The outbreak of hostilities found the RAN composed of two heavy and four light cruisers, four sloops either in service or completing (including *Parramatta*) and the five elderly destroyers of the famed 'scrap iron flotilla' together with a variety of support vessels. The first Australian units reached the Mediterranean theatre in December 1939 and remained there in support of operations ashore until being withdrawn to fight the Japanese in January 1942. During this time the RAN participated in every facet of Mediterranean operations, including the

Parramatta under way in wartime. She was struck on the starboard side amidships by *U559* and sank with heavy loss of life. *BfZ*

Battle of Cape Matapan and other engagements with the Italian navy (notably the sinking of the cruiser *Bartolomeo Colleoni* by the first *Sydney*'s ill-fated successor), the withdrawal from Crete, and the 'Spud Run' – the hazardous supply of Tobruk.

Career

For notes on the sloop type, see HMS *Penzance* (**16**).

One of four Australian-built escort sloops of the Grimsby class, HMAS *Parramatta* was laid down at the Cockatoo Docks and Engineering Co. Ltd in Sydney in November 1938, launched in June 1939 and completed in April 1940. After working up with the 20th Minesweeping Flotilla, RAN, on 29 June *Parramatta* sailed from Fremantle for the Red Sea which she reached a month later. Her service began with the evacuation of British Somaliland during the Italian offensive in the Horn of Africa, but much of her time was spent defending convoys from air attack in the Red Sea. In April 1941 she participated in the British campaign against Eritrea which resulted in the surrender of Italian forces in East Africa on 17 May. Among her last tasks before being transferred to the Mediterranean in May was the towing of HM light cruiser *Capetown* to Port Sudan following damage by an Italian torpedo boat off Eritrea on the night of 7–8 April. No sooner had *Parramatta* reached the Mediterranean than she was flung into the desperate effort to supply Tobruk whose garrison included troops of the Australian 9th Division. On 24 June, during her first 'Spud Run', *Parramatta* found herself rescuing survivors of a fellow escort, HM sloop *Auckland*, after she had been destroyed by German aircraft off Bardia. Escort duties between Alexandria and Tobruk and in support of the British garrison on Cyprus continued until September when she was assigned the task of Duty Sloop at Attaka on the Suez Canal. However, she returned to the fray in November and on the 25th sailed from Alexandria on her fourth mission to Tobruk.

Background of the attack

In February 1941 the arrival of the Afrika Korps in Libya heralded a string of major reverses for British and imperial forces in North Africa. Beginning in March of that year General Rommel launched an offensive that within a few weeks had pushed the British 500 miles east to Tobruk. The enormous strategic importance of Tobruk lay in its status as the only fully equipped port on the 600-mile coastline separating Benghazi from Alexandria herself. On its possession depended the ability of either party effectively to supply and reinforce troops engaged in offensive operations in the desert. The decision was therefore taken to hold Tobruk which was invested by the Axis while Rommel pushed his advance eighty miles east to Salûm (Sollum) in Egypt. Until the siege was lifted in December the responsibility for supplying the beleaguered garrison lay with the Mediterranean Fleet commanded by Admiral Sir Andrew Cunningham and no port can have exacted a greater price for its survival. Over the 242 days of the siege the Navy ferried more than 80,000 men in and out while landing 34,000 tons of stores, guns and tanks for its defence. Against this must be set a total of fifty-four naval and thirteen merchant vessels sunk or damaged by the end of 1941. Hampered by mines and deprived of air support, Cunningham's difficulties were compounded by the arrival of the *U-Boot-Waffe* in the Mediterranean that autumn, with Kptlt Hans Heidtmann's *U559* among the first to force the Straits of Gibraltar in September. On the night of 26 November *U559*, then on her second patrol along the Allied supply route between Alexandria and Tobruk, sighted the SS *Hanne* with a vital cargo of ammunition. Escorting her to Tobruk were the sloop HMAS *Parramatta*, the escort destroyer HMS *Avon Vale* and two converted whalers of the South African 22nd Anti-Submarine Group, HMSASs *Southern Isles* and *Southern Maid*. Heidtmann's first attack early on 27 December wasted three torpedoes against the *Hanne* but a single torpedo fired half an hour later accounted for *Parramatta* in the space of a few minutes.

War Diary of *U559*, patrol of 24 November–4 December 1941: PG 30594, NHB, reel 1,120, p. 156

Date, time	Details of position, wind, weather, sea, light, visibility, moonlight, etc.	Incidents
26.xi		
2000	Qu. CO 5939, wind ESE 3–4, cloud 9, 1,027 mb	
2245		A shadow in sight off to the north-east. We approach. Three steamers of 1,000–3,000 GRT.[1] They have an escort of two destroyers astern and what appear to be two fishing trawlers ahead.[2]
		The conditions of light are wholly unfavourable. I have the bright horizon behind me and am at times directly in the path of the moon. The convoy is set against a backdrop of rain, illuminated every so often by lightning. We run in to attack the destroyer stationed on the port quarter.
2400	Qu. CO 6775, wind ESE 4, cloud 1, 1,025 mb	As we commence attack the destroyer shifts to the starboard quarter. We press home the attack on a 3,000-ton steamer behind which there is a smaller steamer, slightly overlapping.[1]
		Heidtmann
27.xi		
0012		Spread of three torpedoes fired at both vessels; inclination 80°, enemy speed 8 knots, range 2,000 m. All miss. This is inexplicable as the next attack with just a single torpedo involves the same coordinates and this hits from 1,500 m.
		Again we approach to attack. The destroyers make a tempting target but I can't afford to take my time – the convoy must be nearing the approaches of Tobruk.
0046[3]		I fire a single torpedo from a range of 1,500 m, with the same coordinates as before, at a destroyer with just a single funnel.[4] A hit followed by two detonations in quick succession.
		Destroyer breaks up and sinks under the pall of the explosion. Shortly after there is another powerful detonation, presumably her depth charges going up.
		I withdraw to the south-east because I want to use all the time available to put some distance between myself and the scene of the sinking using our one good diesel.[5] The fishing trawlers and destroyer appear to be searching for the position from which we fired. We see them intermittently before they disappear behind a curtain of rain and then for a long time hear depth charges being dropped.
0400	Qu. CO 6788, wind N 3–4, cloud 5, 1,025 mb	

1   The SS *Hanne* was the only merchantman being escorted, making Heidtmann's reference difficult to understand.

2   The 'destroyers' were HMA sloop *Parramatta* and HM escort destroyer *Avon Vale*, while the 'fishing trawlers' were the converted whalers HMSASs *Southern Isles* and *Southern Maid*.

3   Allied sources offer two different times for the attack, one earlier (0035) and one later (0058). It is to be presumed that Heidtmann's, which bisects the two, is the more accurate.

4   Presumably *Parramatta* though *Avon Vale* answers the same description.

5   *U559* had been experiencing problems with her starboard diesel engine for the previous three days.

The sinking

It is curious that Heidtmann's description of his second attack fails to mention the *Hanne*, alongside which *Parramatta* was communicating by megaphone at the time she was hit on the starboard side. Two explosions were recorded by survivors and witnesses in *Avon Vale*, first abreast the wardroom amidships and then under the quarterdeck. Though the Allies concluded that *Parramatta* had been struck by two torpedoes, the hit had in fact brought on a secondary explosion, presumably the detonation of the after magazine (rather than the depth charges suggested in Heidtmann's war diary), to which the dull red flashes seen at the time would lend support. Plunged into darkness, *Parramatta* rolled over to starboard and sank within a matter of minutes, her back broken. This, however, was not the last of HMAS *Parramatta* as both bow and stern sections resurfaced before disappearing. The stern emerged a second time before subsiding once

more, though unsubstantiated reports record it being seen drifting for some time and indeed as many as three days later.

Fate of the crew

Although Cdr Walker was able to pass the order to abandon ship, the speed with which *Parramatta* sank made an orderly evacuation impossible and no more was heard of him. Survivors' estimates suggest that about a third of the ship's company (almost exclusively those on deck watch) escaped the wreck by diving or jumping over the side or, in some cases, stepping into the sea as she went down. The task of rescuing survivors on a particularly dark and squally night fell to Lt Cdr P. A. R. Ward of the *Avon Vale* who was faced with a familiar dilemma. On the one hand it was clear that there were many men in the water though these 'proved to be scattered widely and it was impossible to see them in the darkness', making rescue both slow

Heidtmann seen on *U559*'s conning tower. The donkey emblem of the 29th *U-Flottille* dates the shot to between May and September 1942. *DUBMA*

and difficult, and indeed a number of survivors recalled bumping into friends during the night. On the other, Ward was concerned for his ship's safety, *Southern Isles* and *Southern Maid* having been sent on to escort *Hanne* into Tobruk leaving *Avon Vale* alone on the scene. In the event he needn't have worried since *U559* had long since beaten a retreat. Fifteen or sixteen survivors were initially plucked from among the debris followed some hours later by four from a Carley float, though of these one died immediately upon rescue. Two more (Stoker Fred Greenfield and O.Sig. Harvey Stewart) managed to swim to *Avon Vale* from a float containing thirty men before Ward felt compelled to quit the scene at daybreak (0300 GMT). No other survivors were picked up though Ward did signal the hospital ship *Ramb IV* (seen proceeding west as *Avon Vale* headed for Alexandria) to continue the search. Although *Avon Vale* dropped a number of floats for the survivors, *Ramb IV* found nothing but patches of oil and sorties by Sunderland flying boats from Alexandria the following morning also drew a blank.

However, not all had perished. Three men – AB Fred Tysoe, O.Sig. A. N. Miller and AB Alec Ladhams – managed to board a whaler amply stocked with water and bully beef which had been abruptly left at the scene by *Avon Vale* after a false submarine sighting during the night. A fourth man was pulled aboard but died soon after, the others making for the Barbary Coast which they reached without difficulty. They rejoined the Allies after spending a couple of weeks being hidden by a group of Berbers within two miles of a German encampment. Another who apparently also made it ashore was AB George A. Smith, though under very unusual circumstances. His story was among those gathered by survivor Terry Currie between 1994

and 2003 and preserved in a dossier lodged in the Australian War Memorial in Canberra (see below). No first-hand account survives, Smith having related his story to Stoker Greenfield whose retelling runs like this: Having abandoned ship Smith (who apparently could not swim) eventually found an uncomfortable berth on *Parramatta*'s upright stern section together with about twenty others. After several hours the detonation of a depth charge on its thrower left Smith the only survivor. Parting company with the wreck and clinging to some flotsam, Smith found himself swept towards the coast, coming ashore about twenty-five miles from the position of the sinking. Here he was discovered by a unit of the New Zealand Army with which he stayed a month before reporting back to Alexandria. The circulation of this story among *Parramatta* survivors half a century later was greeted with some incredulity, not least with respect to Smith's depth-charge detonation. A *prima facie* analysis might interpret it as a cover-up for some earlier misdemeanour (such as his having gone adrift before *Parramatta* sailed from Alexandria, for instance), though it should be noted that O.Sig. Miller recalled speaking to him on the stern section before himself striking out to find another berth. Whatever the credibility of his story, Smith would bring the roster of survivors to approximately twenty-five men (accounts differ). Not a single officer survived, most no doubt perishing in the wardroom or in their cabins aft. The rest, including Lt R. H. S. Litchfield RN, a passenger, were eventually pronounced Missing, Presumed Killed.

Admiral Sir Andrew Cunningham, Commander-in-Chief of the Mediterranean Fleet, was a great admirer of the fighting spirit shown by the Royal Australian Navy in the Mediterranean and in his memoirs paid HMAS *Parramatta* his highest compliment: 'The *Parramatta* was a great loss. She had a good record of fine service.' High praise from a notoriously hard taskmaster.

U559 and Hans Heidtmann

Built by Blohm & Voss of Hamburg and commissioned in February 1941, *U559* made ten frontline patrols, all under Oblt.z.S. (Kptlt from October 1941) Hans Heidtmann. On her third patrol *U559* was one of six U-boats of the *Goeben* group (including *U331*; see 41) to pass through the Straits of Gibraltar in late September and early October 1941. A month after despatching *Parramatta* Heidtmann sank the PoW ship SS *Shuntien* with heavy loss of life, many of the rescued perishing after HMS *Salvia* was in turn destroyed by *U568* (see 44). *U559*'s career continued at a modest pace until 30 October 1942 when she was sighted north-east of Port Said and overwhelmed by five British destroyers supported by aircraft. Forced to surface, *U559* suffered the loss of eight of her forty-five crewmen, but the most damaging blow came in the form of the code books and cipher material recovered from her before she sank. Though two members of the boarding party from HMS *Petard* went down with *U559* while trying to salvage her M4 enciphering machine, the material obtained was instrumental in allowing Bletchley Park to break the more complex four-rotor Enigma code introduced earlier that year. Heidtmann survived to spend four years in Allied captivity (during which he was awarded the Knight's Cross in March 1943) before being released in May 1947. Joining the Bundesmarine following its inception in 1956, Heidtmann retired a Kapitän zur See in September 1972. He died in April 1976.

Sources

Admiralty, *Enemy Submarine Attacks on H.M. Ships: The Sinking of H.M.A.S.* Parramatta (TNA, ADM 199/160)

HMAS *Parramatta*: survivors' records (assorted memoirs and material compiled 1994–2003 by Terry Currie, a survivor) (Australian War Memorial, Canberra, PR03300)

U559 file (DUBMA)

Letter containing HMAS *Parramatta* casualty list from Miss M. W. Thirkettle to Cdr G. L. Sheridan RAN, Australian High Commission, London, 8 May 1981 (typescript, NHB, S.10046)

Cunningham of Hyndhope, Admiral of the Fleet Viscount, *A Sailor's Odyssey* (London: Hutchinson & Co., 1951)

Gill, G. Hermon, *The Royal Australian Navy, 1939–1942* (Adelaide: Griffin, 1957)

Hague, Arnold, *Sloops: A History of the 71 Sloops Built in Britain and Australia for the British, Australian and Indian Navies, 1926–1946* (Kendal, Cumbria: World Ship Society, 1993)

McGuire, P., and F. M. McGuire, *The Price of Admiralty* (Melbourne: Oxford University Press, 1954)

Stevens, David, ed., *The Australian Centennial History of Defence*, II: *The Royal Australian Navy* (Melbourne: Oxford University Press, 2001)

Career history of HMAS *Parramatta*:
  http://www.navy.gov.au/HMAS_Parramatta_%28II%29

---

43   HMS *AUDACITY* (ex MS *HANNOVER*)

Cdr D. W. MacKendrick, RN†

Sunk by *U751* (Type VIIC), Kptlt Gerhard Bigalk, 21 December 1941

North Atlantic, 470 nm W of La Coruña (Spain)

Audacity at sea during her operational life of fourteen weeks, ended by three torpedoes from *U751*. Note the Martlet fighters ranged aft in the absence of a hangar below deck. Rudimentary though she was, *Audacity* represents a key development in naval power. *BfZ*

Theatre North Atlantic (Map 1)		*Displacement* 8,600 tons	
Coordinates 43° 45' N, 19° 54' W		*Dimensions* 467.25' × 56.25' × 18.25'	
Kriegsmarine code Quadrat BE 8719		*Maximum speed* 14.5 knots	
U-boat timekeeping differential +1 hour		*Armament* 1 × 4" AA; 4 × 3" AA; 4 × 20 mm AA; 6 × .303" AA	
Fatalities 73 *Survivors* 225+		*Air wing* 6 aircraft (Grumman Martlet Mk IIs – F4F Wildcats); no lift or catapult	

Career

The career of HMS *Audacity* was as brief as it was eventful and few ships can have had so great an impact in the short span of time vouchsafed them. Laid down in 1938 for Norddeutscher Lloyd and launched in March 1939, the German motor ship *Hannover* was completed at the Bremer Vulkan yard at Vegesack on 10 May that year and entered service as a refrigerated cargo liner. The outbreak of war found *Hannover* in South American waters where she led an itinerant existence before sailing from Curaçao on 5 March 1940 in company with two other freighters, *Mimi Horn* and *Seattle*. Their

intention was to return to Germany but on 8 March the trio ran into the British blockade, intercepted by the light cruiser *Dunedin* (**40**) and the Canadian destroyer *Assiniboine* in the Mona Passage off Santo Domingo. *Mimi Horn* and *Seattle* got away but *Hannover*'s crew took steps to scuttle their ship and abandoned her in flames. However, a boarding party from *Dunedin* succeeded in bringing the engine room flooding under control and containing the fire, and together with *Assiniboine* brought her still burning into Kingston, Jamaica on 13 March. Christened *Sinbad*, that summer *Hannover* sailed for Britain where she was taken over by the Ministry of Shipping and renamed

Empire Audacity. Earmarked for conversion to an ocean boarding vessel, she was transferred to Blyth Shipbuilding and Dry Dock Co., Northumberland in November 1940.

Meanwhile, the Admiralty had begun to address the threat posed by German air attack and reconnaissance to the convoy system and consequently the need for a continuous air presence at sea. The fighter catapult ships and catapult-armed merchantmen had already proved their worth (see HMS *Springbank*, **33**) but their limitations were all too apparent and attention therefore focused on the 'trade protection' or 'escort' carrier first mooted in the mid-1930s. In December 1940 the Admiralty proposed the conversion of a small merchantman to an escort carrier and on 2 January 1941 *Empire Audacity* was selected for this purpose. The choice was an obvious one. Not only did her MAN diesel engines offer an adequate turn of speed, but their exhausts were easily trunked away from the flight deck which was planned to replace the fire-damaged superstructure. Work began at Blyth on 13 January and involved the installation of a 453-foot wooden flight deck on piers above the shelter deck along with one of the early air-warning radar sets, and the addition of 3,000 tons of ballast to preserve stability. Flight arrangements might best be described as rudimentary. There was no island, no accelerator to assist take-off and only two arrester wires to restrain landing. Above all there was neither hangar nor lift so the six Grumman Martlets embarked had to be parked and serviced at the after end of the flight deck when not aloft.

HMS *Empire Audacity* was commissioned on 20 June 1941 under a veteran Swordfish pilot, Cdr D. W. MacKendrick, though it was not until 31 July that she acquired her final name: *Audacity*. The six Martlets of 802 Squadron were embarked in August and on 13 September *Audacity*, by now assigned to Western Approaches Command, joined the first of her four Gibraltar convoys, OG74. By the time of her loss fourteen weeks later *Audacity*'s air group had accounted for five Focke-Wulf Kondors, damaged three more and driven off four others, along with a share in sinking one U-boat (*U131*) and damaging two others. Moreover, they had reported the positions of nine submarines and by obliging U-boat commanders to dive had frequently prevented them engaging the convoy. Indeed, from the U-boat perspective, the near-permanent presence of aircraft eroded the element of surprise upon which the submarine had always relied for its tactical effectiveness. *Audacity* therefore brought the reality of close air support to convoy operations for the first time, and in offering a platform to which aircraft could return the escort carrier enormously enhanced not only their operational flexibility but the role of air power at sea as a whole.

Background of the attack

Alerted by local agents to the impending departure of convoy HG76 from Gibraltar to Britain, in December 1941 B.d.U. formed the *Seeräuber* ('buccaneer') group into a patrol line to intercept it. This consisted of six U-boats to which another five were added in due course, among them Kptlt Gerhard Bigalk's *U751*. Anticipating a major attack, the Admiralty delayed the sailing of HG76 until a sufficiently powerful escort group had been mustered to deal with the threat. The convoy finally weighed anchor on the 14th with a thirteen-strong escort centred around the 36th Escort Group of the remarkable Cdr F. J. 'Johnnie' Walker, whose first convoy this was. (For more on Walker, see HMS *Woodpecker*, **97**.) This comprised HM sloops *Stork* (Senior Officer of the Escort) and *Deptford*, seven Flower-class corvettes, the destroyers *Blankney*, *Exmoor* and *Stanley* from North Atlantic Command, Gibraltar, and the luxury of daylight air cover provided by HMS *Audacity*'s air wing, even though this was reduced to four serviceable aircraft. Though limited to 7½ knots, HG76 stole a march on the *Seeräuber* group by sailing south along the Moroccan coast and it was not until the 16th that the Germans made contact. Even then the upper hand lay with the British as the size of the escort, the aggressive tactics adopted by Walker and *Audacity*'s Martlets limited the attacking boats to very few opportunities. Casualties came thick and fast but initially it was the German side that sustained them: two Kondors fell to *Audacity*'s Martlets; *U131* was scuttled under heavy fire from the escort on the 17th following damage by the Martlets, one of which was shot down; *U434* was depth charged to the surface and abandoned the following morning, and though the *Seeräuber* group hit back by sinking HMS *Stanley* early on the 19th (**G18**), the perpetrator, *U574*, was similarly blasted to the surface and then rammed and sunk by HMS *Stork*. Back at Kernevel, B.d.U. was convinced that the carrier (subsequently interpreted as HMS *Unicorn*, which embarked thirty-six aircraft) was the chief obstacle and exhorted those entering the fray to make her their main priority. Informed by the Admiralty that no fewer than six U-boats were in contact with HG76, on the evening of the 21st Walker ordered four of the escorts to stage a mock battle astern using starshell, snowflake and depth charges to distract the pack while the convoy executed a major alteration of course. The tactic backfired, however, as one of the merchantmen began firing snowflake, thus illuminating the now weakly defended convoy. Kptlt Engelbert Endrass struck first in *U567*, disposing of the Norwegian freighter SS *Annavore* and her cargo of iron ore just before 2030 British time. The light of the snowflake then fell on *Audacity* some miles to starboard, a circumstance which the Board of Enquiry concluded had given her position away to the enemy. However, as Kptlt Bigalk's log reveals, *U751* had already spotted *Audacity* when a burst of artificial light left him in no doubt as to the nature of his quarry.

War Diary of *U751*, patrol of 16–26 December 1941: PG 30730, NHB, reel 1,137, pp. 714–5

Date, time	Details of position, wind, weather, sea, light, visibility, moonlight, etc.	Incidents
21.xii		
2100	[Qu.] BE 8743[1]	A large shadow at 180°.[2]

1 Manuscript addition in pencil.
2 HMS *Audacity*.

Date, time	Details of position, wind, weather, sea, light, visibility, moonlight, etc.	*Incidents*
2121		We alter course towards the shadow, which has performed a pronounced zigzag to the east, and prepare to attack. Assume the shadow is a large tanker.
2130		A huge amount of starshell covers the whole horizon from south to west to north-west. Our boat lies between enemy and starshell, bathed in bright light. Am forced to fire immediately – before enemy is aware of my presence. I decide to fire a spread of four as I haven't quite fixed all the firing coordinates yet.
2137	[Qu.] BE 8719	Spread of four, enemy speed 10 knots, inclination 80°, bows left, depth 3 m, range 1,200 m.[3]
2140		After running time of 3 min. 20 sec. we see a detonation against the stern of the enemy – this also turned out to be clearly audible in the forward compartment.
2141		Enemy alters course away from us to port. The light produced by some extremely bright starshell reveals her beyond all doubt to be an aircraft carrier. Now I understand why I got her range and speed so wrong.[4]
	Very dark night, overcast, wind E 2–3, sea 2, moderate swell, strong sea phosphorescence	I withdraw somewhat to reload torpedoes, keeping a close watch on the carrier all the while. After her course alteration to port (south) the carrier slows to a halt. At intervals of about 10 min. carrier fires red flares every so often; these light up the area most unpleasantly. I find it difficult to understand why the carrier has stopped. The first torpedo hit [*at 2140*][1] must have shattered her rudder and propellers because carrier seems powerless to manoeuvre herself out of an unfavourable position beam to wind.[5] With just a <u>single</u> torpedo – all that remains loaded in my stern tube – there's little chance of my sinking her. I'll have to wait until at least two bow tubes have been reloaded.
2230		A shadow approaches the aircraft carrier and appears to be closing her starboard side. Meanwhile our reloading process has been very slow due to the large number of provisions stowed in the forward compartment.[6]
2240		At last two tubes are ready. I take advantage of the opportunity provided by the current morse signalling to approach immediately as any destroyers bearing down on me might rob me of this unique opportunity. I approach on electric engines only so as not to be heard. Any number of depth charges being dropped and starshell fired. And sea phosphorescence!
2255		The shadow is so monstrously large that its breadth covers at least two periscope glass widths. Line of bearing 0°, range 800 m, enemy speed = 0. Running time 50 sec, depth 4.5 m. Twin salvo from Tubes I and III. Tube I hits 25 m from the stern, Tube III 10 m forward of midships. Shortly after these hit there is a third powerful detonation accompanied by flames and a substantial quantity of smoke close to where the forward torpedo struck. I immediately turn about to starboard to give her a stern shot.
2257		Torpedo fired from Tube V. Line of bearing 180°, enemy speed = 0, depth 4.5 m. Torpedo veers off to port despite my having set a straight course, running as if it had an aim-off of 20° and passing 20 m astern of the carrier. Carrier is firing red distress signals. Two destroyers approach at high speed. As one of them heads straight towards me I am forced to withdraw.
2310		Carrier is so far down by the head that her upper deck seems to be almost awash. Stern is tilted up accordingly at an angle of 20–25°.
2312		Carrier now out of sight. I stop so as to be able to reload torpedoes in peace and quiet.
		Bigalk
22.xii		
0007		We can discern many small lights in the direction of the carrier as well as detecting morse traffic. Several destroyer silhouettes can be seen. Two torpedoes now reloaded. We head back to the scene of the attack which is well illuminated by these many lights. All we can make out as we close are the two to three destroyers' silhouettes which promptly turn away and head off to the west.[7] We proceed to the scene of the detonations using dead reckoning but can see nothing. All the lights have disappeared.

3   These and all subsequent torpedoes were fired by Oblt.z.S. Hermann Schröder, *U751*'s First Watch Officer.

4   Bigalk's torpedo report notes that the range and particularly the speed of the target were underestimated; all but one of his torpedoes therefore passed astern.

5   *Audacity* had indeed been left dead in the water by Bigalk's first hit, though not for the reasons he thought. Her diesels had stopped after the engine room flooded.

6   Barely five days out of St-Nazaire, *U751* was fully laden with supplies to support a patrol of many weeks, and it was standard practice to use the bow torpedo compartment to accommodate the surplus. In the event, *U751* was back in harbour by the 26th having used seven of her eleven torpedoes against *Audacity*..

7   HM corvettes *Pentstemon*, *Marigold* and *Convolvulus*

0233		After a fruitless search I haul away to the east against the sea to reload the remaining torpedo tubes. From close inspection it must have been an aircraft carrier of the Formidable class because from bow to stern the deck was completely flat with no superstructure.[8] And extraordinarily long, with raked stem and stern. In my estimation the carrier very probably sank.
0340		Outgoing W/T transmission 0256/22/145 to B.d.U.: *2300 Qu. 8719 3 torpedo hits on Formidable-class aircraft carrier. Sinking very probable. At 2310 carrier was well down by the bows. Sinking not observed as we were chased off. Searched later without result. Bigalk.*
0400	[Qu.] BE 8728	We set course 0° to pursue convoy.

8 While a Formidable-class carrier (23,207 tons) remained the official propaganda line, B.d.U. decided the victim to have been the light carrier *Unicorn* (16,510 tons), this despite Bigalk's being quizzed at some length as to the silhouette before being credited with the sinking. It should be noted that none of these vessels can remotely be described as having the flat outline accurately described here by Bigalk, while his identification of a Formidable-class carrier is a considerable exaggeration, *Audacity*'s final displacement being just 8,600 tons.

The sinking

Of the four torpedoes fired at 2137 on the 21st, only one found its mark, detonating abaft the engine room at 2035 British time (*Audacity*'s reckoning running a few minutes behind that of her attacker). The rest all passed astern. Significant damage was done to *Audacity*'s unprotected hull, but the ship was in no immediate danger of sinking while the engine room bulkhead held. There are reports that, though down by the stern, *Audacity*'s Port No. 1 and No. 2 guns opened fire on a surfaced U-boat close on her port beam, though this is corroborated neither in official sources nor in Bigalk's log. However, within a matter of minutes a small bulkhead in the shaft tunnel had collapsed, flooding the diesels and causing a complete failure of electrical power. Her inability to manoeuvre once the engines stopped made *Audacity* an easy target for a second attack and Cdr MacKendrick's decision to man the boats suggests he had few illusions as to what lay in store. *U751*'s next attack, recorded at 2145 ship time, sealed her fate, the two torpedoes detonating forward within a few seconds of each other and breaking her back. Though Bigalk records a subsequent detonation, there is no corroboration of this unless the twenty-second gap between explosions recorded by Ch.Yeo.Sigs. T. Pearson is taken as evidence for a torpedo hit followed by a sympathetic detonation forward. In any event, *Audacity* sank at around 2210, her stern rising high out of the water.

Two aspects of *Audacity*'s sinking have been the subject of debate, both in the Board of Enquiry and in subsequent assessments of the event. The first of these was MacKendrick's decision to remove his ship from the main body of the convoy despite the absence of an escort. Although this action was in keeping with Western Approaches Convoy Instructions, the as yet unpractised Cdr Walker, who held six years' seniority over MacKendrick, regretted not having ordered *Audacity* onto the port side or into the centre of the convoy and questioned the advisability of permitting such a valuable ship to become separated at night. This view was endorsed by the Captain (D) in Liverpool but the suggestion was dismissed both by the Board and by Admiral Sir Percy Noble, Commander-in-Chief Western Approaches. The latter reiterated the fact that *Audacity*'s tactical dispositions were a matter for her commanding officer while the Board endorsed MacKendrick's decision to leave the convoy after much of its escort had departed. Nor, as Noble made clear, was remaining in the convoy any guarantee of safety: 'It is interesting to note that during a previous attack when *Audacity* was

in convoy, a torpedo passed twenty-five yards astern of her, and while she was out of convoy the merchant ship in her position was sunk.' The wisdom of Walker's diversionary manoeuvre and the illumination of the convoy caused by it was another aspect to attract attention, though the Board concluded this to have been an unfortunate but inevitable turn of events. In fact, Bigalk's war diary shows that snowflake played no part in alerting him to *Audacity*'s position since he already had her in his sights. Indeed, in obliging him to fire before he was quite ready the incident caused several key coordinates to be underestimated and sent three of his first four torpedoes wide of the mark.

Though Bigalk was awarded the Knight's Cross on his return to St-Nazaire, any satisfaction at his success had to be set against the loss of five U-boats (including Endrass in *U567*, sunk by HMSs *Deptford* and *Samphire* at the same time as *Audacity*) with only two merchant sinkings and a second warship (HMS *Stanley*) to show for a week's struggle during which a dozen commanders had been committed to battle. Worse still from the German perspective was the precedent set by *Audacity*'s role in the four convoys escorted by her, a development with far-reaching consequences for trade protection in the Battle of the Atlantic.

Fate of the crew

So helpless was *Audacity* following *U751*'s first hit that MacKendrick had no alternative but to order abandon ship stations, the Carley floats and ship's boats being lowered fully manned on their falls. As the ranking survivor (Lt Cdr W. E. Higham) later reported, by the time the second and third torpedoes struck the bulk of the crew had got clear of the ship for the loss of just one man. However, this second attack was of a different order to the first. Ch.Yeo.Sigs. T. Pearson had just fired a rocket from the bridge when he espied his ship's nemesis:

> I heard two torpedoes approaching reported from the flight deck. I saw the submarine almost on the beam about 3½ to 4½ cables away. I could see the two torpedoes coming towards the ship so I jumped down into the starboard bridge because I thought the flight deck would crumple, which it did.

Shattered by a major hit forward, *Audacity*'s stern reared up sharply and those still aboard began to abandon ship. Their lashings severed, *Audacity*'s Martlets were now sent skidding down the misshapen flight deck, forcing men to leap overboard. Within about fifteen minutes of Bigalk's second attack it was all over, those who had remained

Bigalk (in white cap) greeted at St-Nazaire by Kptlt Herbert Sohler, commanding the 7th *U-Flottille*, on return from a patrol in *U751* in the winter of 1941–2. *DUBMA*

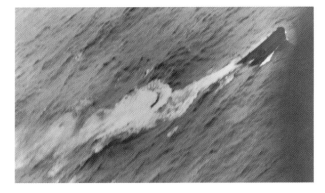

The end of *U751*, destroyed by RAF bombers off Cape Finisterre on 17 July 1942. *IWM*

aboard drawing much the shortest straw in terms of survival. By the time *Pentstemon*, *Marigold* and *Convolvulus* had picked up the last survivor two hours later on an exceptionally dark night, over seventy crewmen had lost their lives, most presumed drowned, with only two of *Audacity*'s pilots surviving. One of the casualties was Cdr MacKendrick, though he came within an ace of being rescued. Seeing him approach *Pentstemon*'s side, the First Lieutenant clambered down to secure him to a line but the ship rolled as he did so, striking MacKendrick a blow to the head which caused him to drown. However, MacKendrick's sacrifice was not forgotten and in 1943 one of the new merchant aircraft carriers, HMS *Empire MacKendrick*, was named in his honour.

U751 and Gerhard Bigalk

Built by the Kriegsmarinewerft at Wilhelmshaven and commissioned in January 1941, *U751* spent her entire operational career in the Atlantic under Kptlt Gerhard Bigalk, an officer with combat experience in naval air reconnaissance during the Spanish Civil War. His award of the Knight's Cross in 1941 was exceptional for an officer with such a reduced tonnage to his name, though it provides an indication of the importance given to carrier sinkings by the German propaganda machine, particularly in light of the loss of HMS *Ark Royal* (**39**) in November. The concession of the award may well be explained by propaganda claims that the victim was a Formidable-class carrier rather than the smaller *Unicorn* which B.d.U. concluded Bigalk to have despatched. *U751* went on to further successes off the eastern seaboard of North America in early 1942, but this run ended on 17 July when she was sunk off Cape Finisterre by RAF Lancaster and Whitley bombers at the beginning of her seventh patrol. There were no survivors.

Sources

Admiralty, *HG Convoys, 1941–1942: Reports of Proceedings* (TNA, ADM 199/932)

—, *Loss of HMS* Audacity *on 21/12/41: Board of Enquiry* (TNA, ADM 1/11895)

—, *Analysis of U-Boat Operations in Vicinity of HG76, 14–23 December 1941* (TNA, ADM 199/1998)

Goetze, Karl-Heinz, U-751 *versenkt den Flugzeugträger* Audacity (typescript, DUBMA, *U751* folder)

Blair, *Hitler's U-Boat War*, I, pp. 410–18

Brown, Capt. Eric M., *Wings of the Luftwaffe: Flying German Aircraft of the Second World War* (London: Macdonald & Janes, 1977)

Burn, Alan, *The Fighting Captain: Frederic John Walker RN and the Battle of the Atlantic* (Barnsley, S. Yorks.: Leo Cooper, 1993)

Heitmann, Jan, 'The Frontline: Convoy HG76 – The Offence' in Stephen Howarth and Derek Law, ed., *The Battle of the Atlantic, 1939–1945: The 50th Anniversary International Naval Conference* (London: Greenhill Books, 1994), pp. 490–507

Hobbs, Cdr David, *Royal Navy Escort Carriers* (Liskeard, Corn.: Maritime Books, 2003)

Nailer, Roger H., 'HMS *Audacity*' in *Warships*, Supplement no. 90 (Autumn 1987), pp. 9–12, and Supplement no. 91 (Winter 1987), pp. 41–5

Poolman, Kenneth, *The Winning Edge: Naval Technology in Action, 1939–1945* (Stroud, Glos.: Sutton Publishing, 1997)

—, *Allied Escort Carriers of World War II* (London: Blandford, 1998)

Roskill, *War at Sea*, I, pp. 478–9

Sainsbury, A. B., 'The Frontline: Convoy HG76 – The Defence' in Stephen Howarth and Derek Law, ed., *The Battle of the Atlantic, 1939–1945: The 50th Anniversary International Naval Conference* (London: Greenhill Books, 1994), pp. 508–15

Wemyss, Cdr D. E. G., *Relentless Pursuit: The Story of Capt. F. J. Walker, CB, DSO***, RN – U-Boat Hunter and Destroyer* (London: William Kimber, 1957)

Career history of HMS *Audacity*:
    http://www.naval-history.net/xGM-Chrono-05CVE-Audacity.htm

Convoy HG76 webpage:
    http://www.uboat.net/ops/convoys/battles.htm?convoy=HG-76

Fleet Air Arm Archive webpages: HMS *Audacity*:
    http://www.fleetairarmarchive.net/Ships/Audacity.html

802 Squadron:
    http://www.fleetairarmarchive.net/Squadrons/802.html

44   HMS *SALVIA*
Lt Cdr J. I. Miller, DSO DSC* RD RNR†
Sunk by *U568* (Type VIIC), Kptlt Joachim Preuss, 24 December 1941
Eastern Mediterranean, 40 nm NW of Sîdi Barrâni (Egypt)

Salvia, probably in the Mediterranean in late 1940 or some time in 1941. She and her entire company were lost to a torpedo from *U568* which also claimed the lives of at least a hundred Axis PoW survivors from the SS *Shuntien*. BfZ

Theatre   Mediterranean (Map 3)
Estimated coordinates   32° 09' N, 25° 20' E
Kriegsmarine code (probably incorrect)   Quadrat CO 6878
U-boat timekeeping   identical
Fatalities   59 and 100+   *Survivors*   none

Displacement   940 tons
Dimensions   205.25' × 33' × approx. 11.25'
Maximum speed   16 knots
Armament   1 × 4"; 4 × .303" AA

Career

For design notes on the Flower-class corvettes, see HMS *Picotee* (**29**).

Among the first of her type, the Flower-class corvette *Salvia* was laid down at William Simons & Co. of Renfrew, Scotland in September 1939, launched in August 1940 and completed that September after an unusually long gestation. She was to have a particularly active career, beginning with a prolonged U-boat hunt with her sister *Nasturtium* while working up at HMS *Western Isles*, the anti-submarine warfare training school at Tobermory. After five days aground off Harwich, in early November she sailed for Liverpool where she was assigned to the Mediterranean theatre with three of her sisters: *Gloxinia*, *Hyacinth* and *Peony*. Reaching Gibraltar on 23 November, this quartet served as escort to Operation COLLAR, one of the great Malta convoys, proceeding to Alexandria thereafter. Here they were formed into the 10th Corvette Group (Mediterranean) and began increasingly arduous convoy, minesweeping and anti-submarine duty in support of British and imperial forces in the Eastern Mediterranean. On 23 February 1941 *Salvia* and the sloop *Fareham* attempted to take the monitor *Terror* in tow after she had been bombed off Derna but to no avail as she sank the following day. It was during the German attack on Crete that *Salvia* sustained her first serious damage, being bombed at Suda Bay on 18 May with the loss of two men killed and eight wounded.

Five days later she reached Alexandria on one boiler. After repairs and a brief interlude at Famagusta on the Cypriot coast, *Salvia* entered the final phase of her career, supporting the British 8th Army in Cyrenaica in the teeth of enemy air superiority. That August she took the stricken netlayer HMS *Protector* under tow after the latter had been torpedoed by Axis aircraft, and her last months were spent on convoy operations between Alexandria and ports on the African coast. HMS *Salvia* was evidently as heavily engaged as any vessel on her station, and the decorations awarded her only CO, Lt Cdr John Miller RNR, provide some idea of his ship's wartime record.

Background of the attack

The afternoon of 23 December 1941 found HM destroyers *Heythrop* (Senior Officer of the Escort; **55**), *Hasty* and *Hotspur* and HM corvette *Salvia* escorting convoy TA5 between Tobruk and Alexandria, composed mainly of empty merchantmen. An exception was the SS *Shuntien* (3,059 GRT) with around a thousand German and Italian prisoners of war embarked. Less than three hours after leaving Tobruk, at around 1900 convoy time, *Shuntien* was attacked and sunk by *U559* (Kptlt Hans Heidtmann; see **42**) in position 32° 06' N, 24° 46' E, twenty-five miles north of Bardiyah (Bardia), Libya. The only escort in sight, *Salvia*, stopped to rescue survivors as the rest of the convoy sailed on, being joined by *Heythrop* in response to *Shuntien*'s distress signal. Decades later Ordinary Signalman Bob Parfitt of *Heythrop* recalled the scene:

> On arrival at the scene we found the corvette HMS *Salvia* with her sea boat away and already picking up survivors. The sea was one huge mass of floating heads and bodies emersed [sic] in an awful lot of oil. *Salvia*, who had already picked the Captain of the *Chungsan* [i.e. *Shuntien*] reported there could be an estimated four thousand [sic] men in the water as there had been a most orderly evacuation of the ship before she sank. Unfortunately for them, *Heythrop* picked up a very strong Asdic signal showing a U-Boat lurking right below these men in the water. Lt Comdr Stafford, not wanting to endanger his ship, did not put a boat away, but continued to hold the contact, while cruising at nine knots around the perimeter of survivors. Lines and grappling nets were down but the picking up of men from the water was, due to the heavy amount of oil, almost impossible. I remember myself fruitlessly holding hands with several men on the net, but to see and feel them slip away though the oil and probably though exhaustion, back into the sea from whence they had come. I do not remember how long we tried, but it was approaching dusk when the Captain (who was of course Senior Officer) felt it was time to call off the rescue operation and ordered *Salvia*, on return of her sea boat, to leave and make for Alex. She had by then over 100 survivors on board and we had eight: a ninth, an Engineer Officer from the *Chungsan* was picked out of the water 30 minutes later.

Although he may have intended to write 'four hundred', it should be noted that Parfitt's figure of 'four thousand men in the water' is a gross exaggeration; reports vary between 850 and 1,100 men under guard in addition to the crew. Moreover, his description of the sinking as having occurred in daylight is contradicted by German and British sources which agree that *Shuntien* was sunk after dark – as indeed the season and time of sinking would suggest. A message from Admiral Sir Andrew Cunningham (Commander-in-Chief Mediterranean Fleet) to the Admiralty on the 26th alludes to a last signal from *Salvia* at 2200 in which she reported being still on the scene having rescued a hundred survivors, though it has not proved possible to establish how many had been rescued by the time she turned for Alexandria. Whether this signal coincides with the order supposedly given by Lt Cdr R. S. Stafford in *Heythrop* for *Salvia* to quit the scene (see Parfitt above) cannot be established on the evidence so far uncovered, though witness testimony suggests that *Heythrop* was on the scene for no longer than about an hour. Whatever the case, no more was ever heard from *Salvia*. In the absence of any further information it must be supposed that midnight on the 23rd found her heading east towards Alexandria, her decks strewn with oil-soaked survivors of the *Shuntien*. At 0135 on the 24th, in a position now estimated to be approximately thirty miles east of the wreck of the *Shuntien*, she crossed the path of Kptlt Joachim Preuss' *U568*, then making her first war patrol since entering the Mediterranean. Already at 2330 on the 23rd Preuss had sighted a destroyer that may well have been *Heythrop* proceeding to Alexandria ahead of *Salvia*, but which disappeared out of range before he could acquire a firing position. This time, however, Preuss was not to be denied, and taking no chances fired a spread of four torpedoes from a range of 1,500 metres.

War Diary of *U568*, patrol of 4 December 1941–17 January 1942: PG 30604, NHB, reel 1,122, p. 760

Date, time	Details of position, wind, weather, sea, light, visibility, moonlight, etc.	Incidents
23.xii		
2237		Incoming W/T transmission from U-Boat Command:[1] *Heidtmann to maintain contact. Ringelmann, Kaufmann, Preuss to intercept convoy.* Beacon signal on 390 kHz.
2330		We see nothing at the rendezvous point and as we receive no further contact reports I decide to carry out a sweep further east at 10 knots for a while.[2] While thus engaged a destroyer heaves into sight off the port quarter making about 14 knots.[3] However, she soon disappears to the north-east. Due to a problem with one of the vents the tubes were not flooded from No. 3 tank and the destroyer had disappeared to the north-east before we could do so externally. Based on the course of the destroyer I assume the convoy lies in that direction. I alter course to 90°.
2400	[Qu.] CO 9211	*Preuß*
24.xii		
0135	[Qu.] CO 6878, wind NW 3, sea 3, overcast	A shadow in sight on the port quarter. Another destroyer.[4] Spread of four torpedoes fired, range 1,500 m, enemy bows right, [inclination] 100[°], speed 12 knots.[5] One hit after 78 sec. Oil spilling out catches fire, several detonations in the after part of the ship, fo'c's'le floats for a few more minutes while stern of ship sinks quickly. I want to approach to determine the name but suddenly the still-floating

---

1   In addition to *U568*, this signal from *F.d.U. Italien* (Korvkpt. Victor Oehrn; see **16**) was intended for *U559* (Kptlt Hans Heidtmann, who had sunk HMAS *Parramatta* a month earlier; **42**), *U75* (Kptlt Helmuth Ringelmann) and *U79* (Kptlt Wolfgang Kaufmann). *U79* had been scuttled earlier that day following damage by *Hotspur* and *Hasty*, while *U75* was sunk off Mersa Matrûh by HMS *Kipling* before the week was out.

2   The position of this supposed rendezvous is not known.

3   This may well have been HM escort destroyer *Heythrop* making her way to Alexandria having assisted in the rescue of *Shuntien*'s survivors.

4   Presumably HM corvette *Salvia*.

5   The brackets indicate a mistranscription in the log of *Länge* (length) for *Lage* (relative inclination of the target to the U-boat in degrees), the key coordinate required for the torpedo data computer. This error is confirmed by the torpedo report. The torpedoes were fired not by Preuss but by his First Watch Officer, Oblt.z.S. Gerhard Thäter, as was standard practice for night-time surface attacks.

foʼcʼsʼle is seen to be a second destroyer now bearing down on us.[6] I withdraw and head east to reload torpedoes because there must soon be a sighting of this convoy, or a report or beacon signal.

0024[7]	[Qu.] CO 6885	Now retrace my course to the west as I can see flashing lights far off in that direction. On closer inspection, however, this turns out to be sheet lightning. I also want to find out the name of that destroyer if possible though.
0613		Incoming W/T transmission from Heidtmann: *Convoy dispersed, one steamer sunk, another damaged.*[8]
0625		Reverse course and head east as there is nothing more to be seen.
⤢		
1445[9]		Navigational correction: 253°, 16 nm.
1600	[Qu.] CO 6887	
1623		Christmas radio message from B.d.U.
1745		Navigational correction: 330°, 6 nm.
2000	[Qu.] CO 6895	
2400	[Qu.] CO 6895	*Preuß*
25.xii		
0400	[Qu.] CO 6885	
0650[9]		Navigational correction: 243°, 10 nm.

---

6 Since *U568* was the only witness to *Salvia*'s loss it is plain that the bridge watch confused her 'still floating foʼcʼsʼle' for a second vessel.

7 Since the events described in this entry clearly succeed those described at 0135, it can be assumed that the time stated (0024) is an error of transcription, presumably 0224.

8 This from Kptlt Hans Heidtmann in *U559*. The 'steamer sunk' was the *Shuntien*. TA5 suffered no casualty at this time that would correspond with Heidtmann's 'damaged' vessel.

9 This entry and that for 0650 on the 25th are significant since they indicate that the attack on *Salvia* took place further west than Preuss's grid coordinate of 0135 on the 24th would suggest. This is as well since the 0135 quadrant raises the question as to how *Salvia* could have sailed the 55 miles separating the two sinking positions in the two to three hours available. In correcting his position by 16 miles to the west Preuss's entry of 1445 places his attack on *Salvia* just 40 miles east of *Shuntien*'s sinking, while a further positional adjustment of 10 miles to the west at 0650 on the 25th separates the two sinkings by under 30 miles

The sinking

The first inkling the British had of the loss of the *Salvia* came with her failure to respond to signals after her last transmission, supposedly at 2200 on the 23rd. An air search was instigated on Christmas Day with no success, the Admiralty War Diary for 26 December recording the possibility that she had been overpowered by her prisoners of war and the crew captured. This opinion was amended on 29 December following a signal from HM corvette *Peony* reporting oil and wreckage in position 31° 46' N, 28° 00' E on the 25th, approximately 165 miles east of the loss of the *Shuntien* and 110 miles east of *U568*'s attack coordinate. On this basis it was assumed probable that *Salvia* had been torpedoed by a U-boat on 24 December while returning to Alexandria with survivors from the *Shuntien*. This assessment of *Salvia*'s position, which would correspond with her supposed course towards Alexandria, has now permeated most secondary accounts of her loss but it does not tally with German records. Even with the slight easterly current, *Salvia* could not have covered 160 miles in the few hours that separate her leaving the scene of *Shuntien*'s sinking late on the 23rd and *U568*'s attack of 0135 early on the 24th. Nor is there anything in German records to corroborate the Admiralty's interpretation. The coordinates given at the head of this entry are therefore those corresponding with *U568*'s quadrant of 0135 as corrected at 1445 that day and at 0650 on the 25th (see below), not those recorded in Allied and other secondary sources. The wreckage discovered by *Peony* would appear to belong to a ship as yet unidentified.

Nor, it should be added, is the question of *Salvia*'s sinking position settled on a *prima facie* reading of Preuss's log. Assuming that *Salvia* did in indeed turn for Alexandria some time after 2200 on the 23rd,

the positions of both *Shuntien*'s and her own sinking as originally plotted would have required *Salvia* to maintain a speed of over twenty knots (four knots in excess of her best speed) in order to zigzag the fifty-five miles separating the two quadrants in the space of little more than three hours. Yet Preuss's attack at 0135 on the 24th was delivered against a target making only twelve knots, though the accuracy of the log transcription does not inspire confidence even on that point (see note 7). However, at 1445 on the 24th Preuss makes a navigational correction in his log of sixteen miles to the west, followed by another of

Preuss poses beside the conning tower of *U568* on 17 January 1942, the date she reached La Spezia from the patrol during which *Salvia* was sunk.
DUBMA

ten miles to the west at 0650 on the 25th thereby reducing the distance between the two sinkings to around thirty miles. The positional data for *Salvia*'s sinking provided at the head of this entry therefore corresponds to a quadrant twenty-six miles west of Preuss's 0135 plot and should not be regarded as more than an extrapolation from the available evidence.

Fate of the crew

Salvia is recorded by the Admiralty as having lost fifty-nine of her ship's company, a figure which does not include any she rescued from *Shuntien*. Though *Salvia* was recalled by O.Sig. Parfitt of *Heythrop* as having picked up at least a hundred men by the time his ship left the scene, the final figure may well have been much greater. Great enough, indeed, to make foundering through excessive topweight a possible contributory factor in her loss. However, although research has established the cause of *Salvia*'s sinking beyond reasonable doubt, nothing has emerged to shed light on the fate of her ship's company or those she rescued.

U568 and Joachim Preuss

For details of Preuss's and *U568*'s earlier career, see HMS *Picotee* (**29**).

The sinking of *Salvia* within two weeks of *U568* entering the Mediterranean was no harbinger of success for Preuss, and two further

patrols from La Spezia proved fruitless. In the early hours of 29 May 1942 *U568* was sunk by depth charges from the destroyers *Hero*, *Eridge* and *Hurworth* north-east of Tobruk, remarkably close to the position in which she may have despatched *Salvia* five months earlier. Her crew was more fortunate than *Salvia*'s, however, surviving the ordeal to a man. Kptlt Preuss was released in November 1947 after spending over five years in captivity. He died in May 1985.

Sources

Admiralty, War Diaries for 17–31 December 1941 (TNA, ADM 199/2219), pp. 761, 781, 839, 866 and 947
—, War Diaries for 1–6 January 1942 (TNA, ADM 199/2220), pp. 94 and 285
—, *Enemy Submarine Attacks on H.M. Ships, 1941* (TNA, ADM 199/160)
—, *Enemy Attacks on Merchant Shipping, 1941–1945* (TNA, ADM 199/1198)
Letter from O.Sig. Bob Parfitt (ex HMS *Heythrop*) to W. Betts recounting the sinking of SS *Shuntien*, High Wycombe, Bucks., 3 October 1992 (typescript, DUBMA, *U568* file)
Ruegg, R. A., *Flower-Class Corvettes* (typescript, IWM, 13(41).245/5, 1987)

Admiralty, *Naval Staff History, The Second World War: The Mediterranean*, II: *November 1940–December 1941* (London: HMSO, 1957)
Preston, Antony, and Alan Raven, *Flower Class Corvettes* [Ensign, no. 3] (London: Bivouac Books, 1973); reprinted as Man o'War, no. 7 (London: Arms and Armour Press, 1982)

45   *M-175* (ex *M-92*)

klt M. L. Melkadze, VMF†
Sunk by *U584* (Type VIIC), Kptlt Joachim Deecke, 10 January 1942
Barents Sea, 25 nm NW of Rybachy Peninsula (Russia)

Not *M-175* but her sister *M-174*, seen in the Kola Inlet in January 1943. *Miroslav Morozov*
Klt M. L. Melkadze, commander of *M-175*. *Miroslav Morozov*

Theatre Arctic (Map 2)		*Displacement* 210 tons surfaced 261.5 tons submerged	
Coordinates 70° 09' N, 32° 50' E		*Dimensions* 146' × 10.75' × 10'	
Kriegsmarine code Quadrat AC 8493		*Maximum speed* 13.5 knots surfaced 7.7 knots submerged	
U-boat timekeeping differential unknown		*Armament* 2 × 21" tt (2 torpedoes carried); 1 × 45 mm AA; 1 machine gun	
Fatalities 20 *Survivors* none			

Career

For background on the Soviet navy and details of the Malyutka class, see *M-99* (**27**).

Like her sisters *M-94* and *M-99* (**28** and **27**), the coastal submarine *M-92* was built at Leningrad's Sudomekh yard where she was launched in October 1937. Assigned to the *Krasnoznammenny Baltiiskii Flot* (Red Banner Baltic Fleet) in June 1938, she commissioned in October of that year. In May 1939 *M-92* was one of a number of submarines transferred via the White Sea Canal to the *Severny Flot* (Northern Fleet) based on Polyarny just north of Murmansk, her designation changing from *M-92* to *M-175* accordingly. Initially under the command of kapitan-leitenant (lieutenant-commander) P. N. Drachenov, she gained her first operational experience to the north of the Rybachy Peninsula during the 'Winter War' with Finland, though did not see action. The outbreak of war with Germany found *M-175* attached to the Northern Fleet's 4th Submarine Division and under the command of starshii leitenant (senior lieutenant; later kapitan-leitenant) M. L. Melkadze who had succeeded Drachenov in February 1941. *M-175*'s first four frontline patrols under Melkadze yielded no confirmed sinkings, though he claimed to have despatched a merchantman in the Norwegian port of Havninberg in October 1941 during the last of these. For this, however, no corroboration has been found in either German or Norwegian sources.

Background of the attack

The conflict in the northern theatre of the war at sea – encompassing the Barents Sea and parts of the Arctic Ocean – afforded the Soviet submarine service much greater freedom of movement than was the case in the Baltic (see *M-99*, **27**). The fifteen units based at Polyarny were joined on the outbreak of war by eight larger vessels from the Baltic and subsequently by a pair of British boats, HMS/ms *Tigris* and *Trident*. This submarine force was augmented by a number of auxiliary surface craft (essentially converted fishing vessels) and an increasing number of cruises were made into the Barents Sea and eventually as far as the Norwegian fjords. However, like the Germans, the Soviet navy found these northern waters to be a challenging environment for submarine operations. Although the Northern Fleet enjoyed year-round access to the Barents Sea from Polyarny, conditions were harsh with extreme cold, poor visibility and heavy seas the rule rather than the exception. Results were therefore always hard to come by, and though the Soviet naval command eventually claimed a million tons of German shipping for the Northern Fleet's submarine force between 1941 and 1944, post-war records indicate 100,000 tons to be closer to the mark. As early as 6 January 1942 Admiral V. I. Kuznetsov, Chief of Staff of the Soviet navy, was claiming forty-eight enemy merchantmen sunk without loss, but the most reliable modern source of data for this theatre corroborates only thirteen victims. Kuznetsov was, however, correct in stating that the Northern Fleet had yet to suffer the loss of a single submarine, though this statistic was not to stand for very much longer. Two days later *M-175* set out on her fifth frontline patrol. Early on the morning of 10 January a submerged *U584*, then en route from Niedenfjord to Kirkenes on her second patrol in northern waters, detected the presence of an enemy submarine on her hydrophone equipment.

War Diary of *U584*, patrol of 25 December 1941–11 January 1942: PG 30616, NHB, reel 1,125, p. 507

Date, time	Details of position, wind, weather, sea, light, visibility, moonlight, etc.	Incidents
10.i		
0000	[Qu.] AC 8547, wind NW 2, overcast, slightly agitated sea, visibility 2–3 nm	0110 dive to listen through hydrophones.
0400	[Qu.] AC 8493	At 0400 we hear the noise of engines, presumably a submarine. At 0550 engine noises are again audible, this time louder and gradually closing. Submarine is proceeding along a predetermined patrol line as is clear from her moving away and then back towards us. We get the contact repeatedly at similar ranges, increasing in intensity and then decreasing, gradually fading out altogether. We go to periscope depth. Submarine identified at a range of 1,000 m but disappears from our field of view. We go to T = 10 m to benefit from better hydrophone conditions and to await her return.[1] At 0640 we go to Battle Stations; engine noises are increasing once again, as expected. We go to periscope depth. Submarine is approaching us. I order a spread of four to be prepared, enemy speed 8 knots (data acquired from hydrophone readings). At 0722 we fire and 65 sec. later we hear two powerful detonations. Periscope was unfortunately awash at this point. We surface immediately; a pall of smoke still hangs over the scene and there is nothing more to see. No further hydrophone effect after the shot. The attack had the advantage of being made in good visibility, brightly moonlit night; submarine had a tall and lengthy

---

1 By 'T = 10 m' Deecke seems to be recording a dive not of 10 metres (33 feet, which would equate to a negligible and unremarkable ascent of 3 meters above the standard periscope depth recorded earlier), but a much greater one of 150 metres (492 feet). Such a dive would not only be more appropriate for hydrophone purposes but would be consistent with his recording *U584*'s return to periscope depth two lines later. For a full discussion of the 'T =' notation, see Reading the *Kriegstagebücher*, p. xxxvii.

Date, time	Details of position, wind, weather, sea, light, visibility, moonlight, etc.	Incidents
		conning tower with a small deck, and with no gun apparent.[2] Nor could we make out a deck gun for'ard – it was too dark for that, and the periscope was constantly awash in the swell. We set course for home.
0800	[Qu.] AC 8491, wind WSW 3, 4/10 overcast, light fog, rough sea, visibility 1 nm	Between 0917 and 1045 we proceed submerged due to thick fog. Hydrophones manned.

---

2 Deecke's description is accurate with the probable exception of *M-175*'s armament, the Malyutka-class boats carrying a 45-mm anti-aircraft gun together with a machine gun.

The sinking and fate of the crew

The circumstances of *M-175*'s sinking initially left the Northern Fleet command with little indication as to her fate. Failing to respond to repeated radio signals and long overdue at Polyarny, *M-175* was presumed lost with all hands, though the possibility of her having been accounted for by a U-boat was only entertained once the Soviets obtained copies of a Finnish newspaper issued on 18 January reporting a German submarine as having sunk a Russian submarine. While there can be no conclusive proof regarding the identity of *U584*'s victim, the fact that *M-175* went missing at this time in an area patrolled by no other submarine of the Northern Fleet makes the circumstantial evidence overwhelming.

Klt Melkadze and his nineteen crewmen presumably died instantly in the powerful detonations described in Deecke's war diary. Among them was the chief engineer of the 4th Submarine Division, inzhener-kapitan-leitenant (engineer lieutenant-commander) V. S. Shilyaev, assigned to *M-175* in a non-functional capacity. Commended for his heroism following the sinking of *M-94* (**28**), Shilyaev had now fallen victim to a second submarine disaster.

U584 and Joachim Deecke

Built by Blohm & Voss at Hamburg and commissioned in August 1941, *U584* carried out eleven frontline patrols, all but one under the command of Kptlt Joachim Deecke. After four patrols in the northern theatre and with *M-175* her only victim, *U584* was transferred to the Atlantic in May 1942 where she managed to notch up just five sinkings in as many patrols. In June 1942 *U584* put a party of four German agents ashore on the North Carolina coast in a rubber dinghy, their remit to carry out sabotage operations against key US installations. The infiltration was not a success and all were executed after being betrayed by two agents landed earlier by *U202*. *U584* went on to take part in a number of major pack operations but her career ended in the spring of 1943 just as the balance of power in the Battle of the Atlantic was about to shift decisively in favour of the Allies. On 31 March she was caught on the surface by Avenger torpedo bombers from the escort carrier USS *Card* while refuelling from *U91*. Both boats dived but *U584* was bombed and sunk with her entire crew. Joachim Deecke was the second member of his family to perish in command of a U-boat, an older brother Jürgen being lost when *U1* apparently struck a mine off the Dutch coast in April 1940.

An undated shot of Joachim Deecke. *DUBMA*

Sources

Basov, A. V., *Flot v Velikoi Otechestvennoi Voine 1941–45* (Moscow: Akademiya Nauk SSSR, 1980)

Bendert, Harald, *U-Boote im Duell* (Hamburg: Mittler, 1996)

Ignatyev, E. P., *Podvodniye lodki XII Serii* (St Petersburg: Izdatel'stvo Gangut, 1996)

Maksimov, Y. A., and S. N. Khakhanov, *Bor'ba za zhivuchest' podvodnikh lodok SF SSSR v Velikoi Otechestvennoi voine 1941–1945 pri vozdeistvii oruzhiya protivnika*, Part II (Moscow: Minister'stvo Oborony [Ministry of Defence] [restricted circulation], 1958)

Piterskij, N. A., *Die Sowjetische Flotte im Zweiten Weltkrieg* (Hamburg: Gerhard Stalling, 1966)

Platonov, A. V., *Entsiklopediya sovetskikh podvodnykh lodok, 1941–1945* (Moscow: Izdatel'stvo Poligon, 2004)

Polmar, Norman, and Jurrien Noot, *Submarines of the Russian and Soviet Navies, 1718–1990* (Annapolis, Md.: Naval Institute Press, 1991)

Rohwer, Jürgen, with J. S. Kay and I. V. Venkov, *Allied Submarine Attacks of World War Two: European Theatre of Operations, 1939–1945* (Annapolis, Md.: Naval Institute Press, 1997)

Rohwer, Jürgen, and M. S. Monakov, *Stalin's Ocean-Going Fleet* (London: Frank Cass, 2001)

Vinogradov, Admiral N. I., *Voennye Memuary: Podvodny Front* (Moscow: Voennoe Izdatel'stvo, 1989)

Webpage devoted to *M-175*:
   http://www.town.ural.ru/ship/ship/m175.php3

46 HMS *GURKHA* (ii)

Cdr C. N. Lentaigne, DSO RN
Sunk by *U133* (Type VIIC), Oblt.z.S. Hermann Hesse, 17 January 1942
Eastern Mediterranean, 20 nm N of Sîdi Barrâni (Egypt)

Gurkha, possibly at Alexandria in December 1941 or January 1942. Hesse's torpedo wrecked the stern section of the ship as far
forward as the after superstructure. *BfZ*

Theatre	Mediterranean (Map 3)	*Displacement*	1,920 tons
Coordinates	31° 50' N, 26° 15' E	*Dimensions*	362.25' × 37' × 10'
Kriegsmarine code	Quadrat CO 9224	*Maximum speed*	36 knots
U-boat timekeeping	identical	*Armament*	8 × 4" AA; 4 × 40 mm AA; 4 × 20 mm AA; 8 × .5" AA; 8 × 21" tt
Fatalities 9	*Survivors* 235+		

Career

Ordered from Cammell Laird of Birkenhead under the 1937 estimates, HMS *Gurkha* was the third unit of the 'L'-class destroyers. They were products of the debate concerning the relative merits of the large Tribal-class destroyers on the one hand and the smaller 'J' and 'K' classes on the other, along with assessments of the tactical requirements likely to be placed on the Royal Navy in the coming war. These boiled down to improved firepower in enclosed 4.7-inch mountings on the smaller hull of the traditional fleet destroyer, a solution which it was hoped would allow the resulting units to give a better account of themselves in a surface action while permitting of more rapid construction. In the event, enemy action and production shortages meant that few took less than two years to complete while most required around thirty months to enter service. Even then four units of the class, *Gurkha* included, were completed with the older 4-inch mounting, though this represented a significant improvement to their anti-aircraft armament.

The ship was laid down as the *Larne* in October 1938 but renamed at the instance of the Brigade of Gurkhas following the loss of the Tribal-class destroyer *Gurkha* off Bergen in April 1940, the Brigade subscribing a day's pay towards her construction. The fact that *Gurkha*'s first and only CO, Cdr C. N. Lentaigne, had a brother in the Brigade (Lieutenant-Colonel 'Joe' Lentaigne) may not have been unconnected with the decision. The new HMS *Gurkha* was launched

in July 1940 and completed the following February. After working up at Scapa Flow *Gurkha* was assigned first to the 11th and then to the 9th Escort Group of Western Approaches Command, but on 26 March 1941 was involved in a major collision which kept her at Rosyth until the end of June where she was fitted with the prototype of the FH3 high-frequency direction-finding set, the first carried at sea. From now on she was hardly to know a moment's rest. In July and August 1941 she served as local escort for convoys WS9C, WS10 and WS10X in their passage to the Middle East, being detached from the latter on 19 August to bolster the defence of the Gibraltar-bound OG71 which had lost HNorMS *Bath* (**30**) to U-boat attack. Allocated to the 4th Destroyer Flotilla at Gibraltar in early September, *Gurkha* was soon pitched into the maelstrom of Mediterranean operations. Towards the end of that month she and her sister *Legion* participated in Operation HALBERD, one of the major convoys to Malta, these two despatching the Italian submarine *Adua* off Algeria on the 30th. After a spell with Force H (during which she stood by the crippled *Ark Royal* following *U81*'s attack on 13 November; **39**), *Gurkha* sailed for a month's refit and repair at Devonport, returning to Gibraltar with convoy WS14 in mid-December. Assigned to the Mediterranean Fleet, *Gurkha* quit Gibraltar for Alexandria on the 22nd, reaching that port by way of Malta on the 29th. The association lasted less than three weeks.

Background of the attack

The mining of the battleships *Queen Elizabeth* and *Valiant* by Italian frogmen in Alexandria on the night of 19 December 1941 left the British Mediterranean Fleet at a low ebb and the defence of the Eastern and Central Mediterranean to the 15th Cruiser Squadron and a handful of destroyers. Not only had the strength of the Fleet been reduced by war attrition, but the scale of its commitments remained undiminished with Malta besieged and the British Army in North Africa relying on the Navy for essential supplies. It was to replenish Malta that convoy MW8B left Alexandria on 16 January 1942. This consisted of SSs *Clan Ferguson* and *City of Calcutta* escorted by HMSs *Gurkha* (Senior Officer of the Escort), *Legion* and *Maori* together with

HrMs *Isaac Sweers* (**74**). At daybreak on the 17th the destroyers took up their positions for the usual dawn air attack, *Gurkha* less than half a cable off *City of Calcutta*'s starboard bow where her powerful anti-aircraft armament could be used to best advantage. However, the real danger this morning came not from above the waves but beneath them, and in an area where the U-boat arm had already claimed HMS *Salvia* (**44**) three weeks earlier. Steaming at just under eighteen knots some twenty miles north of Sîdi Barrâni, at 0738 (Zone B time, in which British timekeeping coincided with German) *Gurkha*'s Asdic operator reported a non-submarine echo to starboard, qualifying it as 'a very small extent of target – moving rapidly right'. He had detected one of a spread of four torpedoes fired by *U133*.

War Diary of *U133*, patrol of 1–22 January 1942: PG 30123, NHB, reel 1,083, pp. 663–4

Date, time	Details of position, wind, weather, sea, light, visibility, moonlight, etc.	Incidents
17.i		
0400	Qu. CO 9215, wind W 4, sea 3–4, cloud 7, good visibility	
0610		We dive and proceed underwater.
0710		Hydrophone effect at bearing 107° true, we go up to periscope depth. Noise first starts with a propeller of a steamer, 70–80 revolutions. These are soon drowned out by propeller noises of first one destroyer and then a second. Through the periscope I can make out the slender mast tips of two destroyers – they're proceeding on a westerly course in relatively close order. Range about 4,500 m. From about 0725 we receive impulses from the *S-Gerät*.[1] As the destroyers are heading directly towards me at an inclination of 0° I alter course to the south and then turn about. One of the destroyers, proceeding on a south-westerly course at an inclination of 80°, bows right, is some 2,500 m away. I prepare to attack this destroyer. As I am turning as part of my attacking manoeuvre the other destroyer suddenly looms large in the left-hand side of the periscope, range 1,000 m, inclination 90°, bows right, speed 15 knots.[2] A spread of four torpedoes is ready to go. The inclination increases further to 100° by the time I get the shot away. We keep the boat from surfacing by running the engines at ¾ speed and ordering 'all men forward'. Boat then begins to dive. After 48 seconds we hear the torpedoes hit, then a few seconds later a secondary detonation (boilers, depth charges on deck or magazine).[3] Two to three minutes after that we hear the typical noises of a ship sinking, like pebbles falling through water. It was a destroyer of the Jervis class that we hit.[4]
0735		After diving we go to 160 m and head off to the north. At about 0800 an intensive hydrophone and echo-sounding pursuit begins. Twenty-two depth charges are dropped, some of which are extremely well aimed, and in one approach dropped right overhead. For a brief period there are three destroyers working together though for most of it we had only two to endure. The men conducted themselves irreproachably and were proud to have got through their 'baptism of fire'.[5] There were no adverse effects that could be described as serious. The depth charges were dropped in patterns of five, though also individually on occasions.

---

1   The *S-Gerät* (*Such-Gerät* – 'search apparatus') active sonar device enabled U-boats to detect minefields or targets.

2   HMS *Gurkha*. The convoy was in fact steaming at 18 knots.

3   Equates to a range of 720 metres.

4   Hesse's attack sketch depicts him firing his spread at a 'Jervis-class destroyer' with a Tribal beyond and slightly further ahead. This is curious since the vessel to port of *Gurkha* was the freighter *City of Calcutta* and the torpedo running time of 48 seconds (720 metres) suggests that it was the nearer of the two vessels which was hit. The lack of confirming data raises the question as to whether Hesse was not in fact aiming at *Legion* and *Isaac Sweers* which together answer the description of a Jervis- and Tribal-class destroyer rather better than *Gurkha* and *City of Calcutta*. However, from the testimony of *Gurkha*'s Asdic operator it appears that *U133*'s other three torpedoes passed astern, an observation that accords with Hesse's underestimation of the target's speed. This appears the most likely scenario in the absence of fuller information.

5   As indicated by Hesse, this was *U133*'s first and indeed only experience of Allied counter-attack.

1020		Hydrophone noises now receding. As they do so we can also hear the odd depth charge still being dropped.
1105		We surface and transmit following short signal: *Convoy Qu. CO 9214, westerly course.*[6] This short signal is retransmitted that evening as *Convoy CO 90, 214 degrees west.* A shame that shore-based radio operators can't even manage to decode a short signal correctly.
1120		We dive and resume underwater cruising.
1200	Qu. CO 9222, wind W 2, sea 2, cloud 2, good visibility	
1600	Qu. CO 9223	A few more depth charges heard at extreme range, almost indistinguishable, very slight hydrophone effect.
1815		We surface and resume cruising on the surface. Pointless trying to catch up with the convoy as it must be at least 80 nm ahead now. This is a head start we can't hope to make up in a single night, even with all engines at full ahead. To continue cruising on the surface by day is not possible given the air cover.
2000	Qu. CO[7]	
2038		Outgoing W/T transmission 0730/17: *Qu. 9224 attacked two destroyers. One sunk. Depth charges. Still two Etos forward and two aft – Hesse.*[8]
2145		Incoming W/T transmission 2114/17: *To Reschke and Hesse.*[9] *Reschke operate using hydrophones, Hesse ditto, report your intentions if situation still looks promising. F.d.U.*[10]
2235		Incoming W/T transmission 2204/17: *To Hesse. Keep it up. Give the English a beating! F.d.U.* What a proud and happy day for our boat!

6 This entry and the corresponding one in the torpedo report no doubt explain why the Kriegsmarine quadrant for this incident is sometimes given as 9214. However, both Hesse's signal of 2038 and his plot of the attack record it as 9224. The latter is preferred as it equates more closely to the Allied coordinates of the attack.

7 Quadrant code incomplete.

8 'Eto' is Kriegsmarine shorthand for the electric G7e torpedo.

9 Kptlt Franz-Georg Reschke was patrolling the same waters in *U205* (see **63**).

10 This and the following signal were sent by *F.d.U. Italien* (Officer Commanding U-Boats, Italy), in this case Korvkpt. Victor Oehrn (see **16**).

The sinking

Though both Cdr Lentaigne and a large number of ratings testified to a double explosion, it appears that *Gurkha* was struck by only one of *U133*'s torpedoes, to which Hesse's own interpretation of a secondary explosion lends support. This was later asserted by Lentaigne to have been the detonation of the after magazine. The damage was extensive, the torpedo blasting a hole some twenty-five feet across at the waterline and flooding all compartments abaft the engine room. The after superstructure partly collapsed, the starboard propeller shaft snapped, the lubrication pumps and steam dynamos were put out of action and the fire main fractured. This last prevented action being taken against the two fires which now broke out – 'the first an oil fuel fire both inside the hull and spreading outward and to windward on the surface of the water; the second a fire both inside and outside the after superstructure mainly fed by the ready-use ammunition on deck'. Any chance of bringing the conflagration under control was dashed by the inability of the crew to reach the seventy-ton portable pump which lay at the heart of the inferno. With no power, a wrecked switchboard and most compartments abaft the engine room flooded, little could be done to quell the blaze which raged out of control fuelled by a combination of depth charges, 4-inch and Oerlikon ammunition. Though topweight was jettisoned and efforts made to close all watertight doors within reach, the battle to save *Gurkha* became increasingly futile. As Cdr Lentaigne recalled, 'at approximately 0820 the ship was showing definite signs of foundering, and the fire had, if anything, increased

and was spreading for'ard, and I considered the chance of saving the ship so reduced that it was necessary to consider saving life'. Though a nine-inch manila line was swum over to *Isaac Sweers* by a volunteer and *Gurkha* towed clear of the blazing oil, the ship's reserve of buoyancy had been lost and the end was nigh. Lentaigne again: 'The ship took a heavy list to port – then flung her bows upward and sank at 0909.'

The Board of Enquiry held seven weeks later in HMS *Sikh* criticised the lack of direction in the aftermath of the blast, particularly with respect to the engine-room personnel. However, no blame was apportioned, it being recognised that the loss of the Chief Engineer and the First Lieutenant in the initial detonation had deprived the ship of the two officers best equipped to lead the damage-control effort. It also accepted that fires had broken out in the area in which damage control was most essential, and that these could not have been effectively combated in the circumstances.

Fate of the crew

Gurkha lost a total of nine men, all in the wardroom when the torpedo exploded beneath them. Five officers who were at breakfast and four of their stewards were killed outright. The only survivor from the wardroom was Sub-Lt Keal RNVR who had been in an armchair when the blast occurred. Shielded from the worst of the blast but having nonetheless suffered two broken legs, he escaped by paddling his armchair across the now flooded wardroom and diving out of the hole on *Gurkha*'s starboard side. Lentaigne recalled that 'there was about

Hesse (in white cap) with his officers on the casing of *U133* in November or December 1941. The conning tower sports the famous snorting bull first worn by Günther Prien's *U47* (see **2**) and taken as the device of the 7th *U-Flottille* after her loss in March 1941. *DUBMA*

a yard of clear water between the ship's side and the burning water. A young New Zealand AB saw this officer and went over the side and dragged him forward when he was hoisted on deck – a very brave act for which the AB was awarded the BEM and he certainly saved this officer's life, though unfortunately this officer lost one leg.' Surgeon Lt Maurice Brown RNVR, the ship's medical officer, was in the foremost cabin flat when *Gurkha* was hit and found himself trapped by fire in the flat itself and by wreckage covering the hatchway above. He was saved by the secondary detonation which not only flooded the flat but created a hole in the deckhead through which Brown gained the duplex pistol room and then the open deck, which, to the astonishment of onlookers, he reached by crawling through a vent. A number of ratings were trapped on the quarterdeck, which was awash, to be rescued by *Gurkha*'s whaler which navigated the oil fire and took them off. Shortly before 0830 the non-swimmers and the injured were transferred to *Isaac Sweers* in the port motor boat and the whaler. Retaining thirty-five ratings and two officers, Lentaigne ordered the other 155 to ensure that their lifebelts were inflated and abandon ship over the port bow. From there they swam to *Isaac Sweers*, then lying about two cables to the north-west. The rest followed half an hour later with the exception of Lentaigne who was still on board when *Gurkha* sank though

survived to be rescued. When all survivors, including six seriously injured men, were aboard *Isaac Sweers* at 0950, a muster was called which confirmed the nine wardroom fatalities – a remarkably small toll in the circumstances. All but the injured were landed at Tobruk on the 18th, to be picked up later by HM corvette *Gloxinia*.

The loss of two *Gurkhas* in as many years made the Admiralty reluctant to revive the name and the Brigade of Gurkhas unwilling to press the matter, and it was not until the 1960s that another was commissioned, the fourth to enter service in the Royal Navy since 1907.

U133 and Hermann Hesse

Built by Bremer Vulkan at Vegesack and commissioned in July 1941, *U133*'s career consisted of just four frontline patrols. The first of these took her to the North Atlantic under Oblt.z.S. Hermann Hesse, but *U133* enjoyed no success while part of the *Stosstrupp*, *Raubritter* or *Störtebecker* groups. Her second patrol in December 1941 brought her into the Mediterranean, Hesse taking her through the Straits of Gibraltar shortly before Christmas. With *U133*'s third patrol in January 1942 came her only victim, HMS *Gurkha*, command of the boat then passing to Oblt.z.S. Eberhard Mohr in March 1942. In what would prove one of the shortest operational careers of any U-boat commander, *U133* was lost with all hands within two hours of leaving Salamis having struck a German-laid mine after Mohr deviated from his prescribed route.

Hermann Hesse was promoted Kapitänleutnant in February 1942 and held three staff positions before taking command of the Type-IXC *U194* in January 1943. Located by a US Catalina south of Iceland, *U194* was sunk on 24 June, just days into her first patrol. There were no survivors.

Sources

Admiralty, *Enemy Submarine Attacks on H.M. and Allied Warships, January–June 1942* (TNA, ADM 199/162)

Arthur, Max, ed., *The Navy: 1939 to the Present Day* (London: Hodder & Stoughton, 1997)

English, John, Afridi *to* Nizam: *British Fleet Destroyers, 1937–43* (Gravesend, Kent: World Ship Society, 2001)

Smith, Peter C., *Fighting Flotilla: HMS* Laforey *and Her Sister Ships* (London: William Kimber, 1976)

Career history of HMS *Gurkha*: http://www.naval-history.net/xGM-Chrono-10DD-41L-Gurkha2-ex-Larne.htm

47   HMS *MATABELE*

Cdr A. C. Stafford, DSC RN†

Sunk by *U454* (Type VIIC), Kptlt Burkhard Hackländer, 17 January 1942

Barents Sea, 20 nm ENE of Kil'din Island (Russia)

May 1940 *Matabele* entering the anchorage at Hvalfjörður, Iceland in the second half of 1941.
A terrible fate awaited her and her men in the Barents Sea. *IWM*

Campaign Arctic convoys (Map 2)		*Displacement* 1,960 tons	
Coordinates 69° 21' N, 35° 24' E		*Dimensions* 377' × 36.5' × 9'	
Kriegsmarine code Quadrat AC 8945		*Maximum speed* 36 knots	
U-boat timekeeping differential –1 hour		*Armament* 6 × 4.7"; 2 × 4" AA; 4 × 40 mm AA; 8 × .5" AA; 4 × 21" tt	
Fatalities 236 *Survivors* 2 (possibly 3)			

Career

For design notes on the Tribal-class destroyers, see HMS *Cossack* (**37**).

HMS *Matabele* was laid down at Scotts of Greenock as the eighth unit in the famous Tribal class of fleet destroyers in October 1936. Launched in October 1937 and completed in January 1939, she was commissioned into the 2nd Tribal Destroyer Flotilla (subsequently renumbered the 6th Destroyer Flotilla) Home Fleet with which she remained for the rest of her career. Among her first and saddest duties was to join in the desperate efforts to rescue those trapped in the submarine *Thetis* after she sank to the bottom of Liverpool Bay on 1 June 1939. The outbreak of war found *Matabele* with the Home Fleet at Scapa Flow, her first action coming during the rescue of HMS/m *Spearfish* (**14**) in the North Sea on 26–27 September. Patrol and blockade duty in the Atlantic and the North Sea continued until turbine defects brought her into Devonport in January 1940 where the opportunity was taken to carry out degaussing work. Rejoining the Home Fleet in March, *Matabele* was soon flung into the Norwegian Campaign which began on 9 April and gave the Royal Navy its first taste of sustained air attack. On the night of 17–18 May she and the cruiser *Effingham* grounded on the Foksen shoal while ferrying troops and equipment between Harstad and Bodø. Both were heavily damaged but *Effingham* could not be salvaged and had to be despatched by gunfire and torpedoes from *Matabele*. Repairs at Falmouth continued until August during which 'X' 4.7-inch turret was replaced by a twin 4-inch high-angle mounting, a recognition of the need for improved anti-aircraft defence shared by all British pre-war destroyer construction. Rejoining the Home Fleet, *Matabele* fell into a routine of escort and patrol duty punctuated with occasional sweeps off occupied Norway, one of which resulted in the sinking of a 400-ton coaster off Åndalsnes during an attack on a German coastal convoy on the night of 23–24 October. January 1941 found her covering a minelaying operation off Norway before briefly forming part of the escort for the battleship *King George V* on her passage to the United States with the new British ambassador, Lord Halifax. A refit at Barrow-in-Furness in April and June was prolonged until August by her running aground outside that port on 5 June, severe damage being done to brackets, shafts and propellers. Rejoining the Home Fleet, in late August and early September she was involved in the delivery of Hurricane fighters to Russia which took her as far as Murmansk. Service continued off Norway and in the North Sea until 11 January 1942 when *Matabele* and her sister *Somali* (**70**) were ordered to join the escort for convoy PQ8 to Murmansk.

The Arctic convoy campaign and background of the attack

The entry of the Soviet Union into the war on the Allied side in June 1941 opened another theatre for the Royal Navy at a time when her resources were stretched to the limit. Russia was to receive the majority of her wartime supplies from the US via the Persian Gulf, but the 'Kola Run' as it became known proved a critical means for supplying the embattled northern front. In August of that year the Admiralty instigated a convoy route to North Russia designated PQ (later JW) in its eastbound and QP (later RA) in its westbound phase. During the summer and autumn these convoys used the port of Archangel on the White Sea, but after QP4 became icebound in November they were rerouted to Murmansk at the head of the Kola Inlet. The initial convoys got through without loss but the Kriegsmarine could

not allow this endeavour to go on unchecked and responded with increasingly ferocious attacks by air, surface and submarine units as the winter of 1941–2 wore on. The *U-Boot-Waffe* opened its account in these waters with the *Ulan* (Uhlan) group (*U134*, *U454* and *U584*), the first to be formed in the northern theatre. On 2 January 1942 *U134* attacked PQ7A, accounting for SS *Waziristan* and her cargo of military supplies. Eight days later *U584* sank the Soviet submarine *M-175* (45) in the Barents Sea. The next eastbound convoy, PQ8, was intercepted by Kptlt Burkhard Hackländer's *U454* on 17 January while under escort by HM cruiser *Trinidad*, the destroyers *Somali* (70) and *Matabele*, and the minesweepers *Harrier* and *Speedwell*. In two attacks that evening *U454* struck both the convoy commodore's vessel (the SS *Harmatris*) and *Matabele*, whose end foreshadowed the terrible ordeal awaiting any whose ship sank quickly at such latitudes.

War Diary of *U454*, patrol of 25 December 1941–20 January 1942: PG 30507, NHB, reel 1,110, pp. 663–4

Date, time	Details of position, wind, weather, sea, light, visibility, moonlight, etc.	Incidents
17.i		
1500	Qu. AC 9773	Plumes of smoke at bearing 250° true. We set off in pursuit; it is the convoy proceeding on a westerly course in its previous formation.[1]
1542		Outgoing W/T transmission: *Enemy convoy in sight Qu. AC 9771, proceeding on westerly course.*
1600	Qu. AC 9747, wind NW 2, sea 1, clearing from the west, visibility W 6–7 nm, E and N 2–3 nm	I now presume the convoy is bound for Murmansk. We haul ahead.
1623		Outgoing W/T transmission: *Take note of beacon signals.* Beacon signals sent at 1659, 1720, 1750 and 1820. Previous radio transmissions have not been acknowledged by HQ. Given our experience to date, however, I reckon that the other two boats (*U134* and *U585*) can hear me even if HQ cannot.
1837		Outgoing W/T transmission: *Three destroyers, five steamers, convoy steering 270°.* This W/T transmission is the first to be acknowledged by HQ.
1831[2]	Qu. AC 8952, clear, bright night, no moon, starlit, Northern Lights, visibility 6–7 nm	I run in to attack starboard side of convoy. Attack will have to be executed with the Northern Lights behind me; hauling round to the south would waste too much time. Besides, this would place the boat between the convoy and the shoreline, limiting our freedom of movement. Convoy is proceeding in a ragged broad formation, with the three destroyers positioned one ahead, one on the starboard bow and the other on the port quarter.[3]
1846	Qu. AC 8952	Spread of two torpedoes fired from Tubes II and IV at the steamer on the extreme right of convoy. Range 4,600 m, inclination 90°. Another spread of two fired from Tubes I and III at destroyer on starboard side, range 3,000 m, inclination 100°.[4] We turn about.
		Shot fired from Tube V at the same destroyer. Inclination 100°, range 2,000 m.
		5 min. 7 sec. after firing the first spread a hit amidships on the steamer initially targeted.[5] A tall grey-black explosion column, vessel is set ablaze and stops. No further observation possible as another steamer then crosses our line of sight.
		2 min. 5 sec. after stern shot a hit on the destroyer witnessed by I.WO, *Obersteuermann* and the after lookout; I was busy keeping an eye on the other picket.[6] Powerful detonation audible throughout

---

1   Hackländer had already sighted PQ8 at 1040 and then again at 1255, identifying six steamers in line abreast escorted by what he interpreted as three 'V & W'-class destroyers, one stationed ahead of the convoy and the other two on its port and starboard beams. Though its dispositions are not known at either of these junctures, the escort in fact consisted of the cruiser *Trinidad*, the Tribal-class destroyers *Somali* and *Matabele*, and the minesweepers *Harrier* and *Speedwell*.

2   The break in the chronological sequence here reflects the original.

3   See n. 1 for the actual composition of the escort. Only the identity of the 'destroyer' on the starboard bow is clear: HM cruiser *Trinidad*.

4   HMS *Trinidad*.

5   This was SS *Harmatris* (5,395 GRT), the commodore's vessel, which reported that she had struck a mine. She eventually reached port under tow.

6   Despite the witnesses cited by Hackländer, *Trinidad* was not in fact struck. The first of those mentioned, First Watch Officer Lt.z.S. Dauter, fired all of *U454*'s

the boat. A column of water spurting up to mast height and a blaze of flame. However, the destroyer doesn't list at all but continues to steam slowly on. The forward picket turns sharply, steams past the torpedoed destroyer and closes us at a very sharp inclination. We haul away to the north with both engines at utmost speed. The stern escort causes us no difficulty; the subsequent counter-attack is derisory with no starshell and just three depth charges dropped.

1920		Destroyer alters course away from us, disappears from sight.
1930	Qu. AC 8952	We alter course to 270° so as to remain close to the convoy. Reloading Tubes II, III and V.
1955		Outgoing W/T transmission: *Attacked, have lost contact.*
2000	Qu. AC 8952, wind NW 3–4, sea 3, clear. Visibility 6 nm.	
2017		Incoming W/T transmission: *KrKr Hackländer from Admiral Arctic Waters. Report last position of convoy.*[7]
2035		Outgoing W/T transmission: *Last sighted position of enemy Qu. AC 8952, enemy steering westerly course, 10 knots.*
2130	Qu. AC 8916	Have headed south to re-establish contact with convoy. After a short time the coastline appears dimly some 12–15 nm off. This means boat is positioned further south than we thought.
2141		Incoming W/T transmission: *Lohse from Admiral Arctic Waters.*[8] *Probable destination of convoy Murmansk.*[9]
2204	Qu. AC 8945	Ship's position calculated according to radio signal from Teriberski-Kharlov.[10] Vessels sighted steering 270°: the convoy. We are in a favourable position. Seven to eight vessels in a ragged broad formation though the individual units are hard to discern against the dark coastal horizon. We run in to attack.
2220	Qu. AC 8945	Spread of two fired from Tubes II and III at the destroyer stationed on the convoy's starboard beam which has just steamed up from the rear.[11] Inclination 90°, range 4,000 m.
2223		Shot fired from Tube V at a 2,000-ton steamer to the left of the targeted destroyer. Inclination 100°, range 4,000 m.
2224[12]		A hit aft on the destroyer, a detonation which causes a high column of water and a great blaze of flame. The stern section of the ship rears up vertically and sinks within 30 sec. The fo'c's'le disappears in the cloud of smoke.
2225		Stern shot hits steamer.[13] A huge detonation ensues, accompanied by a column of flame 200–300 m high. Presumably a fuel explosion. Steamer is blown to smithereens.
2226		Hit on a steamer positioned in the middle of the convoy. Explosion cloud with bright blaze of fire. Steamer stops in a cloud of smoke. Not possible to observe any further developments.
2230		Withdraw to NNE at utmost speed. Counter-attack this time is considerably more energetic than after our first attack. Covering forces have apparently been strengthened. Rockets and a star signal [*sic*] fired from the leading vessel are repeated by two others in the convoy. Five depth charges; 35–40 bursts of starshell, but they fall short. Further away on land we can see searchlight beams, and more starshell and rockets.
2228[2]		Outgoing W/T transmission: *KrKr Admiral Commanding Northern Waters from Hackländer. Convoy Qu. AC 8945, course 270°.*

torpedoes on the night in question. The identity of the 'other picket' is not known. The *Obersteuermann* was the chief navigator, usually a warrant officer.

7   *KrKr* was standard Kriegsmarine signal code for 'Urgent Priority'. *Admiral Nordmeer* (Admiral Commanding Northern Waters, Admiral Hubert Schmundt) had operational control of U-boats in this theatre until the office of *F.d.U. Norwegen* (Officer Commanding U-Boats, Norway) was created in January 1943, being redesignated *F.d.U. Nordmeer* – Northern Waters – in September 1944.

8   Kptlt Ernst-Bernhard Lohse commanding *U585*, then positioned to the west of the convoy.

9   This was indeed the case.

10 Hackländer has fixed his position from weather reports signalled by the Soviet weather stations on Cape Teriberski and Kharlov Island, respectively north-east and east of Murmansk on the Kola Peninsula.

11 Presumably HMS *Matabele*.

12 Manuscript addition in pencil.

13 Despite the target identifications recorded here and at 2226, *Matabele* was in fact the only vessel struck at this juncture though it is conceivable that she took another hit from *U454*. The detonations recorded in *U454* were probably connected with *Matabele*'s demise.

The sinking

The Board of Enquiry that followed the loss of *Matabele* questioned her two survivors at some length, but it was the testimony of officers on *Somali*'s bridge which most influenced its conclusions. The latter's Gunnery Officer, Lt Cdr J. G. B. Cooke, recalled seeing a flash at the stern of the tanker SS *British Workman* and assumed she had been hit but then noticed that the ship lying beyond, *Matabele*, appeared to be 'illuminated'. As *Somali* (Senior Officer of the Escort) increased speed to pass the tanker Cooke saw an Aldis lamp flashing from *Matabele*'s starboard side and steam apparently issuing from the engine room. The rest of his account bears citing:

> About three minutes after that she was quite clear and appeared to be very nearly stopped. Due to her white colour she was easy to see, and the whole ship seemed to jump slightly out of the water but remained whole and then she just split right open. It appeared that B magazine had gone up. The actual explosion extended aft – I should say to the No. 2 boiler room and right for'ard to the bows, and all the upper works fell down through the bottom of the ship.

Somali's Navigator, Lt W. Whitworth, noted that *Matabele* had previously fired two white Very lights northward over her starboard side, and that following a violent explosion in the vicinity of the bridge 'the next thing I noticed was that her stern was sticking up in the air, that she had broken her back and that the whole of the fore part was ablaze and I couldn't even see the outline of her'. Though his observation was not corroborated by Whitworth, the Board leant heavily on Cooke's memory of a gap of about a second 'between the ship's jumping and the flames bursting out' in concluding that *Matabele* blew up as a result of 'a second torpedo hit in or in the vicinity of a magazine'.

Where *Matabele*'s survivors were concerned, the Board dismissed their testimony (and especially that of Ordinary Seaman Higgins) as being of little value, due both to their position aft and because they 'gave the impression to the Board that they had been considerably "rattled" at the time'. Higgins heard the approach of a torpedo and both he and Ordinary Seamen Burras agreed that the initial detonation amidships caused *Matabele* to lurch violently to starboard, righting herself soon after. Neither made any reference to a second torpedo hit. Like Lt Cdr Cooke, Higgins recalled a period of about three minutes between the initial hit and the explosion that destroyed *Matabele*, but both survivors attributed this – one actively, the other implicitly – to the fire raging aboard. Burras was one of a number of men ordered forward after the initial detonation to close watertight doors but was driven back by flames bursting out of the galley and spreading along the deck. When *Matabele* began to list to starboard once again Burras took to the water, recalling that 'the whole ship seemed to be on fire' before the last explosion. Higgins recalled somebody shouting that there was a 'fire for'ard' before the ship blew up and himself saw that the 'middle part of the ship round the bridge and the for'ard funnel were all alight, as if it was luminous'. He was also adamant that *Matabele*'s First Lieutenant was concerned about the magazines, passing the order to 'Go down aft and close the magazine doors!' As the magazines were reached through hatches rather than doors and since Higgins recalled being ordered to close watertight doors, the Board attached little importance to his testimony and dismissed the suggestion of a major conflagration, noting that officers on *Somali*'s bridge four cables away saw no more than escaping steam before the final explosion.

In a note appended to the Board's findings, the Deputy Director of Training and Staff Duties, Capt. R. Oliver-Bellasis, made the case for an internal explosion, noting that 'there seems to be no conclusive evidence whether *Matabele* blew up due to being hit by a second torpedo, or due to an oil vapour explosion'. Though the latter scenario was deemed 'most improbable' by the Engineer-in-Chief, Vice-Admiral Sir George Preece, the ambiguities surrounding *U454*'s various targets and the evidence of the survivors makes an internal explosion the more probable scenario. Whatever other problems and shortcomings were experienced with the G7e torpedo, the speed at which it ran was a uniformly efficient 30 knots over 5,000 metres, and it is therefore extremely unlikely that *Matabele* was hit at three minutes' remove by a second torpedo of Hackländer's spread. As even those in *Somali* initially believed a tanker to have been hit, it can readily be understood how Hackländer, much further away on a very dark night, attributed the succession of explosions to further torpedo hits. Indeed, it must be concluded that his observations of 2224, 2225 and 2226 were all witness to *Matabele*'s catastrophic destruction, though it is not beyond the bounds of possibility that she was finished off by *U454*'s shot of 2223, aimed at a nearby freighter.

Fate of the crew

Though some sources record three survivors from *Matabele*, the only ones mentioned in official sources are the two who testified at the Board of Enquiry. Ordinary Seamen Burras and Higgins were stationed at 'X' mounting aft at the time of the first detonation and both recalled frantic efforts to release Carley floats frozen in their lashings. Burras and others abandoned ship as *Matabele* resumed her list to starboard but Higgins was one of many still on board when 'the ship seemed to blow up altogether'. Though blasted against the guard rail, he just had time to remove his sheepskin coat and jump clear before the ship foundered. There were perhaps sixty men in the water at this point, all from the stern section, but as *Somali* and *Harrier* had to conduct an Asdic sweep to locate the submarine no immediate steps could be taken to assist them. A lifebelt might keep a man afloat but it could not save him from the numbing cold of the Barents Sea in winter, and the majority succumbed to hypothermia. Others were accounted for by detonating depth charges. The four men rescued were *in extremis* by the time *Harrier* appeared and only Burras and Higgins seem to have survived the ordeal. Though Burras subsequently recalled that it was over an hour and a quarter before he reached *Harrier*'s side, it seems improbable that more than ten or fifteen minutes can have elapsed before they were plucked from the water since none were wearing immersion suits. In this respect the Board's concern over the survivors' ability to judge time correctly with regard to what happened during *Matabele*'s last few minutes could perhaps also be extended to their ordeal in the water.

U454 and Burkhard Hackländer

Built by Deutsche Werke at Kiel and commissioned in July 1941, *U454* spent the duration of her two-year career commanded by Kptlt Hackländer. The patrol of December 1941 to January 1942 was the only one in which she enjoyed any success, with successful attacks on the Soviet minesweeper *RT-68*, *Harmatris* and *Matabele*, though only the latter failed to reach port. Neither the experience gained in subsequent

U454 (foreground) seen returning to St-Nazaire from her seventh frontline patrol on 7 December 1942. Beyond is the Type-XIV supply tanker *U462*, one of the ten *Milchkühe* ('milk cows') which the Allies made a priority of sinking. *DUBMA*

patrols nor a shift of operational theatre to the Atlantic in July 1942 brought any further laurels, despite her operating in packs which collectively took a heavy toll of Allied shipping. *U454*'s career ended on 1 August 1943 when she was caught on the surface by an RAAF Sunderland in the Bay of Biscay. Though her return fire accounted for the Sunderland, *U454* was destroyed by bombs with the loss of thirty-

two men. Kptlt Hackländer was one of fourteen survivors picked up by HM sloop *Kite* (**G96**), spending the rest of the war in captivity. He died in January 2001.

Sources

Admiralty, *Enemy Submarine Attacks on H.M. and Allied Warships, January–June 1942* (TNA, ADM 199/162)

—, *Loss of HMS* Matabele *17th January 1942: Board of Enquiry* (TNA, ADM 1/11951)

—, *PQ and QP convoys: Reports, 1942–1943* (TNA, ADM 199/758)

Brice, Martin H., *The Tribals: Biography of a Destroyer Class* (London: Ian Allan, 1971)

Edwards, Bernard, *War of the U-Boats: British Merchantmen Under Fire* (Barnsley, S. Yorks.: Pen & Sword, 2006)

English, John, *Afridi to Nizam: British Fleet Destroyers, 1937–43* (Gravesend, Kent: World Ship Society, 2001)

Roskill, *War at Sea*, I, pp. 492–6, and II, pp. 119–20

Ruegg, Bob, and Arnold Hague, *Convoys to Russia, 1941–1945* (Kendal, Cumbria: World Ship Society, 1992)

Wadsworth, Michael, *Arctic Convoy PQ8: The Story of Capt. Robert Brundle and the SS* Harmatris (Barnsley, S. Yorks.: Pen & Sword, 2010)

Career history of HMS *Matabele*:
http://www.naval-history.net/xGM-Chrono-10DD-34Tribal-Matabele.htm

Defunct website containing recollections of convoy PQ8:
http://web.ukonline.co.uk/ron.greenwood/graf/3.PDF

48 USS (ex USCG) *ALEXANDER HAMILTON*

Cdr A. G. Hall, USCG
Sunk by *U132* (Type VIIC), Kptlt Ernst Vogelsang, 29–30 January 1942
North Atlantic, 6 nm WNW of Skagi Light (Iceland)

Alexander Hamilton seen shortly before her loss to a single torpedo from *U132*. *IWM*

Theatre North Atlantic (Map 1)		*Displacement* 2,216 tons	
Coordinates (of attack) 64° 10' N, 22° 56' W		*Dimensions* 327' × 41' × 15'	
Kriegsmarine code (of attack) Quadrat AE 4756		*Maximum speed* 19.5 knots	
U-boat timekeeping differential +2 hours		*Armament* 3 × 5"; 3 × 3" AA	
Fatalities 26 *Survivors* 185 and 2			

The US Coast Guard

Established by amalgamation with the Life-Saving Service in 1915, the United States Coast Guard traces its origins to the Revenue-Marine (later Revenue Cutter Service) founded for the protection of US interests at sea in 1790. In line with its constitutions, the Coast Guard, which operated under the Department of the Treasury in peacetime, was subsumed into the US Navy between 1 November 1941 and 1 January 1946, though a number of ships – *Alexander Hamilton* included – had come under naval control before that date. Its mission as an anti-contraband, rescue, ice-breaking and patrol force has traditionally required well-found vessels of good endurance, modest armament and reasonable turn of speed, and to these – in whatever era – the designation 'cutter' has been given. The cutter type, which embraces a wide variety of ships, was and remains the mainstay of the US Coast Guard and some 400 served during the Second World War, many with all-CG crews.

Career

The Coast Guard cutter *Alexander Hamilton* (CG-69) was laid down at the New York Navy Yard in September 1935, launched in November 1936 and commissioned on 4 March 1937, one of seven units of the Treasury class. Assigned to Oakland, California in the US Coast Guard's 12th District and renamed *Hamilton*, her first extended deployment came in July 1938 when she sailed north to perform the Coast Guard's annual Bering Sea patrol in Alaskan waters. This took her as far as Unalaska near the western end of the Aleutian chain, her remit extending from medical and humanitarian work to fishery protection duties before returning to Oakland in early November. On 19 July 1939 *Hamilton* was selected for a year-long scientific expedition in the central and southern Pacific under the sponsorship of the National Geographic Society and the University of Virginia. However, the outbreak of the Second World War on 3 September and the formation of the Neutrality Patrol by President Roosevelt two days later caused *Hamilton*'s involvement to be cancelled and the ship ordered to Norfolk, Virginia where she was allocated to the Navy's Destroyer Division 18. The purpose of the Neutrality Patrol was to report and track any belligerent air, surface or submarine activity off the eastern seaboard of the United States and in the West Indies, and on 5 October *Hamilton* began the first of four patrols off the Grand Banks. In February 1940 came a change of role with the establishment of ocean weather stations in the Atlantic, *Hamilton* being earmarked for meteorological duty between the Azores and Bermuda. This continued until November 1941 when she was taken in hand for refitting at Norfolk. From this *Hamilton* emerged in late December to find the United States at war, being immediately assigned to convoy escort duty where her two years' service in the Atlantic stood her in good stead. Already on 11 September 1941 the US Coast Guard had been placed under Navy jurisdiction, a circumstance that required *Hamilton* to revert to her original name to avoid confusion with the fast minesweeper *Hamilton* (DMS-18). It was at this time too that her hull number was changed to WPG-34 and her designation to gunboat. On 30 December the USS *Alexander Hamilton* sailed for Casco Bay, Maine for training with Commander Task Group 4.4 before proceeding to the US Naval Operating Base at Argentia, Newfoundland.

Background of the attack

On 14 January 1942 *Alexander Hamilton* sailed from Argentia in company with the destroyers *Niblack*, *Tarbell* and *Overton* with orders to rendezvous with convoy HX170 off Newfoundland on the evening of the 15 January. They were to escort HX170 as far as the Mid-Ocean Meeting Point (MOMP) south-west of Iceland at which point they would turn her over to the British to complete the voyage to Liverpool. The escort was briefly augmented by the destroyers *Ellis* and *Greer* and the gunboat *St Augustine* until these were detached on the 16th. The convoy reached the MOMP on 22 January in the teeth of a huge storm that delayed the arrival of the British escort force. Low on fuel, *Tarbell* and *Overton* were obliged to make for Iceland leaving the convoy with only *Alexander Hamilton* and *Niblack* for protection until the British arrived two days late on the afternoon of the 24th. Their mission completed, *Alexander Hamilton* and *Niblack* turned for Iceland but were diverted to assist the disabled storeship USS *Yukon* which had suffered engine trouble while en route to join convoy ON57. Reaching the scene on the 25th, *Alexander Hamilton* took *Yukon* in tow and shaped a course for Reykjavik with *Niblack* as escort. On the 26th *Niblack* was relieved of her screening duties by the destroyer USS *Gwin* and the towing party continued its laggardly progress towards Iceland. However, on the afternoon of 29 January, with the swept channel leading to Reykjavik only four miles off and the British tug *Frisky* having relieved *Alexander Hamilton* of the tow, the group was sighted by Kptlt Ernst Vogelsang's *U132* which had been patrolling these waters since the 21st. Her towing duties at an end, *Alexander Hamilton* began working up to fifteen knots with a view to refuelling and reprovisioning at Hvalfjörður before sailing to pick up her next convoy, ON57. But Vogelsang maintained contact and shortly after 1600 (1400 US time) *Alexander Hamilton*, then just three miles ahead of *Frisky*, *Yukon* and *Gwin*, became the target of a spread of four torpedoes.

War Diary of *U132*, patrol of 15 January–8 February 1942: PG 30122, NHB, reel 1,083, pp. 546–7

Date, time	Details of position, wind, weather, sea, light, visibility, moonlight, etc.	Incidents
29.i		
1200	Qu. AE 4756 upper middle, sea 2–3, wind NE 4, overcast with snow and hail, 1,008 mb. Poor visibility.	Day's run: 93.5 nm surfaced, 22.4 nm submerged.
1209		Alarm dive. Coast has suddenly appeared, bursting right through the driving snow.
1341		Cloud of smoke in sight at bearing 242° true; three fishing trawlers.
1420		Escort vessel in sight at bearing 5° true. Range 6,000 m.
1422		Battle Stations. Escort vessel resembles *Brideford*, *Bridgewater* and their ilk.[1] She keeps altering course, giving me no opportunity to fire.
1432		She seems to be carrying out a hydrophone sweep. We go to silent speed.
1505		Cease silent speed. Vessel retires to the south. At the same time destroyers and other vessels appear through the mist, the former zigzagging occasionally.
1530		Convoy identified. One steamer of roughly 3,000 GRT, two destroyers (one 'D' class, the other single-funnelled but class not identified), one motor boat, two patrol vessels and the escort vessel previously sighted.[2] We run in to attack but can't reach the steamer.
1600	Qu. AE 4756 upper middle	
1610	Qu. AE 4756	Spread of four torpedoes fired at single-funnelled destroyer. <u>Shot coordinates</u>: range 2,000 m, inclination green [i.e. starboard] 90°, enemy speed 12 knots, angle of dispersion 2.8°, aim-off green [starboard] 23.5°, own course 350°.[3]
		Boat's conning tower breaches surface. There is a patrol vessel 500 m off, ship's bearing 200°. We quickly dive to T = 20 and after 3 min. 10 sec. hear the impact of a detonation.[4]
1615		Two depth charges dropped about 1,500 m off.
1620		Noises of echo-ranging apparatus; we are overrun from the port side.
1625		We go to 13 m.[5] At a bearing of 70° true we can see a destroyer, range 700 m, which gradually disappears from periscope view; the motor boat and the steamer are lying stopped.
1637		Stern shot at the destroyer. Shot coordinates: range 1,000 m, inclination red [i.e. port] 90°, enemy speed 3 knots, aim-off red [port] 6°, own course 270°.
		Immediately after we fire the destroyer accelerates and alters course towards us.[6] A miss. We go to T = 20.[4]
1640		Echo-ranging apparatus noises; we are overrun from the starboard side.
1642		Depth charge dropped about 2,000 m off. We withdraw, maintaining silent speed until 1812.
1825		We go to 13 m.[5]

1   Vogelsang is apparently referring to the British escort sloops *Bideford* (*sic*) and *Bridgewater*. Although these were comparable in size and silhouette to the *Alexander Hamilton*, she seems not to be the vessel so identified. It must be supposed that this 'escort vessel', which is mentioned again at 1530, was one of the fishing trawlers recorded then and earlier at 1341.

2   Vogelsang describes the 'convoy' as consisting of seven ships when *Yukon*'s group numbered only four. It is to be assumed that he added the three fishing trawlers recorded at 1341 to the strength of the group, vessels which may subsequently have assisted in the rescue of survivors. The identifiable vessels are, respectively, the storeship USS *Yukon* (12,546 tons displacement); the destroyer USS *Gwin* of the Gleaves class (with a silhouette comparable to the British 'D'-class destroyers); *Alexander Hamilton* corresponding to the 'single-funnelled' destroyer; and HM tug *Frisky* the 'motor boat' (see also entry for 1625).

3   *Alexander Hamilton* was estimated to have been making about 15 knots so the rest of salvo presumably passed astern.

4   By 'T = 20 m' Vogelsang seems to be recording a dive not of 20 metres (66 feet – an unconscionably shallow depth for him to take *U132* in the face of an approaching destroyer) but of 160 metres (525 feet); for a full discussion of the 'T =' notation, see Reading the *Kriegstagebücher*, p. xxxvii.

5   Periscope depth.

6   One of this pair of G7e torpedoes was sighted by its target, the USS *Gwin*, which avoided the threat by turning 'hard right rudder to parallel torpedo'. It was then seen to pass abeam of the *Yukon* on a diverging course.

The sinking

Some secondary sources describe Vogelsang as firing his spread of four torpedoes at the storeship *Yukon* and that *Alexander Hamilton* was merely the unfortunate recipient of a stray torpedo, but *U132*'s log makes it clear that this was not the case. Although only one of his spread hit *Alexander Hamilton* at 1412 ship time, it was sufficient to leave her dead in the water. The Court of Inquiry found that damage to the ship, which was struck on the starboard side abreast the stack, included 'fire room flooded; engine badly wrecked and flooded; two boats destroyed; second deck passage immediately abaft engine room bulkhead damaged and watertight door in forward bulkhead blown off'. The torpedo detonated beneath the main electrical switchboard, caused two boilers to blew up, wrecked two auxiliary generators and destroyed the starboard turbine leaving the ship 'immediately deprived of all means of propulsion and of all sources of power and lighting'. *Alexander Hamilton* settled a few feet by the stern but without taking on an appreciable list. However, with the ship dead in the water, his Executive Officer reporting extensive flooding abaft the engine room and the vessel in imminent danger of capsizing, Cdr Arthur G. Hall gave the order to abandon ship at about 1445, by which time she had settled some eight or ten feet by the stern.

But *Alexander Hamilton* did not capsize or sink that day. By the time the British tug *Restive* arrived to take her in tow at 2030 that evening the weather had taken a turn for the worse and plans for a boarding party to be transferred from *Gwin* to *Restive* and then to *Alexander Hamilton* herself had to be abandoned. With none aboard to assist the process, attempts to take her in tow failed and efforts at salvage ceased for the night at 2240. Only at 1015 the following morning did the weather moderate sufficiently for towing to commence, this time undertaken by HM tug *Frisky* which had reached the scene having brought *Yukon* into Reykjavik. By this time *Alexander Hamilton* was listing twenty degrees to starboard with seas breaking over the starboard side aft. Moreover, wind drift had been adding to the distance between her and Reykjavik at the rate of approximately a knot. Nonetheless, a number of ships were now in attendance including the Coast Guard tug *Redwing*, the seaplane tender *Belknap* and the destroyers *Ericsson* and *Livermore*, and hopes were high that she could be brought in. It was not to be. At 1720 that evening having been towed approximately 18 miles the ship gave a sudden lurch to starboard and at 1728 capsized in position 64° 32' N, 22° 58' W. For some time *Alexander Hamilton* 'floated bottom up and was then sunk in about forty fathoms of water, by gunfire from the USS *Ericsson*, the last sight of her being recorded at 1957 on January 30, 1942'.

The Court of Inquiry found that 'the ship's company conducted themselves in a creditable manner', noting a number of examples of 'conspicuously courageous' behaviour. By contrast, both senior officers were the target of severe criticism. The Court recommended that Cdr Hall be reprimanded 'for having entirely abandoned his ship before there were conclusive indications that she could not be kept afloat'. A similar reprimand was recommended for the Executive Officer, Lt Cdr Beverly E. Moodey, for 'his failure to determine the extent of flooding of compartments below the second deck, his failure to institute adequate measures for control thereof, and for his ill-founded reports to the commanding officer of imminent danger of the ship's capsizing or sinking in the face of considerable evidence to the contrary'.

Crewmen of the *Alexander Hamilton* seen abandoning ship in a photo taken from the USS *Gwin* at about 1530 on the 29th, approximately an hour after the attack. The boat is being lowered at exactly the point Vogelsang's torpedo found its mark, on the starboard side abreast the stack. *US Coast Guard*

Reviewing the Court's findings, the commander of the Atlantic Fleet's Battleship Division 5, Rear Admiral Alex Sharp went even further, finding Cdr Hall's action 'neither seamanlike, nor in keeping with the best traditions of the naval service. By delaying any decision to return to his ship while sea conditions permitted, he was subsequently prevented from returning to the *Alexander Hamilton* due to increased wind and roughening of sea after dark'. Sharp also found Lt Cdr Moodey guilty of negligence and of making an inspection of only 'a hasty and superficial nature, as a result of which he reported in fact to the commanding officer that the ship would capsize in a half-hour'. On the basis of the information submitted, Sharp recommended that both officers be brought to trial by general court martial for 'culpable inefficiency in the performance of duty', Hall for 'suffering a vessel of the Navy to be hazarded', and Moodey for 'negligence in obeying orders'. With this assessment Admiral Royal E. Ingersoll, Commander-in-Chief of the Atlantic Fleet, declared himself in agreement, but no record of any court martial survives in the archives of the US Navy's Judge Advocate General, all proceedings not resulting in a punitive discharge being destroyed after fifteen years.

Fate of the crew

The destruction of the ship's vital machinery was also a death sentence for those who operated it. As the Court of Inquiry found, 'there were no survivors among the seven members of the watch in the fire room, engine room and auxiliary engine room'. The boiler explosion also claimed victims beyond these spaces as the blast not only destroyed the bulkhead separating the fireroom from the second deck but lifted the deckhead separating it from the compartments above. Hissing clouds of steam and splinters took the death toll to twenty with another score badly injured, mostly from severe burns. Six of these did not survive. The injured and sixty others were evacuated into the four surviving ship's boats, and though one of these capsized its occupants clung on until they were picked up by one of the Icelandic fishing trawlers – probably those mentioned in Vogelsang's log – shortly before 1600. Two more trawlers arrived on the scene and rescued the remainder of the boats' occupants before taking them to Reykjavik. By 1547 *Gwin*

A studio portrait of Ernst Vogelsang, *c.*1942. He wears the Spanish Cross in
Bronze or Silver with Swords together with the
Iron Cross First and Second Class. *DUBMA*

had taken off the rest of *Alexander Hamilton*'s men, Cdr Hall being the
last to leave.

U132 and Ernst Vogelsang

Built by Bremer Vulkan at Vegesack and commissioned in May 1941,
U132's four frontline patrols were all carried out under Kptlt Ernst
Vogelsang, a decorated veteran of the Spanish Civil War. She soon
claimed her first pennants, sinking the Soviet steamer *Argun* and the
auxiliary patrol craft *SKR-11* (**G13**) in the Barents Sea on her maiden
patrol in October 1941 before being reassigned to Atlantic operations
the following January. *Alexander Hamilton* was the only victim of her
second patrol which Vogelsang was forced to abort later the same day
after a severe depth-charging by the destroyer USS *Stack*, the damage
keeping *U132* under repair for several months. Nonetheless, B.d.U.
expressed its satisfaction with the 'pluck' shown by Vogelsang in a
patrol that had afforded him few targets. His third patrol was more
impressive. On 13 June 1942 *U132* sustained damage to her periscope
and engine room by gunfire and depth-charging from an unknown
escort vessel, following which B.d.U. ordered her to return to La
Pallice with immediate effect. However, Vogelsang demurred and

instead took his command across the Atlantic and into the Gulf of St
Lawrence. In a sortie up the St Lawrence on 6 July *U132* bagged three
merchantmen from convoy QC15 before enduring another depth-
charge attack at the hands of HMCS *Drummondville*. Unperturbed,
Vogelsang struck again, badly damaging the SS *Frederica Lendsen*
before heading east and passing through the Cabot Strait. A further
merchantman was claimed from ON113 on her return journey to
La Pallice where, following yet another depth-charging en route,
Vogelsang was unsurprisingly the toast of the day.

U132's career ended a month into her fourth patrol in the early
hours of 4 November 1942. In attacks just minutes apart *U132* almost
certainly sank two large merchantmen from SC107 and crippled the
ammunition ship *Hatimura*, the latter being finished off by *U442*
three hours later. Since nothing more was heard from Vogelsang after
this episode it has been conjectured that *U132* was close enough to
Hatimura to have been destroyed in the immense detonation of her
cargo. However, this remains no more than conjecture in the absence
of further evidence.

Sources

US Navy, *Report of Proceedings of Court of Inquiry into Torpedoing and
   Subsequent Loss of the ex-US Coast Guard Cutter* Alexander Hamilton
   on January 31, 1942 (NA, RG 38, Flag File Screening Documents, Box 5,
   370/13/4/7)
U132 file (DUBMA)
DANFS, IA, pp. 169–71; also on:
   http://www.history.navy.mil/danfs/a6/alexander_hamilton-ii.htm
   and
   http://www.uscg.mil/history/webcutters/AlexanderHamilton1937.asp

Johnson, Robert Erwin, *Guardians of the Sea: A History of the United States
   Coast Guard, 1915 to the Present* (Annapolis, Md.: Naval Institute Press,
   1987)
Scheina, Robert L., *US Coast Guard Cutters and Craft in World War II*
   (Annapolis, Md.: Naval Institute Press, 1982)
Willoughby, Lt Malcolm F., *The US Coast Guard in World War II* (Annapolis,
   Md.: US Naval Institute, 1957)

Browning Jr, Dr Robert M., 'The First Loss: The Sinking of the *Alexander
   Hamilton*':
   http://www.uscg.mil/history/articles/Hamiltonsinking.asp
Oral history of BM 3/c Thomas V. Mullings (survivor), US Coast Guard Oral
   History Program, 1985:
   http://www.uscg.mil/history/weboralhistory/MullingsOralHistory.pdf

49   HMS *CULVER* (ex USCG *MENDOTA*)

Lt R. F. Kipling, RN†
Sunk by *U105* (Type IXB), Kptlt Heinrich Schuch, 31 January 1942
North Atlantic, 445 nm WSW of Cape Clear, Cork (Ireland)

The US Coast Guard cutter *Mendota* seen in 1932. She was commissioned into the Royal Navy as HMS *Culver* in April 1941. *BfZ*

Theatre   North Atlantic (Map 1)
Coordinates   48° 43' N, 20° 14' W
Kriegsmarine code   Quadrat BE 2784
U-boat timekeeping differential   +3 hours
Fatalities   136   *Survivors*   13

Displacement   1,975 tons
Dimensions   250' × 42' × 13'
Maximum speed   16 knots
Armament   1 × 5"; 2 × 3" AA; 2 × 57 mm; 4 × .5" AA; 6 × .303" AA

Career

For notes on the cutter type and background on the US Coast Guard, see USS *Alexander Hamilton* (**48**).

The US Coast Guard cutter *Mendota* (WPG-49) was laid down at Bethlehem Shipbuilding Corporation, Quincy, Massachusetts in June 1928, launched in November of that year and commissioned in March 1929. One of a ten-strong class fitted with an innovative turbine-electric-drive power plant of remarkable efficiency, *Mendota* spent her peacetime career in the coastal, polar and inland waters of the United States performing the anti-contraband, ice-breaking, rescue and patrol duties associated with the US Coast Guard. However, by the winter of 1940 events of wider consequence were beginning to take a hand in the fate of *Mendota* and her sisters of the Lakes class. For some time President Roosevelt had been advocating legislation to sell or lend war *matériel* to any country fighting the Axis and on 11 March 1941 Congress passed the momentous Lend-Lease Act enabling this. Among the first results of Lend-Lease was an order of 5 April for the entire class to report fully fuelled, stowed and provisioned at the Brooklyn Navy Yard for transfer to the Royal Navy. After a fortnight's instruction in the workings of the ship by Coast Guard personnel in Long Island Sound, *Mendota* was commissioned into the Royal Navy as HMS *Culver* on 30 April. Her ship's company was drawn largely from the battleship *Malaya*, then refitting at New York Navy Yard. With the last inventory taken and receipt signed,

Culver and three of her sisters weighed anchor and sailed for Halifax, Nova Scotia, which they reached on 6 May, departing for the Clyde the following day in company with the battleship *Revenge* as escort to convoy HX125. Allocated to Western Approaches Command, *Culver* cut her teeth with the Londonderry Sloop Division before being assigned to the 40th Escort Group in August. In September and October a month's refit at North Woolwich saw her fitted with radar and the prototype of the FH4 high-frequency direction-finding set, followed by a spell at HMS *Western Isles*, the anti-submarine training centre at Tobermory, Scotland. With this *Culver* rejoined the 40th EG on convoy duty between Britain and West Africa. Her first taste of action came in defence of convoy OS10 to Freetown, rescuing survivors of the torpedoed Dutch freighter *Bennekom* in the North Atlantic and landing them at Bathurst (now Banjul) in The Gambia on 10 November. Apart from a fortnight in Londonderry and at Greenock in December it was the Britain–West Africa run that remained the focus of *Culver*'s activities.

Background of the attack

On 25 January *U105* sailed from Lorient, one of a number of Type-IXB U-boats sent that month to operate in US waters as part of Operation PAUKENSCHLAG ('drumroll'). On the morning of the 31st Kptlt Heinrich Schuch sighted convoy SL98, then sixteen days out of Freetown and bound for Liverpool with an escort consisting of HM sloops *Londonderry* (Senior Officer of the Escort) and *Bideford*, and the ex-US Coast Guard cutters *Culver*, *Landguard* and *Lulworth*. As *U105* manoeuvered into an attacking position, evening on the 31st found *Landguard* and *Lulworth* stationed on the port and starboard bows of SL98 respectively, *Culver* and *Bideford* on the port and starboard quarters, and *Londonderry* sweeping astern. At 2030, with *Culver* zigzagging at 7½ knots and having fallen slightly astern of station, her Asdic operator reported hydrophone effect off the port beam. Sub-Lt Carlow RNVR, second officer of the watch and then on the lower bridge, immediately spotted a submarine almost bow-on at a range of 2,000–3,000 yards. His instant orders to steer hard aport and for full speed ahead came too late to avoid Kptlt Schuch's salvo.

War Diary of *U105*, patrol of 25 January–8 February 1942: PG 30101b, NHB, reel 1,079, pp. 790–1

Date, time	Details of position, wind, weather, sea, light, visibility, moonlight, etc.	Incidents
31.i		
0208		Transmit brief weather report: *47° N, 19° W, 1,032 mb, +11 deg. C [52°F], stratocumulus, visibility 6–8 nm, wind NW 3, gentle swell.*
0400	[Qu.] BE 5434	
0800	[Qu.] BE 5419	
1020		
1200	[Qu.] BE 5418	Plumes of smoke in sight at bearing 214° true. The early morning gloom is still lifting so I withdraw to an appropriate distance while at the same time manoeuvering into an advance position. I remain south of position 47° 30' N.
	[Qu.] BE 5412, wind WNW 2, sea 2, gentle swell, 9/10 overcast, good visibility	By now I can only make out one plume of smoke with any certainty so I hold off to see how the situation will develop.
1600	[Qu.] BE 5141	By late afternoon we have ascertained the following: we are in contact with a convoy that is zigzagging on a general course of 35°, speed roughly 7–8 knots. We can make out two rows of ships. My intention: to attack after nightfall.
1946		I am in an advance position but inconvenienced by the escort operating on the extreme starboard bow
2000	[Qu.] BE 5122	of the convoy.[1] She forces me to withdraw a considerable distance so that I temporarily lose contact with the convoy.
2047		I alter course to 220° and close the enemy. Once more I encounter the side and forward escorts on
2117		the starboard side.[2] I can make out several escort vessels on this side (four) and assume enemy has concentrated his forces on this side because it is so dark.[3] I therefore work my way round to the north onto the port side of the convoy, avoiding the port escorts by heading north and then west,
2216		with a view to launching an attack on the enemy's port side from the north-west. I am now once more positioned directly ahead of the convoy, which is steering a course of 15°. I would reckon there to be about 15 ships with a powerful side and forward escort group evident (10 escort vessels).[4] Despite the bright night (10/10 overcast but full moon) I manage to circumnavigate the port escorts (four vessels)
2331	[Qu.] BE 2784	between 2255 and 2326 until I'm in a position to fire at the rearmost vessel of the port column.[5] The brightness of the night forces me to fire from longish range so I opt for a spread of four torpedoes. Spread fired from Tubes I–IV with the following shot coordinates: enemy speed 8 knots, range 1,200 m, target breadth 100 m, inclination 80°, bows left.[6] Spread order 3 with an angle of dispersion of 4.5°. After a running time of 1 min. 42 sec. (= 1,574 m) we observe two hits. The vessel is blasted into the air after the second hit. Difficult to identify the vessel type. The silhouette revealed a featureless flush deck that was slightly raised at both bow and stern. Only amidships was any form of superstructure (bridge) discerned, on which a taller mast was superimposed. The vessel was not making any smoke. Her size was estimated to be at least 4,000 tons.[7]

---

1 *Culver*'s sister HMS *Lulworth*.

2 HMSs *Lulworth* and *Bideford* respectively.

3 These were HMSs *Bideford*, *Londonderry*, *Landguard* and *Lulworth*.

4 SL98 was made up of twenty-six ships deployed in four rows (though Schuch appears to have seen just two of these at 1600) and either six or seven columns. There was a five-strong escort (see above) along with the survey ship HMS *Challenger*.

5 HMS *Culver*, which Schuch understandably took to be a merchantmen rather than a warship.

6 *Culver* actually measured only 76 metres (250 feet).

7 Although Schuch doubtless means GRT, *Culver* in fact displaced only 1,975 tons. Nonetheless, with her high freeboard, straight bow, large cruiser stern and sparse silhouette forward and aft *Culver* could readily be mistaken for a small merchantman, as was evidently the case here.

Date, time	Details of position, wind, weather, sea, light, visibility, moonlight, etc.	Incidents
		Shortly after the detonations the convoy sends up snowflake and starshell. The starshell illuminates the entire horizon with the exception of the moonlit sector, into which I initially disappear at high speed without further ado.
2400	[Qu.] BE 2776, wind NW 2–3, sea 2–3, light swell, 8/10, good visibility, moonlit	Day's run: Surfaced = 188.3 nm, Submerged = 0.0 nm = 188.3 nm *Schuch*

The sinking

Schuch's war diary is rather unusual in providing a record of events that concurs with Allied accounts in almost every respect save the number of escorts present. His quadruple salvo was sufficiently accurate for two torpedoes to find their mark, the first detonating in *Culver*'s forward boiler room with a huge shuddering explosion. Moments later the second struck further aft on the port side producing a flash that was clearly seen from HMS *Bideford* eight miles off. This was probably *Culver*'s after magazine going up. The survivors reported a further explosion caused by primed depth charges being blasted over the side. Under these hammer blows *Culver* heeled forty-five degrees to starboard, broke in two and sank in a 'V' shape within the space of a minute. Poor subdivision and the single large boiler room with which she was designed no doubt helped hasten the end.

Fate of the crew

The speed of *Culver*'s demise accounted for much of her ship's company, either killed in the explosions or else dragged down with the wreck. Several more were claimed by the ocean before rescuers appeared. Few of the survivors recalled anything of the sinking beyond their location in the ship at the time of the attack, and the violent heel to starboard and rushing water that immediately followed it. Sub-Lt Carlow, the only officer survivor, remembered nothing between the bridge being wrecked and his regaining consciousness in the water. The first vessel on the scene, HMS *Londonderry*, dropped her boats before joining *Bideford* in an anti-submarine sweep in the presumed direction of the attack. Only two faint traces were detected, one of *U105* retreating at full speed on the surface and the other of *Culver* sinking to the bottom of the Atlantic. Within half an hour of the sinking the thirteen survivors had been picked up by *Londonderry*. They were brought to the port of the same name on 5 February, their approach to the strains of the *Londonderry Air* played whenever *Londonderry* returned to her namesake. This particular homecoming was inordinately sombre, however, as *Culver*'s survivors had to face the waiting girlfriends of their dead shipmates. Among those lost was Lt R. F. Kipling, *Londonderry*'s First Lieutenant who had been given temporary command of *Culver* after Lt Cdr R. T. Gordon-Duff had been taken ill at Bathurst earlier that month.

U105 and Heinrich Schuch

Built by AG Weser at Bremen and commissioned in September 1940, *U105* made her first four frontline patrols under Kptlt Georg Schewe. His tenure was highly successful, accounting as it did for almost 100,000 tons of merchant shipping including an Atlantic patrol

Heinrich Schuch seen following his promotion to Korvettenkapitän. *DUBMA*

between February and June 1941 during which twelve ships were sunk for a total of some 70,000 tons. *U105*'s first patrol under Kptlt Heinrich Schuch yielded HMS *Culver* but the intended passage across the Atlantic failed to materialise as she was ordered to pick up survivors from the blockade-runner *Spreewald*, mistakenly sunk by *U333* (Kptlt Peter Cremer) off the Azores. Schuch's next patrol in *U105* accounted for two vessels off Cape Hatteras in March 1942, but on 7 June she was badly damaged by an RAAF Sunderland off Cape Finisterre and limped into the Spanish port of El Ferrol for repairs. With Schuch replaced by Kptlt Jürgen Nissen, *U105*'s last two patrols took her first to the Caribbean and then to the West African trade routes where on 2 June 1943 she was sunk off Dakar by the Potez-CAMS 141 flying boat *Antarès* of the Free French navy, then escorting convoy SL130. There were no survivors.

Promoted Korvettenkapitän, Schuch undertook one final frontline patrol as commander of *U154* before being appointed to the staff of B.d.U. in February 1943. He died in 1968.

Sources

Admiralty, *Analysis of an Attack by U-Boat on Convoy SL98* (TNA, ADM 199/2000)

—, *Analysis of Attacks on Convoys by U-Boats, 1940–1942* (TNA, ADM 199/2495)

—, *Director of Anti-Submarine Warfare: Monthly Anti-Submarine Report for April 1942* (TNA, ADM 199/2059)

Anon., HMS *Culver* (typescript, NHB, no ref.)

Moore, Capt. W. J., *Tales of a Rookie* (typescript memoir, IWM, 92/33/1)

Hague, A., and J. J. Colledge, 'The Banff Class Escorts of WW.II' in *Warships*, Supplement no. 77 (Summer 1984), pp. 1–11

Reed, Ken, *The Hand-Me-Down Ships: A True Account of the World War II Exploits of Ten Ex-American Coast Guard Cutters and the Officers and Men of the Royal Navy Who Served in Them* (Spalding, Lincs.: privately, 1993)

Scheina, Robert L., *US Coast Guard Cutters and Craft of World War II*

(Annapolis, Md.: Naval Institute Press, 1982)

United States Coast Guard, Research and Statistics Section, Operations Division, *The Accomplishments of Ten Coast Guard Cutters Transferred to the United Kingdom* (restricted circulation, United States Coast Guard, 1941)

Webpage devoted to USCG *Mendota*: http://www.uscg.mil/history/webcutters/Mendota_1929.pdf

Career history of HMS *Culver*: http://www.naval-history.net/xGM-Chrono-16CGC-Culver.htm

50   HMS *ARBUTUS* (i)

Lt A. L. W. Warren, DSC RNR†
Sunk by *U136* (Type VIIC), Kptlt Heinrich Zimmermann, 5 February 1942
North Atlantic, 465 nm W of Islay, Inner Hebrides (Scotland)

A newly commissioned *Arbutus* seen in the autumn of 1940. Her pendant number (M86) has yet to be painted on the hull. *BfZ*

Theatre North Atlantic (Map 1)	*Displacement* 940 tons
Coordinates 55° 05' N, 19° 43' W	*Dimensions* 205.25' × 33' × approx. 11.25'
Kriegsmarine code Quadrat AL 6146	*Maximum speed* 16 knots
U-boat timekeeping differential +1 hour	*Armament* 1 × 4"; 4 × .303" AA
Fatalities 43 *Survivors* 30+	

Career

For design notes on the Flower-class corvettes, see HMS *Picotee* (**29**).

The Flower-class corvette *Arbutus* was laid down at Blyth Dry Dock & Shipbuilding Co., Northumberland in November 1939, launched in June 1940 and completed that October. Having worked up at HMS *Western Isles*, the anti-submarine warfare training centre at Tobermory, she was assigned to the 6th Escort Group of Western Approaches Command at Liverpool and began convoy duty in December 1940. She was to be in the thick of things for the next fourteen months. Her first and only kill came on 7 March 1941 while escorting convoy OB293, *U70* being depth charged to the surface and despatched with gunfire from *Arbutus* and her sister *Camellia*. On 5 April she sent a boarding party to *U76* which had been forced to the surface by HMSs *Wolverine* and *Scarborough*, but their hoped-for prize was found to be partially flooded and untenable with chlorine gas. Attempts to take

her in tow ended in the U-boat foundering and *Arbutus* damaging her steering gear. The great U-boat capture, that of *U110* by HMSs *Bulldog*, *Broadway* and *Aubretia*, would have to wait a month longer. Refitted in Liverpool, *Arbutus* returned to the fray in June but on 11 July was damaged in a collision with the freighter *Blackheath* which sent her back to the Mersey until September. After a brief interlude with the 36th Escort Group she was taken in hand for refit and partial reconstruction at Gordon Alison's yard at Birkenhead in November, her stay prolonged into the new year by suspected sabotage. This completed, *Arbutus* rejoined the 6th EG, weighing anchor for the last time on 18 January 1942.

Background of the attack

On 2 February 1942 convoy Outward North (Slow) 63 sailed from Liverpool into the North Channel and thence to destinations in the

United States and the Caribbean. Serving as local escort was the 6th Escort Group consisting of HM destroyers *Verity* (Senior Officer of the Escort) and *Chelsea* together with the corvette *Arbutus*. Three days later ON63 ran into a patrol line of three U-boats including Kptlt Heinrich Zimmermann's *U136*, then on her maiden cruise. A flurry of radio activity followed *U136*'s sighting of the convoy, signals to and from B.d.U. being transmitted on no fewer than five occasions together with beacon signals from *U136* in an attempt to bring *U213* (Oblt.z.S. Amelung von Varendorff) and *U591* (Kptlt Hans-Jürgen Zetzsche) up to the convoy before dark. However, this constant W/T traffic was picked up by the 6th EG and Zimmermann's beacon signal and radio transmission of 2015–2021 (see below) gave the escort a clear fix on *U136*'s position thanks to the sophisticated high-frequency direction-finding (HF/DF) equipment embarked. Cdr R. H. Mills in *Verity* immediately ordered *Chelsea* and *Arbutus* onto the starboard quarter of the convoy to chase down the contact.

At 1950 *Arbutus* reported a further RDF contact and then sighted what appeared to be a U-boat diving on her port bow. Due to confusion on the bridge the subsequent pattern of depth charges was dropped both prematurely and with too shallow a setting, the detonations causing the dynamo to come off its board in the engine room and plunging the ship into darkness for two minutes. Not surprisingly, Zimmermann's log indicates that this pattern fell well wide of the mark. The hunt continued but with no other firm contact gained *Chelsea* eventually signalled *Arbutus* to close her. Lt A. L. W. Warren, CO of *Arbutus*', ordered the navigation lights switched back on and abandoned the bridge for the comfort of the wardroom, leaving the Officer of the Watch, Lt V. G. Paramain RNVR, in charge and the ship still at Action Stations. At 2127 a further signal was received from *Chelsea* ordering *Arbutus* to join her in returning to the convoy. Paramain passed this signal to Warren in the wardroom who replied by ordering him to bring the ship down from Action Stations to Defence Stations. Two minutes later Paramain was helping the quartermaster steady *Arbutus* onto a new course a few hundred yards off *Chelsea*'s starboard beam 'when for perhaps two seconds I heard what I took to be a torpedo approaching'. Their intended victim had turned predator.

War Diary of *U136*, **patrol of 22 January–1 March 1942: PG 30126, NHB, reel 1,084, pp. 131–2.**

Date, time	Details of position, wind, weather, sea, light, visibility, moonlight, etc.	Incidents
5.ii		
2000	Qu. AL 6152, wind NW 3, sea 3, mist, very variable visibility	
2015–2020		Beacon signal.
2021		W/T report no. 170/2021 transmitted: *Enemy disappeared in fog, Qu. AL 6157. U136.*[1]
2045		Two destroyers astern of me; I must be stationed directly ahead of the convoy.
2104		Three depth charges dropped astern.
2112		Four depth charges dropped 3,000 m astern. Might they have spotted me?[2]
2115		Awaiting complete darkness to launch night attack.
2127		We close to attack but are greeted with empty seas; convoy must have zigzagged away.
2150		I dive and get a hydrophone bearing at 220°.
2203		We surface and set off in pursuit.
2225		Morse signalling intercepted astern to north-east. We turn and head in that direction and come across two zigzagging destroyers.[3]
2237	Qu. AL 6146	Spread of three torpedoes fired at destroyer with two funnels, a hit amidships.[4] Destroyer breaks apart and sinks immediately. Bows right, inclination 90°, enemy speed 12 knots. Running time 52 sec. = 780 m.
2240		I turn away in what I presume to be the direction of the other destroyer in order to dispose of this one too.[5] She soon heaves into sight ahead at an acute inclination, bows right. Can't get the go-ahead from the torpedo data computer yet.[6] Just as we're about to pass her at a range of 150 m we can hear loud shouting up on her deck. Alarm. Destroyer looses off a good salvo of gunfire but no hits (dirt on the guns[7] – at 150 m). As I'm closing the hatch I hear another four salvoes. I go slowly to 160 m.

---

1 This transmission and the preceding beacon signal were responsible for the HF/DF fix reported by the 6th Escort Group at precisely this time.

2 It is hard to know what to make of this entry. Although *U136* had been detected by RDF twenty minutes earlier and depth charges dropped at 2104 U-boat time, it is unclear why Zimmermann should equate this latest pattern with his having been sighted at 3,000 metres in the mist of a February night off Scotland.

3 These two were the ex-American escort destroyer *Chelsea* and the corvette *Arbutus*.

4 *Arbutus* had but one funnel; *Chelsea* had four.

5 HMS *Chelsea*.

6 Zimmermann here explains that the attack angle was too extreme for the torpedo data computer to calculate a firing solution, indicating that *U136*'s bow was pointing more than 90° away from the target.

7 This seems to be an expression for *Chelsea*'s guns being unable to depress sufficiently to bear on their target – quite plausible since the range was only 150 metres.

2301		Five depth charges dropped about 2,000 m away.[8]
2313		One depth charge above the boat at a shallow depth, no adverse effects.
2318		Five depth charges, range increasing.
2335		Five depth charges, range continuing to increase slowly.
		Zimmermann

6.ii

0000	Qu. AL 6148, wind NW 2–3, sea 3, mist	
0058		Surfaced. W/T report 0057/6/238 transmitted: *Two-funnelled destroyer sunk, forced to dive, contact with convoy lost in Qu. AL 6146, in pursuit steering 280°, U136.*[4] Sent three times but not repeated back to us.
0255	Qu. AL 5268	Bright white stars at 280°. I alter course accordingly.

---

8   *Chelsea* did indeed follow up her salvoes with patterns of depth charges, but as Zimmermann noted the settings were too shallow.

The sinking

In the absence of a Board of Enquiry the only official source relating to the loss of *Arbutus* from the Allied side is the report of her sole officer survivor, Lt V. G. Paramain. Paramain recorded a 'terrific explosion as the ship was hit on the starboard side' abreast the forward bulkhead of No. 1 boiler room at 2138 ship time. This opened up the entire forward section of the ship, ripping away deck plating and leaving the upper works 'in a tangled condition'. With the after part of the bridge wrecked, Paramain and others were forced to slide down the mast stays through clouds of escaping steam to survey the damage from the forecastle. *Arbutus* was by now listing to starboard, and if she were not finished off by an internal explosion Paramain considered it unlikely that the ship would remain afloat for very much longer. Amidships 'the deck over the boiler room had been blown out with steam pipes from the boiler room round [the] funnel casing, and wreckage from the starboard side impeded [the] clearing away of [the] port skiff'. Further investigation revealed that steam was billowing out of the port wardroom flat doorway and that water had already reached the main deck. By the time Paramain and those crew members who could be got aft abandoned ship the starboard gunwale was awash. About twenty-five minutes after the attack *Arbutus* capsized and sank rapidly by the bow leaving a thick layer of oil on the surface which immediately caught fire, probably due to the rupture of petrol cans stowed on the upper deck. The explosion of three depth charges marked the end of HMS *Arbutus*.

Lt Paramain's report barely conceals his disdain for Lt Warren's leadership on the night *Arbutus* was sunk. Paramain not only queried Warren's depth-charge procedure, implying that the uncoordinated patterns were responsible for the power failure, but objected strongly to his commanding officer's order to put the navigation lights on once the hunt for *U136* had been abandoned – so much so that Paramain instructed Sub-Lt A. K. Loten RNVR to record his disapproval in the log, indicative of a complete breakdown of respect for Warren. Paramain was then left in charge while Warren headed for the wardroom, an unthinkable place for a commanding officer to seek refuge while his ship was at Action Stations. Perhaps it was mere coincidence or a combination of noise and fear that resulted in Paramain twice being ignored as he was mustering the crew to abandon ship, but the tone and content of his report and its praise for none but the men of HMS *Chelsea* suggests a profound dissatisfaction with the morale of his ship.

Whether this was Lt Paramain's particular grievance or evidence of a wider malaise aboard remains a matter for speculation.

Fate of the crew

For reasons as yet unclear Lt Paramain seems to have had considerable difficulty in persuading survivors to abandon ship in an organised fashion. He could hardly make himself heard when ordering those on the boat deck to go further aft, and even when he eventually got the message across 'no attention was made to this repeated order by those endeavouring to clear the skiff against a starboard list'. He then tried to induce other ratings on the fo'c's'le head to work their way aft to the rafts, but these refused. Having gone aft to assist the Coxswain and others in floating off rafts, Paramain ordered his float to be paddled back to the port side for'ard 'in an attempt to pick up any who may have jumped from the boat deck or forecastle as the ship rolled over, which I was convinced must soon occur'. Three or four men were rescued as a result. Once *Arbutus* had gone a further search was made for survivors and two more hauled onto the rafts which were brought together to improve their chances of rescue. *Chelsea* spent some time hunting for *U136* and according to Paramain it was almost three hours (less than two hours by *Chelsea*'s reckoning) before she returned and lowered scrambling nets in the early hours of 6 February. The business of rescue was complicated by the fact that 'all were more or less saturated by oil fuel which made it extremely difficult to hoist them inboard'. A total of thirty-three men were rescued including nine considered to be in a critical condition, one of whom succumbed during the night. Since the 6th Escort Group was in any case due to part company with ON63 at noon that day it was decided to proceed immediately to Londonderry where the injured were landed on the 7th, the rest reaching Liverpool on the 9th.

The name *Arbutus* was revived in a Modified Flower-class corvette launched at George Brown's yard at Greenock in January 1944 and commissioned into the Royal New Zealand Navy in July of that year.

U136 and Heinrich Zimmermann

Built by Bremer Vulkan at Vegesack and commissioned in August 1941, *U136* spent the duration of her career assigned to the 6th *U-Flottille*. Her three operational patrols were carried out under Kptlt Heinrich Zimmermann, an officer who had won his spurs in the Kriegsmarine's minesweeping service. Despite having no submarine experience,

Letters and flowers for Zimmermann on *U136*'s return to St-Nazaire in March or May 1942. *DUBMA*

Zimmermann bypassed the usual stint as First Watch Officer under a seasoned commander and enjoyed a successful maiden patrol, the sinking of *Arbutus* being followed on 10 February by that of HMCS *Spikenard* (**52**). The rest of *U136*'s career is covered in that entry.

Sources

Admiralty, War Diary for February 1942 (TNA, ADM 199/2236), pp. 127, 138, 174, 209A and 209B
—, *Damage and Losses to H.M. Ships, Miscellaneous Craft and Allied Ships: Reports, 1941–1943* (TNA, ADM 199/802)
—, *Report of Proceedings: Convoy ON63* (TNA, ADM 237/77)
Ministry of Defence, *Convoy ON63* (NHB, ON Convoys Box)
Ruegg, R. A., *Flower-Class Corvettes* (typescript, IWM, 13(41).245/5, 1987)

Preston, Antony, and Alan Raven, *Flower Class Corvettes* [Ensign, no. 3] (London: Bivouac Books, 1973); reprinted as Man o'War, no. 7 (London: Arms and Armour Press, 1982)

---

51   FNFL *ALYSSE* (ex HMS *ALYSSUM*)

L.V. Jacques Pépin Lehalleur, FNFL
Sunk by *U654* (Type VIIC), Oblt.z.S. Ludwig Forster, 8–10 February 1942
North Atlantic, 340 nm ESE of St John's, Newfoundland

Alysse at Saint-Pierre-et-Miquelon in December 1941 or January 1942. *Musée de la Marine, Paris*

Theatre North Atlantic (Map 1)		*Displacement* 940 tons	
Coordinates (of attack) 45° 50' N, 44° 48' W		*Dimensions* 205.25' × 33' × approx. 11.25'	
Kriegsmarine code (of attack) Quadrat BC 5947		*Maximum speed* 16 knots	
U-boat timekeeping differential +2 hours		*Armament* 1 × 4"; 4 × .303" AA	
Fatalities 36 *Survivors* 34			

The Free French navy (Forces Navales Françaises Libres)

With the collapse of France imminent, on 18 June 1940 General Charles de Gaulle issued a broadcast to his countrymen exhorting them to rally to the cause of the Free French government in London. Among those who answered the call was Vice-amiral Émile-Henri Muselier who reached London via Marseille and Gibraltar on 30 June, six days

after the armistice with Germany. On 1 July 1940 the Forces Navales Françaises Libres (FNFL) came into being under Muselier's command, numbering 3,300 men by the end of 1940 and 8,700 in July 1943. A total of sixty-two vessels of all types were commissioned between June 1940 and the reintegration of the French fleet in May 1943. These numbers would no doubt have been much greater had it not been for the events of 3 July 1940 when a British squadron opened fire on the French fleet at Mers-el-Kebir leaving four ships sunk or heavily damaged and over 1,300 sailors and civilians dead. However, small though it was, the Free French navy served with distinction under British operational control, its ships accounting for four U-boats in the Battle of the Atlantic and having in *Rubis* one of the most successful Allied submarines of the war. Nine of its own ships were lost, including *Alysse*'s sister corvette *Mimosa* (**61**).

Career

For design notes on the Flower-class corvettes, see HMS *Picotee* (**29**).

The corvette *Alyssum* was laid down at George Brown & Co. of Greenock in June 1940 and launched in March of the following year. Originally intended for the Royal Navy, she was commissioned with a Free French crew as the *Alysse* on 5 June 1941, second of the nine corvettes to join the FNFL during the war. Following a brief work-up at the anti-submarine school at Tobermory and repairs at Greenock, *Alysse* was assigned to the Canadian 25th Escort Group (EG-C25) of Newfoundland Command based on St John's, the ship joining her first convoy in the Clyde on 22 July. Her first action came on 19 September when she opened fire on a U-boat attacking convoy SC44 on the same night that HMCS *Lévis* was fatally damaged by *U74* (**32**). Escort duty continued until December when *Alysse* joined an all-Free French force consisting of her sisters *Aconit* and *Mimosa* (**61**) – together the 1e division of the FNFL – and the cruiser submarine *Surcouf* in the capture of the Vichy-held islands of Saint-Pierre-et-Miquelon off Newfoundland on Christmas Eve. Delayed at first by poor weather, the operation was unopposed and resulted in seven local men joining the ship as volunteers with the FNFL. January 1942 found *Alysse* refitting on the Clyde before joining Canadian Task Unit 4.1.12 at Londonderry on the 28th. Two days later this force sailed to escort convoy ON60 to Halifax, Nova Scotia.

Background of the attack

Mustered from four ports in the United Kingdom, on 28 January convoy ON60 was joined off Northern Ireland by its escort for the first phase of the Atlantic crossing. This passed off uneventfully but for engine trouble to a single merchantman, and shortly before midday on 2 February ON60's forty-two ships were handed over to its western escort (Task Unit 4.1.12) at the Mid-Ocean Meeting Point (MOMP). All corvettes, TU 4.1.12 consisted of the Canadian *Sherbrooke* (Senior Officer), *Barrie*, *Buctouche*, *Hepatica* and *Moosejaw*, the British *Dianthus*, and the Free French *Alysse*. On the afternoon of the 8th the as yet unmolested convoy was warned by the Admiralty that it had probably been sighted by a German submarine. Sure enough, two boats had established contact that day, *U654* (Kptlt Ludwig Forster) and *U85* (Oblt.z.S. Eberhard Greger), both returning from fruitless patrols in the Cabot Strait separating Newfoundland and Nova Scotia. That night, just as the portion of the convoy bound for the West Indies altered course to the south, Forster attacked an unidentified merchantman at the rear of the port column together with a corvette zigzagging some three cables on her port beam. A salvo of three torpedoes was fired, two at the merchantman and one at *Alysse*, then closing the convoy at reduced speed.

War Diary of *U654*, patrol of 3 January–19 February 1942: PG 30079, NHB, reel 1,134, pp. 228–9

Date, time	Details of position, wind, weather, sea, light, visibility, moonlight, etc.	Incidents
8.ii		
2203	Dusk, very good visibility	Outgoing W/T transmission: *Convoy dispersed, steamers steering independent SW courses. Maintaining contact. Qu. BC 5991 upper left.* The group, which consists of roughly ten vessels, has no particular formation, each steamer is zigzagging independently and irregularly. We can make out three corvettes, which remain stationed for the most part close to two large merchantmen. Slowly it gets dark and we adopt a converging course to attack.
2241		Incoming W/T transmission from B.d.U.: *Forster free to attack.*
2309		Outgoing W/T transmission: *Alpha Alpha Qu. BC 5946 lower right corner.*
2320	Weather: wind SW 1, sea 1, very good visibility, 4/10 overcast, 1,020 mb, +5.4°C [42°F]	For our attack we select a 7,000-ton steamer sailing in the middle of the group, protected by a corvette. My remaining torpedoes: one Eto in the stern tube, one Eto and one Ato in the bow tubes and one reserve stern Ato.[1] As I run in to attack I am several times forced to withdraw by the corvette that would appear to be the convoy's port escort.
9.ii		
0000	Qu. BC 5945	*Forster Oblt.z.S. and Commanding Officer*
0024		Incoming W/T transmission: *Greger requests beacon signal.*[2] My reply: *Am sending beacon signal, enemy position Qu. BC 5866.* Transmitted at 0057.
0028		As a result of a sudden zigzag towards me on the part of the steamer and the corvette I find myself favourably positioned for a shot, only needing the target to continue towards me a little further. Corvette is proceeding some 200 m astern of the steamer but staggered some 500 m on her port quarter.[3] She is gradually closing, inclination 40° bows left.

---

1   'Eto' and 'Ato' were Kriegsmarine shorthand for the electric G7e and compressed-air G7a torpedoes respectively.

2   Oblt.z.S. Eberhard Greger, commander of *U85*.

3   Forster's data is confirmed by Allied sources.

Date, time	Details of position, wind, weather, sea, light, visibility, moonlight, etc.	Incidents
0031 55'[4]	Wind SW 1, sea 1, very good visibility, 4/10 overcast, 1,020 mb, +5.4°C [42°F]	We fire from Tube IV (Eto) at the steamer, torpedo no. 26813, pistol no. 20223. Shot coordinates: enemy speed 9 knots, inclination 90° bows left, depth 2 m, range 1,500 m, point of aim amidships.[5] I immediately turn to fire a stern shot. Due to another vessel bearing down on me to starboard I have to withdraw slightly, which leads to a delay with the second shot. No detonation within two minutes so first shot has missed. I turn about once again for a bow shot. Corvette is now stationed ahead of the steamer and is outlined very clearly against the bright horizon.
0034 50'	Qu. BC 5947	We fire from Tube V (Eto) at the corvette ahead of the steamer, torpedo no. 32398, pistol no. 20647. Shot coordinates: enemy speed 8 knots, inclination 90° bows left, depth 2 m, range 1,500 m, point of aim amidships. I immediately turn about to fire a bow shot from Tube II (Ato).
0036 00'	Wind SW 1, sea 1, very good visibility, 4/10 overcast, 1,020 mb, +5.4°C [42°F]	We fire from Tube I (Ato) at the steamer, torpedo no. 12351, pistol no. 20432. Shot coordinates: enemy speed 8 knots, inclination 95° bows left, depth 2 m, torpedo speed 40 knots, range 1,500 m. Just as we fire the corvette zigzags 30° towards me.
0037 04'		A hit on the corvette amidships. High detonation cloud, dramatic sheet of flame, followed by the detonation of depth charges on her stern. Within two minutes the corvette has completely disappeared beneath the surface.[6]
0037 09'		A hit abreast the after mast of steamer.[7] Steamer lies stopped, firing red, green and white starshell, gradually settling by the stern.[8] Later we see her still motionless with a freeboard of some 2 m aft. Running time of Eto 2 min. 15 sec. (roughly 2,000 m), that of the Ato 65 sec. These timings cannot be verified with certainty as the two detonations followed one another in rapid succession, accompanied by the depth charges of the corvette going up for good measure. Judging from this the corvette's zigzag took her neatly into the line of my Ato and it was the Eto that struck the steamer. As we retire we are constantly having to avoid the other merchantmen, which are now zigzagging wildly around me.
	Becoming hazy, slight surface mist	I have the stern torpedo tube reloaded as we withdraw. The steamer begins to send out morse signals, a number of other vessels fire starshell and a few minutes later I can make out two small vessels, one of which is a corvette alongside the steamer constantly exchanging signals in morse with her lamp.[9] A third vessel joins the group a little later. I remain in the vicinity of the steamer in order to attack her once again with my last Ato. It's a pitch black but clear night, though mist is slowly gathering.
0131	Qu. BC 5947, wind SW 1, sea 1, average visibility, 4/10 overcast, 1,020 mb, +5°C [41°F]	Stern tube is now reloaded. The three escorts are stationed some 500–1,000 m from the steamer. We run in to attack.[10] A stern shot as a *coup de grâce*. Inclination 90°, range 2,000 m, depth 2 m. Misses. Presumably torpedo failure. Torpedo no. 7483, pistol no. 20046. We withdraw.
0235		Outgoing W/T transmission to Greger: *No more torpedoes. Corvette sunk, steamer torpedoed. This steamer in Qu. BC 5866 surrounded by escorts. Convoy dispersed. Am sending beacon signal from vicinity of torpedoed steamer.*

4 Forster has gone to the unusual length of adding seconds to his timekeeping in this and succeeding entries.
5 This and all subsequent torpedoes were fired by *U654*'s First Watch Officer, Oblt.z.S. Werner Schwaff.
6 This was of course not the case since *Alysse* stayed afloat for another thirty-six hours.
7 There is no record of any other ship being struck at this juncture.
8 The starshell was in fact fired by *Alysse*, though in the wrong order sowing confusion among the escort and eliciting criticism in the Board of Enquiry.
9 These two were no doubt HMC corvettes *Moosejaw* and *Hepatica* arriving on the scene of the attack.
10 Presumably fired at *Alysse* as no other vessel was reported in distress at this time.

The sinking

U654's torpedo, picked up on *Alysse*'s Asdic seconds before impact at 2231 on the 8th Allied time, detonated forward leaving her a shattered wreck. In the words of *Hepatica*'s commanding officer, Lt Cdr T. Gilmour RCNR, 'the forward part from stem to mast had been literally demolished'. So far did she settle by the head that the propeller cleared the water leaving no possibility of her getting under way. However, the forward bulkhead of the stokers' mess deck held and an inspection revealed it to be watertight. All non-essential personnel had been evacuated by midnight, but the thirteen-strong salvage party was not long in following, Gilmour deciding that the wreck was too unstable to warrant the danger. By 0115 on the 9th the ship had been completely abandoned, though not before Premier maître mécanicien L'Huillier had taken steps to ensure that there would be sufficient head of steam in the boilers to keep the dynamo turning. At 0200 a hawser was fastened to *Alysse*'s stern but parted half an hour later, with which the salvage effort was left until dawn as *Hepatica* stood by. Attempts to take her in tow were renewed at daybreak, but it was not long before the hawser parted again. At 0930 *Alysse* was reboarded by three of her men together with *Hepatica*'s First Lieutenant, Lt H. McNicholl RCNVR, which found the bulkhead still holding and started up the dynamo without difficulty. However, despite jettisoning some topweight *Alysse* appeared to settle further and McNicholl ordered the boarding party off at around 1100 with a view to scuttling her. Nonetheless, towing was resumed at 1330 on orders from Newfoundland Command, which had dispatched HM rescue tug *Prudent* from St John's escorted by the Canadian minesweeping sloop *Minas*. The towing party had covered no more than fifty-eight miles by daybreak on the 10th but the appearance of *Prudent* at 0625 no doubt raised hopes that *Alysse* might be brought in. It was not to be. At 0745 the tow parted yet again in deteriorating weather and rising seas. *Hepatica* attempted to pass it back but at 0925 *Alysse* 'was observed to roll and lurch violently' listing first to starboard then to port. At 0930, with the key bulkhead evidently having given way, *Alysse* sank with a loud report (probably a boiler explosion) approximately in position 46° 34' N, 44° 10' W.

Forster's account of the attack on *Alysse* tallies closely with Allied sources in many respects, but with some very notable divergences. Firstly, there is no mention in Allied records of any merchantman being hit at this juncture, while *Alysse* took thirty-six hours to sink as against the two minutes noted by Forster, whose subsequent observations are accurate in every respect save in the most patent one of all: the type of ship struck. Though the order of coloured starshell noted by Forster is exactly as reported by the Allied escort, it was *Alysse* which fired them, not any merchantman. Forster's observations of two escorts approaching the stricken vessel equate to HMC corvettes *Moosejaw* and *Hepatica* standing by *Alysse*, but how Forster and his lookouts could have confused her wreck with a 7,000-ton steamer in what he himself describes as good visibility is difficult to explain. Indeed, it is hard to escape the impression of an inexperienced commander unwilling to acknowledge the expenditure of four torpedoes with only a corvette to show for it, a point apparently not lost on B.d.U. (see below).

Nor is the loss of *Alysse* without its share of irony. At 1911 on the 8th, a little over three hours before she was hit, Rear-Admiral L. W. Murray, Flag Officer Newfoundland Escort Force, signalled *Sherbrooke* ordering *Alysse* to be detached to St John's. Assuming this signal was ever received it must be supposed that it had not been deciphered before Kptlt Forster ensured it would never be carried out. A Board of Enquiry convened on the 13th exonerated all parties for the loss of *Alysse*, noting that nothing could have been done to shore up the bulkhead from aft. Formal exoneration of Lieutenant de vaisseau Pépin Lehalleur by a *Tribunal maritime* in the battleship *Courbet* at Portsmouth followed in June 1942.

Fate of the crew

The demolition of *Alysse*'s fore part killed almost half her crew, only one stoker surviving from the seamen's and stokers' mess decks forward. The thirty-six fatalities were French with the exception of the British liaison officer, Sub-Lt L. E. Fisher RNVR, and a Royal Navy Asdic operator, 'Matelot asdic' William Clifton Smee, recently drafted from *Alysse*'s sister *Lobélia*. Most of the officers, including L.V.

Forster (in white cap) and presumably fellow officers of *U654* on return from patrol to Brest in February or May 1942. *DUBMA*

Lehalleur, were dining in the wardroom when the torpedo struck, to be flung into heaps in pitch darkness. Lehalleur himself was knocked unconscious, his inert form carried out by his officers after his absence had been noted. *Alysse* alerted *Hepatica* to her plight by Aldis light, initially to the effect that she had struck a mine, soon corrected to 'Have been torpedoed.' By midnight on the 8th twenty-one of the thirty-four surviving crewmen, Lehalleur included, had got clear of the wreck in the two ship's boats still seaworthy, being picked up by *Moosejaw* shortly after. The other survivors were taken on board *Hepatica* over the next hour or so. They were landed at St John's on the 11th, Lehalleur being transferred to hospital with a fractured scapula.

A memorial service for the dead attended by all the survivors was held on 24 February on the island of Saint-Pierre, home to five of those who had perished. On 4 April 1944 *Alysse* was conferred the FNFL's *Ordre de la division*, an award carrying with it the Croix de guerre with silver star. Her dead are remembered on the Free French naval memorial erected on Lyle Hill overlooking the port of Greenock, Scotland, from which ships of that force often sailed between 1940 and 1945.

U654 and Ludwig Forster

Built by Howaldtswerke at Hamburg and commissioned in July 1941, *U654* carried out three frontline patrols in the North Atlantic under Oblt.z.S. Ludwig Forster, who assumed command after Korvkpt. Hans-Joachim Hesse brought her to Bergen in December 1941. Discounting *U654*'s uneventful transit from Bergen to Brest in that month, the patrol which yielded the sole pennant of *Alysse* in January and February 1942 was Forster's first. Without wishing to bear down too heavily on a novice commander, B.d.U. expressed its concern in its post-cruise assessment that this patrol 'was much impaired by a number of unexplained misses'. *U654*'s second patrol between March and May 1942 yielded two merchantmen between Bermuda and the Carolinas. Her next in the Caribbean brought no further successes, her career ending on 22 August 1942 when she was sunk off Panama by depth charges from a Douglas B18 Bolo bomber of the USAAF. There were no survivors.

Sources

Admiralty, *Damage and Losses to H.M. and Allied Ships, 1941–1943: Reports* (TNA, ADM 199/802)

—, *Reports from Convoy ONS60* (TNA, ADM 237/17)

—, *Convoy ON60* (TNA, ADM 237/118)

—, *ON60: Report of Proceedings* (NHB, ON convoy box)

Anon., *Notice historique sur la corvette* Alysse (typescript, SHM, *Alysse* file)

Ruegg, R., *Flower-Class Corvettes* (typescript, IWM, 13(41).245/5, 1987)

Auphan, Contre-amiral Paul, and Jacques Mordal, *The French Navy in World War II* (Annapolis, Md.: Naval Institute Press, 1959)

Bayle, Capitaine de frégate Luc-Marie, *Les Corvettes F.N.F.L., de leur armement au 2 août 1943* (Vincennes: Service historique de la Marine, 1966)

Bertrand, Michel, *La Marine Française au combat, 1939–1945* (2 vols, Paris: Charles-Lavauzelle, 1982–3)

Chaline, Vice-amiral Émile, and Capitaine de vaisseau Pierre Santarelli, *Historique des forces navales françaises libres* (4 vols, Vincennes: Service historique de la Marine, 1990–2003)

Divine, A. D., *Navies in Exile* (London: John Murray, 1944)

Le Masson, Henri, *The French Navy* (2 vols, London: Macdonald, 1969)

Le Masson, Philippe, *La Marine Française et la guerre, 1939–1945* (Paris: Jules Tallandier, 1991)

Morsier, Pierre de, *Les Corvettes de la France Libre* (Paris: Éditions France-Empire, 1972)

Preston, Antony, and Alan Raven, *Flower Class Corvettes* [Ensign, no. 3] (London: Bivouac Books, 1973); reprinted as Man o'War, no. 7 (London: Arms and Armour Press, 1982)

Salou, Charles, 'L'Alysse' in *Navires et histoire* 10 (February 2002), pp. 14–16

52   HMCS *SPIKENARD*
Lt Cdr H. G. Shadforth, RCNR†
Sunk by *U136* (Type VIIC), Kptlt Heinrich Zimmermann, 10 February 1942
North Atlantic, 505 nm W of Islay, Inner Hebrides (Scotland)

Spikenard seen leaving Halifax, probably in 1941. She was sunk by a torpedo hit from *U136* on the port side amidships. *Naval Museum of Alberta*

Theatre	North Atlantic (Map 1)	*Displacement*	940 tons
Coordinates	56° 08' N, 21° 08' W	*Dimensions*	205.25' × 33' × approx. 11.25'
Kriegsmarine code	Quadrat AL 5235	*Maximum speed*	16 knots
U-boat timekeeping differential	+4 hours	*Armament*	1 × 4"; 4 × .303" AA
Fatalities	57 *Survivors* 8		

Career

For background on the Royal Canadian Navy, see HMCS *Lévis* (**32**). For design notes on the Flower-class corvettes, see HMS *Picotee* (**29**). Notes on the Canadian Flowers are provided in HMCS *Lévis*.

Ordered in January 1940, the Flower-class corvette *Spikenard* was laid down at G. T. Davie of Lauzon, Quebec on 24 February, launched on 10 August and commissioned on 6 December that same year. After just five days' working up at Halifax, Nova Scotia *Spikenard* joined her

first convoy, HX104 bound for the United Kingdom. Two months' fitting out at South Shields on the Tyne was followed between April and June 1941 with training in anti-submarine warfare at HMS *Western Isles*, the shore establishment at Tobermory, Scotland. Convoy duty began in earnest in June, the ship being allocated to the Newfoundland Escort Force on the 25th for service as an ocean escort on the St John's–Iceland run. With the new year came assignment to the Canadian 15th Escort Group (EG-C15) with which *Spikenard* sailed from St John's on 1 February to join convoy SC67, already at sea. It was one of the first 'Newfie–Derry' runs, the escort accompanying the convoy to the Mid-Ocean Meeting Point (MOMP) where it was relieved by a British escort group before itself turning for Londonderry.

Background of the attack

On 30 January 1942 the twenty-two merchantmen of slow convoy SC67 sailed from Halifax, Nova Scotia bound for Liverpool. Accompanying it to the Mid-Ocean Meeting Point at approximately 58° N, 22° W were the six corvettes of the Canadian 15th Escort Group (EG-C15). By the evening of 10 February, with relief by the British 7th Escort Group only hours away, the convoy was 500 miles south of Reykjavik and a similar distance north-west of Londonderry. The escort consisted of HMCSs *Spikenard* (Senior Officer) disposed ahead and towards the starboard side of the convoy, *Chilliwack* on the convoy's port bow, *Lethbridge* and *Louisburg* on the port and starboard beam respectively, and *Dauphin* and *Shediac* astern. By this time, too, the convoy had been sighted by *U591* (Kptlt Hans-Jürgen Zetzsche), low on fuel and returning to St-

Nazaire after a spell on meteorological duty. Fresh from the sinking of HMS *Arbutus* on the 5th (**50**), Kptlt Heinrich Zimmermann's *U136* was brought up to the convoy by beacon signal from *U591*, but neither this nor the radio traffic between them and B.d.U. alerted EG-C15 to the dangers ahead. At 2120 escort time came a first inkling of danger when *Chilliwack* made what she believed to be a submarine sighting and attacked with depth charges after gaining an Asdic contact. What she appears to have spotted was *U591* in the act of unleashing a salvo of torpedoes against her. Neither attack met with any success but *U136* was to enjoy different fortune when she engaged SC67 shortly after. Following a course alteration by the convoy, Zimmermann found himself ahead of the leading ships including *Spikenard*, then blind to submarine attack having lost the use of both her Asdic and her RDF apparatus. Worse, when she and the Norwegian freighter *Heina* were torpedoed by *U136* between 2133 and 2235, the convoy escort failed to appreciate quite which or how many ships had been hit, an oversight with dire consequences for *Spikenard*'s company.

War Diary of *U136*, patrol of 22 January–1 March 1942: PG 30126, NHB, reel 1,084, pp. 138–9

Date, time	Details of position, wind, weather, sea, light, visibility, moonlight, etc.	Incidents
10.ii		
2014		Incoming W/T transmission 128/1930/10/130: *Enemy convoy in sight, AL 5251, easterly course proceeding very slowly. U591.*[1]
		Incoming W/T transmission 1902/10/229: *Zimmermann and Varendorf [sic] to occupy new attack area in northerly AM segment.*[2]
2110		I head in the direction of the convoy indicated by Zetzsche.
		Incoming W/T transmission 230[3]/10/132: *Correct position of convoy is AL 5132, 15 ships, easterly course. Zetzsche.*
		Incoming W/T transmission 2037/10/133: *Zetzsche maintain contact, free to attack, Varendorf and Zimmermann close Zetzsche's convoy. All boats to pull back to designated attack area if counter-attack is robust.*
2225		Incoming W/T transmission 2205/10/134: *Zetzsche reports position in naval quadrant AL 5213 lower middle.* Which means enemy is dead ahead.
2230	Qu. AL 5221	By dead reckoning I must be very close to the convoy.
2255		Two detonations.[4]
2259		Outgoing W/T transmission 218/2250/10/136 to U591: *Send beacon signal. U136.*
		Zetzsche's radio beacon picked up at 234°, I alter course accordingly.
		Zimmermann
11.ii		
0000	Qu. AL 5225, wind NE 2, sea 2, occasional mist, 1,025 mb, bright night, generally good visibility	
0008		Shadows in sight – I proceed directly towards them. It turns out to be the convoy heading east. I haul ahead.
0132	Qu. AL 5235	Am now ahead of the convoy to port when convoy suddenly alters course towards me by 30°.

---

1   Commanded by Kptlt Hans-Jürgen Zetzsche.

2   The Kriegsmarine's AM quadrant was directly to the west of the AL quadrant in which Zimmermann was operating. Oblt.z.S. Amelung von Varendorff (*sic*) was the CO of *U213*.

3   It seems likely that these three digits are a mistranscription for 2030, which equates with the time Zetzsche sent this signal.

4   Since no Allied vessels are recorded as having been struck at this juncture these might be connected with the salvo of four torpedoes fired by Zetzsche's *U591* at 2240, perhaps end-of-run detonations.

Date, time	Details of position, wind, weather, sea, light, visibility, moonlight, etc.	*Incidents*

	Unexpectedly I find myself in the middle, directly ahead of the first row of merchantmen sailing abreast. The escorts are stationed on the port and starboard quarters of this row.[5]
0133	Torpedo fired at freighter from Tube I. Inclination 50°, bows left, enemy speed 8 knots, range 1,000 m, angle of fire 18.7°, aim-off 11°.[6] Misses. Torpedo fired at freighter from Tube II. Inclination 50°, bows left, enemy speed 8 knots, range 800 m, angle of fire 18.7°, aim-off 11°. Hits.[7] Torpedo fired at freighter from Tube III. Inclination 80°, bows left, enemy speed 8 knots, range 1,000 m, angle of fire 359°, aim-off 15°. Hits.
0135	Starboard escort comes very close.[8] Torpedo fired at corvette while turning to port. Inclination 90°, bows left, enemy speed 10 knots, range 1,000 m, angle of fire 340°, aim-off 19°. A hit amidships, running time 40 sec. (600 m). Very powerful detonation, enormous fiery glow, corvette sinks bow first just 300 m away in about 30 sec.[9]
0139	Torpedo fired from Tube V at freighter. Inclination 70°, bows left, enemy speed 7 knots, range 1,000 m, angle of fire 163°, aim-off red [i.e. port] 13°. Misses. Freighter appears to have stopped. Several destroyers and corvettes now emerge from the convoy, coming on at high speed.[10] Countless depth charges dropped astern of me. I withdraw ahead of the convoy to the east, zigzagging all the while. All pursuers apart from one destroyer give up the chase. Noise of depth charges fades away.
0230	Incoming W/T transmission 0158/11/140: *Request permission to break contact as have only 38 cbm of fuel remaining. Qu. [AL] 5235. Zetzsche.*
0235	I withdraw to the south-east; would like to maintain contact but destroyer pursues me with inclination 0° despite strong zigzags. (Radar?) Outgoing W/T transmission 0314/11/142: *0134 Qu. AL 5225 1 corvette destroyed.[11] Hits on 2 merchantmen, one burning, chased off by destroyers, no contact, powerful escort between merchantmen. [Qu. AL] 6143; wind SE 2; sea 2; occasional mist; 1,025 mb. U136.*
0315	We lose destroyer to north-west in the mist and head off in pursuit, course 305°.

5   HMCSs *Spikenard* and *Chilliwack* respectively, which Allied sources place somewhat further ahead than Zimmermann describes.

6   This and all subsequent torpedoes were fired by *U136*'s First Watch Officer, Oblt.z.S. Paul-Friedrich Otto.

7   Either this or Zimmermann's next torpedo struck MS *Heina*, 4.028 GRT.

8   HMCS *Spikenard*.

9   *Spikenard* is reported as having taken not less than two minutes to sink. Curiously, the documentation relating to convoy SC67 records *Spikenard* being hit at 2133 and *Heina* at 2135 whereas Zimmermann's log reverses the order of these attacks. Given the confusion on the Allied side Zimmermann's version is probably the more accurate.

10 Despite Zimmermann's description, the escort consisted of corvettes only.

11 The quadrant code should in fact read '5235' rather than '5225', which would accord with Zimmermann's entry of 0132 and with the torpedo report.

The sinking

Though the order for Action Stations was passed just before *U136*'s torpedo struck, none of *Spikenard*'s survivors (all but one of whom were below deck) ever learnt why it had sounded, though it could be explained by the hit on MS *Heina* (assuming this ship was struck first; see note 9). The few minutes that elapsed between detonation and sinking were chaotic in the extreme and no detailed picture can be formed of *Spikenard*'s last moments. Though the side on which the torpedo hit was a matter of debate at the Board of Inquiry, it was agreed that most of the damage was on the port side where much of the deck and a large section of the hull had been ripped away; Zimmermann's war diary settles the matter. The impact was followed by a blaze which spread rapidly from the break of the forecastle to the funnel, and possibly beyond. Though several believed that the ship had broken her back, *Spikenard* was recorded as having sunk by the head, rent by a second detonation as she went down. This was reckoned to have been a boiler explosion since the depth charges were reported as set to safe.

Survivors recalled *Spikenard* taking between two and five minutes to sink as against the thirty seconds recorded by Zimmermann.

Looking on in *U591*, Kptlt Zetzsche recorded attacks by another boat at around this time while himself claiming a tanker (torpedoes fired between 0144 and 0147 German time), but there is no corroboration for a third ship being lost in this encounter beyond *Spikenard* and *Heina*. Though the order in which these two were hit has been the subject of debate, there is little doubt as to the identity of the perpetrator since Zimmermann made his attacks from ahead of the convoy whereas Zetzsche appears to have been operating on its port side. Moreover, the times given for these sinkings from the Allied side equate with those in *U136*'s log.

Fate of the crew

For *Spikenard*'s survivors the aftermath was as chaotic as the demise of their ship. Of her two boats one was rendered unusable in the blaze while the other broke up as she sank, though frantic efforts to release

A rare shot of *U136* sailing from St-Nazaire in March or June 1942. Note her lobster emblem on the conning tower. *DUBMA*

the port-side Carley float bore fruit when this floated off as the ship went under. Several of the those who managed to get clear of the wreck suffered burns after passing through a wall of fire to make good their escape. The Carley float which they reached was then lashed to a Merchant Navy raft to which they eventually shifted since it promised to keep them drier. Though shouts were heard in the darkness only two other men were rescued from the water before the cries ceased, both the newcomers having suffered severe injuries in the second explosion.

There was, however, to be no quick rescue for these ten survivors. Several units of the escort observed two ships being struck, but while *Heina* was soon spotted issuing smoke no identification could be made of the second burning vessel which was assumed to be a merchantman on fire. When efforts to raise *Spikenard* – the Senior Officer of the Escort – by radio met with no response this was put down to known problems with her equipment. *Dauphin*, whose officers had seen two ships hit, stood by *Heina* for several hours to take off her survivors while *Shediac* was ordered to search to the west for victims of another sinking. The bearing was accurate but though their occupants saw her *Shediac* missed *Spikenard*'s rafts in the water. The convoy ploughed on while the surviving escorts carried out the attacks and sweeps noted by Zimmermann in his log, unaware of their leader's fate. Not until the British 7th Escort Group arrived to assume responsibility for the convoy at approximately 0700 that morning was it apprehended that *Spikenard* may have met with disaster. Attempts by HNorMS *St Albans* to take over as SOE prompted a lengthy exchange of signals with *Louisburg*, *Dauphin* and HMSs *Honeysuckle* and *Gentian* (which had joined the convoy just as *U136* attacked) which established that *Spikenard* was the second vessel seen ablaze. At 0840 *St Albans* ordered *Gentian* to return to the position of the sinking at speed and a raft with survivors was sighted that afternoon in approximately 56° 06' N, 20° 39' W. The two injured men had not survived the night, the rest being obliged by the cold to strip the bodies before slipping them over the side with a prayer. Rescued shortly after 1500 on the 11th, *Spikenard*'s eight survivors were landed at Liverpool on the 14th, four needing hospital treatment for burns.

The ten hours that had elapsed before *Spikenard* was missed by her escort group was among the points examined by the RCN Board of Inquiry into the loss of the ship. After some deliberation it was decided to exonerate the responsible parties in view of the confusion prevailing in the aftermath of the attacks and the temperamental nature of *Spikenard*'s equipment. It also concentrated on the need for improved provision for survivors in the likely event of a corvette's boats being rendered unusable. Not only should rafts and Carleys be provided for the entire ship's company but these should be fitted with flares.

Spikenard was a popular unit and her CO, Lt Cdr H. G. Shadforth, left a poignant memento of his ship in The Crowsnest, the officers' club in St John's which was the heart of the corvette navy. The night before sailing to join convoy SC67 Shadforth had driven a large metal spike – '*Spikenard*'s spike' – into the floor of the club for all to remember her by while the war lasted. B.d.U., meanwhile, showered praise on Zimmermann on his return to St-Nazaire, lauding the 'verve, tenacity and attack-minded spirit' that had yielded *U136* two escorts and two merchantmen on her maiden patrol.

U136 and Heinrich Zimmermann

For details on Zimmermann's and *U136*'s earlier career, including this her first patrol, see HMS *Arbutus* (**50**).

U136's second patrol between March and May 1942 took her to the eastern seaboard of the United States where three merchantmen were sunk and a large tanker damaged. Zimmermann's promising career came to an end on his third patrol while *U136* was operating as part of the *Hai* group north-west of the Canaries. On 11 July 1942 *U136* was located while moving in to engage ships bound for South America once convoy OS33 had dispersed, being quickly sunk in a combined attack by HMSs *Pelican* and *Spey* and the destroyer *Léopard* of the Free French navy. There were no survivors.

Sources

Admiralty, *Analysis of U-Boat Attacks on Atlantic Convoys* (TNA, ADM 199/2495)

—, *Damage and Losses to H.M. Ships, Miscellaneous Craft and Allied Vessels: Reports, 1941–1943* (TNA, ADM 199/802)

—, Department of Anti-Submarine Warfare, *Analysis of Attack by U-Boats on Convoy SC67 on 11th February 1942* (TNA, ADM 199/2001)

—, *Report of Proceedings: Convoy SC67* (TNA, ADM 237/193)

Department of National Defence, *Loss of HMCS* Spikenard: *Reports and Board of Inquiry* (Office of the Naval Historian, Directorate of History, RCN Ship Files, **81**/520/800, Box 100, File #1)

Newfoundland Command Records, *Loss of HMCS* Spikenard: *Reports* (NAC, RG 24, vol. **11930**, file 1156-331/100)

Blair, *Hitler's* **U-Boat** *War*, I, pp. 550–3

Johnston, **Mac,** *Corvettes Canada: Convoy Veterans of WWII Tell Their True Stories* (Toronto and Montreal: McGraw-Hill Ryerson, 1994)

McKee and **Darlington**, *Canadian Naval Chronicle*, pp. 46–9

Macpherson **and Burgess**, *Ships of Canada's Naval Forces* (3rd edn), pp. 86 and 157

Macpherson, **Ken, and** Marc Milner, *Corvettes of the Royal Canadian Navy, 1939–1945* (St Catherines, Ont.: Vanwell Publishing, 1993)

Preston, **Antony, and Al**an Raven, *Flower Class Corvettes* [Ensign, no. 3] (London: Bivouac Books, 1973); reprinted as Man o'War, no. 7 (London: Arms and Armour Press, 1982)

53   USS *JACOB JONES* (i)

Lt Cdr H. D. Black, USN†

Sunk by *U578* (Type VIIC), Korvkpt. Ernst-August Rehwinkel, 28 February 1942

North Atlantic, 25 nm SE of Cape May, New Jersey (USA)

Jacob Jones at an idyllic anchorage in the Pacific between the wars, far from her loss to *U578* in the North Atlantic. *BfZ*

Theatre	US coastal waters (Map 1)	*Displacement*	1,160 tons
Coordinates	38° 42' N, 74° 29' W	*Dimensions*	314.25' × 31' × 9.25'
Kriegsmarine code	Quadrat CA 5458	*Maximum speed*	35 knots
U-boat timekeeping differential	+6 hours	*Armament*	6 × 3"; 5 × .5" AA; 6 × 21" tt
Fatalities	138 *Survivors* 11		

Career

For design notes on the Wickes-class destroyers, of which USS *Jacob Jones* was one of 111 units, see HNorMS *Bath* (**30**).

The USS *Jacob Jones* (DD-130) was laid down by the New York Shipbuilding Corp. at Camden, New Jersey on 21 February 1918 and launched on 20 November that year by Mrs. Cazenove Doughton, great-granddaughter of Commodore Jacob Jones, a hero of the War of 1812 against Britain. *Jacob Jones* was commissioned at the Philadelphia Navy Yard on 20 October 1919, leaving that port for her shakedown cruise on 4 December. Her training completed at Pensacola, Florida on 3 January 1920, *Jacob Jones* sailed for the Pacific where she was to remain for the next ten years. Assigned to the Pacific Fleet's Destroyer Force at San Diego, she spent her first months operating along the California coast on anti-aircraft and firing exercises before entering Mare Island Navy Yard near San Francisco for refit and repair in August. Temporarily placed in reserve, *Jacob Jones* resumed duty with the Destroyer Force on 18 June 1921, with which she remained until decommissioning on 24 June 1922 along with much of her class as a consequence of the recently signed Washington Naval Treaty. This might have been the end for USS *Jacob Jones*, as indeed it proved for many of her sisters, but on 1 May 1930 she was recommissioned after eight years in mothballs and trained as a plane guard for the US Navy's nascent aircraft carrier fleet. Following a refit at Mare Island in

November *Jacob Jones* sailed south for Panama on 4 February 1931 where she undertook plane guard duty for the carrier *Langley* before transiting the Panama Canal for manoeuvres in the Caribbean and then in the Chesapeake Bay. The rest of the summer was spent with Destroyer Division 7 along the New England coast before she made her way to Boston Navy Yard for refitting in October. *Jacob Jones* passed the next three years on fleet duty, mainly in the Caribbean, the highlight being an assignment as escort during President Roosevelt's 'Good Neighbor' visit to Haiti in the summer of 1934. In December she entered Norfolk Navy Yard for refitting, emerging as a training ship for midshipmen from the US Naval Academy, Annapolis in May 1935. Service with the Atlantic Fleet continued, the ship operating first out of New York and then Norfolk from 1937, her officer-training duties interspersed with manoeuvres and exercises off the eastern seaboard of the United States and in the Caribbean.

In October 1938 *Jacob Jones* quit Norfolk to join Squadron 40-T, the force which since September 1936 had been charged with protecting US interests and citizens in Spain during the Civil War. Assigned mostly to the Western Mediterranean, it was not until October of the following year that she returned to the United States, war having by now broken out in Europe. Patrol and escort duty continued along the east coast and in the Caribbean until she was refitted at Norfolk in the spring of 1940. In April of that year she joined the Neutrality Patrol in the Atlantic, being reassigned to officer-training duties in June and then ordered to New London, Connecticut in September for anti-submarine sonar training at the Atlantic Fleet Sound School which was completed at Key West, Florida early in the new year. Returning to the Neutrality Patrol in March 1941, she spent two months in the waters separating Key West and the Yucatan Channel before joining the US Navy's guard of the Vichy-held islands of Martinique and Guadeloupe in the Lesser Antilles. Following a two-month refit at Norfolk, on 1 December *Jacob Jones* sailed for convoy escort training off New England after which she transferred to Argentia, Newfoundland on 12 December for escort duty with Destroyer Division 54 of Destroyer Squadron 27, Atlantic Fleet. Her first action came while escorting the minesweepers *Albatross* and *Linnet* en route to join convoy SC63 on 5 January 1942, an underwater contact heralding a prolonged though unsuccessful depth-charge attack. Her next convoy, HX169 to Iceland, was scattered by a violent storm, *Jacob Jones* proceeding independently to Hvalfjörður which she gained low on fuel and despite compass failure on the 19th. The return voyage with three merchantmen suffered similar tribulations, the convoy becoming dispersed in mountainous seas. *Jacob Jones* reached Argentia on 3 February in company with a Norwegian merchantman, though not before making a second unsuccessful attack on a suspected U-boat contact. Further convoy duty with ON59 at length brought her into Boston for repairs on 8 February, these completed at Norfolk on the 18th. Meanwhile, catastrophic losses of US merchant shipping had caused Vice Admiral Adolphus Andrews, Commander of the Eastern Sea Frontier, to establish a roving anti-submarine patrol off the US coast which in turn brought 'Jakie' to her final assignment. A first sortie on 22 February resulted in an attack on a submarine contact off the Ambrose Lightship during which *Jacob Jones* unavailingly expended her inventory of fifty-seven depth charges. Five days later she sailed from New York for the very last time.

Background of the attack

Among the eighteen U-boats ordered to American waters in February 1942 as part of Operation PAUKENSCHLAG ('drumroll') was Korvettenkapitän Ernst-August Rehwinkel's *U578*. Her maiden success came off New Jersey when the unescorted tanker *R.P. Resor* was sunk east of the Barnegat Light in the early hours of 27 February. The burning wreck was sighted by USSs *Dickerson* and *Jacob Jones* which had left New York that afternoon on a search and patrol mission between Barnegat Light and Five Fathom Bank. *Jacob Jones*, recently assigned to anti-submarine patrol duty, searched the vicinity for two hours but found no survivors. She then resumed her course southward to Cape May and the Delaware Capes, reporting her position on the evening of the 27th before commencing radio silence. Nothing more was heard from her and despite the rescue of a handful of survivors it needed the capture of German records for the precise circumstances of her loss to be revealed. These showed *U578* to have been closed by an enemy vessel at approximately 1025 log time (0425 ship time) on the 28th, thereby affording Korvkpt. Rehwinkel the chance to claim a second victim in twenty-four hours. Still uncertain whether it was a cruiser or destroyer, Rehwinkel brought *U578* into a firing position and shortly before 1100 demolished his target with a double hit.

War Diary of *U578*, patrol of 3 February–25 March 1942: PG 30613, NHB, reel 1,124, pp. 660–1[1]

Date, time	Details of position, wind, weather, sea, light, visibility, moonlight, etc.	Incidents
28.ii		
0800	[Qu.] CA 5456	
0810		A brightly lit steamer heaves into sight on the port bow steering a northerly course. A Swedish vessel, probably the *Gullmaren*.[2] I keep well clear.
0900		Course 180°.
1025		A blacked-out vessel in sight on the starboard bow steering a course more or less reciprocal to our own. We turn to assume a parallel course.
1029		Battle Stations. I haul ahead to carry out a surface attack. We have a favourable position against the backdrop of a dark horizon in the east. The moon is largely obscured by light cloud an hour before it sets. Light is good but a little hazy. Tubes I, III and V ready to fire. I gradually form the impression of a typical cruiser silhouette.[3] The inclination remains too fine to make out any details.
1050		I alter course to 230° to attack with a spread of two torpedoes, depth 3 m as per target assessment. I have brought forward the attack because it will be light in two hours and I want to retire to deeper water in good time. We are now very close as a result of a slight overestimation of enemy inclination. It's now critical that I keep to the pursuit curve at dead slow speed. But she plays into our hands. It is remarkable that the enemy has not spotted us despite our favourable position.

---

1 See p. xv for reproductions of the original log showing Rehwinkel's attack (entries 1050 and 1057) together with the corresponding torpedo report (*Schussmeldung*).

2 A freighter of 3,397 GRT.

3 The confusion is owed to the similarity in proportions and layout between the Omaha-class cruisers (7,050 tons, 556 feet) and the Wickes-class destroyers (1,090 tons, 314 feet). Though of very different size, each class shared the same distinguishing feature of four upright stacks disposed in pairs. See the entry for 1057 and nn. 5, 7 and 9 for more on this.

Date, time	Details of position, wind, weather, sea, light, visibility, moonlight, etc.	Incidents
1057	Qu. CA 5458, wind NW 3, sea 3, almost overcast, moon appearing occasionally between clouds. Fairly good visibility, not altogether clear.	Spread of two fired on attack course 240°.[4] After firing I order both engines utmost speed ahead and hard aport. Doubts arise both before firing and once torpedoes are running as to whether this really is a cruiser. The rather hazy light against us makes identifying details difficult so these can only be made out as the inclination becomes broader. Torpedo officer definitely believes he can make out destroyer features, particularly the island, though this is also a feature of the Concord class.[5] Four funnels can be clearly distinguished. The *Brückenmaat* is convinced it is a cruiser based on her silhouette, size and guns.[6] My impression of a cruiser's silhouette and dimensions remains unaltered although I was unable to concentrate on the details in the last few minutes due to manoeuvring considerations. After a running time of 34 sec. a hit approximately amidships. A powerful explosion follows immediately accompanied by a thick, black, oily cloud of smoke which sprinkles us with oily soot. This is immediately followed by a second hit just forward of the stern which in turn sets off a series of nine very powerful explosions. Presumably either depth charges or mines, these have a powerful effect on our boat and we suffer a number of electrical failures as a result. We are forced to retire through a cloud of smoke. As soon as this has cleared we see small pieces of wreckage still burning. We withdraw, course 120°, at ¾ speed then at half speed.
		Still the doubts persist. Obviously we would love to have sunk a cruiser and the fact that the torpedoes worked with depth settings of 3 m appears to bear this out. According to our Weyher [*sic*], the four-funnelled destroyers have a maximum draught of 2.8 m.[7] On the other hand both range and angle
	Dark once moon has set, good visibility	of spread suggest a destroyer. Torpedo run was timed at 57/100 which is why I first reported 57 sec. running time.[8] This equates to a target range of almost 900 m, which strengthened my original view. However, the running time was actually only 34 sec. – or some 500 m – which ultimately counts for more than any amount of wishful thinking.[9]
1200	Qu. CA 5494	Day's run: surface 85 nm, submerged 24 nm.
1236		Two distant detonations.
1305		Dawn breaking. We dive to proceed under water.

4 The spread was fired by *U578*'s First Watch Officer, Lt.z.S. Raimund Tiesler.

5 The USS *Concord* was a unit of the Omaha-class light cruisers (see n. 3). The torpedo officer was Lt.z.S. Tiesler.

6 The *Brückenmaat* ('bridge mate') was the senior rating of the four-strong bridge watch.

7 Rehwinkel is referring to the Weyer warship recognition manual with which all U-boats were equipped. He may not be accounting for the fact that *Jacob Jones* was fully loaded and her tanks brimful of oil fuel on sailing from New York the previous afternoon.

8 '57/100' refers to 57 per cent of a minute (i.e. 34 seconds), which Rehwinkel initially misinterpreted as 57 seconds.

9 In other words, Rehwinkel and his bridge watchkeeper believed they were seeing a larger vessel further off, but the much shorter running time of 34 seconds supported Lt.z.S. Tiesler's contention that the target was in fact a destroyer at shorter range. As it proved.

The sinking

The first torpedo struck *Jacob Jones* on the port side abaft the bridge, apparently causing a secondary detonation in the magazine. The effect of these two virtually simultaneous explosions was to destroy the chart room, the bridge and the officers' and petty officers' quarters – indeed 'everything forward from the point of impact was sheared off and sank rapidly'. As Rehwinkel corroborates, the second torpedo struck almost simultaneously 'approximately 40 feet forward of the fantail and sheered off everything above the keel plates and shafts [and] destroyed the crews' quarters located in that section'. The overall impression was one of 'unbelievable damage'. In the words of one survivor, 'Number 1 stack and the bridge were gone. Number 2 stack was laying over against the galley deckhouse, and the deck over Number 1 fireroom was rolled up against the galley deckhouse. The deck over the forward compartments was rolled up against the machine gun nest over the top of the engine room.' The condition of the ship left none of the survivors in much doubt that her fate was sealed and the fact that all of her officers were immediately killed or incapacitated put any damage

control measures out of the question. But surprisingly in view of her age and the extent of the damage inflicted, *Jacob Jones* remained afloat for about an hour after the attack and it was not until 0600 that she upended and sank.

An entry in the Eastern Sea Frontier War Diary for March 1942 noted uncertainty as to the circumstances of *Jacob Jones*'s loss and dwelt on the possibility that 'the German[s] picked up a secondary signal from the radio used on the listening watch'. Rehwinkel's log makes no mention of any such assistance but another observation in the War Diary was closer to the mark:

> How much the element of bad luck entered into her sinking, none can be sure. The normal watch was set and 'apparently on the alert.' No man saw any evidence of a submarine and no man saw even the wake of the torpedoes before they struck. It is quite possible that the meeting between the destroyer and the U-boat was simply ill fortune.

It is perhaps ironic that *Jacob Jones* shares with her namesake DD-61 the dubious distinction of being the first American destroyer lost to the *U-Boot-Waffe* following the entry of the United States into the war, the latter having been sunk by the first *U53* on 6 December 1917. DD-130 was also the first US naval vessel lost in combat in Atlantic coastal waters, as DD-61 was the first US destroyer ever lost to enemy action. Their memory was perpetuated in the shape of an Edsall-class destroyer escort of the same name launched in November 1942 (DE-130) together with a USS *Black* and USS *Marshall* of the Fletcher class (DD-666 and DD-676), launched in March and August 1943 in honour of Lt Cdr Hugh Black and Lt Cdr Thomas W. Marshall Jr who lost their lives as commander and executive officer respectively of the second *Jacob Jones*. Her wreck lies in 120 feet of water,

> a mass of twisted wreckage. The stern section is almost unrecognizable. The midsection is sitting upright. The boilers and engine are still visible, although most hull plates appear to have been blown off. The midsection torpedo tubes still have torpedoes in them. Gun shells are often found in the sand and surrounding wreckage. The bow is on its side with a relief of about 10 ft. Visibility is generally very good, sometimes in excess of 100 ft, averaging 30 ft or so. She is routinely visited by sunfish, turtles, and tuna.

Fate of the crew

The vast majority of *Jacob Jones*'s ship's company met a swift end, killed instantly in the primary and secondary detonations caused by *U578*'s two torpedoes or carried to the bottom in the severed bow. The only officer recorded as having survived the explosions, Assistant Engineer Ensign Norman C. Smith, was so badly wounded that 'he was practically incoherent at all times until his death'. Those who survived, all from the midships section with the exception of Machinist's Mate 2/c Thomas R. Moody (the sole escapee from the after engine room), attempted to abandon ship but found it no easy task since there were insufficient able-bodied men available to slip the boats, their efforts hampered by debris, loose rigging and great quantities of oil across the deck. Around thirty men eventually got away in as many as six rafts, though that containing Radioman 3/c Albert E. Oberg and two others narrowly escaped being dragged down with the wreck:

> Near the forward end of what remained of the ship we became caught on jagged metal. In the struggle to get off we lost our paddles and drifted in a semicircle around to what was left of the stern. Just before it sank the stern end started to rise and we drifted toward it. The propeller shafts stuck out above us like giant drumsticks. A piece of hull came up under our raft and started to lift us. We got free a few minutes before it went down. As it went down, the wash pushed us out and free of the wreckage.

However, further calamity awaited the occupants of the most crowded rafts. In testimony provided to the 4th Naval District Intelligence Office at the US Naval Air Station at Cape May, New Jersey the following day (1 March), MM 2/c Moody, who had been flown in on the afternoon of the sinking, stated

> that he abandoned ship in a life raft, which had been thrown over the starboard side; that this raft contained 15 other members of the crew, including Ensign Smith; that when the ship sank this raft was so close to her that when the depth charges went off they were apparently right under the raft; that many of the men on the raft received fatal injuries from these terrific concussions; and that eventually only 3 of the original 15 survived.

The same detonations inflicted casualties on other rafts by blasting their occupants into the water.

No distress signal could be sent before the ship went down and

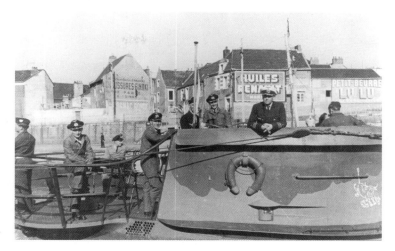

U578 sails from St-Nazaire on her penultimate patrol on 7 May 1942, two months after sinking the *Jacob Jones*. Rehwinkel (in white cap) stands on the conning tower which sports the snorting bull first borne by *U47* (see 2) and adopted by the 7th *U-Flottille* after her demise in March 1941. *DUBMA*

the approach of a weather front that morning would in all probability have doomed the survivors had they not been sighted by a US Army reconnaissance plane at 0810 – three hours after the attack and before *Jacob Jones* was even missed. The pilot reported the sighting and the approximate position of the survivors both to a shore station and to USS *Eagle 56*, a wooden-hulled vessel of the Inshore Patrol (**G132**). Two picket boats were dispatched from Lewes and a lifeboat from Indian River Inlet (both Delaware), but only *Eagle 56* rescued any survivors, picking up twelve men within four hours of the attack, one of whom succumbed before she reached Cape May. Rising seas forced *Eagle 56* to break off the search at 1100 and an operation to locate further survivors over the next forty-eight hours failed to add to the meagre tally of eleven men.

U578 and Ernst-August Rehwinkel

Built by Blohm & Voss at Hamburg and commissioned in July 1941, *U578* made five frontline patrols under Korvkpt. Ernst-August Rehwinkel. The first of these (in the Barents Sea) was unsuccessful, the only episode of note being the ramming of *U578* by the Soviet patrol craft *SKR-25/Briz* off the Kanin Peninsula on 26 November. Her next patrol in the North Atlantic enjoyed no better success, but 1942 saw an upturn in *U578*'s fortunes as part of the *U-Boot-Waffe*'s second 'Happy Time', her third and fourth patrols yielding a total of four merchantmen and the *Jacob Jones* off the eastern seaboard of the United States. These, however, would mark the limit of her success. Having sailed from St-Nazaire for the North Atlantic on 6 August 1942, *U578* disappeared shortly after, presumably while crossing the Bay of Biscay. No explanation for her loss has ever emerged though a mine appears the most likely cause. An attack by an RAF Wellington of 311 (Czech) Squadron against a U-boat off Cape Ortegal (Spain) on 10 August, previously reckoned to have been responsible for *U578*'s loss, is now believed to have been directed against *U135*, which suffered only minor damage. Ernst-August Rehwinkel was posthumously promoted Fregattenkapitän.

Sources

US Navy, Office of the Chief of Naval Operations, *USS* Jacob Jones: *Torpedoed and Sunk* (NA, RG 38, Records of the Chief of Naval Operations, World War II War Diaries, Entry A1 353, War Diary for 4th Naval District, 28 February 1942)

—, Office of the Chief of Naval Operations, Division of Naval History, *History of USS* Jacob Jones *(DD 130)*, together with other material including survivor interviews (NHC, Box 408)

Wilde, Cdr E. Andrew, Jr, USNR, ed., *The USS* Jacob Jones *(DD-130) in World War II: Documents, Photos, Survivors Interviews* (Needham, Mass.: privately, 2006); also on: http://www.destroyerhistory.org/flushdeck/ ussjacobjones/research130.html

Blair, *Hitler's U-Boat War*, I, p. 515

DANFS, III, pp. 484–5; also on:
http://www.history.navy.mil/danfs/j1/jacob_jones-ii.htm
and
http://www.ibiblio.org/hyperwar/USN/ships/dafs/DD/dd130.html

Friedman, Norman, *US Destroyers: An Illustrated Design History* (2nd edn, Annapolis, Md.: Naval Institute Press, 2004)

Morison, *United States Naval Operations*, I, p. 132

Parkin, Robert Sinclair, *Blood on the Sea: American Destroyers Lost in World War II* (New York: Sarpedon, 1995)

Roscoe, *US Destroyer Operations*, p. 74

Webpage devoted to USS *Jacob Jones*:
http://www.destroyerhistory.org/flushdeck/ussjacobjones/index.html

54   HMS *NAIAD*

Rear-Admiral Philip Vian, DSO** RN, Capt. G. Grantham, DSO RN
Sunk by *U565* (Type VIIC), Oblt.z.S. Johann Jebsen, 11 March 1942
Eastern Mediterranean, 30 nm NE of Sîdi Barrâni (Egypt)

Naiad seen during her service with the Home Fleet between July 1940 and April 1941.
Jebsen's torpedo struck her on the starboard side between the funnels. *IWM*

Theatre Mediterranean (Map 3)		*Displacement* 5,450 tons	
Coordinates 32° 00' N, 26° 19' E		*Dimensions* 512' × 50.5' × 14'	
Kriegsmarine code Quadrat CO 9221		*Armour* 3" belt; 1–2" decks and bulkheads	
U-boat timekeeping identical		*Maximum speed* 33 knots	
Fatalities 77 *Survivors* 591		*Armament* 10 × 5.25" DP; 8 × 40 mm AA; 5 × 20 mm AA; 6 × 21" tt	

The Dido-class cruisers

By 1935 it had become obvious that the British fleet had no effective defence against the new and more powerful aircraft that were entering service in Europe, Japan and the United States. To remedy this the Admiralty ordered designs for an anti-aircraft cruiser equipped with the new 5.25-inch dual-purpose gun, a weapon that promised high-angle fire up to seventy degrees on a power-loaded mounting with advanced fire control. The result was the Dido class, of which sixteen

were eventually built to two designs. The Didos were popular in the Service but the class proved poorly suited to the addition of wartime equipment and battle experience revealed serious deficiencies in design, particularly as to subdivision of the engine spaces which contributed to the loss of four of its members to torpedoes, *Naiad* and *Hermione* (**63**) among them. Nor did the 5.25-inch mounting meet expectations, with an operational firing rate of only eight rounds per minute and training and elevating capabilities too slow for effective anti-aircraft fire. For all that, the class had a fine record in the Mediterranean in particular and many an air attack was broken up by barrages of heavy if not especially accurate fire.

Career

Ordered under the 1936 estimates from Hawthorn Leslie's yard at Hebburn-on-Tyne, HMS *Naiad* was laid down in August 1937 as the first member of her class. She was launched in February 1939 but damage sustained during air raids on 10 April and 22 May 1940 delayed completion until July of that year. *Naiad* was immediately assigned to the 15th Cruiser Squadron, Home Fleet which spent the next ten months on patrol and escort duty in the North Sea and the North Atlantic. The highlight of an arduous winter at sea came on 28 January 1941 when she sighted the German battlecruisers *Scharnhorst* and *Gneisenau* south of Iceland but lost contact in bad weather. By the time *Naiad* emerged from a spell under repair on the Tyne that spring she and the 15th CS had been earmarked for transfer to the Mediterranean Fleet. On 26 April *Naiad* joined one of the major trans-Mediterranean convoys, Operation TIGER, escorting it as far as Malta where on 9 May she became Rear-Admiral E. L. S. King's flagship for the desperate defence of Crete. During the latter episode *Naiad* participated in the mauling of a German troop convoy on 22 May before being damaged by air attack later that day. Following repairs at Alexandria *Naiad* resumed the convoy escort and offensive operations in the Red Sea and the Eastern Mediterranean which filled the rest of her days. Among these was her action with the destroyer *Guépard* off

Sidon in June during the British campaign against Vichy Syria, shore bombardments in Lebanon and at Halfaya in support of Operation CRUSADER in July and November respectively, and participation in the brief engagement known at the First Battle of Sirte on 17 December. Meanwhile she had become flagship of Rear-Admiral Philip Vian who assumed command of the 'Fighting Fifteenth' in November 1941.

Background of the attack

On 9 March 1942 the Commander-in-Chief of the Mediterranean Fleet, Admiral Sir Andrew Cunningham, received reports (later proved false) that a cruiser escorting an Italian convoy bound for North Africa had been damaged by air attack off Malta. Accordingly, early on the 10th Rear-Admiral Vian led Force B (*Naiad*, *Euryalus*, *Dido* and nine destroyers) out of Alexandria to attempt an interception. Force B rounded Cyrenaica without incident but when no contact was made Vian turned for home later that day, his force joined by the cruiser *Cleopatra* and the destroyer *Kingston* from Malta. However, the enemy were now fully alerted to the presence of Vian's force which was relentlessly bombed throughout the daylight hours of the 11th though without suffering any damage. Among the shadowers was *U565* which picked up the British squadron on her hydrophones that afternoon and maintained contact until dusk. As darkness fell Oblt.z.S. Johann Jebsen penetrated the destroyer screen, shifting his target continuously. Only a routine zigzag manoeuvre carried out by Force B at 2000 caused a last-minute switch from one of the destroyers to the squadron flagship herself.

War Diary of *U565*, patrol of 21 January–17 March 1942: PG 30601a, NHB, reel 1,121, pp. 535–6

Date, time	Details of position, wind, weather, sea, light, visibility, moonlight, etc.	Incidents
11.iii		
1600	Qu. CO 9213	At 1210 we pick up a hydrophone bearing at 310° which becomes increasingly powerful as the afternoon draws on. As the bearing remains fixed I keep to the same course. As it turns out, we have located the same warship group reported by air reconnaissance in Qu. CO 5384 at 1330. I would estimate the group to be steering a course of 130°.
1809	Qu. CO 9212	We surface as the strength of the hydrophone bearing leads me to believe the group will soon heave into sight. I want to attack on the surface as that gives me the best chance of acquiring the right firing position. I begin by simply tracking what I think to be its easterly course (110°); this is what the hydrophone bearing seems to suggest, and besides it's still too early to attack.
1826		A destroyer appears at a bearing of 190° true, her course taking her towards the main group. At a bearing of 310° true we can see flak and what we presume to be clouds of smoke. We bear north to ensure we remain unobserved.
1845		We alter course to 90°, gradually converging.
1850		Battle Stations!
1921–1924		Dive to listen through hydrophones. Fix obtained at bearing 295° true.
1930		Course altered to 0°.
1946	Qu. CO 9221, easterly wind, mirror-smooth sea, strong sea phosphorescence, misty, visibility approx. 2 nm	To port three shadows appear steering roughly 130°. I try to haul ahead of the group but I daren't attempt it at high speed due to phosphorescence. A large vessel, a cruiser by the looks of it, is heading straight towards me at 0°.[1] As I can neither get free of her nor haul sufficiently far ahead to get a shot in I prepare to attack the next destroyer along on her starboard side, which has an inclination of 60°, bows left.[2] Just as I am turning towards the latter, however, the whole group alters course to port. I turn to port and fire a spread of four torpedoes, but at the cruiser (probably Leander class) because the

---

1 HMS *Naiad*.
2 Apparently HMS *Zulu*.

Date, time	*Details of position, wind, weather, sea, light, visibility, moonlight, etc.*	*Incidents*
		destroyer is now heading straight for me with an inclination of 0°.[3]
		The cruiser appears to be flanked by two destroyers and two torpedo boats on her starboard side, and by a further pair of destroyers on her port side.[4] There appears to be another another large vessel astern of the cruiser.[5]
1959		Spread of four away!
		Inclination 80°, bows right, enemy speed 15 knots, range 2,000 m, angle of dispersion 3°, depth 2 m. This depth setting was that programmed for the attack on the destroyer; we simply didn't have time to readjust it.
		As the destroyer is now at 1,000 m and closing I sound the alarm.
		After 120 sec. running time we hear two torpedo detonations. At 100 m the first depth charges are dropped. Four more patterns of depth charges are dropped between now and 2012 but none of them detonate close enough to endanger the boat. At a depth of between 150 m and 160 m we make off at silent speed, initially in a northerly direction.
2030		We alter course to 310° or thereabouts. The magnetic compass is damaged and gets stuck every so often.
2030–2040		Sinking noises so loud we can't use the hydrophones.[6] Several times we detect echo-ranging apparatus. From hydrophone data we establish that four destroyers are hunting the U-boat. Several times we are overrun but they never get a fix on us.
		At 2157 several depth charges are dropped, estimated range 100 m.
		As no more follow I resume the same course.
12.iii		
0000	Qu. CO 6876	
0048		We surface now that the destroyers are estimated by hydrophone to be around 6 nm distant. We withdraw on approx. course 300°, keeping Castor Pollux dead ahead until compass deigns to start working again.[7]
0131		Outgoing W/T transmission:
		1.) Heading home as condition of CO's eyes continues to deteriorate.[8]
		2.) Mar. Qu. CO 9221 two hits on cruiser likely.
		3.) [Wind] NW 1, 1,010 mb, poor visibility.

3 HMS *Naiad*. Though the hull form of the Dido class was similar to the Leander-class cruisers, the latter were at 7,200 tons not only considerably larger but distinguished from all other British cruisers by possession of a single large trunked funnel. This attack was carried out by *U565*'s I.WO, Oblt.z.S. Ulrich Wörisshoffer.

4 In the darkness Jebsen appears to be confusing *Naiad*'s sisters for destroyers, and the outlying destroyers for smaller craft; the eye complaint referred to at 0131 on the 12th below may have had to do with this.

5 Probably HMS *Cleopatra*.

6 HMS *Naiad*.

7 By 'Castor Pollux' Jebsen is referring to the Gemini constellation.

8 This request was granted by *F.d.U. Italien* (Korvkpt. Victor Oehrn; see **16**), Jebsen being relieved of command on medical grounds on *U565*'s return to La Spezia.

The sinking

No sooner had the 15th Cruiser Squadron (*Naiad* leading *Cleopatra* with *Euryalus* and *Dido* on her port and starboard quarters respectively) altered course from ninety to seventy degrees than depth charges were heard off *Naiad*'s starboard beam. These had been dropped by the destroyer HMS *Zulu* which had sighted *U565* on the surface and gone in for the attack, Jebsen managing to get his torpedoes away just before the depth charges exploded. Vian had earlier ordered any escorting destroyer sighting a submarine to burn a searchlight for a few seconds thereby permitting his force to turn and comb the tracks of any incoming torpedoes. However, *Zulu* had only recently joined Force B from the Home Fleet and raised the alarm by shining a dimmed light which it took some moments to discern. By the time *Zulu*'s position in the escort had been fixed it was too late for *Naiad* to take evasive action, nor is it likely that any more could have been done in the time available once the Squadron began to execute its twenty-degree turn. At 2005 torpedoes were seen passing ahead and astern of *Naiad* but a third struck amidships at Frame 99, the bulkhead separating the Forward Engine Room and 'B' Boiler Room aft. An immediate list of ten degrees to starboard increased to twenty degrees as both compartments flooded. Orders were passed to seal off all internal doors and the flooding was temporarily contained while efforts were made to extricate those inside. Here the design faults of the Dido class began to tell, for though men were saved through manholes illegally cut into the top of these and other compartments by the Senior Engineer, Lt (E) Louis Le Bailly, it had not been possible to make similar provision for other machinery spaces. This meant that trapped men either drowned or were forced to open doors onto adjoining passages, thereby compromising the watertight integrity of the entire ship. Cdr Roy Dowling RAN was later to testify that all accessible watertight doors were closed as a matter of course, but subsequent orders to seal internal doors were not thought to have reached both ends of the ship and at least one was unclipped to permit escape. A further design omission was the lack of an emergency diesel generator. With the four dynamos either destroyed or lacking steam power, efforts at damage control were therefore hampered by a complete failure of electrical power together with a breakdown in *Naiad*'s telephone system as she continued her list to starboard. *Naiad*'s fate was sealed by the flooding of one or both of the wing spaces abreast 'B' Boiler Room, water spreading along the ship via the cable passage. Together with the inrush of water from the speed of the ship, this caused the collapse of the bulkhead separating that space and the After Engine Room, an event that brought *Naiad* onto her beam ends at around 2030, twenty-five minutes after the attack. The order was immediately passed to abandon ship, much of the crew having gathered on the upper deck. *Naiad* capsized and sank by the stern a few minutes later, her bows rearing up against a starry Mediterranean sky.

The Board of Enquiry absolved Capt. Guy Grantham and his officers of responsibility, it being generally agreed that the manoeuvre executed from 2000 onwards made any evasive action almost impossible. Moreover, less than a minute separated the muffled explosions heard to starboard and the torpedo strike. Commenting on the Board's findings, the Deputy Director of the Signal Department, Capt. F. J. Wylie, added that the time span between the submarine sighting by *Zulu* and the hit on *Naiad* (two minutes) nullified any error on her part. Characteristically, Rear-Admiral Vian was not so charitable to *Zulu*, nor could he absolve himself of blame. In his memoirs he cited a moment's delay in his ordering the helm put over after the torpedoes were spotted as being responsible for the hit at Frame 99 – one place a single torpedo could sink the *Naiad*. In retrospect his judgement seems harsh on both counts.

Fate of the crew

Capt. Grantham's order to 'splice the mainbrace' (issue a tot of rum to the ship's company) after eight hours' incessant bombing had just been carried out when disaster overtook his ship. The torpedo that sank *Naiad* struck immediately beneath a bathroom filled with men just off watch, most being either killed or suffering broken legs. Men began making their way up on deck but this was a challenging proposition for many, especially those in the engine spaces. Not long after the bulkhead separating the After Engine Room and 'B' Boiler Room had given way a number of men were seen swimming up to the manhole to escape. It was a different story in the Forward Engine Room and around the workshop flat where water, fuel oil and the heel of the ship rendered the escape hatch almost impassable. Once on deck many chose to abandon ship across the capsized hull but as so often barnacles and the bilge keel accounted for many lacerations and broken limbs, not least Vian who aggravated a large carbuncle on his posteriors. A good number of Carley floats left *Naiad* in serviceable condition but it seems more perished in the darkness than actually

Der kleine Jebsen ('Little Jebsen') as he was popularly known seen while First Watch Officer of *U123* (see **57** and **84**) between May and November 1940. *DUBMA*

went down with the ship. Sixty years later Louis Le Bailly recalled the moment when *Naiad* disappeared and the survivors began to confront the enormity of the event that had overtaken them:

> I found myself swimming in a choppy sea on a dark night as *Naiad* sank stern first to the seabed. There was lots of jabbering and cries for help as we tried to get those who could not swim or were burnt on to the few rafts; and then Leading Stoker Davies, a Welshman with a lovely voice, started to sing *Abide With Me* as he had learnt the hymn in his Methodist Chapel in the Rhondda. Most joined in – and the last line 'In life, in death, O Lord, abide with me', seemed rather appropriate swimming in 600 feet of water 25 miles from shore. The task force – less its Admiral, now in the water with us – had sped on its way.

But help was at hand. Two hours after the sinking nearly 600 oil-soaked survivors were rescued by HMSs *Kipling*, *Lively* and *Jervis* (88, 244 and 260 men respectively) of Force B's destroyer screen, ships well versed in the business of dragging sailors out of the Mediterranean. On rescue Vian shifted his flag to *Dido* and resumed command while the death of Leading Stoker R. T. Davies while coming aboard *Jervis* brought the death toll to seventy-seven men. That so many survived a night-time sinking was owed both to acts of heroism and self-sacrifice aboard and to Jebsen's 'mirror-smooth' sea, even if it appeared choppy to those in the water. As Cunningham, not given to idle flattery, related to the First Sea Lord a few days later, the sinking of *Naiad* had an effect in inverse proportion to her size: 'Such a loss that little *Naiad*. A highly efficient weapon with a ship's company with a grand spirit.'

U565 and Johann Jebsen

Built by Blohm & Voss at Hamburg and commissioned in April 1941, *U565* was the first command of Oblt.z.S. Johann Jebsen who had served as Kptlt Karl-Heinz Moehle's First Watch Officer in *U123* (see **57** and **84**). Her first two patrols thrust her straight into the crucible of Atlantic convoy operations, though without success. In November

1941 *U565* was detached to the Mediterranean as part of the *Arnauld* group, one of ten U-boats transferred from the Atlantic at this time to interrupt British supply lines and counter the depredations of the Royal Navy against Axis convoys. Dönitz, who strongly disapproved of this policy, warned that no U-boat sent into the *Mittelmeer* could very well be expected to return. So it proved, though not before the *U-Boot-Waffe* had taken a severe toll of Allied shipping. *U565* had still to score a success when she quit La Spezia on her second Mediterranean patrol (her fifth in all under Jebsen) on 21 January 1942, though the sinking of *Naiad* signalled a notable change in her fortunes. She spent the rest of her career in the Mediterranean, for details of which see HMS *Partridge* (**79**).

The eye problems referred to in the log excerpt above resulted in Jebsen being assigned to shore duties in April 1942. Promoted Kapitänleutnant in July, he served as an instructor until returning to frontline duty in the Type-IXD *U859* in April 1944. Repeatedly attacked by Allied ships and aircraft on her first patrol in the Indian Ocean, *U859* eventually succumbed to a torpedo from HMS/m *Trenchant* off Penang on 23 September. Twenty crewmen survived, some to be picked up by the British, others subsequently by the Japanese. Johann Jebsen, a recipient of the German Cross in Gold, was not among them.

Sources

Admiralty, *Enemy Submarine Attacks on H.M. Vessels: Loss of HMS* Naiad (TNA, ADM 199/162)

—, *Wartime Damage to Ships: Reports, 1942–1943* (TNA, ADM 199/2068)

Jaksch, Helmut, *Meine Erinnerung an die Versenkung des britischen Kreuzers* Naiad *am 11.3.1942* (typescript, DUBMA, *U565* folder)

Brzeziński, Sławomir, *Brytyjski Krążownik Przeciwlotniczy HMS* Naiad [Profile Morskie, no. 67] (Wyszków: Wydawniczo Handlowa, 2004)

Bush, Capt. Eric W., *Bless Our Ship* (London: George Allen & Unwin, 1958)

Connell, G. G., *Mediterranean Maelstrom: HMS* Jervis *and the 14th Flotilla* (London: William Kimber, 1987)

Cunningham of Hyndhope, Admiral of the Fleet Viscount, *A Sailor's Odyssey* (London: Hutchinson & Co., 1951)

Haines, Gregory, *Cruiser at War* (London: Ian Allan, 1978)

Le Bailly, Vice-Admiral Sir Louis, *The Man Around the Engine: Life Below the Waterline* (Emsworth, Hants.: Kenneth Mason, 1990)

—, 'World Today Sets No Store by Faith' in *The Western Morning News*, 7 June 2003, p. 25

Osborne, Richard, 'A Tale of Two Didos' in *Warships*, Supplement no. 134 (April 1999), pp. 27–33

Raven, Alan, and H. T. Lenton, *Dido Class Cruisers* [Ensign, no. 2] (London: Bivouac Books, 1973)

Raven, Alan, and John Roberts, *British Cruisers of World War Two* (London: Arms and Armour Press, 1980)

Vian, Admiral of the Fleet Sir Philip, *Action This Day* (London: Frederick Muller, 1960)

Career history of HMS *Naiad*:
    http://www.naval-history.net/xGM-Chrono-06CL-Naiad.htm

55   HMS *HEYTHROP*

Lt Cdr R. S. Stafford, RN

Sunk by *U652* (Type VIIC), Oblt.z.S. Georg-Werner Fraatz, 20 March 1942

Eastern Mediterranean, 50 nm NNW of Sîdi Barrâni (Egypt)

An indistinct view of *Heythrop*, probably in the Mediterranean where she spent most of her brief career. Fraatz's torpedo struck her on the port side abreast the after 4-inch mounting which was blasted overboard. *BfZ*

Theatre Mediterranean (Map 3)		*Displacement* 1,050 tons	
Coordinates (of attack) 32° 22' N, 25° 28' E		*Dimensions* 280' × 31.5' × 8.25'	
Kriegsmarine code (of attack) Quadrat CO 6795		*Maximum speed* 27 knots	
U-boat timekeeping identical		*Armament* 6 × 4" AA; 4 × 40 mm AA; 2 × 20 mm AA	
Fatalities 16 *Survivors* about 150			

The Hunt-class destroyers

One of the areas in which the pre-war neglect of the Royal Navy was most keenly felt lay in that of convoy defence. When it was clear that a majority of the Navy's sloops, destroyers and other would-be escort vessels were either ill-suited to the task or likely to be fully committed in home and foreign waters, provision was made in the 1939 Emergency Programme for a substantial class of escort destroyers, the specifications for which were laid down by the then Deputy Chief of Naval Staff, Vice-Admiral Andrew Cunningham. The result was the Hunt class which promised the speed and endurance to undertake convoy operations together with an effective anti-submarine and anti-submarine capability on little more than 1,000 tons. In the event, lack of size and range made the 'Hunts' unsuited to transatlantic escort work though the class gave sterling service in British and Mediterranean waters. A total of eighty-six were completed in four sub-classes between March 1940 and May 1943, nineteen having been lost by war's end.

Career

The fifth unit of the thirty-three-strong Hunt (Type II) class, HMS *Heythrop* was laid down at Swan Hunter of Newcastle upon Tyne in December 1939, launched in October of the following year and commissioned under Lt Cdr R. S. Stafford on 21 June 1941. With an extra thirty inches of beam, the Type-II Hunts enjoyed much improved stability over the first group of the class. After working up at Scapa Flow and temporary attachment to the Irish Sea Escort Force of Western Approaches Command, in August *Heythrop* sailed for the Mediterranean where most of the Type-II Hunts gave war service. Having completed minor repairs at Gibraltar in early September *Heythrop* was given her first assignment, escorting two damaged veterans of the Malta convoy codenamed SUBSTANCE (21–24 July) on the first leg of their passage to the United States, the cruiser *Manchester* and the destroyer *Firedrake* (**78**). On her return she was flung into another convoy to Malta, Operation HALBERD (25–28 September), during which she rescued 300 survivors of the freighter *Imperial Star* on the 28th, subsequently escorting three empty merchantmen from

Malta to Gibraltar. In October *Heythrop* was ordered to join the 2nd Destroyer Flotilla at Alexandria, an assignment which required her to round the Cape of Good Hope to avoid running the gauntlet of Axis air superiority in the Eastern Mediterranean. Reaching Alexandria on 15 November, *Heythrop* immediately joined Operation AGGRESSION, the first of several convoys she escorted to the beleaguered garrisons of Tobruk and Malta, each under heavy air attack. In December she was the last Allied vessel to see HM corvette *Salvia* afloat (**44**) and in January it fell to her to tow the destroyer HMS *Kimberley* into Alexandria after the latter had lost her stern to *U77* off Tobruk. For *Heythrop*, however, the worst was yet to come.

Background of the attack

In early March 1942 the decision was made to pass a supply convoy from Alexandria to Malta, to which operation *Heythrop* was assigned as part of the 5th Destroyer Flotilla. The morning of 20 March found the flotilla under HMS *Southwold* (Cdr C. T. Jellicoe) conducting an anti-submarine sweep in the Gulf of Salûm (Sollum) in advance of the convoy in question, MW10, which had sailed from Alexandria that night. Meanwhile, Oblt.z.S. Georg-Werner Fraatz's *U652* had quit Salamis on the 18th and was operating with *U559* (Kptlt Hans Heidtmann; see **42**) and *U568* (Kptlt Joachim Preuss; see **29** and **44**) between Tobruk and Alexandria. After several efforts to acquire attacking positions against merchantmen on the night of 19–20 March, Fraatz was presented with an inviting though dangerous opportunity later that morning as the masts of the 5th DF appeared over the horizon at 1000. The flotilla was zigzagging routinely at fourteen knots as it proceeded in line abreast at intervals of 7½ cables (1,500 yards), Cdr Jellicoe having just hoisted the signal 'Form single line ahead; speed 20 knots'. Fraatz was able to make his attack with scarcely any need for manoeuvre, but the failure of the destroyers to detect *U652* provides further evidence, already borne out by the sinking of *Barham* (**41**), of the special difficulties attending submarine detection in the Mediterranean and the fact that local escort groups had yet to reach the standard of the best of their Atlantic counterparts.

War Diary of U652, patrol of 18–31 March 1942: PG 30682, NHB, reel 1,133, pp. 597–8

Date, time	Details of position, wind, weather, sea, light, visibility, moonlight, etc.	Incidents
20.iii		
0620–0753	Qu. CO 9138	Alarm dive due to aircraft.
1000	Qu. CO 6795, mirror-smooth sea with a rising breeze during attack	Two plumes of smoke in sight on the starboard beam, then six masts appear, sailing in line abreast and quite far apart. I am forced to dive immediately because their approach is rapid and I am directly ahead of them. Through the periscope I identify them as a reconnaissance group pure and simple, with two modern destroyers proceeding in the centre flanked by 'V & W'-class escorts on either side as well as other smaller types.[1] They appear to reduce speed somewhat before reaching my position.
1054	Qu. CO 6795	A spread of four torpedoes fired at a Jervis-class destroyer (I manage to get between the two medium-sized ones) with twin gun mountings, a single funnel and the letter Fritz with numbers painted on her bows (see Wehyer [*sic*]).[2]

---

1   The escort was in fact made up of seven Hunt-class (Type II) escort destroyers. From Fraatz's periscope viewpoint (port to starboard) these were HMSs *Dulverton, Hurworth, Southwold, Eridge, Heythrop, Avon Vale* and *Beaufort*.

2   Fraatz's identification of his target's pendant number as beginning with 'F' ('Fritz' in German radio communications) is interesting since none of the destroyers present bore this letter. It can be conjectured that in the heat of the moment Fraatz misread *Heythrop*'s actual pendant number – L85 – as beginning

Date, time	Details of position, wind, weather, sea, light, visibility, moonlight, etc.	Incidents

Firing data: torpedo depth 1 m, range 1,000 m, enemy speed 12 knots,[3] inclination 90°, angle of fire 280°. We hear one hit (confirmed by aircraft observation[4]) after a running time of 107 sec. (1,600 m). This is followed by the usual sound pursuit. The first depth charges are not very well aimed but thereafter we are overrun several times with a fair degree of accuracy, though without damage. Our depth varied between 150 m and 170 m.

Overall there were 79 depth charges dropped over the course of six hours. At first there seemed to be three escorts acting in unison, later two. At the beginning, therefore, there was no point in undertaking evasive manoeuvres from our deep position – one of the escorts always restricted itself to sound location, and would have immediately detected any movement on our part. Escorts positioned 240°, 120° and 20° relative to the boat, then just two positioned on precisely opposing sides at approx. 10° and 200°. I also managed to leave these two astern once the third escort appeared to have headed away. What was new to us were the dull gravelly noises – referred to in the Commander's Handbook but then crossed out again – which were quite pronounced, like the sound of pulses from some sort of echo-sounding element (no fixed intervals).[5] The enemy's propellers were extremely strong in what were good hydrophone conditions, so much so that those of a single escort would often take up the entire scale, preventing those of the other escorts being heard (despite the fact that these two were both under way). An observation which struck us as peculiar: the noises of one propeller, heard at high volume, remained fixed for several minutes at a relative bearing of 200° on the quarter, giving the impression of a sounding device above us which we were ourselves circling. But if it had been the noise of a propeller it would have become fainter as the enemy moved away at the same bearing, or weakened on one side as the enemy overran us. But it was as if the noise were simply switched off all of a sudden.

1700 — Sounding pursuit has apparently been abandoned. Boat has sustained no damage and has held up well while we remained deep. A small amount of water penetrated but this was pumped out with the main bilge pump whenever a set of depth charges was dropped. Gyroscope was not switched off; enemy's general withdrawal course to the north.

1200[6] — Day's run: 234 nm on surface, 18 nm submerged = 252 nm.

1929 — Surfaced.

Signal Appendix to War Diary of *U652*: PG 30682, NHB, reel 1,133, p. 603
20.iii

2031   1931/20/559: *Qu. [CO] 6795 at 1054 attacked a six-unit escort group approaching from the east.*[1] *Hit on 'Jervis'-class destroyer (identified by Fritz[2] and twin gun mountings) clearly heard. 79 depth charges over six hours. Boat fine. Pulling back temporarily. Missing signal 541. Fraatz.*

---

with 'F', understandable given that the first two elements were 'L8', readily conflated visually to an 'F' since the target was being observed at a somewhat acute angle. His additional identification of the vessel in question as a 'J'-class destroyer suggests that, after consulting the Weyer ship-recognition manual, he assumed her to be HMS *Jupiter*, pendant number F85 (*Jupiter* had been lost on a Japanese mine off Java three weeks earlier). In any event, these details would confirm that *Heythrop* was indeed Fraatz's initial target.

3   Lt Cdr Stafford's report makes clear that *Heythrop* was in fact making 14 knots, which no doubt explains both Fraatz's underestimation of the range and his having scored just one hit.

4   *Heythrop* and her escorts were attacked by a pair of Italian S.M.79 bombers five hours after *U652*'s strike.

5   Fraatz is describing Asdic which was well known to the Germans by this stage of the war, being discussed in some detail in the 1942 edition of the U-Boat Commander's Handbook (*Handbuch für U-Boot-Kommandanten*) to which Fraatz makes reference.

6   The break in the chronological sequence here reflects the original.

The sinking

Two of *U652*'s torpedoes were seen passing off *Heythrop*'s port quarter, the Officer of the Watch being able to discern the warheads breaching the surface. Barely had the order been given to turn hard astarboard than a third struck the port side abreast No. 3 mounting twenty yards from the stern. The resulting detonation almost severed the stern and flung the mounting bodily into the sea. Also dislodged was an ammunition locker containing two dozen 4-inch shells which sailed over the mast before coming to rest on No. 1 gun shield having taken all the ship's rigging with it. Internal flooding was limited to the after compartments, but the list of the ship was found to have put one of the boilers beyond immediate repair and the other was shut down as a precaution leaving *Heythrop* without power to operate her pumps.

With *Avon Vale* as escort, *Heythrop* was taken in tow by *Eridge* with the aim of bringing her in to Tobruk, to which the rest of the flotilla now headed to refuel before joining the convoy. However, a rising north-westerly wind prevented further progress in that direction and course was altered southward to Bardia. Various hazards in the form of enemy air attack and further submarine sightings were successfully seen off, but *Heythrop* was increasingly down by the stern and making very little headway. At 1600 Lt Cdr Stafford felt obliged to order off the remaining crew and slip the tow, *Heythrop* capsizing within minutes of the last boat getting clear. As the bows remained above the surface *Eridge*'s gunners were obliged to pepper the wreck with pom-pom fire before she vanished for ever in position 32° 13' N, 25° 33' E. Two days later the escort to convoy MW10 beat off an Italian squadron in what came to be known as the Second Battle of Sirte, but only twenty per cent of its cargo survived to be unloaded at Malta. Among the ships left in its wake was *Southwold*, Senior Officer of the 5th DF which was mined and sunk in the approaches to Malta.

The damage report was pored over at some length by the Board of Enquiry which concluded that the Chief Engineer, Lt (E) C. W. Treweeks, showed lack of judgement in not establishing whether the main engines were fit for use. It was recommended that he be informed of this by letter. Aside from the general consensus that the damage-control organisation was not what it should have been, the difficulty of assessing the possibilities of salvaging a ship *a posteriori* were highlighted by reactions to the views of Admiral Sir Henry Pridham-Wippell (acting Commander-in-Chief, Mediterranean Fleet following Cunningham's departure for Washington), who suggested that it would have been preferable had the forward compartments been counter-flooded against the settling of the stern. This suggestion was questioned by the Engineer-in-Chief, Vice-Admiral (E) F. R. G. Turner, and subsequently rejected in no uncertain terms in a follow-up report written by the Assistant Director of Naval Construction, A. P. Cole.

Fate of the crew

There was something distinctly ironic about the timing of the torpedo strike from *Heythrop*'s point of view, occurring as it did while most of the ship's company was mustered on the forward mess deck to be briefed on 'what to expect' on the current convoy. As the torpedo struck aft, however, this did mean that the ship suffered fewer casualties than might otherwise have been expected. All fatalities bar one were caused by the detonation, the entire crew of No. 3 mounting being lost overboard with their guns while four crewmen of No. 2 mounting were blasted onto the forecastle. No casualties were incurred during the transfer of the crew to HMS *Eridge* and none was lost when *Heythrop* rolled over and sank. One of the injured perished en route to Tobruk, *Eridge* briefly stopping her engines while the body was committed to the deep in a brief service read by Lt Cdr Stafford. In the words of one of *Eridge*'s officers, 'the canvas shrouded body hit the water with a gentle splash, but Stafford's voice was suddenly drowned out by the high pitched whine of accelerating turbines' as the Navigating Officer rang down for Full Speed Ahead. As they filed away from the service many of *Heythrop*'s survivors must have cast their minds back to a different muster on a different deck earlier that day, and to those who would never be mustered again.

U652 and Georg-Werner Fraatz

Built by Howaldtswerke in Hamburg and commissioned in April

Fraatz (centre, in full uniform) and his crew on the casing of *U652* at Salamis in February or March 1942. *DUBMA*

1941, *U652* operated under Oblt.z.S. Georg-Werner Fraatz for all of her year-long career. Initially assigned to northern waters, between July and August 1941 *U652* carried out the first U-boat operations off the Kola Coast, sinking the Soviet dispatch vessel *PS-70* off Cape Teriberka on 6 August (**G8**). Her most eventful patrol was that of August–September 1941 during which she was detected and depth charged south-west of Iceland by an RAF Hudson on 4 September. Alerted to her presence by the Hudson, the US destroyer *Greer*, which was proceeding independently to Iceland, began zigzagging and using her echo-sounding equipment to keep *U652* submerged and on her bow. To this threatening posture Fraatz eventually responded by firing a torpedo which missed its target. The *Greer* replied with a pattern of depth charges, provoking Fraatz to launch a second attack. Unable to regain contact, the *Greer* abandoned the hunt after more than an hour, the two vessels going their separate ways. Though the United States had yet to enter the war against Germany, the incident reflects the suspicion and hostility that increasingly characterised relations between the two countries, Roosevelt now issuing a 'shoot-on-sight' policy with immediate effect. On her seventh patrol *U652* passed through the Straits of Gibraltar into the Mediterranean, one of ten U-boats transferred there from the Atlantic in September and November 1941. This policy was strongly disapproved of by Dönitz, for whom the Atlantic was always the decisive theatre of operations and the Mediterranean a trap from which few U-boats were likely to escape. And indeed, *U652*, like every other boat dispatched to *Mittelmeer*, served out her career there. For details of *U652*'s final patrols, see HMS *Jaguar* (**56**).

Sources

Admiralty, *Enemy Submarine Attacks on H.M. Vessels: Loss of HMS* Heythrop (TNA, ADM 199/162)

Graef, Adolf, *Als IWO auf U652 von Oktober 1941 bis Mai 1942*, Jever 1986 (typescript, DUBMA, *U642* file)

Gregory-Smith, Capt. W. F. N., *The Story of HMS* Eridge (manuscript, IWM, 98/1/1)

Blair, *Hitler's U-Boat War*, I, pp. 359–61
Cunningham of Hyndhope, Admiral of the Fleet Viscount, *A Sailor's Odyssey* (London: Hutchinson & Co., 1951)
English, John, *The Hunts: A History of the Design, Development and Careers of the 86 Destroyers of This Class Built for the Royal Navy during World*

War II (Kendal, Cumbria: World Ship Society, 1987)
Morison, *History of United States Naval Operations*, I, pp. 79–80
Piper, N., 'HMS *Grove*' in *Warship*, no. 15 (July 1980), pp. 180–1
Raven, Alan, and John Roberts, *Hunt Class Escort Destroyers* [Man o'War, no. 4] (London: Arms and Armour Press, 1980)

Career history of HMS *Heythrop*:
http://www.naval-history.net/xGM-Chrono-10DE-Heythrop.htm

56   HMS *JAGUAR*
Lt Cdr L. R. K. Tyrwhitt, DSO DSC RN†
Sunk by *U652* (Type VIIC), Oblt.z.S. Georg-Werner Fraatz, 26 March 1942
Eastern Mediterranean, 25 nm NE of Sìdi Barrâni (Egypt)

Jaguar enters the Grand Harbour at Valetta during the sixteen months of arduous service in the Mediterranean which ended in her loss to *U652*. *BfZ*

Theatre	Mediterranean (Map 3)	*Displacement*	1,690 tons
Coordinates	31° 53' N, 26° 18' E	*Dimensions*	356.5' × 35.75' × 9'
Kriegsmarine code	Quadrat CO 9229	*Maximum speed*	36 knots
U-boat timekeeping	identical	*Armament*	6 × 4.7"; 1 × 4" AA; 4 × 40 mm AA; 4 × 20 mm AA;
Fatalities	195 *Survivors* 53		4 × .303" AA; 5 × 21" tt

Career

HMS *Jaguar* was the eighth and final unit of the 'J'-class destroyers, the design of which represented a reversion to the smaller vessels better suited to fleet work than the preceding Tribal class (see **37**). HMS *Jaguar* was laid down at William Denny's yard at Dumbarton on the Clyde in November 1937, launched almost a year to the day later and completed in September 1939. The class entered service as the 7th Destroyer Flotilla, Home Fleet on the eve of the Second World War and spent the first winter of the conflict patrolling the east coast and the Straits of Dover while based on Grimsby. Not so *Jaguar* which ran aground in the Forth soon after commissioning, obliging her to spend much of October 1939 under repair at Leith, while the spring of 1940 found her refitting at Dundee. On 20 May she participated in Operation QUIXOTE during which six under-sea telegraph cables connecting Britain with the German islands of Borkum and Nordeney were severed. Within days she was thrown into the evacuation of British and Allied troops from Dunkirk, rescuing 700 soldiers before bomb

damage on the 29th required her to be towed into Dover. Following repairs on Humberside *Jaguar* rejoined her flotilla on patrol duty at Harwich in June, being assigned to cover the laying of the East Coast Mine Barrier in July and August. On 10–11 October she escorted the battleship *Revenge* on the bombardment of Cherbourg, spending the rest of the month refitting at Devonport Dockyard before transferring to Gibraltar for service with Force H. In late November *Jaguar* joined Operation COLLAR, the delivery of a convoy to Malta and naval reinforcements for the Eastern Mediterranean which resulted in an inconclusive action with the Italian fleet off Cape Spartivento on the 27th. Escort duty continued in December with Operation HIDE, the passage of convoy MG1 from Malta to Gibraltar. In January 1941 she was assigned to the trans-Mediterranean convoy operation codenamed EXCESS which reached Alexandria much depleted on the 16th. With this *Jaguar* joined the Mediterranean Fleet, the beginning of a year of unremitting service with the 14th DF.

Based initially at Suda Bay on the northern coast of Crete, in

February *Jaguar* covered the failed Commando raid on the Italian-held island of Castelorizzo in the Dodecanese, engaging the destroyer *Francesco Crispi* on the 28th, and a month later was present at the Battle of Cape Matapan during which the Mediterranean Fleet accounted for three Italian heavy cruisers. In April came the bombardment of Tripoli and then the sinking of the Italian armed transport *Egeo* off Lampedusa in company with her sisters *Jervis, Janus* and *Juno*. HMS *Jaguar* was among the few ships to emerge unscathed from the evacuation of Crete in May and was soon in action again, engaging the French destroyers *Valmy* and *Guépard* off Sidon on 23 June during British operations against Vichy Syria. Based now at Alexandria, in July *Jaguar* began a routine of shore bombardment and convoy escort duties to Cyprus and Tobruk, and it was while operating off Libya that a 4.7-inch shell accidently fired from *Jervis* struck *Jaguar's* bridge, killing her CO Lt Cdr J. F. W. Hine and one of his men on 1 December 1941. A week later *Jaguar* was at Malta with a new CO and girding herself for surface operations against Italian convoys with Force K. Although it included the brief engagement known at the First Battle of Sirte on the 17th, her first sweep ended in disaster after the squadron ran into an Italian minefield off Tripoli two days later. The cruisers *Aurora* and *Penelope* (**96**) were damaged while a third, *Neptune*, sank with the loss of all but one of her 767 men. A fourth casualty was the destroyer *Kandahar* which had to be scuttled by *Jaguar* the following day once her surviving ship's company had been rescued. *Jaguar* would not be long in following. In January 1942 she resumed the convoy escort duty in the Eastern Mediterranean which claimed her on her fourth voyage.

Background of the attack

March 1942 was a month of severe attrition for the Royal Navy in the Mediterranean. The losses of *Naiad* and *Heythrop* on the 11th and 20th respectively (**54** and **55**) were followed on the 24th by that of HMS *Southwold*, which was mined in the approaches to Malta while escorting convoy MW10. Still patrolling north of Sîdi Barrâni, on the 26th *U652* followed up her success against *Heythrop* by claiming a further scalp on the 'Spud Run', the hazardous supply route between Alexandria and Tobruk: HMS *Jaguar*. *Jaguar* was Senior Officer of a small group completed by the British-built destroyer *Vasilissa Olga* (called *Queen Olga* by the British) of the Royal Hellenic Navy and HM anti-submarine whaler *Klo*. On 25 March they left Alexandria bound for Tobruk with the tanker RFA *Slavol* laden with fuel oil for the 5th Destroyer Flotilla. On the night of the 25th–26th intelligence was received in Alexandria of the presence of a U-boat in the vicinity of the convoy and a warning signalled to the escorts at 0252. This, however, came too late to alter the course of events. Only twenty-five minutes earlier *Jaguar* had fallen victim to *U652*, Oblt.z.S. Georg-Werner Fraatz taking advantage of a favourable zigzag to attack the escort instead of diving beneath the convoy to engage *Slavol* from the rear as originally intended. However, the misunderstandings that followed the loss of the Senior Officer ensured that *Slavol* and her precious cargo would never make Tobruk either.

War Diary of *U652*, patrol of 12–31 March 1942: PG 30682, NHB, reel 1,133, pp. 598–9

Date, time	Details of position, wind, weather, sea, light, visibility, moonlight, etc.	Incidents
25.iii		
2258		Dived to seek hydrophone contact. Contact obtained at bearing 170° true, and then another at 200°. One steamer with either 90 or 180 revolutions, with apparently just the one escort.[1] From the range and hydrophone data we believe enemy is steering a course of 290°, 10 knots.[2]
2330		Surfaced. We attempt to establish visual contact.
2355		A shadow sighted in the anticipated position. We haul ahead but are constantly forced to retire by a large destroyer which comes ever closer on the northern legs of her zigzag.[3] We wait for the moon to set (0200).
		Fraatz
26.iii		
0000	Qu. CO 9262, wind NW 3, sea 2–3, strong swell from the west, bright	We can't discern the formation of the convoy from this range. Once the moon finally disappears (0200) I am at last right ahead of the convoy, only now able to make out what type of vessels are under way. It looks as if there are three escort vessels steaming in line abreast ahead of the convoy. These consist of the large destroyer acting as sweeper off to the side and to the north, a 'V & W'-class escort vessel covering the southern sector and a third escort in the middle.[4] The latter is not so active, but her

---

1 There were in fact three escorts: HMSs *Jaguar* and *Klo*, and HHellMS *Vasilissa Olga*; see n. 4.

2 Fraatz's hydrophone data is impressively accurate, this being exactly the course and speed recorded for *Slavol* by Lt Cole of HMS *Jaguar* at this time.

3 Presumably HMS *Jaguar*.

4 Viewing the approaching line of escorts from the west, Fraatz's assessment of its dispositions (as deduced from his descriptions of the vessels in question) is at variance with British records. The relative positions were as follows: to the north, one mile off *Slavol's* starboard beam, HM anti-submarine whaler *Klo* (which would equate with Fraatz's 'third escort in the middle'); in the centre HM destroyer *Jaguar* (Fraatz's 'large destroyer', later 'Jervis-class destroyer', which he places to the north); and to the south HHellM destroyer *Vasilissa Olga* ('a "V & W"-class escort covering the south'), the last two at unspecified ranges off *Slavol's* starboard and port bow respectively. However, the evidence is that Fraatz initially identified this line as consisting of two escorts and a steamer, and whereas this entry had the benefit of his *a posteriori* reassessment of a steamer and three escorts that of 0235/0238 was not reworded accordingly; see nn. 5 and 13.

Date, time	Details of position, wind, weather, sea, light, visibility, moonlight, etc.	*Incidents*
		behaviour <u>after</u> we fire means that she must be another escort, not the larger merchantman we torpedo later, which must be sailing some way astern.[5] The ships of the escort are in such close order that penetrating from ahead seems to me an impossible task.[6] So I decide to dive beneath the convoy from my position ahead and surface just behind it, from where I can attack the rearmost steamer.[7] But the Jervis-class destroyer now zigzags off to the north so I decide to attack her instead.[8]
0227	Qu. CO 9229	<u>Spread of four torpedoes fired at Jervis-class destroyer.</u> Shot coordinates: torpedo depth 1 m, range 3,000 m, enemy speed 16 knots, inclination 90°, angle of fire 341°. Range was intentionally assessed on the high side with a view to achieving two hits. As visibility improves the great range becomes apparent (as shown by the running time), and it also becomes clear that this was not a Hunt-class escort vessel, with which she could readily have been confused.[9] This is also shown by the width of spread of 100 m, given that the range entered was only 600 m on the long side (angle of dispersion was 2°). Two hits, one on the fo'c's'le and another under the destroyer's bridge, after 145 and 150 sec. *running times respectively (2,250 m)*.[10] Destroyer burns and sinks but flickering lights remain evident for quite a while, either burning wreckage or distress lights being flashed from rafts and boats.
0235/0238		A number of depth charges dropped.[11] We withdraw ahead of the convoy on the surface. Both escorts follow us for a while as we sail at utmost speed, then they fall astern.[12] We reload torpedoes. After reloading we again set off in pursuit of the convoy using dead reckoning and indeed re-establish contact with an unaccompanied merchantman, which we duly overhaul and confirm both previous course and speed. As no escort can be made out I assume that one remained at the scene of the previous sinking to pick up survivors and the other escort vessel I observed must actually have been this steamer, which, hoping that I was still submerged, had mulishly stuck to her earlier course.[13]
0400	Qu. CO 9216, wind NNW 3, sea 2, swell, not that dark, slightly misty	
0437	Qu. CO 9214	Merchantman in sight.[14] <u>Spread of two torpedoes fired at unaccompanied merchantman</u>, estimated 5,000 GRT, modern, thick funnel, five cargo hatches, a cruiser stern, mainmast set very well back, space between bridge and funnel, very large space between funnel and mainmast, straight stem, low deck throughout.[15] <u>Shot coordinates:</u> torpedo depth 2 m, range 3,000 m (so as to achieve two hits despite precise firing data), enemy speed 10 knots, inclination 90°, angle of fire 20°. <u>1 hit</u> in fore part of

---

5   The implication of this sentence is that Fraatz had initially interpreted the vessel he now identifies as a destroyer (presumably *Vasilissa Olga*) as a steamer sailing in company with two escorts. This assumption may have been supported by his *subsequent* observation of a steamer (*Slavol*) sailing unaccompanied at 0235/0238, it being natural for him to suppose that, having disposed of one of the escorts at 0227, the other should turn back to assist survivors while the steamer pressed on alone; see n. 13. His description here of 'a larger merchantman' is evidence of his belief that the convoy comprised more than the one steamer picked up on the hydrophones at 2258 the previous day.

6   Fraatz's 'close order' comment here seems to contradict the widely dispersed stations described in n. 4.

7   RFA *Slavol*, though as Fraatz's signal of 0227 on the 26th indicates (see Signal Appendix below), he had yet to lay eyes on her; see nn. 5 and 13.

8   HMS *Jaguar*. Notice that Fraatz now refines his identification to a 'J'-class destroyer, no doubt on the basis of subsequent information.

9   Here is yet another instance of Fraatz's log showing evidence of *a posteriori* reassessment, the implication being that he had originally identified *Jaguar* as a Hunt-class destroyer.

10   Manuscript addition in pencil.

11   There is no evidence that any depth charges were dropped at this time. Indeed, the failure to make an immediate counter-attack was criticised by Admiral Sir Henry Harwood, Commander-in-Chief Mediterranean Fleet. The noises heard by Fraatz were more likely connected with *Jaguar*'s sinking.

12   This observation is accurate, *Vasilissa Olga* and *Klo* having sailed on after the sinking of *Jaguar* before both turning back to assist her.

13   This sentence reflects Fraatz's initial assumption that the force he attacked consisted of a steamer and two escorts, subsequently amended to a steamer and three escorts but here left in its original form. His remarks in this sentence are based on his observation at the beginning of this entry of two escorts in pursuit (see n. 12). Subsequently finding himself alone with the merchantman (*Slavol*) Fraatz deduces that he had in fact sighted this vessel and an escort which then turned back to assist survivors of the destroyer he sank earlier. What Fraatz did not appreciate until later – but unlike his 0000 entry here failed to amend – was that the convoy in fact consisted of a merchantman preceded by three escorts, two of which turned back while *Slavol* was left to sail to her fate; see nn. 4 and 5. Although Fraatz's assessment of the number of warships in company was inaccurate, his disbelief that a merchantman might be abandoned by its escort in the face of U-boat attack was shared by many.

14   RFA *Slavol*.

15   *Slavol* was in fact of 2,623 GRT.

ship after 158 sec. Running time equivalent to 2,500 m, merchantman settles a little but remains afloat in the swell.

0453   Qu. CO 9214   *Coup de grâce* from Tube V (G7a), a hit amidships, torpedo depth 3 m, steamer is blown to smithereens with a very black explosion cloud and sinks. In the opinion of the II.WO (who observed a slick of oil and smelled petrol) it is possible that the steamer was loaded with fuel, possibly in drums.[16] We withdraw to the north; Reschke has made enemy contact in the same quadrant.[17] As I have only heard or seen one merchantman I have to assume that I have done for this convoy. The tanker that R[eschke] sinks later is presumably that of another convoy, particularly as he reports an easterly course.[18] No other reports from other boats have come in saying that they are searching for me. Return journey commenced.

0700   Qu. CO 6844   Alarm dive to avoid two aircraft.

Signal Appendix to War Diary of *U652*: PG 30682, NHB, reel 1,133, p. 605

26.iii

0227   0227/26/562. *Kr Kr.*[19] *One merchantman picked up by hydrophone but not found, instead three escorts in line abreast, of which one destroyer sunk, two hits. Forced to withdraw into [Qu. CO] 9229, trying to re-establish contact. Fraatz.*

0437   0437/26/565. *Kr Kr. Have just sunk an unaccompanied steamer I came across, 5,000 GRT.*[20] *Convoy disappeared. Returning to La Spezia. Still one Ato.*[21] *Qu. [CO] 9214. Fraatz.*

---

16 She was loaded with fuel oil.

17 Kptlt Franz-Georg Reschke in *U205* (see **63**).

18 The signal from which Fraatz derives this information was not sent by Reschke until 2000 that evening, another example of his tendency to blend *a posteriori* information into 'present' assessment. As a consequence, the sinking of *Slavol* is often attributed to *U205*, though largely because Fraatz himself does not appear to have claimed a tanker despite the observations of his own Second Watch Officer. Whatever the case, Allied sources record *Slavol* as having been sunk at almost exactly the same time as *U652*'s second attack of 0453. Even Reschke, then in the same quadrant as Fraatz, recorded seeing a tanker blow up at an unstated time after 0420. Given Fraatz's entries from 0238 onwards and Reschke's own observation of an *eastbound* convoy (*Slavol* was sailing almost due west towards Tobruk) there can be no doubt that this was indeed *Slavol*, left to her fate in the confusion surrounding *Jaguar*'s sinking.

19 *Kr Kr* (more usually *KrKr*) was standard Kriegsmarine signal code for 'Urgent Priority'.

20 Fraatz's failure to associate this steamer with the convoy is interesting; see n. **18**. *Slavol* was in fact of 2,623 GRT.

21 'Ato' was Kriegsmarine shorthand for the compressed-air G7a torpedo.

The sinking

Jaguar had only just altered course onto the port leg of her zigzag when *U652*'s first torpedo struck between funnel and bridge on the starboard side, followed immediately by another between funnel and pom-pom platform. The ranking survivor, *Jaguar*'s First Lieutenant Lt P. D. F. Cole, was asleep in the chart room below the bridge when the ship was struck, recording later that 'I staggered to the door to be met by flames coming up from the ladder to the chart room. I turned left and went up the ladder to the bridge – at that time the ship was listing badly and I heard the Chief Bosun's Mate say quite calmly "I think she's going" – then I was in the water.' In his official report Lt Cole testified to an immediate list to starboard, following which *Jaguar* broke in two. The fore part of the ship including the mess decks, passages and bridge structure was engulfed in a huge blaze before sinking within about a minute of being struck. The stern section, extending from the after 4.7-inch gun to the ensign staff, remained afloat for another three minutes.

The travails of Lt Cdr Tyrwhitt's force were now compounded by confusion between *Vasilissa Olga* and *Klo* as to which was standing by *Jaguar*, and consequently the diversion of both ships to the task of rescuing her survivors. This inevitably left *Slavol* ploughing on towards Tobruk unescorted, and it was not until Lt Cole was picked up by *Klo* nearly two hours after the sinking that *Slavol*'s dire predicament was apprehended and *Vasilissa Olga* ordered to rejoin their charge forthwith. By the time *Vasilissa Olga* caught up with *Slavol* at 0520 all that remained of her were flickering lights coming from men in boats, Fraatz having despatched her half an hour earlier. Reviewing the episode, Admiral Sir Henry Harwood, Commander-in-Chief Mediterranean Fleet, declared that nothing could have been done to save *Jaguar* once she had been hit, but that *Vasilissa Olga* should have instructed *Klo* to stand by *Jaguar* while she counter-attacked and then rejoined *Slavol*. However, as Harwood concluded in his report to the Admiralty, 'it is not intended to hold an enquiry into this lamentable episode, the facts of which are only too clear', a decision which no doubt owed more to the sensibilities of a hard-pressed ally than any disciplinary consideration.

Clear though the facts may have been to the British authorities, Oblt.z.S. Fraatz plainly found them much less so, a state of affairs all too obvious from the content of his war diary. Indeed, attempting to divine the sequence of Fraatz's interpretation of events from the information provided in his log has proved harder for this entry than for any other in this volume. The reason for this is that Fraatz made a very imperfect job of overlaying his original assessment of the action with the data and deductions subsequently obtained and arrived at. Although *a posteriori* reassessment is a recurrent feature of the U-boat logs (see Introduction, pp. xviii–xix), Fraatz's record of this episode is unusual both as to the extent of the revisions and to the incomplete way in which they were made. The result is a shifting interpretation of events which fails to provide either a coherent account of the action or a clear sense of the evolution of Fraatz's thinking. Small wonder that this attack is sometimes attributed to Reschke in *U205*, but neither

Fraatz's log nor Reschke's for that matter leave much doubt that *U652* accounted for both escort and merchantman.

Fate of the crew

The two torpedoes that struck HMS *Jaguar* exacted a heavy toll of her company and Lt Cole was one of the few men to survive from the fore part of the ship, which was lost with almost the entire off-duty watch. Even fewer can have survived from her engine spaces, while Lt Cdr Tyrwhitt was presumed to have been killed in his sea cabin by the initial detonations. There was no opportunity to launch boats and rafts, leaving the rescue of those who got clear of the wreck to be carried out by *Klo* and *Vasilissa Olga*, which held their courses for around half an hour before falling back to assist the survivors. The fifty-three oil-soaked survivors of *Jaguar* were landed by *Klo* at Mersa Matrûh later that day. Nor was this the end of their troubles, for the hospital train in which they were sent on to Alexandria found itself the target of an air attack en route.

U652 and Georg-Werner Fraatz

For *U652*'s career up to March 1942, see the preceding entry for HMS *Heythrop* (**55**).

U652's two-week cruise of March 1942 received a glowing review by *F.d.U. Italien*, Kapt.z.S. Leo Kreisch commending a 'very well executed, successful patrol, in which yet again the assured, circumspect and single-minded approach of the commanding officer was confirmed'. The pennants of both *Slavol* and *Jaguar* were correctly attributed to Fraatz, but these successes were not to be repeated. On 2 June, a week into her next patrol, *U652* was attacked first by an RAF Sunderland and then by an FAA Swordfish in the Gulf of Salûm (Sollum) northeast of Bardia and severely damaged. *U652* survived a further attack from a Swordfish of the Fleet Air Arm, but Fraatz and his men had to be rescued by Kptlt Friedrich Guggenberger's *U81* (see **39**) and their boat scuttled. Appropriately enough, it was Oblt.z.S. Fraatz who fired the torpedo which sank his former command. Fraatz was subsequently given a shore appointment and promoted Kapitänleutnant, but was lost with many of his *U652* veterans on 15 February 1943 when *U529* disappeared in the Atlantic on her maiden cruise to cause unknown. Fraatz was posthumously promoted Korvettenkapitän on 1 March.

U652 seen at Salamis in February or March 1942, immediately before the cruise during which *Jaguar* was sunk. *DUBMA*

Sources

Admiralty, *Enemy Submarine Attacks on H.M. Ships, 1942* (TNA, ADM 199/162)

—, War Diary for March 1942 (TNA, ADM 199/2237), pp. 766, 796, 820 and 836

Cole, Cdr P. D. F., *Memoirs of a Sailor* (typescript, IWM, 98/1/1)

Connell, G. G., *Mediterranean Maelstrom: HMS* Jervis *and the 14th Flotilla* (London: William Kimber, 1987)

Dance, Lt Cdr F. C., 'HMS *Jaguar*, 14th DF, Malta, 20 December 1941' in *Warship World* 4, no. 12 (Autumn 1994), pp. 24–5

English, John, Afridi *to* Nizam: *British Fleet Destroyers, 1937–43* (Gravesend, Kent: World Ship Society, 2001)

Kinghorn, D., and B. Hargreaves, 'Destroyers of the Royal Navy: "J" Class' [Part I] in *Warships*, Supplement no. 18 (May 1970), pp. 13–20

Langtree, Christopher, *The Kelly's [sic]: British J, K and N Class Destroyers of World War II* (London: Chatham Publishing, 2002)

Payne, Alan, 'The Origin of the J Class Destroyers' in *Warship*, no. 15 (July 1980), pp. 192–8

Career history of HMS *Jaguar*:
     http://www.naval-history.net/xGM-Chrono-10DD-37J-Jaguar.htm

---

57   USS *ATIK* ('SS *CAROLYN*')

Lt Cdr H. L. Hicks, USN†

Sunk by *U123* (Type IXB), Kptlt Reinhard Hardegen, 26 March 1942

North Atlantic, 270 nm ENE of Cape Hatteras, North Carolina (USA)

Theatre	North Atlantic (Map 1)	*Deadweight*	6,610 tons
Coordinates (approximate)	35° 47' N, 70° 04' W	*Gross tons*	3,209
Kriegsmarine code	Quadrat CA 9578	*Dimensions*	328.25' × 46' × 22.75'
U-boat timekeeping differential	+6 hours	*Maximum speed*	9 knots
Fatalities	139 *Survivors* none	*Armament*	4 × 4"; 4 × .5" AA; 4 × .3" AA

Project LQ

'Project LQ', the secret procurement and conversion of merchantmen to operate as decoy ships off the eastern seaboard of the United States, was the result of a meeting on 19 January 1942 between President

Roosevelt and the newly appointed Commander-in-Chief of the US Navy, Admiral Ernest J. King. Concerned at the severe threat to US merchant shipping posed by the new long-range Type-IXB U-boats and aware of the limited resources then at the Navy's disposal for patrolling

SS *Carolyn* seen plying her trade between the wars, a world away from her violent end as the Q-ship *Atik*. *Bruce Taylor collection*

Atlantic coastal waters, Roosevelt suggested trying the hazardous tactic evolved by the British during the Great War of deploying submarine decoys (or 'Q-ships'), one the US Navy had herself briefly employed in the shape of the schooner *Charles Whittemore* in the autumn of 1918. This measure, which involved tempting U-boats into a surface attack and then engaging them with concealed ordnance, was no doubt prompted by the fact that a number of ships were being despatched by gunfire, but the US Navy may not have been aware of the scant success enjoyed by this tactic in the latest conflict (see HMSs *Cape Howe* and *Willamette Valley*, **11** and **12**). Nonetheless, Project LQ was initiated with the intention that such ships would operate between New York and Cape Race under the control of the Commander Eastern Sea Frontier, Rear Admiral Adolphus Andrews. The next six weeks saw the covert leasing of two elderly bulk raw sugar carriers from the A. H. Bull Steamship Company, the SSs *Evelyn* and *Carolyn* of 3,200 GRT. Though the original names were retained, *Evelyn* and *Carolyn* became the USSs *Asterion* and *Atik* (AK-100 and AK-101) for the purposes of personnel records and official station identification. Also converted at this time was the Boston trawler *Wave* which became the USS *Eagle* (later USS *Captor*).

Career

SS *Carolyn* was laid down as the *Parkgate* by the Newport News Shipbuilding and Dry Dock Company in March 1912 and both launched and completed in July of that year. Her peacetime career was spent transporting sugar and passengers between the West Indies and the eastern seaboard of the United States, but she was no stranger to war service. Between June 1917 and November 1918 *Carolyn* was assigned a naval detachment and armed with a 3-inch and a 5-inch gun though without ever coming under direct control of the US Navy. Mercantile service was resumed at war's end. On 12 February 1942 *Carolyn* began a hasty conversion at Portsmouth Navy Yard, New Hampshire which was completed with a discreet commissioning ceremony on 5 March, though it is likely that secrecy

was compromised. Shakedown was limited to two forty-eight-hour sorties in March before *Evelyn* and *Carolyn* sailed for war on the 23rd, their holds packed with dry pulpwood for buoyancy in the event of a torpedo hit. They were expected to be cruising in their assigned areas some 200 miles off the US coast within a few days. As the *Dictionary of American Naval Fighting Ships* relates, 'At the outset, all connected with the program apparently harbored the view that neither ship "was expected to last longer than a month after commencement of assigned duty".' Indeed, 'The commanding officers of the two ships were told they could expect little help if they got into trouble as the situation was critical. Every available combatant ship and plane were [*sic*] being employed to the maximum for convoy and patrol duties.' In the event, *Atik*'s fate trumped even the most dire predictions for her survival.

Background of the attack

On 12 January 1942 Kptlt Reinhard Hardegen struck the first blow of Operation PAUKENSCHLAG ('drumroll'), the German U-boat offensive against Allied shipping off the eastern seaboard of the United States. The sinking of the British SS *Cyclops* that day also marked the beginning of a triumphant patrol during which Hardegen sank nine ships and damaged another in the space of a fortnight, three by means of his deck gun. In early March *U123* sailed from Lorient to resume her depredations in US waters. Fresh pennants were sewn before the month was out, *U123* sinking the tankers *Muskogee* and *Empire Steel* on the 22nd and 24th respectively. Forty-eight hours later the bridge watch sighted *U123*'s next victim: a lone freighter belching large puffs of smoke on the horizon. Hardegen's war diary for the incident, given in full below, is so informed by his later appreciation of the true identity of this freighter that it is difficult to ascertain whether or not he and his men were initially as suspicious as his entry at midnight on the 26th implies. What is clear, however, is that *U123* came very close to falling victim to the USS *Atik*, then just three days into her first Q-ship patrol.

War Diary of *U123*, patrol of 2 March–2 May 1942: PG 30113, NHB, reel 1,081, pp. 737–9

Date, time	Details of position, wind, weather, sea, light, visibility, moonlight, etc.	Incidents

26.iii

| 1600 2000[1] | Qu. CA 9576 | |
| 1903 2303 | | Clouds of smoke on the starboard beam. As we close I initially assume a convoy because we can often make out six or seven individual clouds of smoke far apart on the horizon. It turns out later that this was just the one steamer, issuing very powerful puffs of smoke on a regular basis that were then being carried away on a beam wind. She is steering a steady course, 215°. It transpires later that this was the US steamer *Carolyn*, 3,209 GRT, sailing as a U-boat decoy ship. As she is oil-fired she must have been making this smoke artificially to lure U-boats. Once darkness falls she stops producing so much heavy smoke and suddenly commences zigzagging. |

[27.iii]

| 2000 2400 | Qu. CA 9812 | At first we are suspicious but when we begin our surfaced night approach we identify her as a standard freighter and our suspicions are allayed. She has an ordinary low, smooth stern and level fo'c's'le. There is no indication anywhere of a structure or something similar that might lead us to conclude that she was armed. A large bridge amidships, as is typical of freighter-passenger ships. But what really ought to have struck us is the fact that the ship had a very elevated structure abaft the funnel.[2] The moon is well hidden behind clouds and I fire an Eto from Tube II.[3] |
| 2237 0237 | Qu. CA 9578, wind N 3, cloud 9/10, sea 2/3, visibility 4 nm | Torpedo data: inclination 90°, enemy speed 10 knots, depth 3 m, range 650 m. A hit at the forward end of the bridge which catches fire, vessel settles by the head with a port list. I assume she will sink quickly as she has way on. She transmits a signal giving her name and position.[4] After firing I turn to starboard to pass the vessel's stern. She has lowered one boat into the water, a second is hanging from its davits. It seems a totally straightforward situation and even now there is nothing to arouse our suspicions. But at this point I gain the impression that she is still under way because the range suddenly decreases. I order a course alteration to starboard. But our steamer also alters course to starboard and suddenly turns broadside on (inclination 90°). I turn hard astarboard as flaps and tarpaulins are suddenly lowered and she starts firing with at least one deck gun and two 2-cm machine guns.[5] We are fortunate in that the deck gunfire initially falls short and is then wide of the mark. We can clearly see the fall of shot. The 2 cm [rounds] rain down on the bridge and whistle unpleasantly about our heads. I immediately retire at utmost speed which has the unexpected advantage of producing large clouds of diesel smoke which then obscure us from view. I then see large fragments flying through the air. These are followed by powerful detonations that violently shake the entire boat. My first thought is that we have been hit by a torpedo. All bulkheads secure. I then see great columns of water and the penny now drops that she has fired depth charges at us with throwers.[6] I've fallen for a well-armed U-boat decoy ship like a bloody novice. Fähnrich zur See Holzer was wounded in the first salvo and it is extremely difficult to get him down into the boat through the conning tower hatch.[7] Because of this and due to the many hits and depth charges heard I can't immediately order an alarm dive but have to wait to see if the boat is still fit to do so. We then find ourselves out of firing range and the enemy ceases fire. None apart from Holzer is wounded and a pressure test reveals that the pressure hull is still watertight. We have enjoyed exceptional luck – the next day we count eight 2-cm hits on the bridge. |

---

1 The original times given in this log extract have all been crossed out and amended in pencil to bring them four hours forward. At noon on 24 May Hardegen recorded in the log that he was altering the time from MEZ (*Mitteleuropäische Zeit* – Central European Time) to match the local zone time in the patrol area, which was MEZ –4. However, he was later ordered to reinstate the original times, which explains the handwritten amendment beside each timed entry.

2 This of course contradicts Hardegen's comment two sentences above.

3 Despite Hardegen's use of the first person singular this torpedo was actually fired by *U123*'s First Watch Officer, Oblt.z.S. Horst von Schroeter (see **84**), as was standard practice for surface attacks at night. 'Eto' is Kriegsmarine shorthand for the electric G7e torpedo.

4 This was presumably *Atik*'s signal at 2055 ship time; see below.

5 Hardegen appears to be describing *Atik*'s 4-inch deck guns and .5-inch (.50-cal.) machine guns.

6 *Atik* mounted six depth-charge projectors aft: two on the deck below the after 4-inch guns, two on the after well deck abreast No. 5 hatch, and two on the poop deck, disposed on the port and starboard side in each case.

7 This and subsequent remarks contradict Hardegen's earlier comment that *Atik*'s gunfire 'initially falls short and is then wide of the mark'. The rank of *Fähnrich zur See* equates with the those of US Navy ensign and Royal Navy midshipman.

Once we are out of range I go below to discover that Fähnrich Holzer's condition is hopeless. A 2-cm shell has detonated in his right thigh, devastating the flesh between hip and knee and tearing much of it away. The degree to which the bone is shattered cannot be precisely established, but the leg is hanging together by just tiny scraps of skin. We apply a tourniquet, having to use a towel for the major wound as our bandaging is no good for an injury of this magnitude. It is immediately clear that such a wound could not be successfully treated under U-boat conditions even with a doctor on board, and as we are many days cruising from the nearest neutral port I take the decision to make it as easy for him as possible and inject a substantial dose of morphine. Holzer displays exemplary courage. He remains conscious for another hour, not making any sound that would betray his suffering, although he freely admits on being questioned that he is in almost intolerable pain. At around ~~2400~~ *0400* he loses consciousness.[1]

Hardegen

27.iii[8]		As the *Carolyn* has not sunk – she would appear to have a buoyant cargo – I decide to carry out a submerged attack.[9] She has stopped and the crew has reboarded her.
~~0029~~ *0429*	Qu. CA 9578	I fire a *coup-de-grâce* shot from Tube I at the engine room which strikes after a run of 24 sec.[10] The fore part of the ship settles further and is now awash back to the bridge. I can see the stern out of the water, propeller in the air, still listing to port. The crew gets back into the boats. We retire, still submerged.
~~0127~~ *0527*		We surface. Steamer remains in exactly the same position as last observed through periscope.
~~0150~~ *0550*		Powerful detonations, either boilers or depth charges and magazine. Thereafter the *Carolyn* sinks, no pieces of wreckage can be seen. Fähnrich Holzer passed away quietly during the submerged attack. We have all lost a fine comrade. At around 0800 we commit him to the deep after a short service. He now has a seaman's grave in position 35° 38' N, 70° 14' W.
~~0400~~ *0800*	Qu. CA 9811	We revert to our former course of 270°.
~~0800~~ *1200*	Qu. CA 9722	
~~1200~~ *1600*	Qu. CA 8933, wind NE 2–3, cloud 6/10, sea 2, visibility 15 nm	Day's run: 153 nm (of which 124 submerged), cruise total 3,456 nm.
~~1600~~ *2000*	Qu. CA 8919	
~~1900~~ *2300*		Alarm dive! Large land aircraft.[11]

---

8   Position of date reflects original.

9   The *Atik* was indeed carrying a buoyant cargo of pulpwood logs.

10 This equates to a range of 360 metres.

11 Quite possibly the USAAF bomber ordered to the position given in *Atik*'s distress signal, as *U123* had not altered course significantly to the north or south in the meantime.

The sinking

U123's log provides the only detailed evidence of what befell *Atik* on the night of 26–27 March 1942, making it clear that Lt Cdr H. L. Hicks almost turned the tables on his assailant before succumbing to a second torpedo hit. This, however, is not the only interpretation of the loss of the USS *Atik*. In his volume on US Q-ships of the Second World War, Kenneth M. Beyer (see below) has posited the theory that *U105* (Korvkpt. Heinrich Schuch; see **49**) also carried out an attack on the *Atik* some twenty minutes after *U123*'s first attack at 0237 German time. In his log Korvkpt. Schuch relates how *U105* attacked a ship estimated at 3,000 GRT at 0256 and 0258, observing a port list after hearing the first torpedo hit but not detonate. After making a persuasive argument for *U105* (whose recorded position places her well south of the *Atik*–*U123* encounter) being much further north as a result of a navigational error, Beyer (who was serving in *Atik*'s sister

Asterion at the time) advances the hypothesis that *U105*'s torpedo of 0256 'could have entered *Carolyn*'s hull through the large hole made by *U123*'s first torpedo and come to rest embedded in the exposed hold among the disarrayed [pulpwood] logs without a proper contact with the firing mechanism'. As Beyer continues, the powerful explosions recorded by Hardegen at 0550 German time, eighty minutes after his second torpedo brought *Atik*'s propeller out of the water, could have been the result of the detonation of this torpedo 'as the ship continued to settle by the bow or was rocked by wave action'.

Ingenious though it is, this thesis must at best remain in the realm of conjecture, not least since there is no demonstrable evidence that *U105* was ever on the scene of *Atik*'s demise. Korvkpt. Schuch's war diary makes no mention of *U123*'s first hit or the subsequent hail of gunfire and depth charges that followed, an exchange he could scarcely have failed to notice in view of the fact that he had been tracking whatever target it was for six hours and his supposed attacks on *Atik* came just twenty minutes after Hardegen's. Moreover, *U105*'s attacks of 0256 and 0258 were on a vessel estimated by Schuch to be making eleven knots, whereas *Atik* had a best speed of nine knots – presumably rather less after taking a torpedo. No such doubts surround the 'exceptional good luck' of Kptlt Hardegen, who returned to Lorient in a blaze of glory at the end of a cruise that saw *U123* sink eight vessels and damage three more. Singing Hardegen's praises, Dönitz concluded that 'the Commander displayed exemplary attacking spirit to achieve a magnificent success which – torpedo replenishment cruises aside – is without parallel'. However, Dönitz might have sung an altogether different tune had *Atik*'s gunnery been a shade more accurate.

Despite this miserable turn of events and every indication that the Germans were alive to the use of Q-ships, the US Navy persisted with Project LQ and, *Eagle* apart (see above), commissioned two more decoy vessels in 1942. Unsurprisingly, not a single U-boat had succumbed to this tactic by the time it was abandoned in October of the following year. In ending Project LQ Admiral King condemned it as a waste of money and scarce resources and declared it to have been punctuated not only by incompetence but by abuse of the authority granted its officers in the interests of secrecy, however sincere their desire to contribute to the war effort. Though hardly worth the sacrifice of lives and *matériel*, the efforts of these ships and their crews may not however have been entirely in vain. Summarising the work of the largest of these, the converted tanker USS *Big Horn*, her CO Cdr L. C. Farley stated that

> Evidently the U-boats are wary of attacking an independent tanker. If the Q-ship program has contributed to this wariness, as is suggested in several prisoner-of-war statements, many independent merchant ships may thereby have escaped attack, and the Q-ship program has thus been of value.

Fate of the crew

There were no survivors from the USS *Atik*, nor is it known if any escaped the dramatic detonations that heralded her end. US shore stations were aware of what had initially befallen the 'SS *Carolyn*' since two distress signals received in New Jersey and New York after the first torpedo hit were passed on to the appropriate authorities. The first, sent minutes after the attack and recorded as having been intercepted at 0053 GMT (2053 ship time), read 'LAT 3600 N LONG 7000 W CAROLYN 0055 BURNING FORWARD NOT BAD'. A second, received in slightly corrupt form at 0132 GMT (2132 ship time), stated '36.00 N 70.00 W APPX SS CAROLYN TORPEDO ATTACK BURNING FORWARD REQUIRD SSISTANCE 0055 GMT'. It is conceivable given the timing and language of these signals that they were part of *Atik*'s ruse, an enticement to the U-boat commander to surface and finish her off with his deck armament. Whatever the case, after some delay *Carolyn*'s true identity was recognised in the Eastern Sea Frontier's Joint Operations Control Room in Manhattan and a US Army bomber dispatched to her last reported position on the afternoon of the 27th. However, this aircraft – possibly the same sighted by *U123* in her entry of 2300 – found nothing. The best hope any survivors may have had of rescue probably rested in the destroyer *Noa* (which arrived on the scene late on the 27th and searched until the 30th), and with the *Asterion* (then about 240 miles to the south), which received *Atik*'s distress signals but did not reach her estimated

Hitler presents Hardegen the certificate for the Knight's Cross with Oak Leaves he was awarded in the summer of 1942. *DUBMA*

sinking position until midday on the 28th. Even then she could only search for a day before damage to her steering gear forced her into Hampton Roads for repairs. Another vessel, the Navy tug *Sagamore*, was obliged to return to harbour in mountainous seas. No more was ever heard of *Atik*'s crew and it must be supposed that any survivors perished in the gales that lashed the area on the 28th and 29th. On 30 March wreckage was sighted by two Army aircraft ten miles south of the position given in *Carolyn*'s distress signal but it was never definitively ascertained whether this belonged to her. Ten days later Radio Berlin issued a communiqué which was printed in *The New York Times* the following day, 10 April 1942:

> The High Command said today that a Q-boat – a heavily armed ship disguised as an unarmed vessel – was among 13 vessels sunk off the American Atlantic coast and that it was sent to the bottom by a submarine only after a 'bitter battle.' [. . .] The Q-boat, the communiqué said, was of 3,000 tons and was sunk by a torpedo after a battle 'fought partly on the surface with artillery and partly beneath the water with bombs and torpedoes.'

Atik's covert status prevented any meaningful information being released to next of kin, who were initially informed only that their relatives were 'missing following action in the performance of their duty and in the service of their Country'. It was not until May 1944 that the Navy Department notified relatives that her ship's company was presumed lost to enemy action in the North Atlantic.

U123 and Reinhard Hardegen

Built by AG Weser at Bremen and commissioned in May 1940, *U123* enjoyed a career spanning three commanders and almost four years during which she accounted for over 225,000 tons of shipping. The first of these commanders, Kptlt Karl-Heinz Moehle, had despatched sixteen merchantmen in the Atlantic by the time of his departure in May 1941. However, much of *U123*'s tonnage was notched up by Kptlt Reinhard Hardegen in two patrols off North America during

Operation PAUKENSCHLAG when eighteen ships were sunk for a total of over 120,000 tons. The first of these earned Hardegen the Knight's Cross, the second his Q-ship pennant and the Oak Leaves. Less distinguished was Hardegen's first victim in *U123*, the neutral Portuguese freighter *Ganda* which he sank with torpedoes and gunfire on 20 June 1941, an incident which Dönitz ordered to be purged from the log. *U123*'s triumphal return to Lorient in May 1942 nonetheless marked the end of Hardegen's frontline career, the result of internal injuries from a pre-war air crash as a pilot with the *Marineflieger* (naval air arm). Training duties followed, first with the 27th *U-Flottille* and then at the torpedo school at Mürwik where he was promoted Korvettenkapitän in March 1944 before being appointed a battalion commander in *Marine Infanterie Regiment* 6 in February 1945. Taken prisoner at war's end, he was released in November 1946 and enjoyed a successful civilian career first as an oil trading entrepreneur and then as a member of parliament for the Free Hanseatic City of Bremen.

For the remainder of *U123*'s career, see HMS/m *P615* (**84**).

Sources

US Navy, Records of the Bureau of Naval Personnel, *Casualty File for the USS* Atik (NA, RG 24, Entry 1024 (A1), Personal Affairs Division; Casualty Assistance Branch; Ships, Stations Units and Incidents Casualty Information Records, 1941–1945)

Beyer, Kenneth M., *Q-Ships Versus U-Boats: America's Secret Project* (Annapolis, Md.: Naval Institute Press, 1999)
Chewning, Alpheus J., *The Approaching Storm: U-Boats off the Virginia Coast During World War II* (Lively, Va.: Brandylane Publishers, 1994)
DANFS, I, p. 70; also on: http://www.history.navy.mil/danfs/a/atik.htm
Gannon, *Operation Drumbeat*, pp. 305–7 and 323–9
Hardegen, Kptlt Reinhard, *Auf Gefechtsstationen!* (Leipzig: Boreas-Verlag, 1943)
Morison, *United States Naval Operations*, I, pp. 281–6

Webpage titled 'Q-Ships (Anti-submarine vessels disguised as merchant vessels)': http://www.history.navy.mil/docs/wwii/Q-ships.htm

---

58   HMS *EDINBURGH*

Rear-Admiral S. S. Bonham-Carter, CB CVO DSO RN, Capt. H. W. Faulkner, RN
Sunk by *U456* (Type VIIC), Kptlt Max-Martin Teichert, 30 April–2 May 1942
Barents Sea, 150 nm NNE of Gamvik (Norway)

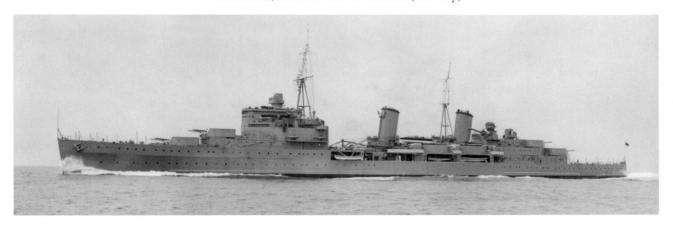

Edinburgh under way early in the war. Teichert hit her twice on the starboard side, first abreast the bridge and then aft, wrecking the stern. Two days later the destroyer *Z25* finished her off with a third torpedo, this time on the port side abreast the bridge. *IWM*

Campaign	Arctic convoys (Map 2)	*Displacement*	10,565 tons
Coordinates (of attack)	73° 08' N, 33° 00' E	*Dimensions*	613.5' × 64.75' × 18'
Kriegsmarine code (of attack)	Quadrat AC 5519	*Armour*	4.5" belt; 1.25–3" horizontal; 2.5" bulkheads; 1–4" turrets
U-boat timekeeping	identical	*Maximum speed*	32.25 knots
Fatalities 57 and 2	*Survivors* 790+	*Armament*	12 × 6"; 12 × 4" AA; 8 × .5" AA; 6 × 21" tt
		Aircraft	2 Supermarine Walruses and catapult

Career

Nameship of the largest modern cruisers built for the Royal Navy, *Edinburgh* and her sister *Belfast* (now preserved on the Thames) represented the third and final development of the Town-class design with increased length and improved horizontal protection over the preceding units. HMS *Edinburgh* was laid down at Swan Hunter and Wigham Richardson's yard at Newcastle upon Tyne in December 1936 and launched in March 1938. Completed in August 1939, she

commissioned into the 18th Cruiser Squadron, Home Fleet and spent the first month of the war patrolling the Iceland–Faroes gap. In October her transfer to the 2nd CS for duty with the Humber Force was delayed by minor damage sustained on the 16th during a German air raid on the Firth of Forth. Patrol and escort duty in the Atlantic, the North Sea and with the Narvik iron ore convoys continued until March 1940 when she began a five-month refit on the Tyne to repair structural flaws in her hull. Emerging from this in October, *Edinburgh* rejoined the 18th CS at Scapa Flow to begin an eventful period of convoy, patrol and offensive duty with the Home Fleet. In March 1941 she participated in the attack on the German-held Lofoten Islands off Norway and in May was involved in the capture of the weather trawler *München* and then in the pursuit of the battleship *Bismarck*, intercepting the supply ship SS *Lech* on the 28th. Patrol and convoy duty in the Atlantic continued through June but in July the desperate need to resupply Malta brought her into the Mediterranean as part of Operation SUBSTANCE which reached the Grand Harbour on the 24th. Having escorted convoy WS10 from the Clyde to Cape Town in August, *Edinburgh* was recalled to the Mediterranean for another Malta convoy, Operation HALBERD, which took place at the end of September. After a further stint on the Iceland–Faroes Patrol she was assigned to escort the first of her six Russian convoys, PQ6, which reached Murmansk without loss in December. Returning with QP4, *Edinburgh* was refitted on the Tyne in early 1942 before rejoining the North Russia run with the first heavily contested convoy, PQ13, and then QP9 which made Scapa on 28 March. On 6 April she sailed to escort PQ14 from Iceland, though one of its twenty-four ships was sunk by *U403* and sixteen more had to turn back owing to ice and bad weather. However, *Edinburgh* battled on and reached the Kola Inlet with the remainder of the convoy on 19 April. The return convoy, QP11, was to be her last.

Background of the attack

For background on the Arctic convoy campaign, see HMS *Matabele* (**47**).

By March 1942 the Kriegsmarine and Luftwaffe had begun a concerted effort to bar the passage of convoys to and from Murmansk. The German occupation of Norway permitted U-boats and aircraft to be deployed at short notice while surface vessels waited their chance to overwhelm a weak escort. With relatively few U-boats assigned to the Arctic theatre Allied losses could not match those in the Atlantic, but there could be no mistaking the trend. Whereas only a single merchantman (SS *Waziristan*) was sunk in convoy between the

introduction of the Russian supply route in August 1941 and the end of February 1942 (see HMS *Matabele*, **47**), six were sunk in March and a further eight in April, with convoy PQ13 being badly mauled.

On 28 April convoy QP11 sailed for Reykjavik from the Kola Inlet with the strongest Arctic escort yet, comprising six destroyers, four corvettes and a trawler. To these the heavy cruiser *Kuibyshev* and the destroyer *Sokrushitel'ny* of the Soviet navy initially added their strength. On the 29th the escort was bolstered by the heavy cruiser *Edinburgh* wearing the flag of Rear-Admiral Stuart Bonham-Carter. That such a significant unit should join the convoy escort was appropriate enough since five tons of gold were packed into one of her bomb rooms. Divided into ninety-three cases, the bullion was being carried to Britain as Soviet payment for US war supplies. When contact was made by the Luftwaffe on the 29th – barely a day into the voyage – it was plain that this would be no easy passage, but few could have imagined the drama the next seventy-two hours would bring. On the evening of the 29th the convoy slowed to little more than four knots and in the early hours of the 30th the escort commander, Rear-Admiral Bonham-Carter, ordered *Edinburgh* to proceed unescorted some twelve miles ahead of the main body, zigzagging in wide arcs at 18–19 knots. Although Bonham-Carter was concerned about the vulnerability of his flagship the decision was nonetheless the cause of some disagreement with his Flag Captain, H. W. Faulkner. Faulkner's fears were to be confirmed for this detachment placed *Edinburgh* in the first line of attack for *U456* (Kptlt Max-Martin Teichert) and *U436* (Kptlt Günther Seibicke), which had sailed from their base at Kirkenes in northern Norway as part of the seven-strong *Strauchritter* ('highwayman') group the previous day. Early on the 30th *U436* aimed four torpedoes at the *Edinburgh*, all of which missed. That afternoon it was *U456*'s turn which attacked having shadowed *Edinburgh* for several hours, crippling but not sinking her with two torpedo hits. The rest of Teichert's war diary records his desperate efforts to deliver the greatest prize yet for the Kriegsmarine in the Arctic theatre into the hands of a trio of pursuing destroyers.

War Diary of *U456*, patrol of 29 April–4 May 1942: PG 30509, NHB, reel 1,111, pp. 333–6

Date, time	Details of position, wind, weather, sea, light, visibility, moonlight, etc.	Incidents
30.iv		
1120	Qu. AC 5554	A cruiser in sight to the south, unquestionably Belfast class.[1]
1200	Qu. AC 5554	Day's run: surfaced 220 nm, submerged 3 nm, total 223 nm.
		Outgoing W/T transmission 1142/701: *Kr Kr*[2] *Qu. [AC] 5582 cruiser, Belfast class, westerly course, high speed, extreme zigzags. Teichert.*
		For a while we lose sight of the cruiser.
1422		Outgoing W/T transmission 1345/703: *Qu. [AC] 5554 no question cruiser Belfast, so far general course 300°, temporarily disappeared to SE, assume in direction of convoy. No attack opportunity. Teichert.*
1510		Cruiser reappears at a bearing 120° true, zigzagging on a course of approximately 300°. With an inclination of 0° she rapidly looms up on the horizon.
1548		Dive to attack. Enemy initially zigzags to the south and after ten minutes alters to a course of *roughly*[3]

---

1 Teichert's identification is correct though *Edinburgh* was in fact the name ship of the class.

2 *Kr Kr* (more usually *KrKr*) was standard Kriegsmarine signal code for 'Urgent Priority'. Teichert consistently leaves out the 'AC' bigram when providing quadrant codes in the 'Incidents' column of this excerpt.

3 Manuscript addition in pencil.

		330°. All this we glean via hydrophones as the attack periscope can hardly be used. We switch to a parallel course.
1610		Cruiser then turns towards us (or away?). She is very hard to make out in the periscope. Inclination 20°, range 4,000 m, so course now 180°. Excellent. We position ourselves for attack. We can only keep the trim by running the engines at half speed.
1618	Qu. AC 5519, wind N 6–7, sea 5–6, visibility 8 nm	Spread of three torpedoes fired from Tubes I, II and IV. Range 1,000 m, enemy speed 15 knots, inclination 60°, torpedo speed 30 knots, depth 4 m, angle of dispersion 4°, point of aim forward funnel.[4]
		Two detonations heard in quick succession after a running time of 80 sec. (= 1,200 m). Boat dips. We can see absolutely nothing through the periscope due to blotches etc. on the lens so I decide to surface briefly.
1632		Surfaced. Cruiser has turned. With an inclination of 30° she is now shrouded in lofty clouds of yellow smoke and listing to port.
1634		Dived. New attack commenced. From what we can hear of her revolutions (80) enemy's speed is now 5–6 knots. We can see nothing through the periscope. Cruiser is heading away from us.
1650		Three destroyers close us at high speed.[5] As I can no longer approach and can see nothing in the periscope I retire under water.
1945		Am free of them and can surface. We set off in pursuit (reported).
2020	Qu. AC 5542	Cruiser with destroyers once more in sight. Outgoing W/T transmission 2102/713: *Cruiser with three destroyers Qu. [AC] 5524, southerly course, barely under way or stopped. Teichert.*[6]
2114		Incoming W/T transmission 2048/710 from Admiral Commanding Northern Waters[7]: *Teichert – 1.) Good. 2.) Immediately report last position and course of cruiser. Try to maintain contact.* I maintain contact with cruiser.
2140	Wind NW 4–5, sea 4, visibility 8 nm, worsening	Destroyer at inclination 0°. We withdraw at maximum speed. When destroyer closes to within 4,000 m we dive.
2215		Two destroyers close by. Echo-sounding and hydrophone pursuit, but their contact is only brief, no depth charges. After an hour one heads off, the other remains in vicinity. Above the surface night has not quite fallen.

Teichert

1.v . . . .

0015	Qu. AC 5524	We surface. And come across Bohmann (0030).[8]
0050		Contact regained with cruiser. Reported.
0216		Outgoing W/T transmission 0157/728: *Cruiser lying stopped Qu. [AC] 5528 in a beam sea. Large patches of oil in her lee. Destroyers surrounding cruiser. Teichert.*
0315		Continual beacon signal 'j' transmitted for the Luftwaffe on 442 kHz in response to W/T 0214/729.
0400	Qu. AC 5527, wind NE 3, sea 2, visibility 4–8 nm, snow showers	Cruiser appears to have got under way again as of 0310. Qu. [AC] 5556, 150°, 6–7 knots reported.
0641		Outgoing W/T transmission 0602/736: *Cruiser steering zigzag course once again Qu. [AC] 5555… Teichert.*
0700		She seems to have stopped once again. Maintaining contact is extremely difficult. Typical Arctic Ocean conditions. We keep on drying and heating up the attack periscope but cannot get rid of the milky film coating the lens. We try everything. Attack on cruiser was also basically guesswork. Cruiser only intermittently in sight.
0800	Qu. AC 5554	

---

4 *Edinburgh* was in fact making 18–19 knots.

5 The timing of this observation by Teichert is not borne out by Allied sources. Capt. Faulkner recorded that the first vessel on the scene was *Forester* at 1730, seventy-five minutes after the initial attack. *Foresight* arrived at 1800 and *Kuibyshev* and *Sokrushitel'ny* at 1832. The first foray by *Forester* to hunt a reported submarine sighting to the north-east was not until later.

6 Interestingly, Teichert's signal makes no mention of his having scored a hit.

7 Operational responsibility for these northerly waters (encompassing the Barents and Norwegian seas, as well as parts of the Arctic Ocean) was held at this time by *Admiral Nordmeer* (Admiral Commanding Northern Waters, Admiral Hubert Schmundt), becoming the responsibility of the newly created *F.d.U. Norwegen* (Officer Commanding U-Boats, Norway) from January 1943, redesignated *F.d.U. Nordmeer* – Northern Waters – in September 1944.

8 Kptlt Heino Bohmann, commanding *U88*, which later picked up survivors from *Hermann Schoemann* (see below).

Date, time	Details of position, wind, weather, sea, light, visibility, moonlight, etc.	Incidents
0824		Outgoing W/T transmission 0752/739: *Qu. [AC] 5555 cruiser, course south, was stopped for 1½ hours. Blizzard, bad visibility. Teichert.* Contact lost until 0930.
0930		Am positioned ahead of cruiser along with Bohmann. Dramatic variations in visibility. Cruiser in Qu. [AC] 5559 zigzags strongly and disappears once again. Blizzard obstructs visibility until midday.
1200	Qu. AC 5591	Day's run: surface 194 nm, submerged 22 nm, overall 216 nm. Cruiser in sight again with one destroyer. Qu. [AC] 5559 lower right corner, estimated speed 2–3 knots. I request permission to attack despite the wretched periscope.
1342		Incoming W/T transmission 1322/755 from Admiral Commanding Northern Waters: *Teichert – first maintain contact for later attack by our destroyers.*
1350		A destroyer emerges from a snow squall at high speed, firing her guns.
1407		When range closes to 4,000 m we dive.
1417		Three depth charges dropped astern, according to *S-Gerät*.[9] Destroyer lingers for a long while. I withdraw.
1600	Qu. AC 5599	
1744		Surfaced. Single destroyer astern, range 4 nm. We monitor her for a long time on the hydrophones. She is stationed ahead of cruiser.
1823	Wind NE 5–6, sea 3, visibility 4–8 nm, variable	Outgoing W/T transmission 1802/772: *1407 forced to submerge by destroyer. Depth charges. Cruiser Qu. [AC] 5596, have contact with destroyer escort. Greatly varying visibility. Teichert.*
1940		Incoming W/T transmission 1612/766: *Teichert – 1.) Provide hourly contact and weather reports. 2.) Report immediately if cruiser's escort exceeds three destroyers. Admiral Commanding Northern Waters.* Since yesterday we have only observed two destroyers in vicinity of cruiser.[10]
2000	Qu. AC 5911	Am now providing hourly contact and weather reports. Cruiser is only intermittently discernible in varying visibility and snow showers. Long-wave transmitter has given up on us. Cruiser appears to be steering on her engines – unable to hold a straight course.
2300		She proceeds southward slowly at 3–5 nm. Cruiser temporarily lost.
2335		Dive to seek hydrophone contact.
2347		We surface. Bearing confirmed via hydrophones.
		Teichert
2.v		
0000	Qu. [AC] 5863	Incoming W/T transmission 2324/788 from Admiral Commanding Northern Waters: *Teichert – free to attack once enemy destroyers are engaged by our own, which should close cruiser at around 0600.*
0100		Cruiser once again in sight.
0200		Cruiser stopped in a beam sea, issuing steam. She is still stopped when I dive.
0400	Qu. AC 5866	Beacon signals sent through master transmitter[11] are not being picked up.
0500		Destroyer group intends to attack from the north. I am stationed to the south.
0548		I am free to attack. I close the cruiser in a blizzard.
0615		Dive as enemy destroyers appear. It is possible that I was seen – still some 6–7 nm from cruiser. This means that I will not be in a position to attack as desired by destroyer group until before 0800. We close at depth of 40 m.
0629		A gunnery duel begins on the surface. Constant salvoes of shells. Am frequently overrun by destroyers. Some of the hits are extremely loud. A hellish symphony.
0702		Major detonation heard.[12] Gunnery duel lasts until 0825.
0800	Qu. AC 5865	I begin by withdrawing somewhat.

9 The *S-Gerät* (*Sondergerät* or *Such-Gerät*) was an early active sonar device fitted to Type-VII U-boats and used to detect minefields or targets.

10 This signal and Teichert's reaction help to explain the confusion that contributed to the German withdrawal in the surface engagement that followed. With only Teichert's reports to go on *Admiral Nordmeer* (Admiral Hubert Schmundt) was confident that his destroyers would face only a weakened *Edinburgh* and two escorts. However, later that night – and unseen by *U456* – *Edinburgh*'s group was joined by the minesweepers *Gossamer*, *Harrier*, *Hussar* and *Niger*. Of marginal value in terms of firepower, the bolstered escort nonetheless unnerved the attackers.

11 The German original is *Steuersender*.

12 This equates with *Z25*'s torpedo hit on *Edinburgh*.

0823	Four depth charges very close by. Powerful repercussions in boat. No damage.
0824	One depth charge. We go deep to 160 m. Echo-sounding pursuit. Three destroyers.[13]
0837	Three depth charges. Well aimed, not deep enough.
0838	Two depth charges.
0848	Two depth charges.
0852	Suddenly we hear powerful noises. Creaking and breaking up then a noise just like that of a sinking ship nearby. Amazing! The cruiser!
0900	Apparently a U-boat hunter group above me. Two different echo-sounding devices – chirping and gravelly sounds.
	I withdraw, course 170°.
1120	Course set 140°.

13 British sources make no mention of any vessel being aware of or attacking a U-boat at this time. It seems that Teichert was in fact hearing depth charges from *Harrier*, dropped alongside *Edinburgh* in an attempt to sink her.

The sinking

Though it is clear from his log that Teichert had underestimated *Edinburgh*'s speed by three or four knots, the relatively close range combined with the length of the target allowed him to score two hits. The first struck abreast the bridge while the second caused such damage to the stern that 'the quarter deck had curled up enveloping the triple guns on the twin turrets, which were protruding through like knives through butter'. Neither affected *Edinburgh*'s ability to raise steam but her two starboard propellers had been wrecked and the rudder ripped away leaving her virtually unsteerable. Once the flooding was contained Capt. Faulkner had no option but to follow *Edinburgh*'s bows at his best speed in order to minimise the chance of further attack. Although HM destroyers *Foresight* and *Forester* added their strength to her escort at 1730 on the 30th (an hour after the attack), *Edinburgh* was in a dire predicament. If *Edinburgh* were to be saved she would have to be escorted back to Murmansk at very low speed while the consequent redistribution of ships weakened the escort for QP11. Worse, as the night wore on *Kuibyshev* and *Sokrushitel'ny* reported that they had to turn back for lack of fuel leaving *Edinburgh* with only *Foresight* and *Forester* for company. Though assisted steering had begun using *Foresight* as a drogue astern, this now ceased as it was considered essential that she and *Forester* be employed for screening purposes. However, with no effective means of controlling the ship against wind and weather Capt. Faulkner was obliged to tack back and forth as best he could. By evening on 1 May barely fifty miles had been covered and a 200-mile voyage separated Bonham-Carter's force from Murmansk. Spirits rose that night with the arrival from Murmansk of the Soviet tug *Rubin* and HM minesweepers *Gossamer*, *Harrier*, *Hussar* and *Niger*. *Rubin* was taken on ahead of *Edinburgh* with *Gossamer* acting as a drogue, Faulkner expressing confidence that the group could proceed at an adequate speed.

However, German surface vessels now began to take a hand in the matter. Thanks to a stream of contact reports from Teichert (see above), *Admiral Nordmeer* (Admiral Hubert Schmundt) was aware that the convoy escort had been reduced by the need to assist *Edinburgh* which was rightly understood to be making for the Kola Inlet. On the night of 30 April–1 May the heavy destroyers *Hermann Schoemann*, *Z24* and *Z25* (the former armed with 127-mm and the latter pair with 150-mm guns) sailed from Kirkenes under Kapitän zur See Alfred Schulze-Hinrichs with the ambitious goal of decimating QP11 before its escort could be reinforced and then destroying *Edinburgh* and her

consorts. They were to enjoy only partial success. At noon on the 1st the German force made contact with QP11 whose outgunned escort of HM destroyers *Bulldog*, *Amazon*, *Beagle* and *Beverley* (**83**) responded aggressively and in a number of separate engagements managed to prevent the Germans getting in among the convoy. On the evening of the 1st, their shell bins low and with only the Russian straggler *Tsiolkovsky* and damage to *Amazon* to show for their efforts, the Germans decided to shift their attention to *Edinburgh* and her escort. As Teichert, still shadowing in *U456*, relates in his log, battle was joined early on the morning of the 2nd.

The first shot seems to have been fired around 0600 by the minesweeper *Harrier* stationed on *Edinburgh*'s starboard quarter. Slipping her tows, *Edinburgh* immediately went on to her best speed of about eight knots which took her into a wide turn to port since she was almost impossible to control. As on the 1st the escort found itself outgunned by the Germans but immediately engaged them in mist and blizzard. Both *Foresight* and *Forester* were soon hit, the latter losing her CO Lt Cdr C. P. Huddart. *Edinburgh*, however, was in no condition to follow them into action. In the words of Rear-Admiral Bonham-Carter, she was 'in a sad state . . . stern gone, no director, no telephones, no R.D.F., no T[ransmitting]S[tation], local power on the turrets and consequently her fighting efficiency was considerably lowered'. Despite this *Edinburgh* managed to open fire with 'B' turret, the only one which could bear. With Capt. Faulkner directing the turret commander by word of mouth from the bridge, *Edinburgh*'s second salvo registered two hits on *Hermann Schoemann* which penetrated the engine rooms cutting all steam and electrical power and leaving her dead in the water. *Z24* and *Z25* responded with a torpedo attack against *Edinburgh*. Unable to take evasive action, she was hit by *Z25* at 0657 on exactly the opposite side to the first of *U456*'s salvo, the approaching tracks watched impotently by many of her ship's company. With the sea entering on either side and the ship in danger of breaking her back, Bonham-Carter ordered *Gossamer* alongside for the transfer of all wounded, passengers and non-essential personnel – a total of 440 men. Still the battle raged, with *Foresight* struck four times while making a torpedo attack on *Hermann Schoemann* in an effort to draw fire from *Forester*, and well-aimed salvoes from *Edinburgh*'s 'B' turret keeping *Z24* and *Z25* from lending assistance to their companion which was by now in a sinking condition. Listing seventeen degrees to starboard and her surviving turret unable to bear, *Edinburgh* was also reaching the end of the line and shortly before

Harrier takes off the last of *Edinburgh*'s men on the morning of 2 May, thirty-six hours after suffering the first of three hits and not long before she was scuttled with five tons of gold still on board. Note her wrecked stern, the quarterdeck peeled back like a sardine can. *IWM*

0800 Bonham-Carter gave Faulkner the order to abandon ship, the remaining 350 men being taken off by *Harrier*. However, *Edinburgh* was reluctant to give up the ghost and eventually had to be despatched by *Foresight*'s last remaining torpedo after 4-inch shells and a pattern of depth charges from *Harrier* had failed to settle the matter. And so it ended. '*Edinburgh*, a thoroughbred to the last, sank gracefully stern first in three minutes.'

Edinburgh's group was now ripe for annihilation by Kapt.z.S. Schulze-Hinrichs but the opportunity was passed up. Desperately low on ammunition and convinced that he was dealing with a force of destroyers, Schulze-Hinrichs turned for Kirkenes leaving around sixty of *Hermann Schoemann*'s men on a raft to be picked up by *U88*. Back in Kirkenes Kptlt Teichert received plaudits from Admiral Schmundt for his dogged tracking of *Edinburgh* in terrible conditions. He was also credited with her sinking as the Germans remained uncertain of the result of their destroyers' torpedo attacks on 2 May. From the Allied perspective a valuable unit had been lost along with a huge amount of gold (inaccessible once the bomb room was flooded after Teichert's attack on the 30th), but the events of the 2nd had put a somewhat different gloss on the matter. The failure of the German destroyers to convert their 'paper advantage' against either QP11 or *Edinburgh*'s group made their achievement in sinking her something of a Pyrrhic victory. That this owed much to the stark courage of those under Bonham-Carter's command was not lost on the onlookers. As the commander of the tug *Rubin* put it, 'Soviets seamens was witness of heroic battle English seamen with predominants powers of enemy'.

Fate of the crew

About fifteen of the fifty-nine fatalities suffered by *Edinburgh* were caused by *U456*'s attack on 30 April. The situation amidships, where the casualties were greatest, is recalled by J. A. P. Kenny, then a young coder:

At that moment [1613], without warning, there was a terrific flash and two

tremendous bangs that almost merged into one and the lights went out. Time seemed to stand still – like a film stopped suddenly – and in the dim light coming from the deck house I saw through the thick smoke a huge, wide crack in the midships bulkhead, which ran from the roof to the floor. For what seemed an age we [sat still] at the table, then the shockwave passed and we were galvanized into action running around the mess deck waking people up – incredibly a large number had slept through the explosion, presumably through exhaustion. One of the torpedoes had hit amidships on the starboard side, one steel plate away from our mess deck – one second away from disaster for us – and it made a hole large enough for a motor coach to pass through. The mess deck next to us which had taken the full force of the explosion was a scene of absolute carnage, many were killed outright, and perhaps they were fortunate for most of the rest fell into the oil tanks below and had lingering deaths.

Having surveyed the damage and flooding, *Edinburgh*'s Executive Officer Cdr J. Jefferis was obliged to seal off the damaged areas so condemning a number of men to death. Among the episodes that haunted survivors was that of eighteen-year-old OD Neville Holt manning the telephone exchange on the platform deck, cut off by flooded compartments but able to communicate with the bridge via voice pipe. Though a number of men including Capt. Faulkner did their best to keep his spirits up there was no way of reaching him and contact gradually ceased as his oxygen ran out over the next two days. Beyond the ongoing battle to bring the ship into harbour in the teeth of German resistance, the main concern of *Edinburgh*'s crew was to keep warm and awake in a ship deprived of heating in temperatures ranging from –5 to –10°C (23–14°F). Draughts of hot soup and cocoa were made available from the Warrant Officers' bathroom and a constant stream of cigarettes and chocolate circulated from the ship's stores.

Over forty lives were claimed by the second torpedo including that of Chief Petty Officer Cook Thomas Gray who 'with limited facilities had fed the wounded and us for the past few days, was last seen being blown out through the side of the ship'. Despite tense moments as thirty stretcher cases from Murmansk were cross-decked to *Gossamer* and *Harrier*, the evacuation of nearly 800 men without loss was a remarkable achievement in the circumstances. The survivors were landed at Polyarnoe in the early hours of 3 May before being dispersed there and to Vaenga and hospitals in Murmansk. Many, however, were destined never to see Britain again, killed in HMS *Trinidad* (lost to air attack on 14 May), HMS *Niger* (lost on a mine on 5 July) and HMS *Marne* (damaged by gunfire from the minelayer *Ulm* on 25 August). The additional two fatalities noted above were both foreigners, one of them Andrzej Powierża, First Secretary at the Polish Embassy in Moscow, who was returning to Britain to join the RAF.

Though the wreck of the *Edinburgh* was declared a war grave, the British government temporarily lifted this decree to permit salvage operations following negotiations with the Soviets, and two dives carried out in 1981 and 1986 recovered all but five of the 465 ingots from a depth of 800 feet. The £45 million proceeds were divided between the salvors (Jessop Marine) and the British and Soviet governments.

U456 and Max-Martin Teichert

Built by Deutsche Werke at Kiel and commissioned in September 1941, *U456* spent her career under Oblt.z.S. (Kptlt from 1 December 1941) Max-Martin Teichert. The majority of her patrols were in northern waters, the sinking of *Edinburgh* being easily her greatest success.

Teichert after his promotion to Kapitänleutnant in December 1941. *DUBMA*

Her other sinking in these latitudes was the tanker SS *Honomu* from the ill-fated PQ17 in early July 1942, with HM minesweeping whaler *Sulla* possibly accounted for in March (**G26**). *U456*'s transfer to the Atlantic in January 1943 doubled her tonnage haul, the patrol of January–February 1943 yielding three merchantmen and a probable hit on HM sloop *Londonderry*. Her next patrol would be her last. Part of the eleven-strong *Drossel* group operating north-west of Cape Finisterre, on 12 May *U456* was attacked by an RAF Liberator shortly after sinking the SS *Fort Concord*. Diving to escape further attack from both ships and aircraft, *U456* was never heard from again. Teichert was awarded a posthumous Knight's Cross in December 1943.

Sources

Admiralty, *Loss of HMS* Edinburgh *through Torpedo Attack* (TNA, ADM 1/12275)

—, *Losses of H.M. Ships to Mines and Submarine Attack, 1942–1945* (TNA, ADM 199/165)

—, *Battle Summary Nr. 22: Arctic Convoys, 1941–1944* (TNA, ADM 234/369)

Kenny, John A. P., *Survival in a Savage Sea* (typescript, IWM, 92/27/1)

Newman, L. D., *Sinking of HMS* Edinburgh (typescript, IWM, P431)

Adrian, Kurt, *Kapitänleutnant Max-Martin Teichert: Mit* U 456 *im Nordmeer und Atlantik. Kreuzer* Edinburgh *Torpediert* (Würzburg: Flechsig Verlag, 2008)

Arthur, Max, ed., *The Navy: 1939 to the Present Day* (London: Hodder & Stoughton, 1997)

Bekker, Cajus, *Hitler's Naval War* (London: Macdonald, 1974)

Higgins, Alan, 'The Sinking of HMS *Edinburgh*: A First Hand Account' in *The Arctic Lookout* no. 37 (2000), pp. 33–7

Jessop, Keith, *Goldfinder: The True Story of One Man's Discovery of the Ocean's Richest Secrets* (London: Simon & Schuster, 1998)

Lanitzki, Günter, *Kreuzer* Edinburgh: *Goldtresor im Nordmeer* (Herford: Koehlers Verlag, 1991)

Moore, David, 'The Loss of HMS *Edinburgh*' in *Warship World* 3, no. 8 (Autumn 1990), pp. 19–20

Napier, J., 'HMS *Edinburgh*/Polyarnoe/Vaenga' in *The Arctic Lookout* no. 32 (1998), pp. 39–40

Pearce, Frank, *Last Call for HMS* Edinburgh: *A Story of the Russian Convoys* (London: Collins, 1982)

Penrose, Barrie, *Stalin's Gold: The Story of HMS* Edinburgh *and Its Treasure* (London: Granada, 1982)

Raven, Alan, and John Roberts, *British Cruisers of World War Two* (London: Arms and Armour Press, 1980)

—, *Town Class Cruisers* [Ensign, no. 5] (London: Bivouac Books, 1975); reprinted as *Man o'War*, no. 5 (London: Arms and Armour Press, 1980)

Ruegg, Bob, and Arnold Hague, *Convoys to Russia, 1941–1945* (Kendal, Cumbria: World Ship Society, 1992)

Sparksman, Norman, *Jottings of a Young Sailor* (Ely, Cambs.: Melrose Books, 2007)

Thwaite, J. N., *A Signalman in HMS* Edinburgh: *The Story of the 'Gold Ship'* (Wantage, Oxon.: privately, 1995)

Watton, Ross, *The Cruiser HMS* Belfast [Anatomy of the Ship] (London: Conway, 1985)

Career history of HMS *Edinburgh*:
http://www.naval-history.net/xGM-Chrono-06CL-Edinburgh.htm

Website devoted to HMS *Edinburgh*:
http://www.hmsedinburgh.co.uk/old/hmsedinburgh.htm

---

59   USS *CYTHERA* (ex SY *AGAWA*)

Lt Cdr T. W. Rudderow, USNR†

Sunk by *U402* (Type VIIC), Kptlt Siegfried Freiherr von Forstner, 2 May 1942

North Atlantic, 135 nm ESE of Cape Fear, North Carolina (USA)

Theatre	North Atlantic (Map 1)	*Deadweight*	1,000 tons
Coordinates	33° 17' N, 75° 24' W	*Gross tons*	602
Kriegsmarine code	Quadrat DC 1591	*Dimensions*	214.75' × 27.5' × 12'
U-boat timekeeping differential	+6 hours	*Maximum speed*	12 knots
Fatalities 68	*Survivors* 2	*Armament*	2 × 3"; 4 × .5" AA

Career

The USS *Cythera* began life as the steam yacht *Agawa* laid down for the New York oil baron William L. Harkness by Ramage & Ferguson of Leith, Scotland, launched on 20 September 1906 and completed in 1907, making her comfortably the oldest and the most elegant vessel treated in this volume. With America's entry into the First World War in April 1917 *Agawa* exchanged the agreeable existence of a luxury yacht for that of a naval patrol vessel when the Harkness family leased

Cythera seen in March 1942, shortly after commissioning as a patrol yacht. Within two months she was no more. *US Navy*

her to the US government. Refitted, she was commissioned as the USS *Cythera* (SP-575) on 20 October 1917 and on 1 November sailed from Newport, Rhode Island for Gibraltar having been allocated to the Patrol Force, Atlantic Fleet. Initially charged with escorting and towing US submarine chasers to European waters, *Cythera* was eventually assigned to escort and patrol duty in the Mediterranean based on Gibraltar. Here she was credited with the rescue of survivors from two steamers, the *Ariel* on 27 May 1918 and the *Uganda* on 3 October, both of which had fallen victim to German U-boats. The war over, *Cythera* returned to New York on 5 February 1919 to be decommissioned on 17 March, being returned to her owners two days later. However, *Cythera*'s naval career was not over and on 31 December 1941 she was purchased from the Harkness family for conversion to a patrol vessel (PY-26). This was completed at Philadelphia Navy Yard on 28 February 1942, the ship commissioning on 3 March. On 1 May she quit Norfolk with orders to join the Pacific Fleet at Pearl Harbor. Laying a course for the Panama Canal, within hours she and the truncated remains of her shapely bowsprit were at the bottom of the Atlantic.

Background of the attack

On 26 March 1942 Kptlt Siegfried Freiherr (Baron) von Forstner's *U402* sailed from St-Nazaire for the first of two patrols as part of Operation PAUKENSCHLAG ('drumroll'), the German offensive against merchant shipping off the eastern seaboard of the United States. On 13 April she sank the SS *Empire Progress* in mid-Atlantic but the next two weeks brought no further success and *U402* was late in taking up her assigned position off Cape Hatteras thanks to a misread signal from B.d.U. On the 27th, his diesel supply dwindling, von Forstner was informed that *U402* would be refuelled at sea along with *U201* (Kptlt Adalbert Schnee; see **33**) and *U572* (Kptlt Heinz Hirzsacker) in early May. Spirits rose when von Forstner added SS *Ashkhabad* to his tally on 30 April but next day B.d.U. cancelled the refuelling, a decision which left *U402* with diesel for only another day's hunting off North Carolina before turning for home. It was during these last hours in her assigned area that *U402* came across the patrol yacht *Cythera* steaming south for the Panama Canal and von Forstner earned his first and only warship pennant.

War Diary of *U402*, patrol of 26 March–20 May 1942: PG 30456, NHB, reel 1,104, pp. 614–5

Date, time	Details of position, wind, weather, sea, light, visibility, moonlight, etc.	Incidents
2.v		
0400	Qu. DC 1537	
0425	Qu. DC 1537	Shadow in sight at 320° true, perhaps 4 nm off. We track her course and speed before hauling ahead. A warship's silhouette but no specific detail discernible. General course of enemy 180°, speed 13 knots, zigzagging.[1]
0617		We dive to carry out a submerged attack but enemy then fails to appear in the main periscope for a long time. We improve our firing position by going on to utmost speed, enemy now appearing smaller than we first thought.
0641	Qu. DC 1591, wind W 2,	A spread of three fired from Tubes I, II and IV, depth 2 m, torpedo speed 30 knots, enemy speed 14

---

1 *Cythera*'s recorded best speed was only 12 knots.

	sea 1–2, good visibility, moonlit	knots, inclination 98°, bows right, range 2,000 m.[1]
		A detonation after 2 min. 9 sec. = 1,850 m, causing a high black explosion column amidships followed shortly after by a number of smaller explosions, presumably depth charges.
		The bow briefly rears up high out of the water but within a minute of the torpedo hit – or by the time the smoke has cleared – there's nothing more to be seen of her.
0644	Qu. DC 1591	We surface and close the scene of the sinking which is identifiable by a substantial slick of fuel oil.
0648		During our search for clues as to the identity of the vessel we come across a float containing two men whom we haul on board. The chances of there being many more survivors would appear slight indeed.
		Statements from the prisoners reveal the following: Patrol Yacht (*Patrouillenjacht*)[2] Py-26 [*sic*] *Cythera* of 850 tons, length 73 m (241 ft), crew 5 officers and 66 men, 2 guns, anti-aircraft armament, 60 depth charges with settings up to 150 ft (45.72 m), just out of Norfolk and bound for the Panama Canal.[3]
0800	Qu. DC 1592	Unfortunately I must now sail for home given the diesel situation. Running on just one engine, 220 revolutions.
		Outgoing W/T transmission regarding our return journey: *Have just sunk patrol yacht* Cythera *of 850 tons in Mar. Qu. Dora Caesar 1591.[4] Course 180°, speed 13 knots,[1] two prisoners taken on board, homeward bound due to fuel situation (44 cbm), 2 + 1 eels,[5] continual high-pressure weather. Request* Pallice.[6] *U402.*
1200	Qu. DC 1646, wind W 2, sea 2, cloud 2	Day's run: 183.4 nm on the surface, 3.2 nm submerged.

2 This parenthetic addition in German follows the original in English.
3 Compare these specifications with those provided above, though that for length may include *Cythera*'s bowsprit which had by now been largely removed. This apart, 73 metres is in fact only 239 feet (not 241), *Cythera* seems to have carried only 50 depth charges, and her complement was 70 officers and men.
4 *Cythera* was in fact of 602 tons. 'Dora' and 'Caesar' represent the letters 'D' and 'C' in the German phonetic alphabet.
5 Translates as two G7e and one G7a torpedoes remaining. 'Eels' (German = *Aale*) was U-boat slang for torpedoes.
6 La Pallice, the deepwater port of La Rochelle, was the most southerly of the frontline U-boat bases on the French Atlantic coast, besides which von Forstner may have wished to shape a course along the Spanish coast to avoid the attentions of Allied aircraft over the Bay of Biscay. Bordeaux was further south, but lay sixty miles up the Garonne and was used mainly for the specialised Type-VIIF, IXD, XB and XIV boats. *U402*'s urgent fuel situation was presumably von Forstner's overriding consideration in making this request, though it was not granted and he put in at St-Nazaire on the 20th.

The sinking

Allied accounts of what befell the USS *Cythera* in the early hours of 2 May 1942 are limited to statements made by Seaman 1/c James M. Brown III as a prisoner-of-war in January 1943 and upon his return to the United States in July 1945. Here he recalls the moments before the attack:

At approximately 0045, 2 May 1942, the *Cythera* was struck by a torpedo. Just previous to that time I was standing watch as a trainer on the forward gun mount. I was looking out to starboard and saw two flashes of white on the water. The full moon was off the port quarter at that time. It was a very clear night and the sea was calm. As soon as I saw the flashes, I gave the warning to the man on the telephone just aft of the gun mount. Immediately after giving the warning, I saw a torpedo wake passing under the bow. I then saw another wake directly approaching the ship. A couple of seconds later the ship was struck about amidships and there was a terrific explosion.

Then *Cythera*'s end:

I was thrown in the air and landed on my knees on the gun mount. I couldn't see the stern but in my opinion the ship broke in two immediately, just aft of the bridge. The forward part of the ship started to sink and heel over to port. The gun was useless and I found it impossible to get to the point of damage. I heard a sound which I took to be machine gun fire, and crouched behind the solid railing (about 2½ feet high) on the deck. At this time I saw the legs of two men going over the side near me. Very shortly thereafter, I heard two muffled explosions. I then went over the side myself. As soon as I broke water, two large waves swept over me. After the waves

passed, I looked around and saw the last part of the ship, the bow-sprit, sink from sight.

As Brown put it when interviewed in Germany in January 1943, 'The ship sunk [*sic*] in about one minute, having broken in half,' a description borne out by von Forstner's observations in the log.

Despite the capture of enemy personnel – the first in US waters – Dönitz was unimpressed by *U402*'s patrol, berating von Forstner for his misinterpretation of 'perfectly clear' instructions that had seen him arrive late in what were at the time 'promisingly congested' shipping lanes off Cape Hatteras. He concluded his report by observing that 'this patrol had more to offer'.

Fate of the crew

US and German sources agree that Brown was one of only two men to survive the sinking of the *Cythera*. Within a minute or so of abandoning ship he spotted Pharmacist's Mate 1/c Charles H. Carter, a survivor of the battleship *Oklahoma* at Pearl Harbor, sitting in a raft some fifty feet off. Swimming over to him with the aid of a life ring he found en route, Brown was helped partially into the raft by Carter whereupon they scoured the vicinity for signs of other survivors. They found none, and only a small circle of flotsam. Discussing the matter with Carter, who had been on the flying bridge at the time of the attack, they concluded that 'the only reason we survived was that we were on parts of the ship last to submerge, and that all other personnel were in the water at the time of the two explosions, caused, we believed, by depth charges from our ship'. Then came rescue from the least-expected quarter:

The crew of *U402* on her commissioning day, Danzig, 21 May 1941.
Von Forstner front centre. *DUBMA*

After a couple of minutes, we heard the submarine surface. We saw it slowly circle around toward us. We attempted to hide in the water but the moon gave away our position and the submarine closed and picked us up. While on the conning tower, Carter and I again looked around for other survivors before we were taken below. The German submarine personnel later told us that they had seen no other survivors or bodies.

It is unlikely that von Forstner would have performed this act of rescue had he not been on the point of turning for France with all but three of his torpedoes expended. Nonetheless, once on board the difference between the propagated image of the enemy and the reality became all too apparent. To the consternation of both commander and crew, a bewildered Brown asked von Forstner why they hadn't been machine-gunned in the water. In lieu of bullets von Forstner not only offered Brown his own sweater but saw to it that both men were given a generous ration of brandy. This set the tone for the next few weeks, with the 'guests' kept well supplied with cigarettes and doses of fresh air on deck between meals with their captors. As von Forstner related in a letter to his wife, 'We should really have kept them locked up and all that, but a U-boat is not spacious as you know and they were nice chaps and friendly – they joined us in our meals, and we brought them home in our own way, and nobody the worse for it.' So cordial were relations, indeed, that Brown and Carter invited their captors to visit them in the United States after the war. Less agreeable was the reception at St-Nazaire on 20 May, where the pair began four years' incarceration as prisoners-of-war, initially in the Marlagmilag Nord camp near Bremen. They were released in May 1945.

In America, meanwhile, the US Navy issued dispatches on 2 June 1942 advising next-of-kin that the crew of the *Cythera* had been classified as missing. It was not until an article appeared some weeks later in the *Deutsche Zeitung in den Niederlanden* announcing that two sailors had been rescued off the United States from a 'Coast Guard cruiser formerly luxury yacht owned by Mr. Harkness' that any news was received of the crew, though letters home from Brown and Carter soon confirmed that they alone had survived the episode. However, the Navy's inability to provide detailed information put relatives through agonies of uncertainty until fuller accounts of the sinking became

available, first following approaches to the International Committee of the Red Cross and the Swiss legation in Berlin in late 1942 and then with the repatriation of Brown and Carter in July 1945. Meanwhile, the sacrifice of *Cythera*'s commanding officer Lt Cdr Rudderow and Ensign Robert E. Brister USNR was commemorated in the naming of two destroyer escorts in 1943, with the name of their erstwhile ship given to another requisitioned yacht, the former *Abril* (PY-31), in October 1942.

U402 and Siegfried Freiherr von Forstner

Built by Danziger Werft at Danzig (Gdansk) and commissioned in May 1941, *U402* undertook a total of eight war patrols in the Atlantic, all under Kptlt (Korvkpt. from April 1943) Siegfried Freiherr (Baron) von Forstner whose wartime career included six months in the light cruiser *Nürnberg* as well as a frontline patrol in Kretschmer's *U99* (see **19** and **20**) as a U-boat commander-in-training. Although von Forstner's record as commander of *U402* up to and including the patrols of Operation PAUKENSCHLAG was unexceptional, his reputation soared on the back of two impressive convoy battles in November 1942 (SC107) and January 1943 (SC118) in which ten merchantmen were sunk and two more damaged. This earned him the Knight's Cross in April 1943, during which month he added two steamers from SC129 to his tally. However, von Forstner's successes were no more than bright glimmers in the blackest period yet for the *U-Boot-Waffe* in the Battle of the Atlantic, Dönitz being compelled to withdraw the U-boats in June until the new T5 *Zaunkönig* acoustic homing torpedo was ready for service. In September 1943 *U402* sailed from La Pallice charged with renewing the assault on the convoy lanes as part of the *Leuthen* group, though no success was achieved either with this or with the subsequent *Rossbach* pack. Harried by aircraft for much of the six weeks she was at sea, *U402* was finally brought to account on 13 October by an Avenger and a Wildcat from the escort carrier USS *Card* in mid-Atlantic. The former waited for *U402* to dive before releasing a Fido acoustic homing torpedo which fulfilled its purpose. There were no survivors.

Sources

Navy Department, Navy Casualty Case Files, USS *Cythera* (NA, RG 24, Box 20, 470/55/03/05)

DANFS, II, p. 227; also on: http://www.history.navy.mil/danfs/c16/cythera-i.htm

Gannon, Michael, *Operation Drumbeat: The Dramatic True Story of Germany's First U-Boat Attacks along the American Coast in World War II* (New York: Harper & Row, 1990)

Sables, Robert P., 'The Armed Yachts of World War II' in *Sea Classics* 34 (December 2000), pp. 34–9 and 60

Waters, Capt. John M., Jr, *Bloody Winter* (2nd edn, Annapolis, Md.: Naval Institute Press, 1984)

McCarthy, Mike, 'USS *Cythera* (PY 26)':
  http://uboat.net/allies/merchants/ship.html?shipID=1586

Sables, Robert P., ' "Overdue Atlantic": USS *Cythera* (PY 26)':
  http://www.navsource.org/archives/12/170575s.htm

Webpage devoted to the USS *Cythera*:
  http://www.navsource.org/archives/12/170575.ht

60   USS *GANNET*

Lt Cdr Francis E. Nuessle, USN
Sunk by *U653* (Type VIIC), Kptlt Gerhard Feiler, 7 June 1942
North Atlantic, 485 nm E of Cape Hatteras, North Carolina (USA)

Gannet decked with flags, possibly while serving as tender to one of a series of aerial survey expeditions to Alaska and the Aleutians between 1926 and 1935. Her loss to *U653* in June 1942 put a strain on Anglo-American relations in the North Atlantic. *Bruce Taylor collection*

Theatre	North Atlantic (Map 1)	*Displacement*	950 tons
Coordinates	35° 50' N, 65° 38' W	*Dimensions*	187.75' × 35.5' × 9.75'
Kriegsmarine code	Quadrat CB 7975	*Maximum speed*	14 knots
U-boat timekeeping differential	+2 hours	*Armament*	2 × 3"; 4 × 20 mm AA
Fatalities 16 *Survivors* 61			

Career

The USS *Gannet* originated as one of the forty-nine Lapwing-class minesweepers authorised by Congress in October 1917 to clear German mines from the approaches to ports along the eastern seaboard of the United States. The resulting vessels, versatile and well found, were also among the last in the US Navy to be fitted with a sailing rig. *Gannet* was laid down by Todd Shipyard Corp. of New York in October 1918, launched in March 1919 and commissioned at New York Navy Yard on 10 July that year under the designation Minesweeper No. 41. Completed too late to fulfil her intended role, *Gannet* instead began her career assigned to the Pacific Fleet, departing New York on 11 August 1919 for her long-term base at San Diego, which she reached on 2 November after shaking down off Guantanamo Bay, Cuba. Given the hull number AM-41, *Gannet* was assigned successively to the Pacific Fleet's Fleet Train, the Aircraft Squadron, Battle Fleet, and later to Base Force, US Fleet. Her service was largely that of tender to aircraft squadrons and related towing, transport and passenger duties along the West Coast and during manoeuvres off Hawaii, Panama and in the Caribbean. The summer months of 1926, 1929 and 1932–5 were spent as tender to aerial survey expeditions in Alaska and the Aleutians. Already designated a minesweeper for duty with aircraft in April 1931, on 22 January 1936 *Gannet* was reclassified a small seaplane tender and assigned the hull number AVP-8. In August 1937 her long sojourn at San Diego ended when she was assigned as tender

for aircraft squadrons of the Scouting Force at the US naval base at Coco Solo on the Caribbean coast of the Panama Canal Zone. Here she remained until ordered to Norfolk, Virginia in June 1939 as tender to Patrol Wing 5, Aircraft Scouting Force based at Key West, Bermuda, St Lucia and Trinidad. In September 1941 she was ordered to establish an advance seaplane base at Kungnait Bay, Greenland, the work carried out in October. *Gannet* was then assigned to Hamilton, Bermuda and it was here that the Japanese attack on Pearl Harbor found her tending the aircraft charged with patrolling local waters and covering the approaches to that base. By January 1942 she was serving not only as tender to the Martin Mariner patrol bombers of Patrol Squadron 74 (VP-74) but also as communications centre for all local air operations.

Background of the attack

On 1 June 1942 the freighter SS *Westmoreland* was torpedoed by *U566* (Kptlt Dietrich Borchert; see **85**) while steaming unaccompanied 250 miles north-east of Bermuda. Before *U566* finished her off with gunfire *Westmoreland* was able to transmit a distress signal which resulted in an air search being instigated from Bermuda lasting several days. On the 2nd USS *Gannet* was ordered by Rear Admiral Jules James, Commandant of the US Naval Operating Base, Bermuda, to rendezvous five miles east of the Mount Hill Light with HMS *Sumar* before proceeding north to join the search. Early the following morning *Gannet*'s commanding officer, Lt Cdr Francis E. Nuessle, was surprised to discover that *Sumar* (Lt G. E. Kernohan RCNVR) was not a corvette as anticipated but a converted yacht capable of no better than ten knots. Moreover, not only had the pair no common signal books and *Gannet* no sonar apparatus, but *Sumar* was in the extraordinary position of having neither radio nor accurate compass. The difficulties occasioned by this situation are recorded by Lt Cdr Nuessle:

> It was found that due to a defective gyro *Sumar* had difficulty in maintaining a base course, deviating as much as 10° to either side. Due to the nature of her machinery it was impossible to maintain position on *Gannet*. The *Gannet* therefore kept station on *Sumar*, and the interval between the ships was closed to 500 yards. Since the two vessels possessed no common zig-zag plan, since the erratic steering of *Sumar* provided the same effect to a moderate degree, and since the lack of an accurate compass would endanger *Gannet* losing contact during dark if more elaborate manoeuvres were employed, no zig-zag plan was ordered.

Lights were rigged on *Sumar*'s stern and *Gannet*'s bow to ensure that contact would not be lost during the hours of darkness. Despite an intensive search with the assistance of aircraft from Bermuda, no survivors from *Westmoreland* were found and at 1300 on 6 June *Gannet* and *Sumar* were ordered to return to Bermuda. By this time, however, they were being shadowed by Kptlt Gerhard Feiler's *U653*. The extract from Feiler's war diary which follows shows how *U653* tracked them through that afternoon and into the small hours of the 7th before launching a pair of torpedoes against each ship at 0420 German time (0220 Allied time). All missed but neither these nor *U653* herself were picked up on *Sumar*'s hydrophones or for that matter by her Asdic equipment, which was by now inoperable. Together this afforded Feiler the opportunity of launching two more torpedoes shortly before dawn.

War Diary of *U653*, patrol of 25 April–6 July 1942: PG 30683, NHB, reel 1,133, pp. 787–9

Date, time	Details of position, wind, weather, sea, light, visibility, moonlight, etc.	Incidents
6.vi		
1200	Qu. CB 4884	Day's run: 153 nm surfaced, 8 nm submerged. Total 161 nm.
1222	Qu. CB 4884, wind NW 5, sea 4–5, swell, cloud 6/10 cumulus, visibility 6–8 nm, 1,014 mb, rising	At bearing 230° true we sight a vessel (navy tender) of around 3,000 tons with a strikingly high and sturdy mainmast.[1] Range 7 nm, steering northerly course, speed 6 knots. She has a large escort on her port bow and to starboard a white-painted destroyer.[2] I haul ahead. The destroyer keeps forcing me off to the east. By 1420 I have been forced so far east that the tender is no longer in sight.[3] We then alter course to search for the enemy, assuming course of 0° and 300°.
1500	Qu. CB 4873	Tender in sight at bearing 234° true. She has now reversed course and is steering 180°, 11 knots. The escort is still ahead of her but for now there is no sign of the destroyer. I initially station myself on her beam so as not to end up astern of her if the group alters course through 180° once more.[4]
1600	Qu. CB 4872, wind NW 4–3 [*sic*], sea 3, swell subsiding, 6/10 overcast	
1800		Group now steering 170°.
2000	Qu. CB 7258, visibility 8–9 nm	
2216	Qu. CB 7526	As we are carrying out advance manoeuvre we sight a steamer at bearing 110° true, inclination 0°, course 280°. I am now positioned exactly between this steamer to the east and the group to the west.
2219		We dive in order to carry out an initial attack on the steamer steering straight towards us. Just as I am preparing to fire I recognise the neutrality markings – she is the Portuguese steamer *Lobito*.[5]
2400	Qu. CB 7539	Our own engine noises are so loud that we can't pick up the steamer in the hydrophones even at a range of 1,000 m. The forward hydroplane is making a particularly loud grating noise which lubrication does nothing to ease.
		Feiler
7.vi	400 nm east of Cape Hatteras	
0011		We surface and resume pursuit of our group.
0113	Qu. CB 7569	Group once again in sight at bearing 185° true. I haul ahead. Speed is 11 knots, course 170°.
0400	Qu. CB 7914	
0405		As we are turning to fire the group disappears in a layer of mist so I move ahead of it. I then approach

---

1   Though Feiler correctly identifies the type, *Gannet* was actually of 950 tons.

2   The 'large escort' apparently corresponds to the armed yacht HMS *Sumar*. Only two ships were present so Feiler's reference to a 'white-painted destroyer' is mistaken; his entry of 1500 acknowledges her absence.

3   These observations provide some indication of how erratic was *Sumar*'s steering.

4   Understandable albeit unnecessary caution since the 180-degree course alteration carried out by *Gannet* and *Sumar* was purely in response to a signal from Bermuda ordering them to abandon their search.

5   SS *Lobito* of the Companhia Colonial de Navegação, 2,720 GRT.

from the west. When I get closer the escort seems to be almost as large as the tender; similar to the dispatch vessel *Grille*, but flatter with a shorter fo'c's'le, a somewhat more raked mast and a funnel abaft the bridge.[6]

The tender has a raked stem, a cruiser stern, foremast and a rather slender funnel abaft the bridge which abuts the midships superstructure. Then on the quarterdeck the tall and notably sturdy mainmast.

The escort vessel is proceeding some 600 m ahead of the tender and is also stationed 400 m further east. I decide to fire a double salvo at each vessel.

0420	Qu. CB 7836, lower right, wind N 1, sea 0, light swell, visibility 1.5 nm, rather murky	04^{H}20^{M}00^S first torpedo fired at escort: G7e, inclination 70°, enemy speed 12.5 knots, estimated range 1,000 m, depth 3 m, right-angled shot.

04^{H}20^{M}08^S second torpedo fired at escort: G7e, shot coordinates as above.

04^{H}20^{M}12^S third torpedo fired at tender: G7e, shot coordinates as above, inclination 57°.

04^{H}20^{M}19^S fourth torpedo fired at tender: G7e, shot coordinates as above.

All miss.[7] My assumption is that all torpedoes have underrun their targets, presumably as the draught of the vessels is probably no greater than 3 m.[8] After 100 sec. we hear a dull detonation in the boat but nothing is seen by anyone on the bridge. So much for our first attack after all this time – four misses! A bitter disappointment. I have the torpedo tubes reloaded, haul ahead and carry out another attack. This time the visibility is such that I can get a little nearer. The two vessels are exchanging morse signals.

0742	Qu. CB 7975, wind N 1, sea 0, light swell, 8/10 overcast, visibility 2,000– 3,000 m, greatly varying degrees of mist	07^{H}42^{M}00^S first torpedo fired at escort: G7e, inclination 85°, enemy speed 12 knots, estimated range 800 m, depth 2 m, right-angled shot. After lookout then reports that escort is altering course towards us.

07^{H}42^{M}20^S second torpedo fired at tender: G7e, shot coordinates as above, inclination 51°. 58 sec. after our first shot a hit on the tender. Running time of torpedo 38 sec. = range of 670 m. Tender blows up immediately, presumably the magazine. Once the explosion cloud has cleared we can see only small pieces of sinking wreckage, debris from the blast is spread far and wide.

65 sec. after the first shot = range of 940 m, a second torpedo detonation is heard both on the bridge and below. (I myself heard this coming from the direction of the escort and also saw some spray over there.) As I didn't see the typical high column of water I assume that the escort was not hit, and that the report and spray were caused by falling pieces of wreckage from the tender.[9] My impression is that the escort has turned towards me as her silhouette has become narrower and clearer. I alter course and withdraw towards the dark horizon (course 300°). The escort is soon lost from sight. She keeps firing emergency signals for about 10 min.[10]

0800	Qu. CB 7948
1200	Qu. CB 7955

Day's run: 261 nm surfaced, 5 nm submerged. Overall 266 nm.

---

6 Completed in 1935 and displacing 2,560 tons, *Grille* was the state yacht of the German government. She was converted to an auxiliary minelayer on the outbreak of war before becoming headquarters ship of *F.d.U. Norwegen* (Officer Commanding U-Boats, Norway) at Narvik from 1942.

7 Neither *Gannet* nor *Sumar* were aware that they had been attacked.

8 *Gannet*'s standard draught was approximately 3 metres (9' 10"), *Sumar*'s presumably less.

9 Feiler is correct.

10 The 'emergency signals' (in this case flares shot by a Very pistol) were fired not by 'the escort' (*Sumar*) but by *Gannet*'s survivors in a desperate effort to attract the former, five before she sank and four from the rafts thereafter.

The sinking

U653's torpedo struck *Gannet* at 0550 Allied time on the starboard side amidships just below the waterline, destroying both boilers and rupturing the forward and after fireroom bulkheads. All machinery and electric power cut out immediately and the engine room, both firerooms and several of the forward compartments began to flood as the ship took on an immediate list of fifteen degrees to starboard. Boatswain J. D. Jeffords (Officer of the Deck from midnight onwards) reported the general situation to Lt Cdr Nuessle when the latter appeared on the bridge a minute or so later and received permission to go below and assess the condition of the ship. His findings over the next two minutes left no cause for optimism: 'the forward bulkhead [of the engine room] was on the point of collapse, it was all bulged

out into the engine room, some of the pumps had been blown down, and great torrents of water were pouring in from the fireroom'. In no doubt that *Gannet* was on the point of sinking, Jeffords stated as much to Nuessle who immediately gave the order to abandon ship. The crew were still getting clear of the wreck when *Gannet* 'rolled steadily to her beam, down slightly by the bow' before sinking bow first, her propeller high out of the water. Just four minutes had elapsed since she was hit.

From the Allied perspective the sinking was notable above all for the disappearance from the scene of HMS *Sumar*, this despite the firing of nine emergency flares for her benefit both before the sinking and from the rafts afterwards. These were noted in *U653* but elicited no response from *Sumar*, which was greeted on her return to Bermuda later that day with an immediate investigation by both British and

American authorities. An enquiry into the event found that her commanding officer, Lt G. E. Kernohan, 'definitely made up his mind that the explosion heard on board his ship was that of a gun being fired', based on his crew obtaining no aural or hydrophone detection of an explosion. Instead, Kernohan 'mistook the pyrotechnics for change of course signals and mistook the torpedo explosion for gunfire'.

Subsequent correspondence between the Commander-in-Chief of the Royal Navy's America and West Indies Command, Admiral Sir Charles Kennedy-Purvis, and the Commandant of the US Naval Operating Base in Bermuda, Rear Admiral Jules James, makes it clear that the event was a source of acute embarrassment to the British, Kennedy-Purvis informing his US counterpart that Kernohan would be 'returning to Canada with a recommendation that he is considered unsuitable to command any of His Majesty's ships'. Indeed, a court-martial was avoided only because *Gannet*'s senior officers – required witnesses in any such process – had been ordered back to the United States. As Rear Admiral James pointed out, only this and Kernohan's departure for Canada saved all concerned from the 'extreme embarrassment of having to have officers and men of the US Navy appear as witnesses for the prosecution of so serious a charge against an officer in the British naval service'. But the dispute rumbled on, revealing the underlying tensions between the two navies on this station above and beyond the sinking of the *Gannet*. A follow-up letter by James observed that 'it would be appreciated if it could be arranged as far as possible for all anti-submarine vessels at Bermuda, or which in the future may be assigned here, to be commanded by officers capable of undertaking any task that may confront us'. When Kennedy-Purvis responded with a suggestion that 'it would be appreciated if, in future, vessels such as *Sumar* should not be detailed for operations for which they are not suitable', James's patience snapped. Not only had a report in April 1942 'distinctly stated that [*Sumar*] was being prepared for this kind of duty', but RN command in Bermuda had 'reported her ready and available for it' prior to the sortie with *Gannet*. Moreover,

> the splendid position of the *Sumar* at the time of the sinking would also further indicate the justification and wisdom of the manner in which she was employed. As a matter of fact she was in a position to attack the enemy and finally to rescue the survivors of her unfortunate consort, and in doing so to cover herself with glory – the ideal position we strive so hard to obtain.

While there is no basis for believing that *Sumar* was capable of detecting *U653* on the morning in question, James's frustration can readily be appreciated.

Fate of the crew

A head count after *Gannet* sank found sixty-two survivors out of a complement of seventy-seven men, though another perished before the episode was over bringing the death toll to sixteen. The official report concluded that 'it is reasonably certain that the greater majority of these, who were in the firerooms or forward living spaces, died instantly from the explosion', though the dead almost certainly included a number of men who were blown off the ship altogether. The speed of the sinking prevented the lowering of the ship's boats, nor did any float clear despite their having been left unfastened in their skids 'and it is believed that all were carried under by the mast and boat boom as the ship rolled over and sank'.

Feiler (front centre) poses with the crew of *U653*. *DUBMA*

Lt Cdr Nuessle, who barely escaped the suction of the wreck, joined the survivors gathered around three life rafts which he immediately ordered lashed together with the wounded hoisted aboard. With *Sumar* having left the scene the survivors found themselves in a serious predicament. By chance they were sighted at 1900 that evening by Lt W. L. Pettingill USN during a routine patrol in Mariner 74-P2, one of the aircraft for which *Gannet* was the tender. Unaware who they were and unable 'to land at sea for rescue purposes without permission from higher authority', Pettingill circled the scene reporting their position to the Naval Operating Base in Bermuda and (as then directed) signalling the survivors that they would be rescued the following day. However, once he became aware from his own observations and the gesticulations of the survivors that there were seriously injured men in the party, Pettingill decided to defy standing orders and put down on the open sea, where he established the identity of the survivors, took eleven men aboard (including the seriously injured, one of them fatally so), and made for Bermuda, reporting his findings en route. Some hours later the rest were sighted by Lt Cdr J. W. Gannon USN in Mariner 74-P7 who guided the nearby fast minesweeper USS *Hamilton* to the scene later that evening where both craft shared the task of rescue before returning the survivors to Bermuda, eleven by air and forty by sea. As the official report of the rescue noted, 'considering the storm that covered the area the following day, it is certain that had rescue operations been postponed, not a man would have survived' – and for many of the injured men Lt Pettingill's decision to defy orders to land had been equally vital. So it was that in USS *Gannet* and Mariners 74-P2 and 74-P7 the roles of tender and tended were reversed to the benefit of both.

The discipline and valour shown by *Gannet*'s ship's company was noted up the chain of command, but the Commander-in-Chief Atlantic Fleet, Vice Admiral Royal E. Ingersoll, rejected the recommendations made for special recognition to all but one man, observing that for the most part he failed to see 'any action which was above and beyond the call of manifest duty'. The exception was Carpenter's Mate 3/c Harry Smith O'Donnell, one of several men blown off the ship by the torpedo detonation. On surfacing, the dazed O'Donnell heard an injured man struggling in the water even further from the ship. Unaware that *Gannet* was doomed, O'Donnell swam off to find Shipfitter 3/c Guilford J. Ruman with multiple fractures and bereft of his lifejacket. For more than half an hour O'Donnell kept Ruman afloat until one of the rafts could be attracted, 'a courageous and unselfish act that resulted beyond doubt in saving Ruman's life'.

U653 and Gerhard Feiler

Built by Howaldtswerke at Hamburg and commissioned in May 1941, *U653* made nine frontline patrols, the first seven under Kptlt Gerhard Feiler and the last two under Oblt.z.S. Hans-Albrecht Kandler. Her slender tonnage, all achieved under Feiler, amounted to *Gannet* and three merchantman sunk with another damaged. In October 1943 Feiler was assigned to a shore appointment for the remainder of the war, but as so often a change in command augured ill for his boat. On 15 March 1944 *U653* was sighted on the surface by a Swordfish from the escort carrier HMS *Vindex* while operating as part of the *Preussen* group in the North-Western Approaches. This aircraft brought up HM sloops *Wild Goose* and *Starling* of Capt. 'Johnny' Walker's 2nd Support Group, *U653* being promptly located by the former and sunk with a single pattern of depth-charges by the latter – Walker's own ship. As the commanding officer of *Wild Goose* (Cdr D. E. G. Wemyss) recalled,

'it may sound quixotic, but it is nonetheless true that Capt. Walker apologized for what he described as "my unwarrantable intrusion", since it was by now the unwritten rule that the first ship to detect had the first bang'. Walker's attack, intended only as a 'softener', had proved lethally accurate and *U653* was lost with all hands.

Sources

Navy Department, Office of Naval Records and Library, *Report of Action and Loss of USS* Gannet (NA, RG 38, June 1942 (tabbed), Box 996, 370/45/4/3)

—, Naval History Division, *Record of Survivors of USS* Gannet *by USS* Hamilton (NA, RG 38, Ser. 022, *Gannet* Survivors (tabbed), Box 1015, 370/45/4/5)

—, Naval History Division, *HMS* Samar [*sic*] *Unity of Command Report* (tabbed) (NA, RG 38, Box 4, 370/13/4/7)

—, Office of the Chief of Naval Operations, Division of Naval History, Ships' Histories Section, *History of Ships Named* Gannet (typescript, NHC, Box 313)

Burn, Alan, *The Fighting Captain: Frederic John Walker RN and the Battle of the Atlantic* (Barnsley, S. Yorks.: Leo Cooper, 1993)

DANFS, III, pp. 17–18; also on: http://www.history.navy.mil/danfs/g1/gannet-i.htm ; and: http://www.hazegray.org/danfs/mine/am41.htm

Pash, Phil, article on Guilford J. Ruman (survivor) in The *Rock River Times* (Rockford, Ill., 10 November 2003)

Wemyss, Cdr D. E. G., *Relentless Pursuit: The Story of Capt. F. J. Walker, CB, DSO***, RN – U-Boat Hunter and Destroyer* (London: William Kimber, 1957)

Webpages devoted to USS *Gannet*:
http://www.navsource.org/archives/11/02041.htm
http://steelnavy.com/ISW%20Avocet-Gannet%20FB.htm

61   FNFL (ex HMS) *MIMOSA*

C.F. Roger Birot, FNFL†

Sunk by *U124* (Type IXB), Kptlt Johann Mohr, 9 June 1942

North Atlantic, 615 nm SE of Uummannarsuaq, Greenland

Mimosa lying at anchor in 1941. She flies the *Tricolore* aft and the ensign of the FNFL at the bow.
Mohr sank her in three minutes with a hit on the port side amidships. *BfZ*

Theatre North Atlantic (Map 1)	*Displacement* 940 tons
Coordinates 52° 12' N, 31° 14' W	*Dimensions* 205.25' × 33' × approx. 11.25'
Kriegsmarine code Quadrat AK 8659	*Maximum speed* 16 knots
U-boat timekeeping differential +3 hours	*Armament* 1 × 4"; 4 × .303" AA
Fatalities 65 *Survivors* 4	

Career

For design notes on the Flower-class corvettes, see HMS *Picotee* (**29**); for background on the Free French navy, see FNFL *Alysse* (**51**).

The corvette *Mimosa* was laid down at Charles Hill & Sons Ltd of Bristol in April 1940 and launched in January of the following year. Originally ordered for the Royal Navy, on 3 May 1941 she became the first corvette to commission into the FNFL. Though her name is occasionally given as '*Mimose*' (possibly because her sister *Alyssum* was rechristened *Alysse*), there is no evidence in either French or British documentation that it was ever anything other than *Mimosa*. June was spent working up at the anti-submarine school at Tobermory and undergoing repairs on the Clyde before she was assigned to the Canadian 20th Escort Group (EG-C20) of the newly formed Newfoundland Escort Force in July. *Mimosa* and her companions were to receive a terrible baptism of fire, several of their early convoys being mauled by concentrated U-boat attack and one of their number, HMS *Gladiolus*, succumbing in defence of SC48 in October 1941 (**35**). Escort duty continued until early December when *Mimosa* hoisted the flag of the Commander-in-Chief of the Free French navy, Vice-amiral Émile-Henri Muselier, and joined her sisters *Aconit* and *Alysse* (**51**) and the cruiser submarine *Surcouf* in the capture of Saint-Pierre-et-Miquelon off Newfoundland on Christmas Eve. One effect of this was to bring a number of local men into *Mimosa*'s ship's company. After escorting HM cable ship *Lord Kelvin* during a lengthy inspection of an undersea cable near St-Pierre, *Mimosa* finally resumed convoy duty in March 1942. On 3 June she quit Londonderry to join the escort of convoy ON100 bound for Halifax.

Background of the attack

On 4 May 1942 *U124* (Kptlt Johann Mohr) sailed from Lorient as part of the six-strong *Hecht* ('pike') group destined for operations off the eastern seaboard of the United States. However, favoured with excellent intelligence the group was soon reassigned to the North Atlantic where early on 12 May *U124* despatched four ships from the Halifax-bound ON92. The *Hecht* group roamed the mid-Atlantic for another month but a combination of bad weather and powerful convoy escort made for slim pickings until ON100 bisected the U-boat patrol line on the afternoon of 8 June. On the face of it a convoy limited to seven knots and defended by only five escorts should have fallen relatively easy prey to a concerted U-boat attack. However, the escort, which comprised the Canadian destroyer *Assiniboine* (Senior Officer) and the corvettes *Dianthus* and *Nasturtium* of the Royal Navy and *Aconit* and *Mimosa* of the FNFL, proved very difficult to penetrate, assisted by the fact that all bar *Mimosa* were equipped with the latest Type-271 radar. Early on the 9th *Mimosa*'s commanding officer, Capitaine de frégate Roger Birot, retired to his cabin believing the convoy's situation to be secure. His timing could not have been more unfortunate for it was at this moment that Mohr, having failed to break through the screen, turned his frustrated attention to the corvette proceeding on the convoy's starboard quarter.

War Diary of *U124*, patrol of 4 May–26 June 1942: PG 30114, NHB, reel 1,082, p. 195

Date, time	Details of position, wind, weather, sea, light, visibility, moonlight, etc.	Incidents
9.vi	Mid-North Atlantic	
0000	Qu. AK 8663	
0050		Hinsch has convoy in sight.[1]
0130		<u>Contact report transmitted</u>. *Convoy [Qu. AK] 8663. 245 degrees. 7 knots. Mohr.*
0140		Twilight is now over. A bright night, Northern Lights. Overcast, flat sea with phosphorescence. Excellent visibility.
0220		Boat is positioned on the convoy's starboard bow. Convoy is escorted on this side by destroyers ahead, abeam and astern.[2] I twice attempt to get past the forward starboard escort but fail both times.
0245		Ites requests beacon signal.[3] As a result of the attacks that follow and subsequent diving I have no chance to comply.
0300		Boat now abreast of the convoy, starboard side. We attempt to penetrate astern of the middle destroyer but have to abort due to the approach of the rearmost destroyer. We turn for a stern attack on the

---

1 Kptlt Hans-Peter Hinsch (see **5**), commander of *U569*.

2 The relative positions of the escort are not specified in any of the sources consulted but it appears that *Mimosa* was on the starboard quarter and *Aconit* on the starboard beam, with *Dianthus* on the port quarter and *Assiniboine* also on the port side, perhaps on the beam to mirror the stations of the starboard escort. *Nasturtium*'s station is unclear though she is presumed to have been sweeping ahead of the convoy, perhaps on the same starboard side as Mohr given the difficulties in penetrating the convoy he goes on to relate. It should be noted that while Mohr refers to the escort as 'destroyers' throughout, only *Assiniboine* was of this type, the rest being corvettes.

3 Oblt.z.S. Otto Ites, commander of *U94*.

		middle destroyer.
0307	Qu. AK 8664	<u>Two single shots</u> from the stern tubes, aimed at a two-funnelled destroyer, inclination 45°, enemy speed 14 and 15 knots, range 2,000 m.[4] Not fired as a spread due to circuitry malfunction. Two misses.
0324		Again we attempt to break through from the side, still no luck. Escorts are too closely bunched and the night is too bright. To the south-west, which is where the merchantmen are, the horizon is black and hazy. I can't make out a single shadow. It is unclear whether this is smoke or a screen. Hinsch reports that he has lost contact.
0340		Boat is now positioned on the starboard quarter of the convoy. We attempt to break through from astern, penetrating the escorts at high speed, but this too fails due to strong zigzags on the part of the destroyer stationed astern. Instead we turn towards this escort for a bow attack.
0410	Qu. AK 8659	<u>Spread of two torpedoes</u> fired at a two-funnelled destroyer, inclination 65°, enemy speed 12 knots, range 2,000 m.[5] Depth set at 3 m.
		A hit just abaft the after funnel. Powerful detonation, broad column of water. This is immediately followed by a boiler explosion, white clouds of steam. A continuous rumble of detonations from both depth charges and magazine. A surface blaze lights up the fore part of the ship which rears up vertically and then sinks in under a minute accompanied by continual depth-charge detonations.
0413		We withdraw to the north-west.
0425		A white bow wave against the dark south-western horizon. A destroyer appears at an acute inclination. We head north at utmost speed then make an evasive manoeuvre to the north-west – boat is hidden behind a cloud of diesel smoke.
0432		Destroyer fires starshell above the boat and alters course towards our position.[6]
0433		Alarm dive. We go to 140 m. No depth charges.
0530		Surfaced. We proceed in direction of convoy, course south-west.
0552		<u>Outgoing W/T transmission</u>: *Convoy [Qu. AK] 8659. 245 degrees. 7.5 knots. Two-funnelled destroyer sunk. Forced to dive, now in pursuit. Mohr.*
0700	Dawn	

---

4   The only member of the escort with two funnels was HMC destroyer *Assiniboine* which Allied sources place on the port side of the convoy rather than the starboard side, as here. Mohr's decision to fire single shots set for different target speeds presumably reflects uncertainty on the latter point.

5   The corvette *Mimosa*, which had only a single funnel.

6   *Aconit* did indeed fire starshell at this time: Lieutenant de vaisseau Jean Levasseur obtained but then subsequently lost an RDF contact on a bearing coinciding with that of Mohr's withdrawal.

The sinking

U124's torpedo struck *Mimosa* on the port side aft close to the engine room at 0122 Allied time, cutting power and causing her to settle by the stern. What Mohr took to be a boiler explosion was assumed by the Officer of the Watch, Aspirant (midshipman) R. Lamy, to have been a second hit, though coming some thirty or forty seconds after the first it must indeed have originated in the ship. Whatever the case, this second explosion brought *Mimosa*'s bow up to an angle of thirty or thirty-five degrees. Lamy then recalled the detonation of a series of depth charges as *Mimosa* stood up in the water, the ship sinking within three minutes of being hit.

B.d.U. was generous in its praise for Mohr whose tally with the *Hecht* group was *Mimosa* and six merchantmen, citing once more his 'tenacity and skill both in maintaining contact with and gaining positions ahead of convoys, and then resolution in attack'. Towards the end of the cruise Dönitz asked Mohr whether the difficulty experienced by the *Hecht* group in approaching escorts at night could be attributed to the Allies' having developed a workable form of shipborne radar. Mohr answered saying that this was unlikely and suggested that instances of destroyers closing him were largely a matter of coincidence. How wrong he was.

Fate of the crew

On the bridge Aspirant Lamy had barely time to register the first torpedo and begin clearing debris when the second explosion occurred. Having vainly attempted to sound the steam siren he turned his attention to sending a distress signal instead. An order to other men on watch to fire two rockets went unheeded as they were already in the process of abandoning ship. Lamy then made for the navigation hut to retrieve the Very pistol only to find himself trapped inside as *Mimosa*'s stern slid under. Not until the hut was fully submerged did he manage to get free, surfacing in time to see *Mimosa* disappear altogether. A further depth charge exploded as Lamy swam clear of the wreck, at length coming across an empty raft. Though too weak to climb onto it, Lamy clung on for over two hours, occasionally hearing the sounds of other men nearby but seeing no-one until joined at around 0400 by Quartier-Maître radio (leading telegraphist) Bracher and Matelot gabier (boatswain) Guégan. Between them they had strength enough to clamber onto the raft. At 0530 they heard the cries of the Officier en second (First Lieutenant), Lieutenant de vaisseau (lieutenant) A. Vissian on a floatanet some 400 yards away. Vissian was hauled onto the raft at 0600, the floatanet being taken in tow bearing the corpses of Enseigne de vaisseau de 2e classe (sub-lieutenant) Daniel Jean Allonier and Matelot asdic (Asdic operator) Hervé Jean Le Dizet.

The two stern tubes from which Mohr missed *Mimosa* during his first attack at 0307 log time. The tubes have been christened as was common U-boat practice. Note *U124*'s edelweiss emblem in the torpedoman's cap, a tribute to the alpine troops of *Gebirgsjäger Regiment* 139; see HMS *Dunedin* (**40**) for the story behind this. *DUBMA*

As with HMCS *Spikenard* (**52**) in February, neither the convoy nor its escort nor in this case the rescue ship *Gothland* apprehended what had befallen *Mimosa* until much later. *Dianthus*, sailing on the convoy's port quarter, heard a series of depth charges after 0215 GMT. She signalled to *Assiniboine* that a ship on the starboard quarter had been seen flashing with an Aldis lamp towards the head of the convoy but decided against leaving her station to investigate an incident outside her remit. L.V. Jean Levasseur, commanding *Aconit*, recorded a succession of underwater explosions, recalling that he

> did not realize that *Mimosa* had been torpedoed. No flame had been sighted and I thought that *Mimosa* had been attacking a contact with a full pattern. The presence of a calcium light floating on the water confirmed my opinion. When I steered to bow 090 at 0234 a strong smell of gunpowder and oil was smelled, but as, [*sic*] at night the merchant ships used to get rid of the oil from their bilges I was not surprised. The smell of gunpowder can be mistaken for the smell of depth charges.

Levasseur therefore attributed *Mimosa*'s subsequent radio silence to her having dismissed the possibility of her contact being a submarine, and a stream of radio signals between the remaining escorts that night succeeded only in establishing that no merchantman had been lost. As with *Spikenard*, it was only as dawn broke that the realisation of *Mimosa*'s probable loss took hold, Levasseur surprised that he could not see her in the gathering light. He immediately signalled *Assiniboine* expressing both his concern and his willingness to turn back and search for survivors, but it was *Assiniboine* that did so, sighting the raft containing Lamy and his three companions shortly after 0800. They were the only survivors of a crew which included six members of the Royal Navy – five communications ratings and the liaison officer,

Sub-Lt R. E. J. Theobald RNVR. There were fifty-nine French fatalities, and the loss of a seasoned officer such as Roger Birot was a severe deprivation for the FNFL. The dead are remembered on the Free French Naval Memorial erected on Lyle Hill near Greenock, Scotland.

U124 and Johann Mohr

For the early part of *U124*'s career, see HMS *Dunedin* (**40**).

The success of *U124*'s *Hecht* cruise continued in her next patrol during which a further 28,000 tons of shipping was sunk in the Caribbean. This not only earned Johann Mohr the Oak Leaves to his Knight's Cross and further plaudits from B.d.U. but cemented a reputation for aggression that supposedly led Dönitz to refer to him in private as 'the favourite horse in my stable'. However, once the technological pendulum had swung the Allied way – as it had by the spring of 1943 – Mohr's tactics were likely to have only one outcome when tested against a well-defended convoy. *U124*'s career ended on the night of 2 April 1943. Apparently sceptical of British radar capabilities to the last, Mohr had just made two successful attacks on convoy OS45 off Oporto when he was detected by HM sloop *Black Swan*, choosing to wait until she was almost upon him before giving the order to dive. Two patterns of depth charges from *Black Swan* were followed by another from HM corvette *Stonecrop*, the loss of Asdic contact being corroborated by a tell-tale slick of oil. There were no survivors.

Sources

Admiralty, *Reports of Proceedings, Atlantic Convoys* (TNA, ADM 199/1338)
—, *Convoy ON100* (TNA, ADM 237/86)
Ministère de la Défense, *Rapport sur le torpillage du "Mimosa" par l'Aspirant LAMY, Officier du Quart au moment du torpillage* (SHM, *Mimosa* file)
Ministry of Defence, *Convoy ON100* (NHB, ON convoys box)
Anon., Mimosa (typescript career history, SHM, *Mimosa* file)
Ruegg, R., *Flower-Class Corvettes* (typescript, IWM, 13(41).245/5, 1987)
Bayle, Capitaine de frégate Luc-Marie, *Les Corvettes F.N.F.L., de leur armement au 2 août 1943* (Vincennes: Service historique de la Marine, 1966)
Blair, *Hitler's U-Boat War*, I, pp. 598–602
Chaline, Vice-amiral Emile, and Capitaine de vaisseau Pierre Santarelli, *Historique des forces navales françaises libres* (4 vols, Vincennes: Service historique de la Marine, 1990–2003)
Gasaway, E. B., *Grey Wolf, Grey Sea* (New York: Ballantine, 1970; London: Arthur Barker, 1972)
Morsier, Pierre de, *Les Corvettes de la France Libre* (Paris: Éditions France-Empire, 1972)
Preston, Antony, and Alan Raven, *Flower Class Corvettes* [Ensign, no. 3] (London: Bivouac Books, 1973); reprinted as Man o'War, no. 7 (London: Arms and Armour Press, 1982)

Webpage devoted to convoy ON100:
    http://www.uboat.net/ops/convoys/battles.htm
Webpage devoted to the career of Capitaine de frégate Roger Birot:
    http://www.netmarine.net/bat/avisos/cdtbirot/celebre.htm

62   HMS *GROVE*

Lt Cdr J. W. Rylands, RN

Sunk by *U77* (Type VIIC), Kptlt Heinrich Schonder, 12 June 1942

Eastern Mediterranean, 35 nm NW of Sîdi Barrâni (Egypt)

Not *Grove* for which no photo has been found but her sister of the Type-II Hunt class HMS *Croome*, seen here in the Mediterranean in 1942. *BfZ*

Theatre Mediterranean (Map 3)	*Displacement* 1,050 tons
Coordinates 32° 05' N, 25° 30' E	*Dimensions* 280' × 31.5' × 8.25'
Kriegsmarine code Quadrat CO 9131	*Maximum speed* 27 knots
U-boat timekeeping differential –1 hour	*Armament* 6 × 4" AA; 4 × 40 mm AA; 2 × 20 mm AA
Fatalities 111 *Survivors* 70	

Career

For design notes on the Hunt-class destroyers, see HMS *Heythrop* (**55**).

Among the last units of the thirty-three-strong Hunt (Type II) class, HMS *Grove* was laid down at Swan Hunter of Newcastle upon Tyne in August 1940, launched in May 1941 and commissioned on 5 February 1942. Her career was to be both brief and eventful. After working up at Scapa Flow, in early March *Grove* joined the force of Home Fleet ships covering both convoy PQ12 to Murmansk and the returning QP8. However, fate disposed her for a theatre other than the Arctic and on 22 March *Grove* quit the Clyde for the Mediterranean as escort to troop convoy WS10 whose route to the Middle East was to take it round the Cape of Good Hope. Off the Azores five days later *Grove* joined with HMSs *Leamington*, *Aldenham* and *Volunteer* in the destruction of *U587*, making this the first U-boat sunk with the aid of High-Frequency Direction Finding apparatus. *Grove* detached from WS10 on arrival at Freetown and took independent passage to Alexandria which she reached on 18 May. She immediately joined the 22nd Destroyer Flotilla, an association which ended with her first major assignment, the escort of a convoy on the Alexandria–Tobruk run.

Background of the attack

Convoy AT49, which sailed from Alexandria bound for Tobruk on the afternoon of 9 June 1942, comprised five merchantmen (most carrying either oil or petroleum) and a six-strong escort led by HMS *Grove*.

Grove's commanding officer, Lt Cdr J. W. Rylands, would later express his dissatisfaction at the relative inexperience of the group, observing that 'this was *Grove* and *Tetcott*'s first run to Tobruk . . . *Peony* had a captain who had not been there [Tobruk], *Hyacinth* had not been there for six weeks and . . . the commodore in RFA *Brambleleaf* had not been to sea since Crete [May 1941] and had never been to Tobruk'. It was to be a difficult passage. At 1950 on the 9th SS *Heron* was discovered to have fallen well astern, it later transpiring that her maximum speed was little better than five knots. *Tetcott* was ordered to fall back and bring her up to the main group. Shortly after, *Hyacinth* and *Grove* both obtained Asdic contacts, *Grove* narrowly escaping a collision with the South African anti-submarine whaler *Parktown* as the latter dropped a pattern of depth changes. At 0320 on the 10th SS *Havre* was torpedoed with a full load of cased petrol and 'immediately burst into a sea of flame', her attacker being either Kptlt Friedrich Guggenberger's *U81* (see **39**) or Kptlt Wilhelm Dommes's *U431* (see **72** and **74**). A few hours later SS *Athene* and *Brambleleaf* were torpedoed by Kptlt Hans Heidtmann's *U559* (see **42**). Both crews immediately abandoned ship, leading to an extraordinary situation as Lt Cdr Rylands requested that survivors reboard *Brambleleaf* to help take her in tow. To Rylands' astonishment 'there was not one single volunteer; not one member of her crew would go'. The slow progress made by the towing party (eventually composed of volunteers from *Grove*) was curtailed later that morning following orders from Rear-Admiral G. H. Cresswell in Alexandria, with which the tow was cast off. The arrival of the tug *St*

Monance permitted *Grove* to rejoin the convoy, now reduced to SSs *Hannah Moller* and *Heron* escorted by *Tetcott* and *Hyacinth*. Further periscopes were sighted and depth-charge attacks carried out before the two surviving merchantmen were taken into Tobruk by *Hyacinth*. But the ordeal was not over for the senior escort. Leaving Tobruk, a navigational error caused *Grove* to run aground at 0124, damaging her port shaft and propeller. This incident impaired her manoeuverability and reduced her speed to just 8½ knots, factors subsequently considered instrumental in the loss of the ship. Cruising north of Sîdi Barrâni, *U77* sighted a 'fast escort vessel' in the half-light of dawn and attacked with a full spread of four torpedoes.

War Diary of *U77*, patrol of 6–17 June 1942: PG 30073, NHB, reel 1,072, pp. 234–5

Date, time	Details of position, wind, weather, sea, light, visibility, moonlight, etc.	Incidents
12.vi		
0300		Surfaced.
0400	Qu. CO 9129, wind N 3, sea 2, clear with sporadic clouds	
0442		As dawn breaks a vessel heaves into sight at a bearing of 290° true. From her low, light-coloured superstructure we assume that she must be a warship, sailing on a pronounced zigzagging course as she approaches. As I have a bright horizon behind me I withdraw to 110° for tactical purposes, by which time I gain the impression that the enemy has altered course to the south.
0449	Qu. CO 6797	We dive as it's getting light. As I'm heading south I see through the periscope that there are now two vessels in sight that look like destroyers, and rather than heading south-east they are heading east. The first one is soon out of range to the east.
0516		We now head north at ¾ speed to intercept the second vessel and take up a firing position. It now becomes obvious that we have before us one of these 'fast escort vessels'.[1] The angle is easy to calculate despite the haze but I have no point of reference for enemy speed. I therefore decide to fire a spread of four.
0537	Qu. CO 9131 HMS GROVE[2]	Spread of four torpedoes fired, aim-off of 23° and a 3° angle of dispersion between each torpedo. Enemy speed 12 knots, inclination 90°, estimated range 2,000 m.[3] After a running time of 63 sec. (equivalent to 945 m) two bright detonations.
0540		Shortly after firing I return to periscope depth and see the following: the enemy's bows have been ripped off forward of the bridge and are rising vertically out of the water. Alongside it the rest of the ship initially seems to be on a totally even keel.
0542	North-East of Ras Azzas	Two minutes later, however, the wreck takes on a heavy list and her stern settles deep in the water. Off to port one can see a lifeboat rowing away from the scene. Despite her foc's'le having been ripped away the enemy sinks stern first which leads me to infer that the second torpedo struck aft.[4] As the stern is now completely awash it's impossible to identify where. In the meantime the other escort has stopped some 1,000 m from her torpedoed companion. But she doesn't give me any chance of a shot from Tube
0543		V. No doubt as a result of my lack of circumspection in raising my periscope we suddenly become the target of aerial bombs and duly submerge to 80 m.[5] We hear no propeller noises. A few more bombs fall but at quite a distance. The stern hydroplane has got stuck in the alarm dive position. Still submerged, I set a southerly course to reload torpedoes. No sinking noises are heard through the hydrophones while reloading the four bow torpedoes but I've no doubt that this can be attributed to our own high speed and trimming, pumping out, etc. I can't see how this light craft, struck by two torpedoes and cut in two, cannot have sunk within a short space

---

1   Schonder is presumably referring to the Hunt-class destroyers which began reaching the Mediterranean in numbers in the autumn of 1941.

2   Manuscript addition in pencil by a British hand.

3   According to Lt Cdr Rylands' report *Grove* had a best speed of just 8½ knots having grounded off Tobruk five hours earlier. Although this was much slower than *U77*'s assessment of 12 knots, modelling of the available attack data reveals that Schonder could not have scored his two hits unless *Grove* had been making at least 10 knots – assuming of course that Schonder's G7e torpedoes ran at their usual speed of 30 knots. The miscalculated range (945 metres as against the 2,000 initially estimated) was relevant only insofar as it actually *increased* the chances of a multiple hit, the salvo having not yet fanned out beyond *Grove*'s length by the time it reached her.

4   Schonder's inference is correct; *Grove* was struck both forward and aft.

5   There were no aircraft on the scene at this juncture and Schonder clearly misinterpreted *Tetcott*'s depth charges as an air attack. In his report Rylands lamented that *Tetcott* had miscalculated the U-boat's probable position and made her attack well wide of the mark. Schonder's log indicates otherwise.

of time. On comparing her to our collection of British warship silhouettes we feel sure she must have been a Hunt-class escort vessel, approx. 1,200 tons.[6] We could clearly discern the marking 'L-77' on her bows, but our vessel bore no resemblance to the Australian escort vessel *Yarra* (= 'L-77') depicted in our Weyer. Presumably wartime markings are different from those used in peacetime.[7]

0800 Qu. CO 9134

0830 Reloading of bow torpedo tubes completed.

---

6 Schonder's description is accurate. His assessment of tonnage bisects *Grove*'s standard and full load displacement of 1,050 and 1,430 tons respectively.
7 Schonder's puzzlement is understandable in view of the fact that both *Grove* and the Australian escort sloop *Yarra* bore the pendant number L77 on their bows. Since *Grove* had only been in commission a little over four months and HMAS *Yarra* had succumbed to Japanese gunfire off Java on 4 March that year it is too much to expect *U77*'s Weyer to have been updated.

The sinking

According to Lt Cdr Ryland's report, the tracks of three torpedoes were sighted off the starboard quarter at 0654 ship time, later amended to 0645 by *Tetcott* and thereby corresponding more closely to the time given for the attack in *U77*'s detailed war diary. The 'hard aport' order issued by the Officer of the Watch failed to bring the ship round in time to 'comb the tracks' allowing Schonder's wide-angled spread to yield the desired result. One torpedo struck the starboard side abreast No. 1 mounting and removed the fore part of the ship back to the bridge while another detonated abreast No. 2 mounting and sheered off the stern. Rylands' observation that 'it was obvious at once that the ship could not remain afloat with such damage' was no overstatement as flooding immediately proved uncontrollable at both ends of the ship. Within a few minutes the order was given to lower boats and prepare all hands for abandoning ship. The wreck of HMS *Grove* disappeared fourteen minutes after the torpedoes struck, two minutes after the last survivors had got clear of the wreck.

Fate of the crew

The detonations claimed almost two thirds of the ship's company, the impact forward such that 'a great deal of unrecognizable human remains was scattered about the decks and bulkheads'. Although *Grove* threatened to founder at any moment there was no panic among the surviving crewmen and almost all made it off safely. An exception was Petty Officer F. W. Smith who heard someone crying out from the still floating bows when he was in the water and returned to save the man in question. His heroism deserved better reward, but in the words of his commanding officer 'he was never seen again as the ship turned over on top of him. A fine coxswain, an excellent seaman; he died a gallant death'. Seventy-three survivors were taken aboard HMS *Tetcott* but several of those rescued were badly injured and three ratings subsequently died of wounds. The remainder were returned immediately to Alexandria.

Though no formal reprimand was issued, the Chief of Staff to the Mediterranean Fleet, Rear-Admiral J. H. Edelsten, was critical of the events which led to the grounding of HMS *Grove*, an accident which made her easy prey for a submarine. He concluded that 'there appears little doubt that Lieutenant-Commander J. W. Rylands, Commanding Officer, and his Officer of the Watch were to blame for this occurrence', a view which was in stark contrast to that of Rear-Admiral Cresswell who was unconvinced as to the reliability of the Admiralty chart for the waters in question, and considered that Rylands had commanded AT49 with 'commendable energy and ability which deserved better

Schonder at Salamis following the award of the Knight's Cross in August 1942. *DUBMA*

fortune'. Timing was everything for this ill-fated convoy, however, and the losses suffered by AT49 were soon overshadowed by the carnage of Operations HARPOON and VIGOROUS over the following days.

U77 and Heinrich Schonder

Built by Bremer Vulkan at Vegesack and commissioned in January 1941, *U77* served four patrols in the Atlantic under Kptlt Schonder for a tally three ships. In December 1941 the last of these brought *U77* through the Straits of Gibraltar and into the Mediterranean where she carried out a further eleven patrols. Schonder commanded the first six of these, damaging HM destroyer *Kimberley* off Bardia in January 1942 before suffering a lean year during which *Grove* and a few small Egyptian sailing craft were his only victims. *U77* enjoyed a brisk run of success after Oblt.z.S. Otto Hartmann assumed command in September 1942 but her career ended on 28 March 1943 following a depth-charge attack by an RAF Hudson off Cartagena. *U77* dived but oil and bubbles were seen and she had evidently suffered severe damage. Some hours later she was found on the surface and destroyed in a depth-charge and strafing attack by a second Hudson. Hartmann and thirty-seven of his crew perished but nine men were rescued by a passing Spanish vessel.

After leaving *U77* Schonder took command of the Type-IXD-2 *U200* in December 1942. *U200*'s first patrol was intended to take her around the Cape of Good Hope to join the *Monsun* group in the

Arabian Sea, but her career ended within two weeks of her sailing from Kiel. On 24 June 1943 she was attacked and sunk by an RAF Liberator of 120 Squadron in the North Atlantic. There were no survivors, the dead including seven members of the Brandenburg Special Forces Unit.

Sources

Admiralty, *Convoy Reports, 27th December 1941–2nd January 1943* (TNA, ADM, 199/1214)

—, *Enemy Submarine Attacks on H.M. and Allied Warships, January–June* 1942 (TNA, ADM, 199/162)

English, John, *The Hunts: A History of the Design, Development and Careers of the 86 Destroyers of This Class Built for the Royal Navy during World War II* (Kendal, Cumbria: World Ship Society, 1987)

Piper, N., 'HMS *Grove*' in *Warship*, no. 15 (July 1980), pp. 180–1

Raven, Alan, and John Roberts, *Hunt Class Escort Destroyers* [Man o'War, no. 4] (London: Arms and Armour Press, 1980)

Career history of HMS *Grove*:
   http://www.naval-history.net/xGM-Chrono-10DE-Grove.htm

63   HMS *HERMIONE*

Capt. G. N. Oliver, DSO RN
Sunk by *U205* (Type VIIC), Kptlt Franz-Georg Reschke, 16 June 1942
Eastern Mediterranean, 100 nm N of Sîdi Barrâni (Egypt)

Hermione under way, probably in the Mediterranean, during her brief year of life. The guns of two of her 5.25-inch mountings are pointed skyward; in the event, her nemesis lay elsewhere. *IWM*

Theatre	Mediterranean (Map 3)	*Displacement*	5,450 tons
Coordinates	33° 17' N, 26° 10' E	*Dimensions*	512' × 50.5' × 14'
Kriegsmarine code	Quadrat CO 6573	*Armour*	3" belt; 1–2" decks and bulkheads
U-boat timekeeping differential	–1 hour	*Maximum speed*	33 knots
Fatalities 88	*Survivors* 498	*Armament*	10 × 5.25" DP; 8 × 40 mm AA; 5 × 20 mm AA; 6 × 21" tt

Career

For design notes on the Dido-class cruisers of which *Hermione* was the fourth unit to be laid down, see HMS *Naiad* (**54**).

Ordered under the 1937 programme from Alexander Stephen's yard at Linthouse, Glasgow, HMS *Hermione* was laid down in October of that year, launched in May 1939 and completed in March 1941. Having worked up in the Clyde off Greenock she was assigned to the 2nd Cruiser Squadron, Home Fleet which she joined in covering operations by the 1st Minelaying Squadron off Iceland and then in the hunt for the *Bismarck* in May. In June she was transferred to Force H at Gibraltar, participating first in operations to fly off aircraft for Malta from the Western Mediterranean and then in the supply convoys to that island known as SUBSTANCE and STYLE in July and August

1941. During the second of these she rammed and sank the Italian submarine *Tembien* in the Sicilian Narrows on 2 August, reaching Malta the following day to find a piece of her victim wrapped around her bows. Patrol and escort duty in the Atlantic and the Mediterranean continued into the spring of 1942, including ten operations to fly off aircraft for Malta and Operation HALBERD, the convoy which brought 85,000 tons of supplies to the beleaguered island in September 1941. In November *Hermione* stood by HMS *Ark Royal* during the desperate efforts to save her off Gibraltar (**39**), while January 1942 found her assisting the damaged submarine *Regent* off the Azores. On 1 April *Hermione* sailed from Gibraltar to participate in Operation IRONCLAD, the capture of Vichy-held Madagascar for which she served as escort to the invasion fleet on its long haul around the Cape. *Hermione* was also present at the assault on Diego Suarez between 5 and 7 May during which she fired on the shore batteries commanding Oronjia Pass. This at length brought her to Mombasa and thence to Alexandria on 7 June with which she joined the 15th CS, Mediterranean Fleet. The association would not be a long one.

Background of the attack

In June 1942 the urgent predicament of Malta, starved of supplies and under constant aerial attack, prompted the British to organise simultaneous convoys to the island from each end of the Mediterranean. Predictably enough, both met the full ferocity of Axis air, surface and submarine attack. The eastbound convoy from Gibraltar, known as Operation HARPOON, managed to get just two of its six merchantmen through while losing the destroyers HMS *Bedouin* and ORP *Kujawiak* of the Polish navy. Worse was the fate of MW11, the westbound convoy codenamed VIGOROUS which assembled off Alexandria on 13 June and to which *Hermione* was initially assigned as radar reporting ship. This consisted of eleven merchantmen and a mixed escort of forty-six ships including eight cruisers under Rear-Admiral Philip Vian in

the *Cleopatra*. Late on the 14th came reports that heavy units of the Italian navy had sailed from Taranto, the convoy by now having lost two merchantmen to repeated air attack. The following morning, with the convoy off Cyrenaica, Admiral Sir Henry Harwood, Commander-in-Chief Mediterranean Fleet, ordered a series of evasive manoeuvres during which so much fuel and ammunition was expended that the goal of reaching Malta had to be abandoned. Reversing course, the cruiser *Newcastle* and the destroyer *Hasty* were hit by torpedoes from German E-boats on the morning of the 15th, *Hasty* having to be scuttled later that day. That afternoon the cruiser *Birmingham* and the destroyers *Airedale* and *Nestor* (RAN) were heavily damaged in air attacks, the last two having to be scuttled over the next few hours. However, MW11's cup of bitterness was not yet full. By the time the survivors made Alexandria on the evening of 16 June their number had been depleted still further. With *Newcastle*'s speed impaired, *Hermione* took her place in the screen and it was here that she was attacked early on the 16th by *U205* in those waters off Sîdi Barrâni which the *U-Boot-Waffe* had turned into a graveyard of Allied ships.

War Diary of *U205*, patrol of 8–23 June 1942: PG 30193, NHB, reel 1,090, pp. 633–4

Date, time	Details of position, wind, weather, sea, light, visibility, moonlight, etc.	Incidents
15.vi		
2258	[Qu.] CO 6572	Dived to seek hydrophone bearing. Contact obtained at 310° true. Immediately surface and set course 310°.
2320	[Qu.] CO 6572	In no time the convoy appears in sight, course 80°. Transmit W/T report to *F.d.U.* accordingly.[1] <u>Battle Stations</u>. A clear starry night with long-range visibility. I alter to a parallel course so as to be able to attack immediately (see attack sketch[2]), namely by firing two torpedoes at each of the two destroyers stationed ahead of the convoy. Other ships in sight include two destroyers and a larger shadow on the port quarter, two further destroyers on the starboard quarter at an inclination of 0°, and two vessels on the starboard bow.[3] All of these are warships, presumably acting as a distant starboard escort for the steamers. I am therefore positioned right in the thick of things, close in, and am forced to shoot from a wide angle, not least because otherwise I will be closed down by the rear destroyers.
2338	[Qu.] CO 6572, wind WNW 3, sea 3, good visibility, cloudless sky	<u>Torpedo from Tube I</u> fired at the lead destroyer. We switch to Tube II. Enemy speed 10 knots, bows left, inclination 80°, range 2,000 m, depth 2 m. We drop back to maintain the parallax.[4]
2340	[Qu.] CO 6573	We target second destroyer.[5] <u>Torpedoes fired from Tubes III and IV</u>. Then another from <u>Tube V</u> on the turn using the same firing data. Then a report comes through from the forward compartment: torpedoes from Tubes *II*, III and IV were never fired; the switchover didn't work.[6] Shots from Tubes

---

1   This refers to *F.d.U. Italien* (Officer Commanding U-Boats, Italy), Konteradmiral Leo Kreisch, with operational control of all U-boats in the Mediterranean. The command was redesignated *F.d.U. Mittelmeer* when the staff evacuated from Rome to Toulon in August 1943.

2   This survives as an appendix to the log.

3   Since *U205* is on the starboard quarter of the convoy the 'larger shadow' mentioned by Reschke would equate to *Hermione*'s sister *Euryalus*. The identity of the destroyers is unclear.

4   The parallax to which Reschke is referring is that applicable to the 'shooting triangle', the trigonometric system on which U-boat attacks carried out with the *Vorhaltrechner* (torpedo data computer) were based. There was always a discrepancy between the point of observation (i.e. the conning tower) and the anticipated point from which the torpedo would start running along its set track (9.5 metres ahead of the bow prior to turning in accordance with pre-programmed gyro angle), for which an adjustment was made via the torpedo data computer. See the Introduction, pp. xxiv–xxvi for more on torpedo firing control.

5   The identity of this destroyer is unclear.

6   The addition of Tube II in pencil should presumably apply to the first line of this entry as well. The tube from which a torpedo was fired was selected via the *Torpedo Schuss-Empfänger* (torpedo fire data receivers) in the forward and after compartments. For whatever reason, the correct procedure appears not to have been followed in the forward compartment which contained four torpedo tubes.

Date, time	Details of position, wind, weather, sea, light, visibility, moonlight, etc.	*Incidents*
		I and V missed the target as enemy speed was underestimated. However, these failures work to my advantage; I remain unnoticed, drop back and watch the large unidentified shadow approach. She is a Glasgow-class cruiser with two destroyers stationed hard on her bow and quarter respectively.[7] We transmit our contact report. The quadrant figure is erroneously keyed in and is given as CO 6472 rather than CO 6572, course 60°, speed 12 knots.
2400	[Qu.] CO 6572	All vessels are zigzagging dramatically. I sail into the gap between the leading four and rear two destroyers and assume a parallel course to the cruiser, gradually closing until I'm within 2,500 m.[8] Then I turn perpendicularly towards her to fire. The rear destroyers are closing but we mustn't let this put us off; I'll never get such a chance again. And indeed I remain unnoticed.
		Reschke
16.vi		
0019	[Qu.] CO 6573	<u>Double salvo fired from Tubes II and IV</u> at the cruiser. Immediately after another <u>torpedo from Tube III.</u> Enemy speed 12 knots, range 2,500 m, target length 150 m, inclination 90°, bows left, depth 2 m.[9] Immediately after firing I turn away and head out through the gap westwards at high speed. This too goes unnoticed – I can scarcely believe it. After 3 min. 29 sec. (a run of 3,000 m) two heavy detonations, and a third in quick succession. A cracking sound ensues accompanied by a 50-m column of fire suggesting that one of the magazines must have gone up. Then in the blinking of an eye the cruiser breaks up amidships. The bows rear up for 30 sec. then there's nothing left to be seen, just clouds of billowing and hanging smoke. A destroyer approaches the scene of the sinking and begins transmitting signals by flashlight.[10] Six minutes later we can hear powerful detonations – depth charges being thrown around in a wild indiscriminate fashion. One of the destroyers closes me from astern but by zigzagging for about 40 min. I manage to avoid being spotted. Then it all goes quiet as if nothing had happened. W/T signal transmitted reporting our success.
0140	[Qu.] CO 6493	Dived to reload torpedoes.

---

7   HMS *Hermione*. The destroyers referred to were two Hunt-class units, one (identity unknown) stationed ahead of *Hermione* and the other, HMS *Dulverton*, on her starboard beam. Though similar in silhouette to the 9,100-ton 'Town'-class cruisers of which *Glasgow* was among the first units, *Hermione* in fact belonged to the much smaller Dido class.

8   Once again, the precise identity of the destroyers is uncertain.

9   Reschke's calculations are accurate, *Hermione* measuring 156 metres and Capt. Oliver recording her speed as 13 knots.

10 The identity of this destroyer and those mentioned below is again unclear though it seems that they may have been Hunt-class units of the 5th Destroyer Flotilla.

The sinking

At 0126 British time *Hermione*'s Asdic operator obtained a new contact and immediately asked whether there was a destroyer stationed on the starboard beam. He was informed that this was the case and nothing suspicious was sighted by the lookouts, visibility being poor due to the funnel haze drifting with the following wind. Within seconds a 'slight swish was heard followed at once by a shattering explosion, accompanied by flash, and the whole ship was violently shaken'. Struck on the starboard side abreast the After Engine Room, *Hermione* listed more than twenty degrees within the space of a minute. Having steadied for about thirty seconds the list resumed leaving Capt. Oliver powerless to take any countermeasures. As he put it, 'the explosion appears to have had a most shattering effect on the ship's structure and bulkheads'. Both the After Engine Room and 'B' Boiler Room flooded immediately, the stern settled rapidly and the quarterdeck was soon awash. The blast wrecked an armoured bulkhead door and both passage doors on the lower deck allowing water to flow along the starboard side as far as the stokers' mess deck, assisted by the flooding of ventilation trunking as the ship capsized. When the list reached thirty-five degrees Oliver ordered all hands on deck and saw to the disposal of confidential books and documents. Two minutes later 'I ordered every man for himself, as it was obvious we could do nothing now to save her'. *Hermione* then 'hung on her beam ends, about three quarters submerged and trimmed by the stern for about 7 minutes' before sinking stern first at 0148 to the determined cheers of her surviving ship's company. As Boy Signalman R. Fleming recalled, 'there was little suction when she went, almost, it would seem, apologetically, as if she had let us down'.

Admiral Harwood was quick to point out the similarities between the loss of *Hermione* and her sister *Naiad* (**54**) 'consequent upon the effects of one, repeat one torpedo explosion in the machinery spaces, and it is felt that certain features in the design of this class need re-consideration'. Various measures including the strengthening of bulkheads, the reduction in the number of doors in transverse bulkheads, and the introduction of additional bulkheads between the lower and upper decks were proposed. Though expert opinion was and remains unanimous that the Dido-class cruisers were much too easily sunk, with hindsight it is by no means certain that *Hermione* was the victim of only one torpedo. While Reschke's implication of three hits may be taking things too far, *Dido* herself observed two distinct flashes from *Hermione* at 0127. Certainly, the damage sustained by *Hermione* and the speed of her sinking would be consistent with a second hit in the same vicinity as the first. Whatever the case, no Board of Enquiry was called, partly as the technical concerns highlighted were considered identical to those of *Naiad* and partly because 'it is considered [that] all possible steps were taken and [the] behaviour of personnel was exemplary'. Describing the loss of this ship in his memoirs, Admiral Vian recalled her 'as one of the most efficient in the Fleet'. Judging by the letter of congratulation he sent Kptlt Reschke from Libya, this was a sentiment with which Field Marshal Erwin Rommel, increasingly starved of fuel and supplies for the Afrika Korps, might not have been in disagreement.

Fate of the crew

Virtually all of *Hermione*'s eighty-eight fatalities were the result of the initial detonation or its immediate effects. The After Engine Room watch was lost to a man and there was but one survivor from the damage-control parties closed up at Action Stations in the office flat directly above it. Nor did any escape from the Central Communication Office or Cypher Office, both of which were cut off by fire and fumes, while only two members of the fire and repair party stationed in the after lobby survived, both with severe burns. The rest of the ship's company abandoned her stoically and without panic. No boats could be lowered but a petty officer managed to cut the lashings of a number of Carley floats and several remained on the surface after the ship went down. The survivors also received the uncovenanted benefit of quantities of 5.25-inch cartridge containers which floated off when the ship sank and demonstrated their value as life-saving devices. A number of broken ankles and minor injuries were sustained as men slid down the port side of the ship or dropped off the bilge keel. The placid waters of the Mediterranean claimed few casualties with the exception of a number who succumbed to oil ingestion along with several killed or seriously wounded by a pattern of depth charges dropped by one of the escorts shortly before *Hermione* disappeared. Aided by calcium lights, torches and life-saving automatic lights, the survivors were soon picked up by HM destroyers *Exmoor* and *Beaufort* in which they reached Alexandria later that day, though five subsequently died of wounds. HMSs *Croome* and *Aldenham* returned to the scene of the sinking at first light but no further survivors were found. Among those borne on the ship's books who never saw land again was Convoy, a feline veteran of many of *Hermione*'s Mediterranean actions. R.I.P.

U205 and Franz-Georg Reschke

Built by Germaniawerft at Kiel and commissioned in May 1941, *U205* spent her first eight patrols under Kptlt Franz-Georg Reschke. After service in the Atlantic *U205* was transferred to the Mediterranean as part of the *Arnauld* group in November 1941 though in neither theatre did she enjoy any run of success. Reschke had a number of unsubstantiated claims, most notably that on the carrier *Ark Royal* some hours before *U81*'s successful attack on 13 November 1941 (**39**) and some sources credit him with SS *Slavol* in March 1942 (see HMS *Jaguar*, **56**) but it seems that *Hermione* was her only sinking in twelve patrols. In October 1942 Reschke was replaced by Oblt.z.S. Friedrich Bürgel who had yet to notch up a single kill when the end came for

Commissioning day for *U205* at Kiel on 3 May 1941. Reschke stands on the *Wintergarten* with the standard 20-mm anti-aircraft gun behind him. The boat's bell has been rigged and her ensign is ready to be broken out on the staff. *DUBMA*

U205 off Cyrenaica on 17 February 1943. Forced to the surface by depth-charge attacks from HM destroyer *Paladin* and a Bristol Bisley bomber of the South African Air Force, she was abandoned by her crew, all but eight of whom survived to be rescued, Bürgel among them. Refusing to sink, *U205* was boarded and taken in tow by HM corvette *Gloxinia* but foundered before she could be brought in to the Libyan port of Derna. Nonetheless, a team of divers later recovered the Enigma enciphering machine from the wreck.

After *U205* Reschke was assigned to shore duties for the duration of the war. He died in December 1996.

Sources

Admiralty, *Wartime Damage to Ships: Reports, 1942–1943* (TNA, ADM 199/2068)

—, *Operation 'Vigorous': Convoy from Eastern Mediterranean to Malta, 11–17 June 1942* (TNA, ADM 199/1244)

Reschke, Korvkpt. Franz-Georg, *Chronik des Bootes* U205 (1948) (typescript, DUBMA, *U205* file)

HMS Hermione, *1937–1942* (unpublished chronology prepared for HMS *Hermione* Association, 1993)

Lee, Eric C. B., *The Cruiser Experience: Life Aboard Royal Navy Cruisers during World War Two* (Fleet Hargate, Lincs.: Arcturus Press, 2000)

Osborne, Richard, 'A Tale of Two Didos' in *Warships*, Supplement no. 134 (April 1999), pp. 27–33

Raven, Alan, and H. T. Lenton, *Dido Class Cruisers* [Ensign, no. 2] (London: Bivouac Books, 1973)

Raven, Alan, and John Roberts, *British Cruisers of World War Two* (London: Arms and Armour Press, 1980)

Roskill, *War at Sea*, II, pp. 63–72

Vian, Admiral of the Fleet Sir Philip, *Action This Day* (London: Frederick Muller, 1960)

Career history of HMS *Hermione*:
    http://www.naval-history.net/xGM-Chrono-06CL-Hermione.htm

HMS *Hermione* Association website:
    http://www.hmshermione.co.uk/

64 HMS *MEDWAY*
Capt. P. Ruck-Keene, CBE RN
Sunk by *U372* (Type VIIC), Kptlt Heinz-Joachim Neumann, 30 June 1942
Eastern Mediterranean, 40 nm NNE of Rashîd (Rosetta) (Egypt)

A pre-war shot of *Medway* wearing the paint scheme of white hull and superstructure with buff funnels favoured by the Royal Navy for service on the China Station, where she spent the whole of her peacetime career. *BfZ*

Theatre	Mediterranean (Map 3)	*Displacement*	14,650 tons
Coordinates	32° 03' N, 30° 35' E	*Dimensions*	580' × 85' × 18.5'
Kriegsmarine code	Quadrat CP 7236	*Armour*	1.5" horizontal; 1.5" bulkheads
U-boat timekeeping differential	–1 hour	*Maximum speed*	15 knots
Fatalities	18 *Survivors* 1,105	*Armament*	1 × 4"; 4 × 4" AA; 2 × 47 mm AA

Career

The first large auxiliary to be purpose-built for the Royal Navy, the submarine depot ship *Medway* was also among its first major vessels to be powered by diesel engines. Designed as the mother ship for eighteen submarines (increased to twenty-one by the time of her loss) of the 'O', 'P' and later 'R' classes, *Medway* was capable of stowing up to 144 21-inch torpedoes together with three spare 4-inch guns and 1,880 tons of diesel fuel. The choice of diesel for her own propulsion appears to have stemmed from a desire to economise on fuel-stowage arrangements but the experiment was not repeated. Beyond the 400 men needed to serve her, the duties of base and repair ship to several submarine flotillas on foreign service required her to provide accommodation and working space for as many as 1,335 additional personnel. HMS *Medway* was laid down at Vickers-Armstrong's yard at Barrow-in-Furness in April 1927 and launched in July 1928. She commissioned at Barrow in July 1929 and after lengthy preparations at Portsmouth sailed east with four 'O'-class submarines in May 1930 to replace the elderly HMS *Titania* and her 'L'-class boats on the China Station. These duties kept her at Hong Kong and Weiheiwei (now Weihai) on the Yellow Sea for the next ten years. The outbreak of hostilities found her under refit at Singapore, on completion of which she was assigned to the Mediterranean Fleet to serve as depot ship to the 1st Submarine Flotilla. On 2 April 1940 *Medway* sailed from Hong Kong for the last time, reaching Alexandria on 3 May where she remained until June 1942.

Background of the attack

By the end of June 1942 Allied fortunes in the North African theatre were at their lowest ebb. To the steady attrition of ships to air and submarine attack was added a series of disastrous reverses on land culminating in the surrender of Tobruk on 20 June and the withdrawal of the British 8th Army to El Alamein, just sixty miles west of Alexandria. Though this turn of events relieved the Royal Navy of the burden of keeping Tobruk supplied, the fall of Alexandria – her principal base in the Eastern Mediterranean – now became a distinct possibility. Accordingly, the decision was taken to begin a preliminary evacuation of the port with the transfer of ships to Port Said, Haifa and Beirut. Among these was HMS *Medway* which sailed for Beirut via Haifa on 29 June with a valuable cargo of ninety torpedoes. With her went the Greek submarine depot tender *Corinthia*, and it is a measure of the value placed on these units that the anti-aircraft cruiser *Dido* and a screen of eight destroyers were assigned to escort them. Next morning their presence was detected via hydrophone by *U372* which had dived a few hours earlier to avoid what she identified as a Hunt-class destroyer. Closing the British squadron, Kptlt Heinz-Joachim Neumann carried out an audacious attack reminiscent of *U331's* on HMS *Barham* (**41**) six months before, breaching the destroyer screen at periscope depth and unleashing a full salvo of four torpedoes at what he initially took to be a range of 1,500 metres. However, when *U372* was convulsed by the first in a succession of detonations just twenty-five seconds later it was plain that Neumann had taken his command to within a suicidally close range of his target.

War Diary of *U372*, patrol of 15 June–12 July 1942: PG 30434, NHB, reel 1,101, pp. 873–4

Date, time	Details of position, wind, weather, sea, light, visibility, moonlight, etc.	Incidents
30.vi		
0800	Qu. CP 7236	At periscope depth.
0806		Hydrophone contact at 290°. Another convoy appears over the horizon, consisting of one large steamer with two funnels, four destroyers and other escort vessels.[1] Battle Stations.
0812		We alter course to 0° for our run-in. Enemy is heading east, average speed. Using the attack periscope is a real problem because the sea is mirror-smooth.
0825		I have now broken through the escort screen. Just the one torpedo boat continues to hinder my attack.[2]
0827	25.5 sec.	Spread of four – fire! Depth 4 m, range 1,500 m.[3] We fire without using the fire-control system since it makes so much noise.
0827	*Submarine depot ship Medway (14,600 tons). Pfeiffer 26/8/54*[7]	Three hits![4] Followed shortly after by collapsing bulkheads and sinking noises.[5] Vessel perhaps Atavea or Niagara class, though possibly also Matsonia class.[6]
0830		At depth of 120 m.
0850–0950		Sporadic depth charges being dropped far away. Perhaps twenty in all. We withdraw and reload torpedoes.
1200	Qu. CP 7233, submerged	Day's run: 86.5 nm on the surface, 10.5 nm submerged = 97 nm.
1258		Surfaced.
1309		Outgoing W/T transmission 1033/30/552: *F.d.U. from Neumann. Qu. 9236 13,000-GRT transport sunk from second convoy. Heavy eastbound traffic.*[8]
1424		We dive to repair gyro compass (new ball bearing required).
1600	Qu. CP 7235, still submerged	
1906		Surfaced.

1 The screen consisted of HM destroyers *Croome, Aldenham, Hero, Sikh* (port beam to port bow respectively) and *Zulu, Dulverton, Tetcott* and *Exmoor* (starboard bow to starboard beam). As *U372* attacked from the south (see 0812 entry), presumably only the starboard destroyers could be made out at periscope depth. Also present were the cruiser *Dido* and the submarine tender *Corinthia* (which Neumann appears not to have seen at 0800 but obliquely acknowledged in his signal of 1309).

2 The screen was composed entirely of destroyers and escort destroyers.

3 The 25.5-second running time recorded for the first torpedo of the salvo in the torpedo report equates to a range of just 400 metres – much too close for comfort. The First Watch Officer, Lt.z.S. Otto Behringer, later recorded *U372* being rocked by the explosions which cut all lighting and brought an inrush of water through the conning tower hatch. Neumann's concern to play down his miscalculation is no doubt responsible for its omission from the log, though the 4½ hours *U372* spent submerged from 1424 onwards presumably entailed more extensive repairs than that to the gyro compass.

4 Manuscript addition in ink by the civilian archivist Walther Pfeiffer who was brought to Britain to work on the logs post-war.

5 The British reported two or three hits against *Medway*.

6 Neumann's torpedo report records a pair of detonations 2 min. 40 sec. after the hits. It is not clear what these were though one or perhaps two end-of-run detonations are a remote possibility. Certainly, the noise of the sinking could not have been heard until after 0840 log time.

7 *Medway*'s twin funnels and high freeboard had plainly confused Neumann as to her identity. The vessels listed are, respectively, the *Awatea* [sic] of the Union Steamship Company of New Zealand (13,482 GRT), the Canadian Australasian Line's *Niagara* (13,415 GRT) and the *Matsonia* (17,226 GRT) of San Francisco's Matson Navigation Co. Though warships are measured by their displacement rather than gross register tonnage, Neumann's assessment certainly equates to the size of his victim.

8 The quadrant given in this signal to Mediterranean U-Boat Command and repeated in the torpedo report is erroneous, CP 9236 being on land. Neumann evidently meant to give the quadrant referred to at 0800: CP 7236. Although the possibility of a typist's error cannot be discounted, this may explain why *F.d.U. Italien* (Konteradmiral Leo Kreisch) replied to the effect that the signal had only been partially intelligible, a problem it attributed to stormy weather in the area.

The sinking

Thirty seconds before his ship was struck at 0925 Capt. Ruck-Keene, then on the lower bridge, 'saw the swirl of discharge of torpedoes, or possibly where the conning tower had broken the surface for a moment, which was approximately 300–400 yards on starboard beam of *Medway*'. Before the screen could be alerted and evasive action taken *Medway* had been hit on the starboard side by two, probably three torpedoes. The first detonated abreast the diesel room, blasting a large hole in the ship's side. The second struck the after end of the engine room together with 'a third probably aft'. Light and power failed immediately with the exception of the low-power circuit as *Medway* listed seventeen degrees to starboard. The engines, stopped by telegraph immediately after the hits, could not be restarted as the engine and diesel rooms filled with water. Attempts to limit the flooding proved fruitless, *Medway* rapidly filling along half her length from the torpedo room forward to the cold rooms aft. Within ten

Medway seen capsizing to starboard within ten minutes of being struck by at least two torpedoes from *U372*. Unavailing efforts have been made to launch a whaler amidships while men can be seen standing on the bilge keel at the waterline. This photo was taken from the destroyer *Hero*, standing by to rescue survivors. *IWM*

minutes the list had progressed first to twenty-four and then thirty degrees with no sign of the ship stabilising. Fifteen minutes after the detonation *Medway* was on her beam ends and she sank bow up two minutes later at 0942. Forty-seven of her load of torpedoes were found floating on the surface and subsequently recovered by the escort destroyer *Aldenham* but much valuable equipment had gone down with her and the 1st Submarine Flotilla, starved of ordnance, claimed just 800 tons of enemy shipping in July 1942.

The large volume of memoranda and reports concerning the sinking of *Medway* never came before a Board of Enquiry. Not only was it obvious that she had been damaged beyond hope of salvage but two key members of the screen, the destroyers *Zulu* and *Sikh*, remained heavily engaged and were eventually lost off Tobruk, succumbing to air attack and shore battery fire respectively on 14 September. However, the loss of the *Medway* was not without controversy. Argument raged about the efficiency of anti-submarine escort in the Mediterranean and the ideal tactics against submarine attack (see HMSs *Barham* and *Partridge*, **41** and **79**). The Admiralty's Deputy Director of Anti-Submarine Warfare, Capt. C. P. Clarke, reacted strongly to the suggestion that the *Medway* incident indicated general incompetence on the part of the British escorts, arguing that this view had 'a ring of "stinking fish" about it: D[irector of]A[nti-]S[ubmarine]W[arfare] is under the impression that in general the British screens have been far more successful than the Italian screens in thwarting submarine attacks. Perhaps the trumpet does not blow loud enough every time the Asdic does its stuff.' He and others reiterated the point that the marked variation in water-temperature layers that characterise the Mediterranean in summer greatly compromised the efficient functioning of the Navy's Asdic equipment, particularly, as here, where the Nile debouched into the sea.

While recalling the impressive record of *Medway* in supplying the 1st Submarine Flotilla, Ruck-Keene also paid fulsome tribute to her nemesis: 'if [*Medway*] had to be sunk it was most fitting that it was done by a submarine, who undoubtedly carried out a very fine unseen attack passing through a strong Asdic screen.' For his part,

Kptlt Neumann's belief that he had sunk a large troop transport remained the German view until *Medway*'s loss was finally announced in September. Her intended place at Beirut was eventually taken by the depot ship HMS *Talbot*, transferred from Malta and subsequently renamed *Medway II* in her honour.

Fate of the crew

When *Medway*'s list reached twenty-four degrees five minutes after the attack HM destroyer *Hero* was ordered along the port side to take off non-essential personnel. *Hero* kept clear of *Medway* as the latter still had some way on and the crew was ordered to jump overboard and drift astern. As the list increased to thirty degrees Capt. Ruck-Keene ordered all men other than the shipwright, electrical and engine-room damage-control parties to abandon ship. In the event, the list continued to increase so dramatically that these too leapt clear only a few minutes later. No boats could be launched and *Medway*'s people got away as best they could while she capsized, most of them from the port side. Taking to the water across the quarterdeck, her chaplain the Rev. Francis Lampen watched the end from a piece of flotsam:

> At that moment he said 'There she goes!' and the ship was turning right over and then put her bows up in the air. It was a tremendous sight and even the exhausted and drowning men seemed quiet for a few minutes. The air hissed out of her. There were two or three men sitting astride her bows – poor chaps, I suppose they couldn't swim – one jumped off as she slipped lower and lower. I expect[ed] an explosion but none came.

But explosions there were – from depth charges dropped perilously close to the survivors by destroyers of the screen. As Lampen recalled, 'The water danced in front of us and it seemed as though one was being hit in the stomach with a knock-out blow.' Despite this and the large numbers of men in the water, practically all of *Medway*'s fatal casualties were reckoned to have come in the torpedo detonations. The final death toll of just eighteen from a ship's company of 1,123 represents an unusually high survival rate for a vessel hit by multiple torpedoes and sunk in under twenty minutes. The calm, warm sea conditions no doubt played their part, together with the fact that a large launch and at least one Carley float were left on the surface after *Medway* went down along with large amounts of flotsam and jetsam. Nor was rescue long delayed, with *Hero* and *Zulu* on hand to pick up survivors. Ruck-Keene noted that 'officers and men behaved in a most exemplary manner, in keeping with the best traditions of the service', though *Medway*'s complement was by no means entirely male since a detachment of WRNS was embarked. Among those picked up by *Hero* was Third Officer Audrey Coningham who received a Mentioned in Despatches for giving her lifejacket to a seaman in distress and supporting him until rescue arrived.

U372 and Heinz-Joachim Neumann

Built by Howaldtswerke at Kiel and commissioned in April 1941, *U372* spent her entire career under Kptlt Heinz-Joachim Neumann who transferred to the *U-Boot-Waffe* after service in the battlecruiser *Scharnhorst*. Three cruises in the Atlantic in late 1941 resulted in as many sinkings but four patrols in the Mediterranean in 1942 yielded only *Medway* on *U372*'s penultimate outing. Five weeks later *Medway* was avenged by four of the destroyers whose screen Neumann had penetrated – *Sikh*, *Zulu*, *Croome* and *Tetcott* – having been directed to her position by an RAF Wellington off Haifa on 4 August 1942. *U372* was sunk in a series of depth-charge attacks but Neumann and his entire crew survived to become prisoners of war. Among them was a Lebanese agent for German intelligence whom it had been intended to put ashore near Beirut.

Sources

Admiralty, *Wartime Damage to Ships: Reports, 1942–1943* (TNA, ADM 199/2068)

—, *Recommendation for Mention in Despatches for Miss Audrey S. Coningham, 3rd Officer WRNS Following the Sinking of HMS* Medway *II* [*sic*] *in the Mediterranean* (TNA, ADM 1/12218)

Lampen, The Rev. Francis, letter to his sister Edith containing an account of the sinking, Warrington, Lancs., 9 November 1942 (IWM, Hilken papers, P137/3)

Connell, G. G., *Jack's War: Lower-Deck Recollections from World War II* (London: William Kimber, 1985)

Joyce, A. H., 'HMS *Medway* – Submarine Depot Ship' in *Warships*, Supplement no. 82 (Autumn 1985), p. 36

Mason, F. A., *The Last Destroyer: HMS* Aldenham, *1942–44* (London: Robert Hale, 1988)

Roskill, *War at Sea*, II, pp. 73–4

Wallingford, Lt Ron V., *HMS Medway, 1927–1942: From the Beginning to the End* (Southampton: privately, 1990; copy in IWM, 95/1865)

Career history of HMS *Medway*:
  http://www.naval-history.net/xGM-Chrono-28Depot-Medway1.htm

65 HMS *EAGLE*
Capt. L. D. Mackintosh, DSC RN
Sunk by *U73* (Type VIIB), Kptlt Helmut Rosenbaum, 11 August 1942
Western Mediterranean, 80 nm NNE of Algiers (Algeria)

Eagle seen off Portsmouth in 1933, probably on sailing for the China Station. *Wright & Logan*

Campaign	Operation PEDESTAL (Map 3)	*Displacement*	22,600 tons
Coordinates	38° 05' N, 03° 02' E	*Dimensions*	667.5' × 105.25' × 21.75'
Kriegsmarine code	Quadrat CH 9119	*Armour*	4.5" belt; 1–1.5" horizontal; 1.5–2" bulkheads
U-boat timekeeping	identical	*Maximum speed*	20 knots
Fatalities 162	*Survivors* 929+	*Armament*	9 × 6"; 4 × 4" AA; 16 × 40 mm AA; 12 × 20 mm AA; 4 × .303" AA
		Air wing	21 aircraft (Swordfish and Sea Hurricanes) served by two lifts

Career

In July 1912 the Chilean government ordered a pair of battleships armed with 14-inch guns from the Tyneside firm of Armstrong Whitworth & Co. After some delay in obtaining the necessary supplies of steel the second of these, *Almirante Cochrane*, was laid down at Elswick on 24 February 1913. By August 1914 the hull and machinery were largely complete but the outbreak of war with Germany brought all work on her to an abrupt halt. Worked resumed a month later by which time the two ships had been taken over by the Royal Navy with a promise that they would be restored to the Chileans after the cessation of hostilities. The first unit, the *Almirante Latorre*, was commissioned as HMS *Canada* in 1915 but the urgent need for heavy weapons resulted in *Cochrane*'s mountings being diverted elsewhere and no further steps were taken to complete her. In 1917, however, the development of air power and the huge expense involved in producing another five 14-inch mountings prompted the Admiralty to purchase the hull outright for conversion to a seaplane carrier. Work resumed in January 1918, the ship being renamed *Eagle* in March of that year. Though launched in June 1918, the pace of work slowed as it became apparent that she could not be completed by war's end and it was not until April 1920 that *Eagle* was ready for preliminary trials as the world's first true aircraft carrier. The trials in question, which included 143 deck landings, established the design feature which has since become standard in carrier construction: that the island should lie on the starboard side of the flight deck. Paid off in November 1920 for completion at Portsmouth Dockyard, *Eagle* did not enter full commission until February 1924.

HMS *Eagle* spent much of the inter-war period on foreign service, initially in the Mediterranean (1924–31) where she rendered notable assistance to victims of the Corinth earthquake in 1928 and then on the China Station (1933–5, 1937–9). In the spring of 1931 she and the destroyer *Achates* made an extended cruise in South American waters in support of the British Empire Trade Exhibition at Buenos Aires. There were refits in 1926, 1929, 1931–2 and 1936. The outbreak of the Second World War found *Eagle* at Singapore from where she and a number of cruisers were assigned to Force I in the hunt for German raiders in October 1939. The assignment took her over 30,000 miles back and forth across the Indian Ocean, which included a brief docking at Durban in December. The early part of 1940 saw her escorting troop transports in the Indian Ocean but on 14 March she suffered an explosion in her forward bomb room which claimed the lives of fourteen ratings and required repairs at Singapore until May. That same month *Eagle* joined the Mediterranean Fleet at Alexandria, the first action for her air wing coming on 5 July with an attack on Italian shipping at Tobruk which resulted in the sinking of the destroyer *Zeffiro* and three merchantmen including the liner *Liguria*. On the 8th *Eagle* was given her first taste of Italian high-level bombing but the following day her aircraft were attacking the Italian fleet off Calabria, though without result. However, an attack on the Sicilian port of Augusta on the 10th claimed the destroyer *Leone Pancaldo* while a second raid on Tobruk on the 20th sank a merchantman and the destroyers *Ostro* and *Nembo*. These successes were followed by the sinking of the submarine *Iride* and her depot ship *Monte Gargano* in the Gulf of Bomba on 22 August. From the end of that month *Eagle* participated in the effort to reinforce Malta and the Mediterranean Fleet from the west codenamed Operation HATS, her planes making a diversionary attack on the Italian airfield at Maritza on the island of Rhodes on 4 September.

In October 1940 came two further attempts to resupply Malta, this time from the east, during which *Eagle*'s air group attacked Italian air bases on Rhodes and the Libyan coast. Then on 11 November five of her Swordfish flew off from HMS *Illustrious* as part of the momentous attack on the Italian fleet at Taranto during which three battleships were put out of action. *Eagle* would have participated in this operation herself had she not been recovering from damage sustained to her aviation fuel system off Calabria in July and in subsequent aerial attacks but not immediately noticed. Convoy cover in the Eastern Mediterranean and in support of Crete together with sorties against Italian airfields and shipping continued until *Eagle* was ordered south through the Suez Canal in March 1941. Ahead of her to Port Sudan went her air wing from where they spearheaded the destruction of Italian shipping at the Eritrean port of Massawa and in the Red Sea on 3 April, an episode which claimed three Italian destroyers and two torpedo boats in collaboration with the RAF and other naval units.

After a spell at Simon's Town in May 1941 *Eagle* proceeded to Freetown, Sierra Leone for operations against German commerce raiders and shipping in the South Atlantic. On 6 June her aircraft bombed the blockade runner *Elbe* which promptly scuttled herself, but nine days later the supply ship *Lothringen* was spotted a thousand miles west of Cape Verde and captured intact by the light cruiser HMS *Dunedin* (**40**). However, on 20 September *Eagle* suffered a major hangar fire which destroyed or damaged thirteen Swordfish and obliged her to put in at Gibraltar for repairs. This together with the need for an overhaul of her engine plant brought her to Birkenhead for refitting at the end of October. In February 1942 *Eagle* returned to the Mediterranean as a replacement for HMS *Ark Royal* (**39**) and resumed the convoy escort duties which define the last phase of her varied career. At the end of that month she began the first of ten aircraft-ferrying operations during which a total of 183 Spitfires were flown off for the defence of Malta. April was spent under repair at Gibraltar but in June *Eagle*'s Sea Hurricanes provided cover for the heavily contested Malta supply convoy codenamed Operation HARPOON during which two destroyers and four of the six merchantmen were lost. For *Eagle* it was but a taste of things to come.

Background of the attack

On 3 August 1942 the fourteen vessels of convoy WS21S sailed from the Clyde, the latest demonstration of the British government's will to resupply the embattled island of Malta. In its final phase through the Western Mediterranean convoy WS21S, now reinforced by a major squadron of British warships and support vessels, became the focus of one of the great naval battles of the Second World War: Operation PEDESTAL. The escort, commanded by Vice-Admiral E. N. Syfret, consisted of the battleships *Nelson* and *Rodney*, the cruisers *Sirius*, *Phoebe*, *Charybdis*, *Nigeria*, *Kenya*, *Manchester* and *Cairo* and no fewer than twenty destroyers, supported by four corvettes, two oilers and a tug, many of which were to go right through to Malta. In addition, air cover was to be provided by the carriers *Victorious*, *Indomitable* and *Eagle* as far east as Bizerte at the entrance to the Sicilian Narrows, the most dangerous part of the voyage. This force, commanded by Rear-Admiral A. L. St G. Lyster in *Victorious*, brought the total number of ships escorting WS21S to forty-one. Other measures were in place as well. Early on the 10th, just as WS21S was passing Gibraltar, a decoy convoy sailed from Port Said into the Eastern Mediterranean. But if a modest amount of confusion was sowed, the Germans and Italians had long since been aware of the planned convoy from the west. Although the main strength of the Axis awaited PEDESTAL south of Sardinia and beyond, *F.d.U. Italien* (Officer Commanding U-Boats, Italy, Konteradmiral Leo Kreisch) had already deployed *U73* (Kptlt Helmut Rosenbaum) and *U331* (Kptlt Hans-Diedrich Freiherr von Tiesenhausen; see **41**) to patrol the waters between Mallorca and Algiers. *U331* was surprised on the surface and damaged by an RAF Hudson on the 8th, but on the morning of the 11th *U73*'s hydrophones picked up the unmistakeable sound of a major force sailing east about eighty miles north-east of Algiers. The following extract from Rosenbaum's log shows once again how an audacious approach by a submarine in the Mediterranean could bear the richest of fruit.

War Diary of *U73*, patrol of 4 August–5 September 1942: PG 30069b, NHB, reel 1,071, pp. 43–4

Date, time	Details of position, wind, weather, sea, light, visibility, moonlight, etc.	Incidents
11.viii		
1045		At periscope depth.
1053		All clear to surface. Hydrophone bearings reported. A quick look around reveals nothing.
1100	Qu. CH 9118	Masts seen through periscope at 180°, destroyers at 5,000 m.
1105		A very long vessel in sight at bearing 200–230° true.[1] Carrier? Freighter? Accompanied by five 'H'- and 'I'-class destroyers as well as another escort vessel.[2] Range 5,000–8,000 m. Zigzagging on a general course of 90°, 12 knots. No opportunity to attack. We shadow them.
1150		A single 'G'-class destroyer approaches from the west at high speed (25 knots), passes us just 400 m to starboard.[3] She is zigzagging towards the first group we saw. In the periscope I can make out a single aircraft far off.
1200	Qu. CH 9119, wind ESE 2, sea 2, 1,021 mb, visibility 10 nm	Day's run: Surfaced: 68.8 nm. Submerged: 44.6 nm. <u>113.4 nm, overall 1,029.2 nm.</u>
1210		Same destroyer turns about and comes back towards us, flashing morse with her searchlight, inclination 0°. Passes 60–80 m astern heading west again.
1224		In the direction she was flashing her light we catch sight of the following with the periscope at 2½ m:
1226		A forest of masts in sight between bearings 270° and 330° true and ahead of these, quite close to us, the escort screen.
1229		Atherstone-class escort vessel passes at 600 m.[4]
1235		Kingfisher-class escort passes us at just 400 m carrying out Asdic sweep.[5]
1236		General periscope impression: warship masts, around eight to ten merchantmen of 7–10,000 GRT, two cruisers, eight destroyers and three other escort vessels, bows right, inclinations varying between 10° and 20°, steering easterly course.[6]
1240		We steer 0° at ¾ speed to get into an attacking position, then alter to a converging course.
1250		I recognise *Eagle* as the rear-most ship of the starboard (southerly) outer column.[7]
1256		To all hands: 'Give your all! Our target is the *Eagle*!'
1300		A destroyer screen of seven destroyers to negotiate.[8] We break through between the third and fourth destroyers with a hard steering manoeuvre from the south, passing them both at a range of 300–400 m. Asdic pulses on all sides.
1302	Western Mediterranean, south of the Balearics	Starboard column now clearly in sight: a Charybdis-class cruiser and *Eagle* in staggered formation, each with a 'V and W'-class destroyer as close escort, at ship's bearing 45° and 135° respectively.[9] Course 100°, inclination 0° (see sketch).[10]
1304		The lead ship of the central column (which comprises eight freighters and transports of 7,000–10,000 GRT) passes 500 m to starboard, followed by the other vessels of this column one after another.[11] If only we had more torpedo tubes!

---

1 Possibly HMS *Eagle* but could equally be *Victorious*, *Indomitable* or even *Furious*, then preparing to carry out Operation Bellows, the flying off of thirty-six Spitfires for Malta.

2 The identity of this group is unclear but if Rosenbaum's description is accurate it would seem not to be *Eagle*'s escort.

3 Possibly HMS *Laforey* of the 'L' class which went on ahead of the screen to refuel having been relieved by HMS *Westcott* at 1100.

4 Presumably one of the Hunt-class destroyers on the northern wing of the screen through which *U73* passed in order to engage *Eagle*, possibly HMS *Wilton*.

5 Possibly another Hunt-class destroyer since no Kingfisher-class patrol sloop took part in Operation Pedestal.

6 Rosenbaum's description of the centre of the convoy is broadly accurate though the numbers of ships are slightly underestimated, the fourteen merchantmen having been under close escort by three cruisers: *Manchester*, *Kenya* and *Nigeria*.

7 Few U-boat commanders were better placed to recognise *Eagle* than Rosenbaum who had attended a reception aboard her at Tsingtau (now Qingdao) in the summer of 1933 while serving as a cadet in the light cruiser *Köln*.

8 *Eagle* had been allocated the following six destroyers as her escort, though their precise dispositions at the time she was sunk are unclear: *Malcolm*, *Venomous*, *Keppel*, *Amazon*, *Wolverine* and *Vidette*.

9 Respectively *Charybdis* of the Dido class, *Eagle* and most likely *Malcolm* and *Venomous*.

10 This survives as an appendix to the log.

11 Possibly MS *Deucalion*, sunk the following day.

Date, time	Details of position, wind, weather, sea, light, visibility, moonlight, etc.	Incidents
1305		Our opportunity comes to attack *Eagle* from within the convoy, range rapidly decreasing. I reduce the
1315	Qu. CH 9119, wind ESE 3, sea 2–3, cloud 2, visibility 10–12 nm, water depth 2,400–2,600 m	angle of dispersion from 14° to 6° for each torpedo and fire a quadruple spread. Firing data: range 800 m, enemy speed 12 knots, inclination 64°, depth 6 m. After 32 sec. running time (= 480 m) a very loud detonation, followed by a second, third and fourth at precisely the intervals at which the torpedoes were fired! Just as planned!
1317		We dip beneath the surface on firing then alter course to 260° and alarm dive to 160 m. All the while we can hear loud sinking, cracking, bursting and roaring noises.
1329		A single dull, powerful explosion (boilers?).
1330		This is followed by the continual dropping of depth charges without any discernible pattern, at first thirteen of them. Also unavailing Asdic pulses.
1350		Another six depth charges, reasonably well aimed. We go to 100 m due to water leak. We pump out. Water entering at a rate of 700 litres per hour through the starboard exhaust valve alone.
1410		We withdraw, initially at 300° then at 0°.
⤢		
1828		Outgoing W/T transmission 1315/516/11: *Convoy of 15 destroyers and escort vessels, 2 cruisers, 9–10 freighters,* Eagle, *probably 1 battleship. Qu. [CH] 9119. 4 hits on* Eagle *from 500 m, loud sinking noises. Depth charges but alright. Rosenbaum.*
⤢		
2256		Incoming W/T transmission from *F.d.U.: Bravo Rosenbaum!!*

The sinking

Rosenbaum may be excused his free use of exclamation marks (a feature of his log generally) as there are no other cases in the Second World War of a U-boat hitting a warship with all four bow torpedoes from the same spread. Not without reason did the convoy escort commander, Vice-Admiral Syfret, consider that there was nothing to be gained from holding a Board of Enquiry into *Eagle*'s sinking. The four torpedoes, which struck with 'heavy muffled explosions' at forty-foot intervals forward between Port No. 3 and No. 2 guns, sealed *Eagle*'s fate in a matter of seconds. Listing five degrees to port after the first torpedo struck, this increased to fifteen degrees with the fourth hit after which *Eagle* 'continued to list rapidly to 30 degrees and then settled bodily'. By this time the list was sufficient to tip the Sea Hurricanes off the flight deck and into the water while men desperately scrambled across her hull. So quickly did *Eagle* founder that only a rough assessment of the damage to key areas could be made through survivor interviews. These revealed that several of the port wing bulkheads had collapsed leading to the complete flooding of the Port Wing Engine Room and 'A', 'C' and 'D' Boiler Rooms. That 'B' Boiler Room had also flooded was deduced from the failure of any of those manning it to survive. The speed with which the port side flooded prevented any damage-control measures being taken and *Eagle* sank in what is variously estimated to be six to eight minutes, although a note on Rosenbaum's plot of the attack estimates fifteen minutes.

HMS *Eagle* was only the most notable casualty of Operation PEDESTAL which lost nine of its fourteen merchantmen together with the cruisers *Manchester* and *Cairo* and the destroyer *Foresight* under relentless Axis air, surface and submarine attack. Damage was also inflicted on the carrier *Indomitable* and the cruisers *Nigeria* and *Kenya*. However, if PEDESTAL is remembered as a strategic victory it is because among the five vessels which battled their way into Malta was the tanker *Ohio* with 10,000 tons of aviation fuel. As Roskill related

in *The War at Sea*, this cargo was to have a significant impact on the course of the war in North Africa: 'The fuel which she carried enabled air strikes to be restarted from Malta just when Rommel was preparing for the offensive intended to drive the Allies firmly out of Egypt. The enemy's shipping losses to air attacks at once increased, and the offensive had to be postponed because of shortage of supplies.' Instead the British 8th Army began in October 1942 the offensive which ended seven months later in the surrender of all Axis forces in North Africa. To that extent HMS *Eagle* was not lost in vain.

For Dr Goebbels, on the other hand, the sinking of *Eagle* was a triumph blessedly free of the embarrassment that had attended the loss of *Ark Royal* the previous November (**39**). Rosenbaum was awarded the Knight's Cross and the Berlin propaganda machine made enormous capital out of the incident, the tenth and last British capital ship to be lost during the Second World War. The only issue from the British side, the failure of the screen to detect *U73*, was not considered worth pursuing as the problems of Asdic detection in the Mediterranean had been documented in a string of sinking reports (see HMSs *Barham* and *Medway*, **41** and **64**), while the noise and speed of the convoy had ruled out the possibility of hydrophone detection.

Fate of the crew

The speed of the sinking and the failure of all means of communication other than word of mouth prevented the order to abandon ship being passed effectively. That so many men survived (over 900 out of nearly 1,100) was due not only to the initiative of her officers who had little hesitation in telling the men mustered at their abandon ship stations to jump for their lives, but also to the fact that the entire ship's company was on the move when the torpedoes struck, being stood down from Action Stations to Defence Stations. Even so, the survival rate was impressively high given that none of the ship's boats were usable, those on the port side being submerged in three minutes and the starboard

Eagle capsizing to port shortly after taking four hits from *U73*. Aircraft are being tipped off the flight deck as the list becomes more pronounced. She had disappeared within six or eight minutes of the attack. *IWM*

ones unlaunchable owing to the list. AB Bill Loades recalls his escape:

> I was on the bridge on the starboard side and we were in great difficulty getting down to sea level to swim for it. As the ship sank in eight minutes it didn't give too much time, although it seemed ages. We waited until she was at an angle of 45° or so to [port] and then slid down the [starboard] side – not so easy as there were numerous openings into the waist of the ship. When we did get down we then had the problem of climbing up the torpedo bulges which were also at 45° but the other way, thus forming a V, and very slimy. Once in the sea we faced fuel oil and patches of aviation fuel, and with no buoyancy, you needed to swim under these patches.

Many were dragged down as *Eagle* sank but resurfaced to tell the tale, the destroyers *Lookout* and *Laforey* joining the tug *Jaunty* in dragging oil-soaked men from the warm waters of the Mediterranean. Most of those picked up were transferred to HMSs *Venomous* (which received 535 officers and men including Capt. Mackintosh), *Malcolm* and *Keppel* and returned to Gibraltar. Four aircraft that *Eagle* had flown off prior to being struck put down on *Indomitable* and *Victorious*, their pilots subsequently awarded DSCs for valiant service over the next few days though one, Sub-Lt (A) M. A. Hankey, was shot down and killed on the 14th.

U73 and Helmut Rosenbaum

Built by Bremer Vulkan at Vegesack and commissioned in September 1940, *U73* enjoyed a lengthy career comprising eighteen frontline patrols. The first six of these took place in the Atlantic under Kptlt Helmut Rosenbaum, previously in command of the Type-IIB *U2*. *U73*'s Atlantic service resulted in the sinking of only four ships (three in her second patrol from convoy SC26) though she participated in more than her fair share of unsuccessful pack operations. In May 1941 *U73* was among the boats assigned to support the battleship *Bismarck* during her ill-fated sortie into the Atlantic. The following January Rosenbaum took *U73* into the Mediterranean where another four patrols completed his tenure. *Eagle* was Rosenbaum's only victim though the same cruise saw an unsuccessful attempt to finish off the cruiser *Nigeria* on 14 August after she had been torpedoed by the Italian submarine *Axum* on the 12th. Eight patrols in the Mediterranean under Oblt.z.S. Horst Deckert yielded just two merchantmen and damage to the British naval oiler RFA *Abbeydale* in June 1943. On 16 December 1943 *U73* was located and depth charged by the US destroyers *Woolsey*. Within an hour she was detected on the surface by radar in USS *Trippe* and attacked with gunfire from both ships. This she returned, causing casualties in *Woolsey* before succumbing with the loss of sixteen of her fifty crewmen. The survivors, Deckert among

Eagle's silhouette being painted onto one of *U73*'s forward torpedo tubes. *DUBMA*

them, were taken on board *Woolsey* and spent the rest of the war as prisoners.

After leaving *U73* in October 1943 Kptlt Rosenbaum assumed command of the 30th *U-Flottille* operating against Soviet forces in the Black Sea. He was killed in an air accident near Konstanza, Rumania in May 1944.

Sources

Admiralty, *Operation 'Pedestal' (Malta Convoy): Reports* (TNA, ADM 199/1242)

—, *Wartime Damage to Ships: Reports, 1941–1942* (TNA, ADM 199/2067)

—, *Operation 'Pedestal': Awards to F. A. A. Personnel for Services Following Loss of HMS* Eagle (TNA, ADM 1/14275)

U73 file (DUBMA)

Arthur, Max, ed., *The Navy: 1939 to the Present Day* (London: Hodder & Stoughton, 1997)

Brook, Peter, *Warships for Export: Armstrong Warships, 1867–1927* (Gravesend, Kent: World Ship Society, 1999)

Brown, David, *Carrier Air Groups: HMS* Eagle (Windsor, Berks.: Hylton Lacy, 1972)

—, *HMS* Eagle [Warships in Profile, no. 35] (Windsor, Berks.: Profile Publications, 1973)

Busch, Harald, '*U73 torpedierte die Eagle*' in *Der Frontsoldat erzählt*, no. 6 (1942), pp. 133–5

Crosley, Commander R. (Mike), *They Gave Me a Seafire* (Shrewsbury, Salop: Airlife Publishing, 1986)

Jones, Geoffrey, *U Boat Aces and Their Fates* (London: William Kimber, 1988)

Roskill, *War at Sea*, II, pp. 302–9

Smith, Peter C., *Pedestal: The Malta Convoy of August 1942* (London: William Kimber, 1970)

—, *Eagle's War: The War Diary of an Aircraft Carrier* (London: Crecy Books, 1995)

War career of HMS *Eagle*:
  http://www.naval-history.net/xGM-Chrono-04CV-Eagle.htm

Fleet Air Arm Archive webpage devoted to HMS *Eagle*:
  http://www.fleetairarmarchive.net/Ships/Eagle1.html

66 USS *MUSKEGET* (ex SS *CORNISH*)

Lt Cdr C. E. Toft, USCG†

Sunk by *U755* (Type VIIC), Kptlt Walter Göing, 9 September 1942

North Atlantic, 425 nm NE of St John's, Newfoundland

The ex-Coast Guard cutter *Muskeget* seen on 17 February 1942, seven months before she was lost with all hands to a pair of torpedoes from *U755*. *BfZ*

Theatre	North Atlantic (Map 1)	*Deadweight*	3,170 tons
Coordinates	51° 41 N, 43° 53' W	*Gross tons*	1,827
Kriegsmarine code	Quadrat AJ 9727	*Dimensions*	250' × 40.25' × 24.25'
U-boat timekeeping differential	unknown	*Maximum speed*	11.5 knots
Fatalities	about 116 and 5 *Survivors* none	*Armament*	1 × 4"; 1 × 3"; 4 × 20 mm AA

Career

For background on the US Coast Guard, see USS *Alexander Hamilton* (**48**).

The auxiliary cutter *Muskeget* originated as the freighter *Cornish* laid down for Eastern Steamship Lines, Inc. at Bethlehem Shipbuilding Corporation, Sparrows Point, Maryland and launched in December 1922. Completed in 1923, the *Cornish* spent her peacetime career in the coastal trade and on the Great Lakes. On 29 December 1941 she was chartered by the US Navy and converted to an auxiliary cutter by the Sullivan Drydock & Repair Co. of New York at a cost of $250,000. Commissioned with the hull number YAG-9 on 3 January 1942 and assigned to the 3rd Naval District, she carried out patrol duty off New York until renamed *Muskeget* (hull number AG-48) on 30 May. Exactly a month later she was transferred to the US Coast Guard which commissioned her on 1 July with the hull number WAG-48, the 'USS' designation being retained per wartime regulations. She was then ordered to Boston in the 1st Naval District for duty with the Weather Observation Patrol, falling under the authority of the District Coast Guard Officer when in harbour and the Commander-in Chief Atlantic Fleet (CINCLANT, CTF 24) when at sea. In July came *Muskeget*'s first assignment to patrol Weather Station No. 2 at 53° 00' N, 42° 30' W, approximately 500 miles north-east of Newfoundland, the

ship returning to Boston on 27 July 1942 before sailing for patrol duty on the same weather station on 24 August. The sea area to which she was assigned as Weather Observation Station Ship – between Halifax, Nova Scotia, Cape Race, Newfoundland, and Iceland – was accurately described as 'a seething and continuous mass movement of convoys and enemy submarines', and it was not long before *Muskeget* attracted the attention of the latter.

Background of the attack

Sailing on her maiden patrol from Kiel on 4 August 1942, *U755* was assigned to the newly formed *Lohs* patrol line in the North Atlantic, so named for Johannes Lohs, a U-boat ace of the Great War. However, unlike Lohs himself more than two months passed without Kptlt Walter Göing notching up any successes either with this or the *Tiger* and *Luchs* ('lynx') groups. But *U755* was not to return to Brest without a pennant. Refuelled by *U462* at the end of August, on the afternoon of 9 September she sighted a steamer which Göing correctly identified as an 'auxiliary naval vessel'. He had come across the USS *Muskeget*, then reaching the end of a weather-reporting cruise and awaiting relief from another requisitioned cutter, the *Monomoy*. By the time the latter arrived on station on the 11th all trace of *Muskeget* and her crew had vanished.

War Diary of *U755*, patrol of 4 August–6 October 1942: PG 30880, NHB, reel 1,138, pp. 383–4

Date, time	Details of position, wind, weather, sea, light, visibility, moonlight, etc.	Incidents
9.ix		
1200	Qu. AJ 9728, wind NW 5, sea 2, cloud 8, 1,018 mb, +11.5°C [53°F]	Day's run: 138 nm on the surface, 0 nm submerged.
1236–1320		Test dive.
1425		The bridge watch reports the tip of a mast emerging from a squall at bearing 50° true. By the time I reach the bridge the masts are already quite prominent on the horizon. Hauling ahead on the surface is no longer an option. I therefore decide to attack immediately and sound the alarm. At first we can see nothing after diving because of the Atlantic swell. The hydrophone operator continues to report hearing propeller noises at ship's bearing 180°. He can also hear Asdic-type impulses that apparently sound like drops of water falling onto a hotplate. I therefore assume a course of 50° and at 1454 re-establish visual contact, inclination 0°. The approach of the vessel in my wake and the fact that the inclination of 0° remains constant leads me to conclude that she picked us up by hydrophone on the surface and is now trying to get an underwater fix. I withdraw at 140° to open some distance on her beam and then alter to a parallel course of 230°. It is extremely difficult to keep the boat steady in the heavy swell so it is only later that I can make out the features of the vessel. She is a cargo steamer with passenger decks. On her fo'c's'le she has two 10.5-cm guns.[1] Forward of the bridge on both port and starboard sides there is a sort of searchlight platform on which anti-aircraft guns are mounted. I can't make out the number of guns aft. When she sinks later I then see she has two further 10.5-cm guns aft.[1] The ship has camouflage painting (mimicry). It is clear to me that we are faced with an auxiliary naval vessel which is presumably stationed here to perform the combined roles of armed merchant cruiser, U-boat hunter and weather-reporting vessel.[2]
1510		At 1510 I alter to an attacking course of 320° – the Asdic pulses have now stopped – and at 1516 we fire a spread of three from a range of 800 m.
1516	Qu. AJ 9727, wind NW 3, sea 3, swell of average severity, cloud 5, 1,020 mb, +12°C [54°F]	The boat dips below the surface completely once we have got the spread away. After 50 sec. we hear two contacts and two detonations.[3] By the time the periscope reemerges only the stern of the steamer can be seen. The boat then dips below the surface once more. At this point there are two powerful detonations 30 sec. apart. The first is probably a boiler explosion after which we can hear the sound of collapsing bulkheads. The second detonation is her armed depth charges going up. This has some minor repercussions for us in the boat. By the time the trim is restored there is nothing to be seen of the steamer, nor any trace of her.
1555		At 1555 I surface and close the scene of the sinking. There's not much floating about. Three men have sought refuge in a rubber dinghy. Some of the crew are struggling for their lives in the water. There is virtually no wreckage to cling to.
1600	Qu. AJ 9727, wind NW 3, sea 2–3, cloud 5, 1,020 mb, +12°C [54°F]	
1627		At 1627 I haul away and once again begin carrying out my patrol sweeps.
2000	Qu. AJ 9728, wind NW 4, sea 3, cloud 8, 1,021 mb, +12°C [54°F]	
2104		At 2104 our boat is once again at the scene of the sinking. There is now a giant oil slick here that extends for several miles. After a great deal of searching I come across two rubber dinghies that have been tied together, containing eight survivors. Just two white men, the others niggers or half-castes.[4] They are all wearing the same type of overalls with built-in lifejackets. For headgear they are wearing

---

1   Such sources as are available suggest that *Muskeget*'s armament was limited to a 4-inch and a 3-inch gun together with four 20-mm anti-aircraft guns. The exact disposition of the larger ordnance is unclear but Göing is correct in identifying two of the latter guns mounted on the bridge structure.

2   Only the last of these assumptions is correct.

3   The running time equates to a range at the point of intersection of approximately 750 metres.

4   See below.

Date, time	Details of position, wind, weather, sea, light, visibility, moonlight, etc.	Incidents
		a sort of car helmet.[5] The uniforms make it quite clear that these are crewmen.[6] We carry out a rather hopeless interrogation attempt – they all try to answer at the same time and shout each other down – which tells me only that this was an American ship that appears to have been called *Muskogee*, *Mukilted* or something like that. When questioned on the tonnage, answers ranged from 7,000 to 3,000 GRT. I would have estimated 3,000 GRT.[7]
2204		At 2204 I move back into position.
2400	Qu. AJ 9489, wind WNW 2–3, sea 2, cloud 3, 1,024 mb, +11°C [52°F]	*Göing*

---

5 The description of their headgear suggests that these men may have formed part of a gun crew.

6 Göing here uses the word *Soldaten*, literally 'soldiers' but Kriegsmarine slang for its crewmen.

7 *Muskeget* was in fact of 1,827 GRT as completed.

The sinking and fate of the crew

In the absence of any survivors, such evidence as exists on the loss of the *Muskeget* is confined to the extract from *U755*'s war diary given above. This indicates that she was struck twice and sank rapidly, her end hastened by secondary explosions which left little debris and few survivors. Whether or not *Muskeget* obtained a fix for *U755* before being struck as Göing suggests remains a matter for conjecture.

The log indicates that very few survived the sinking and that by nightfall their number had dwindled to eight men on two rafts. It should be added that while Göing's epithets might in different circumstances as easily have issued from the mouth of an Allied sailor, there is nonetheless a ruthlessness to his description of men adrift which may reflect the shift in mood by many in the *U-Boot-Waffe* as the Battle of the Atlantic intensified that summer, especially following the *Laconia* incident later that same September (**G34**).

Many years passed before the bereaved learnt anything of *Muskeget*'s end. It was suspected that something was amiss when *Muskeget* failed to report in either later on the 9th or on the 10th, and when signals from her relief, the cutter USS *Monomoy*, went unanswered on the 11th the US Coast Guard began to fear the worst. *Monomoy* continued to sweep the area, attempting to raise *Muskeget* by radio all the while, but in vain. A further search between 15 and 16 September yielded nothing and next of kin (including those of four US Weather Service employees and one Public Health Service officer) were informed on the 25th once it was clear that *Muskeget* would never return to Boston. In an assessment of her fate in May 1943, Capt. C. A. Park, Chief Operations Officer of the US Coast Guard, recorded how 'planes and patrol vessels searched without finding any trace of the vessel. It is assumed the *Muskeget* was probably lost through enemy action, although it may never be definitely known how the loss occurred.' Though official sources qualify her loss to *U755* as only a matter of probability, Göing's log could hardly be more conclusive.

U755 and Walter Göing

Built by the Kriegsmarine Werft at Wilhelmshaven and commissioned in November 1941, *U755* served five frontline patrols under Oblt.z.S. (Kptlt from January 1942) Walter Göing, the first of which accounted for *Muskeget*. *U755*'s second cruise took her to the Mediterranean

Göing seen in command of *U755* in 1942 or '43. *DUBMA*

where no success was enjoyed until her fourth patrol in the spring of 1943 when she sank the Free French anti-submarine trawler *Sergent Gouarne* (**G50**) and a small freighter off Morocco before returning to Toulon. On 28 May, ten days into her fifth patrol, *U755* was sighted off Mallorca by an RAF Hudson which despatched her with two rockets after Göing elected to make a fight of it. Nine men survived to be picked up by the Spanish destroyer *Velasco* and landed at Valencia. Kptlt Göing was not among them.

Sources

Navy Department, Assorted papers concerning loss of USS *Muskeget* (NA, RG 26, Records of the US Coast Guard, general correspondence 1941–53, file 601)

—, Press release concerning loss of USS *Muskeget*, 11 September 1942 (NHC, Box 552)

DANFS, IV, p. 461; also on: http://www.history.navy.mil/danfs/m16/muskeget.htm

Scheina, Robert L., *US Coast Guard Cutters and Craft in World War II* (Annapolis, Md.: Naval Institute Press, 1982)

Webpage devoted to USS *Muskeget*: http://www.uscg.mil/history/webcutters/Muskeget_WAG_48.pdf

Dinsmore, Captain R. P., USCG (Ret.), 'Ocean Weather Ships, 1940–1980' on: http://www.uscg.mil/history/webcutters/rpdinsmore_oceanstations.asp

67   HMCS *CHARLOTTETOWN* (i)

Lt Cdr J. W. Bonner, RCNR†
Sunk by *U517* (Type IXC), Kptlt Paul Hartwig, 11 September 1942
St Lawrence River, 10 nm NNW of Cap-Chat, Quebec (Canada)

Charlottetown under way in about 1942. She was hit by *U517* on the starboard side aft and sank in three minutes. *Naval Museum of Alberta*

Theatre	Canadian home waters (Map 1)	*Displacement*	940 tons
Coordinates	49° 12' N, 66° 48' W	*Dimensions*	205.25' × 33' × approx. 11.25'
Kriegsmarine code	Quadrat BA 3911	*Maximum speed*	16 knots
U-boat timekeeping differential	+2 hours	*Armament*	1 × 4"; 4 × .303" AA
Fatalities	10 *Survivors* about 54		

Career

For background on the Royal Canadian Navy, see HMCS *Lévis* (**32**). For design notes on the Flower-class corvettes, see HMS *Picotee* (**29**). Notes on the Canadian Flowers are provided in HMCS *Lévis*.

The Flower-class corvette *Charlottetown* was laid down at Kingston Shipbuilding Co. of Kingston, Ontario in June 1941, launched in September and commissioned at Quebec City on 13 December that same year. Having worked up at Halifax, Nova Scotia *Charlottetown* joined the Western Local Escort Force with which she remained until increased U-boat activity in the Gulf of St Lawrence brought about her transfer to the Gulf Escort Force in July 1942. She served out the rest of her brief career escorting convoys between Quebec City and Sydney, Cape Breton Island, Nova Scotia.

Background of the attack

As increasing numbers of long-range Type-IX boats emerged in the spring and summer of 1942 so the *U-Boot-Waffe* was able to devote more resources to foraging in the Gulf of St Lawrence and its approaches, namely the Cabot and Belle Isle Straits and the broader reaches of the St Lawrence River leading towards Quebec City. Early successes in May by *U553* (Kptlt Karl Thurmann; see **35**) and July by *U132* (Kptlt Ernst Vogelsang; see **48**) were followed in August by the committing of *U165* (Korvkpt. Eberhard Hoffmann), *U513* (Korvkpt.

Rolf Rüggeberg) and *U517* (Kptlt Paul Hartwig) to these waters. The fact that this was the maiden patrol of each boat and commander proved no disadvantage with *U165* and *U517* enjoying notable success against convoys between Quebec City, Gaspé (Quebec) and Sydney in August and September. In early September these two accounted for four merchantmen from convoy QS33 as well as HMC armed yacht *Raccoon* which was torpedoed by *U165* in the Gulf of St Lawrence on the 7th (**G33**) and lost with all hands. After these successes *U517* moved into the St Lawrence River proper, whose mixture of fresh and salt water rendered Allied Asdic equipment virtually unusable but on the other hand impaired U-boat manoeuvrability and complicated the diving process. Shortly after dawn on 11 September Hartwig sighted HMCS *Charlottetown* sailing downriver in company with the minesweeping sloop *Clayoquot*. They were returning to Gaspé having escorted SQ35 as far as Red Islet at the confluence of the St Lawrence and the Saguenay, the point above which the St Lawrence was considered impenetrable to submarines. With *Clayoquot* low on fuel after the opportunity to oil at Rimouski on the south bank of the St Lawrence had apparently been passed up, neither vessel was zigzagging but sailing in line abreast at a distance of a mile. Despite the early morning fog *U517* was able to carry out a submerged attack, hitting *Charlottetown* with both of her torpedoes.

War Diary of *U517*, patrol of 8 August–19 October 1942: PG 30555, NHB, reel 1,116, p. 77

Date, time	Details of position, wind, weather, sea, light, visibility, moonlight, etc.	*Incidents*
11.ix	**Gulf of St Lawrence**	
0210		Surfaced. Good visibility. Cruising up and down in BA 38 and 39.[1]
0400	Qu. BA 3912	
0800	Qu. BA 3674	
1127		We dive at dawn. It's a foggy day.
1200	Qu. BA 3912	
1250	Qu. BA 3911	Steamer in sight.[2]
1253		Battle Stations.
1258		Vessel successfully hit with spread of two torpedoes. Auxiliary warship of some 3,500 tons, proceeding at 14 knots, course 46°.[3] Two guns, war ensign, camouflage painting, depth charges visible on her stern.[4] Hits not observed as we dip below the surface but two torpedo detonations heard. Periscope depth immediately resumed. Vessel is listing some 20–30° to starboard and down by the stern, having turned perhaps 90° to port. Immediately after the torpedo detonations about four depth charges are dropped somewhere nearby.[5] As I am unsure whether these come from an aircraft or an escort vessel (neither time nor the fog permits a full periscope sweep) I order us to a depth of 120 m.
1300–1600		Constant depth-charge detonations.[6] Either that or ammunition detonating on board torpedoed vessel. Through the hydrophones we clearly identify collapsing bulkheads and vessel sinking into the depths.
1600	Qu. BA 3675	
1900		Flying boat sighted.
2323		Three detonations far off. Presumably depth charges of flooded vessel. Day's run to 1200: 93.6 nm.

Hartwig

---

1 These are the Kriegsmarine grid references for the waters off Cap-Chat on the south bank of the St Lawrence River just before it opens up into the Gulf of the same name. The distance from Cap-Chat to the nearest point on the north bank of the St Lawrence (Pointe-des-Monts) is some thirty miles.

2 HMCS *Charlottetown*.

3 Hartwig repeats this assessment of type and size in the torpedo report, whereas the corvette *Charlottetown* in fact displaced 940 tons. The torpedo report corrects the target speed to 13 knots though this was recorded by the Canadians as having been 11½ knots.

4 *Charlottetown*'s armament consisted of a 4-inch gun forward and a quadruple .303-inch mounting aft.

5 These were *Charlottetown*'s own depth charges exploding. Hartwig appears not to have sighted *Clayoquot*, sailing in line abreast with *Charlottetown* but concealed in the mist a mile on her port beam.

6 These were indeed depth-charge attacks, carried out by *Clayoquot*.

The sinking

U517's first torpedo is recorded as having struck *Charlottetown* on her starboard quarter at 1103 Canadian time. The ship was forced round by ninety degrees, a circumstance also noted in Hartwig's log but which no doubt owed more to the severing of the propeller than the detonation itself, as posited by a number of survivors. Whatever the case, *Charlottetown* was already sinking by the stern by the time Hartwig's second torpedo detonated a few seconds later, probably in No. 2 Boiler Room. No attempt was or could be made to assess the damage and take countermeasures, the movement aft and a heavy list to starboard making a speedy abandon ship the overriding priority. HMCS *Charlottetown* sank stern first within approximately three minutes of being hit.

The Board of Inquiry sat the very next day (12 September) at HMCS *Fort Ramsay*, the naval base at Gaspé. It offered no criticism of those involved, noting the excellent behaviour of *Charlottetown*'s officers and men, the probability that all depth charges had been set to safe (accepting the view offered by the First Lieutenant, Lt George Moors, that the torpedo might have fractured the pistols), and

extolling *Clayoquot*'s commanding officer, Lt H. E. Lade RCNVR for his skill, judgement and seamanship, as well as the bearing of both ships' companies. However, critical voices were subsequently raised in connection with the sinking. With some justification did Rear-Admiral L. W. Murray RCN of Newfoundland Command question whether the depth charges had indeed been set to safe. Moreover, in view of Lade's testimony to the Board and the two hours that *Clayoquot* spent hunting *U517*, Murray concluded this ship to have had sufficient reserve of fuel to have permitted both vessels to be zigzagging, or at the very least proceeding at higher speed, at the time *Charlottetown* was struck.

A combination of minimal detail in the communiqué announcing the sinking on 18 September (stating simply that *Charlottetown* had been lost in Northern Waters where enemy submarines had been active) together with an excess of zeal on the part of certain newspapers gave the impression that she had succumbed during a heroic convoy battle in the Atlantic, her end linked both to the loss of the destroyer *Ottawa* three days later (see next entry, **68**) and *Assiniboine*'s destruction of *U210* on 6 August. Only later was it revealed that she had been sunk in waters very much closer to home than the authorities dared admit.

Paul Hartwig seen in an undated studio photo. *DUBMA*

Fate of the crew

Charlottetown's casualties were remarkably few in view of her rapid sinking, perhaps due to the fact that a change of watch just minutes before she was struck meant that most of her ship's company were in a state of relative preparedness. Even so, sources differ on the number of those killed and at what stage they lost their lives. Only two men are known to have been killed outright by the detonations, the Chief Engineer CERA David Todd in his cabin and AB L. A. Wharton who was blasted off the bridge and into the sea. In no doubt that *Charlottetown* was finished, Lt Cdr Willard Bonner was exhorting his men to abandon ship within seconds of the first hit and both the starboard seaboat and a number of Carley floats were successfully launched. However, attempts to release the port-side boat had to be abandoned owing to the list. With almost all the men off the ship (Bonner being the last) and *Charlottetown*'s bow rising before the final plunge, a depth charge exploded followed a minute or two later by four or five more, most of them noted by Hartwig in his log. The first apparently claimed more lives than Hartwig's torpedoes (including that of Bonner) and injured another thirteen men; Bonner was lashed to the rudder to make space for the living before his weight tore it loose. For all this, the morale of the survivors appears to have been exceptional. Although *Clayoquot*'s unavailing efforts to locate and sink the offending U-boat delayed the work of rescue by several hours, *Charlottetown*'s men cheered her each time she sped past on her anti-submarine sweeps. By midday the survivors were aboard *Clayoquot* to be disembarked at Gaspé at 2030 that evening. Among those

recognised was Sick Berth Attendant C. Bateman of *Charlottetown* who received a Mention in Despatches for tireless work tending the wounded throughout the day despite injuries to himself. One man succumbed in *Clayoquot* and several more perished in hospital ashore bringing the death toll to ten.

Charlottetown's name was revived in the shape of a River-class frigate laid down at Lauzon, Quebec in January 1943 and completed in April 1944, though the concession of the same pendant number – K.244 – was a departure from RCN practice.

U517 and Paul Hartwig

Built by Deutsche Werft at Hamburg and commissioned in March 1942, *U517* was one of the long-range Type-IXC boats to join the fray in August 1942. On 8 August *U517* left Kiel for Canadian waters on her maiden war patrol. This was a notable success, Kptlt Paul Hartwig sinking seven merchantmen, the US troopship *Chatham* and HMCS *Charlottetown* in the space of nineteen days. B.d.U. was elated at this 'outstanding first patrol . . . with a new boat', lauding the 'skill and prowess demonstrated by the Commander', but Hartwig's remarkable debut proved to be the sum of his success. On 21 November 1942, just four days into her second patrol, *U517* was sunk off Cape Finisterre by an Albacore torpedo bomber from the carrier HMS *Victorious*. Only one man was lost but Hartwig and the rest of his crew spent the duration of the war as prisoners. Hartwig went on to join the post-war Bundesmarine, eventually reaching the rank of Vizeadmiral.

Sources

Admiralty, *Enemy Submarine Attacks on H.M. and Allied Warships: Reports, 1941-1943* (TNA, ADM 199/163)

Royal Canadian Navy, Atlantic Command Records, *HMCS* Charlottetown – *Board of Inquiry* (NAC, RG 24, D10, vol. 11108, File 55-2/138)

U517, Torpedo report of 1258 hrs on 11 September 1942 (BfZ, Schussmeldung Collection)

Essex, James W., *Victory in the St. Lawrence: Canada's Unknown War* (Erin, Ont.: Boston Mills Press, 1984)

Greenfield, Nathan M., *The Battle of the St. Lawrence: The Second World War in Canada* (Toronto: Harper Collins Canada, 2004)

Hadley, Michael L., *U-Boats Against Canada: German Submarines in Canadian Waters* (Kingston, Ont. and Montreal: McGill-Queen's University Press, 1985)

Johnston, Mac, *Corvettes Canada: Convoy Veterans of WWII Tell Their True Stories* (Toronto and Montreal: McGraw-Hill Ryerson, 1994)

McKee and Darlington, *Canadian Naval Chronicle*, pp. 68–70

Macpherson and Burgess, *Ships of Canada's Naval Forces* (3rd edn), p. 92

Macpherson, Ken, and Marc Milner, *Corvettes of the Royal Canadian Navy, 1939–1945* (St Catherines, Ont.: Vanwell Publishing, 1993)

Preston, Antony, and Alan Raven, *Flower Class Corvettes* [Ensign, no. 3] (London: Bivouac Books, 1973); reprinted as Man o'War, no. 7 (London: Arms and Armour Press, 1982)

68   HMCS *OTTAWA* (i) (ex HMS *CRUSADER*)

Acting Lt Cdr C. A. Rutherford, RCN†

Sunk by *U91* (Type VIIC), Kptlt Heinz Walkerling, 13 September 1942

North Atlantic, 375 nm E of St John's, Newfoundland

Ottawa seen in her wartime fit. She was destroyed by two torpedo hits on the starboard side,
the first of which removed her bows, the second detonating amidships. *BfZ*

Theatre	North Atlantic (Map 1)	*Displacement*	1,375 tons
Coordinates	47° 55′ N, 43° 27′ W	*Dimensions*	329′ × 33′ × 8.5′
Kriegsmarine code	Quadrat BC 6191	*Maximum speed*	35.5 knots
U-boat timekeeping differential	+3 hours	*Armament*	4 × 4.7″; 1 × 3″; 2 × 40 mm AA; 5 × .303″ AA; 4 × 21″ tt
Fatalities	119 and 17	*Survivors*	about 62 and about 7

Career

For background on the Royal Canadian Navy, see HMCS *Lévis* (**32**).

HMCS *Ottawa* began life as the 'C'-class destroyer *Crusader* which was ordered for the Royal Navy under the 1929 estimates. Though originally conceived as a standard flotilla of eight destroyers and a leader, the 'C'-class was cut to four and a leader as a gesture of disarmament by the Labour government of Ramsay MacDonald in January 1930. HMS *Crusader* was laid down at Portsmouth Dockyard on 12 September that year, making her and her sister *Comet* (later HMCS *Restigouche*) the first destroyers ever built in a royal dockyard. *Crusader* was launched in September 1931 and completed in May of the following year. The class commissioned as the 2nd Destroyer Flotilla, Home Fleet and spent the next three years in home waters before being transferred to the Mediterranean in August 1935 as a consequence of the Abyssinian Crisis. In September the Flotilla was detached for service in the Red Sea where it remained until March of the following year. After a refit, *Crusader* rejoined the Home Fleet, performing evacuation and patrol duty off Spain in the summer of 1936 and eventually serving as attendant destroyer to the carrier *Courageous* (**1**) while under reduced complement between December 1937 and April 1938. As expected, the class failed to fit into the flotilla organisation

by which the Royal Navy operated its destroyers and together with its leader *Kempenfelt* (later HMCS *Assiniboine*) was transferred to the Royal Canadian Navy between 1937 and 1938. *Crusader* was commissioned into Canadian service on 6 April 1938 and renamed *Ottawa* on 15 June, spending the last year of peace on the America and West Indies Station based on Esquimalt, British Columbia. In November 1939 *Ottawa* passed back through the Panama Canal to Halifax, Nova Scotia where she served as local escort to eastbound convoys, though two months were spent in dock following a collision with the tug *Banshee* in April 1940. In September she was assigned to the 10th Escort Group of Western Approaches Command at Greenock and was soon in action as the U-boat offensive gathered pace. Post-war analysis of captured enemy documents has revealed that *Ottawa* shared with HM destroyer *Harvester* (**G49**) in the sinking of the Italian submarine *Faà di Bruno* off Iceland on 6 November 1940, a first for the RCN. *Ottawa* transferred to Newfoundland Command on its formation in June 1941, spending the rest of her career as a mid-ocean escort based on St John's. Her final assignment was to the Canadian 4th Escort Group (EG-C4) in May 1942. *Ottawa*'s last convoy, ON127, proved much the most heavily contested of a busy but comparatively uneventful career.

Background of the attack

Assisted by an unprecedented number of U-boats deployed within the mid-Atlantic 'air gap' and the failure of Bletchley Park to break the four-rotor Enigma code, the German onslaught in the autumn of 1942 presented a severe challenge to convoy defence. However, as Clay Blair points out in his history of the U-boat war (see below), selective accounts of convoy battles in September and October 1942 hardly reflect the overall picture. Despite their advantages the Germans succeeded in attacking just six of the thirty-five convoys at sea in these two months, and total losses amounted to a mere three per cent of the merchantmen involved. But some convoys were badly mauled, including ON127 which left Liverpool on 4 September and ran straight into the powerful *Vorwärts* ('onwards') pack a week into her crossing. ON127's weakness lay less in the size of her escort – the Canadian 4th Escort Group (EG-C4) comprised HMC destroyers *St Croix* (Senior Officer of the Escort; **86**) and *Ottawa*, HMC corvettes *Amherst*, *Arvida* and *Sherbrooke*, and HM corvette *Celandine* – than in the inadequacy of its anti-submarine equipment. None of the ships possessed HF/DF, and only *Celandine* was equipped with the latest Type-271 radar, which in the event broke down at a critical juncture.

On the afternoon of 10 September the *Vorwärts* group began

a succession of attacks against ON127. Over the course of that evening and the early morning of the 11th the escort was almost overwhelmed by attacks from no fewer than seven U-boats. Among the ships accounted for that night was the tanker SS *Empire Oil*, sunk following attacks by *U659* and *U584* (see **45**) leaving two dozen crewmen to be rescued by *Ottawa* on the evening of the 10th. Of the other merchantmen attacked, one was sunk and five more damaged, two of which had to be finished off by *Sherbrooke*. Three more were sunk the following evening and the escort depleted by *Amherst* being detached to despatch MS *Hindanger*. The night of the 12th–13th passed uneventfully as excellent visibility eased the task of the escorts. On 13 September the escort was reinforced by the Canadian destroyer *Annapolis* and HM destroyer *Witch* and boosted by its first air support from Newfoundland. Although a number of boats were driven off, the *Vorwärts* group had not finished with ON127 just yet. Shortly before 2300 *Ottawa* obtained a radar contact on her Type-286P set while proceeding on her own three miles ahead of the convoy. No sooner had *Ottawa* begun a twenty-degree alteration to port to investigate than she took the first of two torpedoes fired by one of the few boats to have remained in contact with the convoy, Kptlt Heinz Walkerling's *U91*.

War Diary of *U91*, patrol of 15 August–6 October 1942: PG 30085, NHB, reel 1,074, pp. 505–6[1]

Date, time	Details of position, wind, weather, sea, light, visibility, moonlight, etc.	Incidents
13.ix		
2200		I establish contact with convoy. As it is slowly getting dark I shape a converging course. Come evening the convoy then alters her zigzag dramatically to the north and I lose contact in the gloom.
2352		Outgoing W/T transmission 2320/13/249: *15 steamers, 2200, Qu. [BC] 6244. Major evening zigzag alteration to the north, contact lost.*
		I am now steering a southerly course as I anticipate the convoy reverting to its general course of 240° at night.
2400	Qu. BC 6191, dark night	*Walkerling*
14.ix		
0150		Several shadows appear – I must be stationed right ahead of the convoy. In the distance I make out a two-funnelled destroyer proceeding very slowly with an inclination of 70°.[2]
0205		Spread of two fired at this destroyer from Tubes I and III. Enemy speed 11 knots, range 1,000 m, inclination red [i.e. port] 70°, angle of spread 4°, side angle 0°, angle of fire 340°, aim-off red [ditto] 20°, parallax adjustment 0.5°, depth 2 m. Two detonations after 1 min. 50 sec.[3] A black and white detonation cloud and bright red tongue of flame. Destroyer stops and lies burning, then fires a shell which splits into five green stars. Starshell is then immediately fired by other vessels. I conclude that the former must have been a distress signal because a second destroyer now closes her stricken fellow.[4] Turning a complete circle on full rudder I now run in to attack the second destroyer which is now lying stopped.
0215		Single shot fired from Tube II, angle of fire 0°.[5] Running time 1 min. 45 sec. A hit amidships. High column of water, a number of successive detonations, apparently detonating depth charges. Destroyer sinks immediately, then a complete firework display of starshell followed by these green five-star

---

1 The page from the original log showing the attack sequence (entries 0150 to 0215) is reproduced in the Introduction, p. xxv.

2 HMCS *Ottawa*.

3 Walkerling's torpedo report records a running time of 1 min. 45 sec. Unusually for a surface attack at night, it was Walkerling himself who fired this salvo and that of 0215 rather than his torpedo officer.

4 HMCS *St Croix*.

5 Despite Walkerling's description, *Ottawa* was again the target of this attack.

Date, time	Details of position, wind, weather, sea, light, visibility, moonlight, etc.	Incidents
		rockets and attempts to illuminate the scene of the attack with searchlights.[6] Three or four escorts show a green-red light at their mastheads and fire red stars. Within about two minutes the lights are switched off again. I am still within the escort screen and proceed at ¾ speed towards the dark horizon. Once again I find myself closing the convoy but am forced away by starshell and searchlights. Then a destroyer approaches in my wake, closing rapidly. I turn hard about and soon she is out of sight. I then witness a torpedo from another U-boat hitting a steamer.[7] The convoy has carried out a dramatic zigzag and I lose contact. I set off in pursuit on a westerly course.
0400	Qu. BC 6148	
0800	Qu. BC 5329, wind SSW 4, cloud 10, sea 3–4, showers, visibility rapidly deteriorating	Outgoing W/T transmission 0602/14/270 sent at 0830: *Spread of two against two-funnelled destroyer, a hit, burning fiercely, a hit on second destroyer coming alongside, hit amidships, sunk immediately.*[8] *Sinking of former not observed due to counter-attack. SSW 3, [1,0]15 mb, falling, light rain. Five eels, 28 cbm, still pursuing.*[9]

6 Jenson (see 'Sources' below) records that the second hit coincided with the firing of a distress signal from *Ottawa*.

7 SS *Empire Sailor*, sunk by *U518* (Oblt.z.S. Friedrich-Wilhelm Wissmann).

8 See below.

9 'Eels' (German = *Aale*) was U-boat slang for torpedoes. '28 cbm' indicates the remaining diesel fuel supply in cubic metres.

The sinking

Walkerling's first torpedo struck at 2305 Allied time (0205 on the 14th German time). Most of *Ottawa*'s survivors recorded this hitting the port side forward though several including the First Lieutenant, Lt (G) T. C. Pullen RCN, believed that it had detonated on the starboard side, an opinion supported by Kptlt Walkerling's sketch of the incident. Whatever the case, *U91*'s torpedo smashed the fore part of the ship, removing the bows back to 'B' 4.7-inch mounting together with most of the forward mess decks. Though *Ottawa*'s engine plant seemed unaffected, proceeding ahead was impossible and it appears that Lt Cdr Rutherford was awaiting a report on the condition of the bulkheads before deciding whether to go astern. As a result, once Walkerling had completed the full circle indicated in his log HMCS *Ottawa* still presented a stationary target though wind and current had conspired to bring her round to port. Though Walkerling appears to have mistaken *St Croix* as the victim of his second attack (which had indeed closed *Ottawa* before going in search of the perpetrator), *Ottawa* was again the recipient, being struck on the starboard side abreast No. 2 boiler room whereupon 'the ship immediately began to break up'. The order to abandon ship was passed though none can have been in any doubt that the end had come. Listing to starboard until she was on her beam ends, *Ottawa* sank bow and stern up at 2330 Allied time, twenty-five minutes after the first attack.

The principal findings of the Board of Inquiry centred on safety, in particular the need to counter the situation that had unfolded in *Ottawa* when ratings on watch had become trapped in the Asdic cabinet and the heads due to debris piled up against the door and, in the latter case, by the door becoming jammed in its frame. Capt. (D) Newfoundland, H. T. W. Grant RCN, also expressed the view that 'it appears possible that earlier action to turn the ship to the estimated bearing of the submarine might have delayed, or possibly avoided a second blow'. Even had this been possible Lt Cdr Rutherford's death prevented further exploration of the matter and Walkerling's

manoeuvres in any case made the point irrelevant. However, the main controversy centred not on the loss of *Ottawa* herself but the conduct of the Canadian 4th Escort Group (EG-C4) in general. The tactics of ON127's escort (led by Lt Cdr A. H. Dobson RCNR in *St Croix*) were questioned by the Americans and especially by the British who were highly critical of his decision to detach escorts to finish off damaged merchantmen astern of the convoy. By contrast the Canadians felt that Dobson and his group had put up a spirited and dogged defence against relentless attack without the benefit of HF/DF or the latest radar. *Ottawa*'s Lt Pullen, who had pointed out to the Board the great lengths to which Rutherford had gone to obtain HF/DF and even an inferior form of RDF in Londonderry, was in no doubt where the escort's deficiencies lay: 'I consider that if we had been fitted with HF/DF and RDF type 271 that in all probability the ship would still be afloat.' There is, however, a coda to Lt Pullen's testimony in the form of a memoir by *Ottawa*'s RDF officer, Sub-Lt Latham Jenson RCNVR who survived the sinking. His memoir, which was published in 2000, reads as follows:

> In Londonderry just before our last trip a lovely new 271 radar set appeared on the jetty next to *Ottawa*. The captain had not been informed of this major change to his ship, and when I told him what was planned, he was furious. He had been given no authority to accept this and I was to tell them that they were not to install it.

The fog of war?

For his part, Walkerling claimed two destroyer sinkings on reaching Brest in the first week of October, with which B.d.U. credited him in the absence of better information, noting that he had exploited the opportunity in question to maximum effect. *St Croix* lived to fight another day but her turn would come a year later at the hands of *U305* (**86**).

Fate of the crew

U91's first torpedo claimed dozens of lives. The evidence of Lt T. C.

Pullen, the first officer to venture forward to investigate, makes grim reading in this respect:

> The upper mess from number One gun was just wreckage, bodies, etc. There were several ratings pinned down in the after end of the upper mess deck. I could see that efforts were being made to try and extricate them. I went down to the stokers' mess deck, which was piled high with wreckage and bodies. I climbed over this about five feet and shone my flash light forward to see what was left and there was nothing there. There were two men alive that I could see who were there, whose legs were pinned.

Those on the bridge had to endure the screams of men trapped in the Asdic cabinet issuing up the voice pipes. Efforts to free them and others trapped by wreckage or jammed doors in the heads and elsewhere had hardly begun when *Ottawa* was struck for the second time, condemning them to a gruesome end. Nor was there much comfort in the water. Though Acting Gunner (T) L. E. Jones had set the depth charges to safe after the first hit and the suction of the wreck was slight, it was later estimated that as many men lost their lives in the water as had succumbed aboard to the torpedoes. Those floats that had been launched were overcrowded and not all who made it to one were equipped with lifejackets. Each time a float overturned there were fewer men left clinging to it once it had been righted. Lt Cdr Rutherford, whose last words to Pullen before leaping from the keel were 'She was a good ship, Number One', lessened his chances of survival by handing his lifejacket to a rating, though the Board of Inquiry attributed his death and that of Surgeon Lt G. A. Hendry RCNVR 'largely to exhaustion caused by little or no rest for some days previous', the latter having worked ceaselessly tending injured survivors of SS *Empire Oil*. The convoy swept past leaving the work of rescue to be performed by *Celandine* and then *Arvida* which inched as close as they dared and dropped scrambling nets to parties of survivors, many of which did not hang low enough for them to gain a foothold. Though *Ottawa* was sunk in the warmer waters of the Gulf Stream (some men were stung by jellyfish), heavy seas, injury, exhaustion and the effects of oil had reduced the number of survivors to approximately sixty-nine by the time the last was rescued by *Celandine* at 0535, six hours after the sinking. Among them were seven crewmen from *Empire Oil* who had survived two sinkings in three days.

Ottawa was not forgotten and the name was revived when HMS *Griffin*, one of two survivors of the 'G'-class destroyers, was transferred to the Royal Canadian Navy in March 1943.

U91 and Heinz Walkerling

Built by Flenderwerft at Lübeck and commissioned in January 1942, *U91*'s career comprised six Atlantic patrols. Kptlt Heinz Walkerling commanded the first three of these, but beyond the sinking of *Ottawa* on her maiden patrol *U91*'s entire tonnage came on 17 February 1943 when she claimed five merchantmen from the badly mauled HX229. This was to be Walkerling's last seagoing patrol as he was transferred first to shore appointments with the 9th, 24th and 19th Flotillas and finally to the torpedo school at Mürwik in September 1944 where he spent the rest of the war. He was succeeded in *U91* by Kptlt Heinz Hungershausen who assumed command in April 1943 but enjoyed no success. She was sunk during his third patrol on 25 February

A shot of *U91*'s conning tower taken off the Azores around the time of *Ottawa*'s sinking in the autumn of 1942. *DUBMA*

1944 while part of the *Preussen* group in the North Atlantic. Depth charged to the surface by HM destroyers *Gore*, *Affleck* and *Gould*, *U91* was abandoned with the loss of sixteen of her fifty-two men. Hungershausen survived to be made a prisoner of war.

Sources

Admiralty, *Report of Proceedings for ON127* (TNA, ADM 237/90)
—, *Convoy ON127* (NHB, ON Convoys Box)
—, Trade Division, Reports of Attacks on Convoys, *Report of an Interview with the Master, Captain E. Marshall, S.S.* Empire Oil (TNA, ADM 199/1710)
Newfoundland Command Records, *Board of Inquiry into Loss of HMCS* Ottawa (NAC, RG 24, D12, vol. 11930, file 1156-353/17)

Blair, *Hitler's U-Boat War*, II, pp. 23–32
English, John, Amazon *to* Ivanhoe: *British Standard Destroyers of the 1930s* (Kendal, Cumbria: World Ship Society, 1993)
Jenson, Cdr Latham B., *Tin Hats, Oilskins & Seaboots: A Naval Journey, 1938–1945* (Toronto: Robin Brass Studio, 2000)
Kinghorn, D., and B. Hargreaves, 'Destroyers of the Royal Navy from 1926. Part IV: "Crescent" Class, 1929–30 Estimates' in *Warships*, Supplement no. 3 (June 1966), pp. 5–10
McKee and Darlington, *Canadian Naval Chronicle*, pp. 71–4
Macpherson, Ken, *The River Class Destroyers of the Royal Canadian Navy* (Toronto: Charles J. Musson, 1985)
Macpherson and Burgess, *Ships of Canada's Naval Forces* (3rd edn), p. 35
Pullen, T. C., 'Convoy O.N.127 and the Loss of HMCS *Ottawa*, 13 September, 1942: A Personal Reminiscence' in *The Northern Mariner/Le Marin du Nord* 2, no. 2 (April 1992), pp. 1–27
Skillen, C. R., 'Sinking of the *Ottawa*' in Thomas G. Lynch, ed., *Fading Memories: Canadian Sailors and the Battle of the Atlantic* (Halifax, Nova Scotia: The Atlantic Chief and Petty Officers' Association, 1993), pp. 116–19

Career history of HMS *Crusader*/HMCS *Ottawa*:
   http://www.naval-history.net/xGM-Chrono-10DD-17C-Crusader-Ottawa1RCN.htm

69 HMS *LEDA*

Lt Cdr A. H. Wynne-Edwards, RN
Sunk by *U435* (Type VIIC), Kptlt Siegfried Strelow, 20 September 1942
Greenland Sea, 175 nm W of Sorkappfallet, Spitsbergen

A newly commissioned *Leda* in 1938. She was struck on the starboard side amidships by a torpedo from *U435* and rolled over twenty minutes later. *P. A. Vicary*

Campaign	Arctic convoys (Map 2)	*Displacement*	875 tons
Coordinates	72° 26' N, 04° 15' E	*Dimensions*	245.25' × 33.5' × 7.25'
Kriegsmarine code	Quadrat AB 2272	*Maximum speed*	16.5 knots
U-boat timekeeping differential	+1 hour	*Armament*	2 × 4" AA; 4 × .5" AA; 4 × .303" AA
Fatalities 44 and 2	*Survivors* 72 and 16		

Career

For notes on the sloop type, see HMS *Penzance* (**16**).

The Halcyon-class minesweeping sloop *Leda* was laid down at Devonport Dockyard in November 1936 and launched in June 1937. In May 1938 she was commissioned into the Fishery Protection Squadron as a tender to HM sloop *Hastings* but the outbreak of war found her with the 5th Minesweeping Flotilla at Harwich, to which she had been assigned in August 1939. Transferred to Nore Command in October and then to Rosyth Command in January 1940, the 5th MF spent the first months of the war engaged in routine minesweeping duty off the East Coast. *Leda*'s first blooding came during Operation DYNAMO when she evacuated over 3,000 British and French troops in eight harrowing trips between Dunkirk and the Kent ports of Margate and Sheerness in late May and early June 1940. Bombed, strafed and damaged by several collisions, *Leda* required dockyard attention at Sheerness before returning to duty. Subsequently she participated in Operation BS37, the laying of the East Coast Mine Barrier, and from now on *Leda*'s career was devoted largely to minesweeping operations along with spells of convoy duty. Until the autumn of 1941 these were performed largely in British coastal waters, and not without incident. In early September 1940 *Leda* was instrumental in rescuing the destroyer *Ivanhoe* after she had been crippled during an abortive minelaying operation off the Texel. While escorting a coastal convoy on 30 October *Leda* was involved in a collision with one of her charges during a severe gale off Rattray Head which kept her in dock in Aberdeen until 16 November. Emerging from a period of refit and repair at Leith and Rosyth between April and June 1941, *Leda* was allocated to the 6th MF, then assigned to local escort of Atlantic convoys while based on Stornoway in the Hebrides. In September 1941 the instigation of a convoy route to North Russia brought *Leda* into Arctic waters and the first of four voyages to Archangel and the Kola Inlet where she devoted part of October 1941 and the summer of 1942 to minesweeping and anti-submarine duties in local waters. Having refitted at Rosyth to acclimatise her for Arctic duty and correct boiler trouble in the spring of 1942, *Leda* joined PQ15 which reached Murmansk after a comparatively easy passage on 5 May, but much of July and August was spent searching the Barents Sea for stragglers and survivors from an altogether more disastrous convoy: PQ17. The next return convoy, QP14, would claim *Leda* in her turn.

Background of the attack

For background on the Arctic convoy campaign, see HMSs *Matabele* and *Edinburgh* (**47** and **58**).

As the Arctic summer of 1942 brought improved weather

conditions and near-permanent daylight to northern waters, so the attrition of Allied convoys to Russia from surface, air and submarine attack increased markedly. In early July came the nadir of Allied fortunes in this theatre when the Murmansk-bound PQ17 was ordered to scatter against the possibility of an attack by the battleship *Tirpitz* and proceeded to lose twenty of its thirty-five ships to air and U-boat attack in the space of forty-eight hours. The disaster that befell PQ17 had a number of repercussions among which was the provision of greater resources to Arctic convoy protection once the 'Kola Run' was resumed in September. The next convoys – PQ18 and the overlapping QP14, which sailed from Archangel on 13 September – were escorted by a total of over forty warships including the escort carrier *Avenger* (75), sixteen destroyers, five corvettes, two submarines and an assortment of anti-aircraft ships and trawlers. Despite these

measures PQ18 reached Archangel on the 17th having lost thirteen of its forty-four ships, mostly to air attack, and the escort now devoted itself to QP14. Assisted by bad weather (which hindered German air reconnaissance) and the summer retreat of the polar ice pack (which allowed the convoy to sail north of the 75th parallel and so beyond the range of German bombers), QP14 managed to escape the attentions of the enemy for almost a week. However, by 20 September no fewer than seven U-boats were closing in across the Greenland Sea. Among these was Kptlt Siegfried Strelow's *U435*, three days out of her Norwegian base at Skjomenfjord when she sighted QP14 and shadowed it for thirty-six hours before drawing first blood. Unusually, the log extract which follows is written largely in the perfect and pluperfect tenses, direct evidence of composition somewhat later in the patrol or upon *U435*'s return to Skjomenfjord.

War Diary of *U435*, patrol of 16–29 September 1942: PG 30489, NHB, reel 1,108, pp. 373–4

Date, time	Details of position, wind, weather, sea, light, visibility, moonlight, etc.	Incidents
20.ix		
0400	Qu. AB 2258	
0405		Convoy at bearing 60° true, range 10,000 m.
0415		Outgoing short signal transmitted: *Qu. AB 2256. U435.*
0430		Convoy at bearing 60° true, range 15,000 m.
0500		Convoy at bearing 60° true, range 15,000 m.
0515		Outgoing short signal transmitted: *Convoy of more than 30 steamers Qu. AB 2282. U435.*
0525		We dive with a view to penetrating convoy.
		During the previous night's shadowing I had come to the conclusion that the relatively bright night-time conditions (contact was maintained at an average range of 10,000 m) and the very strong side and forward escort made a surface attack impossible. On the other hand, hauling ahead of the convoy during daylight hours had been foiled by a combination of air reconnaissance and the great distance at which the escort was operating from the convoy. I therefore decided to haul ahead of the convoy during the hours of darkness and then carry out an underwater attack at dawn. We penetrated the very powerful forward escort on a reciprocal course at a depth of 20 m, the latter consisting of three destroyers in an arrowhead formation sweeping with Asdic at the front followed by two more destroyers zigzagging very sharply and at high speed.[1] The boat then found herself between two columns right in the middle of the convoy. Despite being in a favourable firing position I didn't press home an attack on the first big ships that presented themselves as I wanted to attack the aircraft carrier and had not yet sighted her.[2] When I had established that the carrier was in all likelihood out of range I fired at a steamer of 6,000 GRT at an inclination of 80° and range of 800 m, and at two steamers lying at obtuse inclinations. As the third torpedo fired was a surface runner I let loose another at the same target, the surface runner having passed astern. Only now did I spot the carrier, stationed a long way off in the port columns and at an obtuse angle. After turning the boat about I then fired a stern torpedo at the destroyer stationed astern of the convoy and sank her. (Probably Jervis class as J93 could be clearly made out in large black letters on the ship's side.)[3]
0625		Tube I: inclination green [i.e. starboard] 80°, speed 9 knots, aim-off green 17°, range 800 m. A hit after 46 sec. on a steamer of 6,000 GRT.[4]
0626		Tube II: inclination green 100°, speed 9 knots, aim-off green 16.5°, range 900 m. Detonation after 4 min. 10 sec.[4]
0628		Tube III: inclination green 120°, speed 9 knots, aim-off green 14°, range 1,200 m. Surface runner.

1 Strelow's description would equate to the stations of HMSs *Fury*, *Malcolm* and *Meteor* ahead, and *Impulsive* and *Opportune* astern.

2 HMS *Avenger*, which Rear-Admiral Robert Burnett had detached from the convoy together with HM cruiser *Scylla* at almost exactly this time.

3 Strelow has correctly identified *Leda*'s pendant number but his extrapolation that she was a 'J'-class destroyer is incorrect. By this stage in the war British destroyers were assigned the flag superior 'I', 'G', 'L' or 'R', whereas 'J' was reserved for minesweeping and surveying craft.

4 No hit is corroborated in Allied sources.

Date, time	Details of position, wind, weather, sea, light, visibility, moonlight, etc.	Incidents
0629		Tube IV: inclination green 125°, speed 9 knots, aim-off green 13°, range 1,200 m. Detonation after 4 min. 30 sec.[4]
0631		Tube V: inclination green 130°, speed 9 knots, aim-off green 13°, range 1,200 m. Detonation after 1 min. 25 sec. Destroyer sunk.[5]
0753		Boat surfaced after a few deterrent depth charges had been dropped.
0800	Qu. AB 2271, wind N 2, sea 2, overcast, 1,013 mb, visibility 10–15 nm	
0830–0845	*Minesweeper Leda*[6]	Wreck of destroyer in sight, her bow still sticking up out of the water.[7] I try to get a few pieces of wreckage so as to establish her name and size.[8]
0958		Incoming W/T transmission: *Please send beacon signal F for aircraft BV128 approaching area. Admiral, Northern Waters.*[9]
1008		Outgoing short signal transmitted: *Convoy Qu. AB 2189. Stay alert for beacon signal. Strelow.*
1000–1050		Beacon signal sent.
1037		Convoy temporarily lost from sight in snow showers at bearing 241° true, distance 10 nm.

Signal Appendix to War Diary of *U435*: PG 30489, NHB, reel 1,108, p. 382

20.ix

1950	1025/740
	To Admiral, Northern Waters:[9] *5 single shots at 3 steamers and 1 destroyer, 1 surface runner, 1 steamer of 6,000 GRT probably sunk. Hit after 46 seconds. 1 destroyer sunk, hits probable on 2 further steamers. Detonations after 4 min. 10 sec. and 4 min. 30 sec. 0627 Quadrat AB 2272.* *Strelow.*

5 HM sloop *Leda*, which despite the claims made in the preceding entries was the only vessel struck at this time. Quite apart from *U435*'s timekeeping being an hour in advance, Strelow's chronometer seems to have been set twelve minutes ahead of its British equivalents which recorded the hit at 0520.

6 Manuscript addition in pencil, possibly by the civilian archivist Walther Pfeiffer who was brought to Britain to work on the logs post-war.

7 HM trawler *Ayrshire* reported having sunk the wreck a full hour earlier.

8 Strelow does not state whether this attempt was successful. Certainly, it seems an unusual risk to take in the wake of a large convoy with air cover.

9 *Admiral Nordmeer* (Admiral Commanding Northern Waters), Konteradmiral Otto Klüber, had operational control of U-boats in this theatre until the office of *F.d.U. Norwegen* (Officer Commanding U-Boats, Norway) was created in January 1943.

The sinking

Unseen by her four lookouts, Strelow's torpedo struck *Leda* on the starboard side between the boiler rooms at 0520 ship time, the main detonation being followed by two smaller explosions thought to be ruptured boilers. The effect was shattering: 'The hull structure, starboard side amidships, from the boat deck to below the waterline, and the boat deck from the Commanding Officers [*sic*] cabin to the motor boat, were completely blown away', while the ship's funnel 'was split on the starboard side for its entire length'. *Leda* was immediately deprived of all steam, electrical power and communication between bridge and engine room as fires broke out both below and on deck. Having assumed a twenty-degree list to port, *Leda* 'settled in the water and gradually heeled over until she was on her beam ends'. At around 0540 'she turned completely over and floated with bow and stern out of the water, her back broken'. The official report goes on to state that 'at 0630 the wreck was sunk by gunfire by HMS *Ayrshire*', an assertion that sits in stark contrast with Strelow's record of the bow section being still afloat at 0730–0745 British time.

The Board of Enquiry declared itself satisfied that 'there was never any possibility of the ship being saved', but also expressed the view – concurred in by the Commander-in-Chief Home Fleet, Admiral

Sir Bruce Fraser and Rear-Admiral Robert Burnett commanding the Home Fleet's destroyers – that *Leda* should have been zigzagging. Fraser recommended that Lt Cdr A. H. Wynne-Edwards be informed of his error of judgment but spared any further censure as he had been under the impression that *Leda* was forming a close screen with HM anti-submarine trawlers *Ayrshire* and *Northern Gem*, neither of which had sufficient fuel to permit zigzagging. Meanwhile, Strelow returned to Skjomenfjord the undisputed ace in the pack that assailed QP14, adding three merchant pennants in the space of two minutes later on the 20th while *U703* accounted for HM destroyer *Somali* (see the next entry, **70**). There is, however, no corroboration for the hits on merchantmen claimed by Strelow during the attack sequence that accounted for *Leda*.

Fate of the crew

The majority of *Leda*'s casualties were incurred below decks amidships in the torpedo detonation and subsequent explosion. Up on the bridge command devolved on the Officer of the Watch, Lt H. R. Pratt RNVR, while Lt Cdr Wynne-Edwards spent five minutes battling to free himself from the chart house where he had been trapped by a jammed door. Under questioning, Lt Pratt freely admitted that he had issued

Strelow (in white cap) seen on *U435*'s conning tower. The two victory pennants flying from the attack periscope date the photo to her arrival at Kiel on 26 April 1942, five months before *Leda* was sunk. Between the two crewmen on the left can be seen the UZO target bearing indicator; its binoculars are not fitted. *DUBMA*

no orders to abandon ship as the vessel 'was very nearly in two and there was no communication between forward and aft. It was evident that the ship could not be saved and life-saving gear was cleared away automatically.' With the motorboat and the starboard whaler wrecked, the port whaler 'irreparably damaged by the mast collapsing across it, and the starboard foremost Carley float . . . blown out of the ship and broken in two halves' the outlook for the surviving ship's company appeared bleak. However, orders to jettison anything that might aid buoyancy and the speed with which *Northern Gem*, *Ayrshire* and HM sloop *Seagull* closed the wreck meant that many more were saved than might have been expected. *Northern Gem* was on the scene within minutes of the abandon ship and rescued thirty-three men, but as former Coxswain Sid Kerslake recalled her efforts were not universally welcomed:

> We had the rescue nets over the side for them to climb up as quickly as possible, and as they did so a destroyer came up our starboard side and shouted through the loud hailer for our skipper to get back to the convoy, for we were not supposed to stop to pick up survivors on the run back. Our skipper told him to f**k off, whereupon the destroyer's CO said he would report him when we arrived back in port, though as far as I know nothing came of it.

A total of ninety-four men were rescued from the water including sixteen survivors of the SSs *River Afton* and *Navarino*, both casualties of the earlier PQ17. However, six succumbed to the effects of burns and hypothermia on the voyage home, bringing the death toll to forty-six men: an officer, forty-three ratings and two survivors of the *River Afton*. They are remembered on a crest in the Maritime Museum at Salcombe in Devon, which town together with nearby Kingsbridge had *Leda* as their adopted warship.

U435 and Siegfried Strelow

Built by F. Schichau at Danzig (Gdansk) and commissioned in June 1941, *U435* carried out four frontline patrols in northern waters and three in the Atlantic, all under the command of Kptlt Siegfried Strelow. Strelow had no previous combat experience as a submarine commander but as a career torpedo officer had seen extensive service in the battleship *Schleswig-Holstein*, the 'pocket battleship' *Admiral Graf Spee*, the destroyer *Richard Beitzen* and the light cruiser *Leipzig*, together with command of a number of torpedo boats both before and during the war. *U435* notched up some impressive successes in the Arctic during 1942, sinking five merchantmen and the Royal Fleet Auxiliary oiler *Gray Ranger* (**G36**) besides *Leda* herself. She was reassigned to Atlantic operations in September 1942. For details of her subsequent career, see HMS *Fidelity* (**80**).

Sources

Admiralty, *Convoys to Russia 1942: QP14 and PQ14* (TNA, ADM 237/177)

—, *Enemy Submarine Attacks on H.M. and Allied Warships: Reports, 1941–1943* (TNA, ADM 199/163)

—, *PQ and QP Convoys: Reports, 1942–1943* (TNA, ADM 199/758)

—, *Ship's movements: HMS* Leda (NHB)

Ministry of Defence, *Damage Report on HMS* Leda (NHB, T.20388)

—, *HMS* Leda: *Summary of Service* (NHB, S.10377)

Cocker, M. P., *Mine Warfare Vessels of the Royal Navy, 1908 to Date* (Shrewsbury, Salop: Airlife Publishing, 1993)

Hague, Arnold, 'What Ship?' in *Marine News* 45, no. 6 (June 1991), pp. 343–4

Kerslake, S. A., *Coxswain in the Northern Convoys* (London: William Kimber, 1984)

Ruegg, Bob, and Arnold Hague, *Convoys to Russia, 1941–1945* (Kendal, Cumbria: World Ship Society, 1992)

Career history of HMS *Leda*:
http://www.naval-history.net/xGM-Chrono-22MS-Halc-Leda.htm

70   HMS *SOMALI*

Lt Cdr C. D. Maud, DSC RN

Sunk by *U703* (Type VIIC), Kptlt Heinz Bielfeld, 20–24 September 1942

Greenland Sea, 270 nm SW of Sorkappfallet, Spitsbergen

Somali at sea shortly after the outbreak of war in 1939. Three years' arduous war service ended with a torpedo from *U703* in the Arctic. *BfZ*

Campaign Arctic convoys (Map 2)		*Displacement* 1,960 tons	
Coordinates (of attack) 75° 12' N, 01° 00' W		*Dimensions* 377' × 36.5' × 9'	
Kriegsmarine code (of attack) Quadrat AB 1836		*Maximum speed* 36 knots	
U-boat timekeeping differential +1 hour		*Armament* 6 × 4.7"; 2 × 4" AA; 4 × 40 mm AA; 8 × .5" AA; 4 × 21" tt	
Fatalities 82 *Survivors* 155+			

Career

For design notes on the Tribal-class destroyers, see HMS *Cossack* (**37**).

A unit of the Tribal class of fleet destroyers, HMS *Somali* was laid down at Swan Hunter & Wigham Richardson's yard at Wallsend-on-Tyne on 26 August 1936 and launched almost a year to the day later. Completed in December 1938, she was commissioned as the lead ship of the 2nd Tribal Destroyer Flotilla (subsequently renumbered the 6th Destroyer Flotilla) in the Home Fleet, with which she remained for the rest of her career. Her first months were marked by ill fortune, being struck by the Dutch liner *Sibajak* while anchored at Gibraltar in February 1939 and emerging from repairs at Portsmouth to find herself as headquarters ship during the desperate efforts to rescue those trapped in the submarine *Thetis* after she plunged to the bottom of Liverpool Bay on 1 June. In August *Somali* was deployed on blockade and interception duty in the North Atlantic and within two hours of the outbreak of hostilities on 3 September had taken the first prize of the war, the German freighter *Hannah Böge* which she intercepted 350 miles south of Iceland. Service with the Home Fleet continued, notably the rescue of HMS/m *Spearfish* (**14**) in the North Sea on 26–27 September and the escort of the first Canadian troop convoy in December. Following turbine and evaporator repairs

at Smith's Dock Co. of Middlesbrough between January and March 1940, *Somali* rejoined the Home Fleet in time to participate in the Norwegian Campaign which began on 9 April, the ship serving for some time as General Sir Adrian Carton de Wiart's headquarters at Namsos. Varied duties in support of troop movements and operations ashore continued until 1 May when *Somali* was damaged in a series of air attacks on Åndalsnes which required her to make for Scapa Flow for repairs. However, she was back on station on the 8th just as military developments ashore were making the Allied position untenable and German air superiority was posing an increasing hazard to naval operations. On the 15th *Somali* steered to provide anti-aircraft support for the Polish troopship *Chrobry* which had been bombed in the Vestfjord the previous day with elements of the 1st Battalion Irish Guards embarked. Later that day *Somali* and her companion the French destroyer *Foudroyant* were themselves dive-bombed in Traenfjorden, the former struck on the waterline right forward and both subsequently taking passage to Scapa Flow. Following repairs at Liverpool *Somali* rejoined the 6th DF in September and spent the winter of 1940–1 operating with the Home Fleet. In March 1941 she participated in the raid on the Lofoten Islands during which cipher material of great importance to the breaking of the Enigma code was recovered from the requisitioned trawler *Krebs*. Then on 7 May *Somali* spearheaded the capture of the German weather trawler *München* off Jan Mayen in the Greenland Sea resulting in another significant haul of documents for the codebreakers at Bletchley Park. Before the month was out she was in action against the battleship *Bismarck*, leading the 6th DF in torpedo attacks on the 26th.

Having spent the summer of 1941 refitting at Southampton *Somali* returned to northern waters, the beginning of a year of intense activity which ended in her loss. August saw her escorting the battleship *Prince of Wales* to Placentia Bay, Newfoundland for the meetings between Churchill and Roosevelt which resulted in the Atlantic Charter, before participating in the dispatch of Hurricane fighters to Archangel at the end of the month. In December she took part in a second raid on the Lofoten Islands and in January joined the first of her ten Russian convoys, PQ8, during which her sister *Matabele* blew up having been torpedoed by *U454* (**47**). On 15 May 1942 *Somali* embarked Rear-Admiral Stuart Bonham-Carter from the crippled cruiser *Trinidad* after she had been bombed in the Arctic Sea and two months later participated in the fiasco of convoy PQ17. It is a measure of how stretched were the resources of the Royal Navy that August found her as escort for Operation PEDESTAL in the Mediterranean, *Somali* being again called upon to rescue survivors of another stricken vessel, this time the cruiser *Manchester*. Returning to northern waters,

on 2 September *Somali* sailed from Loch Ewe as close escort to convoy PQ18, being detached on the 16th to a homeward-bound convoy already at sea: QP14. It was to be her last assignment.

Background of the attack

For background on the Arctic convoy campaign, see HMSs *Matabele* and *Edinburgh* (**47** and **58**). For background on convoy QP14, see the preceding entry for HMS *Leda* (**69**).

Though QP14 had crossed the Greenwich Meridian with her journey to Loch Ewe half complete, by the evening of 20 September a number of U-boats were effecting a slow attrition of the convoy and its escort, including Kptlt Reinhart Reche's *U255* (see **100**) which torpedoed the freighter *Silver Sword* at approximately 1715 convoy time, and Kptlt Heinz Bielfeld's *U703* which had sailed from Skjomenfjord in northern Norway on the 14th. As Bielfeld's log demonstrates, the presence of the escort carrier *Avenger* (**75**) had obliged *U703* to a frustrating afternoon of diving to evade patrolling aircraft which relented only as dusk fell. At this juncture the escort commander, Rear-Admiral Robert Burnett, ordered *Avenger* and his own cruiser *Scylla* to be detached from the main body of the convoy while shifting his flag to the destroyer *Milne*, and it was while these orders were being executed that Bielfeld caught sight of *Somali* on the port bow of the convoy and moved in to attack.

War Diary of *U703*, patrol of 14–26 September 1942: PG 30711, NHB, reel 1,136, pp. 28–30

Date, time	Details of position, wind, weather, sea, light, visibility, moonlight, etc.	Incidents
20.ix		
1315–1339	Northern Waters Qu. AB 1632	Alarm dive due to aircraft from carrier.
1504–1532	Northern Waters Qu. AB 1654	Alarm dive due to aircraft from carrier.
1600	Northern Waters Qu. AB 1649	
1632–1702	Northern Waters Qu. AB 1649, bright, 9/10 overcast with occasional breaks, wind WNW 2, sea 1–2, visibility 12–15 nm, 1,023 mb	Alarm dive due to aircraft from carrier. By dead reckoning and in view of the continual alarms from aircraft approaching from the carrier I must be positioned approximately ahead of the convoy. Intention: to dive at around 1830 with a view to attacking.
1745		Navigational correction: 201.5°, 15.5 nm.[1]
1815		Outgoing W/T transmission 1720/737: *Thrice forced under by aircraft from carrier. Currently Qu. AB 1674. Bielfeld.*
1825	Northern Waters Qu. AB 1838	We dive to attack.
1845		At periscope depth: nothing to be seen.
1915		At periscope depth: convoy appears. Unfortunately I am not positioned sufficiently far ahead but stationed off to port and can thus only get a shot away at one of the escorting destroyers. Convoy is proceeding in typically wide formation, with the carrier – apparently *Furious* given flat deck – right in the centre.[2] The destroyers form a complete screen. The number of destroyers present is remarkably

---

1   In other words, Bielfeld's navigator had requested that the plotted position of *U435* be moved to the south-east, as is evident from the sudden shift from the AB 16 quadrant here to the AB 18 quadrant at 1825.

2   Though not dissimilar in silhouette and each the product of conversions from other types, the escort carrier *Avenger* was at 12,150 tons a much smaller vessel

Date, time	Details of position, wind, weather, sea, light, visibility, moonlight, etc.	Incidents
		large; I can't make out any corvettes or other escorts.[3] Those that I can see clearly are either Tribal class, 'J' class, Athertone [*sic*] class or 'V & W' class.[4]
		We run in to attack a Tribal-class destroyer.[5]
1955	Northern Waters Qu. AB 1836, 10/10 overcast, misty blurred	Spread of three torpedoes fired from Tubes I, II, III; enemy speed 12 knots, inclination red [i.e. port] 61°, range 2,500 m, aim-off red 22.5°, mean angle of fire 300.6°, angle of dispersion 3°, parallax adjustment red 1.8°, depth set at 3 m.
1956	horizon, visibility 5 nm, showers, wind WNW 2, sea 1–2, 1,020 mb	A hit after 1 min. 32 sec., or 1,330 m. The run ended right at the forward end of the second funnel. I witness a very high white explosion cloud; target is broken apart and sinks quickly though I couldn't witness her demise. As well as the initial impact two further detonations were clearly audible in the boat. The second is assumed to have been a boiler explosion.[6]
2003	Northern Waters Qu. AB 1839	Two destroyers bear down on me, still zigzagging. One then makes for the position of the sinking to pick up survivors. We dive to 120 m. Depth charges now start coming in the usual patterns but with no great accuracy. There appears to be a separate stratum of water at 80 m which makes proper echo-sounding pursuit impossible.[7] Every so often they drop another few, probably just to make themselves feel better. But there is also the possibility that they are after someone else – and indeed it turns out later they were after Reche.[8]
2235	Northern Waters Qu. AB 1835	We surface and withdraw to reload torpedoes. Then resume pursuit, course 250°.
2350		Outgoing W/T transmission 2250/746: *1955 Qu. 1836 AB sank Tribal-class destroyer. Now Qu. 1835 AB. 63 cbm, in pursuit, my last report no. 737.*[9] *Bielfeld.*
2354		Outgoing W/T transmission 2315/747: *Convoy consists of more than 20 steamers, full screen of escort destroyers. Aircraft carrier in the centre, probably* Furious.[2] *Bielfeld.*
		Bielfeld
21.ix		
0000	Northern Waters Qu. AB 1831	
0150		Incoming W/T transmission 0050/721: *With effect from 0500, Bielfeld to occupy Qu. 4120, Esch Qu. 4160 AB.*[10] *Until then keep trying to establish contact. Reche to seek contact independently. Anyone establishing contact to send beacon signal. Admiral [Commanding] Northern Waters.*[11]
		I won't quite make that; 0530 in attack area at the soonest.

than *Furious* (22,450 tons).

3   Though they may not have have been visible to Bielfeld at this juncture, there were in fact corvettes and 'other escorts' aplenty sailing with QP14, including the corvettes *Dianella*, *Lotus*, *Poppy* and *La Malouine*, the anti-submarine trawlers *Ayrshire*, *Lord Austin*, *Lord Middleton* and *Northern Gem*, and the minesweeping sloops *Bramble*, *Gleaner*, *Harrier* and *Seagull* (another, *Leda*, had been sunk by *U435* earlier that day; **69**). Also there were the converted anti-aircraft ships *Alynbank*, *Palomares* and *Pozarica*.

4   Several of the classes listed here were indeed represented in the escort including the Tribal-class destroyers, fleet destroyers of the 'F', 'I', 'M' and 'O' classes, and Hunt-class escort destroyers of the Type-II 'Avon Vale' group rather than the Type-I 'Atherstone' (*sic*) sub-class identified by Bielfeld. Beginning with the rearmost ships, the port outer screen of the convoy consisted of the following: *Gleaner*, *Eskimo*, *Ashanti*, *Lord Austin*, *Tartar*, *Somali* (occupying the extreme port station, 6,000 yards from the convoy), *Harrier*, *Intrepid*, *La Malouine*, *Faulknor*, *Lord Middleton*, *Fury* and, leading the convoy, *Blankney*. The port inner screen, beginning once again with the rearmost vessel, consisted of *Wheatland*, *Wilton* and *Impulsive* (on port bow of convoy), though the first two were at this time detached to escort *Avenger* and *Scylla*.

5   HMS *Somali*.

6   Possibly Bielfeld heard end-of-run detonations for his two misses. Whatever the case, his assertion that *Somali* 'breaks apart and sinks quickly' could hardly be further from the truth as she did not founder for another three days.

7   The problem of Asdic pursuit in waters with different temperature layers was well known to the Allies, particularly in the Mediterranean; see HMS *Barham* (**41**). Here the proximity to the Arctic ice pack may have had some bearing on Bielfeld's observation.

8   Kptlt Reinhart Reche, commander of *U255*. Reche had attacked the convoy at 1815, crippling the SS *Silver Sword*, and counted 86 depth charges dropped against him over the next few hours.

9   '63 cbm' indicates the remaining diesel fuel supply in cubic metres.

10   Kptlt Dietrich von der Esch, commander of *U586*.

11   *Admiral Nordmeer* (Admiral Commanding Northern Waters), Konteradmiral Otto Klüber, had operational control of U-boats in this theatre until the office of *F.d.U. Norwegen* (Officer Commanding U-Boats, Norway) was created in January 1943, being redesignated *F.d.U. Nordmeer* – Northern Waters – in September 1944.

0205   Incoming W/T transmission 0143/752: *Bravo Bielfeld. Admiral [Commanding] Northern Waters.*
0400   Northern Waters
            Qu. AB 1767

The sinking

Perhaps because *Somali* was in the process of altering to the starboard leg of her zigzag only one of Bielfeld's spread struck her, the hit recorded on the port side 'at about 1856½' British time. This detonated abreast the engine room, the largest compartment in the ship, damaging the bulkheads of the adjacent spaces (No. 3 Boiler Room and the gearing room) all of which flooded within minutes. In addition to the failure of electrical power *Somali* rapidly assumed a fifteen-degree list to starboard and settled by the stern until the quarterdeck was awash. Having inspected the blast himself and consulted his Chief Engineer, *Somali*'s CO Lt Cdr C. D. Maud expressed misgivings about her fitness for towing but nonetheless agreed to a hawser being passed to *Ashanti*, an evolution which began within an hour of *U703*'s attack. A steaming party of about seventy men remained on board, the after part of the ship was battened down and abandoned, topweight jettisoned and damaged bulkheads shored up insofar as this was possible. For just over three days the tow continued, traversing 450 of the 650-odd miles that had to be covered if *Somali* were to reach Akureyri in northern Iceland where *Ashanti*'s Capt. R. G. Onslow intended to beach her. *Ashanti* was refuelled by the auxiliary *Blue Ranger* on the 22nd, the towing effort escorted throughout by *Eskimo, Intrepid, Opportune* and *Lord Middleton*. On the 23rd, however, the weather turned, the temperature dropped and the wind freshened from the west. Onslow began pumping *Ashanti*'s oil overboard at a rate of a ton an hour to keep a moderate beam sea from breaking over *Somali*'s listing starboard side (literally pouring oil onto troubled waters). But as evening approached the stiff breeze turned into an Arctic gale whose ferocity Onslow later recalled in memorable prose:

> It came without warning – no sudden fall in the barometer, no storm clouds ahead of it. It came like a raging dervish, shrieking and howling in the rigging, whipping off the crests of the rising waves and driving them to leeward in an unbroken sheet of spindrift. The slide of air down Greenland's ice slopes and glaciers had become a torrent, an avalanche, a hurricane of cold.

Though it was still day, driving snow reduced visibility to a hundred yards and the change in conditions heralded the end for *Somali*. At 0230 on the 24th the tow parted, *Somali*'s back breaking simultaneously. The fore and after ends rose up, each assuming an almost vertical position. The stern section sank immediately but the fore part remained afloat until about 0250. Her official sinking position was cited by the Admiralty as 69° 11' N, 15° 32' W, approximately 180 miles north of Raufarhöfn in north-eastern Iceland.

The Admiralty wrote to Maud (promoted commander in December 1942) informing him of 'Their Lordships' warm appreciation of the determination and resource shown on this occasion by him and his whole ship's company'. The only technical criticism was that jettisoning weight from the extremities of the ship had perhaps contributed to the strain amidships.

Fate of the crew

Lt Cdr Maud estimated that only five men were killed in the initial explosion, four from the Engineering Department and one ordinary seaman 'who was probably on the upper deck'. However, given the discrepancy between the number of those recorded as having perished in the actual sinking three days later (fifty) and the final casualty list held by the Admiralty's Naval Historical Branch (eighty-two) the initial toll was probably very much higher. Some had an exceptionally lucky escape: three ratings on the pompom deck were blown overboard by the force of the blast but were able to clamber onto a Carley float which had suffered a similar fate. The starboard watch was ordered off the ship into the trawler *Lord Middleton* which had come along the starboard quarter, and more were evacuated within the hour leaving Lt Cdr Maud and his steaming party of seventy men. When *Somali* sank in the early hours of the 24th a number of rafts and floats were successfully launched. Indeed, all men were ready to abandon ship immediately, having survived three days under a tarpaulin on deck after Maud had forbidden any from venturing below except under strict necessity. However, the conditions in which the rescue took place were so appalling that only seventeen or so survived to be picked up in a 'very steep and very angry' sea. *Lord Middleton, Ashanti* and *Eskimo* had the near-impossible task of getting close enough to rescue men without running them down. *Lord Middleton*, first on the scene, rescued most of those who survived, but for *Ashanti, Eskimo* and *Opportune* it was 'heartbreaking work' in air temperatures of a degree Celsius (30°F) and waters recorded as four degrees (40°F), seasonally warm but still bitterly cold. As Capt. Onslow in *Ashanti* recalled,

> The ship was rolling drunkenly and we were drifting so fast that inevitably some of those in the water were trapped under our bilge keel before we could grab them. And a few swept past our bow or stern when to have moved would have meant losing those we nearly had. We could only pray that the ships to windward would see them in the blinding snow and spindrift. I was proud of our men that night. Many of them showed great courage and endurance, particularly those who went over the side at the risk to themselves of being caught under the bilge keel. But their courage was of little avail. Of those they [*Ashanti*'s men] brought aboard, none were still breathing, and only one responded to artificial respiration. He was the Captain.

Frigid and unconscious, Lt Cdr Maud appeared to have succumbed but was brought round. Nonetheless, *Somali*'s demise sat heavily on Onslow's conscience. Aware that her hull had been groaning piteously as the sea got up on the 23rd, Onslow later

> cursed myself for not having ordered [*Somali*'s men] to abandon ship while the going was good. I told myself that no one could have foreseen the sudden onset of the storm. But then I thought that after more than 20 years at sea – most of them in destroyers – I should by now have been seaman enough to have done so.

U703 and Heinz Bielfeld

Built by H. C. Stülken at Hamburg and commissioned in October 1941, *U703* gave 2½ years' unbroken service in the Northern Theatre

An indistinct but rare photo of a wartime burial at sea, in this case that of
Acting PO Norman McKie of *Somali* who died of wounds in *Ashanti* on 24
September, three days after the attack. Capt. R. G. Onslow has momentarily
slowed *Ashanti*'s engines while the body is committed to the deep.
Bruce Taylor collection

An undated wartime photo of Heinz Bielfeld. *DUBMA*

operating mainly out of Trondheim, Bergen and Narvik. In sixteen
months under Kptlt Heinz Bielfeld she sank just three merchantmen
in addition to HMS *Somali*, including two stragglers from PQ17 in
July 1942. *U703* then operated for a further fourteen months under
Oblt.z.S. Joachim Brünner during which two merchantmen and the
Soviet minesweeping trawler *T-911* (**G54**) were sunk before she went
missing in heavy seas east of Iceland in late September 1944. Neither
the position nor the cause of her loss is known. Bielfeld himself enjoyed
no better fortune. On his first patrol the *Schnorchel* of *U1222* (one of
the new Type-IXC-40 boats) was sighted by an RAF Sunderland in the
Bay of Biscay on 11 July 1944 and the submarine hit with a pattern of
depth charges which dispersed her wreckage over a wide area. There
were no survivors.

Sources

Admiralty, *Convoys to Russia, 1942: QP14 and PQ14* (TNA, ADM 237/177)
—, *Enemy Submarine Attacks on H.M. and Allied Warships: Reports,
1941-1943* (TNA, ADM, 199/163)

—, *PQ and QP Convoys: Reports, 1942–1943* (TNA, ADM 199/758)
Sullivan, Edward, letter to Admiral of the Fleet Lord Lewin of Greenwich, 5
    December 1997 (manuscript, IWM, Misc. 200 (2930))
U703 folder (DUBMA)

Blair, *Hitler's U-Boat War*, II, pp. 18–22
Brice, Martin H., *The Tribals: Biography of a Destroyer Class* (London: Ian
    Allan, 1971)
English, John, Afridi *to* Nizam: *British Fleet Destroyers, 1937–43* (Gravesend,
    Kent: World Ship Society, 2001)
Kinghorn, D., and B. Hargreaves, 'Destroyers of the Royal Navy: Tribal Class
    (Part III)' in *Warships*, Supplement no. 16 (November 1969), pp. 27–33
Onslow, Admiral Sir Richard, 'A Long Tow' in Peter C. Smith, ed., *Destroyer
    Action: An Anthology* (London: William Kimber, 1974), pp. 162–78
—, 'A Tale of Two Tribals' in *The Arctic Lookout*, no. 27 (1997), pp. 17–24
Ruegg, Bob, and Arnold Hague, *Convoys to Russia, 1941–1945* (Kendal,
    Cumbria: World Ship Society, 1992)

Career history of HMS *Somali*:
    http://www.naval-history.net/xGM-Chrono-10DD-34Tribal-Somali.htm

---

71   HMS *VETERAN*
Lt Cdr T. H. Garwood, RN†
Sunk by *U404* (Type VIIC), Kptlt Otto von Bülow, 26 September 1942
North Atlantic, 505 nm W of Port Noo, Donegal (Ireland)

Theatre   North Atlantic (Map 1)
Coordinates   54° 53' N, 23° 03' W
Kriegsmarine code   Quadrat AL 5473
U-boat timekeeping differential   +3 hours
Fatalities   160 and 77   *Survivors*   none

Displacement   1,120 tons
Dimensions   312' × 29.5' × 8.5'
Maximum speed   34 knots
Armament   2 × 4.7"; 1 × 3" AA; 2 × 40 mm AA; 2 × 20 mm AA;
            3 × 21" tt; 1 × Hedgehog ATW

Career

For design notes on the 'V & W'-class destroyers, see HMS *Whirlwind*
(**13**).

The destroyer *Veteran* was laid down at John Brown of Clydebank
in August 1918, launched in April 1919 and completed on 13

November that year. Despite her name, *Veteran* belonged to the
second group of the Modified 'W' class destroyers, of which she was
one of seven completed units. Commissioned for the 3rd Destroyer
Flotilla, Atlantic Fleet, *Veteran* served with this force in home waters
until it was assigned to the Mediterranean to police the aftermath of

Veteran emerging from her conversion to short-range escort on the Thames in February 1942. She was lost with all hands to one or two torpedoes from *U404*.
IWM

the Greco-Turkish War in December 1922, remaining 'up the Straits' until ordered to the China Station in 1926. The close of 1928 found her back with the Mediterranean Fleet with which she remained until paid off into reserve at Chatham in April 1930 – temporarily as it turned out since she was recommissioned for the 8th DF on the China Station in December 1931. *Veteran*'s second sojourn in the Orient lasted from February 1932 until December 1934 when she sailed for the Mediterranean to join the 1st DF. When *Veteran* finally returned to Britain in July 1936 it was to pay off at Spithead after a brief stint off Spain following the outbreak of the Civil War. A short period as a training vessel ended with her laid up at Chatham but September 1939 found the ship refitting while allocated to the 16th DF, then assigned to Western Approaches Command at Plymouth. Reboilered and commissioned with a crew composed largely of reservists, *Veteran* completed trials off Portland in November and the following month was allocated to the 18th DF in the same Command. *Veteran* spent the next few months escorting convoys in the Channel and South-Western Approaches, the first of over eighty that she would escort during her wartime career. In April 1940 *Veteran* was ordered first to the Clyde and then to Scapa Flow from where she participated in the Norwegian Campaign, serving as an escort, supporting operations ashore and finally assisting in the evacuation of Allied troops from the end of May. Following a refit at Chatham in June, *Veteran* was transferred to Harwich against the possibility of a German invasion, the ship patrolling the east coast and the Channel and participating with HM destroyers *Malcolm* and *White Swan* in an attack on enemy shipping off Ostend on 11 September. On 30 September *Veteran* was assigned to convoy duty with the 6th Escort Group at Londonderry and immediately pitchforked into action in the North Atlantic, where she served until the following January.

So ended the first half of *Veteran*'s war career, one that brought an extraordinary catalogue of accidents in addition to the episodes

described above: on 7 February 1940 she was in collision with HMS/m *H43* off Portland; on 11 March a similar encounter with the tanker *Horn Shell* required repairs at Devonport; on 29 May it was the turn of the coaster *Ngakoa*, repairs this time being performed at Rosyth; then on 29 September *Veteran* was mined off the Barrow Deep Light Vessel, being repaired at Barrow-in-Furness. Then came yet another collision, this time with her sister *Verity* on 19 January 1941, the damage made good during a refit at Vickers, Barrow. Nonetheless, the most accident-prone destroyer in the Navy re-entered the fray in March and spent the rest of her career on increasingly arduous service in the Atlantic. In the summer of 1941 she was briefly transferred to the Iceland convoy route, being reassigned to the 2nd EG in August. *Veteran*'s only kill came on 11 September when she joined the 'four-piper' HMS *Leamington* in destroying *U207* while escorting SC42 in the Denmark Strait. In December she was earmarked for conversion to a short-range escort, one of thirteen 'V & Ws' so selected, the work carried out on the Thames over the winter. After a spell working up at HMS *Western Isles*, the anti-submarine training establishment at Tobermory, *Veteran* returned to action in March 1942, being ordered to Newfoundland for detached convoy duty off the eastern seaboard of the United States and Canada. This assignment at length brought her to convoy RB1 which sailed from New York on 21 September.

Background of the attack

Having sunk twelve ships from convoy ON127 including the destroyer HMCS *Ottawa* on 14 September 1942 (**68**), the *Vorwärts* ('onward') group withdrew to reform its patrol line in the central Atlantic. On 23 September *U380* reported sighting an eastbound formation of passenger liners which was interpreted as a troop convoy. So tempting a prize brought not only the *Vorwärts* boats but also those of the *Pfeil* ('arrow') and *Blitz* ('lightning') groups converging on the probable position of these 'transports'. What the Germans had actually encountered was RB1, a fast convoy consisting of eight small American river boats and coastal steamers being transferred from New York to Britain via Halifax and St John's for use as hospital and accommodation ships. Sailed by reduced crews and defended by just two escorts, HM destroyers *Vanoc* (Senior Officer) and *Veteran*, RB1 presented the Germans with an attractive and vulnerable target. To begin with, however, the convoy appeared to lead a charmed life. Engine trouble prevented *U96* and *U380* taking up firing positions, *U211*, *U260* and *U607* failed to make good their attacks, and *U91*, *U410* and *U584* were driven off by the two destroyers. But this could not last

and on the afternoon of the 25th the bloodletting began. SS *Boston* was sunk by two torpedoes from *U216* and SS *New York* despatched by *U96* that evening, *Veteran* being detached to rescue survivors while the rest of the convoy was ordered to scatter and reform at daybreak. An exchange of signals with *Vanoc* on either side of midnight on the 25th in which *Veteran* reported having rescued survivors from the *New York* (in addition to those picked up earlier from the *Boston*) and was rejoining the convoy at sixteen knots was the last the Admiralty knew of her until the capture of *U404*'s war diary for the morning of the 26th.

War Diary of *U404*, patrol of 23 August–13 October 1942: PG 30458, NHB, reel 1,105, pp. 101–2

Date, time	Details of position, wind, weather, sea, light, visibility, moonlight, etc.	Incidents
26.ix	North Atlantic	
0400	Qu. AL 4469 middle	Course 90°, ¾ speed
0800	Qu. AL 4565 lower right, wind SW 6.5, high swell, banks of fog, wildly variable visibility, 2–5 nm	Course altered to 105°. Still at ¾ speed. By dead reckoning the convoy must be close by to the south.
0925		Large single-funnelled steamer in sight at bearing 130° true. Inclination 120°, bows left, range 8,500 m. Zigzagging strongly, general course roughly south-east. We set off in pursuit with all engines at utmost speed.
0936		Destroyer on our starboard quarter, same course as steamer.[1]
0940		We dive to attack destroyer. Due to the high swell and banks of fog we can't get any sort of view through the periscope. No firing opportunity.
1012		Surfaced. At bearing 180° true on the starboard bow there are two large box-shaped steamers, each with a single funnel and a single short thick mast. Bows right, inclinations 40° and 80°, range 6,000 m.
1013		Dive to attack.
1018		Course altered to 300°. Half speed. Enemy visible only intermittently through the periscope.
1024		Enemy bearing 195° true, clearly proceeding quite slowly. Alter course to 230°, half speed. I think I can make out the convoy, now being reassembled by the aforementioned destroyer after being scattered by the fog.[2]
1035		Two-funnelled destroyer on the starboard bow, inclination 90°, bows left, range 6,000 m, proceeding slowly.[3] Favourable firing position.
1036	Qu. AL 5473 Lat.: 54° 51' N Long.: 23° 05' W	Course 228°, half speed. Spread of torpedoes fired from Tubes I, II, IV at destroyer. Torpedo speed 30 knots, enemy speed 10 knots, depth 3 m, 4 m and 3 m, inclination 90°, range 2,600 m.[4] Point of aim 40 m from stern (compensation for over-assessment of enemy speed). The boat, which has been held at 12 m against the heavy swell to allow the periscope to be used, breaches the surface after firing the torpedoes. Trim is regained immediately thanks to precautionary flooding of the quick-diving tanks. We dive to 140 m as the consequences of this unfortunate development are unclear.
1037		Two hits, detonations heard at 53 sec. and 57 sec., range 700 m. These are followed by hissing and breaking sounds in the hydrophones, also audible by naked ear.
1038		Third detonation heard after 104 sec. As we descend we hear rapid propeller noises approaching from the port quarter.

1 Presumably HMS *Vanoc*.

2 Von Bülow's description suggests that this was *Vanoc*, then reorganising the convoy after it had lost formation during the night.

3 Supposing *Vanoc* was the destroyer sighted at 1024 then this can only have been *Veteran*. If so, this indicates that *Veteran* was on the point of rejoining RB1 after rescuing survivors of SSs *Boston* and *New York*, something not appreciated at the time nor confirmed since.

4 As the entry for 1037 indicates, von Bülow's assessment of the range was overestimated by a factor of nearly four, even allowing for the difference (slight in this case, given the beam-on inclination of 90 degrees) between range at point of firing and point of intersection.

1045   Course 320°, depth 140 m. Two very strong detonations that shake the boat followed by *strong*[5] hissing and breaking heard through hydrophones. We at first take these to have been depth charges, despite their sounding quite different to the various depth-charge attacks we have been subjected to thus far. On further consideration of all circumstances and observations, however, it is assumed that the third torpedo hit was on one of the box-shaped steamers observed at the same bearing, which perhaps had a cargo of ammunition. This may have gone up eight minutes later, blasting the vessel to pieces with two detonations.[6]

1056   Hydrophone effect on both port and starboard beams.

1132   Course alteration to 300°.

---

5 Manuscript addition in pencil.

6 Despite von Bülow's *a posteriori* analysis, the only likely scenario here is of *Veteran* sinking or suffering further detonations following the hits at 1037. The optimistic claim of a more distant steamer might be interpreted as his attempt to mask a significant overestimation of target range in the 1036 attack.

The sinking

Although Kptlt von Bülow was unable to identify his victim with certainty, post-war examination of his log left the Admiralty in little doubt that his attack at 0736 convoy time had accounted for HMS *Veteran*. The detonations heard nine minutes later in the now submerged *U404* are consistent with boiler or magazine explosions, or possibly depth charges that had not been set to safe. Nonetheless, though the perpetrator was identified, *U404*'s log leaves significant questions as to the circumstances of *Veteran*'s sinking and the fate of her people. Von Bülow's plausible observations of *Vanoc* shepherding her charges together just twelve minutes before making his attack indicates that *Veteran* was on the point of rejoining RB1 when she was struck, though nothing was reported by the British at this juncture. Indeed, no more was heard from *Veteran* after her signal exchange with *Vanoc* at 0038, seven hours before the attack which destroyed her. The assertion by Lawton (see below) that an abrupt end to this transmission prompted *Vanoc* to retrace her course and begin a search for *Veteran* is supported neither in official sources nor indeed by chronological comparison with von Bülow's log. The best guess is that *Veteran* was hopelessly shattered by the detonation of von Bülow's two torpedoes and sank before any distress signal could be transmitted, her few survivors cast adrift on the Atlantic while their companions in RB1 sailed on none the wiser.

The exultation at B.d.U. – and subsequently broadcast on German radio – after the combined attacks on RB1 was due to the successful boats all overestimating the tonnage of their victims. The three steamers were claimed to represent a combined total of 48,000 GRT, but the reality was that *Boston*, *New York* (both 4,989 GRT) and *Yorktown* (1,547 GRT, sunk later on the 26th by *U619*) together displaced less than a quarter of that figure. Von Bülow reached St-Nazaire to claim a Knight's Cross for his career tonnage though despite his claims had sunk only *Veteran* on this patrol.

Fate of the crew

It is unclear at what stage *Veteran* was first missed but initially at least the Admiralty had neither the resources nor the inclination to launch a hunt for a destroyer which could not be raised by radio. No official corroboration has been found for the claim by Reed (see below) that an aircraft of RAF Coastal Command was signalled to search for *Veteran* at around noon on the 26th. Later that day *Veteran* was unavailingly signalled to break radio silence and report her position. However,

when two days had passed without news of her it became obvious that this was no ordinary mishap. Shortly before midnight on the 28th the Commander-in-Chief Western Approaches, Admiral Sir Percy Noble, diverted HM frigate *Exe* from her course to join ON132 and ordered her to position 54° 34' N, 24° 44' W on the assumption that *Veteran* had been attacked shortly early on the 26th (corresponding to her last reported signal). Joined by the corvette *Gentian*, *Exe* reached this position by dead reckoning at 1000 on the 29th and began a gradual eastward search along the course taken by RB1. A position roughly at the longitude at which *Veteran* was sunk was not reached before early evening on the 29th, more than eighty hours after *U404*'s attack. Nothing was sighted. The pair continued their hunt, sweeping eastward then southward until the search was finally abandoned on the evening of 3 October.

No trace of *Veteran* was ever found and nothing is known of what befell her men after she was hit. Among the 160 crewmen classified as Missing, Presumed Killed were Surgeon Lt Francis M. Hayes and Sub-Lt Michael J. Carter, two of the twenty-three US citizens who lost their lives in the Royal Navy having joined the RNVR before America's entry into the war. Also lost were forty-eight survivors of the SS *Boston*, the Chief Officer of the *New Bedford* (who, for reasons unknown, was transferred along with the *Boston* survivors) and twenty-eight from the SS *New York*. Unsurprisingly, the circumstances under which the defence of this convoy had been left to just two escorts were being raised in the American media by war's end. It has been claimed that RB1 was in fact a decoy for a much more valuable convoy though no documentary evidence has ever been adduced in support of this. The circumstantial evidence rests on awards and decorations granted to the masters and chief engineers of practically every merchantman in the convoy (including posthumously), and on compensations of £10 and £20 respectively for those seamen and officers who completed the voyage. More likely the diminished escort reflects both the desperate shortage of such vessels at this stage in the Battle of the Atlantic and the low value of the convoy, with compensation being offered for the motley assemblage of ships involved. Whatever the case, the precise fate of those sailing in *Veteran* seems likely to remain a mystery.

U404 and Otto von Bülow

Built by Danziger Werft at Danzig (Gdansk) and commissioned in August 1941, *U404* did not become operational until January 1942. Her first six patrols in the Atlantic under Kptlt (Korvettenkapitän

Von Bülow and his First Watch Officer seen on the conning tower of *U404*
on her return to St-Nazaire on 3 May 1943. Among the victory pennants
is one claiming the US carrier *Ranger* on the strength of which von Bülow
was awarded the Oak Leaves to the Knight's Cross. He had in fact engaged
the British escort carrier *Biter*, missing her with four torpedoes on 23 April.
DUBMA

from April 1943) Otto von Bülow yielded fifteen vessels, the majority
of which were sunk in the relatively unprotected waters off the United
States during the second 'happy time' of early 1942. These successes
were recognised with the Knight's Cross in October 1942 to which
the Oak Leaves were added in April 1943 thanks to his claim (later
proved false) to have accounted for the US carrier *Ranger*. By contrast,
U404's operational career under von Bülow's successor, Oblt.z.S. Adolf
Schönberg, lasted just four days. Sighted off Cape Ortegal, Spain on 24
July 1943, *U404* was attacked and probably damaged by a US Liberator.
Despite replying with anti-aircraft fire, the arrival of a second Liberator
sealed *U404*'s fate and she was lost with all hands.

On leaving *U404* von Bülow was appointed commandant of the
newly established 23rd *U-Flottille* at Danzig, a school for trainee U-boat
commanders. In March 1945 he took command of the new Type-XXI
U2545 which, however, never saw action. Joining the Bundesmarine in
1956, von Bülow ended his naval career as a Kapitän zur See in 1970.
He died in January 2006 at the age of ninety-four.

Sources

Admiralty, *Reports of Proceedings, 1942* (TNA, ADM 199/618)
—, *Mercantile Convoy Reports, December 1941–December 1942* (TNA, ADM
     199/719)
—, *War Diary Summaries, September/October 1942* (TNA, ADM 199/2249
     and 2250)
—, *Information from Captured Records Regarding Warships, H.M. Trawlers
     and Merchant Vessels Lost Without Trace During the War* (NHB,
     Information Abstract AB.233)
—, *HMS* Veteran: *Torpedoed and Sunk by* U404, *29th September 1942* (NHB,
     S.7130)
Ellis, William, *Convoy R.V.1* [*sic*] (manuscript memoir, Bruce Taylor
     collection)

Bibby, K., 'Convoy RB.1 (16–25 September 1942)' in *Warships*, Supplement
     no. 82 (Autumn 1985), pp. 331–3
Blair, *Hitler's U-Boat War*, II, pp. 32–4
Bülow, Kapt.z.S. Otto von, 'The Sinking of HMS *Veteran*' in Fairweather, ed.,
     Hard Lying, pp. 223–4
Fairweather, C. W., Editorial in *Hard Lying: The V & W Magazine*, no. 17
     (June 2004), pp. 1–3
—, ed., *Hard Lying: The Story of the "V & W" Class Destroyers and the Men
     Who Sailed in Them* (Chelmsford, Essex: Avalon Associates, 2005)
Kirkby, Hilary, 'Wartime Memories of a Merchant Mariner' in *The Tiverton
     Gazette* (Tuesday, 14 June 2005), p. 20
Lawton, John, *The Proudest of Her Line: The Story of HMS* Veteran
     (Wrexham, Clwyd: privately, 2006)
Preston, Antony, *'V & W' Class Destroyers, 1917–1945* (London: Macdonald,
     1971)
Raven, Alan, and John Roberts, *'V' and 'W' Class Destroyers* [Man o'War, no.
     2] (London: Arms & Armour Press, 1979)
Reed, James, *Convoy 'Maniac': R.B.1* (Lewes, Sussex: The Book Guild, 2000)
—, 'Convoy Maniac – RB1' in Fairweather, ed., *Hard Lying*, pp. 216–20
Smith, Peter C., *HMS* Wild Swan: *One Destroyer's War, 1939–42* (London:
     William Kimber, 1985)
Stokes, Jack, 'My War' in *Hard Lying: The V & W Magazine*, no. 16
     (December 2003), pp. 6–16; also in Fairweather, ed., *Hard Lying*, pp. 70–7
     and 224
Urbanke, Axel, „U404 – das ‚Wikingerboot' auf Feindfahrt mit der
     Unterwasserkamera" in *U-Boot im Focus*, no. 6 (2010), pp. 22–32

War career of HMS *Veteran*:
     http://www.naval-history.net/xGM-Chrono-10DD-09VW-Veteran.htm
Webpage containing details of convoy RB1:
     http://ahoy.tk-jk.net/Letters/HaroldLesliePapworthwasCh.html
Scan of undated wartime article from *The People* titled 'How Lake Steamers
     Fought a U-Boat Pack':
     http://ahoy.tk-jk.net/Letters/FatherlostonHMSVeteran.html

72   HMS *MARTIN*
Cdr C. R. P. Thompson, DSO RN†
Sunk by *U431* (Type VIIC), Kptlt Wilhelm Dommes, 10 November 1942
Western Mediterranean, 80 nm NE of Algiers (Algeria)

Martin seen on completion in April 1942. Six months later she was no more, the victim of three torpedo hits on her port side from *U431*. *BfZ*

Campaign	Operation TORCH (Map 3)	*Displacement*	1,920 tons
Coordinates	37° 53' N, 03° 57' E	*Dimensions*	362.25' × 37' × 10'
Kriegsmarine code	Quadrat CH 9247	*Maximum speed*	36 knots
U-boat timekeeping differential	+1 hour	*Armament*	6 × 4.7"; 1 × 4" AA; 4 × 40 mm AA;
Fatalities	159 *Survivors* 63		2 × 20 mm AA; 12 × .5" AA; 4 × 21" tt

Career

The 'M'-class destroyers of the 1939–40 programme, of which *Martin* was the first unit to be laid down, were virtual repeats of the preceding 'L' class (see HMS *Gurkha*, **46**).

Laid down at Vickers-Armstrong's yard at Walker-on-Tyne in October 1939, HMS *Martin* was launched in December 1940 but not completed until April 1942. Assigned to the 17th Destroyer Flotilla, Home Fleet, *Martin* was immediately assigned to Russian convoy duty, joining PQ15 which sailed for the Kola Inlet on 26 April. Her first taste of action came at the end of May as part of the close escort for convoy PQ16 to Murmansk during which three U-boats were engaged without success and bomb damage inflicted by German aircraft. In late June she joined the fateful convoy PQ17, escorting it until it was ordered to scatter on 4 July, whereupon it was savaged by German air and U-boat attack. Having returned independently to Scapa Flow *Martin* sailed for the Kola Inlet once again on 20 July, this time with supplies and ammunition for the return convoy, QP14, then taking shape at Archangel. On 24 August *Martin* left Archangel in company with HM destroyers *Marne* and *Onslaught* and the cruiser USS *Tuscaloosa* for a sweep along the coast of northern Norway. This force appears to have been acting on Allied signal intelligence and duly encountered the German minelayer *Ulm* south-east of Bear Island on the 25th, sinking her and rescuing fifty-four survivors. Returning to Scapa at the end of August, on 4 September *Martin* sailed to escort

her fourth eastbound Russian convoy, PQ18. For the fate of this and the westbound QP14 which *Martin* subsequently joined, see HMS *Somali* (**70**). After allocation to the 3rd DF Home Fleet and a month at Scapa the order to sail for the balmy waters of the Mediterranean on 30 October must have come as a blessed relief in *Martin* but the change of climate heralded a terrible reversal in her fortunes. Having refueled at Gibraltar on 5 November *Martin* took her place in the destroyer screen for Force H, then patrolling off Algeria in support of Operation TORCH.

Background of the attack

On the evening of 5 November 1942 Italian spies near Gibraltar observed an armada of over ninety ships passing the Straits into the Mediterranean, the first inkling received by the Axis of Operation TORCH, the Allied landings in Algeria and Morocco which sounded the death knell for the *Afrika Korps*. The *U-Boot-Waffe*'s commander in the Mediterranean, Konteradmiral Leo Kreisch (*F.d.U. Italien*), deployed the nine boats he had immediately available into three lines south of the Balearics with a view to interdicting landings on the Algerian coast. They were joined some days later by *U431* (Kptlt Wilhelm Dommes) which had returned from patrol to La Spezia on the 5th only to be hastily resupplied and sent back to sea. Returns against the TORCH convoys were initially dismal with few sightings and no successes. Reinforced by boats passing through the Straits of Gibraltar, Kreisch redeployed his force into the *Hai* ('shark') and *Delfin* ('dolphin') groups off Algiers and Oran. Even then the Germans enjoyed scant success, and though *U81* and *U331* sank SS *Garlinge* and the US troop transport *Leedstown* (G37) off Algeria, Kreisch's exhortations to engage the enemy 'without consideration for crew or boat' failed to generate the results expected of such a concentration in busy waters. However, the *U-Boot-Waffe* had not quite done with TORCH yet. Shortly after midnight on the 10th *U431* gained her first opportunity as lookouts sighted a group of seven cruisers and destroyers heading west. This was the screen for Force H which had sailed east of Algiers the previous evening before reversing course towards Bougie at midnight. Unable to close the group due to mechanical problems which limited his speed to ten knots, Dommes was obliged to fire a spread of four torpedoes from a range of over 3,000 metres. A short while later the unsuspecting destroyer *Martin* was shattered by three torpedoes from this salvo which is plotted and discussed in detail in the Introduction, pp. xxiv–xxv.

War Diary of *U431*, patrol of 7–22 November 1942: PG 30485, NHB, reel 1,107, pp. 608–9

Date, time	Details of position, wind, weather, sea, light, visibility, moonlight, etc.	Incidents
10.xi	Western Mediterranean	
0243	Qu. CH 9247, lower right	Several shadows appear at bearing 30° true. A group made up of seven warships proceeding in a westerly direction at average speed. There appear to be four destroyers and three cruisers. I initially adopt a parallel course and then make every effort to close (port electric engine at ¾ speed, starboard diesel at half speed, my maximum speed being 10 knots).[1] Although we must present quite a silhouette for the warship squadron given the strong prevailing sea phosphorescence, we remain unnoticed. I estimate the squadron's speed to be exceeding my own by about 5 knots.
0352		I turn to fire.
0354		A spread fired at the larger unit stationed on the squadron's port quarter.[2] At the very moment of firing the bows of a destroyer further away emerge from behind those of the cruiser.[3] Depth 2 m, enemy speed 15 knots, inclination red [i.e. port] 80°.[4] The progress of the spread can be easily followed thanks to the sea phosphorescence. It runs well. We hear hits after 3 min. 25 sec., or 3,100 m.[5] Cruiser is blown into the air in a huge blaze of flame. An astoundingly large mushroom-shaped cloud of smoke and flame rises up into the sky.
		I head off to the east and then behind the squadron to the north-east. As we are withdrawing on this north-easterly course, to the right of the great cloud of billowing smoke and flame from the exploding vessel, another further tall mushroom cloud several hundred metres high appears, at the base of which a shadow is visible, at times accompanied by a great blaze of flame. This occurred 500–1,000 m to the north-west of where the vessel sank.
		As several destroyers are now closing I withdraw even further which means that I observe no subsequent developments. Plenty of morse traffic exchanged between the different ships of the group but no counter-attack.
		I take the first ship we hit to have been a cruiser of the Leander class. I think I saw that the rather wide funnel (a bit like *Leipzig*'s) was higher than the bridge.[6] The second unit we hit was probably a destroyer.
0400	Qu. CH 9247, right edge, wind NE 2–3, almost overcast, sea 2, 1,029 mb. Sea phosphorescence.	

---

1 Dommes had previously reported clutch problems with the port diesel engine and was obliged to use the electric engine instead. This not only reduced *U431*'s maximum speed but limited her ability to dive.

2 It is not known which ship was being targeted here.

3 HMS *Martin*.

4 The ranking survivor of HMS *Martin*, Lt Kavanagh, recalled a speed of 16 knots, but see n. 5.

5 Three hits from a spread of four fired by *U431*'s First Watch Officer, Lt.z.S. Friedrich Weidner. This remarkable result at such a range demonstrates the accuracy of Weidner's and Dommes's calculation of the key variables of inclination and speed (80 degrees and 15 knots respectively). Indeed, their assessment of *Martin*'s speed may have been more accurate than the 16 knots recalled by Lt Kavanagh himself. With such precision, underestimating the range by nearly 1,000 metres actually worked to *U431*'s advantage since the salvo reached *Martin* long before it had dispersed to the extent envisaged at the calculated point of intersection, thereby allowing three torpedoes to strike the target.

6 The absence of details on the composition of the escort makes it unclear which cruiser Dommes is referring to here; certainly none was torpedoed at this juncture. The only single-funnelled cruisers in the Royal Navy belonged to the Leander class of 7,200 tons but none were present on this occasion. The light cruiser *Leipzig*, with a trunked funnel similar to that of the Leanders, displaced 6,619 tons.

0430	As we haul away the boat is suddenly shaken by a powerful underwater explosion. The bridge watch can see nothing in the way of visual phenomena that would explain this. Presumably the depth charges of the destroyer we hit went off as she sank. The warship squadron is now out of sight, last seen at bearing 285° true.
0504	Outgoing W/T transmission 0354/10/567: *Qu. CH 9247. Spread fired at light warship group. Course 300°, 15 knots. Three detonations, one unit blown up, another giving off substantial clouds of smoke.*[7]

7   Dommes later observed that the enemy had been keeping a more southerly course than that reported in this signal, and indeed Lt Kavanagh recorded that *Martin* was steering 270° at the time.

The sinking

HMS *Martin* has the unfortunate distinction of being the only Allied destroyer of the war to suffer three torpedo hits in a single attack, meeting a predictable fate as a consequence. The first struck at 0259 ship's time abaft the forward cabin flat, setting fire to this space and to the wardroom. The second torpedo struck 'between 20 and 27 bulkheads, blowing off A turret and the forecastle, and causing extensive fires in the remaining mess decks,' no doubt as a result of the detonation of the forward magazine. The third torpedo was believed to have struck close to the engine room, causing the immediate flooding of this area and the failure of all lighting. Within two minutes of the first explosion the bridge was under water and the fore part sinking. The stern floated at an angle of about sixty degrees for another twenty minutes or so, a depth charge detonating as it went under and noted by Dommes in his log entry for 0430.

As neither hydrophone effect nor Asdic contact had been gained by *Martin* or any other vessel in the screen and as nothing could have been done to save her from 900 kilograms of explosive, a Board of Enquiry was waived. However, while the cause of the sinking was never in doubt, it was not clear on which side *Martin* was struck. The principal official source on the loss, a brief report by the ranking survivor, Lt Charles Kavanagh, records that 'all torpedoes appeared to come from the starboard side' and that *Martin* listed heavily to starboard after the third detonation, a view supported by survivor recollections. However, this is contradicted by Kptlt Dommes's torpedo data and his sketch of the episode which indicate that the attack was made on *Martin*'s port side, *U431* being positioned to the south of the group as it sailed west. This is corroborated by Chief Yeoman of Signals Harry Plaice who recalled (admittedly many years later) *Martin* listing to *port* after the second hit, though his description could equally be equated with the impact of a hit on the starboard side.

Despite his claims, *Martin* was Dommes's only success during this action, though she was the first of two destroyer kills for *U431* over seventy-two hours (see HrMs *Isaac Sweers*, **74**). Nonetheless, this was scant consolation for *F.d.U. Italien* which suffered the shattering loss of five *Mittelmeer* boats in as many days in return for just eight sinkings from the Allied fleets.

Fate of the crew

HMS *Martin* was one of a number of British ships lost or damaged during Operation TORCH and little detailed information on her sinking has been found in Admiralty sources. It is not known how many men initially got clear of the ship though it is clear that many lost their lives in the detonations and fires that destroyed her. The fact that Cdr Thompson had stood the men down from Action

Dommes takes his place on the *Wintergarten* for *U431*'s commissioning at Danzig on 5 April 1941. *DUBMA*

Stations to Defence Stations shortly before the attack seems to have contributed to the number of casualties, Lt Kavanagh noting that 'with a few exceptions, the only survivors are from the watch on deck' and survivor testimony attributing the high death toll to the parties of men who had gone below after that order was passed. Apart from Kavanagh's report, the only written source of note so far uncovered is that of Ch.Yeo.Sigs. Harry Plaice who recalled making his way onto the wrecked bridge to find the dejected figure of Cdr Thompson: 'Only our captain remained in his chair and I asked him for permission to abandon ship, but he didn't answer me. I think he was still in a state of shock having realised that a great number of his crew were already lost.' The survivors clung to the few floatanets that had drifted clear of *Martin* as she sank, but it took HM destroyer *Quentin* (herself lost to air attack three weeks later) the best part of five hours to rescue them in the darkness. Many were both in an advanced state of exhaustion and saturated with fuel oil from the *Martin*'s freshly replenished tanks. The last man was recovered at approximately 0800 British time making a total of sixty-three survivors from a ship's company of 222. They were quickly returned to Gibraltar from where most reached Britain in the battleship *Duke of York*.

U431 and Wilhelm Dommes

Built by F. Schichau at Danzig (Gdansk) and commissioned in April 1941, *U431* spent most of her frontline career under Kptlt Wilhelm Dommes. Her first two patrols, which were carried out in the Atlantic, yielded only one merchantman but a transfer to the Mediterranean in November 1941 improved matters considerably (a rare exception to the rule) with Dommes revealing a penchant for attacks on naval and auxiliary vessels. His seven Mediterranean patrols accounted for three merchantmen (with a fourth damaged) together with HM minesweeping whaler *Sotra* in January 1942 (**G20**), *Martin* and another destroyer, HrMs *Isaac Sweers* (**74**), three days later. A salvo of four torpedoes directed at the carrier *Furious* off Cartagena on 29 October 1942 failed to find its mark. For the remainder of Dommes's and *U431*'s career, see HrMs *Isaac Sweers*.

Sources

Admiralty, *Damage to H.M. Ships by Torpedo and Mine, 1941–1943* (TNA, ADM 267/94)

—, War Diaries for 1–15 and 16–30 November 1942 (TNA, ADM 199/2251 and 2252), pp. 370, 394, 403 and 703

Dommes, Fregkpt. Wilhelm, correspondence with Ch.Yeo.Sigs. Harry Plaice (DUBMA, *U431* file)

Tenholt, Paul, *Chronik des deutschen Unterseebootes* U-431 *und seiner 16 Feindfahrten* (typescript, DUBMA, *U431* file)

Admiralty, *Operation Torch: The Invasion of North Africa, November 1942– February 1943* [Battle Summary no. 38] (restricted circulation, Admiralty, 1948)

English, John, Afridi *to* Nizam: *British Fleet Destroyers, 1937–43* (Gravesend, Kent: World Ship Society, 2001)

Kinghorn, D., and B. Hargreaves, 'Destroyers of the Royal Navy: "M" Class' in *Warships*, Supplement no. 22 (May 1970), pp. 13–21

Roskill, *War at Sea*, II, pp. 312–37

Schneider, Werner, *12 Feindfahrten. Als Funker auf* U-431, U-410 *und* U-371 *im Atlantik und im Mittelmeer. Ausbildung, Einsatz, Gefangenschaft, 1940– 1946* (Weinheim: Germania Verlag, 2006)

Career history of HMS *Martin*: http://www.naval-history.net/xGM-Chrono-10DD-43M-Martin.htm

73   HMS *HECLA* (i)

Capt. S. H. T. Arliss, DSO RN
Sunk by *U515* (Type IXC), Kptlt Werner Henke, 11–12 November 1942
North Atlantic, 200 nm W of Tangier (Morocco)

Hecla in the final stages of fitting out at John Brown's yard, Clydebank, around January 1941. Towering over her is one of Sir William Arrol's Titan cranes. Within two years she had been undone in a relentless attack by Werner Henke in *U515*. *BfZ*

Campaign Operation TORCH (Map 1)	*Displacement* 10,850 tons
Coordinates 35° 42' N, 09° 55' W	*Dimensions* 623' × 66' × 16'
Kriegsmarine code Quadrat CG 8830	*Armour* 2" horizontal; 1.5" bulkheads
U-boat timekeeping differential +1 hour	*Maximum speed* 17 knots
Fatalities 281 *Survivors* about 545	*Armament* 8 × 4.5" DP; 8 × 40 mm AA; 6 × 20 mm AA

Career

The destroyer depot ship *Hecla* was laid down at John Brown of Clydebank, Scotland in January 1939, launched in March 1940 and completed in January 1941. Designed as the mother ship to a flotilla of eight or nine destroyers on detached duty, *Hecla* not only provided accommodation and working spaces for the personnel required to keep her charges operational, but also stowed up to eighty 21-inch torpedoes and 150 depth charges. *Hecla* spent the first months of her career at Hvalfjörður in Iceland where she tended *U570* (subsequently HMS/m *Graph*) following her capture on 27 August 1941. Early in 1942 she was transferred to the Eastern Fleet and was on passage to join that force in the Indian Ocean when she struck a mine off Cape Agulhas, South Africa on 15 May. The mine, part of a field sown by the German minelayer *Doggerbank* on 16 April, cost the lives of twenty-four men and wounded 112 others. Torpedoes and depth charges were scattered by the blast but none exploded and the ship was brought into Simon's Town under two from the cruiser *Gambia*. *Hecla* immediately went into the Selborne Dock where repairs continued until September. After trials in False Bay *Hecla* sailed north, her assignment to the Eastern Fleet forgotten.

Background of the attack

For additional background on Operation TORCH, see the preceding entry for HMS *Martin* (**72**).

When the Germans got wind of Operation TORCH (the Allied landings at Vichy-held Casablanca, Oran and Algiers on 8 November 1942), pressure was quickly applied on B.d.U. to provide a substantial U-boat force on either side of the Straits of Gibraltar. Under no illusions that the passage of a submarine eastwards into the Mediterranean could ever be reversed, a reluctant Dönitz concentrated thirty-five U-boats west of Morocco. As it turned out, the overall returns for such a large force were no better than those in the Mediterranean itself. In addition to the British escort groups based at Gibraltar and in North Africa, fresh squadrons of US Navy Catalinas had by now been deployed and proved a constant thorn in the side of the first wave of U-boats of the *Schlagetot* ('death blow') group. However, successes were scored by three boats: *U173* (Oblt.z.S. Hans-Adolf Schweichel) and *U130* (Korvkpt. Ernst Kals) which slipped through the defensive screen to sink four large US troop transports off the Moroccan port of Fédala on 11th and 12th November respectively, thereby forcing the Allies to shift their unloading operations to Casablanca (**G38–41**); and Kptlt Werner Henke's *U515* which on the evening of the 11th sighted a group of British warships in the final stages of its passage from Freetown to Gibraltar. This consisted of the converted cruiser *Vindictive*, the depot ship *Hecla* (which Henke mistook for a cruiser) and the destroyers *Marne* and *Venomous*. Henke's attacks on the night of the 11–12th, recorded in a log marked by unusual understatement, were spread over seven hours and punctuated with depth charging and gunfire from the British. They would earn the highest respect from B.d.U. and British alike.

War Diary of *U515*, patrol of 7 November 1941–6 January 1942: PG 30553, NHB, reel 1,115, p. 524

Date, time	Details of position, wind, weather, sea, light, visibility, moonlight, etc.	Incidents
11.xi		
1753	[Qu.] CG 8770	Surfaced.
1915	[Qu.] CG 8780	Cruiser group in sight. Two cruisers of the Birmingham and Frobisher classes respectively, as well as ~~2~~ three 'K'-class destroyers.[1] Steering an easterly course, cruising speed 15 knots. Every so often radar warning readings on 139 cm.[2]
		Henke
12.xi		
	West of the Spanish coast	I haul ahead at utmost speed but am several times forced to retire by the destroyers. I run in to attack the Birmingham-class cruiser in the rear.
0015	[Qu.] CG 8830	<u>Spread of four torpedoes fired from Tubes I–IV</u>: depth 2 m, enemy speed 15 knots, bows right, inclination 95°, range 1,500 m. Running time 70 sec., one surface runner and one circular runner, a single hit abreast the engine room. Ship slows and stops, escorts gather round while the other cruiser makes off to the east at high speed.
0128		I have penetrated the escort.
		Coup-de-grâce <u>shot from Tube I</u>: depth 2 m, range 1,500 m, hits amidships, running time 2 min. 25 sec.
0149		*Coup-de-grâce* <u>shot from Tube V</u>: depth 2 m, range 2,000 m, a hit 40 m from the stern, running time 2 min. 4 sec. Cruiser is listing heavily to port.
0201		<u>Shot from Tube VI</u>: aimed at 'K'-class destroyer passing alongside, range 1,000 m, depth 2 m, hit

---

1 These were, respectively, HM depot ship *Hecla*, HM cruiser *Vindictive* and HM destroyers *Venomous* of the 'V & W' class and *Marne* of the 'M' class. Henke's misidentification of *Hecla* is understandable in view of the similarities in turret arrangement, hull design and size between her and the Southampton-class cruisers (to which *Birmingham* belonged). He is, however, quite correct in identifying *Vindictive* – then fitted out as a repair ship – as a member of the 'Elizabethan' class of heavy cruisers (of which *Frobisher* was a unit). The fact that the number '2' is crossed out and replaced by the word 'three' in the typed-up version of the log is evidence of a degree of confusion as to the number of destroyers, though only *Venomous* and *Marne* were present.

2 This refers to the Metox centrimetric-wavelength radar-screening device with which *U515* was fitted.

Date, time	Details of position, wind, weather, sea, light, visibility, moonlight, etc.	Incidents
		25 m from the stern.[3] Powerful detonation, broad explosion column, depth-charge detonations under destroyer's stern.
0206		*Coup-de-grâce* <u>shot from Tube IV</u>: at cruiser, depth 2 m, hit 30 m from bows, ship doesn't sink. Am now spotted and pursued by a destroyer firing starshell.[4] Steering failure, switchboard fire.
0217		Alarm dive, depth charges at 120 and 160 m.[5] We reload torpedoes.
0431		Surfaced. We approach the cruiser again which has now settled deep in the water. She is being slowly towed stern first by a destroyer lying alongside [*sic*].[6] Suddenly the destroyer fires a salvo of gunfire at us, then another is fired from the cruiser's forward turret.
0538		Alarm. Countless depth charges. Asdic noises.
0613		We surface and approach the cruiser. More gunfire from the destroyer.
0650		<u>Spread of two torpedoes from Tubes II and IV</u>: aimed at different points on the target, enemy speed five knots, a hit heard after about two minutes, depth 3 m.[7] Depth charges, hydrophone pursuit, *Bolde* successfully deployed.[8]
1200	[Qu.] CG 8890 Lat.: 35° 14' N Long.: 9° 34' W	Day's run on surface: 120 nm. Day's run submerged: 30 nm. Throughout the rest of the day hundreds of depth charges rain down; at periscope depth I can make out aircraft and a U-boat hunting group.[9]
1919	[Qu.] CG 8870	Surfaced. Outgoing W/T transmission to B.d.U.: *This morning Qu. CG 8830 four hits on Birmingham-class cruiser, a fifth heard, sinking not observed, a hit on 'K'-class destroyer, sinking probable. 190 cbm, 5 + 8 eels.*[10] *Henke.*

Henke

---

3   HMS *Marne*, whose stern was blown off in this attack.

4   HMS *Venomous*, which sighted *U515* at 1,500 yards, closed at twenty-four knots and dropped a pattern of five depth charges.

5   Though Henke did not know it, this entry coincides with the time *Hecla* disappeared so it is possible that *U515* was actually listening to her sinking. There is little to choose between German and British timekeeping at this juncture.

6   Still unaware that his 'cruiser' had sunk more than two hours earlier, Henke had actually spotted *Venomous* attempting to take *Marne* in tow.

7   Henke plainly believed that he was again attacking *Hecla* though his target was in fact *Marne*, then lying stopped Though a hit may have been heard in *U515* none was in fact registered by the British.

8   *Bolde* was the calcium-zinc discharge that replicated the echo produced by an Asdic submarine contact by generating large masses of bubbles. This device was also known as the *Pillenwerfer* ('pill-thrower') after the ejector fitted for this purpose in the stern of the U-boat.

9   This was no exaggeration. The arrival on the scene of destroyers and strafing aircraft at dawn kept *U515* submerged for many hours. Mulligan (see below) quotes a member of the crew in the control room who recalled Henke announcing at one point to his men: 'What are you looking at me for? What can I do about it?'

10   Translates as 190 cubic metres of diesel fuel with a probable mix of five G7e and eight G7a torpedoes remaining. 'Eels' (German = *Aale*) was U-boat slang for torpedoes.

The sinking

At 2311 on the 11th British time (0011 on the 12th German time) *Vindictive* sighted a wake on her starboard beam which she took to be *Venomous* rejoining the group after detaching to investigate an RDF contact an hour earlier. This was in fact *U515* running in to attack and five minutes later *Hecla* shuddered under the impact of two explosions. Though Henke noted only one detonation against the 'cruiser', Capt. S. H. T. Arliss later reported *Hecla* being simultaneously struck by two torpedoes amidships, causing an immediate list to starboard and extensive flooding of the boiler rooms and other spaces. However, since Henke recorded that one of his torpedoes had assumed a circular trajectory and the remaining two were accounted for by *Vindictive* it is difficult to see how *Hecla* can have suffered more than one hit at this juncture. For her part, *Vindictive*, then three cables off *Hecla*'s port beam, escaped being hit thanks to a routine alteration of course onto

the next leg of the zigzag, a manoeuvre interpreted by Henke and most onlookers in *Hecla* as her disappearing to the east at high speed. As a result, 'when steadied on the new course of 090° [*Vindictive*] observed two torpedoes on a parallel course overtaking the ship, one on each side'. Though Cdr H. W. Falcon-Steward of *Venomous* closed *Hecla* and offered to take her in tow, Capt. Arliss instead ordered the two destroyers to form an anti-submarine screen in view of his greatly reduced speed.

Meanwhile, *Hecla* 'paid off to starboard, lost way, listed rapidly to 7½ degrees starboard, and then slowly to 11 degrees starboard, where she hung'. The ship went over to auxiliary power, emergency cables were rigged to keep the pumps working and efforts made to right the trim of the ship but *Hecla* was evidently in extreme danger and Henke not long in responding. His next torpedo, fired an hour after the first and watched as it approached by many of *Hecla*'s men, struck forward on the port side with an explosion that was 'very violent, large quantities of oil and debris being thrown into the air'. Lt H. H. McWilliams describes the scene from the boat deck:

> There was a terrific orange flash, shooting up as high as the mast, above which rolled a huge billowing cloud of ruddy smoke studded with flying debris. Then a great column of water went up and presently bits of steel and wood began raining down all round with fearful clattering sounds. We shrank against the overhanging boat until this was over, then ventured out to be caught in a shower of water coming down like rain.

What had been a starboard list suddenly became a seventeen-degree list to port. When this increased to twenty-five degrees over the next ten minutes Arliss gave the order to abandon ship. *U515*'s next torpedo, fired ten minutes later according to Arliss and twenty-one minutes later according to Henke, struck *Hecla* on the port side abreast 'X' turret. This accelerated the list to port (again contradicting Henke's observation), the ship settling 'until the quarter deck and port waist were awash'. But Henke was not finished. At 0100 on the 12th British time (0201 log time) – an hour and three quarters after his first attack – HMS *Marne* had her stern blown off by Henke's seventh torpedo while she was standing by *Hecla*; thirteen crewmen were killed but she eventually made Gibraltar under tow from HM tug *Salvonia*. Henke's eighth torpedo, fired five minutes later, struck *Hecla* on the starboard side aft, hastening what was already a foregone conclusion. However, *Venomous* now obtained a hydrophone fix and then visual contact and set off in pursuit at twenty-four knots, opening fire with her forward guns. Characteristically, Henke did not dive until the range had closed to 200 yards, his periscope being observed to pass ten yards down *Venomous*'s port side while she dropped five depth charges. As Henke records in his log, these caused some damage to *U515* while *Venomous* herself suffered the temporary loss of a dynamo. Henke therefore missed the last of *Hecla* which capsized onto her beam ends and sank stern first at 0116 British time, two hours after taking the first of four or five hits.

The Admiralty's Anti-Submarine Warfare Division concluded that the offending U-boat had probably been sunk by *Venomous* but acknowledged the exceptional boldness of her opponent. Indeed, Henke's remarkable persistence, which brought him back for the *coup de grâce* after ninety minutes of depth charging, has no parallel in the history of U-boat engagements with Allied anti-submarine escorts. This much was acknowledged by B.d.U.'s Chief of Operations, Konteradmiral Eberhard Godt, who in his review of *U515*'s patrol considered Henke's actions worthy of the 'highest recognition', distinguished as they were by 'quite exceptional audacity and pluck'. All the more impressive, indeed, since the feat had been achieved in a relatively large and unwieldy Type-IX boat, much less suited to agile jousting with escorts than the Type VII. Henke was awarded the Knight's Cross while still on patrol, Dönitz's memoirs recalling the episode as deserving the 'highest praise'. Predictably enough, Admiral Sir Andrew Cunningham, Commander-in-Chief Mediterranean Fleet, was scathing of the British performance, criticising Capt. H. G. D. Acland of *Vindictive* (the Senior Officer present) for failing to arrange proper RDF coordination and then mistaking the offending U-boat for one of his own destroyers. He also described the escort's preemptive anti-submarine measures as 'thoroughly unsatisfactory until the enemy had betrayed his presence by firing torpedoes'. However, Henke's

HMS *Venomous* reaches Casablanca loaded with survivors of *Hecla* and *Marne* on the morning of 13 November 1942. An abundant reception awaited them from the escort carrier *Chenango* and the heavy cruiser *Augusta* of the US Navy. *NARA*

determination to sink *Hecla* at all costs was sufficiently apparent from Allied reports for the Admiralty to conclude that no useful purpose would be served by holding a Board of Enquiry into her loss.

Fate of the crew

Only 'a small number' of *Hecla*'s men were lost as a direct consequence of the first two hits, whether killed in the blasts or as a result of debris landing on deck. However, any chance of a great majority of the crew surviving the sinking was dashed by the destruction or effective loss of all her boats, those on the starboard side being wrecked by the first blast at 2316 and the rest rendered unusable once the second torpedo deprived *Hecla* of sufficient power to operate the 10-ton crane at 0028. The starboard sea boat was lowered despite the heavy list to port but 'may have been damaged in the process as she later capsized'. The order to abandon ship was passed after the second hit but there could be no organised evacuation without boats and it was largely a case of every man for himself. Although the majority of *Hecla*'s ship's company had got clear of her before Henke's two final hits at 0100 and 0105, the blast from these killed or fatally injured a number of men in the water while several Carley floats were sucked into the torpedo holes. A number of men were lost as they struck out towards *Marne* in the expectation of early rescue, being claimed instead by the demolition of her stern by Henke's seventh torpedo. Others died under a rain of debris and exploding ordnance or in the detonation of a succession of *Marne*'s depth charges. Lt H. H. McWilliams SANF was one of two *Hecla* survivors to be rescued by a boatload of men who had abandoned *Marne* after she was hit, being eventually taken on board *Venomous*.

Most of those who survived spent the rest of the night and much of the next morning clinging to Carley floats which drifted over a wide area. *Venomous*'s attempts to rescue them 'were broken off on several occasions to investigate RDF contacts and to drop depth charges periodically', though one such attack accounted for another group of men in the water. Many more perished through exhaustion or the

An undated studio portrait of Werner Henke. *DUBMA*

effects of fuel oil during the twelve hours it took *Venomous* to complete her work. Stoker Charlie Brierley was one of twenty-four men clinging to each other or to ropes trailing from a three-foot square biscuit float; just four remained by the time *Venomous* found them after midday on the 12th, the last crewmen to be rescued. For the rescue teams it made for 'depressing work' and more than thirty of those taken on board were found to have succumbed. Sadly, the work of rescue also claimed the life of Boatswain Herbert Button of *Venomous* who repeatedly swam out to secure exhausted survivors before collapsing himself. This was the second time in three months that *Venomous* had been called upon to care for hundreds of survivors (see HMS *Eagle*, **65**) and many of the 500 men she picked up on this occasion paid tribute to 'the unfailing humanity of matelots in times of stress'. Les Rawles has this memory:

> I remember trying to climb aboard but was slipping back. Someone said 'Grab him!' and I was hauled aboard where I just flaked out. Standing over me was a couple of *Venomous* lads with a tot, which was pushed down me. I had no choice. Then cigarettes, followed by corned beef straight out of the tin with fingers – not enough knives to go round. It tasted good.

Packed with men and desperately low on fuel after a prolonged anti-submarine hunt and sweeps for survivors, Cdr Falcon-Steward of *Venomous* decided to make for Casablanca on learning that it was in American hands. It was to prove a fortunate turn of events. Among the US ships in harbour was the light cruiser *Augusta* together with the escort carrier *Chenango* which provided 500 showers and breakfasts, and handed out shoes and clothes to all in need of them before accommodating most of the survivors for a night's sleep in the latter's hangar. Generously refuelled, *Venomous* reached Gibraltar on the afternoon of the 14th. More fortunate still were the sixty-four men who abandoned *Hecla* after the final hit and swam over to the crippled

Marne, completing a journey that had claimed the lives of many who had decided to abandon ship earlier. After a nervous night they were safely transferred to HM corvette *Jonquil* which reached the scene at 1700 on the 12th and immediately turned for Gibraltar.

Some 281 men were lost with *Hecla*, over a third of her ship's company. Though four died in *Venomous* on the 12th and another in *Augusta* despite the best efforts of her medical staff, Capt. Arliss reported with some justification that 'the loss of life cannot be regarded as unduly heavy' in the circumstances. The name was revived in 1944 for a repair ship loaned from the US Navy.

U515 and Werner Henke

Built by Deutsche Werft at Hamburg and commissioned in February 1942, *U515* undertook six frontline patrols under Kptlt Werner Henke. A combination of rich hunting grounds and her commanding officer's unbridled aggression yielded twenty-six ships for a total in excess of 150,000 tons, including the RAF flying boat tender *Dumana* in December 1943 (**G68**). Her career ended in April 1944 when she was sighted south-east of the Azores by an Avenger from the escort carrier USS *Guadalcanal*. An eighteen-hour hunt ensued during which patrolling aircraft were joined by ships from *Guadalcanal*'s escort group, USSs *Flaherty*, *Pillsbury*, *Chatelain* and *Pope*. Attacks by *Chatelain* and *Pope* early on the afternoon of 9 April so damaged *U515* that her crew could not prevent her breaching the surface where she was immediately sunk by *Chatelain* and circling aircraft. Henke and forty-three of his fifty-nine men survived to be incarcerated at Fort Hunt, Virginia, but he was shot and killed during an escape attempt on 15 June 1944. This singular incident and the chain of events leading up to it are treated in detail in Dr Timothy Mulligan's biography of Werner Henke (see below).

Sources

Admiralty, Director of Anti-Submarine Warfare, *Analysis of U-Boat Attacks on HMS* Hecla *on 11–12 November 1942* (TNA, ADM 199/2013)
—, *Operation Torch: Reports, 1942* (TNA, ADM 199/869)
—, *War Diary, 1–15 November 1942* (TNA, ADM 199/2251), pp. 486, 499, 500, 501 and 508
Assorted recollections of the loss of HMS *Hecla* and rescue of her survivors (undated typescript material, Charlie Brierley collection)

Blair, *Hitler's U-Boat War*, II, pp. 107–15
Coleman, Edward, *Navy Days: Recollections of Navy Days by a Veteran of World War II* (Budleigh Salterton, Devon: Andrew Books, 1999)
Dönitz, *Memoirs*, pp. 276–82
McWilliams, H. H., 'The Loneliness of the Long-Distance Swimmer' in *Sea Breezes* 66, no. 553 (January 1992), pp. 11–19
Moore, Robert J., and Capt. John A. Rodgaard, *A Hard Fought Ship: The Story of HMS* Venomous (2nd edn, St Albans, Herts.: Holywell House Publishing, 2010; 1st edn, Loughborough, Leics.: privately, 1990)
Mulligan, Timothy P., *Lone Wolf: The Life and Death of U-Boat Ace Werner Henke* (Westport, Conn.: Praeger, 1993)
—, 'Forcing a U-Boat Ace to Surface: Source Materials in a Biography of Werner Henke' in *Prologue* 27, no. 3 (Fall 1995), pp. 249–57

74   HrMs *ISAAC SWEERS*

Ktz. W. Harmsen, KM

Sunk by *U431* (Type VIIC), Kptlt Wilhelm Dommes, 13 November 1942

Western Mediterranean, 60 nm NW of Algiers (Algeria)

Isaac Sweers enters the Grand Harbour, Valetta in December 1941. The depredations of Axis bombing are apparent on all sides. *IWM*

Campaign	Operation TORCH (Map 3)	*Displacement*	1,604 tons
Coordinates	37° 23' N, 02° 12' E	*Dimensions*	351' × 34.75' × 9.25'
Kriegsmarine code	Quadrat CH 8324	*Maximum speed*	36.5 knots
U-boat timekeeping differential	+1 hour	*Armament*	6 × 4" AA; 4 × 40 mm AA; 4 × 20 mm AA; 8 × 21" tt
Fatalities 138 *Survivors* 84+			

The Royal Netherlands Navy (Koninklijke Marine)

Although the Dutch navy's age of greatness had long since passed the Koninklijke Marine remained a first-class fighting force with a small but well-equipped fleet of ships all of which were built in home yards. The focus of inter-war naval planning was the preservation of the oil-rich Dutch East Indies against the Japanese, and the Netherlands was the one colonial power whose overseas fleets outnumbered those retained for the defence of the metropolis. As with other Allied navies the process of rearmament did not begin in earnest until the 1930s and the German attack of May 1940 caught the Koninklijke Marine in the early stages of a major expansion. In the event, some twenty-one units reached Britain including two cruisers, a destroyer (*Isaac Sweers*) and nine submarines, many of them incomplete, while the East Indies Squadron consisted of approximately thirty ships including four cruisers, seven destroyers and fifteen submarines. A number of the escapees entered Allied service but their effectiveness was often limited by non-standard equipment and a chronic lack of spares, while the East Indies Squadron was virtually wiped out in early 1942. Reassigned mostly to British and US ships, the men of the Koninklijke

Marine fought on to the end but a special place will always be reserved for the one unit of its own construction to have enjoyed a sustained battle career: the destroyer *Isaac Sweers*.

Career

Designed for operations in the Dutch East Indies and ordered under the 1938 programme, HrMs Torpedobootjager *Isaac Sweers* was laid down at the KM 'De Schelde' dockyard in Vlissingen (Flushing) on 26 November 1938, the second unit in the Gerard Callenburgh class of fleet destroyers. Launched on 16 March 1940, *Isaac Sweers* was fitting out at Flushing at the time of the German attack on the Netherlands on 10 May, the ship immediately setting out for England under tow from the tug *Zwarte Zee*. Making the Downs on the 11th, the pair reached Spithead the following day from where *Isaac Sweers* entered Thornycroft's yard at Woolston, Southampton. A year's work brought *Isaac Sweers* to completion with standard British armament in place of the advanced equipment and fire-control envisioned by her designers. She was the only member of her class to serve under the Dutch ensign, *Tjerk Hiddes* and *Philips van Almonde* having been scuttled and

Gerard Callenburgh being completed for the Kriegsmarine as *ZH1* in 1942. *Isaac Sweers* commissioned with a Dutch crew on 29 May 1941 and sailed from Southampton on 24 June. After working up in the Bristol Channel and at Scapa Flow she was assigned to the British 19th Destroyer Flotilla at Greenock. A spell escorting troop convoys into the Bay of Biscay was followed in September by action in Operation HALBERD, one of the major supply convoys to Malta. Reaching Gibraltar on 24 September, *Isaac Sweers* was allocated to Force A to escort the battleship *Nelson* into the Mediterranean where the main body of the convoy was joined on the 25th. Two days later the convoy came under heavy air attack, *Isaac Sweers* suffering a near miss which left two men wounded by shell splinters and *Nelson* taking a torpedo hit forward. On the 28th Force A reversed course for Gibraltar which was reached on 1 October.

After a further spell of convoy duty *Isaac Sweers* returned to the Mediterranean in November 1941 with Operation PERPETUAL, the dispatch of forty-four aircraft to Malta from the carriers *Ark Royal* and *Argus*. The aircraft were successfully flown off but *Ark Royal* was sunk by *U81* on the voyage back to Gibraltar (**39**), much to the chagrin of her Dutch escort. A series of anti-submarine patrols west of Gibraltar ended on 11 December when *Isaac Sweers* was ordered to Alexandria to reinforce the Mediterranean Fleet. Sailing as part of the four-strong 4th Destroyer Flotilla, on the night of 12–13 December this force intercepted the Italian light cruisers *Alberico da Barbiano* and *Alberto di Giussano* off Cape Bon, Tunisia and sank them both with torpedoes and gunfire. No sooner had the 4th DF reached Malta than it was heading east with the cruisers and destroyers of Force K to bring in the transport *Breconshire* which had sailed from Alexandria on the 15th. Early on the 17th Force K fell in with the *Breconshire* and her own escort, the 15th Cruiser Squadron under Rear-Admiral Philip Vian, and began the run in to Malta. That evening, after several hours' aerial attack during which *Isaac Sweers* brought down an aircraft, an Italian battle squadron was sighted on the northern horizon. Ordering *Breconshire* to alter course to the south with two destroyers, Vian turned to engage the Italians with the rest of his force, *Isaac Sweers* included. Faced by a mass torpedo attack, the Italians turned away and the convoy reached Malta on the night of 18–19 December without further incident. So ended the First Battle of Sirte.

The last days of 1941 found *Isaac Sweers* at Alexandria under a new commander, the redoubtable Kapitein Luitenant ter Zee Willem Harmsen. She was soon in action again, joining the escort for the Malta-bound convoy MW8B on 16 January 1942. The following day HMS *Gurkha* (Senior Officer) was torpedoed by *U133* and set ablaze with oil from ruptured fuel tanks (**46**). *Isaac Sweers* stood by, towing her clear of a patch of burning oil and eventually rescuing all but nine of her ship's company. Within days *Isaac Sweers* was ordered to the Far East where Allied resistance was collapsing before the Japanese onslaught and the Dutch colonial empire lay under mortal threat. Reaching Colombo on 8 February, *Isaac Sweers* went into drydock for repairs before sailing for the Dutch East Indies on the 28th. However,

the annihilation of Allied naval power in the Java Sea and Sunda Strait battles between 27 February and 1 March meant that no good purpose would be served by her arrival and on 15 March she was attached to the British Eastern Fleet. *Isaac Sweers* joined the Eastern Fleet's foray into the Indian Ocean in April and its eventual withdrawal to the east coast of Africa in May before returning to Britain for a refit at Thornycroft's, the ship working up at Scapa Flow before turning south once again in October 1942. Having escorted the carrier *Furious* to Gibraltar, *Isaac Sweers* steered for the Azores with the intention of joining the escort of KMF1, one of the troop convoys bound for North Africa as part of Operation TORCH, but the rendezvous on 2 November was missed due to an error deciphering a signal and the ship allocated instead to escort Force H in the Mediterranean. On the 11th she and HM destroyer *Porcupine* were detached to rescue survivors of the troopship *Nieuw-Zeeland* sunk by *U380* off Morocco that day. Some 241 survivors were safely landed at Gibraltar but it was while sailing to rejoin Force H that *Isaac Sweers* met her end off Algiers.

HrMs Torpedobootjager *Isaac Sweers* stands with the Free French minelaying submarine *Rubis* and the Greek destroyer *Vasilissa Olga* as the most distinguished unit of the Allied navies in exile to see action in the Second World War. Her fighting career stands comparison with that of any destroyer of the period.

Background of the attack

For background on Operation TORCH, see HMSs *Martin* and *Hecla* (**72** and **73**).

No sooner had *U431* sunk the destroyer *Martin* on 10 November 1942 than the opportunity arose for Kptlt Wilhelm Dommes to claim a second warship in her patrol area off Algeria. In the early hours of 13 November she sighted Force R which had left Gibraltar the previous day and was heading east to refuel Force H, itself six days out of Gibraltar. Force R originally comprised the tankers *Dingledale* and *Brown Ranger* escorted by HM corvette *Coreopsis* and the trawlers *Imperialist*, *St Nectan*, *Loch Oskaig* and *Arctic Ranger*. Late on the 12th the escort was augmented by the destroyers *Porcupine* and *Isaac Sweers* which had been detached from Force H to rescue survivors from the troopship *Nieuw-Zeeland* and were now heading east having landed them at Gibraltar. Their intention was to refuel at sea from Force R and rejoin Force H when these met off Algeria on the morning of the 13th. Having refuelled from *Brown Ranger* just before midnight on the 12th *Isaac Sweers* took station approximately 1,000 yards on the latter's starboard beam. Shortly after 0500 this group sighted three members of Force H's outer screen, the anti-aircraft cruiser HMS *Scylla* and the escort destroyers *Farndale* and *Puckeridge*. However, Force R was still under observation by *U431* and Dommes's attack of 0515 Allied time (0615 log time) targeted both *Brown Ranger* and the overlapping *Isaac Sweers* which was by then off the tanker's starboard bow. *Isaac Sweers* was the only victim of Dommes's salvo of four torpedoes but the subsequent inferno convinced him and many in Force R that it was a tanker which had exploded.

War Diary of *U431*, patrol of 7–22 November 1942: PG 30485, NHB, reel 1,107, pp. 613–4

Date, time	Details of position, wind, weather, sea, light, visibility, moonlight, etc.	Incidents
13.xi	Western Mediterranean	
0600	Visibility improving, rain ceasing, clearing gradually	
0605	Qu. CH 8324	Bow waves in sight at bearing 0° true. Then a shadow followed by several more. A large convoy with tankers and steamers. I approach.
		Cannot get a proper idea of group's formation. It would appear that we are positioned on the convoy's starboard bow and that it is proceeding in a south-easterly direction.
0612		Convoy is a group of steamers proceeding in irregular line abreast; out on the right flank there is a Tribal-class destroyer whose course brings her ever closer to us.[1] I must try to pick off both this escort and one or more of the steamers behind.
0615	Qu. CH 8324 Pronounced sea phosphorescence	A spread of four fired just as the fo'c's'le of the destroyer is overlapping the stern of a large tanker proceeding beyond.[2] The streaks of the torpedo tracks can be seen all the way to the target. Inclination 70°, enemy speed 12 knots, range 3,000 m.[3] Width of spread a uniform 10 m.[4]
		After 70[5] sec. (= 900 m) two hits on the target 40 m from the bow and 20 m from the stern. Destroyer is blown to smithereens. The entire convoy starts screeching with sirens and steam whistles.
		I turn hard aport and withdraw. About two minutes later a hit on the large tanker. An oil fire lights up the entire area.[6] Shortly after this a fourth torpedo detonation is heard both on the bridge and below. Just at this moment a destroyer closes at high speed from the north-west; from her perspective we were silhouetted directly against the blaze.[7]
0620		Alarm! We dive to 160 m and withdraw to the south-west, later to the west. No fix obtained on us. Between 0635 and 0740, 21 depth charges. Not well aimed. We are not damaged but as a result of the alarm dive the forward hydroplane gets jammed and refuses to go above the 10° diving-angle position. After much massaging we eventually regain full manoeuvrability.
0650	Qu. CH 8316, upper right edge	
0850		We go to periscope depth. Periscope is misting up worse than ever making detailed observation quite impossible, this despite employing the drying apparatus for three hours last night, which in turn involved an extra degree of complication every time an alarm dive was required. We have now spent ten hours drying out the periscope within the space of a few days. Fruitlessly.
0859		We surface to transmit W/T report.
0929[8]		Outgoing W/T transmission 0615/13/5: *From Dommes: 0615 Qu. CH 8324 eastbound convoy. A 'Tribal'*

1   Force R's formation was relatively flat as Dommes describes it, though the 'Tribal-class destroyer' was in fact HrMs *Isaac Sweers*, of comparable size and silhouette. He appears not to have seen the other two escorts on this starboard side of the convoy, HM trawlers *St Nectan* and *Loch Oskaig*. A diagram of the group at this time, drawn by Lt Cdr A. N. Davies RNVR of *Coreopsis*, places *Isaac Sweers* 1,000 yards off *Brown Ranger*'s starboard bow, with *St Nectan* a similar distance on *Isaac Sweers*'s starboard beam and *Loch Oskaig* 2,000 yards on *St Nectan*'s starboard quarter. However, the Commander-in-Chief Mediterranean Fleet, Vice-Admiral Algernon Willis, observed that 'with the lapse of time [not much] heed should be paid to the diagram of ships' relative positions, which is at variance with other reports made soon after the occurrence'. Indeed, *Loch Oskaig*, allegedly 3,000 yards on *Isaac Sweers*'s starboard quarter, reported that 'at the time of being struck *Isaac Sweers* was overtaking *Loch Oskaig* on the starboard beam distance 500 yards approx.'

2   The torpedoes were fired by *U431*'s First Watch Officer (I.WO), Ltz.S. Friedrich Weidner.

3   Dommes's next entry confirms that *Isaac Sweers* was much closer, and indeed the estimated range in the torpedo report is given as 1,000 metres; the figure of 3,000 metres was presumably that calculated for the tanker (almost certainly *Brown Ranger*). Although Force R was proceeding at 8 knots, Dommes's observation is confirmed by survivor reports which record *Isaac Sweers* zigzagging at 12 knots.

4   The German original has *Steuerbreite* ('steering width') which must be reckoned a mistranscription of *Streubreite* (width of spread). That apart, Dommes's observation of a 10-metre spread does not tally with his subsequent observation that there appeared to be 40 metres between the two hits on *Isaac Sweers*, so this may be his recollection of the relative positioning of the torpedo tracks at some stage during their run.

5   Manuscript addition in pencil. It should be noted, however, that 900 metres more nearly equates to a running time of 60 seconds than 70.

6   Despite Dommes's assertion, *Isaac Sweers* was the only vessel hit in this salvo though his conclusion that a tanker had been struck was shared by many observers on the Allied side.

7   Either *Farndale* or *Puckeridge*, both of which immediately carried out a sweep for the offending U-boat on this side of the convoy.

8   Entered out of chronological sequence, presumably to convey the fact that (as implied in Dommes's entry of 0919) they had attempted to send this signal earlier.

Date, time	Details of position, wind, weather, sea, light, visibility, moonlight, etc.	Incidents
		sunk, tanker left burning, further detonations heard. Two eels remaining, dockyard repairs needed soon.[9]
0919	Poor visibility, 1,000–2,000 m	Before we can transmit the report an escort appears at bearing 0° true, westerly course, low speed. Range 3,000–4,000 m.
0921		Alarm!

9 'Eels' (German = *Aale*) was U-boat slang for torpedoes.

The sinking

Isaac Sweers suffered two hits on her starboard side, the first abreast the bridge and the second close to the after funnel a few seconds later. The first struck a full tank of fuel oil while the second was reckoned to have ignited the after oil tank, with the result that 'within two minutes *Isaac Sweers* was enveloped in flames from her bridge aft' – a state of affairs which no doubt explains Dommes's claim to have hit a tanker. Listing rapidly to starboard, *Isaac Sweers* settled by the stern, her broken foremast visible through a curtain of flame to those gathered on the fo'c's'le. This disaster unfolded not only in the eyes but also in the ears of the crew who were deafened by the 'terrible wail' of the ship's steam siren as she began to sink. *Isaac Sweers* seems to have had her back broken but the bow section remained buoyant, 'showing perpendicularly above the surface' for long enough after the last man had been rescued for the ranking officer, Cdr D. P. Trentham in *Farndale*, to order *Puckeridge* to sink her by gunfire. This was done at 0830, more than two hours after *Isaac Sweers* was hit.

Dommes's achievement in sinking two valuable destroyers in the space of three days was rewarded with the Knight's Cross on 2 December, two weeks after *U431* docked at Pola in the Adriatic. However, this success could not mask the meagre returns achieved by the substantial force deployed against Operation TORCH in the Mediterranean which achieved only eight sinkings (including *Martin* and *Isaac Sweers*) for the loss of no fewer than five U-boats within a week, including von Tiesenhausen's *U331* (see **41**). From the Dutch perspective the issue of whether *Isaac Sweers* had been sunk by a German or Italian submarine was settled only in 1949 following a request from the Koninklijke Marine's historical section for an investigation into German naval records in possession of the British Admiralty.

Fate of the crew

U431's first torpedo accounted for much of the ship's engineering staff, while the second detonated near the wardroom and officers' cabins killing thirteen of the latter immediately. The fact that both torpedoes had either struck or ignited two recently replenished oil tanks condemned more than half the ship's company to the kind of death more often reserved for the crew of a stricken tanker. Not only was *Isaac Sweers* engulfed in flame but leaking fuel spread around the ship causing a lake of fire which few of those stranded aft could hope to survive. *Loch Oskaig* and *St Nectan* did their best to pick up as many as possible from the edge of the fire before turning to those either well away from the blaze or else safely on Carley floats. A number of men did not abandon the wreck and clung to the bow section, but *Loch Oskaig*'s attempt to approach these was abandoned due to exploding ammunition and depth charges. Many of those who took to the water

Dommes (bareheaded) seen with the bridge watch on one of *U431*'s Mediterranean patrols in 1942. His cap is resting on the UZO target bearing indicator whose binoculars are not fitted. *DUBMA*

were nonetheless rescued swimming to windward in a desperate attempt to get clear of the flames and exploding depth charges. An impressive number of men survived to be rescued given the circumstances of the sinking, with fifty-two recorded as having been picked up by *Loch Oskaig* and thirty-two by *St Nectan* – something over a third of her ship's company. The majority, including thirteen severe burn cases, were transferred to *Puckeridge* and *Farndale* which had better facilities to treat them. Among them was Kapitein ter zee Willem Harmsen whose burns to chest, back, arms and face had to be scraped and cleaned in *Farndale*. Despite being in considerable pain his first enquiry was for the welfare of his men. His second was for a beer, but when this was refused by the surgeon a row ensued which threatened the patient's wellbeing and obliged Cdr Trentham to intervene in Harmsen's favour. *Farndale*'s official report observed of this beer that 'unless it came quickly there was little chance of recovery'. A second bottle duly followed and Harmsen's recovery was assured.

Isaac Sweers's contribution to the war in the Mediterranean had been a handsome one and the resolution of her men was demonstrated when the unwounded insisted on taking their turn keeping watch on the voyage to Gibraltar. Trentham's recollection of the spirit of those in *Farndale* bears repeating: 'Their only wish was to get another ship and have a crack at the Hun. The Dutch cheered us. The last memory of this resolute and ready band is one of beaming faces, cheers, wavings and the V sign. Most impressive!'

U431 and Wilhelm Dommes

For details of *U431*'s and Dommes's earlier career, see HMS *Martin* (72).

After the success of this his tenth patrol in *U431*, Kptlt Dommes was replaced by Oblt.z.S. Dietrich Schöneboom whose five patrols in 1943 were emblematic of U-boat fortunes in the Mediterranean at large, the sinking of a single merchantman and four minor sailing vessels being followed by unsuccessful attacks on several Royal Navy warships and a large number of claims uncorroborated in Allied records. On 21 October 1943 *U431* was caught on the surface and destroyed by an RAF Wellington within a hundred miles of the position in which she had sunk *Isaac Sweers*. There were no survivors. Despite his scant success Schöneboom was a posthumous recipient of the Knight's Cross.

Dommes was subsequently appointed in command of the Type-IXD-2 *U178* which he took on a single six-month patrol from Bordeaux to Penang in Japanese-occupied Malaya. He spent the rest of the war as a submarine base commander both there and at Singapore from where he assumed command of U-boat operations in South-East Asia. Like many Germans in the Far East at the end of the war, Dommes was destined for a long period in captivity, being released only in October 1947. He died in January 1990.

Sources

Admiralty, *H.M. Ships, Miscellaneous Craft and Allied Ships Damaged and Lost: Reports, 1939-1943* (TNA, ADM 199/837)

—, Admiralty War Diary, 1–15 November 1942 (TNA, ADM 199/2251), pp. 541, 547 and 605–6

Assorted post-war correspondence concerning the fate of HrMs *Isaac Sweers* (NHB, S.2133)

Tenholt, Paul, *Chronik des deutschen Unterseebootes* U-431 *und seiner 16 Feindfahrten* (typescript, DUBMA, *U431* file)

Anon., *Queen Wilhelmina's Navy* (London: HMSO, 1944)

Bezemer, K. W. L., *Zij vochten op de zeven zeeën: Verrichtingen en avonturen der Koninklijke Marine in de Tweede Wereldoorlog* (Utrecht: W. De Haan, 1954)

Bosscher, Ph.M., *De Koninklijke Marine in de Tweede Wereldoorlog* (3 vols, Franeker: T. Wever, 1984–90)

Divine, A.D., *Navies in Exile* (London: John Murray, 1944)

Mark, Chris, *Schepen van de Koninklijke Marine in W.O.II* (Alkmaar: Uitgeverij de Alk BV, 1997)

Olivier, Marinus, *Olie en vuur op de golven: Het enervend verhaal van een beroeps-marineman voor, tijdens en na Tweede Wereldoorlog 1938–1970* (Kapelle: Herselman, 1996)

Schneider, Werner, *12 Feindfahrten. Als Funker auf* U-431, U-410 *und* U-371 *im Atlantik und im Mittelmeer. Ausbildung, Einsatz, Gefangenschaft, 1940–1946* (Weinheim: Germania Verlag, 2006)

Biography of Ktz. Willem Harmsen:
http://www.netherlandsnavy.nl/Men_harmsen.htm

75   HMS *AVENGER* (ex MS *RÍO HUDSON*)

Cdr A. P. Colthurst, RN†
Sunk by *U155* (Type IXC), Kptlt Adolf Piening, 15 November 1942
North Atlantic, 125 nm W of Gibraltar

Avenger in July 1942, possibly in the Clyde, with two of her Swordfish torpedo bombers on deck.
Only a handful of men escaped the holocaust which followed Piening's torpedo hit on the port side. *BfZ*

Campaign	Operation TORCH (Map 1)	*Displacement*	12,150 tons
Coordinates	36° 15' N, 07° 54' W	*Dimensions*	492' × 69.5' × 21'
Kriegsmarine code	Quadrat CG 8665	*Maximum speed*	17 knots
U-boat timekeeping differential	+1 hour	*Armament*	1 × 5"; 2 × 3" AA; 11 × 20 mm AA
Fatalities	516 *Survivors* 12	*Air wing*	15 aircraft (12 Sea Hurricanes and 3 Swordfish) served by one lift and one catapult

Career

For the development of the escort-carrier type, see HMS *Audacity* (**43**).

HMS *Avenger* belonged to the generation of escort carriers which followed the progenitor of the type, the shortlived *Audacity*. Like *Audacity*, *Avenger* and her three sisters (along with their earlier near-sister *Archer*, which gave her name to the class) were the product of mercantile conversions, but unlike *Audacity* their construction and repurposing was carried out entirely in the United States. HMS *Avenger* originated as the cargo liner *Río Hudson* of the Mooremack South American Line, being laid down at Sun Shipbuilding of Chester, Pennsylvania on 28 November 1939. Launched almost a year to the day later, the *Río Hudson* was requisitioned by the US Navy only to be purchased by the British government on 31 July 1941 with a view to conversion to an escort carrier. Renamed *Avenger*, she was completed by the Bethlehem Steel Corporation's shipyard at Staten Island, New York on 1 March 1942 and commissioned into the Royal Navy the following day. Following sea trials, during which her Doxford diesel engines broke down, *Avenger* sailed from New York on 30 March with troop convoy AT15 bound for the Clyde. Here she was taken in hand for modifications, including lengthening the flight deck by forty-two feet so that Swordfish could take off fully armed and fuelled.

Allocated to the Home Fleet and equipped with three Swordfish torpedo bombers of 825 (later 833) Squadron and twelve Sea Hurricanes from 883 and 802 Squadrons, *Avenger's* brief operational career began on 2 September when she sailed from Loch Ewe to escort convoy PQ18 to north Russia. It was to be a grim baptism of fire. By the time she reached Scapa Flow on 3 October having escorted the overlapping convoy QP14, *Avenger's* Swordfish had flown thirty-two sorties, shot down five German aircraft (for the loss of six of her own) and attacked six of the sixteen U-boats sighted on passage. Among these was *U589* which had made an unsuccessful attack on her on the 13th. It was to prove a costly miss for *U589* was spotted by one of *Avenger's* Swordfish the following day and her position marked by a smoke float. Though the Swordfish was driven off by a Junkers Ju88 bomber, *U589* had been delayed sufficiently for HM destroyer *Onslow* to come up and despatch her with depth charges. *Avenger's* Sea Hurricanes, meanwhile, made fifty-nine sorties during which twenty-six German aircraft were destroyed or damaged, though she was herself the target of air attack and near-missed by two bombs.

Having endured two Russian convoys the news that *Avenger* was headed south was no doubt received with some jubilation by her ship's company. On 22 October she sailed from the Clyde with her sister *Biter* and the fleet carrier *Victorious* to join the slow assault convoy KMS1, its destination the landings at Algiers that were to be part of Operation TORCH. Assigned to the Eastern Naval Task Force, on 7 November *Avenger* was detached to join the elderly converted carrier *Argus* to provide fighter cover for the landings planned at Algiers for the following day. In the event *Avenger* was troubled less by Vichy aircraft than chronic problems with her Doxford engines, and on the 10th she put in at Algiers for repairs after her best speed had been reduced to fourteen knots. By 12 November she was heading west to Gibraltar and what would prove her final assignment: convoy MKF1Y.

Background of the attack

For background on Operation TORCH, see HMSs *Martin* and *Hecla* (**72** and **73**).

Just as the Allies had deployed considerable resources to protect the KMF convoys heading from Britain to North Africa as part of Operation TORCH, so too were the returning vessels (under the code MKF) stoutly defended. The Clyde-bound convoy MKF1Y, which left Gibraltar on 14 November, consisted of half a dozen troop transports and merchantmen protected not only by a five-strong escort (HM destroyers *Wrestler* and *Amazon*, the escort destroyer *Glaisdale*, and the frigates *Exe* and *Swale*) but also by the carriers *Argus* and *Avenger*. B.d.U., for its part, was spoiling for action having failed to make any great impact on the main Allied invasion fleet and MKF1Y's departure on the evening of the 14th was reported to all U-boats west of Gibraltar. Within ten hours of putting to sea the convoy had been sighted by Kptlt Adolf Piening's *U155*. At around 0300 Allied time (0400 German time) an RDF contact was obtained on an unknown U-boat by *Wrestler* which opened fire before launching a depth-charge attack while the convoy made an emergency course alteration to starboard. Though *Wrestler* had been drawn away and *U155* left free to attack, this development was nonetheless a nuisance for Piening as it increased the range from which he had to fire. However, the densely packed convoy still represented a most inviting target and within three minutes *U155* had emptied all her six tubes, four torpedoes from the bow followed by two from the stern. Too late did *Avenger's* Asdic office send warning of an approaching torpedo.

War Diary of *U155*, **patrol of 7 November–30 December 1942: PG 30142, NHB, reel 1,085, pp. 48–9**

Date, time	Details of position, wind, weather, sea, light, visibility, moonlight, etc.	Incidents
15.xi		
0000	Qu. CG 9444	
0255	Qu. CG 8666, dark night, wind SW 4, sea 3, occasional showers	Two shadows (destroyers) in sight at bearing 80° true. Speed 15–20 knots, strong zigzags, general course west, range 3,000 m.
0345	Qu. CG 8665	Convoy in sight at bearing 75° true, range 6,000 m, inclination 10°, eight large shadows, broad formation (two lines abreast), speed 15 knots. On my preferred attack side there are two escort vessels beam on to me, 5,000 m ahead of convoy.[1]

---

1   Presumably HM frigate *Exe*, 5,000 yards ahead of the convoy, and HM destroyer *Wrestler*, 5,000 yards off its port bow.

0405		Forward escort is burning searchlight in all directions, firing tracer to outer side and dropping depth charges.[2] I am now between the escorts and the convoy. Shortly after the escort's gunfire the convoy ships alter course 40° to starboard which means my range at time of firing becomes 2,500 m instead of under 1,000 m.
0414		A spread of four torpedoes fired at the mid-point of two overlapping troop transports followed shortly after by a further spread of two. Inclination between 60° and 90°, range 1,500 m (as originally entered[3]), angle of dispersion 5°, enemy speed 13 knots, depth 4 m. Shortly after firing the second spread the second escort vessel closes burning her searchlight.[4] Her range is now 1,500 m and there's no way of getting past her on the surface.
0418		Alarm dive. We go to 130 m. Shortly after we dive, after a run of 3 min. 20 sec., two torpedo detonations five seconds apart (from the spread of four), and after running time of 2 min. 40 sec. a further torpedo detonation (from the spread of two).[5] No question that all three were torpedo detonations as in each case pistol strike was heard just before explosion.
0440		Some twelve depth charges dropped far away, might have been intended for another boat. In my view this was the convoy reported in W/T transmission: *To all boats in Caesar Gustav, at 1800 14.11, convoy sailed for Atlantic consisting of aircraft carrier, merchantman, two auxiliary cruisers, two destroyers, two corvettes and five large transports.*[6] We couldn't observe to what extent the transports (large passenger liners) were damaged or sunk (depth setting 4 m) due to counter-attack, so I am relying on *B-Dienst*.[7] According to subsequent reckoning convoy must have been proceeding at around 15 knots.[8] I estimate torpedoed tonnage to have been in the region of *35,000–40,000 GRT.*[9]
0615		We surface.
0628		Alarm dive following readings on the 122-cm wave (presumably a destroyer).
0800	Qu. CG 8666	Outgoing W/T transmission via dipole antenna: *0400 Mar. Qu. Caesar Gustav 8665 three torpedo hits on three large transports. Forced to submerge after firing, depth charges. Convoy heading west at 15 knots, broad formation, 9 + 8, 190 cbm.*[10] *Piening.*
	Convoy MKF1(Y), *'Almaak' [sic] damaged,* *P&O liner 'Ettrick' (11,000* *tons) sunk, auxiliary* *aircraft carrier 'Avenger'* *sunk. Pfeiffer 30/11/56.*[11]	
0915		Twin-engined aircraft in periscope at bearing 180° true, altitude 500 m, northwesterly course.

---

2   This attack corresponds with that made by *Wrestler* following an RDF contact. While Piening looked on from afar *Wrestler* reported sighting a U-boat diving just 100 yards off and followed it with a depth-charge attack.

3   In other words, Piening originally entered 1,500 metres and then set the torpedo data computer to *Lage laufend*, or automatic inclination update mode; see Introduction, p. xxvi. As the torpedo running times given at 0418 make clear, the actual range upon firing was much greater.

4   HM frigate *Exe*.

5   The first salvo consisted of the four bow tube torpedoes at 0414, the second of the two stern tube torpedoes at 0417. What Piening had heard were detonations against the naval transport USS *Almaack*, the escort carrier *Avenger* and the transport *Ettrick* respectively. The ranges equate to 3,000 metres and 2,400 metres respectively.

6   'Caesar' and 'Gustav' represent the letters 'C' and 'G' in the German phonetic alphabet, 'CG' being the Kriegsmarine's quadrant code for the waters west of Spain and Portugal and either side of the Straits of Gibraltar. The signal was directed only at boats on the Atlantic side.

7   *B-Dienst*, the Kriegsmarine's radio monitoring and intelligence service, was essential in allowing B.d.U. to establish which ships had actually been sunk by the *U-Boot-Waffe*. Here Piening was hoping it would confirm his tonnage claims. In the case of *Avenger* he would be frustrated as her loss to a U-boat did not become known to the Germans until after the war.

8   Piening's estimate is close to the mark as the convoy was making 13½ knots at the time.

9   Manuscript addition in pencil, with the range shown replacing an original typed figure of 40,000 GRT which has been crossed out. Piening's estimate is not far from the actual figure, which Allied sources record as 32,000 tons of shipping sunk or damaged; see below.

10   The '9 + 8' refers to a probable mix of G7e and G7a torpedoes remaining, '190 cbm' to the available diesel fuel in cubic metres.

11   Manuscript addition in pencil by the civilian archivist Walther Pfeiffer who was brought to Britain to work on the logs post-war. The liner *Ettrick* had belonged to Barclay, Curle & Co. of Glasgow, not P&O, before being requisitioned by the Admiralty as a troop transport.

The sinking

Forced to dive by *Wrestler*, Piening had no visual evidence of the results of his two salvoes. Though his claim to have struck at least 35,000 tons of shipping might appear typical U-boat commander's optimism, on this occasion the reality was close to the truth with the British troop transport *Ettrick* (11,279 GRT; **G42**) and the carrier *Avenger* (12,150 tons) lost to a torpedo each and the naval transport USS *Almaack* (8,600 tons) damaged. But it was *Avenger* that captured the attention of the convoy. Shortly after the initial detonation officers in the landing ship *Ulster Monarch*, then stationed on *Avenger*'s port quarter, recorded 'a vivid red flash on the starboard side of *Avenger* stretching the whole length of the ship and lasting for about two seconds. This flash made a perfect silhouette of the ship and was followed by a pall of black smoke.' By the time *Ulster Monarch* passed the scene of the disaster three minutes later *Avenger* had disappeared. Others noted a more substantial explosion which demolished the central section of the ship: witnesses in the Norwegian-manned escort destroyer *Glaisdale* recorded that *Avenger* simply 'disintegrated'.

The precise cause of the explosion that broke *Avenger* in two was the subject of an 'informal enquiry' conducted by J. L. Bartlett, Assistant Director of Naval Construction. Testimony from the survivors included a number of conflicting statements and threw little light on the issue. Most of the survivors recalled a blast of air wafting aft accompanied by the smell of burning oil, though two were convinced that this followed rather than preceded the explosion. The enquiry concluded that *Avenger* had been struck on her port side and that splinters from the torpedo had detonated bombs and depth charges in the bomb room directly inboard. Bartlett set out a number of reasons why the alternative explanation of a petrol explosion was not viable, not least that four of the survivors were above the aviation petrol stowage area at the time. Aware of the circulation of wild rumours and the fact that 'the loss of *Avenger* has caused a certain uneasiness amongst the officers and men of escort carriers', in January 1943 the Admiralty took the unusual step of ordering the findings of this enquiry to be communicated to the fleet at large. A tangible consequence of the *Avenger* disaster was the installation of longitudinal bulkheads in the four surviving units of the class to ensure that charges were stowed not less than ten feet from the ship's side, a development that kept them out of service until the spring and required design alterations to vessels under construction. However, Bartlett's hypothesis proved unconvincing to those onlookers who could not equate the relatively limited size of the blast which sank the ship with the detonation of a fully stowed bomb room, and the destruction of *Avenger*'s sister HMS *Dasher* while at anchor in the Clyde on 27 March 1943 prompted both a wider investigation into petrol stowage and handling procedures in the Royal Navy's escort carriers and a reappraisal of the earlier disaster. The enquiry into the *Dasher* catastrophe, which claimed 379 lives, attributed her loss to petrol ignition thanks to an unguarded cigarette but pointed the finger at poor stowage and distribution in the US design. With some justification the US Navy responded by citing lax handling procedures by the British. Both were right, and petrol stowage was capped at 36,000 gallons in the RN, a reduction of nearly sixty per cent in the survivors of the Archer class and over fifty per cent in the rest. The USN followed suit, though to a less stringent degree.

Piening's frustration at having to dive before seeing the fruit of his

Piening seen before the award of the Knight's Cross in August 1942. *DUBMA*

attacks was compounded by the fact that the loss of *Avenger* to a U-boat seems never to have been ascertained by the Germans despite details of the sinking being disclosed by the Admiralty. In a letter written in 1964 to H. M. Irwin RNVR, a lieutenant in *Ulster Monarch* at the time of the sinking, Piening observed that 'nobody on the German side knew that your aircraft carrier *Avenger* was sunk by a submarine. I did not get this information until after the war in the year of 1948 when a special group was comparing the war diaries of your Admiralty with my war diary.'

Fate of the crew

Avenger came to a sudden and violent end. All the survivors but one were stationed in the after section of the ship and all but two escaped by diving over the stern as it began to rear up. The exception in the former case was AB C. J. Brackie who was in the starboard gunnery control position beside the flight deck, immediately abreast the torpedo hit to port. Engulfed by the flash of the secondary explosion, Brackie found himself pitched into the sea, recalling that the part of the structure he had vacated 'appeared to break away from the ship'. But most enjoyed no such fortune, the freighter *Macharda* recording that 'Men were seen jumping through the flames into the sea and others sliding down the flight deck into the flames'. Once in the water most of the survivors recalled seeing *Avenger*'s stern lit up by rockets and smoke floats from other vessels before she subsided for good. Unable to stop, *Ulster Monarch* passed the scene of the disaster to find nothing but the glow of oil on the surface and twinkling lights from the lifejackets of survivors. It seems that quite a number of men were able to get clear of the wreck but not until a thunderstorm ushered in the dawn could HNorMS *Glaisdale* go about the business of rescue, the last survivor being picked up approximately three hours after the sinking. That these numbered but a dozen men from a ship's company of 528 places HMS *Avenger* among the heavier losses suffered by the Royal Navy in the war at sea.

Among the casualties was Leading Telegraphist Alan O. Long, winner of the Distinguished Service Medal for his part in the recovery of the Enigma machine and related cipher material from *U110* after she had been forced to the surface by HM destroyers *Bulldog* (his ship) and *Broadway* and HM corvette *Aubretia* on 9 May 1941.

U155 and Adolf Piening

Built by AG Weser at Bremen and commissioned in August 1941, *U155* shared some of the spectacular success typical of the Type-IX U-boats sent to the western Atlantic and the Caribbean in early 1942. Commanded by Kptlt (Korvkpt. from April 1943) Adolf Piening, between February 1942 and December 1943 *U155* sank twenty-six ships for a total of some 140,000 tons during which the former not only won the Knight's Cross but also fame as the pioneer of the 'Piening Route', whereby outgoing U-boats hugged the coasts of France and Spain to avoid the depredations of radar-equipped Allied aircraft over the Bay of Biscay. *U155* enjoyed no success after Piening's departure but survived the war to be scuttled as part of Operation DEADLIGHT in December 1945. In March 1944 Korvkpt. Piening assumed command of the 7th *U-Flottille*, which position he held until war's end. Released from captivity in 1947, Piening joined the Bundesmarine in 1956, retiring a Kapitän zur See after thirteen years' service. He died in May 1984.

Sources

Admiralty, *Loss of HMS* Avenger *by Torpedo: Report of Enquiry* (TNA, ADM 1/12605)

—, *Enemy Submarine Attacks on H.M. and Allied Warships: Reports, 1941-1943* (TNA, ADM 199/163)

—, *Analysis of U-Boat Attacks on Convoy M.K.F.1.(Y) on 15 November 1942* (TNA, ADM 199/2013)

Piening, Kapt.z.S. A. C., correspondence with Lt H.M. Irwin, November–December 1964 (DUBMA, *U155* file)

Brown, David K., Nelson *to* Vanguard: *Warship Design and Development, 1923–1945* (London: Chatham Publishing, 2000)

Hobbs, Cdr David, *Royal Navy Escort Carriers* (Liskeard, Corn.: Maritime Books, 2003)

Jones, Geoffrey, *U Boat Aces and Their Fates* (London: William Kimber, 1988)

Poolman, Kenneth, *Allied Escort Carriers of World War II* (London: Blandford, 1998)

Career history of HMS *Avenger*:
   http://www.naval-history.net/xGM-Chrono-05CVE-Avenger.htm

Fleet Air Arm Archive webpage devoted to HMS *Avenger*:
   http://www.fleetairarmarchive.net/Ships/Avenger.html

Webpage devoted to Sub-Lt (E) John Sidney Brew (fatality):
   http://brew.clients.ch/Avenger.htm

---

76   HNorMS *MONTBRETIA*
Kapt.Lt H. Søiland, KNM†
Sunk by *U262* (Type VIIC), Oblt.z.S. Heinz Franke, 18 November 1942
North Atlantic, 415 nm SE of Uummannarsuaq, Greenland

Montbretia at sea in 1942, the probable victim of two torpedo hits from *U262* which claimed nearly two-thirds of her crew. *IWM*

Theatre North Atlantic (Map 1)	*Displacement* 940 tons
Coordinates 53° 37' N, 38° 15' W	*Dimensions* 205.25' × 33' × approx. 11.25'
Kriegsmarine code Quadrat AK 4877	*Maximum speed* 16 knots
U-boat timekeeping differential +3 hours	*Armament* 1 × 4"; 4 × .303" AA
Fatalities 47 *Survivors* 27	

Career

For background on the Royal Norwegian Navy, see HNorMS *Bath* (**30**). For design notes on the Flower-class corvettes, see HMS *Picotee* (**29**).

The Flower-class corvette *Montbretia* was laid down at Fleming & Ferguson's yard at Paisley on the Clyde in November 1940, launched in May 1941 and completed that September as one of five corvettes commissioned into the Royal Norwegian Navy, then serving under operational command of the Admiralty in London. After working up at HMS *Western Isles*, the anti-submarine training establishment at Tobermory, HNorMS *Montbretia* was assigned to the 7th Escort Group of Western Approaches Command at Liverpool, joining her first convoy on 23 October. Relentless duty in the Atlantic continued until 20 January 1942 when she ran aground in Strangford Lough on the coast of Northern Ireland, an accident that kept her in dock at Belfast until 15 May. Allocated to the 6th EG at Londonderry, no sooner had she returned to Tobermory to work up than she grounded again, this time needing ten days at Liverpool to make good the damage. Rejoining her group, *Montbretia* began a second period of duty in the North Atlantic which saw the 6th EG evolve into a fully trained unit, winning its spurs in the ferocious battle for convoy SC104 on 12–16 October 1942. During this engagement SC104 suffered the loss of seven merchantmen at a cost to the Kriegsmarine of three U-boats, *Montbretia* almost adding a fourth on the night of the 14th when *U615* was driven off at close range with her 4-inch gun. Nonetheless, it was a rather reduced 6th EG that joined ON144 from Londonderry around 7 November; by the time it reached St John's two weeks later it had been depleted still further.

Background of the attack

The concerted blockade of the Straits of Gibraltar as the Kriegsmarine attempted to counter the Allied landings in North Africa in early November 1942 left Dönitz with few U-boats to attack the Atlantic convoys. Not until the middle of that month was it possible to form the *Kreuzotter* ('viper') group, which by the 15th numbered thirteen boats. With Bletchley Park still several weeks away from cracking the four-rotor Enigma code, the slow ON144 convoy sailed right into the *Kreuzotter* line in the 'Black Gap' some 800 miles south-east of Greenland. Though fitted with the latest centimetric wavelength radar, the 6th Escort Group was significantly weakened by the absence of its two destroyers, HMSs *Fame* and *Viscount*, both undergoing repairs after ramming U-boats in defence of SC104 in October. This reduced it to five Flower-class corvettes, consisting of *Potentilla* (Senior Officer of the Escort), *Rose*, *Eglantine* and *Montbretia* (all of the Royal Norwegian Navy) together with HMS *Vervain* of the Royal Navy as replacement. The ensuing battle reached a climax on the night of 17–18 November as no fewer than twelve U-boats closed in on ON144, the corvettes limiting attacking opportunities by running down contact after contact. *Montbretia* was in the thick of the action for most of the night, narrowly missing a torpedo from *U624* (Kptlt Ulrich Graf von Soden-Fraunhofen) at 0300 Allied time. At 0540 *Montbretia*'s radar operator reported a submarine contact sixty degrees off the starboard bow at a range of 4,200 yards. Five minutes later, with the contact range down to 3,600 yards, Kapteinløytnant H. Søiland ordered the ship to close at full speed. Within minutes the range was down to around 1,200 yards and at 0550 a second firm contact was obtained by the Asdic operator on the port bow at a range of 2,000 yards. However, when the first of two torpedoes struck *Montbretia* seconds later it apparently did so on the *starboard* side of the ship.

War Diary of *U262*, patrol of 5 November–9 December 1942: PG 30238, NHB, reel 1,095, p. 17

Date, time	Details of position, wind, weather, sea, light, visibility, moonlight, etc.	Incidents
18.xi		
0800	[Qu.] AK 4877, wind SW 2, sea 1–2, very dark night, 1,026 mb, 9.5°C [49°F]	
0830	[Qu.] AK 7670[1]	A light shining from a vessel at 270°. Presumably morse traffic between the escorts. At the same time we make out a long black shadow in the same direction – a freighter, I assume. We alter course 40° towards it.
0834		Two shadows ahead, one larger than the other; at first I assume freighter and escort, both bows right. We alter course to 220° so that the shadow is now on our port beam. The larger shadow now reveals itself to be a warship. Beam on, her pyramidical outline, raked funnel and lofty foremast all lead me to conclude that she is a small cruiser.[2] The vessel then alters course towards me. I assume I have been sighted. We withdraw at ¾ speed, our stern towards the enemy, turning further so that enemy bows are to the left, then still further so that enemy bows are once again to the right. We then alter course to port to attack, proceeding dead slow.
0851		Three-strong spread fired, inclination 90°, bows right, enemy speed 12 knots, range 800 m.[3] A hit

1 This grid reference, added in manuscript by a person unknown, is wholly inconsistent with the coordinates provided at 0800 and 1200, and indeed with all attacks on ON144 by the *Kreuzotter* group.
2 This vessel is almost certainly HNorM corvette *Montbretia*. Even had a cruiser been present, which there was not, Franke's description is well wide of the mark since *Montbretia* had no funnel cap and displaced a quarter of the smallest operational cruiser in the Allied fleets.
3 This spread and the following *coup-de-grâce* torpedo were fired by *U262*'s First Watch Officer, Lt.z.S. Hans Hellmann.

amidships: a tall sheet of flame rises up, vessel heels heavily. I order hard aport at utmost speed, presenting my stern to her. A *coup-de-grâce* shot from Tube V in order to sink her quickly. Before the shot can be fired an escort vessel appears at 200°, inclination 20°, bows right, and manoeuvres into line of fire. A hit forward on this ship: column of flame rises some 50 m in the air, vessel is blown to smithereens. Shortly thereafter the first vessel sinks too.[4] We withdraw from the scene of the sinking at high speed.

0920	We alter course to 330°.
0939	Incoming W/T transmission 085/18/267: *Franke, Kremser, Hackländer and Uphoff to report positions immediately.*[5]
1052	Dived. Practise alarm test dive. We reload torpedoes.
1635	Outgoing W/T transmission 1156/18/284:

1. 2110 spread of three at 7,000 GRT. Hit observed, sinking not witnessed, forced under by escorts.[6]
2. 18.11. 0851 spread of three at large destroyer or light cruiser, sunk. 0853 single at destroyer or other escort coming to assist, sunk.
3. Mar. Qu. [AK] 4796, wind SSW 2, slight swell, [1,0]27 mb, rising, visibility 15 nm, 4 + 2, 72 cbm.[7]
Franke

---

4 Franke's assessment of two vessels sunk in this engagement is reasserted in his signal to B.d.U. at 1635 that day. This was at best an erroneous observation by Franke and/or his lookouts on a very black though calm night. Franke later ceded in his memoir of *U262* (see below) that he had only accounted for *Montbretia*.
5 Intended for Franke in *U262* as well as fellow *Kreuzotter* commanders Oblt.z.S. Horst Kremser (*U383*), Kptlt Burkhard Hackländer (*U454*; see 47) and Kptlt Horst Uphoff (*U84*) respectively.
6 Franke reports making this attack on ON144 on the evening of the 17th though there is nothing in Allied records to corroborate a hit.
7 The '4 + 2' refers to a probable mix of G7e and G7a torpedoes remaining, '72 cbm' to the available diesel fuel in cubic metres.

The sinking

The ranking survivor, Löytnant A. Tenvik KNM, was stationed by the depth-charge rails aft and had just received the order to set the detonators to safe given that *Montbretia*'s quarry was still on the surface when she was rocked by a major explosion. The torpedo struck abreast the mess decks on the starboard side forward shortly before 0600 Allied time, the detonation tearing away the plating on the port side beneath the 4-inch gun mounting, igniting ready-use ammunition there and demolishing much of the wheelhouse and the Asdic hut. Already well down by the bows, *Montbretia* was still proceeding at full speed when the second torpedo apparently struck on the *port* side amidships, approximately a minute after the first. As Lt Tenvik recalled, 'The funnel was split in two and the aft part of it was thrown into the water. The ship was still going full speed ahead with the propeller in the air; it did not list and was on a straight course. Black smoke rose to the air and the ship sank very fast. I estimate the ship sank within thirty seconds after the second torpedo.' Allied witnesses were unanimous that *Montbretia* did not so much sink as power beneath the waves at high speed and on an even keel.

The war diary documenting *U262*'s attack on *Montbretia* is confusing in that it describes the sinking of two vessels (both attacked from their starboard side) whereas Allied records indicate that only *Montbretia* was hit at this time, though once on each side. The surviving evidence points to *U262* as the perpetrator of both attacks, with Oblt.z.S. Heinz Franke failing to identify *Montbretia* correctly in the second instance having turned to fire a stern shot. However, there are significant problems with this scenario, assuming as it does that *Montbretia*'s own bearing changed diametrically relative to her assailant in the minute separating the two attacks, either through her own movements (of which there is no evidence), through *U262*'s manoeuvring to port

as she presented her stern to the target, or through a combination of both. Although *Montbretia*'s survivors have categorically denied that she made any turn following the first hit, there are strong indications that she may have been either listing or heeling to starboard at the time of the second hit, thereby altering her positioning with respect to *U262* as she pressed on at high speed. Another explanation is that a second U-boat was involved, to which the Asdic contact made at approximately 0550 would lend support. However, this theory, favoured by survivors and indeed by the Board of Enquiry, finds no support in surviving German records. Many U-boats fired torpedoes at ON144 during the night in question but only *U262* is recorded as having done so at this time. It is conceivable that the answer lies in the war diary of *U184*, now at the bottom of the Atlantic with Kptlt Günther Dangschat and his crew, the supposed victims of a depth-charge attack by HNorMS *Potentilla* forty-eight hours after *Montbretia* was destroyed. However, the absence of any sinking report by Dangschat makes this improbable, the more so since he sent a dozen radio signals to B.d.U. after *Montbretia*'s sinking without once referring to an attack at this juncture. The picture therefore remains obscure.

Fate of the crew

So alarming was the ship's progress below the surface following the first hit that Kapt.Lt Søiland immediately passed the order to abandon ship. Some of those on the starboard side found the easiest means of escape to be through the gaping hole produced on the ship's port side by the first torpedo. Attempts to lower the port sea boat ended when it landed on deck, proving too heavy to be pushed overboard. Lt Tenvik and others managed to release a Carley float from the port side while the Asdic operator, Utskreven dekksmann (Ordinary Seaman) G. A. Steimler, found himself clambering over the deck stanchions as the next torpedo approached: 'I remember swearing, but I never heard the explosion. The next thing I remember is I was somersaulting into the water, and when I surfaced I saw the stern of *Montbretia* going down with the flag still flying.' Steimler had to gather his wits in a rain of red hot steel followed immediately by an excruciating succession of depth-charge detonations:

> Next the depth charges, which were set, started to explode. I remembered being told that should one be in that position you should turn on your back, fold your arms under your stomach and hold your breath, which I did. I knew, sitting in the Asdic hut, that six charges had been set, so I counted the explosions which stopped at five. (Later I learnt that one of the crew had pulled out one primer). Perhaps the worst was now to hear all the crying for help, calling their families, calling to God for help from my shipmates close to where the depth charges were exploding.

Many of *Montbretia*'s ship's company got clear of the wreck before she sank but depth-charge detonations and the limited number of floats, rafts and rescue mats took their toll as time passed. As Kapt. Lt Christian Monsen of *Potentilla* recalled, 'a number of crew died in the water, freezing to death in under an hour'. Lt Tenvik was one of a dozen men who managed to lash some rescue mats and a Carley float into a single unit. Though the lights and cries of their shipmates were seen and heard in the darkness, exhaustion and exposure kept Tenvik's group from providing any assistance. Efforts to signal a nearby corvette (presumably *Potentilla*) were initially in vain, and it was not until two hours after the sinking that she manoeuvred alongside the rafts while her dinghy rescued those still in the water, the last man being picked up at 0830. Of twenty-nine men brought on board *Potentilla*, two died almost immediately leaving twenty-seven survivors to be taken initially to St John's and then to Halifax. The death toll included forty men of the Royal Norwegian Navy (including Kapt.Lt Søiland) and seven of the Royal Navy.

The contribution made by *Montbretia* to the Battle of the Atlantic was widely acknowledged, the new Commander-in-Chief Western Approaches, Admiral Sir Max Horton, commenting that 'the loss of this gallant ship which played such a distinguished part in recent convoy battles [. . .] will be greatly felt in both navies'. Admiral Sir Charles Kennedy-Purvis, Commander-in-Chief America and West Indies Command, sent a letter of condolence to Kontreadmiral Elias Corneliussen, commanding the Royal Norwegian Navy in exile, declaring that '*Montbretia* fully maintained the high standards of keenness and efficiency that is invariably associated with ships of the Royal Norwegian Navy'.

U262 and Heinz Franke

Built by Bremer Vulkan at Vegesack and commissioned in March 1942, *U262* spent most of her operational career with the 3rd *U-Flottille* operating out of La Pallice. Her tally of *Montbretia* and three merchantmen sunk in nine frontline patrols may have been modest, but her service under Oblt.z.S. Heinz Franke (Kptlt from April 1943) between October 1942 and November 1944 was anything but uneventful. *U262* was damaged on several occasions, and not only by air attack and shipborne depth charges. On the night of 26–27 April 1943 Franke found his progress to the coast of Prince Edward Island blocked by pack ice in the Cabot Strait. Forced to submerge, *U262* spent almost a day trapped under the ice before surfacing the following

Franke being decorated with the Knight's Cross by *F.d.U. West*, Kapt.z.S. Hans Rudolf Rösing (left), following *U262*'s return to La Pallice on 7 December 1943, a year after the sinking of *Montbretia*. DUBMA

night after repeated attempts during which severe damage was done to the boat and her armament left unserviceable. *U262* managed to reach the appointed position in time but her expected passengers, a party of escaped naval prisoners-of-war, failed to materialise having fallen foul of a heightened security regime at Camp 70, Fredericton, New Brunswick. Even so, Franke's efforts no doubt contributed to his being awarded the Knight's Cross in November of that year on a low tonnage score. Three patrols under Kptlt Karl-Heinz Laudahn in 1944 brought scant success to *U262* whose career ended when she was heavily damaged in an air raid on Gotenhafen (Gdynia) in December 1944.

Franke, a career officer who had served two years in the battlecruiser *Gneisenau* before joining the *U-Boot-Waffe*, spent 1944 in a variety of shore appointments including command of a midget submarine unit, and though given command of two Type-XXI boats in the last months of the war saw no further frontline action. A period in captivity was followed by service in a minesweeping unit before Franke entered civilian life. However, he rejoined the newly formed Bundesmarine in 1957, retiring in the rank of Fregattenkapitän in 1972. He died in April 2003.

Sources

Admiralty, *Enemy Attacks on H.M. Ships* (TNA, ADM 199/163)
—, *Director of Anti-Submarine Warfare: Monthly Reports, 1943* (TNA, ADM 199/2060)
—, *Anti-Submarine Warfare Division: Analysis of U-Boat Operations in Vicinity of ON144, 15–20 November 1942* (TNA, ADM, 199/2014)
Franke, Kptlt Heinz, *Bootsgeschichte des Ubootes „U-262"* (typescript, DUBMA, *U262* file)
Ruegg, R., *Flower-Class Corvettes* (typescript, IWM, 13(41).245/5, 1987)
Steimler, Kontreadmiral G. A., letter to Daniel Morgan, Sandvika, 16 March 2003 (typescript/manuscript, Bruce Taylor collection)

Abelsen, Frank, *Norwegian Naval Ships, 1939–1945* (Oslo: Sem & Stenersen AS, 1986)

Blair, *Hitler's U-Boat War*, II, pp. 118–20
Preston, Antony, and Alan Raven, *Flower Class Corvettes* [Ensign, no. 3]
(London: Bivouac Books, 1973); reprinted as Man o'War, no. 7 (London:
Arms and Armour Press, 1982)

Webpage devoted to HNorMS *Montbretia*:
   http://www.warsailors.com/singleships/montbretia.html
Career of Kontreadmiral Gustav Steimler (survivor):
   http://www.nssr.no/binary/2413/file

77   HMS *BLEAN*

Lt N. J. Parker, RN†

Sunk by *U443* (Type VIIC), Oblt.z.S. Konstantin von Puttkamer, 11 December 1942
Western Mediterranean, 55 nm WNW of Oran (Algeria)

Blean shortly before commissioning in July 1942. Within five months she was at the bottom of the Mediterranean thanks to two torpedoes from *U443*. *BfZ*

Campaign Operation TORCH (Map 3)		*Displacement* 1,050 tons	
Coordinates 35° 51' N, 01° 47' W		*Dimensions* 280' × 31.5' × 8.25'	
Kriegsmarine code Quadrat CH 7675		*Maximum speed* 27 knots	
U-boat timekeeping identical		*Armament* 4 × 4" AA; 4 × 40 mm AA; 3 × 20 mm AA; 2 × 21" tt	
Fatalities 89 *Survivors* 94			

Career

For design notes on the Hunt-class destroyers, see HMS *Heythrop* (**55**).

HMS *Blean* belonged to the Hunt (Type III) class whose twenty-eight units followed the design of the Type IIs while sacrificing a 4-inch mounting to ship a pair of torpedo tubes on the quarterdeck. *Blean* was laid down at Hawthorn Leslie's yard at Hebburn-on-Tyne in February 1941, launched in January 1942 and commissioned on 23 August that year. After working up at Scapa Flow in August and September *Blean* was assigned to convoy duty in the North Sea though October found her under repair on the Thames. At the end of that month she joined the Gibraltar convoy run, reaching the Rock on 2 November just as Operation TORCH (the Allied landings in North Africa) was getting under way. Quickly assigned to the 58th Destroyer Division at Algiers, *Blean* spent the rest of her career – the briefest of any of the Hunt class – escorting convoys in the Western Mediterranean.

Background of the attack

For background on Operation TORCH, see HMSs *Martin* and *Hecla* (**72** and **73**).

Oblt.z.S. Konstantin von Puttkamer's *U443* was one of a number of boats sent to reinforce the *U-Boot-Waffe* in the Mediterranean after the losses suffered during Operation TORCH in November 1942. Forcing the Straits of Gibraltar on the night of 4–5 December, *U443* took up a patrol position west of Oran but it was not until the 10th that she encountered any worthwhile targets. That afternoon von Puttkamer had the unusual experience of sighting not one but two large convoys passing him on opposing courses in the space of an hour. Despite counting an almost identical number of merchantmen and transports, von Puttkamer seems never to have entertained the notion that these two convoys might be one and the same but this was indeed the case. What *U443* had spotted was fast convoy MKF4 en route from Algiers to the Clyde sailing first west and then east. At 1530 Vice-Admiral Sir G. F. B. Edward-Collins, Flag Officer North Atlantic at Gibraltar, had ordered MKF4 to reverse course for three hours in order to avoid it catching the slower westbound convoy MKS3Y. However, the order was unnecessary since MKF4 had been delayed two hours off Oran while it was joined by ships sailing from that port – a development of which Edward-Collins was unaware. Patrolling some 2,000 metres from the body of the convoy, *U443* took advantage of a weak zigzag and *Blean*'s station on its starboard beam to hit her with two torpedoes in as many minutes.

War Diary of *U443*, patrol of 29 November–22 December 1942: PG 30497, NHB, reel 1,109, pp. 661–2

Date, time	Details of position, wind, weather, sea, light, visibility, moonlight, etc.	Incidents
11.xii		
0400	[Qu.] CH 7911, wind NE 2, sea 0–1, cloud 5, 1,024 mb, visibility 3 nm	
0730		We dive and proceed under water. It's a mystery to me where these big groups constantly reported as leaving Gibraltar are to be found. With the fabulous hydrophone conditions prevailing it should be impossible for large groups of ships to pass through the patrol line currently formed by our boats in daylight.
0800	[Qu.] CH 7913, wind NE 1, sea 0–1, cloud 8, 1,023 mb, visibility 8 nm	We go to periscope depth a number of times but see nothing.
1200	[Qu.] CH 7684	Day's run: submerged 35 nm, surfaced 110 nm = 145 nm.
1430		Faint propeller noises. A convoy 4 nm to the north, heading west, inclination 60°.
1435		Battle Stations. I count fourteen large transports including one *Monarch of Bermuda* type with three funnels and several two-funnel types, almost all passenger liners.[1] On my side there is just a single-funnelled destroyer zigzagging at high speed, range 3,000 m.[2] I run in to attack this escort as there is no point in trying to attack the steamers from this kind of range, but we get no opportunity to fire even at this target as the entire group – including the destroyer whose inclination had been favourable prior to the manoeuvre – suddenly zigzags 40–50° to starboard. It would have been an excellent opportunity had our boat been stationed more favourably *vis-à-vis* the enemy from the start since the escort was a weak one.[3]
1500		Crew stood down from Battle Stations.
1525		Propeller noises from our last convoy bearing suddenly get louder again.
1530		Battle Stations. An eastbound convoy heaves into sight with an inclination of about 30°. Again we count fourteen large merchantmen. The starboard defence consists of one destroyer and one escort. Her speed is not so great as that of the westbound convoy, I'd estimate 15 knots. The transports again comprise one large three-funnelled vessel and several with two funnels, but I have no clear shot at them because the range is 4,000–5,000 m on my beam. The group's escort on this side consists of one single-funnelled destroyer and one other escort.[4] We set our sights on the destroyer which has now come within about 2,000 m of us. She is proceeding at moderate speed with minimal, barely perceptible zigzags.
1625	[Qu.] CH 7675	A spread of two torpedoes fired from Tubes I and III, inclination 90°, enemy speed 14 knots, range 2,300 m.[5] A hit after a torpedo run of 2 min. 42 sec. = 2,400 m.
1627		A further double spread launched from Tubes II and IV aimed at a single-funnelled transport that was overlapping the destroyer, albeit an extra 1,000 m off. After 2 min. 21 sec. (= 2,100 m) another hit on the destroyer, whose speed had probably been severely reduced by the first torpedo strike. A huge explosion. Nothing more to be seen of the destroyer other than a yellow, red and white fountain. We dive. The destroyer had perhaps been proceeding in a rather incautious and careless manner. She was not sailing at high speed, was barely zigzagging and never once appeared to pick up the torpedoes

1   *Monarch of Bermuda* (22,424 GRT) was indeed the largest of several big liners sailing in MKF4, the composition of which (front row, port to starboard) was *Dempo*, *Monarch of Bermuda*, *Letitia*, *Stratheden*, *Durban Castle*, *Samuel Chase*; (second row) *Tawali*, *Derbyshire*, *Orbita*, *Bulolo*, *Reina del Pacífico*, *Batory*, *Samaria*, *Maloja* and *Sobieski*. *Antenor* probably also present.

2   Possibly HMS *Blean*.

3   Although von Puttkamer seems only to have spotted three, MKF4 in fact had a six-strong escort at the time of the attack (see n. 4), the frigate *Exe* and escort destroyer *Tanatside* having been detached to Gibraltar an hour earlier.

4   The 'single-funnelled destroyer' was evidently *Blean*, sailing on the convoy's starboard beam. HM escort sloop *Egret* was ahead of the convoy in the centre, with the destroyer *Wishart* on the port bow. The positions of the others are not recorded in British sources, but the second escort referred to must have been either *Egret* (one of the first on the scene of the sinking), the frigate *Swale*, the cutter *Banff* or the escort destroyer *Calpe*.

5   Von Puttkamer's torpedo report states that the range was assessed as 3,000 metres though this may have been the figure entered into the torpedo data computer at the start of the attack sequence before it was set to *Lage laufend* (automatic update mode); see Introduction, p. xxvi.

on hydrophones, even though we could hear these for a long time with the naked ear, and most unpleasantly loud they were too.

She can hardly have been an English 'J'-class since:

    a) I wasn't able to observe any twin gun mounting, and

    b) to my mind an English destroyer would have been proceeding with far more effective anti-submarine measures.

So my view is that she was a US destroyer of the Craven class.[6]

1645	The first depth charges are dropped, aim so-so, *Bolde* expelled twice at depths of 150 m and 180 m respectively.[7] After 2½ hours the noises fade away to the east.
1940	Surface and head off on a south-westerly course.
1946	Outgoing W/T transmission: *Marine Qu. [CH] 7675. 1) 1430 westbound convoy sighted, 14 large transports, high speed. 2) 1630 eastbound convoy, 15 large transports, 14 knots, US single-funnelled destroyer sunk with two hits. Depth charges. Still 8 + 2, 81 c[b]m.*[8] *Puttkamer.*
2000 [Qu.] CH 7912, wind W 2, sea 1, cloud 9, 1,126 mb, visibility 3 nm	For a while we retire from the area of the attack towards Cabo Tres Forcas. Then we return to the same area.

---

6   Though rather larger at 1,590 tons and carrying two mountings forward (as against just one in the Type-III Hunts), the US Gridley class (of which *Craven* was a unit) did indeed bear a close resemblance to *Blean*.

7   *Bolde* was the calcium-zinc discharge that, by generating large masses of bubbles, replicated the echo produced by an Asdic submarine contact. This ruse was also known as the *Pillenwerfer* ('pill-thrower') after the ejector fitted for this purpose in the stern of the U-boat.

8   The '8 + 2' refers to a probable mix of G7e and G7a torpedoes remaining, '81 c[b]m' to the available diesel fuel in cubic metres.

The sinking

Blean's survivors had little time to absorb the event which destroyed their ship, whose end is best described by Cdr H. G. Scott of HMS *Wishart* (Senior Officer of the Escort):

> She was struck by one torpedo right aft, and about twenty seconds later, by another further forward, both Starboard side. She was enveloped in a pall of smoke and then later was seen to have rolled over to Port and then to sink by the stern, 40 feet of her bow rising vertically for a full minute before finally sinking. The total time from first torpedo to final disappearance was not more than 4 minutes and the initial capsizing of the ship was very quick indeed.

The sinking throws up but one mild controversy, the discrepancy between the two primary sources as to the time elapsed between the two hits. Von Puttkamer's log and torpedo report record him firing two spreads of two torpedoes resulting in a hit from each spread roughly two minutes apart. This contrasts with the twenty seconds between hits recorded by Cdr Scott in *Wishart*. Whatever problems the Germans had previously suffered with their torpedoes, be it pistol failure, hydrostatic error or gyroscopic malfunction, the speed of a G7e torpedo was a very reliable thirty knots, making a twenty-second gap between hits of the same spread a most improbable scenario. The likelihood, then, is of an error of observation on the British side, Cdr Scott and his men suffering the time compression often experienced by those overtaken by great events.

No Board of Enquiry was held into the sinking of HMS *Blean*. Had one been called it would no doubt have dwelt at some length on the unfortunate situation which led MKF4 to reverse course having just navigated waters which Scott qualified as 'the area which, from the promulgated U-boat situation reports, appeared to be the most dangerous and which we were congratulating ourselves to have passed through unscathed'. Evidently, a breakdown in communication prevented news of MKF4's delay off Oran being transmitted from Sir

Von Puttkamer (right) shooting the sun from *U443's* conning tower some time between October and December 1942, the period during which *Blean* was sunk. In the centre is the UZO target bearing indicator; its binoculars are not fitted. *DUBMA*

Harold Burrough, Vice-Admiral Commanding North Africa, to Vice-Admiral Edward-Collins in Gibraltar, and no sooner had the convoy emerged from waters known to be patrolled by U-boats than the order to turn about sent it – and *Blean* – back into the arms of *U443*.

Fate of the crew

That a slender majority of *Blean's* ship's company managed to survive such a rapid sinking was not lost on those present, Cdr Scott observing that 'it is satisfactory that so many as ten officers and eighty-four men were saved'. Though *Wishart* managed to lower her whaler and two Carley floats, those who got clear of the wreck had to wait while she and *Egret* searched for the perpetrator. They returned about thirty minutes later, *Wishart* spending an hour rescuing the main group of men while *Egret* performed a sweep for those who had drifted off into the gloaming. The survivors were landed at Gibraltar the following day.

U443 and Konstantin von Puttkamer

Built by F. Schichau at Danzig (Gdansk) and commissioned in April 1942, *U443*'s career comprised three patrols under Oblt.z.S. Konstantin von Puttkamer. Her first frontline patrol yielded two large merchantmen while operating with the *Puma* group in the North Atlantic in October 1942. Her second took her into the Mediterranean where she sank first *Blean* and then SS *Edencrag* off Algiers on 14 December. However, this was the sum of *U443*'s success. The end came a week into *U443*'s third patrol not far from where *Blean* had met her fate. On 23 February 1943 she was located by the Hunt-class destroyers *Bicester*, *Lamerton* and *Wheatland* who avenged their sister in a combined depth-charge attack. There were no survivors. Von Puttkamer was posthumously promoted Kapitänleutnant with retroactive effect from 1 February 1943.

Sources

Admiralty, *Enemy Submarine Attacks on H.M. and Allied Warships: Reports, 1941-1943* (TNA, ADM 199/163)

—, *Reports of Mercantile Convoys: Mediterranean–UK, 1942–1943* (TNA, ADM 199/1216)

—, *War Diary for December 1942* (TNA, ADM 199/2253), pp. 361, 375, 418 and 431

Kriegsmarine, *U443*, Torpedo reports of 1625 and 1627 hrs on 11 December 1942 (BfZ, Schussmeldung Collection)

English, John, *The Hunts: A History of the Design, Development and Careers of the 86 Destroyers of This Class Built for the Royal Navy during World War II* (Kendal, Cumbria: World Ship Society, 1987)

Raven, Alan, and John Roberts, *Hunt Class Escort Destroyers* [Man o'War, no. 4] (London: Arms and Armour Press, 1980)

Smith, H. A., *Tales of a* Ganges *Bloater* (London: Minerva, 1998)

Career history of HMS *Blean*:
    http://www.naval-history.net/xGM-Chrono-10DE-Blean.htm

78   HMS *FIREDRAKE*
Cdr E. H. Tilden, DSC RN†
Sunk by *U211* (Type VIIC), Kptlt Karl Hause, 16–17 December 1942
North Atlantic, 590 nm W of Cape Clear, Cork (Ireland)

Firedrake seen completing her refit and repair at Boston in January 1942.
Before the year was out she was struck by *U211* amidships on the starboard side and sunk with heavy loss of life. *BfZ*

Theatre North Atlantic (Map 1)		*Displacement* 1,405 tons	
Coordinates 50° 50' N, 25° 15' W		*Dimensions* 329' × 33.25' × 8.5'	
Kriegsmarine code Quadrat BD 3335		*Maximum speed* 35.5 knots	
U-boat timekeeping differential +3 hours		*Armament* 3 × 4.7"; 8 × .5" AA; 5 × .303" AA; 8 × 21" tt; 1 × Hedgehog ATW	
Fatalities 171 *Survivors* 25+			

Career

Ordered under the 1932 estimates, the 'F'-class destroyer *Firedrake* was laid down at Vickers-Armstrong's yard at Walker-on-Tyne in July 1933, launched in June of the following year and completed in May 1935. A repeat of the 'E' class (see HMS *Exmouth*, **3**), *Firedrake* and her sisters entered service as the 6th Destroyer Flotilla, Home Fleet in the autumn of 1935. Refits apart, *Firedrake* spent her peacetime career largely on patrol duty in Spanish waters, remaining here while the Civil War lasted. On 23 April 1937 she participated with the battlecruiser *Hood* in raising the blockade of Bilbao, arrogantly brushing aside efforts by units of the Nationalist navy to bar the entry of three British merchantmen into that port. Renumbered the 8th DF in April 1939, the outbreak of war found the flotilla on patrol and escort duty with the Home Fleet at Scapa Flow. *Firedrake* was soon in action, the beginning of an exceptionally busy war. On 11 September she sailed with the carrier *Ark Royal* (**39**) as part of one of the Admiralty's ill-conceived anti-submarine 'hunter-killer' groups. Three days later an unsuccessful attack on *Ark Royal* by *U39* resulted in her being depth charged to the surface by *Foxhound*, *Faulknor* and *Firedrake* and her crew taken prisoner as the Royal Navy notched up its first U-boat sinking of the war. At the end of that month *Firedrake* was involved in the operation to bring the damaged submarine *Spearfish* (**14**) home from the North Sea. With the exception of a refit on the Clyde in November, patrol and escort duty with the Home Fleet continued until 28 March 1940 when *Firedrake* was damaged coming alongside the destroyer *Icarus* at Invergordon, an accident that kept her under repair at Cardiff through much of April. *Firedrake*'s return coincided with the Norwegian Campaign during which she participated in the capture of Narvik, acted as convoy escort and finally assisted in the evacuation of troops from Bodö and Harstad. Bomb damage required repairs on the Clyde in mid-June following which she was temporarily allocated to the 4th DF, Home Fleet, with which she covered the extension of the East Coast Mine Barrier across the Moray Firth by the 1st Minelaying Squadron.

Back with the 8th DF, at the end of August she joined the escort for Operation HATS, the passage of war *matériel* and naval reinforcements from Britain to Malta and Alexandria, *Firedrake* accompanying the convoy as far as Gibraltar. Here she remained as part of Force H, patrolling the coast of Vichy-held North Africa against the passage of French shipping, escorting convoys and taking the fight to the Axis until the summer of 1941. On 18 October 1940 while escorting convoy HG45 she participated with HM destroyers *Hotspur* and *Wrestler* and two Saunders-Roe London flying boats in a successful attack on the Italian submarine *Durbo* which was abandoned and then boarded east of Gibraltar. That a second Italian submarine, the *Lafolé*, was claimed south-east of Alborán Island on the 20th was due to the initiative of men from *Firedrake* and *Wrestler* who managed to recover confidential documents showing Italian dispositions before *Durbo* foundered. Within a few weeks *Firedrake* was involved in Operation COLLAR, the passage of a convoy to Malta and further naval reinforcements for the Eastern Mediterranean which resulted on 27 November in the inconclusive Battle of Cape Spartivento. On 1 January 1941 *Firedrake* assisted in the interception of a four-strong Vichy supply convoy which was captured intact and escorted into Gibraltar. Later that month she participated in the trans-Mediterranean convoy operation codenamed EXCESS, and then joined Force H for RESULT, the bombardment of

Genoa on 9 February. However, on 1 March she ran aground in heavy fog off Málaga, losing her Asdic dome and causing damage to her propellers which required her to be refloated and docked at Gibraltar before sailing for permanent repairs at Chatham at the end of April. No sooner had she completed these at Devonport and returned to Gibraltar at the beginning of July than she was pitched into Operation SUBSTANCE, the first heavily contested convoy to Malta. Reaching the Sicilian Narrows, on the evening of the 23rd *Firedrake* was near-missed by an Italian 100-kilo bomb which exploded on the starboard side amidships causing severe structural damage and flooding No. 1 and No. 2 boiler rooms, the boilers themselves being lifted off their beds. *Firedrake* crawled into Gibraltar under tow from HMS *Eridge* on the 29th where preparations were made for her to cross the Atlantic for full repairs in Boston. On 13 September she sailed from Gibraltar for the last time.

By the time *Firedrake* emerged from her latest refit and repair in January 1942 circumstances had disposed her for convoy duty in the Atlantic. Escort work began with Western Approaches Command and continued with periodic refits on the Clyde until early May when she joined the 7th Escort Group at Londonderry. After repairs at Belfast in late July and early August *Firedrake* escorted the first in a series of ON and SC convoys which ended in her loss in December.

Background of the attack

On 11 December 1942 slow convoy ON153 sailed from Liverpool bound for New York. Having passed through the North Channel it was joined by the British 7th Escort Group comprising the destroyers *Firedrake* (Senior Officer of the Escort) and *Chesterfield* and the corvettes *Alisma*, *Pink*, *Snowflake* and *Sunflower*. Its passage over the next few days was to be impeded first by one of the worst Atlantic storms in recent memory and then by the twelve-strong *Raufbold* ('ruffian') group waiting some 450 miles west of Ireland. ON153 was sighted on the 15th by *U609* (Kptlt Klaus Rudloff) which was stationed in the centre of the *Raufbold* patrol line and succeeded in bringing half a dozen boats up to the convoy during that night. The U-boats were as troubled by the weather as ON153 but once they had established contact they proved difficult to shake off since Asdic was virtually useless in such conditions and visual sighting improbable. Three ships were lost on the 16th: the Norwegian motor tanker *Bello* and the British SS *Regent Lion* to *U610* (Kptlt Walter von Fryberg-Eisenberg-Allmendingen) and the Belgian SS *Émile Francqui* to *U664* (Oblt.z.S. Adolf Graf). *Bello* and *Émile Francqui* sank immediately but *Regent Lion* remained afloat and as darkness fell on the 16th *Chesterfield* and *Alisma* remained astern of the convoy, presumably to render assistance. At 1705 the convoy was again attacked, prompting the order to be passed for Operation RASPBERRY, the firing of a barrage of starshell or snowflake in an attempt to force U-boats to submerge where they could be hunted by Asdic or perhaps lose contact altogether. Alerted to U-boat activity to the north, Cdr E. H. Tilden brought *Firedrake* into a solitary position about four miles off the convoy's starboard beam in mountainous seas and a raging force 9–10 gale. Shortly before 2200 on the 16th Allied time (0100 on the 17th German time) the sound of *Firedrake*'s propellers was picked up on the hydrophones of a submerged *U211* (Kptlt Karl Hause). Surfacing to investigate, *U211* sighted *Firedrake* making just four knots in a head sea.

War Diary of *U211*, patrol of 16 November–29 December 1942: PG 30199, NHB, reel 1,091, p. 292

Date, time	Details of position, wind, weather, sea, light, visibility, moonlight, etc.	Incidents
16.xii		
2000	Qu. [BD] 7796, wind WNW 8–9, [1,0]55 mb[1]	
2140		Dived to listen through hydrophones. Hydrophone effect at 140° true.
2215		Surfaced.
2250		Incoming W/T transmission 2103/16/275:[2] *Raufbold Group cling on tenaciously to convoy. Escorts are powerless in this weather. Attack wherever possible as opportunities to attack are extremely favourable and experience shows torpedoes run true even in worst conditions.*
2400	Qu. BD 3333, wind WSW 9, sea 8, occasional hail showers, 959 mb	
17.xii		
0049		Dived to listen through hydrophones. Fix obtained at bearing 150° true.
0102		Surfaced.
0114	Qu. BD 3335	A destroyer in sight proceeding dead slow, head on to the sea.[3]
0115	Wind WNW 9, sea 8, high swell from the west	Spread of two torpedoes fired. Enemy speed four knots, inclination 80° bows right, aim-off 8°, angle of spread 5.4°, range 1,000 m, depth 2 m.
0117		A hit (after 124 sec.) below the after funnel.[4] A thick black explosion column, accompanied simultaneously by a glowing white cloud of steam. After firing we initially turn away, but after the detonation we turn bow on to her once more. But destroyer has sunk in the meantime.[5] After a short while we are sighted by a second destroyer, starshell is fired and we are forced to withdraw.[6]
0245		Despite further searching we see no merchantmen.
		Outgoing W/T transmission 0210/17/280: *0115 Mar. Qu. [BD] 3335, spread of two against two-funnelled destroyer, sunk. Forced to withdraw, in pursuit.*
0331		Dived to listen through hydrophones. Fix obtained at bearing 140° true.
0400	Qu. BD 3334	

1   The weather conditions recorded here give an idea of the hardship endured by both sides. Force 10 winds were regularly recorded during the three days of this storm.

2   Sent by B.d.U.

3   HMS *Firedrake*.

4   Survivors recalled the torpedo striking beneath the forward not the after funnel. The wide angle of spread selected by Hause suggests an understandable degree of uncertainty in the conditions, but though the range was underestimated the crucial assessment of target speed was accurately gauged.

5   *Firedrake* broke in two, the fore part sinking within twenty or thirty minutes, the after section not for another two hours.

6   There is no record of any escort sighting *U211*. The starshell was fired by *Firedrake* herself to alert *Sunflower* to her predicament. Entries such as this no doubt reinforced B.d.U. in its opinion that Hause had a greater sense of self-preservation than was desirable in a U-boat commander; see below.

The sinking

Striking the starboard side abreast No. 1 Boiler Room at 2210 on the 16th Allied time, *U211*'s hit caused *Firedrake* to list heavily to starboard. Within the space of a minute she had righted herself and then broken in two at the forward bulkhead of No. 3 Boiler Room, the fore part capsizing to starboard before being swept still floating past the rest of the ship. Protruding twenty feet above the surface, it remained afloat for another twenty or thirty minutes while survivors of the after section looked on aghast at the disembodied remains of their ship. Alive to their predicament, the survivors made efforts to shore up the forward engine room bulkhead which was all that kept them from sharing the fate of those in the bow section. Torpedoes, depth charges and other topweight was jettisoned from the after section which remained on an even keel, but the end could not be long in coming. At 0045 on the 17th the elements claimed their victim as the bulkhead collapsed and what remained of *Firedrake* sank within minutes, two and a half hours after the attack. The ranking survivor, Lt D. J. Dampier, gave it as his opinion that the stern section could have remained afloat for days had the weather been less severe but that chances of salvage were nil in the prevailing conditions.

Hause's sinking of a destroyer was acknowledged by B.d.U. but the latter's verdict on *U211*'s second frontline patrol was far from complimentary. The report bemoaned Hause's timidity on other occasions, allowing himself to be chased away from convoys or remaining submerged far longer than was necessary. By way of conclusion, B.d.U. expressed the hope 'that [*U211*'s] welcome destroyer success will have strengthened the assurance, confidence and attack-mindedness of her commanding officer'.

Fate of the crew

The detonation and subsequent disintegration of *Firedrake* accounted for most of her ship's company including Cdr Tilden and left just thirty-five men in the after section. Men were seen clinging to the bow section until it disappeared but there was no possibility of rendering any assistance and none survived from this part of the ship. The corvette *Sunflower*, then on the opposite side of the convoy, went to investigate after being unable to raise *Firedrake* by radio and eventually came across the stern section at around 0015 on the 17th. Capt. J. T. Jones RNR refused to countenance the risk involved in bringing his ship alongside the wreck in the prevailing swell (many survivors recalled '60-foot waves') and decided to circle her until daybreak in the hope that the weather would abate. But *Firedrake* would not see another hour, let alone another dawn. At 0045 the engine room bulkhead collapsed and the thirty-five survivors abandoned ship using the Carley floats. The chances of getting them aboard appeared doubtful in the prevailing conditions until a Newfoundland rating, Able Seaman George Furey, tied a line around his chest, climbed down *Sunflower*'s scrambling net and plunged into the maelstrom in an effort to reach them. Having gained a floating cork net to which a number of survivors were clinging, Furey entwined himself in the netting and so permitted those on board *Sunflower* to haul them alongside the scrambling net. Furey remained in the water, swimming out time and again to isolated individuals and being dragged back to *Sunflower*. That as many as two dozen men were rescued was owed largely to the efforts of this man whose only recollection of the event was regret at not being able to save more. Furey received a Mention in Despatches.

Lt Dampier concluded his official report on the sinking by expressing the survivors' keen 'admiration for the seamanship and skill displayed by [*Sunflower*'s] Commanding Officer under very difficult conditions'. Not for the first or the last time the Admiralty chose to waive a Board of Enquiry as there were no outstanding questions to which answers could be expected.

U211 and Karl Hause

Built by Germaniawerft at Kiel and commissioned in March 1942, *U211* undertook five frontline patrols under Kptlt Karl Hause. *Firedrake*, sunk during her second cruise, was *U211*'s only unassisted sinking. The rest of her slender tonnage came during her first patrol in September 1942 when three merchantmen were damaged including

U211 seen immediately after launching at the Krupp Germaniawerft yard at Kiel on 15 January 1942. *DUBMA*

two from convoy ON127 which were finished off by *U608*. *U211*'s last three patrols were carried out under the shadow of Allied air superiority and nothing more was added to her tally. Though fitted with new anti-aircraft armament, *U211* was heavily damaged by a US Liberator in the Bay of Biscay on 20 February 1943 and forced to return to Brest just a week into her third cruise. The end came on 19 November when she was sighted off the Azores by an RAF Wellington and sunk with a single pattern of depth charges. There were no survivors.

Sources

Admiralty, *Losses of Ships by Mines and Submarine Attacks: Reports, 1942–1945* (TNA, ADM 199/165)

—, *Losses of H.M. Ships and Other Vessels by Enemy Action: Reports, 1942–1945* (TNA, ADM 199/621)

Schmidt-Rösemann, K. H., correspondence with D. Coombes and M. J. Reynolds (typescript and manuscript, DUBMA, *U211* file)

Blair, *Hitler's U-Boat War*, II, pp. 128–9

Divine, A.D., *Destroyer's War: A Million Miles by the Eighth Flotilla* (London: John Murray, 1942)

English, John, Amazon *to Ivanhoe: British Standard Destroyers of the 1930s* (Kendal, Cumbria: World Ship Society, 1993)

Kinghorn, D., and B. Hargreaves, 'Destroyers of the Royal Navy: "F" Class' in *Warships*, Supplement no. 7 (March 1967), pp. 19–30

War career of HMS *Firedrake*:
   http://www.naval-history.net/xGM-Chrono-10DD-23F-Firedrake.htm

HMS *Firedrake* Association website:
   http://www.hmsfiredrake.co.uk/

79 HMS *PARTRIDGE*

Lt Cdr W. A. F. Hawkins, DSC OBE RN
Sunk by *U565* (Type VIIC), Kptlt Wilhelm Franken, 18 December 1942
Western Mediterranean, 45 nm W of Oran (Algeria)

Campaign   Operation TORCH (Map 3)
Coordinates   35° 50' N, 01° 35' W
Kriegsmarine code   Quadrat CH 7673
U-boat timekeeping   identical
Fatalities   38   *Survivors*   about 183

Displacement   1,640 tons
Dimensions   345' × 35' × 9'
Maximum speed   36.75 knots
Armament   5 × 4" AA; 4 × 40 mm AA; 4 × 20 mm AA; 2 × .303" AA; 4 × 21" tt

Partridge seen during her year of life in 1942, most of it spent in the Mediterranean. She was sunk by a single hit aft from *U565. IWM*

Career

The 'P'-class destroyers, of which HMS *Partridge* was among the last units to be completed, were repeats of the preceding 'O' class, the first true destroyers in the Royal Navy to be designed principally for escort rather than fleet duties. *Partridge* was laid down at Fairfield's yard at Govan in June 1940, launched in August 1941 and commissioned for service with the 12th Destroyer Flotilla in February 1942. Her career was to be brief but tumultuous. Having worked up, *Partridge* sailed from the Clyde on 15 April charged with escorting the carrier USS *Wasp* on an aircraft-delivery mission to Malta. Retained at Gibraltar for screening duties in the Mediterranean, on 15 June *Partridge* was heavily damaged in action with Italian cruisers and destroyers south of Pantelleria during Operation HARPOON, the latest attempt to resupply Malta. The convoy and its escort continued towards Malta leaving *Partridge* and the Tribal-class destroyer HMS *Bedouin* alone on the battleground. Having got under way *Partridge* took *Bedouin* in tow but had to slip the cable when the Italian squadron returned and took the pair under fire. *Bedouin* was eventually despatched by an Italian torpedo bomber but *Partridge*, though further damaged by aircraft, made a miraculous escape to reach Gibraltar on the 17th. After two days being patched up she sailed for permanent repairs on the Tyne which lasted until August. Following a brief spells with the Home Fleet at Scapa Flow and on convoy escort duty in West African waters,

Partridge returned to the Mediterranean theatre where she joined the 3rd DF at Gibraltar in early November in support of Operation TORCH, the Allied landings in North Africa. On the 8th she was assigned to the Eastern Task Force for the assault on Algiers, being allocated to screening duties with Force H thereafter.

Background of the attack

For background on Operation TORCH, see HMSs *Martin* and *Hecla* (**72** and **73**).

The morning of 18 December 1942 found HMS *Partridge* performing an anti-submarine sweep eastward on the Gibraltar–Oran run near the Habibas Islands off Algeria. She was sailing on the starboard wing of a line completed by HM destroyers *Penn* (port wing), *Milne* and *Meteor*. That these waters were patrolled by enemy submarines was fully apprehended by the sinking of HMS *Blean* in virtually the same position a week before (**77**). In an attack which recalls that on HMS *Heythrop* earlier that year (**55**), the flotilla was sighted and tracked at periscope depth by Kptlt Wilhelm Franken in *U565* as it closed his position. Although errors and inconsistencies in Franken's log make it hard to equate his observations with the stationing of the British force, at 0806 *Partridge*, then the nearest vessel to *U565*, became the target of a single torpedo.

War Diary of *U565*, patrol of 23 November 1942–1 January 1943: PG 30602b, NHB, reel 1,121, p. 690.

Date, time	Details of position, wind, weather, sea, light, visibility, moonlight, etc.	Incidents
18.xii	**North of Algeria**	
0400	Qu. CH 7677, good visibility, sea 3–4, sea phosphorescence	Surfaced.
0530–0730	Qu. CH 7678, 7679, [76]73[1]	Cruising up and down, alternating courses.
0720		Dived.

---

1 Quadrat CH 7673, here given in abbreviated form, was some distance to the north and not contiguous with the other two quadrants. It was, however, that in which *Partridge* was later sunk.

0730		Three destroyers heave into sight at a bearing of 330° true.[2] They are sailing in line abreast, zigzagging frequently. Average speed. I assume this is the search group referred to in a number of W/T transmissions. It is good attacking weather, sea 3–4. First destroyer passes on our starboard side, minimum range 3,000 m, second passes close by on port side, minimum range 800 m, and the third also to port but at a range of 4,000 m.[3] Their general course is 35°.
0806		Torpedo fired from Tube V at the second destroyer.[4] Inclination 120°, bows left, aim-off 28°, enemy speed 16 knots, depth 3 m, range 850 m. Destroyer has single funnel, simple mast, no inscription.[5] Two guns one above the other on the fo'c's'le, another on the destroyer island.[6] English flag. After two minutes' running time (a run of 1,800 m) a hit.[7] Destroyer stops while her fellows increase their speed.[8] A minute later there is another detonation, probably boilers or magazine.[9] We go to 140 m. The two other destroyers close the scene of the incident and remain there until 0930, sometimes stopped, sometimes dropping depth charges. Presumably rescuing survivors. At 0930 destroyers head away from the scene at a bearing of 140°. I withdraw to the north.
1130		Another destroyer appears and remains in my vicinity for the rest of the day and the following night. Every hour – precise to the minute – she drops a single depth charge. Sometimes she is within visual range, at other times further away, but always audible.
1200	Qu. CH 7672	Alter course to 270°. Day's run: 43.46 nm on the surface, 35 nm submerged. Total 78.76 nm.

2   Although the data provided under 0730 seems plain enough on a *prima facie* reading, it raises many questions in the light of Franken's course observation at the close of this entry and throughout that for 0806 (see nn. 4, 6, 7 and 8). Essentially, the positioning and ranges of the destroyers relative to *U565* cannot be equated with the torpedo information subsequently provided, nor is it clear at what point or points between the initial sighting (0730) and the attack (0806) this data was recorded. Moreover, it is hard to imagine how *U565* can have been overrun by a line of destroyers proceeding at a brisk 16 knots on a general course of 35 degrees (i.e. NNE) having initially been sighted at 330 degrees (i.e. NNW), even allowing for the group's regular 40-degree zigzags. In view of this it must be supposed that Franken was in fact to the *north* of the group and that his first observation of the British force at '330° true' should in fact be understood as 330 degrees *relative* bearing.

3   These are HMSs *Milne*, *Meteor* and *Partridge* respectively, which Franken, awaiting their approach, is seeing in the reverse of their actual stations. According to British reports the distance between each member of the quartet (including *Penn*) at 0800 (and by implication for the 24-hour sweep generally) was approximately 2,500 yards.

4   Based on the description provided at the end of the previous entry (see n. 3), this 'second destroyer' – the middle of the three ships sighted – corresponds to *Meteor*, not *Partridge*. Whatever the case, it is clear that *Partridge* was the ship actually targeted by Franken; see n. 7.

5   By 'inscription' (*Beschriftung* in the original) Franken is presumably referring to the vessel's pendant number, invariably painted round the stern and on the ship's sides forward. In *Meteor*'s case this was G73; *Partridge*'s was G30.

6   By 'destroyer island' (*Zerstörerinsel* in the original) Franken is referring to the after superstructure. While this description is consistent with both *Partridge* and *Meteor*, it more closely describes the latter with her three prominent twin 4.7-inch mountings, two forward and one on the after superstructure. *Partridge*, by contrast, had five of the smaller 4-inch guns in single mountings, two forward, one amidships and two aft. Nonetheless, *Partridge* was the ship actually targeted; see n. 7.

7   The torpedo report gives the running time as 2 min. 20 sec. (2,100 metres). Though well over double Franken's original estimate of 850 metres, a significant increase in range at point of intersection is consistent with the oblique inclination of the target at the time of firing (120 degrees). Once again, it is clear that *Partridge* was the ship actually targeted since an attack on *Meteor* would have required a significantly longer torpedo run to miss her and then go on to score a lucky hit on *Partridge*.

8   Though still at the surface, the strong swell (swell code 5) recorded in the torpedo report suggests that this and the comment which follows it was based on hydrophone data rather than actual observation. Franken's torpedo report contains no visual observations of the hit and its consequences, and as these were normally included (with gusto) as a matter of course their omission is significant.

9   Franken's torpedo report records two further detonations, not one.

The sinking

Lt Cdr W. A. F. Hawkins, who was below deck at the time, recorded that the detonation occurred on the port side aft abreast the wardroom at 0806 (another report suggests 0809), igniting a fuel tank and causing a secondary explosion and fire which was immediately doused by the geyser of water thrown up by the explosion. The blast was sufficient to fracture both propeller shafts and split the keel across the after bulkhead of the gearing room, leaving the ship supported by little more than her deck structure. *Partridge* immediately took on such a heavy list to starboard that Hawkins, convinced that 'the end could not be long in coming', quickly passed the order to abandon ship. Once in the water Hawkins recalled that 'the ship settled amidships

. . . righted herself and then proceeded to lift her stern and forefoot almost vertically in the water, finally submerging when the fore part of the keel was still vertical'. This impression was confirmed by the Chief Engineer, Commissioned Engineer C. H. R. Davis DSC, who got clear of the stern section in time to observe the fore part falling back and actually making contact with the after part before the two halves sank. No sinking time is given in British records but it seems that *Partridge* succumbed within ten minutes of being struck.

The depth at which *U565*'s torpedo had detonated led both the Board of Enquiry and Capt. C. P. Clarke, the Admiralty's Deputy Director of Anti-Submarine Warfare, to conclude that it had been a mine which claimed *Partridge*, a thesis apparently borne out by the absence of either hydrophone effect or Asdic contact in what were reckoned 'very good' conditions for the latter. A subsequent sweep by *Meteor* on *Partridge*'s starboard beam yielded nothing – no surprise in view of the failure of Asdic to detect the original attack and given that *U565* had engaged from the port side. However, the argument for a mine was disproved by intercepts of German radio traffic, among them Franken's sinking reports. Reviewing the episode, Admiral Sir Andrew Cunningham, Commander-in-Chief Mediterranean Fleet, once again expressed disappointment that no Asdic contact had been made either on the submarine or on the torpedoes fired. However, it is probable that *Partridge* was another in a long list of British ships lost as a partial consequence of the shortcomings of Asdic in the high salinity and variable water-temperature layers characteristic of the Mediterranean (see HMSs *Barham* and *Medway*, **41** and **64**).

Unusually, a comparison of Allied and German sources throws up a rather more confused picture of the incident than either provides on its own. In particular, the data fails to resolve the issue of how Franken could have identified his victim as the second in a line of three destroyers sighted at 0730 when this cannot possibly have been *Partridge* on the starboard wing of the group. As this relative positioning is stated categorically in all British reports (including that of *Partridge*'s commanding officer), it must be supposed that Franken erred both in his observations and in his recording of the event.

Fate of the crew

Most of *Partridge*'s casualties were sustained in the stern section where *U565*'s torpedo 'ignited the fuel in no. 8 tank and caused a fire which caused considerable injuries to several officers and ratings'. This blaze not only cost the lives of over twenty men but left many survivors with severe burns. In no doubt that she was finished, Lt Cdr Hawkins gave the order to abandon ship within minutes of the detonation. Once the salvageable Carley floats had been cut free much of the crew was able to scramble down the fo'c's'le and get clear of the ship. Shortly after she disappeared those still in the water were shaken by an explosion which was assumed to have been a depth charge, though Lt Cdr Watkins insisted that all had been set to safe per standard procedure. Whatever the case, help came swiftly in the shape of HMS *Penn* which picked up over 180 survivors, Hawkins's official report extolling the 'wonderful hospitality and assistance by all officers and men'. However, even the best efforts of *Penn*'s Principal Medical Officer and his Sick Berth Attendants could not save all the rescued. Two proved beyond help and another pair succumbed before the injured were transferred to HM Hospital Ship *Oxfordshire* at Gibraltar later that day. The final death toll came to thirty-eight men.

U565 and Wilhelm Franken

For the early part of *U565*'s career under Oblt.z.S. Johann Jebsen, see HMS *Naiad* (**54**).

U565 had one of the longest unbroken careers of any U-boat in

Franken seen wearing the Knight's Cross in May 1943. *DUBMA*

the Mediterranean, serving in this theatre from November 1941 until September 1944. Separating those of Jebsen and Kptlt Fritz Henning, the tenure of Kptlt Wilhelm Franken lasted from March 1942 to October 1943 during which two steamers and a sailing vessel were sunk in addition to *Partridge*, together with three ships damaged. These successes combined with a number of claims for which there is no corroboration in Allied sources sufficed to earn Franken a Knight's Cross in April 1943. In October 1943 he joined the staff of B.d.U. but perished in the same fire that claimed Siegfried Lüdden (see **83**) in the accommodation ship *Daressalam* at Kiel on 13 January 1945.

Pickings were slim for *U565* during the tenure of her third commander, Fritz Henning, though it was long believed that he had added HMS/m *Simoom* to her tally on 15 November 1943. However, recent research suggests that *Simoom* was probably lost in a minefield in the Aegean ten days earlier (**X4**). *U565*'s career ended off Skaramangas, Greece during a USAAF raid on 19 September 1944. Five men were killed and the damage such that *U565* had to be scuttled at Salamis five days later.

Sources

Admiralty, *Enemy Submarine Attacks on H.M. and Allied Warships: Reports, 1941–1943* (TNA, ADM 199/163)

—, *H.M. Ships Lost to Torpedo Attack and Mines, 1941–1943* (TNA, ADM 267/94)

English John, Obdurate *to* Daring: *British Fleet Destroyers 1941–45* (Gravesend, Kent: World Ship Society, 2008)

Kinghorn, D., and B. Hargreaves, 'Destroyers of the Royal Navy: "P" Class' in *Warships*, Supplement no. 26 (May 1972), pp. 19–31

Career history of HMS *Partridge*:
     http://www.naval-history.net/xGM-Chrono-10DD-49P-Partridge.htm

80   HMS *FIDELITY* (ex SS *LE RHIN*)

L.V. C. A. M. Peri, C. de G., pseud. Temp. Cdr Jack Langlais, RN, pseud. Ensign Costa†
Sunk by *U435* (Type VIIC), Kptlt Siegfried Strelow, 30 December 1942
North Atlantic, 180 nm N of Graciosa, Azores

SS *Le Rhin* lies peacefully at Marseilles in 1926. War and a remarkable personality brought her into the Royal Navy as HMS *Fidelity*. *BfZ*

Theatre North Atlantic (Map 1)	*Deadweight* 3,120 tons
Coordinates 42° 05' N, 28° 05' W	*Gross tons* 2,456
Kriegsmarine code Quadrat CE 3178	*Dimensions* 270' × 41' × 20'
U-boat timekeeping differential +1 hour	*Maximum speed* 9.5 knots
Fatalities 328 and 45 *Survivors* (10)	*Armament* 4 × 4" AA; 4 × 40 mm AA; 4 × 21" tt
	Motor torpedo boat MTB 105
	Landing craft LCV 752, LCV 754
	Aircraft 2 aircraft (Vought Kingfishers) handled by crane

Career

Completed for M. & C. Grayson by MacKie & Baxter of Glasgow in 1920, the freighter *Le Rhin* was acquired by the Compagnie de Navigation Paquet of Marseilles in 1923, being assigned successively to its Dakar, Casamance, Black Sea and Morocco routes. On the outbreak of war she was chartered by the French Colonial Intelligence Service, performing several operations in Indo-China before returning to the Mediterranean in the spring of 1940. Still commanded by her long-time master, Capitaine René Cannebottin, a decidedly motley crew by now included one Lieutenant de Vaisseau Claude Peri, ostensibly the W/T officer but actually an 'adventurer of Corsican origin' and a member of the French special intelligence service, together with his alleged mistress Madeleine Guesclin, an explosives expert supposedly succumbing to lung disease. In May 1940, with *Le Rhin* lying at Las Palmas in the Canaries, Peri and a fellow operative fixed plastic explosive (acquired from the British, and then a very new invention) to the hull of the German freighter *Corrientes*, leaving her severely damaged. However, Peri's defining moment was still to come. Learning of the fall of France in Marseille on 19 June, he took control of *Le Rhin* and sailed for Gibraltar together with those willing to continue the war against Germany. Among these was Cannebottin, subsequently Peri's navigation officer. For good measure Peri also appropriated whatever stores, dockside cargo and ammunition he could find, 'using rather forceful arguments such as hand grenades and revolvers to overcome the uncooperative spirit of the port officials and dockers'. In Gibraltar Peri found a willing ear for his defection in the person of the Vice-Admiral Commanding Force H, Sir James Somerville, whom he persuaded of his burning desire to throw in his lot with the British. Wearing the Blue Ensign of the Royal Naval Reserve, *Le Rhin* reached Barry Docks, South Wales on 4 August. Invited by Vice-amiral Émile-Henri Muselier to join the Free French forces, Peri refused point blank, adamant that *Le Rhin* would fight under the White Ensign and no other. Peri was a man accustomed to getting his way and a meeting with Muselier resulted in an 'amicable settlement' that saw *Le Rhin* commissioned into the Royal Navy on 24 September 1940 as HMS *Fidelity*. Peri and his officers all adopted pseudonyms, the former becoming Temporary Lieutenant-Commander Jack Langlais ('Jack the Englishman'); other names proffered to the Admiralty included a Drake and a Marlborough 'but the RN drew the line when one described himself as Horatio Nelson'. In other ways too Peri got his way. His refusal to put to sea in *Fidelity* without Madeleine Guesclin (renamed Madeleine Barclay) required the Admiralty to send her on a WRNS officer course at Greenwich. Barclay subsequently returned to *Fidelity* with the rank of First Officer (equivalent to Lieutenant-

Commander, RN), earning her the distinction of being the only Wren assigned to active duty at sea during the Second World War.

After an initial conversion in 1940–1 *Fidelity* returned to the Mediterranean in the summer of 1941, undertaking several missions in September and October to land agents on the shores of Algeria and southern France and rescue British airmen from the latter. At the end of 1941 she was earmarked for amphibious operations in the Indian Ocean following Admiral Somerville's appointment in command of the Eastern Fleet. However, mechanical defects and a further conversion involving the addition of twin gun mountings, Oerlikon guns, torpedo tubes, Asdic and radar kept her in harbour for another year. Meanwhile, the eccentric behaviour of her commanding officer continued to raise eyebrows. *Le Rhin*'s original cargo of tea, coffee, cement and sugar had been sold, the proceeds being assigned to Peri. Insistent that 'not a penny was to go to General de Gaulle', Peri eventually waived the majority in favour of the RAF Spitfire Fund, retaining a small amount for his personal use. Moreover, a year's enforced idleness did nothing for Peri's temper or the morale of a highly motivated crew anxious to get on with the war. Reports of beatings, solitary confinement without food or water, a man chained naked to a working boiler as punishment, a most questionable suicide (found in the water and deemed to have taken his own life by drowning despite being riddled with bullet holes, Peri opining that 'the dead man must have shot himself in mid-air') and a brawl between Peri and his Chief Bosun in which the latter was very nearly killed resulted in an Admiralty recommendation that *Fidelity* embark only on operations 'in keeping with the temperament of her commanding officer'. It must therefore have been with a mixture of relief and trepidation that HMS *Fidelity* was given orders to sail for the Indian Ocean on 18 December 1942, the outgoing Liaison Officer, Lt P. Whinney, being presented an engraved cigarette case by Peri 'As a souvenir of the black character of Jacques Langlais'. Before long she had joined the southbound convoy ON154 with a mainly British crew of 276 men, fifty-one Royal Marine Commandos and First Officer Barclay.

Background of the attack

Shortly before Christmas 1942 the *Ungestüm* ('impetuous') and *Spitz* ('spike') groups were formed into a single patrol line to intercept the latest slow outbound convoy ON154. The U-boats had a tedious time of it as the convoy was badly delayed by weather and mechanical problems to the Canadian 1st Escort Group's (EG-C1) two destroyers, HMCS *St Laurent* and HMS *Burwell*. But the U-boats' patience in vile conditions would be amply rewarded. *Burwell*'s defects were such that she never sailed at all leaving the defence of the convoy to *St Laurent* (Senior Officer) and five Canadian corvettes (*Battleford*, *Chilliwack*, *Kenogami*, *Napanee* and *Shediac*) which possessed neither HF/DF nor expert operators for their new Type-271 radar sets. The strength of the attacking force (which closed in once ON154 had been sighted by *U664* on 26 December), the slow speed of the convoy, the absence of air cover and the inexperience of a depleted escort group turned ON154's passage into an ordeal suffered by few other convoys in the war. Three merchantmen were sunk on the night of the 27–28th with a fourth succumbing to damage later that day. Though *St Laurent* accounted for *U356*, these attacks were only a forerunner of the havoc wreaked the following night when nine vessels were sunk or damaged,

the latter being finished off by the rest of the pack. Though ON154 was reinforced by HM destroyers *Milne* and *Meteor* on 29 December, much of the escort was desperately short of fuel and girding itself for a repeat of the previous night. To their great relief this scenario never came to pass as Dönitz called off the attack. Despite having the Type-XB tanker and resupply boat *U117* just 130 miles to the north, many U-boats were themselves so low on fuel as to make withdrawal the most prudent option.

Initially HMS *Fidelity* had no more than a spectator's role in this one-sided battle but this was not to last. Sailing at the rear of the fifth column, on the afternoon of 28 December she was closed by *St Laurent* with a desperate request to provide air cover using one of her two Vought Kingfisher seaplanes. However, the attempt to launch an aircraft in heavy seas almost cost the lives of its two crewmen and set HMS *Fidelity* on the road to disaster. While *Fidelity* turned into the wind in an effort to flatten the sea to assist take-off, the Kingfisher caught its wing in *St Laurent*'s wake as it was being swung out and immediately capsized. The loss of the plane was no more than a disappointment but the explosion of its shallow-set depth charge caused severe damage to *Fidelity*'s condensers and left her dead in the water, the first of many breakdowns over the next few days. For several hours *Fidelity* was screened by *Shediac*, but the latter was ordered to rejoin the convoy in the early hours of the 29th and dawn found Peri's ship alone and with steam for no more than two knots. She was sighted in this predicament at 0623 by *Milne*, then proceeding at full speed through the wake of the previous night's carnage to reinforce the escort of ON154. The Admiralty and many of the escorts picked up a number of radio transmissions from *Fidelity* over the next twenty-four hours during which time her two landing craft rescued an estimated forty-five survivors from *Empire Shackleton* (finished off by *U435* on the 29th) including the convoy commodore, Vice-Admiral Wion de Malpas Egerton. Intermittent breakdowns, the launch of the ship's motor torpedo boat (*MTB 105*) on night anti-submarine patrol, U-boat sightings and her desire to fly the Axis ensign were all signalled, the last prompting a response from the Admiralty forbidding her to do anything of the sort. Abandoning any hope of rejoining the convoy, Peri steered *Fidelity* south towards the Azores. One can only imagine the frustration with which he did so.

MTB 105, suffering engine trouble of her own, was close enough to witness an attack on *Fidelity* by *U615* (Kptlt Ralph Kapitzky) shortly before midnight on the 29th, the second commander to have her in his sights that day after Oblt.z.S. Wolfgang Leimkühler (*U225*) had curiously decided that this 'U-boat decoy' was not worth the trouble. Defeated perhaps by *Fidelity*'s anti-torpedo nets – no doubt rigged by Peri in view of his ship's reduced speed – five torpedoes from *U615* failed to have any effect though a separate explosion (possibly *Fidelity* dropping depth charges) was noted both by *U615* and *MTB 105*. Disconcerted by the waste of so many torpedoes, Kapitzky broke off the action but *Fidelity* was now living on borrowed time. On the afternoon of the 30th she was sighted making no more than five knots by Kptlt Siegfried Strelow's *U435*, her anti-torpedo nets presumably stowed. Wary of this unusual vessel and correctly identifying her as the 'decoy ship' reported by *U225* the previous day, Strelow fired two torpedoes within the space of a minute, ending *Fidelity*'s extraordinary career.

War Diary of *U435*, patrol of 30 November 1942–10 January 1943: PG 30489, NHB, reel 1,108, pp. 440–1

Date, time	Details of position, wind, weather, sea, light, visibility, moonlight, etc.	Incidents
30.xii		
1214		Incoming W/T transmission: *M.Qu. CE 3157 U-boat decoy, course SW, speed 5 knots, making black and white smoke alternately, fires starshell, assume have been sighted. Wind S 4, sea 3, good visibility, stratocumulus, 1,034 mb, falling. Intended rendezvous position CE 2334. Kapitzky.*[1]
1227		Incoming W/T transmission: *Boats of Spitz group waiting to refuel to use minimum fuel as past experience shows that delays in refuelling can occur in bad weather.*[2]
1310		Unaccompanied vessel sighted in M.Qu. CE 3173.
1315		Outgoing W/T transmission: *Unaccompanied vessel sighted M.Qu. CE 3173. Diving to attack. Strelow.*
1410		Boat dives to commence attack.
1638		Torpedo fired from Tube IV. Running time 23 sec., hits under the bridge.[3]
1639		Torpedo fired from Tube I. Running time 15 sec.[4] Likewise strikes the fo'c's'le.
1642		We hear a powerful detonation.
1646	M.Qu. CE 3178[5]	One depth charge falls extremely close. Vessel has a large aircraft crane aft and an aircraft.
		<u>12th shot</u>:[6] relative bearing 346.5°, aim-off green [i.e. starboard] 9°, inclination green 81.5°, angle of fire 355°, range 800 m, enemy speed 5 knots.
		<u>13th shot</u>:[6] relative bearing 348°, aim-off green 6.8°, inclination green 83°, angle of fire 354.5°, range 800 m, enemy speed 5 knots.
1715		Surfaced.
1740		At scene of sinking we encounter drifting wreckage and numerous survivors.
1948		Outgoing W/T transmission: *M.Qu. CE 3178 Leimkühler's U-boat decoy sunk with two single torpedoes, Eto and Ato, 23 and 15 sec. running time.*[7] *Course 180°, speed 4 knots. Seaplane embarked, appearance indicated warship. Similar to* Waldemar Kophamel.[8] *Hundreds of survivors at scene of sinking. Two depth charges dropped following torpedo hits, one very close. When we surface a hemp line 15 cm thick is found lying athwart the boat with a heavy object. 1 + 0.*[9] *10 cbm.*[10] *Transmission no. 754/29 not received properly. Time of sinking 1638.*[11] *Strelow.*
1952		Incoming W/T transmission: *Strelow to report whether survivors are in boats or whether their destruction can be counted on given the state of the weather.*[12]
2000	M.Qu. CE 3147, wind SE 2–3, sea 2, cloud 8, showery, light swell, 1,031 mb	
2100		Alter course to 270°.
2200		Both engines stop.

---

1 Signal from Kptlt Ralph Kapitzky of *U615* which had fired five torpedoes against *Fidelity* without effect the previous evening. *Fidelity* had however already been sighted by *U225*; see n. 7.

2 Signal from B.d.U. to *Spitz* group referring to refuelling from *U117* which eventually took place on 1–2 January 1943; see n. 13.

3 The running times of this torpedo and that which follows it at 1639 are much less than would be expected had the original range assessment (800 metres or around 55 seconds) been accurate, the 23 seconds stated here equating to 345 metres. Strelow's torpedo report admits his having underestimated the speed of the target, but aiming amidships still struck *Fidelity* twice.

4 The running time equates to a range of just 225 metres, much the shortest recorded in this book. Although the firing data provided in the entry for 1646 indicates that Strelow had simply miscalculated the range, firing from such close quarters was in contravention of The U-Boat Commander's Handbook (*Handbuch für U-Boot-Kommandanten*) which stated that 'No torpedo attack should […] be carried out at a range under 300 metres.'

5 Manuscript addition in pencil.

6 Unusually for a war diary entry, Strelow takes care to record the number of torpedoes fired since leaving Bergen on 30 November, though in this case does so at 1646 rather than at the time of firing (1638 and 1639 respectively). The attack left him with one remaining torpedo; see n. 9.

7 Oblt.z.S. Wolfgang Leimkühler of *U225* which had sighted *Fidelity* on the morning of the 29th. 'Eto' and 'Ato' was Kriegsmarine shorthand for the electric G7e and compressed-air G7a torpedoes respectively.

8 A U-boat tender of 4,700 tons.

9 Probably indicates a single G7e torpedo and no further G7a torpedoes remaining.

10 Indicates ten cubic metres of diesel fuel remaining.

11 The stated time is an error or mistranscription since Strelow's second torpedo had yet to be fired at that juncture.

12 See below.

Date, time	Details of position, wind, weather, sea, light, visibility, moonlight, etc.	Incidents
2344		Incoming W/T transmission: *Zetzsche, Strelow, Hunger, Hasenschar, Leimkühler to refuel from Neumann on 31/12 from midday Qu. BD 9482.*[13] *In event of more than 24 hours' delay report time of arrival. Only take on minimum for return journey, max. 25 cbm if necessary. First boat refuelled to report after having withdrawn, Neumann to report supply situation after operation complete. Above boats to switch to Ireland after midnight today.*
2400	Qu. CE 2363	***Siegfried Strelow***
31.xii		
0007		Outgoing W/T transmission: *300–400 survivors on overladen floats as well as in the water. No boats. Assume there must be crews from merchantmen among them.*[14] *Wind SSE, sea 2, 2/10 overcast, 16°, 1,032 mb and falling. Strelow.*
0115		Proceeding slowly at diesel-electric speed on port engine towards refuelling position, course 349°.[15]
0400	Qu. BD 9797	

---

13 The commanders of *U591, U435, U336, U628* and *U225* are directed to refuel from Korvkpt. Hans-Werner Neumann's Type-XB *U117* in that order.

14 Although his signal at 1948 on the 30th records his impression that his victim was a man o'war, Strelow was clearly surprised at the number of men in the water and correctly surmises that her complement had been swelled with survivors from other vessels.

15 Effective at low speeds, diesel-electric propulsion involved the use of just one diesel engine driving its own shaft and motor while the other was used to charge the batteries. The most economical way of making progress, but slower than cruising speed.

The sinking

Strelow's log apart, nothing is known of *Fidelity* once she lost contact with *MTB 105* shortly after *U615*'s unsuccessful attacks on the evening of the 29th. Radio transmissions from *Fidelity* were picked up by *MTB 105* during the course of that night and the next morning but too faintly to be decipherable. As no survivors from *Fidelity* herself were ever rescued the information concerning her demise is limited to Strelow's war diary. This reveals only that *Fidelity* suffered two torpedo hits forward within the space of a minute followed by a major detonation three minutes later, and that she sank soon after leaving several hundred survivors in the water.

When news of *Fidelity*'s sinking reached London the Free French forces were quick to assert the achievements of the former 'trap ship *Rhine*', noting in a despatch that 'all men and material on board gloriously disappeared in the area of the Azores in December 1942 while she was escorting a convoy attacked by German submarines'. This, however, was not quite all from the FNFL where *Fidelity* was concerned. Shortly after her loss Amiral Philippe Auboyneau of the FNFL approached the Admiralty regarding *Le Rhin*'s original cargo, disposed of in 1940 by 'Jack Langlais' for the benefit of the RAF and his own pocket. An internal memorandum from April 1943 prompted by this request and seemingly written by no francophile captures the ambiguity of *Le Rhin*'s legal status, her relationship with the Royal Navy, and indeed the Admiralty's exasperation with the whole *Fidelity* affair: 'No useful purpose will be served by splitting hairs now to decide whether or not any particular sort of French have a right on behalf of an undefined kind of France to benefit from what may or may not have been a robbery carried out by an unusual kind of Frenchman against another sort of French.'

Fate of the crew

Though no survivors of the actual sinking were ever picked up, the pilot and observer of *Fidelity*'s second Kingfisher and eight crewmen from *MTB 105* were rescued by HMC corvette *Woodstock* during the search for survivors and derelicts some days later. *Fidelity*'s mystique, the eccentricities of her commanding officer and the fact that there were survivors from her ancillary craft ensured that tongues wagged, so much so that the Admiralty's terse report on *Fidelity*'s presumed loss served only to fuel the speculation. Press articles published in March and October 1943 and a public letter written by the widow of the convoy commodore, Vice-Admiral de Malpas Egerton, caused the Admiralty to issue a further letter to next of kin in November 1943 with the aim of dispelling some of the wilder rumours then circulating. The problem for the Admiralty, however, was that no one on the Allied side was in possession of any but the barest facts concerning *Fidelity*'s loss. Not only had the nature of her demise prevented *Fidelity* reporting the attack, but Strelow's radio transmission of 1948 on the 30th was one of dozens relating to the decimation of ON154 deciphered by Bletchley Park over the next forty-eight hours. Nor did Strelow's reference to a 'U-boat decoy' prompt the Admiralty to draw a connection between her and *U435*. All the Admiralty could muster from its own intelligence, extracted from survivors of Kptlt Ralph Kapitzky's *U615* after she scuttled herself in the Caribbean in August 1943, was that *Fidelity* had been sunk on 31 December by *U435*, though even this was wrong insofar as the attack had actually taken place on the 30th. Not until German records were examined after the war did the Allies obtain specific information on the date, position and circumstances of the sinking.

The signal received by *U435* from B.d.U. at 1952 on the 30th is by some way the most sinister in any U-boat log excerpted in this volume. Not surprisingly the suggestion has been made on at least one occasion that it was effectively an order to massacre the survivors of what had earlier been identified as a 'U-boat decoy'. Questions remain as to Strelow's almost total silence with regard to *U435*'s movements between 1646 and 2100 along with other anomalies such as the time difference between the entries of 1948 and 1952, it being beyond the bounds of possibility that *U435*'s message of 1948 was sent, received, decrypted, cogitated and replied to in code within the space of four minutes. However, with no evidence to substantiate it the notion of an atrocity belongs in the realm of conjecture, which the loss of Strelow together with his entire crew in July 1943 no doubt makes definitive.

U435 and Siegfried Strelow

For details of *U435*'s and Strelow's earlier career, see HMS *Leda* (**69**).

Transferred to Atlantic operations during the patrol which accounted for *Fidelity* in December 1942, pickings proved more slender than they had in the Arctic. The attack on *Fidelity* was preceded by two other successes against ON154, the SS *Empire Shackleton* finished off by gunfire on 29 December (forty-five survivors were picked up by *Fidelity*) and the derelict SS *Norse King* which was despatched with the deck gun and torpedoes later that day. Two further patrols in the Atlantic yielded damage to a single merchantman, the US Liberty ship SS *William Eustis* which had eventually to be scuttled. *U435*'s career ended on 9 July 1943 while part of the *Geier* patrol line some seventy-five miles west of Cabo Mondego (Portugal). Sighted on the surface by an RAF Wellington, she was attacked and destroyed by a pattern of depth charges. There were no survivors.

Strelow seen on his return from a patrol in command of *U435*. The U-Boat War Badge on his breast together with the absence of the Knight's Cross (which he won later) together date the photo to between April and September 1942. Note the fish emblem on his cap. *DUBMA*

Sources

Admiralty, *War History: French Armed Merchant Ship "Le Rhin" (later HMS* Fidelity*)* (TNA, ADM 199/1320)

Ministère de la Défence, *Notice historique sur HMS* Fidelity (SHM, *Fidelity* file)

Ministry of Defence, *Loss of HMS* Fidelity (NHB, S.10591)

Whinney, Cdr P. F., *HMS* Fidelity (typescript, June 1977, IWM, 78/50/1)

Burn, Alan, *The Fighting Commodores: Convoy Commodores in the Second World War* (Barnsley, S. Yorks.: Leo Cooper, 1999)

Hampshire, A. Cecil, *On Hazardous Service* (London: William Kimber, 1974)

—, 'The Fighting "Fidelity"' in *Nautical Magazine* 216, no. 3 (September 1976), pp. 154–6

Jullian, Marcel, *HMS* Fidelity (Paris: Amiot-Dumont, 1956; Eng. trans. London: Souvenir Press, 1957)

Kingswell, Peter, Fidelity *Will Haunt Me till I Die* (3rd edn, Portsmouth, Hants.: Royal Marines Historical Society, 2003)

Marriott, Edward, *Claude and Madeleine: A True Story* (London: Picador, 2005)

Norbury-Williams, Lawrence, 'The Mystery of HMS *Fidelity*' in *Marine News* 46, no. 11 (November 1992), pp. 663–4

Revely, Henry, *The Convoy that Nearly Died: The Story of ONS 154* (London: William Kimber, 1979)

Webpage devoted to the sinking of HMS *Fidelity*: http://www.wartimememories.co.uk/ships/fidelity.html

81   HMS *WELSHMAN*
Capt. W. H. D. Friedberger, DSO RN
Sunk by *U617* (Type VIIC), Kptlt Albrecht Brandi, 1 February 1943
Eastern Mediterranean, 45 nm ENE of Tubruq (Tobruk) (Libya)

Theatre Mediterranean (Map 3)		*Displacement* 2,650 tons	
Coordinates 32° 12' N, 24° 52' E		*Dimensions* 418' × 40' × 11.25'	
Kriegsmarine code Quadrat CO 6776		*Maximum speed* 39.75 knots	
U-boat timekeeping differential –1 hour		*Armament* 6 × 4" AA; 4 × 40 mm AA; 7 × 20 mm AA; 156 mines	
Fatalities about 155 *Survivors* 118+			

Career

The fourth unit of the Abdiel class of fast cruiser minelayers, HMS *Welshman* was laid down at Hawthorn Leslie's yard at Hebburn-on-Tyne in June 1939, launched in September 1940 and completed in August 1941. The cruiser minelayer type had made its introduction with HMS *Adventure* in 1922 but only with the six-strong Abdiel class did a truly capable design enter service. With a maximum speed approaching forty knots, the Abdiels were designed to sow minefields

at speed and unescorted in enemy waters, the weapons in question being stowed on an enclosed mining deck and discharged through a pair of laying ports in the stern. But it was as fast transports that the class became famous, their speed and anti-aircraft armament making them ideally suited for the supply of Tobruk and particularly Malta during the sieges of 1942.

Having worked up at Scapa Flow, in September 1941 *Welshman* joined the 1st Minelaying Squadron in the Kyle of Lochalsh with

Welshman glides into the Grand Harbour at Valetta after a high-speed supply run in May 1942. She has been disguised as a Vichy destroyer with the addition of funnel caps and a *trompe-l'œil* break in the forecastle. *IWM*

which she sowed an anti-submarine field off the Butt of Lewis as part of the Northern Barrage and then three defensive fields off the East Coast. In December she laid anti-submarine fields in the Bay of Biscay before making a supply run to Gibraltar, Freetown (Sierra Leone) and Takoradi (Gold Coast) in January 1942. Further offensive minelaying operations in the Channel and the Bay of Biscay in February were followed by a refit on the Tyne and then by layings off northern France in April. In May *Welshman* made the first of three supply runs from Britain to Malta, two of them disguised as a Vichy destroyer thanks to the three funnels which made the Abdiel class unique among British ships of their size. The ruse was bought but *Welshman*'s paravanes detonated two mines on entering the Grand Harbour on 10 May which required repairs at Scotstoun on the Clyde. In early June *Welshman* returned to Gibraltar in time to participate in the supply convoy codenamed Operation HARPOON during which vital stores were landed at Malta. A second brief refit at Scotstoun was followed by Operation PINPOINT in July with similar purpose and then PEDESTAL in August and TRAIN in October. On 11 November *Welshman* took passage to Algiers in support of Operation TORCH, the Allied landings in North Africa, followed by a further supply run to Malta. Returning to Gibraltar, on the 27th she sailed for Haifa from where she returned to the Grand Harbour on 1 December brim-full with food and much-needed spares and torpedoes for the 10th Submarine Flotilla. A return trip to the Algerian port of Bône with submarine and MTB spares brought her back to Malta on 4 January 1943. Apart from an interlude ferrying troops between Beirut and Cyprus, *Welshman* spent the rest of that month on minelaying duty in the stategically vital Sicilian Narrows separating Tunisia and Sicily. However, a notable career was drawing to a close. No sooner had *Welshman* returned to Malta from a minelaying sortie in the Skerki Channel on 31 January than she weighed anchor for Alexandria at 1700 that same evening. A day later she was no more.

Background of the attack

Kptlt Albrecht Brandi's *U617* was one of seven U-boats to enter the Mediterranean in November 1942 to bolster the strength of *F.d.U. Italien* (Officer Commanding U-Boats, Italy) in its efforts to counter the Allied landings in North Africa. Konteradmiral Leo Kreisch had every reason to be pleased with *U617* whose commander claimed eleven Allied merchantmen and warships sunk or damaged for a total of over 70,000 tons during his first two patrols between November 1942 and January 1943. However, only three successes are borne out by Allied records and the actual tonnage equates to barely 7,000 tons, a fact not appreciated by Kreisch who authorised the award of the Knight's Cross to Brandi in late January. Despite his penchant for optimistic interpretation of visual and acoustic data, Brandi proved a thorn in the side of the Allied navies, and never more so than on 1 February 1943 when he sighted a 'cruiser' off Tobruk. This was in fact the fast cruiser minelayer *Welshman*, sailing independently between Malta and Alexandria. With 'nautical twilight at an end' and Capt. Friedberger's ship making about twenty-five knots on a four-minute zigzag, Brandi was presented with a fair test of his marksmanship, even if *Welshman*'s course took her within approximately 1,200 metres of *U617*'s position. No surprise, therefore, that Brandi resorted to a full spread of four torpedoes to maximise his chances.

War Diary of *U617*, patrol of 27 January–13 February 1943: PG 30648, NHB, reel 1,130, pp. 756–7

Date, time	Details of position, wind, weather, sea, light, visibility, moonlight, etc.	Incidents
1.ii		
1600	[Qu.] CO 6753	
1605		Hydrophone effect at 355°.[1]
1735		An unescorted cruiser at bearing 350° true.[2] Inclination 5°, bows left, range 3,000 m. I manoeuvre into an attacking position. Her shadow is still very faint in the periscope.
1745	[Qu.] CO 6776, wind NW 3, sea 2, 6/10 overcast. Visibility 2,000 m. Almost completely dark.	Spread of four torpedoes fired.[3] After 88 sec. two heavy detonations followed by a third.[4] Probably her boilers going up.[5]
1755		Surfaced. Cruiser capsized, sinking stern first.[6] Several searchlights on land at a bearing of 180° true. We withdraw, course 0°.
1813		Radar-warning readings of a number of ships on the 140-cm wave, volume 5. Alarm dive.
1825		Surfaced. Several more radar readings. A land-based station that sweeps in our direction every so often.
2000	[Qu.] CO 6743, wind NW 3, sea 2, rain, visibility 500 m	I haul off to the north to reload and transmit W/T report.
2112		Outgoing W/T transmission: 1.)[7] *At 1745 in position Qu. [CO] 6776 hit cruiser with two torpedoes, depth 4 m, capsized and left sinking. 'Dido' type probably, but in darkness not sure.[8] Brandi.*
2305	2305 [*sic*]	Dived to reload.
2400	[Qu.] CO 6475	

Brandi
Kptlt and Kmdt.

---

1 Provenance unknown; certainly not *Welshman*.
2 HM fast minelayer *Welshman*.
3 The torpedo report adds the following firing data: target inclination 93.5°, target speed 20 knots, range 1,200 metres. Brandi believed that the middle two torpedoes of the spread had struck the target, though the Board of Enquiry concluded that only one had done so; see below.
4 Equates to a range of 1,320 metres.
5 Brandi's description of a third detonation is corroborated but this did not affect *Welshman*'s boilers.
6 Although this is an accurate description of *Welshman*'s sinking, it did not occur until nearly two hours later.
7 It is not clear why this number has been inserted.
8 Though not dissimilar in their proportions, at 5,600 tons the Dido-class cruisers had more than twice the displacement of the fast minelayer *Welshman*, and at 512 feet were nearly 100 feet longer. What set the Abdiel class apart, however, was their three upright funnels; the Dido class had two raked ones.

The sinking

Capt. Friedberger, on the bridge with his executive officers when the ship was struck at 1845, left this record of his impressions:

> I felt two explosions right aft. I observed flame and sparks on both sides of the stern, but no gear from the ship appeared to be thrown into the air, nor was I disturbed by blast or my stance affected in any way. Both engines stopped and the ship turned to the Northward, losing headway, with a list of five degrees to starboard. Almost immediately I received a report that the starboard shaft would not turn, and the port propeller had probably gone; but boiler rooms were correct and lighting and power in the ship could be continued.

Though not noted by Friedberger, Brandi's assertion of a third detonation is corroborated by a passenger aboard, Capt. G. W. G. Simpson RN, who was walking between Friedberger's day and sleeping cabins when the ship was struck and noted a final explosion five seconds after the second. Initial reports indicated that the main and lower decks were flooded from stern to wardroom, that the wardroom flat bulkhead was in the process of being shored up and

major leaks stopped, and that a store-room fire was being combated with foam. Most significantly in view of subsequent events, any 'slight quantity of water, projected onto the starboard side of the mining deck by the explosion, was being dealt with by submersible pumps'. Half an hour later matters appeared to be under control. Power and lighting remained unaffected, the fire had been put out and 'the situation as regards flooding was very satisfactory; in fact the condition of the ship was excellent, except for her helplessness'. The Chief Engineer, Cdr (E) H. E. C. Hims, continued to supervise the operation of the submersible pumps on the mining deck, fuel oil was transferred from the starboard to the port tanks to offset a slight increase in list to eight degrees, and a party mustered to see *Welshman* taken in tow by the escort destroyer *Tetcott*, expected on the scene at 0030. Gun crews were closed up in case the offending U-boat should return. However, Friedberger's assessment of *Welshman*'s condition was to prove optimistic in the extreme. Deliberations with Capt. Simpson in the charthouse as to the cause of the explosions were interrupted at 2035 when HMS *Welshman* gave an alarming lurch of thirty degrees to starboard. Barely had Capt.

Friedberger reached the bridge and given the order to abandon ship than *Welshman* was on her beam ends. Over the next few minutes she sank stern first, her bows standing up before disappearing at around 2040, two hours after the attack.

The Board of Enquiry found that one of the torpedoes had detonated beneath the stern and the other two nearby or in the ship's wake. Though Brandi's torpedo report does not settle the matter, this would be consistent with *U617*'s torpedoes having been fitted with magnetic pistols set at a depth to sink a cruiser; as Capt. Friedberger, Capt. Simpson and the Board of Enquiry agreed, three contact detonations on *Welshman* would almost certainly have blown off her stern completely. The Board accepted that neither Friedberger nor any of his officers should be held responsible for the loss 'as it is improbable, from the evidence available, that the ship could have been saved'. Nonetheless it expressed concern that Friedberger and Cdr (E) Hims made a 'grave error of judgment in believing their ship to be in a safe condition'. The Board found that there had been a complete failure to appreciate that the detonation had almost certainly left the mining deck open to the sea, and that 'in the absence of any sub-division between the upper and mining decks over a larger part of the ship's length, the mining deck was in effect the ship's upper deck as far as stability was concerned'. Though Hims was confident that steady pumping was gaining on the water on the mining deck, 'he seems to have mistaken a surge of water aft, due to slight motion of the ship, for a definite receding of the water under the suction of the pump'. While this misjudgment had no bearing on the fate of the ship, it did mean that there were far more men below decks than was safe in the circumstances. Though it exonerated the officers of any moral responsibility for the ensuing loss of life given 'their belief that the ship was absolutely safe', the Board expressed its dismay that this misapprehension had prevented boats being put out or orders passed for those not vitally employed elsewhere to remain on deck.

The unanswered question from Capt. Friedberger's perspective was why *U617* had not finished off her crippled victim under the cloak of darkness. Brandi's log entry for 1755 gives two possible answers to this question: first, that he observed *Welshman* capsized and in a sinking condition, and second that the area was being lit up from the coast and *U617*'s safety thus compromised. Nothing exists to shed any light on the second point, *U617*'s position being at least ten miles offshore. On the other hand, *Welshman* had no more than a five-degree list at the time Brandi was recording her as sinking by the stern. However, timing apart, this description – repeated in Brandi's W/T transmission of 2112 and in the torpedo report – is borne out in British records of her demise.

Fate of the crew

Nine men were lost in the initial detonations, namely two officers in their cabins, the depth-charge sentry, the Steering Engine Room watchkeeper and five stewards in their flooded mess. Given the misplaced confidence in *Welshman*'s stability, many were below deck when she gave her dramatic lurch to starboard and consequently failed to make it off the ship as she turned onto her beam ends. Despite orders to set all depth charges to safe a number of men in the water were killed by the detonation of one of these before the ship went down. The survivors gathered on and around half a dozen Carley floats and

Hitler presents Brandi with the certificate of the Knight's Cross with Oak Leaves awarded him in the summer of 1943, though on the basis of an inflated tonnage score. *DUBMA*

floatanets which had been cut from their lashings but no boats were lowered before she sank. Despite it being the southern Mediterranean the waters were seasonally cool and many failed to survive the four or five hours that elapsed between the sinking and the arrival of HM destroyers *Belvoir* and *Tetcott*. Capt. Friedberger also noted that 'a slight sea got up at about 2300 which exhausted many men, who drowned'. Over half the ship's company and passengers perished in the sinking, two ratings and a US naval correspondent being added to the toll in *Belvoir* during the night. However, it has not been possible to establish the exact number of passengers on board, nor how many were lost. The survivors were disembarked at Alexandria where the wounded were transferred to hospital. Thirteen bodies were eventually found washed ashore.

Condolences for *Welshman*'s loss echoed through naval circles and in the Admiralty, with one of the more elegant obituaries written in the margins of the Board's findings by Capt. J. S. Cowie, Deputy Director of the Operations Division (Mining): 'The loss of *Welshman* is a serious blow, and D.D.O.D.(M)'s sole consolation lies in the knowledge that the unspectacular nature of her services has not prevented a proper appreciation of her value.' A memorial erected by the Fast Minelayers Association in Milford Haven, Wales records the service of *Welshman* and her sisters together with that of the earlier *Adventure*.

U617 and Albrecht Brandi

Built by Blohm & Voss at Hamburg and commissioned in April 1942, *U617* made seven frontline patrols under Oblt.z.S. (Kptlt from October 1942) Albrecht Brandi. As mentioned above, *U617* enjoyed some success in the Mediterranean but her claimed tonnage grossly outstripped actual sinkings, and by the time Brandi was awarded the Oak Leaves to his Knight's Cross in April 1943 this exceeded that sunk by a factor of more than five. However, a good proportion of his confirmed sinkings were warships, including HM tug *St Issey* off Benghazi in December 1942 (**G44**), *Welshman* and HM escort destroyer *Puckeridge* in September 1943 (**G59**), days before *U617*'s career ended though not before Brandi had claimed an uncorroborated brace of destroyers. On the 11 September *U617* was damaged by a pair of RAF Wellingtons off Alborán Island and pursued by surface units to the coast of Spanish Morocco where she beached herself near Sîdi Amar on the 12th. *U617* was destroyed by gunfire and her entire crew interned by the Spanish authorities before being repatriated to Germany.

Brandi's return to Germany was somewhat different to that of his crew. Transferred to an officers' internment camp near Cadiz, he succeeded in escaping and made his way home via France with the assistance of a car and bogus papers provided by German consular officials in Cadiz and Madrid. By November 1943 he was back in the Mediterranean and in command of *U380* with which he completed only one patrol. *U380* was first damaged and then sunk in US bombing raids against Toulon on 4 February and 11 March 1944 which cost the lives of two of her crewmen. For the rest of Brandi's career, see USS *Fechteler* (**101**).

Sources

Admiralty, *Loss of HMS* Welshman: *Board of Enquiry and Report of Findings* (TNA, ADM 1/13090)

—, War Diary for February 1943 (TNA, ADM 199/2255)

U617, Torpedo report of 1745 on 1 February 1943 (BfZ, Schussmeldung collection)

U617 file (DUBMA)

Anon., Research notes concerning the loss of HMS *Welshman* (typescript, IWM, Misc. 204 (2968))

Blair, *Hitler's U-Boat War*, II, pp. 208–9

Burton, Tom, *Abdiel-Class Fast Minelayers* [Warships in Profile, no. 38] (Windsor, Berks.: Profile Publications, 1973)

Dodson, Aidan, 'The Fast Minelayers' in *Ships Monthly* 27 (May 1992), pp. 14–17

Fraschka, Günter, *Mit Schwertern und Brillanten: aus dem Leben der siebenundzwanzig Träger der höchsten deutschen Tapferkeitsauszeichnung* (Baden: E. Pabel, 1958)

Hargreaves, Brian B., 'Abdiel Class Fast Minelayers' in *Warships*, Supplement no. 134 (April 1999), pp. 1–15

Kurowski, Franz, *Jäger der sieben Meere: die berühmtesten U-Boot-Kommandanten des II Weltkrieges* (Stuttgart: Motorbuchverlag, 1998)

Roskill, *War at Sea*, II, pp. 427–30

Wright, Richard N. J., 'Abdiel Class Fast Minelayers at War' in *Warship* 18 (1994), pp. 104–12

Career history of HMS *Welshman*: http://www.naval-history.net/xGM-Chrono-07ML-Welshman.htm

82   HrMs (ex MS) *COLOMBIA*

Ktz. J. L. K. Hoeke, KM
Sunk by *U516* (Type IXC), Korvkpt. Gerhard Wiebe, 27 February 1943
Indian Ocean, 30 nm E of Port Alfred, Eastern Cape (South Africa)

The Koninklijke Nederlandsche Stoomboot Maatschappij's liner *Colombia* seen in the 1930s.
Wiebe sank her with a single torpedo on the starboard side just forward of the bridge. *BfZ*

Theatre	Southern Ocean (Map 1)	*Deadweight*	6,648 tons
Coordinates	33° 36′ S, 27° 29′ E	*Gross tons*	10,782
Kriegsmarine code	Quadrat KZ 1792	*Dimensions*	457′ × 61.25′ × 26.5′
U-boat timekeeping differential	–2 hours	*Maximum speed*	12 knots
Fatalities 8	*Survivors* 312+	*Armament*	4 × 3″; 8 × 20 mm AA; 6 × .5″ AA; 4 × .303″ AA

Career

For background on the Royal Netherlands Navy, see HrMs *Isaac Sweers* (74).

Ordered by the Koninklijke Nederlandsche Stoomboot Maatschappij (Royal Netherlands Steamship Co.), the motor liner *Colombia* was laid down at P. Smit Jr of Rotterdam, launched in 1929 and completed in 1930. *Colombia* spent her peacetime career cruising on the company's routes between north-western Europe and the Caribbean, and it was in the West Indies that she was requisitioned into the Royal Netherlands Navy on 8 November 1940. Brought to Britain and earmarked for conversion to a submarine depot ship, the work was carried out by the Caledon Shipbuilding & Engineering Co. of Dundee between March and September 1941, *Colombia* being commissioned into the Dutch submarine service on 20 May that year. On 5 January 1942 she sailed from Dundee to join convoy WS15 bound for the Far East, reaching Colombo on 4 March as Allied resistance was collapsing in the face of the Japanese offensive. Assigned to the British Eastern Fleet, she remained in Ceylon until ordered to Bombay in May upon being relieved by another converted liner, HrMs *Plancius*. In August *Colombia* was transferred to East London in the Cape Province to provide support and maintenance facilities to Dutch submarines on passage to and from the Far East. However, in February 1943 a routine voyage to Simon's Town for what was no doubt an overdue spell in dry dock was destined never to be completed.

Background of the attack

At dawn on 27 February 1943 HrMs *Colombia* sailed from East London bound for dry dock at Simon's Town on the Cape of Good Hope. An acute shortage of escort vessels while no fewer than seven convoys were at sea left her with only HM corvette *Genista* for company, though RAF air cover was to be provided throughout the day as far as Port Elizabeth, where *Colombia* was due to anchor inshore for the night. It was not to be. As midday approached on the 27th – just four hours after clearing the breakwater at East London – *Colombia* and her escort were zigzagging at *Colombia*'s best (current-assisted) speed of 12½ knots some ten miles offshore. This route was the result of a compromise between the British naval authorities at East London, who would have preferred her to be sailing five miles offshore, and Kapitein ter zee John Hoeke of the *Colombia* who wanted to keep at least twenty miles off the coast. Though conditions were later described by Hoeke as 'most favourable for observation, the atmosphere being very clear and the sea calm', neither aircraft, escort nor *Colombia*'s twenty-five lookouts spotted the periscope of Korvettenkapitän Gerhard Wiebe's *U516*, whose second patrol had brought her south to the Cape trade routes where Allied shipping had hitherto plied a prolonged but relatively safe route to the Indian Ocean and the Middle East. Operating as part of the *Seehund* ('seadog') group between Port Elizabeth and East London, *U516* sighted *Colombia* at 1000 Allied time and tracked her for the next hour and a half. The failure of both *Genista* and *Colombia* to pick up hydrophone effect led the Allies to conclude that the attack had been made from long range. Wiebe's spread of three torpedoes was fired from a good 1,500 metres, but it is questionable how favourable the conditions were for hydrophone detection in vessels making twelve knots.

War Diary of *U516*, patrol of 23 December 1942–4 May 1943: PG 30554, NHB, reel 1,115, pp. 646–7

Date, time	Details of position, wind, weather, sea, light, visibility, moonlight, etc.	Incidents
27.ii		
0400	Qu. KZ 1794, wind NW/W 1, sea 1, cloud 1, good visibility, slight sea phosphorescence	
0422	Qu. KZ 1794	We dive for daytime cruising. Alternately at 35 m and periscope depth.
0800	Qu. KZ 1792	To periscope depth for a full sweep of the horizon. A steamer in sight together with a corvette; range 7,000 m, inclination 30°.[1] We assume attack course. Steamer is zigzagging up to 60°, corvette providing protection ahead. Steamer riding high in the water. A 'Blue Star Line' passenger liner. A cruiser bow and stern. Estimated 10,000 tons.[2]
0938	Qu. KZ 1792	Spread of three, range 1,500 m, inclination 60°, angle of dispersion 3°. A hit amidships. Steamer immediately lists heavily.
0940	Qu. KZ 1792	Corvette alters course and closes us at high speed, inclination 0°. We go to 60 m and to leeward of the steamer at ¾ speed.
0944	Qu. KZ 1792	One depth charge.[3]
0946	Qu. KZ 1792	Two further depth charges.[3] We go to silent speed, corvette passes astern.

---

1 HrMs *Colombia* and HMS *Genista*.

2 *Colombia* had in fact been completed for the Koninklijke Nederlandsche Stoomboot Maatschappij though Wiebe's identification is otherwise unusually accurate, *Colombia* being of 10,782 GRT and having the hull form described.

3 Dropped by HMS *Genista*. However, as Lt Cdr R. M. Pattinson's report of the event makes clear, this was purely an attempt to scare off the offending U-boat; no contact had been obtained.

0956	Qu. KZ 1792	Noises of sinking and collapsing bulkheads from the steamer.
1011	Qu. KZ 1792	Corvette approaches at ship's bearing 65° and then moves away again.
1050	Qu. KZ 1794	Noises at 90°, high revolutions.
1105	Qu. KZ 1794	Hydrophone effect at 65°, high revolutions. Enemy has switched on Echolot at 360 impulses per min.[4] Gradually fades astern, impulses continuing all the while.
1108	Qu. KZ 1794	Noises get louder and louder but then quickly fade astern.
1111	Qu. KZ 1794	Lot switched off, enemy bearing 170°. She then shifts round to port as far as 210° before turning about. Corvette must have overrun boat's position just astern. Our depth 110 m.
1119	Qu. KZ 1794	Enemy no longer audible, last bearing at 155°. We withdraw, course 100°.
1200	Qu. KZ 1797	Day's run: 98 nm.

4   Here and in his entry of 1111 Wiebe is using the terms by which the echo-sounding device patented by the Atlas-Werke firm was known, though the subject of these observations is evidently Asdic. The Echolot was used to measure the distance from keel to seabed in unfamiliar waters.

The sinking

Only one of Wiebe's spread of three torpedoes hit *Colombia*, though another was seen to pass three or four yards astern immediately after the detonation. The blow fell on the starboard side just forward of the bridge, destroying the bulkhead separating Nos. 1 and 2 holds and giving little chance of assessing the damage let alone countering it. As Ktz. Hoeke related to the Board of Enquiry a month later, 'The ship just filled up . . . and when no. 2 filled the whole ship would be open to the sea over the tops of the bulkheads which extended only as far as the main deck.' Given the heavy list to starboard, Hoeke ordered both engines stopped and passed the word to abandon ship, sending the Officer of the Watch below to ensure that the engine watch complied with the latter. The order was also given for *Colombia*'s boats to be lowered and it was while this was being carried out that the list stabilised and the ship began to go down by the head until the bridge was virtually awash. Twelve minutes after the attack 'the ship stood up vertically in the water, stern high with rudder and propellers approx. 90 feet out of the water'. A minute later *Colombia* had disappeared. *Genista* spent two hours circling the position of the sinking in an attempt to get an Asdic fix on the perpetrator. A contact was gained at 1311 (1111 German time), but as Wiebe relates in his log, *Genista* passed astern of *U516* without attacking. Meanwhile, the RAF escort, fifteen miles away at the time of the attack, sighted nothing beyond a school of porpoises.

An exhaustive Board of Enquiry accepted that damage control was impracticable in the circumstances and was satisfied that 'no steps were possible to prevent the loss of the ship after the damage sustained'. It also went to great lengths to investigate the compromise route followed by *Colombia* and *Genista* towards Port Elizabeth, eventually concluding that it was justifiable in the circumstances. The Board's findings in this respect were based on Ktz. Hoeke's insistence that the route be at least twenty miles off the coast, and the fact that he had spent fifteen years in submarines. Reviewing the findings prior to submission to the Admiralty, the Commander-in-Chief South Atlantic, Vice-Admiral W. E. C. Tait gave it as his opinion that Hoeke's rejection of the coastal route had been a mistake, noting that ships sailing independently between East London and Port Elizabeth had always been so routed and that 'no such routed ship had yet been attacked, nor has been since'. Be that as it may, *U516*'s log makes it plain that Wiebe had attacked from the *landward* side having clearly been cruising inshore – close enough, indeed, to have witnessed a lights-out exercise in East London the previous night and to have

Wiebe (left) seen celebrating Christmas 1942 in the officers' mess aboard *U516. DUBMA*

calculated her position from Great Fish Point that morning. Hoeke's hunch that any U-boat would be likely to keep close to the shore was therefore more accurate than Tait's *ex post facto* criticism. Incidentally, the Board's line of questioning on the issue evidently exasperated Vice-Admiral Tait's Staff Officer (Operations), Cdr L. P. Skipwith RN. Replying to one of its questions, Skipworth snapped that 'it was obvious that she would not have sailed via the South Pole from East London to Port Elizabeth – therefore she would go coastal'. The Board reserved its strongest language for this officer, whose 'manner… when answering questions was most offensive and discourteous'. Elsewhere in his report Tait acknowledged the disrespect shown by Cdr Skipwith, but added that 'it must be stated in fairness that he reported sick with a high temperature shortly after his examination by the Board. He has not yet returned to duty; I shall deal with him when he does.'

Fate of the crew

Though no member of *Colombia*'s ship's company was observed to have been killed in the detonation, a roll taken after the sinking revealed that eight men were missing from below decks. These were presumed killed in the explosion or flooding that immediately ensued. The rest got away in nine boats without loss, with Ktz. Hoeke, intent on being the last to abandon ship, waiting until the bridge was awash before leaping clear. They were brought aboard *Genista* two hours after the sinking with the exception of a whaler containing fifty-six men who were picked up by an RAF rescue launch. The survivors were back in East London that evening, barely thirteen hours after sailing.

U516 and Gerhard Wiebe

Built by Deutsche Werft at Hamburg and commissioned in March 1942, *U516* served her first two frontline patrols under Korvkpt. Gerhard Wiebe. The first of these was spent in the Atlantic and the Caribbean between August and November 1942 where, twice refuelled, *U516* enjoyed the success expected of a Type-IX U-boat in distant waters, five ships being sunk for a total of nearly 30,000 tons. *U516*'s second patrol yielded *Colombia* and three merchantmen off Southern Africa for a total of over 25,000 tons before she turned for France after severe corrosion of the pressure hull was discovered near the battery compartment. Leaving *U516* on health grounds in June 1943 and promoted Fregattenkapitän in November, Wiebe went on to a series of shore appointments culminating in a senior posting to the naval school at Mürwik in Schleswig-Holstein in late 1944. He was taken prisoner in May 1945 and not released until August 1947.

U516's remaining frontline service brought her back to the South Atlantic and Caribbean under Kptlt Hans-Rutger Tillessen, six merchantmen being sunk over four patrols. The last of these ended in October 1944 with the boat rerouted to Kristiansand in Norway owing to the Allied blockade of the Bay of Biscay. The odd twenty-four-hour voyage between Norwegian and North German ports aside, *U516*'s last wartime sortie come on 5 April 1945 when she put to sea to transport supplies to St-Nazaire, an assignment which found her in the Atlantic at war's end a month later. She surrendered at Loch Eriboll on 14 May and was sunk off Malin Head as part of Operation DEADLIGHT by the Polish destroyer *Piorun* on 2 January 1946.

Sources

Admiralty, *Enemy Submarine Attacks on H.M. Ships, 1943* (TNA, ADM 199/1321)

Bosscher, Ph. M., *De Koninklijke Marine in de Tweede Wereldoorlog* (3 vols, Franeker: T. Wever, 1984–90)

Mark, Chris, *Schepen van de Koninklijke Marine in W.O.II* (Alkmaar: Uitgeverij de Alk BV, 1997)

Turner, L. C. F., H. R. Gordon-Cumming and J. E. Betzler, *War in the Southern Oceans, 1939–1945* (Cape Town: Oxford University Press, 1961)

Webpage devoted to HrMs *Colombia*:
    http://www.dutchsubmarines.com/tenders/tender_colombia.htm

83   HMS *BEVERLEY* (ex USS *BRANCH*)

Lt Cdr R. A. Price, RN†

Sunk by *U188* (Type IXC-40), Kptlt Siegfried Lüdden, 11 April 1943

North Atlantic, 540 nm E of Belle Isle, Newfoundland

USS *Branch* seen during her brief service with the US Navy between 1920 and 1922. Transferred to Britain and renamed HMS *Beverley*, she was sunk by *U188* in the Atlantic more than twenty years later. *BfZ*

Theatre   North Atlantic (Map 1)
Coordinates   52° 19' N, 40° 28' W
Kriegsmarine code   Quadrat AJ 9661
U-boat timekeeping differential   +2 hours
Fatalities   151   *Survivors*   4

Displacement   1,190 tons
Dimensions   314.25' × 31.75' × 9.25'
Maximum speed   35 knots
Armament   1 × 4"; 1 × 3" AA; 2 × 20 mm AA; 3 × 21" tt;
      1 × Hedgehog ATW

Career

For the circumstances under which HMS *Beverley* joined the Royal Navy, see HNorMS *Bath* (**30**). For design notes on the US Clemson-class destroyers of which USS *Branch* was a unit, see HMS *Broadwater* (**36**).

USS *Branch* (DD-197) was laid down at Newport News Shipbuilding Co., Virginia in October 1918, launched in April of the following year and commissioned into the US Navy on 3 April 1920. After a shakedown cruise off Norfolk, Virginia, *Branch* joined Squadron 3, Division 37,

Destroyer Force, Atlantic Fleet with which she served until laid up at Philadelphia in accordance with the terms of the Washington Treaty in June 1922. Here she remained on 'Red Lead Row' until recommissioned in December 1939 and taken in hand for refitting at Philadelphia Navy Yard. Assigned to Destroyer Division 68, in January 1940 *Branch* joined the Neutrality Patrol first in the Florida Strait and then off Puerto Rico following a month undergoing repairs to her propeller shafts at Philadelphia in March. After a spell at Norfolk Navy Yard and tactical exercises off Hampton Roads, *Branch* was earmarked for a series of training cruises for reservists between July and September. On 8 October 1940 *Branch* became one of the fifty US destroyers transferred to British service at Halifax, Nova Scotia, being renamed *Beverley*. After a refit at Devonport and brief service in local waters, December saw *Beverley* assigned to the 6th Escort Group of Western Approaches Command charged with escorting outbound and inbound convoys between British ports and the sea area north of Ireland.

As with many of the 'four-pipers', boiler trouble soon had *Beverley* in dock, the ship spending three months under repair on the Tyne between March and May 1941. In *Beverley*'s case her boilers had a history of problems going back to *Branch*'s full-power trials in December 1920 when two of the units had to be shut down with buckled brickwork. After a brief spell with Iceland Command, a stint on the Britain–Gibraltar run which included taking the abandoned French freighter *Isac* in tow off Gibraltar on 19 July 1941, and a further period in dockyard hands at Belfast, *Beverley* joined the 8th EG in September, this time for service in the North Atlantic. An arduous spell of duty included the escort of five troop convoys over the winter of 1941–2 before she was assigned to the 1st EG in January 1942. In this company she sailed on two Russian convoys, the embattled PQ14 and QP11 in April and May 1942 during the last of which she was in close action with three German destroyers (see HMS *Edinburgh*, **58**). Following three months' refit and repair at Belfast *Beverley* joined the 4th EG in August but suffered heavy damage in a terrible Atlantic storm that December, limping into St John's on the 17th with only five tons of fuel in her bunkers. Her damage made good, *Beverley* returned to the fray in the new year and it was while escorting SC118

to Londonderry that she made her only U-boat kill, sharing in the sinking of *U187* with HMS *Vimy* on 4 February 1943. In March she took part in one of the critical convoy battles of the war, the defence of HX229 and SC122, but though dawn was breaking HMS *Beverley* did not live to savour victory in the Battle of the Atlantic.

Background of the attack

On 1 April 1943 the forty-one merchantmen of slow convoy ON176 were joined off Rathlin Island, Co. Antrim by the 4th Escort Group comprising the destroyers *Highlander* (Senior Officer), *Beverley* and *Vimy* and the corvettes *Abelia*, *Anemone*, *Asphodel*, *Clover* and *Pennywort*. For a week ON176 made its way towards Canada and the US without incident, except that on the evening of the 5th *Vimy* and *Beverley* were obliged to turn for Iceland after heavy seas had prevented them refuelling from the oilers *Luminetta* and *Bente Maersk* which were sailing with the convoy for this purpose. They were back by 8 April but for *Beverley* this was only the first in a series of mishaps which culminated in her loss. The following evening *Beverley* closed HMS *Clover* in dense fog to transfer some urgently needed diphtheria serum and was returning to her station when at 2210 she reported being in collision with the SS *Cairnvalona*. Neither ship was immediately imperiled by the incident, *Beverley* still capable of fifteen knots despite being holed on the starboard side forward. However, her Asdic and hydrophone equipment had been damaged beyond repair and her tactical capability significantly impaired. The timing could not have been worse since ON176 was now beyond the range of air cover and at its most vulnerable to U-boat attack. On 10 April the convoy was finally sighted by Kptlt Otto von Bülow's *U404* (see **71**), part of the nine-strong *Adler* ('eagle') patrol line. Among the first to respond to *U404*'s beacon signal was Kptlt Siegfried Lüdden in *U188*. The excerpt from Lüdden's log which follows offers a highly detailed account of his approach, penetration and attack on the convoy but the uncorroborated nature of his claims and his wayward description of events (including the sinking of *Beverley*) make it among the most suspect in this volume.

War Diary of *U188*, patrol of 4 March–4 May 1943: PG 30175, NHB, reel 1,088, pp. 443–6

Date, time	Details of position, wind, weather, sea, light, visibility, moonlight, etc.	Incidents
11.iv		
0012	[Qu.] AJ 9391	Convoy at bearing 16° true – range 12 nm.
0023		Outgoing short signal transmitted: *Enemy in AJ 9364, course 240°. Speed 8 knots. Lüdden.*
0025		As darkness falls visual contact with convoy is lost in a squall. We press on through the wall of rain.
0055	[Qu.] AJ 9383	As wall of rain suddenly lifts we identify one shadow after another at bearings 20°–45° true. I infer a southerly zigzag.
0117		Outgoing short signal transmitted: *Enemy in sight AJ 9383, enemy altering course, I think to south. Lüdden.*
		I am now directly between the convoy and the moon. I retreat from the path of the moon at utmost speed and position myself on the convoy's starboard bow, inclination 0°–5°.
0123		Starshell on both sides of the boat. Detonations can be heard at the same time. As no starshell is fired astern of us I remain on the surface, withdrawing at utmost speed for some distance.
		The cloud cover is clearing steadily. Moon now only obscured for brief periods. To track over to

Date, time	Details of position, wind, weather, sea, light, visibility, moonlight, etc.	Incidents
		leeward of the moon would take too long so I decide to remain on the starboard bow, bring up other boats and attack when conditions of light are favourable.
0243		Outgoing short signal transmitted: *Enemy in AJ 9386, course south, speed 7 knots. Lüdden.*
		Bright moonlight prevails, lighting up the westerly, northerly and easterly horizons and enabling us to improve our contact position *vis-à-vis* the convoy and establish that convoy course is now 180°, speed 8 knots.
		Convoy is proceeding in broad formation. We can't make out the columns from our advance position. Three destroyers operating ahead of convoy.[1] As we approach later we see two more to starboard and another astern.[2]
0347		Outgoing short signal transmitted: *Convoy AJ 9631, course 180°, speed 8 knots. Lüdden.*
0400	[Qu.] AJ 9629	
0514		Outgoing short signal transmitted: *Convoy AJ 9637, course 180°, speed 8 knots. Lüdden.*
		Prolonged observation of the starboard destroyer ahead of the convoy reveals that she zigzags off to starboard, away from the convoy, at more-or-less regular intervals of 10 minutes.[3]
0520		To Battle Stations – all tubes ready.
0524		I run in – moon has disappeared behind a low-lying bank of cloud. The horizon behind me is dark and hazy. We await the starboard zigzag of our destroyer, initially proceeding at ⅗ speed on a parallel course of 250°–270° then breaking through to the north after destroyer zigzags back again.
		Another destroyer is stationed between the first and second columns, never budging from this position.[4] After a brief evasive manoeuvre we have her astern of us. Nothing to be seen ahead – that's where Rahe got his depth-charge barrage, putting them on their guard.[5] I therefore select several shadows from the last column for my target with an inclination of about 30°.[6]
		I attack: as we turn to run in we see yet another destroyer on exactly the same bearing as the group we have selected.[7] We remain bow on to her and she quickly passes us. A rapid and violent turning manoeuvre and we slip by astern.
		I turn to attack. A glorious spectacle: ahead of us lies a wall of overlapping merchantmen. In the middle a fat tanker, to her right – still visible in her entirety from this inclination – a steamer, overlapping to the left (but subsequently detached) a further steamer. In the rear, lagging behind at a considerable distance, another steamer. Off to the side of our main group we discern further shadows. Our earlier evasive manoeuvre to get round the destroyer means that the inclination of targets as we turn to attack is around 50°, range between 2,500–3,000 m. To exploit this unusually favourable opportunity to the full I close the group at half speed (with a following sea). No reaction on the part of the destroyer.
		Second Watch Officer reports a new destroyer 50° on our port bow: must be the rear sweeper but luckily for us her inclination is broad, bows right, range some 3,000 m.[8] I must continue to close the group as the tanker's range is still 2,000 m. Second Watch Officer keeps rear destroyer under observation, *Brückenmaat* the starboard destroyer.[9]
0549	[Qu.] AJ 9661, wind SSW 2, sea 2, ¼ overcast,	Multiple torpedoes fired from Tubes I–IV. I = right-hand steamer, II and III = tanker, IV = left-hand steamer. <u>General shot coordinates:</u>

---

1   Lüdden is here describing HM corvette *Asphodel* (port bow), HM destroyer *Highlander* (leading the convoy) and HM corvette *Abelia* (starboard bow).

2   *Beverley* abeam of the first row, *Clover* abeam of the last row, *Anemone* astern.

3   Presumably HM corvette *Abelia*.

4   This would equate to *Beverley*'s station. Although Lüdden employs the word *Kolonne* ('column') he seems in fact to be referring to the first and second rows of the convoy.

5   Kptlt Heinz Rahe of *U257*. This sentence provides an example of the *a posteriori* nature of U-boat *Kriegstagebuch* composition since the signal upon which Lüdden's information is based was not sent by Rahe until 0729 – two hours later.

6   As before, though Lüdden uses the word *Kolonne* ('column') he seems actually to be referring to the last row of the convoy.

7   This appears to have been HM corvette *Clover*, stationed on the starboard beam of the last row.

8   HM corvette *Anemone*.

9   Presumably HM corvettes *Anemone* and *Abelia* respectively, though the accuracy of Lüdden's timekeeping is less certain. The *Brückenmaat* ('bridge mate') was the senior rating of the four-strong bridge watch.

good visibility, strong northern lights

Convoy course 180°, speed 8 knots. Individual shot data: I = bearing 85° true, inclination 85°, aim-off 15.5°. II & III, bearing not recorded, inclination updating automatically, range 2,000 m.[10] IV = bearing 80°, inclination 80°, aim-off 15.5°. Running times and true range: I = 118 sec., range 1,820 m, II & III = running time 94 sec., true range 1,450 m, IV = running time 131 sec., range 2,030 m.

We then turn about for a stern attack. After 94 sec. a hit (T3) on the tanker in her stern section.[11] A mushroom-shaped detonation cloud from which a further high white explosion column rises up into the sky. Tanker breaks her back aft and sinks stern first within 45 sec. Second torpedo misses. The tanker filled almost two glass widths even at a range of 1,500 m (as per torpedo run) – an estimated 8,000 GRT. A mast forward and amidships. Behind her single slender funnel she had (for a tanker) a relatively long stern.

A second hit on the merchantman overlapping to the right, running time 118 sec. Another thick, dirty mushroom-shaped detonation cloud and sheet of flame abaft the foremast. Due to our violent manoeuvre to port the steamer was hidden soon after the detonation so her subsequent fate could not be observed. As we withdrew later the flames were no longer to be seen and I consider a rapid sinking likely given the hit forward. She was a medium-sized merchantman, an estimated 5,000 GRT. Not reported sunk in W/T transmission, only hit.

A third hit after 131 sec. on the merchantman overlapping on the left which breaks in half amidships (I assume the second T3). Bow and stern rise up steeply and sink together after another 90 sec. An estimated 5,000 GRT.

0552

A spread of two torpedoes fired from Tubes V and VI at the lone merchantman that is lagging behind, points of aim the fore and mainmasts. Bearing 83° true, inclination 83°, aim-off 15.5°, range 2,000 m. Running time 117 sec. = 1,800 m. Our laborious hauling ahead has paid off. After 117 sec. a hit abreast the bridge followed shortly after by a hit aft. Steamer goes down by the head after the first hit (T3). The second hit causes a fire aft. Steamer initially remains afloat as we withdraw, holed forward and with the blazing stern of the ship rising out of the water.

0559

. . . the blazing stern suddenly rises up further and the merchantman sinks bow first into the depths.[12] Then a detonation-type bang and an eruption of white steam suggesting a boiler explosion.[13] What was particularly striking about this last ship was the relatively even height of her superstructure.

We withdraw diagonally astern at 4/5 speed, attempting to flee the area lit up by starshell as quickly as possible.

0602

As no counter-attack transpires and no destroyers can be seen I alter course parallel with the convoy, reload torpedoes and begin a fresh advance manoeuvre. I could never have dared hope that my first attack on a convoy would run so smoothly with neither starshell nor escort counter-attack.

0645

Starshell observed at bearing 110° true – exactly where the convoy lies.

0651[14]

Outgoing short signal transmitted: *Convoy AJ 9664, course 180°, speed 8 knots. Lüdden.*

---

10 By 'inclination updating automatically' Lüdden is referring to the *Lage laufend* setting (automatic update mode) of the torpedo data computer; see Introduction, pp. xxv–xxvi.

11 This is the attack which, by description at least, most corresponds with the sinking of HMS *Beverley*. The T3 was the latest version of the standard G7e torpedo. No tanker is recorded as having been sunk or struck at this juncture.

12 The ellipsis at the beginning of this sentence reflects the original.

13 This could well correspond with the underwater explosion recorded by survivors and nearby ships after *Beverley* went down.

14 Manuscript addition in pencil.

The sinking

HMS *Beverley* met a very sudden end and it was left to the ranking survivor, Petty Officer C. G. Braillard, to provide the only shipboard testimony of this event in official sources. Braillard, who was on watch when *Beverley* was torpedoed, recalled having checked the watertight doors and bulkheads forward just ten or fifteen minutes before the ship was struck. At a time he later estimated as 0340 (though 0352 and 0358 were given by other Allied sources; the most likely of Lüdden's attacks came at 0549 German time), *Beverley* was 'hit by one torpedo on the port side between the forward and aft boiler rooms'. Evidence provided by at least one other survivor and apparently witnessed in *Abelia* and *Clover* suggested that *Beverley* had been hit by two torpedoes, one forward and a second in the boiler room. Either way, the effect was catastrophic, a complete power failure being followed by a violent lurch to port. Other than Braillard's recollection of *Beverley*'s bows briefly standing up in the water before sinking nothing is known of her end save that less than a minute separated the hit and her disappearance. The last of HMS *Beverley* came in the form of a heavy underwater explosion after she went down.

The detailed claims made in his log ensured that Lüdden's return from patrol would be greeted with fulsome praise by B.d.U. which purred over the 'tactical acumen' and 'attack-mindedness' with which he had seized his 'big chance'. He was eventually credited with the haul of the tanker and three merchantmen described above for a combined total of 23,000 GRT. However, Lüdden's claims do not stand up to corroboration. Allied records demonstrate that *Beverley* was the only vessel in convoy ON176 to be struck at this time, her demise perhaps corresponding with the hit on the 'tanker' described in the entry for 0549. Nor for that matter does Lüdden's detailed description of a manoeuvre to the rear of the convoy explain how he can have hit *Beverley* in her station abeam the leading row of ON176. Given the 'good visibility' recorded in *U188*'s log and subsequently confirmed in the memoirs of one of those on the conning tower, Anton Staller, grave doubts must surround the honesty or eyesight of Lüdden or his bridge watch on the night in question.

Though he failed to elaborate, the Senior Officer of the Escort, Cdr E. C. L. Day of HMS *Highlander*, bitterly regretted that the escort had been penetrated 'owing to a bad appreciation on my part', adding that 'the loss of *Beverley* is deeply felt by us all'. Indeed, *Beverley*'s yeoman service on the convoy routes was sufficient to earn a note of condolence from the Commander-in-Chief of the US Navy, Fleet Admiral Ernest J. King, who wrote to the First Sea Lord, Admiral of the Fleet Sir Dudley Pound, to convey 'our appreciation of the services of HMS *Beverley* and our regret for her loss with so many of her gallant company'.

Fate of the crew

Only seven members of a ship's company of over 150 men were picked up by *Clover* and *Abelia* over the next hour. Two of these were discovered to be dead while a third, ERA B. A. R. Crabbe, died soon after rescue leaving just four survivors to relate the end of their ship. One of these, PO Braillard, attempted to release Carley floats in the seconds available to him, but those on the port side were awash by the time he reached them and the ship went down before he could set the starboard ones adrift. Dragged down with the ship, Braillard surfaced to find '*Beverley*'s bows sticking up out of the water and as if about to come down on him; the bows then went under'. From the twenty or so men in the water near Braillard a group formed around a calcium flare attached to a raft which kept together until being separated by a large portion of wreckage. Others were claimed by a pattern of depth charges dropped by *Clover* among a group of men within ten minutes of the attack. Their screams were heard aboard *Clover* as she did so though the contact in question was more likely *Beverley*'s hull than any U-boat. After this dispiriting episode *Abelia* and *Clover* searched until well after daylight in the hope of rescuing further survivors. They did so in vain.

U188 and Siegfried Lüdden

Built by AG Weser at Bremen and commissioned in August 1942, *U188*'s career comprised three lengthy patrols under a single commander, Oblt.z.S. (Kptlt from 1 April 1943) Siegfried Lüdden. Returning to Lorient after his maiden patrol in May 1943, Lüdden was praised not only for the sinkings claimed in the extract above but also for his coolness in getting *U188* back at all, his command having been subjected to air attack in the Bay of Biscay on the 2nd which left Lüdden and one of his men badly injured. In June *U188* sailed for the Indian Ocean as part of the nine-strong *Monsun* group, sinking the US steamer *Cornelia P. Spencer* off Somaliland on 21 September and

Lüdden seen aboard *U188* some time between March 1943 and June 1944, the period during which he sank *Beverley* in the North Atlantic. *DUBMA*

damaging the tanker MS *Britannia* in the Gulf of Oman on 5 October. *U188* reached Penang in late October 1943, remaining there until sailing for France on 8 January 1944 loaded with raw materials vital to the German war effort including tin, tungsten, rubber and quinine. The journey home took *U188* first to the Arabian Sea where she sank six ships in a fortnight for a total of over 35,000 tons and then round the Cape having refuelled from the supply ship *Brake* on 11 March. Lüdden was awarded the Knight's Cross while still at sea.

Triumphant though it was, *U188*'s arrival in Bordeaux on 19 June 1944 coincided with the collapse of German arms in western France and the Kriegsmarine's inability to ready her for sea in time required her to be scuttled there on 25 August. She was raised in 1947 and subsequently scrapped. Lüdden, meanwhile, had shared the same fate as *U565*'s Wilhelm Franken (see **79**), succumbing in a fire on the accommodation ship *Daressalam* at Kiel on 13 January 1945. He was posthumously promoted Korvettenkapitän.

Sources

Admiralty, *Enemy Attacks on H.M. Ships, 1943* (TNA, ADM 199/956)

—, *Convoy ON176* (TNA, ADM 237/98)

—, *Loss of HMS* Beverley *on Convoy Duty: Letter of Appreciation and Condolence from C-in-C, US Fleet and Chief of Naval Operations* (TNA, ADM 1/13098)

Blair, *Hitler's U-Boat War*, II, pp. 279–81

Blewett, Geoffrey, *HMS* Beverley: *A Town Afloat and the Town Ashore, 1940–1943* (Beverley, E. Yorks.: Allan Twiddle, 1998)

DANFS, I, pp. 150–1 (USS *Branch*); also on: http://www.history.navy.mil/danfs/b9/branch-i.htm

Hague, Arnold, *Destroyers for Great Britain: A History of 50 Town Class Ships Transferred from the United States to Great Britain in 1940* (London: Greenhill Books, 1990)

Willmann, Klaus, *Das Boot U188: Zeitzeugenbericht aus dem Zweiten Weltkrieg* (Rosenheim: Rosenheimer, 2007)

Career history of HMS *Beverley*:
    http://www.naval-history.net/xGM-Chrono-11US-Beverley.htm

84 HMS/m *P615* (ex TCG *ULUÇALIREIS*)

Lt C. W. St C. Lambert, DSC* RN†
Sunk by *U123* (Type IXB), Oblt.z.S. Horst von Schroeter, 18 April 1943
Central Atlantic, 145 nm WNW of Monrovia (Liberia)

P615 seen during her year of life between April 1942 and April 1943. She met a swift end to a single torpedo from *U123*. IWM

Theatre	Central Atlantic (Map 1)	*Displacement*	624 tons surfaced 861 tons submerged
Coordinates	06° 49' N, 13° 09' W	*Dimensions*	201.5' × 22.25' × 10.5'
Kriegsmarine code	Quadrat ET 6537	*Maximum speed*	13.75 knots surfaced 8.5 knots submerged
U-boat timekeeping differential	+2 hours	*Armament*	5 × 21" tt (9 torpedoes carried); 1 × 3" AA;
Fatalities	44 *Survivors* none		1 × 20 mm AA; 1 × .303" AA

Career

With few shipbuilding facilities of its own, the Turkish Republic had, like her Ottoman predecessor, to turn to the Western powers to equip her navy, a circumstance which left it prey to the vagaries of international politics. The outbreak of the First World War had resulted in Britain confiscating two battleships then completing for the Turkish navy, an experience that was to be repeated on the commencement of the Second though admittedly on a much smaller scale. In Germany the minelaying submarine *Batiray* was taken over by the Kriegsmarine and commissioned as *UA*, subsequently accounting for the armed merchant cruiser *Andania* in June 1940 (**10**). In Britain, meanwhile, an order placed in March 1939 with Vickers-Armstrongs of Barrow-in-Furness for four scaled-down versions of the Royal Navy's 'S'-class boats was only partially fulfilled. On the outbreak of war the British government exercised its option to purchase two of the four boats, the other pair being completed for the Turks in May 1942. Named for the great Ottoman commander of the sixteenth century, *Uluçalireis* was laid down at Barrow on 30 October 1939, launched as *P615* in November of the following year and completed on 3 April 1942. *P615* and her sister *P614* (ex *Burakreis*, completed in March 1942) spent ten weeks working up in the Clyde during which time they co-starred with John Mills in the feature film *We Dive at Dawn* (1943). Assigned to the 3rd Submarine Flotilla and earmarked for escort duty, on 15 June 1942 *P615* sailed for Iceland, the starting point of the Russian convoys. After prolonged anti-submarine exercises off Reykjavik, on 27 June *P615* and *P614* joined the ill-fated PQ17 as ocean escorts, finding themselves reduced to an ineffectual covering patrol after the convoy had been ordered to scatter on 4 July. Early September again found *P615* serving as ocean escort, this time for PQ18 and the overlapping QP14 which were badly mauled by German naval and air attack (see HMSs *Leda* and *Somali*, **69** and **70**). By the end of 1942 *P615* and *P614* were in the middle of several months of anti-submarine training with surface escorts, first at Scapa Flow and then off West Africa in preparation for service against U-boats off the Cape. Though *P614* eventually joined the Turkish navy under her original name in 1946, her sister was destined never to return to European waters.

Background of the attack

On 17 April 1943 HMS/m *P615* sailed from Freetown, Sierra Leone to take up a patrol position off the Cape of Good Hope. Vice-Admiral H. B. Rawlings, then commanding the West Africa Station, had planned the first leg of *P615*'s journey to take her to Takoradi on the Gold Coast with the motor minesweeper *MMS 107* as escort. However, these two were barely twelve hours into their passage when they were sighted in the early hours of the 18th by Oblt.z.S. Horst von Schroeter's *U123* which spent the rest of the morning in pursuit. His initial target was not *P615* but *MMS 107*, against which he had already made one attack when his second salvo was spotted by the Officer of the Watch passing under her from port to starboard at 0450 British time. This was immediately reported to Lt Lambert in *P615* whose garbled reply indicated his suspicion that this was no more than a porpoise, though

he offered to send an enemy report if *MMS 107* was convinced that it had been a torpedo. *P615* then took loose station on the starboard quarter of *MMS 107* (which had no anti-submarine capability) and reportedly ceased zigzagging, no doubt intending to employ her Asdic equipment. Whatever the case, *P615* now became *U123*'s target, von Schroeter's fourth attack of the morning meeting with success at 1000 (1200 German time).

War Diary of *U123*, patrol of 13 March–8 June 1943: PG 30113, NHB, reel 1,081, pp. 828–9

Date, time	Details of position, wind, weather, sea, light, visibility, moonlight, etc.	Incidents
18.iv	**West of Liberia**	
0000	[Qu.] ET 6128, wind WSW 1, sea 0, 1/10 overcast, visibility 4 nm, bright moon	
0344	[Qu.] ET 6129	Two shadows appear at a bearing 340° true but then disappear in a squall.
0417	[Qu.] ET 6153	Contact re-established, we run in to attack. It is completely overcast which makes for a perfect attacking opportunity as we simply can't be made out in the gloom. The first vessel looks like a steamer. We later discern that she is a hybrid; somewhere between tug, gunboat and fishing trawler, and flying the English war ensign. Size roughly 800 tons.[1] The second shadow is still minute and impossible to make out clearly.[2] At first we considered the first shadow to be a small steamer of about 3,000 tons and decided to target this.
0534	[Qu.] ET 6167	Spread of two torpedoes fired, enemy speed 10 knots, inclination 56°, bows right, range 3,000 m, depth 3 m. We fire quickly and immediately alter to parallel course as second shadow is approaching rapidly from astern. Identified tentatively as a submarine. No hits. Again we manoeuvre ahead. The shadows are exchanging morse signals.
0647	[Qu.] ET 6193	Another spread of two fired. Enemy speed 11 knots, inclination 83°, bows left, range 1,500 m, depth 2 m. This time there can be no doubt about the coordinates and the range is rather closer. A very dark night, moon totally obscured by cloud. And I don't see how the eels can have underrun their target.[3] But again no hits. The thought now strikes us that the vessel may be shorter than 100 m (the length setting entered), and that the eels may have passed either end of the ship.[4]
0800	[Qu.] ET 6275	We withdraw as dawn breaks, reload torpedoes and then haul ahead again.
1101	[Qu.] ET 6534	While we are hauling ahead a cloud of smoke appears in sight at a bearing 120° true. As the masts are emerging on the horizon we dive prior to attacking.
1114	[Qu.] ET 6534	Our two targets are proceeding at an inclination of 30°. We run in to attack. Through the periscope I can now clearly make out a submarine behind the steamer. A gun on the conning tower, its plating projecting forward onto the casing, no striking periscope standard. According to Weyer she is of the Taku class.[5] It looks like there are three figures written on the conning tower, 966 as far as I can make out.[6] She is zigzagging around the warship; when first sighted submarine is stationed on her starboard quarter, then shifts to the port bow, only to return to an astern position later.[7]
1153	[Qu.] ET 6537	Tube III (with Type-II pistols) fired at warship. Enemy speed 10.5 knots, inclination 103°, bows left,

1 This was the motor minesweeper *MMS 107* of 225 tons, though as von Schroeter points out two sentences down his figure of 800 tons was not arrived at until later that day. Otherwise his description is not inaccurate.

2 HM submarine *P615*.

3 'Eels' (German = *Aale*) was U-boat slang for torpedoes.

4 One torpedo of this spread was observed to pass under *MMS 107*. Even so, von Schroeter is correct in suspecting that he had overestimated her length; *MMS 107* was only 119 feet (36 metres) long.

5 In his report to B.d.U. von Schroeter suggested that *P615* was a 'Triton-class' submarine, *Triton* being, like *Taku*, a member of the first group of the 'T'-class boats. This is understandable given that, though the design of *P615* and her sisters was based on that of the 'S' class, they shared with the 'T'-class boats the feature of having their forward mounting faired into the conning tower.

6 Von Schroeter's misreading of '966' for 'P615' can readily be explained by the acute angle of observation (30 degrees).

7 This description of *P615* zigzagging is contradicted in *MMS 107*'s report which records her having simply taken station on the latter's starboard quarter.

1154	[Qu.] ET 6537	range 1,500 m, depth 6 m.[8]
		Spread of two fired at submarine. Enemy speed 10.5 knots, inclination 90°, bows left, range 2,000 m, depth 3 m. Just as we fire the submarine looks as if she is turning to starboard to track back behind the warship.
		After firing I shift periscope back to the warship, assuming that hits will be registered on her first. But when the hit comes there is nothing to be seen there. Over towards the submarine a medium-sized explosion column rises up and great fragments fly through the air. No sign of the submarine thereafter; she must have gone straight to the bottom.
1200	[Qu.] ET 6537	Day's run: surfaced = 140.22 nm, submerged = 3.97 nm.
	Lat.: 06° 42.5' N	The tug is steaming gently on, appearing to pay no attention to the explosion. She herself is leading a
	Long.: 12° 56' W[9]	charmed life (though depth 6 m was probably overdoing it) and has cost us five torpedoes in all.
		A cloud of smoke made out in the periscope; we observe it for a while.[10] Off to the east, heading northwest. We opt for a converging course of 40°.

8   A curious depth setting for such a small target, even one still presumed to be of 3,000 GRT. Predictably enough the salvo underran its target, von Schroeter acknowledging his miscalculation in the entry for 1200.

9   These coordinates differ slightly from those given by *MMS 107* (see head of entry), though such discrepancies were to be expected from smaller vessels on the high seas.

10   SS *Empire Bruce* (7,459 GRT), eventually sunk by *U123* at 1419 log time.

The sinking and fate of the crew

P615 was in visual contact with *MMS 107* prior to the detonation and the signal which she began transmitting at around 0950 either to *MMS 107* or SS *Empire Bruce* (recently appeared fine on the port bow) was the last that was heard from her. The hit was observed from *MMS 107*'s bridge, witnesses recording that *P615* 'blew up with a violent explosion and sank in five seconds' at almost exactly 1000 British time. According to the official report, 'the Commanding Officer of *MMS 107* did not see the explosion as he was winding the deck watch at the time, but observations suggest that *P615* was struck by one torpedo under the conning tower, starboard side'. However, at no stage did the minesweeper see any torpedo tracks, and *U123*'s log ('bows left') makes it clear that the hit was in fact on the same port side from which von Schroeter attacked.

The observations made from *MMS 107* largely bear out those recorded in von Schroeter's log: *U123*'s torpedo destroyed *P615* instantaneously and no trace of her company was ever found. In his own report on the sinking, Vice-Admiral Rawlings noted that the area in question had been searched by an RAF Catalina the previous day with 'negative results' and that the 'general trend of U-boat dispositions from the tracking plot suggested that the area was clear'. Of greater concern to the Flag Officer Submarines, Rear-Admiral C. B. Barry, was the assertion by *MMS 107* (though contradicted by *U123*'s entry of 1154) that *P615* had ceased zigzagging shortly before being attacked: 'This is in direct contravention to normal submarine practice and it is considered that probably it contributed in no small degree to her loss.' A paragraph was added to C.A.F.O. (Confidential Admiralty Fleet Order) 1064/42 to the effect that submarine Asdic was 'not designed for high performance on the surface' and that 'no great reliance should be placed on it as a defence against U-boat attack'.

U123 and Horst von Schroeter

For details of *U123*'s career up to May 1942, see USS *Atik* (**57**).

Oblt.z.S. Horst von Schroeter assumed command of *U123* in June 1942 having been successively her Second and then First Watch

Von Schroeter seen following the award of the Knight's Cross in June 1944.
DUBMA

Officer under Karl-Heinz Moehle and Reinhard Hardegen since April 1941. Of the five patrols under his command the most successful was that in which *P615* was sunk, five merchantmen also being claimed in the waters off Liberia and Sierra Leone. Though decommissioned in June 1944 and relegated to duties as a generator boat, *U123*'s aggregate of over 225,000 tons of Allied shipping places her among the most successful U-boats of the Second World War. At war's end she was transferred to France where she was refitted and commissioned as the *Blaison*. She was eventually expended as a target in the Gulf of St Tropez in September 1959.

Oblt.z.S. von Schroeter was one of the few naval officers of his rank to be awarded the Knight's Cross (June 1944). Promoted Kapitänleutnant, he commissioned the Type-XXI *U2506* in August 1944 though no frontline patrol took place. In the last days of the war he sailed her from Hamburg to Bergen where she surrendered to the British on 9 May 1945. Released from captivity in June 1947, von Schroeter joined the Bundesmarine in 1956, enjoying a successful second naval career which saw him appointed Commander of NATO Naval Forces in the Baltic Sea Approaches, the most senior post attained by an officer of the former *U-Boot-Waffe*. He retired a Vizeadmiral in 1979 and died in Bonn in July 2006.

Sources

Admiralty, *Submarine Patrols: Summaries, Losses, Dispositions etc.* (TNA, ADM 199/1340)
—, *Attacks on Allied Submarines and British Submarine Losses in World War II* (TNA, ADM 199/1925)
HMS/m *P615* file (RNSM)
NHB, typescript reply by M. R. Wilson to enquiry from F. Wright Jr regarding submarines ordered from British yards by the Turkish government, dated 12 August 1981 (NHB, S.10006)
U123 file (DUBMA)

Anon., 'Ex-Turkish Submarines in the Royal Navy' in *Warships*, Supplement no. 81 (Summer 1985), p. 24

Bendert, Harald, *U-Boote im Duell* (Hamburg: Mittler, 1996)
Evans, A. S., *Beneath the Waves: A History of H.M. Submarine Losses, 1904–1971* (London: William Kimber, 1986)
Hezlet, Vice-Admiral Sir Arthur, *The History of British and Allied Submarine Operations During World War II* (2 vols, Gosport: Royal Navy Submarine Museum, 2002; published as *British and Allied Submarine Operations in World War II* on CD-ROM, 2003)
Jones, Geoffrey, *Submarines Versus U-Boats* (London: William Kimber, 1986)
Poolman, Kenneth, *Allied Submarines of World War Two* (London: Arms and Armour Press, 1990)
Turner, L. C. F., H. R. Gordon-Cumming and J. E. Betzler, *War in the Southern Oceans, 1939–45* (Cape Town: Oxford University Press, 1961)

85   USS *PLYMOUTH* (ex MY *ALVA*)

Lt Ormsby M. Mitchel, Jr, USNR
Sunk by *U566* (Type VIIC), Kptlt Hans Hornkohl, 5 August 1943, North Atlantic
80 nm ENE of Cape Henry, Virginia (USA)

Plymouth under way in August 1942 following her conversion to patrol gunboat. Hornkohl's attack set the bridge structure ablaze and sank her in three minutes. *BfZ*

Theatre	North Atlantic (Map 1)	*Deadweight*	1,500 tons
Coordinates	37° 22' N, 74° 25' W	*Gross tons*	2,265
Kriegsmarine code	Qu. CA 8152	*Dimensions*	264.5' × 46.25' × 19'
U-boat timekeeping differential	+6 hours	*Maximum speed*	15 knots
Fatalities	95 *Survivors* 84	*Armament*	1 × 4"; 4 × 3" AA

Career

The USS *Plymouth* originated in circumstances rather different from those in which she was sunk. She was laid down at the Krupp Germaniawerft yard at Kiel as a luxury yacht for William K. Vanderbilt II of New York and launched in 1931 as the *Alva* in honour of Vanderbilt's mother, the tireless supporter of the American woman's suffrage movement. Although designed for pleasure, *Alva* was nonetheless a stoutly built ship with powerful diesel engines and an

endurance of 15,000 miles. The quality of her construction and power plant were soon put to the test, Vanderbilt taking her round the world without mishap and recording the experience in a privately printed volume (see below). With war clouds gathering, *Alva* was presented to the US Navy by her owner on 4 November 1941 and after brief spells at Jacksonville, Florida and Washington Navy Yard arrived at Norfolk Navy Yard on 22 January 1942 for conversion to a patrol gunboat. Renamed *Plymouth* and assigned the hull number PG-57, on 20 April she was placed in full commission and assigned to escort duty with the Inshore Patrol Squadron, 5th Naval District based at Norfolk from where she joined her first convoy to Key West, Florida on 8 May. *Plymouth* was to spend the rest of her career on the New York–Norfolk–Key West run with the exception of a stint on the New York–Guantanamo Bay convoy route between August and October 1942. She was converted to a motor torpedo boat tender in 1943.

Background of the attack

On the morning of 4 August 1943 convoy NK557 sailed from New York bound for Key West comprising six merchantmen together with *FT.22*, a small coastal transport of the Royal Navy on passage to the West Indies. Its escort, Task Unit 2.9.10, consisted of three ex-Coast Guard cutters redesignated as submarine chasers in US Navy service – *Pandora* (Senior Officer), *Calypso* and *Nemesis* – along with the MTB tender USS *Plymouth*. The afternoon of the 5th found the escorts zigzagging irregularly around the convoy base course of 205 degrees at a speed of twelve knots, some eighty miles east of Cape Henry at the mouth of the Chesapeake Bay. The escort was alive to the possibility of submarine attack as a U-boat had been sighted and attacked by aerial reconnaissance some 150 miles east of this position three days before. At 1540 convoy time a sonar contact was obtained by *Plymouth* 1,200 yards on the port beam. Although her commanding officer, Lt Ormsby M. Mitchel USNR, was sceptical about it being a submarine he ordered *Plymouth* hard aport to bring the target ahead. However, the contact was more real than Mitchel could possibly have imagined for no sooner had *Plymouth* begun this manoeuvre than she was hit by a torpedo from Kptlt Hans Hornkohl's *U566* – the same sighted on the 2nd – fresh from a minelaying mission in the approaches to the Chesapeake Bay.

War Diary of *U566*, patrol of 5 July–1 September 1943: PG 30599, NHB, reel 1,122, p. 399

Date, time	Details of position, wind, weather, sea, light, visibility, moonlight, etc.	Incidents
5.viii		
1955		Full periscope sweep.
2118		Full periscope sweep.[1]
2127	[Qu.] CA 8152	Destroyer in sight at bearing 26° true, range 2 nm. Another appears at 350°, range 3–4 nm.[2] To Battle Stations.
2137		Spread of two torpedoes fired from Tubes I and III, both Etos with Pi-2 pistols, at Somers-class destroyer, 1,850 tons.[3]
2138		A first hit after running time of 50 sec. I immediately dive to 140 m, as the other destroyer is very close. Depth 4 m, enemy speed 12 knots, inclination 70°, range 800 m.
2139		A second hit after running time of 120 sec. This torpedo did not leave the tube in the usual manner but had to be expelled after a delay of some 30–50 sec. with additional mine expulsion procedure. The torpedo began running in the tube and therefore must already have edged forward somewhat. However, due to possible damage caused to either the bow cap or the tube itself by our minelaying, it appears to have then reverted to its original position.
		This second hit cannot be easily explained.[4] It must have been purely fortuitous. I don't think it was a case of the torpedo detonating prematurely as the sounds accompanying the explosion were exactly the same as for the first hit. Immediately after the second hit we hear dramatic sinking noises very close by, making the destroyer's sinking a certainty.[5] We retire at a depth of 140 m, course 90°.
2235		Five depth charges dropped far astern. So only now are the Americans doing anything about it!
2325		Asdic noises.
2336		*Bold* released.[6]

1 *U566*'s war diary has the unusual complement of a memoir by an engineering rating, Werner Neis (see below), who recalled Hornkohl's extensive use of the periscope not only as a precaution against air attack but because the powerful *Gruppenhorchgerät* (GHG – 'group listening apparatus') hydrophone was out of action.

2 Task Unit 2.9.10 was disposed as follows: *Pandora* on the convoy's port beam, *Plymouth* on the port bow, *Calypso* on the starboard bow, *Nemesis* on the starboard beam. Since Hornkohl encountered the convoy approaching from the north the implication from his subsequent attack on *Plymouth* is that he sighted first that ship and then *Calypso*.

3 Neither in size nor profile is it possible to find any similarity between *Plymouth* and the Somers-class destroyers, which though longer by nearly 120 feet had a much lower freeboard and less prominent stack. 'Eto' is Kriegsmarine shorthand for the electric G7e torpedo. The Pi-2 pistol was the Kriegsmarine's standard torpedo detonator, introduced in December 1942 in response to problems that had plagued its predecessor, the Pi-1.

4 Allied sources offer nothing to corroborate Hornkohl's record of a second hit two minutes after the first.

5 *Plymouth* sank within three minutes of first being struck.

6 *Bold* (usually known as *Bolde*) was a calcium-zinc discharge that by generating large masses of bubbles replicated the echo produced by a sonar submarine contact. This ruse was also known as the *Pillenwerfer* ('pill-thrower') after the ejector fitted for this purpose in the stern of the U-boat.

Date, time	Details of position, wind, weather, sea, light, visibility, moonlight, etc.	Incidents
6.viii		
0000	[Qu.] CA 8153	I resolve to retire from this area as my loaded Etos have been used up and all the evidence suggests that there is no night-time traffic here. As I have only 52 cbm of fuel left and refuelling is not something I can count on, I decide to head back to base.[7] Torpedo situation: two bow Atos, one stern Ato, one reserve stern Eto.[8]
0110		Hydrophone effect at 70° and 130°.

---

7   The base in question was Brest.
8   'Eto' and 'Ato' were Kriegsmarine shorthand for the electric G7e torpedo and the compressed-air G7a torpedo respectively.

The sinking

There was a significant divergence of opinion on the American side as to whether *Plymouth* was hit by one or two torpedoes, and on which side these had struck. Hornkohl's log settles neither point. As regards the number of detonations, the German data indicates two hits approximately two minutes apart yet those *Plymouth* survivors who testified to two explosions spoke of between one and six seconds between them. As for the side attacked, the log contains neither a diagram nor the 'bows left'/'bows right' aiming data that would resolve the matter. In line with the sonar bearing obtained for the U-boat and a majority (though not all) of survivor testimony, the Board concluded that *Plymouth* had been hit on her port side, which would not be inconsistent with *U566*'s relative position. By contrast, all witness testimony from *Calypso*, *Pandora* and *FT.22* placed the detonations on *Plymouth*'s starboard side, though the motion of the ship on being struck suggests that the Board reached the correct conclusion.

Either way, Hornkohl's attack had a shattering effect on *Plymouth* which lurched to starboard under the force of the explosion before taking on a heavy list to port. The first recorded hit came abreast the pump room between the engine room and the magazines and caused an immediate failure of electric power, rupturing the forward engine room bulkhead and stopping the port screw, with which *Plymouth* began circling slowly. Within seconds a fire had broken out on the boat deck, 'presumably caused by the ignition of the diesel oil in the port D tank', though survivor testimony does not agree on the seat of the blaze, which was variously described as being 'all over the bridge', 'along the entire port side of the vessel forward of amidships', 'in the amidships area of the ship from the engine room level to the bridge' and 'in the engine room'. In any event, the bridge was soon engulfed and before long *Plymouth*'s topsides were well alight and a plume of smoke was towering above the ship. With the fire raging unchecked and the ship sinking by the head, damage control efforts were limited to passing orders for engines to be stopped and depth charges set to safe. At around 1545 convoy time, within three minutes of being struck, the ship was engulfed not by fire but by water as she began her descent to the bottom of the Atlantic.

Lt Mitchel's injuries prevented him filing his own report to the Board of Investigation (which opened the day after the sinking) and it fell to *Plymouth*'s executive officer, Lt R. K. Wing USNR, to comment on the behaviour of her crew in the aftermath of the torpedoing. Based on his report and other witness testimony, the Board absolved the crew of any blame in the sinking and concluded that the conduct of both officers and men had been 'fully in keeping with the highest traditions of the Naval Service'.

Fate of the crew

It is not known how many succumbed in the initial detonations but there can be little doubt that a majority of *Plymouth*'s casualties were sustained in the inferno that followed. Very few survived from the fore part of the ship and only along stretches of the starboard waist and on the fantail was there any shelter from the blaze, many crewmen having to pass through walls of flame to gain sanctuary. A number of men caught fire and there was little their shipmates could do to douse the flames with the available facilities. The composure shown by the victims left a lasting impression on Lt Francis F. Taylor:

> The injured men were crying in agony. You could tell them where to go or stand still and they would do it and acknowledge it. In fact one man who died on the way in said 'Mr. Taylor, would you please put these flames out,' which I was already helping to do with the aid of some other men.

Taylor also recalled the sacrifice of Ensign R. Keltch, 'fully dressed and unhurt', who after helping to put out the flames of the men on fire announced that he was 'going forward to see if I can get some more fellows out'. Neither he nor hydrophone operator Sonarman 3/c Franklin Alexander McGinty were ever seen again, the latter perishing in an attempt to rescue a burning man trapped in the magazine area.

Within two minutes of the initial detonation *Plymouth* had taken on a pronounced list and was settling by the head. As it became clear that she was foundering both the burnt and unburnt began to leap overboard and make their way to three rafts and the remains of a ship's boat. Two rubber life rafts and a number of lifejackets were dropped by a circling Mariner patrol bomber of the US Navy. From 1630 onwards sixty-two survivors were rescued by *Calypso* and twenty-six by *FT.22*, an exercise complicated not only by oil, wind and heavy seas but by sharks which *Calypso* kept at bay with her 3-inch deck gun. Many were partially or completely naked by the time they were hauled aboard the rescuing ships, while for those who had drifted downwind it required the launching of one of *Calypso*'s boats for them to stand any chance of being picked up. Shortly before 1800 both vessels turned for Norfolk which they reached through fog and minefields at 0715 and 0830 respectively the following day. Medical personnel did their best for the injured but four men died en route, three in *Calypso* and one in *FT.22*, 'all from multiple burns and shock'. Despite refusing a place on a raft on the grounds that 'others were more injured than himself', Lt Mitchel was among the more badly wounded survivors, having been thrown against a bulkhead in the blast and suffered injuries to his left leg which required amputation above the knee. The last to leave the ship (indeed he went down with her before being shot to the surface thanks to his lifejacket), he was awarded the Navy Cross for extraordinary heroism, as were Keltch and McGinty posthumously.

U566 and Hans Hornkohl

Built by Blohm & Voss at Hamburg and commissioned in April 1941, *U566* spent her first year under Kptlt Dietrich Borchert with four patrols in the Northern Theatre and the Atlantic resulting in four sinkings. Another two patrols under Oblt.z.S. Gerhard Remus in the second half of 1942 yielded a merchantman in each with two more hit, but the first was curtailed by ramming and the second carried out under the shadow of Allied air attack, *U566* being damaged by an RAF Hudson on 17 December. Once repairs were completed at Brest in January 1943 command devolved upon Oblt.z.S. (Kptlt from April 1943) Hans Hornkohl whose four patrols that year were all punctuated by encounters with Allied aircraft. On the third of these she gained her last pennant, that of USS *Plymouth*, while two Lockheed Ventura bombers of the US Navy were accounted for forty-eight hours later and others beaten off. However, *U566* had by now expended her nine lives against attacking aircraft and on 24 October, six days into her fourth patrol under Hornkohl, she was sighted by an RAF Wellington off Porto. By the time the Wellington turned for home, damaged by flak and low on fuel, her six bombs had inflicted sufficient damage for Hornkohl to give the order for *U566* to be scuttled. Taking to dinghies, the crew was picked up by a Spanish trawler and landed at Vigo from where they were ushered back to France. Hornkohl made an uneventful patrol in command of *U1007* before being assigned successively to *U3152*, *U2502* and *U3041* in the last few months of the war. None of the latter ever became fully operational.

Sources

US Navy, War Diary of the Eastern Sea Frontier, entry for 5 August 1943 (NA, RG 38, Records of the Chief of Naval Operations, World War II War Diaries, Entry A1 353)

—, 10th Fleet Convoy and Routing Files, Form 'D' for convoy NK-557, August 1943 (NA, RG 38, Records of the Convoy and Routing Division, Entry A1 348, Convoy NK-557)

Navy Department, Office of the Judge Advocate General, *Board of Investigation into the Loss of USS* Plymouth *at Sea* (JAG, A17-25/PG57)

Hornkohl seen on *U566*'s conning tower some time between February and August 1943. *DUBMA*

—, Office of the Chief of Naval Operations, Division of Naval History, *History of USS* Plymouth *(PG 57)* (NHC, Box 627)

Neis, Werner, *Bootsgeschichte von* U566 (1980) (typescript, DUBMA, *U566* file)

Anon., '*U566*'s Successful Fight Against Allied Aircraft' in *The U-Boat Archive* no. 1 (October 1998); reprinted in Jak P. Mallmann Showell, ed., *The U-Boat Archive: Early Journals Reprinted (1998–2000)* [U-Boat Archive Series, vol. 6] (Milton Keynes, Bucks.: Military Press, 2004), pp. 18–12

Chewning, Alpheus J., *The Approaching Storm: U-Boats off the Virginia Coast During World War II* (Lively, Va.: Brandylane Publishers, 1994)

DANFS, V, p. 332; also on: http://www.history.navy.mil/danfs/p8/plymouth-iv.htm ; and: http://www.ibiblio.org/hyperwar/USN/ships/dafs/PG/pg57.html

Morison, *United States Naval Operations*, X, pp. 184–5

Sables, Robert P., 'The Armed Yachts of World War II' in *Sea Classics* 34 (December 2000), pp. 34–9 and 60

Vanderbilt, William K., *West Made East with the Loss of a Day* (privately, 1933)

Memoirs of Phillip B. Hatcher (survivor): http://phatcher1.blogspot.com/

86   HMCS *ST CROIX* (ex USS *McCOOK*)

Lt Cdr A. H. Dobson, DSC RCNR†
Sunk by *U305* (Type VIIC), Kptlt Rudolf Bahr, 20 September 1943
North Atlantic, 440 nm ESE of Uummannarsuaq, Greenland

St Croix seen shortly after being transferred from the US Navy in September 1940. She was lost three years later to a new weapon, the *Zaunkönig* acoustic homing torpedo; a second *Zaunkönig* against HMS *Itchen* three days later left just one survivor from her ship's company. *BfZ*

Theatre North Atlantic (Map 1)		*Displacement* 1,190 tons	
Coordinates 57° 20' N, 30° 35' W		*Dimensions* 314.25' × 31.75' × 9.25'	
Kriegsmarine code Quadrat AK 0218		*Maximum speed* 35 knots	
U-boat timekeeping differential +2 hours		*Armament* 1 × 4"; 1 × 3" AA; 2 × 20 mm AA; 3 × 21" tt	
Fatalities 67 in *St Croix,* 80 in *Itchen* *Survivors* 1			

Career

For background on the Royal Canadian Navy, see HMCS *Lévis* (**32**). For details of the circumstances under which HMCS *St Croix* joined the RCN, see HNorMS *Bath* (**30**). For design notes on the US Clemson-class destroyers of which USS *McCook* was a unit, see HMS *Broadwater* (**36**).

USS *McCook* (DD-252) was laid down at the Bethlehem Steel Corporation shipyard at Quincy, Massachusetts in September 1918, launched in January 1919 and commissioned into the US Navy on 30 April that year. Following her shakedown cruise *McCook* was assigned to Destroyer Force, Atlantic Fleet with which she served along the east coast until being decommissioned under the terms of the Washington Treaty in June 1922. *McCook* spent the inter-war years laid up at Philadelphia along with most of her classmates before rejoining the Atlantic Fleet in December 1939. Here she remained until turned over to the British at Halifax, Nova Scotia in September 1940. Renamed *St Croix*, she and six other 'flush-deckers' were commissioned into the Royal Canadian Navy on 24 September, cutting her teeth on local escort duty. The following month *St Croix* was earmarked for conversion to a long-range escort at Devonport Dockyard. Sailing for Britain on 30 November, *St Croix* was not far out of St John's, Newfoundland when she ran into a hurricane which forced her back into harbour and eventually to Halifax, Nova Scotia for repair and refit. From this she emerged in March 1941, being assigned first to local escort duties at Halifax and then in April to the Canadian 21st Escort Group (EG-C21) of the Newfoundland Escort Force with responsibility for shepherding convoys between St John's and Iceland. The full refit eventually took place at Saint John, New Brunswick between September 1941 and April 1942 after which *St Croix* was assigned to duties with the Mid-Ocean Escort Force. On 24 July 1942 came her first kill when *U90* was sunk while attacking convoy ON113 but in September *St Croix*, recently assigned to the Canadian 4th Escort Group (EG-C4), was present at the destruction of HMCS *Ottawa* by *U91* (**68**) while escorting ON127. In October she was allocated to the Canadian 1st Escort Group (EG-C1). A further refit at St John's in November and December was followed in January and February 1943 by intensive training with EG-C1 at HMS *Western Isles*, the anti-submarine school at Tobermory, Scotland. Dividends were reaped on 4 March when *St Croix*, then escorting KMS10 off Portugal, shared in the destruction of *U87* with HMC corvette *Shediac*. After repairs at Halifax in June *St Croix* returned to the fray, being allocated in July to the newly formed Canadian 9th Support Group (SG-9) based on Londonderry. Although intended for operations against U-boats transiting the Bay of Biscay, this unit seems to have been confined to convoy duties in the Atlantic which by the end of September had claimed two of its number: *St Croix* and HMS *Itchen* (**88**).

Returning to the fray

By the early summer of 1943 the struggle between the *U-Boot-Waffe* and the Allied forces in the North Atlantic had become a one-sided affair. Though U-boats continued to slip down the ways no less than fifty-three were lost in the Atlantic in April and May, a devastating blow that brought home to all at B.d.U. the advances made by the Allies both in tactics and technology, even if much of the latter remained unknown. The U-boats were withdrawn from their key battleground and little was sunk by them in the North Atlantic between June and late September 1943. However, the Battle of the Atlantic was by no means over. A new weapon was entering its final stages of development in Germany: the T5 acoustic homing torpedo, known by the Germans as the *Zaunkönig* ('wren') and to the Allies by the acronym GNAT (German Naval Acoustic Torpedo). In obviating the need for a U-boat commander to acquire a favourable inclination (relative angle) on his target, the *Zaunkönig* for the first time gave him an effective means of engaging a fast-approaching escort. With a range of 5,700 metres and a speed of nearly twenty-five knots, the *Zaunkönig* presented its greatest danger to vessels sailing between eight and twenty knots; slower and they generated insufficient noise to attract the torpedo; faster and they tended to defeat the sinuous course of the T5.

Background of the attack

In September B.d.U. formed the *Leuthen* group (named for a famous victory of Frederick the Great) comprising twenty-one boats sailing from French and Norwegian bases equipped with the *Zaunkönig* torpedo and charged with reopening hostilities against Allied convoys. Among them was Kptlt Rudolf Bahr's *U305*, equipped not only with four T5 torpedoes but also the latest *Wanze* ('bug') radar-warning system together with twin and quadruple flak guns to offset the decisive air advantage enjoyed by the Allies. The first convoy located by the group was westbound ON202. *U270* (Oblt.z.S. Paul-Friedrich Otto) recorded the first operational use of the *Zaunkönig*, wrecking the stern of HM frigate *Lagan* in the early hours of 20 September. Together with two further hits on merchantmen later that morning, this confirmed to Admiralty intelligence that the U-boats had embarked on a major offensive with the benefit of new technology. The decision was therefore taken to merge ON202 with the slower ONS18, a laborious process requiring many hours to form an unwieldy mass of seventy ships but which nonetheless ensured the presence of an extremely powerful twenty-ship escort. This comprised the Canadian 2nd Escort Group (EG-C2; two destroyers, three corvettes – including HMS *Polyanthus*, **87** – and a trawler), the British 3rd Escort Group (five corvettes and a destroyer, frigate and trawler) and the Canadian 9th Support Group (SG-9; two destroyers including *St Croix*, three corvettes and the frigate HMS *Itchen*, **88**) along with air cover provided by the merchant aircraft carrier HMS *Empire MacAlpine*. At dusk on the 20th HMCS *St Croix* was detached with *Itchen* and HM corvette *Narcissus* to hunt a U-boat sighted by an RCAF Liberator astern of the convoy. Guided to the position by this aircraft (to which Bahr makes reference in his log entries for 2105, 2108 and 2230) and now out of sight of the remaining escort, *St Croix* closed a submerged *U305* shortly before 2000 Allied time (2200 U-boat time).

War Diary of *U305*, patrol of 23 August–22 October 1943: PG 30388, NHB, reel 1,097, p. 377

Date, time	Details of position, wind, weather, sea, light, visibility, moonlight, etc.	Incidents
20.ix		
1720	Qu. AK 3914	Aircraft at bearing 290°, range roughly 12,000 m. Inclination 0°. Hasn't seen me. Alarm dive!
1745		Surfaced.
1905	Qu. AK 0261	Steamer in sight at bearing 200° true, range some 25,000 m. I haul ahead. We soon make out a destroyer acting as advance escort for the steamer.[1]
1922		Outgoing W/T transmission 1922/20/111: *One destroyer, one steamer Qu. AK 0259. U305.*[2]
2000	Qu. AK 0252, wind W 2, sea 2, cloud 2, 1,024 mb	Enemy is proceeding on a westerly course. I haul ahead to gain an attacking position.
2105	Qu. AK 0218	At bearing of 250° true an aircraft flies in to attack straight out of the sun, range some 5,000 m. Seen too late by lookout, AA guns clear. We make emergency turn, flak guns deployed, port twin AA guns fire 80 rounds at the target, well aimed. No effect observed. The quadruple AA mounting doesn't get going in time. Aircraft opens up with gunfire and drops four bombs, the latter hitting the water on our starboard side.[3] No particular effect.
2108		Once aircraft has passed over, alarm dive! We go to 100 m. At about 80 m a depth charge detonates astern of the boat. The hydrophone operator can now pick up the noise of propeller screws.
2133		We go to periscope depth. In the periscope we make out a destroyer (Churchill class) with an inclination of 0°, range 6–8,000 m.[4] We prepare to make a T5 attack.
2151	Qu. AK 0218	Torpedo (T5) fired from Tube II. Range 1,500 m, inclination 60°, bows left, enemy speed 12 knots, depth 4 m.

---

1 These may have been HM corvette *Polyanthus* (**87**) and the rescue ship *Rathlin* which had remained astern of the convoy following the torpedoing of SSs *Theodore Dwight Weld* and *Frederick Douglass* earlier that day.

2 Note the slight differences in the way this signal was recorded by *U952* priot to her attack on HMS *Polyanthus* (**87**).

3 The RCAF Liberator in question then proceeded to guide *St Croix* to *U305*'s position; Bahr refers to this aircraft again in his entry for 2230.

4 HMCS *St Croix*. The fifty 'four-stackers' transferred from the US Navy in 1940 were known to the Kriegsmarine as the 'Churchill class'. Note the inclination of 0°, implying that the target was in a bow-on position. The T5 torpedo for the first time made this a viable position from which to launch an attack.

Date, time	Details of position, wind, weather, sea, light, visibility, moonlight, etc.	Incidents
		After firing we go to 160 m. After 2 min. 30 sec. a loud torpedo detonation (one clear explosion and one hollow thud). Then a number of very loud detonations. It sounds like a number of depth charges exploding at the same time followed by a few isolated detonations. Propeller screws can no longer be heard.
2230		To periscope depth. It is dusk.[5] Destroyer is lying motionless with a slight list to port, smoke billowing out. The after mast is leaning towards the stern so this is clearly where torpedo struck. An aircraft is circling above the destroyer. I close to deliver a *coup-de-grâce* shot.
2240		Hydrophone operator reports propeller screws. Another destroyer appears at 280° true, range some 6,000 m.[6]
2244	Qu. AK 0218	*Coup-de-grâce* shot from Tube III (T3), depth 4 m, range 1,000 m, fixed angle of fire 0°.[7] After 1 min. 2 sec. a hit 10 m from the stern. A high red mushroom-topped pillar of flame, dramatic quantities of smoke, thereafter nothing more to be seen of the stern section of the ship.
		In the meantime the second destroyer (Jervis or Hunt class) has closed.[6] It is now genuinely dark. I turn about to deliver a stern attack.
2253	Qu. AK 0218	Torpedo (T5) fired from Tube V. Enemy speed 10 knots, bows left, inclination 143°, depth 4 m, range 1,500 m. A tube runner![8] Enemy turns towards us, I can make out flecks of sea spray on her stern. We can't dive as torpedo is half out of the tube. We eventually get the torpedo away when destroyer has closed to 500 m. Inclination now 70–80°. I order a rapid descent to a great depth. After 57 sec. a torpedo detonation.[9] No depth charges.
2310		Sinking noises picked up on the hydrophones at 20° and 145°.[10] I decide to withdraw submerged as I imagine the aircraft is still searching the area. We reload torpedoes.
21.ix	North Atlantic	
0000	Qu. AK 0218	Asdic pulses. From hydrophones we reckon three destroyers. Boat is overrun on a number of occasions but depth charges are very inaccurate. No ill effects!
0400	Qu. AK 0241	

5 Though Bahr's log entry is timed at 2230 it should be borne in mind that *U305* was keeping German Summer Time (GMT +2 hours), which apart from the latitude explains dusk being recorded at such a late hour.

6 HMS *Itchen*, a River-class frigate (**88**).

7 The T3 was the latest version of the standard G7e torpedo.

8 *Rohrläufer* in the original, referring to a torpedo not properly expelled from its tube.

9 This torpedo did not sink *Itchen* as Bahr's next entry implies but exploded in her wake. *Itchen* was accounted for three days later by *U666* (**88**).

10 The noises were probably owed in part to the sinking of *St Croix*'s bow section.

The sinking

It is difficult to establish any accurate picture of what befell HMCS *St Croix* as a result of *U305*'s torpedo since virtually none survived long enough to tell the tale. Such evidence as does exist, however, corroborates Bahr's record of a double explosion. This was reasonably but erroneously assumed by the RCN to have been two torpedoes detonating aft, though both German and Allied accounts make reference to depth-charge explosions which evidently added to the damage. From the testimony of the sole survivor, Stoker William Fisher, *St Croix* listed immediately with her engines stopped. The damage was clearly sufficient for a majority of the crew to be ordered into the destroyer's whaler, motor boat and Carley floats, but according to Fisher it was clear that Cdr Dobson still had some hope of getting *St Croix* under way:

> We had quite a few of the boys in the boat when we saw smoke rising from 1 and 2 funnels. No one could understand why smoke should be rising from them as they had both been shut off before we had been hit. I was later told that the captain had given orders to get up steam and see if they could make way.

But the attempt was soon brought to a halt by Bahr's *coup de grâce*, fired at 2244 German time (2044 Allied time), almost an hour after his first:

> The smoke had been rising for about three minutes when the *Itchen* came over the horizon. A few minutes later there was a terrific explosion and flames leaped into the air . . . [The] stern of the ship disappeared quickly, but from amidshipforward [i.e. the forward section] stayed up from three to five minutes, then she turned her bow into the air and went down.

The latter point bears out the accuracy of Bahr's description in his entry for 2244, and though Fisher's chronology deviates from *U305*'s log it seems likely that at least some of the noises heard by her hydrophone operator at 2310 were of *St Croix*'s bow section on its way to the bottom of the Atlantic.

Bahr's strike illustrated the potential of the T5 torpedo and B.d.U. expressed its approval of his having surfaced to assess its effect before delivering the *coup de grâce*. However, even this brief excerpt from *U305*'s log reveals the shortcomings of the *Zaunkönig* since Bahr's 2253 attack against *Itchen* detonated not on her hull but in her wake, a persistent sensitivity fault that would never be properly corrected.

Influenced no doubt by the reports of his hydrophone operator, Bahr concluded that a second warship had been sunk. Bahr was credited with this kill, the first in a long line of misinterpretations of acoustic data that characterise German assessments of T5 attacks. The critical problem was that of visual corroboration, since a U-boat would usually dive having launched a *Zaunkönig* to avoid becoming the target of its own weapon.

See HMSs *Polyanthus* (**87**) and *Itchen* (**88**) for more on the aftermath of the *Leuthen* group's attack on convoy ON202/ONS18.

Fate of the crew

From the testimony of Stoker William Fisher, the only member of *St Croix*'s company ever to see dry land again, it appears that no more than a handful of men succumbed to *U305*'s initial attack. Most of these were on the quarterdeck, being either killed outright or blasted into the sea. As Fisher related, over the next half hour the ship's whaler was lowered, Carley floats pitched over the side and the injured lowered into *St Croix*'s motor boat:

> The captain, several officers and ratings were still with the ship when she was hit the third time [i.e. the second attack] and some of them managed to get off before she went down. As we kept picking survivors out of the water the oil was so thick that we could hardly recognise some of the boys.

Aware that there had been an explosion in her wake, Lt Cdr C. E. Bridgeman of *Itchen* dared not stop for survivors but made the following signal to the Senior Officer of the British 3rd Escort Group, Cdr M. J. Evans in HMS *Keppel*: '*St Croix* torpedoed and blown up, forecastle still afloat and survivors in rafts and boats, torpedoes fired at me. Doing full speed in vicinity, will not attempt to pick up survivors until *Polyanthus* arrives.' However, *Polyanthus*'s arrival heralded not the rescue of *St Croix*'s men but her own destruction at the hands of *U952* (**87**). The survivors of both ships had now to wait until it was safe enough for *Itchen* to rescue them the following morning. As Fisher recalled, those in the whaler and the four Carley floats secured to it fared best, losing not a single man through the night. Less fortunate were those in the motor boat commanded by the First Lieutenant which became swamped having taken too many men on board, prompting several to panic and abandon her, never to be seen again. Screened by *Narcissus*, *Itchen* picked up a total of eighty-one survivors but their deliverance had all too short a lease. In the first minutes of 23 September *Itchen* was struck by a *Zaunkönig* from *U666* and blew up, a disaster from which there were only three survivors (**88**). One of them was Stoker Fisher of *St Croix*, rescued by the Polish steamer *Wisła* a few hours later and eventually landed at Brooklyn, New York. Beyond the human tragedy, the sinking of *St Croix* deprived the Allies of a seasoned veteran of the Battle of the Atlantic and her loss dealt a heavy blow to the Royal Canadian Navy.

U305 and Rudolf Bahr

Built by Flenderwerft at Lübeck and commissioned in September 1942, *U305*'s only commander was Oblt.z.S. (Kptlt from December 1942) Rudolf Bahr, who had been awarded the Iron Cross Second Class for service in *Prinz Eugen* during Exercise RHEIN, the sortie which resulted in the sinking of the battlecruiser *Hood* and the battleship *Bismarck* in the Atlantic in May 1941. *U305*'s first two cruises yielded a pair of merchantmen, but the second of these resulted in serious

Bahr seen prior to the award of the Iron Cross First Class in June 1942.
DUBMA

damage at the hands of the destroyer USS *Osmond Ingram* and aircraft from the escort carrier USS *Bogue*. Returning to Brest in June 1943, Bahr was among the U-boat commanders sent to the Bay of Danzig in July to observe demonstrations of the new *Zaunkönig* torpedo, with which he disposed of HMCS *St Croix* during his third patrol. Nor was she *U305*'s only warship prize: on 7 January 1944, a month into his fourth and last patrol, Bahr sank HM frigate *Tweed* north-east of the Azores (**G69**).

Until recently Bahr and his entire crew were believed to have perished following a series of depth-charge attacks off Ireland by HM destroyer *Wanderer* and HM frigate *Glenarm* on 17 January 1944. However, research by Dr Axel Niestlé (see below) not only casts doubt on whether *U305* was in the area at all but indicates that the vessel sunk on this occasion was in fact *U377*. Moreover, Niestlé suggests that the key to *U305*'s end lies in a garbled emergency signal received both by B.d.U. and Bletchley Park the previous day. This signal, sent by a U-boat reporting her imminent demise from a torpedo hit, raises the possibility that *U305* was in fact accounted for by one of her own *Zaunkönige*. Whether *U305* met her end in this or some other way must remain a mystery until her wreck comes to light.

Sources

Admiralty, *Analysis of U-Boat Operations: Convoys ONS18 and ON202, 19–24 September 1943* (TNA, ADM 199/2022)

—, *Enemy Submarine Attacks on H.M. Ships, 1943* (TNA, ADM 199/956)

Royal Canadian Navy, Newfoundland Command, *Board of Inquiry – Loss of HMCS St Croix* (NAC, RG 24, D12, vol. 11930, file 1156–354/23)

Office of the Naval Historical Section, *Report on Loss of* St Croix (original in Office of the Naval Historical Section, Department of National Defence, Ottawa; copy in BfZ, Sammlung Rohwer, T-5 Auswertungsdokumente)

Rohwer, Jürgen, *Analyse der T-5 („Zaunkönig")-Schüsse von U-Booten gegen Geleitfahrzeuge. U305: HMCS St Croix* (Report for Federal Office of Weapons Technology and Procurement, 1964) (BfZ, MaS 8/2.07)

—, *Die Entwicklung des Zaunkönigs: die Kriegsgeschichte als Hilfswissenschaft der Wehrtechnik, dargestellt am Beispiel der zielsuchenden Torpedos* (BfZ, Sammlung Rohwer, „T-5: Manuskripte und Auswertung" folder)

Bercuson, David J., and Holger H. Herwig, *Deadly Seas: The Duel between the* St Croix *and the* U305 *in the Battle of the Atlantic* (Toronto: Random House of Canada, 1997)

DANFS, IV, pp. 292–3 (USS *McCook*); also on: http://www.history.navy.mil/danfs/m7/mccook-i.htm

Fisher, William, 'The End of HMCS *St Croix*' in *Canadian Military History* 8, no. 3 (Summer 1999), pp. 63–9

Hague, Arnold, *Destroyers for Great Britain: A History of 50 Town Class Ships Transferred from the United States to Great Britain in 1940* (London: Greenhill Books, 1990)

Jones, Geoffrey P., 'Bahr's Busy Boat' in his *Defeat of the Wolf Packs* (London: William Kimber, 1986), pp. 177–91

Lynch, Thomas G., ed., *Fading Memories: Canadian Sailors and the Battle of the Atlantic* (Halifax, Nova Scotia: The Atlantic Chief and Petty Officers' Association, 1993)

McKee and Darlington, *Canadian Naval Chronicle*, pp. 101–4

Macpherson and Burgess, *Ships of Canada's Naval Forces* (3rd edn), p. 41

Rohwer, Jürgen, and W. A. B. Douglas, 'Canada and the Wolf Packs, September 1943' in W. A. B. Douglas, ed., *The RCN in Transition, 1910–1985* (Vancouver, BC: University of British Columbia Press, 1988), pp. 159–86

Career history of HMCS *St Croix*: http://www.naval-history.net/xGM-Chrono-11US-StCroix.htm

Naval Museum of Manitoba webpages devoted to HMCS *St Croix*: Sinking of HMCS *St Croix*: http://www.naval-museum.mb.ca/battle_atlantic/st.croix/tragic-saga.htm

Memoirs of Stoker William Fisher (survivor): http://www.naval-museum.mb.ca/battle_atlantic/st.croix/survivors-account.htm ; also in *Winnipeg Free Press*, 1 October 1943

Biographies of Manitobans lost in HMCS *St Croix*: http://www.naval-museum.mb.ca/battle_atlantic/st.croix/manitobans.htm

Niestlé, Axel, 'Re-assessment of German U-Boat Losses in World War II: The Loss of *U305*, *U377* and *U641*', posted 23 December 2004: http://www.uboat.net/articles/index.html?article=57

87   HMS *POLYANTHUS*

Lt J. G. Aitken, RNR†

Sunk by *U952* (Type VIIC), Oblt.z.S. Oskar Curio, 20 September 1943

North Atlantic, 435 nm ESE of Uummannarsuaq, Greenland

Polyanthus under way in unusually calm conditions in July 1942. Her sinking by *U952* on 20 September 1943 and then *Itchen*'s by *U666* three days later wiped out her ship's company. *BfZ*

Theatre North Atlantic (Map 1)		*Displacement* 940 tons	
Coordinates 57° 23' N, 30° 48' W		*Dimensions* 205.25' × 33' × approx. 11.25'	
Kriegsmarine code Quadrat AK 2962		*Maximum speed* 16 knots	
U-boat timekeeping differential +2 hours		*Armament* 1 × 4"; 2 × 20 mm AA; 4 × .303" AA; 1 × Hedgehog ATW	
Fatalities 84 in *Polyanthus*, 2 in *Itchen* *Survivors* none			

Career

For design notes on the Flower-class corvettes, see HMS *Picotee* (**29**).

HMS *Polyanthus* was laid down at Henry Robb Ltd of Leith, Scotland in March 1940 and completed in April of the following year. Her working-up period at HMS *Western Isles*, the anti-submarine warfare training school at Tobermory, was delayed by a collision with HM trawler *River Esk* on 1 May 1941, the first incident in a somewhat chequered career. She became operational at Liverpool on 11 June and by month's end had been assigned to the 17th Escort Group of the Newfoundland Escort Force. Convoy duty continued until a boiler-room fire sent her to Charleston, South Carolina for ten days' repair in October. After further service in the Atlantic *Polyanthus* made her way to Galveston, Texas where her fo'c's'le was extended to improve habitability in March and April 1942. *Polyanthus* battled on with the NEF until January 1943 when she was reallocated to the Canadian 2nd Escort Group (EG-C2) at Londonderry, one of fifteen British ships placed under RCN control during the Second World War. Her first crossing with this force was marked by engine problems which reduced her speed to seven knots and by mountainous seas which scattered convoy ON160. There followed a two-month refit on the Tyne during which a Hedgehog spigot mortar, first in a line of lethal Allied anti-submarine weapons, was fitted abaft the 4-inch gun. From this she emerged in April but *Polyanthus* was soon back in dockyard hands. On 5 May she grounded while leaving St John's with convoy HX237, requiring a month's repair at Baltimore during which HF/DF equipment was probably fitted. North Atlantic escort duty resumed in July in seas largely cleared of the enemy, but for HMS *Polyanthus* the holiday was not to last.

Background of the attack

The reopening of hostilities by the *U-Boot-Waffe* in September 1943 and the *Leuthen* group's attack on merged convoy ON202/ONS18 are covered in the preceding entry for HMCS *St Croix* (**86**).

On 15 September convoy ON202 sailed from Liverpool bound for North America. Before long it was joined by the Canadian 2nd Escort Group (EG-C2) which consisted of two destroyers, a trawler and three corvettes including HMS *Polyanthus*. In the early hours of 20 September the torpedoing of *Frederick Douglass* and *Theodore Dwight Weld* by U-boats of the *Leuthen* group caused *Polyanthus* to be detached to screen the rescue ship *Rathlin* as she went about picking up survivors. This took several hours and the pair required the rest of the day to regain the now merged convoy ON202/ONS18. As they neared the convoy that evening *Polyanthus* was ordered to perform a similar function for HM frigate *Itchen* (see next entry, **88**) while she picked up survivors of *St Croix*, finished off by *U305* at around 2045 on the 20th (Allied time). A signal sent at 2230 by Lt Cdr C. E. Bridgeman (Senior Officer of the British 9th EG in *Itchen*) to his counterpart in the 3rd EG (Cdr M. J. Evans in HMS *Keppel*) reported 'four U-boats in vicinity of wreck, *Polyanthus* in company'. But change was afoot even as this signal was being transmitted. *Polyanthus* had sighted and obtained an Asdic contact on a U-boat which was then seen submerging at a range of 2,500 yards. Zigzagging on the line of contact at her best speed of sixteen knots, *Polyanthus* had observed an alarm dive caused not just by her approach but by Oblt.z.S. Oskar Curio of *U952* having launched a *Zaunkönig* acoustic torpedo against her.

War Diary of *U952*, patrol of 6 September–23 October 1943: PG 30787, NHB, reel 1,140, p. 301

Date, time	Details of position, wind, weather, sea, light, visibility, moonlight, etc.	Incidents
20.ix		
1832		Incoming W/T transmission 1813/20/106: *To Leuthen. Once Kinzel's short signal has been received, all boats to remain on surface and sail towards convoy at best speed. Boats around convoy must take action to alleviate the punishment being meted out to others. Only two aircraft with convoy so far, according to B-Dienst.*[1]
1922		Incoming short signal transmission 1922/20/111: *One destroyer, one steamer, my position AK 0259.*[2] Details of position strike me as navigational error, as I am right there myself but can see nothing of either Bahr or the reported vessels.
2000	Qu. AK 0259, wind W 2, sea 0–1, cloud 1, very good visibility	
2140	Qu. AK 0242	Man the guns! Liberator appears at bearing 10° true, average altitude, extreme range, trying to keep the sun behind it. The attack comes as boat is turning about.
2145		Gunfire and four bombs which fall very close. Whole boat leaps up, briefly goes down heavily by the stern and is then drenched in falling columns of water. Attack was made from the port quarter but as a result of violent manoeuvring all bombs fell on starboard side. Rudder failure, gyro compass out, Junker compressors have jumped free of their beds and there is a 2-cm hit between the two twin flak guns. No casualties, boat able to dive.
2154		Outgoing short signal transmission: *Attacked by aircraft, position AK 0242. U952.*

---

1   Kptlt Manfred Kinzel, commanding *U338*, had earlier signalled his intention to remain on the surface and take on enemy aircraft with his new anti-aircraft armament. Ironically, B.d.U.'s exhortations to other boats to relieve the pressure on him by following a similar strategy came as *U338* disappeared without trace, sunk by the Canadian corvette *Drumheller*. As many *Leuthen* commanders no doubt appreciated, B.d.U. underestimated the extent of the convoy's air cover which was supplied by the merchant aircraft carrier HMS *Empire MacAlpine* and long-range aircraft from Iceland. *B-Dienst* was the Kriegsmarine's radio monitoring and intelligence service.

2   Sent by Kptlt Rudolf Bahr of *U305* whose transmission of this signal is recorded in the preceding entry for HMCS *St Croix* (**86**). It is unclear whose was the 'navigational error' but such discrepancies were to be expected of smaller vessels after weeks on the high seas. Indeed, there are a number of different coordinates from the Allied side for the longitude and latitude in which both *St Croix* and *Polyanthus* were sunk.

Date, time	Details of position, wind, weather, sea, light, visibility, moonlight, etc.	Incidents
		With some crude steering and all engines at utmost speed I keep the aircraft astern of me at all times so as to have all guns bearing in the event of another attack. Aircraft once again attempts to attack from the sun but then fails to follow through. It is impossible to keep our bearings as we swing around with both compasses broken, the magnetic compass completely and the gyro compass for 45 minutes. Steering failure is quickly dealt with.
2230		Outgoing short signal transmission: *Aircraft maintaining contact. U952.*
2314		Aircraft lost from sight in the twilight. Head towards convoy at utmost speed.
2320		Incoming W/T transmission 2254/20/120: *To Leuthen: 1.) Contact reports suggest that convoy is proceeding in great circle. Bahr's sighting probably part of convoy. 2.) Continue search at best speed assuming enemy course between 280° and 240°. Starting point ?93°[3] 3.) Consider ways of using Hagenuk to detect vessels using radar and thereby maintain contact with convoy.*[4]
2354		Infrared searchlight in sight at bearing 110° true. At first we take it to be from an aircraft.
21.ix		
0011		Again we see red searchlight. But no radar traces. She must be one of the convoy escorts – probably sent our way by the earlier aircraft.[5] As she approaches, using the searchlight only sparingly, we identify her as a destroyer, inclination 0°, closing in our wake at high speed. Torpedo crew to Battle Stations.
0022	Qu. AK 2962, wind WNW 3, sea 2–3, cloud 5, good visibility	We fire a T5 torpedo from Tube V. Enemy speed 18 knots, range 5,000 m, depth 5 m.[6] Prior to firing we reduce speed in order to close the range and wait for the searchlight to come back on so as to fire straight at the source of the infrared light.[7] Alarm dive!
0025		An extremely powerful detonation.[8]
0027		Sinking noises that can be clearly heard in our boat with the naked ear. These are followed by a dull cracking sound like that of collapsing bulkheads. No propeller noises or depth charges; I believe the destroyer must have sunk. Boat can't surface directly because the damage caused by the aircraft bombs means that we would not be in a condition to dive again immediately in an emergency. The starboard electric engine is out, so too the group hydrophone apparatus, two cells from Battery 1 are ruptured, cold water intake of starboard diesel is damaged, and the pintle holders of the starboard main clutch are also damaged. I order reloading and repairs under water. Course 270°.
0135		A number of depth charges in vicinity of boat.
0137		Hydrophone apparatus up and running. Two hydrophone bearings at 80° and 290°, volume 4 and 5. Boat is overrun by hunting party on several occasions but they get no fix.

---

3   The original has the '93' preceded by an illegible blacked-out digit. It is not clear what is being referred to here.

4   B.d.U. is referring to the *Wanze* radar-warning device recently introduced by the Hagenuk company.

5   HM corvette *Polyanthus*, which was in fact on the scene to cover *Itchen*'s efforts to rescue survivors of the *St Croix*.

6   *Polyanthus* was in fact recorded as proceeding at her best speed of sixteen knots. Unlike conventional weapons, the meandering course characteristic of the *Zaunkönig* acoustic homing torpedo when the close or remote fire settings were actuated makes it impossible to derive the exact range of a detonation from the running time.

7   As Curio recognises, the red light was owed to the infrared screen which the Allies began fitting to their searchlights in the summer of 1943 in an effort to minimise the visibility of the beam itself.

8   *Polyanthus* exploding. The time given coincides exactly with Lt Cdr C. E. Bridgeman's original assessment of the sinking from *Itchen* (2225), later modified by him to 2236 following discussions with Sub-Lt F. J. Young of *Polyanthus* (see below). The Board of Enquiry favoured the latter timing.

The sinking

The fact that not one survivor of the sinking of HMS *Polyanthus* lived to see dry land explains the scant information concerning her loss in Allied records. That any detailed information survives at all from the Allied side is owed to the fact that Lt Cdr C. E. Bridgeman, commanding HMS *Itchen* (see next entry, **88**), had the opportunity both to interview the sole survivor, Sub-Lt F. J. Young RNVR, and signal a digest of their discussion to Cdr Evans in *Keppel* the following day before both Bridgeman and Young were killed on the 23rd. It

therefore bears repeating in full:

> Hit 2236Z right aft, two to three minutes after U-boat dived. Asdic contact ahead 2,500 yards, ship zigzagging on line of Asdic contact 16 knots, no shots fired. Full rudder on when hit. No H[ydrophone]E[ffect] heard.

The speed of her demise is borne out by Curio's aural impression of the episode which records his victim sinking within two minutes. Nor is the cause far to seek. Curio's depth-setting was five metres, a metre or so below *Polyanthus*'s mean draught, but a magnetic pistol detonation under the keel would have had a devastating effect. The signal sent to all escorts by Lt Cdr Bridgeman in *Itchen* at 2245 Allied time stating that 'Think *Polyanthus* torpedoed. Radar contact faded' indicates that her loss had not been witnessed from her companion.

Fate of the crew

Having received *Itchen*'s signal of 2245, Cdr Evans of *Keppel* immediately ordered the corvette *Narcissus* to join the former in searching for survivors from both *Polyanthus* and *St Croix*. However, Lt Cdr Bridgeman concluded that the risk of doing so at night was too great in the circumstances and decided to wait until morning. By now about twenty-four miles astern of the convoy, *Itchen* and *Narcissus* instead began a steady sweep over a wide area of ocean, carrying out a series of unsuccessful attacks against U-boat contacts before proceeding to the scene of the torpedoing of *St Croix* shortly after daybreak. Given the number of *St Croix*'s survivors needing rescue and intent on not abandoning the scene until they were quite certain that none had been missed, *Itchen* and *Narcissus* did not reach the position in which *Polyanthus* was reckoned to have been sunk until 0945 on the 21st, more than eleven hours after the attack. By 1015 *Itchen* had picked up only two men of whom one died shortly after leaving Sub-Lt Young as the sole survivor. In an exchange of signals between *Keppel* and *Itchen*, Cdr Evans inquired of Bridgeman whether 'any purpose would be served in carrying out further search for survivors', to which he received the stark reply 'None whatever'. The commanding officer of *Narcissus*, Lt W. G. H. Bolton, subsequently informed the Board of Enquiry that 'there was not even a piece of wreckage any larger than an ashtray'. Any prospect of the Allied authorities learning more about *Polyanthus*'s fate was dashed two days later when *Itchen* blew up following a torpedo hit from *U666*, a disaster that left three survivors from three ships' companies (**88**). Sub-Lt Young was not among them.

U952 and Oskar Curio

Built by Blohm & Voss of Hamburg and commissioned in December 1942, *U952* entered the fray under Oblt.z.S. Oskar Curio in May 1943, the worst month experienced by the *U-Boot-Waffe* in the entire Battle of the Atlantic. On the 19th *U952* was depth charged by HM frigate *Tay* while attempting to intercept eastbound SC130, suffering damage which obliged her to turn for France. Her next operational sortie was aborted three times due to technical problems before she joined the *Leuthen* group south-east of Greenland in September. Here she was in the thick of the action, sinking *Polyanthus* on the 20th and narrowly escaping a ramming by HM trawler *Northern Waters* two days later. Undaunted, Curio made an unsuccessful *Zaunkönig* attack on the Free French corvette *Renoncule* and the following day (23rd) sank the US freighter *Steel Voyager* and damaged the SS *James Gordon Bennett*. For this patrol he received the Iron Cross First Class and was promoted Kapitänleutnant. *U952*'s third cruise took her into the Mediterranean where three more sorties based on Toulon yielded a single merchantman off the Sicilian coast in March 1944. Damaged at Toulon by US bombers in July 1944, she was destroyed in a further raid on 6 August. After a spell of training Curio was appointed in

Curio sports a bow tie on returning to La Pallice in *U952* from the patrol during which *Polyanthus* was sunk. *Dr Friedrich Curio*

command of *U2528* which like so many of the Type XXIs never became operational. The last days of the war found Curio a passenger in *U2503* as she made her way from Germany to Norway. On 4 May 1945 *U2503* was attacked by a pair of RAF Beaufighters one of which struck the conning tower with a rocket that killed Kptlt Karl-Jürg Wächter and twelve of his crewmen. Curio took command, finding himself obliged to run *U2503* aground on the Danish coast where local people refused all requests for assistance. So ended his war. He died in Cologne in 1981 after a successful career in media marketing.

Sources

Admiralty, Director of Anti-Submarine Warfare, *Analysis of U-Boat Operations: Convoys ONS18 and ON202, 19–24 September 1943* (TNA, ADM 199/2022)

—, *Enemy Submarine Attacks on H.M. Ships, 1943* (TNA, ADM 199/956)

Curio, Oscar [*sic*], *Die Stunde Null* (typescript, U2503 file, DUBMA)

Ministry of Defence, Polyanthus, *HMS, and Convoys ONS18 and ON202* (NHB, S.7977)

Rohwer, Prof. Jürgen, *Analyse der T-5 („Zaunkönig")-Schüsse von U-Booten gegen Geleitfahrzeuge. U952: HMS Polyanthus* (Report for Federal Office of Weapons Technology and Procurement, 1964) (BfZ, MaS 8/2.07)

—, *Die Entwicklung des Zaunkönigs: die Kriegsgeschichte als Hilfswissenschaft der Wehrtechnik, dargestellt am Beispiel der zielsuchenden Torpedos* (BfZ, Sammlung Rohwer, T-5 Auswertungsdokumente)

Ruegg, R. A., *Flower-Class Corvettes* (typescript, IWM, 13(41).245/5, 1987)

Fisher, William, 'The End of HMCS *St Croix*' in *Canadian Military History* 8, no. 3 (Summer 1999), pp. 63–9

Macpherson and Burgess, *Ships of Canada's Naval Forces* (3rd edn), p. 186

Preston, Antony, and Alan Raven, *Flower Class Corvettes* [Ensign, no. 3] (London: Bivouac Books, 1973); reprinted as Man o'War, no. 7 (London: Arms and Armour Press, 1982)

88   HMS *ITCHEN*

Lt Cdr C. E. Bridgeman, DSO RNR†
Sunk by *U666* (Type VIIC), Kptlt Herbert Engel, 23 September 1943
North Atlantic, 430 nm SSE of Uummannarsuaq, Greenland

Not *Itchen,* for which no photo has been found, but her River-class sister HMS *Helford. BfZ*

Theatre North Atlantic (Map 1)		*Displacement* 1,370 tons	
Coordinates 53° 30' N, 39° 45' W		*Dimensions* 301.25' × 36.5' × 9'	
Kriegsmarine code Quadrat AK 7147		*Maximum speed* 19.5 knots	
U-boat timekeeping differential +2 hours		*Armament* 2 × 4" AA; *c.*4–10 × 20 mm AA; 1 × Hedgehog ATW	
Fatalities 148 and 80 and 2 *Survivors* 2 and 1			

The River-class frigates

Successful as they were, the Flower-class corvettes (see HMS *Picotee*, **29**) had neither the endurance nor the speed, armament or seakeeping qualities to serve efficiently in the Atlantic and already by 1940 the expected German onslaught against the convoy system was urging the provision of a purpose-designed unit. The result was the River class to which the misleading designation of 'frigate' was given. If not 'the eyes of the fleet' of Nelson's time, the Rivers were nonetheless the first truly capable ocean-going escort vessels to enter service in the Second World War and represent the beginning of an important line of warship development which continues to this day. Embodying the lessons of the first stage of the Battle of the Atlantic, the design was based on a 300-foot hull (the shortest able to cope with the long Atlantic seaway) with a new twin-screw arrangement capable of twenty knots. Oil bunkerage, which eventually reached 650 tons (though only 440 in *Itchen's* case), permitted an endurance of 9,500 miles at ten knots. Add to this much improved habitability and armament (eighty depth charges versus forty) when compared with the Flowers. What did not change from the Flowers was the simplicity of the design which allowed vessels to be built in many yards with no experience of warship construction, and 151 units had been completed in Canada (82), Britain (57), and Australia (12) by the time they were in turn superseded by the Loch-class frigates from 1943.

Career

HMS *Itchen* belonged to the first group of River-class frigates ordered for the Royal Navy in February 1941. She was laid down at Fleming & Ferguson's yard at Paisley on the Clyde in July of that year, launched in July 1942 and completed that December. After working up at Tobermory and a brief refit on the Clyde, *Itchen* joined the Canadian 1st Escort Group (EG-C1) as Senior Officer's ship on the Newfie–Derry run in March 1943, one of fifteen British ships placed under RCN control during the Second World War. She remained with this force until transferred to the Canadian 9th Support Group (SG-9) at Londonderry in August, her first taste of action coming on 19 September when *Itchen* and her brood were ordered to assist merged convoy ON202/ONS18 south of Iceland. Four days later she was no more.

Background of the attack

The reopening of hostilities by the *U-Boot-Waffe* in September 1943 and the *Leuthen* group's attack on merged convoy ON202/ONS18 are covered in the entries for HMCS *St Croix* and HMS *Polyanthus* (**86** and **87**).

On the morning of 21 September 1943 *Itchen* and HM corvette *Narcissus* rejoined the merged convoy ON202/ONS18 and its depleted escort after the former had rescued eighty-one survivors of the destroyer *St Croix* and two from the corvette *Polyanthus*. The appearance of a thick blanket of fog at midday provided a welcome respite for the convoy since many of the *Leuthen* U-boats now lost contact and the escort proved equal to the few attacks made that evening. In the early hours of the 22nd *U229* (Oblt.z.S. Robert Schetelig) was picked up on HMS *Keppel's* centimetric radar and then hunted down and sunk by gunfire, ramming and depth charges at 0542 Allied time. However, the fog lifted that afternoon and a crescendo of HF/DF bearings heralded the return of the wolfpack. As night fell the escorts ahead of the convoy began chasing down contacts. Shortly before midnight *Itchen* and the Canadian corvette *Morden* both obtained a contact on Kptlt Herbert Engel's *U666* which had manoeuvred ahead of the convoy and was closing from an advance position. This, however, was no tactical disadvantage since the new *Zaunkönig* T5 acoustic torpedo gave the U-boats a viable option in end-on attack which they had not previously enjoyed. Accordingly, on either side of midnight Engel unleashed a T5 from each end of his boat in the hope of despatching two 'tin cans' in one engagement. *Morden* he missed (though a sinking was claimed based on acoustic data) but *Itchen* was struck having just caught *U666* with her searchlight and two well-aimed rounds on the conning tower.

War Diary of *U666*, patrol of 31 August–16 October 1943: PG 30696, NHB, reel 1,135, pp. 181–2

Date, time	Details of position, wind, weather, sea, light, visibility, moonlight, etc.	Incidents
23.ix		
0005		Hydrophone effect at 160° true.
0020		Surfaced. Head towards hydrophone contact at ¾ speed, course 160°. Nothing to be seen.
0105		We haul ahead slightly, course 270°.
0120		Course alteration to 85° towards convoy.
0145	Qu. AK 7147	Shadows appear at bearing 120° true. We discern them to be two escort destroyers.[1] Vessels' course appears to be south-west. Initial range roughly 6,000 m, speed 12–14 knots. Presumably this is the advance close escort. We turn about for a stern shot.
0147	Qu. AK 7147	Battle Stations.
0156		Stern shot (T5) at the destroyer stationed to starboard.[2] Shot coordinates: inclination 0°, enemy speed 15 knots, range 4,000 m, torpedo depth 4 m, remote fire setting.[3] We remain on the surface, turning to fire a bow shot at the second destroyer.[4] Destroyer initially has inclination of 110°, bows right, range 2,000 m, enemy speed 12 knots. From hydrophone operator we get a report of radar-warning readings on 140 cm just as the destroyer turns towards the boat and accelerates.
0201	Qu. AK 7147	Bow shot (T5) from Tube II. Shot coordinates: inclination 0°, enemy speed 15 knots, range 1,500 m, torpedo depth 4 m, remote fire setting.[3] Destroyer switches on searchlight and immediately picks up our boat. She opens up with gunfire, two hits on the conning tower.
0202		Alarm! As boat sinks to 20 m we hear an exceptionally loud detonation on the starboard bow. Running time of second torpedo 1 min. 10 sec.[5] Shortly afterwards a heavy detonation to port. Running time of first torpedo 8 min. 21 sec.[6] No further sounds of propellers. Five depth-charge detonations heard off to port, presumably the sinking destroyer's own charges. Then all is silent. Sinking noises can be heard on both sides, to starboard by naked ear throughout the boat, and to port via the group listening apparatus.[7] I assume the second torpedo resulted in a direct hit since range at time of strike was under 1,000 m.[8]

---

1   HM frigate *Itchen* and HMC corvette *Morden*.

2   *Morden*.

3   'Remote fire' (*Weitschuss*) was one of the three run settings of the *Zaunkönig* torpedo and was primarily for use against approaching targets, or those with a relative inclination of up to 110°. This involved the *Ente* ('duck') torpedo control mechanism being set to assume a labile or erratic snaking track towards its target; compare with *Nahschuss* in USS *Buck* (**90**), n. 3, and HMS *Mahratta* (**99**), n. 5.

4   *Itchen*.

5   This is the fatal hit on *Itchen*. The running time equates to a range of 1,050 metres though account must be taken of the indirect course of the *Zaunkönig* torpedo and Engel estimates it at under 1,000 metres at the end of this entry; however, see n. 8.

6   Unlike conventional weapons, the meandering course characteristic of the *Zaunkönig* acoustic homing torpedo when the close or remote fire settings were actuated makes it impossible to derive the exact range of a detonation from the running time. In any event, and despite Engel's claim to the contrary, his T5 had in fact exploded harmlessly in *Morden*'s wake.

7   The 'noises' belonged to *Itchen* and *Morden* respectively. As *Morden* was several thousand metres off, Engel's claim was based on acoustic data acquired by the *Gruppenhorchgerät* hydrophone apparatus.

8   As related in n. 5 above, this second torpedo is that which destroyed *Itchen*. Engel's reference to a range 'under 1,000 m' is interesting since it might offer a clue to the length of the *Sperrstrecke* (lit. 'blocked stretch') with which the *Zaunkönig* torpedo was set. In order to minimise the risk of the firing U-boat becoming the target of its own weapon the *Sperrstrecke* provided for a straight run after the torpedo was launched and before the acoustic mechanism was actuated. Although this was initially fixed at 400 metres and only increased in late 1944, it might be possible to interpret Engel's comment as suggesting that this distance was in

Date, time	Details of position, wind, weather, sea, light, visibility, moonlight, etc.	Incidents
0245	Qu. AK 7147	Overrun by the convoy.
0400	Qu. AK 7147	
0410		Overrun by the rear escort. Asdic and loud propeller noises. Boat taken down to 120 m. No depth charges.
		It seems as if the convoy only had a single destroyer astern, zigzagging wildly across the entire area. Surfaced. The detonation on our starboard side has resulted in various malfunctions in the boat. A trace of oil on the starboard side from Tank No. 4. The hits from the gunfire have caused damage to the plating. We find various objects on the bridge, including a can of food with English labelling and two English coins dated 1942 and 1943 respectively.
		We withdraw to carry out repairs.
0606		Outgoing W/T transmission 0201/23/871: *Just sank two leading destroyers in Qu. AK 7147. Overrun by convoy at 0245 steering course 225°.*
0740		We dive and proceed at Battle Stations at a depth of 60 m. Reload torpedoes.

fact already 1,000 metres, or at least considerably further than the design specification. That said, it is possible that Engel is simply confusing the specifications of the T5 with its predecessor, the T4 *Falke* ('falcon'), which had a *Sperrstrecke* of 1,000 metres.

The sinking

As *Itchen* sank almost immediately in pitch darkness and with only a handful of survivors it comes as no surprise that there is little to document her end among Allied sources. The event noted by Engel at 0202 (0002 Allied time) was described by *Itchen*'s fellow escorts as a 'terrific explosion', a 'blinding flash', and by the US steamer *James Smith* as a 'violent explosion' followed at once by 'terrific flames and smoke'. The detonation, which apparently broke her back between bridge and funnel, was reckoned by some observers to have been produced by her depth charges and by others her magazine. It was quite likely both. The only known survivor testimony is that of Stoker William Fisher who had been rescued following the loss of HMCS *St Croix* two days earlier. Fisher recalled being blasted thirty feet against the bulkhead of one of the gun supports. Staggering to his feet a few seconds later he found the ship listing as water roared into her hull and promptly dived overboard, *Itchen* being by rent by another explosion as he did so. By the time Fisher regained the surface it was to see her propellers disappearing. He estimated *Itchen* to have 'gone down in about forty seconds'. The fact that cans of food and money were found on *U666*'s bridge about a thousand yards distant and that splinters and debris reached *Morden* (further still) gives a fair impression of the force of the explosion which destroyed her. In the absence of survivor testimony the Board of Enquiry into her loss held at St John's two weeks later could do little more than confirm the identity of the vessel concerned.

In an analysis written after the battle for convoy ON202/ONS18 and subsequently broadcast in part, Grossadmiral Dönitz expressed his satisfaction at the achievements of the *Leuthen* group and the new technology deployed, exulting in the sinking of no fewer than twelve escorts and nine merchantmen. Where technology was concerned he was of course referring chiefly to the T5 (*Zaunkönig*) acoustic homing torpedo. A report on the same action written by the Admiralty's of Anti-Submarine Warfare Division with the benefit of Dönitz's broadcast remarked that this was 'interesting to note' since the actual figure was four escorts (three sunk and the frigate *Lagan* left a constructive total loss) and six merchantmen. As the Allies soon realised, U-boat

commanders including Engel in *U666* and Bahr in *U305* (see HMCS *St Croix*, **86**) tended to claim sinkings based on misleading acoustic data. Analysis after the war by Professor Jürgen Rohwer has revealed that the actual strike rate of the T5 against escorts was little more than sixteen per cent. This was due both to an oversensitive mechanism that frequently detonated the charge in the intended victim's wake and the rapid introduction of the British Foxer, US FXR and Canadian CAT noise-making devices which proved effective in luring the T5 away from the propellers of their would-be targets. Hindsight shows that the technological battle had swung irrevocably in the Allies' favour, but the loss of four escorts and over 400 sailors in seventy-two hours after months during which none had been sunk in the North Atlantic told the convoy men an altogether different story.

Fate of the crew

Itchen's end came so violently that a majority of those aboard (some 230 men) must have perished immediately. Fisher recalled seeing men leap overboard but noted that most soon drowned. The few who got clear of the wreck found themselves ahead of a column of merchantmen whose passing presented a mortal danger without any prospect of rescue, several being run down or sucked into a vortex of propellers. Stoker Fisher recalled how 'the wash from the ships would wash us back and forth; we would choke and there was a lot of oil and small boards that would slap us in the face'. The first to pass was the SS *James Smith* which had witnessed the event and observed men on either side as she sailed by. In a moment of excitement 'one merchant seaman yelled to them [the survivors] "Are you Americans?"'. The response to this rather unhelpful question was complete silence, leading Ensign W. M. Partlow USN to report his suspicion that these were Germans from the submarine caught in the searchlight and subsequently fired upon, but as neither *U666* nor any other was lost in this encounter the men were unquestionably survivors of *Itchen*. Nonetheless, the life-rings dropped by *James Smith* proved crucial for Fisher who reached one shortly after the convoy had passed. He and two others were rescued three hours later by the Polish merchantman *Wisła* which broke all

An undated photo of Herbert Engel. *DUBMA*

The bridge watch on the conning tower of *U666* seen some time between February and October 1943. Engel at left in white cap. In the centre under a crewman's hand is the UZO target bearing indicator; its binoculars are not fitted. The crewman behind clutches the attack periscope. *DUBMA*

regulations by stopping to do so. A search by HMC corvette *Sackville* and RAF aircraft the following day yielded only flotsam and empty rafts.

Just three men survived the sinking of HMS *Itchen*. From her own crew of 148 men only two were saved but the death toll was greatly increased by the fact that *Itchen* was carrying eighty-one survivors from *St Croix* and the sole survivor from *Polyanthus*, with Stoker William Fisher of *St Croix* the only one of this band to survive a second time. Perhaps due to the fact that only one man (Sub-Lt F. J. Young RNVR) had survived the sinking of *Polyanthus* on the 20th, many secondary sources have recorded and continue to record that one of the survivors from *Itchen*'s sinking was also from *Polyanthus*. This was not the case.

U666 and Herbert Engel

Built by Howaldtswerke at Hamburg and commissioned in August 1942, *U666* sailed from Kiel on her maiden patrol in February 1943. Commanded by Oblt.z.S. Herbert Engel, *U666* headed for the North Atlantic to form part of the *Ostmark*, *Stürmer* and *Seewolf* patrol lines. A six-week sortie brought only a hit on the Greek freighter *Carras* (finished off by *U333*) while herself suffering damage at the hands of an RAF Fortress on 19 March. *U666*'s next sortie in May and June 1943 (when assigned to the *Oder*, *Mosel* and *Trütz* patrol lines) yielded nothing beyond an RAF Hudson she shot down in the Bay of Biscay at the beginning of the patrol. Promoted Kapitänleutnant as he sailed to join the *Leuthen* group at the beginning of September, Engel scored his maiden victory with HMS *Itchen* but she remained *U666*'s only unassisted kill. On 11 January 1944, three weeks into her fourth patrol,

U666 was sighted off Ireland and sunk with all hands by a Swordfish from the escort carrier HMS *Fencer*.

Sources

Admiralty, Director of Anti-Submarine Warfare, *Analysis of U-Boat Operations: Convoys ONS18 and ON202, 19–24 September 1943* (TNA, ADM 199/2022)

—, *Enemy Submarine Attacks on H.M. Ships, 1943* (TNA, ADM 199/956)

—, Ship's movements: HMS *Itchen*, February–September 1943 (NHB)

Rohwer, Jürgen, *Analyse der T-5 („Zaunkönig")-Schüsse von U-Booten gegen Geleitfahrzeuge. U666: HMS* Itchen (Report for Bundesamt für Wehrtechnik und Beschaffung [Federal Office of Weapons Technology and Procurement], 1964) (BfZ, MaS 8/2.07)

—, *Die Entwicklung des Zaunkönigs: die Kriegsgeschichte als Hilfswissenschaft der Wehrtechnik, dargestellt am Beispiel der zielsuchenden Torpedos* (BfZ, Sammlung Rohwer, T-5 Auswertungsdokumente)

Cocker, M. P., *Frigates, Sloops, & Patrol Vessels of the Royal Navy 1900 to Date* (Kendal, Cumbria: Westmorland Gazette, 1985)

Fisher, William, 'The End of HMCS *St Croix*' in *Canadian Military History* 8, no. 3 (Summer 1999), pp. 63–9

Lavery, Brian, *River-Class Frigates and the Battle of the Atlantic: A Technical and Social History* (Greenwich: National Maritime Museum, 2006)

Memoirs of Stoker William Fisher (survivor):
http://www.naval-museum.mb.ca/battle_atlantic/st.croix/survivors-account.htm ; also in Winnipeg Free Press, 1 October 1943

89   USS *SKILL*

Lt Cdr E. J. Kevern, USNR†
Sunk by *U593* (Type VIIC), Kptlt Gerd Kelbling, 25 September 1943
Gulf of Salerno, 17 nm W of Punta Tresino (Italy)

The only known photo of USS *Skill*, seen on her launching day at Lorain, Ohio, 22 June 1942.
She blew up following a hit from *U593* on the starboard side forward. *US Navy*

Campaign   Operation AVALANCHE (Map 3)
Coordinates   40° 19' N, 14° 35' E
Kriegsmarine code   Quadrat CJ 6794
U-boat timekeeping   identical
Fatalities   76   *Survivors*   29

Displacement   890 tons
Dimensions   221' × 32.25' × 10.75'
Maximum speed   18 knots
Armament   1 × 3" AA; 2 × 40 mm AA; 8 × 20 mm AA

Career

The USS *Skill* (AM-115) was one of the Auk-class auxiliary mine-sweepers, a development of the pre-war Raven class with facilities for minelaying and improved anti-submarine capability. Powered by diesel-electric engines, she was laid down by the American Shipbuilding Co. at its Lorain, Ohio yard on Lake Erie in November 1941, launched in June 1942 and entered service on 17 November that year. Following her shakedown cruise she was assigned to Mine Squadron 6 of the Atlantic Fleet's Mine Division 17 and spent the first months of her career on anti-submarine duty off the eastern seaboard of the US. Although published sources (*DANFS*) have her operating along the North African coast in preparation for Operation TORCH in November 1942, *Skill* did not in fact reach the Mediterranean until 1943 where her first minesweeping duties were carried out in the run-up to Operation HUSKY, the invasion of Sicily on 10 July. The finest hour of a short but active career came off Porto Empedocle, Sicily on 15 July when *Skill* towed her sister *Staff* out of the minefield in which she had been crippled. Then on the 26th she helped the destroyer USS *Mayrant* (commanded by the president's son, Franklin Delano Roosevelt Jr) into Palermo after the latter had been heavily damaged in a German dive-bombing attack. *Skill* was subsequently damaged by a near-miss during an air raid on Palermo harbour that night, having to be patched and sent for dry docking in Algiers. Repairs were completed in time for her to participate in Operation AVALANCHE, the landings at Salerno which began on 9 September 1943, after which she was assigned to the patrol and convoy duties in local waters where she met her fate.

Background of the attack

On 15 September 1943 Kptlt Gerd Kelbling's *U593* sailed from Toulon charged with harrying Allied shipping in the Gulf of Salerno following the landings there six days earlier. Despite ongoing problems with two of his torpedo-firing mechanisms, on the 21st Kelbling sank the freighter *William W. Gerhard* as well as claiming damage to a second ship for which there is no corroboration. On the morning of the 25th, while cruising in almost exactly the same position as his success four days earlier, Kelbling sighted a pair of 'destroyers' through his periscope. These were the minesweepers *Seer* and *Skill*, then patrolling the Gulf of Salerno with their sisters *Speed* and *Pilot* of Mine Squadron 6. Though one of *Skill*'s crewmen recalled sighting torpedo tracks two minutes before the impact at 1140 (a doubtful observation given a total running time of ninety-six seconds and the alleged tracks being sighted just 150 yards from the vessel) most had no inkling that disaster was upon them until their ship was rent asunder. Indeed, so devastating was Kelbling's attack that most of *Skill*'s crewmen can never have known what hit them.

War Diary of *U593*, patrol of 15 September–5 October 1943: PG 30625, NHB, reel 1,127, pp. 593–4

Date, time	Details of position, wind, weather, sea, light, visibility, moonlight, etc.	Incidents
25.ix	Gulf of Salerno	
0000	Qu. CJ 6786	Surfaced.
0438	Qu. CJ 6794, wind SE 1, sea 0, 3/10 stratus, moon-lit, average to good visibility	
0502	Qu. CJ 6794	Dived.
0800	Qu. CJ 6794	
1110	Qu. CJ 6794	A destroyer patrolling back and forth to the south, another patrolling to the west.[1] The former is moving into a good firing position.
1140	Qu. CJ 6794, wind SE 0–1, sea 0, good visibility	Spread of three torpedoes fired from Tubes I, III, IV. Inclination 79°, bows right. Enemy speed 10 knots, range 1,500 m, angle of dispersion 3.5°, depth 4 m, Pi-2 pistols.[2] A hit after 96 sec. (= 1,500 m). For a short time a thin column of smoke around 40 m high is visible above the surface, then all that remains of the destroyer is a residue of mangled sheet metal.[3] This also sinks after a few seconds. The second destroyer now alters course towards us and closes at high speed. We go deep and withdraw to the north-west, towards Capri. Two more escorts arrive on the scene but they are hunting without Asdic, every so often dropping a few random patterns of depth charges nowhere near us.[4]
1200	Qu. CJ 6794	Day's run: 18.5 nm on the surface, 14 nm submerged = 32.5 nm.
1600	Qu. CJ 6791	
2106	Qu. CJ 6791, wind SE 1, sea 0–1, 4/10 stratus, good visibility	Having retired to the north-west we recharge our batteries off Capri. We are then picked up on radar by a destroyer immediately upon surfacing. We launch two *Aphrodites*.[5] Radar-warning readings gradually become fainter.
2245	Qu. CJ 6781	We carry out a test firing of all guns. No problems. Once again we shape a course for the middle of the bay.
2309 ⚋	Qu. CJ 6784	Dived.
26.ix	Gulf of Salerno	
0457		Outgoing W/T transmission 0235/26: *1140 Mar. Qu. CJ 6794 destroyer walloped. Still 3 + 1.*[6] *Kelbling.*

1 US minesweepers *Skill* and *Seer* respectively.

2 The standard torpedo detonator introduced in December 1942 in response to problems that had plagued its predecessor, the Pi-1 pistol.

3 Since both halves of the ship remained afloat for at least twenty minutes Kelbling was either mistaken in his observations or else decided to extrapolate a sinking in order to ensure his being credited with the pennant. By contrast, it seems likely that a zero was left off in the transcription of Kelbling's estimate of the height of the explosion column, which was adjudged to have reached 450 metres by observers in USS *Pilot*, then eight miles off. However, the limited field of vision afforded by his attack periscope may not have allowed Kelbling to appreciate the full ferocity of this event.

4 US minesweepers *Speed* and *Pilot*. The former dropped seven patterns of depth charges.

5 *Aphrodite* was a primitive radar decoy consisting of hydrogen-filled balloons streaming aluminium- or tin-foil strips. However, Kelbling's following sentence suggests that on this occasion they fulfilled their purpose.

6 Kelbling is listing his remaining torpedoes, probably three G7es and a G7a, but a reference to FAT or T5 torpedoes is also possible.

The sinking

Striking abaft the forward magazine, the torpedo explosion was followed immediately by a second of exceptional magnitude, it later being assumed that the warhead had detonated both the forward magazine and possibly also the forward fuel tanks. As Cdr A. H. Richards, CO of MinRon 6, recalled from the bridge of the USS *Pilot*, then eight miles distant, a 'tremendous column of white smoke . . . was followed almost instantly by brilliant, yellow and gold flames which completely consumed the white smoke and mounted upward to an estimated 1,000 to 1,500 feet'. The combined effect was to break the ship in two, though neither section sank as quickly as Kelbling claimed. The after section remained on a fairly even keel for a while, though the fire that engulfed its forward part not only prevented any form of damage control but gradually swept aft until it was completely ablaze. The stern section sank following a heavy explosion at 1200, twenty minutes after the attack. The forward section capsized immediately after the initial detonations and remained bows up before disappearing at around 1210.

Fate of the crew

The loss of USS *Skill* is unusual in that not a single officer or chief petty officer was seen after the initial blast. Such was the violence of the detonation and the speed with which the forward section capsized

Kptlt Kelbling (left) seen with Jürgen Könenkamp of *U375* at Salamis
in March 1943. *DUBMA*

that only five men survived from this part of the ship: a man at the bow, two on the flying bridge and two on the boat deck aft. The first of these, Seaman 2/c Henry R. Beausoleil, was standing mine watch and was blown into the sea about 100 yards from the ship. Many only realised what had befallen them on regaining consciousness in the water. Soundman 3/c Frank M. Lombardo was busy eating lunch in the packed mess hall aft:

> It was exactly 11:40. I bent over to take a bite . . . and that is the last thing I remember. The next thing I can recall is a feeling of going down, deeper and deeper into the water, and I instinctively turned around and pulled for the surface. I must have been 20 or 25 feet under, judging by the time it took to get to the top.

Reaching the surface about fifty yards from the ship and reboarding the after section, Lombardo saw a number of men struggling to release the rafts as the fire took hold. One of these was S2/c Joseph E. Garnier who had suffered two broken legs having been blown off the bridge yet was assisting with the release of the rafts. Carpenter's Mate 1/c Everett B. Reed was awarded the Silver Star for tireless efforts to assist wounded men trapped by fire or drowning near the wreck. Men in the water without lifejackets were provided them by those still aboard the ship, notably by Gunner's Mate 1/c Harry W. Bataille, though the survivors on the port side soon faced an even graver threat. Lombardo:

> But now the diesel oil caught fire, and with a roar it burst into a flame fifty or sixty feet high, a great red, crackling wall of fire that began to bear down on us. The raft was a trap. We couldn't move it, and though many of us were badly wounded we had to leave it and strike out on our own. I watched that fire, and my mind seemed numbed into blankness. I wondered if I could dive when it reached me and swim under it to safety and knew that there wasn't a chance of that. As it moved forward the area behind it kept burning, so that I would have to swim fifty yards underwater to get beyond it. The gentle breeze pushed it down the port side of the vessel and spread it deeper across the water. There was only one way for me to go, straight before the fire toward the stern of the ship. Movement was painful and I didn't seem to make headway at all. I could feel the terrific heat of the flame, and it gained relentlessly on me. There were several agonizing minutes when I thought I was gone, and then I had reached the stern of the ship and swam around it, shielded from the searing heat. The fire did not

follow me, for the wind pushed it away from the port side and all on the starboard side was clear water.

Others who struck out in the wrong direction or could not keep ahead of the blaze were engulfed while the rest of MinRon 6 looked on powerless to intervene. One who could count himself particularly fortunate was Electrician's Mate 2/c Edgar P. Lesperance, the last to abandon ship having given his lifejacket to a wounded comrade despite himself being a non-swimmer. Jumping from the after section shortly before it exploded, Lesperance was amazed to find that necessity had gifted him an unsuspected skill and he swam in improvised fashion a hundred yards to the nearest raft.

Over the next ninety minutes thirty-three dazed survivors – fewer than a third of the ship's complement – were hauled from the water by *Seer* and *Speed*, practically every one of them a stretcher case. Not a single survivor was unwounded. Four succumbed to their injuries either in *Speed* or subsequently aboard the US Army hospital ship *Acadia*. Among these was S2/c Garnier whose insistence on staying behind to help with the rafts prevented him getting sufficiently clear of the wreck before the after section exploded.

U593 and Gerd Kelbling

Built by Blohm & Voss at Hamburg and commissioned in October 1941, *U593* enjoyed a successful operational career under Kptlt Gerd Kelbling which saw her account for nine merchantmen (over 40,000 GRT) and five naval vessels in a twenty-one-month period. For all this, the first of her three patrols in the Atlantic in March 1942 was none too auspicious, *U593* narrowly escaping destruction at the hands of HM escort destroyer *Tynedale* off Ushant, though that particular score was to be more than settled at the end of the following year. Kelbling went on to sink three merchantmen off the eastern seaboard of the US and Canada before slipping into the Mediterranean in October 1942 where *U593*'s exploits rival those of any U-boat in that theatre. Three merchant kills in March 1943 were followed by another in April, the US *LST-333* in June (**G52**), a further merchantman in July, and then *Skill* and two more merchantman between September and October 1943. *U593*'s final patrol off Algeria in December 1943 brought her career to a climax, Kelbling accounting for *Tynedale* and her sister *Holcombe* on the 12th (**G66–67**), a feat which in turn heralded her own demise. After a prolonged hunt she was located by the destroyers USS *Wainwright* and HMS *Calpe* on the 13th and subjected to a relentless depth-charge attack. *U593* surfaced but was immediately taken under fire from her pursuers, leaving Kelbling no option but to scuttle his vessel. Unusually in such circumstances *U593*'s crew was rescued without the loss of a single man. Kelbling, who had been awarded the Knight's Cross in August 1943, was transported to a prisoner-of-war camp in Canada where he remained until September 1947. He died in August 2005.

Sources

US Navy, Action reports on loss of USS *Skill* by Cdr W. L. Messmer (30 September 1943) and Cdr A. H. Richards (7 October 1943) (NA, RG 38, World War II Action Reports, Entry A1 351); also on: http://home.earthlink.net/%7Eam115/navyrpt.html

Brooks Tomblin, Barbara, *With Utmost Spirit: Allied Naval Operations in the Mediterranean, 1942–1945* (Lexington, Ky.: University Press of Kentucky, 2004)

DANFS, VI, p. 526; also on:
> http://www.history.navy.mil/danfs/s13/skill-i.htm and
> http://www.hazegray.org/danfs/mine/am115.htm

Fay, Robert C., [with Soundman 3/c Frank M. Lombardo], 'Just an Auxiliary: When There's a Tough Job Ahead It's, "Send for the Sweeps" ' in *Our Navy* (mid-April 1944), pp. 4–6 and 60–1

Lott, Arnold S., *Most Dangerous Sea: A History of Mine Warfare, and an*

Account of US Navy Mine Warfare Operations in World War II and Korea (Annapolis, Md.: US Naval Institute, 1959)

Webpages devoted to USS *Skill*:
> http://home.earthlink.net/%7Eam115/
> http://www.navsource.org/archives/11/02115.htm

Webpage devoted to *U593*:
> http://home.earthlink.net/%7Eam115/u593.htm

90   USS *BUCK*

Lt Cdr M. J. Klein, USN†
Sunk by *U616* (Type VIIC), Oblt.z.S. Siegfried Koitschka, 9 October 1943
Tyrrhenian Sea, 50 nm S of Capri (Italy)

Buck under way in May 1942. Hit forward and wrecked in a secondary detonation, she was the first victim of the *Zaunkönig* acoustic homing torpedo in the Mediterranean. *BfZ*

Campaign	Operation AVALANCHE (Map 3)	*Displacement*	1,720 tons
Coordinates	39° 57' N, 14° 28' E	*Dimensions*	348.25' × 36' × 17.25'
Kriegsmarine code	Quadrat CJ 9128	*Maximum speed*	35 knots
U-boat timekeeping	identical	*Armament*	4 × 5"; 4 × 40 mm AA; 4 × 20 mm AA; 8 × 21" tt
Fatalities	about 150 *Survivors* 94 and 1		

Career

The Sims-class destroyers, of which USS *Buck* was the last of twelve units to be completed, were based on the design for the preceding Benham class though with the addition of a fifth 5-inch mounting and the new Mk-37 fire-control system, the first gunnery computer ever installed in a destroyer. However, the first units to be completed were found to be dangerously unstable and nearly 120 tons overweight, a situation remedied by the removal of the fifth mounting, a bank of four torpedo tubes, the searchlight tower aft and other top-hamper together with a redistribution of deck fittings and equipment. The result was a large and well-armed destroyer which gave sterling service in the Pacific and, in the case of *Wainwright*, *Roe* and *Buck*, in the Atlantic and Mediterranean theatres.

The USS *Buck* (DD-420) was laid down at Philadelphia Navy Yard in April 1938, launched in May 1939 and commissioned on 15 May 1940. Having shaken down, *Buck* spent the rest of that year with the

Atlantic Fleet before a spell with the Pacific Fleet in February 1941. From this she returned in June and 1 July found her as part of Task Force 19 en route for Argentia, Newfoundland where she joined a convoy carrying the 1st Marine Brigade to Reykjavik as part of the US occupation of Iceland. This accomplished, *Buck* began convoy escort duty between Iceland and the United States on 7 July, having several encounters with U-boats in the North Atlantic in the months before Pearl Harbor. Without altering her duties, the entry of the United States into the war nonetheless expanded *Buck*'s radius of operations to ports in Northern Ireland, North Africa and the Caribbean, and it was during one of these convoys, AT17, that she was joined by Lt Cdr (later Rear Admiral) Samuel Eliot Morison USNR to draw material for what became the official history of the US Navy in the Second World War. Her first brush with disaster came on 22 August 1942 while escorting convoy AT20 from Halifax, Nova Scotia to Scotland when she was struck on her starboard side aft by the British liner *Awatea* with 5,000 Canadian troops embarked. The collision, which occurred while *Buck* was attempting to shepherd another British troopship, the *Letitia*, to her proper station in dense fog, severed the keel and sliced through most of the fantail. With the starboard propeller wrecked and the port unit damaged, *Buck* had considerable difficulty maintaining steerway as her men battled to secure the wrecked fantail with lines and cables. The salvage effort had to be abandoned when the port propeller dropped off a few hours later, leaving *Buck* helpless in rising seas and her commander with no option but to cut the fantail loose together with seven men trapped in the steering compartment. Worse, the destroyer *Ingraham* was run down and sunk by the naval oiler USS *Chemung* as she closed to render assistance. Once *Chemung* – herself heavily damaged – had completed the rescue of *Ingraham*'s eleven survivors (later transferred to the USS *Bristol*, **92**) she took *Buck* in tow until relieved by the fleet tug USS *Cherokee*. *Buck* reached Boston on 26 August where repairs were not completed until November.

Atlantic convoy duty resumed that winter and continued until *Buck* was ordered to the Mediterranean in June 1943. Assigned to the Western Naval Task Force and operating from ports in Tunisia and Algeria, *Buck* performed bombardment, screening and patrol duties in the run-up to Operation HUSKY (the invasion of Sicily) and escorted a convoy of LCTs to the beachhead on D-Day itself, 10 July 1943. On 3 August, while escorting a return convoy from Sicily to Algeria, *Buck* sighted the Italian submarine *Argento* and blew her to the surface with three patterns of depth charges. *Argento* was abandoned under heavy fire, *Buck* taking forty-five prisoners. Having escorted a convoy to the United States *Buck* returned to the Mediterranean in late September in support of Operation AVALANCHE, the landings at Salerno.

Background of the attack

From July 1943 the Allied landings in Italy required the transport of an increasing volume of troops, supplies and equipment first to Sicily and then to the Italian mainland following the landings at Reggio di Calabria, Otranto and Salerno in early September. This state of affairs not only required US and British destroyers to perform continual escort duty across the Western Mediterranean but also to patrol the beachhead approaches against the possibility of submarine and torpedo boat attack. On 8 October the USS *Buck* took up a solitary patrol off the Gulf of Salerno south of Naples, not far from where the US destroyer *Rowan* had succumbed to an E-boat torpedo with the loss of over 200 lives on 11 September. At approximately 0030 on the 9th a firm radar contact was obtained by *Buck* at a range of 14,000 yards, Lt Cdr M. J. Klein immediately sounding the alarm for General Quarters and ordering a course alteration towards the contact. Increasing speed to twenty-five knots, Klein ordered a full pattern of depth charges to be set for 150 feet. His would-be target was Oblt.z.S. Siegfried Koitschka's *U616*, six days into a patrol off Salerno. The following excerpt from Koitschka's log not only reveals the advances made by the Germans in radar-warning apparatus but also the offensive capabilities of a new anti-escort weapon, the T5 *Zaunkönig* acoustic homing torpedo.

War Diary of *U616*, patrol of 3–15 October 1943: PG 30647, NHB, reel 1,130, pp. 609–10

Date, time	Details of position, wind, weather, sea, light, visibility, moonlight, etc.	Incidents
8.x		
1830		Surfaced.
2000	[Qu.] CJ 9161	
2005	Wind [?] 2, sea 2, bright moon, visibility 4 nm	We evade *S-Boot* group at bearing 20° true.[1]
2020		*S-Boot* group at bearing 40° true. We withdraw to the south-west.
2335		Radar-warning readings on 170-cm and 136-cm waves.
9.x	SW of Salerno Bay	
0000	[Qu.] CJ 9128, wind [?] 2, sea 3, cloud 5, visibility 2 nm, intermittent moon	Radar-warning readings on 136-cm wave, becoming very loud, continuous tone. A destroyer with inclination 0°, Hunt class or perhaps 'J' & 'K' class (two-gun fo'c's'le, single funnel).[2] We turn away but destroyer alters course towards us, still holding us.
0036		Torpedo fired from Tube V; a *Zaunkönig*. Depth set at 4 m, torpedo speed 40 knots, inclination 50°.[3] Fixed angle of fire 180°, range 3,000 m. Destroyer closes to within 2,000 m, then torpedo hits after 4 min. 15 sec.[4] Several high tongues of

---

1 *S-Boot* (short for *Schnellboot* = 'fast boat') was the German term for motor torpedo boat. Kriegsmarine examples of the type were known as E-boats by the Allies.

2 USS *Buck*. Convinced his target was British, Koitschka's torpedo report settled on her as being a 'J'- or 'K'-class destroyer. Although the mountings and stack were larger in the Sims-class destroyers than they were in the 'J' and 'K' classes, the three types were otherwise very similar in layout and proportions.

3 The speed of 40 knots recorded by Koitschka is an error since the T5 was capable of only 24.5 knots. However, the source of his confusion is clear: the 'close fire' setting (German = *Nahschuss*) he selected was common both to the *Zaunkönig* and to the older G7a torpedo, for which it indeed equated to a speed of 40 knots. Together with the fact that the *Zaunkönig*'s *Nahschuss* setting was intended for use against retiring targets with a relative inclination of between 110° and 180° (whereas *Buck* was in fact *closing* bow-on at speed), Koitschka's error raises the question of his familiarity with the capabilities of a weapon the Kriegsmarine had rushed into frontline service; see Introduction, pp. xxvi–xxvii.

4 Unlike conventional weapons, the meandering course characteristic of the *Zaunkönig* acoustic homing torpedo when the close or remote fire settings were actuated makes it impossible to derive the range at which *Buck* was hit from the running time.

flame accompanied by loud detonations (depth charges). This is followed by a billowing column of oil smoke some 200 m high. By the time the smoke has cleared there is nothing more to be seen of the destroyer. Radar-warning readings on 136-cm wave disappear. Readings appear on 170 cm. We launch two *Aphrodite* balloons and these radar readings then disappear as well.[5] We reload Tube V and withdraw to the west.

0050	Outgoing W/T transmission 0050/9/534: *0036 Mar. Qu. CJ 9128 destroyer sunk. Koitschka.*
0253	Radar-warning readings on 170 cm, two *Aphrodites* launched. Readings disappear.
0340	Radar-warning readings on 170 cm, two *Aphrodites* launched. Readings disappear.
0350	A hospital ship at bearing 290° true, heading east.
0400	[Qu.] CJ 9141

---

5 Koitschka is referring to hydrogen-filled *Aphrodite* radar decoy balloons which in his assessment permitted *U616* to elude further detection from an unidentified vessel. There is, however, no evidence that any other Allied vessel was in the vicinity at the time of the sinking.

The sinking

The ranking survivor, Lt J. A. Hoye USNR, who was stationed on the port side of the after deckhouse when the ship was hit, recorded that 'there seemed to be two explosions forward, occurring nearly simultaneously. *Buck* heeled to port and then immediately began to settle by the head.' Others also testified to a major secondary blast, suggesting a detonation of the forward magazines. One of the few witnesses to the effect of these explosions was Lt E. J. Cummings who 'went forward on the starboard side until I saw that everything forward of the stack had been blown away on the starboard side. I knew now that there was no possibility of saving the ship.' With any chance of further inspection forward barred by piles of wreckage on the port side, Lt Hoye 'passed the word to put all depth charges on safe and cut all rafts loose' before issuing the order to abandon ship. Barely had this order been passed than the sea began to wash over what remained of the main deck forward. The party charged with setting the starboard charges to safe was immediately engulfed, though those stowed aft and on the port side had by this time been made safe. Seconds later *Buck* plunged beneath the waves, Lt Hoye gaining one last sight of her: 'I turned and looked back. I saw the stern sticking up at about a 75° angle. She slid straight into the water as I watched. I estimated the time between the explosion and the sinking to have been about 4 minutes.' This assessment tallies precisely with the additional data provided in Koitschka's torpedo report: 'nothing more to be seen of destroyer after four minutes'.

Assessing *U616*'s cruise in Berlin, Konteradmiral Eberhard Godt purred over what he considered a 'model example of a *Zaunkönig* shot', the first to claim an Allied warship in the Mediterranean theatre. But though the effectiveness of the new T5 torpedo was here made quite apparent, such results were in fact the exception rather than the norm. Not only was visual evidence of the sort provided by Koitschka something of a rarity (most U-boat commanders preferring to go deep in order to avoid being targeted by their own weapon), but many end-of-run detonations were interpreted as hits. Moreover, orders that escorts close the enemy at slower speeds and the introduction of decoy noise-makers further diminished the already modest strike rate of what the *U-Boot-Waffe* had hoped would be a decisive weapon (see HMS *Itchen*, **88**). For USS *Buck*, however, the potency of the T5 was all too real and the measures to counter it not soon enough.

Fate of the crew

Most of those stationed on or forward of the bridge were accounted for by the blasts which rocked the ship at around 0040. An exception was Lt D. T. Hedges USNR, an officer taking passage in the *Buck*. Though having no official battle station, Hedges was permitted to observe events from the port wing of the bridge and had just heard the order for depth charges when *U616*'s torpedo hit. Left unconscious by the force of the blast, Hedges had no further recollection of the incident until he came to some way from the ship: 'When I regained consciousness I found myself some distance under water.' The blast was also felt by those further aft, Machinist Lester McGee (then beside the after deckhouse) noting the passage of 'several seconds before the force of the explosion knocked me down. When I ended up I was in front of gun 4.' No sooner had *Buck* gone down than a depth charge from the starboard racks detonated, wreaking havoc among the survivors most of whom were still within seventy yards of the sinking. Some were killed outright and others left fatally injured, while most of the rest reported being numbed from the chest or waist down for periods varying from a few seconds to ten minutes. Many had their lifejackets blasted off and rafts were overturned, at least one having its bottom blown out by the explosion.

Nor was the ordeal of *Buck*'s surviving crewmen over. Though the Mediterranean was relatively warm, a shortage of large flotsam, the almost complete absence of provisions, the extent of oil contamination and the number of those injured made for a dismal night, morale lowered still further by the certain knowledge that *Buck* had gone down too quickly for any SOS to be transmitted. Dawn found groups of men spread over a wide area, many trying to support injured comrades and encourage them not to give up. Spirits rose between 1000 and 1100 when they were sighted by a US Dakota transport plane which dropped three life rafts, but there was to be no immediate rescue. It was not until 2000 that the survivors were found by the US destroyer *Gleaves* and the British tank landing craft *LCT 170*. A total of ninety-five men were rescued, the majority by *Gleaves*, to be landed the following day at the Sicilian port of Palermo.

Buck was gone and her company killed and scattered but her memory lived on. When Samuel Eliot Morison completed the final volume of his monumental *History of United States Naval Operations in World War II* in 1960, his mind turned back with sadness and

Koitschka seen on *U616*'s return to Toulon on 15 October 1943, six days after sinking *Buck*. DUBMA

gratitude to the ship in which he and his project had first embarked eighteen years before. The name was revived in the shape of a Sumner-class destroyer launched in March 1945.

U616 and Siegfried Koitschka

Built by Blohm & Voss at Hamburg and commissioned in April 1942, *U616* did not become operational until February 1943 when she sailed from Kiel for the first of nine patrols under Oblt.z.S. (Kptlt from January 1944) Siegfried Koitschka. This first sortie apart, *U616*'s career was spent in the Mediterranean which she reached after forcing the Straits of Gibraltar in May 1943. Koitschka claimed many hits against enemy shipping in 1943 and early 1944 but post-war analysis revealed *Buck* and the British *LCT 553* (**G62**) two days later on the 11th to be his only confirmed sinkings. On the night of 13–14 May 1944 *U616* damaged a pair of merchantmen from convoy GUS39 off Algiers but the end was nigh. British escorts called up air support as well as surface assistance from the US Navy which committed no fewer than eight destroyers to the scene. *U616* was damaged by

the USS *Macomb* on the 14th and the resulting oil slick allowed the group to prolong the hunt for nearly three days, the longest against a single U-boat of the entire war. After a relentless pursuit with RAF air support, *U616* was eventually forced to the surface and scuttled under heavy fire on the 17th, though her crew all survived to be picked up by the USS *Ellyson*. Though they could not know it, for two of the hunting destroyers this success represented a settling of scores: it was *Hilary P. Jones* that rescued survivors from the *Reuben James* (**38**) after she had fallen victim to Koitschka's marksmanship when he was First Watch Officer of *U552*, and *Gleaves* which had rescued the majority of *Buck*'s surviving company seven months earlier. Koitschka remained in captivity until June 1946.

Sources

Navy Department, Office of Naval Records and Library, *Action Report: Sinking of USS Buck, 9 October 1943, off Salerno, Italy* (NA, No Serial, Box 871, 370/45/1/6)

—, Office of Naval Records and Library, Ships' Histories Section, *USS* Buck; and *USS* Buck *(DD-420)* (NHC, Box 140)

Rohwer, Prof. Jürgen, *Analyse der T-5 („Zaunkönig")-Schüsse von U-Booten gegen Geleitfahrzeuge. U616: USS* Buck (Report for Bundesamt für Wehrtechnik und Beschaffung [Federal Office of Weapons Technology and Procurement], 1964) (BfZ, MaS 8/2.07)

DANFS, I, p. 169; also on: http://www.history.navy.mil/danfs/b10/buck-ii. htm

Friedman, Norman, *US Destroyers: An Illustrated Design History* (2nd edn, Annapolis, Md.: Naval Institute Press, 2004)

Morison, *United States Naval Operations*, I, pp. 107 and 327; IX, pp. 42–3, 61–91; XIV, xii

Parkin, Robert Sinclair, *Blood on the Sea: American Destroyers Lost in World War II* (New York: Sarpedon, 1995)

Roscoe, *US Destroyer Operations*, p. 333

Webpage devoted to USS *Buck*:
http://www.destroyerhistory.org/goldplater/ussbuck.html

Webpage devoted to collisions during convoy AT20:
http://www.daileyint.com/seawar/apejtwas.htm

91   HMS *HYTHE*

Lt Cdr L. B. Miller, RN†

Sunk by *U371* (Type VIIC), Kptlt Waldemar Mehl, 11 October 1943

Western Mediterranean, 20 nm N of Béjaïa (Bougie) (Algeria)

Theatre Mediterranean (Map 3)	*Displacement* 656 tons
Coordinates 37° 04' N, 05° 00' E	*Dimensions* 174' × 28.5' × 8.25'
Kriegsmarine code Quadrat CH 9553	*Maximum speed* 16 knots
U-boat timekeeping identical	*Armament* 1 × 3" AA; 1 × 40 mm AA
Fatalities 62 *Survivors* 20	

Career

For notes on the sloop type, see HMS *Penzance* (**16**).

Laid down as the *Banff* at the Ailsa Shipbuilding Co. of Troon, Scotland in July 1940, the Bangor-class minesweeping sloop *Hythe* was launched in September 1941 and completed in March 1942. The Bangor class, of which over 160 units were laid down in British,

Canadian, Indian and Hong Kong yards, was a response to the Royal Navy's pressing need for minesweeping and escort vessels capable of being built in large numbers by civilian yards and powered by a range of reciprocating, diesel and turbine machinery. The result was a small vessel which, though ill-suited to the accretion of minesweeping technology, nonetheless gave valuable service all over the world.

Hythe, probably soon after completion in the spring of 1942. She was struck abreast the bridge by a *Zaunkönig* torpedo from *U371* and sank in four minutes with much of her crew. *IWM*

Career details for *Hythe* are few, but after working up in Scottish waters she sailed for Gibraltar in mid-May 1942 and remained in the Mediterranean theatre for the rest of her career, which included duty with the Malta convoys.

Background of the attack

On 4 October 1943 convoy MKS27, consisting of twelve ships arranged in five columns, sailed from Alexandria bound for Gibraltar, a passage that was expected to take ten days. Her escort was made up of HM sloops *Hythe* (Senior Officer) and *Rye*, along with two converted whalers of the South African 22nd Anti-Submarine Group, HMSASs *Southern Isles* and *Protea*. By 0100 on the 11th the convoy had reached

the waters north of the Algerian port of Bougie then being patrolled by Kptlt Waldemar Mehl's *U371*. Just before 0112 ship time *Hythe's* Asdic operator picked up what he believed to be a submarine echo at 2,000 yards on the port bow, course being altered accordingly. *Hythe's* commanding officer, Lt Cdr L. B. Miller, reached the bridge to find the range reduced to an estimated 400 yards and was later reported to have brought his ship round to starboard to pass ahead of the submarine in order to attack with depth charges. Mehl had missed an eastbound convoy the previous evening but this time was not to be denied and *Hythe* was hopelessly shattered by an acoustic homing torpedo before she could deliver her attack.

War Diary of *U371*, patrol of 7–28 October 1943: PG 30433, NHB, reel 1,101, pp. 559–60

Date, time	Details of position, wind, weather, sea, light, visibility, moonlight, etc.	Incidents
10.x		
0536	Qu. CH 9537	Dived.
0628	Qu. CH 9537	Unaccompanied destroyer heaves into sight at bearing 15° true, proceeding west at 25 knots. She passes us at a range of 5,000 m. American Livermore class. We had only picked her up on the hydrophones 10 min. earlier.
		We spend the rest of the day lying motionless.
1606	Qu. CH 9529	At bearing 320° true four destroyer masts in sight. Very far off. They've already passed me. Heading west. Barely picked up by hydrophone.
1835	Qu. CH 9529, bright moonlight, intermittently overcast, slightly agitated sea	Hydrophone effect at 228° true, presumably the anticipated convoy, hugging the coast as she approaches.[1] We position ourselves ahead of the convoy course line with the intention of carrying out a submerged attack by moonlight.
2030		However, she passes us to the south without ever coming into sight.
2145		We raise the round dipole; aircraft warning readings are piercingly loud.[2]

---

1 Convoy KMS31G. Mehl had been alerted to its approach the previous day.

2 The *Runddipol* was the antenna of the recently introduced *Naxos* radar detector, effective against both airborne and seaborne apparatus. Mehl refers to this device by name in his signal of 2211 on the 11th. The *Runddipol* replaced the so-called Biscay Cross, a rudimentary wooden cross strung with wires which had to be dismantled before diving.

Date, time	Details of position, wind, weather, sea, light, visibility, moonlight, etc.	Incidents
2250		Fresh hydrophone effect at bearing 102° true, presumably the westbound convoy.[3] We haul ahead on the basis of hydrophone data to carry out a submerged attack.
11.x		
0045	Qu. CH 9553	Westbound convoy in sight. She approaches, bows right. Attack carried out using night search periscope. Around eight vessels with one destroyer operating ahead of the convoy.[4] We pick up the starboard side escort by hydrophone but initially cannot sight her in the pale moonlight.[5] Asdic noises are piercingly loud; I've probably been detected and no doubt by the side destroyer which I can now see through the periscope. Narrow silhouette. The leading destroyer is zigzagging normally but then reduces speed. She is 1,000 m off, inclination 20°.
0109	Qu. CH 9553	I order a *Zaunkönig* fired at this escort from Tube II, inclination 20°, bows right, speed 12 knots, depth 4 m, range 1,000 m but entered as 2,000 m.[6] Angle of fire 0°. Immediately after we fire the side destroyer looms up close by, inclination 0°, substantial bow wave.[7] I order us deep. As we are going down a very clear contact detonation after 63 sec. running time. At 180 m five very well aimed depth charges cause major reverberations but only minor damage – remarkable that a boat like this pulled through.[8] Further noises, presumably relating to the sinking of the destroyer we hit. Another phase of Asdic hunting; we hear the convoy receding through the hydrophones, nothing more.
0345		Back to periscope depth.
0350		Round dipole raised.[2] Aircraft warning readings on 170-cm wave, volume 3.
0430	Qu. CH 9537	As 0350. We remain submerged. CO_2 level brought back down to 3.5 % and held there. We stay put, lying motionless.
↗ 2211		Outgoing W/T transmission 1745/LL/582: *0109 westbound convoy [Qu. AB] 9553, Zaunkönig fired at lead destroyer, depth 4 [m], inclination 70°, speed 12 knots, range 1,000 m.[9] Contact detonation heard after 63 sec. No further observations due to immediate counter-attack. Punishing depth charges.* Naxos *warning readings.[2]* Mehl.

---

3   Convoy MKS27.

4   The 'destroyer' ahead of the convoy was HM sloop *Hythe*. MKS27 in fact consisted of twelve merchantmen and four escorts.

5   *Hythe* apart, the dispositions of the escort cannot be discerned from the available data, though as HMSAS *Southern Isles* launched an immediate counter-attack (see the entry for 0109) she may well have been the vessel sighted.

6   Mehl's decision to enter a range greater than that estimated is unclear though may be motivated by the estimated range being the same as the initial straight run or *Sperrstrecke* of the T5; see HMS *Itchen* (**88**), n. 8.

7   Presumably HMSAS *Southern Isles*, which went on to make the depth-charge attack recorded at 0109.

8   Though Mehl's comment might be taken as a criticism of the Type-VIIC boats, he is no doubt confining himself to *U371* which had put in two years' arduous war service and had suffered a severe depth-charging during her first Mediterranean patrol in October 1941.

9   The inclination of 70 degrees given here contradicts the 20 degrees stated earlier in the attack sequence and in the torpedo report; quite possibly a typist's error.

The sinking

No Board of Enquiry was called for HMS *Hythe* and in the absence of any officer survivors official information concerning her loss appears to be limited to a succinct two-page report prepared by Lt J. A. Pearson DSC RNR, CO of HMS *Rye*, based on his own observations and with information gleaned from survivors. The torpedo which struck *Hythe* at 0112 detonated below the bridge on the port side between the forward boiler room and forward provision room. The bow section was sheared off forward of the bridge while 'the after part of the ship still being propelled by the engines ran down on her fore part'. Both mast and funnel collapsed onto the bridge which 'was completely wrecked and apparently on fire'. Settling rapidly, what remained of HMS *Hythe* 'sank on an almost even keel in about four minutes'.

The Director of the Admiralty's Anti-U-Boat Division, Capt. C. P. Howard-Johnston DSO DSC, ventured that *Hythe* had either 'inadvertently crossed the track of torpedoes fired at the convoy, or presented the boat with an inviting target when it threw off to starboard in the latter stages of the attack', the reported hit amidships no doubt concealing the fact that *Hythe* had fallen victim to a new weapon: the acoustic torpedo. Altogether clearer was the fact that the *Zaunkönig* offered new possibilities to the *U-Boot-Waffe* in the Mediterranean, the sinking of *Hythe* coming hard on the heels of that of USS *Buck* (**90**). Indeed, within forty-eight hours Mehl had struck again with the same weapon (see the subsequent entry for USS *Bristol*, **92**).

Fate of the crew

Virtually no information has emerged to shed light on the situation aboard during *Hythe*'s last moments or on the plight of her men in the water. Given the manner of her sinking it must be supposed that the great majority of the survivors, who represented less than a quarter

Waldemar Mehl suitably accoutred in scarf, *Arbeitspäckchen* ('working suit') and commander's white cap, probably at the start of one of his patrols in command of *U371* between May 1942 and March 1944. *DUBMA*

of her complement of eighty-two men, were stationed aft when the torpedo hit, while few if any can have survived from the bow section in view of what befell it. Able Seaman S. J. Roxburgh recalled the situation on the bridge immediately before the detonation in which Lt Cdr Miller and his bridge watch perished to a man, the former having by this time taken up his depth-charge station aft. Arriving on the scene shortly after, HMS *Rye* sighted a handful of Carley floats containing a score of dazed and oil-soaked men, most of whom were carrying injuries. Lowering her boats, *Rye* circled the position while *Southern Isles* led the work of rescue, the last man being hauled aboard at 0148

– little more than thirty minutes after the sinking. The survivors were landed at Gibraltar on 14 October.

U371 and Waldemar Mehl

Built by Howaldtswerke at Kiel and commissioned in March 1941, *U371* had a long and relatively successful career under four commanders between May 1941 and May 1944. *U371*'s first Kommandant, Kptlt Heinrich Driver, claimed three merchantmen in the Atlantic before taking her into the Mediterranean on his third patrol in September 1941. Two further cruises proved fruitless and Driver was succeeded by Kptlt Heinz-Joachim Neumann (see **64**) as acting Kommandant in the spring of 1942, a single patrol yielding no pennants. In July Kptlt Waldemar Mehl sailed on the first of eleven patrols in command. His record was an impressive one for the Mediterranean, *U371* sinking or damaging eight merchantmen and accounting for three escorts including HM minesweeping trawler *Jura* on 7 January 1943 (**G45**), *Hythe* and the US destroyer *Bristol* two days later on 13 October (**92**).

For details of *U371*'s and Mehl's subsequent careers, see USS *Bristol*.

Sources

Admiralty, *Enemy Submarine Attacks on Merchant Shipping, 1943: Reports* (TNA, ADM 199/441)
—, Ship's movements: HMS *Hythe*, March 1942–September 1943 (NHB)
U371 file (DUBMA)

Cocker, M. P., *Mine Warfare Vessels of the Royal Navy, 1908 to Date* (Shrewsbury, Salop: Airlife Publishing, 1993)
Schneider, Werner, *12 Feindfahrten. Als Funker auf U-431, U-410 und U-371 im Atlantik und im Mittelmeer. Ausbildung, Einsatz, Gefangenschaft, 1940– 1946* (Weinheim: Germania Verlag, 2006)
Stern, Robert C., *Battle Beneath the Waves: U-Boats at War* (London: Arms and Armour Press, 1999)

---

92   USS *BRISTOL*

Cdr J. A. Glick, USN
Sunk by *U371* (Type VIIC), Kptlt Waldemar Mehl, 13 October 1943
Western Mediterranean, 15 nm NW of Cap Bougaroun (Algeria)

Theatre   Mediterranean (Map 3)
Coordinates   37° 19' N, 06° 19' E
Kriegsmarine code   Quadrat CH 9631
U-boat timekeeping   identical
Fatalities   52   *Survivors*   241

Displacement   1,839 tons
Dimensions   348.25' × 36' × 17.5'
Maximum speed   37.5 knots
Armament   4 × 5"; 4 × 40 mm AA; 7 × 20 mm AA; 5 × 21" tt

Career

The Bristol-class destroyers, of which the subject of this entry was the leading unit, were a sub-group of the Benson and Gleaves classes, themselves based on the design for the preceding Sims class (see USS *Buck*, **90**). These ships differed from the Sims class in the addition of quintuple torpedo tubes and a fourth boiler, which required the placing of a second stack. The Bristol sub-group owed its origin to the decision by the General Board of the US Navy to complete units of the Benson and Gleaves classes with an improved anti-aircraft armament. The new design, which was approved in May 1940, provided for the replacement

of one of the 5-inch mountings and a bank of quintuple torpedo tubes with 40- and 20-mm guns. Though 40-mm guns were initially in short supply, *Bristol* was the first of sixty-eight vessels so completed.

The USS *Bristol* (DD-453) was laid down by the Federal Shipbuilding and Drydocking Company, Kearny, New Jersey in December 1940, launched in July 1941 and commissioned on 21 October 1941. *Bristol* was in the middle of her shakedown cruise in the Chesapeake and Casco Bay areas when the Japanese struck Pearl Harbor and the rest of December was spent on training duties based on Norfolk, Virginia. In January 1942 she was allocated to plane

Bristol under way in the Atlantic in April 1943. She had her back broken by a *Zaunkönig* acoustic homing torpedo from *U371* and sank in twelve minutes. *BfZ*

guard duty for the carrier *Wasp* before serving a brief stint with the South Atlantic Patrol between February and March. *Bristol* was then assigned to convoy escort duty in the Atlantic, on which she served between New York, Boston, Nova Scotia and Londonderry until September 1942. Encounters with the enemy were few but *Bristol* had twice to rescue survivors from the Atlantic, first from the US steamer *West Imboden* on 21 April and then from the destroyer *Ingraham* after she had been run down and sunk by the naval oiler USS *Chemung* on 22 August while escorting convoy AT20 from Halifax to Scotland (see USS *Buck*). Refit and repair were carried out at Boston in June and then in New York between September and October where she was earmarked as an escort for Operation TORCH, the Allied landings in North Africa. On 24 October *Bristol* joined the Western Naval Task Force destined for French Morocco, being allocated for the landings at Fédala east of Casablanca. Although the invasion convoy achieved complete surprise, the Fédala landings on 8 November met sufficient opposition to require the Task Force to open fire on Vichy positions ashore. *Bristol* began the day by taking the French trawler *Poitou* (see **G43**) as a prize but later saw action in earnest as units of the Vichy navy steamed from Casablanca to contest the landings. Together with other units of the Center Attack Force, she engaged the destroyer *Milan* which was driven ashore under heavy fire and then opened up on the 100-mm guns of the Batterie du Port on Cap Fédala which was shelling the landing beaches. Before the day was done *Bristol* had not only resumed fire on the fort but joined the pursuit of a force of Vichy ships back to Casablanca. But it was submarines that presented the greatest danger to Operation TORCH and on 11 November *Bristol* led the counter-attack on *U173* after the latter had torpedoed three US Navy ships outside Casablanca harbour (including the troop transport USS *Joseph Hewes*, **G38**), opening up with her forward 5-inch gun and landing numerous 20-mm rounds on the conning tower while attempting to ram. Two patterns of depth charges were also dropped but *U173* escaped to damage the Navy transport *Electra* on the 15th, *Bristol* being ordered to assist the salvage effort. Already on the 12th *Bristol* had rescued survivors from the troop transport *Tasker H. Bliss*,

torpedoed by *U130* during a telling attack on the anchorage at Fédala (**G41**). On 17 November *Bristol* was assigned to escort a convoy back to Norfolk, which she reached without incident on the 30th.

Following a refit in New York, *Bristol* resumed escort duty in the Caribbean and in the Atlantic, making two return trips to Casablanca and being briefly assigned to TG 21.14, a hunter-killer group centred on the escort carrier USS *Card*. Early July 1943 found *Bristol* back in the Mediterranean where on the 7th she sailed from the Tunisian port of Bizerte as part of the Navigation Group charged with guiding the US 7th Army to Licata, one of the landing places selected for the Allied invasion of Sicily codenamed Operation HUSKY. With the assault imminent, *Bristol* was ordered to stand off and provide fire support against shore batteries, which she did under increasingly heavy air attack at dawn on the 10th – D-Day. Except for refuelling, *Bristol* remained off Licata for the rest of July before moving to the north side of the island where she shot down three German aircraft off Capo d'Orlando between 8 and 11 August. On 6 September *Bristol* sailed from North Africa to participate in Operation AVALANCHE, the US landings at Salerno. Her duties as part of Fire Support Group 2, Southern Attack Force on D-Day, 9 September 1943, mirrored those during HUSKY: escorting the assault forces inshore and providing fire support as needed, in this case against German armour. Two days later she had the melancholy duty of rescuing survivors from the US destroyer *Rowan* which had succumbed to an E-boat torpedo off the Gulf of Salerno. The seventy survivors were landed at Oran on the 14th, *Bristol* resuming her patrol duties in the Salerno area for the rest of the month.

Background of the attack

Two days after sinking HMS *Hythe* (**91**) Kptlt Waldemar Mehl's *U371* struck again in the same waters, thereby claiming a second US Navy destroyer for the *U-Boot-Waffe* in 100 hours (see USS *Buck*, **90**). Midnight on 12 October 1943 found the USS *Bristol* screening fast troop convoy SNF5 between Naples and Oran in company with USSs *Wainwright* (Senior Officer), *Rhind*, *Trippe*, *Benson* and *Nicholson*.

Occupying Position 4 on the port bow of the convoy, *Bristol* was steaming at fifteen knots some 4,000 yards from the nearest ship of the main body. At 0409 on the 13th the base course of the convoy was adjusted and a new zigzag commenced a few minutes later. No sooner had *Bristol* settled on this course than the junior officer of the watch, Ensign N. F. Taylor, heard a suspiciously loud noise emanating from the ship's hydrophone apparatus. The time was 0422. Hurrying back to the Sound Unit hut, Taylor, who was *Bristol*'s sound and radar officer,

'found the Sound Operator training back and forth trying to find the bearing of the point of highest noise intensity. By this time, however, the noise was coming in from all around the forward part of the ship; and it was impossible to obtain a bearing on it.' Taylor immediately reached for the phone to alert the bridge but before he could place his hand on the receiver *Bristol* was shattered by a T5 acoustic torpedo from *U371*.

War Diary of *U371*, patrol of 7–28 October 1943: PG 30433, NHB, reel 1,101, p. 562

Date, time	Details of position, wind, weather, sea, light, visibility, moonlight, etc.	Incidents
13.x	North of Cap Bougaroni[1]	
0128	Qu. CH 9631	A destroyer on a westerly course, proceeding at 19 knots, passes at a range of about 5,000 m. We had previously heard her approach through the hydrophones and started an attack run.[2] From the hydrophone bearings it sounded as if there was another destroyer as well.[3]
0235		Destroyer picked up at different hydrophone bearing of 95° true, also doing 19 knots. Run-in carried out with attack periscope because of depth-keeping problems.
0410	Qu. CH 9631	Destroyer in sight at bearing 56° true, turns out to be the lead destroyer of a westbound convoy.[4] The moon is now low as well as being behind me so I can only make them out as vague silhouettes. I am situated directly ahead of the port escorts. It's too dark to fire at the merchantmen so I decide to attack the destroyer stationed on the port bow of the convoy. The lead destroyer has now stopped a few hundred metres abeam of me.[5] No Asdic pulses.[6]
0417	Qu. CH 9631	*Zaunkönig* fired at the large destroyer from Tube V. Inclination 20°, bows left, depth 5 m, speed 17 knots, range approximately 1,000 m but 3,000 entered, angle of fire 155°.[7]
		After 2 min. 43 sec. a hit amidships on the starboard side. A contact detonation both from the way it looked and sounded.[8] Isolated blazing pieces of wreckage, dark but small detonation clouds, a white mushroom cloud of steam.
		Given the uncertainty of the situation we go very deep. Powerful sinking noises and cracking sounds, no depth charges. The other destroyers seem to have assumed a surface attack and are sweeping the area at high speed. On one occasion I am overrun.
0720		To periscope depth. Two destroyers in sight at bearing 240° true, 8,000 m off. A hunting group, occasional Asdic noises.[6] We withdraw. Sporadic depth charges.
1330		Full sweep of horizon – nothing. We noted the two American Sims-class destroyers, 1,570 tons.[9] It is to be assumed that the vessel sunk belonged to the same class.[10]

---

1 Mehl here uses the French name for Cap Bougaroun.

2 There is no earlier log entry to shed light on this.

3 There were six destroyers in all: USSs *Bristol*, *Wainwright*, *Rhind*, *Trippe*, *Benson* and *Nicholson*.

4 It is not clear which member of the screen this was though *Bristol* can be discounted since Mehl correctly identifies the targeted vessel as being on the port bow of the convoy.

5 Mehl appears to have interpreted either the convoy base course alteration at 0409 or the change of zigzag pattern at 0411 as the ship having stopped, of which there is no mention in US sources.

6 Mehl here uses the English term 'Asdic'.

7 Mehl's decision to enter a range greater than that estimated is unclear though may be motivated by the estimated range being the same as the initial straight run or *Sperrstrecke* of the T5; see HMS *Itchen* (**88**), n. 8.

8 In other words, the torpedo had struck *Bristol*'s hull rather than detonating magnetically beneath it. Mehl might reasonably have expected the latter given his depth settings.

9 These are presumably the same destroyers as those referred to at 0720.

10 Though incorrect, this is still a commendable piece of ship recognition by Mehl, *Bristol*'s design owing much to the Sims class.

The sinking

Bristol was struck on the starboard side abreast the forward engine room, 'and in view of the fact that the ship broke into two parts the impact is believed to have been made close to the keel'. No subsequent explosions or fires were reported, nor was any water column observed by other vessels in the screen. Briefly stunned by the force of the explosion, by the time Cdr Glick reached the bridge from the Emergency Cabin his ship was in her death throes. No more than a minute or so had passed since the detonation:

> The ship already had buckled in the vicinity of the forward smoke pipe. Both the bow and the stern were angled upward. The mast was inclined aft and the forward smoke pipe was inclined forward. The main deck at the break of the fo'c'sle was under water and it was believed that the forward smoke pipe was being carried away slowly. Steam was escaping from the machinery spaces and a grating sound was heard as metal members and plating ruptured progressively.

A momentary lull in the grinding of metal encouraged Glick in the hope that *Bristol* might remain afloat a while longer. 'This impression was not of long duration, however, for soon the breaking of metal was heard again and the forward half of the ship increased its angle from the horizontal rapidly to approximately 30°.' With power, steering, steam and communications lost, Glick passed the order to abandon ship and watched as the two extremities increased 'their angle from the horizontal and settled into the water slowly'. Her back broken, *Bristol* sank in two parts, the stern section eight minutes after the blast and the bows plunging out of sight three or four minutes later after reaching an angle of eighty degrees. Within twelve minutes of being struck the USS *Bristol* was no more.

Fate of the crew

Despite the effect of the detonation and the fact that a good part of the crew was asleep, only fifty-two members of *Bristol*'s complement of 293 men perished in the sinking and its aftermath. Virtually all the fatalities were incurred among the duty watches in the forward fire room, forward engine room and after fire room which took the brunt of the blast. That so few were lost in the aftermath was owed to the launching of eight life floats and two rubber life nets, the 'surprisingly small amount of fuel oil on the surface of the water after the ship sank', the 'high state of training which existed and resulted in the orderly abandoning of the ship', in addition to the speed with which USS *Trippe* was on the scene to rescue survivors. Though *Trippe* could not commence this task until *Wainwright* arrived to screen her, the first men were being rescued forty minutes after the sinking and the rest had been recovered within two hours of that event. The vast majority (234) were rescued by *Trippe*, though one officer and seven men were picked up by *Wainwright*, which had time to commit a body to the deep before the rescue vessels turned to rejoin the convoy. The survivors were landed at Algiers later that day and the wounded, most suffering from lacerations, placed in the care of a US Army hospital.

Though the loss of a valuable and battle-hardened unit was felt to be 'a matter of great regret', Vice Admiral H. Kent Hewitt, Commander of US Naval Forces in North West African Waters, was quick to praise the rescue operation, noting that 'the fact that so many of her officers and men were rescued is a matter of profound gratification. This gallant and well trained crew is a valuable asset and will continue to do

The bridge watch of *U371* seen off Tobruk in May 1942. *DUBMA*

valiant service in the days that lie ahead. It is hoped that they can be kept together to man another destroyer.' It is not clear whether Hewitt's wish was realised, but both Cdr Glick and his Executive Officer, Lt Cdr Lederer received high praise for their conduct, the former having remained aboard until the last possible minute.

U371 and Waldemar Mehl

For details of *U371*'s and Mehl's early career, see the preceding entry for HMS *Hythe* (**91**).

The sinking of the USS *Bristol* brought Kptlt Waldemar Mehl's tally in *U371* to eight merchantmen and three escorts, though she was to be his last success. In March 1944 command of *U371* devolved upon Oblt.z.S. Horst-Arno Fenski (see HMS *Penelope*, **96**) who accounted for two more ships including the trooper *Dempo* of 17,024 GRT before the end came on 4 May. A hit on the US destroyer *Menges* in the Gulf of Bougie off Algeria early on the 3rd led to an unrelenting pursuit by an assortment of Allied vessels and aircraft including the destroyer escorts *Pride* and *Joseph E. Campbell* of the US Navy, the escort destroyer HMS *Blankney*, the destroyer *L'Alcyon* and escort destroyer *Sénégalais* of the Free French navy, and the US minesweeper *Sustain*. For a day Fenski kept *U371* on the seabed in the hope that the hunters would quit the scene. However, their patience was rewarded on the morning of the 4th when *U371*, by now desperately low on oxygen and power, was obliged to surface. Though immediately spotted and forced to scuttle herself under heavy fire from *Sénégalais*, Fenski had a parting shot up his sleeve in the shape of a *Zaunkönig* torpedo which he unleashed even as his men were abandoning ship. This struck *Sénégalais* though without causing sufficient damage to sink her. All but three of *U371*'s crew were captured, Fenski among them.

In recognition of his achievements Waldemar Mehl was awarded the Knight's Cross on leaving *U371* in March 1944, being transferred to the first of a series of shore appointments with *F.d.U. Mittelmeer* and then B.d.U. itself. He was promoted Korvettenkapitän shortly before the end of the war and spent three months in a minesweeping unit following the German surrender. Mehl, who became an architect in civilian life, died in retirement in March 1996.

Sources

Navy Department, Office of Naval Records and Library, *Action Report of Torpedoing and Loss of the USS* Bristol, *13 October 1943* (NA, No Serial, Box 866, 370/45/1/5)

—, Office of the Chief of Naval Operations, Division of Naval History, *History of USS* Bristol *(DD 453)*; and *USS* Bristol *(DD 453)* (NHC, Box 130)

Mehl, Waldemar, typescript letter to Herrn Erich Schwarzer, 7 May 1988 (DUBMA, *U371* folder)

Rohwer, Prof. Jürgen, *Analyse der T-5 („Zaunkönig")-Schüsse von U-Booten gegen Geleitfahrzeuge. U371: USS* Bristol (Report for Bundesamt für Wehrtechnik und Beschaffung [Federal Office of Weapons Technology

and Procurement], 1964) (BfZ, MaS 8/2.07)

DANFS, I, p. 159; also on: http://www.history.navy.mil/danfs/b9/bristol-i.htm

Friedman, Norman, *US Destroyers: An Illustrated Design History* (2nd edn, Annapolis, Md.: Naval Institute Press, 2004)

Morison, *United States Naval Operations*, II, pp. 19–114 and 157–74; IX, pp. 71–91, 170–209, 254–70, 295–301 and 310–14

Parkin, Robert Sinclair, *Blood on the Sea: American Destroyers Lost in World War II* (New York: Sarpedon, 1995)

Schneider, Werner, *12 Feindfahrten. Als Funker auf U-431, U-410 und U-371 im Atlantik und im Mittelmeer. Ausbildung, Einsatz, Gefangenschaft, 1940–1946* (Weinheim: Germania Verlag, 2006)

93   USS *LEARY*

Cdr J. E. Kyes, USN†
Sunk by *U275* (Type VIIC), Oblt.z.S. Helmut Bork, 24 December 1943
North Atlantic, 580 nm WNW of La Coruña (Spain)

Hunter turned hunted: *Leary* seen on 20 December 1943, just four days before she succumbed to a *Zaunkönig* acoustic homing torpedo from *U275*. BfZ

Theatre	North Atlantic (Map 1)	*Displacement*	1,160 tons
Coordinates	45° 15' N, 21° 40' W	*Dimensions*	314.25' × 31' × 9.25'
Kriegsmarine code	Quadrat BE 7343	*Maximum speed*	35 knots
U-boat timekeeping differential	+3 hours	*Armament*	6 × 3"; 4 × .5" AA; 6 × 21" tt
Fatalities 97	*Survivors* 59		

Career

For design notes on the Wickes-class destroyers, of which USS *Leary* was one of 111 units, see HNorMS *Bath* (**30**).

The USS *Leary* (DD-158) was laid down by the New York Shipbuilding Corp. of Camden, New Jersey in March 1918 and launched in December that same year. *Leary* was commissioned on 5 December 1919 and departed Boston for her shakedown cruise on 28 January 1920. After a year's training at Guantánamo, Cuba and in northern waters, *Leary* transited the Panama Canal to join the Battle Fleet in the Pacific in January 1921. She participated in the fleet manoeuvres off Peru in February but USS *Leary* was already nearing the end of her first period of service. On 29 June she was decommissioned in accordance with the terms of the Washington Naval Treaty and laid

up in reserve at Philadelphia Navy Yard. The reprieve came on 1 May 1930 when she was reactivated and allocated to the Atlantic Fleet based at Newport, Rhode Island. *Leary* spent the rest of the inter-war period on fleet duties in the Caribbean and in the Pacific where joint manoeuvres took her to California every other year, though training cruises for reserves and midshipmen took up an increasing proportion of her time after 1935.

The outbreak of war in Europe in September 1939 brought *Leary* and her sister *Hamilton* to the lower New England coast on anti-submarine patrol. Converted to a destroyer escort during 1941, *Leary* joined the increasingly hazardous Iceland convoy run in September of that year. Already in April 1937 she had made history by becoming the first US warship to take a search radar to sea; now on 19 November

1941 *Leary* became the first US vessel to make radar contact with a U-boat. In February 1942 *Leary* began escorting convoys between the Mid-Ocean Meeting Point and Iceland, remaining on this duty until refitted at Boston in February 1943 where she lost one of her fours stacks. After anti-submarine training out of Guantánamo and a stint escorting convoys to Trinidad, *Leary* sailed for New York in June where convoys were mustering in preparation for the Allied invasion of Sicily. Between July and October *Leary* completed two return voyages escorting supply convoys between New York and Algiers, being assigned in November to the hunter-killer group TG 21.14 centred on the escort carrier *Card*. It was a hunt from which she would not return.

Background of the attack

In mid-December 1943 B.d.U. dissolved the *Weddigen* group in the North Atlantic and replaced it with the *Borkum* pack (named for one of the East Frisian Islands in the North Sea) to attack the convoy route joining Sierra Leone, Morocco and Gibraltar. Using Enigma decrypts the Allies were not only able to reroute convoys MKS33 and SL142 around the *Borkum* patrol line, but also to send out the hunter-killer group TG 21.14 to intercept the German blockade runner *Osorno* as it approached the Bay of Biscay. However, TG 21.14 – which consisted of

the escort carrier USS *Card* and three 'tin-can' destroyers of DesRon 27, *Schenck, Decatur* and *Leary* – soon found itself as much hunted as hunter, *Osorno* having slipped away to be replaced by a still more elusive underwater foe. On 22 December a Luftwaffe sighting of *Card* prompted B.d.U. to order the *Borkum* pack to sink her, making it only a matter of time before battle was joined by two sides spoiling for a fight. The key engagement took place in the early hours of the 24th and in a fairly even contest the losses were a vessel from each of the participating navies: *U645* (presumed), USS *Leary* and HMS *Hurricane* later that day (**94**). At around midnight on the 23rd *Schenck* had picked up the radar signature of a vessel now reckoned to be *U645* (Oblt.z.S. Otto Ferro). This resulted in *Schenck* and *Leary* being detached from *Card* to run down the contact. At 0458 on the 24th German time *Leary* acquired a further radar contact to the north-east and immediately began streaming her anti-*Zaunkönig* FXR gear. A little after 0500 *Leary* fired starshell (described in the log below) after a second firm contact was obtained off her starboard bow. However, noise from the FXR and the shelling prevented *Leary* picking up any but the faintest of sound contacts and by the time Cdr James E. Kyes received word of an approaching torpedo it was too late. At 0510 on Christmas Eve *Leary* was struck by a *Zaunkönig* acoustic torpedo fired from her intended quarry, Kptlt Helmut Bork's *U275*.

War Diary of *U275*, patrol of 29 November 1943–11 January 1944: PG 30366, NHB, reel 1,096, pp. 599–600

Date, time	Details of position, wind, weather, sea, light, visibility, moonlight, etc.	Incidents
24.xii		
0029		Incoming W/T transmission 0029/24/703: *Two destroyers in BE 7328. U305.*[1]
0040		Incoming W/T transmission 0042/24/704: *Enemy aircraft carrier in BE 7325.*[2] *Course SW. U305.*
0050		We alter course to 270° and head towards Bahr's sighting.
0114		Incoming W/T transmission (passed on) 0114/24/705: *Intend to attack with FAT. U415.*[3]
0154		Incoming W/T transmission 0130/24/707: *Am driven off by cruiser.*[4] *Enemy steering 250°, high speed. Bahr.*[1]
0158		Incoming W/T transmission 0131/24/706:[5] *1) Borkum Group to close Bahr's position at maximum speed. Go for the kill. 2) Bahr check grid coordinates, report again.*
0400	Qu. BE 7351, wind N 3, sea 2, decreasing swell, changing cloud cover, good visibility, 1,040 mb	
0428[6]		Incoming W/T transmission 0403/29/709: *Hydrophone effect at 210°, high speed, course SW, am positioned BE 7266, 25 cbm. Schröteler.*[7]
0423		*Wanze* readings on 131 cm, *Naxos* pulses, continual tone on 131 cm, high 3–4-cm oscillation.[8]

---

1 Kptlt Rudolf Bahr (see **86**). Almost certainly *Schenck* and *Leary*.

2 USS *Card*.

3 Kptlt Kurt Neide warning fellow *Borkum* boats before firing a spread of three FAT torpedoes at 0143. The FAT (*Federapparat-Torpedo*), which was employed against large formations of ships, followed a preset straight run before pursuing a meandering trajectory of 800 or 1,600 metres with course alternations of 180 degrees. This spread missed the carrier *Card* and her escort the USS *Decatur* though Neide scored a fatal hit on HM destroyer *Hurricane* with a *Zaunkönig* later that day (**94**).

4 No Allied cruiser was present, TG 21.14 consisting of the escort carrier USS *Card* and three 'flush-decker' destroyers of the Wickes and Clemson classes: *Leary, Schenck* and *Decatur*. It is possible that Bahr's confusion was owed to the similarity in proportions and layout between the Omaha-class cruisers and the flush-deckers.

5 Signal from B.d.U.

6 The break in the chronological sequence here reflects the original.

7 Kptlt Heinrich-Andreas Schroeteler, commander of *U667*.

8 Both *Wanze* and *Naxos* were U-boat radar-detection devices.

0439–0453[6]		*Naxos* readings volume 1 increasing to volume 5.
0435		A shadow at ship's bearing 270°. We turn hard astarboard and go to utmost speed as shadow is closing rapidly and is identified as a destroyer.[9]
0449		Outgoing W/T transmission 0449/24/711: *One destroyer BE 7354. U275.*
		Destroyer closes at inclination 0° until she is some 1,000 m off and then veers away to starboard until she is at inclination 90°, bows left. However, the range does not increase much as she appears to have greatly reduced her speed or stopped altogether. She then alters course again and towards us but keeps on turning until she is at inclination 90°, bows right. She repeats this manoeuvre twice and then retires at relative bearing 180°, firing at us with her guns from a range of some 5,000 m. While I am still deliberating whether or not to turn the boat about to launch a bow attack, a second shadow is reported by the watch approaching rapidly at relative bearing 250°, inclination 0°.[10] She is identified as a destroyer and fires several well-aimed starshells over the boat followed by one which falls short. The effect is to light up the watch on the conning tower completely. At 0505 we fire a torpedo from Tube V as starshell falls into the water astern of the boat. Inclination 0°, range 2,000 m, enemy speed 12 knots.
0506	Qu. BE 7343	Alarm dive. We go to 140 m. We hear depth charges followed shortly after by . . .
0512		. . . a torpedo detonation. Our hydrophone fix on the torpedo disappears following the detonation. At ship's bearing 100° we now pick up the other destroyer on the GHG.[11] Silent speed.
0520		Five depth charges.[12] We hear continual thudding and Asdic noises between the next series of depth charges.
0550		Sinking noises can be heard throughout the entire boat (strong creaking, cracking and roaring).[13]
0605 & 0613		Destroyer overruns the boat. Thudding noises, no depth charges. During the listening pursuit we steer alternating courses at 180 m, ensuring that our stern is always towards destroyer. The noises gradually become weaker and then disappear.
0800	Qu. BE 73[?]9,[14] wind N 3, sea 2, flat swell, good visibility, 1,040 mb	
0801		We go up to [W/T] reception depth then reload Tube V.
0810		Incoming W/T transmission 0524/24/713: *Starshell in BE 7348. U270.*[15]
0917		We surface to air the boat and transmit W/T report.
0925		Incoming W/T transmission 0844/24/715:[5] *To Borkum. Dive at dawn. Proceed submerged towards patrol line positions ordered for 1000 on 23 December.*
0929		Outgoing W/T transmission 0435/24/717: *Two destroyers Qu. 7343, starshell fired, 0505 stern T5, inclination 50°, Emil 20.*[16] *Detonation after 7 min., sinking noises 38 min. later. A few depth charges from first destroyer. 107 cbm.*[17] *Bork.*
0935		Dive to continue passage submerged.

---

9 USS *Schenck*. Unbeknownst to Bork, *Schenck* was in action with *U645* (Oblt.z.S. Otto Ferro) and the gunfire referred to in the following entry presumably relates to that engagement.

10 USS *Leary*.

11 GHG was short for the *Gruppenhorchgerät* ('group listening apparatus') hydrophone array. This was *Schenck*, about five or six miles off at the time of the attack but which reached the scene shortly before *Leary* sank having despatched *U645*.

12 Presumably *Schenck*'s final and possibly decisive attack on *U645*.

13 The sinking of *Leary* was reported to have taken place at 0241 US time (0541 German time) by her survivors but at 0250 by *Schenck*, the same time at which *U382* (Oblt.z.S. Rudolf Zorn) reported hearing sinking noises.

14 The third digit of the quadrant is illegible. The most probable figure is '7319', which happens to be adjacent to the quadrant recorded at 0506 (7343).

15 Kptlt Paul-Friedrich Otto.

16 'T5' refers to the *Zaunkönig* acoustic homing torpedo. 'Emil' represents the letter 'E' in the German phonetic alphabet, in this case an abbreviation of *Entfernung* (range) in hectometres, so that 'Emil 20' denotes a range of 2,000 metres.

17 This refers to *U275*'s remaining diesel fuel in cubic metres.

The sinking

The official report on the sinking records that *Leary* was hit twice in quick succession at 0210 ship time, first on the starboard side abreast the after engine room and then supposedly by a second torpedo further aft five seconds later. The ship immediately lost way and settled by the stern with a 20–25-degree list to starboard. All main power was lost, steam pressure dropped rapidly with the rupture of both main and auxiliary steam lines, the after deckhouse was demolished and the stern left a tangled wreck of steel and severed limbs. Flooding of the after engine room gradually spread to the forward engine room through a ruptured bulkhead. Efforts to get *Leary* under way were soon abandoned and at 0225 Cdr Kyes turned his attention to abandoning ship. Disembarkation began once all floatable gear had been tossed over the side, the process punctuated by a pair of violent explosions separated by 'an interval of two or three seconds' at 0237 (though recorded by *Schenck* at between 0245 and 0250) on the starboard side in the vicinity of the forward engine room. The official report attributed this to a third hit, recording that the ship then 'listed so heavily to starboard that footing could not be gained on the main deck'. *Leary* was soon in her death throes and by 0241 had disappeared altogether, sinking by the stern with her bow vertical before all of her surviving crewmen had got clear.

As a result of the official report noting three torpedo hits (two at 0210 and a third at 0237), *Leary* is now usually reckoned to have fallen victim not only to *U275* but also to another *Borkum* boat, *U382* (Oblt.z.S. Rudolf Zorn). The argument for *U382*'s involvement is *prima facie* perfectly reasonable. At 0220 *U382* fired a *Zaunkönig* at a US destroyer followed by a second a minute later when it was suspected that the first was a dud, Oblt.z.S. Zorn recording a pair of explosions twenty seconds apart at 0225 and 0226. However, a closer reading of German sources raises significant problems with any such attribution. While *U275*'s war diary closely matches US reports on the sinking, *U382*'s log does not obviously relate to the same incident. In order for *U382*'s torpedo to have struck *Leary* at almost exactly the same moment as *U275*'s – itself no small coincidence – it would need to have done so between 0210 and 0213 (the maximum variation between the times recorded by *Leary* and Bork in *U275*) whereas Zorn's detonations are not recorded before 0225. The contention that *U382*'s timekeeping was simply at variance with those of *U275* and *Leary* is countered by the fact that Zorn goes on to record the noises attending the sinking in entries which tally perfectly both with US reports and with *U275*'s log. A more likely scenario is that tabled by Professor Jürgen Rohwer (see below) who, beyond noting the frequency with which *Zaunkönig* hits were followed by a secondary detonation, suggests that the second explosion at 0210 may have been no more than a primed depth charge blown overboard by the first explosion. Even greater problems are raised by attributing the detonations of 0237 (or 0245–0250 according to *Schenck*) to *U382*. Not only is there still at least twelve minutes' difference between *U382*'s detonations and those recorded by *Leary* and *U275* (or twenty minutes if, as a comparison of all sources suggests, *Schenck*'s later time is the more accurate), but Zorn records firing at a moving target whereas *Leary* was by now dead in the water. Moreover, it is unlikely that an acoustic torpedo would have been attracted to a vessel whose engine plant was idle, and Zorn's 'hit' of 0225 can more readily be equated to the concurrent depth-charging of a U-boat (reckoned by Prof. Rohwer to be Kptlt Otto Ferro's *U645*) by USS *Schenck* a few miles to the north than to any success of her own.

Denying *U382* a role in *Leary*'s end does however leave unresolved the agency of the explosion(s) amidships at 0237. Given the problems raised by Zorn's log it seems equally possible that *U645* played a role in the sinking before succumbing to *Schenck*, or that the explosions in the flooded engine room were somehow internally generated, as these were only 'believed' to have been caused by a torpedo. However, the possibility of *U645*'s involvement is disputed by Dr Axel Niestlé (see below) who not only places the encounter with *Schenck* between 0220

and 0230, but underlines the absence of evidence that *U645* was there at all. Indeed, Niestlé goes on to posit that this encounter, if such it was, could as easily have been with *U275* herself, though her log provides no indication that she was surfaced as *Schenck* reported. Whatever the case, though the number and origin of the torpedoes that claimed the USS *Leary* will probably never be known for certain, only *U275*'s log gives her an indisputable hand in the sinking.

Fate of the crew

The two explosions that wrecked *Leary*'s stern at 0210 ship time accounted for 'between 40 and 50 men' according to the official report, and the five sailors who survived from this part of the ship owed their lives to having been blown forward onto the main deck. An entire gun crew was tossed overboard and the decks littered not only with dead and wounded men but also gloves, tins of peaches and a batch of freshly baked Boston cream pie blasted from the ship's stores and galley. Still, the damage and casualties might have been greater had a party of seamen not promptly set the remaining depth charges to safe. Fifteen minutes after the attack Cdr Kyes passed the order to abandon ship, his men obeying with the same steady bearing that characterised them throughout: 'There was complete order. Silence predominated. Only now and then orders were heard, and everyone did as he was told.' A distress signal was sent while a majority of the survivors concentrated on assisting the trapped or injured and releasing the remaining ship's rafts. This task was complicated by the increasing list and only three rafts had been launched before the order came to abandon ship. These were overcrowded and many men were kept afloat by lengths of shoring timber provided for damage-control purposes. Most crewmen were wearing lifebelts by the time they went over the side and it is a measure of the discipline shown by *Leary*'s men that many added to the row of shoes left neatly along the well deck before abandoning ship. Shortly before the second pair of detonations dealt *Leary* the *coup de grâce*, Kyes discovered a black mess attendant whose jacket had been shredded by one of the blasts and immediately presented him his own kapok lifejacket. This action may explain why Kyes, last seen leaving the sinking *Leary* via the sea ladder on the port side, was never picked up. He was posthumously awarded the Navy Cross for 'heroic conduct and fearless spirit of self-sacrifice'. Another who distinguished himself was the ship's doctor, Lt (jg) Anthony Kerasotes, who helped to disembark the wounded and continued offering medical attention and encouragement to men in the water until he himself drowned.

Schenck arrived on the scene shortly before *Leary* sank and immediately began recovering survivors, but Lt Cdr Earl W. Logsdon could not hazard his vessel with U-boats in the vicinity and left the ship's whaleboat with a crew of four to continue the work of rescue while he went in search of the enemy. Twice *Schenck* was obliged to chase down contacts and drop depth charges and it was not until four hours after the sinking that the last man was brought aboard. In the intervening period another fifty or so men had succumbed to injury, oil and exhaustion in squally conditions, while several had the misfortune of being sucked into *Schenck*'s propellers. A total of ninety-seven men were lost with the *Leary* and on board the *Schenck*, the fifty-nine survivors being transferred to the USS *Card* on Christmas morning. A day earlier *Schenck* had cruised past the scene of the sinking to find it scattered with bodies, the gratitude of the survivors to their rescuers

Bork seen in an undated shot at sea. *DUBMA*

charged with countering the Allied landings in Normandy (see HMS *Blackwood*, **103**). She had no success but reached Brest unscathed on 25 June. Bork was then retired from operational duty, serving out the rest of the war on the staff of a succession of *U-Flottillen*.

U275 returned to the English Channel for two patrols under Oblt.z.S. Helmut Wehrkamp, neither of which enjoyed any success. Three more sorties under Wehrkamp finally yielded *U275* her first merchant pennant, that of SS *Lornaston* on 8 March 1945. Two days after this success, however, *U275* was no more. She disappeared in the English Channel on or around 10 March, the presumed victim of a mine in the British Brazier E field.

Sources

Navy Department, Office of Naval Records and Library, *Report of Anti-Submarine Action by USS Leary on 24 December 1943 and Subsequent Sinking* (NA, Box 1142, 370/45/7/3)

—, *History of USS Leary (DD 158)* (NHC, Box 466)

Rohwer, Prof. Jürgen, *Analyse der T-5 („Zaunkönig")-Schüsse von U-Booten gegen Geleitfahrzeuge. U275: USS Leary & U382: USS Leary* (Report for Bundesamt für Wehrtechnik und Beschaffung [Federal Office of Weapons Technology and Procurement], 1964) (BfZ, MaS 8/2.07)

—, *Die Entwicklung des Zaunkönigs: die Kriegsgeschichte als Hilfswissenschaft der Wehrtechnik, dargestellt am Beispiel der zielsuchenden Torpedos* (BfZ, Sammlung Rohwer, T-5 Auswertungsdokumente)

Blair, *Hitler's U-Boat War*, II, pp. 452–5

DANFS, IV, p. 78; also on: http://www.history.navy.mil/danfs/l5/leary-i.htm ; and: http://www.ibiblio.org/hyperwar/USN/ships/dafs/DD/dd158.html

Friedman, Norman, *US Destroyers: An Illustrated Design History* (2nd edn, Annapolis, Md.: Naval Institute Press, 2004)

Morison, *United States Naval Operations*, I, pp. 225–6; X, pp. 171–6

Morrison, Brig. Gen. John H., Jr, and Alan Scott Robinson, eds., *The Night We Lost the USS Leary DD-158, 24 December 1943: Personal Stories from Survivors and Others Who Were There* (n.p.: USS Schenck (DD-159) and USS Leary (DD-158) Association, 1994)

Niestlé, Dr Axel, *German U-Boat Losses During World War II: Details of Destruction* (Annapolis, Md.: Naval Institute Press, 1998)

Parkin, Robert Sinclair, *Blood on the Sea: American Destroyers Lost in World War II* (New York: Sarpedon, 1995)

Roscoe, *US Destroyer Operations*, pp. 293–4

Webpage devoted to Lt (jg) Anthony Kerasotes (fatality): http://www.uiaa.org/illinois/veterans/display_veteran.asp?id=158

being all the greater. When *Schenck* closed *Card* to refuel a week later it was to find herself showered with candy bars tossed down from *Leary* survivors lined up on the flight deck. They were landed at Norfolk, Virginia on 2 January 1944, three days before the loss of the *Leary* was officially announced by the Navy.

Leary was gone but the selfless efforts of *Schenck*'s crewmen in rescuing and caring for her survivors cemented a bond between the two ships that long outlasted the war, and which at length bore fruit in the USS *Schenck* and USS *Leary* Association. That apart, the courage, skill and resolution shown by both ships' companies on 24 December 1943 marks a high point in the wartime service of the US Navy's venerable flush-deck destroyers, one to match the savage close-quarters encounter between the *Borie* and *U405* on 1 November that year (**G65**).

U275 and Helmut Bork

Built by Bremer Vulkan at Vegesack and commissioned in November 1942, *U275*'s career began with three lengthy frontline patrols under Oblt.z.S. Helmut Bork. The first of these, in September 1943, saw her join the *Leuthen* group which had such success in reigniting the U-boat war (see HMCS *St Croix* and HMSs *Polyanthus* and *Itchen*, **86–88**), though *U275* did not draw blood either as part of this or the subsequently formed *Rossbach* group. Bork's second patrol brought the sinking of the *Leary* together with claims of another two destroyers sunk, though there is nothing to corroborate the latter. In June 1944 *U275*'s third patrol saw her assigned to the *Landwirt* group

94 HMS *HURRICANE* (ex CT *JAPARUA*)

Cdr J. R. Westmacott, RN

Sunk by *U415* (Type VIIC), Kptlt Kurt Neide, 24–25 December 1943

North Atlantic, 600 nm WNW of La Coruña (Spain)

Hurricane seen in a dazzle camouflage shortly after completion in June 1940. She was struck aft and sunk by a *Zaunkönig* acoustic homing torpedo from *U415*.
IWM

Theatre	North Atlantic (Map 1)	*Displacement*	1,350 tons
Coordinates	45° 10' N, 22° 05' W	*Dimensions*	323' × 33' × 8.5'
Kriegsmarine code	Quadrat BE 7321	*Maximum speed*	35.5 knots
U-boat timekeeping differential	+1 hour	*Armament*	2 × 4.7"; 1 × 3" AA; 4 × 20 mm AA; 4 × 21" tt; 1 × Hedgehog ATW
Fatalities	5 *Survivors* about 200		

Career

Ordered in 1937 as part of a flotilla of six destroyers for the Brazilian navy, the *Japarua* was laid down at Vickers-Armstrongs, Barrow-in-Furness in June 1938 and purchased together with her sisters by the British government on 4 September 1939. She was launched as HMS *Hurricane* on 29 September and completed in May 1940. The choice of name reflects the similarity in design between these ships and the 'H'-class destroyers ordered for the Royal Navy under the 1934 estimates. Fitted out for anti-submarine operations, the class entered service as the 9th Destroyer Flotilla, Home Fleet, *Hurricane* being immediately flung into convoy duty in the North Atlantic, initially as Local Escort to troop convoys. The unfolding of the U-boat offensive towards the end of the year caused the 9th DF to be redesignated the 9th Escort Group in November, though this phase in *Hurricane*'s career is notable less for operations against the Germans than for her rescue efforts after the U-boats had done their work. Her finest hour came on 18 September 1940 when she was called upon to rescue survivors of the liner *City of Benares* and the freighter *Marina*, both torpedoed by *U48* the previous day. Around 140 people were rescued, including a number of child evacuees from the *City of Benares* which made her sinking one of the most notorious of the war. On 30 April 1941 *Hurricane* picked up no fewer than 451 survivors from the liner *City of Nagpur*, sunk by *U75* the previous day. *Hurricane*'s first stint of escort work came to an abrupt end on the night of 7–8 May when she was bombed and sunk in the Gladstone Dock during an air raid on Liverpool, the ship sustaining damage aft which kept her out of the war until the following January. *Hurricane* spent 1942 with the 28th EG as part of Western Approaches Command based on Liverpool before becoming leader of the 1st EG in December. Apart from a spell detached for special joint operations with RAF Coastal Command in the Bay of Biscay in June and July 1943, *Hurricane* spent her final year with the 1st EG, one that included the culminating battles in the Atlantic campaign. Beneath these bare facts lies the reality of thirty convoys escorted over three years, placing HMS *Hurricane* among the stalwarts of the Battle of the Atlantic.

Background of the attack

At 2200 on 17 December 1943 the British 1st Escort Group sailed from Lough Foyle, Northern Ireland with instructions to join the merged convoy ON62/KMS36 in the Atlantic. The group consisted of HM destroyers *Hurricane* (with the recently appointed Senior Officer of the Escort, Cdr J. R. Westmacott), *Wanderer* and *Watchman*, and the frigate *Glenarm*. Shortly after joining this convoy on the 19th the 1st EG was rerouted first to convoy SL142 and then to ON216 on the 22nd following intelligence reports of U-boat dispositions in the Atlantic. As these evolved over the course of the next twenty-four hours so the 1st EG was reassigned to ON62/KMS36 as originally planned, regaining contact with its charge at 0930 on the 24th. However, no sooner had *Hurricane* and *Glenarm* begun sweeping ahead of the convoy than they were ordered to proceed at their best speed to position 45° N, 22° W where the USS *Leary* had been torpedoed by *U275* of the *Borkum* pack (see preceding entry, **93**). Reaching the scene of the sinking, *Hurricane* and *Glenarm* began a search for the perpetrator and any other U-boat in the vicinity. At 1902 that evening their efforts were rewarded with an HF/DF contact at a range of approximately twenty miles, both ships altering course accordingly. A separate radar contact was obtained in a different position at 1945, *Glenarm* being ordered to investigate while *Hurricane* closed the earlier contact. Sighting a U-boat shortly before 2000 GMT, Cdr Westmacott elected not to illuminate the area or open fire but to continue closing the range before slowing to fifteen knots as he approached within 1,000 yards of the enemy. However, it was not *Hurricane* but Kptlt Kurt Neide's *U415* which landed the first blow in the shape of a *Zaunkönig* acoustic homing torpedo.

War Diary of *U415*, patrol of 21 November 1943–6 January 1944: PG 30473, NHB, reel 1,106, p. 743

Date, time	Details of position, wind, weather, sea, light, visibility, moonlight, etc.	Incidents
24.xii	North Atlantic	
1300		Course 213°.
1525		Incoming W/T transmission 1148/24/722:[1]
		Borkum Group: 1). After surfacing proceed at cruising speed to occupy new patrol lines from BE 7128 to 7339 in rearranged order: Brans, Otto, Petersen, Ferro, Neide, Bahr etc.[2]
1600	Qu. BE 4989	Set course 255° for new position.
1932		Surfaced. Twilight over.
2000	Qu. BE 4988, wind SW 3, sea 2, 8/10 overcast, visibility reasonable though sometimes misty, 1,040 mb	
2055	Qu. BE 7321	Shadow of destroyer sighted at a bearing 265° true (ship's bearing 10°), range 3 nm, closing rapidly, bows left, inclination 5°.[3] Presently she fires starshell on her port beam. No evidence of radar detection.
2056		Single torpedo (*Zaunkönig*) fired from Tube III with a fixed angle of fire of 2°. Depth 4 m, remote fire setting.[4] Aimed using the boat's net deflector.[5] Destroyer now has an inclination of exactly 0°. Alarm! We dive to a depth of 160 m.
2058		Sharp detonation close to the boat. The loud noise of propellers comes to an abrupt halt. This is followed by breaking and cracking sounds, then the sound of three depth charges, then all goes quiet. As we have no other *Zaunkönig* ready to fire and since I suspect that there are other destroyers nearby we withdraw at silent speed.[6]
2125		Ongoing sounds of echo detection nearby; I assume this is the search group.
2130		Propeller noises approaching from bearing 250° true, 180 rpm.[7]
2142		Six depth charges, not that close.
2145		Another propeller noise at bearing 120°. No Asdic pulses can be heard.[8] The destroyers are sweeping back and forth.[9]
25.xii	North Atlantic	
0000	Qu. BE 4987	

1 From B.d.U.

2 Commanders of *U801*, *U270*, *U541*, *U654*, *U415* and *U305* (see **86**) respectively, all part of the sixteen-strong *Borkum* group. Despite the '1.' at the beginning of the transmission, this is the extent of the signal as recorded by Neide.

3 HM frigate *Glenarm*. Neide's log implies that this destroyer continued to be monitored but at some point his bridge watch clearly confused her with *Hurricane*, the target of *U415*'s attack of 2056.

4 'Remote fire' (*Weitschuss*) was one of the three run settings of the *Zaunkönig* torpedo and was for use against approaching targets. On this setting the torpedo ran straight before adopting a snaking trail until it picked up a noise contact, altering course accordingly.

5 The 'net deflector' took the form of a jumping wire stretching from the bow to the conning tower. Despite the name, these were in fact used as radio aerials and particularly as safety harness anchors for those working on the casing. Neide is here using it as a rudimentary sight against a target at 0° inclination.

6 HM frigate *Glenarm* was the only vessel present apart from *Hurricane*.

7 *Glenarm*.

8 Mehl here uses the English term 'Asdic'.

9 Neide has again overestimated the number of warships present, here interpreting *Glenarm*'s movements as those of two destroyers. It was not until the following morning that *Glenarm* and the stricken *Hurricane* were joined by a third vessel, HM destroyer *Watchman*.

0022		Propeller noises can no longer be heard. We go to 60 m and remove the torpedo from Tube V. We manage to get both the torpedo and the tube itself operational again; the eel was initially stuck.[10]
0400	Qu. BE 4984	
0425	Wind SW 3, sea 2, 9/10 overcast, average visibility, 1,040 mb	We surface once torpedo work is complete. My intention: to head in the direction of the most recent hydrophone bearings with a view to possibly gaining another shot at a destroyer.
0502		<u>Outgoing W/T transmission 2011/24/731</u>: *2056 in BE 7321 T5 at destroyer heading east. A hit after two minutes, sinking heard; depth charges, apparently hunter group.*[11] *Still one* Zaunkönig *ready, Tube II out of action. Wind SW 3, sea 2, overcast, 40 mb, +16°[C; 61°F].* Neide.
0600		Search for destroyer broken off. Course set for position in patrol line.
0800	Qu. BE 7233	

---

10 'Eel' (German = *Aal*) was U-boat slang for torpedo.

11 Despite Neide's claim, it would be another eight hours before *Hurricane* sank.

The sinking

U415's torpedo is recorded as having struck HMS *Hurricane* aft at 2002 British time (2102 German time). The damage was recorded by Cdr Westmacott as being 'less than might have been expected from a contact torpedo', his submission to the Board of Enquiry reiterating his belief that *Hurricane* had not been hit by a torpedo at all. By contrast, the more detailed report of *Hurricane*'s Chief Engineer, Lt (E) K. P. Clarke, left little doubt that the damage aft was both substantial and quite compatible with an acoustic torpedo detonation: 'The Quarterdeck was lifted to about forty-five degrees from 159 bulkhead aft, stern being blown away. 159 bulkhead was torn open on port side and ship side holed at water line about 156 frame, port, these causing fairly rapid flooding. After magazine and shell room were open to sea and flooding rapidly.' Flooding was also noted in the port gland, the former torpedo warhead magazine, the office flat and through the after engine room bulkhead. The port engine stopped and would not budge even with a full head of steam, while the starboard turbine, though still functioning, had to be shut down once it became apparent that the shaft and propeller were fouling the wreckage aft. With all doors and hatches sealed and *Hurricane*'s pumps working Lt Clarke believed that 'there was sufficient margin of stability for the ship to remain afloat in reasonable weather', Cdr Westmacott signalling Western Approaches Command at 2240 to the effect that conditions were suitable for towing. But it was not to be. Aware of her vulnerable condition and the risks posed to the convoy by the absence of most of its escort (*Watchman* having been detached to assist *Glenarm* in shielding *Hurricane*), Admiral Sir Max Horton, Commander-in-Chief Western Approaches, ordered her scuttled next morning unless she was able to raise steam. This could not be accomplished and at 0945 the order was passed to abandon ship, the ship's company transferring to *Glenarm* by sea boat. With every hatch, door, scuttle, valve and hull aperture left open, *Hurricane* sank by the stern at around 1215 on Christmas Day, sixteen hours after the attack.

Konteradmiral Eberhard Godt was delighted with Neide's patrol, extolling his 'ruthlessness' and crediting him with the sinking not only of *Hurricane* but also of the US destroyer *Decatur* earlier on the 24th. However, the patrol was not quite the success B.d.U. imagined, *Decatur* having been missed by a *Zaunkönig* and *Hurricane* sinking long after *U415* had left the scene.

Hurricane abandoned on Christmas morning 1943. The photo, taken from *Glenarm*, shows the damage resulting from Neide's *Zaunkönig* hit aft. *IWM*

Fate of the crew

Only four lives were claimed by Neide's attack, one rating killed outright by a depth charge dislodged in the explosion, a second left mortally injured by the same cause, and two members of the depth-charge party presumed blasted overboard. Fourteen others were injured by the detonation, including several with fractures caused by whiplash from the explosion. These were transferred to *Glenarm* in boats along with the rest of the ship's company from 1000 onwards on the 25th. However, an accident on board *Glenarm* brought the death toll to five. Orders by her commanding officer, Lt Cdr W. R. B. Noall, to the effect that *Hurricane*'s abandoned motor boat be sunk at point-blank range

Commissioning day for *U415* at Danzig on 5 August 1942. *DUBMA*

Neide brings *U415* back to Brest on 6 January 1944 flying pennants for HMS *Hurricane* (which he sank) and USS *Decatur* (which he did not). *DUBMA*

brought his port after Oerlikon gun crew into action and numbers of *Hurricane*'s men to the rail to watch the spectacle. Unfortunately, one of the 20-mm high-explosive shells struck the gauge rail of the Oerlikon platform and detonated on impact, Stoker H. B. Ferrie being killed in a hail of splinters which injured six others.

As the decision to scuttle *Hurricane* came from the top, the Board of Enquiry concerned itself almost exclusively with the speed at which she had closed *U415*. As set out in a recent amendment to Atlantic Convoy Instruction No. 138, ships within range of a GNAT (as the *Zaunkönig* was known to the Allies) were to avoid those speeds between eight and twenty knots at which the torpedo's homing device was reckoned to be most effective. The Board therefore concluded that Cdr Westmacott had committed a clear error in slowing to fifteen knots though it was subsequently disputed whether this had affected the issue. Commenting on the findings of the Board, G. W. G. Simpson, Commodore (D) Western Approaches, gave it as his opinion that

> the action taken in the engine-room was to throttle down, allowing the propellers to trail, and according to the evidence of a majority of personnel in the engine-room it appears that the throttle was not reopened to admit steam to establish a steady speed of 15 knots. In fact, the ship was still decelerating when hit. Thus, it appears that had the Captain ordered 7 knots instead of 15 on this occasion, the result would have been the same, and *Hurricane* would have been struck.

Having considered the matter Admiral Horton decided to exonerate Westmacott, adjudging him 'to have handled every situation with marked ability, and in spite of his misinterpretation of Atlantic Convoy Instruction 138 on this occasion I consider that he is worthy of further employment as Senior Officer of an Escort Group'.

U415 and Kurt Neide

Built by Danziger Werft at Danzig (Gdansk) and commissioned in August 1942, *U415* did not sail on her maiden operational cruise until March 1943. Commanded by Oblt.z.S. (Kptlt from June 1943) Kurt Neide, *U415* immediately found herself in the thick of convoy action. Her first patrol yielded two merchantmen from ONS3 though damage

from three RAF aircraft brought her limping back into Brest on 5 May. However, the Allies by now had the upper hand in the Battle of the Atlantic and four further patrols under Neide added only the pennant of the destroyer *Hurricane*, though a spread of three torpedoes aimed at the escort carrier USS *Card* narrowly missed its target just hours before this encounter, while a *Zaunkönig* failed to connect with the destroyer USS *Decatur*.

Neide left *U415* in March 1944 following which she made three brief sorties from Brest under Oblt.z.S. Herbert Werner. The first of these resulted in serious damage from a Wellington and two Liberators of the RAF on 7 June, though both of the latter were shot down. A second sortie in early July lasted just two days, but her third under Werner was no more than a few minutes old when she struck a mine in Brest harbour on 14 July 1944 and sank with the loss of two crewmen.

After leaving *U415* Neide took up a position in B.d.U.'s Operations Division in which he remained until serving a brief period in captivity at war's end. He died in September 1980.

Sources

Admiralty, *Enemy Attacks on H.M. Ships: Losses and Damage, 1943* (TNA, ADM 199/958)

—, *Enemy Submarine Attacks on H.M. Ships, 1943: Reports* (TNA, ADM 199/1321)

Dickens, Capt. Peter, *HMS* Hesperus [Warships in Profile, no. 20] (Windsor, Berks.: Profile Publications, 1972)

English, John, Amazon *to* Ivanhoe: *British Standard Destroyers of the 1930s* (Kendal, Cumbria: World Ship Society, 1993)

Kinghorn, D., and B. Hargreaves, 'Destroyers of the Royal Navy: "H" Class (ex Brazilian) and "I" Class (ex Turkish)' in *Warships*, Supplement no. 10 (September 1967), pp. 15–26

Career history of HMS *Hurricane*:
http://www.naval-history.net/xGM-Chrono-10DD-33Brazil-Hurricane.htm

95 HMS *HARDY* (ii)

Capt. (D) W. G. A. Robson, DSO* DSC RNR
Sunk by *U278* (Type VIIC), Oblt.z.S. Joachim Franze, 30 January 1944
Barents Sea, 90 nm SSE of Bear Island

Hardy at speed, possibly while running trials in the autumn of 1943. A few months later she lost her stern
to a *Zaunkönig* acoustic homing torpedo from *U278*. *IWM*

Campaign Arctic convoys (Map 2)		*Displacement* 1,808 tons	
Coordinates 73° 37' N, 18° 56' E		*Dimensions* 362.75' × 35.75' × 10'	
Kriegsmarine code Quadrat AB 6383		*Maximum speed* 36 knots	
U-boat timekeeping identical		*Armament* 4 × 4.7"; 2 × 40 mm AA; 8 × 20 mm AA; 8 × 21" tt	
Fatalities 35 *Survivors* 214			

Career

The destroyer leader HMS *Hardy* was laid down at John Brown of Clydebank in May 1942, launched in March 1943 and completed in August of that year after delays in the installation of the new Mk-VI fire control director. One of the 'V'-class destroyers of the emergency war programme, she was named after the leader of the 2nd Destroyer Flotilla which was lost at the First Battle of Narvik on 10 April 1940, an action which won Capt. (D) Bernard Warburton-Lee a posthumous Victoria Cross. Most of the 'V' class (*Hardy* included) commissioned as part of the 26th DF, Home Fleet in the autumn of 1943, its units dividing their time between Arctic convoy duty and escorting carrier raids against Axis shipping off Norway. In October *Hardy* escorted the relief garrison to Spitsbergen before being assigned with other elements of the 26th DF to her first Russian convoy in November: JW54B. However, *Hardy* was long gone by the time her flotilla performed its greatest exploit, the sinking of the Japanese heavy cruiser *Haguro* in the Malacca Strait on 16 May 1945.

Background of the attack

For background on the Arctic convoy campaign, see HMSs *Matabele*, *Edinburgh* and *Leda* (**47**, **58** and **69**).

As 1943 drew to a close the war at sea looked to have swung overwhelmingly in favour of the Allies in the Northern Theatre. Though the Luftwaffe and U-boat threat remained, Allied losses in the second half of 1943 could be counted on the fingers of one hand

while heavy damage to the *Tirpitz* in September and the sinking of the *Scharnhorst* in December removed the main surface threats to the Russian convoys. However, as the British suspected, convoys JW56A and JW56B, which sailed from Loch Ewe two weeks apart in January 1944, were always likely to have a harder time of it than their immediate predecessors. On Hitler's direct orders Dönitz bolstered the forces available to *F.d.U. Norwegen*, all newcomers being equipped with the T5 acoustic homing torpedo and the latest *Naxos* radar detectors. Though Enigma decrypts allowed the Admiralty to reroute JW56A north of the anticipated patrol line, the northernmost boat in the *Isegrim* (a wolf in Germanic mythology) group, *U956* (Mohs) was sufficiently out of position to sight the convoy at noon on 29 January and bring up eight more boats. False claims aside, the night of 25–26 January brought the first German successes against Russian convoys since October, with the sinking of two large merchantmen from JW56A together with damage to a third and to HM destroyer *Obdurate*. The Allies were therefore alive to the threat lurking between North Cape and Spitsbergen and the sailing of the return convoy RA56A was delayed to allow its intended escort to add its strength to JW56B as it approached the *Werwolf* and *Wiking* patrol lines. The combined escort, totalling fifteen ships at one point, was commanded by W. G. A. Robson, Captain (D) of the 26th Destroyer Flotilla in HMS *Hardy*. The U-boats closed in *en masse* on the night of 29–30 January with *U278* (Franze), *U313* (Schweiger), *U472* (von Forstner), *U601* (Hansen) and *U957* (Schaar) each launching *Zaunkönig* torpedoes against the escort. Many hits were claimed based on misleading acoustic data but only one vessel was in fact struck: HMS *Hardy* in the early hours of the 30th. The attack came as she, *Venus*, *Virago* and the Norwegian destroyer *Stord* were chasing down an HF/DF contact along the starboard flank of the convoy. Two U-boats were detected by *Virago* on *Hardy*'s port bow but of these the flotilla leader knew nothing until her stern was blown off and the ship set ablaze.

War Diary of *U278*, patrol of 29 January–19 February 1944: PG 30369, NHB, reel 1,096, p. 348

Date, time	Details of position, wind, weather, sea, light, visibility, moonlight, etc.	Incidents
30.i		
2400	Qu. AB 6614, wind [?] 1, sea 1, overcast (with snow), poor visibility	
0016		Shadow at bearing 230° true, probably a fellow U-boat, which then disappears in the mist.
0124	Qu. AB 6653	U-boat surfaces 1,000 m away, bearing 245° true. We carry out an identity signal exchange. I want to get within hailing distance to ask about hydrophone bearings but the boat heads off at utmost speed. Morse communication forbidden as enemy is believed to be nearby.
0220		Starshell seen at bearing 330° true.
0244		Incoming W/T transmission 0244/743: *Starshell bearing 40° true, Qu. [AB] 6555. U636.*[1] When compared with my own this observation gives a workable combination to use as a basis for the position of the enemy. Therefore:
0246		Outgoing W/T transmission 0246/745: *Starshell bearing 330° true, Qu. [AB] 6628. U278.*
0344		Shadow off to port at bearing 325° true, range 2,500 m. Battle Stations.
0347	Bärenenge[2]	Outgoing W/T transmission 0347/749: weather report. Shadow subsequently identified as destroyer, two more shadows then heave into sight astern.[3] First destroyer is converging on our own course, inclination 30°. I turn about and present my stern to her. Inclination of destroyer becomes finer.
0357	Qu. AB 6383	Both engines stopped, torpedo fired from Tube V. A T5, inclination 15°, bows left, enemy speed 15 knots, range 2,500 m, depth 4 m, point of aim stern. We withdraw for 1 min. at slow speed, 1 min. at half speed, then utmost speed, attempting to get away on the surface.[4]
0358		After 1 min. 45 sec. a detonation far off that has no effect on the target, no column of water that would have to be evident in the event of a hit. As it turns out later from W/T transmission 1319/786 this detonation was most probably the first hit by Schaar, who is nearby.[5] The attacked destroyer opens up with her quick-firing gun on her starboard quarter (I am on her port beam by now) and begins a sweep with a red light from her mast (detection mechanism).[6]
0404		A hit on the destroyer beneath her after superstructure, glowing red fragments of wreckage fly up to twice the height of the mast. Barely a minute later yet another detonation on the destroyer, producing a large cloud of dark smoke. When this clears there is nothing more to be seen of the ship.
0411		The other two destroyers zigzag wildly around the area, dropping depth charges and searching with their red lights.
0422		We launch *Aphrodite*; the strips of tin foil end up in the water, balloon fails to rise.[7]

---

1 Kptlt Hans Hildebrandt.

2 Literally 'Bear Straits', this apparently refers to the body of water separating North Cape and Bear Island at the entrance to the Barents Sea. There seems not to be an English equivalent.

3 *Hardy* and two of HMS *Venus*, HMS *Virago* and KNM *Stord*.

4 The gradual nature of Franze's withdrawal was designed to avoid *U278* becoming the target of her own *Zaunkönig*.

5 Oblt.z.S. Gerd Schaar, commander of *U957*. As Franze indicates, this entry was composed with information gleaned from a signal subsequently transmitted by Schaar at 1319 that day, which expanded on his transmission of 0429 (see above). The 1319 signal read as follows: 'AB 6381 [fired] at two destroyers, 0346 T5 hit after 11 min., cloud of smoke, sank. 0354 destroyer with T5 after 12 min., blew up.' This was no doubt sent in response to Franze's signal of 0912 (see above) claiming a sinking at 0357, evidence of the concern by each party that a valuable pennant might be claimed by the other. In the event, *F.d.U. Norwegen* (Officer Commanding U-Boats, Norway) credited Franze with the kill.

6 Despite Franze's suspicions of a detection device, the red light was probably no more than the infrared screen which the Allies began fitting ahead of their searchlights in the summer of 1943 to avoid the beam itself being seen.

7 The *Aphrodite* radar decoy system involved the launching of a hydrogen-filled balloon streaming four-metre strips of aluminium or tin. It was designed to

Date, time	Details of position, wind, weather, sea, light, visibility, moonlight, etc.	Incidents
		With both diesels at emergency speed and the electric engine connected for good measure we get clear of the destroyers and disappear into the mist.
0429		Incoming W/T transmission 0405/751: *Two destroyers done for in Qu. AB 6381. Schaar.*
0912		Outgoing W/T transmission 0830/765: *Three destroyers Qu. AB 6383. T5 fired at 0357, a hit astern after 7 min. Ship blew up a minute later. Query relative timing of Schaar's attack. Listening pursuit, last W/T 0530.*[8] *Franze.*

hover above the water secured by a sheet anchor but in this instance the necessary lift appears not to have been achieved.

8   By 'listening pursuit' (*Horchverfolgung* in the original) Franze is referring to Asdic.

The sinking

The hit on *Hardy*'s stern was followed by a second detonation, reckoned by Capt. Robson and the Admiralty to have been the after magazine going up. Accounts vary as to when this took place, ranging from 'almost immediately' in the recollection (many years later) of Lt C. J. R. Whittle, through Franze's 'barely a minute later' (see the entry for 0404) to Robson's 'three minutes later'. These discrepancies would not matter except that, as discussed below, *Hardy*'s sinking was claimed by no fewer than three U-boats. Whatever the case, after the first explosion 'the Ship shook violently twice, trimmed by the stern and listed 5°–10° to Starboard'. The port engine stopped immediately and the starboard engine was found to be revolving at very high speed, the shaft having broken. After the second explosion the Chief Engineer, Cdr (E) Ernest Mill, evacuated the engine room and reported to Capt. Robson that the ship was flooded up to the after engine room bulkhead with both turbines disabled. Aware that *Hardy* was doomed, Robson passed the order to abandon ship, whereupon the surviving ship's company was transferred to HMSs *Virago* and *Venus* (see below). On board HMS *Venus* Robson agreed with his rescuer, Cdr J. S. M. Richardson DSO, that towing would not only leave the escort force severely depleted but imperil both vessels involved for no certain gain. Offered the task of despatching her, *Hardy*'s torpedo officer declined and at 0551 it fell to his counterpart in *Venus* to fire a *coup de grâce* torpedo from a range of approximately a mile. 'There was the devil of an explosion slap between the mast and the funnel. *Hardy* blew up spectacularly and sank in two halves in approximate postion 73° 37' North, 18° 56' East.' This event, which brought Robson to tears in *Venus*'s wardroom, coincided with *U601* firing a T5 at her, Oblt.z.S. Otto Hansen subsequently claiming a hit based on acoustic data.

F.d.U. Norwegen faced a difficult task unravelling the various hits claimed by the *Werwolf* and *Wiking* groups at this juncture. Aside from *U278*'s attack of 0357 and *U601*'s two hours later, *F.d.U.* had also to evaluate the claims of Oblt.z.S. Gerd Schaar's *U957* (torpedoes fired at destroyers at 0354 and 0356 with running times of 11 min. 45 sec. and 12 min.) and Oblt.z.S. Wolfgang-Friedrich Freiherr von Forstner's *U472* (fired at a destroyer at 0357, running time 2 min. 30 sec.). Based on a comparison of the war diaries, the Germans credited Franze with the kill, a view confirmed in post-war analysis by Professor Jürgen Rohwer and by the British Naval Historical Branch. Rohwer attributes Schaar's claims to end-of-run detonations (eleven to twelve minutes being typical of these) and von Forstner's to an unsuccessful attack on

the nearby *Stord*. These assessments are beyond dispute but attributing *Hardy*'s sinking to *U278* cannot represent more than a balance of probability. Quite aside from the question mark hanging over the second detonation in *Hardy* there are irreconcilable issues with respect to the positions of the various U-boats (their own coordinates putting them many miles apart) and the relative timekeeping of four different chronometers (*Hardy*'s and those of the three U-boats just mentioned). The British themselves estimated that at least two and possibly as many as four U-boats were in striking distance. The file on the loss of HMS *Hardy* is therefore unlikely to be fully closed.

Fate of the crew

Neither official nor personal accounts uncovered by the authors shed any light on how many of *Hardy*'s men were lost in the detonations that wrecked her stern. Capt. Robson ordered all men to the forecastle after the second explosion while *Virago* was signalled by *Venus* to close *Hardy* and take off survivors. Though several were brought off, *Virago* damaged her bows coming alongside for the third time, with which Robson ordered *Venus* to finish the job and *Virago* to join *Stord* in covering them. Cdr Richardson of *Venus* then brought his ship along the starboard side of *Hardy* in a scene vividly recalled by Lt Whittle:

> There followed an eerie and unforgettable scene: the two ships locked together, rolling and grinding in the Arctic swell, men in the water between the two ships, others lowering themselves on bow-lines to pull them out or onto the scrambling nets and in imminent danger of being scrunched, the whole scene awesomely lit up by flickering illumination of the Northern Lights.

Sub-Lt L. T. Stainer made a hair-raising escape:

> I made my way to the rail and climbed over it, ready to drop onto the *V[enus]*'s deck but at that moment she yawed away and I hung onto the rail for dear life. That rail was as cold as ice – in fact I am not at all sure that it was not thinly coated with ice as many parts of the ship were. It passed through my mind that my skin could freeze to the metal but instead my hand seemed to start sliding and it was with some relief that I saw *V[enus]*'s deck pass below me as I let go and fell in the heap on it.

Scorning rescue, Cdr (E) Ernest Mill, a product of the Royal Navy's Mate Scheme for promotion from the lower deck, freed a Carley float and set off to recover those in the water. Stainer recalls his adventure:

> He had paddled to the nearest red light and had found a young rating calling for help . . . he hauled him on board and set off for the next light visible but the insistent cries for help from the one already rescued sapped his

Franze (second from right) and his senior officers gathered on the casing to celebrate *U278*'s commissioning at Vegesack on 16 January 1943. *DUBMA*

patrols was that against JW56A (see above) in January 1944 during which *U278* scored one of the *Isegrim* group's four successes. Having refuelled at Hammerfest, Franze then added *Hardy* to his tally though this was to be the extent of *U278*'s success beyond the destruction of an abandoned Russian radio station in the Arctic Sea in September. The end of the war found *U278* at sea, Franze bringing her into Narvik from where she was escorted to Loch Eriboll and eventually scuttled by the Polish destroyer *Błyskawica* as part of Operation DEADLIGHT on 31 December 1945. Joachim Franze died in March 1984.

Sources

Admiralty, Anti-Submarine Warfare Division, *Analysis of Operations: Convoys JW56A, JW56B and RA56* (TNA, ADM 199/2027)

—, *H.M. Ships Lost or Damaged: Reports, 1944* (TNA, ADM 199/957)

—, *Naval Staff History No. 22: Arctic Convoys, 1941–1945* (TNA, ADM 234/369)

—, *North Russia Convoys JW and RA: Reports, 1943–1944* (TNA, ADM 199/77)

—, *Convoy JW56B and the Loss of HMS* Hardy (NHB)

Rohwer, Prof. Jürgen, *Analyse der T-5 („Zaunkönig")-Schüsse von U-Booten gegen Geleitfahrzeuge. U278: HMS Hardy; U472: H.No.M.S. Stord; U601: HMS Hardy; U957: H.No.M.S. Stord* (Report for Bundesamt für Wehrtechnik und Beschaffung [Federal Office of Weapons Technology and Procurement], 1964) (BfZ, MaS 8/2.07)

Stainer, Sub-Lt L. T., private papers (typescript, IWM, 05/80/1)

U278 file (DUBMA)

English John, Obdurate *to* Daring: *British Fleet Destroyers 1941–45* (Gravesend, Kent: World Ship Society, 2008)

Ruegg, Bob, and Arnold Hague, *Convoys to Russia, 1941–1945* (Kendal, Cumbria: World Ship Society, 1992)

Syrett, David, 'Communications Intelligence and Murmansk Convoys JW56A, JW56B and RA56: 12 January–9 February 1944' in *The American Neptune* 58, no. 4 (Fall 1998), pp. 369–81

Whittle, Lt Cdr C. J. R., 'The Sinking of HMS "Hardy", January 30th 1944' in *The Arctic Lookout*, no. 20 (Spring 1995), pp. 20–4; also in *Warship World* 5, no. 6 (Spring 1996), pp. 24–5

Career history of HMS *Hardy*:
http://www.naval-history.net/xGM-Chrono-10DD-60V-Hardy2.htm

concentration so he hit him over the head with his paddle after two or three shouts to silence him had failed. In comparative peace he paddled on only to find that he was chasing after men already dead so with that he turned back to the two ships [*Hardy* and *Virago*] and as he approached his passenger came to and pleaded 'Can I shout now, Sir?' Amidships the *V[enus]* had put a scrambling net overside as one or two had dropped between the two ships and the net gave those trying to save them something to hang on to over the water. Commander (E) put his arm through the net to hold his raft while eager hands hauled the rescued man aboard. Unfortunately before he could follow a kick of *V[enus]*'s screw sent a wave to upset the raft and pitched him into the sea. Two men, clinging to the net but themselves clear of the water, finally managed to grab him and haul him aboard.

The survivors reached the Kola Inlet on 1 February without further incident.

U278 and Joachim Franze

Built by Bremer Vulkan at Vegesack and commissioned in January 1943, *U278* served seven frontline patrols under Oblt.z.S. (Kptlt from April 1944) Joachim Franze. All were carried out in the Northern Theatre under operational command of *F.d.U. Norwegen*, with *U278* based variously on Bergen, Narvik and Hammerfest. The first of these

---

96   HMS *PENELOPE*

Capt. D. G. Belben, DSO DSC AM RN†

Sunk by *U410* (Type VIIC), Oblt.z.S. Horst-Arno Fenski, 18 February 1944

Tyrrhenian Sea, 45 nm WSW of Naples (Italy)

Campaign Operation SHINGLE (Map 3)		*Displacement* 5,270 tons	
Coordinates 40° 55' N, 13° 21' E		*Dimensions* 506' × 51' × 14'	
Kriegsmarine code Quadrat CJ 5934		*Armour* 2.25" belt; 1–2" decks; 1" bulkheads	
U-boat timekeeping identical		*Maximum speed* 32.25 knots	
Fatalities 419 *Survivors* 206		*Armament* 6 × 6"; 8 × 4" AA; 8 × 40 mm AA; 6 × 20 mm AA; 6 × 21" tt	

Career

The Arethusa class of light cruisers, of which *Penelope* was the third of four units, were scaled-down versions of the Amphion class which had preceded them. Whereas the latter had the endurance to operate against enemy trade on the high seas, the smaller Arethusas were designed for fleet work in more confined waters and as such gave

valuable service in the Mediterranean. The London Naval Treaty of 1930 had restricted the Royal Navy to 91,000 tons of new cruiser construction and as the Admiralty was more concerned to increase the number of hulls than produce powerful examples of the type, the design legend of the Arethusa class was pared down to just 5,220 tons standard. This tonnage could only be obtained through the application

Penelope seen in December 1942 following repairs at New York and Portsmouth to damage sustained at Malta in the spring. Fourteen months later two torpedo hits from *U410* on the starboard side aft accomplished what hundreds of bombs could not. *BfZ*

of new building techniques and the Arethusas made much more extensive use of welding than with one or two exceptions had been the case in previous British naval construction. The result was an elegant and capable ship, though as with most British cruiser designs of the 1930s with too great a vulnerability to underwater damage; examples are HMSs *Naiad* and *Hermione* (**54** and **63**) together with *Penelope*'s sister *Galatea*, sunk by two torpedoes from *U557* with heavy loss of life in December 1941 (**G17**).

HMS *Penelope* was laid down at Harland & Wolff of Belfast in May 1934, launched in October 1935 and completed in November 1936, being immediately assigned to the 3rd Cruiser Squadron, Mediterranean Fleet with which she saw service during the Spanish Civil War and where she remained until recalled to Britain in January 1940. Transferred to the 2nd CS, Home Fleet in February, *Penelope* spent the next two months on patrol and escort duty in the North Sea and the North Atlantic. Her first taste of action came during the Norwegian Campaign when she grounded off Fleinvær in the Vestfjord on 11 April, requiring her to be beached at Harstad and then towed first to Skjelfjord in the Lofoten Islands and finally to Greenock on 16 May during the Allied evacuation of Norway. Repairs at Palmer's shipyard at Hebburn-on-Tyne lasted until July 1941, *Penelope* rejoining the 2nd CS a month later for service with the Home Fleet. In October she and her sister *Aurora* were transferred to the 3rd CS and ordered to the Mediterranean to form the nucleus of Force K, charged with harassing Axis supply convoys to North Africa. Reaching Malta on 21 October and augmented by the destroyers *Lance* and *Lively*, Force K made its first interception on the night of 9 November when a convoy of seven Italian merchantmen and a destroyer of its escort was wiped out in the space of three-quarters of an hour. The destruction of a second convoy on the 24th and another on 1 December brought the Luftwaffe's supplies of aviation gasoline in North Africa to a critical level. There followed the brief engagement known at the First Battle of Sirte on 17 December but Force K was itself undone in an Italian minefield off Tripoli on the 19th which claimed the cruiser *Neptune* and the

destroyer *Kandahar*, and left *Aurora* crippled; *Penelope* escaped with minor damage.

This disaster brought *Penelope* to Rear-Admiral Philip Vian's 15th Cruiser Squadron and the Malta convoy run. Over the next three months six convoys were escorted to and from Malta in the teeth of Axis air attack. On 22 March 1942 the last of these, MW10 from Alexandria, precipitated the Second Battle of Sirte during which Vian's cruisers and destroyers beat off an Italian squadron including the battleship *Littorio*. Three of the four merchantmen reached Malta which then came under ceaseless bombardment, *Penelope* being holed forward by a near miss on the 26th. On 27 March she entered dry dock in an attempt to make her seaworthy, the beginning of a twelve-day ordeal during which 2,100 Axis sorties were flown in an attempt to finish her off. Punctured by shrapnel and debris, *Penelope* earned the nickname 'HMS *Pepperpot*', but not until 8 April was the decision taken to run the gauntlet to Gibraltar, leaking, listing and unseaworthy though she was. The 9th brought wave after wave of attacks at sea but *Penelope* survived to reach Gibraltar and then New York for repairs at Brooklyn Navy Yard which continued until August. These were completed at Portsmouth that autumn but it was while *Penelope* was in the United States that the author C. S. Forester visited her and subsequently based his novel *The Ship* on her exploits at Second Sirte.

Early 1943 found *Penelope* back in the Mediterranean where she joined the 12th CS as part of Force Q at the Algerian port of Bône. Over the next few months she operated in support of military operations ashore as the Afrika Korps retreated through Libya and Tunisia while severing its supply lines with Italy. In June *Penelope* participated in the assault on Pantellaria and Lampedusa and then in the landings on Sicily in July and at Salerno in September, providing gunfire support in each case. Next came the Aegean where on 7 October she and the cruiser *Sirius* intercepted a German troop convoy bound for the British-held island of Leros. A single troop barge survived a holocaust that claimed five others, an ammunition ship and half a battalion of men. However, *Penelope* was not to emerge unscathed. Later that morning she and

Sirius were jumped by eighteen Stuka dive bombers as they raced back to Alexandria through the Scarpanto Strait, *Penelope* suffering damage from several near misses and an unexploded hit. The damage was made good at Alexandria, *Penelope* returning to Levant Command based in November. The abandonment of the Aegean campaign brought *Penelope* to Gibraltar and a brief period hunting German blockade runners in the Bay of Biscay in December. However, the new year saw her back with the 15th CS in the Mediterranean and to the last episode in a great fighting career: the landings at Anzio (Operation SHINGLE).

Background of the attack

The Allied landings at Anzio on the western coast of Italy on 22 January 1944 were accompanied by heavy bombardment of German positions from a combined naval force under the command of Rear Admiral F. J. Lowry USN. However, overcaution on the part of the military commander, Major General John P. Lucas (US Army), and ferocious German resistance thereafter prevented any quick breakout from the beachhead and kept Lowry's ships on station for far longer than anticipated. On the evening of 17 February *Penelope* secured after nearly two days' continuous shelling and turned for Naples to resupply. Following news that the cruiser HMS *Dido* had collided with a US landing craft in Naples Bay *Penelope* was ordered to return to Anzio immediately after refuelling to take up her duties. However, a shortage of escorts meant that this journey would have to be undertaken alone. Steering a northwesterly course as she entered the waters between the islands of Ischia and Palmarola, *Penelope* was zigzagging at twenty-six knots when she was sighted by *U410* at dawn on the 18th. Having just passed up the chance of attacking an unaccompanied Allied landing craft, Oblt.z.S. Horst-Arno Fenski could hardly believe his luck when an unescorted cruiser first filled his sights and then obligingly zigzagged into a perfect position for him to deliver an attack. Though *Penelope*'s high speed called for careful calculation she nonetheless provided a relatively straightforward target.

War Diary of *U410*, patrol of 3–28 February 1944: PG 30468, NHB, reel 1,106, p. 307

Date, time	Details of position, wind, weather, sea, light, visibility, moonlight, etc.	Incidents
18.ii		
0400	Qu. CJ 5952	
0553		Landing craft in sight, course 290°. I can't bring myself to attack; all it would do is betray our presence prematurely and scare off what I expect to be more worthwhile targets.
0626		It's already fairly light, so we dive. Just as we do so we sight a mast tip at bearing 110° true. We quickly trim the boat and go to periscope depth. Enemy approaches rapidly; at first we think she's a destroyer but later we identify her as a cruiser. Approach for a bow-on attack, two tubes ready with a T5 and a T3 respectively.[1] Tube III is out of action and after yesterday's experiences I've no confidence in Tube I.[2] Our cruiser is zigzagging, changing course every 2–5 min. by between 40 and 60 degrees. I estimate her speed to be 24 knots.[3] At a range of 4,000 m, bows right, inclination 70°, enemy suddenly alters course by 30° to starboard, bringing her towards us. Now she's ours for sure. At 0658 + 35 sec. a single torpedo (T3) fired from Tube IV. Enemy speed 24 knots, inclination 70° bows right, range 6000 m, depth set at 6 m.[4]
		A hit 40 m from the stern after 35 sec.[5] The cruiser, now unmistakably identified as being Aurora class, stops with steam billowing and settles further by the stern.[6] At 0712 + 10 sec. I fire a *coup-de-grâce* shot from Tube I, depth set at 6 m, 0° angle with no aim-off. The same firing failure as yesterday. Torpedo gyroscope starts up, torpedo won't budge. We drain the tube and stop the gyro. At 0716 + 30 sec. I fire a T5 *coup-de-grâce* shot from Tube II, quick fire setting.[7] 0° angle as before. Enemy is still just under way, so point of aim at forward control tower. Depth 6 m, range 600 m. A hit amidships after 55 sec. Cruiser capsizes and sinks stern first within two minutes. We head off to the south-west. Later we see two landing craft at the position of the sinking.[8]
0800	Qu. CJ 5937	

1 T5 was the *Zaunkönig* acoustic homing torpedo; the T3 was the latest version of the standard G7e torpedo.
2 At 1016 on the 17th *U410* had attacked an escort with a torpedo which turned out to be a 'tube runner' and could not be expelled from Tube I.
3   British sources record a speed of twenty-six knots though some deceleration is to be expected as the ship changed course with each zigzag.
4   The final zero has been struck out in pencil to correct an obvious typist's error.
5   The running time equates to a range of 525 metres.
6   Fenski's identification is correct, though the class to which *Penelope* and *Aurora* belonged was in fact named for the lead ship *Arethusa*.
7   'Quick fire' (*Schnellschuss*) was one of the three run settings of the *Zaunkönig* torpedo. This involved disarming the acoustic mechanism to permit the T5 to function like a conventional straight-running torpedo.
8   These were the British *LST 165* and *LST 430*.

The sinking

U410's first torpedo was adjudged by the British (agreeing the point to within twenty seconds of Fenski) to have struck *Penelope* at 0659½, 'slightly abaft 134 bulkhead, thereby fracturing the oil tanks immediately abaft the engine room, flooding the after engine room, the wardroom flat and compartments below, and the centre cabin flat abaft 144 bulkhead'. Listing nine degrees to starboard and settling by the stern, *Penelope* was heavily but not yet fatally damaged. However, Capt. Belben's ability to influence events was limited by the failure of all main lighting and telephones. Reports gradually filtered through that the after engine room was completely out of action, that only one of the two turbines was serviceable in the forward engine room, and that the steering had gone. Following further reports from the damage control centre, Belben ordered the ship to be counter-flooded, all starboard torpedoes to be fired and topweight on the starboard side jettisoned. Having failed to elicit any response to a general distress signal, Belben signalled two nearby LSTs to close *Penelope* and ordered the crews of 'A' and 'B' turrets to prepare for towing. Barely a minute after this message had been sent *U410*'s second torpedo struck close to the bulkhead separating 'B' boiler room and the after engine room. Once again, events demonstrated the susceptibility of British pre-war cruiser designs to underwater attack. If, as seems probable, Fenski's second torpedo detonated in the area of the starboard wing space abreast 'B' boiler room, the almost inevitable consequence would be an immediate flooding not only of these two spaces but also of the engine rooms on either side. The fact that *Penelope* capsized onto her beam ends within the space of a minute lends credence to this scenario. Nor was the end long in coming. 'The bows were then high in the air and the ship sank by the stern almost immediately at approx. 0718½ (estimated).' Fenski's observation that *Penelope* sank within two minutes of the second detonation is endorsed by all but one of the reports submitted to the Board of Enquiry.

Fate of the crew

HMS *Penelope* went down with more than two-thirds of her wartime complement of over 600 men. The first torpedo appears not to have accounted for many but the response of a highly experienced ship's company in closing up at Action Stations and assuming their damage-control positions below decks set the scene for the tragedy which followed. When *U410*'s second torpedo hit *Penelope* nineteen minutes later the immediate capsize of the ship doomed most of those stationed below. Others, though caught by the second hit in the comparative safety of the open deck, gave their lives in a vain attempt to save their shipmates. Not for the first time a ship's chaplain of the Royal Navy died trying to assist the wounded, and the Rev. P. A. Munby RNVR was last seen struggling to open the hatch leading from the fo'c's'le to the sick bay. Asked where he was going, he replied 'Where I'm needed.' Those who did get clear of the wreck had a long wait in waters thick with fuel oil and with little to aid buoyancy. Though one landing craft (*LST 165*) had received *Penelope*'s signal to 'Close me' at 0702, neither she nor *LST 430* were in a position to begin picking up survivors for about an hour, many having to wait over two hours for rescue. Valiant efforts were made by both landing craft crews, embarked soldiers of the Queen's Regiment and particularly Lt Morrison RNR of *LST 165* who dived overboard to help exhausted and fuel-laden men up the

Fenski addressing the crew of *U410* at La Spezia some time between May and August 1943. *DUBMA*

scrambling nets, but the ordeal was more than many could endure. One of these was Capt. Belben, seen encouraging his men in the water but found to be unconscious by the time he was hoisted aboard *LST 165*. He and thirteen others who could not be resuscitated or died later were buried in Naples.

The loss of life weighed heavily on the Board of Enquiry and at the Admiralty. The Director of Operations Division (Foreign) Capt. A. D. Nicholl, who had commanded *Penelope* with distinction between April 1941 and May 1942, observed that 'there seems little doubt that the fact that the ship's company was closed up at action stations contributed to the heavy number of casualties'. Nicholl agreed with the Board's suggestion that hands should 'not be sent to action stations in an emergency of the type that will not require the ship to go into action'. However, the Board exonerated Capt. Belben from any blame in *Penelope*'s loss, accepting that he had adopted 'such damage control action as could possibly be taken after the first explosion'. He was awarded a posthumous DSO for his leadership during *Penelope*'s exploits in the Aegean and a Mention in Despatches for her work off Anzio. Famous out of all proportion to her size, *Penelope* received fulsome tributes from many quarters. Those who perished in her on 18 February 1944 are remembered on a plaque in St Ann's Church, Portsmouth.

U410 and Horst-Arno Fenski

Built by Danziger Werft at Danzig (Gdansk) and commissioned in February 1942, *U410*'s operational career began with two patrols in the Atlantic under Korvkpt. Kurt Sturm. These yielded a single merchantman but Sturm's tenure is notable for an unusual mission to escort the blockade runner *Rhakotis* into Bordeaux from a position south-west of the Azores at the end of December 1942. Shadowed and attacked by RAF and RAAF aircraft, *Rhakotis* was eventually sunk on 1 January 1943 by the cruiser HMS *Scylla* leaving *U410* with the problem of dealing with 155 crewmen and prisoners of war. Half reached the Spanish coast in boats but the rest were taken aboard *U410* which twice came close to destruction by British aircraft, on the latter occasion sinking to the bottom. In an episode that reflects the cool relationship that many in the *U-Boot-Waffe* had with the German political establishment, Sturm refused to dock at St-Nazaire until the SS troops lined up on the quay were dismissed and he had received assurances that the prisoners he was carrying would be treated befitting their status.

His replacement, Oblt.z.S. Horst-Arno Fenski, was thrown straight into the maelstrom of Atlantic convoy operations, sinking two merchantmen on his first patrol but suffering damage in depth-charge attacks by Catalina aircraft and HMCS *Shediac* on 6 March 1943. *U410*'s next patrol took her into the Mediterranean on the night of 5–6 May, though she was damaged by air attack before reaching La Spezia on the 13th. There followed a highly successful period by Mediterranean standards, Fenski sinking nearly 40,000 tons of merchant shipping together with *Penelope* and the US *LST-348* two days after on 20 February 1944 (G72). This, however, proved to be *U410*'s last success as she was wrecked during a US air raid on Toulon on 11 March which also claimed the life of one of her crewmen. Nonetheless, Fenski's war was not over. Taking command of *U371* (see HMS *Hythe* and USS *Bristol*, 91 and 92), on 3 May 1944 he damaged the US destroyer *Menges* off Algeria, an action which prompted a relentless pursuit by US, British and Free French escorts and aircraft lasting more than a day. Eventually forced to surface on the morning of the 4th, *U371* was sunk by gunfire from the waiting French escort destroyer *Sénégalais* but not before Fenski had hit her with a final T5. Most of *U371*'s crewmen, Fenski included, were picked up inshore near Bougie, the latter spending two years in captivity. As the *U-Boot-Waffe* was destined to do, Fenski had fought to the bitter end. He died in February 1965.

Sources

Admiralty, *Enemy Attacks on H.M. Ships: Reports, 1943–1944* (TNA, ADM 199/959)
U410 file (DUBMA)
Short, Don, *My Navy Days* (typescript, IWM, 02/2/1)

Bee, Mike, HMS Penelope: *Her Life and Times* (author, ongoing)
Brown, David K., Nelson *to Vanguard: Warship Design and Development, 1923–1945* (London: Chatham Publishing, 2000)
Forester, C. S., *The Ship* (London: Michael Joseph, 1943)
Gordon, Ed, HMS Pepperpot*! The* Penelope *in World War Two* (London: Robert Hale, 1985)
Haines, Gregory, *Cruiser at War* (London: Ian Allan, 1978)
'Her Company', *Our* Penelope: *The Story of HMS* Penelope (London: Harrap, 1941)
Johnson, Bill, 'HMS *Penelope*' in *Warship World* 6, no. 6 (Spring 1999), pp. 18–19 and 25
Lamb, R. A., and R. H. Osborne, 'Arethusa-Class Cruisers' in *Warships*, Supplement no. 47 (August 1977), pp. 3–22
Lee, Eric C. B., *The Cruiser Experience: Life Aboard Royal Navy Cruisers during World War Two* (Fleet Hargate, Lincs.: Arcturus Press, 2000)
Raven, Alan, and John Roberts, *British Cruisers of World War Two* (London: Arms and Armour Press, 1980)
Schneider, Werner, *12 Feindfahrten. Als Funker auf U-431, U-410 und U-371 im Atlantik und im Mittelmeer. Ausbildung, Einsatz, Gefangenschaft, 1940–1946* (Weinheim: Germania Verlag, 2006)

War career of HMS *Penelope*:
   http://www.naval-history.net/xGM-Chrono-06CL-Penelope.htm
HMS *Penelope* Association website:
   http://homepage.ntlworld.com/mike.bee/Index.htm
Webpage devoted to HMS *Penelope*:
   http://www.wartimememoriesproject.com/ww2/ships/penelope.php

97   HMS *WOODPECKER*

Cdr H. L. Pryse, RNR
Sunk by *U256* (Type VIIC), Oblt.z.S. Wilhelm Brauel, 19–27 February 1944
North Atlantic, 530 nm WSW of Cape Clear, Cork (Ireland)

Woodpecker in December 1942, shortly before commencing escort duties in the Atlantic.
Fourteen months later she was undone by a *Zaunkönig* acoustic homing torpedo from *U256*. *BfZ*

Theatre North Atlantic (Map 1)		*Displacement* 1,475 tons	
Coordinates (of attack) 48° 49' N, 22° 38' W		*Dimensions* 299.5' × 37.5' × 9.5'	
Kriegsmarine code (of attack) Quadrat BE 1843		*Maximum speed* 19.75 knots	
U-boat timekeeping differential +2 hours		*Armament* 6 × 4" AA; 8 × 40 mm AA; 6 × 20 mm AA; 1 × Hedgehog ATW	
Fatalities none *Survivors* 213 and 17			

Career

For notes on the sloop type, see HMS *Penzance* (**16**).

Ordered under the 1940 war emergency programme as a unit of the modified Black Swan class, the escort sloop HMS *Woodpecker* was laid down at William Denny's yard at Dumbarton on the Clyde in February 1941, launched in June 1942 and completed that December. After working up at HMS *Western Isles*, the anti-submarine school at Tobermory, Scotland, *Woodpecker* joined the 7th Escort Group at Londonderry in January 1943. Service in the North-Western Approaches and then in support of the North African Campaign continued until April when she was assigned to the newly formed 2nd Support Group under Capt. F. J. 'Johnnie' Walker. (For more on Walker, see HMS *Audacity*, **43**.) Her appearance coincided with a decisive turn in Allied fortunes in the Battle of the Atlantic and in the year before she was sunk Walker's ships destroyed no fewer than twelve U-boats, *Woodpecker* sharing in five of them: *U449* (24 June 1943), *U504* (30 July), *U762* (8 February 1944), *U424* (11 February) and *U264* (19 February, just hours before she was herself mortally wounded). Walker's 'relentless pursuit' of the enemy, amounting to a personal obsession, took the 2nd SG across the Atlantic, onto the Gibraltar route, through the Bay of Biscay offensive in the summer of 1943 and then back to Western Approaches Command and the Mediterranean supply run at the end of the year. Refitted at Avonmouth between August and November 1943, in the new year *Woodpecker* deployed with the 2nd SG for anti-submarine operations in the North Atlantic, this time with air support provided by HM escort carriers *Activity* and *Nairana*. *Woodpecker* was the first and as it turned out the only casualty suffered by the 2nd SG, which had accounted for three more U-boats by the time Walker succumbed to a stroke in July 1944 and another eight by war's end to become the most successful anti-submarine unit of the Second World War.

Background of the attack

In the first years of the war limited resources and rudimentary tactics had restricted the Allied navies to defensive escort of convoys. By 1944, however, an increased supply of ships, close air support, improved intelligence and refinements in ordnance, tactics and technology made possible the formation of offensive hunting groups with the capacity to detect, run down and destroy U-boats, usually in tandem with one or more escort carriers. The most formidable of these was Capt. F. J. Walker's 2nd Support Group which consisted of HM sloops *Starling* (Senior Officer), *Kite*, *Magpie*, *Wild Goose*, *Wren* and *Woodpecker*. On 29 January 1944 the 2nd SG sailed from Liverpool to take up a patrol area south-west of Ireland in which U-boats were reported gathering to intercept convoy traffic. It was one of the cruises that established Walker as the most successful U-boat killer of the war. Over a three-week period Walker's group (supported for the first week of operations by HM escort carriers *Activity* and *Nairana*) sank six U-boats with *Woodpecker* sharing the credit for three of these. The last, *U264*, was claimed on 19 February, two days after the 2nd SG had joined the escort of convoy ON224, then threatened by the *Hai* ('shark') group. Kptlt Hartwig Looks and fifty of his crewmen were picked up by *Starling* and *Woodpecker* between 1800 and 1900 that evening. At 2155 that night Walker's group obtained an HF/DF bearing for *U608* (Oblt.z.S. Wolfgang Reisener) while she was transmitting a signal fifteen miles to the north. Increasing to seventeen knots, the 2nd SG closed the position in line abreast, the order (port to starboard) being *Wild Goose*, *Woodpecker*, *Starling*, *Magpie* and *Wren*. Several miles short of the area indicated by the HF/DF fix the 2nd SG was sighted by Oblt.z.S. Wilhelm Brauel's surfaced *U256*. As the line overran his position Brauel fired bow and stern shots at the sloops overtaking him on either side, aiming first at *Starling* and then at *Woodpecker* in quick succession. A brief Asdic contact was obtained by *Woodpecker* 600 yards off her starboard quarter just before she was struck by one of Brauel's *Zaunkönig* ('wren') acoustic homing torpedoes.

War Diary of U256, patrol of 25 January–22 March 1944: PG 30232, NHB, reel 1,094, p. 401

Date, time	Details of position, wind, weather, sea, light, visibility, moonlight, etc.	Incidents
20.ii		
0000	Qu. BE 1843, wind SE 2, sea 1, cloudy, visibility 3 nm, light swell	
0004		A shadow on the starboard quarter at bearing 120° true, range 5,000 m. It is the shadow of a large two-funnelled destroyer.[1] She closes slowly on our starboard side with a broad inclination. Battle Stations!
0007		Shadow at bearing 220° true. Another destroyer with same silhouette closing on port side, also broad

---

1   HM escort sloop *Starling*. *Starling* and her sister sloops of the 2nd Support Group had only the one funnel, though Brauel may well have been misled by the radar housing atop the bridge of each unit.

		inclination.[2]
0008		*Naxos* pulse readings lasting four to five seconds, volume 5, at intervals of three seconds.[3] Destroyers both proceeding at 15 knots and slowly drawing level, one on either side.[4]
0010		We turn hard aport to fire both a stern and bow shot and switch to slow speed.
0011	Qu. BE 1843	T5 fired from Tube V at starboard-side destroyer, range 3,500 m, inclination 70°, bows left, angle of fire 180°, depth 4 m, fired in line with the stern of the boat.

T5 fired from Tube II at port-side destroyer, range 2,000 m, inclination 80°, bows right, angle of fire 0°, depth 4 m, fired in line with the bow.

Alarm! To 160 m.

After 2 min. 2 sec. first detonation heard to starboard, followed by powerful sinking and breaking noises.[5] Bow eel has found its mark.

After 3 min. 10 sec. a second detonation heard to port with equally loud sinking and breaking noises. These are followed immediately by four further detonations. Stern eel has found its mark.[6]

No further noises, no depth charges. I withdraw, course 170°. Tube II reloaded.

0340	Surfaced! Starshell, course 350° towards position of sinking.
0345	Short *Naxos* pulses.
0347	Alarm! Dive to 80 m, one engine at slow speed, course 270°.
⚡	
2122	Outgoing W/T transmission 2051/20/76: *0011 [Qu.] BE 1843 simultaneous stern and bow T5 at two destroyers, inclinations left 120° and right 130°, speed 15 knots. Detonations after 3 min. 10 sec. and 2 min. 02 sec. Powerful sinking and disintegration noises then no further hydrophone effect. Still one bow T5, 66 cbm.[7] Brauel.*

---

2   HMS *Woodpecker*.

3   The *Naxos* radar-detection system, which appears to have picked up radar pulses from one of the group. These were most likely from HMS *Starling* which obtained a contact off *Woodpecker's* starboard bow after the hit.

4   The 2nd Support Group was in fact proceeding at seventeen knots at this juncture.

5   It must be supposed that this was the hit on *Woodpecker*. The 'starboard' origin of the noises is explained by *U256* having turned about when firing her two torpedoes, something not clear in the log but made apparent in Brauel's own sketch of the incident years later (see below). 'Eel' (German = *Aal*) was U-boat slang for torpedo.

6   *Starling* was not hit, nor did she or any other escort note any explosions beyond those involving *Woodpecker*. Several of *Woodpecker's* dislodged depth charges detonated at 330 metres, which perhaps equates to the 68-second lapse between Brauel's actual hit and his supposed second hit. This was Brauel's own explanation for his misinterpretation of the event after the war, though it is not clear why the log records these explosions occurring on either side of *U256*.

7   By '66 cbm' Brauel is referring to the available diesel fuel in cubic metres.

The sinking

Whichever of *U256's* 'wrens' hit *Woodpecker*, this particular battle of the birds was an unequal one. The torpedo demolished the after part of the ship, wrecking the propellers and steering gear. Some forty feet of the quarterdeck was peeled back over 'X' mounting leaving the deckhead of the after compartments pointing skyward. The ship flooded to the after engine room bulkhead and 'a closer inspection revealed both forecastle and upper deck generally concertinaed and in some cases split'. The port side was badly buckled abreast the funnel and water was entering through a crack in the hull. However, the ship appeared to be in reasonable trim and with lighting and W/T still functioning it was hoped that she might be brought in to Falmouth. Instead of launching a hunt for the perpetrator Capt. Walker decided to close *Woodpecker* in *Starling* with a view to taking her in tow, instructing the rest of the group to stream Foxer decoys in a square patrol around them. However, there was a heavy sea running and towing was abandoned until the next day following two unsuccessful attempts during which *Starling* scraped her way along *Woodpecker's* port side and smashed her seaboat. Once the tow had been passed on the morning of 20 February the pair proceeded at no better than a knot and a half until HM salvage tug *Stormking* arrived to take over on the

21 with which the rest of the 2nd SG gratefully turned for Liverpool. Wreckage below the water and the windage of the damaged stern kept the pair to 4½ knots but matters were proceeding satisfactorily until a weather report from the Admiralty on the 26th forecast a northerly gale and with it the likelihood that *Woodpecker* would founder. Lt Cdr Pryse ordered the remaining men off that evening, ensuring that the ship was pumped as dry as possible and that all doors were secured before she was abandoned. *Stormking* continued to tow through the night, the wind picking up all the while, until on the morning of the 27th she abandoned her attempt to gain the lee side of the Scillies in rising seas. No sooner had *Stormking* cast off at 0715 than *Woodpecker's* true state was revealed; she capsized within a matter of minutes and was seen by those of her ship's company on board HM corvette *Azalea* bottom up, her bow well out of the water. To hasten her end Lt Cdr Pryse requested that *Azalea* and the Canadian corvette *Chilliwack* finish her off with gunfire, *Woodpecker* sinking at 0806 in position 49° 51' N, 06° 43' W.

The loss of *Woodpecker* just sixty miles off the Bishop Rock Light was a blow to Walker and his men but could comfortably be set against the destruction of six U-boats by the 2nd Support Group over the previous three weeks, the latter cheered up the Mersey on their return to Liverpool on 25 February. On the German side B.d.U. made a characteristically over-optimistic assessment of *U256's* success, Brauel being credited with sinking not only *Woodpecker* but also two ships identifiable as *Starling* and the US destroyer *Borie*, neither of which were so much as hit. *Borie*, incidentally, had already been claimed as sunk by *U256* on 31 October 1943; see below.

Fate of the crew

Quite exceptionally, the torpedo that ended *Woodpecker's* career caused neither fatalities nor serious injury to any of her company. First to leave were eleven prisoners from *U264* who were transferred to *Magpie* at daybreak on the 20th. They were followed on the 22nd by four officers, seventy-nine ratings and the six remaining U-boat men to *Magpie* and *Wren*, and on the 25th by an officer and fifty-one ratings to HM frigate *Rother*, leaving a steaming party of seven officers and seventy-one ratings. Informed on the afternoon of the 26th of the likelihood of the stern dropping off (with the consequent collapse of the engine room bulkheads), and ordered by the Commander-in-Chief Western Approaches, Admiral Sir Max Horton, not to risk the crew if her condition appeared precarious, Lt Cdr Pryse ordered the remaining crewmen to be taken off at 1830 on the 26th. This was successfully carried out by *Azalea* and *Chilliwack*. In his official report Pryse was generous in his praise of *Woodpecker's* ship's company: 'No Commanding Officer could wish for a more gallant and efficient company of Officers and men, and on each occasion of reducing complement many of the volunteers to stay behind had to go.' After a spell of survivors' leave many of *Woodpecker's* men found themselves commissioning one of her sisters, the newly completed HMS *Lark*, but she too succumbed to a *Zaunkönig*, torpedoed by *U962* off the Kola Inlet on 17 February 1945. However, here the similarity ends, for though *Lark* survived to be beached at Murmansk as a constructive total loss, three of her men perished in the attack which left many others wounded, old Woodpeckers among them. *Woodpecker's* connections with the Hertfordshire community of Bushey are remembered in the town Museum, the ship having been adopted during Warship Week in February 1942 during which £120,000 was raised towards the cost of building her.

U256 and Wilhelm Brauel

Built by Bremer Vulkan at Vegesack and commissioned in December 1941, *U256* made five patrols under three commanding officers. The first of these under Kptlt Odo Loewe brought her into the *Steinbrinck* and *Loos* patrol lines in August 1942 but earned no pennants. On the 25th of that month she was damaged first by HMNorS *Potentilla* and HMS *Viscount* and then in separate attacks by two RAF Whitley bombers in the Bay of Biscay on 2 September. Refitted as a flak boat, *U256* returned to frontline service only in October 1943, though with her effective range reduced. Commanded now by Oblt.z.S. Wilhelm Brauel, a defensive attack by *U256* against the destroyer USS *Borie* on 31 October was erroneously credited as her first kill. Relieved of her ungainly flak guns after the costly failure of Dönitz's tactic of fighting it out with aircraft in the Bay of Biscay, in January 1944 *U256* sailed for the North Atlantic on a two-month patrol which yielded her only confirmed sinking, that of HMS *Woodpecker*. Brauel's last patrol

Brauel (with white cap) and the crew of *U256* pose under the famous sawfish emblem fixed to the headquarters of the 9th *U-Flottille* at Brest on 22 March 1944. *DUBMA*

ended just a day out of Brest on 7 June when *U256*, sailing in company with *U415* (see **94**), was heavily damaged by a Wellington and two Liberators of the RAF, though the latter were both shot down. *U256* limped into Brest and her final voyage, made under Korvkpt. Heinrich Lehmann-Willenbrock, entailed a transit to Bergen where she was decommissioned in October 1944.

Promoted Kapitänleutnant in April 1945, Brauel was given command of the *Schnorchel*-equipped *U92* (one patrol from August to September 1944, no successes), *U3530* (never put to sea) and finally *U975*. The latter sailed under Brauel just once, being delivered to Londonderry in May 1945 following the German surrender, after which she was scuttled off Bloody Foreland (Ireland) as part of Operation DEADLIGHT. Brauel spent a brief period in captivity in England before returning to Germany. He died in September 2002.

Sources

Admiralty, *Losses of H.M. and Merchant Ships by Mines and Submarine Attacks: Reports, 1944–1945* (TNA, ADM 199/175)

Brauel, Kptlt Wilhelm, letter to ex-crewmen of *U256* regarding the sinking of HMS *Woodpecker* (typescript, April 1990, DUBMA, *U256* folder)

Rohwer, Prof. Jürgen, *Analyse der T-5 („Zaunkönig")-Schüsse von U-Booten gegen Geleitfahrzeuge*. U256: HMS Woodpecker (Report for Bundesamt für Wehrtechnik und Beschaffung [Federal Office of Weapons Technology and Procurement], 1964) (BfZ, MaS 8/2.07)

Blair, *Hitler's U-Boat War*, II, pp. 497–501

Burn, Alan, *The Fighting Captain: Frederic John Walker RN and the Battle of the Atlantic* (Barnsley, S. Yorks.: Leo Cooper, 1993)

Hague, Arnold, *Sloops: A History of the 71 Sloops Built in Britain and Australia for the British, Australian and Indian Navies, 1926–1946* (Kendal, Cumbria: World Ship Society, 1993)

Wemyss, Cdr D. E. G., *Relentless Pursuit: The Story of Capt. F. J. Walker, CB, DSO***, RN – U-Boat Hunter and Destroyer* (London: William Kimber, 1957)

Career history of HMS *Woodpecker*:
http://www.naval-history.net/xGM-Chrono-18SL-Woodpecker.htm

98 HMS *WARWICK*
Cdr D. A. Rayner, DSC RN
Sunk by *U413* (Type VIIC), Kptlt Gustav Poel, 20 February 1944
Celtic Sea, 15 nm WSW of Trevose Head, Cornwall (England)

Warwick in the 1930s, already nearly twenty years old and with four years' war service ahead of her.
The end came after *U413* removed her stern with a torpedo off Cornwall. *BfZ*

Theatre British home waters (Map 2)	*Displacement* 1,207 tons
Coordinates 50° 30' N, 05° 27' W	*Dimensions* 312' × 29.5' × 10.75'
Kriegsmarine code Quadrat BF 2169	*Maximum speed* 24.5 knots
U-boat timekeeping identical	*Armament* 2 × 4.7"; 4 × 20 mm AA; 1 × Hedgehog ATW
Fatalities about 67 *Survivors* 94+	

Career

For design notes on the 'V & W'-class destroyers, see HMS *Whirlwind* (13).

HMS *Warwick* was laid down at Hawthorne Leslie's yard at Hebburn-on-Tyne in March 1917, launched in December of that year and completed on 18 March 1918. She belonged to what was known as the Admiralty 'W' or Repeat 'V' group of the class. Joining the Dover Patrol, *Warwick*'s finest hour came in the earliest days of her career when she served as Vice-Admiral Sir Roger Keyes's flagship at the blocking of Zeebrugge on 23 April 1918, and it was while returning from the second attempt to block Ostend harbour on 10 May that she was mined aft and broke her back. However, she made Dover with her sister *Velox* lashed alongside. Repaired and fitted for minelaying during 1918, she ended the war with the Grand Fleet. Details of *Warwick*'s inter-war service are few but by 1921 she was serving with the 1st Destroyer Flotilla, Atlantic Fleet. This was renumbered the 5th DF in 1925, possibly on being deployed to the Mediterranean, but was back with the Atlantic Fleet (Home Fleet from late 1932) by March 1927. On 31 January 1934 *Warwick* suffered slight damage in collision with her sister *Vortigern* off Gibraltar and was consigned to the Reserve Fleet in February 1936. Recommissioning in August 1939, the outbreak of war found *Warwick* at Plymouth with the 11th DF of the Home Fleet, with which she spent the next year on convoy and anti-submarine patrol duty in the South-Western Approaches. In February 1940 she followed Western Approaches Command to Liverpool, being assigned to the

7th Escort Group in the autumn for convoy duty in the Atlantic. On 23 December *Warwick* sailed from Liverpool to join convoy OB263 off Londonderry but had no sooner passed the Bar Light Vessel than she was holed in the engine room by an acoustic mine, having to be towed back up the Mersey by her sister *Wild Swan* and at length beached in Tranmere Bay.

Once repairs had been completed in the spring of 1941 *Warwick* rejoined the 7th EG in the Atlantic. In early 1942 she was detached for duty with the US Navy in the Caribbean and July found her towing the American tanker *Gulfbelle* first into Port-of-Spain and then to Curaçao after she had been hit by *U126* off Tobago on the 3rd. In December *Warwick* was earmarked for conversion to a long-range escort and took passage for Britain where the work was carried out at Dundee between January and May 1943. The conversion, which was performed on twenty-one of the 'V & Ws', involved the removal of the fore funnel and No. 1 boiler and their replacement with additional oil bunkerage and crew accommodation together with a revised weapons and radar fit. In June *Warwick* began escort duty on the Britain–Gibraltar run, being allocated in July to operations with RAF Coastal Command against U-boats transiting the Bay of Biscay. In October she participated in operations to establish the first Allied air bases in the Azores before resuming convoy work in the South-Western Approaches. Early 1944 found her refitting at Ardrossan from where she sailed for Devonport on 15 February.

Background of the attack

On the evening of 19 February 1944 HMSs *Warwick* and *Scimitar* sailed from Devonport following intelligence reports that a U-boat was operating off the north coast of Cornwall between Pendeen and Trevose Heads. This was indeed the case and the morning of the 20th dawned clear and cold to find Kptlt Gustav Poel's *U413* sizing up an abundance of shipping in the Celtic Sea. However, although the British had been alerted to her presence, circumstances could hardly have been less favourable for making good their intelligence. As Commander Rayner recalled, 'convoys in long lines of two columns were passing up and down the war channel and the sea was littered with fishing vessels of all sizes. As our radar screen was confused with the echoes from the small craft a determined U-boat could have done what he liked.' So it proved. Matters were not assisted by *Warwick* turning off her Asdic set for essential adjustments at 1130, minutes before *U413* unleashed a salvo of two torpedoes at her.

War Diary of *U413*, patrol of 26 January–27 March 1944: PG 30471, NHB, reel 1,106, pp. 592–3

Date, time	Details of position, wind, weather, sea, light, visibility, moonlight, etc.	Incidents
20.ii	West coast of England	
0800	[Qu.] BF 2165	
0845		Battle Stations! A number of hydrophone readings. Two 'S'- and 'T'-class destroyers are proceeding at low speed along the outer convoy route, range 3,000 m.[1] They start carrying out Asdic sweeps. After half an hour they make for the gap in the Trevose minefield having dropped several patterns of depth charges.[2] I can see two fighter aircraft through the periscope and the coastline can be clearly discerned.
1000		Hydrophone readings at bearings ranging from 265° to 310° true. I assume a convoy and head in this direction. But it turns out to be several fishing trawlers.
1045		Back to the expected convoy route. Barrage balloons in sight at a bearing of 160° true. That has to be the anticipated convoy.
1115		Despite our converging at half speed the contact keeps moving away; based on our course towards the convoy the inclination must be around 70°. Range between 7 and 8 nm. We don't go any faster because two of the convoy's destroyers are passing my position, one of them very close, sweeping with Asdic and stopping every so often.[3] I gradually form the impression that the various *Naxos* contact readings do indeed indicate that my presence has become known to them because there is a substantial difference in today's escort screen![4]
1130		Am closed by one of the destroyers whose pristine appearance and twin forward mounting make me think she must be brand new.[5] I don't think it likely that I will get within firing range of the convoy now, and as I consider it probable (at the very least) that the destroyers are on to me, making the prospects for success today very poor, I decide to have a go at the destroyer which is now turning away and heading off. As I ascertain later, she is a fast escort vessel of the 'V & W' class.[6]
1137	[Qu.] BF 2169	A spread of two torpedoes fired at the fast escort vessel from Tubes I and III. Shot coordinates: enemy bows right, inclination 96.5°, enemy speed 12 knots, range 1,200 m, torpedo depth 4 m, magnetic detonator pistols set. A hit after 4 min. 50 sec. followed immediately by a second detonation.[7] Destroyer lies stricken and listing with a column of smoke some 300 m high. I assume an explosion of her boilers or magazine. We can hear loud sinking noises in the boat. Several trawlers appear on the scene but within 15

1 Possibly HMSs *Scimitar* and *Warwick* of the 'S' and 'V & W' classes respectively. The latter recorded obtaining a contact (later classified 'non-sub') and dropping depth charges half an hour earlier at 0815.
2 On 22 July 1940 the British had declared the existence of a minefield stretching across the Celtic Sea from the northern coast of Cornwall to the shores of Waterford and Wexford in Ireland. However, there were numerous channels to permit the passage of shipping, including that off Trevose Head.
3 *Scimitar* and *Warwick*. Though Poel considers the pair attached to a convoy, this was not in fact the case.
4 Poel is referring to *U413*'s *Naxos* radar-detection apparatus which would identify radar sweeps being carried out by nearby Allied vessels. Despite Poel's fears that *U413* had been picked up by these radar sweeps, the British had in fact been alerted to his presence by Enigma decrypts.
5 *Warwick*, for whose smart appearance Cdr Rayner had been praised upon arrival at Devonport on the 19th. She had been painted the previous week at the conclusion of her refit at Ardrossan. Poel might have been surprised to learn that both she and *Scimitar* had over twenty-five years' service behind them.
6 Poel is correct, though the log does not specify precisely when this identification was made.
7 As the recorded range and inclination are inconsistent with straight-running torpedoes (for which 90 seconds would be a more likely running time) and as *Zaunkönige* were not fired in multiple spreads, it must be supposed that Poel had launched FAT torpedoes (*Federapparat-Torpedo*) which after a preset straight run would pursue a meandering course with repeated 180-degree turns. No torpedo report exists to clarify the issue but Grossmann (see below) recalls *U413* firing a single FAT before diving deep, all subsequent observations of *Warwick*'s fate being purely acoustic.

| | | minutes there's nothing more to be seen of the destroyer.[8] Five aircraft of different types (from single- to four-engined) circle the scene. Floats have been launched. |

She's disappeared!

1150 — Second destroyer has approached.[9] She's being very skilful, always proceeding slowly then accelerating in short bursts to drop a few depth charges.

Being so close to the coast in shallow waters this is no place for a *Zaunkönig* attack. I want to save my stern *Zaunkönig* (no T5 left in the bow tubes) solely for defence purposes. Besides, an increasing number of aircraft are buzzing overhead at low altitude.

We head off at periscope depth.

1200 [Qu.] BF 2169 Day's run: 33 nm surfaced, 21 nm submerged = 54 nm.

---

8 *Warwick* disappeared in under ten minutes.
9 HM escort destroyer *Wensleydale*.

The sinking

British sources agree with Poel's assertion that there were two detonations but the cause of the second is uncertain. Poel himself appears to rule out the possibility of it having been his second torpedo and the Board of Enquiry attributed it to the detonation of the after magazine and/or the torpedo warhead magazine. In his memoirs Cdr Rayner recalled the impression this event made on him:

> The sky suddenly turned to flame and the ship gave a violent shudder. Then the flame had gone and as far as I could see everything was strangely the same. Looking ahead, I could see something floating and turning over in the water like a giant metallic whale. As I looked it rolled over still and I could make out our own pennant numbers painted on it. I was dumb-founded. It seemed beyond reason. I ran to the after side of the bridge and looked over. The ship ended just aft of the engine room – everything abaft that had gone. What I had seen ahead of us *had really been the ship's own stern*.

Shattered though she was, *Warwick* remained on an even keel and once the First Lieutenant had seen to the dousing of sporadic oil fires the question of saving her presented itself. Any optimism was shortlived. Four minutes after the secondary detonation *Warwick* gave a sudden lurch to port, probably following the collapse of the after engine-room bulkhead. Having capsized she sank by the stern, her bows remaining above the surface for a few minutes, perhaps resting on the seabed in what was little more than thirty fathoms before gradually slipping under.

In a mistaken appreciation of *U413*'s firing position, the British paid tribute to the skill and cunning with which they reckoned she had mingled with the large number of fishing vessels in the area before making her attack. Though their presence no doubt added to *Warwick*'s and *Scimitar*'s radar difficulties, Poel's log provides no evidence that they played any part in his attack, the success of which probably owed more to ordnance than tactics. Nor were the British alone in misconstruing the evidence before them. Across the Channel Poel received the Knight's Cross for a patrol during which B.d.U. credited him as having sunk three destroyers and a further escort of unknown type. But, *Warwick* apart, these claims were based on misinterpreted acoustic data after lengthy *Zaunkönig* runs and Poel claimed only one victim during this patrol.

Fate of the crew

The few minutes that separated the detonations from her sinking kept the death toll from HMS *Warwick* under seventy men. A majority of these were aft when the ship was struck and none survived from the severed stern section. Despite the few minutes vouchsafed her no orderly evacuation could be effected, efforts to lower the port whaler and the ship's motor boat from the starboard side being defeated by burning oil and jammed davits in each case. As Ordinary Coder S. K. Fawcett recalled, 'the words Abandon Ship, which usually accompanies such incidents, were never heard, as events overtook us and . . . I was shot off into the water'. Narrowly avoiding being dragged under by the mainmast rigging, Fawcett was propelled to the surface to find himself surrounded by debris, corpses and oil. By the time the survivors were scrambling into Carley floats patterns of depth charges were being dropped by the escort destroyer *Wensleydale* which had joined *Scimitar* in the hunt after witnessing the attack. Though some way off, to Ordinary Telegraphist K. G. Holmes the detonation of each charge felt 'like being punched in the stomach'. Help for the oil-soaked remnant of *Warwick*'s crew came over the next two hours courtesy of the fishing fleet, those on Fawcett's float whiling away the time contemplating their good fortune at having earned survivors' leave. By 1300 over ninety men had been brought aboard two trawlers, the aptly named *Lady Luck* and the Belgian *Christopher Columbus* whose formidable skipper, Marcel Bacquaert, endured in the memory of those he rescued. They were landed at Padstow later that afternoon but six men failed to survive the night. Fawcett endured a lengthy spell in hospital as hypothermia turned to pneumonia while his erstwhile shipmates were sent to Plymouth to draw new kit before taking their survivors' leave. *Wensleydale*, meanwhile, was able to avenge the *Warwick* six months later (see below).

The Board of Enquiry considered the conduct of both officers and ship's company to have been exemplary, an opinion concurred in by Admiral Sir Ralph Leatham, Commander-in-Chief Plymouth. Forwarding the findings of the Board of Enquiry to the Admiralty, he expressed his great regret for 'the sinking of this ship after such long and distinguished service'. The dead are remembered by six trees in St Merryn's churchyard, Padstow and by plaques on the harbour wall there and in the church itself. Since *Warwick* was sunk in relatively shallow waters just fifteen miles off the Cornish coast her wreck has been the focus of numerous diving expeditions, not all of which have respected her status as a war grave. In the words of one commentator, 'there isn't much point in taking a wrecking bar onto this wreck, so great has been the pillage'.

U413 and Gustav Poel

Built by Danziger Werft at Danzig (Gdansk) and commissioned in June 1942, *U413* had a busy career marked by the increasingly dangerous conditions faced by U-boats operating in Atlantic and British coastal waters. On 14 November 1942, just two weeks into her first frontline patrol, Oblt.z.S. (Kptlt from February 1943) Gustav Poel sank the troopship *Warwick Castle* of 20,107 GRT. *U413*'s next cruise yielded two merchantmen, but four subsequent patrols as part of the *Meiser, Star, Fink, Donau, Schlieffen, Siegfried, Körner, Tirpitz* and *Eisenhart* groups in 1943 went unrewarded. Her last patrol under Poel yielded only *Warwick* and a change of command in April 1944 availed her little. *U413* twice sailed from Brest under Oblt.z.S. Dietrich Sachser in the summer of 1944. The first of these sorties ended with damage from an RAF Halifax on 8 June. Repaired and equipped with the *Schnorchel* breathing pipe device, *U413* sank the SS *Saint Enogat* off the Isle of Wight on 19 August but a prolonged hunt involving HM destroyers *Forester, Vidette* and *Wensleydale* along the south coast of England ended her career for good. She was sunk off Brighton on 20 August with the loss of all but the Chief Engineer, Oblt (Ing.) Karl Hutterer, who got away through the forward escape hatch before floating ninety feet to the surface where he was rescued by *Wensleydale. Leitender Ingenieur* Hutterer lived long enough to make contact with survivors of the *Warwick* in the 1980s. Kptlt Poel served out the war ashore, first as a unit leader at the *Marineschule* in Mürwik and then as a staff officer at B.d.U. He died in Hamburg in January 2009.

Sources

Admiralty, *H.M. Ships Lost or Damaged: Reports, 1944* (TNA, ADM 199/957)

Survivors' memoirs and letters concerning sinking of HMS *Warwick* (manuscripts and typescripts, 1984–5, IWM, Misc. 159 (2461))

Fawcett, O.Coder S.K., *Sinking of HMS* Warwick *20th February 1944: My Account* (manuscript, c.1984–5, IWM, Misc. 159 (2461))

Grossmann, Fähnrich Gerhard, *Einzelunternehmen von* U413 *im Januar bis März 1944* (typescript, DUBMA, *U413* folder)

Fairweather, Cliff, ed., *Hard Lying: The Story of the "V & W" Class Destroyers and the Men Who Sailed in Them* (Chelmsford, Essex: Avalon Associates, 2005)

Poel seen aboard *U413* some time between November 1942 and March 1944.
DUBMA

Harries, Lt Cdr David, 'HMS *Warwick*' in *Hard Lying: The V & W Magazine*, no. 11 (June 2001), pp. 2–5

Holmes, O.Tel. K. G., 'The Memories . . .' in *Hard Lying: The V & W Magazine*, no. 8 (December 1999), pp. 27–9; also in Fairweather, ed., *Hard Lying*, pp. 274–7

Jones, Geoffrey, *U Boat Aces and Their Fates* (London: William Kimber, 1988)

Preston, Antony, '*V & W' Class Destroyers, 1917–1945* (London: Macdonald, 1971)

Priestley, Reg, 'HMS *Warwick*' in *Hard Lying: The V & W Magazine*, no. 14 (December 2002), pp. 6–7

—, 'HMS *Warwick*' in *Hard Lying: The V & W Magazine*, no. 20 (December 2005), p. 28

Raven, Alan, and John Roberts, '*V*' and '*W*' Class Destroyers [Man o' War, no. 2] (London: Arms and Armour Press, 1979)

Rayner, Cdr D. A., *Escort: The Battle of the Atlantic* (London: William Kimber, 1955)

Smith, Peter C., *HMS* Wild Swan*: One Destroyer's War, 1939–42* (London: William Kimber, 1985)

Career history of HMS *Warwick*: http://www.naval-history.net/xGM-Chrono-10DD-09VW-Warwick.htm

99   HMS *MAHRATTA*

Lt Cdr E. A. F. Drought, DSC RN†

Sunk by *U990* (Type VIIC), Kptlt Hubert Nordheimer, 25 February 1944

Arctic Ocean, 175 nm W of Sørøya (Norway)

Campaign	Arctic convoys (Map 2)	*Displacement*	1,920 tons
Coordinates	71° 17' N, 13° 30' E	*Dimensions*	362.25' × 37' × 10'
Kriegsmarine code	Qu. AB 9423	*Maximum speed*	36 knots
U-boat timekeeping	identical	*Armament*	6 × 4.7"; 1 × 4" AA; 4 × 40 mm AA;
Fatalities	220 *Survivors* 17		2 × 20 mm AA; 12 × .5" AA; 4 × 21" tt

Career

For design notes on the 'M'-class destroyers, of which *Mahratta* was the final unit to be completed, see HMS *Martin* (**72**).

HMS *Mahratta* began life as the *Marksman*, being renamed in recognition of the financial support given to the war effort by the Government of India and as a tribute to the Mahratta Brigade of the Indian Army which had distinguished itself against the Italians in the Abyssinian campaign of 1940–1. She might with equal justice have been named after the city of Walsall whose Warship Week in February 1942 raised part of the £700,000 needed to build her. First laid down at Scotts

Mahratta seen in August 1943, shortly before her first convoy to Russia.
She succumbed to a *Zaunkönig* from *U990* in waters which took a heavy toll of her ship's company. *IWM*

of Greenock in January 1940, *Mahratta* was not launched until July 1942 thanks to bomb damage in May the previous year which required the hull to be dismantled and the keel relaid. By the time she was completed in April 1943 – as long a gestation as any British wartime destroyer – *Mahratta* had been christened 'the Blitz Boat'. After working up at Scapa Flow *Mahratta* was assigned to the 3rd Destroyer Flotilla, Home Fleet, participating in the relief of the British garrison on Spitsbergen in June 1943 and then in the series of feints towards Norway intended to distract attention from the invasion of Sicily in July. In August came her first passage to North Russia, in this case a supply run to the Kola Inlet by the 10th Cruiser Squadron and its escort. Further escort duty brought *Mahratta* into the Bay of Biscay in October from where she accompanied the damaged battleship *Valiant* into Plymouth. A second supply run to Kola permitted her to join the escort for the return convoy RA54A which sailed from Murmansk on 1 November. After refitting at Hull between November and January of the following year, *Mahratta* headed north to escort convoy JW56B to Murmansk and then the return RA56, detaching to join JW57 on 22 February.

Background of the attack

For background on the Arctic convoy campaign, see HMSs *Matabele*, *Edinburgh* and *Leda* (**47**, **58** and **69**).

Despite committing more than two dozen U-boats to the Arctic

theatre – one which, like the Mediterranean, Dönitz considered an unnecessary distraction from the key battleground in the Atlantic – the returns achieved in the first five months of 1944 made grim reading for the German navy. The handful of merchantmen sunk was far outweighed by attrition to *F.d.U. Norwegen* (Officer Commanding U-Boats, Norway) which lost eighteen boats in the same period. The Allied victims of this campaign were increasingly its escorts, which proved too numerous and well equipped for U-boats to circumvent even under cover of darkness. The Murmansk-bound convoy JW57 in February 1944, comprising forty-three vessels and a nineteen-strong escort, was no exception. Though a pack of no fewer than fourteen *Werwolf* boats was formed to hinder its progress, no merchantman was sunk while the Germans lost *U713* (destroyed by HMS *Keppel* on the 24th) and *U601* (bombed by an RAF Catalina on the 25th). Despite numerous claims based on acoustic data following end-of-run *Zaunkönig* detonations, the only loss suffered by the Allies was that of HMS *Mahratta* to *U990*. The episode captures the frustration felt by the *U-Boot-Waffe* at the effectiveness of convoy defence, Kptlt Hubert Nordheimer's war diary recording how he quickly abandoned any hope of getting past the escort and resorted instead to attacking a destroyer on the convoy's starboard quarter. Unlike other *Werwolf* boats, however, Nordheimer remained on the surface to witness the results of his *Zaunkönig* attack.

War Diary of *U990*, patrol of 26 January–28 February 1944: PG 30815, NHB, reel 1,142, p. 448

Date, time	Details of position, wind, weather, sea, light, visibility, moonlight, etc.	Incidents
25.ii	European Arctic Waters	
1944		Just as I am about to dive to carry out a hydrophone sweep we sight a brief exchange of light signals at bearing 80° true, close range. We go to maximum speed, Battle Stations.
2000		A shadow at bearing 65° true, apparently a destroyer. I close her with constant course alterations.

Date, time	Details of position, wind, weather, sea, light, visibility, moonlight, etc.	Incidents
2030		Five destroyers on the port side.[1] I have made contact with the rear of the convoy. My intention: to circumvent the destroyer patrolling furthest to starboard so as to find an unprotected spot on the convoy's flank or bow. But this puts us on the lee side of the convoy which is disadvantageous for the deployment of *Aphrodite* and the lookouts despite the benefits of a dark horizon.[2] Attempt fails.
2106[3]		Outgoing W/T transmission 2038/794: *Convoy AB 9425, course 15°, speed 8–10 knots. Nordheimer.*
2055		T5 torpedo fired from bow at destroyer on extreme starboard quarter.[4] Shot coordinates: depth 4 m; close fire setting, side angle 0°; angle of fire 0°; enemy speed 15 knots; inclination 180°, range 2,000 m.[5] She blows up after 2 min. 16 sec. Neighbouring destroyer fires two red starshells; this is followed shortly after by a further detonation at the scene of the explosion. Must be her depth-charge supply on deck. I turn about, presenting my stern to the detonation so as to be able to fire a T5 from the stern tube should the need arise.
2107		*Wanz* radar readings.[6] Depth charges on all quarters. *Aphrodite* launched. Radar pulses break off.
2117		Outgoing W/T transmission 2159/798: *Look out for Fübos.[7] U990.* About 5 min. after each *Fübo* I launch 1–2 *Aphrodites* in such a way that they will be driven towards the *Fübo*. The scene of the sinking is artificially shrouded in smoke laid by the enemy.[8]
22193		Incoming W/T transmission 2137/796: *Nordheimer: important to maintain contact for other boats closing in. F.d.U.[9]*
2218		Convoy must have zigzagged away to the north. Contact lost. Dive to seek hydrophone contact but then forced to 160 m as I am closed by destroyers. Depth charges.[10]
2400		Head off at maximum speed in direction of last hydrophone bearing.
26.ii	European Arctic Waters	
0029		Outgoing W/T transmission 2325/703: *AB 9197, hydrophone effect for convoy at bearing 15° true. Nordheimer.*
0041		Outgoing W/T transmission 2055/704: *AB 9423, destroyer sunk 2 min. 16 sec. after bow T5 fired. Convoy screened from astern by six destroyers in close order. Nordheimer.* In Qu. [AB] 9431 I can see several flickering lights.

---

1   Four of these were probably HMSs *Serapis* (P. J. L. Gazalet, Captain (D) 23rd Destroyer Flotilla), *Mahratta*, *Vigilant* and *Impulsive*, which together represented the starboard quarter escort of JW57.

2   *Aphrodite* consisted of a hydrogen-filled balloon to which strips of aluminium foil were attached. It was released from the U-boat to act as a radar decoy though never enjoyed great success.

3   The break in the chronological sequence here reflects the original.

4   'T5' refers to the *Zaunkönig* acoustic homing torpedo.

5   Based on the speed at which the escort was proceeding, *Mahratta* was estimated by the Board of Enquiry to have been making twelve knots at the time she was struck. 'Close fire' (*Nahschuss*) was one of the three run settings of the *Zaunkönig* and was for use against retiring targets with a relative inclination of between 110° and 180°. This involved the *Ente* ('duck') torpedo control mechanism being set to pursue a straighter, less erratic track towards the target; compare with *Weitschuss* in HMS *Itchen* (**88**), n. 3. Unlike conventional weapons, the meandering course characteristic of the *Zaunkönig* acoustic homing torpedo when the close or remote fire settings were actuated makes it impossible to derive the range at which *Mahratta* was hit from the running time.

6   Nordheimer is here referring to the *Wanz* radar-warning system; known also by its nickname *Wanze* – 'bug'.

7   *Fübos* is an abbreviation for the *Fühlungsbojen* or *Fühlungshalterbojen* ('contact buoys' or 'contact-keeping buoys') which were dropped by U-boats to mark the position of a convoy. Half an hour after being dropped the buoy would explode in a combination of green, red and yellow stars, neighbouring boats being signalled to be on the lookout for the contact marker.

8   The smoke that shrouded *Mahratta* at this time was either residual from the detonations or a combination of these and severe weather. No smoke screen was laid by the remaining escorts which were still struggling to locate her in blizzard conditions.

9   Sent by *F.d.U. Norwegen* (Officer Commanding U-Boats, Norway), Kapt.z.S. Rudolf Peters.

10 Dropped either by *Serapis* or *Vigilant*.

The sinking

The effect of *U990*'s torpedo, fired at 2055 log time, was perhaps less than might have been expected, the Board of Enquiry recording that 'the shock was slight and caused both engines to stop instantly'. Although there was uncertainty as to the type of torpedo used, the fact that it struck near the propellers raised suspicions that it was a GNAT (German Naval Acoustic Torpedo – the British term for the T5/ *Zaunkönig*), which is confirmed in *U990*'s log. The log also corroborates Allied reports of a violent explosion about five minutes after the first which wrecked *Mahratta*'s stern. Though Nordheimer's thesis of a depth-charge detonation seems unlikely, no firm conclusions were reached by the British as to its cause. The impression gained by those witnessing it from afar was that a magazine had detonated, the ship going up 'like a rocket' in an enormous explosion. Although this view was supported by several of *Mahratta*'s survivors, not all considered the second as powerful as the first, which in turn led Lt Cdr Philip Bekenn (CO of HMS *Impulsive*) to the unsubstantiated conclusion that a boiler had exploded. The available evidence caused the Board of Enquiry to favour a magazine explosion but even this was contradicted by the Director of Naval Construction, Sir Stanley Goodall, who found 'no definite evidence' for such an event. A suggestion by the Board that it was owed to a second torpedo has been perpetuated in subsequent accounts of *Mahratta*'s loss, but the matter is settled in German records which make clear that *U990* not only limited herself to a single torpedo but was the only boat in contact with the convoy at this time.

Whatever its cause, the second explosion 'flooded all the after compartments including the gearing room and possibly the engine room, causing the ship to take a heavy list to port'. Stoker Petty Officer Charles Smith, was on watch in No. 2 Boiler Room:

> I had no sooner left the voice pipe when the second explosion occurred. All the lights in the ship went out and I then took it into my own hands as to the best thing to do. The ship started to list to port and I shut down the boiler room and I came up top. Everything was dark and I couldn't see. There was debris lying everywhere. I then shouted down to the engine room to see if there was anyone on watch. With that the ship was listing more to port.

Heeled over to port and down by the stern, *Mahratta* remained afloat for more than an hour. Though any hope of saving her seems to have been abandoned, circumstances prevented an orderly abandon ship. For one thing, even a stricken hulk was preferable to being cast adrift on the Arctic Ocean on a wild night in winter. Moreover, the fact that surviving records make no mention of the ship's boats suggests that these had either been wrecked or could not be launched, and much of the crew devoted their energies to freeing iced-up Carley floats before the end came. At 2220 HMS *Mahratta* suddenly rolled onto her beam ends and sank stern first, approximately eighty minutes after Nordheimer's hit.

Fate of the crew

The nature of the detonations and the speed with which *Mahratta* eventually capsized made a heavy death toll inevitable at such a high latitude, even after a number of Carley floats were cut free. HMS *Impulsive* reached the scene at 2152 in blizzard conditions and was awaiting 'a suitable moment between snow squalls to pull alongside' when *Mahratta* signalled that the end was nigh at 2219. Lt Cdr Bekenn brought *Impulsive* as close as he dared as *Mahratta* capsized and sank but few men were in the Carleys and rescuing the 'struggling figures, saturated and blinded by oil fuel and rapidly becoming paralysed by the cold' proved very difficult. A heavy swell, biting wind and driving snow made manoeuvring difficult while men succumbed in seas close to freezing and thermometers reading −5°C (23°F). The frustrations attending rescue efforts in such conditions were mused on at length by Lt Cdr Bekenn in his testimony to the Board:

> It was very sad that once in the water no survivor appeared to be able to make any effort to swim towards the ship. Carley rafts were drifted upon, but it transpired that they were very empty with only one or two men in each ... Having completed the first drift to leeward the ship manoeuvred to

Nordheimer relaxing ashore. His rank of Oberleutnant zur See dates the photo to between October 1940 and March 1943. *DUBMA*

windward, but by this time only those actually in Carley rafts were alive. I was astounded when we only counted 17 survivors, but know that those on the iron deck and in the whaler did their utmost. It is difficult to disregard 3 or 4 near ones, and look for 20 but this is possibly a thing to aim at. In our case the visibility was such that one could only go by shouting and the biggest number of red lights.

As Bekenn recorded, *Impulsive*'s ship's company gave of their best to help survivors, climbing down the scrambling nets to assist the very few who had strength enough to reach the ship's side while being washed down as she rolled in the swell. Two men, Able Seamen John Riggs and James Wells, were commended for volunteering 'to be lowered into a carley float in a heavy snow storm to try to rescue survivors, knowing full well that if their ship gained contact with an enemy, they must be left'. Buffeted by icy waves, Riggs and Wells were found to be unconscious by the time they were hoisted on board, virtually the last to be rescued. Both were Mentioned in Despatches.

A grim novelty of the sinking was the fact that the entire episode from attack to capsizing was broadcast to the rest of the convoy via *Mahratta*'s radio telephone. The commentary, presumed to have been made by Lt Cdr Drought himself, ended with the words 'We are abandoning ship. We are sinking. We cannot last much longer.' This transmission, heralding the death of over 200 men (including that of Drought, who made no attempt to leave *Mahratta*'s bridge), persisted in the memory of all who had to endure it. Lt Cdr Bob Whinney, commanding HMS *Wanderer*, later recorded his own impression of the episode: 'Personally, from sheer impotence and rasping anguish, the *Mahratta* incident compared with the terrible moments when the strafing of the *Laconia*'s survivors was taking place near Ascension Island and with the staggering horror at the news of the sinking of the mighty *Hood*.'

U990 and Hubert Nordheimer

Built by Blohm & Voss at Hamburg and commissioned in July 1943, *U990* made five frontline patrols in northern waters, all under Kptlt Hubert Nordheimer. HMS *Mahratta*, sunk on the first of these, was her only victim, though unsuccessful attacks were carried out against the escort of convoy JW58 in April 1944. Together with *U276*, on 24 May *U990* was ordered to stand by *U476* after she had been crippled by an RAF Catalina off the Norwegian port of Kristiansund, twenty-one survivors being picked up by Nordheimer and the wreck despatched with a torpedo. Next day it was *U990*'s turn. Sighted by an RAF Liberator north-west of Trondheim, *U990* was sunk in a depth-charge attack with the loss of twenty of her own men and three of *U476*'s, though Nordheimer survived to be picked up by the German patrol boat *V5901*. He was then given command of the Type-XXI *U2512* which, however, had yet to see active service at the time of her scuttling at Eckernförde in May 1945. Hubert Nordheimer died in 1997.

Sources

Admiralty, *Awards of Mention in Despatches to Two Men of HMS* Impulsive *Following the Sinking of HMS* Mahratta *on 25th February 1944* (TNA, ADM 1/29624)

—, *JW and RA Convoys 1944: Commodores' Reports and Reports of Proceedings* (TNA, ADM 199/327)

—, *Losses of H.M. Ships to Torpedo and Mine, 1943–1944* (TNA, ADM 267/95)

Ministry of Defence, *HMS* Mahratta *and Convoy JW57* (NHB, S.4200)

English, John, *Afridi to Nizam: British Fleet Destroyers, 1937–43* (Gravesend, Kent: World Ship Society, 2001)

Kinghorn, D., and B. Hargreaves, 'Destroyers of the Royal Navy: "M" Class' in *Warships*, Supplement no. 22 (May 1970), pp. 13–21

Ruegg, Bob, and Arnold Hague, *Convoys to Russia, 1941–1945* (Kendal, Cumbria: World Ship Society, 1992)

Whinney, Capt. Bob, *The U-Boat Peril: An Anti-Submarine Commander's War* (Poole, Dorset: Blandford Press, 1986)

Career history of HMS *Mahratta*: http://www.naval-history.net/xGM-Chrono-10DD-43M-Mahratta-ex-Marksman.htm

Website devoted to HMS *Mahratta*: http://hmsmahratta.50megs.com/photo3_1.html

Defunct website devoted to AB Hugh McIntosh (fatality) and HMS *Mahratta*: htttp://www.monkton-farleigh.freeserve.co.uk/hms_mahratta.htm

---

100   USS *LEOPOLD*

Cdr K. C. Phillips, USCG†

Sunk by *U255* (Type VIIC), Oblt.z.S. Erich Harms, 9–10 March 1944

North Atlantic, 365 nm SSW of Grindavik (Iceland)

Leopold launched sideways into the Sabine River at Orange, Texas on 12 June 1943.
Nine months later her back was broken by a *Zaunkönig* acoustic homing torpedo from *U255*. *US Navy*

Theatre North Atlantic (Map 1)		*Displacement* 1,200 tons	
Approx. coordinates 58° 44' N, 25° 50' W		*Dimensions* 306' × 36.75' × 8.75'	
Kriegsmarine code Quadrat AK 3862		*Maximum speed* 21 knots	
U-boat timekeeping differential +2 hours		*Armament* 3 × 3"; 2 × 40 mm AA; 8 × 20 mm AA; 3 × 21" tt; 1 × Hedgehog ATW	
Fatalities 171 *Survivors* 28			

Career

In 1940 the success of the British Hunt-class escort destroyers (see HMS *Heythrop*, 55) prompted the start of design work on an equivalent for the US Navy. However, little enthusiasm was shown for the destroyer escort type in US naval circles and it was only a British order for a hundred units of the resulting design in June 1941 which saved it from being discarded. In the event, the unfolding of the U-boat campaign later that year made convoy defence an urgent priority for the US Navy which belatedly ordered its first destroyer escorts in November 1941. It is a measure of US industrial capacity that by the spring of 1943 the Destroyer Escort Program had a staggering 1,005 ships on order. Of these a total of 563 ships were completed in six sub-classes, the fourth of which was the Edsall class. Of similar hull design and armed to a comparable standard, the principal differentiating factor between the sub-classes lay in propulsion, which in the case of the Edsalls consisted of a 6,000-bhp geared diesel drive ('FMR'). Construction of the entire sub-class of eighty-five units (including *Leopold*) was divided between the Consolidated Steel Corporation at Orange, Texas and the Brown Shipbuilding Co. of Houston between 1943 and 1944.

The USS *Leopold* (DE-319) was laid down by the Consolidated Steel Corporation's yard at Orange in March 1943, launched in June of that year and commissioned with a US Coast Guard crew on 18 October. After structural firing tests at Sabine Pass, Texas, docking at Galveston and a spell at New Orleans, *Leopold* sailed on her shakedown cruise to Great Sound, Bermuda on 7 November where training and exercises continued until the ship turned for Charleston, South Carolina on 9 December. Following destroyer-escort exercises in the Chesapeake Bay *Leopold*, by now assigned to Escort Division 22, joined convoy USG68 which sailed for the Mediterranean from Norfolk, Virginia on 24 December. The convoy and its escort (codenamed Task Force 61) reached the Straits of Gibraltar on 10 January 1944 where the former was turned over to a British escort. After two days' patrolling the Atlantic side of the Straits against the passage of U-boats into the Mediterranean TF61 joined the escort for westbound convoy GUS27

on the 16th. Scattered by a gale, the last of the convoy did not reach New York until 4 February. The second half of that month was taken up with training exercises at Casco Bay, Maine, which *Leopold* carried out in company with CortDiv 22 before returning to convoy duty.

Background of the attack

In March 1943 the CU convoy series was initiated between New York and Liverpool to remedy the depletion of British oil reserves following the Allied landings in North Africa. Escorted by the US Navy and consisting largely of oil tankers, these convoys crossed the Atlantic at a high average speed of fourteen knots, which partly explains why only a handful of vessels were lost from sixty-eight sailings over a two-year period. One of the casualties was the USS *Leopold*, which sailed from New York with the twenty-seven-ship CU16 on 1 March 1944. The escort, codenamed Task Group 21.5, comprised the destroyer escorts *Poole* (Senior Officer), *Harveson*, *Joyce*, *Kirkpatrick*, *Peterson* and *Leopold* herself, the only unit fitted with HF/DF equipment. Though dogged by bad weather, the convoy proceeded largely uneventfully until 9 March. At 1950 that evening *Leopold* reported a radar contact at a range of approximately 8,000 yards and five minutes later Cdr K. C. Phillips signalled the escort to the effect that 'this looks like the real thing'. Phillips was right. *Leopold* had come across Oblt.z.S. Erich Harms's *U255*, then eleven days out of Bergen with orders to attack the Atlantic convoys. General Quarters was sounded and a flare sent up as the order was passed to fire on sight. *Joyce* was immediately detached to assist *Leopold*, the former recording *Leopold* as having fired two starshells and 'about four or five 3-inch shells, and heavy 20-mm fire from forward batteries' at about 2000. When this barrage abruptly ceased it was assumed that *Leopold* had simply broken off the action. It proved otherwise. Though streaming her FXR gear, *Leopold* had in fact been silenced by a *Zaunkönig* acoustic homing torpedo, the impact of which caused a complete loss of power to the ship and her guns. The torpedo had been fired by Oblt.z.S. Harms while *U255* performed an alarm dive to evade *Leopold*'s attentions.

War Diary of *U255*, patrol of 26 February–11 April 1944: PG 30231, NHB, reel 1,094, p. 300

Date, time	Details of position, wind, weather, sea, light, visibility, moonlight, etc.	Incidents
9.iii	North Atlantic	
1935		Hydrophone effect at 300°, fades away to eastwards.
1955		We surface, course 340°, half speed, charging batteries.
2000	[Qu.] AK 3896 upper left, wind WSW 4, sea 3, cloud 8, 9°[C; 48°F], 1,038 mb, visibility 10–15 nm	
2040		Onset of twilight.
2130	[Qu.] AK 3865	We dive to carry out hydrophone sweep. Hydrophone effect at 355°, apparently an unaccompanied vessel.
2142		We surface and head off in pursuit, course 20°, ¾ speed.
2150		A shadow at 350° which then alters course away from us and disappears. To Battle Stations.
2155	[Qu.] AK 3862 lower middle, wind WSW 4, sea 3, overcast, some rain, 1,036 mb, variable	Several shadows suddenly appear at bearing 10° true. Inclination 120°, bows right. The moon then breaks through and I can make out 10 to 15 vessels. As I am positioned behind the convoy on the starboard side I alter course to port away from the convoy with a view to circumventing it and acquiring a position on the dark side. Just as I am altering course I see a destroyer bearing down on

Date, time	Details of position, wind, weather, sea, light, visibility, moonlight, etc.	Incidents
	visibility	us at 10°.[1] It fires starshell, range 1,000 m. Alarm! I want to fire Tube II right away but the torpedo mechanics in the forward compartment are already closing the bow caps. I have them reopened and
2200		manage to get a shot away. Destroyer is now dead ahead, inclination 0°, range 600 m, fixed angle of fire 0°, T5 torpedo from Tube II, depth set at 4 m. A detonation after 27 sec., then a loud breaking and cracking sound audible both in bow compartment and hydrophone room.[2]
		We go to 160 m. No hydrophone effect from the destroyer, no depth charges, nor are we overrun. The destroyer opened fire with her anti-aircraft armament as we dived.[3] Single-funnelled destroyer with apparently just one gun on the fo'c's'le.[4]
2230		Asdic impulses from two vessels.
2256		One depth charge, numerous double thuds. It appears that two destroyers are searching for us, stopping alternately.[5] They overrun us several times.
2330		Several double thuds. Based on hydrophone data the convoy would appear to be moving away at 70° true.
2355		We release *Bolde* decoy.[6]
10.iii	North Atlantic	
0000	[Qu.] AK 3862 upper right	
0100		Destroyers retire at bearing 60° true.
0120		We surface and set off in pursuit of last hydrophone bearing (60°).
0132		Short signal transmitted: *Convoy AL 17.*[7] *U255.*

1   USS *Leopold*.

2   The torpedo running time is brief enough to indicate that it was a direct hit, there being insufficient time for the acoustic homing mechanism to have taken effect. A remarkable piece of marksmanship given that *Leopold* was apparently closing at a bow-on inclination (0°).

3   The original has *Flawaffen*, the abbreviation for *Fliegerabwehrwaffen* (lit. 'air-defence weapons').

4   Harms's description is correct except that *Leopold* had a Hedgehog spigot mortar mounting fitted forward beside a 3-inch gun.

5   USS *Joyce* was in fact the only other vessel on the scene.

6   *Bolde* was the calcium-zinc discharge that replicated the echo produced by an Asdic submarine contact by generating large masses of bubbles. This device was also known as the *Pillenwerfer* ('pill-thrower') after the ejector fitted for this purpose in the stern of the U-boat.

7   Kept submerged by *Joyce*, Harms could not provide a full three- or four-digit grid coordinate of the convoy's position, limiting himself instead to informing B.d.U. that CU16 had continued her easterly course from AK to the neighbouring AL sector.

The sinking

Leopold's gunfire had been sufficiently intense to mask the torpedo detonation and *Joyce* was initially unaware of what had befallen her. Only when *Leopold* failed to respond to radio and light signals did she investigate further, closing to within 1,500 yards to find her 'dead in the water with hole in port side in compartments B-1 and B-2, and with her back broken; screws out of water; and crew abandoning ship'. The time was 2015, approximately fifteen minutes after the hit. At 2028 *Joyce* was forced to make an emergency manoeuvre to evade a torpedo reported approaching before leaving the scene to commence a search of the surrounding area. However, she did so needlessly since not only was *U255* the sole U-boat in touch with the convoy but there is no record of her firing a second torpedo that night, nor did Harms – then submerged at a great depth – surface for over three hours after the attack. Returning at 2106, *Joyce* discovered that *Leopold* was 'now broken in half, bow and stern section separating with the stern section drifting downwind'. Survivors recalled the two halves parting at approximately 2100, an hour after the attack. At 2132 a lookout in *Joyce* 'sighted torpedo track on port beam', again needlessly forcing her to defer the work of rescue which did not begin for another three-quarters of an hour. When *Joyce* returned to the scene in hope of

picking up more survivors at 0145 on the 10th it was to observe the stern section sinking following the detonation of a number of depth charges. However, the bow section remained afloat and at 0710 *Joyce* again closed the wreck, this time with orders to sink it by gunfire. In the event, it took over half an hour and nearly a thousand rounds of assorted ammunition before the bow section succumbed to a pair of *Joyce*'s depth charges.

The lack of any officer survivors prevented the drafting of an official report and consequently the recording of any detailed information on the damage sustained by *Leopold*. Even after interviewing the survivors the commanding officer of USS *Joyce*, Lt Cdr Robert Wilcox, reported that 'there is some question whether the *Leopold* was struck by the torpedo from the port or starboard side. From personal observation, I can only say there was a much larger hole on the port side than there was on the starboard side of the *Leopold*.' For his part, Seaman 1/c Richard R. Novotny, then manning a 20-mm gun on the starboard side amidships, distinctly recalled the detonation occurring on the port side. Harms's log does not settle the matter – no surprise since *Leopold* was struck in a bow-on attack. At B.d.U. Operations, meanwhile, Konteradmiral Eberhard Godt noted with satisfaction that 'the convoy was energetically attacked in a determined manner, and although the boat was chased away the offending destroyer had to pay the price with her own sinking'.

Fate of the crew

It is not clear how many lives were claimed by *U255*'s torpedo. The detonation had a powerful effect topsides, Cdr Phillips being blasted off his bridge into the sea while Seaman 1/c Troy S. Gowers recalled being blown out of his shoes from his gun station into a life net a few yards away. From the testimony of former Seaman Novotny, it appears that one of the ready-use 20-mm ammunition lockers may have detonated following the torpedo hit. Though the order to abandon ship will have come too late for many below decks, it nonetheless seems likely that most of *Leopold*'s fatalities were caused by the bitter waters of the Atlantic. Of the men who abandoned ship, even those fortunate enough to secure a place on the rafts endured a prolonged ordeal in heavy seas. Seaman Gowers recalled that of eighteen or nineteen men on his raft only three or four survived to be rescued. The rest had either been washed away or succumbed to hypothermia. Gowers and Seaman 1/c Joseph N. Ranyss tried to keep their companions awake 'but those that were freezing knew it. One boy said "I'm dying, I can't hold out any longer" and in a minute he was gone.' Seaman Novotny told a similar tale:

> The tendency would be to simply just fall asleep and pass on. Shipmates were trying to hang on themselves, and hang on to their buddy next to them in order to keep them around the raft. But there were so many that were expiring from the cold water, you couldn't hold on to all of them. You had to let go and hold on yourself.

Elsewhere a number of men were sucked into *Joyce*'s screws when she turned away from the wreck the first time.

However, not all *Leopold*'s men obeyed the order to abandon ship. Around forty remained on the stern section, their number added to by several men hauled from the water, Cdr Phillips among them. Blankets and whisky were recovered from below decks and efforts made to free a man who had been pinned under a heavy galley range. As *Joyce* closed the wreck hopes rose of an immediate rescue, but much to their despair the only message bellowed across via megaphone was 'We're dodging torpedoes. God bless you. We'll be back.' Shortly after, the stern capsized to port pitching most of the men into the water including Cdr Phillips who was never seen again. Though it remained afloat for another hour and a half, the stern section gradually settled under the assault of fifty-foot waves which washed the remaining men off one by one. Perhaps the only survivor was Seaman 1/c W. G. O'Brien who was brought to the surface by his lifejacket after the stern section sank and eventually reached a raft. Not until 2218, more than two hours after the attack, did *Joyce* commence picking up survivors, recovering twenty-eight men and three corpses over the next three hours. These were eventually landed at Londonderry after *Joyce* rejoined the convoy. The death toll was all thirteen officers and 158 of *Leopold*'s complement of 186 enlisted men. Based on his experience of this operation, Lt Cdr Wilcox recommended that all floater nets be replaced with life rafts as 'from testimony from survivors and from the fact that no survivors were recovered from floater nets, I am of the opinion that they are dangerous to the safety of the men who use them'.

U255's crew celebrate their return to St-Nazaire on 11 April 1944, a month after sinking the *Leopold*. DUBMA

U255 and Erich Harms

Built by Bremer Vulkan at Vegesack and commissioned in November 1941, *U255* spent almost her entire career in Arctic waters, mainly under Kptlt Reinhart Reche. Her first operational patrol in June and July 1942 coincided with the ferocious combined air and submarine attack on convoy PQ17, *U255* claiming four merchantmen within a week for a total of over 25,000 tons. Reche continued his vein of success in four subsequent frontline patrols, sinking another five merchantmen and a Soviet ice-breaker before handing over command of *U255* to Oblt.z.S. Erich Harms in June 1943. After a final patrol in the Barents Sea during which the Soviet hydrographic vessel *Akademik Shokal'ski* was sunk by gunfire on 27 July (**G53**), *U255* transferred to Bergen where she spent the winter of 1943–4. In March she sailed from Bergen on her first Atlantic cruise though only *Leopold* had been accounted for by the time she docked at St-Nazaire six weeks later. The Normandy landings of 6 June brought *U255* to the defensive *Landwirt* line in the Bay of Biscay (see HMS *Blackwood*, **103**), but she returned to St-Nazaire on the 12th once it became clear that the U-boat bases were not in imminent danger of capture. *U255* was decommissioned following damage in August 1944 and spent the rest of the year under repair. She returned to the fray with a minelaying sortie off Les Sables d'Olonne on 18 April 1945 but the last days of the war were spent shuttling between La Pallice and St-Nazaire under Oblt.z.S. Helmut Heinrich. *U255* was surrendered to the British at Loch Alsh in May 1945 and disposed of later that year as part of Operation DEADLIGHT.

Leaving *U255* in August 1944, Erich Harms began training for the new Type-XXI boats and in January took command of *U3023* which, however, was scuttled at Travemünde in May 1945 without ever seeing frontline service.

Sources

US Navy, *Action Report: Escort of Convoy CU-16, 1–11 March 1944* (NA, RG 38, TG 21.5, 3/15/44, Box 100, 370/44/21/1)

—, Commander Task Force 21.5, *Reports of USS's* Poole *and* Joyce *Following Torpedoing of USS* Leopold (BfZ, Sammlung Rohwer, T-5 Auswertungsdokumente)

US Coast Guard, Historical Section, Public Information Division, *USS Leopold*; and *USS Leopold (DE-319)* (NHC, Box 469)

Hengen, Dieter, memoir of the attack on the USS *Leopold* (undated manuscript by former First Watch Officer of *U255*, DUBMA, *U255* folder)

Rohwer, Prof. Jürgen, *Analyse der T-5 („Zaunkönig")-Schüsse von U-Booten gegen Geleitfahrzeuge*. U255: *USS* Leopold (Report for Bundesamt für Wehrtechnik und Beschaffung [Federal Office of Weapons Technology and Procurement], 1964) (BfZ, MaS 8/2.07)

Andrews, Lewis M., Jr, *Tempest, Fire and Foe: Destroyer Escorts in World War II and the Men Who Manned Them* (Victoria, BC: Trafford Publishing, 2004)

DANFS, IV, p. 92; also on:
http://www.history.navy.mil/danfs/l5/leopold.htm
and
http://www.ibiblio.org/hyperwar/USN/ships/dafs/DE/de319.html

Davis, Martin, ed., *Destroyer Escorts of World War Two* (Missoula, Mont.: Pictorial Histories Publishing Co., 1987)

Epperson, W. Scott, 'Survivor of the *Leopold*: Retired Coastguardsman Tells of WWII Coast Guard Experience' in *River Currents* (Second Coast Guard District, St Louis, Mo.) (June 1994), pp. 1–14

Friedman, Norman, *US Destroyers: An Illustrated Design History* (2nd edn, Annapolis, Md.: Naval Institute Press, 2004)

Price, Scott, 'Final Voyage' in *Commandant's Bulletin* (USCG) (April 1994), pp. 19–21

Scheina, Robert L., *US Coast Guard Cutters and Craft in World War II* (Annapolis, Md.: Naval Institute Press, 1982)

United States Coast Guard, *The Coast Guard at War*. V: *Transports and Escorts*, vol. I (Washington, DC: Public Information Division, Historical Section, US Coast Guard Headquarters, 1949), pp. 122–3

Webpage devoted to USS *Leopold*:
http://www.uscg.mil/history/webcutters/Leopold.asp
Listings of casualties and survivors of the sinking of the USS *Leopold*:
http://www.uscg.mil/history/webcutters/Leopold_Casualties.pdf
http://www.uscg.mil/history/webcutters/Leopold_Survivors.pdf

101   USS *FECHTELER*

Lt Calver B. Gill, USN
Sunk by *U967* (Type VIIC), Kptlt Albrecht Brandi, 5 May 1944
Western Mediterranean, 25 nm SE of Isla de Alborán

Commissioning day for the *Fechteler* at Norfolk Navy Yard, 1 July 1943.
Within a year she and twenty-nine of her men were at the bottom of the Mediterranean. *US Navy*

Theatre	Mediterranean (Map 3)	*Displacement*	1,400 tons
Coordinates	36° 07' N, 02° 40' W	*Dimensions*	306' × 36.75' × 13.5'
Kriegsmarine code	Quadrat CH 7543	*Maximum speed*	24 knots
U-boat timekeeping differential	+1 hour	*Armament*	3 × 3"; 2 × 40 mm AA; 8 × 20 mm AA; 3 × 21" tt; 1 × Hedgehog ATW
Fatalities 29 *Survivors* 185+			

Career

For background on the US Navy's Destroyer Escort Program, see the preceding entry for USS *Leopold* (**100**). The USS *Fechteler* belonged to the second (Buckley) sub-class of the Destroyer Escort Program whose 102 units were powered by a 12,000-shp turbo-electric drive ('TE').

The USS *Fechteler* (DE-157) was laid down at the Norfolk Navy Yard in February 1943, launched in April of that year and commissioned on 1 July. Between September and December 1943 she escorted two tanker convoys on the New York–Dutch Antilles–North Africa run. After refitting at New York, *Fechteler* participated in experimental anti-submarine exercises in Narragansett Bay following which she sailed independently for the Azores and Londonderry on 28 February 1944. Arriving on 6 March 1944, *Fechteler* joined the escort of a New York-bound convoy after which she was assigned to USG38 which sailed from Hampton Roads, Virginia for the Tunisian port of Bizerte on 1 April 1944. This reached its destination on 22 April though only after coming under heavy air attack off Cap Bengut, Algeria on the 20th during which *Fechteler* shot down a German He111 bomber against the loss of two merchantmen and two more damaged.

Background of the attack

On 1 May 1944 convoy GUS38, comprising no fewer than 107 merchantmen, sailed from Bizerte bound for Hampton Roads. While the bulk of the convoy reached its destination unscathed a month later, the same could not be said for its escort (Task Force 66, comprising sixteen US escorts and the anti-aircraft cruiser HMS *Delhi* in the Mediterranean) which lost the services of the destroyer escort *Menges* to a T5 *Zaunkönig* acoustic torpedo from *U371* (see **91** and **92**) in the Gulf of Bougie on 3 May and was twice attacked by Kptlt Albrecht Brandi's *U967* as it approached the Straits of Gibraltar in the early hours of the 5th. At 0225 the USS *Chase* reported a surface radar contact 6,000 yards ahead of the convoy which was subsequently confirmed by the cutter *Taney* (Commander Task Force) and the destroyer *Laning*. Closing the contact, *Laning* reported it as a probable submarine after members of her bridge watch spotted the target dive. The escort was immediately ordered to stream their anti-*Zaunkönig* FXR gear while USSs *Lowe*, *Fechteler* and *Fessenden* were detached to cover the port bow of the convoy 'which would be the earliest target the submarine could reach'. At around 0312 the escorts all recorded a heavy explosion, the result of Brandi's first torpedo of the night detonating harmlessly in the vicinity of the convoy. Still undetected by the hunting quartet, at 0330 convoy time *U967* sighted a destroyer which Brandi interpreted as lying stopped at a range of approximately 2,000 metres. Eleven minutes later Brandi fired a *Zaunkönig* at a second destroyer his log similarly describes as hove to, but this time at a range of 5,000 metres. No unit of Task Force 66 is recorded as having stopped at this juncture nor does Brandi's log permit a ready identification of which vessel he had sighted in each case. Nonetheless, *Fechteler* had just carried out a turn to starboard when she was struck by this second torpedo after a run of 1,400 metres, its course undiverted by the FXR gear she was streaming.

War Diary of *U967*, patrol of 11 April–17 May 1944: PG 30800, NHB, reel 1,141, pp. 630–1

Date, time	Details of position, wind, weather, sea, light, visibility, moonlight, etc.	Incidents
5.v		
0226	[Qu.] CH 7544, wind SW 1, sea 0–1, cloud 7, 1,008 mb, visibility 4,000–5,000 m, misty, moonlit	Surfaced. Intermittent *Naxos* readings.[1]
0323	[Qu.] CH 7542	Positional correction 268° true, 5.5 nm.
0343	[Qu.] CH 7542	Radar-warning readings become regular, increase in volume. Presumably shipborne. Then the shadow of a medium-sized steamer appears in sight at bearing 85° true, inclination 10° right. We dive.[2]
0354	[Qu.] CH 7542	Torpedo fired from Tube V – a *Zaunkönig* – based on hydrophone bearings. Enemy speed 15 knots, remote fire setting, inclination 0°, depth 4 m, range 3,000 m.[3] A hit heard after 11 min. 58 sec.[4] Gurgling noises but no sound of bulkheads collapsing. Boat goes to night search periscope depth but there is nothing to be seen.[5] No further hydrophone effect other than noise buoys.[6]
0400	[Qu.] CH 7542	

---

1 *Naxos* was a U-boat radar-detection device.

2 This timing coincides precisely with Allied accounts, the USS *Laning* reporting the disappearance of her radar contact at 0244 convoy time. A number of *Laning*'s crewmen also saw *U967* dive at this moment.

3 'Remote fire' (*Weitschuss*) was one of the three run settings of the *Zaunkönig* torpedo and was primarily for use against approaching targets, or those with a relative inclination of up to 110°. This involved the *Ente* ('duck') torpedo control mechanism being set to assume a labile or erratic snaking track towards its target.

4 This was Brandi's torpedo but the 'hit' was at best a wake or end-of-run detonation. The minesweeper USS *Steady*, patrolling astern of the convoy, reported the explosion as being close by her but the same detonation was also reported to have jarred the *Laning* some miles ahead of the convoy.

5 The German original is *Nachtzielsehrohr*, more commonly known as the *Luftzielsehrohr* or sky search periscope.

6 The original is *Heulbojen* which is the standard German term for nautical whistling buoys, though Zimmermann is here referring to the FXR noise-making device. The FXR was towed by escort vessels to deflect homing torpedoes away from their propellers.

Date, time	Details of position, wind, weather, sea, light, visibility, moonlight, etc.	Incidents
0430		Hydrophone effect, a destroyer with slow revolutions, now stopped. She is in sight at periscope depth, estimated range 2,000 m, inclination 30–40°, bows right.[7]
0441	Alborán waters, [Qu.] CH 7543	Torpedo fired from Tube II – a *Zaunkönig*. Enemy speed 15 knots, remote fire setting, inclination 0° (entered as she has stopped), range 5,000 m, depth 4 m.[8] A hit after 2 min. 2 sec., clearly direct.[9] Followed by sinking noises and dull explosions, presumably her boilers.[10]
0502–0510		Several depth charges with shallow depth settings at rapidly changing ranges and bearings. In the absence of any hydrophone effect assume they must have been dropped by aircraft.[11]
0627		A very powerful explosion, sounding as if it was made up of several individual detonations occurring in immediate succession. This is followed by the loud collapsing of bulkheads. I presume this was the final effect of our Tube-V attack of 0354.[12]
0800	[Qu.] CH 7549	
1200	[Qu.] CH 7573	Day's run: 21.4 nm on the surface, 34.3 nm submerged, total 55.7 nm.
1600	[Qu.] CH 7576	
2000	[Qu.] CH 7579	Tubes II and V reloaded.

7   Though the identity of this destroyer cannot be stated with certainty, the range differential between it and the vessel sighted eleven minutes later at 0441 (3,000 metres) suggests that different ships were targeted in the first instance (presumably *Fechteler* and *Lowe* respectively). By extension, the fact that Brandi's attack of 0441 ended with a hit on *Fechteler* after a run of 1,400 metres (see nn. 8 and 9) makes it probable that she and the vessel targeted at 0430 were one and the same, the range differential being accounted for by converging inclination and a course alteration to starboard. There is no record of any unit of Task Force 66 being stopped at this time, though Brandi may have been confused by the major course alteration to port which was ordered at precisely this juncture.

8   Once again, the identity of this destroyer is uncertain though the outcome of this attack (*Fechteler* hit after a run of 1,400 metres) and the presumed dispositions of the three escorts based on their stations in the screen at 0200 (*Fessenden* 3,000 yards on *Fechteler*'s starboard beam, then *Fechteler* herself and finally *Lowe*, furthest from *U967* 3,000 yards on *Fechteler*'s port beam) suggests that *Lowe* had been Brandi's original target. The discrepancy between a target speed of fifteen knots and the same vessel subsequently being described as stopped is explained in the torpedo report. Although the data originally fed into the torpedo computer included a target speed of fifteen knots and an inclination of forty degrees, once Brandi decided that the vessel was stopped the simplest method of overriding the gyro angle of forty degrees for the initial torpedo course was to set the target inclination to zero degrees, a bow-on position which would nullify the target speed entered into the computer.

9   This running time equates to approximately 1,400 metres rather than the 5,000 initially estimated. It can be inferred that Brandi had targeted *Lowe*, approximately 3,000 yards on *Fechteler*'s port beam (assuming the group had retained its stationkeeping since 0200), and ended by hitting the latter as the convoy's course alteration brought her closer to him. Brandi's 'direct hit' remark reflects his belief that the T5 had detonated following a straight run towards a static target, thereby obviating the need for the acoustic sensor to be activated. However, the targeting discrepancies alluded to elsewhere together with the fact that TF66 was recorded as proceeding at not less than twelve knots mean that this could hardly have been the case.

10 Despite Brandi's description, *Fechteler* did not in fact sink for another hour and a half.

11 An anti-submarine sweep was carried out by several vessels, evidently somewhat to Brandi's confusion. Two Liberator bombers were sent to assist in the hunt but did not arrive until an hour after this entry at 0612 log time.

12 The timing of this entry can be equated with the detonation of *Fechteler*'s depth charges as she went down. Nonetheless, Brandi's readiness to ascribe this to the steamer supposedly hit in his attack of 0354 is consistent with his notorious tendency to claim sinkings on unsubstantiated evidence. In this case, having wrongly deduced a near-immediate sinking from acoustic evidence at the end of his 0441 entry (see n. 10), Brandi demonstrates some audacity in deploying this much later data as evidence for the sinking of the vessel attacked at 0354. It should be added that *Fechteler* was the only vessel struck by *U967* in this Brandi's sole cruise in command.

The sinking

Although it can be no more than a supposition, the inference to be drawn from Brandi's log is that the vessel sighted at 0430 log time was *Fechteler*, then 2,000 metres off. At 0441 Brandi made a further destroyer sighting, this time at a range of 5,000 metres, which he proceeded to attack with his second *Zaunkönig* of the night. Assuming that the relative stationkeeping of the US group was unchanged from its dispositions at 0300 log time, it appears probable that this was the *Lowe*, some 3,000 yards to port of the *Fechteler* and proceeding, like her, at approximately fifteen knots. In the event, it was *Fechteler* which detonated Brandi's torpedo after a run of just 1,400 metres, the reduced range compared with the 0430 data presumably accounted for

by converging inclination and a course alteration to starboard.

The blast from the detonation was variously described by survivors as 'considerable', 'violent' and 'terrific'. Immediately after the explosion on the port side amidships *Fechteler*'s gunnery officer, Lt R. H. Mason, recorded that the ship had 'heeled to starboard, listed to port for a few minutes then put itself on an even keel. We were apparently dead in the water, out of trim with an angle between the bow and the stern of approximately 15°'. By this time *Fechteler* had settled amidships and 'an inspection of damage showed deck plates cracked amidships at about Frame 90, no. 1 and 2 engine rooms and no. 2 fire room flooded, decks awash. Water tight integrity was preserved forward and aft'. Steam was billowing out of the machinery spaces but exchanges with the nearby

Laning briefly raised the prospect that *Fechteler* might be saved and the assistance of a tug was requested from Gibraltar. However, her condition had become irreversible by the time HM salvage tug *Hengist* (in the rear of the convoy) reached the scene an hour later. *Fechteler's* commander, Lt Calver B. Gill, soon received a number of damage-control reports to the effect that the ship's back was broken. All floats and life rafts were put out, depth charges set to safe and the order passed to abandon ship. 'At this time, the angle of the bow and stern had reached about 30° and the deck plates amidships were cracking ominously.' With all survivors clear of the ship, *Fechteler*, 'broken in the middle, was heard to crack and the bow and stern came together in perpendicular about 125 feet out of the water where she steadied for about five minutes'. The stern section sank just before 0515, the bow followed it a few minutes later, approximately an hour and a half after the attack. The disappearance of the stern was accompanied by a large explosion initially believed to have been *Laning* – then closing to rescue survivors – taking a torpedo hit of her own, though later attributed to the detonation of a few of *Fechteler's* depth charges. In the event, *Laning* suffered only minor damage and the work of rescue proceeded without interruption.

Reviewing Brandi's cruise in Toulon, *F.d.U. Mittelmeer* (Officer Commanding U-Boats, Mediterranean) Kapt.z.S. Werner Hartmann noted that 'the sinkings of all targets fired at are acknowledged based on the observations of the commanding officer. These successes all provide convincing evidence of the faultless reliability of *Zaunkönig* torpedoes.' Although *Fechteler's* fate demonstrates its capabilities, Hartmann's remarks nonetheless reflect the vicious circle of wishful thinking that pervaded all levels of the *U-Boot-Waffe* where the *Zaunkönig* was concerned: detonations would be heard and sinking noises reported, thereby bolstering the misplaced confidence of shore-based staff in the T5's strike rate. Indeed, as time passed it became common for such noises to be reported in U-boat logs whenever a *Zaunkönig* was fired.

Fate of the crew

Striking approximately abreast No. 1 engine room, *U967's* torpedo claimed virtually the entire engine room watch as well as a number of men in adjacent spaces. A total of twenty-nine men were killed (including one each on 6 and 7 May) and twenty-six injured. Although a number of men had taken to the water in the aftermath of the explosion, the fact that *Fechteler* remained afloat for another hour and a half permitted an orderly evacuation to take place during which few if any additional casualties were incurred. As well as her own salvageable boats and floats, the survivors were able to make use of a boat and further rafts and floats dropped by *Laning* twenty-five minutes after the detonation. However, most of *Fechteler's* men would have to wait a little longer for rescue. Having picked up seven swimmers at 0415 *Laning* was ordered by the commander of Task Force 66, Cdr William H. Duvall in the *Taney*, to join *Lowe* and *Mosley* in the hunt for the offending submarine. At 0520 *Laning* returned to find the tug *Hengist* closing the wreck. Between them the two vessels picked up approximately 185 survivors (primary sources differing as to the exact number), though two men may have swum as much as a mile for rescue in another ship. Their work complete, *Laning* and *Hengist* turned for Gibraltar at their best speed. After spells in rest

Officers and warrant officers of *U967* enjoying tea, beer and cigars on their return from patrol some time between December 1943 and May 1944.
DUBMA

camps at Algiers and Oran the survivors were returned to the United States.

The outstanding episode in the sinking of USS *Fechteler* was the rescue of three men trapped aft by a party led by Lt (jg) William H. Bowman. *Fechteler's* CO, Lt Calver B. Gill, a survivor of the carrier *Yorktown*, left it to Lt Bowman to perform a final search of the wreck while he supervised the loading of the injured into the ship's boat. It was to be a momentous assignment. Hearing voices from the machine shop, Bowman and Chief Boatswain's Mate Read initially found it impossible to reach this compartment, but by approaching from the deck side and wading through the water 'discovered a small space of approximately a foot by foot and a half wide leading into the machine shop'. Despite *Fechteler's* increasingly precarious condition Read 'crawled through the small aperture and handed out one man with difficulty'. However, a second man was trapped under displaced equipment and it required Electrician's Mate E. R. Miller to join Read in the compartment to extricate him. As Lt Bowman's report states, they succeeded in freeing him and 'with difficulty handed him through the hole to me and we carried him down the side to the ship's boat'. Another whose luck was in was Ship's Cook 2/c Pons, discovered in an ammunition stowage space forward of the machine shop 'buried under 20 mm magazines with water up to his chin'. Help was summoned, the magazines removed one by one and a bowline eventually fastened round Pons's shoulders allowing him to be hauled out in dazed condition. These three were then placed in the care of Lt Gill in the injured boat where much morphine was dispensed that night.

U967 and Albrecht Brandi

Built at Blohm & Voss at Hamburg and commissioned in March 1943, *U967's* career was limited to just three operational patrols. The first of these, under Oblt.z.S. Herbert Loeder in October and November 1943, saw *U967* assigned to the *Siegfried*, *Körner*, *Tirpitz*, *Eisenhart* and *Schill* patrol lines, though none of these groups managed to locate the HX and SC convoys then at sea. Still under Loeder's command, on 20 January 1944 *U967* sailed from St-Nazaire for the Mediterranean, negotiating the Straits of Gibraltar on 13 February. On the 23rd she put in at Toulon where command passed to Kptlt Albrecht Brandi whose earlier career in *U617* and *U380* is covered in HMS *Welshman* (**81**). *U967*'s sole pennant – *Fechteler* – was gained during Brandi's only patrol in command, her last as it turned out, the boat being damaged in US bomber raids over Toulon on 5 July and 6 August. The latter claimed the lives of two of her crewmen and required *U967* to be scuttled on 19 August 1944 to prevent her falling into Allied hands.

Brandi's verified career total is twelve ships for 32,000 tons, but his accredited tonnage was far greater and his various exploits in the Mediterranean raised him high in the esteem of U-boat command. He was promoted Korvettenkapitän after the sinking of *Fechteler* and then Fregattenkapitän just six months later as *F.d.U. östliche Ostsee* (Officer Commanding U-Boats, Eastern Baltic). Two weeks prior to this promotion he was awarded the Diamonds to his Knight's Cross to complement the Oak Leaves and Swords acquired in April 1943 and May 1944 respectively. Together with Wolfgang Lüth (see **6**) this made Brandi the *U-Boot-Waffe*'s most decorated officer, though with only thirteen per cent of the tonnage of the former. Released from captivity in September 1945, Brandi became an architect and eventually governor of the province of Westphalia. He died in January 1966.

Sources

Navy Department, Office of Naval Records and Library, *Sinking of USS Fechteler, North-West of Oran, Algeria, as a Result of Underwater Explosion while Engaged in Escorting Convoy, Mediterranean Area, 5 May 1944* (NA, TF66, Serial 01, Box 241, 374/44/23/7)

—, *Sinking of USS* Fechteler (NA, Box 982, 370/44/4/1)

—, Office of the Chief of Naval Operations, Division of Naval History, *History of USS* Fechteler *(DE 157)*; and Fechteler *(DE-157)* (NHC, Box 284)

Rohwer, Prof. Jürgen, *Analyse der T-5 („Zaunkönig")-Schüsse von U-Booten gegen Geleitfahrzeuge. U967: USS* Fechteler (Report for Bundesamt für Wehrtechnik und Beschaffung [Federal Office of Weapons Technology and Procurement], 1964) (BfZ, MaS 8/2.07)

Anon., 'Six Who Served' [memoirs of Lt Joe Coffee (survivor)] in *Columbia* [Columbia University alumni magazine] (Fall 2005), p. 29; also on: http://www.columbia.edu/cu/alumni/Magazine/Fall2005/WW2.pdf

Andrews, Lewis M., Jr, *Tempest, Fire and Foe: Destroyer Escorts in World War II and the Men Who Manned Them* (Victoria, BC: Trafford Publishing, 2004)

DANFS, II, p. 399; also on: http://www.history.navy.mil/danfs/f2/fechteler-i.htm and: http://www.ibiblio.org/hyperwar/USN/ships/dafs/DE/de157.html

Davis, Martin, ed., *Destroyer Escorts of World War Two* (Missoula, Mont.: Pictorial Histories Publishing Co., 1987)

Friedman, Norman, *US Destroyers: An Illustrated Design History* (2nd edn, Annapolis, Md.: Naval Institute Press, 2004)

Grover, Lt Cdr David, 'Loss of the USS *Fechteler*' in *Sea Classics* 39 (April 2005), pp. 38–41 and 64; also on: http://www.findarticles.com/p/articles/mi_qa4442/is_200504/ai_n16057826

Morison, *United States Naval Operations*, X, p. 257

Roll of Honor of USS *Fechteler*: http://www.desausa.org/de_photo_library/uss_fechteler_de157.htm

102   HMCS *VALLEYFIELD*

Lt Cdr D. T. English, RCNR†

Sunk by *U548* (Type IXC-40), Oblt.z.S. Eberhard Zimmermann, 6 May 1944

North Atlantic, 45 nm SE of Cape Race, Newfoundland

Valleyfield whose brief career was ended by a *Zaunkönig* acoustic homing torpedo from *U548* in the approaches to St John's. *BfZ*

Theatre	North Atlantic (Map 1)	Displacement	1,445 tons
Coordinates	46° 03' N, 52° 24' W	Dimensions	301.25' × 36.5' × 9'
Kriegsmarine code	Quadrat BB 6964	Maximum speed	20 knots
U-boat timekeeping differential	+5 hours	Armament	2 × 4" AA; 1 × 3" AA; 8 × 20 mm AA;
Fatalities	123 and 2 Survivors 38		2 × .303" AA; 1 × Hedgehog ATW

Career

For background on the Royal Canadian Navy, see HMCS *Lévis* (**32**). For design notes on the River-class frigates, see HMS *Itchen* (**88**).

HMCS *Valleyfield* was laid down at Morton of Quebec on 30 November 1942, launched on 17 July 1943 and commissioned on 7 December that year. After working up at Halifax and Bermuda *Valleyfield* was assigned to the Canadian 1st Escort Group (EG-C1) with which she joined her first convoy, SC154, en route to Britain at the end of February 1944. Diverted to Horta in the Azores, *Valleyfield* eventually reached the Clyde with convoy SL151 from Sierra Leone towards the end of March. Two more convoys brought her to Londonderry, from where she sailed with ONM234 bound for North America on 27 April.

Background of the attack

On 23 March 1944 *U548* (Oblt.z.S. Eberhard Zimmermann) sailed from Narvik on her maiden operational patrol, charged first with meteorological duty south of Iceland and then with offensive operations on the Newfoundland Bank. If weather reporting had earlier been regarded as a thoroughly tedious assignment, by the spring of 1944 it carried with it the near certainty that Allied direction-finding apparatus would not only gain a fix on the boat in question but send an aircraft to silence her transmissions once and for all. So it proved in this case, though it was *U342* (Oblt.z.S. Albert Hossenfelder) not *U548* which took the consequences. On 16 April *U548* was relieved by *U342*, which was lost with all hands shortly after transmitting her first weather report on the 17th. Meanwhile *U548* was heading west but the eastern seaboard of North America was now a dramatically different

proposition to that off which Zimmermann had enjoyed such easy pickings as Second Watch Officer in *U130* two years earlier. Dogged continually by aircraft and hunting groups, *U548* was forced to spend much of her time submerged, an unsuccessful attack on the damaged SS *Baltrover* off Cape Broyle on 3 May 1944 bringing the attentions both of HM frigate *Hargood* and an RCAF Liberator, with which she exchanged machine-gun fire.

But *U548*'s luck was about to change. Heading for waters south of Cape Race in order to obtain better navigational data via dead reckoning, Zimmermann spent three days with hardly a ship registered before the tedium was lifted first by a signal from B.d.U. congratulating him on the birth of a daughter and then by the sight of an enemy warship unwittingly closing *U548*'s position. This was HMC frigate *Valleyfield* (Lt Cdr D. T. English RCNR) sailing with the Canadian 1st Escort Group (EG-C1) comprising the corvettes *Edmundston*, *Frontenac*, *Giffard* and *Halifax*. The force, commanded by Cdr John Byron RNR in *Valleyfield*, was returning to St John's having turned convoy ONM234 over to the Western Local Escort Force. Exhausted by ten days of convoy duty and latterly by constant vigilance against small icebergs and 'growlers' of submerged ice, both Lt Cdr English and Cdr Byron were fast asleep as *Valleyfield*'s brief career neared its end. With no U-boats suspected in the vicinity and the performance of Asdic known to be adversely affected by the CAT anti-acoustic device, not a single escort was streaming its noise-making gear to deflect homing torpedoes. It was to prove a costly mistake. Unseen and undetected by defective radar in both *Valleyfield* and *Frontenac*, *U548* was about to use a *Zaunkönig* acoustic homing torpedo to claim the only success of a three-month patrol. For Zimmermann it crowned an auspicious day.

War Diary of *U548*, patrol of 21 March–24 June 1944: PG 30586, NHB, reel 1,117, pp. 743–4

Date, time	Details of position, wind, weather, sea, light, visibility, moonlight, etc.	Incidents
7.v		
0140		Twilight.[1]
0215	[Qu.] BB 6938	Surfaced.
0314		Incoming W/T transmission 1843/6/260: *To Zimmermann. 04/05 a daughter born to the commander. Mother and baby doing fine. Many congratulations. Kom. Adm. Uboote.*[2]
0400	[Qu.] BB 6967, wind N 3, sea 2, patches of cloud, hazy, average visibility, bright moonlight, 1,032 mb	
0403		Shadow in sight at ship's bearing 280° or 160° true. Bows left, inclination 15–20°. Approaches rapidly. We go to utmost speed and adopt parallel course. Shadow can now clearly be identified as US destroyer escort, zigzagging around a mean course of 0°.[3] Despite our making maximum speed she closes rapidly so we quickly manoeuvre into advance position abeam her course line. I order an alarm dive for the attack as there is an extremely bright moon.
0418		Battle Stations. All tubes ready for submerged attack. We run in towards the destroyer at periscope depth. Further hydrophone effect at ship's bearing 330° and 25° but I can't make out any other vessel

1 Zimmermann was keeping German Summer Time (GMT +2), hence the onset of twilight at such a late hour.
2 Not a coded signal but a genuine message of congratulation from Admiral Hans-Georg von Friedeburg, *Kommandierender Admiral der Unterseeboote* (Admiral Commanding U-Boats) following Dönitz's appointment as Commander-in-Chief of the Kriegsmarine in January 1943.
3 Actually the River-class frigate HMCS *Valleyfield*. However, this class (two of whose units served in the US Navy) had more than a passing resemblance to US destroyer escort designs.

Date, time	Details of position, wind, weather, sea, light, visibility, moonlight, etc.	*Incidents*
		through the periscope.[4]
0432	[Qu.] BB 6964	T5 fired from Tube II at destroyer. Shot coordinates: enemy bows left, inclination 5°, enemy speed 14 knots, range 1,500 m, depth 4 m, point of aim the bow. Just as we fire the destroyer zigzags to an inclination of 0°. Boat taken deeper after firing and we turn away to starboard. A hit after 3 min. 12 sec.[5] Very loud, dull detonation then no further propeller noises. Powerful breaking and cracking sounds. For 1 min. 32 sec. there is prolonged roaring, hissing, cracking of bulkheads and the thuds of large sections of the ship reaching the seabed (70 m). It sounded to us as if the destroyer was falling on our boat. We set course 240° and go to 60 m. We pick up the noises of three fast-moving destroyers at ship's bearing 60°, 100° and 160°.
0438		We switch to silent speed. The destroyers are putting out their noise buoys.[6] These have a very loud, monotonous shrill tone like a circular saw.[7] No more propeller noises audible. Destroyers are sweeping the area of the sinking in a coordinated fashion. Two destroyers steam up on either side as far as ship's bearing 80° and 280° respectively, then shift further astern. Occasionally the destroyers switch off their noise-making apparatus, presumably to carry out a hydrophone sweep, and only then can we hear faint noises of their propellers. Followed again by a slow patrol on both sides. No depth charges so far.
0559	[Qu.] BB 6959	Single pattern of depth charges. A fair distance away. Boat touches sea bottom at 83 m. We remain there for the time being. No Asdic noises. Boat is twice overrun by a destroyer trailing a circular saw.[7] Several patterns of depth charges off to starboard in deeper water. I decide to remain on the bank and then withdraw to the south-west.
0818		We lift off the bottom and steer a southwesterly course, silent speed.
0930		Random depth charges dropped in general area by aircraft.

---

4 HMCSs *Giffard* and *Frontenac* on *Valleyfield*'s starboard and port beams respectively, or *Giffard* and *Edmundston* if Zimmermann is referring to the vessels on *Valleyfield*'s starboard side.

5 Unlike conventional torpedoes, the meandering course characteristic of the *Zaunkönig* when the close or remote fire settings were actuated makes it impossible to derive the exact range of a strike from the running time.

6 The original is *Heulbojen* which is the standard German term for nautical whistling buoys, though Zimmermann is in fact referring to the CAT (Canadian Anti-Acoustic Torpedo) noise-making device. Similar to the Royal Navy's Foxer, the CAT was towed by escort vessels to deflect homing torpedoes from their propellers. However, Zimmermann's timekeeping is questionable since *Valleyfield*'s loss was not immediately apprehended, nor was the group at large alerted to the situation until eighteen minutes after the attack at 0001 on the 7th.

7 Like other Allied counter-acoustic torpedo devices, the CAT apparatus was known by the Germans as the *Kreissäge* or 'circular saw' because of its distinctive mechanical sound.

The sinking

Shortly after 2335 (ship time) on 6 May *Valleyfield*'s Officer of the Watch, Lt C. I. P. Tate RCNVR, learnt that the hydrophone operator had obtained a contact on the port bow. Training the oscillator in the direction of the sound and playing it through the loudspeaker yielded a 'ticking sound'. This was quite likely the electric motor of *U548*'s *Zaunkönig* torpedo which struck *Valleyfield* amidships just two seconds after Tate had ordered the operator to investigate further. Tate ventured to the Board of Inquiry that the hit had been on the port side 'a little way below the water line' but other survivors disputed both the side and the point of detonation. Though Zimmerman's log leaves no doubt that he attacked *Valleyfield* from her port side, a magnetic pistol detonation beneath the keel appears the more likely scenario, particularly given the comments of Lt J. H. Warren RCNVR who testified that 'I was thrown about one foot off the deck on a vertical line'. Whatever the case, the effect was devastating. *Valleyfield*'s back was immediately broken, the two halves capsizing in opposite directions in a chaos of tearing metal, escaping steam and collapsing superstructure. The forward section reared up and sank within ninety seconds while the after part went down – stern up – barely five minutes later. Within

seven minutes of the explosion HMCS *Valleyfield* had disappeared leaving a sparse remnant of flotsam, oil and men.

Neither of the ships closest to *Valleyfield* – *Frontenac* and *Giffard*, each about 2½ miles off – had appreciated what had befallen her. *Frontenac* attributed the thud heard from *Valleyfield*'s position and the smoke visible there to a depth-charge detonation, while not even the explosion column that rose twice the height of *Valleyfield*'s bridge succeeded in arousing *Giffard*'s suspicions. Lt Cdr C. Peterson, *Giffard*'s commanding officer, attempted to raise the Senior Officer, Cdr Byron in *Valleyfield* herself, by voice radio several times but received no response. Only when *Edmundston* (which had now unwittingly become the group's Senior Officer) confirmed that she had lost radar contact with *Valleyfield* did *Giffard* close her last known position, at length coming across evidence of the sinking.

The Board of Inquiry, a report based on its findings by J. C. Rowland RCN (Captain (D) Newfoundland) and subsequent debate in the upper reaches of the Royal Canadian Navy produced a number of criticisms and observations concerning *Valleyfield*'s loss. These included the group's lack of vigilance and the implication that too many had already mentally docked at St John's; the failure to resume zigzagging after the worst of the ice was supposed to have been passed (Cdr Byron's order for the whole group to cease zigzagging was made three hours before the sinking, and shortly before he retired to his cabin); the amount of radio chatter between members of the group; the regrettable fact that both *Valleyfield* and *Frontenac* were to all intents and purposes without effective radar; and *Giffard*'s delay in instigating Operation OBSERVANT, the practice of describing a square around a stricken vessel and her rescuer while dropping the odd depth charge for good measure, with all this may have implied for *Valleyfield*'s dwindling band of survivors. Only the radar issue is free of contention though even here Zimmermann's war diary makes it clear that he immediately took *U548* to periscope depth after launching his torpedo, thereby reducing the likelihood of any fix being obtained. Zimmermann would have been amused by the Board's conclusion that the attack and subsequent escape were the work of 'a very experienced Captain [who] took advantage of the situation offered by the presence of numerous bergs, growlers and pieces of ice'. In fact, a novice commander without a pennant to his name had simply fired a homing torpedo at a ship which had unwittingly closed his position without the benefit of radar, this before settling on the seabed until an ineffectual pursuit had subsided.

Although the Board of Inquiry which drew up its findings on 12 May praised the 'prompt action and complete disregard of their own safety exhibited by the Commanding Officer and ship's company of HMCS *Giffard*', the Flag Officer Newfoundland, Commodore C. R. H. Taylor RCN, took a rather different view on the 31st:

> The commanding officer, HMCS *Giffard*, should have realized the ships of the group were well placed to order 'Close and carry out Observant anticlockwise round *Valleyfield* (or my own position)' as soon as he knew that something had happened to HMCS *Valleyfield*. It is considered that in this way there was a very good chance that the U-boat would have been detected by HMCS *Halifax*. It is difficult to understand why, having realized that something had happened at 2343, as shown by his altering course towards *Valleyfield* at that time, the Commanding Officer, HMCS *Giffard* made no signal to institute a search for the enemy until 0001, a matter of eighteen minutes later.

But hindsight, as they say, is 20/20.

Fate of the crew

Though Lt Cdr English made it to the bridge in time to pass the order to abandon ship, the instruction went largely unheard by *Valleyfield*'s ship's company, the remnants of which were taking to waters warmed only by fuel oil spilling from her bunkers. Those in the stern section had slightly longer before being plunged into the Atlantic, but there was only one survivor from this part of the ship. Among the casualties were Leading Seaman D. H. Brown and Ordinary Seamen D. E. Brown and M. H. Woods (all RCNVR), seen hastening to the quarterdeck to set all depth charges to safe. The first two received posthumous mentions in despatches, though it was later pointed out that the new type of pistol with which the charges had been fitted would not have detonated given the shallowness of the water. Then there was Telegraphist Harry Norman RN, who came forward to free the trapped HF/DF operator, 'this being done at the risk and subsequent cost of his own life'.

Crowded in and around three Carley floats and one floatanet, the survivors now faced a battle against hypothermia in waters recorded at freezing point. Attracted by the red lights on their lifejackets, *Giffard*

A US sailor displays wreckage supposedly from *U548* after she was sunk by USSs *Buckley* and *Reuben James* (ii) off Nova Scotia on 19 April 1945. *DUBMA*

was on the scene of the sinking within minutes of the attack but her arrival did not bring rescue for the survivors. Closing the men in the water, Lt Cdr Peterson instead hollered down a question as to whether they had been torpedoed, and following a highly indignant reply in the affirmative proceeded to carry out a search for the offending submarine. Though correct procedure under the circumstances, it was a blow to those in the water, several of whom were *in extremis*. Peterson then waited nearly twenty minutes before signalling the rest of the group to join him in carrying out anti-submarine and rescue measures. Rescue when it came over the next hour or so was too late for many. Though *Giffard* stopped to allow men to grasp the scrambling ropes and ladders lowered over the side, the majority were by now too cold to help themselves. The familiar problem of getting a firm grip on oil-soaked men doomed many despite the heroic efforts of Chief Engine Room Artificer N. Fraser who plunged into the water to secure lines around the freezing survivors. A total of 125 men perished, including Cdr Byron (not seen to emerge from below decks), Lt Cdr English (expired as *Giffard*'s scrambling nets were being lowered), five Royal Navy ratings, *Halifax*'s Surgeon Lt C. E. Irvine RCNVR (who had transferred to *Valleyfield* hours earlier to tend to a case of suspected appendicitis), and Lt (E) J. Storey RCNVR who was returning to Canada after completing an engineering course in Britain. The survivors were all suffering from extreme hypothermia and practically every one 'a stretcher case', with many unconscious or carrying severe injuries. Three were found to be dead and two more succumbed to exposure within the next two hours. The funeral for these five was held at St John's on 10 May.

U548 and Eberhard Zimmermann

Built by Deutsche Werft at Hamburg and commissioned in June 1943, *U548* was assigned to Oblt.z.S. Eberhard Zimmermann who had seen action aplenty as Second Watch Officer in Korvkpt. Ernst Kals's *U130* but whose only other command had been the training boat *U351*.

Other than a transit patrol to Bergen, *U548* served just one patrol under Zimmermann. Though *Valleyfield* was all that Zimmermann had to show for three months at sea, B.d.U. deemed the patrol to have been energetically conducted, acknowledging both the dangers attendant in *U548*'s weather-reporting duties and the consistently poor visibility that dogged her attempts to engage enemy shipping. This, however, was the end of Zimmermann's front-line career. The Allied invasion of France made it impossible for Zimmermann and much of his crew to rejoin their boat at Lorient following a spell of leave, and it was left to Kptlt Günther Pfeffer to bring the boat back to Germany. Commanded now by Oblt.z.S. Erich Krempl, *U548* sailed from Horten on her second war patrol on 5 March 1945. Assigned once more to North American waters, she was apparently sunk in a depth-charge attack by the US destroyers *Buckley* and *Reuben James* (ii) off Sable Island, Nova Scotia on 19 April. There were no survivors.

Zimmermann survived the war to be released from captivity and reunited with his family in December 1947.

Sources

Royal Canadian Navy, Atlantic Command, *Torpedoing of HMCS* Valleyfield: *Board of Inquiry* (NAC, RG 24, vol. 11930, file 1156-381/65)

—, *Report on Loss of HMCS* Valleyfield (Office of the Naval Historical Section, Department of National Defence, Ottawa; copy in BfZ, Sammlung Rohwer, T-5 Auswertungsdokumente)

Rohwer, Prof. Jürgen, *Analyse der T-5 („Zaunkönig")-Schüsse von U-Booten gegen Geleitfahrzeuge. U256: HMCS* Valleyfield (Report for Bundesamt für Wehrtechnik und Beschaffung [Federal Office of Weapons Technology and Procurement], 1964) (BfZ, MaS 8/2.07)

Anon., 'Recent events' in *Royal Canadian Navy Monthly Review*, no. 29 (May 1944), p. 58

Cocker, M. P., *Frigates, Sloops, & Patrol Vessels of the Royal Navy 1900 to Date* (Kendal, Cumbria: Westmorland Gazette, 1985)

Hadley, Michael L., *U-Boats Against Canada: German Submarines in Canadian Waters* (Kingston, Ont. and Montreal: McGill-Queen's University Press, 1985)

Lavery, Brian, *River-Class Frigates and the Battle of the Atlantic: A Technical and Social History* (Greenwich: National Maritime Museum, 2006)

McKee and Darlington, *Canadian Naval Chronicle*, pp. 147–50

Macpherson and Burgess, *Ships of Canada's Naval Forces* (3rd edn), pp. 58 and 230

Naval Museum of Manitoba webpages devoted to HMCS *Valleyfield*:
http://www.naval-museum.mb.ca/battle_atlantic/valleyfield/index.htm
http://www.naval-museum.mb.ca/battle_atlantic/valleyfield/video.htm
(video clips of survivors)

103   HMS *BLACKWOOD*

Lt Cdr L. T. Sly, RD RNR

Sunk by *U764* (Type VIIC), Oblt.z.S. Hanskurt von Bremen, 15–16 June 1944

English Channel, 30 nm NW of Cap de la Hague ('La Hogue'), Manche (France)

Blackwood at sea during her year of life. She was shattered off Normandy by a hit forward from *U764. BfZ*

Campaign Operation NEPTUNE (Map 2)		*Displacement* 1,140 tons	
Coordinates 50° 13' N, 02° 15' W		*Dimensions* 289.5' × 35' × 9'	
Kriegsmarine code Quadrat BF 3513		*Maximum speed* 20 knots	
U-boat timekeeping identical		*Armament* 3 × 3" AA; 2 × 40 mm AA; 9 × 20 mm AA; 1 × Hedgehog ATW	
Fatalities 58 *Survivors* about 105			

The Captain-class frigates

The Captain-class frigates originated in 1940 with a design by the United States Bureau of Construction for a small destroyer escort on the lines of the British Hunt class. In the event, the design was rejected by the US Navy for want of suitable machinery and the project cancelled early the following year (see USS *Leopold*, **100**). However, as 1941 wore on the Royal Navy found itself with an increasingly desperate shortage of escorts in the face of the U-boat offensive in the Atlantic, and in June of that year a request was made to the US government for permission to place orders for escorts in American yards. To this the US agreed and in August 1941 fifty ships were ordered under the Lend-Lease programme based on the aforementioned design. The latter not only suited the Admiralty's requirements but offered the added attraction of being readily constructed using standard US building methods. Though effectively escort destroyers, the British chose the designation of frigate accorded the earlier River class (see HMS *Itchen*, **88**) and appropriately enough named them after distinguished captains of Nelson's time. The Captain-class frigates were divided into two groups, the first, which included *Blackwood*, powered by diesel-electric machinery, and the second, including *Bullen* (**109**), fitted with turbo-electric plant. However, the entry of the United States into the war in December 1941 and the naval commitments that inevitably followed meant that the Royal Navy would take delivery of only seventy-eight of the 300 units eventually ordered (thirty-two of the first group and forty-six of the second), the rest being retained for service in the US Navy as the Evarts- and Buckley-class destroyer escorts respectively (for the latter, see USS *Fechteler*, **101**). Although the Captains soon developed a reputation for being poor seaboats with a tendency to excessive rolling, by war's end the class had been involved in the sinking of thirty-four U-boats for the loss of sixteen units to various causes.

Career

Laid down on 22 September 1942, launched on 23 November and completed on 27 March 1943, HMS *Blackwood* was built at Boston Navy Yard like all but two of her sub-group (see above). Her commissioning was delayed by service as a test bed to solve the thrust-block problems common to the entire sub-group. After working up at Bermuda *Blackwood* joined the 4th Escort Group as Leader, sailing from there with her first convoy on 30 June. Based subsequently on Belfast, the 4th EG's convoy work took it south to Dakar, back to the North Atlantic and then to the Bay of Biscay where *Blackwood* shared in the sinking of *U648* on 23 November and then in that of *U600* two days later. In December she was transferred to the newly formed 3rd Escort Group, also based on Belfast. Convoy duty in the Bay of Biscay and on the Gibraltar run culminated in January 1944 with the escort of capital ships to Port Said via the Mediterranean. After further duty in the Atlantic and a refit at Belfast in March, the impending invasion of France saw April and May largely taken up with anti-submarine sweeps of the Western Approaches and the southern part of St George's Channel, the 3rd EG based at Devonport. With the onset of Operation NEPTUNE, the naval side of OVERLORD, from 7 June (D-Day +1) the

3rd EG was charged with patrolling the sea lanes between Portland and Cherbourg against the expected U-boat onslaught. In the event, the first week of the Normandy campaign afforded them many alarms but no genuine U-boat contacts, and the evening of 14 June found *Blackwood* quietly refuelling in the Portland Roads. At 0700 the following morning she sailed to resume her duties. Seventy miles out of Weymouth Bay disaster struck.

Background of the attack

The German High Command only became aware of the invasion of France in the early hours of 6 June 1944 – D-Day itself. The Normandy landings demonstrated the overwhelming might of Allied naval and air power: more than 4,000 transports and landing craft defended by 1,200 warships, all operating under an umbrella of 6,000 fighters and bombers. With German surface units numbering no more than four destroyers, nine torpedo boats and thirty E-boats, much was expected of the *U-Boot-Waffe*, though not even the new *Schnorchel* technology could give it the hoped-for edge over the Allies. Nonetheless, the *Landwirt* ('farmer') group was assembled totalling forty-three U-boats (including fifteen with *Schnorchel*) to which Dönitz issued these bloodcurdling orders: 'Every vessel taking part in the landings… is a target of the utmost importance which must be attacked regardless of risk… Every boat which inflicts losses on the enemy while he is landing has fulfilled her primary function even though it perishes in so doing.' Within four days, with little to show for their efforts, men in the twenty-eight non-*Schnorchel* boats were indeed perishing – five were sunk within four days and five more so badly damaged that they barely made port. This circumstance led to the suspension of Channel operations for such boats, leaving the burden to be carried by the fifteen *Schnorchel*-equipped vessels which had sailed from French bases. One of these was Oblt.z.S. Hanskurt von Bremen's *U764*, which sailed from Brest on 6 June with orders to attack enemy shipping in the key routes between England and the Baie de la Seine. In the early hours of the 9th *U764* found herself overrun by a large number of vessels, following which von Bremen fired four torpedoes from below periscope depth based on acoustic data. All missed. By the morning of the 15th *U764* had reached a point due north of Cherbourg, just short of the operational area to which he had been assigned, but then abruptly reversed course towards Guernsey, logging the need to recharge batteries and give the crew a much-needed day's rest. However, this action brought *U764* into contact with units of the 3rd Escort Group, comprising HM frigates *Duckworth* (Senior Officer), *Blackwood* and *Essington*. The three were just forming a line abreast to carry out a 'gamma' sweep early that evening when one of von Bremen's torpedoes found its mark.

War Diary of *U764*, patrol of 6–23 June 1944: PG 30738, NHB, reel 1,139, p. 233

Date, time	Details of position, wind, weather, sea, light, visibility, moonlight, etc.	Incidents
15.vi	English Channel	
0444	[Qu.] BF 3522	End schnorchelling.
0600	[Qu.] BF 3522	A flotilla of minesweepers crosses the bows of the boat, heading north.
0800	[Qu.] BF 3523	

Date, time	Details of position, wind, weather, sea, light, visibility, moonlight, etc.	Incidents
1200	[Qu.] BF 3521	Day's run submerged: 40 nm.
1400		Fast escort vessel from the south passes the boat at a range of 4,000 m, northerly course.
1600	[Qu.] BF 3513	
1900		A fast escort vessel and a frigate proceeding astern of the boat to the south.[1] When they are approximately 1,000 m on the port beam the fast escort vessel zigzags through 90° and crosses my bow tubes at a bearing of 330° true.
1907	[Qu.] BF 3513	Spread of two torpedoes fired from Tubes I and IV. Enemy speed 15 knots, range 800 m, inclination 100°, depth 4 m. After 1 min. 34 sec. a loud detonation. Target is shrouded in a large brown cloud. When this clears away we see the vessel – 'Atherstone' class – lying dead in the water.[2] The fore part of the ship has been ripped away as far as the bridge, the mast bent. The stern section of the ship sits higher in the water. The frigate approaches the scene hesitantly.[3] Another vessel also approaches from bearing 300° true.[4]
1930		Our true course 180°. The frigate suddenly increases speed, circles the fast escort vessel and turns towards me. I can't turn fast enough to give her a T5 shot from the stern so we dive to 50 m.[5] Frigate passes us at speed astern; whether or not she saw us is debatable.[6]
1933	[Qu.] BF 3513	Two powerful detonations rock the boat. Presumably bombs to scare us launched by a thrower.[7] Effects: nothing to be seen through the main periscope, torpedo jammed in Tube V. Water-cooling supply of electric engines ruptured in two places, rear hydroplane making very loud noise. Starboard shaft also noisy, *No. 1 Ballast Tank perforated, watertight tail section won't shut properly.*[8] Damage to glass gauges and fuses.
2000	[Qu.] BF 3513	Frigate and the other vessel are steaming madly back and forth up above.
2017		A pattern of depth charges dropped to no effect. We head off to the south at silent speed, course 250°. The onset of the ebb-tide takes us quickly away from our attack position. On the surface an extensive search is taking place but fortunately the conditions for sound detection are extremely poor. All power-consuming apparatus is switched off and we head west at dead slow speed using just the one electric engine. I don't think there's much chance of being able to charge the batteries tonight.
2400	[Qu.] BF 3515	Course 270° true.

1 HMSs *Blackwood* and *Essington*, about to rejoin *Duckworth* and their sister *Domett* for a line-abreast anti-submarine sweep.
2 *Blackwood* was a unit of the Captain-class frigates rather than the Hunt-class escort destroyers of the Type-I 'Atherstone' group identified by von Bremen. Though certainly of a size, *Blackwood* bore little resemblance to the Type-I Hunts with her flush deck and funnel set well back from the bridge and foremast.
3 Presumably HMS *Essington* (if consistent with earlier observations), though von Bremen later implies that this frigate was responsible for the attack of 1933, which was actually carried out by *Duckworth*.
4 Probably HMS *Duckworth*, though the reservation expressed in n. 3 applies. HMS *Domett* also rejoined the group at around this time and participated in the subsequent anti-submarine sweep.
5 By T5 von Bremen is referring to the *Zaunkönig* acoustic homing torpedo.
6 *Duckworth*. Ex-crewman Heinz Guske (see below) records that *U764* breached the surface after firing the two torpedoes, something von Bremen fails to mention beyond this oblique reference. However, *Duckworth*'s attack was based on a firm Asdic contact, not a sighting.
7 Von Bremen is here referring to the contact-fuzed bomblets fired by *Duckworth*'s Hedgehog spigot mortar. Guske makes much of this remark: 'It is difficult to imagine that [von Bremen] could believe that these U-boat hunters would be content with merely scaring off their quarry… It is clear that their intention was to destroy.' Even if von Bremen's was not a throwaway remark, the fact that he goes on in the same entry to relate the damage done to his vessel by enemy action indicates that he had little doubt that the British were in deadly earnest. Moreover, Guske seems not to have appreciated that von Bremen's entry of 1933 is unlikely to have been formulated in its entirety until well after the action was over, and that consequently it was based on a complete rather than a partial appreciation of the episode in question.
8 Manuscript addition in pen.

The sinking

U764's torpedo struck *Blackwood* on the starboard side close to the forward magazine, the time being noted by *Essington* and *Duckworth* as 1909 and 1911 respectively. From the perspective of Lt Cdr W. Lambert RNVR in *Essington*, three miles off on *Blackwood*'s starboard beam, the latter suffered a huge explosion before being obscured by a dense cloud of yellow smoke. Once this cleared it became apparent that *Blackwood* was still afloat despite having her forward section demolished by a magazine detonation. The mast had collapsed, the bridge structure was blasted back, a strong smell of cordite hung in the air and the engines had stopped. However, efforts to initiate damage control measures and then abandon ship were hampered by the absence of qualified men to take command of the situation, most of *Blackwood*'s officers having been killed or incapacitated on the bridge and in the wardroom. Command therefore devolved on Temporary Surgeon Lt R. N. Brosnan RNR who was not only untrained for the task but had only joined the ship from *Essington* the previous evening. That apart, Brosnan had his hands full tending many badly injured men while suffering from shock and head wounds himself. Surviving documentation leaves it unclear who took responsibility for damage control, though an unnamed Chief Engine Room Artificer, himself on his first trip aboard, connected all available pumps in an effort to cope with the flooding of the engine room. Steps were then taken to take off the ship's company and *Blackwood* was fully abandoned by 2100. With a salvage tug on its way from Plymouth, Lt Cdr Lambert considered taking *Blackwood* in tow once the survivors had been removed, but 'with the sagging 'midships and the gathering darkness and rising wind, considered it inadvisable to put a party aboard'. The tug *Miss Elaine* reached the scene at 0415 the following morning but too late: at 0410 'minor explosions accompanied by flashes' had been seen coming from *Blackwood* and the tug was warned off for fear of damage from depth charges. By 0413 *Blackwood* had evidently sunk as *Essington* could no longer obtain a radar fix for her.

No Board of Enquiry was convened for *Blackwood*'s loss in view of Surgeon Lt Brosnan's lengthy report and the inability of any other officer to 'give a lucid account of the occurrence'. A summary report by Cdr R. G. Mills, Senior Officer of the 3rd Escort Group, added that 'inconclusive evidence suggests the attacking U-boat may have been destroyed by HMS *Duckworth*' (his own ship), though hindsight vindicates his caution. Von Bremen steered *U764* back to Brest having sustained some damage from *Duckworth*'s Hedgehog attack of 1933, though if he expected plaudits after sinking *Blackwood* he was destined to be disappointed. On the contrary, B.d.U. inveighed against von Bremen's inexplicable decision not to proceed into his designated operational area, snarling at the commander's lack of 'energy and will to attack' which saw him act counter to instructions and retire towards Guernsey on the 15th 'without being particularly pressured by the enemy . . . to give the crew a rest'. Konteradmiral Eberhard Godt was also incandescent at the 'complete waste' of firing four torpedoes (actually five, as one had been a 'tube runner') on the 9th based on hydrophone data alone. His ire was roused even further by the revelation that von Bremen could not be certain that the vessels attacked were not in fact four German destroyers making their way from Cherbourg to Brest, a movement about which he had been informed hours before his 'random firing'.

Fate of the crew

The detonation that wrecked *Blackwood*'s forward section claimed over fifty lives and injured as many again. The ship was at cruising stations and many were on the mess decks forward when the blow fell, the force of the blast leaving corpses littered about the fore part of the ship, both above and below deck. As Cdr Mills observed in his report, 'it was not . . . realized at the time that out of 105 survivors there were no officers or men fully competent to deal with the emergency'. Of those on the bridge, Lt Cdr Sly survived with severe injuries having been in the charthouse, while Lt Garner, the First Lieutenant, was found to have sustained serious back, head and arm injuries when located

Von Bremen seen after the award of the Iron Cross First Class in 1944. Few commanders received more opprobrium after sinking an enemy vessel than von Bremen did following the patrol which ended *Blackwood*'s career. *DUBMA*

on the boat deck between the Oerlikon guns. Other officers suffered severe concussion, while the Petty Officers' mess forward had been completely destroyed in the explosion. Surgeon Lt Brosnan appears to have been the only officer to survive from the wardroom where the stewards were starting to lay for supper. Coming to his senses under a piece of the wardroom table, Brosnan's attempts to get on deck led him through harrowing scenes of death to match any related in these pages – bodies hanging over the port side issuing blood, dead men strewn around the deck, a corpse near the depth-charge racks with multiple fractures to his arms and legs and another hanging from the Asdic cabinet by his feet. Brosnan ordered a number of stokers to go forward to search for more wounded men. Meeting the Sick Berth Attendant, it was agreed that the latter would concentrate the wounded aft where Brosnan would attend to them. As Brosnan recalled, 'Most of the injuries were either head injuries or broken limbs. They were all cold, shocked, soaking wet and thoroughly miserable.' A search party sent to the seaman's mess deck beneath the wardroom found only three men alive, though one of these died before he could be freed from the wreckage. 'The remainder were floating about and were either dead or drowned.' Shortly after the explosion Lt Cdr Lambert in *Essington* sighted two air-sea rescue launches on the horizon and signalled them to close at their best speed and take off survivors. Though the loading of the injured took some time, the launches managed to get all the survivors on board, a total of around 110 men. The death of three ratings en route to Portland, all victims of 'severe head and other injuries', brought the toll to fifty-eight men.

U764 and Hanskurt von Bremen

Built by the Kriegsmarine Werft at Wilhelmshaven and commissioned in May 1943, the Type-VIIC *U764* made seven patrols under Oblt.z.S. Hanskurt von Bremen. She enjoyed little success in the Atlantic and the English Channel at a time when to survive in a U-boat was an achievement in itself and, *Blackwood* apart, her tally was limited to the British SS *Coral* of 638 GRT and *LCT 1074* (**G98**) on 20 and 25 August 1944 respectively. The surrender order issued by B.d.U. on 4 May 1945 found *U764* at sea, von Bremen bringing her into Loch Eriboll, Scotland on the 14th.

However, one of *U764*'s bitterest battles had still to be contested. This was touched off by a former crewman, Funkmaat (Petty Officer Telegraphist) Heinz Guske, who took it upon himself to write an analysis of *U764*'s war diaries after being denied a copy of the account of *U764*'s career composed by von Bremen in the 1980s, a volume the authors have been unable to locate. As Guske put it, 'the basic purpose of this book is to illustrate the falsifications, both direct and by omission, of *U764*'s war diaries'. According to Guske, von Bremen distinguished himself only through his 'arrogance, superciliousness, incompetence and less than professional bearing, ... had little or no regard for his crew ... and ignored the orders and directives issued by his superiors at U-boat headquarters whenever it served his purpose.' Unsurprisingly, Guske's work caused a furore in U-boat circles. Several former crewmen were quick to repudiate his allegations in equally inflammatory language, damning his book as 'without factual or historical value' and characterising him as 'a nasty snoop and denunciator' who 'based on his inadequate or one-sided technical knowledge is neither qualified nor justified to make such iniquitous accusations, nor to utter the criticism that he has in his book. The motives that drove him to make this publication are base

and dishonest.' One day analysis of the available sources may test the validity of these various assertions.

Sources

Admiralty, *H.M. Ships Lost or Damaged: Reports, 1944* (TNA, ADM 199/957)
—, *Anti U-Boat Operations: Reports, 1944* (TNA, ADM 199/472)
von Bremen, Fregattenkapitän Hanskurt, typescript letter to Dr Jürgen Rohwer, 18 December 1967 (BfZ, Sammlung Rohwer, „T-5: Manuskripte und Auswertung" folder)
In collab., *Erklärung der Besatzung von U-764 zum Buch von Heinz F. K. Guske „Die KTBs von U-764 – Tatsache oder Dichtung?"*, May 1994 (*U764* folder, DUBMA)

Anon., 'Captains [*sic*] Class Diesel-Electric Frigates' [Part I] in *Warships*, Supplement no. 78 (Autumn 1984), pp. 21–6
Blair, *Hitler's U-Boat War*, II, pp. 579–92
Collingwood, Donald, *The Captain Class Frigates in the Second World War: An Operational History of the American-Built Destroyer Escorts Serving Under the White Ensign from 1943–46* (Barnsley, S. Yorks.: Leo Cooper, 1999)
Dönitz, *Memoirs*, pp. 421–4
Fismer, Günter, review of Heinz F. K. Guske, *The War Diaries of U764: Fact or Fiction?* in *Schaltung Küste* 149 (November 1993)
Guske, Heinz F. K., *The War Diaries of U764: Fact or Fiction?* (Gettysburg, Pa.: Thomas Publications, 1992)

---

104   USS *FISKE*

Lt John A. Comly, USNR
Sunk by *U804* (Type IXC-40), Oblt.z.S. Herbert Meyer, 2 August 1944
North Atlantic, 780 nm E of St John's, Newfoundland

Fiske immediately after the attack, her back broken and the forward section capsized to port. A number of men can be seen clinging to the hull while others are gathered topsides on the stern section which is still on an even keel. Twenty minutes later her commander Lt Comly was the last to abandon ship. *US Navy*

Theatre	North Atlantic (Map 1)	*Displacement*	1,200 tons
Coordinates	47° 11' N, 33° 29' W	*Dimensions*	306' × 36.75' × 8.75'
Kriegsmarine code	Quadrat BD 5513	*Maximum speed*	21 knots
U-boat timekeeping differential	+3 hours	*Armament*	3 × 3"; 2 × 40 mm AA; 8 × 20 mm AA; 3 × 21" tt; 1 × Hedgehog ATW
Fatalities	33 *Survivors* 180		

Career

For details of the Edsall class, of which *Fiske* was one of eighty-five units, see USS *Leopold* (**100**).

The destroyer escort USS *Fiske* (DE-143) was laid down by the Consolidated Steel Corporation of Orange, Texas in January 1943, launched in March of that year and commissioned on 25 August. In November she opened her account as an escort with a voyage southward from Norfolk, Virginia to the port of Coco Solo in the Panama Canal Zone and then New York. In early December 1943 *Fiske* sailed from Norfolk on the first of three convoy assignments to Casablanca which kept her busy until May of the following year. By now part of Destroyer Escort Division 9, on 10 June 1944 she joined Task Group 22.6, a hunter-killer outfit formed around the escort carrier *Wake Island* to destroy U-boats in the Atlantic. Five days later this group sailed from Norfolk, putting in at Casablanca after an uneventful crossing on 20 July.

Background of the attack

On 19 June 1944 *U804* left Bergen for the Atlantic where she spent six weeks performing weather-reporting duties between Greenland and the Azores. These reports were all decrypted by the Allies and by 24 July sufficient HF/DF fixes had been gained on her position for the US Tenth Fleet to dispatch Task Group 22.6 from Casablanca to track her down. The latter consisted of *Wake Island* and the destroyers *Douglas L. Howard*, *J. R. Y. Blakely*, *Farquhar*, *Fiske* and *Hill* from CortDiv 9. Unaware that she was being hunted, at 1454 on 2 August *U804* surfaced for the first time since diving at dawn. Within minutes the cloud of diesel fumes she emitted upon reaching the surface was sighted by USSs *Fiske* and *Douglas L. Howard*, stationed on *Wake Island*'s port bow and beam respectively. Oblt.z.S. Herbert Meyer's war diary records his suspicion that *U804* had been spotted, though in this case the visual sighting was immediately confirmed by a radar contact which brought the destroyers to target at their best mutually achievable speed of twenty-one knots, *Fiske* being hampered by an engine defect. Having closed the range to around two miles the pair reduced speed to fifteen knots and began searching for the now submerged *U804* by sonar, *Douglas L. Howard* to port and *Fiske* to starboard. At 1531 log time (1230 US time; their respective timekeeping aside, only a minute's difference separated the two sides), just as the destroyers acquired a clear fix on their intended prey, Meyer fired the first of three acoustic homing torpedoes before taking *U804* deep. One of *U804*'s *Zaunkönige* – the first and third of which were aimed at *Fiske*, the second at *Douglas L. Howard* – hit *Fiske* at 1235 ship time (1536 in the war diary). Though a detonation four minutes later was subsequently attributed by the Americans to an internal explosion in the *Fiske*, the more experienced of *U804*'s crewmen were in little doubt that another of their 'eels' had found its mark.

War Diary of *U804*, patrol of 19 June–12 October 1944: PG 30746, NHB, reel 1,139, pp. 566–7

Date, time	Details of position, wind, weather, sea, light, visibility, moonlight, etc.	Incidents
2.viii	North Atlantic	
1200	[Qu.] BD 5433, wind W 3, sea 2, overcast, good visibility	Day's run: on surface: 31.1 nm submerged: <u>53.2 nm</u> 84.3 nm
1454		Surfaced.
1458		Three destroyers in sight, bearing 90° true, fine inclination. Range approximately 6 nm.[1]
1500		Alarm dive then Battle Stations and to periscope depth. I believe the destroyers saw us at the same time we sighted them.[2] Two destroyers are bearing down on us without any zigzagging or alterations in speed. I can no longer see the third in the attack periscope. My course is 270°. The two destroyers, closing from astern, have me directly positioned between their course lines.
1531		A turning shot from Tube V at the destroyer on our starboard quarter: inclination 45°, bows left, enemy speed 10 knots, range 2,500 m, depth 4 m, remote fire setting.[3]
1533		Turning shot from Tube II at the destroyer on our port quarter: inclination 80°, bows right, enemy speed 10 knots, range 2,500 m, depth 4 m, remote fire setting.[4] As we turn back towards the first destroyer targeted I see that she has recently altered course towards us and is closing our periscope at high speed, inclination 0°. She is already quite close.

---

1 USSs *Fiske*, *Douglas L. Howard* and *Farquhar*, though only the first two closed the object sighted, hence Meyer's subsequent periscope sighting of just two destroyers. The Americans estimated the range to be half as much again – nine miles.

2 Meyer's hunch was correct. The sighting was made at 1157 US time which, given the minute's difference in chronometer between the two sides, indicates that the protagonists spotted each other almost simultaneously.

3 The target was probably *Fiske*. 'Remote fire' (*Weitschuss*) was one of the three run settings of the *Zaunkönig* torpedo and was primarily for use against approaching targets, or those with a relative inclination of up to 110°. This involved the *Ente* ('duck') torpedo control mechanism being set to assume a labile or erratic snaking track towards its target.

4 The target was probably *Douglas L. Howard*. See n. 3 for details of the remote fire setting.

Date, time	Details of position, wind, weather, sea, light, visibility, moonlight, etc.	Incidents
1536		Turning shot from Tube VI: inclination 0°, enemy speed 16 knots, range 1,500 m, depth 4 m, remote fire setting.[3] The range on firing is no more than 1,000–1,200 m. We then dive to 150 m.
		We dive at minimal inclination to ensure that we are not too steeply angled in the event that we are overrun.
		At 40 m I am duly overrun by destroyer. Just before the torpedo of 1536 was released we hear a detonation that is quieter than those of the subsequent depth charges and accompanied by a loud roaring sound. Those crewmen who have experienced several frontline cruises reckoned it was an eel hit.[5] For my own part, I have yet to hear an eel detonate but I could clearly distinguish the difference between this first detonation and those of the depth charges. It must have been the eel from Tube II fired at 1533.[6] At the time this detonation occurred I did see a column of water astern on the starboard side of the approaching destroyer, but had the impression that she was dropping depth charges.[7]
1536		Two (nearby) detonations. Depth charges.
1540		Two detonations further off, of which the first is again considered to be a torpedo detonating.
1542		Two detonations, further off. (Depth charges.)
1549		One detonation further off. (Depth charges.)
1551		One detonation nearby. (Depth charges.)
		This depth charge, whose effect was barely felt on the boat as a whole, caused water to burst into the diesel room via the drain of the air outlet head valve at 160 m. As we later discovered, a number of welded seams had ruptured in the air outlet above the air outlet head valve and the outlet had been compressed over a length of about 1.25 m. We could clearly identify the joint welding as being to blame here. The air outlet pipe has a diameter of 300 mm and is made up of sections of steel plating 5 mm thick. As is evident at the point of rupture, the butt seams in some places have welding just 1 mm thick. In many places the welding turned out to be badly contaminated by scum.[7] The compressed pipe was removed at the point it adjoins the air outlet head valve and a blind flange applied to the point of rupture in the form of overlaid 5-mm plating.
1553 to 1555		We briefly go to ¾ speed. There's no response from above despite appalling noises in the control room. My only explanation for this is that something significant must be going on up there. The position of our boat seems to have been accurately identified by the approaching destroyer and the subsequent overrun was extremely loud. More precise observations cannot be supplied because our GHG has been out of action since 6 July 1944.[8]
1600	[Qu.] BD 5514	

5   This was indeed the case. Meyer here uses the word *Soldaten*, literally 'soldiers' but Kriegsmarine slang for its crewmen. 'Eel' (German = *Aal*) was U-boat vernacular for torpedo.

6   Meyer does not elaborate on why he attributes this to his attack of 1533 rather than that of 1531. From the evidence of the log and the relative positions of the two destroyers, this second torpedo appears to have been fired at *Douglas L. Howard* and missed its target.

7   This poor detail welding is evidence of declining standards in U-boat construction as the war progressed.

8   GHG was short for the *Gruppenhorchgerät* ('group listening apparatus') hydrophone array. It had been out of action since the seventeenth day of what was eventually a patrol of nearly four months.

The sinking

U804's first torpedo struck abreast a bulkhead in the after engine spaces at 1236 ship time. The effect was to lift *Fiske* out of the water, briefly forcing her down by bow and stern as her back was broken by strain on the hull and the force of the detonation. Thereafter the fore part of the ship settled with a list to port of around twenty degrees while the stern remained on an even keel with reduced freeboard, both sections awash amidships. Despite the list, *U804*'s torpedo was officially recorded as a starboard hit. This assessment is supported in Meyer's log though a number of survivors remained adamant that she had been struck on the port side. In fact, the *Zaunkönig* seems to have detonated under the keel, immediately depriving the ship of all power and communication. *Fiske*'s commanding officer, Lt John A. Comly,

made this assessment of the damage sustained: 'ship's back broken; compartments B-3 and B-4 completely blown out port and starboard and flooded; port side main deck torn and holding by few shreds of plating; starboard main deck badly buckled and tearing loose; port and starboard bulkheads to deck house blown out . . . splitting of bottom and flooding at least under compartment C-305 M; numerous personnel casualties.' A second detonation in the vicinity of the Hedgehog magazine at 1240 – four minutes after the first – sealed the ship's fate, though as Lt Comly recalled neither the cause nor the extent of the damage could be assessed:

About 1240 there was a muffled explosion forward which occurred in the vicinity of the paint locker or 7.2 projector magazine (frames 18–35). This was not of the jolting nature of a torpedo but due to some internal explosion for which there was no apparent reason. [. . .] There was a blinding flash in that area followed by dense smoke making it nearly impossible for personnel to make an investigation. It was later revealed that there were two holes about four feet square approximately 5 feet above the keel and a few frames abaft the Sonar dome. There were no fires at any other place on board.

At 1245 *Fiske* broke in two and the order was passed to abandon ship, Lt Comly being the last man off at 1300. Within two minutes of his doing so the bow section was standing vertical in the water and the stern had capsized. The former sank at 1342 but the latter (with little more than the propellers still showing) needed a few shells from *Douglas L. Howard* at 1644 before it joined the stern at the bottom of the Atlantic.

Though Meyer's log supports the possibility of *Fiske* being hit by two of his *Zaunkönige*, the visual and recorded evidence is far from conclusive, not least since it is uncertain which of his torpedoes struck the fatal blow. No consideration was given by US naval authorities to the possibility that *Fiske* had been struck by a second torpedo beyond speculation that a second submarine may have been involved in the sinking. Nor was there any prolonged discussion as to how *Fiske's* fate might have been averted. Though neither *Douglas L. Howard* nor *Fiske* were streaming their FXR counter-acoustic torpedo devices, the authorities accepted Lt Comly's argument that 'FXR gear was not streamed as it was believed it would have had the effect of drawing the torpedo into the ship fired from a submarine dead ahead'. In other respects the episode was commendably well handled by *Fiske's* officers and men, depth charges and Hedgehog mortars being set to safe and the abandon ship carried out in an orderly and disciplined fashion.

Fate of the crew

A comparison of the subsequent muster rolls reveals that thirty-three men died as a consequence of *U804's* attack on the *Fiske*. The majority no doubt perished in the initial blast and the flooding of the engine spaces, though as twenty-six were classified as missing and only later reclassified as 'deceased' the total probably includes several who were blown overboard together with any claimed by the second detonation four minutes after the first. Another sixty were injured, twenty suffering leg fractures when *Fiske* was thrust upwards by the detonation. Most of the injured were placed in floater nets beside the wreck, their uninjured shipmates helping to pull them clear. However, *Farquhar* was soon on hand to begin the task of rescue while *Douglas L. Howard* provided an anti-submarine screen as *U804* quit the scene. A full three hours were needed to complete this operation given the number of casualties, few of whom were capable of getting up netting and ladders unaided. Half had to be reached by swimmers and attached to lines before being hauled aboard. Together with his staff, *Farquhar's* senior medical officer Lt (jg) Frank R. Keith USNR put in nineteen hours straight supervising the care of the wounded. Morphine and dressings were soon exhausted and had twice to be replenished from *Wake Island*, once by air drop, while *Farquhar's* carpenter was kept busy turning out dozens of splints. Four of those rescued were found to be either dead or beyond help and were buried at sea that evening; two more died during the night to be committed to the deep next day.

In an effort to minimise the incidence of fracture injuries in such

The crew of *U804* celebrate their arrival at Flensburg on 12 October 1944 from the patrol during which *Fiske* was sunk on 2 August. *DUBMA*

cases, Lt Comly suggested that 'men stationed on weather decks below superstructure deck be instructed to try to stand on ball of feet with knees bent or in some other manner that will tend to reduce leg fractures'. However, the commanding officer of CortDiv 9, Cdr J. H. Forshew USNR, received this suggestion with some scepticism, observing that it would only work if the men in question were 'forewarned of being torpedoed, a not very likely situation'. The Commander Destroyers, US Atlantic Fleet Rear Admiral J. Cary Jones Jr noted only that Comly's suggestion was 'Impracticable. Repair parties should lie down.'

U804 and Herbert Meyer

Built by Seebeckwerft at Wesermünde and commissioned in December 1943, the *Schnorchel*-equipped *U804* made three frontline patrols in 1944 under her only commanding officer, Oblt.z.S. Herbert Meyer. On 12 June she sailed from Kiel on what would probably have been her maiden operational sortie in the Atlantic. In the event, on the 16th she altered course to render assistance to *U998* which had been disabled off Bergen by a Mosquito bomber of 333 (Norwegian) Squadron RAF. However, *U804* was herself strafed by a Mosquito of the same unit which left eight crewmen wounded and obliged her to turn for Bergen, which both she and *U998* reached the following day. It was a harbinger of things to come. Her second patrol between June and October 1944 was devoted largely to weather-reporting duties, the encounter which claimed *Fiske* being the only incident of note. On 4 April 1945 *U804* sailed from Kiel bound for Norway with *U1065* in company. Five days later they were sighted in the Kattegat by no fewer than thirty-four RAF Mosquitoes, being quickly overwhelmed in attacks by twenty-two rocket-firing aircraft. One of the pair (it is not known which) exploded with such violence that a Mosquito was lost and several others damaged. There were no survivors from either boat. Among the dead was Kptlt Ruprecht Fischer, commanding officer of *U244*, who had been taking passage to Norway in *U804*.

Sources

Navy Department, Office of Naval Records and Library, *Action Report Covering the Loss of* Fiske *on 2 August – A Unit of Task Group 22.6 in Lat 47-11N Long 33-29W – Survivors Rescued by* Farquhar, 8 August 1944 (NA, 8/8/44, Box 983, 370/45/4/1)

—, *Action Report Covering the Rescue of Survivors of* Fiske *on 2 August in Lat. 47-11N Long. 33-29W – A Unit of Task Group 22.6*, 18 August 1944 (NA, Box 983, 370/45/4/1)

—, assorted material concerning the sinking of USS *Fiske* (NHC, Box 286)

Rohwer, Prof. Jürgen, *Analyse der T-5 („Zaunkönig")-Schüsse von U-Booten gegen Geleitfahrzeuge. U804: USS Fiske* (Report for Bundesamt für Wehrtechnik und Beschaffung [Federal Office of Weapons Technology and Procurement], 1964) (BfZ, MaS 8/2.07)

Wilde, Cdr E. Andrew, Jr, USNR, ed., *The USS* Fiske *(DE-143) in World War II: Documents and Photographs* (Needham, Mass.: privately, 2001); also on: http://www.destroyerhistory.org/de/ussfiske/researchde143.html

Andrews, Lewis M., Jr, *Tempest, Fire and Foe: Destroyer Escorts in World War II and the Men Who Manned Them* (Victoria, B.C.: Trafford Publishing, 2004)

DANFS, II, p. 408; also on: http://www.history.navy.mil/danfs/f2/fiske-i.htm ; and: http://www.ibiblio.org/hyperwar/USN/ships/dafs/DE/de143.html

Davis, Martin, ed., *Destroyer Escorts of World War Two* (Missoula, Mont.: Pictorial Histories Publishing Co., 1987)

Friedman, Norman, *US Destroyers: An Illustrated Design History* (2nd edn, Annapolis, Md.: Naval Institute Press, 2004)

Morison, *United States Naval Operations*, X, p. 322

Webpage devoted to the sinking of USS *Fiske*: http://www.desausa.org/de_photo_library/uss_fiske_de143_sinking.htm

'*Fiske* Rescue' page on defunct website devoted to USS *Farquhar*: http://users.erols.com/plhuggins/sisters.html

105   HMCS *ALBERNI*
Lt Cdr I. H. Bell, RCNVR
Sunk by *U480* (Type VIIC), Oblt.z.S. Hans-Joachim Förster, 21 August 1944
English Channel, 25 nm SE of St Catherine's Point, Isle of Wight (England)

Alberni edges into Halifax in May 1941. She was sunk off the Isle of Wight by a Zaunkönig *acoustic homing torpedo from* U480. *Naval Museum of Alberta*

Theatre	English Channel (Map 2)	*Displacement*	940 tons
Coordinates	50° 18' N, 00° 51' W	*Dimensions*	205.25' × 33' × approx. 11.25'
Kriegsmarine code	Quadrat BF 3274	*Maximum speed*	16 knots
U-boat timekeeping	identical	*Armament*	1 × 4"; 4 × .303" AA
Fatalities 59	*Survivors* 31		

Career

For background on the Royal Canadian Navy, see HMCS *Lévis* (**32**). For design notes on the Flower-class corvettes, see HMS *Picotee* (**29**). Notes on the Canadian Flowers are provided in HMCS *Lévis*.

HMCS *Alberni* was laid down at Yarrow's yard at Esquimalt, British Columbia in April 1940, launched that August and commissioned on 4 February 1941. Traversing the Panama Canal with her sister *Agassiz*, *Alberni* reached Halifax, Nova Scotia on 13 April where they remained until being assigned to the Newfoundland Escort Force at St John's towards the end of May. *Alberni* served on the Newfoundland–Iceland

run as a mid-ocean escort until being withdrawn for boiler repairs in May 1942. In October of that year she crossed the Atlantic with HX212 and from then until February 1943 escorted convoys between Britain and the Mediterranean in support of the Allied invasion of North Africa. March found *Alberni* back at Halifax with the Western Local Escort Force from where she was assigned to the Quebec Force in May, spending the next five months escorting convoys between Quebec and Labrador. Repairs at Liverpool, Nova Scotia lasted from November 1943 to February 1944 after which she sailed to Bermuda to work up. Following a brief stint with the 4th Escort Group of the Western

Escort Force (EG W-4) at Halifax, *Alberni* sailed for Britain to join in the planned invasion of France. Having participated in NEPTUNE, she spent a brief period docked at Southampton before emerging for her final turn of duty.

Beyond her stalwart service in the Battle of the Atlantic, HMCS *Alberni* is remembered as the ship which in October 1942 received the youngest commanding officer in the Royal Canadian Navy, Acting Lt Cdr I. H. Bell RCNVR taking up his appointment at the tender age of twenty-four.

Background of the attack

On 21 August HMCS *Alberni* sailed from Spithead to relieve her sister HMCS *Drumheller* on anti-submarine patrol duty, her station lying to the east of one of the swept channels leading from the Isle of Wight to the Normandy beaches. In company with a third corvette, HMS *Pennywort*, *Alberni* stopped at a buoy in the swept channel where she came across a small patrol vessel, *PBR 175*. As *Alberni*'s survivors recalled, *PBR 175* was 'troubled with the heavy weather and wanted us to take them in tow'. After a brief delay during which the crew of *PBR 175* was informed that they would be picked up by *Drumheller* on her way back to port, *Alberni* proceeded down the channel independently. By 1140 the next buoy (no. E2) was estimated to be just 2,000 yards off and *Pennywort* 'could just be seen on the horizon'. Both ships had by now been sighted by *U480* (Oblt.z.S. Hans-Joachim Förster), lying submerged for just such a target. *Pennywort* had hastened by without Förster being able to get into a firing position but twenty minutes later he was given a second chance in the shape of HMCS *Alberni*. At approximately 1140 a slight course alteration by *Alberni* brought her obligingly across *U480*'s path.

War Diary of *U480*, patrol of 3 August–4 October 1944: PG 30529, NHB, reel 1,113, pp. 249–50

Date, time	Details of position, wind, weather, sea, light, visibility, moonlight, etc.	Incidents
21.viii	North of Baie de la Seine	
0240–0440		Proceeding at *Schnorchel* depth with intention of returning to previous hunting area.
0400	[Qu.] BF 3273	
0709	[Qu.] BF 3274	Boat settled on seabed at 67 m.
0800	[Qu.] BF 3274	
1058		Boat lifted from seabed.
1118	Wind NE 5, sea 4, overcast, misty, average visibility	To periscope depth. At bearing 5° (275° true) a frigate, bows left, inclination 70°, enemy course 165°, range 1,500 m.[1] She is proceeding at average speed. As a result of a severe problem with the periscope, which due to the swell is giving no clear view at this high magnification, I am forced to raise the periscope rather high. Frigate withdraws to the south-east.
1134		At bearing 65° (336° true) a second frigate, bows left, inclination 15°, enemy course 170°, range 3,000 m.
1136		Frigate alters course to port and bears down on me with inclination 0°.[2] We alter course to the south in readiness for a stern shot from Tube V.
1140	[Qu.] BF 3274, wind NE 5, sea 4, overcast, misty, average visibility	A shot fired on the turn from Tube V (a T5).[3] Coordinates: inclination 0°, enemy speed 12 knots, range 1,000 m, depth 3 m, remote fire setting.[4] We dive to 30 m.
1141		After 1 min. 19 sec. we hear the torpedo striking the target and then detonating. Enemy propellers, which we had so far been following via the GHG (vol. 5), immediately cease.[5] Loud breaking and cracking sounds are immediately heard, audible in the boat with the naked ear.
1143		Very loud breaking-up sounds heard with the naked ear, then a final thundering sound. As the frigate is sinking it appears that this last breaking-up noise was the sound of her coming apart. As the sinking was ascertained from acoustic data beyond any possible doubt I decide not to return to periscope depth. For one thing the periscope is playing up and there is also no point in courting the risk of being sighted by the frigate seen at 1118, which appears from hydrophone data to be making for the scene of the sinking.[6] We go to 40 m and initially use the easterly current to withdraw from our

---

1   HM corvette *Pennywort*.

2   HMC corvette *Alberni*. It must be assumed that the course alteration of fifteen degrees recorded by Förster was either a standard zigzag or minor course correction since there is no evidence of *Alberni* being aware of *U480*'s presence, nor is any such manoeuvre recorded in official sources at this time.

3   'T5' refers to the *Zaunkönig* acoustic homing torpedo.

4   Lt Cdr Bell recalled a speed of 14 knots. 'Remote fire' (*Weitschuss*) was one of the three run settings of the *Zaunkönig* torpedo and was primarily for use against approaching targets, or those with a relative inclination of up to 110°. This involved the *Ente* ('duck') torpedo control mechanism being set to assume a labile or erratic snaking track towards its target.

5   GHG was short for the *Gruppenhorchgerät* ('group listening apparatus') hydrophone array.

6   *Pennywort* was unaware of the incident and the hydrophone data referred to more likely relates to *MTB 469* and *MTB 470* closing the scene of the sinking.

Date, time   *Details of position, wind,*   *Incidents*
              weather, sea, light, visibility,
              moonlight, etc.

attack position. In lively seas like these I believe I will then be safe from hydrophone and Asdic pursuit. My intention is to turn west again later once the tide turns and then manoeuvre further in that direction for *Schnorchel* cruising.

1200   [Qu.] BF 3275   Day's run: 0 nm on the surface, 28.3 nm submerged. Total 28.3 nm.

The sinking

The effect of Förster's *Zaunkönig* torpedo, which exploded at a time variously recorded as 1141, 1143 and 1146, was such that no conclusive proof could be found either of the cause or the location of the detonation. However, a U-boat torpedo was strongly suspected, *Alberni*'s navigating officer Lt H. W. Akhurst RCNVR recording that 'we had apparently been hit between mid-ships and the stern on the port side', while her commanding officer Lt Cdr I. H. Bell reported that 'the fact that the ship sank so rapidly would indicate that the explosion took place in the after part of the engine room, collapsing all bulkheads from the engine room aft'. *Alberni* was submerged from the funnel aft within seconds, sinking by the stern while listing to port. The survivors were unanimous in recording that she disappeared within thirty seconds of the detonation. Since little more could reasonably be expected to emerge, Admiral Sir Charles Little, Commander-in-Chief Portsmouth, wrote to the Admiralty and the Canadian Naval Mission Overseas stating his opinion that 'it is not considered that a Board of Enquiry could give further information on the loss of this ship'.

Much as *Alberni* was believed to have fallen victim to a torpedo, this could not immediately be verified, particularly as *U480* dared not surface long enough to transmit a sinking report in such perilous waters. Her presence as yet unconfirmed, *U480* returned to the scene of her success the following day and there took another scalp in the shape of the minesweeping sloop HMS *Loyalty* (**106**).

Fate of the crew

As Lt Cdr Bell pointed out, the high death toll suffered by *Alberni* – fifty-nine out of a crew of ninety men – came as no surprise in the circumstances: 'the large percentage of fatalities was no doubt due to the fact that the hands had been piped to dinner and apart from the watch were all on the mess decks and were caught by the sudden inrush of water due to the exceptional speed with which the ship sank.' Those right aft, including officers and stewards in the wardroom, had no chance at all. A few survivors from the mess decks and a single stoker emerging from the engine room painted a grim picture of rushing water and entrapment which claimed the lives of most of their shipmates below decks. Those fortunate enough to escape the wreck had not so much as a Carley float to help keep them above water in a Force 5–6 swell. That any survived at all was due largely to the fact that HM motor torpedo boats *469* and *470* noted the detonation on the horizon while returning from a night-time mission off Normandy and altered course to investigate. Thirty-one survivors were picked up within an hour of the sinking and taken to Portsmouth. Before a week had passed the survivors dispatched a telegram to the Captain of Coastal Forces, Portsmouth, expressing their gratitude 'to the officers & ships companies of MTB's *469* & *470* for their splendid seamanship and rescue work in connection with the recent loss of HMCS *Alberni*'.

Commissioning day for *U480* at Kiel on 6 October 1943. Förster on the right.
DUBMA

Mentioned in all reports was Lt F. R. Williams RCNVR who kept spirits up in the water and saved the lives of three men, including that of his commanding officer. His efforts were rewarded with a Bronze Medal from the Royal Humane Society. Amid the pitiable slaughter and waste of life the official report contains a humorous account of survival from an unnamed rating who was dragged down by the bridge structure:

> While still below the surface [he] had his life jacket, rubber boots and trousers blown off by the boilers which exploded. Actually his trousers were round his ankles and he was trying to kick them off when he remembered that his false teeth were in the pocket. He thereupon tightened his hold on his pants and struggled to the surface. He had a complete set of dentures when interviewed.

And so the war went on.

U480 and Hans-Joachim Förster

Built by Deutsche Werke at Kiel and commissioned in October 1943, *U480* was one of only ten U-boats provided with the anti-Asdic rubber coating known as *Alberich* after the dwarf in the *Niebelungenlied* who possessed a cloak of invisibility. *U480* conducted three patrols in British coastal waters under Oblt.z.S. Hans-Joachim Förster. In the first of these success was limited to the shooting down of a Canso (Catalina) reconnaissance aircraft of the RCAF but her second patrol, which began on 21 August 1944, accounted for four vessels in the space of ninety-six hours, *Alberni* being followed to the bottom by HMS *Loyalty* on the 22nd, with the 7,000-ton SS *Fort Yale* rendered a constructive total loss on the 23rd and the 5,700-ton SS *Orminster* sunk on the 25th. For this extraordinary run of success while the

U-Boot-Waffe's fortunes were at such a low ebb Förster received first the German Cross in Gold and then the Knight's Cross in October 1944. The remainder of *U480*'s and Förster's career is covered in the subsequent entry for HMS *Loyalty* (**106**).

Sources

Admiralty, *H.M. Ships Lost or Damaged: Reports, 1944* (TNA, ADM 199/957)

—, *The Last Patrol of* U480 (NHB, FSDN 1/98)

Department of National Defence, Canadian Naval Liaison Records, material concerning sinking of HMCS *Alberni* (NAC, RG 24, D13, vol. 11735, File CS 161-9-1)

—, Naval Headquarters Records Registry Systems, *Sinkings – Warships. HMCS* Alberni (NAC, RG 24, D1c, vol. 6889, File NSS 8870-331/2)

Rohwer, Prof. Jürgen, *Analyse der T-5 („Zaunkönig")-Schüsse von U-Booten gegen Geleitfahrzeuge.* U480: *HMCS* Alberni (Report for Bundesamt für Wehrtechnik und Beschaffung [Federal Office of Weapons Technology and Procurement], 1964) (BfZ, MaS 8/2.07)

Anon., 'The Loss of HMCS *Alberni*' in *Royal Canadian Navy Monthly Review*, no. 33 (October 1944), pp. 57–9

Hallihan, Paul, 'Canadian Meets His Savior: Sailor Rescued After Warship Hit by Torpedo' in *The Toronto Star* Saturday, 4 June 1994, p. A15

Johnston, Mac, *Corvettes Canada: Convoy Veterans of WWII Tell Their True Stories* (Toronto and Montreal: McGraw-Hill Ryerson, 1994)

McKee and Darlington, *Canadian Naval Chronicle*, pp. 175–7

Macpherson and Burgess, *Ships of Canada's Naval Forces* (3rd edn), p. 68

Macpherson, Ken, and Marc Milner, *Corvettes of the Royal Canadian Navy, 1939–1945* (St Catherines, Ont.: Vanwell Publishing, 1993)

Webpage devoted to HMCS *Alberni*:
http://www.naval-museum.mb.ca/battle_atlantic/alberni/index.htm

Webpage containing biography of Lt Cdr Ian Bell (survivor):
http://www.ica.bc.ca/kb.php3?pageid=1378

106   HMS *LOYALTY*

Lt Cdr J. E. Maltby, RD RNR†

Sunk by *U480* (Type VIIC), Oblt.z.S. Hans-Joachim Förster, 22 August 1944

English Channel, 30 nm SE of St Catherine's Point, Isle of Wight (England)

Loyalty under way, probably soon after completion in the spring of 1943. Förster destroyed her with a *Zaunkönig* acoustic homing torpedo. *IWM*

Theatre English Channel (Map 2)		*Displacement* 850 tons	
Coordinates 50° 15' N, 00° 43' W		*Dimensions* 225' × 35.5' × 8.25'	
Kriegsmarine code Quadrat BF 3278		*Maximum speed* 16.5 knots	
U-boat timekeeping identical		*Armament* 1 × 4" AA; 6 × 20 mm AA	
Fatalities 20 *Survivors* 103			

Career

For notes on the sloop type, see HMS *Penzance* (**16**).

HMS *Loyalty* was one of 105 units of the Algerine class of minesweeping sloops which from 1942 onwards provided the Royal Navy and RCN not only with a fully equipped mine countermeasures vessel but also an effective anti-submarine unit. Construction of this highly successful class continued for the rest of the war in both British and Canadian yards.

Loyalty, which was one of the thirty-one members of her class fitted with geared turbines, was laid down as the *Rattler* at Harland & Wolff of Belfast in April 1942 and launched in December that same year. She was completed as the *Loyalty* in April 1943 and adopted by the Derbyshire town of Ripley whose Warship Week in March 1942 had contributed to the cost of building her. *Loyalty* was commissioned into the 18th Minesweeping Flotilla which she joined in June 1943 after working up at Tobermory and in the Forth. The first months of her operational career were spent in the Channel before the 18th MF was transferred to Harwich for mine clearance and escort duty in the North Sea in August. In the event, *Loyalty* spent most of her time with Dover Command and then docked on the Humber in October before the 18th MF was reassigned to Scapa Flow in November. A month later the Flotilla shifted to Seyðisfjörður for local convoy escort and anti-submarine patrol duties in the Iceland–Faroes gap. However, in March 1944 the 18th MF was ordered south in preparation for Operation NEPTUNE – the Normandy landings. After a refit, *Loyalty* began exercises as part of Force G, charged with minesweeping support for the invasion fleet. Her duties fulfilled on 5–6 June, *Loyalty* spent her remaining months off the Normandy beachhead engaged in convoy defence, minesweeping and protection duties, these broken only by periodic spells in Portsmouth and a refit at Sheerness in August.

Background of the attack

On the morning of 22 August 1944 HMS *Loyalty* quit the Normandy coast to conduct a cross-channel sweep to Spithead with the rest of the 18th Minesweeping Flotilla: HMSs *Hound, Hydra, Rattlesnake* and *Ready*, followed at an unspecified distance by HM trawler *Doon*. At approximately 1515 *Loyalty*, then the port-wing ship of the quintet, was forced to alter course to starboard towards *Hydra* (directly on her starboard beam) 'due to a southbound convoy which would not give way'. As the ship's First Lieutenant, Lt H. Scholes RNVR, recalled at the Board of Enquiry, *Loyalty*'s signal to *Hydra* to yield went unheeded and the sweeps of the two vessels became entangled, 'so that the port sweep of the *Hydra* sheared clean through both our sweeps and our kite, and her Oropesa float [. . .] severed our sweep wires and kite wires.' The timing of this mishap could hardly have been worse from the British perspective for it was at this juncture that the group entered the sights of *U480*, Oblt.z.S. Förster having returned to the same waters in which he had sunk HMCS *Alberni* twenty-four hours earlier (**105**). Having dropped back to recover her wires and sweeps, *Loyalty* then worked up to sixteen knots to regain the Flotilla which was by now several miles ahead. Correctly identifying her as a 'straggler', Förster lost no time in notching up his second warship sinking with a T5 *Zaunkönig* acoustic torpedo.

War Diary of *U480*, patrol of 3 August–4 October 1944: PG 30529, NHB, reel 1,113, pp. 250–1

Date, time	Details of position, wind, weather, sea, light, visibility, moonlight, etc.	Incidents
22.viii	North of Baie de la Seine	
0800	[Qu.] BF 3199	
0847		Boat lifted from the seabed.
1200	[Qu.] BF 3278	Day's run: 0 nm on the surface, 28.4 nm submerged = 28.4 nm.
1207	Wind NE 3, sea 3, overcast, foggy, visibility approx. 2,000 m	
1234		Boat is positioned in the marked channel. We settle on the seabed at 53 m.
1428		Hydrophone effect at 150° true, 'sawing' and 'buzzing' in addition to the sound of high-speed propellers.[1] Also Asdic pulses. I assume a convoy as these features are usually indicative of an escorted group of merchantmen. Boat lifted from seabed and to periscope depth.
1500	Wind NE 2, sea 1, overcast, hazy	Visibility has improved somewhat and is now around 5,000 m. This improvement, together with the fact that the convoy escorts and U-boat hunters are now 'sawing' and 'buzzing', serves to reconfirm my frequent observation that this 'sawing' for the most part only takes place during the day and in good visibility.[1] It doesn't occur at night or when visibility is poor. So the enemy would appear to be confident in his belief that U-boats are reliant on periscope observation. However, these observations of mine apply only to convoy traffic in the operational area in question. Both when approaching and withdrawing from the English Channel 'sawing' U-boat hunters are all I seem to come across at night.
1527		Four frigates appear out of the mist at a bearing of 0° (or 90° true), inclination 70°, bows left, enemy course 340°, sailing in loose formation.[2] All four are evidently sawing and making a hell of a racket.[1] Range 4,500 m. It would appear to be a hunting group, as we continually hear very loud Asdic pulses.[3]

1 Förster is here referring to the Foxer gear streamed by British and other Allied escorts to decoy the T5 (*Zaunkönig*) acoustic torpedo away from its target. Originally thought to resemble a whistling buoy, the sound of this device was subsequently likened by the *U-Boot-Waffe* to that of a circular saw. However, there is no evidence that Foxer was being streamed by any vessel in the flotilla. The noises picked up in *U480* can probably be accounted for by the fact that the flotilla's sweeps were out.

2 These were HM minesweeping sloops *Hound, Rattlesnake, Hydra* and *Ready*.

3 According to British sources, only HMS *Ready* had her Asdic gear deployed at this time.

1552		At 174° (or 264° true) a group of LCTs [*sic*], range 2,500 m, inclination 100°, bows left.[4]
1600	[Qu.] BF 3278	
1603		At 209° (or 119° true) another frigate, bows left, inclination 40°, enemy course 340°, range 3,000 m. She would appear to be a straggler from the earlier hunting group.[5]
1606	[Qu.] BF 3278, wind NE 2, sea 1, overcast, hazy	Single T5 torpedo fired from Tube V at the frigate.[6] Settings: enemy speed 12 knots, inclination 60° bows left, range 2,500 m, depth 3 m, remote fire setting.[7] After firing we go to 30 m.
1609		After 3 min. 1 sec. we hear contact and a torpedo detonation. Followed immediately by breaking, cracking and sinking noises. We quickly return to periscope depth.
1612		At periscope depth we observe a large white-grey steam and detonation cloud above the half-sunken frigate at 150° (or 60° true). The stern of the ship is submerged to a point just abaft the funnel, the bows sticking up out of the water at an angle of about 20°. She sinks by the stern. While carrying out a periscope sweep I observe two landing craft at 290° (or 200° true), inclination 0° degrees, range 200 m.[8] Clearly making for the scene of the sinking. We didn't pick them up on the GHG because of the loud sinking noises that drowned everything else out.[9] We go quickly to 40 m and use the current to withdraw to the west. I intend to return to the marked channel tomorrow, but further to the north.
1800–2140		Multiple hydrophone effect from hunting vessels. Asdic pulses but no depth charges.
2000	[Qu.] BF 3198	
2050		Boat settled on the seabed at a depth of 61 m.

---

4   *LCI 164* together with *LCT 517*, *LCT 827* and *LCT 895*, all returning to Portsmouth from Arromanches. They had no operational connection with *Loyalty* or her flotilla.

5   HM minesweeping sloop *Loyalty*. Though again mistaking the type, Förster is correct in identifying her as a straggler from the group of 'frigates' sighted earlier.

6   'T5' refers to the *Zaunkönig* acoustic homing torpedo.

7   'Remote fire' (*Weitschuss*) was one of the three run settings of the *Zaunkönig* torpedo and was primarily for use against approaching targets, or those with a relative inclination of up to 110°. This involved the *Ente* ('duck') torpedo control mechanism being set to assume a labile or erratic snaking track towards its target.

8   Presumably two out of *LCI 164*, *LCT 517* and *LCT 895*, though minutes later HM trawler *Doon* became the fourth vessel to appear on the scene.

9   GHG was short for the *Gruppenhorchgerät* ('group listening apparatus') hydrophone. Förster's sequence of events differs from British accounts in that *Loyalty* is not recorded as having sunk before 1625 at the earliest – after the aforementioned vessels reached the scene.

The sinking

Lt A. K. W. Hoy RNVR, the ranking survivor capable of drafting an immediate report, recalled *Loyalty* being struck at about 1610, which tallies perfectly with Förster's timing of the event. As Hoy put it, 'there was a violent explosion under the stern of the ship on the starboard side and the ship immediately began to list to starboard rapidly.' On the bridge was Sub-Lt H. Fitton RNVR who offered this testimony to the Board of Enquiry:

> At about 10 minutes past 4 there was a violent explosion astern. I looked aft and I then saw a spume of water, which, deadened by the stern of the ship, would be about 20 foot high. Debris rained down on the bridge and the lookouts disappeared. The Captain tried to get the W/T to send out an S.O.S.; it was evident the vessel was sinking already. The Signalman was shouting down the voice pipe to the W/T to get them to send out an S.O.S. but there was no response.

The starboard list noted by Lt Hoy increased until *Loyalty* capsized within a period estimated at between two and seven minutes, her bows rising out of the water as noted by Förster. The time of sinking is variously cited as falling between 1625 and 1640.

As with the sinking of HMCS *Alberni* the previous day, there was some uncertainty among the witnesses at the Board of Enquiry as to whether *Loyalty* had been accounted for by a torpedo or a mine. However, senior figures on the Board were in little doubt that she had been struck by a torpedo. Both Admiral Sir Charles Little, Commander-in-Chief Portsmouth, and Capt. A. Pritchard, the Director of Anti-Submarine Warfare, were adamant that *Loyalty* should have been using her Asdic equipment after dropping out of the sweeping line, the former commenting that 'the Commanding Officer . . . did not appear to have appreciated the potentialities of the Asdic as a detector to give warning of approaching torpedoes', and the latter that Asdic might have enabled a contact 'to have been obtained in time for *Loyalty* to take anti-Gnat precautions' (GNAT being the Allied term for the *Zaunkönig* acoustic homing torpedo).

On the German side, these sinkings and two other successes during this cruise in dangerous waters earned Förster fulsome plaudits on his return to Trondheim. Konteradmiral Eberhard Godt extolled from afar the 'flawless' nature of this patrol, which had 'made high demands of both the boat and her crew' and been marked by 'skilled and precise navigation under difficult conditions, adept use of the *Schnorchel*, and rigorous internal boat handling' in the teeth of 'extremely powerful defence on the part of the enemy'. Förster was immediately awarded the Knight's Cross.

Fate of the crew

The alarming speed with which *Loyalty* listed to starboard made self-preservation a priority for most crewmen, some of those below deck having to be brought to order as they tried to clamber up a ladder simultaneously. Up on deck attention turned to releasing rafts and floats but there was little time for any orderly drill to be carried out. Within minutes the refrain 'Abandon Ship' was ringing from more than one throat though Lt Hoy's experience suggests that many of *Loyalty*'s men were effectively ejected by their own ship:

> Carley floats, lifebelts, floatinettes and so on were thrown overboard and very shortly afterwards I found that I could no longer stand on the Upper Deck – in fact I was sliding down towards the starboard side and the guard rails were beginning to go under on the Upper Deck so I just went over the side and swam away from the ship.

Those who got clear of the ship, some of them in rafts, were quickly assisted by *LCT 517*, *LCI 164*, *LCT 895* and HM trawler *Doon*, all of which were on the scene within five or ten minutes of the detonation and immediately lowered their boats. Within an hour the latter three had picked up seventy-six, three and twenty-eight men respectively, *LCI 164* also taking on board those rescued by *LCT 517*. Among those picked up by *LCI 164* was an unconscious Lt Cdr Maltby 'who did everything possible for the ship with complete disregard for his own safety. His body was later recovered from the water with a rubber lifebelt on, which was not inflated.' For two hours attempts were made to revive Maltby, initially by artificial resuscitation administered alternately by Sub-Lt Fitton, Surgeon Lt D. A. White RNVR (both of *Loyalty*) and the unnamed Medical Officer of *LCI 164*, and later with oxygen apparatus from a passing corvette, HMCS *Calgary*. However, Maltby's life could not be saved, nor could those of three similar cases in *Doon*. These four brought the death toll from *Loyalty*'s ship's company to twenty. The survivors were disembarked at Portsmouth (*LCT 895* and *Doon*) and Newhaven (*LCI 164*) later that evening.

U480 and Hans-Joachim Förster

For *U480*'s career up to and including the patrol in which *Loyalty* was sunk, see the preceding entry for HMCS *Alberni* (**105**).

U480's third patrol, which began on 6 January 1945, was to be her last. She appears to have gone missing having reached her patrol area in the English Channel on 30 January, after which there is no record of her movements. It was long assumed that she had been destroyed south-east of the Scilly Isles by HM frigates *Duckworth* and *Rowley* shortly after sinking the SS *Oriskany* on 24 February. However, this thesis was undermined by the discovery in 1998 of a U-boat wreck

Förster seen following the award of the German Cross in Gold in September 1944 and the Knight's Cross a month later, both on the strength of the patrol during which *U480* sank HMCS *Alberni* (**105**) and HMS *Loyalty*. DUBMA

with *Alberich* coating in position 50° 22' N, 01° 44' W, some twenty miles south-west of the Isle of Wight and 300 miles from the position of *Duckworth* and *Rowley*'s action, which is now reckoned to have accounted for *U1208* instead. If the wreck is indeed *U480* then she probably met her end in the Brazier D2 minefield between Cherbourg and Southampton some time in February 1945, though the precise date and cause may never be known.

Sources

Admiralty, *H.M. Ships Lost or Damaged: Reports, 1944* (TNA, ADM 199/957)
—, *The Last Patrol of* U480 (NHB, FSDN 1/98)
—, Ship's movements: HMS *Loyalty*, June 1943–August 1944 (with lacunae) (NHB)

Cocker, M. P., *Mine Warfare Vessels of the Royal Navy, 1908 to Date* (Shrewsbury, Salop: Airlife Publishing, 1993)
Maher, Brendan A., *A Passage to Sword Beach: Minesweeping in the Royal Navy* (Annapolis, Md.: Naval Institute Press, 1996)

Career history of HMS *Loyalty*:
    http://www.naval-history.net/xGM-Chrono-22MS-Algerine-Loyalty.htm
Defunct webpage with memoirs of C. W. Brown (survivor):
    http://www.users.globalnet.co.uk/~indigo/glencoe.htm

107   HMS *HURST CASTLE*
Lt H. G. Chesterman, DSC RNR
Sunk by *U482* (Type VIIC), Kptlt Hartmut Graf von Matuschka, Freiherr von Toppelczan und Spaetgen, 1 September 1944
North Channel, 20 nm N of Tory Island, Donegal (Ireland)

D-Day for *Hurst Castle*, seen quietly at anchor on 6 June 1944. Her career ended three months later when her stern was wrecked
by a *Zaunkönig* acoustic homing torpedo from *U482*. BfZ

Theatre North Atlantic (Map 2)		*Displacement* 1,010 tons	
Coordinates 55° 35' N, 08° 12' W		*Dimensions* 252' × 36.75' × 10'	
Kriegsmarine code Quadrat AM 5612		*Maximum speed* 16.5 knots	
U-boat timekeeping identical		*Armament* 1 × 4" AA; 10 × 20 mm AA; 3 × 12" Squid A/S mortars	
Fatalities 17 *Survivors* 102			

Career

In 1942 the appearance of the River-class frigates (see HMS *Itchen*, **88**) at last provided the British and Canadians with a truly capable Atlantic convoy escort, but effective though they were the Rivers and the Loch class that followed were still too large and complex to be built by many of the smaller yards which had hitherto specialised in the Flower-class corvettes (see HMS *Picotee*, **29**). The result was the Castle-class corvette, perhaps the finest small escort design of the Second World War. The design of the Castles owed much to the lessons learnt in the Flower class, with improved habitability and endurance, longer hulls, a forecastle extending to the after superstructure, a large bridge and a heavy lattice mast to carry the sensors and equipment that were taking the battle to the U-boats. Add to this the Squid mortar, the most potent anti-submarine device of the war, and the Castles provided an excellent balance of seaworthiness and offensive capability, even if they could manage no better than 16½ knots. Some ninety-six were ordered but the decisive reversal of German fortunes in the Battle of the Atlantic during 1943 led to the cancellation of all forty-two Canadian orders and the transfer to the RCN of twelve British-built units. A total of thirty-nine Castles saw service before war's end, including one with the Royal Norwegian Navy.

Ordered in February 1943, HMS *Hurst Castle* was laid down at Thornycroft's yard at Woolston, Southampton in August 1943, launched in February 1944 and completed on 9 June that year. After working up off the east coast of Scotland *Hurst Castle* was dispatched to HMS *Western Isles*, the anti-submarine training school at Tobermory where she spent much of July. Based on Londonderry, *Hurst Castle* joined her first convoy, the Gibraltar-bound KMS59, in early August. She was back on the 30th, weighing anchor for the last time that same day.

Background of the attack

On 30 August 1944 HMS *Hurst Castle* and her sister *Oxford Castle* sailed from Londonderry with orders to join Force 33, a hunting group patrolling the North Channel off the north-east coast of Ireland. The rendezvous was reached early on the afternoon of the 31st with which *Hurst Castle* was placed under the command of *Pevensey Castle*, and together with *Launceston Castle* and *Ambuscade* assigned to waters north of Tory Island. Following an aerial sighting of a U-boat early on 1 September the quartet was ordered to proceed east to the position of the aircraft marker. By 0824 that morning *Hurst Castle* was sailing on a course of eighty degrees at fourteen knots, the ship at cruising stations and *Kenilworth Castle* and *Oxford Castle* in sight ten miles to the east. Their quarry was Kptlt Graf (Count) von Matuschka's *U482* which, as his entry of 1200 reveals, spent much of her time submerged.

War Diary of *U482*, patrol of 16 August–26 September 1944: PG 30531, NHB, reel 1,113, pp. 327–8.

Date, time	Details of position, wind, weather, sea, light, visibility, moonlight, etc.	Incidents
1.ix		
0433		A bomber passes very low astern of the boat and on a course perpendicular to our own. It obviously didn't notice us so I don't give the order to open fire. At the same time one of the lookouts reports radar detection on the starboard quarter on the 3-cm wave.[1]
0435		Alarm, continue cruising at depth of 50 m.
0800	Qu. AM 5612	
0812		Hydrophone effect at 12° and 40°. We go to periscope depth. It's the same escort group we saw yesterday morning at 0902.[2]
0819	Qu. AM 5612, sea 2, average swell, sunshine and overcast spells	Torpedo fired on the turn from Tube V (a T5).[3] Shot coordinates: enemy speed 16 knots (judged by propeller revolutions), bows right, inclination 140°, range 5,000 m, depth 4 m, close fire setting.[4]
0822		A hit after 3 min. 13 sec. As the grey-white detonation cloud disperses the mast suddenly disappears and the bows of the vessel rise vertically. There they hang for almost a minute (or perhaps rest on the seabed as depth is only 85 m) before sinking.[5] Our target was a vessel which looked like a destroyer with a pronounced lattice mast and a strikingly large crow's nest. Single funnel. I assume she was a US escort destroyer.[6] We withdraw from the scene of the attack towards deeper water. The other destroyer, which was previously out of range, has obviously set out its noise buoy now.[7] Two more destroyers appear on the scene, one of them also streaming a buoy that gives out a light humming tone not dissimilar to that of a transformer.[8] These destroyers appear to be carrying out a sweeping search, approaching then moving further away. Several patterns of depth charges then follow (up to six at a time), but only one of these is anywhere near us. No sound location pulses heard.[9] I then take the opportunity presented by the destroyers all being on one side to make my escape in the opposite direction.
1200	Qu. AM 5611	Day's run: surfaced 1.5 nm, submerged 43 nm, total 44.5 nm.[10]
↗		
2.ix		
0500		Incoming W/T transmission 1919/1/125: *According to B-Dienst report, possible torpedoing at around 0700 Mar. Qu. 6412, 10 degrees and 11 nm from Skarry Island.*[11] (So *B-Dienst* picked up on this hit too but they obviously meant AM 5612 and 'Tory Island'.)

1 Force 33 was alerted to the presence of an enemy submarine in approximately this area by an RAF Liberator, though the sighting report in question was only intercepted by HM frigate *Helmsdale* ninety minutes after this entry.

2 *U482* had almost certainly sighted ships from Force 33 at this time the previous morning, but the composition of this particular hunting group was different, *Hurst Castle* having joined the group later on 31 August.

3 'T5' refers to the *Zaunkönig* acoustic homing torpedo.

4 'Close fire' (*Nahschuss*) was one of the three run settings of the *Zaunkönig* and was for use against retiring targets with a relative inclination of between 110° and 180°. This involved the *Ente* ('duck') torpedo control mechanism being set to pursue a straighter, less erratic track towards the target.

5 Allied reports confirm that *Hurst Castle*'s stern briefly rested on the seabed, but the depth must have been considerably less than 85 metres since she herself was only 76 metres long.

6 Von Matuschka was presumably thinking of the Evarts- or Edsall-class destroyer escorts, which though larger had a silhouette not dissimilar to the Castle-class corvettes.

7 'Noise buoy' (*Heulboje* in the original) refers to the Foxer gear, a towed device designed to lure the *Zaunkönig* acoustic homing torpedo away from the ship's propellers. The 'destroyer' referred to is HM corvette *Launceston Castle* which appears to have been closest to *Hurst Castle* at the time of the attack.

8 Probably HM destroyer *Ambuscade* and HM corvette *Pevensey Castle*.

9 Von Matuschka is here referring to Asdic.

10 An extreme ratio of submerged to surfaced time that only a *Schnorchel*-equipped boat could manage. Less than ten per cent of *U482*'s maiden patrol (2,279 miles in total) was spent above periscope depth, illustrating clearly the terrible risks to U-boats of remaining surfaced so close to the enemy at this stage of the war.

11 *B-Dienst* was the Kriegsmarine's radio monitoring and intelligence service which on this occasion confused the position of *Hurst Castle*'s sinking.

Von Matuschka shown wearing the Iron Cross Second Class and the Fleet War Badge which he earned in 1941 for service in the heavy cruiser *Prinz Eugen*. To these the German Cross in Gold was added on the strength of the cruise during which *Hurst Castle* was sunk in September 1944. *DUBMA*

The sinking

The time of the explosion was recorded by *Hurst Castle* as 0825, three minutes after that stated in von Matuschka's log. Striking aft on the port side 'probably in No. 14 oil fuel tank', *U482*'s T5 acoustic torpedo 'flooded a number of areas immediately, including the tiller flat, after peak tank, Engineer's store and workshop, main general store and provision room instantly'. It was later established that the after and forward engine room bulkheads had collapsed, 'the former almost immediately' and the latter within about a minute. Listing to port, *Hurst Castle* began to settle slowly by the stern. Her CO Lt H. G. Chesterman did not need long to assess the situation: 'By the time the smoke had cleared it was obvious that the ship was sinking and I gave the order to abandon ship.' Within six minutes of being hit *Hurst Castle* was sinking rapidly by the stern, her bows rising vertically out of the water. Chesterman's account of the incident tallies perfectly with von Matuschka's war diary: the fore part of the ship 'hung for some minutes with about 40 feet of bow above water; probably the stern on the bottom'.

Back at Bergen, von Matuschka's claims of two tankers, two further merchantmen and a corvette were acknowledged by Konteradmiral Eberhard Godt, who immediately awarded him the German Cross in Gold for an outstanding maiden cruise. Such a collection of pennants claimed at this state of the war no doubt raised eyebrows in some quarters but they were in fact quite correct, besides which von Matuschka had significantly underestimated the tonnage.

Fate of the crew

Details of how the seventeen fatalities were inflicted are few though a number must have perished below decks and at least one rating is recorded as having been trapped in the funnel guys. However, the fact that *Hurst Castle* retained her stability for a few minutes after the

detonation permitted an orderly evacuation and ensured the survival of a large majority of her company. PO Telegraphist Fred Kemp had just gone below when the torpedo struck:

> I had just got to the bathroom when we were hit. One hell of an explosion in complete darkness except for a few emergency lights. I ran back to the W/T office and told the lads to get their lifejackets blown up and to BEAT IT. I did not think that she would last long and I also knew that none of them could swim. I went looking for my oiled silk tobacco pouch but I couldn't find the bloody key to the C[onfidential] B[ooks] chest. Then I did what I should have done and got the emergency transmitter working. By the time I got the emergency signal off, I had difficulty getting out of the office and on to the upper deck as the ship was not far from sliding straight under.

But not everything worked in the crew's favour as they followed orders to abandon ship. In the absence of a griping spar the whaler could not be turned out against the list, and although the dinghy was successfully lowered it was quickly awash on the weather side and unusable in a breaking sea. The 102 survivors, most of whom were equipped with inflatable lifejackets, eventually divided themselves between six Carley floats though a number of men were left without a berth and more than one may have drowned. However, help was at hand: HMS *Ambuscade*, 'brilliantly handled, was very soon on the spot and commenced picking up survivors'. Chesterman made particular mention of Stoker PO Jordan of *Ambuscade* who 'repeatedly dived into the sea to rescue exhausted men'. Her rescue mission complete and by now critically short of fuel, *Ambuscade* turned for Lough Foyle where *Hurst Castle*'s survivors disembarked early that afternoon.

U482 and Hartmut Graf von Matuschka

Built by Deutsche Werke at Kiel and commissioned in December 1943, *U482* made just two frontline patrols under the aristocratic Kptlt Hartmut Graf von Matuschka. Though this was his first U-boat command, von Matuschka was not new to action at sea having served three years in the heavy cruiser *Prinz Eugen*, including the Battle of the Denmark Strait in May 1941. Von Matuschka's maiden cruise was exceptional for this period of the war, and her tally of five vessels sunk for a total of over 32,000 tons constituted the most successful patrol by any Type-VIIC boat in 1944, a feat which earned him the German Cross in Gold. B.d.U. had good cause to praise this 'exemplary patrol' but *U482*'s well of luck had already run dry. Her second cruise in November brought her back to the North Channel where she was lost to unknown causes some time in early December, most likely on a mine. There were no survivors.

Sources

Admiralty, *Enemy Submarine Attacks on H.M. Ships, 1943–1944* (TNA, ADM 199/958)
—, Ship's movements: HMS *Hurst Castle*, June–August 1944 (NHB)
U482 file (DUBMA)

Blair, *Hitler's U-Boat War*, II, pp. 630–42
Goodwin, Norman, *Castle Class Corvettes: An Account of the Service of the Ships and of Their Ships' Companies*, ed. Steve Bush (Liskeard, Corn.: Maritime Books, 2007)
White, Douglas, and George Ransome, 'The Castle Class' in *Marine News* 20, no. 9 (September 1966), pp. 277–80

108   HMCS *SHAWINIGAN*

Lt W. J. Jones, RCNR†

Sunk by *U1228* (Type IXC-40), Oblt.z.S. Friedrich-Wilhelm Marienfeld, 25 November 1944

Cabot Strait, about 13 nm SW of Channel Head, Newfoundland

Shawinigan enjoys a placid moment some time in 1942 or 1943. She was lost with all hands to a *Zaunkönig* acoustic homing torpedo from *U1228* in the Cabot Strait. *National Defence*

Theatre Canadian home waters (Map 1)	*Displacement* 940 tons
Estimated coordinates 47° 23' N, 59° 13' W	*Dimensions* 205.25' × 33' × approx. 11.25'
Kriegsmarine code Quadrat BB 5512	*Maximum speed* 16 knots
U-boat timekeeping differential +1 hour	*Armament* 1 × 4"; 4 × .303" AA
Fatalities 91 *Survivors* none	

Career

For background on the Royal Canadian Navy, see HMCS *Lévis* (**32**). For design notes on the Flower-class corvettes, see HMS *Picotee* (**29**). Notes on the Canadian Flowers are provided in HMCS *Lévis*.

HMCS *Shawinigan* was laid down at G. T. Davie of Lauzon, Quebec on 4 June 1940, launched on 16 May 1941 and commissioned on 19 September that same year. Reaching Halifax, Nova Scotia on 27 October, she joined the Sydney Force in November before being transferred to the Newfoundland Command at St John's in January 1942. After five months on the 'Newfie–Derry' run *Shawinigan* was assigned to the Halifax Force to escort the Quebec–Labrador convoys. Joining the Western Local Escort Force in November, she began a refit at Liverpool, Nova Scotia from which she did not emerge until March 1943. In June of that year *Shawinigan* was transferred to the WLEF's newly formed 3rd Escort Group (EG W-3), shifting to the 2nd Escort Group (EG W-2) in April 1944 while undergoing a second refit at Liverpool. On completion of this in June 1944 she sailed for Bermuda to work up before returning to escort duty in Canadian waters. In October she towed the wreck of HMC frigate *Magog* into Godbout Bay, Quebec after she had been torpedoed by *U1223* in the St Lawrence on the 14th.

Background of the attack

In October 1942 the sinking of the ferry SS *Caribou* with 136 passengers and crew by *U69* in the Cabot Strait resulted in the provision of an escort for all subsequent ferry services between Sydney (Cape Breton Island, Nova Scotia) and Port aux Basques (Newfoundland). Just over two years later, on 23 November 1944, HMCS *Shawinigan* and the lighthouse tender USS *Sassafras* left Sydney on the same route, their remit being to escort the passenger ferry SS *Burgeo* northward across the Strait. The passage was uneventful. At 1812 GMT (as kept by the RCN) on the 24th *Shawinigan* sent a signal to the effect that *Burgeo* and *Sassafras* had safely reached Port aux Basques, before proceeding on a lone anti-submarine patrol in the Cabot Strait. Her orders were to rendezvous with *Burgeo* off Channel Head at 1015 local time the following day for the return journey to Sydney. But *Shawinigan* never kept the appointment and her signal on the evening of the 24th was the last that was ever heard of her. The culprit was Oblt.z.S. Friedrich-Wilhelm Marienfeld's *U1228* which had abandoned any attempt to penetrate deep into the Gulf of St Lawrence owing to technical problems but now made her first and only kill.

War Diary of *U1228*, patrol of 12 October–28 December 1944: PG 30867, NHB, reel 1,144, pp. 99–100

Date, time	Details of position, wind, weather, sea, light, visibility, moonlight, etc.	Incidents
25.xi		
0127		End of schnorchelling.
0145		Coast fabulously lit up in the moonlight, Sugar Loaf table mountains, the glow of Cape Ray lighthouse on the horizon, Sugar Loaf at 355° true.[1]
0150	[Qu.] BB 5512, wind NE [?], sea 1, brilliant moon gives very good visibility on moon side	Hydrophone effect at bearing 200° true. We go to periscope depth.
0210		A destroyer at bearing 210° true, zigzagging around north-east base course, range 3,000 m.[2]
0220		We turn to make a stern approach, course altered to 140°.
0230		Turning shot fired from Tube VI, inclination 90°, bows right, enemy speed 10 knots, depth 4 m, remote fire setting, point of aim the stern, estimated range 2,500 m (watchkeeper's range of 1,000 m was left unaltered).[3]
0232		Sound of torpedo running merges with that of the target's propellers.
0234		A hit after 4 min. exactly. A 50-m high detonation column with a dramatic fountain of sparks. Once this subsides there remains a slender plume of smoke just 10 m high. Destroyer has disappeared. Noise of propellers disappeared from hydrophone as torpedo detonated, replaced by a great thundering, rushing sound. Her silhouette suggested that she was a destroyer of the 'S & T' class; two funnels, the after one rather smaller and narrower.[4]
0236		Six depth charges over next 1–3 min. I presume these are the destroyer's depth charges going up as they reach their set depth, or scare charges dropped by another escort nearby, whose propeller noises were reckoned by the hydrophone operator to have been an echo after the experience of this afternoon and were therefore not reported to me.[5]
0242		We go deep and withdraw on course 160° as visibility in the moon sector is only average due to dark cloud.
0303		Loud detonation heard.[6]
0400	[Qu.] BB 5515	Until 1645 a number of different propeller noises picked up at different bearings, often cutting out for long periods.

1 The Sugar Loaf and Table Mountain (*sic*) are two separate topographical features of the region. As Sugar Loaf is due north of Cape Ray, Marienfeld's observations place the distant *U1228* somewhere slightly to the south-east of Cape Ray and to the south-west of Channel Head.

2 HMC corvette *Shawinigan*.

3 'Remote fire' (*Weitschuss*) was one of the three run settings of the *Zaunkönig* torpedo and was primarily for use against approaching targets, or those with a relative inclination of up to 110°. This involved the *Ente* ('duck') torpedo control mechanism being set to assume a labile or erratic snaking track towards its target. It is not clear what Marienfeld is referring to in the parenthetic text but target range was not a key component of the trigonometric calculation generated by the torpedo data computer; see Introduction, p. xxv.

4 Marienfeld seems to be referring to the British 'S'-class destroyers of First World War vintage, eleven of which saw service into the second war and which bore names beginning with both 'S' and 'T'. However, it is hard to find any visual point of comparison between these and the Flower-class corvettes, which were seventy feet shorter and had just the single funnel.

5 An instance of multiple hydrophone effect reported at 1840 on the 24th was agreed by Marienfeld and his operator to have been the propellers of a single small steamer sighted earlier, the echoes caused by proximity to the Newfoundland coast. In this case Marienfeld settled on the presence of a second ship but no other Allied vessel – naval or otherwise – is known to have been in the vicinity when *Shawinigan* was sunk.

6 It is not known whether this was connected with *Shawinigan*'s sinking.

The sinking

Her ship's company wiped out, there is little that can be added to *U1228*'s log which leaves no doubt that *Shawinigan* came to a swift and catastrophic end, probably struck aft by Marienfeld's *Zaunkönig* acoustic homing torpedo and demolished in a secondary explosion. For its part the Royal Canadian Navy had no clear idea of what had befallen *Shawinigan* until the surrender of *U1228* in May 1945 and internment of her senior officers. When interrogated these gave a picture of the sinking subsequently confirmed by capture of the war diary itself. Until then the only information had come in the form of various loud reports heard in nearby Port aux Basques, Grande Bay and Duck Island on the Newfoundland side of the Cabot Strait. Coastal watchers on Duck Island recorded hearing a loud explosion followed by 'roar-like thunder', remarkably similar to Marienfeld's entry of 0234 even if the recorded time (equivalent to 0215 log time) differs somewhat.

As far as the authorities were concerned the guilty party on the Canadian side was the SS *Burgeo*, which contravened written instructions in not reporting the failure of her appointed escort to make the rendezvous at 1015 GMT (approximately nine hours after the attack) and proceeding to Sydney unescorted rather than returning to harbour as mandated by convoy instructions. For his part, the master of the *Burgeo*, Capt. John L. Gullage, countered that darkness and mist had made visibility at the rendezvous extremely poor, that he had no inkling of any mishap that would warrant his breaking radio silence, and that he had concerns about *Burgeo*'s stability if he waited any longer in deteriorating weather conditions. Ironically, he and his wife had been woken by a loud report at home in Port aux Basques the night before but had no reason to connect this incident with the loss of *Burgeo*'s escort of the morrow.

Despite the sinking of *Shawinigan*, Marienfeld's failure to take the battle to the Canadians in the Gulf of St Lawrence was strongly criticised by B.d.U. and led Dönitz to amend her War Orders to counter what was considered excessive caution on his part.

Fate of the crew

None survived the loss of HMCS *Shawinigan* nor can their chances of rescue have been improved by the fact that Capt. Gullage of the *Burgeo* did not alert the naval authorities to her non-appearance until after he made Sydney on the afternoon of the 25th – approximately eighteen hours after the attack. As W. G. Mills, the Newfoundland government's Undersecretary of State for External Affairs put it, 'If any of *Shawinigan*'s crew survived the loss of their ship during the night of 24th to 25th, they may have lived through most of the day but hardly through the following night.' By this time the weather in the Cabot Strait had deteriorated considerably and it was only on the 27th that firm evidence of *Shawinigan*'s fate emerged. At 1020 that morning an aircraft reported a large oil slick to the south-west of Marienfeld's estimated attack position. On reaching the scene the Canadian 16th Escort Group (EG-C16) found that 'oil, apparently boiler fuel, covered a considerable area and on searching further, three bodies wearing RCN lifebelts were located floating in the sea'. The recovery of a portion of *Shawinigan*'s bridge, two Carley floats, a fire extinguisher, a life buoy and three more bodies in different positions by HMCSs *Anticosti*, *Antigonish*, *Charlottetown* (ii) and *Springhill* settled the matter, though the time that had elapsed and the powerful currents running in and out of the Gulf of St Lawrence defied (and continue to defy) any clear pinpointing of where her loss occurred. The latitude and longitude given at the head of this entry therefore equate purely to *U1224*'s quadrant code. The six bodies found were transferred to HMCS *Truro* and landed at Sydney at nightfall on the 27th.

U1228 and Friedrich-Wilhelm Marienfeld

Built by Deutsche Werft at Hamburg and commissioned in December 1943, the Type-IX-C40 *U1228* made three frontline patrols under Oblt.z.S. Friedrich-Wilhelm Marienfeld. The first of these came to grief two nights out of Bergen when *U1228* was depth charged by an RAF Liberator on 18 September 1944. Damage to her *Schnorchel* resulted in several cases of carbon monoxide poisoning including one fatality. *U1228*'s second frontline patrol took her to the Canadian coast in November, yielding both a rebuke from B.d.U. and the only pennant

Marienfeld (second from left) seen relaxing ashore at La Spezia in the spring of 1942 while serving as Second Watch Officer of *U205* (see **63**). *DUBMA*

of her career: HMCS *Shawinigan*. *U1228*'s final cruise was to have brought her back to North American waters but the war ended before she reached her patrol area. She was intercepted by US destroyers on 11 May 1945 and escorted to Portsmouth, New Hampshire where she surrendered on the 17th. *U1228* was scuttled off New England by the US Navy on 5 February 1946. Friedrich-Wilhelm Marienfeld died in August 1973.

Sources

Royal Canadian Navy, Naval Headquarters Records Registry Systems, *Loss of HMCS* Shawinigan (NAC, RG 24, vol. 4108, file 1156-331/93)

U1228 folder (DUBMA)

Rohwer, Prof. Jürgen, *Analyse der T-5 („Zaunkönig")-Schüsse von U-Booten gegen Geleitfahrzeuge*. U1228: *HMCS* Shawinigan (Report for Bundesamt für Wehrtechnik und Beschaffung [Federal Office of Weapons Technology and Procurement], 1964) (BfZ, MaS 8/2.07)

Anon., 'Recent Events' in *Royal Canadian Navy Monthly Newsletter*, no. 35 (December 1944), pp. 56–7

Greenfield, Nathan M., *The Battle of the St. Lawrence: The Second World War in Canada* (Toronto: Harper Collins Canada, 2004)

Hadley, Michael L., *U-Boats Against Canada: German Submarines in Canadian Waters* (Kingston, Ont. and Montreal: McGill-Queen's University Press, 1985)

Johnston, Mac, *Corvettes Canada: Convoy Veterans of WWII Tell Their True Stories* (Toronto and Montreal: McGraw-Hill Ryerson, 1994)

Knight, Arthur, '*Shawinigan* Incident' in Thomas G. Lynch, ed., *Fading Memories: Canadian Sailors and the Battle of the Atlantic* (Halifax, Nova Scotia: The Atlantic Chief and Petty Officers' Association, 1993), pp. 78–80

McKee and Darlington, *Canadian Naval Chronicle*, pp. 183–5

Macpherson and Burgess, *Ships of Canada's Naval Forces* (3rd edn), p. 85

Macpherson, Ken, and Marc Milner, *Corvettes of the Royal Canadian Navy, 1939–1945* (St Catherines, Ont.: Vanwell Publishing, 1993)

Preston, Antony, and Alan Raven, *Flower Class Corvettes* [Ensign, no. 3] (London: Bivouac Books, 1973); reprinted as Man o'War, no. 7 (London: Arms and Armour Press, 1982)

Naval Museum of Manitoba webpage devoted to HMCS *Shawinigan*: http://www.naval-museum.mb.ca/battle_atlantic/shawinigan/

Canadian Broadcasting Corporation TV news clip featuring Tom Simpson (former crewman), 22 May 1996: http://archives.cbc.ca/war_conflict/second_world_war/clips/12688/

109 HMS *BULLEN*

Lt Cdr A. H. Parish, RN†

Sunk by *U775* (Type VIIC), Oblt.z.S. Erich Taschenmacher, 6 December 1944

North Atlantic, 8 nm NNE of Cape Wrath, Sutherland (Scotland)

Bullen in the summer of 1944. Her career was ended by a torpedo on the port side amidships from *U775*. BfZ

Theatre	North Atlantic (Map 2)	*Displacement*	1,400 tons
Coordinates	58° 30' N, 05° 03' W	*Dimensions*	306' × 36.75' × 9'
Kriegsmarine code	Quadrat AN 1541	*Maximum speed*	24 knots
U-boat timekeeping	identical	*Armament*	3 × 3" AA; 2 × 40 mm AA; 8 or 10 × 20 mm AA; 1 × Hedgehog ATW
Fatalities	72 and 2 *Survivors* 97+		

Career

For design notes on the Captain-class frigates, see HMS *Blackwood* (**103**).

HMS *Bullen* was built at Bethlehem Shipbuilding Corporation's yard at Hingham, Massachusetts where she was laid down on 17 May 1943, launched on 17 August and completed on 25 October that same year. Powered by turbo-electric machinery, she belonged to that sub-group of the Captain-class frigates whose US units entered service as the Buckley class. Having worked up at Bermuda *Bullen* was assigned to the 6th Escort Group and joined her first convoy on 11 January 1944. Atlantic and coastal duties were briefly interrupted in February for repairs at Belfast and then in June when she escorted the battleship *Nelson* to her bombardment station off Normandy. In July *Bullen* suffered the unusual experience of having her propellers fouled by an oil line from the escort carrier HMS *Vindex* while refuelling north of Ireland, the ship returning to Liverpool. In October she joined the newly formed 19th Escort Group based on Belfast and charged with support and escort duties off northern Scotland.

Background of the attack

On 5 December 1944 the 19th Escort Group (commanded by Cdr G. V. Legassick RNR in HMS *Hesperus*) was ordered to a patrol area off Cape Wrath following a U-boat sighting by aerial reconnaissance. The night's sweep proceeded uneventfully, with *Hesperus* and HM frigates *Bullen*, *Goodall*, *Antigua* and *Loch Insh* assuming Order No. 4 (single line abreast) through a bitterly cold night. At 0800 on the morning of the 6th *Bullen* was ordered to exchange positions with *Goodall*, then on the landward side of the line. Shortly after this manoeuvre was completed, and with Cape Wrath itself now in sight, *Hesperus* obtained an Asdic contact on the landward side that was initially considered to be of doubtful origin, large rocks on the seabed close to the coastline often being indistinguishable from lurking U-boats. But this was no rock. A little before 1000 *Bullen*, her men at Cruising Stations, was struck amidships by torpedo from Oblt.z.S. Erich Taschenmacher's *U775*.

War Diary of *U775*, patrol of 18 November–12 December 1944: PG 30743c, NHB, reel 1,139, pp. 378–9

Date, time	Details of position, wind, weather, sea, light, visibility, moonlight, etc.	Incidents
6.xii		
0800	Qu. AM 3639, sea 2, overcast, average visibility	
0830		End of schnorchelling.
08937[1]		Dawn breaks. Hydrophone effect at 310°–0°, or 130°–180° true, volume 3–4. Three different sources identified.[2] I take us to periscope depth.
0941		Destroyer at 355° or 94° true. Inclination 90°, bows left, range 3,000 m.
0947		Enemy has zigzagged.
0949	Qu. AN 1541, sea 2–3, overcast, average visibility	Torpedo fired on the turn from Tube II at a destroyer (Jervis class).[3] <u>Shot coordinates</u>: enemy speed 10 knots, inclination 60°, bows left, range 1,000 m, depth 4 m, remote fire setting.[4]
0950		After 1 min. 15 sec. a hit 10 m from the stern.[5] A great column of water with a black cloud of smoke.
0951		Destroyer is on fire. We can hear sinking noises via the group hydrophone apparatus. I take us to 20 m.
0952		I return to periscope depth. Further hydrophone bearing at 250° or 340° true. Volume 3–5. I can't see anything through the periscope, it's extremely misty in this direction. I take the boat to 30 m. A vessel in close proximity switches on her circular saw.[6] I head off at silent speed to the south-east, hugging the coast.
1007		Depth charge detonations.[7]

---

1   The time originally typed was 0837 but the '8' has been crossed out and replaced with a hand-written '9'.

2   Despite the ample testimony given to the Board of Enquiry, no details of the relative stations of the 19th Escort Group are available so this may have been any combination of *Hesperus*, *Bullen*, *Goodall*, *Antigua* and *Loch Insh*.

3   Taschenmacher's description of a 'J'-class destroyer more nearly equates to *Hesperus* than to the Captain-class *Bullen* or indeed any other ship present.

4   The phrase 'bows left' indicates that Taschenmacher attacked *Bullen* from her port side, the latter acknowledging as much in a signal to *Antigua*. Although this tallies with her subsequent list to port, the Board of Enquiry concluded on the basis of near-unanimous survivor testimony that *Bullen* had been hit on her starboard side. One rating claimed to have seen a hole on her starboard side and the torpedo wake leading to it. However, Taschenmacher's depth setting of four metres makes a below-keel detonation the most likely scenario. 'Remote fire' (*Weitschuss*) was one of the three run settings for the G7a torpedo. This was the lowest speed setting but offered the greatest range.

5   *Bullen*'s survivors were as one in placing Taschenmacher's hit amidships.

6   Like other Allied counter-acoustic torpedo devices, the 'Foxer' apparatus was known by the Germans as the *Kreissäge* or 'circular saw' because of its distinctive mechanical sound. Here it is being streamed either by *Goodall*, *Antigua* or *Loch Insh*.

7   Taschenmacher went on to record numerous depth-charge attacks over the next eight hours, none of which presented any great danger to *U775*.

The sinking

U775's torpedo struck HMS *Bullen* in the engine room amidships, producing a detonation that was clearly heard by the entire 19th Escort Group. The ship was plunged into darkness but remained sufficiently stable for the telegraphists to signal *Hesperus* that she had been torpedoed on the starboard side and was sinking fast. However, it soon became obvious that *Bullen*'s back was broken, her precarious stability giving way to 'awful rending sounds from below which seemed to indicate that she was breaking up'. At this point Lt Cdr Parish leant over the bridge and gave the order to abandon ship. Listing to port as well as collapsing amidships, *Bullen* was then seen to jackknife, both sections of the vessel rearing up before sinking partially. Now abandoned, the fore part disappeared within half an hour while the after section remained afloat for a further ninety minutes. The Board of Enquiry apportioned no blame to the late Lt Cdr Parish, noting that 'this class of ship is known for its lack of longitudinal strength' and that 'a severe explosion amidships would therefore cause the ship to break in half'. However, the Board did observe that too many watertight doors had been left open, and that one or both halves of *Bullen* might possibly have been salvaged had these been closed immediately. It also tended to the view that a mine was the most likely cause of the detonation, though a majority of survivors and onlookers harboured little doubt that it was a U-boat torpedo which had accounted for HMS *Bullen*. Indeed, the 19th Escort Group was convinced that *Bullen* had been avenged before the day was out, attacks by *Goodall* and *Loch Insh* on a contact that afternoon yielding both oil and debris. However, this is not borne out in U-boat records. Though *U297* (Oblt.z.S. Wolfgang Aldegarmann) was destroyed on the 6th, the discovery of her wreck in May 2000 demonstrated her to have fallen victim to an RAF Sunderland in waters closer to the Orkneys. The wreck of *Bullen* was located in July 2002 at a depth of ninety metres. According to the dive team, 'An immediate recognition of the wreck being a warship was easy, fire control and range finding equipment jumbled in amongst the compass and telegraphs and further up the wreck were small deck guns and ammunition spewed out over the seabed.'

Fate of the crew

U775's torpedo accounted for the entire engine room watch, any who

Not Erich Taschenmacher but his First Watch Officer, Lt.z.S. Michael Nielson seen in what is apparently the only photo that can be connected with *U775*.
BfZ

survived the initial blast being trapped as the escape hatchway 'was twisted like a figure 8'. Of those killed by the blast outside the engine room, some were seen lying with books and reading matter still in their hands, *Bullen* having been at Cruising Stations and men enjoying a 'Stand Easy' at the time. Three men were too badly wounded to be moved and went down with the ship. When the order came to abandon ship the remainder of *Bullen*'s crew leapt into the sea and made for the Carley floats which had been cut free. However, many of these had landed the wrong way up and in the absence of paddles several had difficulty getting clear of the ship before she sank. One float had a narrow escape after being sucked beneath the bow section, the occupants seeing *Bullen*'s pendant number hurtling towards them as they emerged on the opposite side. Another capsized when the ship's radar broke free and landed on top of it. *Hesperus* came alongside the wreck and unrolled her scrambling nets, and both she and *Goodall* lowered manned whalers to pick up those still in the water. *Goodall* was soon ordered to begin Operation OBSERVANT, an anti-submarine search on an increasing perimeter, but those picked up by her whaler drew the shortest of straws. With about ten survivors and her own crew of six aboard, the whaler came alongside *Hesperus* and threw up her painter to be tied fast before the occupants climbed up the scrambling net on the port side. However, at this point Cdr Legassick elected to hasten the rescue operation, ordering *Hesperus* slowly under way so as to move on to the other whaler and floats. This proved catastrophic for those in the whaler which capsized almost immediately, with the result that two of *Goodall*'s men and approximately seven of *Bullen*'s were either drowned or sucked into *Hesperus*'s propellers.

Of many selfless acts witnessed in the work of rescue none stood out more than the dogged refusal of Lt Cdr Parish to be hauled from the water before all of his men had been rescued. On receiving orders from the bridge of *Hesperus* to 'save *Bullen*'s captain' Parish was thrown a heaving line, but instead of taking it Parish simply swam with the line to another Carley float and passed it to his men. The bridge repeated the order to get Parish aboard, and twice more a heaving line was thrown to him. Ignoring all requests to tie the line to himself, Parish simply passed the line on once again. On the third attempt to pass the line to a rating, however, exhaustion set in and he simply 'turned over and floated away'. The survivors were transferred to an unnamed depot ship at Scapa Flow from where the ablebodied were ordered to the mainland at Thurso for the long journey back to Chatham.

U775 and Erich Taschenmacher

Built by the Kriegsmarinewerft at Wilhelmshaven and commissioned in March 1944, *U775* made two frontline patrols under Oblt.z.S. Erich Taschenmacher. Her maiden cruise between November and December 1944 yielded the sinking of *Bullen* but was aborted soon after due to engine trouble. Although damaged by RAF Lancasters in a sheltered dock at Bergen on 12 January 1945, *U775* was able to sail on her second patrol on 7 February. In seven weeks she sank the SS *Soreldoc* in the Irish Sea and probably damaged the SS *Empire Geraint* in the Bristol Channel, but two other sinkings claimed by Taschenmacher during this cruise have not been corroborated. *U775* was surrendered to the British at Trondheim on 9 May 1945 and escorted to Loch Ryan. She was eventually sunk outside the North Channel as part of Operation DEADLIGHT on 8 December that year.

Sources

Admiralty, *Board of Enquiry into Sinking of HMS* Bullen *December 1944 and Loss of Whaler in Subsequent Rescue Operation* (TNA, ADM 1/18039)
—, War Diary Summary for 1–15 December 1944 (TNA, ADM 199/2307), pp. 124 and 134
U775 file (DUBMA)

Anon., 'Captain Class Turbo-Electric Frigates' [Part I] in *Warships*, Supplement no. 80 (Spring 1985), pp. 23–32
Collingwood, Donald, *The Captain Class Frigates in the Second World War: An Operational History of the American-Built Destroyer Escorts Serving Under the White Ensign from 1943–46* (Barnsley, S. Yorks.: Leo Cooper, 1999)
Ould, Vic, ed., *The Life and Death of HMS* Bullen: *Memories of Some Survivors* (2nd edn, Fleet Hargate, Lincs.: Arcturus Press, 1999)
Skinner, Richard W., *U-297: The History and Discovery of a Lost U-Boat* (Pulborough, W. Sussex: Historic Military Press, 2002)

Wrecks of Cape Wrath website:
http://www.scapaflow.com/wrecks-of-cape-wrath.html

Gazetteer (1936–1945)

The following is a listing of all warships sunk by U-boats for which it has not been possible to provide a full entry in this volume. The criteria for the inclusion of a vessel in the main part of the book was the survival of the U-boat log recording the sinking of *either* (a) any surface unit in excess of approximately 600 tons' displacement (excepting trawlers, navy tankers, landing ships, troop transports and miscellaneous vessels) *or* (b) a submarine of whatever size. This Gazetteer captures all confirmed sinkings not meeting any of those criteria. Note also the following:

- Where a vessel has been excluded from the main part of the book due to the non-existence of the U-boat log, either as a result of the loss of the boat herself during the cruise in question, the breakdown in German record-keeping towards the end of 1944 (see Introduction, p. xvi), or other administrative reasons, this is indicated by a ‡ beside the name of the unit sunk.
- Where a vessel has been excluded from the main part of the book by reason of size or type, this is indicated by a ° beside the name of the unit concerned.
- Some vessels have been excluded on both counts, but all are included in the sinkings graph in the Introduction, p. xxxii.
- Vessels lost on mines laid by U-boats are not included in this listing, nor are those torpedoed and beached or brought into harbour, even when they were subsequently lost or stricken as constructive total losses, nor those landing craft or boats lost while being transported in other ships.
- Cases in which a U-boat has been demonstrated either not to be the perpetrator of a sinking or else cannot with certainty be attributed the pennant are dealt with at the end of this listing under *Excluded Vessels*.
- Under *Remarks* † denotes fatalities and * indicates survivors. Where applicable, the corresponding U-boat data is shown in parentheses.

This listing owes much to existing sources, particularly Professor Jürgen Rohwer and his collaborators on *Axis Submarine Successes of World War Two* (revised edn, 1999), together with Rainer Busch and Hans-Joachim Röll's *Der U-Boot-Krieg, 1939–1945* (vol. III), Kenneth Wynn's *U-Boat Operations of the Second World War* (2 vols) and the constantly updated pages of uboat.net. Allied fatality and survivor figures have in addition been gleaned from the British Ministry of Defence's Naval Historical Branch, naval-history.net and *DANFS*. U-boat fatality and survivor data are from Axel Niestlé's *German U-Boat Losses during World War II*. Soviet entries have been added and/or corrected with the assistance of Miroslav Morozov of Moscow. To all of these our thanks and acknowledgement.

No.	Date	Name	Force	U-Boat (Type)	U-Boat Commander	Type	Remarks
1936							
G1	12 December	C3‡	Spanish Republican navy	U34 (VII)[1]	Kptlt Harald Grosse	Patrol submarine	Torpedoed off Málaga (Spain); 37† 3*; log apparently destroyed by German authorities
1939							
G2	30 October	*Northern Rover°*	RN	U59 (IIC)	Kptlt Harald Jürst	Anti-submarine trawler	Torpedoed 25 nm W of Papa Westray, Orkney (Scotland); 27† 0*
G3	28 December	*Barbara Robertson°*	RN	U30 (VII)	Kptlt Fritz-Julius Lemp	Anti-submarine trawler	Sunk by gunfire 35 nm NW of the Butt of Lewis, Lewis (Scotland); 1† ?*
1940							
G4	13 April	*Froya°*	KNM	U34 (VII)	Kptlt Wilhelm Rollmann[2]	Minelayer	Torpedoed after being beached at Sotvika, Stjørnfjorden (Norway) following damage from aerial and artillery bombardment; 0† 78*
G5	1 June	*Astronomer°*	RN	U58 (IIC)	Kptlt Herbert Kuppisch	Boom carrier	Sunk by gunfire 30 nm SE of Wick, Orkney (Scotland); 4† 101*
G6	19 December	*Rhône°*	MN	U37 (IXA)	Oblt.z.S. Nicolai Clausen	Navy tanker	Torpedoed 80 nm NE of Cap Juby (Morocco); 11† 39*; NF *Sfax* sunk in same attack (21)
1941							
G7	23 June	*M-78‡*	SN	U144 (IID)	Kptlt Gert von Mittelstaedt	Coastal submarine	Torpedoed W of Ventspils (Latvia); 15† 0*; *U144* sunk N of Hiiumaa Is. (Estonia), Gulf of Finland by Soviet *SHCH-307/Treska* on 10 August; (28† 0*)
G8	6 August	*PS-70°*	SN	U652 (VIIC)[3]	Oblt.z.S. Georg-Werner Fraatz	Dispatch vessel	Torpedoed 7 nm off Cape Teriberka, Kola Peninsula (Russia); 45† 12*
1941							
G9	10 August	*SKR-27/Zhemchug°*	SN	U451 (VIIC)	Kptlt Eberhard Hoffmann	Patrol craft	Torpedoed W of Kildin Is., Barents Sea; 61† 0*
G10	25 August	*T-898/Nemets°*	SN	U752 (VIIC)	Kptlt Karl-Ernst Schroeter	Minesweeping trawler	Torpedoed 80 nm E of Cape Cherny, Kola Peninsula (Russia); 41† 2*
G11	12 October	*TLC-2 (A 2)°*	RN	U75 (VIIB)	Kptlt Helmuth Ringelmann	Troop-carrying lighter	*TLC-7* sunk by gunfire, *TLC-2* by gunfire and torpedo in same attack off Sidi Barrâni (Egypt); 16† 0* and 20† 1* respectively
G12	12 October	*TLC-7 (A 7)°*	RN	U75 (VIIB)	Kptlt Helmuth Ringelmann	Troop-carrying lighter	
G13	18 October	*SKR-11°*	SN	U132 (VIIC)	Kptlt Ernst Vogelsang[4]	Auxiliary patrol craft	Torpedoed NW of Cape Svyatoy Nos, Kola Peninsula (Russia); ?† ?*
G14	15 November	*T-889/ Krasnoarmeets°*	SN	U752 (VIIC)	Kptlt Karl-Ernst Schroeter	Minesweeping trawler	Torpedoed 6 nm SE of Ostrye Ludki, White Sea; 43† 0*
G15	11 December	*Lady Shirley°*	RN	U374 (VIIC)	Oblt.z.S. Unno von Fischel	Anti-submarine trawler	Both torpedoed in same attack S of Gibraltar; 33† 0* and 30† 12* respectively
G16	11 December	*Rosabelle°*	RN	U374 (VIIC)	Oblt.z.S. Unno von Fischel	Armed yacht	
G17	15 December	*Galatea‡*	RN	U557 (VIIC)	Kptlt Ottokar Paulshen	Light cruiser	Torpedoed W of Alexandria (Egypt); 472†144*; *U557* sunk W of Crete after accidental ramming by Italian MTB *Orione* on the 16th; (43† 0*)
G18	19 December	*Stanley* (ex USS *McCalla*)‡	RN	U574 (VIIC)	Oblt.z.S. Dietrich Gengelbach	Escort destroyer	Torpedoed E of the Azores; 136† 25*; *U574* immediately rammed and sunk by HMS *Stork* (see HMS *Audacity*, **43**); (28† 16*)
1942							
G19	21 or 22 January	*Rosemonde°*	RN	U203 (VIIC)	Kptlt Rolf Mützelburg	Anti-submarine trawler	Torpedoed NE of the Azores; 25† 0*
G20	29 January	*Sotra°*	RN	U431 (VIIC)[5]	Kptlt Wilhelm Dommes	Minesweeping whaler	Torpedoed NE of Bardia (Libya); 22† 0*

1   See HMS *Whirlwind* (13).
2   See HMS/m *Spearfish* (14).
3   See HMSs *Heythrop* (55) and *Jaguar* (56).
4   See USS *Alexander Hamilton* (48).
5   See HMS *Martin* (72) and HrMs *Isaac Sweers* (74).

No.	Date	Name	Type	Force	U-Boat (Type)	U-Boat Commander	Remarks
G21	31 January	Belmont (ex USS Satterlee)‡	Escort destroyer	RN	U82 (VIIC)	Kptlt Siegfried Rollmann	Torpedoed SSE of Sable Island, Nova Scotia; 138† 0*; U82 sunk NE of the Azores by HMSs *Rochester* and *Tamarisk* on 7 February; (45† 0*)
G22	7 or 8 March	Northern Princess‡°	Anti-submarine trawler	RN; on loan to USN	U587 (VIIC)	Kptlt Ulrich Borcherdt	Torpedoed by S of Newfoundland; 38† 0*; U587 sunk NNE of the Azores by HMSs *Aldenham*, *Grove* (62), *Leamington* and *Volunteer* on the 27th; (42† 0*)
G23	8 March	Notts County°	Anti-submarine trawler	RN	U701 (VIIC)	Kptlt Horst Degen	Torpedoed SE of Iceland; 41† 0*
G24	11 March	Stella Capella°	Anti-submarine trawler	RN	U701 (VIIC)	Kptlt Horst Degen	Torpedoed SE of Iceland; 33† 0*
G25	15 March	Acacia°	Lighthouse tender	USCG	U161 (VIIC)	Kptlt Albrecht Achilles	Sunk by gunfire S of Haiti; 0† 35*
G26	30 March	Sulla°	Minesweeping whaler	RN	U456 (VIIC)[6]	Kptlt Max-Martin Teichert	Presumed torpedoed off Kola Peninsula (Russia); 21† 0*; otherwise lost to unknown cause after the 25th
G27	16 April	Vikings°	Anti-submarine trawler	FNFL	U81 (VIIC)[7]	Kptlt Friedrich Guggenberger	Torpedoed 23 nm off Beirut (Lebanon); 41† 16*
G28	12 May	Bedfordshire°	Anti-submarine trawler	RN; on loan to USN	U558 (VIIC)[8]	Kptlt Günther Krech	Torpedoed 12 nm off Cape Lookout, NC (USA); 37† 0*
G29	13 June	Farouk°	Decoy schooner	RN	U83 (VIIB)	Kptlt Hans-Werner Kraus	Sunk by gunfire off Tripoli (Lebanon); 8† 10*
G30	19 June	YP-389‡	Anti-submarine trawler	USN	U701 (VIIC)	Kptlt Horst Degen	Sunk by gunfire 10 nm off Diamond Head, NC (USA); 4† 21*; U701 sunk off Cape Hatteras, NC by USAAF Hudson on 7 July; (39† 7*)
G31	7 July	Aldersdale°	Navy tanker	RN	U457 (IXC)	Korvkpt. Karl Brandenburg	Sunk by gunfire and torpedo in the Barents Sea having been abandoned following bombing attack by Ju88s on the 5th; 0† 54*
G32	25 July	Laertes°	Minesweeping trawler	RN	U201 (VIIC)[9]	Kptlt Adalbert Schnee	Torpedoed 180 m SSW of Freetown (Sierra Leone); 19† ?*
G33	7 September	Raccoon‡	Armed yacht	RCN	U165 (IXC)	Korvkpt. Eberhard Hoffmann	Torpedoed in the Gulf of St Lawrence; 37† 0*; U165 sunk off Lorient (France) by RAF Wellington on the 27th; (51† 0*)
G34	12 September	Laconia°	Troop transport	RN	U156 (IXC)	Korvkpt. Werner Hartenstein	Torpedoed NE of Ascension Is.; 1,621† 1,111*
G35	19 September	Alouette°	Anti-submarine trawler	RN	U552 (VIIC)[10]	Kptlt Klaus Popp	Torpedoed 10 nm off Cabo Espichel (Portugal); 14† 27*
G36	22 September	Gray Ranger°	Navy tanker	RN	U435 (VIIC)[11]	Kptlt Siegfried Strelow	Torpedoed W of Jan Mayen Is., Greenland Sea; 6† 33*
G37	9 November	Leedstown‡°	Troop transport	USN	U331 (VIIC)[12]	Kptlt Hans-Diedrich Freiherr von Tiesenhausen	Torpedoed in abandoned state off Cap Matifou (Algeria); 59† ?* inflicted during earlier aerial attacks; U331 sunk NW of Algiers by RAF Hudsons and FAA Albacores and Martlets on the 17th; (32† 17*)
G38	11 November	Joseph Hewes‡°	Troop transport	USN	U173 (IXC)	Oblt.z.S. Hans-Adolf Schweichel	Torpedoed in Fédala roads (Morocco); 100+† 258*; U173 sunk off Casablanca by USSs *Woolsey*, *Swanson* and *Quick* on the 16th; (57† 0*)
G39	12 November	Edward Rutledge°	Troop transport	USN	U130 (IXC)	Korvkpt. Ernst Kals	
G40	12 November	Hugh L. Scott°	Troop transport	USN	U130 (IXC)	Korvkpt. Ernst Kals	
G41	12–13 November	Tasker H. Bliss°	Troop transport	USN	U130 (IXC)	Korvkpt. Ernst Kals	All three torpedoed in same attack on Fédala anchorage (Morocco); 15† ?*; 59† 60* and 34† ?* respectively

6 See HMS *Edinburgh* (58).
7 See HMS *Ark Royal* (39).
8 See HMS *Gladiolus* (35).
9 See HMS *Springbank* (33).
10 See USS *Reuben James* (i) (38).
11 See HMSs *Leda* (69) and *Fidelity* (80).
12 See HMS *Barham* (41).

No.	Date	Name	Type	Force	U-Boat (Type)	U-Boat Commander	Remarks
G42	15 November	Ettrick°	Troop transport	RN	U155 (IXC)	Kptlt Adolf Piening	Torpedoed 125 nm W of Gibraltar; 24† 312*; HMS *Avenger* sunk in same attack (75)
G43	17 December	Poitou°	Patrol craft (ex trawler)	FNFL	U432 (VIIC)[13]	Kptlt Heinz-Otto Schultze	Torpedoed off Fédala (Morocco); 20† 2*
G44	28 December	St Issey°	Naval tug	RN	U617 (VIIC)[14]	Kptlt Albrecht Brandi[15]	Torpedoed NE of Benghazi (Libya); 36† 0*
1943							
G45	7 January	Jura°	Minesweeping trawler	RN	U371 (VIIC)[16]	Kptlt Waldemar Mehl	Torpedoed 5 nm E of Algiers (Algeria); 17† ?*
G46	3 February	Dorchester°	Troop transport	USN	U223 (VIIC)	Kptlt Karl-jürg Wächter	Torpedoed WSW of Uummannarsuaq, Greenland; 677† 229*
G47	7 February	LCI(L) 162°	Infantry landing ship	RN	U596 (VIIC)	Kptlt Gunter Jahn	Torpedoed E of Oran (Algeria); 18† 0*
G48	8 February	Bredon°	Anti-submarine trawler	RN	U521 (IXC)	Kptlt Klaus Bargsten[17]	Torpedoed NW of Lanzarote, Canary Is.; 43† ?*
G49	11 March	Harvester‡	Destroyer	RN	U432 (VIIC)[18]	Kptlt Hermann Eckhardt	Torpedoed in the central North Atlantic; 145 + 39† 48 + 12* (+ figures refer to survivors of SS *William C. Gorgas*); U432 immediately sunk by FNFL *Aconit*; (26† 20*)
G50	26 March	Sergent Gouarne°	Anti-submarine FNFL trawler	FNFL	U755 (VIIC)[19]	Kptlt Walter Göing	Torpedoed N of Ceuta (Spanish Morocco); 5† 55*
G51	15 June	T-411/Zashchitnik No. 26‡°	Minesweeper	SN	U24 (IIB)	Kptlt Klaus Petersen	Torpedoed 20 nm W of Sokhumi (Georgia), Black Sea; 26† 26*; log not extant
G52	22 June	LST-333°	Tank landing ship	USN	U593 (VIIC)[20]	Kptlt Gerd Kelbling	Torpedoed off Cap Corbelin (Algeria); beached but sank under tow during attempted salvage on 6 July; 25† 263*
G53	27 July	Akademik Shokal'ski°	Hydrographic vessel	SN	U255 (VIIC)[21]	Oblt.z.S. Erich Harms	Sunk by gunfire NW of Novaya Zemlya, Barents Sea; 11† 14*
G54	30 July	T-911/Astrakhan°	Minesweeping trawler	SN	U703 (VIIC)[22]	Oblt.z.S. Joachim Brünner	Torpedoed S of Novaya Zemlya, Barents Sea; 28† 14*
G55	22 August	DB-36°	Landing craft	SN	U24 (IIB)	Kptlt Klaus Petersen	Both sunk by gunfire, charges and grenades in same attack SW of Gagra Bay, Black Sea; 0† 3* and 0† 3* respectively
G56	22 August	DB-37°	Landing craft	SN	U24 (IIB)	Kptlt Klaus Petersen	
G57	24 August	TSC-578/Shkval‡°	Anti-submarine patrol boat	SN	U23 (IIB)[23]	Oblt.z.S. Rolf-Birger Wahlen	Sunk by gunfire, charges and grenades 22 nm S of Sokhumi (Georgia), Black Sea; 3† 7*; log not extant
G58	29 August	TSC-11/Dzhalita‡°	Minesweeping trawler	SN	U18 (IIB)	Oblt.z.S. Karl Fleige	Torpedoed 25 nm NW of Pot'i (Georgia), Black Sea; 15† 23*; log not extant
G59	6 September	Puckeridge‡	Escort destroyer	RN	U617 (VIIC)[24]	Kptlt Albrecht Brandi[25]	Torpedoed 40 nm E of Gibraltar; 62† 129*; U617 beached near Sidi Amar (Morocco) following damage by RAF Wellingtons on the 11th and destroyed by HMSs *Hyacinth* and *Harlem*, and HMAS *Woolongong* on the 12th; (0† 49*)

---

13 See HMS *Gladiolus* (**35**).
14 See HMS *Welshman* (**81**).
15 See USS *Fechteler* (**101**).
16 See HMS *Hythe* (**91**) and USS *Bristol* (**92**).
17 See HMS *Cossack* (**37**).
18 See HMS *Gladiolus* (**35**).
19 See USS *Muskeget* (**66**).
20 See USS *Skill* (**89**).
21 See USS *Leopold* (**100**).
22 See HMS *Somali* (**70**).
23 See HMS *Daring* (**4**).
24 See HMS *Welshman* (**81**).
25 See USS *Fechteler* (**101**).

No.	Date	Name	Type	Force	U-Boat (Type)	U-Boat Commander	Remarks
G60	1 October	T-896/Krasny Onezhanin‡°	Minesweeping trawler	SN	U960 (VIIC)	Oblt.z.S. Günther Heinrich	Torpedoed NE of Dikson Is. (Russia), Kara Sea; 43† 0*
G61	8 October	Orkan‡	Destroyer	Polish navy	U378 (VIIC)	Kptlt Erich Mäder	Torpedoed SSW of Reykjavik (Iceland); 179† 44*; U378 sunk in the central North Atlantic by aircraft from USS Core on the 20th; (48† 0*)
G62	11 October	LCT 553°	Tank landing craft	RN	U616 (VIIC)[26]	Oblt.z.S. Siegfried Koitschka	Torpedoed SW of Gulf of Salerno; ?† ?*
G63	22 October	Orfasy°	Minesweeping trawler	RN	U68 (IXC)	Oblt.z.S. Albert Lauzemis	Torpedoed 185 nm SE of Freetown (Sierra Leone); 34† 0*
G64	31 October	SKA-088‡°	Patrol cutter	SN	U24 (IIB)	Kptlt Klaus Petersen	Torpedoed S of Gagra (Georgia), Black Sea; ?† ?*; log not extant
G65	1–2 November	Borie‡	Destroyer escort	USN	U405 (VIIC)	Korvkpt. Rolf-Heinrich Hopmann	Scuttled NNW of the Azores on the 2nd after ramming U405 in a mutually fatal encounter the previous day; 27† 127*; (49† 0*)
G66	12 December	Tynedale‡	Escort destroyer	RN	U593 (VIIC)	Kptlt Gerd Kelbling	Torpedoed NW and NE of Bougie (Algeria) respectively; 73† 82* and 84† 90* respectively; U593 sunk by USS Wainwright and HMS Calpe on the 13th; (0† 51*)
G67	12 December	Holcombe‡	Escort destroyer	RN			
G68	24 December	Dumana°	Flying boat tender	RAF	U515 (IXC)[27]	Kptlt Werner Henke	Torpedoed W of Sassandra (Ivory Coast); 31† 138*
1944							
G69	7 January	Tweed‡	Frigate	RN	U305 (VIIC)[28]	Kptlt Rudolf Bahr	Torpedoed NE of the Azores; 83† 44*; U305 possibly sunk SW of Ireland by HMSs Wanderer and Glenarm on the 17th (but see p. 341); (51† 0*)
G70	14 February	Salviking‡	Salvage vessel	RN	U168 (IXC-40)	Kptlt Helmut Pich	Torpedoed 270 nm SW of Colombo (Ceylon); 27† 28*; log not extant
G71	16 February	LST 418°	Tank landing ship	RN	U230 (VIIC)	Kptlt Paul Siegmann	Torpedoed off Anzio (Italy); 21† ?*
G72	20 February	LST-348°	Tank landing ship	USN	U410 (VIIC)[29]	Oblt.z.S. Horst-Arno Fenski	Torpedoed 40 nm S of Naples (Italy); 24† c.30*
G73	20–21 February	LST 305°	Tank landing ship	RN	U230 (VIIC)	Kptlt Paul Siegmann	Torpedoed off Anzio (Italy) and foundered on 21st; ?† ?*
G74	1 March	Gould‡	Frigate	RN	U358 (VIIC)	Kptlt Rolf Manke	Torpedoed NNE of the Azores; 124† 14*; U358 sunk later that day by HMS Affleck; (50† 1*)
G75	2 March	LST 362‡°	Tank landing ship	RN	U744 (VIIC)	Oblt.z.S. Heinz Blischke	Torpedoed SW of Ireland; 88† 94*; U744 captured on the 6th by British-Canadian 6th EG 550 nm W of Dingle Bay (Ireland) but scuttled by HMS Icarus later that day; (12† 40*)
G76	10 March	Asphodel‡	Corvette	RN	U575 (VIIC)	Oblt.z.S. Wolfgang Boehmer	Torpedoed WNW of Cape Finisterre (France); 93† 5*; U575 sunk N of the Azores by aircraft from USS Bogue on the 13th; (18† 37*)
G77	27 March	Maaloy‡°	Minesweeping trawler	RN	U510 (IXC)	Oblt.z.S. Alfred Eick	Torpedoed SW of Ceylon; 17† ?*; log not extant
G78	30 March	Laforey‡	Destroyer	RN	U223 (VIIC)	Oblt.z.S. Peter Gerlach	Torpedoed 60 nm NE of Palermo, Sicily; 179† 69*; U223 immediately sunk by HMSs Blencathra, Hambledon and Tumult; (23† 27*)
G79	9 May	PC-558°	Patrol craft	USN	U230 (VIIC)	Kptlt Paul Siegmann	Torpedoed 28 nm NNE of Palermo, Sicily; c.35† 30*
G80	12 May	SKA-0376‡°	Anti-submarine patrol craft	SN	U24 (IIB)	Oblt.z.S. Martin Landt-Hayen	Torpedoed N of Po'ti (Georgia), Black Sea; ?† ?*; log not extant
G81	29 May	Block Island‡	Escort carrier	USN	U549 (IXC-40)	Kptlt Detlev Krankenhagen	Torpedoed NW of the Canary Is.; 6† 951*; U549 sunk later that day by USSs Eugene E. Elmore and Ahrens; (57† 0*)
G82	13 June	Birdlip°	Anti-submarine trawler	RN	U547 (IXC-40)	Oblt.z.S. Heinrich Niemeyer	Torpedoed off Greenville (Liberia); 37† c.16*

---

26 See USS Buck (90).
27 See HMS Hecla (73).
28 See HMCS St Croix (86).
29 See HMS Penelope (96).

No.	Date	Name	Type	Force	U-Boat (Type)	U-Boat Commander	Remarks
G83	15 June	*Mourne*‡	Frigate	RN	*U767* (VIIC)	Oblt.z.S. Walter Dankleff	Torpedoed SSE of Wolf Rock (England); 111† ?*; *U767* sunk in the Golfe de Saint-Malo by HMSs *Fame*, *Havelock* and *Inconstant* on the 18th; (49† 1*)
G84	24 June	*DB-26*‡°	Landing craft	SN	*U20* (IIB)	Oblt.z.S. Karl Grafen	Sunk by gunfire off Gagra (Georgia), Black Sea; ?† ?*; log not extant
G85	5 July	*Ganily*‡°	Anti-submarine trawler	RN	*U390* (VIIC)	Oblt.z.S. Heinz Geissler	Torpedoed off Utah Beach, Normandy (France); 39† ?*; *U390* immediately sunk by HMSs *Wanderer* and *Tavy*; (48† 1*)
G86	19 July	*Vital de Oliveira*‡°	Auxiliary transport	Brazilian navy	*U861* (IXD-2)	Kptlt Jürgen Oesten	Torpedoed 25 nm S of Farol de São Tomé, Cabo Frio (Brazil); 99† 171*; log not extant
G87	29 July	*Prince Leopold*‡°	Infantry landing ship	RN	*U621* (VIIC)	Oblt.z.S. Hermann Stuckmann	Torpedoed off Normandy (France); 14† ?*; log not extant
G88	30 July	*MO-105*‡*	Anti-submarine patrol cutter	SN	*U250* (VIIC)	Kptlt Werner-Karl Schmidt	Torpedoed N of Primorsk (Russia), Gulf of Finland; 19† 7*; *U250* sunk later that day by *MO-103*; (46† 6*)
G89	30 July	*KT-804/No. 35*°	Anti-submarine trawler	SN	*U481* (VIIC)	Oblt.z.S. Klaus Andersen	Both torpedoed in same attack off Estonia, Gulf of Finland; ?† ?* and ?† ?* respectively
G90	30 July	*KT-807/No. 42*°	Anti-submarine trawler	SN	*U481* (VIIC)	Oblt.z.S. Klaus Andersen	
G91	31 July	*MO-101*°	Anti-submarine patrol cutter	SN	*U370* (VIIC)	Oblt.z.S. Karl Nielsen	Torpedoed in Björkö Sound, E Gulf of Finland; ?† ?*
G92	8 August	*Regina*‡	Corvette	RCN	*U667* (VIIC)	Oblt.z.S. Karl-Heinz Lange	Torpedoed 8 nm N of Trevose Head (England); 30† 66*; *U667* lost on a mine off La Pallice on the 25th; (45† 0*)
G93	12 August	*T-118 (ex USS Armada)*°	Minesweeper	SN	*U365* (VIIC)	Kptlt Heimar Wedemayer	Torpedoed four hours apart N of Mys Kharasavey, Kara Sea; ?† ?* and ?† ?* respectively
G94	12 August	*T-114 (ex USS Alchemy)*°	Minesweeper	SN	*U365* (VIIC)	Kptlt Heimar Wedemayer	
G95	14 August	*LCI(L) 99*‡°	Infantry landing craft	RN	*U667* (VIIC)	Oblt.z.S. Karl-Heinz Lange	Torpedoed off Hartland Point (England); 9† ?*; *LST 921* (USN) left constructive total loss in same attack; 43† 70*; *U667* lost on a mine off La Pallice (France) on the 25th; (45† 0*)
G96	21 August	*Kite*‡	Escort sloop	RN	*U344* (VIIC)	Kptlt Ulrich Pietsch	Torpedoed NE of Jan Mayen Is., Greenland Sea; 217† 9*; *U344* sunk by FAA Swordfish from HMS *Vindex* on the 22nd; (50† 0*)
G97	22 August	*Bickerton*‡	Frigate	RN	*U354* (VIIC)	Kptlt Hans-Jürgen Sthamer	Scuttled off Vannoy (Norway) following attack from *U354*; 38† c.140*; *U354* sunk NW of Bear Is. by FAA Swordfish from HMS *Vindex* and HMSs *Mermaid*, *Peacock*, *Loch Dunvegan* and *Keppel* on the 24th; (51† 0*)
G98	25 August	*LCT 1074*°	Tank landing craft	RN	*U764* (VIIC)[30]	Oblt.z.S. Hanskurt von Bremen	Torpedoed off Normandy (France); 10† 4*
G99	25 August	*KKO-2*°	Survey ship	SN	*U242* (VIIC)	Oblt.z.S. Karl-Wilhelm Pancke	Both torpedoed in same attack in the E Gulf of Finland; 25† 7* and ?† ?* respectively
G100	25 August	*VRD-96*°	Barge	SN		Oblt.z.S. Karl-Wilhelm Pancke	
G101	26 August	*T-45/Antikainen*°	Minesweeping trawler	SN	*U745* (VIIC)	Kptlt Wilhelm von Trotha	Torpedoed off Nerva Is., Gulf of Finland; ?† ?*
G102	26 August	*Nord*°	Survey vessel	SN	*U957* (VIIC)	Oblt.z.S. Gerd Schaar	Sunk by gunfire N of the Taymyr Peninsula (Russia), Kara Sea; 18† 4*
G103	2 September	*T-410/Vrzy*‡°	Minesweeping trawler	SN	*U19* (IIB)	Oblt.z.S. Willy Ohlenburg	Torpedoed off Konstanza (Rumania); ?† ?*; last U-boat sinking in Black Sea; log not extant
G104	23 September	*SKR-29/Brilliant*°	Patrol craft	SN	*U957* (VIIC)	Oblt.z.S. Gerd Schaar	Torpedoed N of Kravkov Is., Kara Sea; 64† 0*
G105	24 September	*T-120 (ex USS Assail)*‡°	Minesweeper	SN	*U739* (VIIC)	Oblt.z.S. Ernst Mangold	Torpedoed NW of Scott-Hansen Is., Kara Sea; 41† 44*; log not extant
G106	17 October	*BMO-512*‡°	Anti-submarine	SN	*U1165* (VIIC-41)	Oblt.z.S. Hans Homann	Torpedoed WNW of Tallinn (Estonia), Gulf of Finland; ?† ?*;

30 See HMS *Blackwood* (**103**).

No.	Date	Name	Type	Force	U-Boat (Type)	U-Boat Commander	Remarks
							log not extant
G107	31 October	SB-2°	Landing craft	SN	U475 (VIIC)	Kptlt Otto Stoeffler	Torpedoed off Osmussaar Is. (Estonia), Gulf of Finland; ?† ?*
G108	18 November	SKA-062‡°	Patrol cutter	SN	U679 (VIIC)	Oblt.z.S. Eduard Aust	Torpedoed NW of Cape Pakri (Estonia), Gulf of Finland; ?† ?*; log not extant
G109	28 November	T-387‡°	Minesweeping trawler	SN	U679 (VIIC)	Oblt.z.S. Eduard Aust	Torpedoed N of Cape Pakri (Estonia), Gulf of Finland; ?† ?*; log not extant
G110	5 December	BO-230 (ex USS SC-1477)‡°	Anti-submarine patrol craft	SN	U365 (VIIC)	Oblt.z.S. Diether Todenhagen	Torpedoed E of Kildin Is., Barents Sea; ?† ?*; log not extant
G111	7 December	BO-229 (ex USS SC-1485)°	Anti-submarine patrol craft	SN	U997 (VIIC-41)	Oblt.z.S. Hans Lehmann	Torpedoed N of Kil'din Is., Barents Sea; 23† 13*
G112	20 December	LST-359°	Tank landing ship	USN	U870 (IXC-40)	Korvkpt. Ernst Hechler	Torpedoed 440 nm SW of Cape Finisterre (France); ?† ?*
G113	21 December	Reshitel'ny°	Motor boat	SN	U997 (VIIC-41)	Oblt.z.S. Hans Lehmann	Sunk by gunfire off Cape Korabelnaya (Russia), Kola Inlet; ?† ?*
G114	24 December	BMO-594‡°	Anti-submarine patrol cutter	SN	U637 (VIIC)	Kptlt Wolfgang Riekeberg	Torpedoed off Cape Pakri (Estonia), Gulf of Finland; ?† ?*; log not extant
G115	24 December	Clayoquot‡°	Minesweeper	RCN	U806 (IXC-40)	Kptlt Klaus Hornborstel	Torpedoed off Halifax, Nova Scotia; 8† 67*; log not extant
G116	26 December	Capel‡	Frigate	RN	U486 (VIIC)	Oblt.z.S. Gerhard Meyer	Torpedoed N of Cherbourg (France); 77† ?*; log not extant
G117	29 December	T-883/Dvina°	Minesweeping trawler	SN	U995 (VIIC-41)	Oblt.z.S. Hans-Georg Hess	Torpedoed SE of Cape Svyatoy Nos, Kola Peninsula (Russia); 49† 0*
1945							
G118	9 January	L'Enjoué°	Patrol craft	FNFL	U870 (IXC-40)	Korvkpt. Ernst Hechler	Torpedoed W of Cape Spartel (Morocco); ?† ?*
G119	11 January	T-76/Koral‡°	Minesweeping trawler	SN	U745 (VIIC)	Kptlt Wilhelm von Trotha	Torpedoed off Aegna Is. (Estonia), Tallinn Bay; ?† ?*; U745 lost to an unknown cause in the Gulf of Finland on 4 February, possibly a mine; (48† 0*)
G120	12 January	Louhi‡	Minelayer	Finnish navy	U370 (VIIC)	Oblt.z.S. Karl Nielsen	Torpedoed off Russarö (Finland); 10† 31*; last U-boat sinking in the Baltic Sea; log not extant
G121	16 January	Deyatel'ny (ex HMS Churchill, ex USS Herndon)‡	Escort destroyer	SN	U286 (VIIC)	Oblt.z.S. Willi Dietrich	Torpedoed NE of the Kola Inlet, Barents Sea; 117† 7*; log not extant
G122	17 February	Bluebell‡	Corvette	RN	U711 (VIIC)	Kptlt Hans-Günther Lange	Torpedoed off the Kola Inlet, Barents Sea; 90† 1*; log not extant
G123	20 February	Vervain‡	Corvette	RN	U1276 (VIIC-41)	Oblt.z.S. Karl-Heinz Wendt	Torpedoed S of Waterford Harbour (Ireland); 60† 33*; U1276 immediately sunk by HMS Amethyst; (49† 0*)
G124	22 February	Trentonian‡	Corvette	RCN	U1004 (VIIC-41)	Oblt.z.S. Rudolf Hinz	Torpedoed 12 nm E of Falmouth (England); 6† 91*; log not extant
G125	24 February	Ellesmere‡°	Anti-submarine trawler	RN	U1203 (VIIC)	Oblt.z.S. Sigurd Seeger	Torpedoed NNW of Ushant (France); 38† ?*; log not extant
G126	2 March	BO-224 (ex USS SC-1507)°	Anti-submarine patrol craft	SN	U995 (VIIC-41)	Oblt.z.S. Hans-Georg Hess	Torpedoed NNE of the Kola Inlet, Barents Sea; 7† 24*
G127	3 March	Southern Flower‡°	Minesweeping whaler	RN	U1022 (VIIC-41)	Kptlt Hans-Joachim Ernst	Torpedoed off Reykjavik (Iceland); 25† ?*; log not extant
G128	10 March	Nordhav II‡	Minesweeping trawler	KNM	U714 (VIIC)	Kptlt Hans-Joachim Schwebcke	Torpedoed off Dundee (Scotland); 6† 17*; U714 sunk by HMSAS Natal off St Abb's Head (Scotland) on the 14th; (50† 0*)
G129	17 March	Guysborough‡°	Minesweeper	RCN	U868 (IXC-40)	Oblt.z.S. Eduard Turre	Scuttled SW of Brest (France) following attack by U868; 52† 38*; log not extant
G130	20 March	Lapwing‡	Escort sloop	RN	U968 (VIIC)	Oblt.z.S. Otto Westphalen	Torpedoed off the Kola Inlet, Barents Sea; 158† 61*; log not extant
G131	16 April	Esquimalt‡°	Minesweeper	RCN	U190 (IXC-40)	Oblt.z.S. Hans-Edwin Reith	Torpedoed off Halifax, Nova Scotia; 44† 26*; U190 surrendered on 11 May; log not extant
G132	23 April	Eagle 56 (PE-56)‡°	Patrol craft	USN	U853 (IXC-40)	Oblt.z.S. Helmut Frömsdorf	Torpedoed off Portland, Me. (U.S.A.); 49† 13*; U853 sunk 5 nm E of Grove Point, Block Is., R.I. by USS Atherton on 5–6 May; (55† 0*)
G133	24 April	Frederick C. Davis‡	Destroyer escort	USN	U546 (IXC-40)	Kptlt Paul Just	Torpedoed SSE of Uummannarsuaq, Greenland; 126† 66*; U546 sunk soon after by USSs Flaherty, Neunzer, Chatelain, Varian,

No.	Date	Name	Force	Type	U-Boat (Type)	U-Boat Commander	Remarks
G134	29–30 April	*Goodall*‡	RN	Frigate	*U286* (VIIC)	Oblt.z.S. Willi Dietrich	Scuttled off the Kola Inlet, Barents Sea following attack by *U286*; 98† *c.*100*; last confirmed U-boat sinking in Northern theatre; *U286* sunk soon after by HMSs *Loch Shin*, *Anguilla* and *Cotton*; (51† 0*)
G135	2 May	*Ebor Wyke*‡°	RN	Minesweeping trawler	*U979* (VIIC)	Kptlt Johannes Meermeier	Torpedoed off Hrafnseyri Light, Skagi (Iceland); 23† 1*; log not extant
G136	7 May	*NYMS 382*‡°	KNM	Minesweeper	*U1023* (VIIC-41)	Kptlt Heinrich-Andreas Schroeteler	Torpedoed ESE of Torbay (England) while *U1023* making for Weymouth to surrender after B.d.U. ends U-boat war; 22† 10*; log not extant

Excluded vessels

The following vessels, occasionally or traditionally reckoned to have been sunk by a U-boat, can either definitely be excluded from the Gazetteer or else cannot be proved to have succumbed to this cause:

No.	Date	Name	Force	Type	Remarks
X1	11 November 1942	*La Sibylle*‡	FNFL	Coastal submarine	Sometimes attributed to *U173* (Oblt.z.S. Hans-Adolf Schweichel), herself sunk off Casablanca (Morocco) by USSs *Woolsey*, *Swanson* and *Quick* on the 16th (57† 0*), *La Sibylle* was either sunk by a US aircraft or else lost in a US minefield off Casablanca; 41† 0*
X2	30 January 1943	*Samphire*	RN	Corvette	Sometimes attributed to *U596* (Kptlt Gunter Jahn), *Samphire* was in fact sunk by the Italian submarine *Platino* off Bougie (Algeria); 45† ?*
X3	17 October 1943	*SKR-14*°	SN	Patrol craft	Sometimes attributed to a mine laid by *U636* (Kptlt Hans Hildebrandt), *SKR-14* was in fact lost by grounding; ?† ?*
X4	15 November 1943	*Simoom*	RN	Patrol submarine	Long presumed torpedoed by *U565* (Oblt.z.S. Fritz Henning[31]), *Simoom* is now reckoned to have been lost in a minefield off Donoussa Is. (Greece), Aegean Sea, or else to an unknown cause between 4 and 6 November; 49† 0*
X5	4 December 1943	*M-36*	SN	Coastal submarine	Sometimes attributed to a mine laid by *U20* (Kptlt Clemens Schöler), *M-36* was in fact lost in an accident in the Black Sea on 4 January 1944; ?† ?*
X6	26 August 1944	*S-51*	SN	Medium submarine	The sinking of this submarine, sometimes erroneously claimed to be *S-56* or *M-108*, is often attributed to *U711* (Kptlt Hans-Günther Lange), though only damage was inflicted in this attack in the Barents Sea; *S-51* was seen trailing smoke as she quit the scene of the engagement
X7	19 October 1944	*KM-321*°	SN	Coastal minesweeper	Sometimes attributed to *U1165* (Oblt.z.S. Hans Homann), *KM-321* was in fact lost in Narva Bay, Gulf of Finland; ?† ?*
X8	5 November 1944	*Spokoiny*	SN	Destroyer	Sometimes claimed to have been sunk by *U997* (Oblt.z.S. Hans Lehmann), *Spokoiny* in fact survived the war to be scrapped in the late 1940s
X9	28 December 1944	*Empire Javelin*‡	RN	Infantry landing ship	Sinking long attributed to *U772* (Kptlt Ewald Rademacher), herself now reckoned sunk off Cork (Ireland) by HMS *Nyasaland* on the 17th (48† 0*): *Empire Javelin*'s loss in the English Channel was probably due to a mine; ?† ?*
X10	5 February 1945	*T-116* (ex USS *Arcade*)‡°	SN	Minesweeper	Sometimes attributed to *U992* (Oblt.z.S. Hans Falke) during an attack off the Kola Inlet, Barents Sea, *T-116* in fact survived the war to be expended as a target after 1963; ?† ?*
X11	23 February 1945	*La Combattante*‡	FNFL	Escort destroyer	Sometimes attributed to *U5330* (Lt.z.S. Klaus Sparbrodt), *La Combattante*'s loss off Cromer (England) was probably due to a mine; 68† 117*

---

31 See HMS *Naiad* (54) and HMS *Partridge*, (79).

Select Bibliography

The following works and websites have been consulted in the preparation of many and in some cases all of the main entries in this book. Among them are works which have been referred to with respect to specific campaigns and theatres of operations, or in connection with a specific navy or warship type. Generally speaking, these sources are not listed in individual entries except where they contain detailed references to the sinking in question. In such cases they appear in abbreviated form in the *Sources* section at the close of each entry, to which readers are referred for material specific to each sinking.

I   The U-Boat War, 1939–1945

General

Blair, Clay, *Hitler's U-Boat War* (2 vols, New York: Random House, 1996–8)

Busch, Rainer, & Hans-Joachim Röll, *Der U-Boot-Krieg, 1939–1945* (5 vols, Hamburg: Mittler, 1996–2003)

Hague, Arnold, *The Allied Convoy System, 1939–1945: Its Organization, Defence and Operation* (London: Chatham Publishing, 2000)

[Hessler, Fregkpt. Günter], *The U-Boat War in the Atlantic, 1939–1945* (3 vols, London: HMSO, 1989)

Howarth, Stephen, and Derek Law, eds., *The Battle of the Atlantic, 1939–1945: The 50th Anniversary International Naval Conference* (London: Greenhill Books, 1994)

Milner, Marc, *The Battle of the Atlantic* (St Catherines, Ont.: Vanwell Publishing, 2003)

Rohwer, Jürgen, *Axis Submarine Successes of World War Two: German, Italian and Japanese Submarine Successes, 1939–1945* (2nd edn, London: Greenhill Books, 1999)

Rohwer, Jürgen, and Gerhard Hümmelchen, *Chronology of the War at Sea, 1939–1945* (2nd edn, London: Greenhill Books, 1992)

Roskill, Capt. Stephen W., *The War at Sea* (3 tomes in 4 vols, London: HMSO, 1954–61)

Schlemm, Jürgen, *Der U-Boot-Krieg 1939–1945 in der Literatur : Eine kommentierte Bibliographie* (Hamburg & Berlin: Elbe-Spree Verlag, 2000)

Campaigns and theatres

Abbazia, Patrick, *Mr. Roosevelt's Navy: The Private War of the U.S. Atlantic Fleet, 1939–1942* (Annapolis, Md.: Naval Institute Press, 1975)

Admiralty, *The Royal Navy and the Mediterranean Convoys: A Naval Staff History* (London: Frank Cass, 2006)

—, *The Royal Navy and the Arctic Convoys: A Naval Staff History* (London: Frank Cass, 2007)

Brooks Tomblin, Barbara, *With Utmost Spirit: Allied Naval Operations in the Mediterranean, 1942–1945* (Lexington, Ky.: University Press of Kentucky, 2004)

Campbell, Vice-Admiral Sir Ian, and Capt. Donald Macintyre, *The Kola Run: A Record of Arctic Convoys 1941–1945* (London: Frederick Muller, 1958)

Gannon, Michael, *Operation Drumbeat: The Dramatic True Story of Germany's First U-Boat Attacks Along the American Coast in World War II* (New York: Harper & Row, 1990)

Hadley, Michael L., *U-Boats against Canada: German Submarines in Canadian Waters* (Kingston, Ont. and Montreal: McGill-Queen's University Press, 1985)

Hickam, Homer H., *Torpedo Junction: U-Boat War Off America's East Coast* (Annapolis, Md.: Naval Institute Press, 1989)

Kelshall, Gaylord T. M., *The U-Boat War in the Caribbean* (Port of Spain, Trinidad: Paria, 1988)

Kemp, Paul, *Convoy! Drama in Arctic Waters* (London: Arms and Armour Press, 1993)

Milner, Marc, *North Atlantic Run: The Royal Canadian Navy and the Battle for the Convoys* (Toronto: University of Toronto Press, 1985)

Morozov, Miroslav, *Podvodniye lodki VMF SSSR v velikoy otetchestvennoy voine 1941–1945. Part I: Krasnoznamenniy Baltiyskiy Flot: Letopis boevikh pokhodov* (Moscow: Izdatel'stvo Poligon, 2001)

Page, Capt. Christopher, *The Royal Navy and the Malta and Russian Convoys, 1941–1942* (London: Frank Cass, 2002)

Paterson, Lawrence, *U-Boats in the Mediterranean, 1941–1944* (Annapolis, Md.: Naval Institute Press, 2007)

Tildesley, Kate, 'Voices from the Battle of the Atlantic' on http://www.war-experience.org/history/keyaspects/atlantic/default.asp

Woodman, Richard, *Arctic Convoys, 1941–1945* (London: John Murray, 1996)

Ships and technologies (general)

Campbell, N. J. M., *Naval Weapons of World War Two* (London: Conway Maritime Press, 1985)

Gardiner, Robert, ed., *Conway's All the World's Fighting Ships, 1922–1946* (London: Conway Maritime Press, 1980)

—, *The Eclipse of the Big Gun: The Warship, 1906–45* (London: Conway Maritime Press, 1992)

Jordan, Roger W., *The World's Merchant Fleets, 1939: The Particulars and Wartime Fates of 6,000 Ships* (London: Chatham Publishing, 1999)

Whitley, M. J., *Destroyers of World War Two: An International Encyclopedia* (London: Arms and Armour Press, 1988)

II   The U-Boot-Waffe and the Kriegsmarine

Dönitz [Doenitz], Grossadmiral Karl, *Zehn Jahre und Zwanzig Tage* (Bonn: Athenäum-Verlag, 1958); English trans.: *Memoirs: Ten Years and Twenty Days* (London: Lionel Leventhal, 1990)

Hadley, Michael L., *Count Not the Dead: The Popular Image of the German Submarine* (Kingston, Ont. and Montreal: McGill-Queen's University Press, 1995)

Mulligan, Timothy P., *Lone Wolf: The Life and Death of U-Boat Ace Werner Henke* (Westport, Conn.: Praeger, 1993)

—, *Neither Sharks nor Wolves: The Men of Nazi Germany's U-Boat Arm, 1939–1945* (Annapolis, Md.: Naval Institute Press, 1999)

Niestlé, Axel, *German U-Boat Losses during World War II: Details of Destruction* (Annapolis, Md.: Naval Institute Press, 1998)

Padfield, Peter, *Dönitz: The Last Führer. Portrait of a Nazi War Leader* (London: Victor Gollancz, 1984)

Rössler, Eberhard, *Geschichte des deutschen Ubootbaus* (2nd edn, 2 vols, Koblenz: Bernard & Graefe, 1986–7); Eng. trans.: *The U-Boat: The Evolution and Technical History of German Submarines* (London: Arms and Armour Press, 1981)

—, *Die Torpedos der deutschen U-Boote : Entwicklung, Herstellung und Eigenschaften der deutschen Marine-Torpedos* (Hamburg: Mittler, 2005)

Rust, Eric C., *Naval Officers under Hitler: The Story of Crew 34* (Westport, Conn.: Praeger, 1991)

Showell, Jak P. Mallmann, *U-Boats under the Swastika* (Shepperton, Surrey: Ian Allan, 1973)

—, *U-Boat Commanders and Crews* (Ramsbury, Wilts.: Crowood Press, 1998)

—, *German Navy Handbook, 1939–1945* (Stroud, Glos.: Sutton Publishing, 1999)

—, *The U-Boat Century: German Submarine Warfare, 1906–2006* (London: Chatham Publishing, 2006)

Stern, Robert C., *Type VII U-Boats* (Annapolis, Md.: Naval Institute Press, 1991)

The U-Boat Commander's Handbook [US Navy trans. of 1942 edn, 1943], ed. Earl J. Coates (Gettysburg, Pa., Thomas Publications, 1989)

Topp, Erich, *The Odyssey of a U-Boat Commander*, trans. Eric C. Rust (Westport, Conn.: Praeger, 1992)

Vause, Jordan, *Wolf: U-Boat Commanders in World War II* (Annapolis, Md.: Naval Institute Press, 1997)

Wynn, Kenneth, *U-Boat Operations of the Second World War* (2 vols, London: Chatham Publishing, 1997–8)

http://uboat.net/

http://www.uboatarchive.net/

http://www.ubootwaffe.net/

III   The Allies

Warship losses

Brown, David, *Warship Losses of World War Two* (2nd edn, London: Arms and Armour Press, 1995)

[HMSO], *British Vessels Lost at Sea, 1914–18 and 1939–45* (Wellingborough, Northants.: Patrick Stephens, 1988)

Hocking, Charles, *Dictionary of Disasters at Sea during the Age of Steam Including Sailing Ships and Ships of War Lost in Action, 1824–1962* (2 vols, London: Lloyd's Register of Shipping, 1969)

Kemp, Paul, *The Admiralty Regrets: British Warship Losses of the 20th Century* (Stroud, Glos.: Alan Sutton, 1999)

Lenton, H. T., and J. J. Colledge, *Warship Losses of World War II: British and Dominion Fleets* (Shepperton, Surrey: Ian Allan, 1964)

McKee, Fraser, and Robert Darlington, *The Canadian Naval Chronicle, 1939–1945: The Successes and Losses of the Canadian Navy in World War II* (St Catherines, Ont.: Vanwell Publishing, 1996)

Royal Navy

Brown, David K., Nelson *to* Vanguard: *Warship Design and Development, 1923–1945* (London: Chatham Publishing, 2000)

—, *Atlantic Escorts: Ships, Weapons and Tactics in World War II* (Barnsley, S. Yorks.: Seaforth Publishing, 2007)

Colledge, J. J., and Ben Warlow, *Ships of the Royal Navy: The Complete Record of All Fighting Ships of the Royal Navy from the 15th Century to the Present* (4th edn, London: Chatham Publishing, 2006)

Elliott, Peter, *Allied Escort Ships of World War II: A Complete Survey* (London: Macdonald & Jane's, 1977)

Friedman, Norman, *British Destroyers and Frigates: The Second World War and After* (Barnsley, S. Yorks.: Seaforth Publishing, 2008)

—, *British Destroyers: From the Earliest Times to the Second World War* (Barnsley, S. Yorks.: Seaforth Publishing, 2009)

Howse, Derek, *Radar at Sea: Royal Navy in World War 2* (Basingstoke, Hants.: Palgrave Macmillan, 1993)

Lavery, Brian, *Churchill's Navy: The Ships, Men and Organization, 1939–1945* (London: Conway, 2006)

Lenton, H.T., *British and Empire Warships of the Second World War* (London: Greenhill Books, 1998)

Roberts, John, *British Warships of the Second World War* (London: Chatham Publishing, 2000)

http://www.naval-history.net/ (for ship biographies and fatalities)

http://www.cwgc.org/debt_of_honour.asp (for individual fatalities)

http://www.unithistories.com (for RN officer biographies)

http://www.fleetairarmarchive.net/ (for aircraft carriers and naval aviation)

Royal Canadian Navy

Douglas, W. A. B., ed., *The RCN in Transition, 1910–1985* (Vancouver, BC: University of British Columbia Press, 1988)

Douglas, William A. B., Michael J. Whitby, Roger Sarty *et al.*, *The Official Operational History of the Royal Canadian Navy in the Second World War*, vol. II, part 1: *No Higher Purpose, 1939–1943*; vol. II, part 2: *A Blue Water Navy, 1943–1945* (St Catharines, Ont.: Vanwell Publishing, 2002–7)

Macpherson, Ken, and John Burgess, *The Ships of Canada's Naval Forces, 1910–1993: A Complete Pictorial History of Canadian Warships* (3rd edn, St Catherines, Ont.: Vanwell Publishing, 1994)

Milner, Marc, *The U-Boat Hunters: The Royal Canadian Navy and the Offensive against Germany's Submarines* (Toronto: University of Toronto Press, 1994)

—, *Canada's Navy: The First Century* (Toronto: University of Toronto Press, 1999)

Schull, Joseph, *Far Distant Ships: An Official Account of Canadian Naval Operations in World War II* (Ottawa: King's Printer, 1950)

http://www.navy.gc.ca/project_pride/home/index_e.asp (for RCN history, data and ship photos)

US Navy

[In collab.], *Dictionary of American Naval Fighting Ships* (9 vols including addendum, Washington, DC: Naval History Division, Department of the Navy, 1959–91); also on http://www.history.navy.mil/danfs/

Alden, Cdr. John D., *Flush Decks & Four Pipes* (2nd edn, Annapolis, Md.: Naval Institute Press, 1989)

Dickey, Lt Cdr John L., II, *A Family Saga: Flush Deck Destroyers, 1917–1955* (Waldoboro, Maine: privately, 2000)

Morison, Rear-Admiral Samuel Eliot, *History of United States Naval Operations in World War II* (15 vols, Boston: Little, Brown, 1947–62)

Roscoe, Theodore, *United States Destroyer Operations in World War II* (Annapolis, Md.: US Naval Institute, 1953); abridged as *Tin Cans: The True Story of the Fighting Destroyers of World War II* (New York: Bantam Books, 1960)

Silverstone, Paul, *The Navy of World War II, 1922–1947* (New York: Routledge, 2007)

Index

Photos in *italics*. No ship prefix has been used for vessels of the German, Soviet, Spanish, Chilean and Finnish navies.

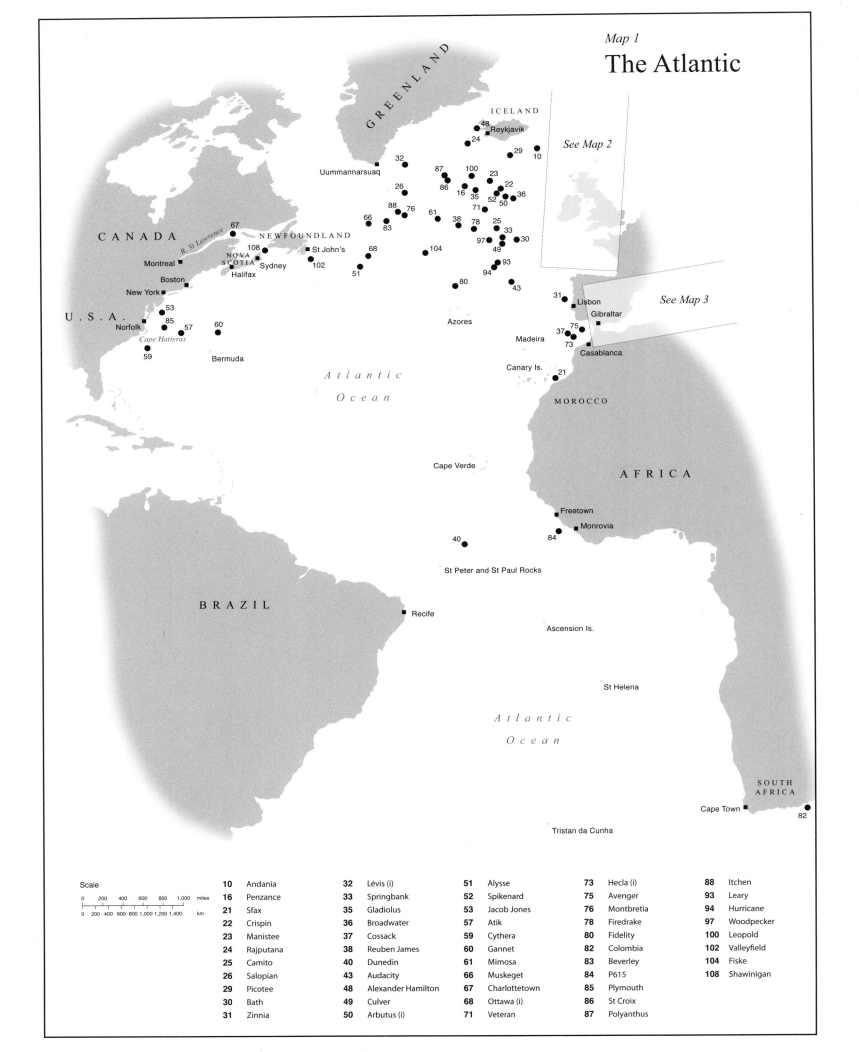

Map 1

The Atlantic

GREENLAND

ICELAND

48 Reykjavik
24
32
29 10
Uummannarsuaq
87 100 23
26 86 22
16 35 52 36
88 76 71 50
66 61 38 78 25
67 83 104 33 30
CANADA R. St Lawrence 97 49
NEWFOUNDLAND 68 94 93
108 St John's 80 43
Montreal NOVA 102 51
SCOTIA Sydney
Boston Halifax
New York
U.S.A. 53
Norfolk 85 57 60
Cape Hatteras Azores
59
Bermuda

See Map 2

See Map 3

31 Lisbon
Gibraltar
75
37 73
Madeira
Casablanca

Canary Is. 21

Atlantic Ocean

MOROCCO

AFRICA

Cape Verde

Freetown
Monrovia
40 84

St Peter and St Paul Rocks

Ascension Is.

BRAZIL Recife

St Helena

Atlantic Ocean

SOUTH
AFRICA
Cape Town 82

Tristan da Cunha

Scale

0 200 400 600 800 1,000 miles

0 200 400 600 800 1,000 1,200 1,400 km

10 Andania	**32** Lévis (i)	**51** Alysse	**73** Hecla (i)	**88** Itchen
16 Penzance	**33** Springbank	**52** Spikenard	**75** Avenger	**93** Leary
21 Sfax	**35** Gladiolus	**53** Jacob Jones	**76** Montbretia	**94** Hurricane
22 Crispin	**36** Broadwater	**57** Atik	**78** Firedrake	**97** Woodpecker
23 Manistee	**37** Cossack	**59** Cythera	**80** Fidelity	**100** Leopold
24 Rajputana	**38** Reuben James	**60** Gannet	**82** Colombia	**102** Valleyfield
25 Camito	**40** Dunedin	**61** Mimosa	**83** Beverley	**104** Fiske
26 Salopian	**43** Audacity	**66** Muskeget	**84** P615	**108** Shawinigan
29 Picotee	**48** Alexander Hamilton	**67** Charlottetown	**85** Plymouth	
30 Bath	**49** Culver	**68** Ottawa (i)	**86** St Croix	
31 Zinnia	**50** Arbutus (i)	**71** Veteran	**87** Polyanthus	